Political Representation
in France

Political Representation in France

Philip E. Converse
and
Roy Pierce

The Belknap Press of
Harvard University Press
Cambridge, Massachusetts, and London, England
1986

This book is printed on acid-free paper, and
its binding materials have been chosen
for strength and durability.

Library of Congress Cataloging-in-Publication Data

Converse, Philip E., 1928–
Political representation in France.

Bibliography: p.
Includes index.
1. Elections—France—Longitudinal studies.
2. Voting—France—Longitudinal studies.   3. France.
Parlement (1946–   ).   Assemblée nationale—Elections
—Longitudinal studies.   4. France—Politics and
government—1958–   I. Pierce, Roy.   II. Title.
JN2959.C65   1986   324.944   85-15789
ISBN 0-674-68660-8 (alk. paper)

This book is for
Jean and Win

Contents

Preface

One of the most fugitive yet oft-cited references in the recent political science literature is an item usually entitled "Miller and Stokes, forthcoming." In the late 1950s our colleagues Warren E. Miller and Donald E. Stokes conducted a novel and exciting study of popular representation in the United States Congress by coupling interview materials drawn from voters in a sample of congressional districts with counterpart information from interviews with their representatives in Washington, along with roll-call votes cast by those representatives on behalf of their districts. In the early 1960s three classic articles were published which described in brief form some of the central findings of the study. Over the course of these articles the reader was referred for details to the much more extended monograph "forthcoming," which would do fuller justice to the richness of the materials.

The three articles occasioned such widespread interest—an interest which we believe remains lively today—that the "forthcoming" reference was eagerly awaited and even given secondary citation. But although the monograph was indeed partially drafted, it never "forthcame." Moreover, interest was so high that the complex multilevel study design was replicated in full in a few instances abroad, along with several duplications of more limited components. Some articles have appeared from these replications, chiefly in Europe, and a monograph or two has appeared from replications limited to one or two of the central design components. But until now no extended monograph has been developed from any replication of the full complex design, although several were originally projected.

We review this eddy in the current of inquiry for two primary reasons. The first reason is that we wish to make it entirely plain that our debt to the inspiration provided by the initial Miller-Stokes study, not only in matters of design and data analysis but also in theoretical underpinnings, is complete. Among other things, the study reported here was first conceived in 1965, in the immediate wake of the first Miller-Stokes products.

The second reason is a little more complex and, in its own way, rather amusing. As outsiders have reviewed the affliction of noncompletion that seems to have surrounded the Miller-Stokes design, one rumor that has surfaced from time to time has been that somewhere in the later stages of monograph preparation Miller and Stokes discovered some deep and fatal flaw in the design which led to a termination of activity and what amounted to a quiet retraction of the whole enterprise. Although few have probably taken this rumor seriously, we contribute this volume as one token of its error. But more especially, the preparation of our own work, which started nearly twenty years ago, with all of the relevant data in hand more than ten years ago, has left us with the deepest sympathy for the completion problem. The full design produces data of a complexity and richness which vastly outstrip anything we have encountered in our social science careers. Bits and pieces may be wrenched out of the central context for articles here and there. But full mastery and reportage of the total design is a project of dimensions which, it is safe to venture, none of the interested parties can ever have foreseen.

Our own replication of the design for France became even more complex because of the sudden intervention, in May and June 1968, of the massive public disorders in France which led among other things to the precipitous dissolution of the French National Assembly, the body that we had so carefully sampled and interviewed less than a year before. These events, coupled with our hasty return to the field in 1968, fortuitously provided us with an unparalleled "before-after" study of the disorders, embedded in an examination of elite responsiveness to popular demands. But this second wave of work, which turned what was already a complex multilevel Miller-Stokes study into a longitudinal one as well, has multiplied our labors by at least another half.

All of this has produced a volume of considerable length despite the fact that, speaking from the inside, we are very nearly embarrassed at how little we have exploited the materials available to us. At many points scattered across our chapters, further analytic gambits were highly indicated theoretically, and were obviously available to us if time cost had been no deterrent. In any ideal world these would have been pursued. But we hurried on, restricting our attention in most instances to the bare essentials.

However hurried we may have felt, the time span occupied by the writing has posed difficulties. The first draft of some of this text was written before

1970, and half or more had been completed by 1975. It has been interesting to us, if perhaps a source of chagrin, to measure the speed of advance of this field against our fixed text. A major part of the final year of work was occupied in returning to early parts of the manuscript to update citations and some of the discussions. We hope our colleagues will be charitable if they find that these efforts to recognize work emerging long after our drafts were laid down are not always so complete as they might be.

Similarly, there are numerous analyses of data in the volume that we might have carried out in a different style had they been designed in 1983 instead of 1969 or 1972. We have reviewed these early analyses and enjoy a clear conscience as to their outcomes: we are confident that newer methodological devices would in no case have changed basic substantive conclusions. The main cost in this department, beyond a certain dated atmosphere to some of the procedures, are insights that newer methods might have permitted but which more primitive operations concealed.

We are also aware that in numerous passages in our text, complexity does battle with aesthetics. One common affliction is that in some instances pages of prefatory explanation about operationalizations and statistical treatment lead to final results which, though pregnant and crucial to the flow of the argument, can be digested in a final paragraph or two. Most of the time we have tried to offer the reader some protection from this complexity by devices such as notes and appendices, along with sterner measures of pure deletion. Indeed, in some of the thornier areas late in the volume, connoisseurs are likely to complain that the details of our analyses are very inadequately explained, despite the many paragraphs given over to this function. Here we can only apologize and promise fuller informal explanations upon request.

We are specially indebted to Warren Miller not only for his creation of the research paradigm used here, but for aid and comfort along the way, and a final insightful review of the full manuscript. Two French colleagues played major roles in the development of the enterprise. Our esteemed collaborator and friend, Professor Georges Dupeux of the University of Bordeaux, aided us at every turn, corrected the French we composed for our interview schedules, and would have been a full participant in the venture but for other major labors in which he was involved at the time. Pierre Weill did the immediate direction of the fieldwork at SOFRES, and as we became familiar with his care, energy, and imagination we began to regard him as the "lucky find" of the study.

For a project which has taken most of twenty years, it is obvious that we have spanned a whole generation of research assistants. Jean Dotson, however, has been with us from the very beginning to the very end, and is as exhausted as we are. Without her endless cheerful help, the work would never have come to fruition. Many, if not all, of our graduate student assistants and advisers have since become professors with careers of their own. Those playing a major role of one type or another along the way include Bruce Campbell, Robert Groves, Jacques Hagenaars, Charles Hauss, Henry Kerr, Michael MacKuen, Michael Robinson, Maria Sanchez, and Jacques Thomassen.

Manuscript work has stretched equally across an evolution of technologies and several excellent secretaries, including Christine Fiore, Verna Washington, Maureen Kozumplik, and Marlene Smith. Coders for the project needed in most cases to be not only bilingual but also capable of coping with an unusual range of material. We thank Marie-José Capelle, Martine J. Delavergne, Charlotte Dufo, Elsa Ettedgui, Lynn Hansen, Mary K. Headley, Barbara Hoerner, Joyce Kaminsky, Carol R. Lyon, Marie-Claire Mostefai, Christine B. Murray, Martine Pineau-Valencienne, Gerda Reppen, Françoise B. DeRocher, Marianne Waterbury, and Rosina E. Wiltshire. Various forms of research, computer, and analytic support have been provided by Frank Baumgartner, Charles Franklin, Christine Guzorek, Peter Joftis, and Brian Wiersema. Leslie R. Thurston prepared the map of French political regions.

Parts of this book have appeared elsewhere, sometimes in versions that have been revised since they were first presented. Portions of Chapter 5 appeared in a paper entitled "Stability and Change in the Sources of French Electoral Behavior," delivered at the 1972 Annual Meeting of the American Political Science Association, at Washington, D.C. Much of Chapter 20 was first presented as a working paper, entitled "Political Representation in France: Exploring Candidate Knowledge of Constituency Sentiment," at the International Political Science Association Round Table on Elections in Complex Societies held at Queen's University, Kingston, Ontario, in June 1975. Parts of Chapter 15 were presented in a paper entitled "Elite Reactions to the May-June Revolt," delivered at the 1977 Annual Meeting of the Society for French Historical Studies, at Berkeley, California.

Portions of Chapter 4 and Chapter 7 were published as "Some Mass-Elite Contrasts in the Perceptions of Political Spaces," in *Social Science Information*, August-October 1975. Much of Chapter 21 first appeared as "Representative Roles and Legislative Behavior in France," in the *Legislative Studies Quarterly* of November 1979; and a substantial portion of Chapter 8 was published in the August 1981 number of the same journal. Parts of Chapter 11 and Chapter 12 appeared in *Political Behavior* in 1981, under the title "Left-Right Perceptions, Partisan Preferences, Electoral Participation, and Partisan Choice in France." We are grateful to the publishers of these journals for permission to reprint.

We are happy also to acknowledge debts of gratitude to other publishers who have kindly granted us permission to reproduce or adapt materials that have appeared elsewhere. We are grateful to the American Enterprise Institute for Public Policy Research, of Washington, D.C., for permission to print Table 1-1; the *American Political Science Review* for permission to print Figure 16-1; the Elsevier Science Publishing Company for permission to print Table 8-6 and Table 8-7; IFOP (Institut Français d'Opinion Publique) for permission to print Table 14-4; the Presses de la Fondation Nationale des Sciences Politiques for permission to print Table 12-4; St. Martin's Press for permission to print Figure 5-1 and Figure 5-2; and SOFRES (Société Française d'Enquêtes par Sondage) for permission to print Figure 5-4, Figure 14-1, and Figure 14-4.

No brief history of our labors would be complete without recognition of a succession of substantial grants from the Ford Foundation in the early part of our work, which supported most of the original data collections and several years of the early data analyses and writing. A grant from the Horace H. Rackham School of Graduate Studies was pivotal in carrying out our 1969 followup interviewing. At a later point, in 1973, further support for writing and analysis was provided by Grant GS-37997 from the National Science Foundation. At the same time, after ten years of work and several grant supplements and renewals it became a problem to return for more help. Thus the second decade of work has gone on largely in a "nights and Sundays" mode, with both authors absorbed chiefly in other projects and duties. During this latter period, however, the administrative patience and support of our colleagues at the Center for Political Studies at the University of Michigan and two delightfully quiet writing spells, made possible first by the John Simon Guggenheim Memorial Foundation and later by the Center for Advanced Studies in the Behavioral Sciences at Stanford, were absolutely crucial. A semester at the University of Oslo and another at the Ecole des Hautes Etudes en Sciences Sociales in Paris provided valuable stimulation and perspective.

As we have pursued this quest over two decades, moments of discouragement have occurred, particularly in the later, unfunded stages. At such times, we the authors felt like linking hands to chant, following the civil rights hymn, "We Shall Forthcome." At last, we have.

Philip E. Converse
Roy Pierce

Ann Arbor, Michigan
June 1985

*Political Representation
in France*

Introduction

This is a book about popular political representation, or the way in which democratic forms, including mass elections, influence the resolution of societal policy disputes in national deliberative bodies. Our ultimate concern is with the degree of fidelity whereby the public will is reflected in the final authoritative decisionmaking of elected representatives.

Our mode of procedure is primarily empirical, resting on data necessarily drawn from particular times and places. Although we shall frequently introduce relevant data from a number of modern democratic countries, most of these will simply form a backdrop for the main study to be reported. This study was carried out in France in the late 1960s and the 1970s. The chief actors consist of the French electorate, on the one hand, and, on the other, of those political elites who competed at the polls in this period to represent the citizenry in the National Assembly. Among the most important members of the latter group are those candidates who won seats and thereby served their constituencies as deputies for one or more terms.

France is in some senses an opportune, and in other senses a difficult, site for such a study. For the last century, with the sole exception of a few wartime years, France has been one of the few nations which has lived consistently under a form of representative government. It was one of the first nations to adopt universal male suffrage and to establish its essential conditions: free primary school education, freedom of organization, and freedom of the press. Threats to representative government and the freedoms which it requires have periodically appeared. Save for the shadow of defeat in

World War II, however, French political leaders successfully overcame them. By any standard of historical practice, France has maintained a long-term commitment to the notion that governors must be responsive to their citizens.

For the same century, however, the word "instability" has probably been used more frequently than any other to characterize French politics. The characterization was often exaggerated, applied in a negative evaluative sense, and not set within a large enough context to be—as it should have been—overshadowed by the great French success in maintaining representative government for almost a century. But there was also a reality underlying the frequent references to instability. Anyone who has spent time trying to help students learn about French politics knows how much difficulty they have in becoming familiar with the broad contours of such apparent manifestations of instability as the succession of regimes, the parade of Premiers and cabinets during the Third and Fourth Republics, the multiparty system with its almost ceaselessly changing labels (and worse, initials), the lack of correspondence between electoral parties and legislative groups, the varied political itineraries of particular leaders, the sometimes surprising choices of the electorate, and the periodic development of what appear, at least from afar, to be major political crises.

These two aspects of French politics—consistency and seeming instability—form the background to this book, although they are expressed in the pages that follow in ways which we could not wholly anticipate when we began our work. In 1967 we set out to try to find an answer to the question: how does representative government operate in the apparently unstable context of French political life? Three years passed before we could even begin to assess our findings. During the intervening period all we could do, almost literally, was to incorporate into our study (which we had already regarded as ambitious in itself) the impact on the representative process of the explosion of public passions which occurred in France in May–June 1968. Our original intention had been to discuss representative government in France on the basis of data collected in 1967. Instead, what we present here is a richer and deeper study based on data collected in 1967, 1968, and to a lesser degree, 1969 as well.

Original Study Design

In the spring of 1967, following the national legislative elections of March, we conducted a survey involving personal interviews with cross-section samples of the French electorate in 86 electoral districts (*circonscriptions*) randomly selected from among the 467 into which the continental portion of the country was divided. At the same time, as a separate but interlocking survey, we also interviewed 272 of the major candidates who had competed at the March 1967 election for seats in the National Assembly for the same

86 sample districts. The candidates interviewed included most of those who had been successful at the polls.

The general goal of the study was to examine the character of the political representation process in France, following a design which has been or is being replicated in nearly a dozen countries with popularly elected legislative representatives.[1] The principal means employed were to obtain the perceptions of both candidates and voters of common topics, wherever possible by identical measures, and to obtain from each group (candidates and voters) an estimate of the other group's perception of those topics. Data were collected from both candidates and voters on a wide variety of topics, but our interests centered on two central and related subjects: the dynamics of the electoral process as a means of selecting deputies, and the relationship between public opinion and the ultimate legislative decisions made by the deputies.

With respect to the electoral process, we naturally collected data from the sample of constituents relevant to the broad determinants of electoral choice which are jointly most potent and most stable over long periods, as well as data from the candidates relevant to their electoral strategies. At the same time, however, we collected data from both candidates and constituents concerning their respective perceptions of and reactions to various aspects of the coalition formation which is made imperative in most districts by the need for a second, run-off ballot.

With respect to the relationship between public opinion and legislative decisions, we ascertained the candidates' positions on numerous prominent issues of public policy, as well as their perceptions of their constituents' positions on those same issues. The survey of the sample of constituents provided independent information concerning the position of the public in the sample districts, thereby making it possible to assess the relative accuracy of the candidates' views as to the distribution of opinion in their districts. Ultimately, we expected to trace the interweaving of constituent demands and the views of their deputies in Paris over several years of roll-call votes cast by those representatives in the National Assembly. Once again, the principal aim of this analysis was, of course, to study systematically the impact of constituency opinion, as perceived by the deputies, upon legislative behavior.

Disorders of May–June 1968

We were in the process of preparing our 1967 data for analysis when France exploded with the disorders of May–June 1968. For a short period, while the world watched with fascination, the fate of representative government in France seemed to hang in the balance, as it had periodically done in the past. But attachments to representative government were sufficiently strong (and fear of or distaste for its alternatives sufficiently great) to permit the mechanisms of representation to be employed in the resolution of the immediate crisis. Once again, France furnished a dramatic illustration of the coexistence of destabilizing forces and the institutions of representative government.

The May–June disorders, which led to the dissolution of the National Assembly and the election of a new one at the end of June, threatened to reduce the usefulness of our study but at the same time provided us with a rare opportunity to enrich it in ways directly relevant to our original objectives.

The potential damage to our study was twofold. On the one hand, some deputies whom we had interviewed in 1967 lost their seats in 1968 and were replaced, in many cases, by candidates who had not been interviewed in 1967. On the other hand, it was reasonable to believe that the popular upheaval of May–June had produced significant changes in the assumptions of many deputies concerning broad-gauged public demands on government and would, therefore, also produce significant changes in their legislative behavior, thereby rendering obsolete the body of candidate opinion we had assembled in the spring of 1967. If we had continued to work with the 1967 data alone, we would have had to choose between two alternate types of analytic work. One alternative would have been to base our analysis on the series of roll-call votes which spanned only the brief, one-year life of the legislature elected in 1967, and to ignore the dramatic turn of events of May–June 1968. The other alternative would have been analytic work based on legislative roll calls taken after the 1968 election, which would necessarily have omitted deputies who had been interviewed in 1967 but not reelected in 1968 and which would not have included direct information about the impact of the upheaval.

Neither alternative was desirable, particularly as the minimal effort required to rescue our study from near disaster provided us also with what seemed to be an unparalleled opportunity to assess in a rigorous fashion the broad political significance of the May–June disorders within the conceptual framework already established for the study for which data had been collected in 1967. However one interpreted the May–June revolt, there was good reason to believe that it had left some marks on the public or their representatives, or both, which would be relevant to their later political behavior.

In one sense, the May–June disorders represented an abnormal intrusion into the normal course of representative government in France. After all, the revolt was the greatest social outburst to occur in a postwar democracy, and whatever the future may hold for the recurrence of such events, within the perspective of the history of representative government in France these disorders were hardly a routine matter. But the effects of extraordinary events may extend to more routine matters. In the case of the May–June disorders, the opposing currents of sympathy and hostility which they generated could reasonably be expected to affect the orientations of the public to the political system in more or less enduring terms and, therefore, to affect the public's modes of political evaluation and their political choices at later, more routine electoral functions. Political scientists have tentatively concluded that basic political orientations are relatively stable, and that enduring shifts in those orientations are likely to occur only in cases of major social upheaval, such as war or depression. The May–June revolt was a major social upheaval. If its life span was fleeting by comparison with those of the wars and depressions which appear to have been critical to changes in basic political orientations in the past, it was nevertheless comparable with war and depression in the apparent clarity of its impression on a large segment of the French population. But the resolution of such speculations about the impact of the crisis in fundamental and enduring terms could, of course, only come about through additional research.

While the revolt was clearly an abnormal event, it was also in a sense a part of the representation process itself. It was the kind of social movement which can submerge some old issues, give greater urgency to others, or generate new issues entirely; and such altered currents of opinion have to be worked out through the mechanisms of representative government just as they would if they had been registered under less dramatic circumstances. Here too, as in the case of the effects of the revolt on more enduring political attitudes, the only way to ascertain whether and in what ways the revolt had altered public opinion, and the disposition or the capacity of legislators to satisfy it, was to extend our original study.

We were fortunate, in this respect, in having originally adopted a design of unusual relevance to the problem of assessing the significance of the May–June revolt. We had, after all, conducted a study of elite responsiveness to public demands on the eve of a major political explosion that involved, inter alia, the very issue of elite responsiveness to public demands. Indeed, we were fortunate also in that we had included in the original design at both elite and mass levels detailed information on some of the more central specific issues of the revolt, such as the educational system and the role of trade unions. Whereas social scientists preparing to study unexpected social or political explosions usually rue the fact that they come to them only after the event, we found ourselves blessed with the kind of measurement which could constitute a "before" measure in a full-fledged "before-after" design. Therefore, we set aside our original plans and returned hurriedly to the field in the summer of 1968.

Ideally, we would have liked to replicate our entire fieldwork of 1967 by returning to interview the same voters who had already been interviewed in 1967, as well as the main candidates for legislative office in the same districts, most of whom had already given us a first interview in 1967. Stern financial limitations ruled out this ideal course, however, and we were able to return to the mass samples in only a randomly selected half of our original 86 districts, plus the 11 additional districts of our original 86 which did not fall into our half-sample but where the deputy elected in 1967 was replaced at the 1968 election. On the mass level, therefore, for 1968 we have a full reinterview in all districts among the original sample of 86 where the incumbent lost his seat, as well as results from a proper half-sample of districts, whether or not they returned new deputies in 1967. On the elite level, we have interviews with 57 candidates from these 54 districts, including 33 candidates who were reelected or elected for the first time in 1968.

Referendum and Presidential Election of 1969

Our second wave of mass and elite interviews was conducted shortly after the legislative elections of June 1968. Within the year following those elections, French voters were called upon twice to cast their votes nationally. The first occasion was the referendum of April 1969, at which they were asked to vote "Yes" or "No" on a complicated question involving both the reorganization of the Senate and the establishment of regional councils. President de Gaulle had urged a "Yes" vote and indicated before the referendum that he would resign if his position were not supported by the electorate. The proposals which de Gaulle backed were rejected by the voters, and de Gaulle promptly resigned from the presidency. There is no vice-president in the French constitutional system, and the President's resignation entailed a new presidential election. This election was held in June, and Georges Pompidou, who had been Premier from April 1962 until July 1968, when President de Gaulle replaced him in the premiership with Maurice Couve de Murville, was elected President on the second ballot.

This new sequence of events did not change the composition of the National Assembly or intrude upon our representation design in the way the May–June revolt had. It did, however, provide us with still another unforeseen opportunity to amplify our earlier work in ways directly relevant both to the main elements of our original design and to those features which were added in 1968 to take into account the impact of the May–June revolt.

Our main consideration was that if we conducted a third wave of interviews with our respondents on the mass level in the fully representative half-sample of 43 districts, shortly after the presidential election of 1969, we would be able to gauge what portion of the changes registered among our respondents between 1967 and 1968, as a result of the May–June crisis, still remained in evidence a year later, after French political life had returned to more routine levels. The timing of the 1969 presidential election was ideal for this purpose, as it fell just one year after the 1968 legislative elections, and those, in turn, had taken place only a little more than a year after the 1967 legislative elections. A followup survey in connection with the 1969 presidential election would provide us with a panel study taken at three points when popular political awareness was at peak levels, due to electoral circumstances in each case, and straddling two roughly equal intervals.

For these and other reasons we returned to the field a third time in the summer of 1969, with the kind of haste to which we were becoming accustomed. We reinterviewed our panel of voters who had already been interviewed twice, and we were also successful in obtaining interviews with a substantial portion of people who fell into our 1968 sample but whom, for various reasons, we had failed to interview at that time. In addition, we interviewed a small but fresh cross-section sample of the electorate in the same 43 legislative districts from which our panel had been drawn, in order to check on the representativeness of our third wave of respondents, which was naturally reduced by the usual attrition to which panel surveys are subject.

It has turned out to be difficult, even in a book of the span of this volume, to do full justice to all of these interlocking data collections.[2] We shall in particular give rather short shrift in these pages to data from the third wave in 1969, although they will make an appearance at a few crucial points and have frequently provided us with background information.

Organization of This Book

To trace influence relationships between mass and elite levels in any complex modern society is a difficult task. To do so for a country like France, with its instabilities and crosscurrents, is more difficult still. Therefore, although our ultimate subject is political representation, we shall approach it gradually. We shall not begin to talk about such complex phenomena in any intensive way until after we pass the halfway point of this volume, in what is the largest but the last of four parts of unequal length. In the interim we shall be assembling the raw materials necessary to make the later stages of our work intelligible. While this review of ingredients has rather the function of an extended preface, it is designed to be of interest in its own right. Indeed, a large number of books, each self-contained, have been written on the general subjects which will occupy our attention in each of our first three parts. Our own materials, as definitive as any extant for this period in French history, will add considerably to our understanding of French political life, even before the subject of representation is fully explored.

Part I of the volume is entitled "The French Voter," and it is limited to our data collections drawn from the common voters. In it we examine the nature of the more abiding political cues which French voters appear to use to make sense of their changing political environment. One of the most distinctive features of that environment is a system of multiple political parties, with a constellation of formations in frequent change. After we review in Chapter 1 the history of this environment in the period leading up to our study, we turn in Chapter 2 to a consideration of what the voter seems to perceive of this party system at a cognitive level. With this landscape in mind, Chapter 3 examines the affective attachments felt toward these political parties, and attempts to account for the fact that such attachments seem diluted in France. In Chapter 4 we move to a competing set of guideposts that might help provide abiding orientation to the French voter, in the form of the classic spectrum of ideological orientations ranging from the extreme left to the extreme right. Chapter 5 concludes Part I with a review of the evidence for a number of other durable anchors or reference points, including religious conviction, social class location, or, in a shorter time frame, feelings toward Charles de Gaulle, the man who dominated the thirty years of French history terminating in the period of our study.

Part II, "Choosing a Representative," is devoted to a consideration of the way in which the abiding cues of Part I intermingle with the more transient features of elections, such as candidates and issues, to determine the composition of specific sessions of the French National Assembly. We first introduce the candidates as we know them from our elite interviews, with descriptions of their social and political backgrounds in Chapter 6, and the ways in which their structuring of political issues contrasts with that of the common citizen in Chapter 7. With these ingredients in hand, we begin to ask in Chapter 8 how visible these candidates are as distinct entities in the minds of the electorate; here a handy foil is our Part I work on the visibility of the several parties. In Chapter 9 we put still more of these elements together, asking after the nature of linkages that are perceived by the voters between political issues, on one hand, and the election options of parties and candidates, on the other.

Legislative elections in France are more complicated than those in most democracies because of the system of two *tours* (rounds of voting): an initial election with a great multiplicity of offerings in some districts, and then a run-off election limited to the more successful candidates, held a week later, in those districts where no clear majority of votes was garnered by any candidate in the first tour. We can exploit this unique system to further our understanding of the dynamics of voter choice. Chapter 10 considers the primary determinants, both abiding and short-term, that seem to govern popular voting in the first tour. Chapters 11 and 12 then consider what happens at the second ballot as a function of the changes in options between the two tours, first to the decision as to whether to vote again a second time, and then to the dynamics of vote transfer among those whose first-ballot preference has disappeared from the options available. Chapter 13 considers the same inter-tour dynamics from the point of view of the candidates revealed by the first ballot to be marginal, who must decide whether to stay in the race and, if they decide to leave it, whether to try to throw their support to some other candidate who is involved in the runoff. The effects of these candidate tactics on voter choice have long been a subject for speculation, and our data permit us to evaluate them uncommonly well.

Part III, which is relatively brief, is devoted to a consideration of the ways in which the massive popular disturbances of May and June 1968 seemed to impact on both voters (Chapter 14) and political elites (Chapter 15) to shift their political perceptions and behaviors. Using our unique "before-after" panel data from 1967 and 1968, we consider some of the factors leading citizens to strike or go out onto the streets in major demonstrations, as well as the reaction of the broader public to these events, registered by marked changes in votes at the elections called to replace the Assembly which was declared dissolved in the wake of these dramatic events. We also consider the perceptions of the 1968 candidates of the student revolt and the strike movement, as well as their more general views concerning the efficacy of such forms of popular political action as a method of enhancing elite responsiveness to popular wishes.

Part IV culminates the volume by putting together elite and mass behavior in full interactive or "linkage" form, thereby permitting us to view the nature of political representation in the French system. Chapters 16 and 17 provide a necessary preface, the first by outlining key theories and models of representation, and the second by reviewing the institutionalized practices of the National Assembly which channel and structure its authoritative decisionmaking on matters of public policy. The next four chapters examine some of the main ingredients of the representation process. Chapter 18 lays out our skein of "linkage issues" and addresses the state of a simple linkage between district opinion and delegate roll-call voting in the Assembly. Chapter 19 focuses on the fit between the personal issue convictions of candidates or deputies and the distributions of policy sentiments in their home districts. Chapter 20 examines one set of conditions which can act to limit the fidelity of popular representation: those governing the accuracy with which the representative perceives policy sentiment in his district. Chapter 21 considers another class of limitation bound up in the representative's conception of his political role, and the degree to which he feels a "will to represent" a district at all.

In Chapter 22 we put all of these ingredients into a more synthetic view of the nature of political representation in France, considering what our data have said about competing models of that process. In Chapter 23 we pursue a set of more particular themes which have long attracted the attention of scholars interested in representation, such as whether representation appears to be more faithful when electoral margins are large or when they are small, and the nature of change in the character of the representation process over time. The final chapter draws together the major findings of the study and considers some of the paradoxes that popular representation in France seems to pose for political theory.

PART I

The French Voter

We start with the voter. By casting a ballot for a legislative candidate, the voter claims his or her share, however infinitesimal, in the determination of the policies that will eventually emerge from the representation system. It is difficult, however, for the average French citizen to follow political affairs. Since the end of World War II, the French political environment has been much less stable than that of most other western democracies. France is unique in that its first postwar constitutional framework, that of the Fourth Republic, collapsed in 1958 and was replaced by a dramatically different structure under the Fifth Republic. Even more important, during both the Fourth and Fifth Republics the party system was both highly fractionalized and unstable. New parties emerged, old ones disappeared, some changed names, almost all experienced widely fluctuating levels of popular support at the polls.

It is important to understand the sources of this electoral instability, as the French voter normally expresses policy claims through political parties, making them the crucial vehicle of popular representation. Does this instability reflect some fickleness of French political temperament at the individual level, or does it flow from the peculiarities of French political institutions? A series of analyses made with comparative panel data from France and the United States points in the latter direction. But this is small comfort for French voters, who consider their party system to be far too complicated. Indeed, the system is so complex that some parties are literally invisible to substantial proportions of the electorate. Pairing off system-level determinants of variations in the visibility of specific parties against individ-ual-level determinants such as education and political involvement indi-cates, again, that it is the system, rather than the voters themselves, that accounts for the phenomenon in question.

How, then, do French voters cope with this kaleidoscopic system? How do they orient themselves within the large and complex electoral field? What underlies such electoral stability as the system does have?

Students of politics in the United States and Great Britain naturally point to habitual party loyalties as the primary stabilizer of mass political attitudes and electoral choices. And there is indeed evidence to show that the same dynamic properties of partisan identifications observed in the U.S. and Britain are at work among those French voters who repeatedly profess a partisan identification. But partisan loyalties remain quite undeveloped in France, relative to countries such as the U.S. and Britain. This weakness of party identification is traceable jointly to the multiplicity and transience of the parties in the system and to a kind of reticence norm that impedes so-cialization into partisanship within French families.

In the absence of fully developed party loyalties, what alternate long-term forces might help to structure popular political attitudes? The left-right continuum could conceivably play such a role in a fluid party system. But although there is widespread familiarity with left-right labels in France, an understanding of what they mean is limited at the mass level. Left-right orientations do help to make the party system intelligible for many voters, but there are no signs that they surpass party identifications as a determi-nant of mass political behavior.

Social-class status, which was a powerful electoral force in Britain dur-ing the period covered by this volume, is a very weak correlate of political attitudes in France. Religion is a much more potent political factor. Not only during the 1950s and 1960s, but down to the mid-1980s, the most de-vout citizens are inclined to the political right, while the more nominally religious and those without any religion at all are most likely to support parties of the left.

During the period under observation, however, there was strong evi-dence indicating that attitudes toward Charles de Gaulle might well be the most powerful alternate to party identification as a more general determi-nant of political outlooks. Attitudes toward de Gaulle differ conceptually from left-right orientations, social class, or religious attachments. But de Gaulle dominated the French political agenda for a quarter of a century and was the pivotal actor when decisive political choices had to be made by the mass electorate. It would not be surprising if attitudes toward de Gaulle, pro and con, proved to be the guiding thread through the French political labyrinth for people not firmly oriented within the system by established party loyalties.

Political representation in France promises to be a complex process if the voters' electoral choices are guided to a large extent by religious outlooks and attitudes toward de Gaulle in spite of the fact that the normal objects of legislative decisionmaking are economic and social problems.

1

The Framework
of French Politics

During the late 1960s Englishmen and Americans looking back
over the previous quarter of a century would have found that
many changes had taken place in the political life of their countries. Between 1945 and 1970, political leaders came and went; new issues
appeared and old issues were transformed; new social forces claimed attention at the forefront of the political scene; wars were fought and an empire
was liquidated; crises of currency and crises of conscience gnawed at the
substance and the spirit of the citizenry.

But Englishmen and Americans would also have found many familiar
and fixed points of reference on the altered landscape of people, issues,
forces, and moods. The constitutional systems of Britain and the United
States remained virtually unchanged. The party systems of the two countries
had also undergone little change. In England the same parties competed at
the elections of 1945 and 1966 with virtually identical results. In the United
States the two major parties that dominated the field in 1968 had also done
so in 1948. There was even the additional parallel of a southern Democratic
third party at each of the two elections. In both countries the content of
political argument changed enormously, but the framework within which
that argument was conducted changed little.

Not so in France. Frenchmen looking back from the same vantage
point would have surveyed a record including major constitutional change,
an unstable party system, and a sharply altered balance of political forces.
The Fourth French Republic, a more or less conventional parliamentary sys-

tem, was replaced in 1958 by the Fifth Republic, a hybrid regime containing elements of both the parliamentary and presidential systems. Some political parties maintained continuity of nomenclature and symbolism throughout the entire period, but others did not. Parties changed their names (but not necessarily their leaders) or joined electoral coalitions bearing transient labels; existing parties disappeared or divided; new ones emerged. These dynamics were not limited to the margins of the system; more often than not they affected it at the core.

The configuration of the party system changed throughout the period as well. Always a multiparty system, it nevertheless assumed a succession of basic forms. The early postwar years were characterized by tripartism, in which three large parties dominated the electoral and parliamentary scene. Later, the party system became highly fractionalized with half a dozen more or less clearly identifiable groups vying for popular support. Still later, under the Fifth Republic, the shape of the party system changed again. This time, the underlying structure became quadripartite, with two large opposing political blocs, each consisting basically of two parties contending for primacy within their respective blocs even as each of the blocs sought dominance over the other. This quadripartite framework was still in its early stages during the late 1960s, the period which receives intensive study in this volume. It achieved clearer expression during the 1970s and 1980s. The reader, however, should have no trouble in following the emergence and development of the basic configuration, or in discerning the reasons why it unfolded as it did.

Amid the changing contours of the French political landscape, however, there was one prominent landmark: the towering figure of Charles de Gaulle. There is some irony here, as de Gaulle himself was the source of much of the fluidity characterizing the other elements of the political system. Wartime leader of the French Resistance and President of the Provisional Government immediately after the war, de Gaulle became an opponent of the Fourth Republic and, eventually, founder and President of the Fifth. The focal point of French political leadership at the start of the postwar era, at the transition from the Fourth to the Fifth Republics, and during the 1960s as well, de Gaulle contributed a personal dimension to French politics that no other contemporary democracy has experienced to the same degree.

Constitutional Changes

France, like other continental European nations whose political systems had been dislocated by the Second World War, adopted a new constitutional framework early in the postwar period. In Germany and Italy political reconstruction meant essentially the liquidation of the recent Nazi and Fascist past and the creation of new democratic institutions linked historically to more distant, earlier liberal eras. The postwar French political leadership naturally disowned the wartime Vichy Regime, which had been established in 1940 in the throes of military defeat and which under Marshal Pétain increasingly collaborated with the German victors. With few exceptions, however, the French political elites that emerged after the war also repudiated the constitutional structure of France's prewar Third Republic, a liberal democratic regime that had existed from 1870 to 1940, longer than any other regime that France had experienced during its checkered constitutional history following the Revolution of 1789.

For some, the rejection of the Third Republic reflected the conviction that the regime had been responsible for France's defeat and had abdicated its responsibilities to Marshal Pétain. For others, policies associated with the Third Republic appeared outmoded or unjust. Leftists thought that the regime had been too conservative; emerging Catholic political leaders resented its anticlericalism.

Still other leaders, most notably de Gaulle but also including Socialists who had been frustrated in their efforts to govern prior to the war, believed that the central weakness of the Third Republic had been lack of executive authority. The Third Republic was controlled by men who opposed the exercise of power. Memories of authoritarian rule by Louis Napoleon were fresh in the minds of the regime's founders, who identified parliamentary democracy with legislative omnipotence and established conventions that the president should be either weak or quickly brought to heel at the first sign of independence, and that the premier and the cabinet should be rotated sufficiently often to ensure that they properly understood their subordination to the legislature. Those unwritten rules of the game, combined with the fluid multiparty system, made policy formation difficult and governments short-lived.

Efforts had been made during the 1930s to strengthen the executive, but these all failed because they emanated from the right, which leftists trusted less than ever in the era of Nazism and Fascism. Yet similar plans for constitutional reform were produced by Resistance groups that were obviously immune to the kinds of criticism that had been directed at the prewar right. The overall result was that in 1945 few members of the French political elite recommended a return to the constitution of the Third Republic. At the same time as France's first elected postwar Assembly was chosen, in October 1945, more than 95 percent of the voters approved a referendum item authorizing that Assembly to prepare a new constitution.

The Fourth Republic

Drafting a new constitution proved to be difficult. The participating parties were in more agreement over what they did not want than over what to put in its place, and an inevitable succession of compromises frustrated the cherished hopes of the more ambitious reformers. In particular, it was clear that there would be no strong and independent executive of the kind preferred by Charles de Gaulle, who signified his disapproval by resigning as President of the Provisional Government in January 1946. Nevertheless, a majority in the Constituent Assembly, consisting of Communists and Socialists, adopted a constitutional text that was submitted for ratification at a referendum in May 1946. This constitutional draft was rejected by the voters, largely because of the opposition of the Mouvement Républicain Populaire (MRP), which at that time had a large electoral following, and also because the Communist party campaigned so vigorously in favor of the draft that anticommunist forces mobilized to prevent what would have looked like a Communist victory.

A second Constituent Assembly was elected in June 1946, and this time the Assembly produced a draft constitution that was satisfactory to the MRP as well as to the Communists and Socialists. The text, which was ratified at a popular referendum in October 1946, became the Constitution of the Fourth Republic.

Charles de Gaulle had remained silent between his resignation in January 1946 and the election of the Second Constituent Assembly on June 2 of that year, but two weeks after the election he made a historic speech at Bayeux in which he set forth his basic diagnosis of France's political weaknesses and outlined his prescription for a constitutional system that would overcome them. The direct source of the problem was the party system, "our old Gallic propensity for division and quarrels." The remedy lay in the separation of powers, in particular in an executive branch independent both of the parties and the legislature. In de Gaulle's view, the French party system expressed too many fundamental conflicts, due at once to "the national temperament, the vicissitudes of history, and the upheavals of the present," to produce cohesive governments or efficient administration and to maintain "the prestige and authority of the state." If the parties continued to be the source of executive power, they would simply transmit their rivalries to that branch of the constitutional system that required unity, cohesion, and internal discipline. It was necessary, therefore, to counteract the divisive qualities of the party system by institutional means. France's new democratic institutions had to compensate for "our perpetual political effervescence." In particular, the chief of state should be "placed above parties," chosen by an electoral college including, but much larger than, parliament, and endowed with a number of important responsibilities, including that of appointing the Premier and the cabinet.

De Gaulle thus expounded the central theme that he was to adhere to without exception throughout the Fourth Republic (which he soon afterwards baptized "le régime des partis") until it became possible for him in 1958 to convert the terms of the Bayeux speech into the Constitution of the

Fifth Republic. That moment, however, was still twelve years distant. The Bayeux speech did not deter the parties from agreeing on a new constitutional draft that was not very different from the first one and presenting it to the voters. Popular ratification was secured because all three of the major parties—Communists, Socialists, and MRP—supported the text; but de Gaulle's opposition to it (as well, perhaps, as a certain amount of poll-weariness on the part of French voters, who had already voted at a referendum and elections in October 1945, a referendum in May 1946, and elections in June 1946) helped to diminish the margin of popular support for the new constitution. More than 30 percent of the voters abstained, and the votes cast for the constitution were actually fewer than those cast for the draft that had been rejected in May.[1]

Shortly after the new constitution was adopted and its institutions launched, de Gaulle formed a new political movement called the Rassemblement du Peuple Français (RPF) in order to build popular support in favor of bringing him back into power and establishing a new constitution along the lines he had outlined in his Bayeux speech.

In one sense, the RPF failed, for it did not succeed in arousing the requisite amount of support to accomplish de Gaulle's aim of forcing the Fourth Republic to capitulate on terms that would permit him to change the constitutional system. De Gaulle disbanded the RPF in 1953 and almost totally withdrew from public life until 1958, when the Fourth Republic, already floundering because of the unsuccessful efforts of its leaders to reach a solution to the conflict with the Algerian independence movement, was confronted with the threat of a coup d'état by the French army in Algeria. But the RPF provided encouragement to de Gaulle's associates and close supporters and inspired them to maintain a skeletal organizational framework which could be (and was) employed in 1958 when the long "crossing of the desert" (Viannson-Ponté, 1963) came to an end.

That moment arrived in May 1958 when French settlers in Algeria revolted in order to prevent the formation of a government in Paris that would try to make peace with the Algerian nationalists. The French army in Algeria remained temporarily in control of the situation there, but it could continue to do so only on the condition that it not appear to accept the authority of the French government, which the settlers on the scene had repudiated. But the army also had little regard for the French colonists, some of whose leaders in May 1958 were more or less fascist in outlook. In this cross-pressured situation, the army threw its support to de Gaulle, whose return to power would fill the political vacuum, permitting the army to avoid accepting the authority of either the discredited government in Paris or the unacceptable leadership of the French colonists.

There was considerable resistance among the politicians in the National Assembly in Paris to recalling de Gaulle to power. He had, after all, been a contemptuous opponent of the Fourth Republic in which they served. But the authority of the government had been undermined.[2] There were signs of an imminent invasion of Metropolitan France by the French army in Algeria, an event which would have placed France in the situation of Spain in 1936. The only force on the mainland that might be able to organize opposition to an invading French army was the Communist party, and a majority of French deputies and political leaders became persuaded that the only way to steer between a military dictatorship and a Communist dictatorship was to bring de Gaulle back to power.[3] On June 1, 1958, de Gaulle was elected the last Premier of the Fourth Republic by the National Assembly. Among his near dictatorial powers was authorization to draft a new constitution for submission to the voters at a referendum.

The Fifth Republic

During the summer of 1958 a constitutional text was drafted that faithfully translated into concrete institutions the constitutional principles that de Gaulle had outlined in his Bayeux speech in 1946. Whereas the Constitution of the Fourth Republic had permitted political power to be largely monopolized by the National Assembly, the new constitutional document gave extensive powers to the President and to the Premier and the cabinet, and it sharply limited the powers of the legislature.

When this new constitutional draft was submitted to a popular referendum in September 1958, the only major party that campaigned against ratification was the Communist party. The other main parties all decided to support the constitution, although some did so less out of enthusiasm for the document than out of their conviction that only de Gaulle could end the Algerian War. Some non-Communist left-wing leaders, such as Pierre Mendès-France and François Mitterrand—the latter to become de Gaulle's principal opponent in later years—opposed the new constitution (as they had opposed returning de Gaulle to power), but they were isolated and lacked major party support. The result was a massive vote in favor of ratifying the Constitution of 1958. More than 65 percent of the registered voters in Metropolitan France cast ballots in favor of what became the Constitution of the Fifth Republic.

According to the Constitution of 1958, the President was elected by a cumbersome electoral college of some eighty thousand electors, consisting mainly of persons selected by France's numerous municipal councils. That kind of electoral college met only once, in December 1958, when to no one's surprise it chose de Gaulle as President of the Fifth Republic. In 1962, after the Algerian War had ended and Algeria had become independent, de Gaulle turned his attention again to constitutional matters and held a referendum on a constitutional amendment providing for the direct popular election of the President. This procedure was of questionable constitutionality, as it bypassed the constitutional provisions that explicitly referred to constitutional amendments, but those provisions required the consent of the legislature. De Gaulle could not have gained legislative support for his amendment, which was opposed by every political party except the Union for the New Republic (UNR), the party that had been formed in the fall of 1958 by de Gaulle's followers specifically to support him. The proposal, however, was popular with the voters. After all, they were being offered the chance to participate directly in the election of the President. Once again, as in 1958, de Gaulle's constitutional recommendation was endorsed by the voters.

By the end of 1962, therefore, France had come full circle with respect to its constitutional structure. In 1946 it had acquired a constitution that was supported by the major parties and opposed by de Gaulle because it vested authority in the legislature and subordinated the executive. In 1958, in the shadow of civil war, most of the parties had accepted de Gaulle's terms for a new constitution that redressed the institutional balance, although they did not do so ungrudgingly. In 1962 de Gaulle had secured the popular ratification of a constitutional amendment that was supported only by the Gaullists and opposed by every other party because it symbolized and institutionalized the aggrandizement of the executive. De Gaulle had won his war against the parties.

Parties and Elections, 1945–1956

De Gaulle did battle against not one but two types of party systems. His first clash with the parties, which produced both his resignation early in 1946 and his Bayeux speech later in the same year, took place during the period of tripartism. During the first few years after World War II, French electoral politics was dominated by three parties, the Communist party, the MRP, and the Socialist party, the latter usually being referred to as the SFIO, after the initials of its official name—Section Française de l'Internationale Ouvrière—from its founding in 1905 until 1969, when it became simply le Parti Socialiste. At each of the first three elections after the war, those three parties together received almost 75 percent of the votes (see Table 1-1). The Radical-Socialists (often called simply Radicals) and the various right-wing groups which the French generally refer to as *modérés* (designated in this book as conservatives), which had been major political forces before the war, were relegated to a minor role during this period.

The Communist and Socialist parties emerged in the postwar period stronger than they had ever been before. The high point of prewar electoral success for these two leftist parties had been 1936, when the Communist party won about 15 percent and the Socialist party about 20 percent of the votes. Socialist party gains were short-lived; in November 1946 the Socialists

Table 1-1. Votes and seats (Metropolitan France, 1945–1962).

Party	October 21, 1945 Votes %	Seats	June 2, 1946 Votes %	Seats	November 10, 1946 Votes %	Seats	June 17, 1951 Votes %	Seats	January 2, 1956 Votes %	Seats	November 23, 1958 Votes %	Seats	November 18, 1962 Votes %	Seats
Communist (PCF)	26.0	148	26.2	146	28.6	166	25.8	97	25.7	145	18.6	10	21.8	41
Extreme left							.08		0.4		1.2		2.3	2
Socialist (SFIO)	23.8	134	21.1	115	17.9	90	14.5	94	14.9	92	15.2	44	12.5	65
Radicals and allies	11.1	23	11.5	39	12.4	55	10.2	77	15.6	77	7.2	23	7.7	42
MRP	24.9	141	28.1	160	26.4	158	12.5	82	11.1	72	10.8	57	8.0	36
Gaullists					1.6	5	21.8	107	4.4	16	21.4	198	35.9	249[a]
Conservatives	13.3	62	12.8	62	12.8	70	12.8	80	14.5	96	19.8	133	10.9	28
Extreme right[b]									13.2	42	2.5		0.9	
Miscellaneous	0.9	14	0.3		0.3		1.6	7	0.2	4	3.3			2
Total	100.0	522	100.0	522	100.0	544	100.0	544	100.0	544	100.0	465	100.0	465

Source: Roy Pierce, "French Legislative Elections: The Historical Background," in Howard R. Penniman, ed., *The French National Assembly Elections of 1978* (Washington, D.C.: American Enterprise Institute, 1980), ch. 1.
    a. Includes 20 Gaullist conservatives (Independent Republicans).
    b. Mainly Poujadists in 1956.

won a smaller proportion of the vote than in 1936, and they never returned
to the 1936 level during the 1950s or 1960s. The Communists, however,
held most of their gains throughout that period; even in 1958, their least
successful electoral year during the era under discussion, they won a larger
fraction of the vote than they had in their best prewar year.

Unlike the Communists and Socialists, the MRP was a new party that
had been formed during the war by Catholic Resistance leaders. Although
the MRP had prewar predecessors in the form of small liberal Catholic parties, these had never achieved anything like the early postwar electoral success of the MRP. The MRP's popular appeal rested mainly on two factors: it
was believed to be the party closest to de Gaulle; and, although its leaders
tended in those years to be more or less socialistic in outlook, it attracted
the support of many rightist voters who regarded it as the most effective
anti-Communist party available. The conservatives and the Radicals, who
might have played that anti-Communist role (the former among Catholics,
the latter among anticlericals), could not do so at the time because they
were discredited by their association with the Third Republic or the Vichy
Regime.[4]

The political characteristics of tripartism were quite unlike any that
France had previously known. The party system of the Third Republic had
been highly fractionalized and, except on the left—which had always been
concerned about maintaining coherence between the parliamentary group
and the party organization as a whole—the links between electoral parties
and parliamentary groups were tenuous, and the parties in parliament were
undisciplined. Parliamentary decisionmaking required intricate bargaining
among numerous groups and individuals, and lines of electoral accountability were often unclear. In the early postwar period these habits were briefly
but dramatically transformed. When Communists and Socialists entered
parliament in increased numbers, they stamped it with parliamentary group
discipline that was displayed by the fledgling MRP as well. The leaders of
the three big parties bargained hard with one another, and when deals were
struck that could be ratified by the respective party machines, their adoption
was ensured by loyal parliamentary majorities. At the same time, the price of
agreement among the warring monoliths was often power-sharing, and each
party carved out as large a private domain within the state machinery as it
could (Williams, 1964, ch. 27).

Tripartism was the system in force when de Gaulle launched his
Bayeux attack, but it soon gave way to partisan behavioral patterns similar
to those of the Third Republic. Two events accounted for the change: the
Cold War and de Gaulle's creation of the RPF. The breakdown of cooperation between the Soviet Union and the Western powers was transposed into
domestic French politics. The Communist party left the government in the
spring of 1947, and the opposition of the Communists meant that the So-

cialists and the MRP had to turn to their right to build parliamentary majorities. That increased the influence of the Radicals and the conservatives, and it complicated the parliamentary game. There were now more players, and the Radicals and conservatives revived many of the individualistic parliamentary habits of the prewar system.

De Gaulle's RPF won more than 20 percent of the votes at the elections of 1951, thereby further fragmenting the party system. The main victim of the Gaullists' relative success was the MRP, which lost more than half of its previous electoral support. The MRP could no longer be considered de Gaulle's party, and rightist voters seeking an anti-Communist party could take comfort in the RPF, as de Gaulle had made opposition to the Communists (whom he called "separatists") one of the pillars of his new movement.

The 1951 election produced a nearly hexagonal Assembly containing six parties of approximately equal size. The Gaullist RPF and the Communists were the largest, but they were as opposed to each other as they were to the other parties—the Socialists, MRP, Radicals, and conservatives—which together held a majority of the seats (and were referred to as the Third Force).[5] "Condemned to live together," as one of their least forceful but most durable leaders had put it, the Third Force parties managed to construct a succession of fragile, short-lived governments that sometimes confronted and often evaded the problems facing the country at home and overseas.

Thus, in the early 1950s, the Third Force parties outmaneuvered their Gaullist and Communist opponents, frustrating for the moment Gaullist expectations that the regime would collapse. Indeed, the RPF cracked before the Fourth Republic did. RPF deputies were absorbed into the parliamentary game, and in 1953 de Gaulle dissolved the RPF and withdrew from public life. But even as de Gaulle suffered this setback, the survival power of the Fourth Republic was eroding and processes leading to the disintegration that de Gaulle had predicted were under way. Divided by doctrine, interest, and personal ambitions, the French party system continued to splinter and became an increasingly less viable mechanism for the conversion of popular opinion into the solution of political problems. For a brief period in 1954, Pierre Mendès-France breathed new life into the system by liquidating the Indochina War, but he also incurred undying enmities and set loose rancorous conflicts by forcing the Assembly to face up to the long postponed issues of European integration, German rearmament, and the growing sentiment in favor of independence in France's North African protectorates of Morocco and Tunisia.

By the 1956 election—the last held under the Fourth Republic—the French parties no longer represented a system but a congeries of warring clans.[6] The Third Force was shattered: the Socialists and MRP had become completely estranged from each other because of legislative battles in 1951 over the issue of state aid to Catholic schools. The Radicals, never more than a splinter group in the popular vote after World War II despite being the main spawning ground of premiers and ministers, were themselves divided into two groups, one led by Pierre Mendès-France and linked with the Socialists in what was called the Republican Front, the other led by Edgar Faure and allied with the MRP and the conservatives. The Gaullists, no longer permitted by de Gaulle to use the RPF label, now called themselves Social Republicans, and they too were divided between the Republican Front and the more moderate MRP, conservative, and Radical forces.

The electoral volatility that de Gaulle's creation of the RPF had unleashed in 1951 was displayed again, in new form, in 1956. In the absence of their leader, now temporarily withdrawn from politics, the Gaullists collapsed at the polls. The Social Republicans, heirs to a party which had won more than 20 percent of the vote in 1951, won some 4 percent of the vote in 1956. But this Gaullist defeat did not really operate to the advantage of any of the remaining parties. Former RPF voters, instead of swelling the ranks of any particular party, dispersed their support throughout a wide range of the party spectrum. The MRP and the conservatives, who had the most to hope for from a Gaullist collapse, were disappointed: the conservatives made only marginal gains and the MRP actually suffered marginal losses. The Communist share of the vote dropped slightly; the Socialist share gained slightly. Mendèsist Radicals made brisk percentage gains, but their vote was still comparatively small, representing about 11 percent of the total.

The main victor at the 1956 election was a new party, officially called Union et Fraternité Française (UFF) and popularly called the Poujadists, after its leader Pierre Poujade. The UFF was originally a sort of demagogic taxpayers' defense organization, formed by Poujade in the mid-1950s, and called the Union de Défense des Commerçants et des Artisans (UDCA). Other parties took the UDCA seriously while it acted as a pressure group but, surprisingly, not when it became an electoral organization under the UFF label. The new party campaigned vigorously, both in public (by using catchy slogans, negative themes, rowdyism, and sometimes violence) and more discreetly (by using storekeepers and deliverymen to gain support through face-to-face appeals). It ended up winning almost 12 percent of the votes, thereby frustrating the hopes of every other party to reap the major share of the harvest of liberated Gaullist voters.

Former RPF voters can have contributed only a fraction of the support gained by the Poujadists in 1956, for the RPF had been strongest in the cities and the north while the Poujadists were strongest in the small towns, countryside, and the south. Much Poujadist support probably came from new voters and former abstainers (there were fewer abstentions in 1956 than at any previous postwar electoral consultation) in rural areas and small towns which were beginning to feel the competitive pressures of French postwar economic modernization.[7] In many respects the Poujadist electorate of 1956 resembled the German Nazi electorate of the early 1930s in that it consisted very largely of normally uninvolved persons who were suddenly mobilized into political action in the face of economic adversity (Converse, 1964).

The Assembly that emerged from the 1956 election was the last of the Fourth Republic. It was as badly splintered as the previous one, and the number of deputies among whom majorities could be built was no larger than before. Despite the near disappearance of the Gaullists, the opposition—composed of Poujadists and an enlarged group of Communists—was virtually as numerous as it had been from 1951 to 1956.[8] The classic maneuvers of bargaining, compromise, combination, and recombination were more necessary than ever for policymaking. Some important measures were enacted concerning both domestic affairs (in the domain of social welfare) and overseas policy (in Black Africa and Madagascar, which were set on the road to genuine self-government). But the leaders and parties of the Fourth Republic could not settle the worsening Algerian question, which had reached the crisis stage. On this overriding issue, the Assembly could not, to use Gaullist language, produce a government that could govern. When the French colonials in Algeria revolted in 1958 and the army called for the return of de Gaulle, the Assembly capitulated and brought de Gaulle back to power.

De Gaulle's confident prediction that the French "régime des partis" would one day collapse was, therefore, fulfilled. Whether the correctness of de Gaulle's prediction also implies the accuracy of his constitutional theory is an issue that can never be decided. Certainly the French party system was ill suited to formulating a policy for Algeria, building popular support for that policy, and implementing it with constancy of purpose, all of which de Gaulle was to accomplish. But given the contrast between the outlook of the advocates of a French Algeria and the real balance of forces in North Africa and the world, and the consequent division of public opinion in the country, it would be foolish to ignore the fact that the nature of the issue itself had much to do with the failure of the Fourth Republic to settle it. After all, it took de Gaulle four years to clear the issue from the national agenda, and not without tolerating and even creating ambiguity about his ultimate purpose.[9] But be that as it may, Algeria brought de Gaulle back to power, and de Gaulle gave France new institutions. These institutions were to stimulate still another major transformation in the French party system. Having passed through tripartism and high fractionalization, it was now to start evolving toward the quadripartite character to which we referred at the beginning of this chapter: a system dominated by two competing political coalitions, each consisting of two parties that were at once allies and rivals.

The Party System in the Fifth Republic

Changes in the French party system under the Fifth Republic occurred in successive stages and were propelled by the dynamics of the new political situation and the new institutional arrangements. First, the return to power of de Gaulle was accompanied by the restoration of a Gaullist party that was to become the dominant party in the system until 1981. Second, a new electoral law placed a premium on electoral alliances (of a very different kind from those permitted by the electoral system used in 1951 and 1956) and encouraged the forging of a leftist coalition including both Socialists and Communists, to which de Gaulle unwittingly contributed by his unilateral termination of the Cold War. Third, the establishment of direct election of the President at the end of 1962 encouraged aspirants to the office to attempt to build broad partisan coalitions directed toward the electorate at large. The premiership was now the gift of the President and could no longer be secured by careful maneuvering in the Assembly. Real power rested with the presidency, a nationally elected office, and advancement to that office required new strategies. Indeed, virtually all of the important developments in the French party system after 1962 can be interpreted in the light of leadership-positioning for a run for the presidency.

Legislative Elections of 1958 and 1962

The first legislative elections of the Fifth Republic took place in November 1958, one month after the referendum at which the new Constitution was ratified by the voters. Gaullists from the Social Republicans and a variety of other organizations which had been hastily thrown together to support de Gaulle in the heat of the colonists' revolt formed a new party called the Union for the New Republic (UNR). Although de Gaulle did not endorse the UNR, and relatively few voters actually associated the UNR with de Gaulle before the 1958 election (Converse and Dupeux, 1966), the new Gaullist party won about 20 percent of the votes. As time went on, however, the UNR (and its successors) became more clearly associated with de Gaulle in the public mind. Thus, the 1958 election marks the beginning of what was to become a remarkable growth in electoral support for Gaullism.

The 1958 election was a watershed event in other ways as well. The electoral strength of the combined left-wing parties fell below 50 percent for the first time since the war (Goguel, 1967), and it was not to achieve majority status again until 1981. Communist support dropped sharply, and so did that of the Radicals, who lost half of their 1956 strength. The conservatives, on the other hand, gained by about a third, achieving in 1958 what they had vainly hoped to win in 1956.

Most striking of all, in terms of electoral volatility, was the almost complete disappearance of the surprise party of 1956, the Poujadists. The organization ran fewer candidates in 1958 than in 1956,[10] but they did compete in 1958 in places where they had been strong two years before. Nevertheless, the Poujadists suffered a complete electoral collapse (Goguel, Lancelot, and Ranger, 1960).

Between the legislative election of 1958 and that of 1962, Frenchmen went to the polls three times to participate in referenda. In January 1961 de Gaulle asked the voters to approve his policy for self-determination of Algeria, and 75 percent of them did so. In April 1962 he asked them to approve the Evian Agreements by which Algeria had become independent, and this time over 90 percent of the voters endorsed his policy. And in October 1962 some 62 percent of the voters approved the President's proposal to amend the Constitution to provide for the direct popular election of the President.

The antagonism was so great between the non-Gaullist parties and de Gaulle over the General's move to amend the Constitution by referendum that for the first, and to date the only, time during the Fifth Republic the National Assembly voted to censure the government for its acquiescence in de Gaulle's initiative. De Gaulle promptly dissolved the National Assembly, and in November 1962, one month after the referendum on the constitutional amendment, new legislative elections were held.

The Communists improved their electoral showing slightly over their postwar low of 1958, but the Socialists' proportion of the vote decreased and that of the Radicals remained about the same; so those leftist parties, taken together, did no better or worse at the polls than they had in 1958. A new, small left-wing party made its first electoral appearance in 1962. This was the Parti Socialiste Unifié (PSU), created in 1960 and the successor to several tiny, ephemeral splinter groups created during the 1950s by leftists disillusioned with the larger parties. The PSU contested only about 20 percent of the seats in 1962 and won but 2 percent of the total vote. Despite this lack of success, the PSU became a permanent fixture of the partisan landscape during the 1960s. It appealed mainly to left-wing Catholics, and during the upheaval of May–June 1968 the PSU was the most revolutionary of the established French parties.

The parties of the left did not increase their total share of the vote in 1962, but at the elections of that year they took the first steps toward building a leftist electoral coalition. The electoral system used during the Fifth Republic makes it possible for parties to ally with one another by withdrawing in one another's favor at the second ballot.[11] In 1958 Socialists and Radicals had cooperated with each other in this manner, but they had competed with the Communists at least as fiercely as they had competed with

the Gaullists or the conservatives. With the left divided at the second ballot, Gaullists and conservatives had had little trouble producing pluralities
and winning seats even where the left was normally strong. In 1962, however, Socialists and Communists withdrew in favor of whichever one of the
two parties' candidates seemed to be the better placed to defeat a Gaullist or
a conservative at the second ballot. In some districts both Socialists and
Communists withdrew at the second ballot to help a Radical candidate.

These second-ballot electoral alliances permitted the left-wing parties to
make more efficient use of their votes than in 1958, and even though they
won about the same proportion of the first-ballot votes as they had won in
1958, they increased their share of parliamentary seats.

Although the left began in 1962 to consolidate, if not strengthen, its
position, the Gaullists were more successful in advancing their electoral and
parliamentary fortunes. The UNR won more than a third of the votes,
sharply increasing its 1958 share.[12] At the same time, the conservatives split
into two different groups. One group, called the Républicains Indépendants
and led by Valéry Giscard d'Estaing, decided to throw in their lot with the
Gaullists. Giscard's Independent Republicans—or Gaullist Conservatives, as
they also may be called—were later to compete with the "pure" Gaullists
for position and power within a combined Gaullist bloc, but during the period treated in this book they remained allied with the UNR (and its successors) on virtually all critical occasions.

The conservatives who remained hostile to de Gaulle were reduced to a
mere splinter group. They won some 10 percent of the votes in 1962, but
they won few seats. The Independent Republicans, on the other hand, won
half as many votes at the first ballot, but they were not opposed at the second ballot by Gaullists and therefore won almost as many seats as the anti-
Gaullist conservatives did. Gaullism was beginning to make serious inroads
into the French right, by winning the support of the Independent Republicans and by directly attracting voters with right-wing political sympathies.

Presidential Election of 1965

The next electoral consultation after the legislative elections of 1962 was the
presidential election of 1965, the first direct election of a French President in
well over a century. Although for a while de Gaulle adopted the not uncommon strategy of United States presidential incumbents of appearing uncertain over whether to be a candidate, it was no great surprise that he
decided to run, thus becoming the standard bearer of the Gaullists, including both the UNR and the Independent Republicans.

De Gaulle's principal opponent at the presidential election of 1965 was
François Mitterrand. Mitterrand had impeccable anti-Gaullist credentials, as
in 1958 he had opposed bringing de Gaulle back into power and had opposed approving the Constitution of the Fifth Republic. Mitterrand an-

nounced his candidacy for the presidency at a time when Communists, Socialists, and Radicals were drawing closer to one another in the hope of defeating de Gaulle, and he had the great advantage of not belonging to any of those three parties, which might well not have been able to agree jointly to support a single candidate coming from any one of them. Communists, Socialists, and most Radicals found Mitterrand acceptable, and they threw their support to him as the sole left-wing candidate. Thus, another step in the forging of a leftist electoral bloc was taken.

A third candidate of some prominence was Jean Lecanuet, an MRP senator and the mayor of Rouen. Lecanuet was supported by the anti-Gaullist conservatives and the withering MRP (which had reached a postwar low in electoral support at the legislative elections of 1962).

Three minor candidates also competed at the election. One was Jean-Louis Tixier-Vignancour, who was the candidate of the extreme right-wing opponents of de Gaulle, including Vichyites and the outraged former North African colonists who had migrated to Metropolitan France after Algeria became independent. Another was Pierre Marcilhacy, a virtually unknown, middle-of-the-road senator. The third minor candidate was Marcel Barbu, a businessman without any political connections, whose motives in running were not easily fathomable.

The results of the presidential election surprised most observers, possibly because of the extent to which they differed from the results of the referenda of 1961 and 1962 (see Table 1-2). De Gaulle failed to win a majority at the first ballot, and it was necessary to hold a run-off ballot between the two

Table 1-2. Results of presidential election, December 1965 (Metropolitan France).

Votes and candidates	First ballot, December 5		Run-off ballot, December 19	
Votes				
Registered voters	28,233,167		28,223,198	
Voting	24,001,961		23,862,653	
Abstentions	4,231,206	(15.0%)	4,360,545	(15.4%)
Blank or void ballots	244,292		665,141	
Valid ballots	23,757,669		23,197,512	
Candidates				
De Gaulle	10,386,734	(43.7%)	12,643,527	(54.5%)
Mitterrand	7,658,792	(32.2%)	10,553,985	(45.5%)
Lecanuet	3,767,404	(15.9%)		
Tixier-Vignancour	1,253,958	(5.3%)		
Marcilhacy	413,129	(1.7%)		
Barbu	277,652	(1.2%)		

front-runners.[13] That meant a straight fight between de Gaulle and Mitterrand, once again pitting Gaullist and anti-Gaullist forces directly against
each other, but this time within the highly charged and sharply focused
context of a presidential election. De Gaulle won at the second ballot, but
his margin of victory was not large. By pooling their efforts, the left-wing
parties (with the help of determined anti-Gaullists from other sectors of
opinion, including the extreme right) had been able to hold de Gaulle's
support well below the levels it had attained at the various referenda. Another major step had been taken toward the unification of the leftist parties
for electoral purposes, and the image of de Gaulle's electoral invulnerability
had been shattered.

Partisan Regrouping, 1965–1967

After the presidential election of 1965, the French party system rapidly took
on the basic characteristics that, with few exceptions, it was to display into
the 1980s. The framework of the new structure was the presence of two
large electoral blocs, each consisting of two main partisan groups. Other
not insignificant political forces were also in the competition during the late
1960s, but the dynamics of the situation were thrusting relentlessly toward a
quadripartite structure.

   One major electoral bloc consisted of the Gaullists, including both the
orthodox Gaullists of the UNR and Giscard d'Estaing's Independent Republicans. The latter had joined forces with the pure Gaullists in 1962, and
they supported de Gaulle for the presidency in 1965. Prior to the 1967 elections, Gaullists and Giscardians agreed to present a single candidate in each
district under the label Ve République. Thus, the components of the Gaullist bloc did not compete with each other at all in 1967, not even at the first
ballot. Of course, the balance of forces within the Gaullist bloc was asym-
metrical at this time; the orthodox Gaullists were dominant. But in districts
where the right was normally strong, the Independent Republicans were assured of electoral victory because they were not opposed by orthodox Gaullists. They were therefore able to maintain their separate identity as a party
and provide organizational support for their leader, Giscard d'Estaing.
Eventually, Giscard relied on that support as the springboard for his
successful race for the presidency in 1974, and the balance between Giscardians and Gaullists approached equality at the legislative elections of
1978. But in the immediate context of our study, all that was still a part
of the future.

   At the same time, equally impressive efforts at partisan regrouping
were being carried out on the left. François Mitterrand pressed forward with
a new group, of which he was president, called the Fédération de la Gauche
Démocrate et Socialiste (FGDS). The Federation was an umbrella organization embracing the Socialist party, the Radicals, and a recently formed
group called the Convention des Institutions Républicaines (CIR), which

itself was a kind of federation of clubs for left-wing intellectuals seeking to breathe new life into French leftist politics (without having to mount the hierarchies of the existing left-wing parties in the customary fashion).

The Federation, which brought new solidarity to the main elements of the non-Communist left, allied with the Communist party and the smaller PSU at the legislative elections of 1967, thus unifying the entire left for the purpose of counteracting the Gaullists electorally. The left-wing bloc was not so disciplined as the Gaullists, but it achieved a degree of cooperation that the left parties had not displayed at any previous election since World War II. The parties of the Federation, like the two Gaullist parties, ran a single candidate in each district that they contested. For the first time in French Republican history, Socialists and Radicals did not compete with each other at the first ballot. The Communists ran a candidate of their own in every district, and the PSU also ran candidates in about one hundred districts. Therefore, left-wing voters had a choice of candidates at the first ballot: Federation, Communist, or, less frequently, PSU. But all three groups agreed to withdraw in favor of their best-placed candidate at the second ballot, in every district where the left had a chance of winning. In that sense, there was a left-wing alliance in 1967 that was more extensive and formalized (and, in the event, more effective) than the limited and informal alliance of 1962. In effect, the leftists displayed the same kind of solidarity at the legislative elections of 1967 that they had shown in 1965 by backing Mitterrand as the single leftist candidate for the presidency.

Although the steps taken by the left-wing parties to pool their electoral resources were impressive, it is also true that there was a fierce element of competition among the leftist parties, particularly between the Federation and the Communist party. Those two groups were much more evenly balanced in terms of popular support than the UNR and Independent Republicans were within the Gaullist bloc, but when the leftist alliance was in its incipient stage, the Communist party had been the dominant electoral force on the left. When the Socialists and Radicals joined forces within the Federation, the balance was significantly redressed. Indeed, in the light of later events, the creation of the Federation appears as the first major step by François Mitterrand to build a non-Communist formation that would surpass the Communist party in electoral appeal. Just prior to the 1967 elections, both the Federation and the Communist party could perceive themselves as entering a test to determine which one would emerge as the major French leftist group.

Both groups had reason for optimism. Mitterrand had done comparatively well at the presidential election of 1965, and his name was associated with the new Federation. The Communists, who had suffered a decline in electoral support under the Fifth Republic, gained in political respectability after the presidential election. Their support for Mitterrand earned them good will among the non-Communist left. De Gaulle's foreign policy, once he was freed from preoccupation with Algeria, turned increasingly toward emphasizing independence from the United States, a theme which the Communists had also consistently broadcast. When, in 1966, de Gaulle withdrew France from the North Atlantic Treaty Organization and visited Moscow in the effort to symbolize French freedom of action, the Communists lost much of the stigma that had attached to them as Russian lackeys. De Gaulle, who had once called the Communists "separatists," now both facilitated the creation of a leftist electoral alliance and contributed to its success.

In that fashion, two broad, competing coalitions were formed, Gaullist and leftist, and these were to dominate French electoral politics during the late 1960s, throughout the 1970s, and into the 1980s.[14] This is not to say that other groups did not compete electorally. At the 1967 election two other clearly distinguishable formations were present as well. One was the Centre Démocrate (CD), led by Jean Lecanuet and consisting of the two parties that had supported his presidential candidacy in 1965. The other was the Alliance Républicaine pour les Libertés et le Progrès (AR), which was led by Jean-Louis Tixier-Vignancour, who had been the candidate of the extreme right at the 1965 presidential election. Thus, in 1967 the voters had a choice among four distinct groups, representing respectively the left, the center, the Gaullists, and the extreme right, each of which had also been represented at the presidential election of 1965. The big battalions, however, were the Gaullists and the left. That had already been demonstrated at the presidential election, and it was to be demonstrated time and again at subsequent elections.

The Twilight of Gaullism, 1967–1969

The late 1960s was a period of turmoil and political transition in several Western democracies, but in none as much as in France.[15] Within a period of two years, France experienced an astonishing gamut of political events: virtual stalemate between the Gaullists and their opponents at legislative elections in 1967; the greatest display of mass discontent in a modern democratic country in May 1968; a Gaullist electoral triumph in June 1968; de Gaulle's defeat at a popular referendum in April 1969, followed immediately by his resignation and slightly later—in June 1969—by the election to the presidency of Georges Pompidou, who had been de Gaulle's aide for many of the postwar years and his Prime Minister from 1962 until 1968.[16]

Part II of this volume presents an extensive account of electoral politics in France, based on data relating to the 1967 legislative elections. The analysis of those elections, however, is not historically oriented, and it will be of help to the general reader if we enlarge somewhat here on their context and character. Part III discusses in comparatively brief compass the mass up-

heaval of May 1968 and the ensuing elections from a more historical vantage point. Here, therefore, we will simply sketch out how those events fit
into the dramatic sequence that crowded the late 1960s in France. Finally,
we will say a few words about the referendum and presidential election of
1969. Although those developments do not fall within the subject matter of
this book, they round out, almost tragically, those that we do treat, and
they draw the final curtain across the remarkable de Gaulle era.

The 1967 legislative elections were the first "normal" elections of the
Fifth Republic, in that they took place at the expiration of the full term of
office of the Assembly elected in 1962.[17] But if 1967 brought quieter times,
they were not to last for long. The 1967 election produced a parliamentary
stalemate, while anti-Gaullist sentiment proceeded invisibly to gather increasing support of uncommon intensity.

In 1967 the Gaullists gained slightly and the leftists lost marginally in
first-ballot votes relative to the elections of 1962, but the leftist parties were
more effective than they had been in 1962 in pooling their strength at the
second ballot in order to win seats. Despite their comparatively favorable
popular showing, the Gaullists lost seats while the left gained more than
forty (see Table 1-3). The result was a National Assembly that was very
difficult for the government of Prime Minister Georges Pompidou to manage.[18] The Gaullists had difficulty producing majorities, and the government resorted frequently to the arsenal of procedural weapons placed at its
disposal by the Constitution of 1958 precisely for the purpose of prying unwanted decisions out of a refractory parliament. Fissures appeared within
the Gaullist bloc as Giscard d'Estaing's Independent Republicans, who had
fared better in 1967 than the Gaullists of the UNR (relative to their show-

Table 1-3. Votes and seats (Metropolitan France, 1967, 1968).

Party	1967		1968	
	% Votes	Seats	% Votes	Seats
Communist (PCF)	22.6	72	20.1	33
Unified Socialist (PSU)	2.2	4	3.9	—
Federation (FGDS)	18.9	116	16.4	57
Democratic Center (1967); Progress and				
Modern Democracy (1968)	12.7	40	10.4	31
Independent Republicans (RI)	5.4	40	6.3	60
Gaullists (UNR, 1967; UDR, 1968)	32.2	190	37.3	282
Miscellaneous	6.0	8	5.6	7
Total	100.0	470	100.0	470

Sources: République Française, Ministère de l'Intérieur, *Les Elections législatives de 1967* (Paris:
Imprimerie Nationale, 1967); and République Française, Ministère de l'Intérieur, *Les Elections
législatives de 1968* (Paris: Imprimerie Nationale, 1969).

ing of 1962), pressed hard to increase their weight in policymaking; Pompidou referred to Giscard as "the cactus" (Alexandre, 1970).

At the same time, the mood of large segments of the public was becoming increasingly anti-Gaullist. Disillusionment with the Gaullist regime
among certain critical groups had already been evident at the 1967 election.
Middle-of-the-road voters, of the kind who had voted for Lecanuet at the
first ballot of the presidential election of 1965 and then voted for de Gaulle
at the second ballot, voted for the Democratic Center at the first ballot of
the legislative elections and then voted for leftists at the second ballot.
Workers became more assertive. Although 1967 was far from a "historic"
strike year, more man-days were nevertheless lost by strikes during 1967
than in any other year of the Fifth Republic except 1963 (which was notable for an unusually long miners' strike). Perhaps the most destabilizing
force was the emergence into adulthood of the vast population born between 1947 and 1951. At the end of 1967, the 16–20 age group was the most
numerous five-year slice of the French population. The flashpoint of these
combustible elements was, of course, the university students. The average
annual growth in the university student population for the five years preceding the academic year 1967–1968 had been more than 12 percent, and
the growth for the single year from 1966–67 to 1967–68 was more than 16
percent.[19] None of this pointed inevitably toward a massive social upheaval,
and still today the lines of causation remain obscure. But we do know that
the French electorate moved sharply leftward between 1965 and 1967. In retrospect, the upheaval of May 1968 seems an outburst born of frustration
among discontented people who had almost, but not quite, defeated their
Gaullist rulers at the ballot box.[20]

The 1968 upheaval began in Paris early in May with student demonstrations and rioting that quickly spread to provincial universities as well.
Prime Minister Pompidou was out of the country when the student revolt
started; ministers on the scene were indecisive or unwise; and de Gaulle does
not appear to have taken the affair seriously. Unions seized the opportunity
to exploit early sympathy for the students by demonstrating and calling 24-
hour strikes, at first only in the western departments, then throughout the
entire country on May 13, the anniversary of the colonists' revolt in Algeria
that had brought down the Fourth Republic. But events slipped out of the
control of the unions as well. Wildcat strikes and factory seizures followed
the organized demonstrations, and by the third week of May the country
was virtually paralyzed.

The strike movement was impressive in its own right, but the distinctive feature of the May upheaval was the proliferation of mass demonstrations, in which there was very substantial middle-class participation. Thus,
French students, workers, and middle-class men and women, particularly
among the young, registered their dissatisfaction massively. But while most
of the demonstrations were peaceful, some turned into riots. Even as the

opposition groups gained courage from their obvious numbers, they were striking fear among the regime's supporters and the disengaged. These were largely invisible during May, but as events turned out, they were more numerous than the regime's opponents.

De Gaulle's behavior during the upheaval was successively disdainful, ineffectual, discouraged, and decisive. Prime Minister Pompidou returned to France soon after the outburst, but de Gaulle visited Rumania for several days during the middle of May, uttering on his return the formula: "La réforme, oui; la chienlit, non." De Gaulle took no initiative until the country was already at a virtual standstill; on May 24 he went on television and announced his intention to hold a referendum on a vague proposal to give the chief of state a mandate to "reconstruct the university system" and to adapt the economy "to the national and international needs of the present." The speech disappointed his followers, failed to rally the uncommitted, and was followed by a night of rioting in Paris and the provinces.

Events were moving toward a showdown, with Pompidou staking the outcome on negotiations with the union leaders (and by indirection the Communist party)[21] and Mitterrand announcing that he would be a candidate at the presidential elections that he confidently expected were imminent, when de Gaulle disappeared for twenty-four hours. He had gone to the headquarters of French forces in Germany at Baden. When he returned to France, he announced over the radio that he was postponing the referendum he had proposed a week earlier and dissolving the National Assembly. The situation became transformed almost immediately. Massive pro-Gaullist demonstrations, sometimes matching in magnitude the largest of the earlier anti-Gaullist ones, erupted the same day in Paris and the following day in the provinces. Counterdemonstrations were also organized, but opposition steam was running out. Electoral traditions are deeply rooted in France even if the referendum is not. Strikers could have prevented de Gaulle from conducting a referendum, but they dared not interfere with constitutionally sanctioned legislative elections. French men and women gradually returned to work, and the parties squared off for the electoral contest to be held at the end of June.

It was widely believed at the time that de Gaulle's disappearance had been a deliberate maneuver, and that he had gone to Baden to assure himself of the loyalty of the French troops stationed in Germany. But Pompidou (1982, pp. 192–199) contended in his memoirs that de Gaulle had left Paris in a mood of deep discouragement, that it was the military commander at Baden who had stiffened his resolve, and that it was Pompidou himself who had insisted that de Gaulle dissolve the National Assembly.[22] Whatever may have happened, the dissolution defused what was still an inflammable situation. The focus of attention shifted from barricades to ballots.

As in 1967, the electoral conflict in 1968 was characterized by the clash between two electoral coalitions: the Gaullists and their Independent Republican allies on one side, and the coalition of leftist parties on the other. But unlike 1967, which was something of a standoff, 1968 produced a right-wing victory of historic proportions. The Gaullists and their partners won some 45 percent of the votes and 70 percent of the seats.[23] The Gaullist party—now called the Union pour la Défense de la République (UDR)—won a majority of the seats by itself, the first time in French electoral history a single party had done so. With the gains of the Independent Republicans added to those of the UDR, the size of the overall Gaullist majority was overwhelming. The leftist parties lost votes, as well as a disproportionately large share of seats. The fears aroused by the demonstrations and violence during the weeks preceding the election had been parlayed by the Gaullists into anti-Communist sentiments that severely weakened the leftist bloc. Non-Communist leftists (and centrists) who had voted for Communists at the second ballot in 1967 in order to defeat the Gaullists did not do so in 1968. The May–June revolt, created by growing leftist antagonism to the Gaullist regime, resulted in a backlash that strengthened the Gaullists and weakened the left. Squeezed by the two large polar blocs, the heirs of the Democratic Center, now called Progrès et Démocratie Moderne (PDM), continued to decline. The extreme right ran very few candidates and won even fewer votes in 1968 than it had won in 1967.

The Gaullists, presenting themselves as the "party of order," emerged from the May crisis stronger than ever, but the standing of de Gaulle himself suffered, first among the elites, later among the electorate as well. The constitutional system that de Gaulle had established survived the shocks of May, but de Gaulle's authority had been diminished. De Gaulle was to suffer still another blow in August, when the invasion of Czechoslovakia by Soviet and other Warsaw Pact troops demonstrated the futility of his opening to the Soviet Union as a way of counterbalancing United States influence in Europe.

In the spring of 1969 de Gaulle pressed forward with plans to hold a referendum on a complicated measure providing for the reorganization of the Senate (France's indirectly elected and largely powerless second chamber) and the establishment of regional councils. Presumably, this was the sort of referendum that de Gaulle had had in mind during May 1968 but had been forced to abandon at that time. The issues, however, lacked the drama and appeal of the questions de Gaulle had brought directly before the voters in earlier years (the Constitution, Algerian policy, direct election of the President). Few Gaullist leaders threw themselves into the fray enthusiastically; Giscard d'Estaing advocated voting "No"; Pompidou campaigned in favor of de Gaulle's position but refused to stake his career on the outcome, as de Gaulle had done. Indeed, Pompidou had already made it known that he was available for the presidency once de Gaulle no longer held the office, thereby blunting the edge of de Gaulle's customary announcement that he would resign if the referendum did not carry. It did not; 53 percent of the voters cast a "No" vote. De Gaulle resigned as soon as the results were known. The de Gaulle era had come to an end.

De Gaulle's resignation made it necessary to hold a new presidential election, which took place in June.[24] The configuration of candidates at the 1969 election was quite different from that of 1965. Georges Pompidou became the single standard-bearer for the Gaullists (including the Independent Republicans). The left-wing parties, however, did not unite behind a single candidate as they had done in 1965, when they jointly supported François Mitterrand. Leftist unity was temporarily broken by the events of May. The Communists were annoyed at Mitterrand because he did not coordinate his activities with them. At the same time, anti-Communism again rose to a high level because of the May upheaval, Gaullist electoral propaganda, and the Czechoslovakian invasion, leaving the non-Communist left anxious—for the moment—not to be closely associated with the Communist party. Accordingly, there were several leftist candidates for the presidency in 1969: Jacques Duclos, a longtime leader of the Communist party; Gaston Defferre, a Socialist and mayor of Marseille; and Michel Rocard, then the leader of the PSU. Another leftist candidate was Alain Krivine, an extreme leftist who ran as a representative of the revolutionary current of May.

With the left divided, the centrists considered that they had a real chance of winning. Their candidate was Alain Poher who, as President of the Senate, had played a leading role in the campaign to defeat de Gaulle at the April referendum, and then had become interim President of the Republic upon de Gaulle's resignation. Poher was backed by a segment of the PDM (some PDM leaders, however, supported Pompidou), the Radicals, and even some Socialist leaders. Another candidate, in the quixotic tradition established by Marcel Barbu in 1965, was a wealthy businessman named Louis Ducatel.

As in 1965, no candidate won a majority at the first ballot (see Table 1-4). Pompidou won about the same proportion of the vote as de Gaulle had won at the first ballot in 1965. This time, however, the runner-up was not a leftist; the fragmentation of the left caused its strength to be dispersed among the several left-wing candidates, even though it added up to almost as large a proportion of the vote as Mitterrand had won in 1965. Poher came in second, although he won less than a fourth of the votes. Duclos came in third and did better than his party had done at the legislative elections of 1968. The remaining candidates, including even Defferre, who had been a nationally known figure for many years, won only small fractions of the vote.

The second ballot was a runoff between Pompidou and Poher. Defferre

Table 1-4. Results of presidential election, June 1969 (Metropolitan France).

Votes and candidates	First ballot, June 1		Run-off ballot, June 15	
Votes				
Registered voters	28,774,041		28,761,494	
Voting	22,492,059		19,854,087	
Abstentions	6,281,982	(21.8%)	8,907,407	(31.0%)
Blank or void ballots	287,372		1,295,216	
Valid ballots	22,204,687		18,558,871	
Candidates				
Pompidou	9,761,297	(43.9%)	10,688,183	(57.6%)
Poher	5,201,133	(23.4%)	7,870,688	(42.4%)
Duclos	4,779,539	(21.5%)		
Defferre	1,127,733	(5.1%)		
Rocard	814,051	(3.7%)		
Ducatel	284,697	(1.3%)		
Krivine	236,237	(1.1%)		

advised his supporters to vote for Poher at the second ballot, but the other three left-wing candidates (including Duclos, acting for the Communist party) advised their supporters to abstain, as they saw no political difference between Pompidou and Poher. Pompidou won handily, obtaining a larger proportion of votes than de Gaulle had won at the second ballot in 1965. But there were fewer voters at the second ballot in 1969 than there had been at the second ballot in 1965; almost a third of the electorate abstained. Many left-wing voters followed the advice of their first-ballot choices and remained aloof from the runoff between a Gaullist and a centrist. But Georges Pompidou had won the election; on June 15, 1969, he became the second President of the Fifth Republic. The post–de Gaulle era had begun.

2

French Voters and Their Party System

We have seen that there are many continuous threads in the history of French party competition since World War II. The three national elections of the late 1960s contained numerous echoes of the 1946 struggle between de Gaulle and the right, on one hand, and the Communist and Socialist left, on the other, over the development of a constitution for the Fourth Republic. Nevertheless, to focus exclusively on these continuities is to ignore what is most distinctive about French politics over this period: the persistent and dramatic flux of the manifest political parties and their fortunes at the polls. Of the three major political groupings which dominated the reconstruction of France after the Liberation, only the Communist party by 1969 remained in anything like its earlier form, and many other parties, even some relatively large ones, had arisen and died in the interim. Indeed, some observers have considered this electoral instability to be one of the prime sources of a more far-reaching instability in the nation's fundamental political institutions.

The role of the political parties over time in France is of intense interest to us, because it is through these vehicles that the French voter expresses his policy demands on government. The party system provides the clearest channels of communication between the mass public and elite decisionmaking. Although political parties more often than not grow up extraconstitutionally in modern democracies, the communication and representation function is basic to their existence. In countries like France, where party discipline in legislative decisionmaking tends to be relatively strict, the shape of the party system, and the nature of the voter's interaction with it, become the more critical as we trace out the processes which lie between citizen preferences and the ultimate decisions of state.

We will spend this and the following chapter examining the interaction between French voters and their national party system in some detail. We shall first review the evidence that France has shown an instability in party voting patterns in recent decades which is truly distinctive compared with the experience of other nations. Then we will turn to a rather elaborate dissection of some of our own data, addressed to the fundamental question as to the source of this instability. Does it arise primarily from some peculiar tendency to fickleness that individual French voters bring with them to the polls, or is it more properly seen as a product of the party and electoral system to which those voters are asked to respond? With initial answers to this question in hand, we will proceed to sketch out some important features of the cognitive maps that French voters hold of their party system. We will wait until Chapter 3 to consider the ways in which French voters relate themselves by emotional ties to particular parties in that system over time.

The Nature of Electoral
Instability in France

The sheer facts of electoral instability in France are not hard to establish. For example, Rose and Urwin (1970, pp. 287–319) analyzed the relative variability in the fortunes of nearly one hundred political parties within nineteen democracies over the quarter of a century after World War II. An index of instability of voter support is on the average two and a half times as great for the six French parties selected by the investigators as for the mean for all the rest of the parties from other countries catalogued. The French instability mean is also more than 50 percent greater than the next most unstable democracy of the nineteen countries.[1] And even these data tend to underestimate the true instability of the voting record in France, since some of the parties monitored were analytically aggregated from party factions that at times had been in bitter competition and presented candidates under different party labels. Moreover, a number of French parties could not be included in the catalogue for the simple reason that they were so short-lived they could not generate time-change statistics.[2]

To document the unique instability of French party support at the polls does not, however, carry us very far toward an understanding either of the phenomenon itself or its implications for the rest of the political system. In fact, it is not clear precisely at what level the unusual variability arises. At first glance, we might conclude that the French voter is uncommonly fickle in his partisan affections. This conclusion, however, is somewhat risky short of further information. Summaries of change in vote totals from election to election focus entirely on *net* change. Although it is clear that French voters must change their parties from election to election at substantial rates to produce so many dramatic shifts in party fortunes, it would be going well beyond these data to argue that *gross* change over time in party voting is unusually high in France simply because it is clear that *net* change is distinctively large relative to other countries. It is conceivable that mass voters in other countries are equally fickle or even more so, but that for some reason their movements between parties tend to cancel one another out, so that a great deal of gross interchange at the individual level fails to register in much of the *net* change of aggregate party fortunes. Or, to take a somewhat different tack, let us consider the frequency with which French voters going to the polls discover that the party which they preferred at the preceding election no longer is offering a candidate in their districts. If they are delighted to change their votes because of the creation and discarding of party formations at an elite level in France, it would be erroneous to accuse them of any extraordinary infidelity.

It is useful to begin our diagnosis of voting variability in France at the individual level, examining in particular whatever evidence we may muster as to the changeability of the French voter himself relative to voters in other countries. If we can establish unusual partisan fickleness at this level in France, then we may be less motivated to look in other directions.

The most detailed inspection of this question at the individual level has been provided by MacRae (1967). For a number of French elections after World War II he compared current party preferences given by French voters with the party which they recollected having voted for at the preceding national election. His measure of individual stability is in effect the proportion of voters whose party preference over two elections remained constant, as opposed to the proportion who made some switch in parties. Restricting his analysis to those French voters supporting parties which showed during this period the least aggregate change in vote proportions over time ("stable parties"), he finds that there is if anything more frequent repetition of votes in France than is reported by respondents in the United States for successive presidential elections. Thus he concludes that in France, at least where stable parties are concerned, there is less underlying individual instability of support than for the two major American parties, also obviously "stable" ones (MacRae, 1967, ch. 8).

These findings are surprising, and if they could be generalized to the total French electorate, they would imply that there is no unusual fickleness of party preference among voters there, and that sources of aggregate vote instability must be sought at other levels. But the exclusion of voters for those very transient parties that represent what is unique about French electoral politics, while useful for MacRae's specific purposes, clearly limits the generality of comparisons between the two electorates in ways that seem likely to overstate stability of party choice on the French side. Moreover, when MacRae was writing, the only way of assessing rates of individual change over time was to depend on rather long-term recall on the part of the voter with respect to the earlier party voting.

We are fortunate in having available for both the United States and France surveys on the same panel of respondents reinterviewed at several points in time, in direct connection with more than one election. Reinterviewing the same persons provides an immediate monitoring of individual constancy of partisanship over time, without dependence on the respondent's ability to recall accurately how he might have felt about party alternatives years back into the past.

Such recall is demonstrably faulty, as our panel studies make clear. For example, in a major national panel survey of the American electorate conducted by the Survey Research Center in the late 1950s, only 83 percent of voters in 1958 recalled their 1956 presidential vote behavior in the same way that they had reported it immediately after that election, with regard to the turnout and party choice decisions. In the more complex and confusing French voting system it is likely that recollection is even more precarious: as little as one and a half years after the 1967 legislative election, only 65 percent of our French panel respondents gave a report identical to that made at the time of the election. Clearly voters in both systems have trouble remembering earlier vote choices with any reassuring degree of accuracy, and as memory erodes, the door is open for all sorts of bias and distortion. Some of these lines of distortion are well-known: in both systems, respondents tend to exaggerate their turnout as time elapses, and also report ever-increasing proportions of votes cast for winners rather than losers.[3] It is also reasonable to expect that such recall overestimates stability of preference for some individuals whose memory is dim but who tend to adjust their reports of past vote to whatever their current party feelings may be.

The MacRae comparisons were also drawn between American presidential voting and French legislative voting. Since net change in U.S. aggregate presidential vote returns runs signally higher than such change in Congressional voting, it would seem useful to shift the comparative base so that legislative voting is treated on both sides, and our American panel data make such comparisons possible.

Controlling Discrepancies in Voting Systems

There remain a number of important conceptual difficulties in making our comparisons as rigorous as possible, because of marked differences between the voting systems of the two countries. One simple example involves the run-off, or two-ballot, system of conducting general legislative elections in France during the Fifth Republic. In order to track constancy of party preference over time in French elections that are most comparable to United

States estimates, should we compare the first ballot in 1967 with the first ballot in 1968, or should we turn to second-ballot results? Most scholarly analyses of French election data are performed on first-ballot material. This is done in part because there is greater dispersion of the results before races are narrowed to a few leading candidates for the second ballot, thereby capturing more nuances of opinion. It is also done because second-ballot results are somewhat incomplete because, as we have seen, there are no second-ballot returns in the minority of districts where the election is decided at the first ballot.

Particularly when the investigator is working across time, including Fourth Republic returns where only a single election was used, the first ballot appears to recommend itself as the proper choice. For our interest in tracing out the full opinion representation process, however, it can be argued that the second ballot, where one is required, is by far the more important of the two, as this determines the actual representation in the National Assembly. What seems to be the happiest solution to this dilemma has been provided by François Goguel, who has used the notion of the "decisive ballot." Thus he mingles data from first ballots that elected a clear winner with data from the second ballot in run-off districts (Goguel, 1946, p. 247; also see Goguel, 1968, pp. 843–844). This obviates the problem of partial second-ballot returns. For our estimation purposes, we shall keep track of party constancy in voting both for first ballots over time and for "decisive" ballots in the Goguel sense.

We have already referred to another difficulty in cross-system comparisons of vote stability: there may be basic differences in the likelihood that any given voter even has the opportunity to vote for the same party alternative at successive elections, quite apart from his preferences in the matter. The vast majority of American voters choosing between the Democratic and Republican alternatives at one election will find exactly the same party alternatives available at the next election. Many French voters, however, will proceed to the polls knowing that the party they voted for in the preceding election is either defunct or at least not offering candidates in their particular districts. Any vote variability that arises from this source is clearly not a matter of the individual fickleness that we are trying to estimate, but rather a source of variation at the system level of elite decisionmaking. Therefore for both the American and French cases, we have examined vote stability across pairs of elections, setting aside those cases in which the choice at the first election was not available for selection in the second election.

It is but a small step to another consideration that involves similar system differences. In some elections, voters find themselves confronted by exactly the same constellation of parties and specific candidates as in the preceding election. As a commonsense matter, it would seem likely that voting choices would tend to be more constant when the party offerings are

exactly the same than when there are different elements in the choice. Moreover, it would be reasonable to imagine that this situational variable might
be quite different in different political systems such as France and the
United States, for reasons independent, once again, of the individual fickleness of the voter. To proceed one step further: between the case where the
individual cannot possibly repeat his vote, and the case where he is confronted by exactly the same set of candidates he evaluated before, lies a
whole continuum of possibilities reflecting the degree to which the local
offerings in the legislative election duplicate or depart from those presented
in the previous election. And again, it would be reasonable to imagine that
there are enough system differences in the constancy of selection offerings
that they must be taken into account in any rigorous effort to sort individual variability from system effects.

Therefore we have commissioned a control variable which reflects the
degree of turnover in election offerings, and which we have maintained
through all of our analyses. In the case where there is complete turnover of
offerings between one election and the next, the index registers .00. Where
the offerings in the second election are identical to those in the first, the
index takes a value of 1.00. It should be clear that such an index can be defined both for constancy of candidate offerings and for constancy of party
offerings, and that generally the index for candidate offerings will be lower
than that for party, where there is less turnover of offering from election to
election. In the American congressional district, the value of the index for
party offerings almost always approaches 1.00. For candidates, however, the
index tends to lie a bit below .50. This reflects the fact that the typical congressional contest involves an incumbent who ran at the preceding election
and gained a majority of the votes (although usually less than 60 percent),
pitted against a challenger who did not run at the preceding election.

Although we are interested in the index of constancy in election offerings less for its own sake than as a control on system differences which
should not be confused with individual propensities, it is of fair interest to
see how the French and American voting systems do differ in the constancy
of alternatives presented from election to election. These data are arrayed in
Table 2-1, where the percentages refer to proportions of individuals encoun-
tering second elections under varying degrees of constancy of candidate or
party offerings, relative to first elections, for the French and United States
panel studies. We see in the first row that total turnover in parties being
represented simply did not occur in either system in this period. In France,
total turnover of candidate offerings never occurred either, although about
one voter in eight in the United States encountered a complete turnover of
congressional candidates in his district. In both systems, however, substantial proportions of voters could not repeat their particular candidate choices
at the second election, and much smaller proportions did not find even the

Table 2-1. Percentage comparisons in constancy of party and candidate offerings in successive legislative elections, France (1967–68) and the United States (1956–1958, 1958–1960).

| | France | | | | | | United States | | | |
| | Decisive ballots, all districts | | Decisive ballots, two-party districts | | First ballots, all districts | | All districts | | Two-party districts | |
Constancy level	Candidate	Party	Candidate	Party	Candidate	Party	Candidate	Party	Candidate	Party
Respondent could not repeat first election choice										
Total change of offerings	0.0	0.0	0.0	0.0	0.0	0.0	13.0	0.0	13.1	0.0
First election choice not offered, second election	25.0	5.4	24.3	2.6	32.6	4.8	25.9	1.2	30.4	0.4
Respondent could repeat first election choice (index of constancy of offering)										
0.30–0.39	0.0	0.0	0.0	0.0	2.2	0.0	0.5	0.0	0.7	0.0
0.40–0.49	0.0	0.0	0.0	0.0	6.2	0.0	0.4	1.0	0.4	0.0
0.50–0.59	14.2	3.0	16.3	4.7	1.8	0.5	22.7	0.2	26.5	0.2
0.60–0.69	10.7	5.0	9.5	3.7	15.0	2.4	14.9	0.8	15.8	0.0
0.70–0.79	4.5	4.0	0.0	0.0	16.2	11.2	5.1	0.6	5.7	0.4
0.80–0.89	2.8	0.0	1.0	0.0	12.7	10.2	1.3	1.0	0.1	0.0
0.90–0.99	3.7	0.0	1.9	0.0	8.8	20.6	2.9	0.6	0.1	0.0
1.00 (direct replication of offerings)	39.1	82.6	47.0	89.0	4.5	50.3	13.3	94.6	7.2	99.0
Total	100.0	100.0	100.0	100.0	100.0	100.0	100.0	100.0	100.0	100.0
N	(394)	(394)	(212)	(212)	(423)	(423)	(1832)	(1750)	(1338)	(1329)
Mean index value	0.631	0.905	0.648	0.940	0.501	0.888	0.435	0.976	0.369	0.993

party they had chosen at the first election represented at the second (see second row, Table 2-1). All of these voters for whom simple repetition of choice was impossible at the second election are disregarded in the subsequent analyses of constancy in candidate and party choice, respectively.

The bottom row of Table 2-1 gives a mean expression for the constancy index encountered by voters in the two countries under the various conditions, where the first two rows have been scored as a .00 circumstance (repetition precluded). As we have anticipated, there is almost perfect constancy of *party* offerings in congressional voting in the American case. It is not surprising, either, that less party constancy is encountered in France, although the values are not so far below those for the United States as might have been imagined. More noteworthy are the data on *candidate* constancy, which runs consistently *higher* for France than for the United States. The difference is not too impressive when constancy is measured from the first 1967 ballot in France to the first ballot in 1968. But the values advance very significantly when decisive ballots are considered. Clearly French parties offer the same legislative candidates in successive elections with greater frequency than occurs in the United States, and the effects of the first-ballot winnowing away of minor, stray candidates is to produce an ultimate constellation of surviving candidates which tends to look much more like the set of surviving candidates in the preceding election than is customary in the United States.

Basically, our interest lies much more in party constancy than in candidate constancy. But enough is known about the independent influence of candidates on voting choice to lead us to expect that where party constancy is high, there will be more switching of votes if there is high candidate turnover than if there is little or none.

Another system difference which makes rigorous comparisons of vote fidelity difficult is the fundamental contrast between the two-party American case and the French system with its multiplicity of competing parties. As MacRae (1967) pointed out in his work, it may not be reasonable to consider the shift of a vote from one party of the left to its next-door neighbor in France as representing quite the same degree of behavioral instability as would be implied by a switch from, say, a Democratic vote in the United States to the only opposition, the Republicans. It is for this reason that we have included in Table 2-1 the data for both countries which apply only to districts involving competition purely between two parties. It will be noted that in such two-party districts in France, confined to decisive-ballot situations and almost always pitting a major party of the left against the Gaullists, constancy in party offerings advances toward the United States value. Candidate constancy, however, advances in these districts as well, departing even more widely than the general French case from the range of situations faced by American voters.

There is one final consideration to be made before we examine the vote stability results. In one sense, the MacRae data are superior to ours, because they cover a larger range of time. That is to say, while there may be characteristically different ranges of vote stability by country, it is reasonable to doubt that vote stability within a single country would show perfectly constant rates over time. For a variety of reasons, including different lapses of times between elections (in France) and variations in change-inducing events between different pairs of successive elections, we would expect any estimates of vote instability of the kind we are about to make to show some intracountry variation from election to election. MacRae brings this variation under reasonable control by sweeping across a number of successive elections for both countries, so that the sampling of elections, if not large, still has a good chance of revealing more characteristic national values. Although we find our panel data much more reliable for such estimates, our panel surveys are far more limited in time: there was only one pair of successive elections available for France (1967–68) in this general postwar period, and two adjacent pairs for the United States (1956–1958 and 1958–1960).[4] If by chance these samples of one and two "cases," respectively, happened to have fallen at elections whose change rates were unrepresentative, our estimates would be correspondingly misleading.

Our only protection against this potential difficulty was to pay attention to any specific peculiarities of these elections in each country. In particular, we considered whether *net* changes in party support, as calculable from aggregate voting statistics, were running unusually high or unusually low for the elections involved in our panel studies, relative to other elections in the same general period in the two countries. Now, as we have seen, there is no necessary correspondence between rates of net and gross change in voting, save for the fact that net change can never exceed gross change. But in a commonsense way, we might as an empirical matter expect enough correspondence between visible net change and underlying gross change to find net-change assessments an important qualification for our panel estimates of stability.

Therefore we made net-change calculations for aggregate vote stability by party over a broader span than the period within which our panel data fall. These data are presented in Figure 2-1. The measure used to compare vote proportions by party in successive elections is the simple cumulated percentage difference; that is, for the aggregate results for any pair of elections we asked by what sum of percentage points the first distribution would have to be "adjusted" to bring it into identity with the second distribution. If the two percentage distributions were already identical, the index would take a value of 0.00, and it would increase as the two distributions became more and more disparate from each other. The calculations were entirely straightforward in the American case because of the stable identities of the two major parties. They became much more discretionary in the French case, for it was necessary to decide, for any given brace of

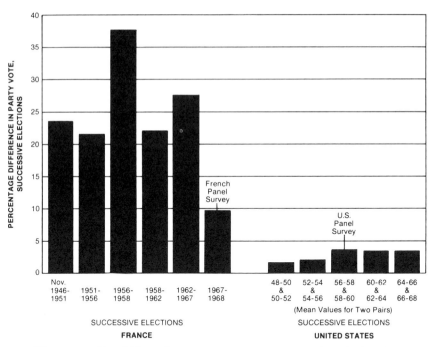

Figure 2-1. Instability of aggregate party vote proportions in legislative elections, France and United States, 1946–1968.

elections, whether various related parties would or would not be considered to be the same.[5]

We discovered, somewhat to our dismay, that our panel surveys happened to have been carried out when net instability in party fortunes was at a very low ebb in France but at a modest high point in the United States. It is not hard to understand why the 1967–68 French transition shows such relative aggregate stability despite the intervention of the large-scale disturbances of May and June 1968 and a substantial change in the party composition of the National Assembly in the second election. The time between these two elections—about fifteen months—was much briefer than any of the other transition periods, and there was no intervening formation or termination of relatively large parties, as had characterized virtually every other transition in the series.

All told, Figure 2-1 indicates that in the degree gross change tends to co-vary with net change, the accidents of our panel timing load the dice toward a considerable overestimate of French voting stability, and at least a slight underestimate of party constancy on the American side. What this means analytically is that if we discover the French voters in our panels to show more stability of party choice than American voters, we will have no way of knowing whether this was a product of the unrepresentative time periods involved or whether it shows some more reliable and meaningful difference between the electorates in their individual dispositions toward party fidelity. Let us keep this problem in mind as we turn to the constancy estimates themselves.

Estimates of Individual
Constancy in Voting Choice

It will be recalled that we have set aside those voters in both electorates who were excluded, by the nature of the party or candidate offerings in the second election, from any possibility of repeating their first-election choice. Thus our measure of individual vote stability is simply the proportion of citizens repeating their vote at the second election, relative to the total set who had the possibility of doing so. Even this operational definition is incomplete: what is to be done with individuals who fail to vote in the second election? We have prepared two sets of estimates: the first is limited to two-time voters who either repeated their first vote or made a distinctly different choice at the polls in the second election; the second adds people who voted at the first election but not the second to the denominator of the proportion, as potential repeaters who chose not to exercise the privilege of repetition.

In Table 2-2 we provide the grand summary of the individual vote stability values for parties and candidates across election situations in the two countries, without any control on differences in the constancy of election offerings. Table 2-3 gives the country comparisons after such controls are applied.[6] These displays represent our most exacting effort to contrast the individual stability of the French and American voter, with the effects of system differences in the structure of the voting situation minimized. Perhaps the most obvious feature in both tables is the relative similarity of the data from the two countries. If the French voter is distressingly fickle, as the changeability of aggregate vote data from France would suggest, it is not overwhelmingly obvious on the basis of these tables alone.

A more searching examination has generated two other broad impressions. First, it is clear, especially from the more important Table 2-3, that vote stability is persistently lower in the French first-ballot context, almost as though there is some tendency for the French voter to approach the first ballot in an experimental mood, especially when that ballot is unlikely to be decisive. At the same time, it would not do to push such an interpretation very far, since other results to be discussed later (Chapter 12) show that when the French voter's first-ballot candidate choice survives for the second round of voting, he or she very rarely switches away from that choice for the second *tour* (round of voting). Nonetheless, we can see from these data that earlier scholarly focus on first-ballot results tends to exaggerate somewhat the instability of partisan choice in the French electorate.

Table 2-2. Individual stability of voting choice at successive elections in France and the United States (unadjusted for election offerings).[a]

Choice	France, 1967-68				United States (1956-1958 & 1958-1960)	
	First ballots: all districts	Decisive ballots: all districts	Decisive ballots: two-party districts		All districts	Two-party districts
Candidate						
Percent repeating vote, based on two-time voters	81.1 (304.5)	87.6 (305.5)	92.8 (153.5)		86.2 (874)	85.8 (639)
Percent repeating vote, based on all voters at first election	75.6 (326.9)	78.8 (339.9)	80.1 (177.9)		76.5 (984)	78.3 (700)
Party						
Percent repeating vote, based on two-time voters	76.8 (429.0)	85.0 (387.4)	93.1 (204.8)		83.3 (1366)	82.7 (1073)
Percent repeating vote, based on all voters at first election	71.0 (463.9)	76.6 (430.1)	80.9 (236.0)		74.1 (1535)	74.9 (1184)

a. Based on panel data; restricted to cases where vote repetition possible. Case numbers are in parentheses (weighted for France, unweighted for the U.S.).

Table 2-3. Individual stability of voting choice at successive elections in France and the United States (with constancy of election offerings controlled).[a]

Choice		France	U.S.
Candidate			
Based on persons voting in both elections	French first ballot all districts vs. U.S. all districts	80.8	86.2
	French decisive ballot all districts vs. U.S. all districts	89.0	86.2
	French decisive ballot two-party districts vs. U.S. two-party districts	91.4	84.8
Based on all voters in first election	French first ballot all districts vs. U.S. all districts	74.7	76.5
	French decisive ballot all districts vs. U.S. all districts	79.9	76.5
	French decisive ballot two-party districts vs. U.S. two-party districts	79.3	77.2
Party			
Based on persons voting in both elections	French first ballot all districts vs. U.S. all districts	73.5	83.1
	French decisive ballot all districts vs. U.S. all districts	85.9	83.2
	French decisive ballot two-party districts vs. U.S. two-party districts	93.5	82.7
Based on all voters in first election	French first ballot all districts vs. U.S. all districts	69.9	75.4
	French decisive ballot all districts vs. U.S. all districts	76.8	74.0
	French decisive ballot two-party districts vs. U.S. two-party districts	81.1	74.9

a. Based on panel data; restricted to cases where vote repetition possible.

The second impression is that the French results, varying from less stable in the first ballot to more stable in the second, actually turn out to bracket the counterpart data from the United States with its less complex simple-plurality system. If first ballots are less stable in France, second ballots appear more stable. The latter differences are not always large enough to seem significant, as in the case, which is ultimately most interesting to us, of candidate choice in matched two-party situations. Moreover, we have already digested a basic message from Figure 2-1, which says that our French panel data come from a transition which was unusually stable for France, whereas our United States panel data come from a transition which was marked by unusual instability in that country's electoral history. Therefore, we would be hard-pressed to argue that the modest signs of greater French stability at decisive ballots, relative to the United States, are more than situational in the most short-term sense of the word.

In any event, one major conclusion emerging from these analyses can be asserted flatly. This is the simple fact that much of the marked partisan instability shown by the French electorate in its natural voting pattern—that is, outside of the highly controlled conditions we have examined—arises from system-level differences in party politics and the organization of voting in France, rather than from any dramatic oddities in the temperament of the individual French voter. Once we go beyond the multiplicity of parties and the inconsistencies in their presentation over successive elections, the peculiarities of the run-off system for polling the public, and the other institutional features we have analytically removed from consideration, the French voter in the microcosm does not appear blatantly different from his American counterpart.

Voter Perspectives on the Total Party System

We have shown that when French voters are confronted by party and election configurations similar to those typical for the United States, they display rates of fidelity in party voting which approach those of American voters. This demonstration is important at a theoretical level. It should not, however, conceal the fact that French voters do not find themselves confronted by election conditions of the American type with any great frequency. Most typically, even at the local level, they are asked to respond to a party system which is large and mercurial. This complexity at an institutional or system level appears to make a very basic contribution to the unquestionable and dramatic aggregate instability of party voting over time in France. Therefore it is now important to ask in more detail how the French citizen sees this customarily kaleidoscopic system of parties.

The size and fluidity of the French party system intrude on any attempt at systematic study of the electorate. In a preceding sample survey conducted during the change in regimes in 1958, respondents were asked in open-ended fashion which of the current political parties they generally preferred. In most countries, such a query produces a very limited array of responses, which can be coded routinely into one or another specific party category. The 1958 French responses, however, posed many coding problems. A substantial fraction of voters gave no single recognizable party at all. Instead, mention was made of admiration for a particular local or national political personality, or solidarity was expressed for some more or less concrete social groupings ("workers," "Catholics," "patriots," and so forth). Other voters responded with labor union affiliations or feelings of broad *tendance* (tendency) on the left-right spectrum.

Even setting aside for the moment these many stray citations of types other than specific party attachments, it still took twenty code categories to capture in any reasonable detail the 1958 references to unique political groupings of that year. In 1967 we repeated the same question, and this time twenty-one distinct party designations were required to represent the mentions of specific parties. Over the period of less than ten years between the two surveys, only nine party names on the two lists were the same. Thus some thirty distinct party designations were actively being used by one voter or another in our samples at the beginning and end of a decade. In between the two surveys other parties had arisen and died. Moreover, for this period there were additional party labels that would have been familiar to the well-informed, but whose support was so esoteric that no sympathizers happened to turn up in our surveys. All told, it would not be an exaggeration to imagine that the close observer of French party politics in this era might have needed to recognize forty to fifty different labels or sets of initials, representing more or less distinct political formations. The foreigner awed by the obscurities of French parties need not be embarrassed: the mental chore involved in keeping track of such a system is not to be taken lightly.

From one point of view, this prolific generation of political parties makes the French system a most commendable one. For whatever else it accomplishes, the system does offer an astonishing variety of choice, and choice is the vital ingredient of democratic theory. To be sure, a great multiplicity of parties poses severe problems of justice and fair representation when it comes to forming decision rules about the way in which actual ballots are to be aggregated into a distribution of legislative seats. But at the grass roots, which is our main focus for the moment, the richness of choice offered by the French party system could be regarded as a voter's delight.

The French voter does not, however, view his party system in exactly this light. Whereas he might be happy in the abstract with an abundance of voting options, he is distinctly discontent in practice with the proliferation of parties. In both 1958 and 1967 respondents were asked whether they thought the number of parties then current in France was too large, too small, or about right, and they were also asked what number of parties they thought would be ideal for the system. The 1958 questions were posed at a time when the collapse of the Fourth Republic had made the public particularly impatient with the Byzantine complexities of multiparty maneuvering in the National Assembly that left the government more often than not immobilized despite the need for rapid action. Therefore it is not surprising that this discontent was registered in popular reactions to the teeming landscape of parties. Nevertheless, the massiveness of the negative reaction in 1958 remains impressive. Less than 3 percent of French voters felt that the number of parties was suitable, and another half percent felt it was too limited. More than 97 percent of citizens expressing opinions indicated that there were too many parties. Since as little as 70 percent agreement on touchy political issues is often thought of as relative "consensus," this degree of unanimity concerning the improper shape of a basic political institution is breathtaking.

By 1967, the development of the Fifth Republic's strong executive powers had drawn some of the public's wrath away from the political parties per se. Moreover, the expansion of the UNR to more than 30 percent of the popular vote, with the Communists remaining generally over 20 percent, meant that over half of the vote spoils in the later 1960s were concentrated within two major parties, a matter which was likely to decrease public sensitivity to party proliferation. Nonetheless, dissatisfaction with the sheer size of the party system remained at what by any absolute standards must be considered high levels. In 1967, almost 80 percent of French voters continued to feel that the party system was larger than it should be.

More interesting still are the data concerning the optimal number of parties for the French nation. In 1958 the modal desire in the electorate was for a three-party system, and the mean number of parties seen as optimal was 2.9. By 1967, despite the mild decrease in annoyance at the size of the party system that had taken place since 1958, the modal view as to the ideal situation for France had shifted to the two-party case, with a mean of only 2.5 parties now seen as optimal. Indeed, the set of 1967 respondents who believed that the number of parties in the system was then "suitable" gave a mean value of 3.0 parties as ideal for France. Thus there is evidence of some perception that the party system had simplified itself over the preceding decade, as it probably had in terms of the concentration of the popular vote within a few large parties. Despite this trend toward concentration and simplification, however, the French electorate continued to complain at rather massive levels about the proliferation of parties.

We can illuminate what underlay this discontent by asking what segments of the electorate were most anxious to have a simpler system. Views as to the optimal number of parties varied rather clearly as a function of other attitudes concerning the party system. Respondents were asked, for example, how important a role they felt the political parties should play in the governing of France. A very substantial majority—nearly three out of four giving opinions—felt that the parties should play at least a fairly important role, representing a significant endorsement of parties in principle, beyond the issue of their proliferation. Not surprisingly, it was among the minority who doubted that the parties should play much of a role that the size seen as ideal for the party system was smallest. Or again, respondents were asked to indicate how different they thought the parties were from one another. Here the call for a simpler system was strongest at the two extremes of judgment: people who felt there were already many important differences between the existing parties, and those who tended to discount the importance of differences between the parties—people undoubtedly skeptical of the role of parties more generally. It was the intermediate group seeing moderate differences—about a quarter of the electorate—that was least unwilling to accept a more complex system.

More important still, perhaps, is the fact that on every attitude item concerning the party system, it was the "don't know" category (typically 10–15 percent of responses on the subject) that showed the smallest mean number of desired parties. In other words, citizens who were most psychologically remote from the party system wished to simplify it most thoroughly. This proposition can be extended: it was the people who were least involved in following politics, generally speaking, who envisioned an ideal French system with the fewest political parties. One would expect a similar relationship with education, and as Figure 2-2 shows, there was indeed a progressive acceptance of a more complex party system as education increased.

Such a pattern of relationships dovetails nicely with a view of the French party system as being something of a comfort and indulgence for the elite. In any country, there are multiple axes of political controversy, and in the simple two- or three-party system this means that many logically possi-

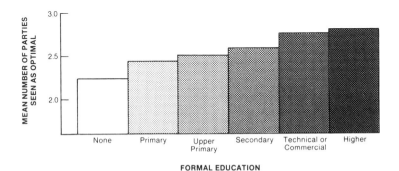

Figure 2-2. Optimal number of parties desired for France, by levels of formal education, 1967.

ble combinations of issue positions cannot be expressed. Politicians in such a system are frequently obliged to accept positions taken by their own party with regard to one or more issues that they personally may not find comfortable. While this happens in France as well, it happened much less frequently in the period of our study. If a prominent French politician found himself strongly out of sympathy with his own party on some new axis of controversy, whether it involved ideological positions, choices of parliamentary or electoral coalitions, or questions of individual leadership, it was not uncommon for him throughout the postwar period to attempt to start a new political party that would express his personal configuration of views precisely and would avoid the awkwardness of compromise and strange bedfellows. Indeed, these were the common sources of party creation in France. In terms of classic normative democratic theory, there is nothing wrong with such party proliferation. If there is a defensible configuration of positions on issues of the day that is not well represented by any existing party, it can be seen as a public service to provide that package of options in a recognizable party.

What such a formulation leaves out, however, is the empirical fact that few members of a national electorate find it very rewarding to spend time following the finer nuances of elite political competition. The formation of a new party is undoubtedly ideologically satisfying to the political elites involved, and it gladdens the hearts of a small stratum of admirers in the mass public who are the most sophisticated and involved. But such events, particularly when they occur frequently, are likely to create a sense of needless complexity and confusion for much of the electorate, which would be quite satisfied with a more limited set of gross options. It is in this sense that the French party system has been tailored more to elite needs than to mass reality. The variation in preferred system size by formal education and political involvement is merely a symptom of this mass-elite discrepancy.

Although the most politically involved members of the French electorate were less extremely discontent with the large party system than other voters, we should not leave the impression that they, at least, were truly contented with the system in that form. Even well-educated activists in the mass electorate tended far more often than not to criticize the proliferation of parties, and their modal preference was for a three-party system, a state of affairs that would have been a radical simplification of the French political reality they faced.

The Visibility of
Specific Political Parties

We are moving toward a consideration of the ways in which our French voters related themselves to favorite parties on the public scene. In most systems we could consider how preferences among party alternatives are established without any further preface. In the French case, however, the size and complexity of party options are such that we are forced to ask a prior question: what party alternatives did the common French voter recognize as being available at the time of our studies? It would not be surprising to find that information about the full range of party alternatives was less than perfect in the electorate as a whole.

Our questionnaire was designed to measure two levels of salience for specific parties in the system. Before the interviewer mentioned any party names, the respondent was asked to cite the names of as many parties as he could. This was the measure of spontaneous recall. Then the respondent was given a list of ten of the most prominent recent French political party formations and was asked whether there were any parties on the list which he knew but had forgotten to include among the party names he had already cited. This was the measure of recognition, or what may be taken as indicative of some cognitive presence of the party in the voter's mind, although at a lower level of salience than for parties recalled spontaneously. There is internal evidence that these measures fall short of perfect validity, since some respondents failed to indicate even recognition of a political party which they later claimed to be their favorite among the alternatives. Nonetheless, we can reasonably expect these measures to yield a rough reflection of the distribution of information concerning components of the party system.[7]

Figure 2-3 summarizes this distribution of information over all parties used and all members of the electorate. We see in the upper-left-hand corner that only 94 percent of the electorate indicated recognition of at least one party, which is to say that 6 percent failed to indicate recognition of any. Nearly three times that proportion—about 16 percent—failed to cite even a single party spontaneously. Moving down the deeply shaded "recall" portion of the graph, we note that the median number of parties cited is less than four, although a small fraction of the electorate spontaneously named virtually all of the parties on our list.[8] Necessarily, a much wider range of parties was at least recognized: the more informed half of the electorate knew almost all of those presented.

What are the implications of these data? It is perhaps easier to begin by reviewing what the implications are not. The existence of a handful of persons who do not appear even to recognize a single party is not in itself shocking: every large electorate contains some chronic nonvoters who simply refuse to participate in the electoral system at all, and France is no exception. Moreover, it goes without saying that where only two or three parties in the system are recalled or recognized, they tend very disproportionately to be the dominant current parties, or what may be loosely seen as the main alternatives, monopolizing 60–80 percent of the popular vote. Recognition of at least these parties might be taken as constituting a rough

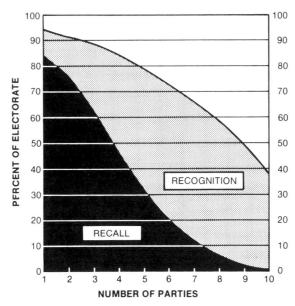

Figure 2-3. Numbers of French political parties cited or recognized by varying proportions of the electorate, 1967.

working knowledge of the party system, enough to make voting choice a meaningful act. Cognitive vagueness about an additional fringe of minor parties on the part of many citizens is no overwhelming indictment of the French party system or of the gross contours of its operation.

But it remains of theoretical interest to us that by no means all of the party alternatives being offered by the French system at a given time have much subjective reality even for the active electorate, much less the non-voters. There are, as it were, empty places here and there in the French voter's cognitive landscape of his or her party system, where the informed outside observer sees a meaningful political alternative. This fact will be important to us as we turn to more systematic models of party choice for France, for it is all too easy to assume perfect information at the outset, and then end up struggling to arrive at tortured explanations of why given voters failed to select a party that seems rationally appropriate for them, when the simpler fact of the matter may be that they are at least vague about, and perhaps completely ignorant of, that party's existence and suitability. Or, to put the matter another way, we would probably evaluate individuals who shifted their votes from the Communist party to the UNR in successive elections, according to whether these were the only parties in the system that had much subjective reality for them, quite differently from those who deliberately sidestepped a large number of intervening parties of which they were well aware.

Differences in the Visibility of Specific Parties

It is of interest to decompose the data of Figure 2-3 to ascertain how widely the major and minor French parties differ in respect to their visibility to the electorate. Clearly the most familiar party to the French electorate in 1967 was the Communist party (PCF): over three-quarters of the electorate cited it spontaneously, and most of the rest indicated recognition when prompted by our list. At the other extreme lay two relatively new splinter parties which, as we shall come to appreciate, shared many parallel characteristics, despite their respective locations at opposing ends of the ideological spectrum: the PSU to the far left and the Alliance Républicaine of Tixier-Vignancour to the far right. The PSU was the older of the two, having already presented candidates at the 1962 legislative elections, and hence it is not surprising that 21 percent of the electorate mentioned it spontaneously, as opposed to only 8 percent for the Alliance Républicaine. Yet the visibility of these two extreme parties differed less than such figures suggest. The PSU was the creation of the New Left, and although prized in intellectual circles as a palatable alternative to the senescent radicalism of the Communist and Socialist oligarchies, had not achieved great national currency in the mass electorate. The Alliance Républicaine was smaller and certainly newer, but it had produced a somewhat greater national splash as the 1967 party of the extreme right. Therefore we find that only 42 percent of the electorate failed to show recognition of the Alliance Républicaine, despite its low frequency of recall, while 47 percent showed no recognition of the PSU.

In a more general way, the correlation between spontaneous recall of parties and their mere recognition is less than perfect across our ten listed parties, although most of the visibility discrepancies between the two levels of salience could readily be understood.[9] Nonetheless, it is worth cumulating the two levels of salience, giving double weight to spontaneous recall, in order to arrive at a rough summary measure of overall visibility by party. In Figure 2-4 the bar for a party would occupy the total space (height of 2.0) if all members of the electorate recalled the party spontaneously; and it would occupy half the space (height of 1.0) if recalls and nonrecognitions balanced off perfectly or if only recognition occurred.

The overall patterns of visibility by party fit commonsense expectations. Generally speaking, the largest active parties in the system were the most salient, while splinter parties or moribund parties prominent in an earlier period were less widely visible. It might seem curious, however, that the Communist party received more frequent recall and recognition than the UNR, which had been winning half again as many popular votes as the

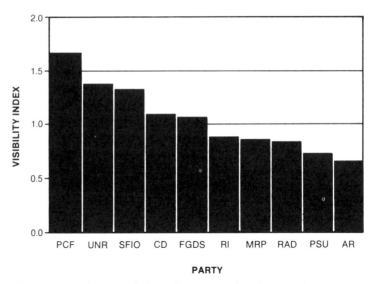

Figure 2-4. Relative visibility of various political party formations to members of the French electorate, 1967. The Visibility Index is formed by scoring the spontaneous recall of a party as two points, its passive recognition as one point, and the absence of either as zero points.

PCF during the 1960s, and had the added advantage of being the party of the governing administration. Similarly, the Socialists (SFIO) were almost as salient as the UNR, despite having drawn little more than one-third as much voting strength in the 1960s. Moreover, in the 1967 election itself the SFIO identity was somewhat blurred by the participation of its candidates under the banner of the Fédération de la Gauche (FGDS).

These patterns are perplexing mainly because we assume that party visibility at any given time is some direct and simple function of party size at that time, or at least of size as measured at the most recent national election. It is obvious that 1967 voting strength was indeed an important determinant of variation in party visibility: the correlation between the 1967 vote size of the various parties and their recall or recognition just after that election is .27.[10] But the data strongly suggest that constancy of a party as an important and stable object of perception over a lengthy period of time increases its visibility in the eyes of the mass public. For example, the voting strength of parties in the 1962 legislative elections actually shows a slightly strong correlation with 1967 party visibility (correlation of .29); and if we average 1962 and 1967 voting strength as our predictor, the correlation rises to .32. Moreover, if we add in computations of voting strength for the 1967 parties at still earlier postwar elections, the multiple correlation advances to .36.

Some joint function of size and historical constancy thus seems important in accumulating high visibility. In these terms, the PCF and the SFIO were by far the "senior" parties among the major ones active in the mid-1960s. Unlike the UNR, they had been prominent among the three or four most dominant parties under exactly those labels in all elections since World War II, and had been on the scene for decades before. Of course, sets of people informally known since the Liberation as "Gaullists" had operated in French party competition. But they had done so under a sequence of different labels, and even in 1967 they were in the process of shifting to yet another designation.

Such purely nominal change may seem very innocuous, but there is reason to believe that it has a dimming effect on party visibility. Until the public becomes adjusted to the new name, for example, references to the party in the media suffer a basic loss of meaning. Of course, this adjustment occurs overnight for the avid followers of the political scene. For the usually inattentive public, however, the penetration process may take a period of years.

Individual Differences in Awareness of the Parties

Attentiveness varies widely across the electorate, as Figure 2-3 has attested. Some French citizens have no difficulty in rattling off the names of ten or more political parties, while a fraction at the other pole does not seem to recognize as much as one party even when prompted by a list. It is obvious that the recognition and recall data can provide us with an excellent individual-level measure of knowledge of the party system, and one which should be highly discriminating. We have in fact built such a measure, which we call "total party visibility." This consists of the sum of each respondent's party visibility scores (as shown in Figure 2-4) across the full array of ten parties, which can, therefore, range from 0 to a maximum of 20.

It is not surprising that the index of total party visibility is correlated both with political involvement more generally and with the respondent's level of education. That fact is worth mentioning, however, inasmuch as the correlations with both terms are quite substantial (over .40) and are higher than the correlation between education and involvement themselves. In fact, since this measure of information has been summed across party citations, so that it involves somewhat equal units, it may not be too fanciful to observe that people of advanced education display two to three times as much information about the parties as the vast majority of the French electorate (about 65 percent), which has only primary education. In part because of the negative association between age and education, the young showed a rather marked tendency to have more knowledge of the parties than the aging.

It also follows consistently that voters more oriented to the party system in their political behavior display more knowledge of the parties. Respondents were asked whether they attributed the greatest importance to the identity of local candidates, the national party leader, or the political party itself in forming their voting decisions. About one respondent in twelve insisted on adding to these fixed alternatives the information that he gave special attention to the issues or policy program involved, and these people show the highest party knowledge of all. But party knowledge is considerably higher in the substantial portion of the electorate (about 40 percent) claiming to focus mainly on the parties than it is among those who give main weight to local candidates or national leadership.[11]

There is also a correlation between knowledge of the parties and the perception that there are more differences between them. The evidence suggests that experience in shopping among parties contributes to familiarity with the system: people who report having voted for different parties in the course of their lives show considerably higher knowledge of them than persons who maintain that they have always voted for the same party.

Finally, we note a strong curvilinear trend in party knowledge when the electorate is sorted according to the number of parties thought desirable for France. The greatest party knowledge is concentrated among advocates of a three-party system, although those wishing a system of four to six parties are fairly knowledgeable as well. The plurality desiring a two-party system is less knowledgeable; more ignorant still are those who call for systems of one party or seven or more parties, and most especially those who say they do not know what size the system should be.[12] All told, we get a picture of some watershed in the electorate between the relatively sophisticated voters, who are oriented to parties as vehicles of popular politics and who keep fairly close tabs on party developments, and another large segment, which displays less interest in politics, follows the party system only vaguely, and pays most attention to the personality aspects of political competition.

Individual versus System
Factors in Party Visibility

We have seen that two quite distinct classes of factors bear on whether an individual will recall or recognize a given party in the French system. One set of factors is composed of what the person brings to the situation as an individual, such as his customary attentiveness or inattentiveness to what is going on in the political world around him. The other set of potent determinants is represented by the parameters of the situation he confronts, such as the size and constancy of the specific party being tested for, along with other system-level attributes of the parties which are, for any individual, "givens." We can decompose our party visibility data, based as they are on about two thousand individuals confronting each of ten parties, into some twenty thousand (nonindependent) instances of the cognition of a single party by a single individual. With the data in this form we can ask which class of factors—the individual or system level—is generally more potent in accounting for whether or not a given party is recalled, is recognized, or passes unperceived by an individual.[13]

It turns out that system-level properties—attributes of parties—are vastly more important in accounting for these responses than measures of individual attentiveness. Any such statement must be made guardedly, since it is always possible that some individual-level attribute we did not think to measure or include in the analysis would, if added, account for sweeping new proportions of variance in recognition of parties. There would be room for such new terms, since system and individual variables put together do not account for quite one-fifth of the total variance. But it is implausible that any simple individual-level predictor that would have enormous importance has been left out.[14]

An assortment of variables at both levels were included in this analysis. On the individual side, predictors like age, education, occupational status, two measures of political interest and involvement, a measure of the individual's left-right location, left-right distance from the party in question, and strength of personal partisanship were all used. On the system side, numerous attributes of the specific parties were employed, including terms representing size (voting strength) and historical constancy, as well as the extremism of the party, its location on the left-right continuum, whether or not the party operates under relatively personalized leadership, whether it ran candidates in the respondent's district in 1967, and so forth.

The two most potent predictors at the individual level turned out to be political interest and education. None of the other individual variables made more than miniscule additional contributions to the prediction, and few of them were even significantly correlated with party recognition in a zero-order sense. Yet education and political interest jointly accounted for little more than 2 percent of the variance in recognition of individual parties.

On the system side, almost any single party attribute we employed accounted in a zero-order sense for significantly more variation than this total effect of education, interest, and all the other individual-level variables combined. By far the most noteworthy determinant, as expected, was the simple expression of party voting strength in the 1960s, although terms representing earlier historical size made a further substantial contribution to the prediction. The likelihood that a given party ran candidates in 1967 in the respondent's district was quite strongly correlated with overall party size; nonetheless, that variable made a further significant contribution on its own to the individual recognition of given parties. Similarly, parties that were true organizations, as opposed to entourages of prominent political leaders, were most likely to be recognized as parties by the public. It is also true that perceptions of parties were clearer when they were extremist than when they were centrist: the PSU and the Alliance Républicaine showed higher levels of recognition than less extreme minor parties of comparable historical constancy.

All told, the set of party attributes accounted for more than eight times the variance that could be associated with all of the individual-level variables put together. It is important not to confuse this kind of contrast with our earlier assertions about the marked importance of education and political involvement in accounting for individual variations in the index of party visibility. Both types of conclusions are true at their respective levels of analysis. The party visibility index sums information held by the individual across all major parties in the system, and thereby excludes from consideration any intrasystem variation in party attributes. Individual differences in education and involvement jointly accounted for almost one-quarter of the variance in this measure, a rather substantial figure. For the second phase of our analysis, however, we disaggregated the party visibility estimates to permit differences in the system-level properties of specific parties to enter into consideration. In effect, we asked how these systematic differences between parties as objects of perception affected the probability that any given individual would recognize any given party, as opposed to the effects on that probability that were tied to individual differences. And we found that when party attributes were permitted to vary in this sense, these system-level factors dwarfed the individual-level effects. While individual voters do differ in their alertness to what is going on in politics, the imperfections in knowledge of the national party system which are so substantial in France can be tied squarely to the unusual proliferation and transience of political parties that characterize the system.

Conclusions

There is more than a little family resemblance between the results of the first large analysis reported in this chapter and the one which we have just encountered. In the first instance, we found that much of the high instability of fortunes that French political parties encounter at the polls seemed to be generated by distinctive characteristics of the national party and electoral system, rather than by any mysterious fickleness on the part of individual voters. Given the limitations of our data bases, which dealt with an unusually stable election transition in France but one of relatively large change for the United States, we could not conclude that all of the manifest party change in France was due to systematic peculiarities. Nonetheless, it was clear that as we limited our examination of the stability of party voting to small subsets of French voters operating under "American" election conditions, there was a convergence toward degrees of partisan constancy similar to those found for the United States.

In like fashion, we have shown that much of the imperfection in information that French voters display at any point in time about their party system can be traced to some of its key peculiarities, such as the variety and fluidity of its party organizations. Thus the institutional arrangements that have surrounded popular voting in France figure prominently in accounting for the channels, so distinctive by cross-national standards, that French behavior at the polls has seemed to follow. It goes without saying that elite actors have been more responsible for these institutional features than the citizenry at large.

Let us keep in mind that our ability to trace much of the distinctiveness of French voting behavior to such system-level factors in no sense changes the distinctiveness of the behavior. When confronted with electoral alternatives most parallel to those of American voters, the French voter may behave in a similar fashion. But the fact remains that few French voters find themselves in a situation of the American type. Similarly, although the imperfect information held by most French voters concerning current party alternatives may be a function of various unusual properties of the party system, the distinctive consequences remain. Depending on the attentiveness of the voter, there are in fact empty spaces in the furnishings of these cognitive maps that must be dealt with in any models of voting choice for France.

Up to now we have considered what the French voter thinks of his party system as a whole, as well as his awareness of specific parties within it. In a later chapter we shall have more to say about his detailed cognitions of those parties which he recognizes. First, however, it is important to ask about the nature of the sentiments and loyalties that he forms toward individual parties, for this is perhaps the most important single feature of the way he relates to national political life.

3

Party Loyalties
in France

In several of the countries where popular voting was first studied by sample surveys, scholars were impressed by the degree to which the emotional attachments formed by voters toward specific political parties seemed to become remarkably durable over time, as well as pervasive in their effects, lending a predictable coloration to all manner of political evaluations. Thus these identifications with parties came to be seen as the chief stabilizing element for voting at a mass level. In view of the relative instability of French voting patterns, whatever stabilizing terms do exist in that political culture are of uncommon interest for us. Now that we have sketched a rudimentary picture of the way in which the French voter envisions his party system, it is important to devote some attention to the role that such loyalties play in France.

In the course of much empirical work with party identification, especially in the United States and Scandinavia, a considerable amount of middle-range theory grew up years ago around the formation and natural history of these individual allegiances.[1] It was recognized, for example, that although knowledge of a person's party attachment is the best single predictor of his voting behavior over time, the identified voter does not necessarily vote for his chosen party under all circumstances. From time to time he may become annoyed at the performance of this chosen party, or be attracted to some glamorous candidate of an opposing party, and therefore decide to defect for that election. Naturally, the piece of empirical theory surrounding the concept of party identification does not in itself predict such defections. But it does say that they will not be terribly common, and that they will become progressively less common, the more strongly developed the sense of identification is. Moreover, there is an important prediction to be made, even when defections do occur. This is simply that the odds strongly favor a return to the party of identification after the immediate pressures which produced the defection have been relaxed.

The phenomenon of party loyalty was also shown to have implications for mass political behavior extending well beyond the details of party voting. Allegiance to a party means that it becomes a positive reference group in judging all manner of political controversy (W. Miller, 1976). Most voters in the mass electorate pay so little attention to politics that they are frequently unaware of detailed issue positions taken by the leadership of their preferred party. But when they are aware of such positions, they are clearly influenced to adopt the same positions. This phenomenon becomes most impressive in the numerous documented instances in which loyal voters take on positions of their preferred party which are counter to what the outside observer would deem to be their rational self-interest. Yet the general acceptance of cues from the preferred party, as well as prejudicial rejection of leaders, positions, and actions associated with competing parties, tends to endow such party loyalties with a central role in the patterned stability which often marks mass political life.

In more recent years the cross-cultural generality of the party identification syndrome as documented for the United States has been severely questioned. Butler and Stokes (1969) found in their longitudinal studies that although British voters gave answers to questions about more generalized party loyalties, these statements were less durable in time than their American counterparts; and in particular, respondents had more difficulty distinguishing between such long-term orientations and how they intended to vote or had voted at the most recent election. These authors hypothesized that differences between voting institutions might create differences between the ways the two electorates thought about politics. In the United States, where voters are confronted with long lists of candidates for a great variety of offices, the guiding commonality is shared party affiliation. The British voter, however, only selects one candidate at a single level of government, thereby plausibly deflating the psychological importance of a repetitive party cue.

The possibility that responses to party identification questions might have rather different behavioral meanings from one political culture to another has attracted a great deal of attention. This insight became particularly important when some of the longitudinal voting studies being made in an increasing range of countries failed to replicate in one way or another the kind of party identification dynamics that had become so familiar for the United States and parts of Scandinavia. Budge and his associates (1976) provided a telling assembly of such negative evidence. Most noteworthy were longitudinal data from the Netherlands (Thomassen, 1976), which appeared to show that responses to an intended measure of party identification were at least as unstable as voting preference, and probably even more so! Recently other serious studies have shown rather different patterns of vote and party identification stabilities from one nation to another (for example, Leduc, 1981).

These discrepant findings make it particularly important to ask what role, if any, long-term loyalties to specific parties play as a stabilizing element in the French voting system. The question merely gains in urgency when asked in the context of popular representation, for the French legislative system is one of strict party discipline. Since the party bloc dominates national policy determination, voters interested in influencing policy must orient themselves to parties fully as much as to candidates.

The Meaning of Party
Identification in France

From one point of view, we already knew before our current research was launched that there was something highly distinctive about the status of party identification in France. Our earlier research there in 1958 had established that reported levels of loyalty were remarkably limited among French voters, relative to all other countries in which the phenomenon had been investigated (Converse and Dupeux, 1962). In part this decrement was represented by the fact, mentioned in the last chapter, that when French voters were asked what parties they generally felt closest to (the standard item for measuring party identification), a substantial number of them cited a variety of objects other than parties, such as prominent political leaders, labor unions, or general locations on the left-right spectrum. More noteworthy still was the extraordinary frequency with which French respondents indicated that they felt close to no party at all. In most countries examined, 75–90 percent of electorates readily report some generally preferred party of identification. The comparable figure for France in 1958 was unquestionably less than 60 percent, and might have been considered to be as low as 45 percent. It was natural to suggest at the time that there might be a functional relationship between this stunted development of conventional partisanship in France and the aggregate instability of party voting strength which had been so dramatic in that country during the postwar period.

Of course, it is quite possible to recognize peculiarly low levels of such reports in France without for a minute granting that expressions of partisanship, when actually offered by our French respondents, had a different meaning from that found in the United States or Scandinavia. On the face of the matter, it is not at all clear why the phenomena surrounding party identification should have either no meaning or a radically different meaning in France, because in a number of other settings these phenomena have been easily tied to very basic psychological processes.

In addition to our knowledge about the cue-giving functions of party as a reference group, a great deal is known about the dynamic patterns associated with party attachments over time. It is clear, for example, that they tend to accumulate in strength over the life cycle, so that old cohorts in electorates show deep-dyed identifications, while the youngest cohorts are much more weakly attached to any parties (Markus, 1983). It is also clear that there is in most countries a critical phenomenon of transfer of partisanship across the generations: young people growing up in partisan homes are very likely to adopt identifications with their "family party," and these feelings tend far more often than not to persist and strengthen. All of these attendant processes seem firmly rooted in the simplest and most universal facts of human experience, from socialization or rudimentary learning. It is not at all difficult to imagine that peculiarities of social and political culture may intrude to intensify or flaw these processes, or to channel them in unusual directions. But if this is the case, we continue to have interesting substantive findings on our hands, and not methodological artifacts, because a commonality of meaning and significance remains. What would be astonishing would be the discovery that a political culture had evolved in such a fashion that it had succeeded in exempting the total electorate from rudimentary processes of socialization or learning, or in some other way had left these processes intrinsically incomparable with the same processes in other countries.

Nevertheless, a growing awareness of politics in which party identification does not seem to have the same meaning as first established, along with the weak levels of response to normal party loyalty items in France, serves to keep the issue of some fundamental displacement of meaning there a lively possibility. Nor are the low levels of response the only signs of deviance. Elsewhere we have modeled the dynamic accumulations of party loyalties across the life cycle and across the generations in a way which, on the one hand, fits learning theory and, on the other hand, suggests that relatively new democracies are likely to have weak aggregate levels of partisanship, until after some generations they "mature" (Converse, 1969). Detailed survey data from the five rather disparate political systems studied two decades ago by Almond and Verba fit this process model quite admirably.[2] But it has also been obvious that France in the period of our early studies did not fit the model at all well. In terms of decades of voting experience—the key predictor—the French system was not much less "mature" than that of Great Britain. Yet the limited development of party loyalties in its electorate as of 1958 would have implied, if the model had been blindly applied, that democratic elections with male suffrage did not begin until the 1920s, instead of in the 1870s, as history assures us it did.

Therefore we must concern ourselves directly with the problem of the meaning of party attachments in France, including the possibility that the measurement operations themselves lack in some fundamental way the meaning they appear to have in countries like the United States. But how can we even approach such a delicate problem as the "fundamental meaning" the items have for respondents in French language and French culture? Let us recognize at the outset that it does not take much metaphysical ingenuity to push the issue of cultural relativism so far that no cross-national empirical confirmation is possible or, for that matter, worth trying. Needless to say, we shall stop short of that point. We will be persuaded that there is no prohibitive problem of the fundamental meaning of the operations if (1) it can be shown that the behavioral implications, correlates, and dynamic patterns of party identification across time are approximately the same for the minority of French voters who report an identification as they are for the majorities in other countries who make similar reports; and if (2) we succeed in demonstrating with some empirical rigor the peculiar factors which have intruded in the French case to leave its overall levels of identification in a state which is cross-nationally deviant. Success in these regards will give us reason to believe we are talking about significant substantive differences, and not mere artifacts of measurements.

Measurement of Party Identification in France

As efforts have been made to replicate the party identification measurement in other political cultures, another more practical difficulty has been encountered. Extreme care must be taken in translation of item wording and in application procedures. Some early casual efforts at duplication of this measurement produced unusual results; and it was established in Germany and elsewhere that what appeared to be small differences in wording and procedures (including the coding of responses) could produce rather remarkable differences in response distributions and other behavioral correlates of the measure (see Kaase, 1976). Indeed, this concern begins to blend with the more exalted question of conceptual meaning, for when data from this or that country are shown which fail to replicate normal dynamic patterns found for the construct in the United States, it is not always certain that the culprit is the underlying *meaning,* as opposed to the "national" differences in translation, interviewing, or coding procedures (see note 7).

However this may be, the lesson is that we must be very explicit here as to how we have gone about measuring party identification in France, and even more especially, perhaps, how the coding has been carried out. The root question has been imbedded in a section of the questionnaire dealing with the role of political parties. It reads: "Quel est le parti dont vous vous sentez habituellement le plus proche?" (To which party do you usually feel closest?) When any relevant object was named, the interviewer proceeded to ask: "Diriez-vous que vous vous sentez très proche de ce parti, assez proche, ou pas très proche?" (Would you say that you feel very close to this party, rather close, or not very close?) Thereby the interviewer provided an additional measure of identification strength. Among other wording requirements, experience has shown that if the notion of custom or generality is not conveyed, as by "habituellement" (usually), the responses reasonably enough lose their long-term meaning. When the phrase "generally speaking" is dropped from the parent United States question, for example, the responses come to behave over time very much as statements of momentary vote preference, thereby obviating the whole point of the party identification measurement.

The importance of an adverb like "usually" in the party identification question was not appreciated at the time of our involvement in an earlier French election study in 1958, a matter which robs us of a perfectly clean time series for French party identification covering more than a decade. Nevertheless, we do have two measurements from the autumn of 1958 which are instructive to compare with our three "readings" from 1967, 1968, and 1969. Although it is important to keep in mind the lack of perfect comparability at one important point, the administration and coding of these items has been identical, so that comparisons over time are less flawed than they would be with any other partisanship items available. Moreover, one of the features of the 1958 data of greatest significance for us is the small fraction of the French electorate professing a party identification; and presumably if the more restrictive adverb had been added to the question, the proportion reporting such an identification would be smaller still. Therefore the comparisons over the decade retain considerable interest. There are, however, still further impediments of a more general and serious kind to making simple statements about the prevalence of party identification in France.

There are three types of reasons for this difficulty. First is the coding problem, frequently mentioned above, occasioned by the variety of responses. Is the respondent a party identifier only if he or she reports attachment to some specific and recognizable political party of the hour, or will any reasonable statement of general political location, such as "I am of the right," serve to qualify? What if the response to the request for the party felt to be closest is "Mitterrand"? Is this a true party identification, or should it be set apart in some special category of personalistic identifications that are distinct from loyalties to a political party? If it is so set apart, what should we do with responses like, "the party of Mitterrand (whatever it is)"? What should we do with respondents who name a pair of parties, especially two with quite discrepant ideologies? As these marginal coding decisions multiply, any simplistic statement as to aggregate levels of party identification takes on some margin of the arbitrary, and should be stated as a range rather than as a single fixed percentage. We shall in fact proceed with such range estimates, giving the proportions making the conventional specific-party response, with additional proportions to convey the other vaguer kinds of political locations.

The second type of problem arises from refusals to answer the question. Should it be assumed that such respondents are actually identified with some party, even though they will not divulge it? We must also address the possibility that some other types of nonresponse, such as "none" or "don't know," might be covert refusals. Where *explicit* refusals are concerned, we discover a considerable decline in such responses since the late 1950s. In the earlier period, refusals ran at 8–12 percent, but they only register 3–6 percent in our data from the late 1960s. This decrease in refusals coincides with an increase in the willingness of Communist sympathizers to identify themselves, and the magnitudes of the two changes match quite nicely as well.[3] Therefore it would seem wise to adjust our 1958 data somewhat to recognize the high likelihood that the missing Communist identifiers did tend to give explicit refusals. For the 1960s, however, the rate of explicit refusals is so limited (especially the 3–4 percent registered in 1967 and 1969) that we can afford to ignore the problem.

The possibility that other kinds of null responses may represent covert refusals is more difficult to dispose of in perfectly convincing fashion. Although we accept the likelihood that some fraction of "don't knows" and "no party" responses are evasions, our best estimate is that this fraction is extremely low, and we shall generally take such responses at face value. The evidence supporting such a posture is of several types. First, voters giving null responses to the party identification question do not show any marked tendency toward null responses when they are asked to report how they voted, although for most people the revelation of vote would be the more sensitive matter. Second, as we shall see, people who give other types of null responses to the party identification item than explicit refusals show themselves in a variety of ways to be relatively marginal to the political system, inasmuch as their expressed involvement with and attentiveness to it are very limited. There is no reason for a person who resents the invasion of privacy involved in revealing his partisanship to resist making purely cognitive reports about the political world, such as listing political parties with which he is familiar. Indeed, all the pressures are to avoid displaying ignorance; yet persons giving nonresponses when asked their party identification perform quite poorly in this "test" of party knowledge (see Figure 2-3). All told, then, it is reasonable to take most of these null responses at face value.

The third class of problems draws us closer to the substance of our discussion. This is the simple fact that if specific partisan feelings tend to be underdeveloped in France relative to other countries, then it is to be expected that responses to our question will show a degree of instability and unreliability which is high by cross-national standards. Since our study provides us with panel data, we can monitor responses of the same individuals over time, and we do indeed find a much greater rate of individual turnover into and out of specific identifications than is usually found. Thus, significant proportions of people who mention a party identification at one time point say they have no party or that they "don't know" at the next; while others who have said "no party" at the first time point venture some party at the next.

This kind of turnover is an annoyance, to say the least, and risks becoming a threat to the very concept of party identification in France, although it is useful to suspend judgment on that issue momentarily. But if such turnover is at least compensating (gross change without net change) in the short term, then we could make somewhat firmer statements as to what the levels of aggregate partisanship in France have tended to be for various periods. But an examination of Table 3-1, showing the general nature of responses to the party identification item over our several available time points, rapidly convinces us that the character of these responses in an aggregate, net-change sense is uncommonly labile as well as sensitive to short-term shifts in the political situation.

Table 3-1. Types of party identification response in France, 1958 and 1967–1969 (percentages).

| | 1958 | | | | |
Type of response	September (Pre-elect.)	December (Post-elect.)	1967	1968	1969
Respondent cites as his "party of identification"					
A normal political party	38.5	47.6	59.5	48.7	45.0
A left-right location only	7.8	4.9	6.3	17.9	17.0
A political leader	3.3	6.3	7.8	12.8	7.4
A vague or uncodable group (not a political party)	3.3	4.9	1.5	4.8	10.1
	52.9	63.7	75.1	84.2	79.5
Respondent says					
"None" or "Don't know"	39.4	24.8	21.5	9.7	17.0
"Refuse"	7.8	11.5	3.4	6.2	3.6
	47.2	36.3	24.9	15.9	20.6
Total	100.1	100.0	100.0	100.1	100.1
N	(1108)	(958)	(1961.2)	(553.5)	(1019)

The variations in Table 3-1 are at many points less haphazard than they may appear. In the United States, for example, it has become clear that party identifications intensify and polarize in the weeks *after* major national elections. This intensification is brief, lasting only a month or two, and then the normal distribution of partisanship is restored, persisting in that form until the next major election. In the American case, where most citizens are identified with a party, the intensification shows itself mainly in increased expressions of strong loyalty. An analogous effect in France might well involve an increase in the proportions reporting identification with some party. This effect does seem clearly expressed in the dramatic change in measurements taken only two months apart in the fall of 1958. Moreover, the 1967 and 1968 measurements were also gathered largely in the zone of intensification just after major national elections. Only the first reading in 1958 and the reading for 1969 lay entirely outside such a zone, and the lesser partisanship expressed in these instances is therefore quite intelligible.

The 1968 distribution seems anomalous, but it can readily be related to the specifics of the political situation in that year. Because of a slight tendency for the less politically involved (and hence the less partisan) to drop out of our panel, both the 1968 and 1969 distributions should be taken as overestimating partisanship slightly—perhaps by 2 percent in 1968 and 1 percent in 1969.[4] More important, however, are the reflections of the political traumas of May and June 1968. The 1968 data suggest that these events combined with the normal post-election intensification effects to raise quite dramatically the proportion of the electorate which felt and reported some political commitment. At the same time, the intensity of the political situation was such that many informants felt more comfortable about retreating to somewhat vaguer statements of their sympathies. We can follow this change in our panel waves, and it fits the known situation rather nicely: that is, partisans of the left were most likely to give vague accounts of their preferences in the 1968 setting, such as mentioning "the left" generally instead of citing their specific leftist party. Meanwhile, many citizens not normally attentive to politics and usually without a party decided under the pressure of events to jump on the Gaullist bandwagon, contributing in an important way to the overall increase in levels of commitment.[5]

Table 3-1 taken as a whole tends to underscore the relative instability of these party identification reports in France, as well as our assertion that it is much more difficult in the case of France than of most other countries to give any single precise estimate as to proportions of identified partisans. If we force ourselves to range estimates, taking into account all we have said about corrections needed for missing Communists, refusals, and the like, then we might guess in a rough way[6] at the following percentages over time:

	In the wake of an election			Outside the election wake	
	1958	1967	1968	1958	1969
Normal party identification	53	61	53	43	47
Some political position	69	76	84	56	72

Although it may be hard to establish any precise or stable values for partisanship in France during this period, at least two key observations can be made. First, the level of partisan response in France was weak relative to that in most other countries. This is very obvious if we insist on some "normal" party response. But it is also true, although much less so, if we include any kind of clear position-taking response, since it is the 1969 column in the tabulation which is most properly comparable to the bulk of published data, including party identification distributions for the United States in this general period.

The second observation could be made only hesitantly on the basis of our own materials, but when it is given some subsequent corroboration and its theoretical importance is acknowledged, it deserves note. This is the hint in the tabulation that levels of partisanship were advancing somewhat in the first decade of the Fifth Republic.[7] Such an advance was very clear where mere position-taking was concerned; it was less clear for party identification more strictly defined, but it still could be imagined, particularly if some of the special circumstances surrounding the 1968 report are discounted. Moreover, we are emboldened to imagine that such an advance in partisanship was already visible in these data because more recent data from France, beyond the view of our own study, seem to speak to a continuing advance (see, for example, Inglehart and Klingemann, 1976; the *Eurobarometer* 5 of 1976; or Capdevielle et al., 1981), although the matter is clouded by lack of standardization in measurement and its timing. These suggestions are of special interest because our empirical theory had created an expectation that levels should be advancing in France, despite marked impediments to partisanship in this form in the political culture. Later in this chapter we shall see that some of these impediments were themselves diminishing in this period as well.

Stability of Partisanship over Time

We have already encountered several facts which are discouraging if we are to imagine that the phenomenon of party identification, when it occurs in France, is essentially the same as party identification in other settings. Chief among these facts is the instability of responses to the party identification item. If the concept of party identification is at all useful analytically, it is so because such attachments can be treated as highly stable over time. The instability of the aggregate distributions (Table 3-1), along with the testimony of our panel data that substantial fractions of the French electorate will cite some party identification at one point in time and then say they have no such attachment a year or so later, can readily be interpreted to mean that the party identification item simply lacks the key characteristics within French political culture that makes it useful elsewhere.

This lability of response, however, is at least congruent with the general proposition that partisan attachments are underdeveloped in France. At this point we arrive at two quite distinct possibilities. One is simply that because of cultural peculiarities, party identification was in this period a meaningless notion in France. The other is that the phenomenon was present in familiar form among some fraction of French voters, but the responses to the item were thoroughly clouded by an unusually large proportion of voters who were trying dutifully to answer the question but who really lacked abiding party loyalties of the kind sought and frequently but not always admitted it.

The second possibility is a more plausible one than may appear, in view of what is known about party identification elsewhere. In the United States, for example, it is clear from long-term panel studies of individual stability in partisanship that any given estimates of such stability—typically, correlations between individual statements of partisanship at two time points—are a compound of two elements: a majority of the electorate, whose party identifications are incredibly stable, even over long periods, and a small fringe of the electorate, usually very marginal to the political process, whose statements of partisanship are quite unstable—little more than a report of how they might vote at the moment (Converse, 1975). This situation in the United States is depicted graphically in Figure 3-1 on the basis of actual panel data from the 1956–1960 period. We see that the stability of party identification, measured by individual correlations over a four-year time lapse, declines steadily as one moves from the most politically involved decile of the population to the least involved. What is important for our purposes, however, is that the stability in the American case remains impressively high for all but the least involved 4 percent of the electorate, who in any event are chronic nonvoters. It is not hard to imagine that although the proportion of the French electorate marginal to the party system and hence giving labile responses was very much larger (hypothetical dotted line), at the upper reaches of involvement or integration into the party system, party identification has the same meaning and stability as in the United States, despite being represented by a much smaller fraction of the electorate.

With our panel data for France, we can make a simple test of this possibility very directly. Let us calculate the cross-time correlation indexing individual stability of partisanship in France, parallel to the United States data on Figure 3-1. To compute such a correlation, all individuals who fail to

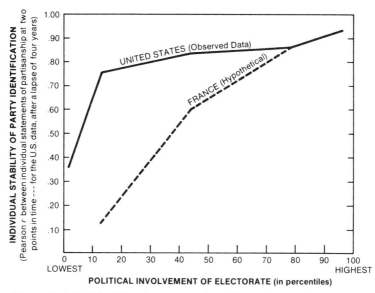

Figure 3-1. Political involvement and stability of party identification, France and the United States.

make a statement of partisanship in *both* 1967 and 1968 automatically fall out as missing data, unlike the American case.[8] Thus in-and-out identifiers, as well as persistent nonidentifiers, are excluded from consideration, a fact which leaves us dealing with what was roughly the most party-involved 40 percent or so of the French electorate. The expected American stability correlation, calculated for 100 percent of the electorate for a time lapse between measurements of fifteen to sixteen months, is 0.848. The *observed* French correlation for the fifteen- to sixteen-month interval between 1967 and 1968 for the most involved 40 percent of the electorate is 0.834.[9]

Thus the empirical state of affairs is very much as we had conjectured in Figure 3-1. When we limit the French data to true identifiers, we have a level of stability which is every bit as satisfying and analytically useful as that which pertains in the United States. It remains quite plausible, therefore, although we have yet to prove it, that the party identification phenomenon, where it did occur in France, may have indeed been essentially the same as that familiar to us from the United States. All the marked signs of instability encountered earlier are simply added evidence that such attachments were relatively underdeveloped in France. At the same time, we are usefully cautioned that when we deal with the set of people who defined themselves as partisans at any single moment in time, our measurement is somewhat more adulterated than usual with people who lacked attachments in the abiding sense intended by the question, and who ideally should not have tried to respond. This means in turn that distributions such as those of Table 3-1 must be read as at least mild overestimates of levels of genuine party identification in France.

Types of Identifiers and Nonidentifiers

Before we begin to examine the dynamic effects of party identification in France, it is worth briefly considering what types of people have sorted themselves into the various kinds of identification we have coded for our 1967 data.

Figure 3-2 overflows with information: it is not easy to read, but will repay careful study. First, the three brackets below the graph set off three

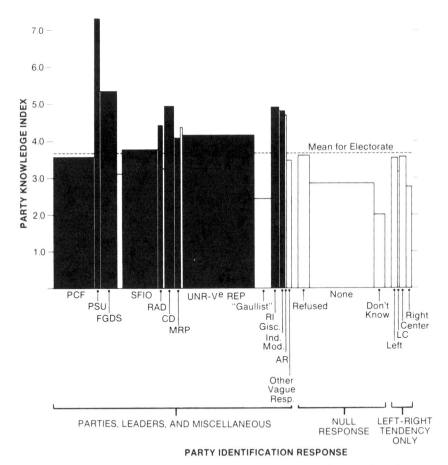

Figure 3-2. Knowledge of the party system, by type of party identification response, France, 1967.

broad types of response, running from the left side of the graph to the right: (1) political positions that can be more or less related to party formations; (2) null responses; and (3) statements of left-right tendency. Second, the *width* (not the *area*) of each vertical bar is an approximate reflection of the frequency of that kind of party response in the French electorate in 1967. Thus the two most frequent responses were "UNR" and "None."

On the party-related left side of the figure the black bars involve responses naming specific parties, while the thin white bars interspersed with the black bars represent the more heterodox references to political figures, labor unions, and the like. These white bars have been positioned to correspond roughly to the left-right region where the objects mentioned appear to fall. The thinnest black bars represent splinter parties; the broad black bars, the major mass parties.

The *height* of each bar reflects the mean for that respective group on the index of party visibility. As already noted, we can see that persons giving null responses to the party identification item generally fall well below the overall mean in knowledge of the party system, and stand in particular contrast to the identifiers with specific parties. But this is least true of explicit refusals, a group which probably is a compound of covert partisans and people attempting to avoid the ignominy of a null response.

It is of some interest that people who give superficially sophisticated left-right responses also tend to show relatively little knowledge of the specific parties in the system. Weak information, with an exception or two, is also shown by those people giving relatively heterodox or vague information about their positions (white bars interspersed among party identifiers). In general, there is a progression in information from the null responses, associated with the greatest ignorance, upward through the vague and heterodox mentions, and then on to the people giving normal party identifications, who are the most knowledgeable about the party system. Differences in political involvement, highly correlated with party knowledge, would show much the same patterns across party identification types.

There are further contrasts of interest to us if we restrict our attention to the more genuine partisans. In a rough way, if we were to organize party types in *descending* order of knowledgeability (or political involvement), we might find:

> Splinter parties of left;
> Splinter parties of right;
> Mass parties of right;
> Mass parties of left.

In other words, the clientele of splinter parties, usually composed of ideological dissidents who have split off from older parties, is uncommonly sophisticated about details of the party alternatives. At the same time, this pattern speaks to the high intellectual heterogeneity of the left, which is undoubtedly a common state of affairs in many countries: a working mass of limited education and political knowledge, championed by a minority of the well-educated who are vitally engaged in politics as a means of improving the lot of the underdog.

Types of party identification responses can be looked at from other points of view. We have noted that respondents were asked whether local candidates, national leaders, or the political parties themselves were most influential in their voting decisions, and this question was posed before the party identification item. The orientations of various types of identifiers differ widely in these regards, usually in ways that can be readily anticipated. Thus, for example, voters identifying with the Communist party are far and away more strongly and exclusively oriented to political parties as criteria for voting than are any of the other types of identifiers or nonidentifiers, although partisans of leftist parties more generally tend to be relatively party-oriented. Sympathizers of the more centrist *partis des notables* (parties based on locally prominent people)—the dying MRP and most especially the Radicals—show much less orientation to parties per se, but a strong focus on local candidates. Among nonidentifiers, the "no party" and "don't know" types give even more exclusive attention to local candidates, while there is a better balance of attention among people who refuse to answer the party identification question.

It would be unwise to conclude that there are unidirectional causal links between these orientations and party choice. There is no reason, for example, to imagine that the Communist party has undue attractiveness for people who are less interested in personalities than in competing party organizations. It would be more plausible to suppose that people who become Communists for other reasons are schooled in the importance of the party over more transient considerations of individual leadership. Nonetheless, the consistency between the statements of party versus personality orientation and the types of response to the party identification item does serve to raise our confidence that with both measurements we are tapping syndromes which differ reliably from each other.

A striking example of these differences is yielded by the detailed responses within the Gaullist camp. As Figure 3-2 has already implied, we differentiated between respondents who indicated that they identified with an actual Gaullist party, such as the UNR, and those who merely said they were "Gaullist" or gave specific references to de Gaulle himself. Among those making actual party responses, a full half had indicated earlier that they attended most to parties in their voting decisions. For persons merely making Gaullist or de Gaulle references, the fraction was less than one-third. Instead, this contingent reported that they gave primary attention to national leaders, in proportions nearly double those for people citing an actual Gaullist party. In one sense, of course, these patterns are again not surprising. But if we refer back to Figure 3-2, we may note that this kind of heterogeneity within the large Gaullist camp has some pervasive correlates: the two groups differ substantially in their knowledge of the party system, and the set of people who make only the more personalized Gaullist response are even less informed about parties than the nonidentifiers.

There is also more general evidence that relatively marginal portions of the French electorate tend to be attracted primarily to a personalistic style of politics. We may hypothesize that features of French political culture at the system level tend to encourage this kind of response, particularly the practice of the prominent political figure who takes his entourage and creates a new "party" with it, one which few would expect to endure beyond the leader's own interest in it. It is intriguing in this regard that a parallel question about orientation to leaders, candidates, and parties which was posed to a national sample in Canada revealed rather substantial differences between respondents of French and of Anglo-Saxon background. French Canadians represent themselves as paying more attention to the personalistic aspects of politics, and less attention to political parties per se, than is true of English Canadians.[10] And historically it seems to have been the case that political parties in French Canada have been more commonly labeled, either formally or in informal discourse, with the names of individual political leaders, usually with good reason.

It also seems reasonable to hypothesize that the system emphasis on parties as personal vehicles in France may rank among the features of the political culture which inhibit the development of strong party identifications. A major feature of those identifications, as we have seen, is that they tend to accumulate and intensify over the adult life of the identifier. There is no reason to doubt that allegiances to individual leaders would also show much the same accumulation and intensification over time. The problem is that the extreme national prominence of an individual figure which is needed to set in motion a political party is likely to be somewhat short-lived by comparison with the full life cycle of most adults in the electorate. If the entourage party does not last more than five, ten, or fifteen years, then the identifier is sooner or later left to find some new object of attachment. Not only does this mean that the identifier starts "back at the beginning," as it were, with initially weak loyalties; but there is also evidence that identifications initiated afresh tend to intensify themselves only at slower and slower rates, the older the individual is at the time of initial adoption.[11] Thus, several effects would combine to impede aggregate levels of party loyalty where identifications are directed to particular leaders rather than to more continuous and enduring party organizations.

Of course, all of these surmises hinge on the assumption that party identification does behave dynamically in France much as it does elsewhere.

Now that we are familiar with some of the static properties of party identification responses in France, let us turn to a critical examination of that assumption.

Dynamic Properties of Partisanship in France

We have indicated that we will be more or less content with the assumption that the phenomenon of party identification in France was essentially the same as in other countries, to the degree that we find that, where it existed, it showed the same dynamic properties over time. One of those dynamic properties is a high level of individual stability in partisan loyalty, and we have already seen that such stability was indeed present in this period, at least in a strictly *locational* sense: that is, provided the French voter stated a party loyalty in two successive interviews, the relative stability of the locations mentioned was almost identical with the United States case. This statement ignores not only that such locations were much less often chosen in France at any one point in time, but also that the likelihood of picking some location at both points in time was much lower in France as well. Thus at any point in time French reports of partisanship are adulterated by unstable mentions, and the contrast with the United States is marked. Yet if by "true party identifiers" we mean the limited fraction of the French electorate choosing one or another party repeatedly, then the stability of the locations chosen was about the same as for the United States. This fact in itself is important, but there are other dynamic tests to be made.

Party Identification and Vote Constancy

In addition to individual stability of identification, perhaps the other sine qua non of the whole notion of party identification is that true identifiers, although they may occasionally defect in a given election, are less likely than nonidentifiers to shift their favors from party to party over time. We can thus return to the issues of vote constancy raised in the preceding chapter, to see how such constancy relates to French party identification.

The joint analysis of constancy in vote and party identification becomes rather more complicated than meets the eye even for countries with simpler party systems than that of France in this period. There is probably no quick reduction of information on the topic that conveys exactly what we might like to know without becoming snarled in artifacts or system-specific configurations that intrude on the data to a remarkable degree. Perhaps the most popular mode for such analysis flows from the original Butler-Stokes comparisons of Britain and the United States, which reduced the information from three-wave panel studies in each country to a simple fourfold table, cross-tabulating "Stable" and "Variable" respondents jointly for party identification and vote.

The main point of the Butler-Stokes analysis was to compare the off-diagonal cells, referring to voters stable in one sense but variable in the other. In the United States, voters stable in partisanship but variable in vote outnumbered those who were stable in vote but variable in partisanship by a ratio of 8 to 1. The same ratio for British voters, however, was only 2 to 1, indicating a greater propensity for Americans to retain their party identifications while changing their vote. The general contrasts between the two tables led Butler and Stokes to conclude that although such identifications certainly contributed to vote constancy in Britain, "the British voter is less likely than the American to make a distinction between his current electoral choice and a more general partisan disposition" (Butler and Stokes, 1969, p. 43).

This analytic paradigm has been increasingly replicated for other times and places for which panel data are available (among other studies, Thomassen, 1976a, 1976b; Norpoth, 1978; Leduc, 1981; Cain and Ferejohn, 1981), and it seems proper to employ our own panel data to locate France in the same firmament.

We do so with some qualms, however. We are impressed by the many complications that the Butler-Stokes simplification necessarily conceals, even for countries of simple political structure. Nor is adapting the format sensibly to the complexities of French politics and voter perceptions an easy task. Therefore we shall indeed examine our French data in this form, but shall also put them subsequently into another comparative format to capture some important features of the situation that the Butler-Stokes paradigm seems to lose or confuse.

One very generic question about the Butler-Stokes type of table has to do with who is to be included and excluded from the calculations. The number of plausible inclusion criteria turns out to be rather large, and one petty version of this issue is that written accounts of paradigm use are often so inadequate as to the decision rules employed that like tables cannot be retrieved even with the same data base. More grave substantively is the sad fact that the general conclusions to be drawn from such tables, especially when contrasted cross-nationally, can often be dramatically modified according to the specific choice of rules for inclusion. Cain and Ferejohn (1981) showed, for example, that the Butler-Stokes table for Britain would have looked a good deal more like that for the United States if the then resurgent Liberal party had been excluded from the calculations.

A broader set of inclusion variations arises from editorial decisions about the handling of voters who are in and out of the active electorate. As Leduc (1981) has shown, summary data for the United States create the impression that it is either among the most stable or among the most unstable of electorates, according to whether or not persons who vote at one election but not at an adjacent one are added to the "Variable" vote cell. This is so for the simple reason that against a backdrop of European comparisons, voting turnout in the United States, especially in off-year national elections, is quite low. From our point of view in this chapter, the inclusion of turn-out variation serves to confuse the issue, since we wish to know whether party identifications tend to stabilize vote preferences when people form them, and not whether people get to the polls or not. But it is a legitimate interest for Leduc, who is attempting to isolate all forms of changeability in electoral outcomes country by country; hence for his purposes turnout variations deserve inclusion.

Butler and Stokes appear to have handled the turnout issue in a fashion more suited to our needs. They tried to rule out turnout variations by re-stricting their contrasting tables for Britain and the United States to the set of people who always voted (and always had some partisanship). People who were stable in partisanship but did not always vote were thus not added to the "Variable" group in either country. Although this treatment is more useful for our purposes, it does not solve the comparability problem. Be-cause of marked Anglo-American turnout differences (especially for U.S. congressional elections), this set of inclusion rules means that over two-thirds of the British electorate contribute data to the table, whereas for the United States only the most politically involved 41 percent of the electorate, who are stable partisans and manage to vote in three consecutive congres-sional elections, are represented. This makes a dramatic difference in the field of view when national tables are to be compared. Moreover, given evi-dence that partisanship is less stable among Americans who are less in-volved, for whom it is likely merely to mirror current vote preferences, we can see that the most crucial Butler-Stokes "nation contrasts" that "prove" less independence of party identification from vote in England are almost certain to be in some degree an exaggeration arising from the comparison of rather different slices of the two electorates.

These comments no more than begin the list of complications which the Butler-Stokes format simplifies and therefore hides from view, even in the general case. The reader can intuit some of the further problems to be resolved as we summarize the decision rules we have used to prepare our French version of the Butler-Stokes comparisons and to rework those origi-nal comparisons, the better to fit our data:

(1) For our own comparisons we have employed only two time points, rather than the three in the Butler-Stokes original. This is because, despite our three panel waves, we have only two normal legislative votes. Of course, Butler-Stokes had but two actual votes as well, with the other wave (1963) being represented only by a current preference, not a vote. Our two actual votes (1967 and 1968) will be matched to the two actual British votes (1964 and 1966), and to the 1958 and 1960 U.S. votes.

(2) We have included only people reporting a specific party identifica-tion *and* casting a vote for the *same* party at the first election. This is more

stringent than the original Butler-Stokes specification, in which identifying with one party and voting for another repeatedly sufficed to class the respondent as "stable."

(3) In the problematic case of France, we have taken identification to signify attachment to a specific political party, not some vaguer reference; and we have included "leaners" for the United States but not for Britain.

(4) We have excluded those people who identified with a real party but had no candidate of that party available to vote for locally, on the grounds that this is a matter of some cross-system variation irrelevant to the behavioral hypotheses involved.

(5) We shall distinguish between those people who switch their vote or party identification between the first and second measurement from those who move from a party identification or vote to no identification or no vote.

Throughout, of course, we have extended these criteria and adjustments to the United States and British data, in addition to our French material. Figure 3-3 shows these turnover tables for all three countries.

The most striking feature of Figure 3-3 is that French respondents were more stable in their voting than in their party identifications, while that comparison is reversed for the United States and Britain, just as in the original observations reported by Butler and Stokes (1969). A related contrast is that a markedly smaller proportion of French than Anglo-Saxon voters were stable in both their party identification and their vote.

The largest single source of these two contrasts is the group of French voters who voted for the same party at the two successive elections, but shifted from having a party identification in 1967 to not having one in 1968. Roughly five times the proportion of French voters as of Anglo-Saxons fall into that category.[12] Of course this motion out of identification would in some degree be balanced off in a fuller tabulation by a flow into identification in 1968 from none in 1967, which fails to show here because the table is limited to those for whom a party identification matches a vote in 1967. As we saw earlier in the chapter, however, the exodus from specific identifications in 1968 does considerably outweigh the influx of new identifiers in that year, a retreat from partisanship into vaguer statements that tended to be concentrated on the left after the embarrassments of the May-June excesses. All of this flux in and out of identification reflects the uncommon lability of these reports in France, which has been mentioned repeatedly in this chapter. It does not in itself tell us whether the sense of partisanship tends to function in familiar ways for at least those French voters who do give stable identification responses.

Yet, as we look at the rest of the figure with the bottom row and right-hand column suppressed, the message continues to be that in France, between 1967 and 1968, stable voters outnumbered stable party identifiers.

FRANCE (1967-1968)

		PARTISAN CHOICE IN VOTING FOR THE NATIONAL ASSEMBLY			
		STABLE	VARIABLE		
			1968 Vote ≠ 1967 Vote	Abstained in 1968	
PARTY IDENTIFICATION	STABLE	56	4	5	65
	VARIABLE: 1968 PI ≠ 1967 PI	8	4	0	12
	VARIABLE: No PI in 1968	14	8	1	23
		78	16	6	100%

Wtd. N = 223.8 (41% of Total Electorate)

GREAT BRITAIN (1964-1966)

		PARTISAN CHOICE IN VOTING FOR THE HOUSE OF COMMONS			
		STABLE	VARIABLE		
			1966 Vote ≠ 1964 Vote	Abstained in 1966	
PARTY IDENTIFICATION	STABLE	80	2	6	88
	VARIABLE: 1966 PI ≠ 1964 PI	2	4	1	7
	VARIABLE: No PI in 1966	2	1	2	5
		84	7	9	100%

Wtd. N = 1075.5 (74% of Total Electorate)

UNITED STATES (1958-1960)

		PARTISAN CHOICE IN VOTING FOR THE HOUSE OF REPRESENTATIVES			
		STABLE	VARIABLE		
			1960 Vote ≠ 1958 Vote	Abstained in 1960	
PARTY IDENTIFICATION	STABLE	74	6	10	90
	VARIABLE: 1960 PI ≠ 1958 PI	2	3	1	6
	VARIABLE: No PI in 1960	3	0	1	4
		79	9	12	100%

Wtd. N = 782 (45% of Total Electorate)

Figure 3-3. Stability of party identification and legislative voting: France, 1967–1968; Great Britain, 1964–1966; and the United States, 1958–1960.

French voters were more likely than British or American voters of the same period to remain constant in their electoral choice while they changed their party identification than they were to maintain their party identification while altering their vote choice. And more generally, even with turnout variability suppressed, the French voter seems more changeable than his Anglo-Saxon counterparts.

The question remains what is to be made of these contrasts. One system-level difference which would certainly lead one to expect more changeability in general in France, relative to the pair of Anglo-Saxon countries, has to do with the sheer fractionalization of its party system. It is difficult, for any system of highly multiple parties, to say just how many parties there are at any point in time. France in the period of our study might have been called a six- or eight-party system, although if all miniscule splinter parties were to be catalogued the count could go considerably higher. Our code book in 1967, for example, was obliged to recognize well over twenty distinct and specific parties with which somebody or other claimed to be identified (setting aside, along with vaguer objects, labels that were simply erroneous), although some of these were obsolete entities. The fractionalization of the French party system in this period was notorious; and it would stand to reason that if one political system packs ten times as many parties into a given political space as another, then one would expect cross-party changes in such a system to be somewhat easier.

A pure two-party system does, after all, have a noteworthy Manichean flavor to it: anybody with political commitments either fights for the Deity or must join the very Devil. Surely it is a less portentous act, in a system of highly multiple parties, to change one's mind concerning which of a dozen apostles will bring heaven to earth most rapidly than it is to abandon Good completely and go over to Evil.

Of course, a model is implicit here which deserves spelling out. One assumption is that political "spaces" cover roughly the same distances in one nation as in another. It is true that the two groupings making up most two-party systems are thought of as "moderate," and that splinter parties at the extremes can signally add to the policy ground (that is, the breadth of options) being represented. But we need not insist that the centers of gravity of two competing parties be as distant from each other as the centers of gravity of five parties in the same system. Instead, our first assumption requires less strenuously that the expected "distance" between any two randomly selected pairs of partisans is roughly the same, whatever the number of parties in the system. And it certainly rejects the simplest opposing postulate, which would be that if system A has ten times as many political parties as system B, then the "distance" separating any two randomly selected pairs of partisans can be expected to be ten times as great.

A second, and to us a more controversial, assumption might be that in the degree people move their personal locations, rates of change will be in-

versely proportional to "distance" traversed. Once we add this assumption
to the first, we can begin to sense the conditions under which party fractionalization can have an enormous impact on the proportions of an electorate changing parties (for *either* identification or vote), and hence on the
whole cast of a Butler-Stokes turnover table.

An easy thought experiment toward this end imagines voters whose
political locations (unidimensional, for simplicity's sake) are measured at
two points in time, as displayed in a scatter diagram. If there is no association between locations at the two points, the "cloud of points" is circular; if
the association is perfect, all points fall on a single line. To represent a two-
party system it is natural to bisect each measurement of locations in some
central way, creating four quadrants. In such a figure, those in the upper left
and lower right quadrants are "stable" and the others are "unstable." But if
instead we want to represent in the same space a twenty-party system, then
we must draw twenty lines in both directions through the diagram, so that
four hundred (twenty times twenty) unique cells are created. It takes little
further thought to realize that if crossing party lines is the issue, it will happen more frequently even for the same underlying cloud of points, and
probably much more frequently, when there are four hundred cells su-
perimposed than when there are only four.

With this picture in mind, we can state the conditions which link
party numbers with expected rates of interparty movement. If voter locations are independent at the two time points, then party size alone creates
enormous differences in expected rates of interparty movement. In fact, in
the independent case, and with equal-sized parties, expected change will be
ten times as frequent where there are ten times as many parties. In the case
of perfect association and stable means, there will be no difference by party
size at all, but chiefly because by construction there is no change at all. A
more realistic case lies between these two logical extremes, and usually toward the side of higher association. Nonetheless, although this "realistic"
zone tells us that expected rates of change are not going to be ten times as
great just because party size is ten times as great, we can still conclude that
change rates should double for reasons of party size which have nothing to
do with behavior differences, "meaning of party identification," or anything
further.

We said, however, that our second assumption, on which the above
conclusions partially rest, was controversial. Now let us say what that controversy is. When we assume that citizens traverse political spaces at rates
inversely proportional to "distance" in the system, it might be remonstrated
that we have thereby discarded any theories of identification with the parties, and have shifted ground to a distance model of change instead. This
would be so because a party is a qualitative category, an organization made
up of leadership, secretariats, and the like. Such organizations have bound-

aries within which sympathizers remain. This does not mean that members cannot leave, if they lose confidence in the organization. Of course they can. But there is nothing in the theory of identification itself which says that the probability of leaving is greater if there are closely neighboring organizations (the twenty-party system) than if there is merely one organization and its opponent. Identification is identification; it does not take cognizance of neighborly relations.

We are in partial agreement with this criticism. We would revise our second assumption to add a ceteris paribus; and we would make it clear that while distances must matter in these systems, as the assumption postulates, so must party boundaries. While movement over short distances is more likely than over long ones, movement is also impeded by the necessity of crossing party boundaries. Realistically, there is no reason why both effects cannot be recognized. What this means, in terms of our thought experiment, is that the difference in expected change rates between large and small party systems is less than we might imagine, even after we have reduced them once to take account of nonindependence of positions. But none of this obviates the initial judgment that party system size must be a basic contributing parameter to estimates of change in assessments of the Butler-Stokes kind.

If this is so, then it is easier to understand why the Netherlands has become a textbook case of chaotic changeability, in which the stabilizing lines of party identification are hard to find, especially when those lines are dependent upon contrasts with the tiny Anglo-Saxon party systems in a Butler-Stokes format. After all, while France has long been a prototype of a fractionalized party system, the Netherlands in recent times has been very considerably more fractionalized. The code book for the Thomassen (1976a) Dutch panel study covering the 1970–1972 period lists thirty-one specific political parties. Two of these are electoral lists headed by political personages, and four others are named umbrella parties uniting other specific parties, so perhaps we should talk of a more modest system of twenty-five parties. But after the thirty-one listed parties there is a code category "Other Parties," which is inhabited by further Dutch voters. Therefore, it is a very large party system indeed.

Actually, there is a much better formal way of measuring the degree of fractionalization in a party system, as suggested by Rae (1967). This index improves upon sheer counts of parties, which fail to distinguish between those twenty-party systems in which no party gets more than 10 percent of the vote (highly fractionalized), and those less fractionalized twenty-party systems where there are two main parties capturing 95 percent of the vote and eighteen other splinter formations. The index, which depends on the probability that the members of any randomly selected pair of voters are of the same party, is simply the sum of squared proportions of party vote (or identification) across all parties in the system.[13] Figure 3-4 shows the results of our calculation of this superior measure for the several countries we are discussing, during the period of study.

Figure 3-4 mainly assures us as to the towering levels of fractionalization in the Dutch party system. On the one hand, it is a bit surprising that the leading discussions of Dutch data put into the Butler-Stokes format fail to recognize the powerful variations that must be touched off in these assessments by huge differences in fractionalization alone, from the United States at one extreme to the Netherlands at the other. On the other hand, party fractionalization better addresses the issue of party changeability (in vote *or* identification), than it does the crucial balance of vote change rela-

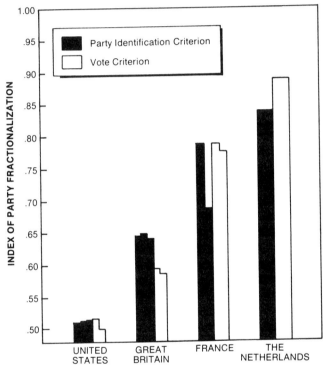

Figure 3-4. Party fractionalization in four countries, 1950s to 1970s. The years in which panel data are available in each country are: the United States, 1956–1960; Great Britain, 1964–1970; France, 1967–1968; the Netherlands, 1970–1972. Slight further variations in heights of bars merely convey election-year differences, unlabeled because, as the figure shows, they are so trivial. The main exception involves the second (1968) party identification reading in France, when professed loyalties to specific parties imploded sharply on the Gaullists.

tive to identification change, one of the chief original motivations of the Butler-Stokes table.

At the same time, the Butler-Stokes paradigm is not entirely satisfying, even where this more focused issue is concerned. This is true because one thing the Butler-Stokes simplification loses is the *fit* between party identification and vote choice. In other words, the "Stable-Stable" cell of their table can logically contain people who identified with one party stably but voted for another stably, a set of heretics who depart widely from the implied composition of the cell, which is imagined by the casual reader to be made up exclusively of strong party identifiers voting loyally over and over. Butler and Stokes recognize this, and point out that the level of adulteration with persistent defectors in both of their Anglo-Saxon systems is "trifling" (1969, p. 42n). We heartily agree, for these systems, and in the years examined. It is well recognized, however, that defections from one's own party that arise because of candidate preferences elsewhere are likely to persist through multiple elections until the defection-producing configuration is dissolved. Thus, for example, a very significant fraction of U.S. Democrats who defected in favor of Eisenhower over Stevenson in 1952 did so again when the same configuration of candidates was presented in 1956. These persistent defectors would look like "Stable-Stable" loyalists in a Butler-Stokes table, but they are quite the opposite.

The issue is less whether persistent defections occur much in limited-party Anglo-Saxon systems, where they do not, than it is whether system variation in such matters cannot become important when we begin to get into highly promiscuous comparisons, as between systems of two parties and thirty-one parties. We have already seen in the preceding chapter that the constancy of candidate offerings is *greater* in France than in the United States, despite lesser party constancy there (see Table 2-1). Since candidate constancy in France is a major source of prolonged defections, there are system-level reasons to expect more such defection in France than in the United States or, probably, Britain. Hence this variation can go beyond the "trifling," especially for cross-national contrasts. The main point is that the simplified statistics of the Butler-Stokes paradigm lose their incisiveness rapidly as they are employed across more and more heterogeneous systems, where other system-level differences, such as those having to do with party fractionalization or constancy of vote offerings, intrude in a vexing way. One major problem, among several, is the failure of those simple reductions to join party identification and vote tightly, as with such concepts as "loyal" and "defecting" votes.

A Further Test of Loyal and Defecting Votes

Therefore we have added another simple test of party identification dynamics in France, intended to be complementary to the Butler-Stokes test. Because it is also simple, it gives only a partial description of the situation as well. But it does tend to address an important facet of the dynamics to be expected if party identification is operative in its classic form, which becomes quite blurred in the Butler-Stokes form.

Mindful of emphasis placed in theoretical discussions of party identification upon concepts of the "homing tendency" after defections have occurred, we have found it useful to divide our voters into three groups, according to the nature of the fit between their partisan identifications and their vote at the first of a pair of successive elections. At this "time-1" election, some voters will be identifiers and some will not. Those who are identifiers subdivide naturally again into those casting loyal and those casting defecting votes at the first election. Thus we have three "conditions" defined for time-1, and the question becomes one of relative vote constancy at the next election.

If party identification is operating as expected, we would of course predict that identifiers voting loyally in the first election would be more likely to repeat their vote in the second election than nonidentifiers. At the same time, however, we would predict that defectors would be even *less* likely to repeat their defecting vote a second time than would nonidentifiers. In addition to tying vote and identification choices more closely together, this analysis format also permits us to keep in view a kind of "control" group of persons without identifications, so that if there are system-level factors which promote or inhibit a lot of party change, the intrasystem contrasts with this "control" help steer us away from misconstructions.

The important point of this format is that it requires party identification as stated at time-1 to have some carry-over meaning at time-2. Thus if some labile respondent who was not clearly identified claimed some identification at time-1 which was no more than his vote intention in the first election, and then gave a different party of identification at time-2 which represented no more than a new vote whim at that time, he would still count against the prediction, since he would rank as a loyally voting identifier at time-1 who changed his party choice at time-2. The fact that he also adjusted his partisanship at time-2 to fit his vote would be ignored, and appropriately so where the party identification concept is concerned.

The data from this analysis are presented in Figure 3-5.[14] Perhaps the most striking impression created by this display is the degree of similarity, in regard to these crucial dynamics of party identification, among these countries, which according to the Butler-Stokes criterion should be quite discrepant where such dynamics are concerned. In every case, the predictions about party change at the second time point are sustained, relative to the "control" provided by the unidentified. And with one exception (the second ballot in France) the differences along the lines of the prediction are quite substantial, ranging from 12 to 22 percent. Here, then, is a resounding

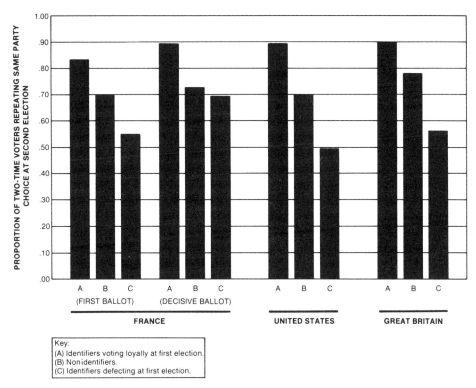

Figure 3-5. The stabilizing effects of party identification on constancy of party voting: France, 1967–1968; the United States, 1956–1960; and Great Britain, 1964–1966.

confirmation of the basic party identification dynamics present in all three countries.

And yet, if we pay attention to much finer detail, there are country differences in the figure, and these tend to follow, albeit rather feebly, the lines we have come to expect in this chapter. The difference in performance by party identification groups is sharpest for the United States, where the whole construct of party identification seems to be most fruitful. It is very nearly as sharp for Great Britain, a country with a party system only slightly more fractionalized than that of the United States. It is somewhat less sharp for the highly fractionalized French system, especially in the unusual second tour. But the pattern is there nonetheless—and quite sharply so for the first ballot.

We assume that the French results show fewer sharp differences for at least two reasons. First, it should be remembered that we are dealing here with persons giving a single report of identification (associated with the first election), and we have seen that in France there is a greater adulteration of these reports by persons who should not have claimed any such identification (as witnessed by in-and-out reports). Moreover, in all the bodies of data the identifiers defecting at time-1, although usually less likely to repeat the same party vote than nonidentifiers, still do repeat their defections at fairly substantial rates. Second, our work with constancy of candidate offerings (Chapter 2) suggests that France is likely to be high in this regard, and hence high in the prolongation of defection, especially where decisive ballots are concerned. Generally, however, our hypotheses concerning the preservative effect of party identification are clearly confirmed for France as well as for Britain and the United States.

Thus the two truly essential properties of the party identification phenomenon—individual stability of identification over time and a marked retardation of change in party voting when an identification is present—turn up unquestionably in the French case. None of these demonstrations guarantees that party identification offers the full analytic utility it provides in other settings, since we might well find other variables in France which are still more stable and more powerful in accounting for political attitudes and voting choice. We will pay fuller attention to this possibility in the next chapter. Moreover, it is beyond question that there is a lability to these responses in France beyond what we find elsewhere, which weakens the variable. But at least we are satisfied that party identifications, where they exist in the harder core in France, show much the same behavioral implications as those that are familiar to us from other settings.

Intensification of Party Identification over Time

In addition to our two key properties, other dynamic patterns that are associated with party identification in societies where it has been investigated have helped a great deal in understanding both the microcosmic processes involved and the macrocosmic implications of the phenomenon. Although we would not regard these as essential defining properties, it is natural to wonder if they are not replicated in France.

One of these patterns involves the intensification of the strength of felt party loyalty on the part of the individual as time passes. This expectation does not demand that once a party loyalist, always a more and more extreme party loyalist. Certainly events occur in individual lives that touch off full-blown conversions, turning individuals away from a strong attachment to one party and toward some nascent but growing attachment to a competing one. But such events and such conversions are demonstrably rare. This means that for most people, most of the time, the grooves of preference and habit wear deeper with practice (Converse, 1969; Markus, 1983). And since few people undergo conversion in this sense in societies with any lengthy history of party competition, we would expect to find a rather clear positive correlation between age and the reported strength of party loyalty. This is true simply because if conversions are rare, then biological age and length of psychological membership in a given political party are bound to be highly correlated. As noted earlier, however, it has been shown that where it is possible to differentiate between an individual's age and the length of psychological membership, as in the case of a man who is converted to a new party when he is fifty, he will take on the new loyalty more slowly than as if he had adopted it at age thirty.

However important conceptually this latter fact may be—and we shall find it is very important in the French case—the simplest test of the expectation is to ask whether indeed it is true in France that strength of party identification is correlated positively with age. Persons who had given some content response to the party identification item were subsequently asked *how* close they felt to whatever political object it was that they had named: very close, fairly close, or not very close. These responses gave three descending levels of identification strength; and if we consider that people who had no identification at all comprise a fourth or "zero" state, we can examine the way such intensity of partisanship behaves as a function of simple biological age.

The first results are somewhat disappointing. There is indeed a little increase in partisanship as age advances, but nobody would be tempted to call it a strong association. The gain by decade is quite faint and irregular, and it is clearly reversed among people over eighty. Such a reversal is not in itself unusual: it has been observed among the extremely old in some other countries as well, and it seems an integral part of the psychological retirement from current events and attention to public life that also produces a decline in voting turnout among even the healthy aged. But over the main portion of the life cycle, the rate of increase in partisan strength, so measured, is much weaker than that usually observed.

A closer examination of the data makes clear, however, what is going on. There is little in the theory surrounding the intensification of identifications over time that would necessarily predict that the probability of developing some sense of loyalty, however faint initially, increases with age. The main prediction is rather that *given* some initial identification, if it remains undisturbed it can be expected to intensify with the passage of time. Therefore we were wrong to include the zero state of no identification as part of our prediction. Indeed, when we examine this zero state taken alone, we find precious little evidence of an increased probability of identification with age for France: if anything, the pattern is faintly negative, another interesting fact to which we shall return.

When we set aside people of no identification and focus on identifiers of greater or lesser strength, the positive relationship with age brightens considerably. It still would not be considered strong by cross-national stan-

dards, but this might simply represent the known adulteration of our measurement with an unusually large fraction of labile respondents who should
not have professed any "general" identification. But there is still another
possibility which is well worth checking out. This involves, on the one
hand, the French anomaly of rapid party creation, so that many of the
French parties available for identification in 1967 were of fairly recent vintage; and on the other hand, the theoretical expectation that if a party is
adopted for identification later in life, the intensification of loyalties is likely
to occur at a visibly reduced rate. In most countries, where the party scenery
has remained fairly constant for more than a generation and conversion is
rare at best, this expectation is almost untestable. But France offers a unique
site for test, precisely because new parties are commonplace.

A good example of this reasoning involves the UNR, or whatever designation is current for the major Gaullist party. It is not hard to imagine
that there existed in this period some remnant of the French electorate that
had become enamored of de Gaulle during World War II, and more especially of Gaullism in the partisan sense soon thereafter, who persisted in loyalty to this perspective throughout the lean years of the General's
retirement, and who saw in the UNR of 1958 a very direct continuation of
the movement. For such a remnant, we can imagine that personal loyalties
had been steadily intensifying for twenty-five years, or a period covering
much of the adult span of many survivors of that remnant. However this
may be, it is incontestable that, for a very substantial portion of the sympathizers of the UNR-UDR in our period, this party had been launched as a
practical political vehicle de novo in 1958. For French citizens then below
their middle thirties, this period may have covered all of their effective voting life, so that normal intensification expectations would apply. But for
any of those who were in, say, their sixties—and many of them were—the
UNR would have become visible and attractive as an object of political
identification only after they had reached middle age; and hence the intensification of their loyalties to the UNR, according to the theory, should have
progressed rather more slowly.

Although we lack sufficient cases for reliable estimates of the progress
of identifications by age cohort within sets of specific-party sympathizers, we
can group together parties of similar longevity to test the central prediction
at issue here. In particular, we shall contrast the growth of identification by
age within the oldest parties in the system, all of them dating back well before World War II (Communists, Socialists, and Radicals), with the identification patterns for the newest party creations of the 1960s. The theory
would not call for any striking difference in identification strength where
the youngest cohort of the electorate is concerned; but it would predict that
the rate of gain in partisanship as we pass upward through older cohorts
should be discernibly more rapid for the oldest parties than for the newest.

One last problem disturbs us, where the newest parties are concerned. This is the now familiar question as to when in fact a nominally new party is perceived as new. This is most problematic for the FGDS, which unfortunately provides us with the majority of our cases of new-party sympathizers. Surely it could be expected, for example, that some longtime identifiers of the SFIO might regard the FGDS as a very direct continuation of their preferred party, and would suffer little discontinuity of identification as a result. Nonetheless, the FGDS was something of a new creation, and it is worth seeing whether the data do fit our theoretical derivations.

The results are presented in Figure 3-6, where the heavy line represents the overall progression in strength of identification for the sample as a whole, and the two lighter lines refer to the old-party and new-party subsets as indicated.[15] There is not much question that our expectations are confirmed.

Surely it is gratifying to discover that derivations from a theory developed with no reference to France at all, yet uniquely testable in France be-

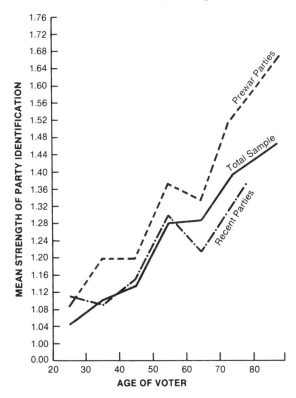

Figure 3-6. Strength of party identification, by voter age, with prewar and recent parties, France, 1967.

cause of the peculiar fondness in that country for the generation of new parties, should show such clear results. Moreover, we have here a rather eloquent rejoinder to any claim that for one or another obscure reason, whatever "party identification" might be extracted from the French electorate would be a phenomenon qualitatively different from anything measured elsewhere.

But our gratification with the theory and its predictions should not obscure what is important in Figure 3-6 for the French case itself. For that figure is our best documentation to date of the argument that the rapid generation of parties in France is of vital importance in inhibiting the development of stronger aggregate party loyalties in the electorate.

The Intergenerational Transmission of Partisanship

Another seemingly ubiquitous dynamic pattern associated with the party identification phenomenon is the fact that people appear to be predominantly socialized into some kind of nascent party preference as they grow up in their family of origin. Hence, there is normally a substantial correlation between the partisan identifications of parents and children.[16]

This correlation calculated for French data is very similar to that found in the United States, when the figures in both cases are based on voters' reports of their parental party.[17] Any such calculation of the parent-child congruence of party choice must, however, be limited to cases in which preferences or identifications are available for both generations. Any instance where *either* the parent *or* the child has no preference is automatically excluded. In our work with the 1958 French sample, we noted that this was a point at which astonishing differences opened up between the two countries. In a United States sample of the adult electorate in 1958, 86 percent of the respondents were able to give some partisan characterization of their father's electoral preferences. The French study of the same year showed that when French respondents were asked to indicate what partisanship or broader political orientation (a *tendance* such as left-right) their father had held while they were growing up, only 26 percent of the electorate could suggest a party, ideological orientation, or even the vaguest of tendances, such as that he "always voted for the fatherland." Although the possibility of a principled evasion of this kind of disclosure could not be ruled out in any definitive way for France, there were various indications that the hiatus in information was largely real. It seemed unlikely, for example, that many French men or women would refuse to disclose their father's partisanship or left-right orientation when they were in fact willing to disclose their own. More important, the flavor of the qualitative responses to the question was quite compelling. The typical respondent said that his or her father had never said anything about his personal relationship to partisan politics within hearing, and it was frequently implied that such reticence was entirely natural.

There were other striking patterns of contrast and similarity between the French and American data. Just as the transmission of particular partisan dispositions seemed to occur at the same general rates in the two countries *where any transmission occurred at all,* so it was also true that a tendency to adopt any kind of partisanship seemed significantly dependent on family socialization. In other words, where voters were able to remember their father's partisanship, about 80 percent in both countries were themselves identified with a party at a comparable threshold. When this knowledge was not present, only about 50 percent of respondents, *again in both countries,* reported some personal partisanship. It would be hard to construct a more delightful example of stunning discrepancy between the two countries in the fundamental "input parameters" of the process. It seemed clear that the cultural patterns which kept French parents from discussing partisan politics with or even in the company of their children was a basic and potent source of the underdevelopment of partisan identifications in that country.[18]

Work published since our 1958 results appeared has been generally supportive, although not unanimously so. For example, Roig and Billon-Grand reported one of the earliest political socialization studies conducted on French school children early in 1963. Their results seem to reinforce the image of French youth who at the time of their study were either remarkably vague about or downright ignorant of the major contours of party competition within their country.[19]

Other attitudinal material drawn from an adult sample in the spring of 1970 seems to bear on the cultural assumptions involved. Respondents were asked what they felt were the earliest ages at which children should be exposed to several sensitive topics. Among adults who thought that religion should be discussed with children at all, the mean age proposed was 5.7. For sex, the appropriate age was seen as 11.0. For politics, however, it was felt that the age of innocence should not be terminated until the child was 15.6 years old.[20] More recently, in 1980, the *New York Times*–CBS News Poll replicated this survey in the United States and found that the mean age at which American adults thought parents should start talking to children about politics was a shade under 11 (*Public Opinion,* August-September 1980). In France, 15 percent of adults thought that parents should never talk to children about politics, compared with only 5 percent in the United States. Or again, cross-national data from the mid-1970's cited by Percheron and Jennings (1981) show France joining Britain to become the two most extreme countries of a six-nation study with respect to infrequency of parental discussions of politics with children.

Why should such unusual reticence occur? Any answer we might give is necessarily speculative. It is quite possible, however, that French parents have tended to perceive politics as within the domain of opinion, as opposed to the domains of knowledge and faith, and that they have shunned political discussion in order to avoid the risk of being contradicted by or in front of their children, just as Crozier (1964) feels that avoidance of what he calls the "face-to-face" in hierarchical relationships is a distinctively French pattern of bureaucratic behavior.[21]

At the same time, certain parts of the picture which we generated for the earlier period have been challenged by Percheron et al. (1978) and Percheron and Jennings (1981), on the basis of Percheron's socialization study of a national sample of 903 parent-child pairs conducted in France at the end of 1975. Although her data reflect limits somewhat similar to ours on intra-familial political discussion, she shows that 70 percent of her children report some left-right orientation for their fathers. She contends that for the reasons of party fluidity we have already discussed, it is bootless to focus upon party identification; the true coin of intergenerational transmission is made up of left-right distinctions. This latter argument is one that has intrigued us, and has led us to invest heavily in such measurements in our 1967 study. We shall turn to these measurements in the next chapter, and indeed the question of party versus left-right orientation as the predominant political cue in mass French political perceptions will occupy us repeatedly over much of the rest of this work.

For now, however, it is our impression that the Percheron data showing substantial knowledge by French children of paternal political orientations in 1975 (albeit quite visibly less than, say, the knowledge American children have about their parent's party identification) represents more a development of the new period than a matter of left-right orientations as opposed to parental partisanship. The most obvious reason for believing so is that, contrary to implications, our 1958 question was not restricted to paternal partisanship, but asked explicitly for either paternal party or orientation (tendance). The very large proportions who said quite plainly that they knew neither one fails to fit at all with the 1975 Percheron data. This is not perplexing, however, because our 1967 replication of the family socialization materials shows clearly that change was occurring in these matters, even in the 1958-1968 period; and ultimately, we shall see that the Percheron data fit quite nicely into a broader time series for such change in France.

In any event, it is evident that French cultural patterns in the early period were sharply inhibiting the flow of political information from parent to child, and that this lack of communication was strongly associated in an empirical sense with an absence of partisan identification after the child had reached adulthood. Thus in a remarkable proportion of cases, the French family was simply not an agency of socialization into political partisanship. The next question is whether or not signs of change were apparent at the time of our second study, conducted nearly a decade later.

On the basis of conjectures drawn from our 1958 data, we asked respondents in 1967 whether they had ever heard their father say anything about his own political preferences while they were growing up (see Table 3-2). Two-thirds of the French electorate said that they had never heard such an intimation, and only 13 percent indicated that their father had mentioned his preferences often. We also asked about the degree of the father's interest in politics, as we had in 1958. The distributions in both cases were very low, with about half the electorate unable to remember that he had had any interest in politics whatever, and only about one in ten reporting any substantial interest. In a society often depicted as crackling with intense partisan conflict, this was surely a remarkable conspiracy of silence.

It is not surprising that reports of conversations with the father and estimates of his degree of political interest are very strongly correlated, as may be seen by examining the distribution of case numbers in the interior of Table 3-2. Moreover, both factors seem very potent in accounting for whether or not the respondent perceived any political coloration for the father, a matter which is the main point of that table, fitting nicely with earlier speculation. Of course, in assessing Table 3-2 it should be kept in mind that 40 percent of the French electorate are crowded into the lower right-hand corner of the table: people whose fathers never spoke of their preferences, and who are not recalled as having had any political interest at all.

Just as paternal communication seems to account, at least in a statistical sense, for much of the variation in whether or not the respondent recalls some political coloration for the father, so these latter differences in recollection remain associated in 1967 with whether the respondent himself expresses some partisan identification. Indeed, we find that the parameters of this transmission in the 1967 study fit at least moderately well with those estimated for 1958 in both France and the United States. Again, roughly 80 percent of sons of aligned fathers have a clear identification themselves, as against only about 50 percent among people who have no partisan recollections of their fathers.

One major change in the contours of the data, however, has arisen between 1958 and 1967. This change is a considerable increase in the proportions of the French electorate who can give some account of their father's partisanship. In 1958, only 25–26 percent provided any such account, by very generous criteria. Although some discrepancies between the coding practices of the earlier study and of that conducted in 1967 make precise comparisons difficult, the 1967 data show about 40 percent making these reports, a gain of well over ten percentage points in a decade.[22]

From one point of view, an increase in the proportion of fathers seen as

Table 3-2. Percentages of French electorate recalling any political tendency for father whatever, as a joint function of his conversations about politics and his reported political interest, 1967.[a]

Question: "Did you hear your father speak about his political preferences in this period?"	Question: "Do you recall how interested your father was in politics (while you were a child)?"					
	Very much interested	Moderate interest	Little interest	No interest at all	Do not recall his interest	Total[b]
Yes, often	96[c] (117.5)	88 (70.7)	96 (14.9)	86 (12.4)	d (0.7)	13
Yes, sometimes	86 (37.4)	81 (162.0)	78 (99.0)	80 (44.2)	54 (12.9)	20
No, never	76 (28.9)	46 (122.8)	46 (157.9)	26 (562.1)	14 (282.8)	67
Total[b]	11	20	16	36	17	100

a. Limited to respondents giving the content responses indicated on the reports of father's interest and of his conversations.
b. Entries in the total row and total column sum to 100% and indicate the overall distribution of interest and conversation responses.
c. Cell entries give the percentage of all respondents (number of cases in parentheses) in the cell who were able to give any kind of information locating their father politically.
d. Cases inadequate for the calculation.

identifying with a party is exactly what the logic of the more general party identification model would predict in the French case. If 80 percent of the children of aligned fathers take on a partisanship themselves, and some 50 percent of those without aligned fathers do so as well, then in any electorate with low initial levels of identification these levels must inexorably rise toward an equilibrium state in which just over 70 percent of the electorate have some clear partisanship, and other things being equal, such a value should be approached quite rapidly. In each succeeding cohort, a larger proportion of individuals can be expected to identify, giving the children of that cohort a larger probability of having aligned fathers, and hence a still greater personal likelihood of identification, and so on until the equilibrium point is reached (Converse, 1969).

Such, at least, would be the argument if there were no further factors actively inhibiting the rate of increase. But we have already contended that there were such factors in France not encompassed by the original model. For example, that original model presumes that when a younger cohort of fathers identifies in higher proportions, the increase will be appreciated in its totality by their ensuing sons. Yet, in France, this would not have been the case if the mores of political reticence on the part of parents characteristic of the 1950s had persisted. Thus, a new set of considerations must be introduced.

In a general way, it is obvious how the reticence norms would affect predictions from the model. Only a part of whatever gains were made by succeeding cohorts of fathers would be transmitted to their children, so that "normal" expectations about the rate of growth in partisanship would have to be correspondingly scaled down. But the addition of this new complexity makes it very difficult to be more precise in our growth predictions. For example, it is possible that such a norm might be either more or less strong in the uninvolved and uneducated strata of the electorate newly taking on partisanship than it had been in strata with earlier partisan involvements. Or again, it is quite possible that the parental reticence norm itself had been undergoing change during this period. Any of these possibilities would have had a potent bearing on the precise rate at which partisanship was spreading in France.

Since the 1958 study lacks anything more direct than side comments as to whether fathers talked about politics during the respondents' childhood, we cannot examine in any incisive way how reticence norms were changing, if at all. Yet with an additional assumption or two, we can make reasonable estimates of trends by subdividing our 1967 reports of paternal communication according to the age of the respondent (or "child"). The first assumption is a highly plausible one. It is that no respondent who had not reported paternal talk of politics at age twenty-one would come to make such a report at a later date. Given that the question refers to whether such talk was heard while the respondent was growing up, this means that a "child" who began to hear his father talk politics only after he himself was twenty-five or thirty would not change on this basis from a negative to a positive report. The second assumption remains plausible, although with a greater margin for error. This assumption is that respondents in the decades after they were twenty would not forget such paternal talk once it had been noticed, so that positive responses to the item would not change to negative ones through memory erosion. In short, we need to assume that any changes by age reflect changes in real events of an earlier vintage, without systematic additions or subtractions as a function of ensuing time.

If these assumptions are granted, then we must conclude from Figure 3-7 that reticence norms have indeed been eroding in recent decades, by comparison with the state of affairs in homes during the first thirty years or so of the Third Republic (1870–1900). The pace of change, at least as reflected in these data, was not perfectly regular, nor has its scope been dramatic enough to bring the youngest generation within the practice that seems "normal" in most other political cultures: the French father of the 1930s and early 1940s remained relatively reticent about politics. Nonethe-

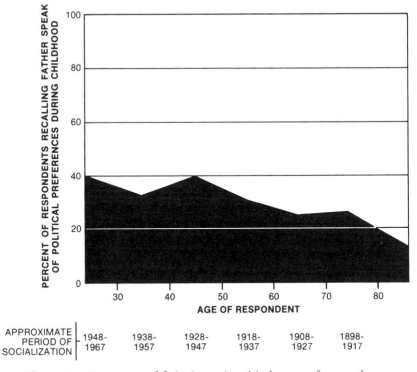

Figure 3-7. Awareness of father's partisanship by age of respondent, France, 1967.

less, it is hard to imagine a progressive "forgetting" mechanism so strong as to account for the data shown.

It is interesting to return to the Percheron parent-child pair data of 1975 while keeping in mind the secular erosion of parental reticence norms. As already explained, in 1958 we found that only about 26 percent of an adult sample could locate their fathers politically for the period of their childhood, but by 1967 the proportion had advanced to a value arguably about 40 percent.[23] In 1975 Percheron found that 70 percent of the children in her sample were able to give a left-right orientation for their fathers. At first glance, this string of numbers suggests that change between 1967 and 1975, if that is the proper interpretation, was implausibly rapid. In other words, if change during the 1967–1975 period had proceeded at exactly the same per annum pace as that during the 1958–1967 period, then by 1975 only about 52 percent of children should have been able to locate their fathers politically, rather than the 70 percent found in the Percheron study.

But this hasty assessment is quite wrong, as a little thought will show. Under simple mechanical assumptions, at least, the Percheron 70 percent can be seen as slightly lower than one might have expected, rather than implausibly higher, especially if we take account of the fact that her percentages refer to fathers located by tendance only, rather than by either tendance or party, and hence should be slight underestimates relative to the 1958 or 1967 figures. This is the case simply because the 1958 and 1967 samples were both of adults, or "children of all ages," whose socialization stretched into the deep past, whereas the Percheron sample is of true children, whose socialization, if any, was occurring in the late 1960s and early 1970s. Thus under rather standard assumptions, the socialization of members of our 1958 sample was occurring in a median sense around 1930, and that of the 1967 sample around 1940. Those times were much more ancient than the year 1970, which is a crude median socialization time under the same assumptions for the Percheron data. Indeed, if we make a simple linear extrapolation from the 1958–1967 gain, the Percheron children might have been expected to show knowledge of fathers in the low 80 percent range, instead of the observed 70 percent. Of course we cannot take such simplistic extrapolation too seriously for any of several reasons, including the reduced currency (tendance only) of the Percheron data and the likelihood that such growth would in any event be more logistic than linear (and hence decelerating in the later stages).

The most important point of all is, of course, that the Percheron data are not only nicely compatible with the hypothesis of a forty-year decline in norms of reticence about politics in the French family, but also that, by leaping forward to a youth cohort, they provide a monitoring of the future which argues forcefully that the trends observed in our 1958–1967 work have persisted and will continue to persist in France.

All told, several roughly hewn observations from our work with paternal partisanship seem quite incontestable. Cultural assumptions about children have in the past created marked blockages of partisan communication within the French family. Although these communication barriers appear to have been eroding progressively over the past several decades, we must remember that many members of current *adult* samples, and certainly those adults of the late 1960s to whom this volume is devoted, failed to receive the kind of partisan political socialization that is very widespread in some other societies. It should not be forgotten that some of this decrement arose not merely because of inhibited communication, although that was important, but also because in point of fact the parental generation itself had fewer partisan preferences to convey, even if it wished to do so. But the important point is that in the past both factors combined to leave many French young people without assumptions, formed early, that they were by birth Communists, or Socialists, or Gaullists. And the absence of these assumptions has meant that as they attained adulthood and participated in electoral politics themselves, they were significantly less likely to display any persisting sense of party loyalty.

Conclusions

Over the course of this chapter we have continued to examine the way in which the French voter relates himself to the national party system that is the chief "conveyor belt" carrying his opinion on public issues of the day upward to political elites and, ideally, into political practice.

As we have proceeded we have made two principal discoveries. The first is that this conveyor belt suffers special uncertainties in France, because the affective bonds between French voters and their political parties have been uncommonly loose. Once again, this is not to say that the French citizen brings to politics any different capacities or expectations from those shown by the common voter in other political systems. Indeed, we have found that where close attachments to specific political parties are well developed, the party identification variable shows much the same set of determinants, process characteristics, and consequences that are familiar from work in other cultures. But it is to say that the institutional and historical configurations confronting the French voter have been visibly displaced in several important regards from those common in many other democracies. Most notably on the institutional side, rapid changes in the manifest identity of parties in the large and fractionalized system make it difficult for abiding loyalties to mature. At the same time, special historical values surrounding political communication within the family, and with children most particularly, have created a reticence about personal partisanship or orientation which has severely diluted the normal intergenerational transmission of party loyalties to the young. These displacements have joined forces to loosen the voter-party bond in France in a very distinctive manner.

The second discovery, very likely to be correct, but more difficult to document, is that change has been occurring in these matters in France in recent decades. The voter-party bond is probably still looser in France currently than in most comparable modern democratic states. But the evidence seems to be that it has been in the process of tightening over the past thirty years or so, and thereby is converging toward a cross-national norm. The reasons for this tightening are probably several, including the logic of the general model of firming partisanship in a maturing system. But they include as well the disappearing of past impediments to partisanship that are more distinctively French. It is even possible that the party system is becoming less chaotic, with few main party formations maintaining their respective identities over longer periods of time, although this continues to be quite arguable. What is much less arguable, but fully as important, is that norms about parental reticence concerning the discussion of politics in front of children have been shifting briskly in the past twenty-five years, once again in the direction of more typical cross-national values. An increase in the number of children aware of parental political orientations means that an increasing number of children will adopt partisan orientations of their own as they mature into adulthood. From this source alone, we should expect levels of partisan loyalty to have been inching forward in France over the past twenty-five years, and although the evidence remains more fragmentary than we would like, the conjecture seems confirmed.

If all of our past theorizing has merit, then the next expectation is that with partisanship levels rising, the highly distinctive volatility of French voting, of the kind documented by Rose and Urwin (1970) for the period through 1968, should have declined in more recent years. This hypothesis is less easy to assess than might appear. The best way to gauge vote volatility is to summarize rates of change in overall percentages of votes cast by party from one election to the next. But these values in most countries show rather marked situational variations in the short term, so that long-term trends are hard to discern without a long time series. There have only been three national legislative elections since 1968 (1973, 1978, and 1981), and hence only three vote transitions if we start with 1968. These three transitions do produce data congenial to the hypothesis: that is, two of the three transitions show greater stability values than any others in the whole series of eleven transitions since World War II.[24] This result is not definitive, but it is surely suggestive.

However interesting these winds of change may be for theory or for France, it is important for the reader to remember that we have been able to chronicle them in part by peeking forward in time, beyond the period of our actual study. This means that our representation study data deal with a period in which voter-party bonds in France remained quite loose by cross-national standards. The resulting diffraction of political cognitions and enduring party loyalties has consequences for the representation process which later parts of this volume will explore.

First, however, there are some other features of French political culture that are commonly assumed to promote greater continuity and stability in the electorate than the kaleidoscopic party system can by itself encourage. It is to these other factors that we shall turn in the last two chapters of Part I.

4

La Gauche et
la Droite

When André Siegfried wrote his classic description of stability in French voting patterns, he paid scant attention to that flux of political parties which we have emphasized in the preceding chapters. Instead, he worked within a fixed firmament bounded at its two poles by the extreme left and the extreme right. Whatever specific political formations might represent these camps in any given election was not of profound interest to him. Quite apart from the ebb and flow of party groups, he was deeply impressed that the same microregions which were supporting parties challenging the status quo in the first years of this century had also supported ideologically comparable parties in the 1870s, or even during the Revolution a hundred years before (Siegfried, 1913).

This fixed firmament paced off from left to right was hardly Siegfried's personal creation. It was deeply imbedded in French political culture and remains so to this day. At the time of the Revolution, the radicals sat to the left of the president's box in the French legislative assemblies, and the conservatives to his right, giving rise to the political connotations of the terms.[1] With the passage of years, increasingly fine gradations in the space between the extreme left and the extreme right have come into general use to express nuances of opinion, so that an informal calibration of the *hemicycle,* or semicircular arrangement of assembly seating, into as many as seven positions or more (extreme-left, left, left-center, center, and so on) have become a familiar part of political discourse, popular in Siegfried's time and continuing in frequent use during the Fourth and Fifth Republics.

This currency of "left," "center," and "right" has of course been widely exported, and is a commonplace for politically sophisticated observers around the world. But there is probably no country in which it figures so centrally in the political vocabulary as in France, and this in turn may go beyond the accident of birth. Such an abiding yardstick against which policy propositions as well as the ideological proximities and driftings of parties and prominent leaders can be plotted in fixed and common terms is a convenience that may be sorely needed in France to give simplicity and order to the flux and complexity of political life.

The prevalence and obvious utility of this coinage, along with Siegfried's observation of basic left-right continuities in the mass voting record, all suggest that our initial emphasis on voter relationships with specific parties as a source of stability in the French electoral process may have been somewhat misplaced. Perhaps in this political culture the personal sense of an abiding location somewhere on the left-right continuum tends to be highly developed among voters, and thus serves as a functional equivalent for the specific-party loyalties common to other political systems. Such fixed orientations could help the common voter to "ride out" the flux of parties, much as a boat at anchor can bob in a fixed position while waves roll beneath.

In their excellent survey research studies of popular French politics in the 1960s, Deutsch, Lindon, and Weill began explorations of left-right orientations in preference to emphasis on party loyalty as the central political attribute of the voter. They showed their national samples a seven-point scale stretching from the extreme left to the extreme right, and asked:

> One usually locates French people, where their political opinions
> are concerned, in terms of a scale like this. As you see, there are two
> main groups, the left and the right. A person can place himself more
> or less to the left or more or less to the right. Where would you put
> yourself personally on this scale?
>
> ⌣   ⌣   ⌣   ⌣   ⌣   ⌣   ⌣
> Extrême-Gauche, Gauche   Droite, Extrême-Droite
>
> —(Deutsch, Lindon and Weill, 1966, p. 13)

Several aspects of their results are of great interest to us. First, these results showed that almost 90 percent of the French electorate typically chose some location on such a scale. This was suggestive, if not definitive, evidence that the key terms did have wide currency at a mass level. Furthermore, such a proportion of self-locations runs far higher than that for party identification in France, and indeed is about the magnitude that one expects to find in other countries for people who at least "lean" toward an enduring attachment with some specific political party. In other words, it appears that large numbers of French respondents who are politically unclassifiable in terms of party loyalty can indeed be given some location with such an approach. Finally, the authors showed that over the course of six surveys conducted within a moderate time period (two years), the aggregate distribution of these identifications across the electorate displayed about the same stability that is often found for party identifications elsewhere.

In view of contemporaneous work indicating that much of the American electorate seemed remarkably insensitive to ideological yardsticks of the left-right kind (Campbell et al., 1960; Converse, 1964), these results hinted at a much more ideological electorate in France, a conclusion retrospectively congenial to Siegfried and fitting other national stereotypes as well. Moreover, evidence concerning restricted party loyalties in France might be written off as having little significance if functionally equivalent anchors on a left-right continuum were customary for most French voters.[2]

In our own surveys of the late 1960s we elaborated somewhat on the procedures used by Deutsch, Lindon, and Weill (1966). We presented *all* of our respondents—including political elites running for Assembly seats as well as the rank-and-file voters evaluating them—with a continuum laid out from "1" ("extreme left") to "100" ("extreme right"), supplemented by intermediary labels distributed at appropriate points along it.[3] Both mass and elite respondents were asked to locate the French political parties on this continuum.[4] After these judgments were made, helping to form an enriched frame of reference for the scale positions, we asked both mass and elite respondents to indicate their own personal positions in the same left-right terms.

This chapter is devoted to an exploration of these left-right perceptions of party locations, in conjunction with self-locations on the same continuum.[5] These materials contribute in several ways to the development of our argument in this volume, and it is obvious that we would be remiss if we tried to describe the political process in France without confronting head-on the chief descriptive currency of the culture. For example, we have been dealing with the voter and his party system, as well as the salience of specific parties to him. But we have as yet said nothing about what particular meanings these parties may hold for him politically. Perhaps the most simple and obvious component of their public images is bound up in perceptions of their left-right positions. Moreover, our most general concern is focused on political representation, a process requiring communication between common voters and their representatives. It is hard to evaluate such a communication process without asking whether some of the key symbols used, such as left-right calibrations, are viewed in the same way by both parties.

The central problem of the chapter, however, remains that with which we began. To what degree do left-right orientations provide French voters with elements of meaning and long-term stabilization which are effective substitutes for party loyalties? Superficially, the data already presented seem to provide some positive answer. As we delve more thoroughly into the properties of these left-right measures, however, we may in part revise our view.

The Perceived Left-Right Locations of the Parties

The impression of ideologized electorates in western Europe has been reinforced not only by the fact that most adults in these countries are willing to locate themselves in left-right terms, but also by the observation that when asked to locate familiar parties in left-right terms, the average of the locations offered for each party seems quite plausible, strongly implying that a consensual meaning for the left-right currency pervades these mass electorates.

Our data from France of the late 1960s reflect both of these properties. But we are in a position to push our inquiry a good deal further. For one thing, the accuracy of a set of average locations attributed to familiar parties may conceal a great deal of individual dispersion of conceptions, and in the limiting case we might encounter a "correct" average compounded of nothing but flagrant errors bracketing the "real" party position. Therefore the dispersion of these estimates is of as much interest as their central tendency. Moreover, since the electoral process is intended to be a communication system, it is of vital interest to know whether the party system in the mind's eye of political elites has the same contours as it does for the public as a whole, even in an average sense. We also can probe questions of substantive meaning and temporal stability which are at issue in imputations of an ideologized French electorate.

Average Party Locations

If we take the numerical locations assigned to each party by our sample of French voters and simply average them, we find for 1967 the attributed left-right party structure shown in Figure 4-1. We see that if the picture is considered broadly enough, citizen perceptions of party locations appear on balance to be reasonable. Certainly the Communists (PCF) are placed at the extreme left, the Alliance Républicaine (AR) of Tixier-Vignancour is at the far right, and the intervening assignments are not bizarre.

It is nonetheless instructive to examine the display in greater detail. Although the ordering of parties is largely what one would expect, the Républicains Indépendants (RI) of Giscard d'Estaing are an exception. The issues on which this group of dissident Gaullists had distinguished themselves from the parent UNR were not at all readily classifiable in left-right terms. It is likely, however, that a panel of expert observers would in this

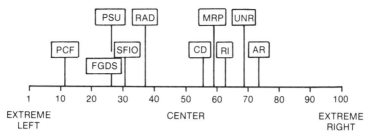

Figure 4-1. Average perceptions of party locations on left-right continuum, French national electorate, 1967.

period have considered them to lie to the right of the UNR, and not to the left, as in the average public perceptions.

A few other details of spacing between the several parties might perplex the knowledgeable observer. For example, the Radical-Socialists (RAD), although once a clear leftist party and even in their moribund state of 1967 located somewhere between the Socialist left and the rightist camp, seem in Figure 4-1 to be considerably closer to the true left than the collective behavior of their *notable* (locally prominent) representatives since World War II would justify. One might also expect the Alliance Républicaine to be located more dramatically to the right than the figure shows. Or again, although it is true that the PSU was mainly a dissident left-wing splinter group from the SFIO, just as Figure 4-1 implies, it is likely that much of that party's leadership would have fancied its policy positions to be more extremely leftist than those of the aging and domesticated Communist party. Many outside observers would have taken that view, though the case depends heavily on what political elements one chooses to emphasize. In any event, very few analysts would have seen the PSU as closer to the SFIO than the Communists by as large a margin as that of the average mass perception.

With these quibbles in mind, it is interesting to compare these mass perceptions with those of the political elite jointly involved in our study. The average locations attributed to the parties by 272 Assembly candidates who ran in our districts in 1967 are juxtaposed with the mass perceptions in Figure 4-2. Here we find, in a degree which is almost amusing, most of the "corrections" which we were tempted to make in Figure 4-1. For the elites, the Giscardian splinter group is seen as lying to the right of the UNR, not to the left. To be sure, the Radical-Socialists are placed by these elite observers farther to the left, by a tiny margin, than was true of the mass voters. But since all other leftist parties are moved still farther to the left in these elite perceptions, the Radicals do end up occupying a more "middling" position between left and center than they were accorded by the common

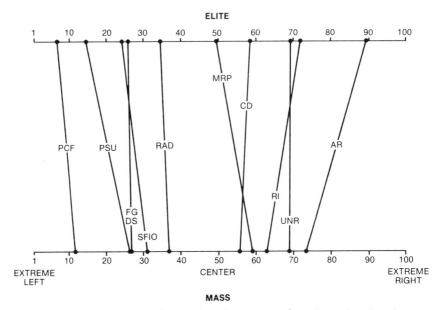

Figure 4-2. Average left-right locations assigned to the major French party formations by mass and elite, 1967.

voter. The Alliance Républicaine is displaced very sharply to the right by the elites. In fact, the general rule is that the elite observers make sharper discriminations more generally, pushing parties of the left further to the left as well as those of the right further to the right. On the left, however, the PSU is moved the greatest distance, so that it is no longer closer to the SFIO than to the Communists, "correcting" another minor oddity in the array of mass perceptions. In sum, while the mass assignments are certainly recognizable, the elite perceptions of party locations are more "familiar."

Can we decide which of these perceptual "maps" is the "right" one? We have already betrayed a temptation to choose the elite version. We can argue, for example, that our politicians are obviously much closer to the situation than the rank-and-file voters, so that they bring much more, and more accurate, information to their judgments. Indeed, when shortly we shall attempt a more systematic diagnosis of the differences between the mass and elite maps, we shall find that we can account for a great majority of the specific discrepancies with a rather parsimonious proposition about imperfect information on the voter's side. Thus, for some purposes, it may be fair to answer that the elite view is the more correct. But there is another sense more germane to our own inquiry in which this answer is wrong, because it is addressed to the wrong question.

It is useful to consider that each map is "right" for the population that generated it. If the mass view of the party system differs from a more informed elite view, this is already an important political datum. The electorate is, after all, making its input to the general communication process on the basis of its own understanding of the situation. That understanding is represented with patently greater accuracy by the mass map than by the elite one.

Why this matters can be made clear through an illustration exploiting the discrepancies between the maps shown in Figure 4-2. Suppose that in a given election the Républicains Indépendants draw some modest groundswell of new votes away from the parent UNR. If the election process is a communication mechanism, as in theory it is supposed to be, then this vote increase for the RI is a message which the citizenry has tried to enter in the political system. According to the mass map, the left-right content of this message (and there may be other overtones, according to the situation) is that more "leftist" positions on the flanks of the UNR have gained in popularity. This must follow if the new RI votes come from people who share the general mass view of the RI as a left-leaning splinter of the UNR. But this is only the input side of the communication process. What happens on the output side, as the message is received by the elite commissioned to act on the basis of the popular mandate? As the elite half of Figure 4-2 attests, the politicians know full well that the RI is a right-leaning splinter of the UNR. Therefore if the message coming through the election channel is that RI votes are increasing at the expense of the UNR, the message as received suggests a popular thrust to the right, which is the political opposite of the intended message.

Whether or not the appropriate elite will in any event be responsive to such a message is obviously a significant further consideration, but one which can be set apart from the question of communication accuracy per se. What is important for our immediate purposes is that we have portrayed a pathology in the communication process, one serious enough to turn a message completely around between the cognitive maps of the senders and receivers. Both maps are "right," in that they are real to the actors using them as a basis for understanding the world. But for any voters trying to send a message and any representatives trying to be responsive to popular sentiment, the consequences turn out to be dysfunctional. It is in this sense that curiosity as to which map is the more accurate can often be quite beside the point. Since a communication process is involved, the significant question may well have to do with the nature of the fit between the maps.

Left-Right Party Perceptions
as a Measurement Tool

Many of the questions one might want to ask of French voting data require some prior determination as to the relative left-right positions of the political parties. If we wish to ask, for example, what relationship exists between the status of landless rural proletariat and leftist voting in France, we cannot even begin to construct an answer without first deciding which party's votes we are going to count as leftist. In the same vein, if we wish to form a correlation between social status and left-right voting, we cannot do so until we have decided what is appropriate as a left-right ordering of the parties.

Since we now know not only the left-right order in which the electorate itself places the various contending parties, but also have quantitative evidence as to the varying distances which separate neighboring parties arrayed in such a left-right order, what would be more natural than to incorporate this information into our analyses, thereby avoiding some decisions which would of necessity be somewhat arbitrary if we made them ourselves?

In the limiting case, we might score the vote of any individual respondent according to the left-right location which he himself assigned to the party he chose. In such a scoring system, a vote for a party like the Radical-Socialists would take on as many different degrees of a left-right position as there were variations in individual supporter assignments for that party. Most Radical-Socialist voters would see it as lying in the left-center zone running roughly from 30 to 50 on our scale, and their votes would be scored accordingly. But if there were any stray Radical-Socialist supporters who located that party on the extreme right, with a value of 80 or 90 on the scale, then their votes in such a scoring system would go into our calculations as far-right votes.

We shall in fact experiment with such a scoring system at a later point. It is important, however, to clarify what such scoring does and does not mean. First, it obviously refers to the vote message as *sent,* and not as *received* by the elite observer. Under all but exceptional circumstances, that observer will implicitly assign to all Radical-Socialist votes the same left-right message, an assignment which, as we have seen, may or may not coincide with the view of the average supporter. Second, we should remember that such a scoring system refers only to the left-right content of the message as sent, and cannot capture any unrelated dimensions of meaning that may have been intended. In election situations where the heart of controversy has come to rest momentarily on some issue which crosscuts normal left-right differences, such scoring would be quite worthless as a tool for analyzing the intent of the vote message. Although we must keep this limitation in mind, it is less oppressive than may appear, for the simple reason that most generic interpretations of French voting outcomes do focus on the left-right content of the popular mandate, and that is what our individual-level scoring system addresses as well.

There is, however, a good reason for discontent with such a scoring system. If we consider what might lead a Radical-Socialist voter to give a perplexing far-right position for this party, one plausible cause might be that he is very inattentive to left-right differences in general. He may have cast his vote for the Radical-Socialist candidate because he is a family friend, and his far-right assignment for the party may be a haphazard shot in the dark, given in thorough ignorance and lacking any functional connection with the reasons for his vote. If it is true that indifference to left-right distinctions does rise significantly the more widely left-right party assignments depart from consensual views of any given party, then our individual-level scoring might have some undesirable features.

Another kind of scoring system—the one which we shall use most frequently in our work—puts more weight on consensus at the mass level in these perceptions. In this version, we propose to score as the left-right meaning of any given party vote the average locations for that party across the electorate, as shown in Figure 4-1. Since these averages conceal a fair amount of individual variation, we would not be too comfortable with such a scoring scheme as being able to capture an intended left-right message without a better sense of the factors that produce this individual variation. For example, it is often argued that there is great heterogeneity of political subcultures across the various regions of France, and that specific parties vary widely in their political meaning—including their left-right position—in different areas. Suppose that much of the individual variation in locations assigned to the Radical-Socialists arises because in the South and Southwest of France the Radicals were in our period a clear leftist party, whereas in other parts of the country they were generally seen as very much to the center or even leaning mildly to the right. In such a situation, both the intended left-right message and the left-right interpretations given to the Radical vote at the elite level might legitimately differ by region in a fashion that our assignment to national-average left-right values would badly obscure. But if the bulk of individual variation in attributed locations of the parties arises because of very deviant guesses from people disinterested in the left-right distinction at the outset, as our preceding example supposed, then a heavier dependence on national-consensus scoring would be warranted.

Individual Variation in Locations
Perceived for Parties

A good deal of individual variation does underlie the assignments of party locations provided by the voters in particular. This dispersion is portrayed in Figure 4-3.[6] In examining this figure, we must keep in mind that party locations were elicited only for parties at least recognized by the respondent. Given vast differences in party visibility, this means that ratings were provided by less than 50 percent of the sample for some of the least visible parties. Since Figure 4-3 is plotted in terms of proportions of the total sample (rather than proportions of the raters of each party), the areas beneath the curves for the most visible parties, such as the Communists and the Social-

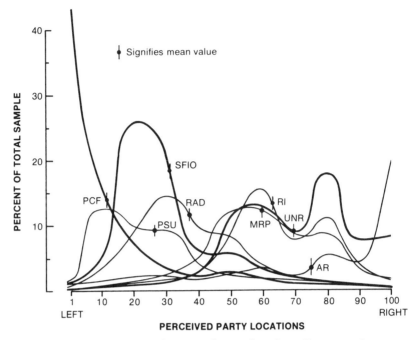

Figure 4-3. Dispersion of perceived party locations, France, 1967.

ists, are much larger than those for the less visible parties, such as the PSU.

Several facts strike the eye immediately. First, there are clearly defined peaks or modal values in the locations assigned for almost every party. At the same time, almost every zone of values is occupied by at least a few respondents in assigning every party. This combination of events means that each distribution is skewed: if the mode is to the right of center, there is a long tail of the distribution stretching off to the left; if the mode is to the left, the long tail stretches to the right. What this implies statistically is that in almost every case the *average* party location as displayed in Figure 4-1 lies closer to the center at 50 than the mode or most commonly assigned score for that party. Moreover, it follows that the more extreme the mode for a party, the longer the tail, and hence the more dramatic the displacement of the average toward the center. By far the most frequent score assigned to the Alliance Républicaine is 100, or the extreme-right value. But a few mass respondents give that party leftist locations of 30, 20, and even one. In the same way, the most common assignment for the Communists is at one, or the leftmost extreme. But the long tail, including some few extreme-right assignments, moves the mean quite notably toward the center.

In a very general way, then, such long tails have the effect of shrinking all the locations portrayed in Figure 4-1 toward the center of the continuum. What is the meaning of these long tails? Surely the people whose responses create these tails are giving very deviant responses to the locations of the parties involved, relative to the way most of their compatriots see the same parties. But that does not entirely answer the question. Why are their responses so deviant?

One hypothesis worth testing is that deviant assignments tend to arise among people who are quite unclear as to the true left-right policy interests of the party they are trying to rate. Such a hypothesis involves two different types of ignorance: first, lack of familiarity with a given party, leading to pure guesswork as to where it stands; and second, a more fundamental lack of clarity as to the meaning of left-right distinctions more generally, so that placement of any party is likely to be somewhat haphazard. Fortunately, we can check both portions of this ignorance hypothesis against our data.

One indicator of party familiarity which we have used before involves the distinction between those respondents who mentioned a party on their own initiative and those who merely recognized it among a residual set of parties displayed after they had conjured up all the parties they could think of spontaneously. It would be reasonable to imagine that parties readily recalled are more familiar to the respondent than those only recognized after prompting. Therefore it confirms the first facet of our ignorance hypothesis to show that the average locations assigned to parties by people merely recognizing them lie significantly *inside* the total-sample means (that is, toward the center at 50) shown in Figure 4-1, relative to the assignments of persons who spontaneously cited the same parties, whose assignments, as a corollary, lie regularly *outside* those same total-population means (see Figure 4-4). Clearly more guesswork and hence more deviant tails result when people try to locate parties they only recognize on a list but have not recalled.

To evaluate the second facet of the ignorance hypothesis, we can turn to a further question which was asked of respondents in the same connection. After we had asked our informants to assign left-right positions to parties they recognized and to choose a position for themselves, we asked them what they considered to be the most important differences between parties of the left and those of the right. This question was designed to find out how meaningful left-right distinctions might be to the respondent, as well as to suggest what meanings were in fact used. Almost one-quarter of the sample indicated that they did not know what differences separated left from right. Now confusion at this level does not necessarily mean that a person cannot give a fairly orthodox left-right assignment to a particular party. After all, if one has heard the Communist party described for many years as "the extreme left," and the Socialist party as merely "left" but not extreme, then he or she is likely to have little difficulty putting these two parties in their "proper" zones on our continuum, even though he or she

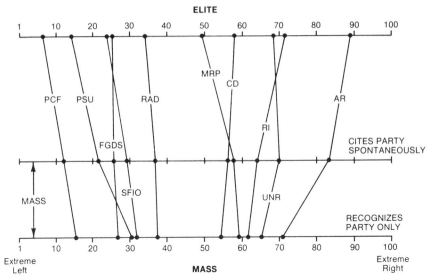

Figure 4-4. Average left-right party locations for elite and mass by party salience, France, 1967.

may be quite unclear as to what kinds of postures a party must take to warrant these conventional left-right labels.[7] Nevertheless, it would stand to reason that the frequency of haphazard guesswork in locating the parties would be higher among people vague about left-right differences than among people who cognize them more thoroughly.

This expectation is handsomely borne out. In the case of every party, including even those usually located rather close to the center (such as the Centre Démocrate), the average locations given by people with some substantive understanding of the left-right continuum are farther outward from the 50-point than they are for raters who appear to lack such understanding.

All of these comparisons are also corroborated by other statistical indicators of guesswork. One such indicator is the pure degree of consensus (or lack of variance) in given groups as to the details of location. If we asked a set of professional geographers point-blank what the longitude of St. Louis, Missouri, is, we would be likely to get some little scatter of responses around a true value of nearly 90°W. This is information for which few would have enough points of reference on tap to ensure thoroughly accurate estimates, but for professionals the scatter of locations in degrees longitude would be quite limited. If we asked a lay population the question, and refused to accept "don't know" responses, the scatter of estimates would be amazing: it would be large even for those who understood the currency of longitude, for they would rarely think in those terms, and for those who did not the resulting number would be essentially random.

Nicely fitting this paradigm, we find a clearer consensus about where the various parties are located among those evincing understanding of the left-right continuum; the dispersion of responses among the less informed tends to be greater, as indexed by the standard deviations of their assignments. The same contrasts occur, in even sharper form, between the assignments of our mass sample as a whole and those of our elite sample. These latter "professional geographers" show much greater agreement as to party locations than is found among the lay public. The standard deviations of their assignments are always less, and often much less: on an average, the reduction in such dispersion is about 40 percent.

All of this evidence makes it clear that guesswork due to imperfect information is a major source of the variation among individual perceptions of party locations. Then what does this mean for our choice of the precise set of average locations to be used as standard "objective" locations in scoring the left-right position of our respondents under varying circumstances? Because variations in information produce uniform shrinkage or expansion of perceived positions for all parties—much like fixed marks on an elastic band—it should make almost no difference whether we borrowed these scores from the more ignorant of our mass respondents or from our elite sample, since the kinds of correlational uses for which the scores are needed are quite insensitive to such routine transformations.

We have seen, however, that a party-specific ignorance term enters in which is associated with differences in visibility among the various parties. In general, the less visible the party, the more guesswork about its location and the more its average assignment will lie toward the center relative to the consensual assignments of the highly informed. A perfect example is provided by our two extreme parties, the highly visible Communist party and the less well known Alliance Républicaine. In the total mass sample (Figure 4-3) the modal Communist assignment is one, and the mean is displaced by a modest dozen points toward the center. But for the Alliance Républicaine, the displacement is by 27 points (to 73, from 100), and in the subgroup of the mass sample most ignorant of left-right differences, the displacement is a full 40 points! These differential displacements remove us from the uniform-shrinkage case, and in some instances actually lead to a shuffling of the left-right order of the parties. Indeed, the increased guesswork occasioned by the less well known Républicains Indépendants is an important reason why the mass sample locates them to the left of the well-known UNR (or "inside" it), whereas the elite sample on the average puts them to the right, or outside that party.

Although these party-specific effects are not overpowering in magnitude, they are sufficient to put some small premium on what average locations are used as a scoring device. Of course, the ignorance effects are real ones, and could be expected to influence choice behavior and the sending of messages upward. Individuals may vote for a party that they consider to be centrist when they might refrain from doing so if they knew that well-informed people considered the party to lie to the extreme right. From this point of view we would be quite justified in using the average locations as seen by the full mass sample, ignorance and all, for our scoring system. But it can be argued cogently that people who give deviant locations for particular parties are usually people for whom that party is not salient in any event, and hence less likely to win their vote. In the degree that the blurring of party locations inward toward the center comes from such people, we might well want to exclude their perceptions and limit our average to people for whom this or that party is a lively possibility as a choice.

This consideration leads naturally to the question: what locations tend to be given for the various parties by their immediate clienteles, those people who express an identification with them? Since guesswork should be minimal for identifiers—occurring only where the voter does not think in left-right terms to begin with—everything we have said up to now would lead us to predict that identifiers of a given party would give average locations which are less displaced toward the center than are the overall mass ratings. But this pattern turns out to be the exception rather than the rule. In seven comparisons out of ten possible parties, the party faithful give an average location *closer* to the center than is true of the mass sample as a whole, although in two or three of these seven instances the differences are entirely trivial, with the identifier ratings nearly identical to the national mass averages. As a clear example of the most frequent pattern, the total mass sample placed the Communist party at 11.6; mass respondents who did not freely cite the Communists but recognized them when mentioned showed the normal displacement of imperfect information, giving them a mean location of 15.4; but the same mean among Communist party sympathizers was 16.1, or more centrist still!

It is not, of course, hard to understand why these patterns are as they are. First, the three exceptions to the rule—those parties whose identifiers do give a more extreme location than is provided by the total sample—form a very coherent set of parties which have the joint properties of novelty and low visibility. The low visibility means that guesswork is running high among "outsiders," so that displacement of the national means toward the center is particularly strong. The novelty, signifying new splinters within the party system, means that identifiers are few and hard-core; they are militants proud of their ideological distinctiveness. Hence their own partisans see these three groups as more extreme than they are rated by the total sample, most of whom are outsiders. These three parties are the PSU, the Alliance Républicaine, and the Républicains Indépendants.

It is among the older mass parties that identifiers tend to see their preference as *less* extreme than the total sample. Here the effects run in the opposite direction. The party is well known to "outsiders," and those to whom it has no appeal tend hostilely to sharpen the contrast between their own position and the position attributed to that party. "Insiders" of such a mass party who have succumbed over time to the broadened appeals necessary for any party to attract a large-scale base are on the average more centrist than the position assigned to the party by elite observers. And if outsiders are prone to *contrast* the party location with their own position, "insiders" tend to *assimilate* such an attributed position with their own. Thus they give it a more centrist location than is assigned by the total sample, most of whom are necessarily "outsiders." At the same time, although we have come to associate relatively centrist assignments of the parties with dispersed responses, it is interesting to note that the centrist locations of their parties offered by identifiers tend more often than not to show *less* dispersion than is true of the total sample: identifiers show some consensus in "pushing" their parties toward the center.

Up to this point we have examined the displacements of perceived party locations in two subgroups that might have some claim to defining a general left-right scoring of party positions. Among the more informed segments of the electorate, these assignments tend to be relatively expanded outward from the center. Among the sympathizers attracted to each party, these assignments tend more often than not to be contracted inward toward the center. In between lie the national averages of Figure 4-1. Thus we become increasingly interested in accepting these latter averages as the best compromise for a scoring system.

Regional Variations in Left-Right
Perceptions of the Parties

There remains, however, the disturbing possibility that national averages might conceal marked regional variations in these perceptual locations of the parties. It is certainly a persistent feature of political lore in France that substantial divergences exist between regional subcultures in the patterning of political competition, including what the various parties are taken to represent.

Although various ways of partitioning France into regions might be used, we have employed nine geographic regions whose boundaries have been chosen specifically to maximize differences in political subcultures across the country (see map, Chapter 5).[8] Our mass samples in these regions do show significant differences in their average self-locations on the left-right continuum, and in predictable directions: the West of France shows the most rightist coloration, with the East close behind; the northern rim of the Massif Central, the Midi, and the North are the farthest to the left. As we shall see later, there are other differences in the determinants of mass political choice across these regions that in some degree support the contentions of distinctive political subcultures.

The left-right positions attributed to the political parties, however, fail to show much regional differentiation. The only noteworthy exception is provided by the Alliance Républicaine, the most recent addition to the party system at the time and hence a group very unevenly recognized across the French domain. Its placement is quite diluted toward the center in some of the more rural of our regions, to the point where it actually falls "inside" the UNR by a slight margin. The MRP and the Républicains Indépendants, already very close together in the average national perceptions, interchange positions by a tiny margin in three regions. Otherwise, the left-right ordering of the parties is identical across all regions, and the general spacing between them is quite similar as well. The dying Radical party, often thought to have quite diverse left-right significance in different regions, always takes up the same relative position, and its nine regional means fall within a narrow absolute range on the continuum (between 34 and 42). All told, although regions may vary substantially in their political habits, their perceptions of the firmament of national parties seem sufficiently homogeneous that our national-average perceptions do little violence to them.[9]

Stability of Party Locations over Time

A final desirable property in any set of average locations that is to be used in a general scoring of the left-right position of the parties is that the specific placements not be subject to violent fluctuations from year to year. In 1968 we asked our respondents once again to give us left-right positions for parties that were prominent in that year. Because of changes both in parties and in some party labels, only three party names were repeated in just the same form in the second year, thereby providing exact comparisons over time. The national-average locations for these three parties came astonishingly close to being identical in the two years: the average difference in placement from one year to the next for the same party barely exceeds one-half of one point on our 100-point scale!

This performance is the more remarkable because of the turbulent events of May and June 1968, which intervened between the two measurements. In fact, our elite respondents did make modest adjustments in their left-right placements of the parties in 1968—especially for the three parties yielding comparisons with the mass sample—which were a clear response to the differential roles played by the various parties during the disturbances. Thus in a sense our national-average locations from the mass sample are almost too inert and unresponsive to events. Yet the inertia observed in these assignments is itself a finding of substantive interest. It appears that party images are more resistant to change among the mass of common voters than they are for elite observers. It is almost as though the voters' images are broad and insensitive stereotypes rather than being fine-tuned to the flow of political events as the elites' images are. We can profit from such inertia by regarding the national-average locations provided by the mass sample in

1967 as a scoring system for the left-right position of the parties which is likely to be quite accurate for the whole general period, rather than for the month of the election alone.[10]

Self-Locations to Left and Right

The fact that most French voters are willing to report personal locations on the left-right continuum, as well as to provide estimates of party locations which are on balance roughly appropriate, undergirds our impressions of an electorate which is relatively sensitive ideologically. Actually, although various studies have shown proportions of French voters as high as 90 percent willing to choose left-right positions, the corresponding figure in our study fell just short of 80 percent. This lower figure is not surprising, since our self-location question was not posed until after the respondent had been obliged to give left-right assignments for all the parties he had recalled or recognized. Other French surveys have dealt with a single, simple question in which it is relatively easy for a respondent vague about left and right to pick a point arbitrarily. The long battery of party placements was undoubtedly intimidating to those with a limited grasp of the dimension involved.[11]

Indeed, of those mass respondents who were subsequently to give clear definitions of what left-right differences meant, a good 90 percent did provide these self-locations. This was true for only 54 percent of those who had trouble supplying a meaning. There was no corresponding attrition, of course, among our elite respondents, virtually all of whom supplied a personal location on the continuum.

As we shall see, the question of meaning weaves through all of these self-location data, for both mass and elite. But let us begin by laying out the basic facts. Figure 4-5 presents a pair of smoothed distributions indicating the way in which the two samples array themselves on the same left-right scale. There are rather marked differences in both form and center of gravity between the two populations on the same numerical scale. The average self-location in the mass sample in 1967 lay just a shade to the left of a perfectly centrist position (a mean of 47.5), whereas the same mean within the elite sample was a rather leftist 30.5. We shall find that this discrepancy requires cautious interpretation. First, however, let us consider the salient features of each distribution taken separately.

Mass Locations

As might be expected, the general form of the mass curve is more nearly bell-shaped than flat or U-shaped: extreme positions attract only a fringe of responses, although both extremes are in fact populated. The distribution is essentially trimodal, with some piling up of cases in the 20–30 range on the left and a smaller mode at 80 on the right. But by far the most prominent

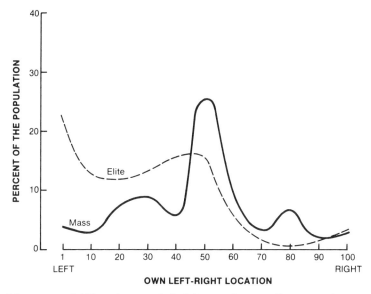

Figure 4-5. Self-locations on left-right continuum, France, 1967.

feature of the distribution is the towering mode in the center. A full quarter of the total mass sample, and almost one-third (31 percent) of those choosing any locations, put themselves exactly at the central point, 50.

It is worth wondering how meaningful as a location this 50 is for the dominant plurality of French voters who choose it. Of course, a centrist or middle-of-the-road position in politics can be a meaningful and dedicated one. Some French parties have erected centrist programs. Truly centrist parties, however, have never been able to claim the resounding voter support that might be expected on the basis of Figure 4-5. And although centrism may well have its true believers in the French electorate, the 50-point location on our scale is an obvious selection for a person who is neutral, uncommitted, or even thoroughly indifferent to or ignorant about this generic axis of political dispute. Therefore those flocking to 50 as a personal location might well resemble voters who have no party identification more than a set of partisans.

Indeed, Deutsch, Lindon, and Weill (1966), working with the dominating mode that also arises at the central position of their left-right distributions, have shown that as a general matter political involvement describes a U-curve from extreme left to extreme right, and that in this heavily populated center category it plunges to its nadir. The self-styled centrists are such a politically apathetic lot that most of them (all but a few who *are* involved politically) are placed by these investigators in a special category off the left-right continuum, appropriately labeled "le marais."[12]

Our own data merely serve to confirm these findings. The large pha-
lanx of respondents at 50 turn out to be less politically involved than their
peers who chose other left-right locations. They also are less likely to give
ideological definitions for the differences between left and right or, for that
matter, to attempt any definitions whatever. And finally, along with those
who do not locate themselves at all, they are disproportionately responsible
for those scattered and idiosyncratic estimates of the left-right locations of
the parties, figuring prominently in the kind of guesswork which deformed
the average locations assigned by mass respondents, as noted in the preceding section.

Finding what underlies these centrist responses casts helpful illumination in several directions. It puts a somewhat different light on the high
levels of willingness to provide these self-locations on the part of the mass
French electorate. It helps to explain why 80–90 percent within these voter
samples will self-classify in left-right terms although, as we shall soon see,
only about 65 percent understand what these terms mean. Indeed, we seem
within reach of a very simple resolution of what threatened to be a major
cross-national anomaly. If we were to add the 20 percent who do not give
locations for themselves in our sample—also a politically uninvolved set of
people—to the 25 percent who locate themselves at the 50 point, then we
are already dealing with nearly half of the total French electorate. This gets
us into a range reminiscent of the nearly 40 percent of the American public
unable to say what the differences between "liberals" and "conservatives"
mean politically. In short, the fact of self-location can be a rather superficial
datum.

Given the low levels of political interest and participation among the
centrists of Figure 4-5, there is a real sense in which the two smaller modes
of the mass distribution, at left of center and at the right, represent much of
the political conflict that exists in France at the mass level. In other words,
it may be both legitimate and fitting to erase mentally most of the central
mode of the distribution as noncombatant, leaving a curve which is nearly
bimodal.

Elite Locations

The elite curve in Figure 4-5 is also bimodal, the chief mystery being why it
is displaced so far to the left. Obviously, by most modes of accounting the
vast majority of French political elites are not left of center. Are we faced
here with a cultural phenomenon of the kind to which Siegfried (1930,
p. 73) called attention more than half a century ago when he wrote that in
French political life one must "never lose contact with the left" and "always
be to the left of one's opponent?" Or is there some more prosaic explanation? In contemplating this mystery, two facts should be kept in mind. One
is that we are dealing here with self-images, and not with policy postures as

external observers might code them. The other is that our panel of elite respondents is scarcely a proper sample of the total universe of French political elites. It *is* a proper national sample of the candidates who ran for Assembly seats in the 1967 legislative election and who were prominent enough to garner more than 1 or 2 percent of their district's votes. That year the leftist opposition to de Gaulle appeared to be riding a crest of some popularity, which may have brought out an unusual number of leftist hopefuls.

Although both of these caveats are apt, it is not clear that they explain these peculiar data. The data seem wrong. Perhaps our elite respondents interpreted our left-right scale running from 1 to 100 in a palpably different way from our mass respondents. But even a moment's thought assures us this cannot have been the case. The elite, like the mass, respondents were only asked their self-locations after they had located the political parties on the same scale. There was no unusual displacement to their party assignments. In fact, we have seen that if we could remove a guesswork factor from the mass ratings, the use of the scale in the two populations would be essentially identical. It was only when the elite respondents were asked to locate *themselves* that a dramatic leftward displacement occurred.

These patterns taken together raise a further intriguing possibility, which is that most of these elite contestants preferred to think of themselves as populating the left wings of their own political parties! This is not a strict corollary of the pattern described up to this point, since it is possible that most elite informants placed their own parties at or symmetrically near their own positions, whereas their opponents from other parties located that party considerably to the right. Fortunately, our data permit us to sort out these possibilities easily.

We find that in every one of the six party comparisons possible at the elite level, the candidates of the given party located it on the average farther to the left than did outside opponents. The effect is slight among parties of the left, in part because there is little room for such displacement. Thus, for example, Communist candidates gave locations for the PCF which average 3.5. Non-Communist candidates located the PCF on the average at a value of 7. As we move to parties and candidates of the right, however, the leftward displacement of estimates for the respondent's own party become quite striking. At the far right, for example, we interviewed only two candidates of the small Alliance Républicaine, but the average left-right position assigned to that party by these two adherents was 35.5, as opposed to an average assignment of 90 by the remaining candidates of other parties.

The classic case of these effects is provided by the Gaullist candidates, of whom we interviewed about eighty persons—the number depending on definitions of membership. These persons, like the other elite respondents, were given three possible Gaullist rubrics to rate in left-right terms: the UNR, the Ve République, and "Gaullists." Gaullist candidates assigned values to all three of these rubrics averaging, in a very narrow range, from

50 to 52 on the scale. Candidates of other parties, however, rated these three groups in a much more rightist 66–74 range.

Thus a very generalized preference prevailed among these elites to envision their own parties as being farther to the left than outsiders would have assumed. It remains possible, however, that in addition, these candidates also tended to consider themselves as personally falling still more to the left of the position they ascribed to their party, a position already left-biased.

This possibility cannot be detected on the far left, where party candidates arrayed their own positions quite symmetrically around the left-displaced position they accorded to their own parties. But as soon as we move even to the parties of the moderate left, there is a slight tendency for candidates to put themselves to the left of the position they ascribe to their parties. And when we move to parties of the center and the right, this personal flight to the left again becomes marked. It is noteworthy even among the Centre Démocrate; it becomes impressive among the Gaullists. Setting aside some Gaullist dissidents who might be discrepant more generally, we find a striking picture. Less than one-third of the mainstream Gaullists placed themselves at a point on the left-right continuum identical with their ratings of their Gaullist party. Of the remaining two-thirds, 96 percent placed themselves to the left of the position they accorded their party, with only 4 percent to the right!

All told, these data are fairly saturated with the felt importance of being relatively leftist, for oneself as well as for one's political party. Given the short-term political tides favoring the left in 1967, it is possible that this "glamor of the left" was a momentary matter. The evidence, however, suggests otherwise. For one thing, although the 1967 political atmosphere favored the left, the short-term bias in this direction was not dramatic. For another, it should be remembered that our interviews with candidates were taken after the election results were in, and under guarantees of anonymity. Eagerness to present oneself as relatively leftist for electoral advantage would have been irrelevant.

The most telling data, however, come from a small reinterview conducted with some of these same politicians after both the disorders of May 1968 and the legislative elections of the following month. As those elections indicated, the May revolt had brusquely shifted the general political climate from the mild leftism of 1967 to an intense rightism. If the elite leftist preference of 1967 is a response to the immediate climate of the period, then we have much more reason to expect a dramatic rightist preference to emerge in the 1968 interviews. But we find nothing of the sort. There is a shifting of one's own left-right locations somewhat to the right in response to events, just as there is in the mass sample reinterviewed in 1968. But the symptoms of the leftist preference, for oneself as well as one's party, are still quite visible.[13]

Hence we must conclude that this curious preference for symbols of the left at the elite level in 1967 and 1968 is a more durable phenomenon, the latter-day expression of Siegfried's (1930, p. 74) "mystical attraction to the left, analogous to that of the Mohammedan to Mecca or that of [Jules Verne's] mad Captain Hatteras toward the North pole"—itself anchored rather deeply in French political culture. We may reflect, along with Siegfried, that the most important historical event in that political culture, ingrained in all well-educated Frenchmen, had pitted a heroic left against a decadent right. The legacy of these values, reinforced by traumas like World War II, has endured in an endless sequence of party rubrics stressing the egalitarian, republican, and democratic virtues of even their rightist proponents. Thus, although somebody must defend the status quo in the eternal political conflict, it may be more comforting in France to do so under the most leftist symbology possible.

The Centrist Preference in Mass Self-Locations

Given the pervasiveness of the leftist preference at the elite level, both for one's preferred party and for one's own location, it is worth asking whether there is any counterpart for such a bias at the mass level. The answer seems to be flatly negative. Where personal locations are concerned, in nine of ten possible party comparisons, identifiers with a given party fix their personal locations closer to the *center* of the left-right continuum than to the positions they assign to their preferred parties.[14] We shall call this a centrist preference.

There are several plausible interpretations of this centrist preference on the part of mass voters, but one interpretation should *not* be put upon it. We saw earlier that mass voters tended to ascribe more centrist positions to the various French parties than were accorded to them by the elites. We discussed this pattern in terms of a statistical artifact, though one permitting a more substantive interpretation as "guesswork." It is tempting to imagine that the centrist preference now being scrutinized is simply another example of the same artifact.

It can hardly be so. The centrist trend in party assignments due to guesswork was most marked where observed parties were least salient. Here, of course, we are dealing with the party of maximal salience for the respondent: the party he claims to be identified with. Hence there should be little if any guesswork involved. Yet he considers the position of his preferred party to be more extreme than his own position.

More tenable interpretations of the centrist preference in these mass self-locations are available. One which appeals to us harks back to the classic McClosky (1960) findings that the issue positions of party elites turn out to be more extreme than is characteristic of their own party's rank and file.[15] From this point of view, the centrist preference observed in the self-locations of the French rank and file may well reflect no more than a simple recognition by the party sympathizer that this is true. The adherent finds the left-right coloration of his particular party to be quite palatable, but he is also aware that his party leaders are more vociferous in their policy positions than it would occur to him to be. Therefore he codes them as a shade more extreme than he feels he himself is, where the left-right continuum is concerned.

In addition to these effects, much the same centrist tendency is visible when we compare the respondent's assignment of a location to his preferred party with the position ascribed to it by others, be they mass or elite. In other words, while the mass voter sees his preferred party as slightly more extreme than he feels himself to be, he also sees it as still more centrist than others consider it.[16]

To summarize, then, when we combine personal locations with perceptions of party locations, we find an intriguing contrast between mass and elites, whereby in two operational senses (personal and preferred-party) the mass sample demonstrates a marked centrist preference, but the elite sample displays a curious preference for the symbols of the left.[17]

Understanding of the Left-Right Distinction

Up to now we have dealt with labels and their uses. We have seen that much of the mass electorate in France can apply the left-right labels to parties in ways that seem quite conventional to the outside observer, and that they can characterize their own positions in these terms. At occasional points we have seen hints, however, that these facts may be rather superficial. Thus there is a significant level of ignorance concerning some of the less visible parties. Moreover, we have developed some suspicions as to the ideological sensitivity of that large plurality of French respondents flocking to locate themselves at the 50-point center of our left-right scale. In other words, where prominent political parties and left-right labels are concerned, a large portion of the French electorate knows "what goes with what." The next question is the degree to which they know "why."

One way of illuminating this matter is very direct. After our mass respondents had located both the parties and themselves in left-right terms, we went on to ask: "People often distinguish between parties of the left and parties of the right. In your opinion, what are the most important differences between the left and the right?" Our elite respondents were posed the same question at the same point, although, for obvious reasons, the initial sentence was deleted.

Such a question is bound to elicit a great range of qualitative responses which can be coded from any number of viewpoints. In fact, we have coded these responses (as many as four per respondent) in more than one way. Our main code, however, was aimed at discerning differences in levels of understanding of these terms, in ways that would bear on the ideological sophistication of the respondent. This code was organized for the French case exactly as it had been when it was applied to answers from American voters concerning the meaning of liberal-conservative differences in the politics of the United States.[18]

These coding rules give first priority to any mention, made in all the answers of one respondent, which invokes broad differences in political philosophy or ideology as the essence of the left-right distinction. This top "ideological" category (our first category) obviously includes discriminations drawn between parties of motion and change, on the one hand, and parties defending the status quo, on the other hand. It also includes contrasts between Communist or Socialist doctrines and capitalism, the republican-antirepublican axis, and even such antinomies as that between pragmatism and ideology. The respondent dealing at any point with such abstract principles of government or society achieves this highest level.

The second category involves persons who make none of the above kinds of responses, but who instead describe the most important left-right differences in terms of differential support given to concrete interest groups which vie over goods mediated by the political system. The most obvious, and always most numerous, responses in this category deal with class conflict: the left supports the workers, or *le petit peuple* (little people), while the right favors the *patronat* (owners), the rich, or the bourgeoisie. But any indication of generalized support to any population, ranging from *commerçants* (business people) to the church, is included in this Group Conflict category.

The third and fourth categories include descriptions which, in their most elevated form, point out disagreements over particular narrow issues, usually current ones. Domestic issues are placed in the third category as slightly more relevant in a conventional sense to left-right distinctions, while foreign policy mentions alone are demoted to the fourth category. The fifth category contains responses that are less issue-oriented than any of the foregoing. This category, not requiring isolation in the American case but warranting attention for the French responses, involves the description of left-right differences purely in terms of current personalities or, at most, leadership styles.

The final category, charitably included at the bottom of the "content" (substantive) responses, encompasses those replies which seem to aim at some substantive point, but one which is quite unintelligible to the coder. Most of these responses simply sidestep the actual terms of the controversy, with pithy observations such as "left and right are different because they do not agree," or "they struggle against each other for power."

Further discriminations can be made among noncontent responses. Probably the most reliable discrimination of all merely separates those who confess that they "don't know" what any important differences between left and right might be from those who give other kinds of noncontent responses, such as the judgment that "no true differences" separate left and right.

Elite Understanding of Left and Right

It may seem absurd on the face of it to ask whether our elite respondents understand left-right differences. Of course they do. Nonetheless, when we set up our code many years ago as a means of evaluating the ideological sophistication of mass publics, we assumed implicitly that political elites would give responses that would be coded quite differently from those given by all but the most ideological of common voters. But the coding is necessarily somewhat crude, and detractors have asked whether thoroughly informed and highly ideological respondents, subjected to the same simple question and summary coding, would in fact look different from the rank-and-file respondents. Therefore we took pains to follow exactly the same interviewing and coding procedures with our elite informants, to see how they would fare.

We were gratified to discover that a full two-thirds of our elite sample gave descriptions of left-right differences which our code classified in the top, or "ideology," category. This proportion is more than five times as great as that falling in any other type of response.

The next most prevalent elite response is of a rather special kind. It involves the 13 percent who claimed there were few important differences between left and right, and hence bypassed any content description. In other work, we have found this "no difference" response to spring from two very different sources. It can be either an effort to conceal ignorance or a response of supersophistication. The latter form is more or less nostalgic: the differences between left and right are "not what they used to be," "it has become hard to distinguish between the performances of leftist and rightist governments," and so on. Of course this response scarcely means that the speaker brings no political substance to the left-right distinction. Indeed, in the American case we append a further probe to ask such respondents what the differences *used* to be, and respondents of any political attentiveness usually have no trouble providing an "ideological" response. It seems likely that if we had added such a probe for our French elites, the responses would have increased the ideology category quite dramatically.

At this point, however, we are less interested in the distribution of these responses from the elite per se, than we are in how the elite responses compare with those from the mass sample. We have used the coding of elite responses to suggest what might be an upper limit or ceiling due to crude

measurement that might hover over any effort to gauge the ideological sensitivity of a mass population. When we make the appropriate comparisons,
however, we find (Figure 4-6) precious little need to worry that we might
mistake the elite population for the mass one because of crude measurement
of the understanding of the left-right distinction. Even ignoring the likelihood that "no difference" responses conceal a perfect ideological understanding in the elite case, the distributions are dramatically different. While
67 percent of the elite sample give incontrovertible ideological responses,
only 11 percent of the mass sample do. Nearly one-quarter of the mass-sam-
ple respondents simply confess that they do not know what the difference
may be between left and right, while only 1 or 2 percent of the elite sample
make such a manifest response. It might not be outrageous to conclude, on
the basis of these loose measurements, that the mass sample as a whole
shows only one-seventh to one-twentieth of the understanding of the left-
right distinction which our elite sample has.

Mass Understanding of Left and Right

It should come as no surprise that the profile of meanings for left and right
emerging for the French mass sample (Figure 4-6) shows a vastly closer resemblance to parallel codings for the American mass electorate than it does

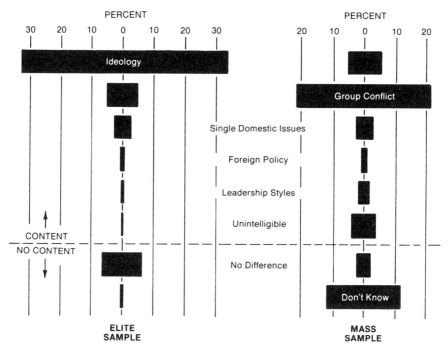

Figure 4-6. Profiles of meaning attributed to left-right differences by
mass and elite samples, France, 1967.

to the French elite profile. On the one hand, fewer Americans (63 percent) can supply any meaning for the liberal-conservative distinction than can the mass French electorate for the left-right distinction (76 percent). Again, this might well be expected in view of the greater frequency of the left-right shorthand in French political discourse. On the other hand, more Americans give descriptions of the meaning of the distinction which are classified as ideological, or more like the modal French elite response (ranging from 17 percent to 25 percent, depending on the period), than we find in the French electorate.

The parallels between the French and American mass distributions continue beyond the gradient of understanding to at least some gross features of substantive detail.[19] The most frequent substantive response in the American case links "liberals" with the working class and sees "conservatives" as defenders of business or the well-to-do. The corresponding group-conflict impressions loom very large in the French responses as well. Between 20 and 25 percent of the total sample, or more than one-third of those giving substantive answers, offered as their primary description of the left that it stood up for the workers, or le petit peuple, and said at the same time that the right represented the bourgeoisie, the rich, capitalists, or management. An additional group approaching the same size either made at least one of these responses or associated the left or right with some closely related class grouping ("the left favors the trade unions").[20]

Thus a major core of these responses is made up of highly conventional links between the two political camps and specific population groupings that concretize a basic status or socioeconomic cleavage. We were interested not only in how prevalent these obvious associations might be in France, but also in whether any competing concentration of such connotations might surface as well. In view of the strong historical ties between the Catholic Church and the political right, and the often bitter anticlericalism of the left, religious references seemed to be a plausible candidate. Furthermore, as we shall see in the next chapter, a religiosity dimension in France predicts more sharply to left-right positioning in the mass sample than socioeconomic differences do. Hence we were quite intrigued to see the incidence of religious connotations cited for left or right, relative to socioeconomic ones.

The results are suggestive, though hardly overwhelming. It is true that significant proportions of our mass respondents do mention religious differences in describing the left-right dimension, and these references constitute about 10 percent of all content responses. In fact, once past ideological descriptions and socioeconomic associations, religious references are about the only other type that registers in any concentration. There would be no comparable admixture of religious explanations in the United States or most other countries.

In addition, the group construing the left-right axis entirely in religious terms, though small, does show characteristic perceptual displacements of particular parties on the left-right continuum that are of a type which seems quite predictable (Converse, 1966). One would not anticipate that their perspective would be totally different from the more purely socioeconomic arrangements of the parties, because there has been a considerable coincidence between the conventional left-right locations of the parties and their postures on the clerical issue. But this coincidence has broken down at some points. As we saw earlier, for example, the MRP was launched after World War II as a Catholic party, yet one supporting the left on social issues. At the opposite extreme, the Radical party, despite its increasingly "middling" posture on socioeconomic issues, retained a considerable legacy of anticlericalism from the period of its leftist youth around the turn of the century. Thus the left-right differences between the MRP and the Radicals should appear to be stronger if one thinks in terms of religious rather than socioeconomic cleavages. And, indeed, while the left-right "distance" put between Radicals and MRP in our total sample averages some 22 points, the distance expands to 34 points, or is more than half again as great, if one sees the left-right cleavage in religious terms. Hence the understanding of the dimension has further consequences.

Nevertheless, to keep matters in perspective it must be recognized that religious references are dwarfed in number by the frequency of socioeconomic connotations registered by the mass sample, as demonstrated by Table 4-1, which focuses on the two types of responses in isolation. We see also in this table that, if anything, elite respondents are more likely than mass respondents to introduce religious references into their descriptions, but this seems to occur simply because they give richer and more comprehensive descriptions of left-right distinctions in general.

In view of the rather stark differences in apparent understanding of the left-right dimension between mass and elite, as captured in Figure 4-6, it is natural to ask how much variation in the quality of such understanding can be unearthed within the mass sample taken by itself. An obvious prediction is that persons who are more involved in politics and more attentive to po-

Table 4-1. Relative preponderance (percentages) of socioeconomic and religious distinctions in left-right descriptions by mass and elite.[a]

Distinctions	Mass	Elite
Socioeconomic only	82	74
Both socioeconomic and religious	12	22
Religious only	6	4
Total	100	100

a. Includes only respondents offering either religious or socioeconomic distinctions between left and right.

litical information are more likely to have a clear sense of the meanings of these basic distinctions.

We wanted to partition the mass sample into three strata to highlight monotonic trends across them, and we have used an index of political involvement for this purpose.[21] The relative sizes of these strata are dictated in some degree by the distribution of index scores, but we had no interest in seeking a division of the sample into equal thirds. In fact, in the light of lore suggesting that avid attention to politics is given only by a rather limited fraction of most electorates, we isolated a mere 15 percent of the sample in our top involvement stratum. A bottom stratum includes 28 percent of the sample whose inattention to politics is nearly complete. This leaves a "middle mass" of about half the electorate (57 percent).

As Figure 4-7 shows, the quality of understanding does vary quite notably across these involvement strata. As we move from the bottom to the top stratum (that is, from right to left on the figure), the proportion of ideological definitions increases by a factor of greater than four, while the proportion straightforwardly confessing ignorance declines by a factor of nearly five. These differences are certainly satisfying in their magnitude. It is instructive to notice, however, that although the most involved 15 percent of the mass sample look considerably more like the elite sample than do the

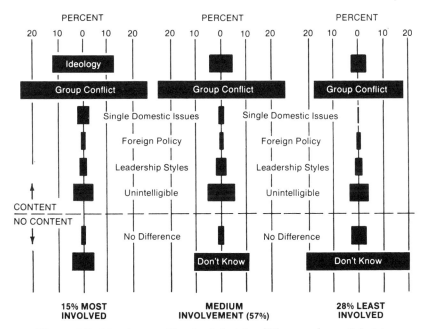

Figure 4-7. Meaning profiles for left-right differences by political involvement within the mass sample, France, 1967.

rest of the mass voters, it is still true that, by any reasonable way of plotting the matter, the elite sample differs from the most involved of the voters by a wider margin than separates the top and bottom strata of the mass sample. Thus, for example, if we calculate a percentage difference index between the various profiles of left-right meaning in Figures 4-6 and 4-7,[22] we find a difference of 77 points between the top and bottom of the mass sample, as opposed to a difference of 110 points between the elite sample and the most involved 15 percent of the mass sample. This is not the only time in this book when we shall be impressed by the greater distinctiveness between the political belief systems of our elite and mass samples than between the belief systems of the upper and lower involvement strata of the mass sample (see, for example, Chapter 7).

Nor are the reasons for such a difference entirely obscure. Presumably we are dealing here with matters of information-processing, and the attentiveness of our political elites to politics is nearly preemptive. It would seem likely that in the general period of our study, these elites would have been averaging at least eight hours a day on political matters, and perhaps more. It is unlikely, on the other hand, that the 15 percent of the mass sample most attentive to politics would have been averaging even as much as an hour a day, as opposed to the likely few minutes a day in the bottom 28 percent of the electorate. Or again, if there were ways to enumerate all the bits of political information held by all of our respondents, mass and elite, it would seem likely that the absolute difference between our elites and the most attentive seventh of the electorate would be much greater than that existing across the involvement strata of the electorate.[23]

The Functional Use of Left-Right Orientations

We have now completed our survey of three sets of raw materials concerning the left-right dimension which our interview schedule afforded us for both mass and elite: perceptions of left-right locations for the many French parties, self-locations on the same continuum, and descriptions as to what the continuum means to these respondents in more substantive political terms. Thus we can return more knowledgeably to the basic question posed at the beginning of this chapter: does the left-right yardstick function as a substitute for party loyalties in lending order and continuity to perceptions and decisions of the French voter? In weighing a response, it is worth keeping in mind what we have learned in the interim about the frequently shallow character of left-right understandings for much of the public.

No question of ultimate function is easy to answer. For one thing, such a question is impossibly broad and vague. We can narrow it somewhat by noting with Downs (1957) that left-right calibrations are supposed to function as a shorthand which reduces information costs. Assessments of competing policy options can be mentally referred to such a continuum and compared with the viewer's sense of personal location on it. More important still, political candidacies which integrate over a large number of postures on specific policies can be similarly located and compared.

We shall certainly be trying to assess the functioning of these frames of reference in terms like this. Nonetheless, even this narrowing fails to bring us to operational tests, and the variety of such tests which we might apply to the problem is still huge. Putnam, Leonardi, and Nanetti (1979) use a small causal analysis, for example, to assess the degree to which party affiliations seem to have functioned over time to stabilize the left-right positioning of their Italian elites on political issues. This analysis gambit, which showed party affiliations to play an important but very far from exhaustive role in such stabilization, was entirely appropriate, particularly since these investigators could profit from a unique six-year panel study. Even this test, however, did not attempt to establish a "horse race" between partisanship and left-right locations as competing frames of reference to produce a more stable political landscape in the minds of the voters. When we focus on the problem in this form, it is clear that many types of analysis would address the issue in one degree or another.

We do not, in fact, expect to arrive at a conclusive answer to this formulation of the problem in this chapter. But we shall make several stabs at the question here, and we shall continue to probe it at several points later in this volume. Those wishing a simple and incontrovertible verdict will be disappointed, even at the end of our labors. Yet we need not apologize because a definite "tilt" in the verdict will emerge. And better still, along the way we shall cast a great deal of illumination on the question of function. Several states of affairs surrounding the function question which are not only plausible conjectures but are commonly assumed to pertain can, in fact, be ruled out quite unequivocally. And by narrowing the possibilities in this way we shall in due time gain a clearer understanding of those that remain.

Idiosyncrasies in Perceptions of Party Locations

Almost any theory which imputes importance to the left-right dimension as an efficient orienting device assumes that specific parties are evaluated by the voter with at least some eye on the fit between their left-right position and his or her own. A whole class of theories of this type would be discredited if it turned out that there was no correlation between voters' self-locations on the continuum and the left-right positioning of the parties for which they chose to vote.

We are not about to report that no such correlation exists. As a matter of fact, if we attribute left-right scores to each of the parties according to their consensual placement in the mass sample (see Figure 4-1), and then examine the correlation between one's own left-right placements and the scores for the party chosen at the polls, we find a substantial value running over $r = .50$.

We recall, however, that there was considerable dispersion of perceived locations of the various parties in the mass sample. One weak brand of litmus paper we can use to detect something about the functioning of these left-right orientations in voting is to ask whether knowledge of these idiosyncrasies of perception helps us in understanding vote choices. In particular, let us rescore the vote choice not with the consensual left-right location for the preferred party, but rather with the score attributed to that particular party by the specific voter preferring it. We would expect that the correlations between own location and vote choice would advance as we take idiosyncratic perceptions into account, if indeed any importance is attached to calibrations of the left-right kind by the common voter.

Since we have various election years and two tours in each, we can check a multiplicity of times for an advance in correlation magnitude. But they all tell about the same story, and we have the largest case numbers for the two vote tours of 1967. The relevant comparisons are shown in Table 4-2. Thus we see that the advances do exist when idiosyncratic perceptions are taken into account, and they are not trivial in size.

The significance of these advances varies according to the level at which they are assessed. At the level of system communication, which is important to the study of representation, this advance is troubling. The elites scrutinizing the vote mandate for its policy significance show substantial consensus as to where the parties are located in left-right terms, and they certainly assume that a vote for a given party reflects a preference for that degree of "left-rightness." The advances in correlations when idiosyncratic perceptions are taken into account mean, for example, that voters who are themselves at 60 on the left-right continuum, that is, who are moderately rightist, may vote for a party which most people, including the elites, see as

Table 4-2. Left-right scoring of the 1967 vote in consensual and idiosyncratic forms.

	1967	
Vote choice scoring	Tour I	Tour II
Average left-right location in mass sample	.56[a]	.53
(Weighted N)	(1202)	(976)
Idiosyncratic location by voter	.64	.60
(Weighted N)	(896)	(742)

a. Correlation (r) between own left-right location in 1967 and the indicated left-right scoring of the vote.

moderately leftist, such as one at 40, but which they themselves place at some moderate-rightist value like 56 or 64. Such people are at the root of a correlation advance, but they also epitomize a gap between the message as sent and the message as received.

At the same time, the advance of correlations when idiosyncratic perceptions are recognized seems to suggest that these perceptions are of some importance to the actors. This lesson is a weak one, because the correlation advance says little about the nature of this importance. In particular, causality remains perfectly ambiguous. Three terms are at issue: the choice of a preferred party, the assignment of a left-right location to it, and one's own left-right location. These may have developed in all possible permutations of a temporal order to produce the observed advance in the vote correlations. Thus, for example, it might be that instead of his own left-right location being primary, the actor first had a party identification, later acquired some rough (but often inaccurate) notion of where that party stood in left-right terms, and finally, when asked by the interviewer, determined that he had to be at a nearby left-right location himself because of his partisanship. Even if this contrary scenario has produced the correlations, however, it is true that the actors feel it is important to tidy up their account with these left-right adjustments; and the correlation advance remains consistent with the possibility that a sense of one's own left-right location is both causally autonomous and of high importance to such voters in other political evaluations.

Therefore, if causality is at issue, we probably need to exploit the longitudinal features of our data set, and we also need to pit these left-right orientations against party identifications in a more explicitly diagnostic manner.

The Parallel Role of Party Identification

In one of the few efforts to confront left-right self-locations with the construct of party identification, Inglehart and Klingemann (1976) surmise that the causal primacy of one or the other of these forms of political self-definition varies across political cultures. In particular, they hypothesize that the relative importance of left-right locations will be greater the more multiparty the system and the faster the historical turnover of major political parties. France is for them the epitome of the situation where left-right primacy seems likely.

There are several reasons why making close comparisons between party identification and the left-right self-locations is inordinately difficult, as we shall soon see. Yet one of the most obvious questions to be asked in a longitudinal mode has to do with the relative stability of these two forms of political self-definition. The main theoretical interest of both constructs stems from their potential role as anchors, or reference points, for political evaluations. Anchors are not of much use unless they are themselves stable.

Unfortunately, in this setting there are two kinds of stability that can be monitored. The self-evident one is stability of self-location. This, however, can only be calculated for those who give themselves some substantive location in two successive panel waves. Thus there is a further question of stability surrounding the very matter of any self-definition. In the preceding chapter we pointed out that there was considerable turnover in whether or not respondents claimed to have some party identification. In the course of the 1967 and 1968 interviews, some 23 percent of the mass respondents participating in both waves professed a loyalty to some specific party in one year but not in the other. In comparison, some 15 percent of the same sample chose some personal self-location on the left-right continuum in one year but not in the other. Of course, larger portions of the sample in *both* years classified themselves in left-right terms than in partisan terms, but it seems fair to conclude that the tendency to make or to sidestep a left-right declaration is somewhat more stable than the tendency to make or avoid a profession of party loyalty.

Yet when we look at the stability of substantive choices among those who do make declarations in both years, the picture becomes rather different. In the preceding chapter we noted that the continuity correlation for party identification between 1967 and 1968 was $r = .834$. The comparable value for left-right self-locations is $r = .620$ ($N = 528$). If we wish to think in terms of proportions of stable variance in these two cases, we may take the square of these values. This suggests that for party identification, the shared (stable) variance is about 70 percent of the total, whereas for left-right locations it is only about 38 percent. Thus it might be possible to claim that for two-time reporters, partisanship is nearly twice as stable as left-right self-location.[24]

Another way in which we might use our longitudinal data to assess the relative efficacy of party identifications and left-right self-locations in providing stabilization for political evaluations would be to contrast the stability of other political orientations and behaviors among (a) those lacking partisanship, but classifying themselves in left-right terms, and (b) those with partisanship, but no left-right position.

We shall in fact complete our current discussion with a few comparisons of this type. But there are some very severe restrictions on what we can do in this mode. One is obvious. Given the somewhat mixed verdict with respect to the stability of these two constructs (the left-right position being more stable over time, but, among those with partisanship, the relative locations being much more stable), it would be ideal to take self-definitions as stated at the initial point in 1967 and, without asking whether or not these self-definitions were restated later, simply to see how well the 1967 data predict other obvious things, such as vote in 1968 or 1969. We are unable, however, to do that comparatively for our two test groups because one group by definition lacks partisanship as a 1967 predictor, and the other lacks 1967 left-right self-locations.

Table 4-3. Percentages reporting party identification and left-right self-location, mass sample, 1967.

Party identification	Left-right self-location		
	Reported (incl. 50)	None reported	Total
Specific party reported	52.4	5.3	57.7
No specific party reported	26.0	16.3	42.3
Total	78.4	21.6	100.0[a]

a. Weighted N = 2007.

Another problem is apparent once we cross-classify our mass respondents according to whether or not they report the possession of these two orientations as of 1967 (see Table 4-3). Possession of these types of political self-definition tend to co-occur: if the voter reports one form, he tends to report both (a tau-b of .35). This may not be surprising substantively, but it means that the number of cases for comparison between the off-diagonal cells (one orientation without the other) are fairly limited. The proportion without a party but with some left-right location appears to be much more ample in numbers, as the logic of the more prevalent self-locations dictates. But some of this advantage is deceptive, since it will be recalled that more than one-third of those who failed to profess allegiance to some specific political party nonetheless cited some object of political identification, such as de Gaulle or a labor union. Finally, if we wish to look at longitudinal data, case shrinkage is more severe, since the 1968 mass study was only a half-sample.

Possession of both of these self-definitions is naturally associated with political involvement, as we have seen. People with attachments to specific political parties are much more involved than those with no attachments whatever, while those with other or vague identifications fall in between. Similarly, those who claim some left or right location are more involved than those who claim none, with those claiming the neutral point of 50 falling in between. But there is a difference of nuance between the two self-definitions and the involvement variable. Symptoms of involvement relationship are stronger for party identification than for left-right location, a fact which produces one intriguing result.

If we attempt to heighten the contrast between our two test groups by isolating persons who reported some partisanship in both 1967 and 1968, but who did not offer a left-right self-location either time, and opposing them to persons choosing a left-right location both times but partisanship neither, we are reduced to very small case numbers indeed (ten to fifteen), but these two extreme groups are quite different from each other. The two-time partisans without left-right locations seem about as involved politically as are the two-time partisans who also give personal self-locations left and right in both waves, given the high level of their reported voting turnout. The opposing group—in neither wave partisan but in both waves reporting a left-right position—is totally different. Its involvement in politics seems even less than that among voters who do not give either self-description in either year, in view of their low rate of turnout at the polls. Thus the left-right labels do seem to provide some flimsy structural basis for those too remote from politics to relate to the party system. Yet the gap in prevalence of self-classification between partisanship and left-right is not so dramatic as it might seem, once attention is restricted to the active electorate engaged in regular voting.

If we regain a few cases by defining our test groups on their 1967 reports alone, predicting across time and letting whatever volatilities of possession and position in these two orientations take their toll implicitly, a few other interesting comparisons can be made. We measured left-right self-locations in 1967, 1968, and 1969. Therefore, even for our test group which gave a partisanship but no left-right location in 1967, it is possible to examine the continuity correlation between the 1968 and 1969 left-right reports, just as it is for the other test group which expressed left-right locations but not party identification in 1967. One expectation might be that those with left-right orientations (but no party) as early as 1967 would show greater continuity in their 1968–69 left-right reports, on grounds that they would be more firmly oriented to left-right cues than our partisans of 1967 who gave no left-right self-location at that time.

This expectation fails rather abysmally, however, if we are willing to attend to small case numbers. Those with 1967 left-right positions but no party show a 1968–69 continuity in left-right self-locations which is only $r = .66$ ($N = 177$). This is below either obvious comparison group: those with both self-descriptions in 1967 show later left-right continuities mounting to $r = .72$ ($N = 279$), while the most sharply contrasting group—those with only partisanship to guide them in 1967—actually show a 1968–69 continuity in left-right self-locations of $r = .87$ (N of only 11), higher than any of the other groups. Among competing explanations for these differences, one would be that party attachments do in fact provide a more stable cynosure for political evaluations than does a sense of location on the left-right continuum. Another is that persons with partisan attachments (alone) are more highly involved in politics than persons with left-right locations (alone), and stronger political involvement usually means more stable political orientations. A third, combined explanation might invoke partisanship and involvement as a joint causal nexus producing more stable evaluations. But the basic fact—that these statements seem more stable for 1967 partisans than for those orienting to left-right without a party—is impressive.

Another longitudinal comparison between these test groups defined by their 1967 reports can be wrenched from continuities in voting choice, 1967 to 1968. Here the two crucial comparisons with the most cases use either the correlation of 1967 and 1968 first-tour votes or the same correlation for decisive-tour votes in the same two years.[25] The verdict in this instance is clouded by small case numbers and empirical differences very limited in magnitude (Table 4-4). Nonetheless, the absolute trends seem to favor party identification as a stabilizing agent over left-right self-location.

We conclude with a final comparison which is conceptually less incisive in that it gives up our small test groups to return to the total sample, yet which is undergirded by much more satisfying case numbers. Let us pose the following hypothetical "desert island" problem. We have interview time to measure one of these political self-descriptions, but not both. We know that both orientations are somewhat unstable, and that both fail to classify many voters. But we want to predict not merely the vote reported in the same interview as the self-descriptions are reported but also a later vote choice. Which self-description should we choose for measurement?

This formulation invites us to compare relationships between self-descriptions given us of partisanship or left-right location in 1967 with voting choices cast at some later time: in this case, 1968. To make all of these entities commensurable, any party cited as an object of loyalty has been assigned a left-right value based on the consensual ratings also used to give a numerical score to the vote choices in 1968.

The results are quite striking. For our panel respondents, 1967 left-right self-locations predict 1968 voting choices in the same mid-.50s range already noted for the prediction to the more proximal 1967 vote. To be precise, the

Table 4-4. Differential continuities in voting choice, 1967 and 1968, by self-descriptions offered in 1967.

Self-descriptions	Tour I	Decisive Tour
Both partisan and left-right	.82[a]	.87
(Weighted N)	(295)	(255)
Party identification only	.67	.72
(Weighted N)	(21)	(19)
Left-right self-location only	.61	.64
(Weighted N)	(104)	(104)
Neither partisan nor left-right	b	b
(Weighted N)	(13)	(14)

a. Correlation (*r*) between the stated parties voted for, scored in terms of consensual left-right locations, in 1967 and 1968.

b. Case numbers of voters too few for the calculation.

correlation with the first tour vote in 1968 is $r = .57$ ($N = 465$), and with the second tour it remains .52 ($N = 270$). If instead we use 1967 *party identification* as a predictor of 1968 voting, the corresponding values are $r = .73$ ($N = 445$) for the first tour and .71 ($N = 259$) for the second. Thus in this longitudinal prediction, where the temporal priority of terms is unambiguous, party identifications in 1967 account for from 60 to 86 percent more of the variance in 1968 voting than do the statements of left-right self-location drawn at the same time.

It might be protested that these differences in predictive power may be somewhat artificial, since self-descriptions in left-right terms are much more prevalent than those in terms of party identification (78 percent to 58 percent, according to Table 4-3). In other words, we may achieve more predictive bite with party identification than with left-right self-locations, but if we are achieving this bite with far fewer people, leaving many more out of our calculations as "missing data," what does it profit us?

As it turns out, this protest has very little merit, for we can see that the numbers of cases predicted to in the 1968 balloting differ only trivially in the two instances. The main reason is that the scoring of party identification in left-right terms which we are using in this instance also makes many assignments for persons beyond the 58 percent who profess a normal loyalty for some specific political party. People whose party is "De Gaulle" are scored as other Gaullists, those who identify with a trade union of leftist stamp are given a middling leftist score, and so on. These additional assignments close what appears to be the classification gap between 78 percent and 58 percent to a much smaller gap, that between about 78 and 71 percent. Moreover, as we have seen, professed partisans without left-right locations vote at high rates, while those with left-right locations but no party turn out poorly. Since in these vote predictions nonvoters drop out as missing data, the gap in classification underlying these vote predictions is reduced further still. Thus there is no ground whatever to discount the large observed differences in predictive capability as some kind of artifact of numbers.

A final critique of these most recent tests might point out that they hinge on simple-minded "zero-order" predictions from one variable (party or left-right) on to later votes. Although this is the sine qua non of any "desert island" problem, it is likely that we would prefer to take more factors into account in assessing the power of these two predictors of later votes. Since we shall have an opportunity to do exactly this in Chapter 10, it seems worth postponing further tests until that point in our work.

Conclusions

We have said that we shall return more than once in this volume to comparisons of the functioning of partisan perceptions and left-right orientations in France. Our "first cut" at the subject here has produced results which are more suggestive than incisive. Most of the time, in the most compelling tests, it appears as though partisanship is a more efficacious frame of orientation than is the sense of one's own left-right position. But at some points the differences are small, and we have seen that the *declaration* of partisanship (if not position once declared) is less stable than that for left-right location.

Nevertheless, such a first glimpse does begin to limit the possible answers to any question of primacy between the two. We began this chapter quite impressed by the weakness of party loyalties in France and very attracted to the possibility that a left-right yardstick in the minds of the French voter substitutes pervasively for those cues of party shorthand that help voters evaluate the political world in some other cultures. Given the flux of actual parties, or party names, in France, it seemed plausible that party attachments were at least derivative if not epiphenomenal, and that the sense of left-right positions might be the true source of such autonomy and continuity as the French system can claim at the level of the common voter.

Whatever else may be said, our results do seem to pose a major challenge to any contention of extreme primacy for left-right orientations. Whereas it is true that in the aggregate the French voter gives a plausible account of the left-right positions of parties in the system he recognizes, there is a good deal of individual dispersion in these views that can be empirically associated both with limited familiarity with some parties and with limited familiarity with the left-right dimension itself. Similarly, although more French respondents locate themselves in left-right terms than in terms of party loyalties, we do not have to go very far beneath the surface to learn that many of these self-placements are of questionable pedigree, since the individuals involved often have but a limited understanding of what the labels "left" and "right" mean politically, and many seem to choose the exact midpoint of the left-right continuum as a means of avoiding a more integral commitment.

Our efforts to examine the comparative functioning of the two forms of political self-description toward the close of the chapter have produced similar results. We have seen nothing, on the one hand, to suggest that the left-right self-locations are meaningless. Indeed, it seems likely that they do indeed play a benign role of orientation for some voters, particularly those apathetic enough about politics to lack much sense of the party system. On the other hand, we have certainly seen nothing to indicate any dominance of these orientations over partisanship in providing system continuity. In the limited set of instances we have generated so far in which the relative potency of these two modes of self-description can be contrasted for the stabilization they appear to lend to political evaluations and behavior, we have seen two kinds of outcome. Either the differences observed are weak enough to be inconclusive, or they seem to attest quite clearly that party attachments lend significantly more continuity and organization to popular political behavior in France than do feelings of location on a left-right continuum. What we have never encountered to date is an instance in which left-right orientations clearly and persistently outweigh partisan attachments. Although this configuration of results still is less than incisive, it would certainly seem to disconfirm the extreme primacy of left-right orientations which originally seemed possible.

In later chapters we shall resume these comparisons from other points of view. For example, we have not as yet examined the relevance of these left-right self-locations to more specific policy issues current in France in the late 1960s. We shall do this in Chapter 7, and can ask at that time about the relative degree to which these left-right orientations compete with party-based programs as cues to voter policy positions. At still later points, we shall have an opportunity to make more stringent comparisons of the use of the party firmament as one reference point, or the left-right continuum as another, in voter judgments as to shifts of choice between the two rounds of voting characteristic of the French electoral system.

Before we proceed with these matters, however, we wish to consider what other sources of stabilization in the political evaluations of French voters deserve to be added to these most obvious factors of party loyalties and feelings of self-location on a right-left continuum.

5

Class, Religion, and Gaullism

We have now considered two factors—party loyalties and left-right orientations—that can help lend order and continuity to politics for the French voter. There is, however, a school of thought (Shively, 1972; Crewe, 1976) which holds that in European polities where party identification is not well developed the prime underpinning of mass political behavior is not party identification but rather attachment to the religious, class, or other social groups that contribute to giving people a sense of collective identity. In this chapter, therefore, we shall explore several potential guideposts to political choice that we have not yet considered, in order to make a preliminary assessment of their relative standing as political forces in France. These will include class status, religion, and attitudes toward de Gaulle. Attitudes toward de Gaulle are of an entirely different order from class or religion, but it seems appropriate that they be treated here. De Gaulle personally ran for election only once (although at the first direct presidential election in over a century), but—as we pointed out in Chapter 1—he dominated the French political stage for more than a quarter of a century in a fashion unique in democratic experience. It would be surprising indeed if de Gaulle himself had not been a central pole of attraction and antagonism for the mass electorate as they were called upon to take sides in the electoral battles of the era. The pro-Gaullist–anti-Gaullist axis may be an even more potent alternative to party identification (or left-right orientation) than class or religion as a central source of political cues for the French electorate. Accordingly, we will address the question of how these other potential political forces interact with one another, and how they might compare with party identification and left-right orientations as determinants of the partisan vote.

Social Class

The central fact about the relationship between social class and electoral behavior in France is the enormous discrepancy between the trivial impact of social class differentials and the expectations generated by the vocabulary, formulas, and interpretive frameworks employed by many if not most elite participants and observers. Empirical studies of class and mass electoral choice have shown that the effect of class on voting varies widely across different countries, and France is by no means the only country in which status polarization is weak.[1] But France stands out because of the sharp contrast between the terms in which electoral conflict is typically described and the reality underlying mass electoral choices. The language of French political commentary is saturated with class imagery. There is small cause for wonder at that. After all, France both enjoys the prototypical revolutionary tradition and displays sharply delineated stratification in actual social life. The French left has been dominated by Marxist-inspired parties for a century, and a basic left-right political differentiation has been central to the mass public and the political leadership alike. What is striking in the light of this environment is that the relationship between social status and partisan preferences in France is as weak as it is.

We do not intend to discuss voting in any detail in this chapter. That will be done in Chapter 10, where we shall focus directly on how the various political forces discussed in the two preceding chapters and this one combine to shape the partisan vote. But it will in no way cloud our later analysis to point out here that if we create a measure of left-right voting, as described in the preceding chapter, by assigning to the parties that competed at the 1967 election the mean left-right locations attributed to them by the mass electorate, we find that whether one employs as the indicator of class status subjective class perceptions or "objective" occupational status, or some broader measure that includes them both, it does not account for more than 6 percent of the variance in left-right voting across France as a whole in 1967. France stands in sharp contrast, in this domain, to such neighbors as Great Britain and the northern countries, where social class has typically been an important factor in popular voting.

Class and Political Preference in France, 1958 and 1967

There is no reason to believe that the feeble performance of social class as a correlate of electoral choice in France in 1967 is a historical exception, tied to the circumstances of that particular year. We are able to compare the relationship between political preferences and social class in both subjective and "objective" form in 1967 and 1958. With regard to subjective class, in both years respondents were asked, "What social class would you say you belonged to?" The 1967 replies were coded according to the same categories employed for the coding of the 1958 responses, and those categories were, in turn, grouped uniformly into several more general categories. Those operations provided a measure of subjective social class for each of the two years. The results of the operations are presented in Table 5-1. It appears clearly that the distribution of aggregate class self-perceptions in France across the decade from 1958 to 1967 was impressively stable. The relationship between subjective social class and political preferences across the same period is not likely to be affected by any large net shifts in the perceived class structure.

For each of the two years, 1958 and 1967, we have cross-tabulated the first three categories of subjective class that appear in Table 5-1 with three groups of basic political preferences ordered in left-right terms.[2] A left-right ordering of the parties active in 1958 had been constructed on the basis of the mean scores attributed to them by a panel of French political experts, and we relied on that same ordering for the 1958 parties for our own analysis here.[3] For the parties active in 1967, the ordering was based on the mean left-right scores attributed to them by the electorate itself, as described in Chapter 4.

In order to ascertain the political locations of a maximal number of cases for both 1958 and 1967, fairly elaborate searching procedures were employed. For the 1958 three-wave panel study, the data were searched first for the respondents' party identification at the first wave and for their recalled vote in 1956. If both of those items of information were missing, the search

Table 5-1. Class self-perceptions, France, 1958 and 1967 (percentages).

Self-perceived class	1958	1967
Bourgeoisie	6.6	4.7
Middle class	29.5	32.4
Working class	45.1	43.2
Rural middle class	0.6	0.9
Rural working class	0.4	0.4
Rural, unspecified	2.8	1.2
Don't know	11.6	12.5
Not ascertained; refuse	3.4	4.7
Total	100.0	100.0
N	(1127)	(2007)

proceeded to party identification at the second wave, then the 1958 vote, and finally party identification at the third wave. Furthermore, in order to avoid contamination by the Gaullist surge that developed after the referendum of September 1958, preference for the Gaullists was recorded only for the first wave of interviews, which took place before the referendum, or for the recalled 1956 vote. Postreferendum Gaullist identifiers or voters were treated as missing data. These operations produced a record of the basic political orientations of the French electorate in 1958, *before* those orientations were affected by the advance of Gaullism.

For 1967 a similar but not identical procedure was followed. The data were searched for party identification, the first ballot vote in 1967, and the second ballot vote in 1967. If only one score emerged, that score was assigned to the respondent. If two or three scores were uncovered, the mean was assigned. That procedure supplied the basic political orientations of the French electorate in 1967.

The results of the cross-tabulation appear in Table 5-2. It can be seen at once that there was little change in the relationship between subjective class and basic political preferences across the decade from 1958 to 1967. Such class solidarity as appears at the end of each decade manifests itself primarily among the bourgeoisie and operates to the advantage of the right-wing parties. But the degree of association between subjective class and political preference is low for both 1958 and 1967, and hardly differs from one point to another.

There was virtually no change either, between 1958 and 1967, in the relationship between *objective* class and basic political preferences. The relevant distributions with regard to objective class are presented in Table 5-3. In preparing that table, we employed exactly the same measures of basic political preferences that we have just described in connection with the cross-time analysis of the relationship between political preferences and subjective class. The measure of objective class used here is simply the occupation of the head of the respondent's household (excluding farmers and farm laborers), as reported by our survey respondents.

The distribution of political preferences among the nonmanual group in 1967 was virtually identical to what it had been in 1958; in fact, the similarity is almost eerie. The distribution of preferences among the manual group shows only a slight variation from 1958 to 1967, all of it consisting of a shift of manual workers' households from the parties of the center to those of the right. In 1967 as in 1958 barely more than one half of the voters of manual workers' households preferred the parties of the left over those of the center or right. As in the case of subjective class, objective class defined in occupational terms is minimally related to political preference in France, and there was virtually no change in that relationship between 1958 and 1967.

Table 5-2. Basic political preferences by subjective class (percentages), France, 1958 and 1967.

Political preference	1958[a]			1967[b]		
	Bour-geoisie	Middle class	Working class	Bour-geoisie	Middle class	Working class
Right	59.7	51.1	29.7	61.7	52.6	36.1
Center	19.3	23.0	22.3	24.0	19.2	15.2
Left	21.0	25.9	48.0	14.3	28.2	48.7
Total	100.0	100.0	100.0	100.0	100.0	100.0
N	(62)	(239)	(323)	(87.0)	(562.2)	(738.4)

a. Tau-b = .24; gamma = .39
b. Tau-b = .21; gamma = .35

Table 5-3. Basic political preferences by nonmanual and manual occupations (percentages), France, 1958 and 1967.[a]

Political preference	1958[b]		1967[c]	
	Non-manual	Manual	Non-manual	Manual
Right	49.9	28.3	49.9	34.9
Center	19.6	20.4	19.7	14.6
Left	30.5	51.3	30.4	50.5
Total	100.0	100.0	100.0	100.0
N	(663)	(382)	(727.6)	(665.2)

a. Farm occupations excluded.
b. Gamma = .38
c. Gamma = .32

Class and Partisan Preferences: France and Great Britain

In order to ensure that data from our study could be used for a cross-national comparison of the effects of class on political preferences in France and Great Britain, we took special pains at the third wave of interviews, conducted in 1969,[4] to replicate as closely as possible the measures of social class and occupational status which had been used previously with striking effect by Butler and Stokes (1969). We employed the same question as they did for the basic measurement of subjective social class.[5] We also made every effort to classify the occupational status of our respondents by the same method as they did, in order to construct a six-point scale equivalent to the one they used. This scale, which is based jointly on occupation and number of employees or subordinates (or, in the case of certain farm occupations, the size of farm), was originally produced to fit the British context, but it contains no status designations for particular occupations which appear to be at variance with conventional perceptions of occupational status within the French social context.[6] This is not to say that a close comparison of perceived occupational status in Great Britain and France would not reveal differences that would occasionally require us to depart from the British model in ranking occupational groups in France. It hardly seems likely, however, that any such differences would significantly affect the proportions of people falling into the six gross categories employed.

In discussing class cleavages in party support, Butler and Stokes (1969, pp. 70-71) chose to relate their measures of class to what they called "party self-image," which corresponds to our measure of identification. Therefore, we shall take our measure of party identification in 1969 as the indicator of political preference to relate to social class. Furthermore, we shall relax somewhat the criteria for party, much as we did toward the end of the last chapter, by including as party identifiers not only the people who identified with a discrete political party, but also those who identified with major party leaders or broad left-right tendencies.

The distribution of party identification in France by subjective social class, compared with the distribution of partisan self-images in Britain by subjective social class, as reported by Butler and Stokes, appears in Figure 5-1. Respondents identifying with the center parties or other centrist political objects have been excluded from the calculations for France in order to make the figures more nearly comparable with those reported by Butler and Stokes, who exclude supporters of the Liberal party from their analysis.

The ratio of right to left partisan identification within the middle class in France is 66:34, and the equivalent ratio for Great Britain (taking the Conservative party as the right and the Labor party as the left) is 79:21. The ratio of left to right partisan identification within the working class in France is 59:41; in Great Britain the equivalent ratio is 72:28. In terms of Alford's (1963) well-known measure of class voting, derived by subtracting the proportion of persons in the middle class voting for the left from the proportion of persons in the working class voting for the left,[7] the index figure for class voting in Britain in 1963 exceeded that for France in 1969 by the difference between 51 and 25.

		SUBJECTIVE CLASS	
		Middle	Working
A. FRANCE			
	Right	66%	41%
PARTY IDENTIFICATION			
	Left	34%	59%
		100%	100%
	N	(233.9)	(372.6)

		CLASS SELF-IMAGE	
		Middle	Working
B. GREAT BRITAIN			
	Conservative	79%	28%
PARTISAN SELF-IMAGE			
	Labor	21%	72%
		100%	100%

Figure 5-1. Party identification by subjective class, France, 1969 (excluding identifiers with center parties), and partisan self-image by class self-image, Great Britain, 1963 (Conservative and Labor parties only). British data from *Political Change in Britain: Forces Shaping Electoral Choice*, by David Butler and Donald Stokes. © 1969 by D. Butler and D. Stokes, and reprinted by permission of St. Martin's Press Inc.

Impressive cross-national differences for Britain and France also appear when one compares the relationship between political preference and the occupational status of the head of household in the two countries. Figure 5-2 shows the percentages of British voters preferring Labor and the percentages of French voters identifying with left-wing parties for each of the six points of the occupational status scale which Butler and Stokes devised and which we replicated. As in the case of Figure 5-1, the British figures are based on proportions of preferences for the two major parties only, and the figures for France exclude identifiers with the center parties.

The marked political solidarity that appears in Britain among the managerial groups and the supervisory nonmanual groups, on the one hand, and the manual groups, on the other, is simply not evident in France. In both countries a majority of the people in the two manual-worker categories identify with the left, but that majority is minimal indeed for French skilled manual workers and barely larger for French unskilled manual workers. The only group in France that contains an overwhelming percentage of people identifying with one of the two main political tendencies is the higher managerial category, which tends to identify with rightist parties, a situation

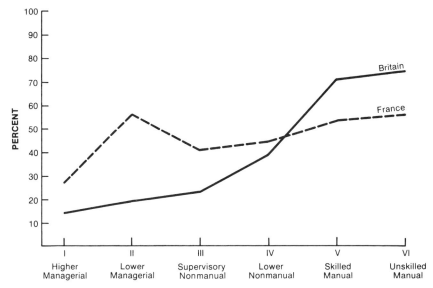

Figure 5-2. Percent of British voters preferring Labor and French voters identifying with the left, by occupational status of head of household, Britain, 1963, and France, 1969. British data from *Political Change in Britain: Forces Shaping Electoral Choice,* by David Butler and D. Stokes. © 1969 by D. Butler and D. Stokes, and reprinted by permission of St. Martin's Press Inc.

that is similar to that for 1967 presented in Table 5.2, where alternate measures of political affiliation and class were employed.

The people who behave most similarly in the two countries are those who come from households where the head has a lower nonmanual occupation. That is the one group which, both in Britain and France, behaves differently from conventional expectations with respect to both class self-identification and partisan political preference. Often researchers seeking an indicator of objective class simply divide the population into two groups by distinguishing between manual and nonmanual occupations. Butler and Stokes showed that such a division fails to reflect the psychological attachment to the working class of a large majority of people in Britain coming from lower nonmanual occupational backgrounds, a phenomenon that we find in France as well. The normal expectation with regard to the relationship between class and partisan preference is that middle-class people will identify with the right and that working-class people will identify with the left. Butler and Stokes (1969, p. 77) showed, however, that in England a majority of the people from households where the head of the family has a lower nonmanual occupation think of themselves as Conservatives. We have found, similarly, that a majority of the same kind of people in France think of themselves as supporters of right-wing parties.

Another instance of inconsistency between reality and the conventional notions about the relationship between class and political preference is found in France but not in Britain. This concerns the behavior of those from lower managerial households. In both France and Britain the great majority of these people think of themselves as middle class. As Figure 5-2 shows, however, the greatest difference in partisan preferences between similar groups in Britain and France appears in the lower managerial category. The overwhelming majority of such people in Britain think of themselves as Conservative supporters, whereas in France a larger proportion of people from that category (which is heavily populated with teachers) identify with the left than with the right. In fact, the proportion of people from the lower managerial group identifying with the left is larger than that from any other occupational group, including the unskilled manual workers, although the margin of difference is minuscule.[8]

Multiple Class Attributes and Partisan Preferences

It is evident from the foregoing that neither objective class nor subjective class, in the ways in which we have measured those attributes, is a good overall indicator of political orientations in France, at least for the period under investigation. There was virtually no change in that regard between 1958 and 1967, and the feebleness of class as a political indicator in France is brought into sharp relief by a comparison with the situation in Great Britain, where class normally counts for a great deal in partisan differentiation.

These overall findings, however, do not mean that social class is irrelevant in French mass politics. For some subgroups of the French population
the association between class and political choice is quite strong by normal
standards. Michelat and Simon (1971) have shown that the effect of class
on political preferences strengthens with the cumulation of class attributes,
and our own independent analysis is not dissimilar to theirs in that regard.
As Figure 5-2 indicates, people from French households where the head is
engaged in a skilled manual occupation or an unskilled manual occupation
identify with the left (as between right and left only, excluding the center)
in proportions of 54 percent and 56 percent respectively. If we combine the
two groups, the proportion of manual workers who identified with the left
in 1969 was little more than 54 percent. Combining the four other occupational groups, those in the managerial and nonmanual categories, we find
that together they identified with the right in the proportion of 59 percent.

If we subdivide those two groups of people (one containing people
from families where the head of household occupies a managerial or nonmanual position, the other containing people from households where the
head is a manual worker) on the basis of subjective class, the influence of
class quickens in the expected direction. The proportion of working-class
identifiers among the manual occupational group who identify with the left
rises from 54 to 62 percent, and the proportion of middle-class identifiers
among the managerial and nonmanual occupational group who identify
with the right rises from 59 to 67 percent. If we push the analysis further,
and subdivide the two groups on the basis of the occupation of the respondent's parents, there is a further gain in the conventional impact of class attributes on political preference. In families where the head of household has
a manual occupation, people who identify with the working class and
whose parents were manual workers identify with the left in the proportion
of 69 percent. Conversely, in families where the head of household has a
managerial or nonmanual occupation, people who identify with the middle
class and whose parents had managerial or nonmanual occupations identify
with the right in the proportion of 70 percent.

There is no doubt that the association between class and political preference strengthens with the cumulation of class attributes. That is particularly the case for working-class people, for whom the gains in propensity to
identify with the left are sharper than the gains in tendency to support the
right are for middle-class people. But it should be noted that the French
working class, even when defined in terms of the three attributes we have
employed above, does not identify with the left in as large a proportion as
the British working class, defined only in terms of the occupation of the
head of household, identifies itself as Labor. Similarly, the French middle
class does not identify with the right in the same overwhelming fashion as
the British middle class identifies itself as Conservative. Class polarization

simply does not exist in France in the same way as it does in Great Britain.

Furthermore, those groups in France for whom multiple class attributes are expressed in political terms represent only portions of the population. The specification of each group in terms of multiple class attributes naturally reduces the size of the group as each successive attribute is added. Such gains as appear in the potency of class as a factor in partisan preferences are compensated for by loss of generality in explanatory power.

Religion

Religion is a far more powerful factor in French political behavior than social class. The relationship between left-right voting and religious practice within the nation's largely Catholic electorate is clear and unambiguous. Devout and obedient Catholics vote to the right; Catholics indifferent to religious practice and people without any religious affiliation vote to the left.

This finding may seem anachronistic, and it is worth our while, in evaluating it, to keep in mind both the intensity of the clerical dispute during the first decades of popular party competition on a regularized basis in France, and the strength of intergenerational transmission not only of political but also of religious orientations (Percheron, 1982). André Siegfried could write in 1930 (p. 62) that the clerical-anticlerical frontier was undoubtedly "the dominant dividing line of all our politics." The importance of that dividing line may have diminished since 1930 (and we shall comment later about continuity and change in that domain), but there is ample evidence that religion is a major factor in shaping French political attitudes. This seems a rather classic case of the perpetuation of first lines of political cleavage long after they have lost their primary relevance (Lipset and Rokkan, 1967).

The importance of religion as a political factor may also seem remarkable because neither the left-right axis nor actual electoral competition is perceived to any major extent in religious terms. We saw in the preceding chapter that the left-right dimension is perceived primarily in social and economic terms, not as an expression of religious differentiation. And while less than one-fourth of the electorate regarded the 1967 election as pitting "the working class against the capitalists," there were more than five times as many references to the election in those starkly class terms than there were acceptances of the notion that the election had been a struggle of *les catholiques contre les laïques* (Catholics versus anticlericals).[9] Yet by every measure we have employed, religion is a more powerful determinant of political orientations in France than is social class.

As our reference to André Siegfried's comment in 1930 indicates, the powerful role of religious differences has been known and described in various ways for a long time. Siegfried's own pioneering work on the politics of western France dates from 1913. During the period after World War II, both French and American scholars called attention again to the importance of religion for French politics: François Goguel (1952) in a brilliant interpretation of the role of religion in shaping the character of French democracy; and Duncan MacRae, Jr. (1958) by giving a quantitative description of the strength of the religious factor through ecological analysis. Later, Michel Brulé (1966) employed sample survey data to assess the importance of religion as a factor in the vote at the French presidential election of 1965. Brulé concluded that the voters' choices at that election could be better accounted for by their religious situation, defined in terms of their religion and degree of religious practice, than by their age, sex, or occupation. Still later, Aver et al. (1970) tested Brulé's conclusion with sample survey data collected in 1966, which contained the respondents' declarations of intended partisan vote at the next, hypothetical, election, and they found it to be generally confirmed. Finally, Michelat and Simon (1977) produced a large-scale study in which they established the existence of a close relationship between religious variables and political variables that just did not disappear even after they incorporated many individual-level and contextual variables into their analysis.

In our own discussion of the relationship between religion and political preferences in France, we shall follow almost the same outline that we followed in connection with the less potent factor of social class. First, we shall put the question into brief historical perspective by examining whether there is reason to believe that the relationship between religion and politics altered across the decade from 1958 to 1967. Then, we shall briefly show how religion was linked with the voters' sense of their own left-right locations in 1967. Finally, we shall consider the impact of religion in the light of broad class distinctions and shall comment on the effects of such a "cross-cutting" cleavage on the representation system.

Religion and Political Preference in France, 1958 and 1967

Just as we were concerned to see whether any change had taken place in the relationship between social class and political preferences between 1958 and 1967, we were also interested in examining whether any change had taken place in the political power of religion across the same period. Unfortunately, the instruments available to us for making such a comparison were not so satisfactory·as those we were able to use for our cross-time study of the political impact of social class. For 1967, we had two direct measures of religious attitudes: a six-point religiosity scale based on the religion and frequency of church attendance of the respondents (excluding the few people professing a religion other than Catholicism);[10] and a pseudo-interval measure of affect for the clergy as registered on a "thermometer" scale running from 0 (signifying complete antipathy) through 50 (signifying indifference or ignorance) to 100 (signifying complete sympathy).[11] We did not have either measure for 1958. Nevertheless, two religion-related questions were asked at the 1958 survey, and we combined the responses to them to form a surrogate clerical-anticlerical variable for that year.[12]

The political preferences of the 1958 respondents were searched in precisely the same fashion described earlier in this chapter in connection with their relationship to social class in 1958; but whereas for that analysis the 1958 parties were arrayed according to how a panel of experts rated them on a socioeconomic dimension, for the purposes of this religious analysis we used the ordering of the parties (by the same panel of experts) on a clerical-anticlerical dimension. Those ordered party preferences were then cross-tabulated with the 1958 surrogate clericalism variable. An analogous operation was carried out for 1967. Basic partisan preferences were searched as they had been in connection with the class analysis. Those were then ordered and crossed with our six-point religiosity scale as the indicator of religious outlook.

The results of the operations are summarized in row A of Table 5-4. The strength of the relationship between our measures of religion and political preferences is greater in both 1958 and 1967 than the strength of the relationship between either subjective class or "objective" class and the same political preferences as reported in Tables 5-2 and 5-3.

The results concerning religion for 1958 and 1967 are not, of course, strictly comparable, but we were sufficiently intrigued by the hint they contain of a slight weakening of the relationship between religion and political preferences between 1958 and 1967 to pursue the matter further, although still imperfectly. In 1967 we had asked a question in the Likert-scale agree-disagree format that was very similar to, although not identical with, one of the two questions that we had incorporated into our surrogate clericalism variable for 1958.[13] Therefore, we cross-tabulated the responses to those near-matching variables for 1958 and 1967 with the respective sets of basic political preferences. The results of that analysis appear in row B of Table 5-4. We cannot draw firm conclusions from them, but they too suggest that there was a modest decline in the political effect of religion between 1958 and 1967.[14] Whatever that short-term trend may have been, however, it re-

Table 5-4. Strength of relationship between religious indicators and basic political preferences (gamma), France, 1958 and 1967.

Religious indicator	1958	1967
A. Surrogate clericalism (1958) and religion and religious practice (1967)	.50	.46
B. Attitude toward aid to church schools	.49	.43

mains clear that religion is a more powerful political influence than social
class.

Class and Religion

Aver et al. (1970) and then Michelat and Simon (1977) found that the relationship between religion and religious practice, on the one hand, and hypothetical vote intentions, on the other hand, was not significantly affected by
controlling for occupation. We find essentially the same thing on the basis
of our somewhat different measures. Whether one controls for occupational
status or for subjective class, there still remains a clear association between
religion and basic political attachments.

Figure 5-3 shows that the tendency to identify with the leftist parties
varies regularly as a function of religiosity among people from both manual
and nonmanual occupational backgrounds, with only one exception. The
exception is that in families where the head of the household has a nonmanual occupation, Catholics who report that they attend church "often"
are marginally more likely to identify with a leftist party than are Catholics
from the same kind of occupational background who report that they attend church only "sometimes." It is likely, however, that this irregularity is
more the result of ambiguity in our measurement instrument than in the
phenomenon itself. There is little difference in the left-right self-locations of
the Catholics who attend church "once a week or more" and those who attend church "often." But the latter category is only half as numerous as the
former, and this disparity takes on greater significance when the set of respondents is divided according to occupational status. If, as seems reasonable enough, the two most religious groups were combined, the curve in
Figure 5-3 would be smoothed.

Figure 5-3 also shows that the strength of the relationship between religiosity and party identification is somewhat greater among people from
manual working-class backgrounds than it is among people from nonmanual occupational backgrounds.[15] That helps to explain why class solidarity
in political terms, as limited as it is in France, is more clearly expressed at
the upper reaches of the occupational hierarchy than it is in its lower range,
as we noted earlier in this chapter.

The political impact of religion within occupational or status groups is
perhaps the prototypical case of a "cross-cutting cleavage" of the kind that
has received considerable attention in the literature concerned with uncovering the factors that contribute toward or impede the maintenance of democratic institutions and processes.[16] On the whole, the work concerning
cross-cutting cleavages tends to view them as helping to reduce political di-
visiveness in a society, although some of the work is careful to specify the
conditions under which such a pacifying effect might actually occur (Dahl,
1966, pp. 371–380). It is possible, however, that the particular juxtaposition

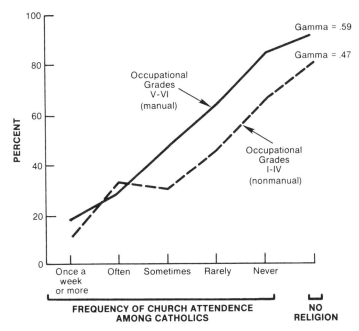

Figure 5-3. Percent of voters who identify with the left, by manual-nonmanual occupational background and religion and degree of religious practice, France, 1967.

of religious and class cleavages found in France may lead to some increase in informal, day-to-day, political conflict and rancor. This would be true if, as is reasonable to expect, most informal communication occurs within broad class lines rather than across them. Where a middle class is homogeneously conservative and the working class homogeneously leftist, the struggle may be bitter as it is projected to the highest levels of national policymaking; but within groups engaging in informal communication there would be marked political consensus. In the French case, however, the members of both the middle and the working class can be seen as divided against themselves by strong left-right partisan differences, bolstered by contrasts in world views that are deeply rooted in a historic religious cleavage.

For the purposes of this volume, however, the more important issue is the effect on the representation process of class divisions within common religious groups. In general terms, the problem is simply this: how directly and faithfully can the economic and social interests of people be represented in a political system where electoral choices are based on religious divisions far more than on economic and social considerations? We are not in a position at this stage to attempt a general reply, but it may be in order to illustrate the problem in empirical terms with respect to a specific group of people who are often assumed to have a common class interest—the industrial workers.

We isolated the people in our 1967 sample who belong to industrial working-class families and stratified them into three groups based on religion and frequency of church attendance.[17] These three groups differ sharply and ordinally with regard to their left-right locations and left-right voting, as well as other clearly political referents, such as attitudes toward de Gaulle. There is, however, little variation among the three groups on economic and social issues, including those issues that may be presumed to lie at the heart of such working-class solidarity as may exist. Religion-related issues, of course, are a different matter, and on these the three working-class groups differ markedly.

To be sure, there are some differences in the characteristics of the French working class, depending on religious outlook. More than 60 percent of the industrial work force are male; but among the most devout industrial workers, women outnumber men by a considerable margin.[18] The most religious workers are much more likely to live in small or middle-sized towns, as opposed to large cities, and they are more likely to work in small plants with fewer than twenty employees and less likely to work in large factories with more than two hundred workers than their less religious counterparts. Sympathy for unions is higher than the national average among the most religious industrial workers, but it is higher still among the middle group and highest of all among the least religious workers. Those differences in sympathy for unions perhaps reflect the differential rates of unionization among the three groups of workers: only 13 percent of the most religious workers belong to unions, while 22 percent of the middle group and 40 percent of the least religious workers are unionized. Yet, except for religion-related issues, there is little difference among industrial workers in their opinions on issues of public policy, including such presumably class-related issues as union rights and the workers' share of the national income.

The most religious and the least religious industrial workers have similar outlooks on issues of economic and social policy, but they vote for different candidates: the devout vote for the right and the indifferent vote for the left. In circumstances such as these, the problems posed for candidates, especially the victorious ones, can be complex indeed, and the ways in which those problems are solved have important implications for the operation of the representation process. Candidates, whether of the right or left, who try to satisfy directly the class interests of their working-class supporters risk damaging the interests of the middle-class voters who have supported them because of religious considerations. But if they ignore the economic and social concerns of their working-class supporters, they will be leaving those voters without any possibility of representation in those issue domains. The conflict is particularly acute for rightist candidates who draw support from the Catholic working class, and the consequences of representational failures are most severe for those Catholic workers. Given the peculiarities of the French party system, devout Catholics are virtually locked into the right-wing parties. Deeply religious workers whose economic interests are ignored by the right have no other place to turn.

Of course, representation is not a simple process. It is an oversimplification to isolate one policy domain (in this case, class-related issues) and exclude others with which it almost inevitably must become entwined, not only as legislators bargain and compromise over specific measures but also in the overall perspectives of the voters. The Catholic working class seeks satisfaction of both its religious and economic concerns, and the fact that its concerns are plural makes possible, and perhaps tolerable, trade-offs between them. Moreover, voters may derive satisfaction from seeing their preferences upheld even when they are not directly transformable into policy outputs which produce concrete rewards. For example, Gaullism—to which we shall turn our attention later in this chapter—was stronger in 1967 and 1968 among the most devout people who considered themselves working class than it was among equally religious voters who regarded themselves as belonging to the middle class. It is not unreasonable to assume that there could have been some sort of psychological trade-off for Catholic workers between satisfaction of their economic interests and the satisfaction of knowing that their chosen candidates were supporters of de Gaulle.

Considerations of the sort we have just mentioned may mitigate the problem of representation for the Catholic working class within the French party system, but they do not eliminate it. Cross-cutting cleavages at the electoral level produce strong cross-pressures on candidates and deputies, and the ways in which the latter respond to these conflict situations have important implications for representation. Indeed, some choices that legislators may make can effectively exclude a whole class of voters from the representation process in certain issue areas, as we have indicated in discussing the situation of the Catholic working class.

Readers may object that our data relating to the political effects of class and religion in France derive from the late 1960s and that the situation has changed in more recent years. Indeed, the experience of Britain since 1963, which we have used as one pole of comparison, is a case in point. Even in 1969 Butler and Stokes devoted a chapter to discussing the factors making for a decline in class-based political alignment in Britain (chapter 5), and in 1976 they reported data illustrative of such a decline from 1963 to 1970 (chapter 9). Särlvik and Crewe (1983, pp. 74–91) document the trend away from class polarization through 1979, and Crewe (1983) reports a further deterioration of the class alignment at the elections of 1983.

SOFRES, which has regularly conducted post-electoral surveys in France for *Le Nouvel Observateur*, has kindly furnished us with copies of its reports, enabling us to track the relationship between occupational status and voting, and between religiosity and voting, from 1973 to 1981. SOFRES reports the proportion of the vote cast for each party (or presidential candidate) by the occupation of the head of household, and four of the occupational categories employed form a fair scale of occupational status: big business and the professions, small business, middle management and white collar, and workers. SOFRES also includes farmers and the retired or inactive, but because they are of indeterminate class status we shall exclude them from our calculations here. Similarly, SOFRES charts the vote by four categories of religion and religious practice, although it changed the meaning of some of the scale positions between 1974 and 1978. We cannot reorganize our 1967 data to match all the later SOFRES occupational and religious categories perfectly, but we can gain some sense of trends since 1967.

We would expect some slow and gradual decline of the historic association of religious fidelity with the right and of anticlericalism with the left, and indeed that is what we find, although the decline is slight and, as we shall see in a moment, the political power of religious attachment has remained impressive. With regard to the effects of occupational status, competing hypotheses are plausible. On the one hand, with the disappearance of de Gaulle, who had a considerable following among the working class, a strengthening of the conventional Marxist-inspired class alignment might occur. On the other hand, the growth of a middle-class radicalism, already foreshadowed in our data on demonstration participation in 1968 (discussed in Chapter 14), could at least counter any such gains by the left among manual workers and perhaps even outstrip them. Through the presidential election of 1981 we only find evidence of the former effect, although it is slight indeed. For the legislative elections of 1981, however, both effects appear unmistakably, with leftist support advancing much more sharply among people of higher-status occupational background than among the working class.

Yet those separate findings are weak estimates at best. What does stand out with striking clarity is that for each of the six electoral consultations from 1973 through May 1981 for which we have SOFRES estimates of the vote both by occupational background and by religion, the slope of the curve is steeper for religion. Figure 5-4 records the mean proportion of the vote for leftist parties or candidates, by occupational background and by degree of religious practice, across the four elections for which we have relevant SOFRES data and for which the code categories are uniform: the first ballot of the legislative elections of 1978, the election of the European Assembly of 1979, and both ballots of the 1981 presidential election. It is ap-

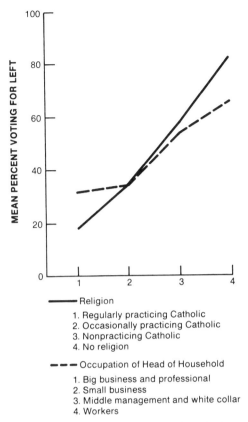

Figure 5-4. Percent voting for leftist parties by religion and by occupation of head of household, France, March 1978 – May 1981. Source: SOFRES.

parent that religion was a more powerful determinant of the vote than occupational background.

Regional Effects of Class and Religion

France is a country with distinct patterns of political regionalism, in the sense that in some sections of the country certain parties and political tendencies are particularly strong, and the balance of political forces changes slowly if at all. Of course, France is not unique in displaying regional political patterns. All democratic nations do so to some extent. An obvious example from United States political experience is the southern states, which, after the reconstruction period following the Civil War, were for a long time virtually one-party states in which the Democratic party prevailed, while the Republican party predominated in somewhat less striking fashion in the New England states. We would not want to claim that regionalism is a more prominent feature of the political landscape in France than elsewhere, but it is one of the better-known aspects of French political life. As a result of the strong French tradition of electoral geography as a mode of political analysis, pioneered by André Siegfried, refined by François Goguel, and ably pursued by other scholars, the continuities in the geographical dispersion of partisan electoral support have been more thoroughly investigated than any other aspect of French political behavior.[19]

We have referred to France's regions several times in this study, and now it is appropriate to describe their boundaries and how these were determined. We approached the problem of delineating regions somewhat differently from the way in which the French school of electoral geography

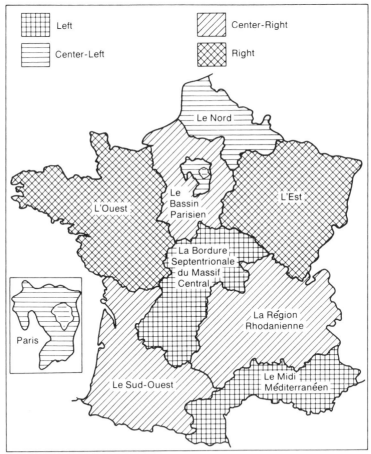

French Political Regions
(1965-1967)

proceeds. French electoral geographers normally establish political regions by using aggregate electoral data. They plot the distribution of the vote by parties or tendencies for given geographic areas, usually the departments; and the regional patterns of electoral support show up across clusters of departments clearly and with historical regularity. The regions referred to in our study were not defined on the basis of aggregate data but rather on the basis of sample survey data. Moreover, the critical variable used was not the partisan vote but rather the self-assigned locations of the respondents on the left-right scale in 1967. We clustered our eighty-six sample districts on the basis of the mean left-right locations of the respondents in such a way as to maximize the variance between clusters. In that manner, we established nine political regions, each of which is comparatively homogeneous in terms of left-right orientations as well as distinct from neighboring regions (see Table 5-5). All the discussions in this volume concerning the regional distribution of various attributes rest on this method of determining the regions.[20]

Earlier portions of this chapter have shown that social class is a weak determinant of political outlooks in France and that religion is a more powerful factor in partisan preference. It should be added that those generalizations hold not only nationwide but also, on the whole, within the French regions. To be sure, regional variations exist in the relative political importance of class and religion, which we shall examine momentarily in some detail. First, however, we wish to stress several broad generalizations.

The first is that all our measures of class and religion have a positive

Table 5-5. French political regions.[a]

Region	Number of sample districts	Mean left-right location
La Bordure (Septentrionale) du Massif Central (the area bordering the Massif Central on the north)	4	40.7
Le Midi Méditerranéen (the Mediterranean coast)	8	41.9
Le Nord (Northern France)	10	44.9
Paris (the Parisian conurbation)	15	45.3
La Région Rhodanienne (et Montagneuse)— (heart of the Massif Central and French Alps)	7	46.8
Le Sud-Ouest (Southwestern France)	10	47.5
Le Bassin Parisien (the Parisian Basin and Seine Valley)	7	49.4
L'Est (Eastern France)	12	52.5
L'Ouest (Western France)	13	52.9

a. Based on the self-assigned left-right location of respondents in our 1967 sample survey.

effect on political preferences, however minimal the effect of class may be in some regions. Although this remark may seem innocuous, it is of considerable importance in pointing up the general weakness of class status as a factor in political choice. There is no question here of the generally low level of status polarization resulting from wide regional variations in the partisan direction of status voting, which tend to average toward zero when aggregated across the nation as a whole. The low national summaries are a compound of some regions where class status predicts to political cleavage modestly and of others where there is almost no predictive power at all.

A second point is that, with one exception, religion is a more powerful political force than social class in each of our nine regions. That exception is the Midi, the well-known leftist belt that borders the Mediterranean Sea from Spain to Italy. In that region, measures of social status predict equally well with religion to political preferences.[21] Nowhere, however, on a regional basis, does class outstrip religion as a political force.

Third and finally, it is important to emphasize the extent to which the political relevance of religious attitudes is a broad cultural phenomenon that cannot be reduced to other conventional sociological factors. Although religion counts very heavily politically in some of the most strongly Catholic, and rural, regions, it is also a potent political influence in the urban and anticlerical Paris region. It is clear that the role of religion as a political force is not limited to rural or "underdeveloped" areas, but extends into the most "modern" and urban areas as well. Furthermore, though it may seem tautological to observe that the weight of religious attachments on political alignments tends to be heaviest in the most devout regions, that statement is less vacuous than it may at first seem. In a region where religious practice is uniformly high, the correlation between devotion and left-right partisan preferences would not tend to be strong. Such correlations gain in robustness only where there are matched polarizations between religious differences and political competition. What the importance of religion for electoral choice in the strongly Catholic regions indicates is that religion is actually more of an issue there than one might suspect, and that contrasting religious outlooks are more closely coupled with political choices there than elsewhere.

Despite the fact that religion generally has a more powerful impact than class status on partisan preferences, there is considerable variation in the way that those two social cleavages jointly fit in with political alignments from region to region. Indeed, the form that this variation takes is a matter of considerable interest in its own right. There appears to be an intelligible pattern in the way those two factors intersect on a regional basis. And that pattern takes us some distance down the road to understanding the underpinnings of political regionalism.

Figure 5-5 shows the relative proportion of variance in left-right voting

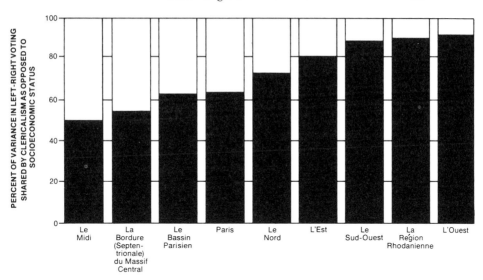

Figure 5-5. Relative importance of clericalism and socioeconomic status as factors in voting (first ballot), by region, France, 1967.

at the first ballot of the 1967 election shared by clericalism as opposed to average socioeconomic status in each of our nine political regions.[22] What Figure 5-5 indicates, though in tantalizingly imperfect form, is that the proportions of variance accounted for by clericalism and socioeconomic status vary with the relative left-right orientations of the regions. On the whole, the more leftist the region, the more relative variance accounted for by socioeconomic status, and the more rightist the region, the more relative variance accounted for by clericalism. (Similarly, the more anticlerical the region, the greater the relative importance of socioeconomic status, and the more clerical the region, the greater the relative potency of religion.) The regions are not ordered in Figure 5-5 in a manner that is literally consistent with their left-right ordering (shown in Table 5-5). But the underlying values correlate on a regional basis at a statistically significant level.[23]

These relationships suggest that political regionalism in France may be to some extent a reflection of variations in the distribution of the political impact of socioeconomic status and religious attachments across the relevant geographical areas. Rosenthal (1967, p. 395) has rightly pointed out that scholars have not succeeded in reducing regionalism to the distributional patterns of other sociological variables. We are far from suggesting here that there is nothing to regional distributions of left-right orientations (and their accompanying electoral patterns) but the regional distributions of social status and religious attitudes. The average proportion of variance across our nine regions that is explained by those two factors together is only a bit more than 25 percent, and seldom rises to more than one-third. It is clear that other factors taken together dominate electoral outcomes on a regional basis. The neatness of the pattern that appears in Figure 5-5, however, furnishes a promising starting point for the fuller decoding of regional political differences in France.

Gaullism

Class status and religious attitudes are factors that can affect people's orientations toward politics virtually anywhere, depending upon a variety of historical and social conditions. Although we have found class to be a comparatively weak force in shaping political outlooks in France, and religion to be a comparatively strong one, the situation may be different in other countries. We have examined the operative force of these two factors in France because local historical and social circumstances point to them as highly plausible political forces, not because of any suggestion that whatever influence they may have might be unique to France.

Now we turn to a force that is endemic to France: attitudes toward Charles de Gaulle. In no other modern democracy have political developments been so intertwined with the activities of a single national leader for so long. To those other complexities that make postwar French politics fascinating, such as the unstable party system, we must add the uniquely central position of Charles de Gaulle.

In Chapter 1 we referred to the unparalleled role played by de Gaulle for three decades: from the summer of 1940, when he issued his historic call from London for resistance against the German invader, until his retirement from politics after his defeat at the referendum of April 1969. First as Resistance leader, then as head of the postwar French government, later as leader of the opposition to the Fourth Republic, eventually as founder and first President of the Fifth Republic, and finally as France's first popularly elected chief of state since 1848, de Gaulle occupied a central role in the politics of his country that has no counterpart in any other nation. De Gaulle's position was so commanding, his presence so enduring, and his visibility so great through all the vicissitudes of postwar French politics that by the time of our investigations in the late 1960s there was ample reason to believe that attitudes toward de Gaulle were a major source of popular orientations toward electoral choice, rivaling in importance all those other factors that we have explored in this and earlier chapters.

It may be said as well that the year 1967, to which our most numerous and most stable measures apply, is nearly ideal for assessing the comparative potency of attitudes toward de Gaulle as a guiding force in French mass politics. The formative years of the Fifth Republic were past, and the explosion of 1968 was yet to erupt. The elections of 1967 took place when Fifth Republic politics stood at a high level of serenity. It can hardly be said that de Gaulle was maintaining a low profile at the time; but the furious battles surrounding the Constitution and decolonization were over, while the outburst of diffuse discontent of 1968 had not yet occurred. Such political resonance as attitudes toward de Gaulle displayed in the comparative calm of 1967 would reflect the accretion of sentiments over time rather than potentially transient positions developed under stress.

There is certainly evidence that generalized attitudes toward de Gaulle were related to the electorate's behavior during the earlier years of the Fifth Republic. Dupeux (1960, pp. 132–133) reported a relationship between mass vote intentions at the constitutional referendum of 1958 and mass belief that the real issue was de Gaulle himself as opposed to the intrinsic merits of the Constitution. Converse and Dupeux (1966) showed that attitudes toward de Gaulle were related to partisan attachments but not to any standard demographic factors, and the scale of attitudes toward de Gaulle constructed by *Sondages* (1963, no. 3) behaved in the same way. The Gaullism–anti-Gaullism scale employed by Michelat (1965, pp. 242–254) was related both to electoral choices at the 1962 referendum on the direct election of the President and to partisan choices at the legislative elections of 1962.[24]

Those findings would surely lead us to expect attitudes toward de Gaulle to be still an important political factor on the mass level in 1967, if not perhaps so powerful as they were to become in 1968; for if 1967 was a sort of return to normalcy, the crescendo of political conflict that mounted during the upheaval of May 1968 reverberated around de Gaulle in an unambiguous fashion. "A bas de Gaulle" (Down with de Gaulle) was the slogan chanted in the streets by the regime's demonstrating opponents, while its silent and fearful supporters looked hopefully toward de Gaulle for a signal that would put things right for them again. They waited for an excruciatingly long time, but when that signal finally came at the end of May, in the form of the dissolution of the National Assembly, de Gaulle's supporters flooded the streets that only a few days earlier had been the exclusive preserve of his opponents. At the elections that followed in June, the dialectic of political forces revolved in no uncertain terms around the figure of the French President.[25] The convulsive events of 1968 put de Gaulle's centrality into uncommonly sharp relief, but his prominence had repeatedly been demonstrated earlier as well, with the result that we would expect attitudes pro and con de Gaulle to rank in political potency with religion and even the left-right dimension.

We are impressed in this regard with the temporal stability of mass reactions to de Gaulle, as well as we can measure them, across the 1967–1968 interval.[26] The continuity correlation for Gaullism is $r = .68$, compared with $r = .62$ for left-right locations. Although both of these values fall below the stability of partisanship ($r = .83$), occupational status ($r = .72$), and perhaps clericalism (for which we have no panel data), they are very high relative to any of the other political attitudes we have measured in these studies.

Furthermore, virtually everyone in our sample electorate expressed an attitude toward de Gaulle, as compared with a missing-data rate for left-right locations of some 20 percent of the respondents (and an even higher missing-data rate for party identification). Remember also that a substantial proportion of people with left-right locations populate the *marais*: that large pool of uninvolved centrists with little or no awareness of what left-right locations signify. The distribution along the Gaullist dimension has no bulge at the indifferent midpoint similar to that which we observe for the left-right axis. And we may reasonably surmise that for uninvolved voters, evaluations of de Gaulle have more real meaning than expressions of left-right locations do. Gaullism is not only a more stable attitude than left-right orientation; it is also more widespread among the mass electorate. Indeed, more people place themselves on our Gaullism scale than on our clericalism scale, for in assessing degree of religious attachment we must perforce confine ourselves to Catholics and nonbelievers, ignoring the small minority of people who profess other religions.

The main political forces we have been considering are correlated with one another, and sometimes at substantial levels, as Table 5-6 indicates. The picture is generally one of mutually supporting influences (with the notable exception of socioeconomic status), but in relation to Gaullism Table 5-6 is of special interest from two points of view. The first concerns the intercorrelations between Gaullism and the other two attitudinal variables, partisanship and left-right orientations. The second relates to the degrees of association between Gaullism and our two sociological variables, clericalism and socioeconomic status.

First, attitudes for and against de Gaulle are fairly robustly correlated with both left-right locations and partisanship, but they overlap less with partisanship than left-right locations do (about 30 percent shared variance on the average, as opposed to some 40 percent). That means that any con-

Table 5-6. Intercorrelation matrix of principal political forces (Pearson's *r*), 1967.

| | Principal political forces | | | |
Principal political forces	Clericalism	Left-right partisan identification	Gaullism	Own left-right location
Left-right partisan identification	.499			
Gaullism	.374	.557		
Own left-right location	.414	.653	.461	
Socioeconomic status	.146	.217	.020	.135

tribution to left-right voting made by Gaullism will be more independent of partisanship than the equivalent contribution of left-right orientations will be. This suggests strongly that Gaullism may well be on a par with left-right locations as an independent determinant of the mass vote.

Second, Gaullism is only modestly associated with clericalism (less than 15 percent shared variance), and the overlap with socioeconomic status is virtually nil. This not only tells us a great deal about the social bases of attitudes toward de Gaulle, but it provides further evidence of the complexities of political representation in France. There is some tendency for pro-clericals to be pro–de Gaulle and for anticlericals to be anti-Gaullist. But the association is not so overwhelming as to preclude numerous cases of admiration for de Gaulle among anticlericals and opposition to him among the religious. And support for de Gaulle (along with opposition to de Gaulle) is not class-based. Gaullist enthusiasts, like Gaullist opponents, are to be found among rich and poor, the middle class and the working class, the comparatively uninstructed and the university graduates. De Gaulle was a polarizing force in all walks of French life and, as we suggested in an earlier comment on the classlessness of French politics, this force may well have been a diffuse social irritant and obstacle to harmonious interpersonal relations. And although there is clear evidence of association between attitudes toward de Gaulle and traditional lines of religious cleavage in France, the overlap is smaller than any other displayed in Table 5-6, barring those involving socioeconomic status. Even common religious outlooks constitute less than a complete barrier to differences of opinion over de Gaulle.

Earlier in this chapter we referred to the problems of representation that can result from cross-cutting cleavages, in particular those stemming from the feeble role of class status as a political force in France, combined with the more powerful political play of religious attitudes. If people from widely varying economic and social circumstances, presumably having conflicting economic and social interests, do not express those interests electorally but rather cast their votes on religious lines, they risk being ill-served in other than the religious domain by the deputies they elect.

To the extent that Gaullism is a major factor in voting, the pattern of cross-cutting cleavages is further complicated and the problem of representation is exacerbated. Attitudes toward de Gaulle are even less class-related than are religious outlooks. Therefore, the voters who are moved primarily by admiration for or hostility toward de Gaulle are even more likely to end up with deputies who are not attuned to their economic and social needs than are the voters who make their electoral choices primarily on the basis of religious attitudes. And although Gaullism is associated with religious outlooks, the link is not particularly close, with the result that voters who are cued to politics through Gaullism may not have their religious interests attended to very notably either. The disjunction between electoral choice and policy satisfaction may be even greater for voters whose political orientations rest on their attitudes toward de Gaulle than it is for those whose electoral choices are based mainly on their religious outlooks.

Conclusions

In this chapter we have explored three factors—class status, religious outlooks, and attitudes toward de Gaulle—as alternates to partisan attachments and left-right orientations in shaping and stabilizing the political choices of the mass electorate. Of the three, we are most impressed with attitudes pro and con de Gaulle. Religion, in the form of locations on the clerical-anticlerical dimension, appears also to be a political factor to be reckoned with, although not on a par with the Gaullist–anti-Gaullist dimension. Class status, in any measurable form available to us, runs a poor third in relevance to mass political attitudes of any kind.

Perhaps the most noteworthy aspect of Gaullism as a political force in France is the breadth of its sweep across the entire electorate. There was almost no one in France during the late 1960s who was indifferent to de Gaulle. As a result, and in contrast to the situation for left-right, not only does virtually the entire electorate place on the Gaullism dimension, but few people take refuge at the indifferent midpoint. Of course, personal reactions to a single, salient national leader probably represent the lowest threshold of political awareness. Some fraction of the people who populate the Gaullism dimension are otherwise so uninvolved politically that they rarely or never vote, and their orientations to de Gaulle therefore become politically irrelevant. But attitudes toward de Gaulle are also impressively stable temporally, which suggests that they reflect more than casual judgments. In the French context, where partisan attachments are not well developed and left-right orientations are neither universal nor wholly free from ambiguity, attitudes toward de Gaulle may well be the most important political force operating on people without party identifications, as well as an independent influence rivaling left-right locations in potency. Those are possibilities to which we shall pay close attention later in this book.

It is important to keep in mind that feelings about de Gaulle have a different conceptual status from the other political determinants we have discussed. Class status and religion are rooted in the social structure. Powerful socializing agencies—the church, the secular school system, and the family—help to perpetuate the political expression of attitudes ranging across the proclerical-anticlerical dimension. Partisan attachments are transmitted from one generation to another when the elites who shape the contours of the party system permit that system to attain sufficient continuity of nomenclature and symbolism (see Chapter 3). Notions of left and right are enshrined in the nation's political vocabulary, and the feeling of belonging to one broad tendency or the other may also be handed down in the family (Percheron and Jennings, 1981).

Attitudes toward de Gaulle are not so institutionalized. The relevance of Gaullism is much more bounded in time than are left-right locations or any of our other more generic indicators. The departure and then the death of General de Gaulle meant the removal of the focal point of Gaullism from the political scene, and with an abruptness that could have no counterpart where the other abiding cleavages are concerned. The impact of Gaullism did not, of course, evaporate overnight in France. The popular attractions of Gaullism as a political alternative survived the General's death quite admirably, much to the benefit of his immediate successors. Nonetheless, the salience of attitudes toward de Gaulle has inevitably diminished with the passage of time, and in this sense Gaullism must rank with the least durable of our correlates of political choice. In fact, it might reasonably be asked why we have even included Gaullism in our catalogue of abiding orientations.

The answer is in some degree one of expediency. It would be hard to categorize reactions to de Gaulle as a short-term intrusion on French political life, in view of the fact that they were continuously potent for decades. De Gaulle wrote the French political agenda for a generation. As long as we bear in mind that Gaullist attitudes must necessarily suffer erosion over the long term, there is no harm in considering them as closer to truly enduring orientations than to short-term influences for the historic period under investigation in this book.

With regard to the more sociological variables we have treated in this chapter, the strong political effects of religious outlooks merit attention. This is especially true when religion is compared with purely socioeconomic cleavages, as reflected by alignments between class status and political preferences. For the homeland of the most famous modern popular revolution, these latter alignments are remarkably feeble, and they are quite overshadowed by the religious factor. The clerical-anticlerical cleavage was a more potent political force than status polarization in 1958, during the late 1960s, and—from what we can tell from other studies—through 1981. Although awareness of and interest in the importance of religious attitudes for political choices has been growing (see Martin, 1978), one cannot help being impressed by the paucity of historically elaborated investigations aimed at theoretical explanations of the effects of religion on mass political behavior, especially in comparison with the amount of effort that is directed toward producing class-based explanations of political phenomena.

The particular cleavage patterns endemic to France meld into a representation system of uncommon complexity, at least by Anglo-Saxon standards. The popular mood depends overwhelmingly on how well the political elites manage the economy and arrange the distribution of income and opportunity; yet in choosing those elites the electorate is guided far more by attitudes toward de Gaulle and stances toward religion than by their immediate economic and social interests. In such a system, the elected representative must steer between trying to promote the welfare of some of his constituents at the risk of offending the interests of others, on the one hand, and doing nothing jarring at the risk of generating diffuse popular discontent on the other hand. And, on the other side of the representation process, even the voter who makes his electoral choices with confidence is prey to frustration and disillusionment as the deputy he has helped to elect, and who is admirable from all the points of view that really count to the voter, appears helpless to improve his daily lot.

In Part IV of this book we shall address the issue of how the French deputy goes about trying to represent his constituency. But before we reach that point, we must gain a better understanding of the forces that determine the average Frenchman's vote at legislative elections. Although we have occasionally had reason to compare some of the political factors we have discussed with actual voting choices, these comparisons have been piecemeal and for limited purposes. In Part II we shall discuss more completely and systematically how the French electorate perceives the choices presented to it. In particular, in Chapter 10, we shall examine how the more potent forces we have explored in this and previous chapters interacted with one another, as well as with other shorter-term considerations, at the elections of 1967, to produce the aggregate choice of a National Assembly designed to represent the voice of the people in the ensuing years.

PART II

Choosing a Representative

It takes two to form a relationship, which is what political representation is. We have looked at the voter who, multiplied by aggregation, becomes one set of participants: the "represented." The other set of participants consists of the fortunate few who survive the hazards of the electoral process and become deputies. Nothing succeeds like success in this process: most of the winners are incumbents. And among the winners, the Communists are disciplined professional partisans, while the others constitute a social and especially an educational elite. There is an unavoidable problem here: will these deputies really know what is on the minds of their constituents?

Candidates and voters differ widely in their approach to the broad issues of public policy which underlie the analysis of political representation in this book. The policy attitudes of the parliamentary elite of candidates are much more structured, stable, and coherent than are those of the mass electorate. This contrast is particularly sharp when issue positions are associated with the left-right dimension. The linkage between policy attitudes and left-right locations is very close among the elite; it is much less so but still apparent among the thin stratum of citizens who are highly involved in politics; but it is less than impressive among the majority of ordinary citizens and fades to the vanishing point among the least involved third of the electorate. Despite these gross disparities, however, there is reason to believe that elite interpretations of left-right cues in terms of issue positions do not distort those of the citizenry, with the result that we shall want to pursue the linkage between left-right positioning and policy outputs as a key to the representation process in France.

By roughly comparable measures, candidates are more visible than parties in France, and they are also more visible to the voters than candidates are in the United States. Once again, we find that these phenomena are more easily explained in terms of institutional arrangements than individual-level voter attributes. But candidate visibility in France does not translate into policy terms as party visibility does. Almost without exception, more French voters assign issue positions to parties than to candidates, which means that parties are the main conveyor belt for mass representation on specific issues. But the extent to which the French electorate speaks with one voice concerning which party stands for any given issue falls far short of unity. As in the case of the linkage between issue positions and left-right orientations, the linkage between issue positions and parties is relatively clear only for the minority of highly involved voters.

How do the potentially orienting forces treated in Part I, along with the perceptions discussed here, fit together when the French voter casts his or her ballot? The issues are complex, and we shall not spoil the fun by giving too much away here. There may be some surprises ahead for readers who are skeptical about the role of party identification in France, and for those convinced that the left-right dimension provides the main clue to French mass electoral behavior. They will also find out the kinds of voters for whom attitudes toward de Gaulle and issue positions were significant electoral influences, independent of partisanship and left-right tendencies.

All this has to do with the comparatively simple first ballot. In almost 90 percent of the electoral districts there was also a second ballot in 1967. That simplifies things in one sense: there are fewer candidates in almost every district. It complicates things in other ways: some candidates have to decide whether or not to drop out and, if they do so, whether to support another candidate. Most voters can repeat their vote for their first-ballot choices, and they do so in overwhelming proportions; but first-ballot supporters of dropout candidates have to decide whether or not to vote and, if they do so, for whom. Dropout candidates and forced-choice voters make these decisions on strikingly similar grounds: party sympathies, however transient, carry more weight than left-right perceptions.

The candidates know more than the voters do about what goes on at the elite level during the hectic week between the two ballots, but—in an aggregate sense—their knowledge of what the voters are doing is considerably less than perfect. Here is another potential pitfall in the representation system. Deputies are being elected who do not fully know who their supporters are.

6

The Candidates

Almost 2200 candidates competed at the legislative elections of 1967 in the 467 districts of continental France. Not all of those candidates seriously believed that they might win seats in the Assembly. To be sure, some candidates who polled only tiny fractions of the vote may have badly misread the political situation in their districts and thought that their chances of election were much greater than they really were. That may well have been the case for certain dissident Gaullists and some candidates of minor parties, such as the PSU and the Alliance Républicaine. But most of the candidates who did poorly knew that their vote-gathering potential was slight and entered the race in pursuit of goals other than election to the Assembly, such as maximizing their party's national vote total, maintaining the visibility of their party with a view to the future, or acquiring leverage with allied parties by demonstrating that their electoral support at the first ballot, however small, could be vital to the success of another candidate at the second ballot.

Moreover, every French election brings out what the French call *candidats fantaisistes*—capricious candidates who are merely indulging personal whims. In order to exclude the latter, as well as candidates who were not likely to have thought that their presence would have any significant effect on the outcome of the election, we based our sample on the universe of candidates who won more than 5 percent of the valid ballots cast at the first ballot in their districts.[1] By setting that threshold we may have excluded some candidates who were quite serious about their potential electoral appeal, but they cannot have been numerous. Even after discounting the candidates who failed to win 5 percent of the vote in their districts, over 1900 candidates remained, an average of more than four per seat. That population constituted the basic pool from which the electorate chose those—less than a fourth of the total—who would represent them as deputies in the National Assembly.

The reduction that we made in the size of the candidate universe for sampling purposes reveals an important, if not surprising, aspect of the process by which the electorate winnows out those candidates who are eventually to become deputies. Candidates of the more visible parties have a much better chance of being elected than do candidates of minor parties or candidates who run *sans étiquette*—without any party label at all. Even before our application of the 5 percent threshold, almost 80 percent of the candidates represented one of the four main political formations of the period: the Communist party, the Federation, the Democratic Center, and the two components of the Gaullist bloc, the pure Gaullists of the UNR and Valéry Giscard d'Estaing's Independent Republicans. After the cut, almost 90 percent of the remaining candidates were representatives of those four major groups. Many more candidates from minor parties, and candidates without any party labels, than candidates from the main partisan groups failed to win 5 percent of the votes. Of the some 250 candidates who did not reach the 5 percent threshold, less than 10 percent were from the major parties; a fourth were from the PSU or the Alliance Républicaine, and more than two-thirds were from other minor parties or were candidates without any party label at all. Endorsement by a major party enormously increases the probability of electoral success.

Election and Prior Electoral Experience

Almost half of the candidates in our sample were running for the Assembly for the first time in 1967. Some three-fourths of the candidates had never previously been elected to the Assembly.[2] Of the fourth who had already served as deputies, most were incumbents, while a small proportion consisted of candidates seeking to regain seats that they had lost at an earlier election.

Incumbents enjoy a tremendous electoral advantage over nonincumbents. Table 6-1 sets out the electoral fortunes in 1967 of our sample of candidates, broken down by gross categories of parliamentary experience. It is evident that incumbents are far more likely to be elected than are nonincumbents.

Three-fourths of the incumbent candidates were reelected in 1967, representing a far higher success rate than that of either nonincumbents with some parliamentary experience or candidates without any parliamentary ex-

Table 6-1. Electoral success, by parliamentary experience (percentages), France, 1967.

		Parliamentary experience	
Electoral success	Incumbent	Former deputy, senator, or former senator	No parliamentary experience
Winners	74	23	9
Losers	26	77	91
Total	100	100	100
Weighted N	(50.7)	(30.4)	(188.9)

perience at all. To describe the electoral achievement of the incumbents in somewhat different terms: although they constituted less than 20 percent of the candidates, they furnished more than 60 percent of those who were victorious.

Former deputies, senators, and former senators did not fare so well as incumbent deputies. The ratio of winners to losers among nonincumbents with some type of parliamentary experience is almost the reverse of what it is for incumbents: less than a fourth of those candidates were successful in their bids for Assembly seats, while almost 80 percent were unsuccessful. Yet even these figures are somewhat misleading, in that they suggest that the electoral chances of nonincumbent former deputies are greater than they actually were in 1967. Our category of nonincumbents with parliamentary experience includes mainly former deputies, along with a sprinkling of senators. But almost as many sitting senators in our sample as former deputies were elected to the Assembly. If we were to combine incumbent senators with incumbent deputies, which is not unreasonable, the success rate of the enlarged incumbent group would increase slightly, while that of the group of former deputies and former senators would decline to 16 percent. That figure is higher than the election rate of the candidates without any parliamentary background at all, less than 10 percent of whom were elected in 1967, but the difference between those two success rates is smaller than one might intuitively expect. There is an electoral advantage to having had parliamentary experience of some kind in the past, compared with not having had any at all; but that advantage is not large, and it is dwarfed in magnitude by the overwhelming advantage held by incumbents over candidates of any other kind.

There was some variation in the success rate of incumbents depending upon how many parliamentary terms they had already served, but this variation was not large. Somewhat less than two-thirds of the first-term incumbents were reelected, while almost 85 percent of the incumbents who tried for a third term were successful. Case numbers are small for the more seasoned veterans, but all of the incumbents in our sample who sought a fourth term were reelected ($N = 5$) and more than three-fourths of the incumbents who were running for at least a fifth term were reelected ($N = 7$). The happy electoral fate of most veteran incumbents contrasted sharply with the experience of the parliamentary veterans who were not incumbents at the time of the election. All of the nonincumbents in our sample who had served at least four terms in the Assembly prior to 1967 lost at the election of that year ($N = 6$). It appears, at least on the evidence of our 1967 data, that long-term parliamentary experience, naturally associated with incumbent status in the past, is not an independent force in electoral victory. The factor that counts the most, and in overwhelming fashion, is incumbency.[3] The conditional probability that an incumbent will be reelected is of the order of 75 percent. Those are good odds by almost any standard.

Political Socialization

We saw in Chapter 3 how important the intergenerational transmission of political information is for the development of political orientations among the citizenry, and we showed how barriers to such familial political socialization are associated with gaps in political awareness among the mass electorate. It will hardly come as a surprise that in 1967 the candidates, intensely absorbed with things political, came from more politicized family backgrounds than did the mass electorate of that year. When asked about the amount of political interest that their fathers had displayed during their youth, more than three times as many voters as candidates, proportionately, replied that they did not know; and among the repondents who did recall the extent to which their fathers had been interested in politics, the candidates reported considerably higher levels of paternal political interest than the voters did. Table 6-2 sets out in comparative form, for those candidates and voters who recalled the extent to which their fathers were interested in politics, the levels of interest that they reported. It is evident at a glance that the candidates come from much more politicized families than the voters do. Almost half of the electorate reported that their fathers had no interest

Table 6-2. Degree of parental political interest reported by candidates and voters (percentages), France, 1967.

Parental political interest	Candidates	Voters
A lot	38	12
An average amount	33	24
Little	13	19
None at all	16	45
Total	100	100

in politics at all, compared with only slightly more than 15 percent of the candidates. More than three times as many candidates as voters, proportionately, reported that their fathers were interested in politics "a lot," and almost half as many more candidates than voters, proportionately, recalled that their fathers had had an "average" amount of interest in politics.

The gross proportions of parental political interest reported by the candidates mask some spectacular cases of familial political tradition at very high levels indeed. Several of the candidates in our sample were the children of deputies or were otherwise related to people who had held major political posts in the past. The fathers of several others had been active in the founding of political movements, and an even larger number of fathers had held high administrative positions.[4] France, like other democracies, has its real or aspiring political dynasties. Some of the personnel of de Gaulle's Republic had a lineage that reached back across *La République des partis* (Priouret, 1947) into *La République des camarades* (de Jouvenel, 1914).

There is some variation by party affiliation in the degree to which the candidates perceived their fathers as being interested in politics. Figure 6-1 sets out in graphic form the mean political interest scores reported by the candidates for their fathers, partitioned by the partisan grouping of the candidates, for those groups for which case numbers are adequate. Because there is virtually no difference between the mean scores reported by the pure Gaullists of the UNR and those reported by the Independent Republicans, those two groups have been combined.

The main messages conveyed by Figure 6-1 are that the PSU candidates reported the highest degree of paternal political interest and the Gaullist candidates (UNR and RI) the lowest degree, while the Communist, Federation, and Democratic Center candidates reported essentially similar degrees of parental political interest falling between the other two limiting levels. Perhaps the explanation for the comparatively high level of paternal politi-

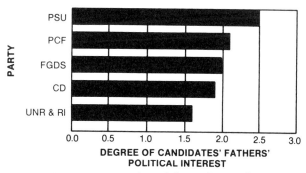

Figure 6-1. Political interest of candidates' fathers, by party, France, 1967.

cal interest recalled by PSU candidates is that it requires intense political so-cialization within the family to adhere to a party such as the PSU, with its deep factional conflicts, frequent schisms, close concern for ideological tenets, and lack of prospects for electoral success (Hauss, 1978).

On the contrary, the Gaullists of the UNR, whose fathers had the lowest level of political interest of those of any of the partisan groups of candidates, belonged to a movement that had been created by Charles de Gaulle in opposition to the Fourth French Republic and that had originally been populated heavily by people from wartime Resistance organizations that had been linked closely to de Gaulle in London. Many of those people had not been active in politics prior to joining the Resistance. Indeed, the Gaullist Resistance movement consisted, *in particular,* of people who had not been among the political elites or even among the politically respectable groups of the Third French Republic: junior officers, young businessmen, and devout Catholics, among others (Dogan, 1960; Hoffmann, 1963; Char-lot, 1971). It would not be surprising if a large proportion of such people had come from families who had little or no interest in politics, because the Third Republic excluded or discouraged them from political participation.

Of course, by 1967 the Resistance component of the Gaullist move-ment had begun to suffer the inevitable attrition of passing years. New peo-ple were entering its ranks who lacked the credentials of the "barons," credentials earned through a common experience of wartime attachment to de Gaulle, shared glory at the Liberation, and gnawing frustration during the long "crossing of the desert" between 1946 and 1958 while the General was out of power (Viansson-Ponté, 1963). But these new men were also, to a considerable extent, political outsiders bent on reform and unencumbered by ties to the political past.[5] Naturally, the Gaullist movement attracted a share of more or less conventional politicians who in other circumstances would have been orthodox conservatives or Radicals. But the more im-pressive aspect is the extent to which the burgeoning Gaullist party, which won two large electoral victories on very short notice, in 1958 and 1962, opened up political opportunities that were seized by people without tradi-tional political vocations.

Although there was some variation by party group in the extent to which the candidates' fathers had been interested in politics, the most strik-ing difference in that regard appears between the candidates as a whole and the mass electorate. That difference between elite and mass was also evident in the extent to which, as well as the precision with which, the candidates and the public at large attributed a political affiliation to their fathers. We saw in Chapter 3 that when asked what the party or tendency of their fa-thers was when they were young, only some 40–44 percent of the electorate gave some account of their father's partisanship. By contrast, when asked the identical question, more than 90 percent of our sample of candidates re-ported what the party or tendency of their fathers had been.

Indications of intergenerational transmission of partisanship are particularly striking among the candidates of the left-wing parties. No less than 90 percent of the Communist, Federation, and PSU candidates reported a left-wing political affiliation for their fathers.[6] The equivalent rate of paternal political affiliation for the Democratic Center candidates was also impressive, and slightly higher even than that for the Federation candidates: 83 percent of the Democratic Center candidates reported a centrist or right-wing affiliation for their fathers. The Gaullists, however, are a distinctive group in this respect. More than 40 percent of the Gaullist candidates reported that their fathers had had leftist political affiliations, and if we separate out the Independent Republicans, whose fathers' political affiliations were very similar to those of the fathers of the centrist candidates, the remaining "pure" Gaullists reported leftist fathers in 45 percent of the cases.

To be sure, the left had included several parties and tendencies in the past—the period to which our candidates were referring when they reported their fathers' political affiliations—just as it still does. The rich assortment within the French historical party spectrum is nicely captured in those reports, with regard to the right and center as well as to the left.

Taking this variety into account, we find that the proportion of candidates' fathers who belonged to one or another element of the left is not the same for each group of partisan candidates. If we consider only the three largest groups of candidates who reported substantial leftist ancestries—the Communists, the Federation, and the "pure" Gaullists—and take them in that order, we find a clear rightward movement of modal tendencies within the reports of leftist parental political affiliation. Among the Communist candidates who reported that their fathers had been leftist, more than a third specified that they had been Communists, Communist sympathizers, "reds," or anarchists; a third indicated that they had been Socialists; more than 15 percent reported simply that they had been on the left; and barely more than 10 percent said that their fathers had been Radicals. Among the Federation candidates reporting leftist fathers, only 6 percent said that their fathers had been Communists, 45 percent said that they had been Socialists, about a fourth referred simply to their having been leftist, and well over a third said that their fathers had been Radicals. Among the Gaullists with leftist fathers, a mere 4 percent specified the Communists or other extreme left groups, some 13 percent mentioned that their fathers had been Socialists, and 70 percent reported that their fathers had been Radicals or center-left in tendency. These distributions are quite clear: among the candidates, defined by partisan group, who reported having fathers with leftist political orientations, the more leftist the group of candidates, the more leftist the affiliations of their fathers.

The candidates' reports of their fathers' political affiliations open up a trail that we shall follow in pursuit of clues to the mystery, noted in Chapter 4, surrounding the striking leftist preference among the candidates as compared with an almost equally pronounced centrist preference among the mass electorate. The clearest expression of those contrasting preferences as between elite and mass is the tendency of the candidates to place themselves well to the left of where the voters place themselves on the left-right dimension. The mean own left-right location of the candidates, it will be recalled, is near 30, compared with a mean of 47 for the public at large. There are other manifestations of elite-mass contrasts in this domain as well. Candidates tend to locate their own parties to the left of where the candidates of the other parties perceive them to be, while the average voter locates his own party closer to the center than other voters do; and candidates routinely perceive themselves as being to the left of their own parties, while the man in the street sees himself as occupying a more centrist position than his party does.

The element of mystery here, on the elite side, is simply the question of why the leftist preference should be so marked. Is it the result of a general displacement to the left of all political objects by the elites because of some structural factor that affects their perceptions of the political world around them? Or is it a general trait of the elite political culture, of the kind described by Siegfried (1930) more than half a century ago, that impels the French politician personally to try to capture the allure of being on the side of progress? In Chapter 4 we opted temporarily for the latter interpretation, mainly because there was good reason to reject the former. French candidates do not perceive the party system as a whole to be systematically displaced to the left of where the mass public locates it. As we have shown, there is considerable concordance in the left-right locations attributed to the various parties by the candidates and by the voters. What is at work appears to be an intensely personal factor. The candidate sees himself as more leftist than his fellow partisans, and by a sort of extension of his ego to his party he also sees it as further to the left than the candidates from other parties do.

With information at hand about the candidates' (and the mass public's) perceptions of their fathers' political affiliations, we can ask whether the candidates' personal leftward preference applies also to their image of their fathers' political locations, or whether they treat their parents' political orientations as part of the "objective" world, as they do the parties of other politicians. On balance, the latter appears to be the case, although the evidence is not wholly conclusive, partly because of measurement problems. We do not have direct estimates from the candidates of the left-right locations of their fathers; so we have substituted for them a variable expressing the candidates' fathers' political affiliations (as recalled by the candidates) in surrogate left-right terms.[7]

The parental mean left-right location that emerges on this basis is almost 41. That is, of course, considerably to the right of the overall mean left-right position—less than 30—of the same candidates. It remains to the left, however, of the mean estimated left-right location (47) of the fathers of the approximately 40 percent of the electorate that attributed a political affiliation to them.[8] That mean of 47 is virtually identical with the mean left-right location of the electorate as a whole. The candidates, therefore, place their fathers to the right of themselves, while the public perceive their fathers, on the average, as occupying the same position on the left-right axis as they do. There is, therefore, some leftward bias in the candidates' perceptions of the political locations of their parents relative to the same class of perceptions on the part of the mass electorate, but it is not so strong as it is in the case of their perceived own left-right positioning.

There are, however, two factors suggesting that some of the leftist fetishism displayed by the French parliamentary elite may affect their perceptions of their parents' political locations. The first is that the parents of all but the youngest candidates in our sample belonged to generations in which the more moderate leftist parties, such as the Radical-Socialists, had wider electoral support than the more extremist ones, such as the Communists; and we would expect some of that "overrepresentation" to show up in any scoring system resting on current perceived left-right locations. The second factor is that our scoring of parents' parties reflects the mean positions attributed to them by all the candidates, and it is that particular set of aggregate perceptions that does not display any leftist bias and does not depart in any regular fashion from the collective perceptions of the voters. The overall mean left-right location of 41 assigned by the candidates to their fathers is, therefore, based on underlying data that would in any event contribute to reducing any systematic perceptual bias in a leftward direction.

Despite these qualifying remarks, which suggest that there may be rather more leftward bias than meets the eye in the candidates' reports of their fathers' political orientations, there is one simple fact that reinforces the notion that most of the leftward bias we have observed, unambiguously in Chapter 3 if more problematically in this chapter, is intensely personal and projected only onto those elements of the "outside world" that are inescapably bound up with the candidate's own political identification, such as his party. When we partition our sample of candidates on the basis of their own party affiliations, we find that each separate group of candidates perceives their parents as having been, on the average, to the right of the group's own average left-right location (see Figure 6-2). In the pursuit of leftist laurels, the French politician yields to no man, not even his father.[9]

As one might expect, given Figure 6-2, there is a tolerably close match in correlational terms between the candidates' own left-right locations and those of their parents. On an individual basis, the correlation is $r = .58$, a comparatively sturdy figure, compared with the $r = .40$ for the minority of the electorate that could recall any parental political affiliation. On a

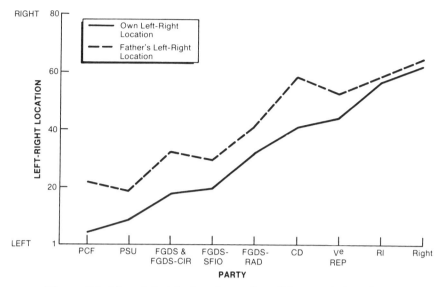

Figure 6-2. Mean left-right locations of candidates and their fathers, by party, France, 1967.

grouped basis, the correlation is $r = .97$, which is highly significant even if it applies to only nine groups.

As Figure 6-2 indicates, the size of the gap between the candidates' left-right locations and those of their parents varies, as between partisan groups. It is largest for the Communists (PCF)—a third of whose parents had been Socialists and, accordingly, to the right of their children—and for the Democratic Center (CD), as befits a hinge party straddling left and right. The smallest differences pertain to the Independent Republicans (RI) and non-Gaullist rightists (Right), which are, along with the PSU, the smallest groups represented. Across the entire party spectrum, however, there are clear indications of familial socialization into particular political outlooks. This phenomenon is all the more impressive because far from all of the candidates became attached to a political party early enough to have been insulated from nonfamily political influences. The Communist and Federation candidates in our sample, constituting half of the total number of candidates who provided us with exact information on this score, did indeed report that they had become attached to a political party, on the average, before they were twenty. The other half of the candidates, however, including those of the PSU as well as of the center and the right, reported that they had not become attached to a political party until the average age of almost twenty-nine. These candidates would have had ample opportunity to absorb political information as young adults and even to shop around among neighboring parties before developing an attachment to one of them. Yet, even later in life, at the time of their candidacies in 1967, their perceptions of their own left-right locations accorded well on a relative basis with their recall of their fathers' political parties or tendencies when they were growing up.

Origins

The candidates were predominantly urban in origin. Almost 40 percent of them had been raised in a big city or the suburbs, while slightly more than 20 percent of them had been raised in a medium-sized city and 18 percent had been raised in a small city. Only some 18 percent of the candidates had been raised in a village, and less than 5 percent had been raised on a farm. In this regard there is virtually no difference between winners and losers.

This distribution of demographic origins among the electoral elite is quite different from that of the electorate at large. Figure 6-3 compares the distribution of responses given by our samples of candidates and voters to an identical question concerning the size of the locality where they had been raised. It is apparent that although the proportions of candidates and voters raised in the suburbs or in small cities is about the same, there are sizable differences concerning the other kinds of localities. Almost one-third more

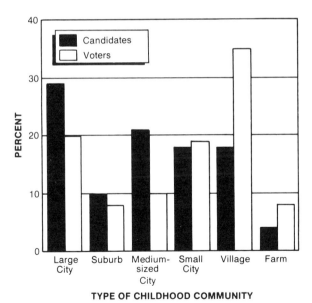

Figure 6-3. Type of childhood community of candidates and voters, France, 1967.

candidates than voters, proportionately, had been raised in big cities; about twice as many candidates as voters came from medium-sized cities; while about half as many candidates as voters had been raised in villages or on farms. In 1967, French candidates were more urban and less rural in background than the electorate as a whole.

The demographic backgrounds of the candidates, however, differed considerably by party. Figure 6-4 sets out the size of the community in which the candidates had been raised, partitioned by party group to include the larger formations for which we have respectable case numbers.

The most striking aspect of Figure 6-4 is the degree to which the demographic backgrounds of the Communist candidates differ from those of the other major groups. Students of French politics are quite familiar with the distinctiveness of the Communist party in terms of its leaders' occupational backgrounds, but here we find a demographic distinctiveness as well. In 1967 more Communist candidates than those of any other major group, proportionately, came from rural backgrounds, and fewer of them than those of any other major group came from heavily urban areas. At first glance, this may appear ironic, as in that year the electorate of the Communist party contained a larger proportion of voters with big city and suburban backgrounds than that of any of the other major groups. In fact, however, the demographic "fit" between the Communist candidates and their voters, taken in the aggregate, was closer than it was for any other

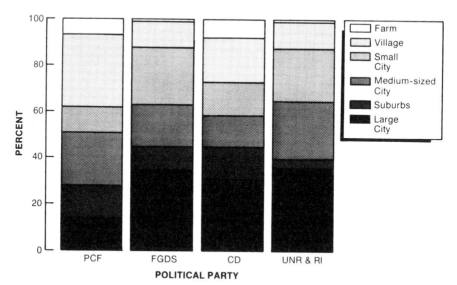

Figure 6-4. Type of childhood community of candidates by party, France, 1967.

party. The match between the Communist candidates and the Communist electorate with regard to rural backgrounds is well-nigh perfect, and far closer than that for the other parties. The Communist candidates did indeed "underrepresent" the Communist voters who had been raised in big cities or suburbs, but Communist underrepresentation of their heavily urban electorate was considerably less marked than the overrepresentation of that same category of voters by the candidates of all the other major political groups.

The partisan groups with proportionately more candidates who had been raised in big city and suburban milieus were the Federation, the Democratic Center and, to a somewhat lesser extent, the Gaullists. Comparatively few Federation and Gaullist candidates had been raised in villages or on farms, but more than a fourth of the Democratic Center candidates had originally hailed from rural areas. That proportion was considerably smaller, however, than the proportion of votes the Democratic Center received from rural voters, who provided more than half of its electoral support.

Although both the candidates as a whole and those who were electorally successful tended to have come originally from different-sized communities than had the electorate, there was nevertheless a considerable element of localism in candidate-selection, at least at the department level. Almost 60 percent of the 1967 candidates ran for office in the same department where they had been raised, and if we exclude the candidates who ran in the homogeneous, urban, Paris region, the figure rises to two-thirds.[10] In fact, outside the Paris region, urbanization was no impediment to this kind of localism. On the contrary, no less than 74 percent of the candidates in the most urban districts, outside of the Paris region, ran in districts in the same departments where they had been raised, a larger proportion than was the case for the medium urban and least urban districts.

On the whole, it made virtually no difference to the electoral success of the candidates whether or not they had grown up in the same district in which they ran for the Assembly in 1967. Excluding the Paris region, about one-fourth of the candidates in each category were winners. There was some variation, however, in the effect of localism according to the nature of the constituency. In the least urban districts (as compared to the most urban and the medium urban ones), localism may have been a positive factor of some importance. In those districts, some 26 percent of the candidates who had been raised in the same department were elected, compared with 19 percent of those who had grown up in a different department.

Sex

The candidates in 1967, as at all previous French elections, were overwhelmingly male. Only 4 percent of our sample of candidates were women, almost all of whom stood for left-wing parties. But if women constituted only a tiny proportion of the total number of serious candidates, the few who did run for legislative office were almost as likely to be elected as the far more numerous male candidates were. Twenty-one percent of our female sample candidates were elected, as compared with 23 percent of the male sample candidates. In 1967 it was twenty-four times more likely that a man would be nominated than a woman, but once nominated, women's chances of being elected were virtually the same as those of men. The French electorate of 1967 showed no bias against women candidates; it was the failure of the parties to nominate more women that produced a National Assembly whose composition was biased sharply in favor of men.[11]

Education

It is common knowledge that the parliamentary elites of Western democracies are, overall, better educated than the electorate as a whole. To some extent, this is due to the different age distribution of the elite as compared with that of the total adult population, but a far more important explanation for the phenomenon is simply that the parliamentary elites, on the average, come from relatively privileged family backgrounds. The French parliamentary candidates of 1967 did not constitute an exception to these general rules. Table 6-3 sets out the educational levels achieved by the entire mass electorate, as represented by our 1967 sample of voters, compared with those achieved by all the candidates and by the candidates who won seats in the Assembly.

As between the electorate and the full complement of candidates, the main differences appear at the two ends of the educational ladder. Two-thirds of the voters had received either a primary school education only or no education at all, compared with only 13 percent of the candidates; only 6 percent of the voters had received higher education, compared with more than half of the candidates. When we compare the electorate with the win-

Table 6-3. Educational backgrounds of voters, candidates, and winners, by percent per educational level, France, 1967.

Education	Voters	Candidates	Winners
No formal	1	0	0
Primary	66	13	14
Upper primary	7	12	4
Secondary	10	15	10
Technical or commercial	10	8	4
Higher	6	52	68
Total	100	100	100
Weighted N	(1956.6)	(269.2)	(61.1)

ning candidates, the bulge in university-trained people on the elite side expands even further. More than two-thirds of the winning candidates in our 1967 sample had been the beneficiaries of higher education.

These differences would have been even sharper if it had not been for the Communist party, more than half of whose candidates had received only a primary school or an upper primary school education, and less than 10 percent of whose candidates had attended an institution of higher learning. Among the remaining political formations, there was some—but not a great deal of—variation in educational background. Sixty percent of the Federation candidates, almost two-thirds of the Democratic Center candidates, and almost 80 percent of the pure Gaullists had attended universities. In terms of educational opportunities, the French deputies of 1967 were a highly privileged group.

Almost 60 percent of the university-trained candidates had received their higher education in Paris, while less than 40 percent had been trained in provincial institutions, and some 5 percent had received their higher education abroad, either in overseas France or a foreign country. There is almost no difference in these frequencies as between all the candidates and the winners only. The location where higher education was received bears no relationship at all to electoral success.

The parliamentary candidates and those who were electorally victorious among them were not only privileged in the extent of their education; they also tended disproportionately to attend elite institutions of higher learning. Table 6-4 presents the proportions of all the candidates, and of the winners only, by the various types of institution of higher learning they

Table 6-4. Types of institutions of higher learning attended by candidates and winners, by percent per type, France, 1967.

Type of institution	All candidates	Winners only
Law (public faculties)	26	30
(private faculties)	1	2
Letters (public faculties)	14	8
(private faculties)	3	6
Grandes écoles	15	17
Other elite schools	9	16
Medicine	12	13
Science	4	0
Pharmacy	3	2
Business	2	0
Other	11	6
Total	100	100
Weighted N	(138.2)	(41.1)

attended. The largest proportion of both groups attended law schools, and of the candidates the second largest proportion attended faculties of letters. But the third largest percentage of candidates, and the second largest percentage of winners, consisted of people who had attended elite institutions that the French refer to as *les grandes écoles,* to which admission is limited in numbers and based on nationwide competitive examinations, preparation for which normally takes two years after the student has graduated from secondary school.

There is no official list of grandes écoles, although everyone agrees that some schools, such as the Ecole Polytechnique, the Ecole Normale Supérieure, and the Ecole Nationale d'Administration (ENA), to name a few, are among them. For that and other reasons, it is not possible to state precisely the proportion of French students in higher education who attend the grandes écoles. We can estimate, however, that during the 1960s between 10 percent and 16 percent of the students in higher education attended the grandes écoles, with the proportion diminishing as university enrollments soared during the decade (Ministère de l'Education Nationale, 1969; Boudon, 1977). The some 15 percent of all the 1967 candidates who had attended institutions of higher learning that are unquestionably grandes écoles are not, therefore, notably out of line with the overall proportion of students attending grandes écoles during the early 1960s. But if we include certain other institutions whose status as grandes écoles is uncertain but which are nevertheless distinguished specialized institutions, such as the Institut d'Etudes Politiques at Paris or the pre–World-War-II Ecole Libre des Sciences Politiques, the proportion of candidates that attended such elite schools rises to almost one-fourth of the total. Among the winning candidates, the proportion that attended the unambiguously grandes écoles is slightly larger than it is among all the candidates, and the inclusion of the other prominent institutions raises the proportion of winning candidates who attended elite schools to almost a third of the total.

Because we were interested in emphasizing the elite nature of the institutions of higher learning attended by large proportions of the candidates and winners, Table 6-4 is not presented in a way that conveys the disciplines in which the university-educated candidates and winners were trained. Accordingly, we set out in Table 6-5 the proportions of candidates and winners who studied certain basic disciplines. It is apparent that law dominates the fields of study of both the candidates and the winners, and by a large margin. After the law, letters is the most popular field of study for both candidates and winners, while medicine (to which we have added the much smaller contingent from pharmacy) occupies third place for both groups. For those three disciplines, there is little difference between the proportions of candidates and the proportions of winners who were attracted to them while at the university, and the same holds true for the less popular field of agriculture (including veterinary medicine).

Table 6-5. Academic disciplines of candidates and winners, by percent per discipline, France, 1967.

Academic disciplines	All candidates	Winners only
Law	43	48
Letters	22	22
Medicine (including pharmacy)	15	15
Science and technology	6	4
Pure science	5	3
Agriculture (including veterinary medicine)	4	4
Business	2	0
Military	1	2
Other	2	2
Total	100	100
Weighted N	(139.0)	(41.2)

When it comes to the fourth most popular broad field of study for the candidates as a whole, the sciences and technology, we find a discernible falloff as between the candidates as a whole and the winners. Some 11 percent of our sample of candidates were trained in those domains, while only 7 percent of the winners were. And at a lower level in terms of proportions, we find a similar falloff for people with university training in business; 2 percent of our sample of candidates who had attended universities had received training in business, but none of them was elected. The French parliament is certainly not unusual among Western legislatures in this regard, but the parliamentary recruitment process in France operates against the selection of people with the kinds of professional expertise that could occasionally be valuable for a business-oriented economy that depends heavily on science and technology for its development. On the contrary, people with professional military training—which is obviously related to domains that are also of great concern to the legislature—although constituting only a tiny proportion of the candidates, were proportionally more numerous among the victors. But even if few people with professional training in business run for the Assembly, and if still fewer are elected, a substantial number of people engaged in French parliamentary politics have some kind of familiarity with business, as an examination of the occupational background of the candidates will demonstrate.

Occupational Background

Just as it is banal to report that parliamentary elites are privileged in educational terms, it is also common knowledge that they come on the average

Table 6-6. Father's occupation, reported by voters, candidates, and winners, by percent per occupation, France, 1967.

Father's occupation	Voters	All candidates	Winners only
Farmers	23	13	17
Farm workers	6	1	0
Big business proprietors	2	11	16
Small business proprietors	16	14	14
Professions	2	17	18
Upper management	3	9	9
Middle management and white collar	13	13	9
Workers	31	18	13
Service personnel	2	1	1
Other	2	3	3
Total	100	100	100
Weighted N	(1858.3)	(265.1)	(61.1)

from occupational backgrounds of comparatively high status. Table 6-6 indicates the occupations of the parents of our sample of the electorate, as well as the occupations of the fathers of both our sample of candidates and subsample of winners.

It is apparent at a glance that there is a gross discordance between the family occupational backgrounds of the population at large and those of our samples of elites. More than a third of the electorate comes from industrial or agricultural working class backgrounds, while well under 10 percent of it comes from big business, professional, or top managerial occupational backgrounds. By contrast, less than 20 percent of the candidates and less than 15 percent of the winners come from working-class backgrounds, while more than 35 percent of the candidates and almost 45 percent of the winners came from big business, professional, or top managerial occupational backgrounds. The only discrete occupational category that is represented more or less equally across Table 6-6 is small business.

In two categories, the differences between the parental occupations of the entire electorate and those of the winning candidates are particularly sharp. Nine times as many winning candidates as voters, proportionately, came from professional family backgrounds, and eight times as many came from "big business" backgrounds. Before the reader jumps to conclusions concerning the latter datum, however, it is important to point out that our use of the expression "big business" should not automatically evoke the image that the term conjures up in English-speaking countries. The occupational categories we employ in Table 6-6 are based on the official French coding conventions, and we have included under "big business" both what the French call *industriels* and *gros commerçants*. Industriels are employers engaged in industrial-type activities who have more than five employees, and gros commerçants are commercial business people with three or more employees.[12] Accordingly, the people who fall within either category operate businesses that can range in size from comparatively small firms to huge enterprises. But even though our big business category is a broad one, the differences between the proportions of voters, candidates, and winners who come from that occupational background are noteworthy, and should be borne in mind with relation to our earlier comments about the small proportion of deputies with professional training in business. Moreover, three times as many candidates (and winners) as voters came from families who held top managerial posts, although not necessarily in private business, as that category also includes people with high-level positions in the civil service.

Essentially the same general message appears when we consider the occupational experience, not of the previous generation, but of the current generation. Table 6-7 presents the occupations of the heads of household among our 1967 samples of the electorate, compared with those of our sample of candidates, both at the time when they "began to be actively engaged in politics" and at the time the candidates were interviewed shortly after the legislative elections of 1967. The relative proportions naturally differ from those reported in Table 6-6 (referring to the occupations of the parents of the voters and the candidates), but we still find a similar discordance between the occupational backgrounds of the electorate as a whole and those of the parliamentary elite.

As we compare, first, the occupations of the mass electorate with those of the candidates when they started out on their political careers, it should be kept in mind that we are comparing the occupational distribution of a complete cross-sectional sample of heads of households with the occupations of the candidates when, in most cases, those candidates were comparatively young.[13] Moreover, while our mass respondents were at least twenty-one years old in 1967, some of our candidates had become active in politics before they were twenty-one and, consequently, they reported their occupations at those earlier ages. The most direct expression of this differences lies in the fact that whereas more than 10 percent of the candidates were students at the start of their political careers, the proportion of students among our mass sample was tiny and therefore has been included within the 2 percent of "other" occupations. Hence we would not in any case expect the distribution of occupations among the electorate to match that among the candidates when they first became politically active.

Nevertheless, the differences between the occupational experiences of the mass electorate and the budding parliamentary political elite are striking. Whereas almost 40 percent of the electorate were industrial or agricul-

Table 6-7. Occupations of mass heads of household and candidates, by percent per occupation, France, 1967.

	Mass heads of household	Candidates	
		At start of political career	Currently
Occupations			
Upper management	5	13	33[a]
Big business proprietors	1	4	6
Professions	5	24	27
Middle management and white collar	21	19	24
Small business	12	3	2
Workers (including agricultural workers)	39	13	2
Service	4	0	0
Farming	11	9	6
Students	0	11	0
Other	2[b]	3	0
None	0	1[c]	0
Total	100	100	100
Weighted N	(1823.9)	(269.2)	(268.3)

a. Includes self-reports of "deputy" or "politics."

b. Includes students.

c. Includes one woman who was raising her family at home, a man who claimed that he had become actively engaged in politics at the age of eight, and another man who had had no regular occupation until comparatively late in life.

tural workers in 1967, only about 15 percent of the candidates had held such jobs when they became active in politics. The other side of this imbalance is that while only slightly more than 10 percent of the electorate either held a top managerial post, was a "big business" proprietor, or practised a profession, over 40 percent of the candidates had been engaged in such activities at the start of their political careers. Indeed, this contrast between the elite and the mass with regard to the comparatively high status occupations becomes even sharper when one takes into account those candidates who had been students when they became politically active. Two-thirds of such candidates were enrolled in higher education and, consequently, were on the way to comparatively high status occupations, even if they had not yet attained them.

These differences between the occupational experiences of the voters and those of the candidates at the start of their careers are widened even further when we compare the voters with the candidates at the time they were interviewed after the 1967 elections. The proportions of candidates with upper managerial occupations is more than double what it was for the candidates at the start of their political careers. For candidates with a big business background the proportion increases by almost a third, while for those from the professions it increases by more than 10 percent. Conversely, the proportion who were workers drops precipitously, that of those in small business drops slightly less, and that of candidates who were farmers drops by a third. The proportion in middle management and white collar occupations increases by more than a fourth, bringing the average proportion of candidates at the time they were interviewed to a level slightly in excess of that for the voters, compared with the slightly lower level that we find when we compare the proportion of voters in such occupations with that of the candidates when they first became active politically. Across the broad occupational categories employed in Table 6-7, the occupational backgrounds of the candidates in 1967 were even less representative of those of the entire electorate than they had been when those same candidates were on the threshold of their political careers.

To some extent, the increased proportions of candidates who reported upper managerial, big business, or professional occupations in 1967 as compared with those reporting similar occupations when they first became politically active reflects the altered status of the candidates who had been university or secondary school students when they became politically engaged. But the big bulge in the upper management category for the candidates in 1967, compared with the earlier period, is due largely to the inclusion in that group of a substantial proportion of 1967 winners who reported that they were engaged full-time in politics.[14] We will have more to say about this phenomenon later in the chapter when we discuss the parliamentary profession. Here we shall only emphasize that the distribution of occupations of the parliamentary candidates when they were interviewed is even less representative of that of the electorate at large than is the distribution of occupations among the candidates when they were at the start of their political careers. The major reason for this is that many of the winning candidates, including a disproportionately large number of those who had earlier engaged in those occupations—manual labor, comparatively low-skilled white collar work, or small personal businesses—in which most of the electorate is engaged, no longer thought of themselves in those occupational terms but rather perceived themselves primarily as deputies.

Early Occupational Basis of Parliamentary Recruitment

In Table 6-7 we have employed a limited number of broad occupational categories. These are quite appropriate for the comparative purpose they fulfill, which is to demonstrate the ways in which the occupational backgrounds of the parliamentary candidates differ from those of the public at large. Now, however, we want to take a closer look at the occupational base of French parliamentary recruitment, and for that purpose a finer classification of occupations is desirable.

Before we can deal properly with that question, a preliminary matter should be mentioned, both because it relates to classifying occupations and because it carries some interest in its own right for the subject of early political recruitment. When the candidates were asked about their occupations at the time they first became politically active, more than 10 percent replied that they had been students. In almost every case, we also know the occupations that they eventually entered, and in examining their occupational background it is obviously more appropriate to count those later occupations than simply to classify them as students. At the same time, the extent to which the eventual parliamentary candidates of the various parties first became active politically as students is not only a datum of some importance, but it is one that is often overlooked in studies of the social background of political elites.

Accordingly, we shall try to make the best of both worlds. First, we shall look at the distribution of parliamentary candidates who were students at the threshold of their political careers, both overall and within the main political formations for which we have adequate case numbers to draw proportions. Then, when we examine the occupations of the candidates more closely, we shall count the candidates who were students when they first became active politically, not as students, but in terms of the occupations they later entered.

Table 6-8 sets out the proportions of all the 1967 candidates, as well as the proportions of the candidates of each of the four large competing partisan groups, who were students when they first entered politics, broken down by educational level at the time. The partisan distribution of the student political neophytes is striking. While somewhat more than 11 percent of all the candidates had been students when they became politically active, more than 20 percent of the Federation candidates and almost 18 percent of the Communist candidates fell into that category, compared with less than 7 percent of the pure Gaullists and none of the Democratic Center candidates. Including PSU candidates not shown separately in the figure, more than 80 percent of those who went into politics while still students became leftist parliamentary candidates some years later. The large proportion of leftist candidates who had been students when they first answered the political call is linked to the fact that the Communist and Socialist candidates became attached to political parties, on the average, about a decade earlier than the Democratic Center and Gaullist candidates did.

Most of the budding politicians who were students were university students. Almost 15 percent of the Federation candidates were university students when they started their political careers, and so were almost 9 percent of the Communist candidates. There is nothing particularly noteworthy about the figures for the Federation; 60 percent of all their candidates had attended institutions of higher learning. The situation of the university

Table 6-8. Proportions of candidates who were students at the start of their political careers, overall and by major party (percentages), France, 1967.

Student level	Communists	Federation	Democratic Center	Gaullists	All candidates
Primary school	2.2	2.9	0	0	1.2
Secondary school	6.7	2.9	0	1.6	3.0
University	8.9	14.3	0	4.9	7.2
Total	17.8	20.1	0	6.5	11.4
Weighted total of all candidates	(67.5)	(56.0)	(50.0)	(54.9)	(269.2)

students among the Communists is more interesting. The Communist candidates who had first become politically active when they were university students are the only Communist candidates in our sample who attended institutions of higher learning. Like the Communist candidates generally, they became attached to the Communist party at a comparatively early age. None of the Communist candidates who had attended universities reported ever having had any political affiliation other than Communist. Very shortly we shall report that the Communist party recruits its parliamentary candidates heavily from the working class, but it is evident that university training is no barrier to becoming a Communist parliamentary candidate. The kind of university-trained person who does so, however, at least on the basis of our sample estimates, is someone who had become attached to the Communist party while still a student, rather than later in life after having entered some comparatively high status occupation for which he or she was prepared by university training.

Having disposed of the parliamentary candidates who had been students when they started their political careers, we can now take a closer look at the occupations of the 1967 candidates when they first became active politically, excluding students as an occupational category and including the occupations that the students went on to pursue. Table 6-9 lists the early occupations of all the 1967 candidates, and for each of the four main political formations for which we have enough cases to permit analysis by political affiliation.[15]

Table 6-9 contains few surprises. The heavily working-class basis of Communist recruitment appears clearly; at least 38 percent of Communist candidates were industrial or agricultural workers when they became active politically, and this proportion should probably be more than 40 percent.[16] Similarly, the historic tendency for the left-wing parties to recruit a substantial proportion of their candidates from the ranks of elementary school teachers is also visible. Nor is it unusual, given the history of the non-Communist left, that the Federation should recruit as many secondary school teachers as it does. Indeed, when we combine the Federation with the PSU (not shown separately in Table 6-9 because of limited case numbers), we find that almost 22 percent of their candidates were employed in secondary education, higher education, or the learned professions when they experienced their political baptism.

Among the pure Gaullist candidates, the relatively large proportions of high civil servants and military people reflect the technocratic outlook with which the Gaullists are often associated, although not always with notable analytic clarity. Gaullist links with business are also manifest, although more in the form of top managerial positions than of proprietorship; 13 percent of the Gaullist candidates had come to politics via such top jobs as corporate directorships (top management), while only about 8 percent of them (proprietors and industrialists) had owned their own businesses. The major source of Gaullist parliamentary candidates, however, was the professions, particularly medicine, which alone accounted for over 18 percent of them. The professions were heavily represented among the Federation candidates as well, although there the dominant professional group consisted of lawyers. It is easy enough to understand why a comparatively large number of professional people seek political careers. They have a greater possibility of working part-time than most people, although factors making for inflexibility are present as well, particularly for doctors. But why doctors should predominate among the Gaullists and lawyers among the non-Communist left is not evident.

The early occupational distribution of the Democratic Center's 1967 candidates is more balanced than that of any other main group. The only significant bulge comes in the 14 percent of Democratic Center candidates who were farmers when they entered politics. Indeed, the rural orientation of the Democratic Center is underlined further by the above-average number of CD candidates who were veterinarians when they began their political careers.

The Communists, however, recruited more heavily among farmers than did any other major partisan group, a fact that is consistent with their heavily rural origins. The Gaullists recruited few farmers, although the proportion of farmers among the larger Gaullist bloc, including both the pure Gaullists and the Independent Republicans, is more than double what it is among the pure Gaullists alone. The Federation candidates in our sample, however, are distinguished by the total absence of anyone who came to politics via farming.

If we confine ourselves, by way of conclusion, to the summation figures for the grouped categories of Table 6-9, we find that no one broad occupational category is represented in even approximately equal proportions among all four major partisan formations. Each major party specializes to some extent in its recruitment of parliamentary candidates. The Gaullists look for civil servants, business managers, and, to a lesser extent, big business proprietors. The Federation, the Democratic Center, and the Gaullists seek professional people in almost equal proportions, but the Communists will have nothing to do with them. The Federation recruits heavily among educators, and the Communists do so somewhat less strongly, while the centrists give them less than average representation and the Gaullists shun them almost as completely as the Communists avoid professionals. The mixed group of middle-level managers, technicians, and journalists strongly resembles the higher managerial and civil service group: recruitment proportions rise as one moves from left to right across the partisan dimension, just as they do for the upper-level group.

The most striking specialization in recruitment effort is evident in the

Table 6-9. Candidates' occupations at the start of their political careers, overall and by major party (percentages), France, 1967.

Candidates' early occupations	Communists	Federation	Democratic Center	Gaullists	All candidates
Farming	15.9	0	14.0	3.3	9.2
Top management and big business proprietors	2.3	15.9	20.0	41.0	20.6
High civil servants		5.8	8.0	14.8	7.3
Military officers				4.9	1.3
Top management (private sector)	2.3	5.8	6.0	13.1	6.9
Big commercial proprietors		2.9	2.0	1.6	2.0
Industrialists		1.4	4.0	6.6	3.1
Professions		26.1	32.0	28.0	20.1
Legal		13.1	10.0	8.2	8.2
Medical		7.2	6.0	18.2	6.8
Pharmacy			2.0		1.0
Veterinary medicine		1.4	6.0		1.4
Engineering		4.4	8.0	1.6	2.7
Education	20.5	34.8	10.0	1.6	17.2
Primary	15.9	17.4	2.0		8.1
Secondary	2.3	13.0	4.0	1.6	5.7
Higher	2.3	4.4	4.0		3.4

Middle management and upper white collar	4.6	8.7	10.0	16.4	9.0
Middle management		5.8	2.0	6.6	4.5
Technicians			4.0	9.8	1.1
Journalists		2.9	4.0		3.4
Workers, white collar, and small business	56.7	14.5	14.0	4.8	22.9
Workers (industrial, agricultural)	38.4	5.8	2.0	1.6	12.7
White collar	11.4	5.8	8.0	1.6	5.0
Small business	2.3			1.6	2.7
Small business or workers	4.6	2.9	4.0		2.5
Other				4.9	1.0
Total	100.0	100.0	100.0	100.0	100.0
Weighted N	(66.0)	(55.2)	(50.0)	(54.9)	(266.9)

extent to which the Communist party recruits its future parliamentary candidates among workers. This emphasis, combined with the party's attention to farmers, white collar employees, and other people from modest occupational backgrounds, makes the Communist party's early recruitment pattern far more representative of the overall national occupational distribution than that of any other party, not excluding the non-Communist left. But when, instead of speaking of the occupations of the 1967 parliamentary candidates when they first became active politically, we turn our attention to the *current* occupations of the candidates—that is, those existing shortly after the 1967 election—we find a rather different situation. The non-Communist parties are no more representative of the national work force than they were in terms of early recruitment, but by this time the Communist party's candidates have lost some of the representative character they had when they first entered politics. Although the Communists are still more broadly representative of the population at large than the candidates of any other group, the large contingent of workers that distinguishes the early recruitment base of the Communist party's parliamentary candidates has been greatly reduced. The workers who joined forces with the Communist party when they were young are no longer workers. They have become professional politicians and party officials.

Current Occupational Base of the Parliamentary Elite

Table 6-10 presents the occupations of our sample of candidates as they were reported to us shortly after the election of 1967, which may be compared with the candidates' occupations at the time they started their political careers as shown in Table 6-9. The great difference between the two situations is that whereas none of the candidates could consider themselves professional politicians at the time of their entry into politics, nearly a fourth of them after the 1967 election described their occupations in political terms. Some of these simply said that they were deputies (or, less frequently, senators or other elective officeholders); others indicated that they were party officials; and still others reported only that they were retired deputies.

The comparatively large number of candidates in this new category of professional politicians is compensated for by a decrease in the proportions of candidates from every other broad occupational category reported by the candidates earlier in their careers. These decreases, however, are not uniform across occupational categories. Virtually as many candidates, proportionately, reported being in the category of top managers (including high civil servants) and big business after the 1967 election as had done so earlier, and the decrease was small for the professionals and for the group of middle managers, journalists, and technicians as well. In the remaining occupational categories, however, the decreases are more striking. Three percent fewer candidates reported being professional educators; another 3 percent

Table 6-10. Candidates' current occupations, overall and by major party (percentages), France, 1967.

Candidates' current occupations[a]	Communists		Federation		Democratic Center		Gaullists		All candidates	
Politicians	51.3		22.8		6.0		21.4		24.7	
Deputies or senators		13.3		15.6		4.0		19.7		12.8
Other elective officeholders		6.7		2.9		2.0				2.8
Party officials		24.6		2.9				1.7		7.1
Retired deputies		6.7		1.4						2.0
Farming	8.9		0		10.0		1.7		6.1	
Top management and big business proprietors	0		20.1		26.0		33.4		20.3	
Professions	0		20.0		30.0		26.7		18.1	
Education	19.9		24.3		10.0		3.4		14.3	
Middle management and upper white collar	4.4		10.0		8.0		10.0		8.4	
Workers, white collar, and small business	15.5		2.8		10.0		3.4		8.1	
Total	100.0		100.0		100.0		100.0		100.0	
Weighted N	(67.5)		(56.0)		(50.0)		(54.0)		(268.3)	

a. Except for Politicians, the broad occupational categories used here include the specific occupations listed under the same headings in Table 6-9.

fewer reported being farmers. The most dramatic decline occurred for the category of workers, white collar employees, and small businessmen, which falls from 23 to 8 percent.

The main reason for the drop in the proportion of workers, white collar employees, and small businessmen is that the great majority of the Communist candidates who had been workers when they first became active politically were no longer workers after the 1967 election. Seventy percent of them were deputies who perceived themselves as full-time deputies, other elected officials, or party officials.[17] The Communists remain the most representative party in an occupational sense, but more Communist candidates, proportionately, were professional politicians or party officials than the candidates of any other party. More than half of the Communist candidates belong in that broad political category, compared with 22.8 percent of the Federation candidates, 21.4 percent of the pure Gaullists, and only 6 percent of the Democratic Center candidates.

The extent to which the parliamentary candidates of the French Communist party consist of professional politicians is quite remarkable. For more than half of them, politics is a full-time occupation. The comparatively large proportion of Communist candidates who are party functionaries is also noteworthy. The importance that the French Communist party attaches to organizational questions is, of course, well known (Kriegel, 1972). The importance of the *permanents*—paid party officials—as a source of parliamentary candidates is, to our knowledge, a less well known indication of the major role that the formal party organization plays in all aspects of the party's political activities.

The Parliamentary Profession

One reason why there were so many professional politicians among our sample of candidates, when they were asked about their current occupations, is that a large proportion of the winning candidates reported that they were full-time deputies, or otherwise indicated that they devoted their attention wholly to political affairs (as in the case of the ministers, for example). The exact proportion of the deputies who perceived themselves primarily as politicians, as opposed to being practitioners of some other occupation, varies depending upon how we classify the deputies who told us simply that they were retired from their former nonpolitical occupations. For those deputies, a case can be made for classifying them either way. On the one hand, the reply referred explicitly to a nonpolitical occupation; on the other, its content suggested that their only current occupation was political. If we count such cases as intrinsically nonpolitical, some 54 percent of the deputies elected in 1967 regarded themselves as full-time politicians; if we count them among the full-time politicians, the proportion of winners in that category rises to almost 60 percent. In either case, a majority of the elected deputies (as opposed to only about a fourth of the candidates as a whole) acknowledged in some fashion the existence of a parliamentary profession.

Whether or not a deputy regards himself as a full-time politician depends on two separate but related factors: partisan affiliation and prior occupational experience. Of the two, prior occupational experience appears to be the stronger; but the issue is complex, and the alternate position is by no means excluded.

Left-wing deputies are more likely than centrists or rightists to regard themselves as full-time politicians. Even if we count as nonpolitical the deputies who simply told us that they were retired from their previous occupations, we find that two-thirds of the leftist deputies regarded themselves as professional politicians, compared with only 44 percent of the centrists and rightists. If we count the ambiguous group (all of whom were leftists) as professional politicians, the proportion of professionals among the leftists rises to more than 80 percent. And, if we exclude cabinet ministers from the calculation, the difference in outlook between the leftists and rightists becomes even greater; in that case, only 41 percent of the centrists and rightists perceived themselves exclusively as politicians. This is strong presumptive evidence that political affiliation colors a deputy's perception of his principal occupation.

At the same time, there is also a strong relationship between the occupational self-perceptions of the deputies and the occupations in which they were engaged prior to becoming deputies. Our analysis in this regard suffers slightly from missing data, as we do not know the last nonpolitical occupation of each of the deputies elected in 1967, but this is not likely to distort our findings. We know the deputies' occupations when they first became active politically, and in many cases—particularly among the professional people—those occupations were not likely to have changed. In some cases, particularly among the deputies who had been students at the start of their political careers, the respondents volunteered information about their later occupations. And we also know the current occupations of the deputies who did not consider themselves to be full-time politicians. Altogether, that leaves few cases for which the relevant information is missing.

The relationship between occupational experience and occupational self-perception among the deputies takes two forms. First, some occupations are simply less compatible than others with simultaneous service as a deputy. Indeed, some occupations, such as positions in the civil service, are legally incompatible with service as a deputy.[18] But even occupations that may legally be engaged in by deputies vary in the extent to which the time and effort they require allow an individual to pursue them and at the same time serve as a deputy. The second consideration is less obvious and slightly more complex. This is the likelihood that a deputy would, if he were to lose his seat, return to the occupation in which he had been engaged prior to becoming a deputy. On the one hand, a deputy (particularly one who had served several terms) who had held an occupation earlier in life that did not bear much relationship to the kind of position he would expect to hold if he left the Assembly, could be expected to think of himself primarily as a deputy rather than as the practitioner of the occupation that he had once held but did not expect to hold again. On the other hand, a deputy whose prior occupation had been one to which he could easily return might well think of himself primarily in terms of that occupation rather than as a deputy. Let us examine these two considerations more closely.

Setting aside for the moment the question of legal prohibitions, the kinds of occupations that would be least compatible with service as a deputy are those requiring regular personal attendance eight or more hours a day, five or more days a week, virtually all year round. In other words, agricultural or industrial labor, salaried white collar occupations, and small personal businesses simply cannot be engaged in by someone who is also a deputy. And that is precisely what we find in our interview data. Depending on how we classify the ambiguous cases (the deputies who were retired from their nonpolitical occupations but did not refer to themselves as professional politicians), either *all* or almost 80 percent of the deputies who had earlier been engaged in those kinds of occupations considered themselves full-time deputies shortly after the election of 1967.[19]

Moreover, manual labor, comparatively low-skilled white collar work, and small personal businesses are not the kinds of occupations to which people are likely to return once they have served as deputies. People in those kinds of occupations cannot go on leave and expect to return to their old jobs after a period of years, nor is it likely that they will want to do so. They have gained experience, skills, and associations that almost surely will lead them into other kinds of work if they should lose their seats while they are still of working age. Indeed, we have already seen how the Communist party, which recruits its parliamentary candidates heavily from people with working-class and white collar occupations, transforms workers into party functionaries.

At the same time, we would expect that deputies who are big business proprietors or corporation directors could arrange their schedules to permit them to attend to their business affairs, at least on a reduced basis, while they are serving in the Assembly. Furthermore, those occupations—which do not even have to be suspended—can be returned to if the deputy loses his seat. Again, we find our expectations confirmed. Less than 10 percent of the deputies who had been industrialists, big business proprietors, or company directors considered themselves primarily as politicians; more than 90 percent of them reported their business activities when asked about their current occupations shortly after they had been elected (or reelected) to the Assembly.

The same phenomenon, slightly attenuated, holds for the deputies from the liberal professions: law, medicine, veterinary medicine, and pharmacy. Slightly more than a fifth of those deputies considered themselves full-time deputies, while almost 80 percent of them cited their professional, rather than their political, status when asked about their current occupations. The opportunity that service as a deputy provides for part-time nonpolitical work appears most clearly among the deputies from the liberal professions. About 40 percent of such deputies who cited the liberal professions as their occupation indicated explicitly that they worked at them only part-time, and virtually everyone who mentioned having a part-time occupation was from the liberal professions.

If we include journalism among the liberal professions, the picture alters somewhat. Then, almost a third of the free professionals consider themselves full-time politicians. On its face, this is something of an anomaly, as journalism would appear to be an occupation that lends itself as well as or better than most to simultaneous service as a deputy. Yet journalism is precisely the kind of occupation by which people whose primary interest is in political affairs can earn a living while they attend to the political activities that most appeal to them. Once these people have achieved high political office, they are not likely to think of themselves primarily in terms of an occupation that was essentially a means to an end that they have now gained. We cannot assert unequivocally that this interpretation fits each of the former journalists among our sample of deputies, but it is consistent with what we know of the careers of most of them.

Civil servants, military officers, and public school teachers constitute a special case within this context. On the one hand, persons from those professions are legally required to go on leave while they are serving as members of parliament.[20] Thus, it is not particularly surprising that between 70 and 80 percent of them in our sample reported themselves as full-time deputies. But civil servants (including teachers) may return to their jobs and simply pick up where they left off if they lose their seats in the Assembly before they reach retirement age. Indeed, civil servants are a privileged group in this respect in that their rights to employment within well-organized corps of public officials are guaranteed. So it is not unreasonable that a minority of the deputies in that category still thought of themselves in conventional occupational terms even though they were legally prohibited from carrying out that occupation at the time. But most deputies from the civil service perceived themselves as full-time politicians.

The deputies from the kinds of occupations that required forty or more hours a week of personal attendance and to which they were unlikely to return, and who overwhelmingly perceived themselves as full-time politicians, were all leftists: Communists if they were workers, Federation deputies if they were white collar employees. The industrialists, big business proprietors, and company directors who tended to think of themselves not as deputies but as businessmen were mainly centrists, Gaullists, or Independent Republicans. Still, since some Federation deputies were businessmen and even more were free professionals, we can make a test to determine whether partisan affiliation or occupational background counts for more in determining a deputy's self-perception in occupational terms. We can compute the proportion of leftist deputies from business and the professions who regarded themselves as full-time politicians and compare it with the proportion of right-wing and centrist deputies from those same occupational categories who similarly perceived themselves as professional politicians. Case numbers are pitifully small, especially among the Federation candidates, but for both the Federation and the centrist-rightist groups, the proportions of those deputies perceiving themselves primarily as businessmen or as free professionals are more than 75 percent. In other words, prior occupational experience appears to count more than political affiliation in explaining why some deputies from the business world or the professional world still considered themselves part of those worlds even though they were deputies.

Conclusions

In 1967 the French parliamentary elite—if we may refer to the candidates for the National Assembly in that fashion—consisted overwhelmingly of male partisans from families in which the fathers had had much more than an average interest in politics and had displayed a political outlook that was, for the times, roughly the equivalent of the partisan position occupied by their sons in the middle 1960s.

Primarily urban in origin, the parliamentary elite was an economic and social elite as well. The candidates came disproportionately from families engaged in what are commonly regarded as high status occupations, and most of them were similarly employed in comparatively high status jobs or were students preparing for such jobs when they first entered politics. Moreover, a large proportion of them were also privileged in the amount of education they had received. In fact, a majority of them had enjoyed higher education, compared with barely more than 5 percent of the adult population as a whole.

This educational advantage looms even larger if we consider that smaller elite, within the larger parliamentary elite, which consists of the electoral winners who became deputies. Here there is a quantitative gain, in that an even larger proportion of the 1967 winners than of the candidates had attended institutions of higher learning, and also a qualitative gain. More deputies than candidates, proportionately, had attended grandes écoles or other elite schools which traditionally furnish the personnel who occupy the highest managerial and administrative positions in France, in both the public and private sectors. The educational privileges enjoyed by deputies probably represent an important factor in the political control of the bureaucracy, the upper levels of which are also recruited from select grandes écoles (Suleiman, 1974, 1978). Deputies with the same educational background can deal on equal terms with an administrative elite whose expertise and social solidarity might otherwise give them as administrators an even greater degree of autonomy than they already enjoy.

Even though the candidates form a privileged group by comparison with the adult population as a whole, the prize that they seek—a seat in the National Assembly—forever eludes most of them, and they do not enter the even more charmed circle of deputies. Half of the 1967 candidates were running for national legislative office for the first time, and that was the only try for a seat in the Assembly that most of them would make. Three-fourths of the 1967 candidates had never served in the Assembly before, and less than 10 percent of those inexperienced hopefuls emerged victorious. The reason for this is that incumbents hold an enormous electoral advantage. Three-fourths of the incumbent candidates won in 1967, even though the previous election had been held fully five years earlier.

The occupational and educational advantages of the candidates and deputies would be even more marked than they were in 1967, relative to the electorate as a whole, were it not for the presence of the Communist party, whose candidates come from more representative (and modest) circumstances than do those of any other French party. But even this contribution to the overall demographic "representativeness" of the parliamentary elite is misleading, for although half of the Communist candidates had been either blue collar or white collar workers when they first became politically active, only some 15 percent of them thought of themselves primarily as blue collar or white collar workers in 1967 at the time they were parliamentary candidates. Instead, more than half of the Communist candidates in 1967 either perceived themselves primarily in political terms—as deputies or other elected officials—or were paid party workers.

These "professional politicians" were more numerous proportionately among Communist candidates than among the candidates of the other groups, but each of the main political formations included a certain number of them. Indeed, whether a candidate perceives himself primarily as a professional politician or in more conventional occupational terms depends at least as much upon the occupation that the person had or was preparing for at the start of his political career as it does upon the candidate's partisan affiliation. Candidates from a profession that can be exercised part-time, or to which a person can return more or less easily after being away from it for some years, are likely to consider themselves in conventional occupational terms, even if they are elected deputies. Candidates from occupations which cannot be engaged in on a part-time basis, or to which an elected official at the national level is not likely to be permitted, or want, to return after his elective mandate has expired, tend to perceive themselves primarily in political terms.[21]

This duality of background and self-perception is a potential source of both richness and distortion in the deputies' understanding of the preoccupations of ordinary French men and women. On the one hand, the deputies with the most direct personal experience of the lot of the common citizen are also those who are most likely to interpret that experience according to the rigid and uniform requirements of party discipline. On the other hand, the deputies who retain links with the outside, nonpolitical world are likely to be confined to that world's most privileged sectors. The professional politicians live in an environment that can be just as insulated from the "real" social world as the environment of the generally privileged part-time politicians whose channels of communication remain open but lead only to partial sources of information. Later on, in Chapter 20, we shall discuss in detail the extent of candidate knowledge of the opinions of their constituents. It will be well to bear in mind at that time the extent to which the social background and self-perceptions of the parliamentary elite may distort their understanding of the popular mind. However much the parliamentary politician may try to remain of the people, he cannot help failing.[22] We turn now to another domain in which the contrast between mass and elite is no less striking than it is in terms of personal backgrounds: the structure of their attitudes toward public policy.

7

Policy Attitudes of Mass and Elite

I n introducing our sample of candidates in terms of their social backgrounds and political experiences, we used the distribution of social and political attributes in our mass sample as a foil. It was clear that our candidates, taken as political elites, were a rather rarefied set of actors in terms of their social class background and political socialization, and we used the mass sample as a backdrop to help indicate just how rarefied a group they were.

In this chapter we shall consider the contrasts between the ideational worlds of politics inhabited by our aspiring candidates, on the one hand, and by the common voters, on the other hand. In particular, we shall focus on the structures of policy preferences in these two samples. It should be obvious that such comparisons are absolutely central to the study of political representation, since this process obliges a representative to perceive and understand the policy sentiments of his constituents and somehow to take them into account, along with his own judgment of policy options. Since the representative only rarely possesses an up-to-date direct measurement of his constituents' policy preferences, he must try to estimate the sentiments of his district from the bits and pieces of information that he has about his constituents. In this estimation process, he is very likely to assume that belief elements which go together neatly in his own mind also tend to co-occur among his constituents. If, for example, he thinks of his district as leftist, he is likely to imagine that when an issue like the development of a nuclear strike force (*force de frappe*) emerges on the political scene, sentiment in his constituency will be negative toward the idea. Comparing the structures of policy preferences in the two samples can throw direct light upon assumptions of this kind.

The Set of Linkage Issues

Our interviews at the mass and elite levels in 1967 and 1968 embraced a wide variety of questions delving directly or indirectly into all of the major policy cleavages which were central to political competition in this period. But one major subset of these policy items became sanctified in our design as "linkage issues," because they involved policy matters which could be probed in both the mass and elite samples. Since these linkage issues will be of central concern to us not merely in this chapter, but also later in our evaluations of the policy representation process in France, it is necessary to begin by describing them and explaining how they were chosen.

Our primary goal, of course, was to pick a set of issue domains which would fairly represent the scope of the principal policy cleavages surrounding the 1967 election. At the same time, because we were interested in following the performance of the winning candidates during their subsequent period of incumbency (expected at this time to be at least five years), we slanted the choices in some degree to fit our best guesses as to which issues were likely to remain in the forefront of public discussion for some years to come.

The linkage issues were divided into two generic forms: conventional "position" issues, and "agenda" or "importance" items. The latter battery was included because, when the interview was being designed, it was often argued that priorities established in the public agenda which kept some issues in the public eye while demoting others could be as important politically as actual pro-con position-taking (see Bachrach and Baratz, 1962). We made no effort to ensure that conventional positions and priority importance were measured for all policy domains, although we did complete this match in some cases. In other cases, such as the issue of government stability, no match seemed appropriate; that is, only the presiding Gaullists went into the 1967 elections stressing the importance of government stability. Although the opposition could scarcely seek governmental "instability" as an end in itself, particularly in view of the unfortunate history of the late Fourth Republic, it doggedly ignored the stability issue. This issue, among the most prominent in the 1967 campaign, was thus broached only in "importance" ratings, or "agenda" form. And, conversely, some other issues were broached only in "position" form.

One unanticipated property of the agenda items, which is worth emphasizing, is that such items clearly suffer more measurement "noise," and are generally less effective measures, than the more conventional "position" issues. This is not to say that the agenda items do not "work": they do indeed show correlations with other issue positions and personal characteristics that might be expected on common-sense grounds. The problem is that the measures seem inert: expected correlations are small in magnitude, and usually are much smaller than those produced by "position" measures for the same policy domain. The reason for this relatively weak performance is simply that most of our politically involved respondents, such as the elite sample or the most involved of the public, rated almost all of the issues that we had chosen as "very important," that is, in the top category of the scale. This was a gratifying endorsement of our decision to include the relevant items; but it left most of the working variance in the responses to those in the mass sample who were less involved in or less attentive to politics. This fact in turn produced some unusual effects which will preoccupy us later in this chapter and will ultimately affect our representation results.

We also attempted to distribute our linkage issues equitably between domestic and foreign policy concerns, as shown in our summary of linkage items (Tables 7-1a and 7-1b). But the single, more extended battery of items on European integration, all in the position form and added for reasons beyond those of our immediate study, tilts the balance somewhat toward a greater concentration on foreign items that are posed as position issues.

Question Identicalness across Samples

Tables 7-1a and 7-1b are organized in such a fashion as to permit rapid assessment of these distinctions as well as of one or two others. Throughout, linkage issues in the agenda format are distinguished from the more conventional position issues by the prefix "Imp" (importance). The tables are also designed to underscore the pattern of identical questions. Whether we expect to compare issue measurements between mass and elite samples, or, as in the case of either type of sample, between the 1967 and 1968 data, it is clear that our comparisons will be tightest when question wording is identical.

The reasons for giving up wording identicalness in some circumstances were diverse. Where the two years 1967 and 1968 were concerned, the same rush of events that had dissolved the 1967 Assembly and produced our 1968 reinterviews often seemed to call for wording adjustments, as well as additions and deletions. Thus, for example, although we were happy that one of the major themes of the 1968 disorders had been anticipated by our 1967 questions in both position and agenda form concerning the priority accorded the education system by government, it seemed wise in 1968 to adjust the question to ask about the priority of "university reform." A bill popularly labeled in this way was being prepared under the supervision of Edgar Faure in response to the student uprisings, and it promised to be subject to debate in the ensuing years, as indeed it was more than once.

Table 7-1a. Schema of linkage issues, mass and elite, France, 1967.

Policy domain	Mass form	Both forms identical	Elite form
Domestic			
Income distribution	Distr. of income equitable	Imp: Income distribution	Distr. of income equitable
Union rights	Protect union rights		Union role in plants
Church and state	Gov't. aid to church schools	Imp: Defense of public schools	Gov't. aid to church schools
			Pay church school salaries
			Aid church school parents
			No gov't. aid to church schools
Education	More gov't. aid to education	Imp: Educational development	Budget priority for education
Economic development		Imp: Economic development	
Foreign			
European integration		French army in European army	
		France accept European foreign policy	
		France remains in Common Market	
		Free movement, European workers	
		France aid poor Europe	
		Imp: Building Europe	
Foreign aid	Foreign aid		Foreign aid
Military expenditure	Force de frappe		Force de frappe
Independent foreign policy	French foreign policy independent of U.S.	Imp: foreign policy independent of U.S.	French foreign policy independent of U.S.
Domestic and foreign			
Government-opposition		Imp: Government stability	
Left-right		Left-right self-location	

In regard to identicalness of wording between mass and elite samples, it seemed important upon occasion to ask our elite respondents somewhat more specific versions of the items posed to the mass sample, and to do so in a more open-ended fashion.[1] The actual wording of all of the items may be found in Appendix D.

One major imbalance apparent from a cursory reading of Tables 7-1a and 7-1b is that apart from the battery of five position questions on European integration, our identical questions for both the mass and elite samples are almost exclusively of the weaker agenda form, rather than the conventional position issues. The only exception is a glorious one, located on the bottom line of both tables: we did ask the "super-issue" of left-right location in the same form for both samples at both time periods.

Keying Issue Responses

Since we shall be spending much of the rest of this chapter, and no small part of the rest of this book, dealing with the interrelationships between these issues, or at the very least relating them to other measurements, such as deputy votes in the National Assembly, it should be made clear what relative "keying," or direction of scoring, we have established between responses to various issues.

The measurement problem involved in a "keying" decision is usually so trivial as to require no comment at all. For example, Tables 7-1a and 7-1b show that the mass sample in 1967 and 1968 was posed two questions about the relationships between parochial and public schools. The "position" question asked whether the government should subsidize parochial church schools, and a first response of "strongly agree" would be expected of persons of some religious devotion, typically Catholic, anxious to preserve a sanctuary against the onslaughts of merely civil education. The agenda question asked how important it was to preserve the civil education system (against budgetary incursions from parochial schools), and the first response was "very important." If we correlate these two measures of what is pretty much the same dimension, the relationship in the mass sample in 1967 is a modest negative value (to be exact, a value of $-.28$). The negative relationship smacks of inconsistency. But, of course, there is none: persons most anxious for government subsidy of the parochial education system are least concerned about the preservation of the public school system, and vice versa. The only reason for a negative sign in the relationship is an artifact in the way the questions happened to be posed. We need merely to reverse, or "change the keying of," one set of responses relative to the other, and the proper positive substantive relationship appears.

The point here is so obvious that most investigators would move to the "proper" substantive keying without bothering to comment. But we are dealing with a long list of diverse political issues, with little in common

Table 7-1b. Schema of linkage issues, mass and elite, France, 1968.

Policy domain	Mass form	Both forms identical	Elite form
Domestic			
Income distribution	Distr. of income equitable		Distr. of income equitable Imp. Income distribution
Social welfare	More gov't. social welfare	Imp: Develop soc. welfare Imp: Fight unemployment	Budget priority, soc. welf.
Union rights	Protect union rights	Imp: Union role in plants	Union role in plants
Church and state	Gov't. aid to church schools	Imp: defense of public schools	Gov't. aid to church schools Pay church school salaries Aid church school parents No gov't. aid to church schools
Education	University reform	Imp: University reform	Budget priority for education Imp: Educational development University reform
Economic development			Imp: Economic development

		Imp: Building Europe
Foreign		
European integration	Speed Common Market	French army in European army
		France accept European foreign policy
		France remains in Common Market
		Free movement, European workers
		France aid poor Europe
Foreign aid		Foreign aid
Military expenditure	Reduce military expenses	Force de frappe
Independent foreign policy		Foreign policy independent of U.S.
		Imp: Foreign policy independent of U.S.
Domestic and foreign	Imp: Government stability	
Government-opposition	Left-right selflocation	
Left-right		

save for the fact that they had all surfaced into hot public debate in France by the latter half of the 1960s. The expected directions of their interconnections between samples and time points are often quite unclear.

We naturally sought a keying scheme which was as objectively determined as possible. Therefore we have keyed our various issues according to the way their response distributions correlate with left-right self-locations. For a goodly share of our issue domains this one simple decision rule suffices to produce very satisfying keyings. Thus, for example, people who favor greater distribution of wealth, stronger union rights, more social welfare measures, and less government support of Catholic schools are generally leftist, while rightist respondents lean in opposite directions in all these domains.[2]

These domains, however, had obvious keyings to begin with. In other domains, especially that of foreign policy, correlations with left-right locations are very feeble and, particularly in the mass sample, hover around zero. Then our simple decision rule is not enough, because discordant signs of relationships with the left-right dimension arise between samples or across years. Obviously none of these inconsistencies involves correlations of any magnitude, and it may seem pointless to deliberate long over whether we shall key an issue item so that its correlation with left-right is plus or minus .02. This decision, taken alone, would indeed be trivial. But it may also determine whether some other larger relationship involving this issue, such as a magnitude of .30, is to be construed as a positive or negative one. This is no longer a trivial matter.

Where discordant signals have been present, our keying decisions have followed the lines of the weight of the evidence, once past a basic rule that a single substantive keying direction must be maintained for all items within any given policy domain. In practice, this "weight" rule means that more importance is attached to the signs of larger correlations than to those of smaller ones, and that evidence from our larger samples of 1967 is seen as more conclusive than that from the smaller samples of 1968. When these further keying assignments have been made on the basis of evidence which is inadvertently weak or mixed, we find that the left, in addition to showing clear support for labor and social welfare measures and distinct antagonism to church school subsidies, was in this period also faintly more favorable than the right to development of the education system and to economic development, where domestic issues were concerned. In foreign affairs, the left was decidedly more hostile to the force de frappe than the right; faintly less enthusiastic about European integration or foreign aid; and somewhat more concerned to keep French foreign policy as independent of United States policy as possible.

One other matter involving these issues and left-right self-locations warrants comment as well. We did not wish to take for granted that postures in all of these policy domains necessarily were related to left-right lo-cations in a simple linear fashion. Therefore we checked these functions across both samples. The linear form seems to be a reasonable approxima-tion for relationships in all of these domains save one, and that exception is observed clearly only in the elite sample. Although the linear approxima-tion says that our rightist candidates were more favorable to European inte-gration than those of the left, the true underlying relationship is quite curvilinear: that is, enthusiasm for European integration reached its maxi-mum among candidates of relatively centrist persuasions. The far left was very hostile, and among the limited number of candidates willing to place themselves far to the right, doubt was rampant about the wisdom of giving up any normal national sovereignty. This departure from linearity is suffi-ciently marked in the elite sample, and seems meaningful enough, that we have modeled the relationship with a quadratic rather than a linear equa-tion. The observed function linking these same variables in the mass sample, although faintly bowed in the same direction, departs from linearity so modestly that we would not normally have bothered to respecify the form of the function. Inasmuch as we are comparing results from the two sam-ples in what follows, however, both samples will be treated in the same way.[3]

Mass and Elite Belief Systems

Our linkage issues provide the raw material for a comparative assessment of the structure of policy preferences in a common cross-section population and a population of political elites. When in the preceding chapter we compared these populations with regard to their demographic characteris-tics, we certainly expected that the elite sample would in a variety of other ways show signs of privilege, in addition to the defining characteristic of po-litical prominence which we obviously knew them to hold. We have equally clear expectations as to the differences worth predicting between our two samples with regard to the structuring of policy preferences, but these expectations are considerably more controversial.

The controversy was touched off many years ago when, confronted with quite substantial empirical differences in certain properties of belief systems displayed by persons highly informed about politics (candidates for the U.S. Congress) and those much less informed (a common cross-section of the American electorate), we attempted to erect a theoretical rationale for the observed differences (Converse, 1964). The puzzle had been initiated in 1961 when we had first seen that our cross-time data from a sample of the mass American electorate showed remarkably low correlations between pol-icy preferences expressed at one point in time and those expressed by the same persons two or four years later. Our embarrassed verdict as of 1961 was that these correlations were as low as they were because our opinion questions were vaguely worded. Hence it was not surprising that our respondents had trouble answering them with much consistency over time.

This 1961 resolution seemed quite satisfying until we began to discover signs within our mass sample that some of our respondents who were most knowledgeable about politics did not find our questions vague or confusing at all, but were quite able to respond to them incisively and to repeat their responses in equally incisive ways two years later. This raised the possibility that the problem might reside less with our question wording than with differences in the richness of meaning, and the crystallization of attitudes, that various people might bring to these questions.

Our detection of these differences within a mass sample was indirect and presumptive. Therefore, it became imperative to find some sample of persons whose deep immersion in politics could hardly be questioned. This need seemed to be filled by the Miller-Stokes study of U.S. congressmen, carried out in 1958 in connection with the same research that produced the estimates of cross-time stability of mass responses to policy questions, and part of the study which is a prototype for the inquiry reported in this book. This elite sample had no longitudinal component; so we were unable to compare the stability of attitudinal reports among these political "experts" with that found among rank-and-file voters. We were, however, able to compare the apparent tightness of attitude organization, or degree of "constraint," between belief elements in the two samples. And surely enough, the levels of constraint in the elite sample were considerably greater than those low levels in the mass sample which had originally seemed an integral part of the evidence that our issue questions were shot through with unreliability.

Since people most familiar with the subject matter of the items could respond to them in ways that were incompatible with assertions of massive unreliability, even if people less familiar with the subject matter could not, it seemed desirable to reject our original, simplistic assumption that the questions were just vaguely worded. In fact, it seemed important to develop a view whereby measurement reliability was not a generic property of the measuring instrument (the questionnaire item), but rather could be expected to vary as a function of the interaction between the topic of the instrument and what various (types of) respondents bring to that topic in terms of prior information, or what would more recently be called schemata relevant to the policy dispute (Converse, 1970).

All of our issue items are such commonplaces that none of them would ever catch an active politician by surprise: they invariably tap dimensions which have been vivid in his mind for as long as they or he have existed on the public scene. His attitudes on the topics involved, though often subtle and nuanced, are nonetheless sharply crystallized, forged in public explanation and public commitment, and frequently rehearsed. At the other extreme, we know that some respondents in a mass sample have never even been aware of some of the referents of these issue items, and certainly have not formed clear attitudes about them. We know this because now and again a respondent will overcome his embarrassment and tell us so; and it seems likely that a larger number have difficulties of this sort than are up to confessing them. In between these extremes, of course, there is bound to be a lengthy gradient of more or less partial familiarity and attitude crystallization.

The vaguer the familiarity with the issue domain, and the more impoverished the cognitive associations with governing schemata or other more robust attitudes the topic calls up, the less certain respondents are likely to feel about which response alternative is appropriate for them to choose. This uncertainty may cloud their responses in several ways. These responses are likely to show more feeble connections with other attitudes they hold, some of which may in fact be much more clearly crystallized. And the odds that they will give the same response to the item at some later point in time would seem to be quite reduced.

The foregoing account is a rather brief digest of the original formulation, with emphasis on the proximal portions linking cognitive states, such as richness of familiarity with a specific topic, to the nature of survey responses to items addressing these topics. But space does not permit a complete rehearsal, and we can introduce a few other features subsequently as they become relevant. We have certainly seen enough to get a reasonable feel for the underlying argument.

Numerous scholars have accepted this general argument and have found it useful in understanding contours in their own data. This has been especially true of scholars in elite studies, who have repeatedly found much more consistent structuring of political attitudes among their respondents than is customary from mass interviews (see Putnam, 1973). At the same time, ambitious challenges to the argument from one point of view or another have appeared in great number for more than a decade. Any adequate review of this persistent discussion would carry us far afield from our topic of political representation. Nonetheless, one difficulty encountered by investigators trying to disconfirm the argument is worth mentioning, if only to whet our appetite for what is to come. This is the simple fact that very few bodies of attitude data on closely matched mass and true elite samples exist, so that adequate tests of the kind originally laid out by Converse (1964) have not been easy to come by, although more are now beginning to emerge.

The dearth of such comparison points has probably affected the course of the discussion rather vitally. Thus, for example, in one of the most frequently cited efforts to disconfirm our 1964 formulations, Achen (1975) concluded that the low reliabilities appearing in the political attitudes of mass samples arise merely because the questionnaire items are vaguely worded. This is essentially where we started with the problem in 1961; and his conclusion is not particularly astonishing in view of the fact that he had no further data from genuine political elites to lay against his mass sample material, and he ignored such data from true elites as have been published. Like virtually all of the other major efforts at disconfirmation, from Brown (1970) to Judd and Milburn (1980), Achen worked within a mass population and took some of the more educated or politically involved of these citizens as equivalent to the political "elite." Although this fiction is understandable when the desired counterpart data are simply not available from what might more compellingly be called "political elites," it takes little thought to realize that such a discrepancy in data source should go a long way toward emasculating the differences originally observed.[4]

The important point is that our data permit the proper comparisons to be made, and this is rare. In fact, on at least two grounds they can claim to be quite superior to the comparisons originally published. One of these we have already mentioned: unlike the situation with the original study, a significant number of the questionnaire items were posed in exactly the same form to both mass and elite samples. These exact matches can be used to examine the remote but often cited possibility that the original mass-elite contrasts arose because of differences in item wording, which rendered the elite responses more reliable for reasons of measurement artifact, and not because the elites brought more to the issues involved.

The second improvement is more important still. In the original study we were able to examine the degree of constraint between policy attitudes as it stood at a single point in time for both the mass and elite samples. We were also able to assess the stability of these responses over time in at least the mass sample. What eluded us were estimates of stability within the elite sample, since there were no elite reinterviews. This lacuna meant that although the mass attitudes seemed in an absolute sense to be quite unstable, we had no outside reference point from which to judge the estimates, and were left merely supposing that our elite informants would have given more stable responses over comparable lapses of time. But this was pure guesswork. Our French data include longitudinal components at both levels, such that those earlier surmises can be evaluated. In permitting all four directions of comparison at once, the data set may be unique.

In the intervening period, some evidence about attitude stability at elite levels has grown up (see most especially Putnam, Leonardi, and Nanetti, 1979), and these materials have confirmed the original argument as clearly as it could be confirmed, given a lack of a tightly matched set of mass samples as a "control." The happy fact is that our French data include longitudinal components at both mass and elite levels.

Before passing to the actual analyses, let us say a few summary words concerning the expectations about these data which our original formulations (Converse, 1964) would create. First and foremost, we would predict that our elite informants would normally show signs of higher constraint, or tighter attitude organization, within any point in time than would our mass sample. We would also expect that the elite sample would normally show greater stability in given single attitudes over time than would emerge from the mass sample. At somewhat greater risk, because the differences necessarily will be smaller, we might offer a prediction that if we partition the large mass sample into strata from highly involved to poorly involved in politics, as we have done before (Chapter 4), some semblance of the elite-mass differences in constraint and stability should be recapitulated, although we would not expect the differences from top to bottom in the mass sample to be of the same magnitude as those separating the elite sample from the mass sample taken as a whole.

We have modified the preceding predictions with terms like "normally" because under some circumstances the underlying theory does predict inversions of these normal expectations. In other words, one of the conventional means of gauging constraint between attitudes in two samples is to look at relative levels of intercorrelations within the same grid of attitudes in the two samples.[5] Greater constraint is expected to register in higher levels of intercorrelation. What this means in the "normal" case is that our elites should show stronger intercorrelations than the mass sample as a whole; and that within the mass sample, intercorrelations should be higher for the more involved politically than for the less involved. At the same time, even at the outset it seemed apparent that under special circumstances the theory would predict an inversion of these effects. One class of such expected inversions was described at some length in the original formulation (Converse, 1964, pp. 234–238), in relation to stereotypical group conflict issues, and has subsequently been observed in nature. In the case of our French data we shall encounter another class where strong forces pushing toward inversion are obviously to be predicted.

Constraint between Policy Attitudes

Conventionally, constraint is examined by surveying all coefficients of association in a matrix of intercorrelations of policy attitudes. We shall in fact move in this general direction. But such a total matrix in our case has a number of interesting "regions," or submatrices, reflecting differences in the conceptual status of some of the attitudes to be compared across samples. In some cases, these differences lead to variants on our "normal" predictions, and these are interesting to isolate.

Left-Right Locations and Specific Policy Attitudes

One particularly crucial "strip" of such an intercorrelation matrix is the row or column relating left-right self-locations to all of the other more specific policy attitudes in the matrix. These coefficients are of special interest be-cause of the status of the left-right dimension as a "super-issue."

In our original 1964 formulation, this kind of abstract dimension (left-right in Europe, liberal-conservative in the United States) was accorded a central role. It was postulated to provide an efficient if abstract shorthand for organizing a very wide variety of more concrete political information. Like any dominant schema, it was suggested that familiarity with the cog-nitive yardstick implied by the dimension would greatly increase the capac-ity to make sense of incoming political information and hence to organize it cognitively and to retain it more effectively in accessible memory. As an empirical matter, however, we introduced a fair amount of evidence to sug-gest that substantial portions of the American public in the 1950s were un-familiar with the meaning of liberal and conservative in terms of other policy differences; and that a larger portion still had no more than a limited grasp of the meaning, and hence did not appear to use this abstract notion in evaluating politics with the frequency one takes for granted among the more politically sophisticated.

In Chapter 4 we delved in parallel fashion into the familiarity of our French mass sample with the left-right dimension. Although sheer recogni-tion of labels like "left" and "right" is probably more prevalent in France than is recognition of terms like "liberal" and "conservative" in the United States, when we probed underneath as to the understanding of the political meanings of these terms, we found that such understanding seemed to fall away about as rapidly, once beyond a thin layer of the most politically in-volved of the citizenry, in France as in the United States.

Of course it is meaning which is functionally important here, not just label recognition. We said earlier that some respondents are likely to answer some of our policy items relatively incisively because they "bring a lot" to the subjects involved. That crucial phrase is vague, and must be left so, be-cause what is actually "brought" in any given case is enormously person- and topic-specific. Nevertheless, one thing some respondents can bring to certain policy items is a knowledge of which of the two competing posi-tions is leftist and which is rightist, in terms of the understandings of that particular nation and period. If in addition they bring to the interview a more general sense that they themselves feel more sympathetic to the left or right, they already have a head start on a palatable response to the issue item, even if the policy involved is sufficiently remote from their daily con-cerns that they would never have formed much of a self-starting opinion about it. A total population which brought this much information to each policy item, and no more, might be expected to show a perfect correlation between their personal issue positions and their left-right self-locations, pro-vided all agreed as to which issue positions were left and which were right.

In real life, of course, a variety of other considerations intrude. Many of these involve the person's substantive reactions to the details of the proposal, apart from his or her codings of the left-rightness of the options. But another consideration that intrudes is that not all respondents bring to the question a prefabricated understanding of which policy option is leftist and which is rightist. In fact, we have already seen that nearly one-quarter of our mass respondents point out that they have no idea what the difference between the labels "left" and "right" means with respect to any competing policy options. Thus if we had asked twenty policy items in 1967, these respondents would presumably have thrown up their hands all twenty times if, in trying to formulate their own positions, they had asked themselves "which answer is leftist and which rightist," thus ruling out guesswork. (Of course, more realistically they would have had no reason to ask themselves such a question, much less to feel motivated to guess!) And a further substantial fraction would have understood the left-right difference in such limited terms that they might have retrieved an answer three times out of twenty, or seven times. All of our elites would have had this information at their fingertips for all twenty of the kinds of central issues we would have asked, and so would most of our mass respondents who were extremely involved in politics, following it avidly from day to day. But to say any of this is to recognize that there are basic differences in what various respondents "bring" to these policy alternatives, and it would be surprising indeed if these basic differences did not leave some imprint on the nature of the responses.

The prime interest of the strip of correlations relating left-right self-locations to more specific policy attitudes does not arise, therefore, simply because of the expectation that specific policy preferences will be more tightly linked to the individual's sense of left-rightness among more involved than among less involved persons, although this expectation is clearly present. The original formulations also imply a prediction that the differences in the general levels of these correlations along this strip as we move from highly involved to less involved samples should be more dramatic than anywhere else in the matrix of issue intercorrelations, because of the peculiar sophistication required by the super-issue involved. One of the few things that competing formulations have in common is the assertion that there is no reason to expect such multiplicity of differences, because the original reasoning was faulty. Indeed some, like Achen (1975) or Judd and Milburn (1980), have progressed to empirical demonstrations that differences of this kind cannot be found, at least within the mass samples they have examined. Hence we have here something of a crucial test in its most extreme form.

There are several alternate ways of analyzing and presenting the relevant idea. Figures 7-1 and 7-2 come closest to presenting the appropriate comparisons in relatively raw form, so that the reader need not worry about what is being swept under the rug in the course of more elegant chains of

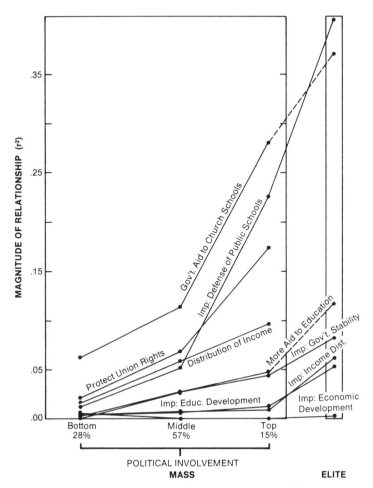

Figure 7-1. Links between own left-right position and domestic policy positions for mass (by political involvement) and elite, France, 1967.

statistical manipulation. In these figures, we have divided the mass population into groups according to the same strata of political involvement which we used in Chapter 4 in discussing variations in understandings of left-right differences. The ordinate is cast in terms of r^2, rather than r, because it is appropriate to make the ratio comparisons between samples which interest us in terms of proportions of covariance.

The general cast of all of these relationships is as expected, and for most of them the differences between the groups are very impressive in magnitude.[6] In both figures it appears to be only the top 15 percent of the sample which bear any resemblance at all to the elite sample, where the tightness of these linkages is concerned. Indeed, in most instances it seems as though this stratum is almost uniquely responsible for whatever mild relationships between left-right locations and policy positions can be detected in the mass sample as a whole, much as our original theory and our work with the left-right dimension in Chapter 4 would have led us to expect.

Figure 7-1 focuses on domestic issues. It is interesting to note that the two items referring to the clerical controversy over the school system stand out with great prominence, despite the lack of much mention of religion in descriptions of left-right differences. Moreover, the apparent prominence of these items, in their associations with left and right, continues among the

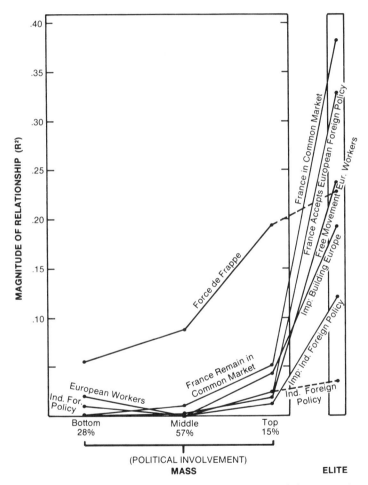

Figure 7-2. Links between own left-right position and foreign policy positions for mass (by political involvement) and elite, France, 1967.

top 15 percent of the mass population and among the elite. It will be important to us later in this book that although not too many informed people *define* "left" and "right" in religious terms, the underlying connotations seem as sharp here as they did in the voting choice case described in Chapter 5.

In Figure 7-2 the foreign issues displayed (with the exception of force de frappe) show modest differences in patterns relative to Figure 7-1. The fit of these items with left-right positions among the elite is quite similar to that for domestic issues. Within the mass sample, however, the evaporation of these linkages is almost complete. A few vestigial linkages remain within the most involved 15 percent, but they are weak; and for the other 85 percent of the electorate there seems to be little connection.

These figures, as we have noted, are not restricted to instances in which identical items were posed to both the mass and elite samples. If we limit our attention now to this subset of twelve coefficients, and summarize the data by averaging covariance proportions (r^2) within the groups isolated in Figures 7-1 and 7-2, we find the following results:

Mass by involvement			Total mass	Elite (1967
Bottom 28%	Middle 57%	Top 15%	sample	candidates)
.006	.009	.070	.015	.247

These are exceedingly imposing differences. The most involved 15 percent of the mass sample show linkages involving left-right locations that are nearly ten times as strong as those among the remaining 85 percent of the electorate. Despite the presence of this 15 percent in the mass sample, however, the elite sample shows linkages which are over sixteen times as great as those for the total mass sample, or some thirty times those for the vast majority of the electorate (85 percent) after the most involved mass stratum is set aside. Although it is popular to contend that these differences do not exist, it would surely take great statistical ingenuity to obscure such vivid contrasts.

Moreover, it is easy to see that these ratios are, in general, underestimates of any predictions the theory would actually make. This is so because the twelve coefficients just examined involve totally unselected issue items. Actually there is nothing in the theory that requires correlations with left-right positions to emerge with *all* policy positions even in the elite sample. Whether particular policy cleavages are aligned with left-right differences in any given policy and era depends upon situations in the real world which the theory simply does not address, although of course most policy cleavages in most times and places do come into alignment sooner or later. What the theory does say is that when such linkages exist in the minds of the well-informed, they are likely to be more dimly reflected among those who are less well informed. Thus if any issues among our unselected twelve are orthogonal to left-right locations even in the elite sample, they act to attenuate empirical contrasts between our sample partitions, even though they are irrelevant to the actual predictions. There are in fact such issues among our twelve. In the most noteworthy example, the covariance proportions linking left-right positions with the agenda priority for economic development are .00, not only for all involvement segments of the mass sample but for the elite sample as well. A couple of the other issues among the twelve approximate this state. Thus if these coefficients irrelevant to the underlying theory were to be set apart, the covariance ratios of 16 and 30 cited earlier and favoring the elite sample would simply advance further still.

The cascade of declining correlations does not in itself answer some further diagnostic questions which might be fruitfully posed, such as whether the correlations are low among the uninvolved because of responses which are quite haphazard and hence tend to look like unreliability or measurement error, or because the uninvolved show less variance in their positions, being more likely to cling to the null center positions, such as "pro-con," "don't know," or "it depends," while the elite are taking actual positions on the issues. But there is probably less difference between these syndromes than appears at first glance, and further work suggests that the true reasons for the varying correlations involve a blend of syndromes in any event.

At this level of approximation, then, the particular strip of the issue intercorrelation matrix involving left-right positions seems to support the basic theory magnificently. But the theory also indicates that the contrasts along this strip should be at a maximum relative to the rest of the entries in the total matrix. To evaluate this prediction, we must look at other regions of the matrix as well. If we wish to remain for a while with the subset of issues asked of both populations in identical form, Table 7-1 suggests that there are two other principal submatrices beyond the left-locations on the left-right continuum. These are the set of five fixed-alternative "position" issues asked about forms of European integration and the set of seven "agenda" items probing the importance of seven different issue domains. An important overlap of one item exists between these two otherwise distinct sets, because one of the seven agenda items asks about the priority of achieving European integration. To prevent duplicate counting, therefore, we shall leave the European integration item with the other agenda issues and shall deal first with the five-item submatrix of integration positions.

The European Integration Submatrix

For reasons that have to do more with common sense than with prior theory, we would expect this submatrix to show higher correlation values than any other region of comparable size in the total matrix, because all items are addressed to what would seem to be the same policy domain, that concerning the desirability of furthering European integration, though by different modalities. At the same time, however, there is nothing new here to suggest that the differential predictions of our belief system theory should not hold as well, although not so dramatically as with the left-right linkages.

The data do in fact confirm this whole cluster of expectations. Averaging across the ten relevant coefficients for each partition of the samples, we find:

	Mass by involvement		*Total mass*	*Elite* (1967
Bottom 28%	Middle 57%	Top 15%	*sample*	*candidates*)
.043	.067	.107	.071	.372

All of these covariance proportions for the somewhat redundant measurements of European integration postures are very much higher than the values for the left-right linkages. At the same time, the general cascading pattern from high values for the more involved groups to lower values for the less involved is still vividly apparent, although the contrasts are indeed somewhat less sharp. Within the mass sample, the most involved 15 percent do not show linkages nearly ten times as strong as the rest of the electorate, but only about twice as strong. And the elite linkages do not average more than sixteen times those for the mass as a whole, but only a little more than five times as great.

The Submatrix of Agenda Items

The last submatrix of a homogeneous sort involving items posed to both samples in identical form is made up of the seven importance or "agenda" items. We have already seen that these items are flawed by a problem of ceilings on the measurement. Most politically involved respondents place most of the seven issues in the maximally important category, so that there is very little true variance with which to work either in the elite sample or among the most involved of the mass respondents. Variance of responses only begins to expand among those whose attention to politics is scanty.

It is worth stressing that such an inverse correlation between political involvement and variance in these agenda ratings is far from a trivial phenomenon. We find, for example, that the standard deviations in importance ratings are greater for the least involved 28 percent of the electorate than for the most involved 15 percent in every one of the seven agenda comparisons available. These standard deviations range from 7 percent greater to 259 percent greater, depending on the importance item involved; on the average they are 185 percent greater, or nearly double in size. If, instead of these comparisons across involvement strata within the mass sample, we compare elite sample data with those from the mass sample as a whole (including the highly involved as well as the less involved), it turns out that these standard deviations for the mass sample are more than twice as great as those in the elite sample. The low ceiling on the agenda items which leaves most involved observers making little differentiation between policy domains is a problem which could have been solved by requiring all respondents to rank the issues for relative priority, rather than to rate them absolutely. As things stand, however, we have only the absolute measurements.

Moreover, when we examine the responses of the less involved members of the electorate to these importance items, a further corollary problem arises in striking form. It is conclusively clear that those less involved respondents who monopolize much of the variance in these absolute importance ratings are also responding to them in a peculiarly simplistic way. In a nutshell, they appear to be responding repetitiously to the global form of the question, rather than to the distinct issue content of each agenda item taken separately: that is, some people who are personally uninterested in politics seem to assume that national politics is nonetheless a very serious matter, and hence they give high importance ratings to virtually all of the issue domains, much as the involved do. Others seem to express their general indifference toward politics by reporting that most of these issue domains are not too important. These conflicting patterns among the poorly involved are directly responsible for the fact that most of the working variance generated by the items shows up in the more apathetic strata of the electorate; yet it is a working variance which is peculiar in that the responses are given with remarkably little discrimination between one policy domain and another, so that what appears to be working variance at first glance turns out on more careful inspection to be distressingly "content-free."

This unsettling diagnosis can be documented quite convincingly if we pay attention to some few reversals that exist in the content keying of our agenda items. On the one hand, we have noted that the maintenance of government stability was an issue to which Gaullist propaganda, and the right in general, attributed great importance, while the left preferred to see it as a non-issue. On the other hand, the secular left attributed great importance to the preservation of public schools, while the clerical right could be expected to find this issue less gripping. Hence these two items provide a situation in which a manifest correlation from the raw data should be negative in formal terms, although, taking content into account, we would want to reverse such a superficial negative correlation to be substantively positive.

In fact, with most of our informed respondents rating most issues as extremely important, the expected negative correlation is rather weak. In other words, most informed leftists did not deny that governmental stability was extremely important, and most informed rightists did not deny that preservation of public schools was extremely important, although presumably if a higher measurement ceiling had been made available, they would have shown a divergence in relative priority. Nonetheless, even in the elite sample the stability and public school items are indeed inversely correlated, although faintly ($r = -.19$), where sheer sense of importance is concerned. This means that when properly re-keyed to take account of content meaning rather than pure form, the corrected correlation is $+.19$. The same signs pertain for the most involved 15 percent of the mass population, although the association is slightly weaker: the raw correlation keyed to question form alone is $-.13$, but when corrected to recognize the underlying content reversal, the association can be seen as $+.13$.

As we move into the less involved reaches of the mass sample, however, the signs of these associations are dramatically reversed. In the moderately involved majority, the sign of the raw association is positive: those who feel governmental stability is relatively important also feel that the defense of the public schools is relatively important. But this means that if we continue to re-key these questions to take account of question substance, the correlation is negative ($-.13$), which implies a kind of substantive inconsistency. This state of affairs becomes still more extreme in the least involved stratum, where the correlation keyed to form alone is $+.32$, whereas keyed to content instead it is $-.32$.

This means that we are confronted with a sequence of correlations linking the stability and public schools agenda items which looks like this:

	Elite sample	*Mass sample by involvement*		
		Top 15%	Middle 57%	Bottom 28%
Correlation keyed to				
Item form	$-.19$	$-.13$	$+.13$	$+.32$
Item substance	$+.19$	$+.13$	$-.13$	$-.32$

To the casual eye, this would seem to be a highly meaningful progression, whichever line we choose to read.[7] We have betrayed a preference for lending primary attention to the keying by question substance. But this preference produces a sense of substantive inconsistency among the uninvolved members of the electorate which many scholars feel approaches libel: who are we to decide, they ask, which configuration of political beliefs is or is not substantively consistent?

This is a concern to which we are sympathetic, and it is certainly not beyond the ingenuity of any scholar to summon up substantive reasons why some voters might be jointly concerned with the importance of governmental stability and public schools, and other voters might be jointly unconcerned with these two issue domains. We are not motivated to expend much thought on this matter, however, since we already know that these correlations, which are positive by form but negative by substance among the uninvolved, recur in all instances in the issue importance submatrix for the mass sample where reversed and unreversed items intersect! The average correlation at the nine relevant issue intersections is as follows:

	Elite	*Mass sample by involvement*		
	sample	Top 15%	Middle 57%	Bottom 28%
Correlation keyed to				
Item form	−.06	+.06	+.30	+.38
Item substance	+.06	−.06	−.30	−.38

What this diplay means is that if we were asked to understand unique configurations of beliefs in a substantive way, we would not be dealing merely with one bivariate oddity, but rather with a five-dimensional policy space in which all associations for the less involved would go against the grain of common political understandings in the late 1960s in France. Taken wholly as a substantive problem, the rationalization necessary to explain this idea structure would be so fiercely complex as to boggle the mind. It is much easier to understand this pattern in terms of politically uninvolved citizens who are admirably consistent in responding to the form of these items, if not to their content. Some respondents feel that political issues are generically important, however limited their personal interest in politics may be, whereas others who are also uninterested regard these issues as generically unimportant. The fact that the absolute magnitudes of the covariation are so slight among the well-informed may partly be understood in terms of the fact that five very heterogeneous policy domains—both domestic and foreign—are involved in these figures. But it is also true, as we have noted, that the univariate variances are very small in these groups because of measurement ceiling artifacts.

With all this said, if we were to take the average of the *squared* correlations underlying the preceding data display, to put it into the form being used earlier, the two rows would be identical. Furthermore, we might conclude that "constraint" is almost nonexistent for these items in the elite sample or among the mostly highly involved of the citizenry, but that it increases progressively as political involvement fades. This is exactly the opposite of the pattern normally predicted by our underlying theory, but we know by now that the source of the "constraint" being displayed here by the poorly involved is quite different from that which we observed in our earlier submatrices.[8]

We mentioned earlier that the original statement of the theory (Converse, 1964) had predicted inversions of the normal ordering of constraint across involvement groups under special circumstances. The case we now face in these agenda items is of a different type entirely from that initially envisioned. Nevertheless, what the original theory would have to say about a situation like this is overwhelmingly obvious. What we have here is a situation in which responses to item form can inflate correlations in one direction while responses to content are pushing in an opposite direction. The original theory is most vitally concerned with differences between individuals and what they bring to the topics of attitude items by way of content recognition, familiarity, and attitude crystallization. Certain practical predictions from the theory proceed on the assumption that, on balance, persons who are more politically involved are likely to bring more content to political issues than those who are less involved. Where form is at war with content, as it is with these item reversals, the ensuing prediction is painfully obvious: the more involved will tend to side with item content, while the less involved will respond along lines of item form. As soon as we are in a setting where large correlations are more likely to arise from form responses than from content ones, as is the case here, then the same theory would predict the kind of inversion of patterns that we have in fact observed.[9]

With this expectation in mind, we may move to the full issue-importance submatrices in these samples, where each submatrix has twenty-one coefficients, rather than the mere nine entries involving content reversals which we have observed before. For a reason which by now is apparent (the presence of large negative correlations in the matrices of the uninvolved), it is misleading to examine the covariance proportions in the form in which they have been presented for the other submatrices. But since the reader is by now aware of what actually underlies them, we shall for completeness show these average squared correlations for the full submatrix:

Mass by involvement

Bottom 28%	Middle 57%	Top 15%	*Total mass sample*	*Elite (1967 candidates)*
.182	.102	.029	.135	.031

The expected inversion of order comes through very clearly in this array. But we may push the matter one step further in order to double-check our reasoning. We have indicated, with the benefit of hindsight, our regret at not having obliged our respondents to rank the issues in terms of their relative priority. This would have preserved response variance in all subsamples, since our politically engaged respondents could not have placed all issues in the "very important" category. More significant still, such a tactic would have been more in the true spirit of the theoretical discussion underlying the notion of issue agendas: governments cannot see to everything at once, but must pick and choose and take things in some order of priority, even though, as our informed respondents tend to say, everything is "very important."

Now there is no methodological magic which will permit us to reconstruct how our respondents would have ranked these seven items. Nevertheless, we can get a step closer to relative priorities, respondent by respondent, if we convert our importance ratings to an "ipsative" base. In other words, we can recalculate the importance ratings given by each person as a deviation upward or downward from the mean rating which that person assigned to the seven issues as a set. What this form of normalization does is to erase those differences between persons which arise merely because one person tends to use the upper part of the scale for most issues, while another tends to use the middle or lower part. It is these differences which we have called "responses to item form," and which we have assumed are responsible for the inversion of correlation magnitudes we have just witnessed as characterizing the issue-importance submatrix. We would expect this inversion to disappear with ipsative scoring.

This is exactly what happens. The average covariance proportions (r^2) over twenty-one coefficients for the most involved 15 percent of the mass sample now advances to a value of .057 instead of the .029 displayed for the raw scoring; and both segments of the less involved 85 percent of the electorate now show values of .034, an enormous deflation from the values of .102 and .182 we observed with the raw importance scoring. Although these new empirical differences by political involvement within the mass sample are not large, the general contours of difference for the issue-importance submatrix begin to look more like those we found in other regions of the issue intercorrelation matrix.

As we leave the issue-important submatrix, we can see why it has been important to proceed by dealing with separate regions of the matrix, rather than some blind summarization for the matrix as a whole. The fact of the matter is that the underlying theory we are testing makes differential predictions from region to region. Sometimes these differences are merely matters of degree; but for the importance submatrix cast in terms of raw scores, the difference is one of direction as well. Hence a prediction for the matrix as a whole is conceptually trivial. Without knowledge of specific item composition, one would gamble that the intersample comparisons would show "normal" differences, with average intercorrelations declining as involvement declines. In fact this *is* true of the issue matrix taken as a whole. But we can see that if 80 percent of the issue items in the matrix had been in agenda form, rather than position form, and we had used raw scoring, the theory would have predicted on balance an *inverse* progression.

Given such differential expectations by item type, and the corollary that what is found to be true of the matrix as a whole is an obvious function of the mix of item types, it is far more satisfying intellectually to trace out the fate of these expectations from region to region over the matrix than to deal with the matrix as a whole.

The Submatrix of Issue Positions

The last major homogeneous submatrix is made up of the other foreign and domestic issues probed in position form, beyond the extended set of European integration items that we have already covered. Since each of these seven items is addressed to a different issue domain, there is no reason to expect strong linkages over the submatrix. Furthermore, it should be kept in mind that we are no longer dealing with issue items posed identically to the mass and elite samples. In this submatrix, the mass questions were closed items, while the elite questions were open-ended.

Nonetheless, there is no reason not to expect the "normal" signs of declining constraint with declining political involvement. That is once again what the averages of twenty-one squared correlations show across these samples:

Mass by involvement

Bottom 28%	Middle 57%	Top 15%	*Total mass sample*	*Elite (1967 candidates)*
.023	.031	.051	.029	.055

Although the ordering fits the theory perfectly, the linkages in the elite sample are only about double those in the mass sample as a whole, and the value for the top 15 percent of the mass sample is only about double that for the less involved remainder of the electorate. These are not trivial differences, but they are pale in comparison with some of our earlier displays.

Looking back over the ground we have covered, we recollect that the differences associated with left-right positions have indeed been the most dramatic we have seen, as the underlying theory predicted they would be. In fact, every prediction made from the theory has been confirmed in these data, and usually by differences that are quite extravagant in their magnitude. It may occur to the reader that now we could proceed to apply the same round of tests to our study conducted in 1968, where the data base would not be inferior to that explored here except in having considerably fewer cases. But where theoretical predictions are concerned, the 1968 results simply duplicate those of the 1967 study. Therefore we shall move on.

A Summary Factor Analysis

Although it has been useful to us to examine our issue intercorrelations by piecemeal "regions," we might have proceeded in a more global fashion with comparative factor analyses of these policy preference structures over the three mass involvement strata and the elite sample. It is, however, of questionable value to perform such comparative analyses except on the subset of issues which was identically posed to our respondents. Unfortunately, the fact that this subset has an overabundance of foreign policy items in general, and of European integration items in particular, tends to give these factors a prominence in the solution structures which is both utterly misleading and a pure artifact of the substantive mix of the measurements available.

Nonetheless, if the reader will keep in mind that these factor structures are hardly representative of the universe of major political issues in France during this period, the results do bring out a few points which are illuminating in this form (Table 7-2). These factor analyses were carried out on data in which the raw scoring of the issue-importance battery was used, rather than the ipsative scoring. The common loading of all the substantively diverse agenda items on a single factor which has no content interpretation is the methods factor that we purged with the ipsative scoring. It may not seem surprising that this is the dominant factor in the "policy preference structure" of the least involved quarter of the French electorate. Yet it may seem shocking that it is the *first* factor for almost the entire electorate (85 percent of it).

By the time we reach the top 15 percent of the electorate, however, there is no sign of this methods factor at all, and of course it is absent within the elite. At these upper levels, responses to the importance items clearly follow the lines of policy content rather than of question form. Thus, for example, the item concerning the importance of preserving public schools tends to load appropriately with the position concerning the role of government in aiding church schools. Similarly, the agenda item on the priority of European integration tends to load with the other European community items. Thus policy content is the guiding principle, rather than question form.

The other feature worth noting in Table 7-2 is the shifting role of the left-right dimension across these involvement strata. In the bottom mass stratum, left-right positions emerge as the fifth factor in the solution, and then only as an isolated structure, representing the sole measurement to load on the fifth factor above our criterion (.50). In the vast middle of the electorate the left-right dimension emerges a bit sooner (as the fourth factor), and it begins to cohere significantly with the religious dimension and the force de frappe. The same cluster becomes the first factor in the most engaged one-seventh of the electorate, the only stratum which seems to conform to a naive understanding of public opinion. By the time we reach the elite sample, it becomes hard to split the left-right positions apart from most of the other chief policy clusters.[10]

Stability of Policy Attitudes

As we have already noted, the nature of our design permits us to make unique mass-elite comparisons in regard to the temporal stability of policy

Table 7-2. Tableau of factor structures based on left-right locations and policy issues, mass and elite, France, 1967 and 1968.

	Mass		Elite
Least involvement (28%)	Medium involvement (57%)	Most involvement (15%)	
1st: "Methods" factor	1st: "Methods" factor	1st: LEFT-RIGHT + church + force de frappe	1st: European integration + LEFT-RIGHT
2nd: European integration	2nd: Social class + education	2nd: European integration	2nd: LEFT-RIGHT + church + force de frappe
3rd: Independence of U.S.	3rd: European integration	3rd: Independence of U.S.	
4th: Social class	4th: LEFT-RIGHT + church + force de frappe	4th: Education + economic development	
5th: LEFT-RIGHT	5th: Independence of U.S.		

attitudes, as well as their apparent constraint. At a conceptual level, of course, we should recognize that constraint and stability are quite different notions. Plausible scenarios can be developed to account for isolated beliefs that are quite impervious to change, and other scenarios can be written describing how certain thoroughly constrained attitudes may be attacked in such a way as to suffer a good deal of instability. Nonetheless, it would seem most reasonable to see this kind of anchoring of particular beliefs (the notion of constraint) as a source of stabilization for them. Hence, though constraint and stability are hardly identical properties, it is conventional to expect some correlation between them. Yet we know of no direct tests of this expectation in a strict mass-elite context, mainly because matching questions have not been posed in longitudinal form to elite respondents, although, as we have seen, signs of the existence of high elite attitudinal stability have been found (Putnam, Leonardi, and Nanetti, 1979).

We are indeed equipped to test this expectation, even though we are limited in two directions that require mention. First, such a test is naturally most satisfying when carried out on items asked in identical form of both samples at both points in time. We have seen that the between-sample identicalness requirement, even for 1967 alone, is quite a limiting one, and such items repeated for both samples in 1968 are few indeed. For example, the battery of European integration position items was asked of both samples in 1967 but only of the elite sample in 1968. Nonetheless, about five items still survive, and they display some variety in terms both of question mode and of the domestic versus foreign policy arena.[11] Most fortunately, they include the "super-issue" of left-right locations.

The other limitation concerns case numbers. The mass wave in 1968 was only a half-sample, and it suffered some panel attrition to boot (see Appendix A). If in addition we continue to partition it into three involvement strata, stability correlations rest on a few more than 100 cases of the most involved; some 420–430 of the middle stratum; and 170–180 of the least involved. On the elite side, there were no reinterviews in 1968 with unsuccessful candidates. All reinterviews were thus with deputies, where the longitudinal N was just over thirty cases.

The reason for our particular interest in the comparative stability of the left-right locations is obvious. Our prior theorizing had suggested that differences in levels of apparent *constraint* across our sample strata would be at their maximum for these left-right reports. In the preceding section of this chapter we found this to be the case, and by a handsome margin. The sense of a left-right positioning proved for the least involved portion of the mass sample to be a feeble and isolated structure, quite unlinked to any of the other major policy concerns measured. When we arrived at the elite sample, the connections were dense and stretched in almost every policy direction. Both prior theorizing and the empirical results in this special case lead to a

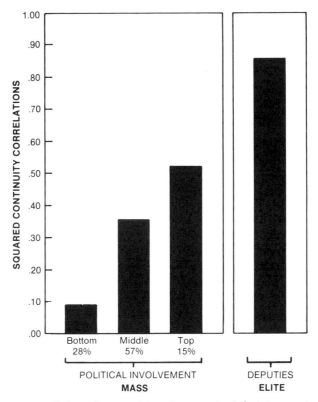

***Figure* 7-3.** Stability of personal locations on the left-right continuum for mass by political involvement, and elite, France, 1967.

very clear expectation that although policy attitudes will in general be more stable among the more informed, the differences in stability will be at their very steepest, relative to our full portfolio of policy measurements, for the left-right self-locations.

These stability coefficients are displayed in Figure 7-3, which is aesthetically as well as scientifically pleasing. The coefficients are, of course, bounded between zero and one. Our four sample partitions come close to occupying the total space from low to high. The least involved 28 percent of the mass sample show almost total instability in their reports of left-right positions after a lapse of little more than a year, whereas our elite sample reports approach total stability. The two intervening groups are appropriately spaced between them.

It is also true, as predicted, that this gradient is steeper for the left-right locations than for any of the other more specific issues for which these strict comparisons are possible, and the margin of difference is quite substantial.

Nonetheless, some such gradient is clear for every issue, and even the weakest instance (that for the poorest match, the church school position item) shows elite responses running nearly two and a half times as stable as those for the least involved of our mass respondents. Although this ratio is rather small compared with the parallel figure of nine and a quarter times greater stability in the left-right location case, it still is a very strong difference by normal social science standards.

If we wish to summarize these stability estimates by averaging as usual across the squared stability correlations (five coefficients) in each sample, we have a choice to make because three of the strict-match stability items are from the importance battery and we can use either the raw or the ipsative forms of scoring those responses.

There is no reason why we should not consider both:

	Mass by involvement				
	Bottom 28%	Middle 57%	Top 15%	*Total mass sample*	*Elite (deputies)*
Raw importance scoring	.172	.275	.349	.230	.607
Ipsative importance scoring	.111	.226	.346	.171	—

Thus we see that whichever version we read, the change in stability is impressively associated with variations in political involvement in just the way the theory predicts. Hence our indicators of stability in these policy preferences over time have behaved in exactly the same way as our indicators of constraint between such policy positions at particular points in time.

Policy Preference Structures and Representation

One of the several purposes we have in examining the nature of these policy preference structures comparatively between mass and elite flows from our concern about political representation, which involves a deputy, on one hand, and, on the other, varying sentiments on policy matters in the district he is mandated to represent. The comparative properties of these structures is bound to affect what he can infer about the nature of opinion in his district on the basis of very limited cues.

One cue he is most likely to possess is a sense of some greater or lesser leftist or rightist coloration in his district. He deals in this shorthand currency all the time, and knows the code well. Suppose a new issue emerges, such as the question of the force de frappe which arose in France in the mid-1960s. Now if he is an acute observer of this elite political milieu in early 1967, he will know that among his politician friends, the fact that somebody is to the right of center will mean better than 3 to 1 odds (from our data) that he is also favorably disposed to the development of such a capability. Actually, by this stage, he will have a much firmer basis for such a guess, since it is clear what positions each party caucus in the National Assembly will take in any debates on the issue, with the Communists vehemently opposed from the left, the Socialists dubious, and the Gaullists committed to support.

While all of this may be common knowledge within the elite level, the actual disposition of citizen sentiment in the home district will not be so well known, except in the rare case in which the representative has mounted opinion polls, for there has been no referendum on the issue. What can the deputy assume? He may have received mail or other constituent communication on the subject, but he can never be sure how representative it is. Obviously, if he knows his district is relatively rightist, he will assume from his experience that it is likely to be favorable to the force de frappe as well. But always there is the nagging question of degree of confidence, particularly if this verdict fails to coincide with his mail. If he has lunch with a colleague whose position is otherwise unknown, our deputy can guess from knowledge of his partner's left-right sentiments, with 3 to 1 odds of being correct. If he has lunch with a randomly selected constituent, are the odds the same? Our data have made manifestly clear they are not, but rather are very much lower.

At least two features which are built into the structure of this complex situation can provide the representative with greater assurance about his estimates than our illustration has thus far implied. One is that he is even more likely to have cues as to the party composition of his district from recent elections than he is likely to have generic left-right coloration data. And second, his most pressing task is to form a broad sense of district sentiment in the aggregate, rather than to predict constituent preferences individual by individual. At a much later point (Chapter 20) we shall work more directly with "linkage" information involving the realities of constituent opinion and what deputies perceive constituency opinion to be. We shall measure the accuracy of these perceptions and some of its determinants. It is appropriate now, however, to ask more generally how party cues and the factor of district aggregation can serve to sharpen the representative's understanding of the policy preferences of his constituents.

Partisanship as a Cue to Mass Issue Positions

Voting returns are the main source of updated information about political trends in a district. A district with an uncommonly large Communist plurality or majority will be thought of as leftist. But even without this intervening step, it would probably be assumed that such a district would oppose the force de frappe, for example, because that is "the Communist position." More generally, district issue positions may be inferred primarily from knowledge of district party composition, rather than from some projection onto an all-purpose left-right continuum. Hence it is important to ask whether guesswork about district issue positions is more accurate when it is based on partisan cues than on generic left-right impressions.

One way to answer this question is to score voters according to the consensus left-right location of the party with which they identify, and then to ask whether such scores are on balance more or less strongly associated with positions on our linkage issues than are the respondents' own choices of left-right locations.

This examination is relevant to much more than questions about deputy estimates of district policy preferences. It carries us back directly to some of our concerns in Chapter 4 as to the relative potencies of party identification and the sense of left-right positioning as aids in organizing and understanding the political world. In that chapter we saw that many citizens make reasonable associations between the major French political parties and various zones on the left-right continuum. This is one kind of "meaning" the continuum may have for the man in the street in France. But when we shifted in that chapter to the *policy* meaning of the continuum, as asked for directly of the voter, we found that the policy connotations of "left" and "right" were quite vague beyond a limited minority of the most politically involved observers in the mass sample. And our demonstrations here, in this chapter, of the feeble linkages between personal left-right positions and policy preferences among the less involved majority (see the factor structures of Table 7-2) can be seen as indirect but confirming measures of the negligible policy connotations of the continuum for many voters.

At the end of Chapter 4 we compared the roles of personal partisanship and left-right locations in generating voting decisions. Now we are proposing to ask whether positions on specific policy issues are better predicted from a knowledge of the voter's self-location on the left-right continuum or from a knowledge of his main party sympathies. Any verdict here, while relevant to deputy estimation of district sentiment, would also appear to suggest whether the voter is more likely to take policy positions because of their appropriateness to his sense of left-right positioning, or because they are appropriate for the "good Communist" or the "good Socialist" or the "good Gaullist."[12]

The actual test is complicated by the fact that many respondents lack partisanship or, to a lesser degree, fail to report left-right location. But if we hold composition constant by examining relationships among the slight majority of the mass sample who express both partisanship and a left-right location, we find that partisanship is a slightly better predictor of issue positions than is left-right location. The differences are not great: the average covariance proportion over the whole issue matrix in this subpopulation is .036 for the left-right measure, but .048 for the partisanship measure (these values correspond to correlations of .19 and .22). Nonetheless, there is a gain in clarity of about one-third in using the party cues, and in view of their accessibility it is likely that they are basic to the estimation process. The data also hint that in this subpopulation, party cues may be more potent in influencing policy attitudes than is a person's sense of left-right positioning, although just how far we should carry this conclusion must depend on what we learn in later chapters (most notably, Chapter 9) about public knowledge of the policy programs of the parties.

The Clarifying Effect of District Aggregation

If district partisanship is one useful cue in guessing district sentiment on policy issues, the fact that much idiosyncratic variation boils away in the process of aggregation is another. We know that the deputy's ability to guess the preferences of given constituents about more specific decisions from the basis of their left-right feelings or even their partisanship is severely limited because these terms are very poorly correlated at the individual level, especially in the vast six-sevenths of the electorate that is not uncommonly attentive to politics. This does not mean, however, that such terms are equally uncorrelated at the aggregated level of representation districts. In fact, strictly speaking, it would be possible to encounter a situation in which specific policy preferences were totally uncorrelated with left-right positioning at the level of individual constituents, but which might show a *perfect* correlation at the level of district means on both variances.[13]

This exact configuration is not, of course, very plausible. Nonetheless, we are operating in a setting where one can plausibly imagine that aggregate correlations between policy preferences might considerably exceed those found at the individual level. Indeed, this is very nearly a corollary of our preceding theory and findings (see Converse, 1975). Let us imagine a few hundred political districts in which most citizens know nothing about ideology, and either fail to respond to questions about left-right positioning or sprinkle themselves haphazardly and symmetrically around due center on the continuum. Some small fraction of these citizens (say 15 percent in each district) are, however, pure ideologues with dedicated left-right positions, although the proportions left and right vary from one district to the next. These ideologues also subscribe to positions on some policy dimension which are a pure function of their positions on the left-right continuum, so that within this small minority the correlation of issue position and left-right is perfect. Within the remaining majority, however, the parallel correlation is by construction zero. For all individuals in the district taken together, the correlations of issue position with left-right differences would be very weak, similar to those we have actually witnessed. But the aggregate district-level correlations in such an instance would be perfect.

Although our data will not be so dramatic as this hypothetical case suggests, we certainly will not require a perfect correlation in one group and no correlation at all in the remainder to imagine that district-level correlations might be noticeably amplified relative to their individual-level counterparts, even though this would mean that only a small minority of politically involved persons were responsible for most of the correlation magnitude. Naturally, profound normative questions would accompany any proof that what a representative is able to deduce about sentiment in his district hinges on patterns created by a very limited minority of the highly involved, and that, by default, the vast majority of the less involved contribute nothing to the "signal."[14] For the moment, however, our interest lies in the more limited existential question as to the degree of amplification of district-level correlations between these policy preferences, relative to their weak magnitudes when calculated for individuals.

As it turns out, the amplification in magnitudes is most impressive, especially if we correct our district-level estimates for measurement error due to the small sample on which each district mean is based.[15] If, for example, we take the squared correlations linking left-right locations with each of our nineteen mass linkage issues at the individual level, the average proportion of covariance is .029.[16] Recalculating over the same coefficients at the district level, the parallel value is .271, or a value nearly ten times as large. This corresponds to an amplification of correlations from about .17 to .52.

The same contrasts calculated over the full matrix of linkage issue intercorrelations for the mass sample (some 190 coefficients, including the left-right variable) are not quite so sharp, but they remain very imposing nonetheless. The average proportions of covariance are .037 at the individual level and .188 at the district level. These coefficients correspond to correlations of .19 in the individual-level calculation and .43 in the district-level case.

Thus the shift in one's sense of the interconnectedness of things as one moves from individual-level to district-level calculations is not unlike the difference between looking at a dull photographic emulsion and then seeing it after the chemical magic of development has taken place. When the individual-level correlation is negligible to begin with (such as less than .03), the district-level correlations typically show no amplification whatever. But as soon as there is any distinctive "signal," aggregation amplifies it; and the clearer the signal, the stronger the amplification that aggregation produces.

Indeed, the whole situation becomes somewhat ironic when we reflect that, apart from one exception that must be understood in other terms,[17] the change from individual-level to district-level correlations draws the magnitudes of association for the mass sample into those amplified ranges which we have found in the elite sample at the level of individual correlations! This rough parity may help to explain why some observers find it so hard to believe that the general level of connectedness of political ideas in the mass public is notably weaker than that within the political elite. They observe that conservative politicians tend with certain high probabilities to take conservative stances on specific issues, just as they observe that conservative regions tend to support conservative candidates or vote the conservative side of referenda with roughly the same high probabilities. Our data testify that a sense of rough parity between these two levels of probabilities is entirely appropriate, for such political beliefs are about as connected for mass publics taken aggregatively in geographic districts as for political elites taken individually. Unfortunately, however, these rough judgments of parity blithely ignore the fact that the two calculations stand on very different bases. If we proceed to the individual level for the mass public as well, we get a rather different picture, one which quite appropriately raises concerns as to the results of large-scale de facto disenfranchisement within the representation process.

However this may be, it is manifestly clear that the fact of aggregation can inject an enormous element of clarification into the deputy's efforts to make inferences about policy sentiments in his district. This does not completely solve the assessment problem, as we shall see in a later chapter when we use our data, district by district and politician by politician, to evaluate their perceptual accuracy. But it certainly serves to bring within reach what could otherwise be an impossible perceptual task.

Conclusions

The basic purpose of this chapter on policy attitudes in France has been to compare the structure of policy preferences in the minds of our mass sample with that found among the political elites vying to represent them, in order to imagine what these elites might tend to deduce about sentiments on specific policies felt by common voters within their districts, given their own perceptions of "what goes with what" politically.

As expected on the basis of earlier work, we found that policy preferences were much more tightly organized or constrained in the belief systems of our elite informants than among our mass sample, and that the separate attitudes within these belief systems of the elite were also much more stable across time. The likelihood that these mass-elite differences have roots in variations in political attentiveness and involvement is suggested by the fact that a considerable semblance of the same contrasts in attitude stability and constraint can be found within the mass sample partitioned according to the degree of their political involvement.

These contrasts are particularly sharp where the left-right dimension is concerned, and this fact is politically significant because of the frequency with which press and politicians alike use this dimension to describe their perceptions of the shifting moods of the public, or to guess the reactions of particular districts or regions to new policy cleavages. Except for a rather thin stratum of the most highly involved voters whose apparent associations for left and right are a reasonable shadow of those found in the elite, politicians would be unlikely to gauge the sentiments of their constituents with any accuracy whatever on the basis of even perfect information as to their left-right positions.

But if the public is not likely to be served with much precision by elite assessments using such tools, neither is it likely to be seriously harmed. The stratum of highly involved citizens lends enough shape to attitude relationships in the mass public, particularly after partisanship cues and district-level aggregation have helped to amplify the "signals," that some reasonable deductions can be made. What is important for the system as a whole is that although these cues from the most involved may say little about the preferences of the less involved majority, we have encountered no evidence to indicate that such cues from the highly involved are positively *misleading* with respect to the preferences of the less involved. In other words, lines of structure in the policy preferences of the majority seem merely to dissolve into a noise of noncorrelation, rather than changing into more active reversals of correlations that might produce erroneous deductions. Some observers prefer to interpret this seeming noise as the result of highly idiosyncratic combinations of cherished beliefs, rather than lack of involvement or attention, even though it is very hard to reconcile this interpretation with the stability evidence we have adduced. Whether idiosyncrasy or inattention is at stake, however, the result is the same for the performance of the system as a communication device.

In Chapter 9 we shall turn the problem around and ask what the common citizen is likely to know about the policy preferences of elite actors vying for his vote at the polls, on the basis of what is known among the public about individual policy postures of the candidates, or what can be deduced by the voter about those postures on the basis of knowledge of the party to which the candidate adheres. This question is every bit as fundamental to the representation problem, since in theory the candidate who succeeds in winning the legislative seat which empowers him to "represent" a given district has been singled out by a plurality of his constituents as an advocate of a preferred policy program, chosen from among the alternatives offered to the public at that election.

Before we proceed to ask what the voter knows about the policy positions of candidates, however, let us first consider how visible individual candidates may be to their electorates as specific political entities, in the more general sense of that term.

8

Candidate
Visibility

In Part I of this study, we discussed the relationship between the
French electorate and their party system. In the course of that discussion we pointed out that, by cross-national standards, French attachments to political parties are comparatively weak. We also determined that
the size and complexity of the party system contribute to the creation of
substantial gaps in the average French voter's knowledge of the parties that
compete for his or her vote. It would be incorrect to think of a French election as a competition in which every party starts with an equal chance of
being chosen by any given voter. There is in fact considerable variation in
the extent to which the various parties are visible to the voters. Indeed, for
many French voters, some parties are quite literally invisible.

In this chapter, we shall pursue our examination of the relationship
between French voters and the objects of their electoral choice by surveying
the extent to which they are familiar with the candidates for legislative office. The ballots that French voters cast always contain the name of a candidate; and almost all of them also contain the name of a party, although
there are some candidates who prefer to run either without a party label
(*sans étiquette*) or with some political designation that does not involve association with any of the main political formations. When voters make electoral choices, even though in most cases they must vote simultaneously for
both a candidate and a party, some may actually be voting primarily for the
candidate while others may primarily be selecting a party.

Whether voters are oriented toward candidates or toward parties when they make electoral choices is an important factor in assessing the representative system as a whole. If the voters are oriented more toward candidates than toward parties, a legislative system characterized by individualistic behavior on the part of the deputies would seem to fit popular expectations better than one based on highly disciplined group voting behavior in the legislative assembly. Conversely, if the voters are oriented more toward parties than toward candidates, they would not be served wholly faithfully by their deputies if these regularly breached parliamentary group discipline.

The purpose of this chapter is to ascertain whether the candidates or the parties are more salient to the French voter when he or she goes to the polls. We shall approach this problem first by introducing a measure of candidate visibility and the factors associated with it, and then by using this measure to assess the relative visibility of candidates and parties. Next, in order to provide a more solid base for interpreting our findings, we shall compare candidate visibility in France with that in the United States, using various measures and applying them under various assumptions. Last, in order to suggest how coherent the French and United States representative systems are in the light of that comparison at the level of the mass electorates, we shall compare French and American parliamentarians' perceptions of the comparative weights of partisan attachments and candidate reputations in their own electoral success.

Factors in Candidate Visibility

In order to capture the extent to which the French public was familiar with the individual candidates in the 1967 election, our mass respondents were first asked to name those candidates who had run for the National Assembly at the first ballot in their electoral districts. They were not asked simply to name the candidate for whom they had voted; our purpose was to determine how many of the candidates in their districts they could name. Then, for each candidate who was correctly named or otherwise accurately identified, the respondents were asked to give the party or tendency of the candidate and whether they had ever read or heard anything about him or her.[1]

On the basis of the answers to these questions, we generated a candidate visibility index that expressed the various degrees of knowledge each voter had about each of the candidates who ran in his or her district.[2] This measure, like the index of party visibility used in Chapter 2, has the advantage of being assignable to both elements of the candidate visibility relationship: the voters and the candidates. Assigned to the voters, it is a measure of their familiarity with each candidate. Assigned to the candidates, in the form of the mean score given to them by the voters in their districts, it becomes a measure of their visibility to their constituents.

Visibility as a Candidate Attribute

In considering visibility as an attribute of the candidates, we have taken into account such factors as the parliamentary experience of the candidates (including incumbency), whether or not they were victorious electorally, the nature of their electoral districts, and their partisan affiliations.

Incumbency is an important determinant of candidate visibility: incumbents had a mean standardized visibility score of 0.90, compared with scores of 0.14 for former deputies and −0.27 for candidates who had never served in the Assembly. Immediate electoral success is also a factor in candidate visibility. Winners had a mean standardized visibility score of 1.06, while losers scored −0.31. Neither of these findings is in the least surprising. Intuitively, we would expect the voters to be more familiar with incumbents than with their challengers; and among the challengers, it is reasonable to expect that people who had once served in the Assembly would be better known than people who had not. Similarly, it is not surprising that winners are more visible than losers. We do not mean to suggest that causality cannot run in both directions here; people may very well vote for familiar faces. But on the whole, once an election is over, attention almost always centers on the winners.

When we examine the joint effect of parliamentary experience *and* electoral success on candidate visibility, however, we find a phenomenon that is by no means obvious. Among the losers, the same relationship between visibility and parliamentary experience that we reported for all candidates, regardless of the electoral outcome, continues to hold: incumbent losers are more visible than losing former deputies, while the latter are more visible than the losers who have never served as deputies. But among the winners there is virtually no difference at all between the visibility of incumbents and that of former deputies and candidates who have never previously served in the Assembly. The determining force affecting candidate visibility among winners appears to be the fact of electoral victory itself, and that force completely washes out the effects of differences relating to previous parliamentary experience.

Indeed, there is very little difference between the degrees of familiarity that the voters have with different types of victorious candidates, even when they are classified in ways that would be expected to reveal differences between their levels of public visibility. For example, we sorted all eighty-six winners in our sample of electoral districts, first into incumbents and former deputies on the one hand and new deputies on the other, and then into "stars" and "ordinary" candidates. The stars differed from ordinary candidates in that they held positions that attracted publicity on a continuing basis, quite independent of a parliamentary connection. The stars included those winning candidates who were internationally prominent, recent ministers, mayors of cities embracing at least 50 percent of the registered voters in their electoral districts, presidents of departmental councils (*conseils généraux*), or some combination thereof. When the winning candidates are sorted on this basis, we find that the public is more familiar with the stars who are incumbents or former deputies than with any of the three other categories of winners, but the margins of difference are surprisingly small. On the average, the voters are almost as familiar with ordinary candidates who are entering the Assembly for the first time as they are with prominent reelected incumbents or former deputies who are returning to the Assembly.

Moreover, there is no indication that the voters' familiarity with elected deputies increases with the length of time the deputy has served. For our sample of interviewed incumbents, there is virtually no correlation between their visibility and the number of elections they won prior to 1967 ($r = .011$) or the number of years they served in parliament prior to 1967 ($r = -.004$). The voters' familiarity with their deputies does not increase incrementally with each election that the deputies contest successfully. On the average, all incumbents are nearly equally visible to the voters at each election.

When an incumbent loses his seat, however, he suffers an instant loss in visibility. It appears that the loss will be regained if he wins back the seat at a later election.[3] If he tries his chances again and fails, however, he will suffer a further decline in recognition by the public which once knew him better than any other class of candidate. For former deputies, the correlation between their visibility and the number of elections they won before 1967 is virtually zero ($r = -.004$), and there is a slight negative correlation between their visibility and the number of years they served in parliament before 1967 ($r = -.132$). The public not only tends to forget losing candidates but it also remembers least the losers who served the longest.

We have set out in graphic form, in Figure 8-1, the visibility cycle of a hypothetical French legislative candidate, based on the mean visibility scores of the respondents in our sample of candidates. When our hypothetical candidate, without any prior experience as a deputy, tries his luck and loses, he is not very visible to the voters in his district. If he tries again and wins, however, the public's familiarity with him increases markedly. If he runs again, this time as the incumbent, and retains his seat, he achieves the same level of visibility that he had reached at his earlier election, but he does not surpass it. If he decides to run as the incumbent once again, but this time is unsuccessful, his visibility diminishes, although not to the low point at which it rested when he was an unsuccessful candidate without any prior parliamentary experience. If he tries his chances again, but this time only with the status of a former deputy, and is successful in his bid, his visibility apparently rises once again to the high level it had already reached twice before.[4] If, as the incumbent, he loses the next election, his level of public recognition drops to where it had been the first time he became a defeated

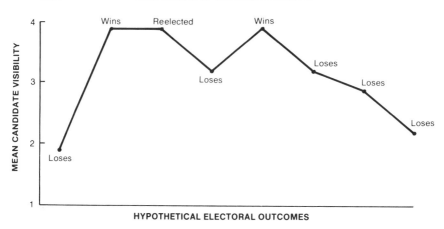

Figure 8-1. Visibility cycle of a hypothetical French legislative candidate.

incumbent. If our friend, who is now an electoral veteran, tries once again and for the first time loses two elections in a row, his visibility declines further, although not precipitously. And if, aging but determined, he makes another try at a comeback and fails again, his level of public recognition falls further, this time more steeply and to a level only slightly higher than that which he attained when he began his electoral career some quarter of a century earlier.

In addition to the electoral experience of the candidates, the nature of their districts also affects their visibility to the public. The least visible candidates are those from the most rural districts. The most visible candidates come from the districts in the "middle range," those that are neither highly urbanized nor predominantly rural.[5] This may result from the better fit in these mixed districts between the channels of political communication, particularly the press, and the size of the district than exists in the other two kinds of district. The big-city press and the regional press, which serves many rural areas, have circulations that encompass numerous electoral districts. For those papers, the electoral district has no meaning as a framework for the organization and presentation of information.[6] But the mixed districts, often consisting of a small-sized town with some surrounding rural areas for which the town is the main commercial center, are likely to be more coherent, self-contained units—what Stokes and Miller referred to as "natural communities" when they reported a related finding for the United States (1966).

Finally, candidate visibility in France varies by party. The most visible candidates in 1967 were Gaullists and Independent Republicans, followed by Communists, then by Federation candidates, and then by the trailing candidates of the Democratic Center and other minor parties. We have here some indication of a right-wing *notable* phenomenon—candidates who are prominent personalities in their own right—although Gaullist and Independent Republican visibility is also associated with the highest rates of electoral success within our sample of candidates. As for winners (or incumbents) alone, leftists were more visible than non-leftists.

Visibility as a Voter Perception

If we shift our attention from visibility as an attribute of the candidates to visibility as a voter perception, we find, as might be expected, that the candidates who were most visible to the voters were those for whom they had voted at the first ballot of the election. That was true of the voters for each of the main electoral formations that competed in 1967: the Communist party (PCF), the Federation (FGDS), the Democratic Center (CD), the Gaullist Union for the New Republic (UNR), and the Giscardian Independent Republicans (RI). The electorates of the minor parties, however, were less familiar with the candidates for whom they voted than they were with the candidates of the competing major parties. Thus the supporters of the Unified Socialist party (PSU) were more familiar with the Communist candidates who ran in their districts than they were with their own PSU candidates; the voters for independent Socialists were less familiar with their own electoral candidates than they were with those of the Federation and Gaullist parties; the UNR candidates were more visible to the supporters of the dissident Gaullists than the dissident Gaullist candidates were; and the electorate of the various independent nonparty candidates knew less about them than they did about the UNR candidates with whom the nonparty candidates competed.

In the discussion of the determinants of *party* visibility in Chapter 2, systemic factors were found to be more important than individual attributes in accounting for the extent of the voter's familiarity with the parties. In particular, the combined size and duration of the parties, expressed as their proportion of the popular vote across several recent elections, accounted for more variance in the individual voter's awareness of the parties than such personal factors as the voter's level of education or degree of political involvement. We have not made a similar exhaustive test with respect to candidate visibility, but our more limited evidence also suggests that systemic factors are more important than individual attributes in determining individual-level variations in candidate visibility.

This is particularly clear at the first and most decisive stage of candidate visibility: the capacity to identify the candidates by naming or accurately describing them. On the average, French voters can accurately identify somewhat less than half of the candidates who run for the Assembly in their districts, and that proportion varies more directly with the number of candidates running in the district than with such personal characteristics as education or political involvement. Education accounts for a bare 1 percent of the variance in the proportion of candidates identified, and political involvement explains only 2.5 percent of the variance. The sheer complexity of the system, expressed in terms of the number of candidates running in the district, accounts for more than twice as much variance in candidate identification as political involvement does. The larger the number of candidates running in a given electoral district, the more difficult it is even for politically involved citizens to identify them.

If we move on from the mere identification of the candidates and take average candidate visibility as our measure,[7] the importance of the number of candidates declines somewhat relative to the importance of education and political involvement. Education accounts for slightly more than 2 percent of the variance in average candidate visibility, and political involvement explains almost 5 percent of the variance. But the number of candidates running in the district accounts for slightly more of the variance than political involvement does. Personal characteristics explain more of the variance in average candidate visibility than in the simple capacity to identify the candidates, but the systemic factor represented by the number of candidates running is still more important than the characteristics of the voters in accounting for both dependent variables.

These findings are quite intelligible. Regardless of one's level of education or degree of political involvement, it is more difficult to remember three names than two, four names than three, and so on. In a system where the average number of candidates per district is almost five, it is not particularly surprising that the proportion of candidates that the voters can identify varies with the number of candidates running. When a voter does know a candidate's name, however, education and political involvement plausibly assume a more important role in accounting for any additional information—such as his party—that the voter may have about the candidate. The sheer number of candidates about whom the voter must assemble that information does not, however, become irrelevant. It is still more difficult to keep track of more candidates than fewer candidates. But once over the hurdle of the initial identification of the candidate, for which the system itself is a much more decisive factor than the voter, the personal characteristics of the *voter* begin to have more weight in determining the amount of knowledge he will have about the candidate. In fact, if we were to stiffen our test of candidate visibility by incrementally adding all sorts of difficult questions about the candidates—such as their age, occupation, or prior electoral experience—the voters' scores on the new index of candidate visibility would increasingly be determined by their own personal characteristics, such as education and political involvement. But for our measure of average candidate visibility, which is appropriate for what can reasonably be expected of the public at large by way of political attentiveness, the complexity of the system plays a more important role than the voters' own personal characteristics do.

Candidate Visibility and Party Visibility

Our measures of party visibility, introduced in Chapter 2, make it possible for us to consider the relationship between candidate visibility and party visibility. The correlations between the visibility of each party and the visibility of candidates of that same party are not particularly impressive at the individual level, but at the aggregate level the correlation between mean candidate visibility (by party) and mean party visibility is a respectable $r = .672$ ($p \leq .05$). This suggests that, on the average, association with a visible party increases the visibility of a given candidate, just as sponsorship by one of the less visible parties diminishes the visibility of that candidate.

The ordering of the parties and the candidates of those same parties on their respective indices of visibility is not the same. In Table 8-1 we set out the mean visibility scores for the French parties,[8] as well as the mean visibility scores for the candidates presented by the same parties. Two points about Table 8-1 should be kept in mind. First, the party visibility scores are national means, while the candidate visibility scores are means for respondents in only those electoral districts where candidates of the various parties actually ran. (Nevertheless, the party visibility scores calculated only on the basis of responses of electors in districts where the various parties ran candidates are virtually the same as those presented in the table.) Second, the measure of party visibility is not identical with the measure of candidate vis-

Table 8-1. Comparison of rank order of party and candidate visibility in France, 1967, by party (mean values).[a]

Party	Party visibility	Candidate visibility
Communist party (PCF)	1.67	2.65
Union for the New Republic (UNR)	1.38	3.33
Socialist party (SFIO)	1.32	2.44
Democratic Center (CD)	1.10	1.75
Federation (FGDS)	1.08	2.19
Independent Republicans (RI)	0.89	2.98
Popular Republican Movement (MRP)	0.87	2.09
Radical party	0.85	2.02
Unified Socialist party (PSU)	0.73	1.02
Republican Alliance (AR)	0.68	0.56

a. Because the national mean index scores for party visibility are computed differently from those for candidate visibility, the two columns may not be directly compared.

ibility and, therefore, absolute index scores may not be compared between columns. But the internal ordering of the scores of one column may be compared with that of the other, and that is what interests us here.

The Communist party is the most visible French party, but Communist candidates are not so visible as UNR or Independent Republican candidates. The reason for this is that candidate visibility, which is necessarily local to those districts where candidates of a given party ran, is highly sensitive to the size of the vote for those candidates in those districts. The correlation between the visibility of the various groups of partisan candidates and the proportion of the votes each group received in the districts where it ran candidates is $r = .916$ ($p \leq .001$). UNR and Independent Republican candidates received more votes in the districts where they ran than Communist candidates received, and that is reflected in the greater visibility of UNR and Independent Republican candidates than of Communist candidates. Candidate visibility tends to co-vary with party visibility, but it moves even more closely in harmony with the size of the vote a candidate receives. Whether the more visible candidates win more votes than the less visible ones because of their greater visibility, or whether they are more visible because they have won more votes, is something that cannot be decided here.

Which object is more visible to the voters, the party or the candidate? That is the very question with which we began this chapter. The answer is related to the significance of the voting act in representational terms. Information about the comparative visibility of candidates and parties is an important element in understanding how the channels of communication between the voters and the legislative decisionmaking process actually operate. In addition, if one of the objects of electoral choice is markedly more visible to the voters than the other, that is a vital item of information for assessing how closely the representative system is matching implicit popular expectations.

Unfortunately, as so often happens with important questions, we do not have the means of providing a definitive answer. Our indices of party visibility and candidate visibility are not identical, and therefore no single summary statistic can be given for both phenomena. We cannot compare total party visibility with average candidate visibility.[9] There is, however, a more limited comparison that can be made, on whose basis a tentative conclusion can be reached.

We know how many people can spontaneously recall the names of the parties, as well as how many people can name or accurately describe the candidates who ran in their districts. We do, therefore, have comparable measures of the extent to which the voters can recall, unaided, the names (or, in the case of candidates, accurate descriptions) of the two objects of electoral choice. Although it is not possible to derive a single summary statistic from these measures that will express the entire sample's ability to recall all the parties or all the candidates, we can compare the proportions of people who can recall certain matching categories of parties and candidates. When we do so, we invariably find that—in terms of unaided recall—the candidates are visible to more voters than the parties are.

The simplest expression of this indication is that whereas almost 80 percent of the first-ballot voters in 1967 identified the candidate whom they told us (later in the interview) they had voted for,[10] less than 60 percent spontaneously recalled the name of the party they later reported they had voted for. Among the voters for the seven main national parties that competed in 1967, only the Communist supporters recalled their preferred party in a larger proportion than their preferred candidates. In the case of every other bloc of partisan voters, the candidates were more salient to the voters—in the terms we are employing here—than the parties were. With regard to this test, as well as others to which we shall refer in a moment, it is important to emphasize that there was nothing in our survey instrument that gave candidate visibility an advantage over party visibility. Respondents were required, unaided, to recall the names of the candidates who ran in their districts (or adequately to describe them), just as they were required to recall the names of as many parties as possible.

A second way of trying to determine which of the two objects of electoral choice is the more visible to the electorate is to estimate the proportions of voters to whom their preferred party, but not their preferred candidate, was visible—and the reverse. When we do this, we find that for about half of the voters, both the party and the candidate for whom they voted were visible in that they were both spontaneously recalled. Another 10 percent of the voters did not recall either the party or the candidate they voted for. But while some 10 percent of the voters recalled their preferred party but not their preferred candidate, one fourth of them could identify the candidate they voted for but did not spontaneously recall their preferred party.[11]

A third way of looking at the problem takes into account candidates and parties for which the respondents did not vote, along with those for which they did cast their ballots. In Table 8-2 we compare party visibility with candidate visibility on this broader basis, still defining visibility as unaided recall of a party's or candidate's name (or, in the case of candidates, an accurate description). The categories included in Table 8-2 represent a descending scale of comprehensiveness in visibility.

Once again we find that candidate visibility has the edge over party visibility as we have been defining visibility. A slightly higher percentage of voters recalled all the candidates than recalled all the parties. Almost twice as many people, proportionately, recalled at least the candidate they voted for, and that candidate's main opponent, as recalled the party they had voted for and that party's principal rival. By grouping the first three categories to-

Table 8-2. Party visibility and candidate visibility in France, 1967, by category of party or candidate (percentages).

Visible parties (or candidates)	Party (N = 2006)	Candidate (N = 1947)
All parties (or candidates) running in district	17	21
Not the above, but at least own electoral choice and main opponent	14	25
Not the above, but at least own electoral choice	14	15
Not the above, but at least one party or candidate	37	23
No party (or candidate)	18	16
Total	100	100

gether, we demonstrate that less than half of the electorate could recall at least the party they voted for, while more than 60 percent of the voters were familiar with the candidate they had voted for.

Candidate Visibility in France and the United States

We are able to determine whether levels of candidate visibility in France are high or low by cross-national standards, because sufficiently matching United States data exist to permit us to make a French-American comparison on that dimension. At post-election sample surveys conducted in the United States in 1958 and 1964, respondents were asked the same three basic questions that we asked in France in 1967: whether they remembered the names of the congressional candidates who ran in their districts, whether they knew which party they belonged to, and whether they had ever heard or read anything about the candidates.

Overall Cross-National Comparisons

In comparing levels of candidate visibility in France and the United States, we shall employ a somewhat different measure of candidate visibility from the one we have used so far.[12] We shall compute, for each country, the proportions of voters who identified the candidates of each party, knew the candidates' parties, and reported having heard or read about the candidates.[13]

In the United States in 1958, in districts where Democrats opposed Republicans, 20 percent of the electorate named the Republican congressional candidate, knew the candidate's party, and claimed to have heard or read about him; and the same proportion of respondents displayed the same level of familiarity with the Democratic candidate. In 1964, the comparable figures were 26 percent for the Republican candidate and 33 percent for the Democratic candidate. Three aspects of these figures are of particular interest. First, there was no difference in visibility between the candidates of the two major U.S. parties in 1958. Second, the levels of visibility of the candidates of both parties were considerably higher in the presidential election year of 1964 than they had been in the off-year of 1958. Third, the visibility of the Democratic candidates increased more sharply than that of the Republican candidates. Whereas almost a third more voters identified the Republican candidates in 1964 than had done so in 1958, two-thirds more voters identified the Democratic candidates.

In Table 8-3 we combine the results for 1958 and 1964, thereby averaging out the different visibility levels for those two years, and show the proportions of the American electorate that correctly identified the candidates of the two major parties (by name and party), and who claimed to have heard or read about them, broken down according to the congressional and electoral status of the candidates. The set is limited to districts in which both major parties competed; unopposed incumbents are excluded. We have, therefore, victorious and defeated incumbents, victorious and defeated challengers, and victorious and defeated candidates of the two parties who opposed each other in districts where no incumbent ran.

It is apparent from Table 8-3 that the most visible candidates were incumbents, whether they won or lost, and that the least visible candidates were the losing challengers and the losing candidates in open races. These data help to explain why Republicans, who proved to be as visible as Democrats in 1958, were much less visible in 1964. In 1958, 42 percent of the Democratic candidates and 44 percent of the Republican candidates from our sample of districts were incumbents. In 1964, however, 55 percent of

Table 8-3. Proportions of U.S. electorate identifying major party candidates, by their congressional experience and electoral outcome, 1958 and 1964 combined (percentages, contested districts only).[a]

Type of candidate	Winners	Losers
Incumbents	34	29
(N)	(1995)	(331)
Challengers	24	15
(N)	(331)	(1995)
Candidates in open races	28	17
(N)	(320)	(320)

a. The electorate identified candidates by name and party and by having heard or read about them.

the Democratic candidates were incumbents while only 39 percent of the Republicans were.

We have accounted for the equivalence in visibility of Democratic and Republican candidates in 1958, as registered in the 1958 sample survey, as well as for the greater visibility of Democratic than Republican candidates in 1964. It remains for us to account for the third phenomenon to which we called attention earlier: the considerable increase in the level of visibility of the candidates of both parties in 1964 as compared with 1958.

The most credible reason for the general increase in candidate visibility between 1958 and 1964 is that the political interest generated by a presidential race rubs off on the congressional candidates. At least one of two things happens. Either the interest aroused by a presidential election leads people to absorb more information about congressional candidates than they do in the absence of a presidential election, or more information is supplied about congressional candidates in a presidential election year than in an off-year, or both. That is not, of course, the only relationship between a presidential election and congressional candidate visibility that one might intuit. It is plausible that a presidential election might eclipse information about congressional candidates by diverting attention away from them, and that public attention would focus more directly on congressional candidates during an off-year election. We shall have more to say about the eclipsing phenomenon later. At this point, however, we can state emphatically that no such eclipsing pattern occurred during the ideologically oriented presidential election of 1964, which was accompanied by a marked rise in candidate visibility relative to the off-year congressional election of 1958.

For the purpose of comparing candidate visibility in France and the United States, we shall combine the United States samples for 1958 and 1964, as we did in compiling Table 8-3. On this basis, 23 percent of the American electorate were familiar with the Republican candidate and 26 percent were familiar with the Democratic candidate, in terms of candidate identification, correct assignment of party, and having heard or read about the candidate. Those proportions are quite within the range of proportions of French voters having the same degree of familiarity with the candidates of the various French parties, as indicated in Table 8-4. Nevertheless, fewer American voters, proportionately, were familiar with the candidates of the two major United States parties than were French voters with the candidates of the two largest French parties, the Gaullist UNR and the Communist party.

Controlling for Institutional Factors

What we have just done is to make a gross comparison of the levels of candidate visibility for the various parties in France and the United States. In the aggregate, when averaging out a presidential election year and an off-

Table 8-4. Proportions of French and U.S. electorates identifying candidates, by their party affiliation, in France, 1967, and in the United States, 1958 and 1964 combined.[a]

Party	Percent	N
Union for the New Republic (UNR)	38	1731.8
Independent Republicans (RI)	33	275.2
Communist party (PCF)	30	2007.0
Democratic party (U.S.)	26	2642.0
Federation (FGDS)	24	1811.7
Republican party (U.S.)	23	2642.0
Democratic Center (CD)	17	1537.1
Minor French parties	9	2010.9

a. The electorate identified candidates by name and party and by having heard or read about them.

year in the United States, we find that although the range of candidate visibility levels is similar in the two countries, the two largest French parties have a certain edge over the two major U.S. parties.

We would not want to conclude from this, however, that French voters are more attentive than U.S. voters to legislative candidates. In making the comparison, we have simply taken each political system as it is in its entirety, which means that at this point we cannot determine what share of the differences in candidate visibility between the two countries may be due to voter attributes and what share is attributable to institutional factors.

We have already seen that, for France, a major factor in candidate visibility is the party system, as expressed in the sheer number of candidates available at each legislative election: candidate visibility varies inversely with the number of candidates running in the voter's district. On the not unreasonable assumption that the same force operates in the United States and in the same manner, we would want to control for the number of candidates competing for the attention of the voters in each country. When we turn to that problem, we find that the number of candidates running simultaneously in any given legislative electoral district is a function of both the party system, narrowly construed, and the electoral system, broadly conceived.

On the one hand, the number of candidates is affected by the number of parties. On this score, the French voter should be handicapped in the domain of candidate visibility compared with the American voter, as France has a multiparty system while the United States has basically a two-party system. On the other hand, despite the greater number of French legislative candidates relative to the number of U.S. congressional candidates in the average electoral district, more candidates compete for the attention of American voters at the time of a congressional election than compete for the attention of the French electorate at a French legislative election. There the only offices at stake are seats in the Assembly, while at a U.S. congressional election there may also be senatorial, gubernatorial, and state legislative and other statewide elections, to say nothing of statewide referenda and even local elections, although the latter are less likely to be held at the same time as national elections in many and perhaps most localities. Assuming that our finding that candidate visibility varies with the number of competing candidates applies also to the United States, it must apply in slightly modified form. The operative factor would not be simply the number of congressional candidates but rather the total number of candidates for all offices at stake at that particular time, including statewide, local, and national offices.

Furthermore, at a French legislative election all the candidates are on a par with one another with respect to the status of the office they are seeking. At a U.S. congressional election, however, there may also be elections for other offices that are generally perceived as more prestigious than congressional seats, such as senatorial seats and governors' chairs. Indeed, it is not unlikely that in the subjective hierarchy of importance perceived by some voters, even state legislative seats may rank higher than congressional seats. If the average American voter knows something about only one or two candidates, these are more likely to be gubernatorial or senatorial candidates than congressional candidates.

We shall take these considerations into account, as fully as we can, in two stages. First, we shall simulate the U.S. two-party system in the context of French multiparty politics, and compare levels of candidate visibility in the two countries, disregarding for the moment that in the United States there may be elections for other, more prestigious offices. Then taking into account the concurrence of senatorial, gubernatorial, and presidential elections in the United States, we shall compare legislative candidate visibility in France and the United States, still maintaining our simulation, for France, of a two-party system. This latter device has the additional advantage of permitting us to arrive at more summary scores for comparing candidate visibility in the two countries than we have produced so far.

We have simulated a two-party system for France by limiting our analysis to those electoral districts where only two candidates competed at the second ballot. When we perform that operation, the proportions of French voters whose knowledge of the candidates includes the three components of our measure of candidate visibility—identification of the candidate, awareness of his party, and having heard or read about him—rise, in some cases quite sharply, for every partisan group reported in Table 8-4 except the Gaullist UNR, for which it remains the same, and the Independent Republicans, for whom it drops slightly (from 33 percent to 30 percent). The proportion of voters familiar with the Communist candidates rises from 30 percent to 41 percent, that familiar with the Federation candidates increases from 24 percent to 36 percent, that familiar with Democratic Center candidates increases from 17 percent to 34 percent, and the proportion of people familiar with the minor party candidates rises from 9 percent to 24 percent.

The increases registered in the visibility of most of these more restricted groups of candidates are readily understandable. These groups contain a heavy concentration of incumbents and, by definition, half of the candidates involved were winners. We would also expect the voters to be more familiar with candidates who, in effect, ran twice, at two ballots held one week apart, than they would be with candidates who ran only once (other things being equal). The reasons why there was little change in the visibility of the Gaullists and Independent Republicans on this new measurement base are that such large proportions of those groups' candidates ran at the second ballot that there was little difference between their first-ballot and second-ballot candidate contingents, and that some of their candidates who did not run at the second ballot were not obscure but well-known vote-getters who had won the election at the first ballot.

Now that we have reduced the set of French candidates whose visibility is being measured to two candidates per district, it is possible to group them again into only two broad party-related categories: left and right. Once that is done, as Figure 8-2 indicates, we find that in French electoral districts where there were straight fights between leftist and right-wing candidates at the second ballot in 1967, 39 percent of the voters in those districts were familiar with the leftist candidates (in the triple terms of our measure), while 36 percent of the electorate in the same districts had the same degree of familiarity with the right-wing candidate. Those figures may be compared with the 26 percent of the American electorate who were familiar with the Democratic candidates and the 23 percent who were familiar with the Republican candidates, averaging our data for the congressional elections of 1958 and 1964.

Thus far, candidate visibility is greater in France than in the United States. Most of the French gain in candidate visibility reported in Figure 8-2 occurs in the first component of our measure: the simple identification of the candidates.[14] In both countries, about the same proportion of the electorate that has identified the candidates then assigns them their correct party (some 80–85 percent). There is no difference in this regard between the candidates of the two American parties, but there is considerable variation among the French candidates. More than 90 percent of the French respondents who name a Communist candidate and almost 90 percent of those who name a Gaullist candidate can assign his party correctly; the proportions drop to about 80 percent for Federation candidates and to 60 percent for Democratic Center candidates.[15]

Once they have both named and assigned correct parties to the candidates, French respondents are more likely than the Americans to report that they have heard or read about them. In France, the proportion is slightly

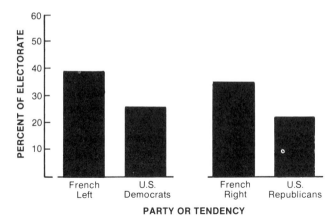

Figure 8-2. Percent of electorate familiar with legislative candidates in France, 1967, and the United States, 1958 and 1964, in two-party contests, by party or tendency.

less than 75 percent, with little variation by party. In the United States, while there is also no variation by party, there is a noticeable variation depending on whether we are considering 1958 or 1964. In the off-year, less than 60 percent of the people who knew the names and parties of the candidates claimed that they had heard or read about them, while in 1964 the proportion was in the French range of 70–75 percent. Once again, we find evidence of more information flow in a presidential year than in an off-year, an important point to which we shall return.

We are now in a position to take our final step in trying to match French and U.S. electoral conditions by taking into account the presence in the United States of candidates for other offices. We cannot do this across the entire array of potential candidates who might compete for the attention of the voters, but we are able to do so for gubernatorial and senatorial candidates. We have computed the levels of partisan congressional candidate visibility in the United States depending upon whether or not there was a senatorial and a gubernatorial election at the same time as a two-party congressional race. Our expectations here are twofold. First, we would predict that congressional candidate visibility will be highest where there is no other election at the same time, next highest where there is only one other election, and lowest where there are two other elections. Second, we would expect that where there is neither a senatorial nor a gubernatorial election to divert the voters' attention from the congressional candidates, the levels of congressional candidate visibility in the United States will approach the levels of candidate visibility in France in districts where there are straight fights at the second ballot.

For this test, which represents our closest most similar systems comparative design, we have employed a measure of candidate visibility that differs from the one used in our simpler two-party comparison. Now we shall consider only the proportions of the electorate that could both identify the candidates and assign the correct party or tendency to them. We use this measure in order to enlarge the basis of comparison by including data for the 1978 U.S. congressional election, as well as data for the elections of 1958 and 1964. The 1978 U.S. Election Study elicited the respondents' ability to recall the name and party of the candidates running in their districts, but it did not contain a simple "heard or read" question in the same form as that employed in 1958 and 1964.[16] We shall also separate the presidential election year of 1964 from the off-years of 1958 and 1978.

The results of this comparison, which are set out in Table 8-5, are mixed. For the U.S. presidential year of 1964, they fit our expectations tolerably well. Congressional candidate visibility declines regularly as the number of other, prestigious candidates increases. Case numbers are small for respondents in districts where there were neither senatorial nor gubernatorial candidates, but there the visibility of Republican candidates was the same as that of French rightists in two-party districts, while the visibility of Democratic candidates surpassed that of French leftists, contrary to what we found when we grouped the 1958 and 1964 elections and did not take senatorial or gubernatorial candidates into account (see Figure 8-2). This indicates that under similar conditions candidate visibility is not normally higher in France than in the United States, as our previous analyses would have led us to believe. If we average the Democratic and Republican visibility levels where there were only congressional races, and do the same for the French left and right, the difference in overall visibility rates for the two countries is insignificant.

For the off-year of 1958, however, congressional candidate visibility was lowest where, according to our hypothesis, it should have been highest; and for the off-year of 1978, although candidate visibility was highest where our hypothesis predicts that it should be, the results are so flat across all three categories of district that insofar as there is variation, it is not significant.[17] Moreover, for both off-years the levels of congressional candidate visibility, without regard to whether there were also senatorial or gubernatorial candidates present, are uniformly lower than the French levels, and almost always so by a wide margin.

The relative success of our predictions for 1964, combined with their resounding failure for 1958 and 1978, raises problems of interpretation that we are not able to resolve definitively. The differences between 1964, on the one hand, and 1958 and 1978, on the other, indicate that the role of a presidential race in stimulating attention to and promoting information about other candidates is even more important than we had expected it to be. A

Table 8-5. Proportions of U.S. and French electorates identifying legislative candidates, by party or tendency and by presence of candidates for other offices, between 1958 and 1978 (percentages).[a]

Candidates on ballot	United States[b]						France[c]	
	1958		1964		1978		1967	
	Democrats	Republicans	Democrats	Republicans	Democrats	Republicans	Left	Right
Congressional race only	29	29	63	49	27	24	54	49
(N)	(121)	(121)	(76)	(76)	(202)	(202)	(1379)	(1379)
Congressional race plus senatorial or gubernatorial race	42	41	46	40	20	15	0	0
(N)	(402)	(402)	(823)	(823)	(974)	(974)		
Congressional race plus senatorial and gubernatorial races	33	34	39	27	22	19	0	0
(N)	(851)	(851)	(369)	(369)	(627)	(627)		
Turnout[d]	43.4		57.8		35.2		—	

a. The electorate identified candidates by name and party.
b. In districts where Democrats opposed Republicans.
c. In 59 districts where the second ballot was a straight fight between a leftist and a Gaullist, Independent Republican, or Democratic Center candidate.
d. Percentage of persons of voting age.

presidential race appears not only to lift the visibility of congressional, senatorial, and gubernatorial candidates, but also to lift those levels of visibility to their "proper" places in a hierarchy of political prestige. A presidential election seems both to heighten the visibility of the candidates for other major offices and to do so in ways that convey to the voters a sense of the differential importance of those other candidates within the larger political system.

There may appear to be a contradiction between the argument that congressional and other candidate visibility rises in presidential election years because of increased attention and greater information, and the argument that congressional candidate visibility suffers from the presence of other candidates for prestigious offices. But there is, in fact, no logical conflict between these two propositions. By presenting them both we are suggesting that a presidential election generates a vast increase in public attention and political information above the levels that are characteristic of off-year elections. At the start of a presidential election campaign, it is probable that the attention which is focused almost exclusively on the presidential candidates does eclipse all the other candidates for major offices. As the campaign proceeds, however, and those other candidates become active in ways and across areas corresponding to their responsibilities and resources, the political awareness stimulated by the presidential campaign diffuses across the entire field of candidates and comes to rest shortly after the election at levels that are more or less consistent with the relative location of each office on the scale of political importance.

Elite Perceptions of Electoral Appeal

French and American legislative candidates, at least the reelected incumbents, seem to have some appreciation of the comparative levels of gross candidate visibility in their respective countries—that is, of the somewhat higher levels of candidate visibility in France as compared with the United States, within the particular institutional frameworks of the two countries.

In their path-breaking 1958 survey of U.S. congressional candidates, Stokes and Miller (1962) asked the successful incumbents in their sample how important they thought their personal record and standing had been as a factor in their reelection. In our own 1967 survey of French legislative candidates we asked all of our respondents how important they thought their personal reputations had been in gaining them votes at the first ballot. The results of the two surveys—including French data for victorious incumbents only, in order to match the U.S. data—are set out in Table 8-6.

This comparison should be treated with more than customary caution, as the closed-end response categories employed in the two surveys were not identical, and it has been necessary to group some categories according to

Table 8-6. Relative importance of personal reputation as a factor in the vote, as perceived by reelected incumbents in France, 1967, and the United States, 1958 (percentages).

France			United States		
Decisive	31				
Very important	42	73	Very important		57
			Quite important	28	
Quite important		27	Somewhat important	9	37
Not very important		0	Not very important		3
Not important at all		0	Not important at all		3
Total		100			100
N		(42)			(76)

Source: For the United States, Donald E. Stokes and Warren E. Miller (1962).

our best estimates of their equivalence. For the French survey, the respondents could select "decisive" as a response category, but that option was not available to the American respondents. As that category surely means "very important," a category that was available to both French and American respondents and one that appears to have the same meaning in French and English, we have grouped together the "decisive" and "very important" French responses, and matched them with the "very important" American responses. American respondents could choose either "quite important" or "somewhat important," response categories that seem quite (somewhat) similar in meaning, and we have grouped them together as the match for the single category of "quite important" on the French side of the comparison. The remaining categories, "not very important" and "not important at all," were identical in the two surveys.

Table 8-6 shows that while more than 70 percent of the reelected French incumbents believed that their personal reputations had been either "decisive" or "very important" factors in their reelection, only 57 percent of the U.S. incumbents thought that their personal record and standing had been "very important." This difference in proportions, though not large, suggests that the difference in outlook between French and American incumbents concerning the relative importance of their personal appeal as vote-getters tends to reflect the empirical reality. As we saw in Table 8-4, after the U.S. presidential election years and off-years had been averaged, the candidates of the major French parties were visible to more voters than the candidates of the two main U.S. parties. Although it is possible that both the U.S. and French incumbents exaggerated the relative importance of their personal reputations in winning them votes,[18] the gross evidence available suggests that the French incumbents were more justified in their claims.

If the somewhat different perceptions of French and U.S. legislators concerning the relative importance of their reputations as an electoral factor have some grounding in reality, their perceptions of the relative importance of party loyalties in winning them votes are characterized by differences that may be less justified empirically. In their 1958 survey Stokes and Miller (1962) also asked the reelected American incumbents about the relative importance of traditional party loyalties as a factor in their reelection. We asked our 1967 respondents about the relative importance of their party labels in winning votes at the first ballot. The response categories for the two surveys differed in the same ways as they did for the question concerning the relative importance of personal reputation, and therefore we have grouped some of those categories as we did earlier.

Table 8-7 presents the results of the two surveys with regard to candidate perceptions of the relative electoral importance of party. The percentage of reelected French incumbents who regarded their party label as "decisive" or "very important" is more than twice that of their American counterparts who considered traditional party loyalties to be "very important." Moreover, almost twice the percentage of Americans as French reported that their party affiliation was "not very important" or "not important at all." We have yet to consider in detail how partisan attitudes mesh with other long-term forces in shaping the popular vote in France. That discussion will appear in Chapters 10, 11, and 12. But it does not prejudge the French case to say that on the U.S. side there appears to be a misperception of some magnitude. Partisanship is a major factor in U.S. electoral behavior, even for the election of congressmen, and it seems anomalous that victorious incumbents should rate it as less important than French deputies do.

Of course, we have no way of knowing in an absolute sense what proportions of the responses for each category and for each set of candidates would most accurately reflect the empirical reality. Indeed, we know from

Table 8-7. Relative importance of party affiliation as a factor in the vote, as perceived by reelected incumbents in France, 1967, and the United States, 1958 (percentages).

France			United States		
Decisive	21				
Very important	33	54	Very important		25
			Quite important	21	
Quite important		30	Somewhat important	24	45
Not very important		16	Not very important		18
Not important at all		0	Not important at all		12
Total		100			100
N		(43)			(73)

Source: For the United States, Donald E. Stokes and Warren E. Miller (1962).

Table 8-8. Reelected incumbents' perceptions of the relative importance of personal standing and party affiliation as a factor in the vote, France, 1967, and the United States, 1958 (mean scores).

Relative importance	France	United States
Personal standing	2.73	2.48
N	(42)	(76)
Party affiliation	2.38	1.83
N	(43)	(73)

our extended account of candidate visibility in the two countries how elusive and complex the "empirical reality" can be. It is possible that the imbalance of perceptions results as much from overestimates of the importance of party on the French side as from underestimates of its importance on the American side. Yet, given the importance of party as a factor in the congressional vote, combined with the comparatively low levels of congressional candidate visibility in off-years, it is difficult not to conclude that the data reported in Table 8-7 reflect greater misperception on the American than on the French side, if indeed there is any misperception on the French side at all.[19]

The data contained in Table 8-6 and Table 8-7 also make it possible to compare the successful French and American incumbents with regard to the relative importance they each attribute to personal reputation and party loyalties in explaining their electoral success. Because those tables do not lend themselves easily to such a comparison in their present form, we have converted the proportions reported in each table into mean scores in order to facilitate the comparison.[20] These mean scores are presented in Table 8-8.

Table 8-8 illustrates clearly the two sets of French and American perceptions we have already discussed: French incumbents attribute somewhat greater importance to their personal reputations than American incumbents do, while they assign considerably more importance to party than the American congressional elite does. In addition, whereas successful French incumbents attach somewhat more importance to their personal reputations as a factor in the vote than they do to party labels, American incumbents attribute even greater relative importance to their personal standing than they do to partisan loyalties.

Conclusions

French voters can identify somewhat less than half the candidates who run for the Assembly in their electoral districts, and that proportion drops when the test of candidate visibility is stiffened to include also knowledge of the candidates' parties and having heard or read something about them. Incumbents and successful challengers are more visible than their unsuccessful opponents; and all candidates, on the average, are more visible if they run in mixed-population districts than if they run in districts that are either mainly rural or mainly urban.

French voters are more familiar with the candidates for whom they vote than they are with the remaining candidates, except in the case of those who vote for minor party candidates or candidates who run without any party label. The number of candidates whom the voters can identify depends more on the number running in the voter's district than it does on the level of political involvement of the voter, although political involvement counts for more in determining the finer aspects of candidate visibility (such as knowledge of the candidate's party and having heard or read about him) than it does in affecting the simple identification of the candidates. Candidate visibility varies with the partisan affiliation of the candidates and is related to party visibility at the aggregate level; but in terms of simple unaided recall, candidates are more visible to the French electorate than their parties.

The parliamentary candidates of the main French parties are more visible to the voters in their districts than U.S. congressional candidates are to their constituents, when presidential election years are averaged with off-years. Congressional candidate visibility, however, appears to rise sharply in a presidential year relative to off-years. That visibility is also greatly affected, though apparently only in presidential election years, by the simultaneous presence of senatorial or gubernatorial candidates, who tend to eclipse the congressional candidates. The latter two phenomena suggest strongly that a presidential election generates an enormous increase in information relative to off-years.

When one controls for such institutional factors as the French multiparty system and the eclipsing phenomenon in the United States, the levels of candidate visibility in France and the United States tend to converge, suggesting that candidate visibility is far more a function of institutional than of personal factors. There is something humanly satisfying about this result. People are pretty much the same in their orientations toward politics when they are in their "natural" state: it is the political institutions surrounding them that produce such behavioral differences as appear when we make gross comparisons without regard to institutional differences. Naturally, we do not want to generalize this finding. We have examined here only one limited aspect of political behavior. But this is not the first time we have encountered such a situation,[21] and its implications are so important for the basic assumptions of political theory that it deserves mention in that larger context.

This is not to say, of course, that politics in France and politics in the United States are pretty much the same once we scratch a bit below the sur-

face. They are emphatically not the same. The institutional differences that
we control away for diagnostic purposes are not controlled away in real political life. They are present, real, pervasive; and, presumably, they have real
effects on people's behavior, thereby shaping political systems in different
ways in different places.

When asked about the relative importance of party affiliation and personal reputation in accounting for their vote-gathering ability, victorious
incumbents in both France and the United States assign greater weight to
personal standing than to party labels, but the French incumbents attach
more importance to party labels than the Americans do. Given the greater
gross visibility of French than American candidates and the documented importance of long-standing mass partisan attachments in the United States, at
least during the period under observation, the American incumbents would
seem to be less justified than the French in holding such opinions. In their
legislative behavior, however, French deputies do not act in conformity
with their perceptions of the relative importance of reputation and party as
factors in their electoral appeal, while U.S. congressmen do. An even superficial acquaintance with voting in the French National Assembly, which we
shall discuss in detail in Chapter 17, indicates that it is more disciplined
along party lines than voting is in the U.S. House of Representatives.

It seems, therefore, that American incumbents have a less accurate view
of the relative importance of party and personal reputation as factors in the
popular vote than French incumbents do. Contrariwise, the parliamentary
behavior of French deputies is less consistent with their perceptions of the
relative importance of party and personality than is the legislative behavior
of American congressmen with regard to their perceptions of these two factors in the popular vote. American congressmen, thus, act in a manner consistent with perceptions that are inaccurate, while French deputies behave in
a way inconsistent with perceptions which we believe to be closer to reality.

Finally, our finding that in France candidate visibility is greater than
party visibility bears the germs of important implications for the representation process, for it suggests that French voters are more oriented toward
candidates than toward parties. This conclusion would not be surprising.
We saw in Chapter 2 that there is more constancy of candidate offerings
than of party offerings from one election to another in France. Thus there is
an "institutional" explanation for the higher level of candidate visibility relative to party visibility in France. French voters have more opportunity to
become familiar with candidates than with parties at successive elections.

But before jumping to any conclusions about the broad meaning in
representational terms of candidates versus parties as objects of electoral
choice, we need to examine more fully the kind of knowledge that the average French voter has of candidates and parties. In comparing candidate visibility and party visibility we have employed a very simple and limited

definition of visibility. It conveys nothing of what the voter may know about a candidate or a party except the name (or, for candidates, other accurate identification). It may be that once the threshold of mere recall is crossed, the voters have more information, relevant to the representative process, about the parties than about the candidates. One class of information about candidates and parties that is highly relevant for the representative process is where they stand on major public issues. If the voting act is to have any meaning as a form of communication concerning matters of public policy, it is essential that the voters distinguish among candidates or parties in terms of issue positions. Whether French voters perceive candidates or whether they perceive parties more clearly in those terms is the next question to which we shall turn.

9

Issues, Parties, and Candidates

I n Chapter 7 on the policy positions of the mass electorate and the parliamentary elite, we found that at the individual level the degree of association between left-right self-perceptions and positions on specific political issues is woefully weak among the public at large. Only in the comparatively thin stratum that is highly involved in politics do we find approximations to the policy content of left-right locations that is displayed at the elite level. What little structure can be perceived in popular preferences seems to depend mainly on that minority of highly involved voters, whose voices are amplified when mass opinion is aggregated to the level of the electoral district.

Issues will also be a central focus of this chapter, but here our perspective will shift from the bird's-eye view of the political elite to the ground-level view of the system as seen by the ordinary voter. Earlier we looked at issues from the point of view of the parliamentary candidates by asking what they can deduce about district policy preferences from such indicators as the left-right coloration of the district and the distribution of long-standing partisan preferences within it. Here we shall ask what issues or policy positions the voters associate with the various parties and candidates that compete for their electoral support.

There are both practical and theoretical reasons for taking this direction at this time. Although the role of left-right orientations in underpinning the French representation process is an abiding concern of this book because of the ubiquity of left-right imagery in French political discourse, the public is not asked at an election to express itself directly in left-right terms. People are not asked where they stand on the left-right axis, nor are they asked if they have moved to the left or to the right since the last election and, if so, by how much. At election time the voters choose among candidates and parties.[1] Left-right terminology is only injected into the communication process by journalists and politicians seeking to summarize and interpret the meaning of the discrete electoral choices made by the voters. Our work would be sadly incomplete if we concerned ourselves only with such attempts at synthesis and ignored the basic mass electoral choices on which they rest.

Moreover, the utilitarian component of democratic theory implies that voters will support at the polls that candidate or party whose program most closely approximates their own policy preferences. It is, therefore, important to know what the voters' perceptions of the parties' and candidates' policy positions are, as such perceptions are logically prior to voting in accordance with positions that match their own.

Although we have shifted our starting point from that of Chapter 7 by focusing on mass views of the elite instead of comparing the structural foundations of both mass and elite policy positions, there is a certain parallelism between the implications of that chapter and of this one. In Chapter 7 we found that a reading of electoral outcomes in left-right terms falls far short of being an accurate guide to mass-level policy preferences, even if the elite is not likely to misinterpret completely the policy implications of a perceptible shift toward the left or toward the right at a given election. In this chapter, we shall ask whether French voters associate certain policy positions with particular candidates or parties in sufficient numbers and with sufficient clarity to enable the political elite reliably to interpret support for those candidates or parties as implied support also for specific policy preferences or priorities.

In order to assess the electorate's perceptions of the issue positions of the various parties (and candidates), it would have been ideal if we could have asked the voters to locate each party (and each candidate) on an axis for each issue on which we had already obtained the personal opinions of the voters and the candidates. But given the large number of parties and candidates, and the numerous issue domains we were canvassing, it was not possible to proceed in that fashion. Instead, we limited the issue battery in this context to our seven "agenda" or "importance" items (see Chapter 7) and asked our respondents to tell us which one of a list of ten political parties more or less current in France at the time fought "hardest" for each of the various issue goals involved. Later in the interview, the respondents were asked an identical question, this time related to the individual candidates who had run for the Assembly in their districts.[2] There was no need, in replying to these questions, for the respondents to rely on their memories to recall any party or candidate. They were handed a list of the parties, and later a list of the candidates who ran in their districts, which they could consult while the interviewers read each of the seven policy domains to them.

We shall proceed first to examine the voters' perceptions of the positions of the various *parties* on our central linkage issues, and then compare our findings in that regard with the voters' estimates of the positions of the competing *candidates* in their districts on those same issues. Our objective will be to determine whether parties or candidates are the main channels for issue representation—the same question that ended our discussion of candidate visibility in Chapter 8. Along the way, we shall also explore the correlates of voter linkage of issues with parties and candidates and the extent to which the voters are consistent in associating a given issue with a party and the candidate of that same party. Lastly, we shall ask whether the electoral orientations of the voters, that is, their tendency to be oriented more toward parties or more toward candidates as objects of electoral choice, are related to the extent to which they associate issues with parties and candidates. That analysis will aid us in formulating a final statement about the way in which issues were perceived by the French electorate as part of the electoral stakes of 1967.

Mass Perceptions of Party-Policy Linkages

In considering the extent to which the party system has meaning for the voters in terms of political issues, the most striking finding is the large proportion of people who report that they do not know which party tried hardest to accomplish the specified policy goals. Throughout the entire electorate, the proportion of voters who could not link any of the ten parties listed with the policy areas mentioned ranged from 34 percent in the case of governmental stability to 47 percent for European integration.[3] Given the gaps in the average French voter's knowledge of the party system that we outlined in Chapter 2, as well as the minimal amount of issue content associated with left-right positioning by the mass electorate, we should be prepared for this indication that, for large numbers of French voters, the choice of a party at election time carries with it little in the way of policy awareness. Of course, some of the policy domains tested, such as the priorities for education or economic development, had not been historically associated with any French party or party cluster, and they were not polarizing issues at the election of 1967. But in view of the historic clash between clericals and anticlericals over the character of the public school system, and the perennial importance of the distribution of income as a source of political conflict, the fact that 38 percent of the electorate did not link any party with the defense of the public school system and 40 percent did not associate any party with an equitable distribution of income indicates the limited penetration of these party disputes into the cognitive field of the mass electorate.

Correlates

The ability to associate parties with policies is distributed differentially across the electorate. Reducing our set of respondents to the 70 percent of our mass sample who gave a valid reply to all seven components of the party-policy linkage battery,[4] we find that almost a quarter of them linked a party with each of the seven issue domains probed, and another 13 percent cited parties for all but one policy area. At the other extreme, however, more than a quarter failed to link any issue with a party, and another 7 percent managed just one citation. The French electorate, therefore, is roughly divided into thirds on this score, with the top third linking parties to almost all of the issues and the least-informed third making no more than one such link.

Awareness of the issue-relatedness of the parties faithfully reflects the levels of political involvement within the mass public. As we saw in Chapter 7, the association of left-right locations with specific issue content varies with the degree of political involvement of the voters. The same phenomenon appears with regard to the voters' ability to associate parties with issues. As Table 9-1 shows, almost everyone in the most involved 15 percent makes a substantial number of such linkages, with about two-thirds making almost all of them. In the least involved stratum, however, almost two-thirds make virtually no such associations.

Political involvement is not the only factor that vitally affects the ability of the mass public to attach policy meaning to the French political parties. Differences in the visibility of specific parties are bound to matter as well, since a person cannot associate an issue with any party that he or she simply does not "see." We computed a summary measure of the breadth of party recall based on the degree of visibility to our respondents of all ten parties for which policy linkages were tested.[5] Table 9-2 shows the relation-

Table 9-1. Percentages of voters linking issues with parties, by political involvement, France, 1967.

Number of linkages	Level of Political Involvement		
	High	Medium	Low
6–7	68	40	14
2–5	31	31	21
0–1	1	29	65
Total	100	100	100
Weighted N	(201.9)	(811.8)	(389.0)

Table 9-2. Percentages of voters linking issues with parties, by breadth of party recall, France, 1967.

Number of linkages	Breadth of Party Recall		
	High	Medium	Low
6–7	64	35	17
2–5	30	34	20
0–1	6	31	63
Total	100	100	100
Weighted N	(380.0)	(535.7)	(487.2)

ship of this measure to party-policy linkages in a manner similar to the display in Table 9-1.

The results of Table 9-2 are almost identical with those of Table 9-1. This similarity arises in part because party recall and political involvement are associated with each other. They are not, however, so closely associated with each other as each of them is with the ability to link issues with parties. We saw in Chapter 2 that personal factors such as political involvement account less for party visibility than do systemic factors such as recent party size and prominence. Therefore, although the relationship between breadth of party recall and the perception of party-policy linkages subsumes the effects of political involvement, it includes some modicum of the effects of other distinct factors as well. In fact, breadth of party visibility correlates somewhat more closely with the number of issues associated with a party ($r = .54$) than political involvement does ($r = .42$), and that is what we would expect.

A still more striking relationship is generated if we consider the pattern of parties actively recalled—not just recognized—among those running candidates in each respondent's own district. Table 9-3 relates the pattern of local party recall to the policy linkage variable. The more familiar the voters are with their local parties, the more likely they are to view them in terms of public policy, and the differences progress with considerable regularity across the range of party familiarity.

In sum, the French electorate is clearly stratified in regard to the extent to which the party system is surrounded by policy connotations. The most involved voters, those who are highly familiar with the parties, associate virtually all of our issues with a party. Others—the most numerous group—with only a moderate sense of involvement and a partial view of the party system, associate some but by no means all policy matters with a party. The disinterested remainder, while still accounting for more than a quarter of the electorate, sees little or no connection between the parties and policy options.

Table 9-3. Percentages of voters linking issues with parties, by pattern of local party recall, France, 1967.

	Pattern of local party recall				
Number of linkages	All parties visible	Partisan electoral choice and main opposing party visible	Partisan electoral choice visible	At least one party visible	No party visible
6–7	64	53	37	35	9
2–5	26	32	38	32	13
0–1	10	15	25	33	78
Total	100	100	100	100	100
Weighted N	(197.0)	(195.0)	(208.5)	(516.7)	(285.7)

Extent

Earlier in this discussion, we referred to the large proportions of French voters who did not associate certain specific issues with any political party. By returning to our discrete linkage issues, we can portray more fully the ways in which matters of public policy are associated with the parties in the minds of the voters.

Table 9-4 sets out the proportions of French voters who associate each of the linkage issues with either a single party, more than one party (but not all of them), all the parties, or none at all ("don't know"). The proportions of people who link the issues with a particular party range from 61 percent in the case of government stability as an issue to 43 percent for educational development and an independent foreign policy. About 1 or 2 percent of the electorate typically associate each issue with more than one party. Somewhat larger proportions reply that "all the parties" are associated with each given issue. And the proportions of people who acknowledge that they cannot associate an issue with any party vary from 47 percent in the case of European integration to 34 percent in the case of government stability.

It is apparent that government stability, defense of secular schools, and distribution of income are the linkage issues most widely perceived in partisan terms. This selection is not surprising. Distribution of income is a partisan issue in all democratic societies; the conflict over secular and religious schools is probably the single most important and durable issue in modern French political history; and Charles de Gaulle and his followers did all they could after World War II to make government stability a central political issue.

Another point of interest in Table 9-4 concerns those who link an issue with "all the parties." These proportions are not negligible: they range from 2 to 13 percent, with the modal proportion being about 5 percent of the

Table 9-4. Percentages of voters associating selected issues with parties, France, 1967.

Issue	A single party	More than one party	All the parties	Don't know
	Issue linked with			
Government stability	61	0	5	34
Defense of the secular schools	56	2	3	39
Equitable distribution of income	54	2	5	39
Economic development	52	1	2	45
European integration	46	1	6	47
Educational development	43	1	12	44
Independent foreign policy	43	1	13	43

voters. Some of these responses may conceal uncertainty or ignorance, but internal evidence raises doubt that most of them do. Explicit responses of "don't know" to the linkage questions advance very sharply as political involvement declines, and if references to "all the parties" merely camouflaged ignorance, we would expect to find a comparable progression by political involvement in those cases as well. We do not find any such pattern. In almost every case, highly involved voters were at least as likely to see all the parties pursuing the specific policy goal as uninvolved voters were.

The two issues drawing the largest proportions of "all the parties" responses are educational development and the independence of French foreign policy. For both issues, the highly involved were as likely as the less involved to make this broad association, suggesting that they were not regarded by even the well-informed as subjects of party conflict. This is not surprising in the case of educational development, an issue which apart from its connection with religion did not loom large as a partisan matter in the years immediately preceding the 1967 election. That so many of the most politically involved citizens—some 18 percent of them by our estimate—felt French independence was not a partisan issue is a more interesting revelation. De Gaulle and his followers had made independence their central position since 1940, and the Communist party had been promoting the same theme for almost as long. The fact that these two most visible parties had been outdoing each other in their efforts to stand as champions of French independence from the United States served to transform it into a nonpartisan issue for a substantial proportion of the electorate, including the most involved voters.

European integration and economic development are the issues which the largest proportions of the electorate claimed to be unable to link with any political party. An oddity arises, however, when we look at the "don't know" proportions for these two issues among the politically involved. Involved voters had more difficulty in associating European integration with a party than they did any other issue except independence in foreign policy. Thus the involved fitted the general pattern on this issue. Where economic development is concerned, however, fewer of the involved failed to link a party with it than any other issue. The less involved found it hard to locate economic development in partisan terms, but the most involved clearly regarded it as a partisan issue.

Consensus

Thus far we have only treated the *extent* of party-issue linkages among the electorate. Also crucial is the degree of consensus concerning *which* parties are associated with each issue. If politicians or pundits are to interpret electoral results correctly in terms of the public's policy expectations, they must have a tolerably accurate sense of how much agreement there is among the voters over which parties stand for particular issue positions. For example, the foreign policy implications of changes in the Gaullist vote would be reasonably clear if the electorate perceived the Gaullists as the party most attached to French independence. A surge in the Gaullist vote would be a signal to press on with that policy; a decline would be a warning that it was not paying off. But if the voters did not perceive the Gaullists to be any more attached to French independence than the other parties, one could hardly conclude that the voters were flashing a foreign policy message to the Gaullists one way or the other.

In order to arrive at a simple but effective measure of the degree of consensus over the party linkage of each issue, we have used the proportions of the electorate linking an issue with each of the various parties (among those actually linking it to any single party) to compute the probability that any two voters will link the same party to a given issue.[6] This measure has a range between some value approaching zero and one, and it serves nicely as a means of comparison of the degree of consensus about party positions across our seven linkage issues. For purposes of this comparison, which appears in Table 9-5, we have simplified the party system somewhat. Instead of listing separately all ten parties to which reference could be made, we have listed seven, including under the heading of the Federation not only specific references to that organization but also references to its constituent parties, the Socialist party (SFIO) and the Radical party. Similarly, we have classified as Democratic Center both the references to it and those to the MRP. All other partisan distinctions have been maintained.

Table 9-5 shows, for each linkage issue, the proportion of voters linking the issue with a single party who associated that issue with each of our primary party groupings. The summary consensus score for each issue appears in the bottom row of the table. We see that consensus was greatest for economic development and next greatest for government stability. There is considerably less consensus about the party linkage of the remaining five issues. The scores for four of them—defense of secular schools, independent foreign policy, equitable distribution of income, and European integration—tend to cluster within a comparatively narrow range. And finally, the consensus over educational development was less than that over any other linkage issue.

The main body of the table indicates that the two issues ranking highest in consensus—economic development and government stability—are preponderantly linked with the Gaullist UNR in the minds of those who associate those issues with any individual party. Self-professed leftists, it should be added, are less inclined to link either issue with the UNR than are centrists, rightists, or the *marais;* but even among leftists, some 60 percent of those making links do associate these issues with the UNR.

Among issues showing less consensus in relation to party linkage, two

Table 9-5. Percentages of those voters linking issues with parties who associated selected issues with particular parties, France, 1967.

Parties	Issues						
	Economic development	Government stability	Secular schools	Independent foreign policy	Distribution of income	European integration	Educational development
Communist (PCF)	13	8	39	13	41	4	22
Unified Socialist (PSU)	1	0	2	1	2	1	3
Federation (FGDS)	6	12	49	21	37	17	36
Democratic Center (CD)	3	4	3	5	4	23	4
Union for the New Republic (UNR)	75	69	6	54	13	49	32
Independent Republicans (RI)	2	6	1	5	2	5	2
Republican Alliance (AR)	0	1	0	1	1	1	1
Total	100	100	100	100	100	100	100
Consensus score	.58	.50	.39	.35	.33	.32	.28

are markedly associated with the main left-wing parties. Defense of secular schools and an equitable distribution of income are overwhelmingly associated with the Communist party and the Federation. Income redistribution tends to be associated more with the Communists, and secular schools more with the Federation, but the two leftist parties together are associated with both issues by the great majority of people who see any link at all between these issues and the parties. The main reason why these issues are comparatively low on consensus, of course, is the division of the left into two large party groups. If we were to count the Communist party and the Federation together as a single party, consensus over party linkage for the two issues would increase considerably. It would be greatest for defense of the secular school system and next greatest for income redistribution among all seven linkage issues. But consensus is smaller over these issues than over economic development or government stability because the Gaullist UNR enjoys a near monopoly of the latter issues, while the left is divided between a Communist and a non-Communist party. One could, of course, argue that the Communists and the Federation should be counted as a single party because of their electoral alliance. But Communist and Federation candidates opposed each other at the first ballot and, as we shall see in Chapter 12, a substantial proportion of first-ballot Federation voters refused to vote for Communist candidates at the second ballot. Because there is little doubt that the Federation and the Communist party were perceived as distinct parties by the electorate, it seems appropriate to treat them in that fashion here.

The two other issues showing similar levels of consensus relate to foreign policy: independence of the United States and European integration. Independence in foreign policy is most often associated with the UNR, but it is often linked with the main leftist parties as well. These particular perceptions are strongly affected by left-right locations. The UNR link is made by very large majorities of centrists, rightists, and the marais, but by barely more than a quarter of the leftists. Most of the leftists claim a link with the left, favoring the Federation over the Communists by almost a two-to-one margin despite the unremitting effort of Communists to appear as defenders of French national independence.

There is comparatively little consensus as to which party does most to promote European integration. It is most often linked with the UNR, but substantial fractions of the electorate associate it instead with the Democratic Center or the Federation. In fact, European integration is the only one of the seven linkage issues that is associated with the center to any appreciable degree, a matter which helps to explain the curvilinear relationship noted earlier in this book between left-right locations and positions on our European integration items. Thus the efforts of French centrists at the elite level to carve a distinctive position for themselves as champions of European integration did meet with some resonance in the mass public. Nonetheless, almost twice as many voters associated European integration with the more visible UNR than with the Democratic Center.

The last of the seven issues, the development of education, showed the least consensus in 1967. A majority of those linking it with any single party associated it with the left-wing parties, and a plurality associated it with the Federation. Nonetheless, the differences are small and the distribution of references to the parties is exceptionally flat.

Clarity

Our discussion thus far has revolved around two principal dimensions: variations in the likelihood that parties will be associated with given issues, and the degree of consensus over which parties are linked with each issue. These two phenomena can combine in different ways. For some issues, both the incidence of and consensus over party linkage may be comparatively slight; for other issues both may be comparatively great. For another class of issues, the incidence of party linkage may be high but consensus low; for other issues, the situation may be the reverse. It is, therefore, useful to combine the two measures of incidence and consensus into a single summary score that expresses them jointly. We shall refer to that synthetic measure as clarity, because it summarizes in directly comparable fashion how clearly the electorate perceives the party system in terms of the issue domains we have canvassed.[7]

Table 9-6, which presents the clarity scores for each of the linkage issues, serves as a useful summary of this section of the chapter. The values are highest for the issue of government stability, where the Gaullist claim to the issue is paramount, although economic development comes in a close second. The values drop off rapidly thereafter. In an "ideal" system where

Table 9-6. Clarity of party-issue linkage, by issue, France, 1967.

Issue	Extent of party-issue linkage[a]	Consensus on party-issue linkage	Clarity of party-issue linkage[b]
Government stability	61%	.50	.305
Economic development	52	.58	.302
Defense of the secular schools	56	.39	.218
Equitable distribution of income	54	.33	.178
Independent foreign policy	43	.35	.150
European integration	46	.32	.147
Educational development	43	.28	.120

a. Percentage of voters associating the issue with an individual party.

b. The clarity score consists of the score in the first column, expressed in decimal form, multiplied by the score in the second column.

political options are clear-cut in the mind of the common voter, these values would approach 1.00, since citizens would make consensual associations between particular parties and particular policy options. The fact that these probabilities are usually under .20 underscores the feeble levels at which policy choices are commonly tied to party programs in the mind of the voter.

In conclusion, when we ask what the ordinary citizen is likely to know about the policy stances of the political parties, we encounter a considerable degree of ignorance and confusion. To be sure, some structured and consensual perceptions do emerge. Moreover, these perceptions are quite recognizable to the informed observer: the public is clearest in associating goals of economic development and government stability with the Gaullist UNR, and reasonably clear in associating the defense of the secular school system and the quest for an equitable distribution of income with parties of the left.

Nonetheless, even at their clearest these perceptions would not rank as very strong in the aggregate. Never do most of the citizens see party links for given issues and cast them in the same way. Not much more than half of the public report awareness of party-policy links, even in the "clearest" cases; and when links are reported, there is less than full consensus as to what they are. This blur of uncertainty surrounding even the clearest lines of plausible perception is reminiscent of the weak structure of policy preferences in the mass public. The sense of that similarity is enhanced when we note that a very disproportionate share of such clarity as exists in these perceptions of party-issue linkages in the public is contributed by the same thin stratum of these who are most highly involved in politics.

Popular votes are, however, cast most directly for specific candidates, and the winners become the actual agents of representation in the National Assembly. Our results in the preceding chapter have suggested that candidates are more salient to French voters than parties are. Perhaps voters are clearer as to what policies they are supporting with their votes when they choose between candidates than when they choose between parties. We shall examine this possibility in the next section.

Candidate-Issue Linkage and Party-Issue Linkage

On the surface, there is virtually no difference between the proportions of people who link parties with issues and of people who link candidates with issues. In each case the electorate is roughly divided into thirds. Somewhat more than a third of the voters associate at least six of the seven issues with a candidate.[8] Slightly more than a third of the voters do not associate more than one of the seven issues with a candidate. Somewhat less than 30 percent of the voters fall between the other two groups, associating between two and five of the issues with a candidate.

There is reason, however, to question this apparent equivalence. As a matter of fact, more people are likely to have associated issues with parties than with candidates. This is the case because our interviewing procedure made it possible for respondents to link issues with candidates because of the party affiliation of the candidates, but it did not make it possible for them to associate issues with parties because of the candidates of the parties.[9]

In view of this confounding of candidate-issue linkage with party-issue linkage, the estimates we reported at the beginning of this section of the proportions of people who associate various issue positions with candidates are probably inflated and should be adjusted downward; unfortunately, we are not able to specify by what amount. We have estimated that somewhat less than 15 percent of the people who could not name any candidate that had run in their districts linked candidates with issues solely because of their party labels,[10] but we have no way of estimating what proportion of the rest of the electorate may have linked issues with candidates about whom they knew nothing except their party labels.

In fact, there is reason to believe that even people who were familiar with the candidates linked them with issues because of their party affiliations and not because of independent information about the stands taken on the issues by the candidates. When we discussed party-issue linkage, we pointed out that there is a respectable correlation between breadth of party visibility and party-issue linkage. The more parties the respondent was familiar with, the more issues he or she was likely to associate with a political party. We do not, however, find the same kind of close relationship between average candidate visibility and candidate-issue linkage. There is a modest positive correlation between the two; but whereas overall party visibility accounts for 30 percent of the variance in party-issue linkage, average candidate visibility accounts for less than 10 percent of the variance in candidate-issue linkage. Indeed, party visibility is more closely related to candidate-issue linkage than candidate visibility is. People who know something about the parties are more likely to link issues with candidates than are people who know something about the candidates. Familiarity with the party system is more important than familiarity with the candidates in determining the extent to which the French electorate perceives candidates for the Assembly in terms of public policies.

To a large extent, the people who link the candidates with issue positions are the same ones who link the parties with issues, just as the people who fail to associate the candidates with issues also fail to see any connection between parties and issues. The correlation between candidate-issue linkage and party-issue linkage at the individual level is quite strong ($r = .77$).[11] Of course, there are a few people, amounting to less than 5 percent of the sample under consideration, who link all or almost all the issues with parties but do not link more than a single issue with a candidate, or, conversely, who perceive the candidates but not the parties in terms of central policy positions. But those anomalous cases are far outnumbered by the voters whose perceptions of the candidates and the parties are similar. Once again, we find the population divided roughly into thirds. Somewhat less than 30 percent of the voters perceive both parties and candidates in terms of at least six of the seven linkage issues, while another 30 percent do not link more than one issue with either a party or a candidate. The remaining 40 percent of the electorate fall somewhere between—and they include that small fraction of voters who are exclusively oriented toward either parties or candidates for most of the issues.[12]

This distribution of the population according to perceptions of both parties and candidates in terms of public issues is strongly polarized. What it means, in effect, is that some 30 percent of the population are highly sensitive to the real or potential issue content of electoral choices, while for almost as large a percentage an election has little or no meaning in terms of public policy. Insofar as an election is a means by which the electorate communicates views on issues, or public policy, to the parliamentary elite, the various segments of the electorate differ widely in the amount of information that they are able to communicate to the elite. For some people, about 30 percent of the electorate, an election has meaning across a wide range of issues, and it is these people who provide the minimum level of justification for interpretations of electoral outcomes as expressions of popular support for some policies and popular opposition to others. Another 40 percent of the population have some but less information about the issue content of electoral choices, and therefore to interpret the votes they cast as endorsements of certain elite policy preferences may be chancy indeed. Finally, for somewhat less than a third of the electorate, an election has virtually no meaning in terms of issues. They associate few issues (or none at all) with either parties or candidates, and it would be highly questionable to interpret their votes as broad messages to the elite concerning specific policies.[13]

At this point, the reader may begin to wonder whether there *is* such a phenomenon as candidate-issue linkage, independent of party-issue linkage. We have emphasized certain gross similarities in the extent to which the voters perceive the candidates and parties in terms of central issue positions. We have pointed out that an unknown but not necessarily negligible proportion of the voters probably links candidates with issues because of the parties with which those candidates are affiliated. We have reported that there is an impressive correlation between candidate-issue linkage and party-issue linkage; and we have indicated that the relationship between political involvement and candidate-issue linkage is virtually the same as that between political involvement and party-issue linkage. Is there, then, really much difference between candidate-issue linkage and party-issue linkage? May not what we are referring to as candidate-issue linkage be simply the transposition onto the candidates of the voters' perceptions of the issue positions of the parties?

We hasten to answer the final question in the negative by insisting that candidate-issue linkage *is* independent of party-issue linkage. If it were not—that is, if candidate-issue linkage amounted to the same thing as party-issue linkage—we would find that every person who linked a given issue with both a candidate and a party would link that issue with the candidate of the same party that he or she associated with the issue. In other words, the party affiliation of the candidate chosen would be consistent with the party chosen. In actual fact, across our entire set of respondents the consistency between candidates and parties selected as representative of the various policy domains is far from perfect. The overlap in choice ranges from a high of more than 80 percent for governmental stability to a low of slightly more than 60 percent for economic development, with the average being some 70 percent across the whole set of seven linkage issues. Substantial proportions of the people who associate both a candidate and a party with the various linkage issues are not consistent in their choice of the candidate and the party most devoted to a given position on the same issue.[14] Some voters apparently see a difference between the issue positions of the parties and the positions, on those same issues, of the candidates who represent those parties. It is, therefore, entirely appropriate for us to consider candidate-issue linkage as an independent phenomenon and to compare its properties with those of party-issue linkage.

The Extent of Candidate-Issue Linkage

Between one-third and one-half of the French electorate do not associate our linkage issues with the candidates, depending on the issue area involved. To put the matter positively, between one-half and two-thirds of the electorate do associate issue positions with one or more candidates for legislative office, again depending on the issue concerned. These proportions are not sharply at variance with the proportions of people who associate each of our linkage issues with the parties.

In order to place the extent of candidate-issue linkage into comparative relief, we have set out in Table 9-7 the proportions of our respondents who linked or failed to link each of the seven issues with candidates and with parties. Table 9-7 shows the proportions of our respondents who associated each of the linkage issues with an individual candidate, with more than one candidate, or with all the candidates, as well as the proportions who replied that they did not know which candidate had fought hardest for each particular policy domain. Similar information is reported for party-issue linkage.[15]

The columns of Table 9-7 displaying the percentages of voters who associate the linkage issues with a single candidate and a single party, respectively, show that fewer people link five of the seven issues with a single

Table 9-7. Candidate-issue linkage and party-issue linkage by voters, by issue (percentages), France, 1967.

| | Candidate-issue linkage | | | | Party-issue linkage | | | |
| | Issue linked with | | | | Issue linked with | | | |
Issue	A single candidate	More than one candidate but not all	All the candidates	Don't know	A single party	More than one party but not all	All the parties	Don't know
Government stability	58	3	4	35	61	0	5	34
Defense of the secular schools	51	7	4	38	56	2	3	39
Equitable distribution of income	48	6	5	41	54	2	5	39
Educational development	45	5	11	39	43	1	12	44
Economic development	43	3	11	43	52	1	2	45
Independent foreign policy	43	3	3	51	43	1	13	43
European integration	41	3	5	51	46	1	6	47

candidate than with a single party. Only in the case of educational development is this tendency reversed, while in the case of an independent foreign policy, parity is evident. With government stability as the issue, the difference between the extent of candidate linkage and that of party linkage is slight, lying within the limits of sampling error. For the four remaining issues, however, the lesser extent of candidate linkage relative to party linkage is quite substantial. For three issues—defense of the secular schools, European integration, and an equitable distribution of income—the differences in the proportions of people linking them with candidates and with parties is about 5 percent; while for economic development some 9 percent fewer people associate it with an individual candidate than with an individual party.

Turning to the columns of Table 9-7 that show the proportions of people who linked each issue with *more than one* candidate (but not all) and with *more than one* party (but not all) we find that in every case more people associate the issues with multiple candidates than with multiple parties. When we discussed party-issue linkage earlier, we omitted the phenomenon of voters associating the issues with more than one (but not all) of the parties, because the proportions involved never rose above 2 percent and were negligible. For each of our linkage issues, however, about three times as many voters linked the issue with more than one candidate as linked it with more than one party, and the proportions of voters involved in the case of candidate-issue linkage range from 3 to 7 percent. The phenomenon, therefore, deserves our attention.

In discussing party-issue linkage we did point out that there was as strong a tendency for the most involved as for the least involved voters to link the issues with *all* the parties. When we examine the voters who link the various issues with *more than one* candidate (but not all) with regard to their levels of political involvement, we find a regular tendency for association of the issues with multiple candidates to increase with the level of political involvement. For almost every issue, more of the most involved voters, proportionately, associate the issue with more than one candidate than the medium-involved voters do, and more of the medium-involved voters, proportionately, link the issue with more than one candidate than the least involved voters do.[16] Essentially the same pattern appears with regard to party-issue linkage, although it is not so regular as it is for candidate-issue linkage, perhaps because the overall proportions of voters involved are about a third as large.

This suggests that many of the people who link the issues with more than one candidate or more than one party perceive the array of competing candidates or parties in terms of substantive issue content just as clearly as do the people who link the issues with a single candidate or a single party. In fact, some of them may very well have a more informed perception of the issue content of the electoral choices they make than the people who select a single candidate or party do. Their linkage of more than one candidate or party (but not all of them) with the issues suggests a sophisticated reading of the candidates' and parties' stands on the issues.

Accordingly, it is appropriate to combine the proportions of people who associate the issues with a single candidate and those who associate them with more than one candidate, as well as to perform the same operation with respect to party-issue linkage. When we do this, we find that the proportions of people who link the issues with candidates (in the broadened sense) are actually or virtually the same as the proportions of people who associate the issues with parties (again in broadened terms) for five of the seven linkage issues. For two of those five issues—government stability and defense of the secular schools—the proportions turn out to be identical, while for the three others—an equitable distribution of income, an independent foreign policy, and European integration—they are very similar. For the two remaining issues, however, there is a substantial difference between the extent of candidate linkage and the extent of party linkage. Almost 15 percent more people associate educational development with candidates than with parties, while almost as many more people link economic development with parties than with candidates.

In the preceding chapter, we concluded that candidates are more visible to French voters than parties are, at least in terms of the voters' ability to identify them by name (or, in the case of candidates, by an accurate description other than party). At the same time, however, we cautioned that this phenomenon might not have a major bearing on the respective roles of candidates and parties as channels of representation for the voters. It now appears that this caveat was well advised. For five of our seven linkage issues, about as many people perceive the parties in terms of policy content as perceive the candidates as standing for those same issues. In the case of economic development as an issue, parties are the potential vehicles of representation for more people than the candidates are. Only for one issue—educational development—can we say that the candidates appear to carry issue content for more voters than the parties do.

Consistency of Candidate-Policy Linkages and Party-Policy Linkages

Now that candidate-issue linkages and party-issue linkages have been compared in aggregate terms, we shall see how these two forms of perception of the policy implications of electoral choices combine at the level of the individual voter. These combined perceptions are expressed in the extent to which the voters are consistent, in partisan terms, in the candidate and party that they associate with each issue (when they do associate any given issue with both a candidate and a party).

Table 9-8. Consistency in party linkage and candidate linkage by voters, by issue, France, 1967.

Issue	Consistent voters as percentage of those ratable for consistency	Ratable voters as percentage of total electorate
Government stability	82.5	37.9
European integration	75.7	24.4
Distribution of income	71.7	32.5
Independent foreign policy	70.8	23.9
Educational development	70.1	25.9
Defense of the secular schools	67.2	36.4
Economic development	63.5	27.3
Mean	71.1	29.8

The consistency rates for each of our seven linkage issues are presented in Table 9-8.[17] They range from somewhat more than 80 percent in the case of government stability to slightly more than 60 percent in the case of economic development, with the average rate being about 70 percent across the seven linkage issues. These figures, of course, represent comparatively small fractions of the entire electorate, as the ratable proportions of the electorate reported in Table 9-8 indicate. Before a voter can be rated for linkage consistency on any given issue, he or she must associate both a party and a candidate with the same issue, and the incidence of this joint linkage is always less than the extent of either party linkage or candidate linkage for the same issue. As a result, the number of people who can be rated for consistency ranges from a high of almost 40 percent of the electorate for government stability to only about a fourth of the electorate for an independent foreign policy or European integration.

Consistency rates not only vary with the particular issue. They also vary as a function of the number of issues on which the voters can be rated for consistency, as indicated in Table 9-9, which sets out the proportions of voters who were consistent in their candidate and party linkages on various numbers of issues, according to the number of issues on which they could potentially be consistent. Table 9-9 is not easy to read, but the overall pattern shows a tendency toward consistency. The largest proportions of voters who were consistent fall at or near the tops of the columns, indicating that voters tended to be consistent on the maximal number of issues on which they could be consistent.

Moreover, consistency increases with the number of ratable issues. Moving across the columns of Table 9-9, we find that the proportion of people in each group that is consistent, on at least as many issues as the pre-

Table 9-9. Percentages of voters consistent on party-issue linkage and candidate-issue linkage, by number of issues on which voters are consistent and number on which they could be consistent, France, 1967.

Number of issues on which voters are consistent	Number of issues on which voters could be consistent						
	1	2	3	4	5	6	7
7							23
6						21	19
5					21	23	16
4				32	26	20	8
3			40	23	17	12	13
2		56	27	20	12	13	8
1	66	28	21	16	17	8	7
0	34	16	12	9	7	3	6
Total	100	100	100	100	100	100	100
Weighted N	(216.2)	(184.6)	(180.0)	(156.0)	(162.3)	(157.0)	(171.0)

ceding group *could* be consistent on, is always larger than the proportion of people in the preceding group that was consistent on the maximum number of issues. While 66 percent of the people who could be rated for consistency on only one issue were in fact consistent on that issue, 84 percent of the people who could be rated on two issues were consistent on at least one issue. Similarly, 56 percent of the voters who could be rated on two issues were consistent on two issues, while among the people who could be rated on three issues, 67 percent were consistent on at least two issues—and so on, across the remaining columns.

The obverse of the tendency for consistency to increase with the number of issues available is, of course, the tendency for inconsistency to be greatest among people for whom few issues are ratable. The bottom row of Table 9-9 shows almost monotonically that the fewer the issues available to people, the more likely those people were to be inconsistent. More than a third of the persons who were ratable on only one issue (and they include the least involved politically) were inconsistent in their party and candidate linkages of that issue.

Some amount of inconsistency among the least involved voters, based on ignorance, is inevitable. So, too, is a certain amount of inconsistency on the part of highly involved voters, based, in their case, on knowledge. But these forces making for some inconsistency coexist with a tendency toward consistency. Just as it would be unrealistic to expect to find complete consistency, complete inconsistency would be untenable. If inconsistency predominated, votes would have little meaning as expressions of popular policy expectations; and attentive voters would experience tensions destructive of their sense of participation in a system of representative government. Consistency is a method, fostered by parties and probably also self-induced by voters, for avoiding the tensions inherent in dividing linkages between candidate and party for the same issues. We have no way of knowing what the tolerable limits of such inconsistency are for any given political system, or even—for lack of comparative studies—what the empirical ranges of inconsistency are in different systems. All we can say at this point is that the data for France reveal an intelligible tendency toward consistency.

Consensus on Candidate-Issue Linkage

When we compare the amount of consensus over candidate-issue linkage with that over party-issue linkage (see Table 9-10), we find that for six of the seven linkage issues there is less consensus about candidate linkage than about party linkage. For economic development as an issue the difference in the levels of consensus is dramatic. There is more consensus over which *party* is associated with that issue than there is for any other, but when it comes to *candidate* linkage, the consensus score is below the mean for the set of issues. The decrease in consensus for the other issue for which it is comparatively high for party linkage—government stability—is much less abrupt. Government stability ranks second on consensus over party linkage, and it ranks highest on consensus concerning candidate linkage.

The only issue for which consensus on candidate linkage is greater than it is on party linkage is that of foreign-policy independence from the United States. There is somewhat more agreement among French voters over which party's candidates try hardest to maintain French independence in foreign affairs than there is over which party does so. For all six of the other linkage issues, however, there is more consensus over which party stands for which issue than there is over which candidate stands for which issue.

Table 9-10. Consensus scores on candidate-issue linkage and party-issue linkage, by issue, France, 1967.

	Consensus scores	
Issue	Candidate-issue linkage	Party-issue linkage
Economic development	.28	.58
Government stability	.44	.50
Defense of the secular schools	.32	.39
Independent foreign policy	.41	.35
Equitable distribution of income	.27	.33
European integration	.28	.32
Educational development	.23	.28
Mean	.319	.393

Partisan Content of Issue Linkages

At this point, it is helpful to present in tabular form the proportions of voters, among those who associated the various linkage issues with an individual candidate or an individual party, that linked them with each particular party or group of partisan candidates. This information appears in Table 9-11, which sets the data related to party-issue linkages (already contained in Table 9-5) against the equivalent data concerning candidate-issue linkages. The proportions arrayed in Table 9-11 underlie the sets of consensus scores that appear in Table 9-10, and enable us to observe in concrete partisan terms why the consensus scores for party-issue linkages differ from those for candidate issue-linkages.

Reading across the columns of Table 9-11 from left to right, we see first that government stability as an issue is associated strongly with both the UNR as a party and with UNR candidates; hence consensus is high on both items. Our measure of consensus, however, which is arrived at by summing squares, is more sensitive to relatively small differences between large proportions than it is to comparatively large differences between small proportions. Therefore, the fact that slightly more people proportionately associated the issue with the UNR as a party than with UNR candidates produces a distinctly higher consensus score for party linkage than for candidate linkage.

For economic development, the steep decline in consensus over candidate-issue linkage as compared with that over party-issue linkage is due to the fact that while three-fourths of the voters who associated that issue with an individual party associated it with the UNR, less than half of the people who associated the same issue with a candidate associated it with UNR candidates. Analysis of these distributions according to perceptions of self-locations on the left-right scale shows that although voters of all tendencies contributed to this difference between candidate linkage and party linkage, the leftists contributed disproportionately heavily to the shift. More than 60 percent of French leftists who linked economic development with a party linked it with the UNR, but only 20 percent of the leftists associated the same issue with UNR candidates. At the same time, while a mere 6 percent of the voters who linked economic development with a party linked it with the Federation, almost four times as many voters proportionately associated that issue with Federation candidates. That shift in the direction of candidate-issue linkage is not enough, however, to compensate for the larger proportion of people who associated economic development with the UNR as a party, compared with the percentage that linked it with UNR candidates.

With regard to independence in foreign policy, the pattern is virtually the opposite of that for economic development. This is the only issue on which consensus over candidate linkage is greater than it is over party link-

Table 9-11. Parties and party affiliations of candidates associated with selected issues by voters (percentages), France, 1967.

Party		Government stability	Economic development	Independent foreign policy	Secular schools	Distribution of income	Educational development	European integration
Communist (PCF)	(P)a	8	13	13	39	41	22	4
	(C)b	10	16	18	42	40	27	7
Unified Socialist (PSU)	(P)	0	1	1	2	2	3	1
	(C)	0	1	1	3	3	2	1
Federation (FGDS)	(P)	12	6	21	49	37	36	17
	(C)	13	22	10	36	29	29	18
Democratic Center	(P)	4	3	5	3	4	4	23
(CD)	(C)	4	7	3	4	6	6	19
Union for the New Re-public (UNR)	(P)	69	75	54	6	13	32	49
	(C)	63	45	61	12	18	29	46
Independent Republicans	(P)	6	2	5	1	2	2	5
(IR)	(C)	8	6	5	1	2	4	6
Republican Alliance	(P)	1	0	1	0	1	1	1
(AR)	(C)	0	0	0	0	0	1	0
Other	(C)	2	3	2	2	2	2	3
Weighted N	(P)	(1195.7)	(1023.6)	(841.3)	(1097.6)	(1029.7)	(840.6)	(905.0)
Weighted N	(C)	(1104.8)	(828.0)	(837.2)	(978.8)	(916.0)	(823.7)	(790.0)

a. Party chosen.
b. Candidate of that party chosen.

age. While more than half of the relevant population associated the issue with the UNR as a party, an even larger proportion of voters linked it with UNR candidates. Again, the shift in association is due disproportionately to the behavior of leftist voters; almost twice as many leftist voters proportionately associated an independent foreign policy with UNR candidates as with the UNR as a party. Twice as many voters proportionately linked that same issue with the Federation as a party as with Federation candidates; but, again, that difference is not enough to offset the proportionately smaller difference, at a higher absolute level, between linkage of the same issue with the UNR as a party and linkage with UNR candidates.

For three issues—defense of the secular school system, income distribution, and educational development—there is less consensus over candidate linkage than over party linkage because fewer people proportionately associated those issues with Federation candidates than with the Federation as a party. Two of those issues, defense of secular schools and educational development, were linked by more voters proportionately with Communist candidates than with the Communist party, and twice as many people proportionately associated UNR candidates with defense of the secular schools as associated the UNR as a party with the same issue; but, again, these differences are not enough to offset those involving the Federation and Federation candidates.

Lastly, there is less consensus over candidate linkage than over party linkage for European integration because fewer people proportionately linked the issue with UNR candidates than with the UNR as a party, and because fewer voters proportionately associated it with Democratic Center candidates than with the Democratic Center as a party. Almost twice as many voters proportionately associated European integration with Communist candidates as with the Communist party. The absolute proportions are so small that they have no effect on the consensus scores, but the percentage difference is the most striking among the several instances of a common phenomenon relating to the Communist party: for every issue except the distribution of income, more people proportionately associated the issues with Communist candidates than with the Communist party, although the differences are slight except for the issue of European integration.

Despite variations in the extent to which French voters associated particular issues with parties and with candidates of the same parties, certain issues are characteristically linked with distinctive political tendencies. Government stability, economic development, independence in foreign policy, and, to a lesser extent, European integration are associated in the observant public's view with the Gaullists, while secularism for the public schools and income redistribution are broadly perceived as leftist positions. Perceptions of the position of educational development are less clear-cut. More voters associated that issue with the left than with the Gaullists; but the public splits in three ways, more or less equally, among the Communists, the Federation, and the Gaullist UNR.

Consensus and Consistency

Having discussed consensus over party and candidate linkages with issues and, separately, consistency in party and candidate linkages for the same issue, we may now consider the relationship between consensus and consistency. Are people who are consistent in party and candidate linkages more likely to display consensus in the partisan content of those linkages than the voters as a whole?

The answer is yes. With few exceptions, the consensus scores for candidate-issue and party-issue linkages that appeared in Table 9-10 were not particularly sparkling. Those scores brighten, however, sometimes impressively, when we consider only those voters who were consistent in their perceptions of the party-relatedness and the candidate-relatedness of any particular issue. We have set out in Table 9-12 the consensus scores of the voters who were consistent in their issue-linkage perceptions, as well as the overall consensus scores for party-issue linkage and candidate-issue linkage that have already appeared in Table 9-10. The consensus score for the consistent voters is greater than the higher of the other two consensus scores in the case of every issue except economic development, for which overall party-issue consensus matches that of the consistent portion of the electorate. With that one exception, there is more agreement among voters who are consistent in their perceptions concerning which party stands for which issue and which candidate stands for the same issue than there is throughout the electorate as a whole.

Table 9-12. Consensus scores on candidate-issue linkage and party-issue linkage for voters consistent in candidate-issue linkage and party-issue linkage, and for electorate as a whole, by issue, France, 1967.

	Consensus scores		
	Voters consistent in candidate-issue linkage and party-issue linkage	Electorate as a whole	
Issue		Candidate-issue linkage	Party-issue linkage
Government stability	.70	.44	.50
Economic development	.58	.28	.58
Independent foreign policy	.52	.41	.35
Defense of the secular schools	.43	.32	.39
Equitable distribution of income	.39	.27	.33
European integration	.38	.28	.32
Educational development	.32	.23	.28
Mean	.474	.319	.393

The greater amount of consensus among consistent voters concerning government stability and independence from the United States in foreign policy is particularly sharp. That is because a larger proportion of those voters than of the electorate as a whole associated these issues with the Gaullist UNR. Similarly, consensus concerning European integration is greater because a healthy majority of the consistent voters associated that issue with the UNR, while less than half of the voters as a whole associated it with the Gaullist party or Gaullist candidates.

For the two leftist issues, defense of the secular schools and the distribution of income, more of the consistent voters see links with leftist parties than the voters as a whole do with either leftist parties or leftist candidates. Indeed, more than half of the consistent voters link income distribution with the Communist party.

Lastly, despite the slight increase in the consensus score among the consistent voters concerning educational development, those voters are almost as divided as the whole electorate over which parties and candidates stand for that particular issue.

It is important to remember that although the amount of consensus among the portion of the electorate that is consistent in its party-issue and candidate-issue linkage is often much greater than it is among the electorate as a whole, the consistent voters constitute a comparatively small fraction of the electorate. Even in referring to the electorate as a whole, we are only talking about the 40 to 60 percent of the voters, depending on the issue involved, who associate that issue with a single candidate or party. The voters whose issue-linkage perceptions are consistent in partisan terms represent even smaller proportions of the electorate. Less than a third of our sample electorate is consistent in its linkage of government stability with parties and candidates, about a fourth is consistent concerning the defense of the secular schools and the distribution of income, and less than a fifth is consistent concerning the other linkage issues.

Clarity of Candidate-Issue Linkages

Having compared party-issue linkages with candidate-issue linkages in terms of both extent and consensus, we are able to focus directly on the main objective of this chapter, which is to determine whether parties or candidates are the main vehicles for issue representation in France, by comparing the *clarity* of the two kinds of linkage. Clarity, again, is the summary measure combining both the incidence of linkage for a given issue and the amount of consensus concerning the party (or candidate) with which the issue is linked.[18] To the extent that the ebb and flow of electoral choices in France express mass considerations of basic issues, is it through voting for parties or voting for individual candidates that the voters implicitly convey their messages?

Table 9-13. Clarity of party-issue linkage and candidate-issue linkage by voters, by issue, France, 1967.

Issue	Party-issue linkage			Candidate-issue linkage		
	Extent[a]	Consensus	Clarity[b]	Extent[a]	Consensus	Clarity[b]
Government stability	61%	.50	*.305*[c]	58%	.44	.255
Defense of the secular schools	56	.39	*.218*	51	.32	.163
European integration	46	.32	*.147*	41	.28	.115
Equitable distribution of income	54	.33	*.178*	48	.27	.130
Educational development	43	.28	*.120*	45	.23	.104
Independent foreign policy	43	.35	.150	43	.41	*.176*
Economic development	52	.58	*.302*	43	.28	.120

a. Percentage of voters associating the issue with an individual party (or an individual candidate).

b. The clarity score consists of the score in the extent column, expressed in decimal form, multiplied by the score in the consensus column.

c. Italic numbers indicate the higher of the two clarity scores for each issue.

As Table 9-13 shows, for six of our seven linkage issues there is greater clarity on the party-linkage side than on the candidate-linkage side. Usually the margin by which clarity on party-issue linkage exceeds that on candidate-issue linkage is substantial, although it is rather trifling in the case of educational development, the issue whose relationship to both parties and candidates is perceived least clearly by the electorate. The only issue that the voters relate more clearly to candidates than to parties is independence in foreign policy, although here too the difference is trifling. Overall, the clarity with which the public perceives the parties in terms of issues is greater than that with which it perceives the array of candidates in those terms. Thus far, at least, it appears that the partisan vote, as compared with the vote for particular candidates, contains whatever issue messages the voters may want to convey.

It is possible that the results we have reported concerning the relative clarity of candidate-issue and party-issue linkages are misleading in that they rest on the assumption that all French voters are likely to direct equal amounts of attention toward parties and candidates with regard to their issue positions. It may well be, instead, that some French voters are more oriented toward parties than toward candidates, while for others the reverse is the case, and that these different electoral orientations have a significant effect on the clarity of party-issue and candidate-issue linkages. The clarity of candidate-issue linkages may be heightened for candidate-oriented voters, while that of party-issue linkages is similarly enhanced for party-oriented voters. Such distinctive effects may be washed out of the clarity scores that we have so far presented, which assume that all voters are candidate-oriented when the clarity of candidate-issue linkages is computed and that all voters are party-oriented when party-issue linkages are under examination.

We pursued this line of reasoning by partitioning our mass sample into three groups: party-oriented voters (37 percent), candidate-oriented voters (25 percent), and mixed or unknown (38 percent).[19] Then, for the two groups of voters with clear electoral orientations, we computed fresh clarity scores for the party-issue and candidate-issue linkages. The results showed that different electoral orientations do not have the hypothesized effect on the clarity of issue linkages.

If party-oriented voters differed from candidate-oriented voters according to our hypothesis, the relationships between the clarity of the party-issue linkages and the candidate-issue linkages of each group of voters would necessarily take the forms indicated in Figure 9-1. As shown by the solid signs, the party-issue linkages of the party-oriented voters should be clearer than their candidate-issue linkages for the same issues, and the candidate-issue linkages of the candidate-oriented voters should be clearer than their party-issue linkages for the same issues. And, as indicated by the dashed signs, we would expect the party-issue linkages of the party-oriented voters to be clearer than those of the candidate-oriented voters for the same issues, and vice versa.

The fresh clarity scores, however, do not display the expected relationships. Instead, the clarity of the issue linkage perceptions of both party-oriented voters and candidate-oriented voters is ordered in essentially the same way as for the electorate as a whole. Party-issue linkages are not only clearer than candidate-issue linkages for party-oriented voters in six cases out of the seven, but they are also clearer than candidate-issue linkages for candidate-oriented voters in five cases out of the seven. Moreover, for all seven issues, the candidate-issue linkages of the party-oriented voters are clearer than those of the candidate-oriented voters. We were, therefore, compelled to reject the hypothesis that the overall clarity scores reported in Table 9-13 are not more sparkling because in computing them we combined candidate-oriented and party-oriented voters rather than employing only the candidate-issue linkage scores of candidate-oriented voters and only the

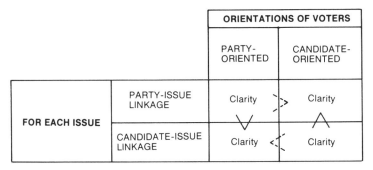

Figure 9-1. Expected relationships concerning linkage clarity, assuming determining influence of voter orientation.

party-issue linkage scores of party-oriented voters. The wholly reasonable proposition that party-oriented voters would be clearer in their perceptions of party-issue linkages than in their perceptions of candidate-issue linkages, while the reverse would be true for candidate-oriented voters, is simply not borne out empirically.

The reason for this almost surely lies in the fact, reported earlier in this chapter, that party visibility and candidate visibility are of unequal importance in affecting party-issue linkages and candidate-issue linkages. While party visibility and candidate visibility are positively correlated with party-issue linkage and candidate-issue linkage, respectively, party visibility is considerably more closely associated with party-issue linkage than candidate visibility is with candidate-issue linkage. Furthermore, *party visibility is more closely associated with candidate-issue linkage than candidate visibility is.* Therefore, party-oriented voters, for whom parties are more visible than candidates, are likely to be clearer with regard to both party-issue linkages and candidate-issue linkages than are candidate-oriented voters, for whom candidates are more visible than parties. That is precisely what we found in the great majority of cases when we computed the clarity scores for the party-issue linkages and the candidate-issue linkages of party-oriented and candidate-oriented voters. Candidate-oriented voters just do not perceive the issue positions of the candidates so clearly as party-oriented voters do. Such clarity as there is in candidate-issue linkages derives more from familiarity with the parties than from familiarity with the candidates.

The reason, then, why the overall clarity scores that we reported in Table 9-13 are not livelier is not because in computing them we crudely mixed the issue-linkage perceptions of candidate-oriented and party-oriented people. It is, rather, because familiarity with the parties is comparatively weak in France. Among voters who are familiar with the parties, the clarity of both party-issue linkages and candidate-issue linkages is higher than it is among people who are familiar with the candidates. But, as we showed in Chapter 8, the candidates are more visible to the French electorate than the parties are. The heightened visibility of candidates relative to that of parties tends to obscure party-issue linkages but contributes little to the clarity of candidate-issue linkages.

Conclusions

In conclusion, there are severe limitations to the clarity with which the French public associates the competing parties and candidates with major issues; and, to the extent that they perceive parties and candidates in terms of public policy, they link issues with parties more clearly than with candidates in almost every case.

Almost a third of the electorate either associates the choice of parties or candidates with policy programs only minimally or does not do so at all. The proportion of French voters that does *not* link issues with either parties or candidates varies with the issue and depends upon whether the presumed linkage is with a party or a candidate; but, with regard to our battery of linkage issues, that proportion is never less than one-third, and in some cases it is more than one-half.

Even among those voters who do associate an issue with a party or a candidate, more often than not there is little consensus concerning which party or candidate is most closely associated with each issue. Consensus over issue linkage, like the extent of issue linkage, varies with the particular issue and depends on whether one is considering party-issue linkage or candidate-issue linkage. Among our seven linkage issues, there is only one (government stability) for which consensus is relatively high about both party-issue linkage and candidate-issue linkage. Consensus is also comparatively strong about which party is associated with economic development; but it is weak, even among the most highly involved voters, over which candidates stand for that issue. There is considerable consensus about which candidates stand for an independent foreign policy, but that consensus breaks down sharply when it is a question of which parties most support that position. For each of those three issues, when consensus is comparatively broad the Gaullist UNR is the party (or the party of the candidates) around which it centers. The remaining four issues show considerable dispersion in the voters' perceptions of which parties or candidates are most closely associated with them, although the main left-wing parties and candidates are most associated with secularism in education and income redistribution.

When we take into account simultaneously the proportions of voters that associate the issues with parties or candidates and the amount of consensus that they display concerning which party or which party's candidate stands for each issue, by computing summary scores for what we have called clarity, we find that, while perfect clarity would be represented by 1.00, the highest clarity score we encounter is .305 (for the party-relatedness of government stability), while the mean of all fourteen clarity scores is a mere .18.

For all our linkage issues except one (independence in foreign policy), the electorate's associations of issues with parties are clearer than their linkages of issues with candidates. The greater clarity of party-issue linkages holds even when we control for the electoral orientations of the voters by taking into account that some voters are candidate-oriented while others are party-oriented. Even the candidate-oriented voters are more likely to associate issues with parties than with candidates. Candidates may be more visible to the French voters than parties, as we saw in the previous chapter, but parties mean more to the voters in terms of specific policies than candidates do.

The extent to which electoral gains and losses for various parties signify implied support for given policy options, therefore, is far from evident. The French electorate tends to identify the Gaullist UNR with government stability and with economic development, and to a lesser extent it links the secular school system and an equitable distribution of income with the main left-wing parties; but, beyond that, even the most astute politician would be hard put to predict the policy expectations of a public that throws its support to one major party or another. Although issues play a role in a French legislative election for highly involved voters, and some issues are more salient to them and are more easily associated with given parties than others, for the bulk of the French electorate we must look elsewhere for the underlying springs of electoral behavior.

10

The First-Ballot Vote

Our survey of the guideposts by means of which the average French voter can find his or her way through the thicket of electoral options is now complete. We have examined the basic political orientations that are likely to be the most stable and enduring cues available to the voter: party identification, self-locations on the left-right dimension, attitudes toward de Gaulle, and positions on the clerical-anticlerical scale. We have investigated the extent to which the competing parties and candidates are visible to the voters who are called upon to choose among them. And we have explored how the voters perceive the candidates and parties in terms of the broad public issues that provide the framework for more specific legislative enactments by the victorious candidates who become the nation's legislators. It is time to assemble these elements, which we have considered separately until now, into a coherent view of how they jointly affect the public's electoral choices.

We shall do so by applying a simple multivariate voting model to the French legislative elections of 1967. Multivariate models, sometimes of considerable complexity, have been applied to voting in the United States with increasing frequency, although more often for presidential elections than for legislative elections (Jackson, 1975; Markus and Converse, 1979; Page and Jones, 1979; Fiorina, 1981). Such models have similarly been applied to voting outside the United States (Schleth and Weede, 1971; Tate, 1980). For French legislative voting in particular, two multivariate models—quite different in basic form—were designed comparatively early.[1]

One of these, produced by Lindon and Weill (1974), is a sequential model that proceeds in six steps, first to eliminate various candidates from the field of possible choice of each voter and then to predict the candidate selections of each voter on the basis of various summed scores. The model rests on a comparatively large number of variables, including four respondent-party proximity scores relating to basic attitudes, eleven respondent-party proximity scores relating to major issues, three sets of candidate evaluations, and a measure of the respondent's degree of general satisfaction. Although, as we shall see later, this model produced satisfactory results when applied to reports of intended partisan vote at the French legislative elections of 1973, it is not parsimonious; and it lies outside the broad methodological framework of the models created for the analysis of voting in the United States.

The other model of French electoral behavior was produced earlier by Campbell (1971). This model, which rests on essentially the same data set as this book does, is so methodologically sound and substantively discerning in its treatment of French legislative voting that in this chapter we shall hew tightly to the path which Campbell first laid out. Indeed, our debt to Campbell is so great that we would be content simply to summarize his account here, were it not that related work done subsequently has inevitably suggested occasional departures from his treatment on points of detail. We have profited greatly from his pioneering work, which we follow in basic outline, although he can in no way be held responsible for the findings we report below.

The Campbell model rests ultimately on the distinction made some time ago between the effects of long-term forces and those of short-term forces on the elector's voting decision (Campbell et al., 1966). For elections in the United States, which is the context within which that distinction was first applied, only one long-term force—party identification—was implied. In the French context, as we have seen, there is good reason for also including other factors in the category of abiding political cues. Our preliminary investigations have pointed to party identification as the dominant force in French voting behavior, but we know that party identification is not so fully developed in France as it is in the United States, and other influences may be powerful in cases where party identification is lacking. These other factors are, of course, left-right positioning, attitudes toward Charles de Gaulle, and degrees of attachment to the Catholic Church. Each of these has been found separately to be a potentially powerful influence on French voting choices. These three factors, along with party identification, constitute our battery of long-term determinants of the vote.

While the inventory of long-term forces that we will apply to France is considerably larger than that which usually applies in the United States, the situation concerning short-term forces is just the reverse. Numerous factors that might have a transient effect on the way people cast their ballots can be imagined, and various combinations of these have been included in models of voting behavior in the United States. We shall confine ourselves to two classes of short-term factors. One of these concerns the voter's position on major issues. Earlier, we explored voters' perceptions of the issue positions of the parties and the candidates. Now we shall investigate the extent to which issue positions have an independent effect on voting choices after the impact of the long-term forces has been taken into account. The other short-term force is made up of affective reactions, favorable and unfavorable, to the various parties. There has been no reason to discuss such measures up to this point, but the multiple indications that we have encountered of the importance of partisan attitudes as a major factor in shaping people's electoral orientations lead us now to investigate the extent to which such transient party reactions may play a role in voting decisions in France in the absence of more enduring partisan attachments.

Following Campbell (1971), therefore, we view the voting act as a simultaneous decision process consisting of two components. The first includes the long-term forces that shape the individual's vote and give the overall electoral process whatever stability it has from one election to another. The second consists of the short-term forces that operate in addition to the long-term forces and contribute to the variations in electoral outcomes from one period to another. We shall employ multiple regression in order to determine initially how much of the variance in left-right voting at the first ballot in France in 1967 was due to the long-term forces, and then to determine how much of the residual variance in the vote can be attributed to the short-term forces after the effects of the long-term forces have been removed. We shall proceed with the analysis in two stages, dealing first with the variables that constitute the set of long-term forces, and then with those making up the short-term forces.

Long-Term Influences on the Vote

The four long-term forces are not, of course, equally distributed throughout the French electorate. Virtually every one of our mass respondents may be placed upon the Gaullism and clericalism scales, but that is not the case for left-right party identification or left-right location. We saw in Chapter 3 that the incidence of party identification in France falls far short of blanketing the entire electorate, even when one includes references to political leaders, left-right tendencies, or groups that are not literally parties although they have some political relevance. Indeed, the shortfall in that regard is at its most severe for our analysis in this chapter, because here we define party identification as including only attachment to "true" political parties. References to political leaders are excluded on the ground that most of them refer to de Gaulle and may be considered as subsumed in our virtually universal

Gaullism measure. References to left-right tendencies are not counted as partisan identifications because they presumably receive expression in the left-right location variable. We lose virtually no information by giving a strict interpretation to party identification, and by doing so we not only make that variable more comparable with its counterpart in other countries, but we also avoid counting certain references twice.

The only definitional problem associated with left-right locations is whether to include the *marais*, those people who assign themselves a centrist location (50) but who have no interest in politics. In this case (and contrary to our strict construction of party identification) we have adopted a relaxed definition by including the marais. The main reason for doing so is to maximize case numbers. This does no harm. Scores of 50 are so close to the mean for both the self-assigned left-right variable and the dependent variable with which it is being associated in the regression analysis (the left-right vote at the first ballot in 1967) that it can have little effect on the results other than to dampen the coefficients slightly, and that suits our conservative evaluative outlook nicely. But we know from Chapter 4 that not everyone in the French electorate can be located on the left-right axis, even when we include the marais. And there is much less than a complete overlap between party identification and left-right positioning. Some people who identify with parties do not assign themselves left-right locations, and even more people who do think of themselves in left-right terms do not at the same time identify with political parties.

In order to get as fine an estimate as possible of the joint effects of the long-term forces on French voting decisions, we must partition the voting population according to the distribution of those forces. Table 10-1 shows that this division results in seven groups, four of which will occupy our attention. Group 1, which consists of people who have all four of the attributes constituting long-term electoral forces, is the largest. This group represents only slightly more than half of the entire electorate, but it includes the most politically involved people in France and embraces almost two-thirds of the people who actually cast a partisan vote at the first ballot in 1967. Group 2, consisting of people with three of the long-term attributes, but not with a self-location on the left-right scale, is the smallest of those we shall discuss. This group, the next most involved politically, constituted some 5 percent of both the total electorate and the actual voters in 1967. Group 3 includes people who have all of the long-term orientations except party identification, while Group 4 consists of people who have only the two near-universal long-term attributes: attitudes toward de Gaulle and degree of attachment to the Catholic Church. Group 3 is the third most politically involved of our groups and represents almost as large a proportion of the voters as of the entire electorate. Group 4 is less involved politically, on the average, and although it includes 12 percent of the electorate, it contributes only 6 percent of the actual voters. Groups 5–7 represent a miscella-

Table 10-1. Distribution of long-term electoral orientations across total electorate and 1967 voters (first ballot), France, 1967.

Voter group	Long-term electoral orientations				Percentage of total electorate	Percentage of 1967 voters (first ballot)
	Party identification	Left-right location	Gaullism	Clericalism		
1	$+^a$	+	+	+	53	65
2	+	0	+	+	5	6
3	0	+	+	+	24	22
4	0	0	+	+	12	6
5	0	0	n.a.	n.a.	b	b
6	0	0	n.a.	+	b	b
7	n.a.	c	c	c	6	1
Total					100	100
Weighted N					(2007.0)	(1373.4)

a. Indicates possession of long-term attribute.
b. Less than ½ of 1 percent.
c. All cases were excluded when party identification was not ascertained, regardless of whether other attributes were present.
n.a. = not ascertained

neous category consisting almost wholly of people who are classified as missing data on the party identification variable. This category is, on the average, more involved politically than Group 4, but though it includes more than 5 percent of the electorate, it contributes less than 1 percent of the active voters. As we are concerned only with actual voters, we shall not discuss Groups 5–7 in this chapter.

Multiple regressions were run, with the left-right vote at the first ballot of 1967 as the dependent variable, for each of the four groups containing two or more long-term voting attributes, and for all four of them combined.[2] Recall that the left-right vote is the respondent's partisan choice expressed as the mean left-right value assigned to that party by the entire sample (see Chapter 4 for the logic of the operation and Appendix B for operational details). The principal results appear in Table 10-2. These go a

Table 10-2. Relative effects of long-term electoral orientations on left-right vote in France, 1967 (first ballot).[a]

Voter group	Party identification	Left-Right location	Gaullism	Clericalism	Multiple R^2
1 (881)					
Coefficient	0.641	0.102	0.116	0.069	.686
Beta	0.621	0.107	0.137	0.075	
T-ratio	22.554	4.178	5.734	3.305	
2 (82)					
Coefficient	0.666	0	0.175	0.083	.666
Beta	0.635	0	0.189	0.073	
T-ratio	8.048	0	2.378	1.004[b]	
3 (306)					
Coefficient	0	0.233	0.186	0.182	.201
Beta	0	0.226	0.209	0.197	
T-ratio	0	5.290	4.925	4.666	
4 (83)					
Coefficient	0	0	0.195	0.058	.037
Beta	0	0	0.174	0.050	
T-ratio	0	0	2.670	0.767[b]	
1–4 (1352)					
Coefficient	0.624	0.151	0.157	0.120	.566
Beta	0.489	0.139	0.176	0.123	
T-ratio	24.858	7.479	9.660	7.081	

a. Numbers of cases are in parentheses.
b. Not significant.

long way toward demonstrating the relative importance of party identification among the long-term factors that pertain to the partisan vote in France.
The decisive consideration lies in the difference between the results for
Groups 1 and 2, on the one hand, and Groups 3 and 4, on the other hand.
Where party identification is present, as in Groups 1 and 2, the long-term
factors together account for two-thirds or more of the variance in the left-
right vote. Where it is absent, as in Groups 3 and 4, the amount of variance
accounted for drops to 20 percent or less.

Furthermore, when party identification is present, its great potency relative to that of the other long-term forces is not an artifact of collinearity
among the independent variables. Though our independent variables inter-
correlate with one another at comparatively high levels, that intercorrelation is not such as to degrade the regression estimate by the presence of
collinearity.[3] The relative importance of party identification as a long-term
factor in the vote is, therefore, apparent not only from a between-group
comparison, but also from a comparison of the effects of party identification
with those of the other long-term forces within each of the groups. When
party identification is present, it is by far the major correlate of the vote.
And whether party identification is present or not, the other abiding electoral influences cut a comparatively narrow swath.

Predictive Power of Long-Term Forces

The predictive power of the long-term electoral forces depends, of course,
on how many of them are present and whether party identification in particular is among them. But even across the entire set of voters, taking into account the "actual" measures of the long-term influences where they are
present and substituting essentially average values for them when they are
missing,[4] our simple additive linear model accounts for some 57 percent of
the variance in the left-right vote. That value compares quite satisfactorily
with those reported by Fiorina (1981) for the six instances in which he applied models of "retrospective voting" to elections for the House of Representatives in the United States. The mean variance accounted for across
Fiorina's six tests was .56.[5] Of course, Fiorina's objective was to demonstrate
that the concept of retrospective voting could be supported empirically, and
not to maximize the amount of variance accounted for in the congressional
vote. Yet it is not without theoretical interest that the concept of retrospective voting is in a general sense no more powerful a predictive tool for congressional voting in the United States than a simpler model of long-term
influences is for legislative voting in France.[6]

Although "variance accounted for" is a perfectly legitimate measure of
the predictive power of a model such as ours, for which the dependent variable consists of a multiplicity of scores representing the locations of various
political parties on a metric scale, it is less applicable to situations such as
those that prevail in the United States, where electoral choices (and conse-

quently the dependent variable) are dichotomous. In that case a more appropriate criterion of success is the proportion of cases "correctly" predicted. Indeed, for the Lindon and Weill (1974) model, which predicts to nominal categories, the proportion of cases correctly predicted is the only applicable method of validation.[7]

When we apply the criterion of the proportion of cases correctly predicted to Groups 1 and 2 combined (those groups that include party identifiers), our simple model based exclusively on long-term factors stands comparison nicely with both Fiorina's model of retrospective voting and the Lindon-Weill model. Fiorina tested his predictions against reports of actual votes; Lindon and Weill tested theirs against reports of vote intentions. The mean proportion of cases correctly predicted by Fiorina's model across his six tests of legislative voting in the United States is 77.7 percent. The Lindon-Weill (1974, p. 86) model correctly predicted 75 percent of the cases, although the base of the calculation is not wholly clear. Our long-term model correctly predicted 73.9 percent of the cases.[8]

This citing of comparative proportions, as satisfactory as it is, presents the results of our long-term model in somewhat weak form. Fiorina's model predicts votes in a two-party system, for which chance alone would correctly predict close to half the votes, while we are predicting votes cast for candidates represented by no fewer than fifteen different scores on our dependent variable (see Table B-4 in Appendix B).[9] Even Lindon and Weill (1974), whose model was prepared within the context of French legislative elections, predict only to the four major party groups that competed at the election of 1973. If, still including only Groups 1 and 2, we consider just the predictions of the vote for the four major groupings that competed at the 1967 election, our success rate rises slightly to 75.5 percent, thereby matching that reported by Lindon and Weill, although the two figures may not be literally comparable.

Lindon and Weill (1974, p. 188) also supply the proportions of predictions that were confirmed by expressions of vote intention for each of the four main competing political formations in 1973. It is interesting to array these alongside the predictive "success" rates of our own model for essentially the same four party groupings in 1967 (see Table 10-3).[10] What is of interest here is not the "between-model" differences of proportions correctly predicted for each party, for they may not be strictly comparable, but rather the difference in "within-model" variations in predictive accuracy. There is considerably more variation in the success rates of our model across the four partisan groupings than there is for the Lindon-Weill model. Our model's predictions of Communist and Gaullist votes are confirmed at much higher rates than are its other predictions, those of Federation or centrist votes. The Lindon-Weill model predicts vote intentions for all four groups more or less equally well.

This difference in variability of results almost surely stems from differ-

Table 10-3. Percentages of predicted votes confirmed by reports of vote intention or of actual vote, by party, France, 1967 (first ballot).

Predictive model	Party			
	Communist party	Socialist party	Reformist movement	Majority (Gaullist)
Lindon-Weill (for 1973)	74	74	68	81
	Communist party	Federation	Democratic Center	Gaullists
Converse-Pierce, long-term forces only, Groups 1 and 2 (for 1967)	89	56	52	87

ences between the two models in regard to the character and distribution of the predictor variables employed. The Lindon-Weill model relies heavily on measures of proximity between the voter and discrete parties, and that procedure allows broad scope for the expression of all forms of partisan attitudes, from strong and enduring partisan identification to current vote preference. The model sums so many scores reflecting attitudes toward partisan objects, which are designated nominally in the survey instrument, that partisanship, broadly construed, may be said to be its dominant predictor variable. The relative accuracy of the model's predictions reflects the association between partisan attitudes and the partisan vote, the closeness of which our own model confirms. And as the association between partisanship and the vote is more or less constant regardless of party, a model that rests on partisanship as the predictor will produce essentially the same results for each party tested.

Our own model, though more parsimonious than the Lindon-Weill model, nevertheless takes into account more of the factors that structure the vote in France. We include party identification, of course, but that is only one factor among four. Attitudes toward de Gaulle, left-right locations, and attitudes toward religion are also included among the predictor variables. Thus the model allows for the interplay of all four of those orienting forces, whatever form that interplay takes.

The variation in the results across the parties suggests what some of those forms may be. The high confirmation rates for the predictions of Communist and Gaullist votes indicate that there are two polar groups of French voters, each of which fits the terms of the model quite well by clustering at one extremity or the other of the scale of predicted values. We can reasonably assume that one of these groups tends to identify with a leftist party, be hostile to de Gaulle, feel leftist in general sentiment, and be anti-clerical; while the other tends to be its polar opposite—attached to a rightist party, pro-Gaullist, rightist in left-right orientation, and proclerical.

The situation is more complicated for the people whose scores on the basic predictor variables do not tend to co-vary in one polar direction or the other, but rather to express the "cross-cutting" possibilities of our multiple measures. Thus we may have anticlerical rightists, pro-Gaullist leftists, or any one of a whole gamut of possible combinations. Our model ultimately places these people somewhere along the inner segments of the scale of predicted values; but the margin of predictive error is larger for the people who fall within that range, because of the ambiguities of their attitudinal mixtures, than it is for those who fall closer to the extremities.

Whatever the reason for the differential accuracy of our model's prediction of votes for the various parties, it cannot be the complexity of the electoral field. Indeed, the success rate of our long-term model (combining Groups 1 and 2) *increases* with the complexity of that field. The proportion of "correct" predictions (across all electoral alternatives) in districts where only three parties competed is 69 percent; in four-party districts it is 73 percent; and in districts with five or more parties it is 77 percent. And when, still combining Groups 1 and 2, we take into account only the votes for the four main competing partisan groups of 1967, the variation in "success" rates in districts with three, four, and five or more parties, respectively, sharpens still further: 68 percent, 75 percent, and 79 percent. As simple as it is, our long-term model acts as a fine-edged cutting tool.

Of course, all of these comparatively comforting results depend on our restricting the analysis to the voters in Groups 1 and 2, the approximately 70 percent of the actual voters reporting a true party identification. Our "success" rates attenuate considerably when we apply the long-term model to the entire electorate. Across the electorate as a whole, the model correctly predicts only 61 percent of the votes. This reduced level of accuracy is directly attributable to the necessity to substitute surrogate scores for the respondents who lacked either a party identification, a left-right location, or both. The scores we employed when those variables were missing—the mean left-right party identification score (44.1) and the score of 50 for left-right locations—are perfectly reasonable, but they are not really neutral. They push the great majority of voters to whom they apply too far toward the lower range of the scale of predicted vote values (which, it may be recalled, tends to match the votes for leftist parties). When we consider only the people with a party identification (Groups 1 and 2), the same proportion of incorrect predictions errs toward the right as toward the left; but when we take the entire electorate into account, 65 percent of the incorrect predictions err by indicating votes to the left of those actually cast by the relevant respondents. This result shows up plainly in the proportions of correct predictions for each of the main party groups. These remain the same for predictions of Communist votes (88 percent), whether we consider the entire electorate or only voters with true party identifications. But the proportions of correct predictions of votes for the other main party groupings drop sharply when we consider all the voters rather than party identifiers only. Correct predictions of non-Communist left votes drop by more than 10 percentage points, and those for centrist or Gaullist votes fall by 20 percentage points.

Moreover, the graduation in proportions of cases correctly predicted in relation to the complexity of the party system attenuates markedly across the entire electorate. Traces of it remain, but the three steps (54 percent, 61 percent, and 62 percent) based on the number of parties running impress much less than they do when the analysis is confined to voters having a party identification. Nevertheless, the overall results of our long-term model are positive, statistically significant, and generalizable across the entire French electorate.

A Closer Look at Party Identification

We have seen that party identification is much more closely associated with left-right voting in France than are any of the other long-term forces we incorporated into our model. There remains uncertainty, however, about the nature of the causal relationship between these two variables. Does party identification command the vote, or is the relationship the other way around, with the vote causing the partisan attachment? Or do the two variables simply co-vary in common reaction to the play of other, unmeasured forces?

Questions of this sort do not concern us with regard to the other long-term forces we have been considering. It is highly implausible that the electorate's attitudes toward religion are the effect, rather than the cause, of their partisan votes. It is not likely, either, that the voters' current electoral preferences account for their attitudes toward de Gaulle or their sense of left-right positioning.[11] The causal problem is central only for party identification.

The reasons for this were set forth at some length in Chapter 3, which contains our most extended discussion of party loyalties in France. On the one hand, we found evidence that the phenomenon of party identification does indeed exist in France, in that where it is present it performs the same stabilizing electoral role as it does in the United States and other countries where its existence is less problematical than it is in France (see Figure 3-5). We found also that for French voters who claimed to have a partisan identification in both 1967 and 1968 the cross-time stability correlation was quite respectable ($r = .83$), by all odds the strongest we have encountered in this study for any political attitude.

On the other hand, we also know that cultural and political obstacles to the development of strong party loyalties exist in France, and that the incidence of party identification is not so high as it is in various other democracies. Even more important, we know that there is considerable movement in and out of a professed party identification in France, and that a substantial amount of that movement is accompanied by changes in the partisan vote (see Figure 3-3).

All this suggests that our 1967 party identifiers include a mix of people evidencing two distinct types of behavior. First, some profess a party identification not only in 1967 but again in 1968. We shall call them "repeated identifiers." This does not mean that they necessarily choose the same party in both years. That many of them do, however, is captured by the high continuity correlation for party identification of $r = .83$ which we have cited for this group. Within the group, which seems an apt counterpart for identifiers in the United States, it is reasonable to imagine that the causal flow is predominantly from identification to vote.

Second, our 1967 professed party identifiers include an uncommon mixture of persons whose claimed attachments are so slight that they report none at all in 1968. We shall call them "intermittent identifiers," to distinguish them from the repeated identifiers. Why they produce such casual reports is not clear, but it would not be surprising if their statements expressed current vote intentions, rather than abiding partisan loyalties. For this group, we could expect that the causal flow would be predominantly from vote to identification.

Of course, it is impossible to establish such causal relationships definitely with our instruments. We can, however, look separately at the repeated and intermittent identifiers to see whether certain differences in their behavior might lend plausibility to the suggestion that two different causal patterns are concealed within the overall association, displayed by our regression model, between party identification and the vote.

Accordingly, we partitioned our 1967 party identifiers into two groups, depending upon our 1968 data to make the crucial discrimination. Then we reran our regression model separately for the repeated and the intermittent identifiers, including the same familiar set of four predictor variables, with the left-right vote in 1967 as the dependent variable. We also performed a variant of an operation reported in Chapter 4, used when we were trying to estimate whether party identification or sense of own left-right location was the better predictor of the partisan vote. At that time, we asked ourselves which of those two variables, as measured in 1967, predicted better to the 1968 vote (and we found that party identification in 1967 correlated marginally more closely with that vote than 1967 left-right location did). The problem cast in this form helps to explain causal confusions, since any variable that is volatile in the short term will predict to the vote much more poorly after a year's time lapse than it may to the contemporaneous vote, whereas one with a longer-term meaning will hold up well. Therefore, for the present analysis, contrasting repeated and intermittent identifiers, we predicted to the 1968 vote as well as to the more routine 1967 vote.

The model performs very differently for these two types of identifiers, as Table 10-4 indicates. Among repeated identifiers, the association between party identification and the 1967 vote is very close, and that between 1967 party identification and the 1968 vote is also impressive. For the intermittent identifiers, the picture is quite different. There is considerable attenuation of the association between 1967 party identification and the 1967 vote, and the association between party identification in 1967 and the 1968 vote fades dramatically, toward statistical insignificance, just as we would expect in view of our more skeptical causal hypothesis for this group.

This analysis indicates that most of the overall association between party identification and the vote—especially the more telling 1968 vote—is generated by the repeated identifiers. These people constitute a large pro-

Table 10-4. Relative effects of long-term electoral orientations on left-right vote, by type of party identifier, France, 1967 and 1968 (first ballots).[a]

Identifier type	Long-term electoral orientations				
	Party identification (1967)	Left-right location (1967)	Clericalism (1967)	Gaullism (1967)	Multiple R^2
Predictions to the 1967 vote					
Repeated identifiers (238)					
Coefficient	0.775	0.061	−0.042	0.104	.765
Beta	0.768	0.065	−0.043	0.120	
T-ratio	15.335	1.519[b]	1.116[b]	2.699	
Intermittent identifiers (99)					
Coefficient	0.578	0.147	0.110	0.148	.614
Beta	0.543	0.148	0.112	0.177	
T-ratio	6.163	1.722[b]	1.409[b]	2.186	
Predictions to the 1968 vote					
Repeated identifiers (240)					
Coefficient	0.603	0.163	−0.007	0.127	.748
Beta	0.625	0.184	−0.008	0.153	
T-ratio	12.007	4.099	0.198[b]	3.336	
Intermittent identifiers (84)					
Coefficient	0.210	0.171	0.089	0.265	.416
Beta	0.214	0.188	0.099	0.346	
T-ratio	1.981	1.772[b]	1.016[b]	3.469	

a. Numbers of cases are in parentheses.
b. Not significant.

portion of the active voters. They include everyone who had a true party identification both in 1967 and 1968, even if the party of identification changed between those two years; and they were a comfortable majority of the people who actually cast ballots in 1967. For these people we cannot say unequivocally that the party identification produced the vote, rather than that the vote produced the party identification. Indeed, for some of the repeated identifiers the vote did cause the expression of party identification. But where we have repeated identifiers whose party identifications at time-1 predict their votes at time-2 more than tolerably well, there are grounds for presuming that the party identification is logically prior to the vote at both time-1 and time-2, particularly when there is evidence (see Chapter 3) that party identification is in fact associated with stabilizing the vote.

The intermittent identifiers are another matter. Their professed attachment to a political party is more of a temporary shelter than a firm anchorage. Whatever partisan attachments these people had were weak, and their value as predictors even of the vote at time-1 is limited, as Table 10-4 shows. Just as some of the repeated identifiers may have confounded their partisan attachments with their current electoral preferences—although we believe most of them did not—some intermittent identifiers may indeed have had partisan attachments that determined their votes. But it is likely that when asked to which party they habitually felt closest, most of those intermittent identifiers merely stated their electoral preference at the moment. There was also, of course, a good deal of casualness in their declarations of party identification. If there had not been, the association between expressed partisan attachment and electoral choice would have been closer.

What is it, then, that accounts (in a causal sense) for the electoral behavior of the intermittent identifiers? On the evidence presented in Table 10-4, it is attitudes toward de Gaulle. For intermittent identifiers, attitudes pro or con de Gaulle in 1967 were the best predictor of their 1968 vote. In Chapter 5 we suggested that Gaullism as a political force belongs to the class of attitudes that is most likely to affect the behavior of people who are otherwise lacking in basic political orientations. The behavior of these intermittent identifiers, whose reality as identifiers may even be cast into doubt, provides stark evidence of the extent to which Gaullism did play a residual, guiding electoral role.

So far, it is clear that for the some 70 percent of actual French voters who professed a true party identification in 1967, partisan attachments correlate closely with electoral choices, even after the effects of the other main long-term political forces have been discounted. Nevertheless, the picture is blurred in causal terms. For more than two-thirds of the identifiers, those who were repeatedly identified with some party, the correlation of those attachments with the vote is quite robust, and it is likely that those partisan attachments shaped electoral choices in a causal sense. But the intermittent identifiers who contribute to the healthy overall relationship between partisanship and the vote probably reflect the opposite causal ordering; their expressed party identification is simply an alternate statement of their current party preference.

Because our voting model expresses both of these contrasting causal orderings, it cannot serve as a summary statement of the relative extent to which party identification in France (along with the other long-term forces) shapes the partisan vote in a manner that is consistent with the theory underlying party identification. Our decomposition of the identifiers into repeated and intermittent categories, however, enables us to make some reasonable estimates. The best estimate is that repeated identifiers, who constituted more than half of the people actually voting in 1967, are driven far more powerfully by partisanship than by the other long-term forces. Furthermore, for those people, party identification is not only a relatively powerful electoral force; it is impressive in an absolute sense. In fact, the translation of *repeated* party identifications into electoral votes in France appears to be so direct as to suggest that party identification might actually be a more powerful electoral force in France than in the United States, where the theory underlying this force has been most widely accepted and most regularly applied. This possibility is not without a certain irony, in view of the skepticism expressed toward the notion that party identification plays the same stabilizing electoral role in France as in the United States.

France and the United States Compared

We tested a parallel long-term model of voting for the U.S. House of Representatives, using the data from the U.S. National Election Study of 1980.[12] The four independent variables employed were party identification, attitudes toward Ronald Reagan as registered on the standard thermometer scale, locations on the liberal-conservative dimension, and positions toward aid to minorities. These variables, of course, are not identical with the independent variables included in our long-term French model. The U.S. party identification variable combines the strength and direction of partisanship and includes both those who only "lean" toward the Democrats or the Republicans and those without any partisan attachments at all, whereas the French variable reflects only the direction of partisanship, and nonidentifiers do not have valid scale scores. Ronald Reagan had not dominated the politics of his country or even of his party for three decades, as de Gaulle had, and hence attitudes toward Reagan properly belong in the short-term category of candidate evaluations. The liberal-conservative dimension does not have the centuries' old centrality in elite political discourse that left-right terminology has in France. And voter position on the issue of government aid to minorities is not the same kind of stable condition as the degree of attachment to a church.

Yet for our purposes the U.S. variables are all tolerable equivalents of the French variables. The U.S. party identification variable can be adjusted to bring it closer to the French one. Reagan's mean thermometer score in 1980 (59.5) was not far distant from that of de Gaulle in 1967 (62.9). The liberal-conservative dimension captures much the same range of outlooks as the left-right dimension does. And the issue of aid to minorities can produce an emotional resonance not unlike that prompted by religion. The correspondence between the two sets of variables is far from ideal, but it is close enough; indeed, similar if not identical forces are being captured.

Three sets of regression analyses were run on the U.S. data. The first, designed to parallel the analysis of the four groups of French voters combined (Groups 1–4), included all those U.S. voters who cast a ballot for a Republican or Democratic candidate for the House of Representatives in 1980 in districts contested by the two major parties, and who were coded on one of the standard scale positions used in the U.S. national election studies to summarize party identification.[13] Missing data relating to party identification were excluded along with the stray off-scale cases. Where data were missing on attitudes toward Reagan, the mean score of 59.5 was substituted. Where data were missing on the liberal-conservative dimension and on attitudes toward aid to minorities, the neutral midpoint scores were incorporated. This substitution procedure, aimed at maximizing cases, paralleled the one we used when combining Groups 1–4 of the French data. Since nonidentifiers as well as identifiers are included, we have virtually all legislative voters for both countries.

The second set of U.S. analyses was designed to approximate the analysis of Group 1 of the French voters, which included only people who had a "true" party identification as well as valid scores on the other three vote predictors. Here, we included as true identifiers all respondents who expressed some form of attachment to one of the major parties, including "leaners" as well as both strong and weak Democrats and Republicans. Only pure independents were excluded.

The third set of analyses also included people with scores on all four independent variables, but counted as identifiers only those who spontaneously described themselves as Democrats or Republicans (whether weak or strong) and excluded the leaners (who described themselves as independents but admitted to thinking of themselves as closer to one of the major parties than to the other), along with those who firmly insisted that they were independents. That set will serve as our match on the U.S. side for the French "repeated identifiers," in the absence of a more direct measure of stable identification for the U.S. respondents in the 1980 study.

Two forms of regression analysis were run for each of these three sets of U.S. respondents. Inasmuch as the dependent variable was dichotomous (1 for a Republican vote; 0 for a Democratic vote), we first ran a logit model regression in order to ascertain the significance levels of the various independent variables and to determine the proportions of votes "correctly" predicted. Then we ran an ordinary least squares regression to estimate the relative importance of each of the significant independent variables in ways permitting direct comparison with the power of the equivalent variables in the French context.

The logit model regressions indicate that the four long-term forces correctly predict about three-fourths of the votes cast for major party candidates for the House of Representatives, with some variation depending upon which set of voters is included in the analysis. That approximates the success rate reported by Fiorina (1981) and Lindon and Weill (1974), and also achieved by our model for people with true party identifications (Groups 1 and 2). Yet only two of the four independent variables contained in the model are significant in the U.S. context: party identification and attitudes toward Reagan. Neither the liberal-conservative dimension nor the position on aid to minorities is significant for any of our three applications of the model.[14] It is not surprising that aid to minorities should have turned out to have no independent effect on the vote; the issue is a weak U.S. surrogate for religious attachments in France. The lack of potency of the liberal-conservative dimension is of more interest. It illustrates the paucity of long-term political forces in the United States, other than party identification, as compared with France, where left-right locations, attitudes toward de Gaulle, and religious outlooks all had a share, along with party identification, in fashioning voting decisions.

As we would expect, party identification proved to be a more powerful influence on the House vote than attitudes toward Reagan, in all three tests (see Table 10-5). Two other aspects of the analysis, however, are less predictable and therefore more interesting. On the one hand, the beta weights for party identification in all three regressions are uniformly smaller than the corresponding betas for party identification in the French analyses (see Tables 10-2 and 10-4), even when we standardize the party systems by dichotomizing the French vote results into the left and the right.[15] On the other hand, the effect of party identification on the House vote for our surrogate group of repeated identifiers is not very different from its effect for all party identifiers taken together. When we segregated out the repeated French identifiers, there was a healthy increase in the apparent influence of party identification on the vote, compared with that displayed by the same variable for all identifiers combined. The difference between the repeated identifiers and the intermittent ones is still more striking. Even allowing for differences between the ways in which we construed stability of party identification for the two sets of voters, French and American, the difference in results is noteworthy.

These various outcomes, for both France and the United States, admit

Table 10-5. Relative effects of long-term electoral orientations on major party vote for U.S. House of Representatives, by distribution of orientations, 1980.

Voter group	Beta	T-ratio	Percentage of cases correctly predicted
All with scalar code on summary party identification (N = 743)			
Summary party identification (PI)	0.373	12.44	74
Attitude toward Reagan	0.156	5.22	
Liberal-conservative location	0.071	n.s.	
Position on aid to minorities	0.061	n.s.	
All identifying strongly or weakly with major party or leaning toward major party (N = 513)			
Summary PI	0.382	9.15	74
Attitude toward Reagan	0.138	3.31	
Liberal-conservative location	0.066	n.s.	
Position on aid to minorities	0.016	n.s.	
All identifying strongly or weakly with major party (N = 366)			
Summary PI	0.400	8.02	78
Attitude toward Reagan	0.193	4.01	
Liberal-conservative location	0.066	n.s.	
Position on aid to minorities	0.016	n.s.	

n.s. = not significant.

of a common interpretation. Party identification is the only long-term political force of any magnitude in the United States that operates throughout the entire electorate. Its potency as an electoral force naturally varies with its strength and stability, but it is generally more stable in the United States than in France, and it operates as an electoral influence more uniformly in the U.S. than in France. Therefore, for the United States, it makes little difference, in regard to the coefficients reflecting the relative strength of party identification as a factor in the House vote, whether or not we base our analysis on the total electorate, on party identifiers only, or on some subset of presumed "stable" identifiers. They all act in more or less the same way (at least for congressional voting), and we may assume with some confidence that for each group the causal direction of the variables in question runs, for most voters, from party identification to electoral choice.

In France, the situation is more complex. Party identification is not well developed there because partisan objects are obscured by the instability of the party system; the intergenerational transmission of partisan attachments is further inhibited by cultural factors; and the incentive for developing party identifications is reduced by the presence of other long-term electoral cues (attitudes toward de Gaulle, left-right orientations, and religious attitudes). Fewer French than U.S. citizens profess to have partisan attachments, and fewer still actually develop stable party attachments.

When stable party identifications do develop in the face of all these obstacles, they have a major effect on electoral choice. They quite submerge the other long-term forces, and they also surpass the power of party identification in the United States, or at least they did in the 1980 House voting. We cannot demonstrate conclusively that here partisanship is the cause and electoral choice the effect. But our considerable circumstantial evidence suggests very strongly that, for the great majority of stable identifiers, this is the true causal relationship. We saw in Chapter 2 that voting stability in France matches normal U.S. levels (controlling for relevant probabilities of vote repetition in the two countries). Chapter 3 showed the contribution that partisan attachments make to voting stability in France as well as elsewhere. There is more "noise" in the relationship between partisanship and voting in France than in the United States because unstable identifiers are more numerous in France. But there is no reason to believe that when conditions are equivalent, party identification plays a less stabilizing role in France than in the United States.

To sum up this section on long-term influences on the vote, party identification is "dear" in France and "cheap" in the United States. In France, it is not come by easily, it is hard to develop, and it suffers from competition with other powerful social and political forces. When it does develop, however, it has an uncommonly powerful effect on electoral choices. In the United States, party identification is almost automatically acquired, easily maintained, and largely independent of social forces. It is the single most important factor in the vote for most citizens, and over time such an attachment can become well-nigh impregnable. But, as our brief examination of voting for the House of Representatives in 1980 has shown, the electoral effects of party identification, though real, can also be no more than modest. Short-term forces can also play an important role in shaping electoral choices in the United States, as they do in France.

Short-Term Forces

Following Campbell (1971), our overall model includes not only the four long-term forces but also two classes of short-term forces: the voters' position on major issues; and party reactions, that is, the play of partisan sympathies other than those subsumed under party identification itself. These are not, of course, the only short-term forces that might affect the way in which people cast their votes, but they were not casually selected for examination. Whereas issue positions as a quintessential short-term force are incorporated into virtually every model of legislative or presidential voting, residual partisanship has not, to our knowledge, been considered separately in any previous voting model.[16] In France, however, where party identification is not well developed, short-term reactions to the various parties can be expected to play an important role in shaping votes.[17]

Issue Positions

The voters' positions on five issues were incorporated into the model: government subsidies for religious schools, inequality in the distribution of income, greater government effort in favor of education, independence from the United States in foreign policy, and European integration. The first four issue positions were measured by single questions, while attitudes toward the fifth, European integration, are scale scores based on five questions.[18] We chose these five issues because they are all directly related to the "linkage issues" that we employed in Chapter 9 when investigating the extent to which the electorate linked parties and candidates with issues. We have therefore limited the analysis to positions on those issues for which we also have information concerning whether and how the voters linked them with candidates or parties.

Following Campbell (1971), our analysis treated the voters' positions on the five issues as independent variables in stepwise regressions for which the dependent variable was the residual variance in the left-right vote at the first ballot of 1967 after the effects of the long-term factors in the vote had been removed. Two separate regressions were run for each of the four main voter groups described in Table 10-1. One form of regression included the voters' issue positions without regard to whether they linked the issues with candidates or parties. Cases of "no opinion" or "don't know" were coded at the indifference point, so that missing data are minimal. The second form of regression took the voters' associations of issues with parties or candidates into account. Nonneutral positions on a given issue were counted only if the respondent associated the issue with a party or a candidate; otherwise, the respondent was scored as indifferent, even if he or she had actually expressed a nonneutral attitude. The reason for this was that if voters' positions on issues are to have some effect on their vote, they need to have at least a minimal notion of the positions of the parties or candidates on those issues.

The results of the analyses can be summarized easily. Of the forty coefficients obtained (four groups times five issues times two definitions of issue position), only seven proved to be statistically significant; the betas for the significant issues are recorded in Table 10–6. Among the voters in Group 1, which contains those involved people with valid scores on all our long-term predictors, issue positions accounted significantly for less than 2 percent of the *residual* variance, regardless of whether the voters linked a party or a candidate with the issues involved. Because issue positions, whether linked

Table 10-6. Independent effects of issue positions on the left-right vote, France, 1967.[a]

| Voter group | Issues | | | | Multiple R^2 |
	Educational development	European integration	Distribution of income	Independent foreign policy	
1					
Issue positions only	—	−0.091	0.083	—	.016
Issue positions and links to parties or candidates	0.106	−0.088	—	—	.020
3					
Issue positions only	—	0.090	—	—	.008
4					
Issue positions and links to parties or candidates	—	—	0.288	−0.191	.128

a. Betas given for significant issue positions only.

or not, had no significant independent effect at all on the votes cast by the people in Group 2, they are not included in the table. Positions on one issue had a minuscule influence on the vote among people in Group 3 who did not link that issue with a party or candidate, but not on the vote of people in the same group who made such a linkage.

Issue positions only had a substantial, significant effect on the vote among the comparatively small number of voters in Group 4, which contains those whose storehouse of abiding political cues is particularly impoverished. For these people, positions on two of our five issues had a relatively important impact on their electoral decisions, *provided they not only had a position on the issue but also associated the issue with at least one party or candidate.* For those comparatively few people, two issue positions accounted for almost 13 percent of the residual variance. As long-term factors accounted for very little of the variance in their left-right voting in the first place, that figure translates into almost the same proportion of *total* variance accounted for by the long-term forces and issue positions combined. Nevertheless, the amount of total variance in their vote that is accounted for by the long-term and short-term forces combined is still less than that explained by the long-term forces alone for Group 3, and much less than that explained by the long-term forces alone for Groups 1 and 2.

The particular issues that moved (or failed to move) Group 4 are of some interest. Attitudes toward the distribution of income were the principal force at work, expressing the conventionally expected polarization in left-right voting terms. Independence from the United States in foreign policy was a less important, but still significant, factor. For this issue, opinions in favor of national independence were associated with rightist voting, and those less concerned about independence with leftist electoral choices. Thus, for this small and minimally involved segment of the electorate, leftist voting was associated with support for redistribution of income and cooperation with the United States, while rightist voting was associated with the distributive status quo and national independence. This combination of issue positions and electoral orientations does not reflect any common, coherent ideological conflict.

For the great majority of French voters, therefore, positions on the issues chosen as most central to the policy cleavages of this period have virtually no operative effect on electoral choices apart from their integration into partisan attachments and left-right orientations. The independent effect of issue positions on electoral choices is negligible for people who claim to identify with parties, or who perceive themselves to be located on the left-right axis, or both. Whatever the pull of issue positions may be for these voters, it is inextricably woven into the other, presumably enduring political orientations.

The only people for whom issue positions play a visibly guiding role are those who lack party identifications or left-right locations. In the absence of these basic steering mechanisms, some issue positions play an observable, though not large, electoral role.

A further condition of the effectiveness of issue positions is that the voter have some ability to locate the issues within the field of competing parties and candidates. We have applied only a minimal requirement in that regard—that the voter associate the issue with any candidate or any party—but even that limited qualification produces clearly observable results consistent with logical expectations. The fact remains, however, that considering the electorate as a whole, the play of specific issue positions as independent determinants of the vote approaches the vanishing point.

Party Reactions

The analysis to test for the influence of the more transient reactions to various parties followed the same basic procedure as the investigation of the effects of issue positions. For each of our four groups of French voters, a regression was run in which the dependent variable was the residual variance of the left-right vote after the effects of the long-term forces had been removed. The predictor variable was a new term expressing net partisan sympathy, defined as the respondent's sympathy for the most favored rightist party available at the first ballot in the respondent's district, less his or her sympathy for the most favored leftist party available.[19]

Somewhat surprisingly, net party sympathy proves to be statistically significant for Group 1 of the French voters, although—quite unsurprisingly—it accounts for a bare 1 percent of the residual variance in the left-right vote. As one would expect, the partisan sympathies of these voters are already virtually exhausted by their professed partisan identifications. For Group 2, net party sympathy is not statistically significant. But for Groups 3 and 4, which include voters without habitual partisan attachments, net party sympathy is both statistically significant and accounts for about 5 percent of the residual variance in the vote. For Group 4, this is a less powerful effect than was produced by the two issue positions that were significant for that group when we tested for the impact of issues after the long-term forces had been taken into account. Nevertheless, net party sympathy is as important in shaping the votes of the people of Group 4 as is Gaullism, the only long-term force applicable to Group 4 that we found to be significant. If we abandon the distinction between long-term and short-term forces, and simply run a stepwise regression of the left-right vote on net party sympathy and Gaullism (the two significant factors in the vote for Group 4), net party sympathy enters the regression first, accounting for more than 7 percent of the variance, and Gaullism enters second, raising the total amount of variance explained to somewhat more than 9 percent. The voters in Group 4 have little to guide them through the electoral labyrinth, but partisan sympathies (however transient they may be) serve as a surer thread than attitudes toward de Gaulle.

The relative potency of party preferences is of less theoretical interest among the Group 4 voters than it is among the more numerous voters of Group 3, who share three long-term electoral orientations—all but party identification. This group raises in a new form the issue first discussed in Chapter 4 concerning the relative impact of left-right locations and partisanship on the vote. Our examination in this chapter of the influence of various combinations of long-term forces suggests strongly that party identification surpasses left-right positioning as a determinant of left-right voting, although this is probably true only of that segment of voters who express a partisan attachment repeatedly in the interview situation. Our investigation of net party sympathy indicates that partisan preferences apart from those subsumed by party identification may also outstrip left-right locations in shaping electoral choices. If, once again, we make no distinction between long-term and short-term forces, and regress the left-right vote of the people in Group 3 on net party sympathy, own left-right location, clericalism, and Gaullism, we find that those predictors enter the equation in the same order and that net party sympathy alone accounts for more than 20 percent of the variance in the vote, while all four independent variables together account for about 28 percent of the variance. Here, however, we run up against the causal problem in its most severe form. Partisan sympathies, as registered on the "thermometer" scale, are never more than one-third as stable as expressions of habitual party attachments; and if some of these attachments may actually be the effects of electoral choices rather than their causes, this is even more likely to be true of party sympathies. Thus the causal property of these transient reactions to the parties is suspect. But for people without regular party attachments, the steering capacity of the other potential electoral forces—whether long-term or short-term—is not particularly impressive; for some people, at least, party sympathy may be prior to the partisan vote, and may even be the embryo of a more enduring partisan attachment.

Conclusions

In this chapter, we have adopted a model and a method first employed by Campbell (1971) to measure the impact of various influences on the partisan first-ballot vote in France. The model rests on the distinction between long-term and short-term forces. The method involves partitioning the French electorate according to the number and combination of long-term electoral orientations which they share. First, the relative effects of the long-term forces on the vote are determined. Then, the effects of the short-term forces on variations in the vote not already "explained" by the long-term forces are computed. Thus, the impacts on the vote of both the long-term and the short-term forces are measured wholly independently of each other.

With regard to the long-term forces, the principal finding is that party identification registers as far more closely associated with the partisan vote than any of the other factors tested. Left-right locations, Gaullism, and religious attitudes count for little when party identification is present; indeed, they fail to impress even in the case of voters who do not claim to be attached to any particular party.

It is doubtful, however, that party identification is such a powerful direct cause as it appears to be of the votes cast by all the people who profess a partisan attachment in an interview situation. When all such French "identifiers" are grouped together (even when the category is confined to people expressing an identification with a "true" political party), the association between party identification and the vote is driven up because of the combination of persons who repeatedly express some identifications, whose electoral choices are in all probability motivated by their partisan attachments, and the "intermittent" identifiers, whose sporadically stated partisan attachments, when given, are often only alternate expressions of their current electoral preferences. Consequently, it is not possible to reduce the electoral impact of party identification in France to some single summary statistic. A reasonable estimate, however, is that for repeated identifiers, who comprise somewhat more than half the people who actually cast a ballot, party identification is by far the most powerful electoral force, one that stands comparison with the operative effect of party identification on legislative voting in the United States, which we also investigated in order to acquire a basis of comparison for our French findings.

We concluded from this work that persistent party identifications provide most of the long-term stability which exists in French mass electoral choices, assisted, at a lower level of effectiveness, by attitudes toward de Gaulle, sense of left-right location, and—least powerful of the long-term forces when taken in conjunction with the others—religious attitudes. When partisan attachments do develop in France in the face of competing influences, they appear to grow harder and stronger by absorbing and subsuming those rival forces.

Following the Campbell (1971) model, we also tested the role of issue positions as a short-term force, and found that for the great majority of the electorate they have virtually no independent impact on the vote, apart from long-term orientations. For one small group of voters, that containing the least politically involved people in the electorate, including those least affected by long-term electoral forces, positions on two of the five issues considered had a substantial effect on their votes, although only among those who had at least some minimal perception of which party or candidate was associated with these issues. It is not enough that voters simply have positions on the issues; logically enough, they must also have some sense of how the issues fit into the field of electoral choice. But more important than the finding that presumably short-term issue positions affect the electoral choices of somewhat more than 5 percent of France's voters is the finding that they have virtually no effect on the overwhelming majority of the electorate after the impact of the long-term forces has been taken into account. It should be clear that we are *not* saying that issues do not count for French voters who have true party identifications or self-assigned left-right locations. What we *are* saying is that whatever the role issue positions may have for such voters, it is already mediated through those other long-term electoral influences.

Lastly, we examined the second short-term force, relative partisan sympathies other than those expressed through true party identification, and found that they had some impact on the residual variance in the vote after the effects of the long-term forces had been removed for the two groups of voters who were without true party identification. The magnitude of that impact was not great, but neither was that of the long-term forces themselves for those particular groups of voters. We dropped the distinction between long-term and short-term forces, and investigated the relative effects of those long-term forces that had proven to be statistically significant and our presumably short-term measure of relative partisan preferences, which we labeled net party sympathy. Here we found that net party sympathy outstripped the importance of any of the long-term forces, including both left-right locations, for the voters who admitted to having any, and attitudes toward de Gaulle. These additional results suggested that party reactions, distinct from party identification, may have a more powerful effect on French electoral behavior than do self-assigned left-right locations, although the causal relationship between simple reactions to parties and electoral choices cannot be established. We shall return to this question of the comparative importance of affective outlooks on the parties and a sense of left-right locations as factors in French voting in the next chapter, which focuses on mass behavior at that almost uniquely French electoral institution, the second ballot.

11

The Second Ballot: Electoral Participation

F rance is the only country with a long record of democratic legislative elections that has recently provided for two ballots at the election of the popularly selected national legislative chamber. In the past, other countries employed electoral systems allowing for two ballots, but they abandoned the two-ballot system in the late nineteenth or early twentieth centuries (Duverger, 1965). Although run-off elections are held for primary elections in some of the states of the United States, they are almost never used for the elections themselves.

In France, however, the two-ballot system is a time-honored aspect of electoral procedure. The notion that an elected official must be the choice of a majority of the voters appears to be an inheritance from the practices of the Roman Catholic Church, passed on first to electoral systems of the Old Regime and then to post-revolutionary France, most of whose early electoral laws provided for two or even three ballots (Campbell, 1958).

French use of the two-ballot system for the election of deputies has not been continuous. Occasionally during the Third Republic and throughout the Fourth Republic, various forms of single-ballot electoral systems were employed, although a two-ballot system was used for by-elections during the Fourth Republic after 1951. But the two-ballot system was used for most of the elections to the Chamber of Deputies during the Third Republic, and with the advent of the Fifth Republic in 1958 virtually the same system was resurrected for the election of the National Assembly.[1]

Under the French electoral system, the election of members of the National Assembly is decided at the first ballot only in districts where a candidate wins a majority of the valid ballots cast and his total vote amounts to at least 25 percent of the number of registered voters in the district. If these conditions are not fulfilled, there is a second ballot. In 1967 the election was decided at the first ballot in only 70 of the 467 districts of continental France forming the universe from which our sample of 86 districts was drawn.[2] In 1968 a larger proportion of the continental seats was won at the first ballot, but a second ballot was still necessary in two-thirds of the districts.

In almost every district, there are fewer candidates at the second ballot than at the first ballot. In 1967 the same candidates competed at both the first and second ballots in only five districts; in 1968, in only one district. Candidates who do not receive a certain proportion of the votes at the first ballot are automatically eliminated from the seond ballot (except where the application of this rule would leave only one candidate at the second ballot).[3] Other candidates who are eligible to run at the second ballot may choose to withdraw from the race, usually in order to lend their support to one of the remaining candidates.

The French electoral system, therefore, places different groups of voters in different situations. Some voters are called upon to vote only once (where the election is decided at the first ballot). Others may vote twice, once at the first *tour*, and again at the run-off ballot (the second tour). But the position of two-time voters differs depending on whether or not the candidate for whom they voted at the first tour also runs at the second.

When a voter's preferred candidate runs at the second ballot, the voter can simply repeat his first-ballot electoral choice. That is what the overwhelming majority of voters do. On the basis of our 1967 survey data, we estimate that about 94 percent of the first-ballot voters who could repeat their vote returned to the polls, and of those who did, more than 98 percent cast their vote for the same candidate.[4]

The voters who cannot repeat their first-ballot electoral choice are in an entirely different situation. They have three alternatives. One is to go to the polls and vote for a different candidate at the second ballot. We estimate that this was the course followed in 1967 by about three-fourths of the first-ballot voters who were placed in a forced-choice situation for the second ballot. A second alternative is to stay away from the polls—to abstain. Somewhat less than half of the remaining fourth of the forced-choice citizens appear to have done that in 1967. The third alternative is to return to the polls, but to register a protest at the new situation by deliberately spoiling one's ballot. According to our estimates, there were somewhat more spoilers than abstainers in 1967 among first-ballot voters who were not able to repeat their choices at the second round of voting.[5] Therefore those voters who cannot repeat their first-ballot choice opt either to vote for another candidate, to abstain, or to spoil their ballots. What criterion do they use when they choose among these alternatives?

Electoral Participation and Partisan Preferences

The evidence available to us indicates that the forced-choice voters' forms of participation at the second ballot in 1967 reflected rational choices based on relative partisan preferences. Those who cast their ballots for another candidate did so because one was available who was not too distant, on the scale of party sympathy, from the candidate of their first-ballot choice. Those who chose instead to spoil their ballots, or deliberately to abstain, did so because they actually felt hostile toward the partisan alternatives available to them.

The data supporting this interpretation are set forth in Table 11-1.[6] It can be easily seen that in the first ballot the "voters" and the "spoilers" each had, on average, an equal amount of sympathy for their choices, but that at the second ballot, although the voters also had a favoring attitude toward the closest (next preferred) party available to them, the spoilers actually

Table 11-1. Mean sympathy for first-ballot partisan choice and for most preferred party available at second ballot, by second-ballot electoral behavior, among voters unable to repeat their first-ballot partisan choice at second ballot, France, 1967.[a]

Second-ballot electoral behavior	Mean sympathy		
	A For first-ballot partisan choice	B For most preferred party available at second ballot	C Difference between A and B
Voted for a candidate	70.4 (186) 20.8	59.9 (193) 18.4	10.4 (185) 24.6
Cast a spoiled ballot	69.4 (22) 19.3	39.4 (29) 20.5	28.5 (22) 30.0
Abstained deliberately	63.7 (9) 17.2	31.2[b] (9) 23.5	32.5[c] (9) 35.1
Abstained randomly	56.5 (16) 25.9	56.8[b] (18) 22.4	0.8[c] (16) 37.1

a. Numbers of cases are shown in parentheses. Standard deviations are in italics.
b. p ≤ .01.
c. p ≤ .025.

disliked the closest available party. The voters who cast their ballots for another party had some motive for voting at the second ballot even though they could not vote for their chosen party. The ballot spoilers had no such motive; they had, on average, a hostile outlook toward what we might more appropriately call, in their case, the "least disliked" rather than the "next preferred" available parties.

The situation of the abstainers, though somewhat more complicated, still supports the case for partisan sympathies as the determining factor in decisions about electoral participation at the second ballot. We have divided the forced-choice abstainers into two categories: those who abstained deliberately (thereby resembling the ballot spoilers) and those who abstained randomly.[7] We have seen that one can expect a base abstention rate of about 6 percent even among people who normally vote. These people—the random abstainers—should not have any distinctive attributes relating to partisan preferences. Their behavior is random, and so should their party sympathies be. But we also know that more than 6 percent of the first-ballot voters in forced-choice situations failed to vote at the second ballot; our estimate is that the proportion abstaining was more than 11 percent. Thus, roughly half of the abstainers were deliberate, and their partisan attitudes should be very similar to those of the ballot spoilers.

Our expectations about both groups of abstainers are confirmed by Table 11–1. Case numbers drop perilously low, but the significance tests for the groups with the fewest cases are all encouraging. The deliberate abstainers look very much like the ballot spoilers. They, too, had no incentive to vote at the second ballot.[8] There is no indication, however, that party sympathies account for random abstentions.

To sum up our findings in this chapter so far, we can say that when French voters cannot repeat their first-ballot partisan choice at the second ballot, they will vote for another party only if one is available for which they feel a certain amount of sympathy. If they regard the only parties available with disfavor, they will either spoil their ballots or abstain. We have demonstrated this unambiguously in the case of the voters and the spoilers. The case of the abstainers is more complex, because all abstainers are not disaffected voters. Only about half of the abstainers in forced-choice situations are deliberate; the other half are random. We have been able, however, to distinguish between these two groups and to show how the deliberate abstainers resemble the ballot spoilers.

Electoral Participation and the Left-Right Dimension

One of the abiding purposes of this book, to which we have given attention whenever it was relevant and possible to do so, is to determine the extent to which conventional left-right categorizations may be considered the equivalents of discrete partisan attachments as mechanisms by which French voters orient themselves to their complex and, in some ways, unstable party system. The problem is a large one, and as we pointed out in Chapter 4, there are a variety of litmus tests that may be applied in the search for elements of its solution; some of these were employed in that chapter, while others were used in Chapter 10. Indeed, it is best not to assume at the start that there is any single solution to the problem, in the sense that one of the two orienting mechanisms is uniformly more important than the other. It is at least as reasonable to envisage the possibility that the relative importance of the two orienting devices may shift, depending upon the use to which they are being put by the voters.

In Chapter 4, one basic litmus test that we applied (in several variants), was to measure how well party identification and left-right self-locations predicted both the current and later partisan choices of the electorate. Depending upon the particular measurement technique, the results ranged from showing a weak and inconclusive superiority of partisan identification over left-right positioning to a less ambiguous and more positive indication that party identification was the stronger indicator. Chapter 10 pointed to a more predominant role for party identification, although problems of causal ordering prevented us from making any exaggerated claims for party identification across the entire electorate. We are now in a position to make another test of the relative strength of left-right locations and partisan attitudes by asking whether the voters' perceptions of the left-right locations of the parties affect their electoral participation in forced-choice situations at the second ballot as clearly as partisan attitudes do.

Of course, the measure of partisan attitudes that we have employed in this chapter is not the same as the measure used in Chapter 4 and Chapter 10. There we compared left-right locations with party identification. Here we have considered partisan sympathy as registered on the "feeling thermometer." It is apparent that in this chapter we could not take party identification directly into account: we have been trying to explain electoral participation at the second ballot by the subset of voters who could not repeat their first-ballot partisan choice at the second ballot; and inasmuch as most French voters who identify with a party will vote at the first ballot for that party, the subset of voters with which we are concerned is precisely the group for which electoral participation at the second ballot *cannot* be explained in terms of partisan identification. Therefore, it would not be far from the mark to restate our problem as being that of trying to discover what force governs electoral participation when party identification is excluded.

There is, however, a relationship between party identification and partisan affect which makes the latter a reasonable surrogate for the former when it cannot be operative. Among the people in our sample who identify with a party for which we have direct sympathy scores, the mean level of affect for the party with which they identify is always higher than it is for any other party; and the same phenomenon holds true when we extend the list of sympathy scores to include those of the leaders of certain groups, such as the Federation, with which some of our sample voters identified but for which we do not have direct sympathy scores. Across an array of nine parties, the mean difference between the mean affect registered by identifiers for the party with which they identify and the mean affect shown for the next best liked party is 14.3, with comparatively little variation between pairs.[9] Therefore, the effort we shall now make to compare the effects of sense of left-right locations on electoral participation at the second ballot with those of partisan attitudes, which we have just examined, has a more than casual link with the analysis near the close of Chapter 4 and in Chapter 10.

In order to test the role of left-right locations in determining electoral participation, we computed scores relating to party distances that are analogous to the scores relating to party preferences recorded in Table 11-1. These party distance measures are presented in Table 11-2. It is apparent that the data do not support the hypothesis that left-right distances account for the various possible decisions about electoral participation at the second ballot. There is no systematic variation in the mean scores in either Column B or Column C analogous to the intelligible patterns of variation that we

Table 11-2. Mean distance on left-right dimension between voters and their first-ballot partisan choice, and between voters and closest party available at second ballot, by second-ballot electoral behavior, among voters unable to repeat their first ballot partisan choice at second ballot, France, 1967.[a]

Second-ballot electoral behavior	Mean distance		
	A Between voter and first-ballot partisan choice	B Between voter and closest party available at second ballot	C Difference between B and A
Voted for a candidate	12.0 (154) *17.2*	18.8 (150) *13.1*	7.7 (141) *23.6*
Cast a spoiled ballot	15.0 (21) *16.0*	19.6 (25) *14.2*	4.4 (19) *21.8*
Abstained	18.1 (20) *17.7*	27.1 (18) *18.4*	8.7 (17) *29.9*

a. Numbers of cases are in parentheses. Standard deviations are in italics.

found in Table 11-1. Such variation as exists is not in the expected direction. Column B shows that the absolute distance between the respondents' own left-right location and the location they assigned to the closest party available at the second ballot was virtually identical for people who voted for a candidate at the second ballot and for those who deliberately spoiled their ballots. Column C indicates that the distance between the left-right location of the voters' first-ballot choice and that of the closest available party was least for the spoilers, the group for which one would expect it to be greatest. The only items that appear in Table 11-2 in expected form are the comparatively large standard deviations for the abstainers in Columns B and C, indicating the presence of the two kinds of abstainers—random and deliberate—that we have already discussed.[10]

Perceptions of left-right locations do not, therefore, account for the form of electoral participation at the second ballot. This negative finding is all the more resounding because it is based not only on the voters' own self-assigned left-right locations but also on their purely idiosyncratic left-right placement of the various parties. In Chapter 4 when we compared the predictive power of left-right self-locations with that of party identifications, we found that the former typically rose as we employed idiosyncratic left-right partisan locations and that they declined when we employed partisan locations based on means across the sample. In this chapter, we find that the mode of scoring which in the earlier chapter strengthened the case for left-right positioning as the prime organizing concept for French voters as they approach their party system produces no evidence that perceptions of left-right locations explain electoral participation at the second ballot. Partisan preferences do account for electoral participation, but partisan proximities on the left-right scale, expressed in the form presumably most likely to enhance their operative power, do not do so.[11]

This unambiguous result is particularly striking for another reason as well. Across our entire mass sample the absolute differences that people perceive between their own left-right location and that of the various parties are uniformly correlated in the expected direction with the amount of sympathy they feel for the same parties, and sometimes at levels that are impressive in social science research ($r = .58$ for the UNR; $r = .56$ for the PCF).[12] This suggests that any phenomenon that can be accounted for by partisan sympathies should also be explicable in terms of party distances. But our "experiment" relating to electoral participation shows that this is not the case.

The reason for this is that even though partisan sympathies vary regularly with left-right distances, the voters distinguish more finely between neighboring parties in terms of party sympathies than they do in terms of left-right distances. It is a well-known historical phenomenon that the elites of ideologically related parties can generate greater antagonisms toward each other than toward opponents whom they know to be more distant from them in ideological outlook. In France, this has been true particularly for Communist-Socialist relations, but the phenomenon is not limited either to France or to the left. Heretics of various sorts have often been treated more harshly than nonbelievers. A similar phenomenon appears to operate throughout the French mass electorate. By placing certain parties relatively close to one another on the left-right scale, French voters acknowledge the ideological proximity of those parties, but they may nevertheless have very different attitudes toward them. Some voters may look on ideologically related parties with more or less equal favor, while for other voters the perceived ideological proximity of the parties is accompanied by feelings of fear or hostility toward one or another of them.

We can demonstrate this phenomenon by examining separately the intercorrelations between sympathy scores for the main leftist parties or leaders (Communists, Socialists, Mitterrand), between sympathy scores for the main rightist parties or leaders (UNR, Giscard d'Estaing, Lecanuet), between left-right distances between self and the main leftist parties (Communists, Socialists, Federation), and between left-right distances between self and the main rightist parties (UNR, Independent Republicans, Democratic Center). The relevant correlation coefficients are set out in Table 11-3, which shows that the correlations for the left-right distance scores are uniformly stronger than the correlations for the sympathy scores for the equivalent matching pair of political objects.[13] This tendency is somewhat more marked with regard to the left-wing parties than it is for the right-wing parties, but it occurs clearly for both types of party clusters.

These figures mean that the voters come closer to regarding the main leftist parties (or the main rightist parties) as interchangeable in left-right terms than they do in terms of partisan sympathy. Across the electorate as a

Table 11-3. Zero-order correlations (r) between attitudes toward selected pairs of partisan objects, France, 1967.

Left-right distance between self and party	r	Partisan sympathy	r
Communists-Federation	.69	Communists-Mitterrand	.54
Federation-Socialists	.60	Mitterrand-Socialists	.45
Socialists-Communists	.58	Socialists-Communists	.30
UNR (Gaullists)–Democratic Center	.42	UNR-Lecanuet	.29
Democratic Center–Independent Republicans	.55	Lecanuet–Giscard d'Estaing	.38
Independent Republicans–UNR	.64	Giscard d'Estaing–UNR	.54

whole, French voters see less difference between the main leftist parties when they consider them in spatial left-right terms than when they consider them in terms of their rankings on the feelings thermometer, and the same holds true for the main right-wing parties as well. The voters simply distinguish more sharply between the main parties along the sympathy-hostility dimension than along the left-right dimension. Their decisions concerning electoral participation, therefore, are more sensitive to partisan attitudes than they are to the sense of left-right distances.

This interpretation is reinforced when we subdivide our sample of respondents into three groups, according to the party they voted for at the first ballot in 1967. Even though our sample as a whole indicates that partisan feeling is uniformly more powerful than sense of left-right distance in discriminating between the major parties, we are particularly interested in the behavior of the subsets of voters who are most likely not to be able to repeat their first-ballot choice at the second ballot. Accordingly, we isolated three groups of first-ballot voters: those who voted for the Communist party, those who voted for the non-Communist left (the Federation or the PSU), and those who voted for the Democratic Center. We ignored the people who voted for the UNR or the Independent Republicans, because those voters were seldom faced with having to choose a different candidate at the second ballot, as well as the voters for the smaller parties or unaffiliated candidates, because they were comparatively few in numbers.

For each of the three groups, we ran the same correlations that appear in Table 11-3. This produced eighteen matching pairs of correlations relating to partisan feelings, on the one hand, and to left-right distances, on the other. Of these eighteen matching pairs of correlations, those relating to left-right distances were stronger than those relating to partisanship in twelve cases. In two cases the correlations were the same (after rounding to the second decimal). Only in four cases out of the eighteen did the voters for any of the three partisan groups distinguish more sharply between the main party clusters on the basis of left-right distances than on the basis of partisan sympathy.

The breakdown of the analysis by party groupings strengthens the argument that electoral participation at the second ballot depends more on partisanship than on sense of left-right distance, because French voters distinguish more sharply between parties on grounds of partisanship than on grounds of left-right distance. More first-ballot voters who could not repeat their partisan choice at the second ballot had voted for the non-Communist left than for any other partisan group (36 percent). Among Federation or PSU voters, all six correlations were stronger on the left-right distance side than on the partisanship side. The first-ballot voters who were more likely than any other group to be faced with the problem of whether or not to vote again at the second ballot uniformly distinguished between the main leftist and rightist parties more in terms of partisan sympathy than in terms of left-right distance.

Among Democratic Center voters, who furnished about a fourth of the voters who could not repeat their first-ballot choice at the second ballot, party sympathy was a clearer discriminator between related parties than were left-right distances in five of the six matching cases.

Only first-ballot Communist voters, who supplied a fourth of the voters who were not able to repeat their first-ballot choice at the second ballot, failed to distinguish between the major parties more often by partisanship than by left-right distance. They did so in only one case out of the six. In three other cases the Communist voters saw more difference between parties in terms of left-right distance than in terms of partisan feeling, and in two cases there was no difference in the strength of the two factors as a criterion of party difference.

We can now explain why French voters' decisions concerning electoral participation at the second ballot can be accounted for in terms of partisan sympathies but not by sense of left-right distance. The electorate distinguishes more sharply between the main left-wing parties and between the main right-wing parties in terms of partisan sympathy than in left-right terms. Among the main groups of partisan voters who are most likely not to be able to repeat their first-ballot partisan vote at the second ballot, this tendency to regard ideologically related parties as "unfriendly neighbors" is most clearly displayed by non-Communist leftists. In that sense the historic rivalry between the two main branches of the Marxist movement in France, the Socialist party (SFIO) and the Communist party (PCF), is reflected in the partisan attitudes of the non-Communist left electorate, and so is the "new left" challenge of the PSU to both of these larger leftist parties.

The non-Communist left furnished more voters than any other voting group to the pool of people who were faced with forced choices at the second ballot in 1967. Centrists and Communists each supplied smaller groups of forced voters, but centrists display the "unfriendly neighbor" phenomenon almost as clearly as the non-Communist leftists do. Communist voters do not display the same tendency, but neither do they behave in a directly contrary fashion; their behavior comes closer to being random in this regard. The overall result of this admixture of forces is that French electoral participation at the second ballot is explicable in terms of partisan attitudes, but not in terms of a sense of party distances on the left-right dimension.

The Rosenthal-Sen Analysis

These findings differ from those suggested by the pioneering work of Rosenthal and Sen (1973), who tested several models of electoral participation at the second ballot in France by analyzing variations in abstentions and spoiled ballots between the two ballots of the elections of 1958, 1962, 1967, and 1968. One generally successful model they tested was a spatial model that they refer to as the alienation model. Derived from the Davis, Hinich, and Ordeshook (1970) notion of the relationship between alienation and electoral participation, it operates on the assumption that "the utility that a voter receives from a candidate is a monotonically decreasing function of the distance between the voter and the candidate" (Rosenthal and Sen, 1973, p. 31).

Rosenthal and Sen were primarily interested in discovering whether spatial models could be useful in explaining French electoral behavior, and not in closely examining the spatial dimensions themselves. But their work is of interest to us because they found that the alienation model was generally satisfactory whether they operationalized space in terms of party sympathies or of left-right locations. Sometimes the alienation model gives somewhat better results when distance is interpreted in party preference terms, and sometimes it produces better results when distance is measured in terms of left-right locations; but the differences in results are not great. Both measures give satisfactory results, without either measure having any systematic superiority over the other.[14]

The basic reason why the Rosenthal-Sen findings differ from ours is that they employ aggregate data and we use individual-level data. Rosenthal and Sen cannot disaggregate their data in order to isolate specific groups of voters whose behavior at the second ballot could be compared and, by inference, explained. They cannot separate the people who could repeat their first-ballot vote at the second ballot from those who could not, and they cannot separate the people who abstained or spoiled their ballots at both the first ballot and the second ballot from those who did so only at the second ballot. Furthermore, our measures were all taken at the individual level while theirs are estimated aggregates. Whereas we read the individual's own left-right self-location and the particular left-right location that he or she attributed to each relevant party, Rosenthal and Sen must assume that all the voters place all the candidates of the same party in the same left-right location, and they must attribute to all the voters for a given party the same position on the left-right dimension that they (Rosenthal and Sen) assign to that party. They based their left-right party locations on the mean values attributed to them by the respondents in our 1967 survey.

In order to determine the extent to which each of these methodological differences, or both together, contributed to the differences between the Rosenthal-Sen findings and our own, we reran our computations, originally reported in Table 11–2: first, on the assumption that all voters perceived the location of each party uniformly and that they placed themselves at the same left-right location as that of the party for which they had voted; second, without distinguishing the voters who could not repeat their first-ballot choice at the second ballot from those who could repeat it; and third, by combining these two characteristics of the Rosenthal-Sen analysis. The results of these operations, compared with our original results as reported in Table 11-2, appear in Table 11-4.

The upper-left section of Table 11-4 (through Column C) reproduces our original findings, and shows that, among voters who could not repeat their first-ballot electoral choice at the second ballot, spatial measures based on individual-level perceptions of self and partisan left-right locations do not distinguish between voters who voted for another candidate at the second ballot, voters who cast a spoiled ballot, and voters who abstained. The upper-right section of Table 11-4 (Column D) reproduces the analysis reported in the upper-left section, but instead of being based on exact individual-level perceptions, it is based on the uniform scores, derived from national means, that are employed by Rosenthal and Sen. The lower-left section (through Column C) reproduces the analysis, employing individual-level perceptions of spatial locations, and applies them not to the limited set of voters who could not repeat their first-ballot choice at the second ballot but rather to everyone who voted at the first ballot, whether or not they could repeat their electoral choice at the second ballot. Lastly, the section on the lower-right (Column D) combines both of the elements involved in the difference between Rosenthal and Sen's work and our own, by including in our basic analysis everyone who voted at the first ballot and employing uniform mean left-right scores rather than exact individual-level perceived scores.

Neither the data in the upper-right portion nor those in the lower-left portion of the table show any major improvement over our original findings concerning the effect of left-right perceptions on participation at the second ballot. It appears, therefore, that neither the Rosenthal-Sen "clumping" of left-right locations, compared with our assignment of exact individual-level perceptions, nor the inability to disaggregate their data, accounts by itself for the difference between their findings and ours.

The lower-right portion of Table 11-4, which incorporates *both* of the ways in which the Rosenthal-Sen analysis differs from our own, contains the best results by far. It reveals a sharp distinction between the voters and the ballot spoilers. The closest available party for the people who spoiled their ballots is seven times as far from them as the closest available party is from the people who voted for another candidate. Furthermore, the abstainers occupy a reasonable position *between* the voters and the spoilers; their closest available party is almost two and a half times as distant from them, on the average, as the closest available party is from the second-ballot voters. Therefore, neither Rosenthal and Sen's "clumping" of left-right locations nor their inability to disaggregate the voters, *alone,* explains why their spatial analysis, based on left-right locations, accounts satisfactorily for electoral

Table 11-4. Mean distance on left-right dimension between voters and their first-ballot partisan choice, and between voters and closest party available at second ballot, by second-ballot electoral behavior, France, 1967.[a]

	A Distance between voter and 1st-ballot partisan choice	Individually assigned left-right locations		Uniform mean left-right locations
		B Distance between voter and closest party available at 2nd ballot	C Distance between closest party available at 2nd ballot and 1st-ballot partisan choice	D Distance between voter and closest party available at 2nd ballot
Voters' second-ballot electoral behavior				
First-ballot voters unable to repeat first-ballot choice at second ballot				
Voted for a candidate	12.0 (154) 17.2	18.8 (150) 13.1	7.7 (141) 23.6	15.9 (186) 6.5
Cast a spoiled ballot	15.0 (21) 16.0	19.6 (25) 14.2	4.4 (19) 21.8	19.6 (23) 13.4
Abstained	18.1 (20) 17.7	27.1 (18) 18.4	8.7 (17) 29.9	18.9 (25) 10.8

All persons voting at first ballot

Voted for a candidate	14.2 (782) *16.0*	13.0 (704) *12.6*	− 1.0 (693) *13.9*	2.8 (1026) *6.6*
Cast a spoiled ballot	15.0 (21) *16.0*	19.6 (25) *14.2*	4.4 (19) *21.8*	19.6 (23) *13.4*
Abstained	19.9 (53) *20.3*	17.2 (48) *19.4*	− 1.9 (47) *22.3*	6.4 (73) *10.9*

a. Numbers of cases are in parentheses. Standard deviations are in italics.

participation at the second ballot, while our own analysis, employing comparable data, does not do so. *Both* of their restrictions must be taken together and in a highly interactive sense in order to explain why the outcome of their alienation model differs from our own when left-right perceptions are employed as the base measure of distance.

Alternate Models of Electoral Participation

Rosenthal and Sen investigate two other spatial models of electoral participation: what they call the furthest-candidate model and the indifference model. Neither of these is very satisfactory in itself, but both make some additional contribution to the explanation of electoral participation when they are combined with other models. The furthest-candidate model operates on the assumption that the voter's primary incentive for participation is to defeat the least desirable candidate; we shall refer to this motivation as negative voting. The indifference model assumes that nonvoting is a function of the voter's indifference to the available alternatives. We shall examine each of these models in turn, to see what light our individual-level analysis can throw upon them.

Negative Voting and Indifference

Observers of French politics have often suggested that voters may cast their ballots in opposition to certain candidates as much as in favor of others (Waterman, 1969). Indeed, the conventional saying that "at the first ballot, they choose; at the second, they eliminate," suggests that second-ballot voting is exclusively a negative matter.[15] At our mass survey of 1967, we attempted to get a firm measure of the extent to which that might be so by asking all respondents who voted for a candidate at the second ballot whether they had voted for that candidate because they liked him, because they did not want one of his opponents to be elected, or for another reason. Among the voters who could repeat their first-ballot electoral choice at the second ballot, almost 60 percent replied that they had voted for their chosen candidate because they liked him, while somewhat more than a fourth placed the emphasis on defeating his opponents. Among the voters who could not repeat their first-ballot choice, however, little more than 20 percent reported that they had voted for their second-ballot choice because they liked him, while more than two-thirds said that they had voted for him in order to defeat his opponents. (The proportion of voters who took refuge in our vague reference to "another reason" was about the same for both groups.) Negative voting, therefore, does occur at the second ballot in France, although it is heavily concentrated proportionately among voters who cannot vote at the second ballot for the candidate for whom they had voted at the first ballot.

Both party sympathies and left-right distances contribute to the negative voting among people who cannot repeat their first-ballot partisan choice at the second ballot. But, counterintuitively, the voters in that category who emphasize defeating their candidate's opponent do not do so because they dislike that opponent more (or feel more distant from that opponent) than do the voters who report that they voted for their second-round choice because they liked him. Rather, the negative voters differ from the positive voters in that the former have more sympathy for (and feel closer to) their first-ballot choice, for whom they cannot vote at the second ballot, than the latter do. Among French voters who cannot repeat their first-ballot choice at the second ballot, negative voting is a function of the high regard for (and closeness to) the voter's first-ballot choice rather than of particular hostility toward (or distance from) the candidate whom they oppose at the second ballot.

This phenomenon suggests that negative attitudes are not likely to be a determinant of electoral participation, at least in the sense that the more one is opposed to a given candidate (or the further one feels oneself to be from a candidate), the more likely one would be to vote for that candidate's opponent. And, indeed, that is what we find when we make a more direct test of this hypothesis. Among voters who could not repeat their first-ballot choice at the second ballot, there is not a great deal of difference between those who chose to vote, those who abstained, and those who spoiled their ballots, with regard to their attitude toward the party available at the second ballot that they liked the least (disliked the most). Moreover, such differences in party sympathy as do exist do not point toward negativism as an incentive to voting.

Indifference toward the two leading alternatives at the second ballot is somewhat harder to assess as a motivation for second-ballot voting, at least when the measure employed is the degree of party sympathy. The main reason for this is that we have no criterion by which to determine how similarly the voters would have to regard two parties in order to permit us to say that they are indifferent toward them. The ordering of the relevant party sympathy scores for each of our three groups of voters among those who could not repeat their first-ballot choice at the second ballot—those who voted for another candidate, those who spoiled their ballots, and those who abstained—is consistent with indifference as a motivation for electoral participation. The difference between the degree of sympathy felt for the closest available party and that felt for the second closest available party at the second ballot was largest, on the average, for the people who voted (30.7), next largest for the abstainers (25.6), and least for the ballot spoilers (17.4). But is the smallest of these differences (17.4), which amounts to almost a fifth of the entire length of the party sympathy scale, small enough to be described as representing indifference? There is just no criterion that warrants us to answer that question one way or the other, but we are doubtful that the data support the indifference model. As for measuring indifference in terms of distances on the left-right dimension, our 1967 data certainly do not validate this model.

The Rosenthal-Sen Heuristic Model

Our main purpose in comparing the Rosenthal-Sen work with our own is to throw light on the relative importance of partisan attitudes and sense of left-right locations as factors in electoral participation. These variables are employed by Rosenthal and Sen in spatial models. But Rosenthal and Sen also examine a nonspatial model of electoral participation, which they call the heuristic model, and we have tested it against our survey data as well. It hypothesizes that electoral participation at the second ballot depends primarily upon two factors: availability of choice and competition. The notion is that participation increases as a function of the closeness of the competition at the first ballot (operationalized as the ratio of the electoral strength of the leading candidate to that of the second leading candidate) and the degree of choice available to the voter at the second ballot (operationalized as the number of candidates). In the Rosenthal-Sen tests, the heuristic model emerged as the best single model of electoral participation.

In order to test the competition component of this model, we divided our sample electoral districts into three groups, based on the appropriate operationalization of competition, and then ran out for each group (most competitive, medium-competitive, and least competitive) the proportions of people who, at the second ballot, voted for a candidate, cast a spoiled ballot, or abstained. We performed that operation not only for all first-ballot voters, thereby approximating the constraints of aggregate data of the kind employed by Rosenthal and Sen, but also for those voters who could not repeat their first-ballot partisan choices at the second ballot. In both tests, districts where there was no left-wing candidate at the second ballot were excluded because our data show that in those districts leftist voters abstain or cast spoiled ballots in abnormally large proportions. The results of these operations appear in Table 11-5.

The upper portion of Table 11-5, which includes all first-ballot voters, offers no support for the hypothesis that participation increases with competition. Some 90 percent of the voters in each group, based on the degree of competition in their districts (as defined by Rosenthal and Sen), cast a valid ballot at the second round of voting. At the same time, we can see why this element of the heuristic model might contribute to an explanation of spoiled ballots. There is not a regular increase in the proportion of ballot spoilers as competition decreases, but the largest proportion of ballot spoilers appears in the least competitive districts. Abstentions, however, do not vary in an intelligible pattern.[16]

Table 11-5. Second-ballot electoral behavior by competitiveness of electoral district, defined as ratio of votes won by leading candidate at first ballot to votes won by second leading candidate (percentages), France, 1967.

Voters' second-ballot electoral behavior	Competitiveness of district		
	Most	Medium	Least
All persons voting at first ballot			
Voted for a candidate	89.1	92.4	91.9
Cast a spoiled ballot	2.5	1.2	3.7
Abstained	8.4	6.4	4.4
Total	100.0	100.0	100.0
Weighted N	(375.7)	(283.5)	(413.6)
First-ballot voters unable to repeat their choice at second ballot			
Voted for a candidate	72.7	87.7	77.2
Cast a spoiled ballot	11.3	5.8	16.8
Abstained	16.0	6.5	6.0
Total	100.0	100.0	100.0
Weighted N	(83.0)	(58.6)	(90.1)

In a separate analysis, we also tested the choice component of Rosenthal and Sen's heuristic model. We did this by measuring the incidence of the various forms of second-ballot electoral behavior depending on whether there were only two or more than two candidates at the second ballot. Here we similarly discovered that there was little difference between the two groups in the proportions of people casting valid ballots, but the effect of the number of candidates on spoiled ballots is quite clear. Four times as many people, proportionately, spoiled their ballots where there were only two candidates at the second ballot as spoiled them where there were more than two candidates available. Consequently, we can understand that when Rosenthal and Sen combine their indicators of competition and choice in a model that employs aggregate data they can account for spoiled ballots, although the choice indicator probably contributes more heavily to the joint result than the competition indicator does.

The competition component of the model works nearly as well when we strip our cases down to the critical segment of the first-ballot voters whose preferred candidate dropped out of the race at the second ballot. The lower portion of Table 11-5 shows more ballot spoilers, proportionately, in the least competitive districts than in the most competitive ones, although there is still no progression in the proportion of spoilers as competition decreases.[17]

Competition has a more marked effect on null ballots when a definition different from Rosenthal and Sen's is used. The Rosenthal-Sen mode of operationalizing competition, as the ratio of the votes cast for the leading candidate to those cast for the runner-up at the first ballot, is probably the best one available for their purpose, which was to test models of electoral participation with aggregate data for the French elections of 1958, 1962, 1967, and 1968. It is, however, more suitable for the elections of 1958 than for the others.

If one hypothesizes that competition is a stimulus to voting at the second ballot, the measure of competition should have a direct bearing on the characteristics of the competition at the second ballot to which the voters can reasonably be expected to respond. In this regard, the Rosenthal-Sen indicator of competition has two weaknesses, one minor and the other more fundamental. The minor element is that although the front-runner at the first ballot almost always runs at the second ballot, the runner-up fails to do so in about 10 percent of the cases.[18] This proportion of districts is sufficiently small that it probably does not have a significant effect on the outcome of the analysis, but it is evident that the measure is inappropriate in such cases. Indeed, it might operate counter to the governing hypothesis, as voters for the runner-up might be alienated by their inability to vote for their favored candidate at the second ballot.

The more fundamental weakness of the definition of competition is that whereas the second ballot at the 1958 election was something of a free-for-all, the second ballot in 1962 marked the emergence of an informal left-wing electoral alliance that was formalized and generalized at the elections of 1967 and 1968. The characteristic structure of the second-ballot electoral competition in 1967 and 1968, and to a lesser extent also in 1962, was a bipolar conflict between a single left-wing candidate and a Gaullist (or a Giscardian). The great majority of the contests at the second ballot in 1967 and 1968 were straight fights between the leftist candidate best placed to win the seat and a Gaullist or Independent Republican candidate. Normally, the two leading candidates at the first ballot also ran at the second ballot only if they came from opposing electoral coalitions. Accordingly, one would expect interest in the second ballot in 1967 and 1968 to be stimulated less by the closeness of the vote between the two first-ballot leaders than by the closeness of the vote between the two electoral coalitions.[19]

In order to test this different indicator of competition, we commissioned a measure based on the proportion of first-ballot votes won by the three left-wing parties that were allied at the 1967 elections—the Communists, the Federation, and the PSU. In this formulation, the most competitive districts were those where the combined leftist vote was between 45 and 55 percent of the total at the first ballot; the least competitive districts were those where the leftist parties together won less than 40 percent or more than 60 percent of the vote; and the medium-competitive districts were those where the leftist vote fell in between these two sets of limiting proportions. As we have regularly done in these analyses, we excluded the districts where there was no left-wing candidate at the second ballot.

Table 11-6 indicates the behavior of the electorate at the second ballot, within each of these three groups of districts based on our revised interpretation of competition, not only for all persons who voted at the first ballot (our aggregate data approximation), but also for those first-ballot voters who could not vote again for their first-ballot choice at the second ballot. For all first-ballot voters, the results of the analysis are somewhat better than those reported in Table 11-5, for which competition is differently defined. Participation rates do not vary with competition, but spoiled ballots vary monotonically in the expected direction.

The result for spoiled ballots is even livelier for the set of first-ballot voters who could not repeat their first-ballot choice at the second ballot. The proportion of people casting valid ballots does not vary significantly with the degree of competition, but there is a regular and marked increase in the proportion of ballot-spoilers as the competitiveness of the districts decreases. Twice as many people, proportionately, in the medium-competitive districts spoiled their ballots as did so in the most competitive districts, and almost twice as many voters, proportionately, spoiled their ballots in the least competitive districts as did so in the medium-competitive districts.

This finding suggests strongly that spoiled ballots do indeed vary inversely with the degree of competition in the district at the second ballot,

Table 11-6. Second-ballot electoral behavior by competitiveness of electoral district, defined as proportion of votes won by leftist parties at first ballot (percentages), France, 1967.

Voters' second-ballot electoral behavior	Competitiveness of district		
	Most	Medium	Least
All persons voting at first ballot			
Voted for a candidate	90.6	91.6	90.9
Cast a spoiled ballot	1.6	1.9	3.6
Abstained	7.8	6.6	5.5
Total	100.0	100.0	100.0
Weighted N	(228.3)	(362.1)	(482.4)
First-ballot voters unable to repeat their choice at second ballot			
Voted for a candidate	76.6	87.0	73.6
Cast a spoiled ballot	5.0	10.4	18.7
Abstained	18.4	2.6	7.7
Total	100.0	100.0	100.0
Weighted N	(74.0)	(64.2)	(93.5)

when competition is defined in terms of the closeness of the first-ballot vote between electoral blocs. The result, however, is more suggestive than definitive, as the proportions of abstainers do not vary systematically (even when we reduce them to known deliberate abstainers).

Therefore, with regard to competition and choice as explanatory factors for electoral participation at the second ballot, we can arrive at only tentative conclusions. Neither factor seems to affect the proportion of people that cast valid ballots. If we take all first-ballot voters into account, the element of choice (defined as the number of candidates at the second ballot) accounts very well for spoiled ballots, but we are unable to determine how well it accounts for spoiled ballots among forced-choice voters. Competition (defined as the ratio of the votes cast for the front-runner at the first ballot to those cast for the runner-up) accounts only moderately well for spoiled ballots. When competition is defined as the closeness of the first-ballot vote as between leftist and rightist electoral blocs, it explains spoiled ballots better than the Rosenthal-Sen definition of competition explains them. Still, there are elements of mystery in this domain, not only because neither competition nor choice appears to affect the proportion of people that cast valid ballots, but also because neither factor enables us to interpret abstentions as intelligibly as we would like. There is room here for further research.

Conclusions

We have covered considerable ground in this chapter. The core of our analysis, however, has been the determination that participation at the second ballot of French elections is explicable in terms of partisan preferences but not in terms of a sense of left-right distance between the voter and the objects of electoral choice. This finding runs counter to the work of Rosenthal and Sen (1973), who find support for a spatial model of electoral participation that employs sometimes partisan preferences and sometimes left-right distances to operationalize the spatial dimension. The difference between their results and ours turns out to be perfectly intelligible, however. They are forced by the nature of their data to make assumptions that are distant from the empirical reality that our individual-level data capture.

In our continuing effort to compare the role of partisan attachments with that of left-right positioning in organizing the French voter's perception of the political world surrounding him, we have just encountered an unambiguous indication that left-right locations fall short of partisanship. But the case is certainly not closed. With respect to the second ballot, we have so far considered only electoral participation. It remains now to turn our attention to how those voters who do participate at the second ballot divide in their partisan choices, and to assess once again the relative force of partisanship and left-right location in determining electoral choices.

12

The Second Ballot:
The Flow of the Vote

In the preceding chapter, we asked how French voters respond when they find themselves unable to vote at the second ballot for the candidate for whom they have voted at the first ballot, because that candidate is no longer in the electoral race. In particular, we asked what determines whether such voters vote for some other candidate, or instead decide not to vote for any candidate at all, either by spoiling their ballots or not going to the polls. Our principal findings were that partisan preferences account neatly for this difference in continued electoral participation at the second ballot, but that a sense of left-right location does not.

In this chapter we shall focus on those voters who, unable to repeat their first-ballot choice, do in fact make some new candidate choice. Given the remaining alternatives, for which ones do these "rebuffed" voters cast their second ballots? And, more important, what are the factors determining these substitute choices? With regard to this latter problem, we shall continue to track the comparative effects of partisan attitudes and sense of left-right location. But first it will be useful to set out a complete tableau of the various configurations of partisan competition at the second ballot.

Patterns of Second-Ballot Voting

Within our sample of eighty-six districts, the 1967 election was decided at the first ballot in ten districts, leaving seventy-six districts in which there was a second ballot. Of the people who had cast a ballot at the first round of voting in those seventy-six districts, fully three-fourths were able to vote for the same party at the second ballot. And of these, more than 90 percent did indeed vote again for the same party. A tiny fraction (2 percent) saw fit to vote for a different party, and some 6 percent abstained from voting (representing the base rate of abstention to which we referred in the preceding chapter).

This chapter deals only with those voters, constituting almost one-fourth of the first-ballot electorate, who could *not* repeat their first-ballot electoral choice at the second ballot. They were therefore placed in forced-choice situations at the second ballot, and their decisions are of special interest to us because of the light they shed on the wellsprings of electoral behavior in France.

In the seventy-six districts where there was a second ballot, the patterns of partisan offerings varied, depending upon which parties stayed in the race and which parties dropped out. These patterns are displayed in Table 12-1. The eight types of competitive configuration are arrayed across the lettered columns of the table, each of which represents a different pattern. By reading down each column we can see which parties did run and which did not run at the second ballot in that type of district. By reading across each row we can see the types of districts in which the first-ballot supporters of the party listed in that row were faced with a forced choice at the second ballot. In order to simplify a complex situation, we have reduced the party spectrum to a limited number of reasonably coherent party groupings.[1]

The most common kind of second-ballot contest was a straight fight between a leftist and a Gaullist, which occurred in more than two-thirds of the districts where there was a second ballot. About half of these pitted a Communist against a Gaullist (Type A districts); in the other half a non-Communist leftist carried the banner against a Gaullist (Type B districts). But there were half a dozen other configurations as well. Thus voters who

Table 12-1. Patterns of second-ballot party competition, France, 1967.[a]

Party grouping	Competitive patterns (district types)								Index of constraint[b]
	A	B	C	D	E	F	G	H	
Communist	X	O	X	X	O	O	O	O	0.26
Federation or PSU	O	X	O	O	X	X	O	O	0.33
Centrist	O	O	X	X	X	X	X	O	0.46
Gaullist	X	X	O	X	O	X	X	X	0.02
Rightist	O	O	O	O	O	O	O	X	0.59
Other	O	O	O	O	O	O	O	O	1.00
District N	(27)	(26)	(3)	(5)	(4)	(6)	(3)	(2)	

a. X = party ran at second ballot. O = Party did not run at second ballot.
b. Proportion of first-ballot voters for party grouping in forced-choice situation.

Table 12-2. Leftist electoral choices in forced-choice situations at second ballot (percentages), France, 1967.

First-ballot Communist voters in districts where Federation or PSU ran at second ballot		First-ballot Federation or PSU voters in districts where Communist party ran at second ballot	
Voted for Federation or PSU	86.2	Voted for Communist party	63.0
Voted for another party	5.9	Voted for another party	16.6
Abstained	4.2	Abstained	8.3
Spoiled ballot	3.7	Spoiled ballot	12.1
Total	100.0	Total	100.0
Weighted N	(54.6)	Weighted N	(73.3)

cast their ballots for the Communist party at the first ballot faced forced choices at the second ballot not only in Type B districts, but in E, F, G, and H districts as well. Similarly, first-ballot supporters of the non-Communist left (Federation or PSU) could not repeat their partisan votes in districts of Type A, C, D, G, and H. Centrist voters were constrained in their second-ballot choices in Type A, B and H districts; rightist supporters could vote for their preferred candidate at the second ballot in only Type H districts; and people who had voted at the first ballot for any of the miscellaneous candidates not included in the major party groupings shown in Table 12-1 could not vote again for those candidates anywhere. First-ballot Gaullist voters were most favored in their options; they faced forced choices only in Type C and E districts. Because limited case numbers prevent us from considering the reactions of each group of partisan voters to each pattern of second-ballot options, we shall discuss mainly the behavior of Communist voters in districts where non-Communists were the only left-wing candidates at the second ballot (B, E, and F), of non-Communist leftist voters where Communists were the only leftists available (A, C, and D), and of centrist voters in districts where only a leftist and a Gaullist candidate confronted each other at the second ballot (A and B). These voters are by far the most numerous of those who could not repeat their first-ballot choice at the second ballot.

Table 12-2 records the second-ballot electoral behavior of Communist and non-Communist voters in districts where the left-wing candidate available at the second ballot was not the candidate for whom they had voted at the first ballot. The first important point to note is the greater propensity for first-ballot Communist voters to support the Federation or PSU at the second ballot than for non-Communist left voters to support Communist candidates. More than 85 percent of the Communist voters switched their support to non-Communist leftists, but less than 65 percent of Federation and PSU voters threw their support to Communists.

It is evident that a large minority of non-Communist leftist voters could not bring themselves to vote for Communist candidates at the second ballot. It is of equal interest that among those who did not vote for Communists, a substantial proportion did not vote for any party. Somewhat more than 15 percent of the total group shifted to a Gaullist or a centrist candidate; but abstentions exceeded the base rate, and more than 10 percent of the Federation or PSU voters spoiled their ballots where the only leftist candidate at the second ballot was a Communist. By contrast, few Communist voters supported a non-leftist candidate where a leftist was available, and fewer still spoiled their ballots, while abstentions appear to have been wholly random.[2]

Centrist voters found themselves in forced-choice situations in the large number of districts where there were straight fights at the second ballot between leftist candidates (whether Communist or non-Communist) and Gaullists (districts A and B). They were also unable to repeat their choices in the few right-wing districts where a Gaullist confronted a rightist candidate (Type H), but we shall ignore those in order to concentrate on the classic dilemma of the centrist voter faced with the polar choices characteristic of most second-ballot competition in France.

According to our sample estimates (see Table 12-3), about half of the centrists threw their support to the Gaullists at the second ballot, whether the leftist candidate was a Communist or a non-Communist. Centrists, however, were four times more likely to vote for a non-Communist leftist than for a Communist; less than 10 percent of them voted for a Communist, while almost 40 percent of them voted for a non-Communist leftist. The remaining centrist voters either abstained or spoiled their ballots. Almost 40 percent of the centrists failed to cast a valid ballot when the left-wing candidate was a Communist, compared to only some 12 percent who abstained or spoiled their ballots when the left-wing candidate was not a Communist.[3]

One other group of voters, represented in virtually all the types of districts we are considering, deserves separate mention. This group, the first-

Table 12-3. Centrist electoral choices in forced-choice situations at second ballot (percentages), France, 1967.

In districts where Federation or PSU ran against a Gaullist at second ballot		In districts where Communist party ran against a Gaullist at second ballot	
Voted for Federation or PSU	38.3	Voted for Communist party	9.4
Voted for Gaullists	50.1	Voted for Gaullists	51.5
Abstained	3.3	Abstained	23.7
Spoiled ballot	8.3	Spoiled ballot	15.4
Total	100.0	Total	100.0
Weighted N	(24.0)	Weighted N	(44.8)

ballot rightist voters, appears only in small case numbers, but one aspect of its behavior is of historical interest. Not one of the thirteen right-wing voters in our sample who was in a forced-choice situation at the second ballot cast a vote for a Gaullist candidate. In 1967 Charles de Gaulle's oldest and most unforgiving enemies, the followers of Marshal Pétain, along with the die-hard defenders of a French Algeria, either cast their votes for leftists or centrists or did not vote at all.

This survey of the flow of the vote, concentrating on the behavior in forced-choice situations of Communist voters, Federation or PSU voters, and centrist voters, has revealed wide variations in second-ballot electoral behavior. First-ballot Communist supporters act very differently from people who prefer non-Communist leftists. Among the typical supporters of the non-Communist left there are intriguing variations in second-ballot choices. And the behavior of first-ballot centrist voters varies at the second ballot, depending on whether the left-wing candidate available is a Communist or a non-Communist. In the next section of this chapter, we shall decipher these different patterns of behavior. But first let us consider the dynamics of public-opinion formation during the week between the two ballots.

In discussing abstentions in the preceding chapter, we referred to two other estimates of the flow of the vote between the ballots in 1967. One of these was based on an IFOP national sample survey conducted between the two ballots (Mothe, 1967).[4] The other was based on multiple regressions performed at SOFRES by Lancelot and Weill (1970), employing the actual aggregate results of the 1967 election.[5] The portions of these two sets of estimates that can be directly compared with our own are presented in comparative form in Table 12-4.[6]

In Table 12-4 the largest differences among the various estimates of the flow of the vote from the first to the second ballot appear in part (a), which refers to Type A districts, where a Gaullist (Ve République) dueled with a Communist at the second ballot. The estimates in part (b), referring to Type B districts, where the second ballot was a contest between a Gaullist (Ve République) and a non-Communist leftist(Federation or PSU), are strikingly similar.

It is not immediately obvious why the Lancelot-Weill analysis, which is methodologically quite different from both the IFOP (Mothe) analysis and our own, should produce results similar to IFOP's and ours for one set of districts but not the other. It is easy to explain, however, why the estimates made by IFOP differ from ours for districts where Gaullists faced Communists, but are similar to ours for districts where Gaullists faced the non-Communist left. The IFOP estimates, which are based on a sample survey conducted between the two ballots, reflect expressed vote intentions; our estimates, which are based on a post-electoral survey, reflect expressed vote reports. Differences between the IFOP estimates and our own, therefore, al-

Table 12-4. Comparative estimates of flow of vote from first to second ballot (percentages), France, 1967.

(a) Flow of vote in districts where second-ballot competition was between Communist party and Ve République

| 2nd-ballot vote | 1st-ballot vote | | | | | |
| | Federation or PSU | | | Centrist | | |
	C-P[a]	M[b]	L-W[c]	C-P	M	L-W
Communist	61	70	59	9	25	26
Ve République	18	16	38	52	58	60
Abstained	7	14	} 3	24	17	} 14
Spoiled ballot	14	—		15	—	

(b) Flow of vote in districts where second-ballot competition was between Federation or PSU and Ve République

| 2nd-ballot vote | 1st-ballot vote | | | | | |
| | Communist | | | Centrist | | |
	C-P	M	L-W	C-P	M	L-W
Federation or PSU	87	82	80	38	37	45
Ve République	8	9	10	51	55	49
Abstained	3	9	} 10	3	8	} 6
Spoiled ballot	2	—		8	—	

a. Converse-Pierce estimates.
b. Mothe (1967, p. 98).
c. Lancelot and Weill (1970, p. 375).

most surely reflect changes in electoral opinion during the last few days prior to the second ballot. Where the IFOP results and our own are similar, it is likely that there was no last-minute shift in voting decisions. It is perfectly plausible that numerous changes occurred in partisan vote intentions during the period between the ballots in districts where Gaullists faced Communists, but that second-ballot vote intentions remained quite stable in districts where Gaullists competed against non-Communist leftists.

As Table 12-4, part (a), indicates, in districts where Gaullists competed with Communists at the second ballot, fully a fourth of the centrist voters in IFOP's sample indicated, before the election, that they would vote for a Communist, while less than 10 percent of our sample of centrists reported, after the election, that they had voted for a Communist candidate at the second ballot. Similarly, though less notably, there is a gap between IFOP's report of the proportion of non-Communist leftists who intended to vote Communist and our own estimate of the proportion of non-Communist leftists that actually did vote Communist. With regard to both the centrists and the non-Communist leftists, the difference between pre-electoral vote intentions and post-election vote reports is reflected in the much larger proportions of abstentions and spoiled ballots registered in our estimates than in IFOP's.

This pattern of last-minute change in electoral opinion is quite intelligible. Those centrist and non-Communist leftist voters who were both anti-Gaullist and anti-Communist at the same time were tempted shortly before the second ballot to cast their votes for Communist candidates out of anti-Gaullism, but when election day arrived their anti-Communist sentiments surfaced sufficiently to drive them into abstention or ballot-spoiling.

Among Communist and centrist voters in districts where there were duels between the non-Communist left and the Gaullists, as reported in Table 12-4, part (b), there was no such sequence of pre-electoral anti-Gaullism followed by retreat into nonparticipation. Communist voters were more committed to the left-wing alliance at the second ballot than non-Communist leftists were. Communist support for the non-Communist left mobilized at a high level before the second ballot and remained constant through election day. Centrist voters in those same districts divided between the non-Communist left and the Gaullists, but for those voters, too, the levels of support registered in the IFOP pre-electoral survey were about the same as those reported in our post-electoral survey.

These indications of constancy within the two main blocs of forced-choice voters in districts where the second ballot involved a straight fight between a non-Communist leftist and a Gaullist are as understandable as the second thoughts displayed by non-Communist leftists and centrists who were tempted to vote Communist if the choice was between a Communist and a Gaullist. The non-Communist left does not arouse the same kind of fear and hostility as the Communist party does. Communist voters were overwhelmingly committed to the left-wing alliance and supported it from the start. A much larger proportion of anti-Gaullist centrists was willing to vote for the non-Communist left than to support the Communists, and these voters did not—in the aggregate—recoil at the last minute from their pre-electoral determination.

So far, we have underscored the differences between the various estimates of the flow of the vote between the two ballots in 1967. We should not, however, overlook the similarities. In broad terms, the three sets of estimates converge on several central points. All three indicate that proportionally more Communist supporters voted for the non-Communist left at the second ballot than non-Communist left supporters voted for Communists. The majority of the non-Communist left voted for the Communists, but a substantial minority voted for Gaullists. Although the largest proportion of centrists in forced-choice situations voted Gaullist, a smaller group voted for the non-Communist left, and some even voted for Communists.

On these points, the three sets of estimates are in accord. The question to which we shall now turn takes this broad area of agreement as its point of departure: why do French voters, in forced-choice situations at the second ballot, divide as they do?

Long-Term Factors Affecting Forced Choices

Our central problem now is to account for the patterns of change in electoral choice that occur between the first and second ballot among voters who cannot repeat their first-ballot partisan vote. This problem is analogous to that of identifying the long-term determinants of electoral behavior, as normally expressed in the first-ballot vote, which we discussed in earlier chapters. Trying to understand the logic of vote changes is similar to trying to understand the basic reasons for vote preferences, because we would expect the same, or at least comparable, factors to influence both patterns. In analyzing first preferences we examined such factors as party identification, perceptions of self and partisan locations on the left-right dimension, religion and degree of religious practice, and attitudes toward General de Gaulle. Now we shall examine the extent to which all but one of those factors explains how the first-ballot voters for any given party divide their votes at the second ballot when they are forced to make a different partisan choice or not to vote at all.

The one major long-term factor in structuring the partisan vote that we cannot rely upon in investigating vote change is party identification. Party identifiers normally vote at the first ballot for the parties with which they identify, while the group of voters we are considering includes only people who could not vote at the second ballot for the party for which they had voted at the first ballot and with which, in a large proportion of cases, they identified. Indeed, the problem before us amounts to explaining why people of the same partisanship cast their second-ballot votes differently when they cannot vote for the party with which they identify.

Fortunately, another factor related to electoral choice has a conceptual status similar to that of party identification. This is the scale of party preferences, expressed in sympathy or antipathy scores on the feeling thermometer, to which we referred in Chapter 10 and also in Chapter 11, where we found it to be at the root of voter decisions concerning whether to participate at the second ballot when first-ballot partisan choices could not be repeated. Such a powerful determinant of electoral participation is likely also to be a major factor in partisan choice. We shall therefore add partisan sympathies to our other measures—left-right location, religious practice, and attitudes toward de Gaulle.

Two groups of voters are represented in large enough numbers in our sample to permit us to examine, separately, their electoral behavior in forced-choice situations. The first consists of people who voted for Federation or PSU candidates at the first ballot in districts where the second-ballot contest was between Communists and Gaullists. The second consists of centrist voters who had to choose between a leftist, whether Communist or non-Communist, and a Gaullist at the second ballot. We shall also examine Communist voters in districts where the second-ballot choice was between the non-Communist left and the Gaullists, although here case numbers are woefully small.

Forced Choices by Non-Communist Leftists

Our discussion of forced choices by non-Communist leftists will be limited to the voters in Type A districts, where the second-ballot choice was between a Communist and a Gaullist. Case numbers are largest for this group of districts, and within it the question as to why non-Communist leftists divide as they do at the second ballot is raised in its starkest form. How to vote when the only partisan alternatives are a Communist or a Gaullist is the classic dilemma that frequently faces non-Communist leftists in France.

It is almost embarrassingly easy to explain why some non-Communist leftists opt for the Communists while others choose the Gaullists in forced-choice situations at the second ballot. Deutsch, Lindon, and Weill (1966, p. 34) have pointed out that the moderate left in France is profoundly divided on almost all major issues: "the voters of the moderate left agree on practically nothing." We have found ample evidence to confirm that judgment in the context of second-ballot partisan choices. *All* of the long-term determinants of voting behavior to which we referred earlier serve to distinguish between the Federation and PSU voters who chose Communist candidates and those who threw their support to the Gaullists. Table 12-5 shows how these two groups of non-Communist leftists, as well as the Federation and PSU voters who abstained or spoiled their ballots, differ with regard to clericalism, attitudes toward de Gaulle, self-location on the left-right dimension, distance from their own left-right self-location and the locations they attributed to the party that they chose and the party they rejected, and the degree of sympathy that they felt for the party they chose and the party they rejected.[7]

In every case, the measures are consistent with what one would expect given the partisan choice made by the voters in question at the second ballot. The non-Communist leftists who voted for Gaullists were strongly proclerical, as indicated by a mean clericalism score of more than 70, while those who chose the Communists were anticlerical, with a mean score barely above 40. Those who opted for the Gaullists had favorable attitudes toward de Gaulle (Gaullism). Those who voted for the Communists were opposed to de Gaulle. The Federation and PSU voters who selected Gaullist

Table 12-5. Mean scores on various attitude dimensions of first-ballot Federation and PSU voters, by second-ballot choice, in districts where only Communists and Gaullists ran at second ballot, France, 1967.[a]

| Attitude dimension | Second-ballot choice | | |
	Communist	Abstention or spoiled ballot	Gaullist
Clericalism	41.2 (38)	40.4 (10)	72.5 (9)
Gaullism	44.5 (38)	25.5 (10)	78.9 (9)
Own left-right location	31.2 (38)	27.0 (10)	54.1 (7)
Perceived distance of Communist party from own left-right location	−15.7 (36)	−8.6 (9)	−34.9 (7)
Perceived distance of Gaullists from own left-right location	40.2 (36)	35.0 (9)	14.0 (6)
Sympathy for Communist party	54.0 (38)	30.1 (10)	39.0 (9)
Sympathy for Gaullist party	28.0 (37)	18.4 (10)	63.9 (9)

a: Numbers of cases are shown in parentheses.

candidates located themselves right of center, at a mean location of about 54; those who preferred the Communists placed themselves left of center, at a mean location of 31. Gaullist supporters perceived the Communist party to be almost 35 points to the left of their own mean self-ascribed location on the left-right dimension; Communist supporters considered the Communist party to be much closer to them on the same scale. Communist supporters, however, perceived the Gaullist party to be even further to their right than Gaullist voters regarded the Communists as being to their left. The Gaullist supporters, on the contrary, considered the Gaullists to be just about as far to their right as the Communist voters felt the Communist party to be to their left. Lastly, the non-Communist leftists who voted for Communist candidates at the second ballot had a somewhat favorable view of the Communist party, as reflected in a mean thermometer score of 54, while they had a distinctly negative view of the Gaullists, to whom they awarded a mean score of 28. Those who preferred the Gaullists, by contrast, disliked the Communist party, to which they gave a mean sympathy score of 39, while they took an emphatically favorable view of the Gaullist party, as expressed in a mean sympathy score of almost 64.[8]

No such neat multivariate explanation of voter behavior emerges, however, when we turn to the non-Communist leftists who abstained or spoiled their ballots. This group of voters clusters within the general category of abstainers and ballot-spoilers discussed in the preceding chapter, where we demonstrated that although partisan attitudes accounted for decisions concerning whether or not to vote at the second ballot, perceptions of left-right locations did not do so. This general finding applies strikingly to the special case of non-Communist leftists.

The non-Communist leftists who abstained or spoiled their ballots are not pallid middle-of-the-roaders, indifferent to the church and de Gaulle, and equidistant from the Communists and the Gaullists on the left-right scale. They are dyed-in-the-wool left-wingers. In a general sense, they resemble the non-Communist leftists who voted for Communist candidates at the second ballot, but their left-wing credentials are even more impressive than that group's. The abstainers and spoilers are still further to the left, and they perceive themselves to be closer to the Communist party on the left-right scale. They are ferociously anti-Gaullist, with regard to both the General himself and the Gaullist party; indeed, on this dimension, they exceed the Communist supporters by a wide margin.

The one measure that distinguishes the abstainers and spoilers most sharply from the Communist supporters, however, is their attitude toward the Communist party. These abstainers and spoilers are even more anti-Communist than the non-Communist leftists who voted for the Gaullists. Just as in the general case discussed in the preceding chapter, the non-Communist leftists who abstained or spoiled their ballots at the second round of voting did so because they intensely disliked both of the partisan alternatives available to them.

There are, therefore, three distinct types of non-Communist leftist voters. One type, the most numerous, consists of people who will vote for Communist candidates at the second ballot in forced-choice situations. These voters regard themselves as leftists; they are anticlerical; they have an unfavorable attitude toward de Gaulle and are quite hostile to the Gaullist party; they regard the Gaullist party as being much further to their right than they perceive the Communist party to be to their left; and they have a mildly favorable attitude toward the Communist party.

A second type of non-Communist leftist voter, less than one third as numerous as the first type, is almost its mirror image. These voters, who will support Gaullist candidates at the second ballot, perceive themselves to be slightly right of center; they are proclerical; they are strongly favorable to de Gaulle and quite markedly favorable to the Gaullist party as well; and they are hostile to the Communist party, which they perceive as being more than twice as far to their left as they perceive the Gaullist party to be to their right.

The third type of non-Communist leftist, about as numerous as the second type, is very much like the first type: leftist, anticlerical, anti-Gaullist, and comparatively close to the Communists on the left-right scale. Yet, in contrast to the first type, this brand of leftist is strongly anti-Communist. As a result, he or she has no incentive to vote either for Gaullist or Communist

candidates and, when faced with that choice, either stays at home or goes to
the polls only deliberately to spoil his or her ballot.[9]

The most important attribute possessed by all three of these groups is
that they prefer the Federation (or PSU) to any of the other parties, and
will vote for it when they are free to do so. When, however, they must
make some other choice because their preferred party is simply not available,
they divide three ways, depending on the kind of match there is between
the available alternatives and their particular mix of partisan attitudes, left-
right sentiments, and attitudes toward de Gaulle.

Forced Choices by Centrists

Centrist voters found themselves in forced-choice situations at the second
ballot even more often, proportionately, than the non-Communist leftists
did. Centrist candidates ran at the second ballot in only twenty-one of our
seventy-six sample districts where there was a second ballot. Everywhere
else, centrist voters had to choose between candidates from other parties, in
most cases between a Gaullist and a single left-wing candidate, who was a
Communist in about half the cases and a non-Communist leftist in the
other half.

It should be recalled that in Type A districts, where the choice was between a Gaullist and a Communist, about half of the people who had voted
for centrists at the first ballot shifted their support to the Gaullists, less than
10 percent voted for the Communists, and the remainder—almost 40 percent of the total—either abstained or spoiled their ballots. In Type B districts, where the second-ballot competition was between a Gaullist and a
non-Communist leftist, about the same proportion of centrist voters shifted
to the Gaullists, more than a third voted for the non-Communist left, and
only slightly more than 10 percent abstained or spoiled their ballots.

In order to enlarge the number of applicable cases, we have pooled the
first-ballot centrist voters in both Type A and Type B districts, broken them
down by their second-ballot electoral behavior, and computed their mean
locations on each of the dimensions that we employed in our analysis of the
forced-choice behavior of non-Communist leftist voters in Type A districts
alone. The results of this operation appear in Table 12-6, which is analogous
to Table 12-5.

Table 12-6 shows that centrist voters who supported a leftist candidate
do not differ systematically, on every dimension, from those who voted for a
Gaullist, in the way that non-Communist leftists who voted for a Communist differ from those who supported a Gaullist. The centrists who voted for
Gaullists are somewhat more proclerical than those who voted for a leftist
candidate, but the latter are also proclerical, and the difference is not large.
Counterintuitively, the centrists who voted for leftists perceived themselves
as slightly right of center, while those who voted Gaullist considered them-

Table 12-6. Mean scores on various attitude dimensions of first-ballot centrist voters, by second-ballot choice, in districts where only Leftists and Gaullists ran at second ballot, France, 1967.[a]

Attitude dimension	Second-ballot choice					
	Leftist[b]		Abstention or spoiled ballot		Gaullist	
Clericalism	56.4	(13)	61.2	(18)	62.8	(34)
Gaullism	41.2	(13)	54.8	(18)	69.2	(34)
Own left-right location (excluding marais)	52.6	(8)	56.2	(10)	43.5	(15)
Perceived distance of leftist party from own left-right location[b]	−21.5	(12)	−36.7	(15)	−29.2	(27)
Perceived distance of Gaullists from own left-right location	26.2	(10)	31.5	(15)	24.0	(25)
Sympathy for leftist party[b]	54.8	(13)	36.5	(18)	39.5	(34)
Sympathy for Gaullist party	43.6	(13)	42.4	(18)	58.5	(34)

a. Numbers of cases are in parentheses.
b. Communist party, Federation, or PSU.

selves on the average to be distinctly left of center. The Gaullist supporters, however, perceived the particular leftist party that ran in their district to be further to their left than the leftist supporters did, but the two groups of voters regarded the Gaullist party to be about equally distant to their right.

The only dimensions in Table 12-6 that account for the different partisan choices made by centrist voters at the second ballot are attitudes toward Gaullism and partisanship. The Gaullist supporters were distinctly favorable to Gaullism, held a favorable opinion of the Gaullist party, and were hostile toward the leftist party in their district. The leftist supporters, on the contrary, were anti-Gaullist, negative toward the Gaullist party, and moderately favorable toward the leftist party they voted for.

With regard to those centrist voters who abstained or spoiled their ballots, partisan attitudes clearly play a role—as we would expect from the findings of the last chapter. That group of voters was, at the same time, more hostile to the available leftist party than the centrists who voted Gaullist were, and more hostile to the Gaullists than the centrists who voted leftist were. They just did not like either the available leftist party or the Gaullists.

Perceived distances between the available parties and the voter on the left-right scale may also have been a factor in the decision of centrist voters to abstain or spoil their ballots, despite our general finding in the last chapter that such distances do not determine nonparticipation at the second ballot. Even if they were decisive in this special case, it is clear that they did not affect the partisan choices of those centrist voters who chose to cast valid ballots. Unlike partisan attitudes, therefore, perceived left-right distances did not, even in the case of this limited subset of centrist voters, have a generally determining effect on electoral behavior.

Forced Choices by Communists

Limited case numbers have been a serious problem in our effort to analyze the behavior of Communist voters in forced-choice situations. In those districts where a non-Communist leftist ran at the second ballot, almost 90 percent of the first-ballot Communist voters supported him, leaving only a small number of absolute cases divided fairly equally between support for the Gaullists and one of the forms of nonparticipation. Hence, in Table 12-7, we can compare only those Communist voters who supported a non-Communist leftist at the second ballot with all the other first-ballot Communist voters in the same districts, whether they voted for Gaullists, abstained, or spoiled their ballots. This procedure has obvious shortcomings, but it at least serves to distinguish between those Communists who shifted their support to the non-Communist left and those who did not.

Table 12-7 indicates that the only dimension accounting for the different behavior of the two sets of Communists is Gaullism. The Communist

Table 12-7. Mean scores on various attitude dimensions of first-ballot Communist voters, by second-ballot choice, in districts where non-Communist leftists ran at second ballot, France, 1967.[a]

	Second-ballot choice	
Attitude dimension	Voted for non-Communist left	Did not vote for non-Communist left
Clericalism	31.9 (54)	31.9 (6)
Gaullism	34.6 (54)	61.1 (6)
Own left-right location	17.1 (47)	16.0 (5)
Perceived distance of non-Communist left party from own left-right location	20.6 (43)	b
Perceived distance of closest non-left party from own left-right location	57.5 (39)	b
Sympathy for non-Communist left party	61.5 (54)	57.4 (6)
Sympathy for most preferred non-left party	24.7 (54)	40.8 (6)

a. Numbers of cases are in parentheses.
b. Fewer than five cases.

voters who threw their support to the non-Communist leftists had all the familiar leftist characteristics, including a strongly negative attitude toward Gaullism. The Communists who did not support those candidates had similarly impeccable left-wing credentials, except for their favorable attitude toward Gaullism. This element of Gaullism among Communist voters was apparently strong enough to outweigh both their generally favorable attitude toward the non-Communist left parties and their generally unfavorable attitude toward the available non-leftist party that they disliked the least. Here is a suggestive indication of the attraction de Gaulle had for a small minority of Communist voters.

Overall View of
Second-Ballot Partisan Choice

So far we have dealt only with selected groups of voters in particular types of second-ballot circumstances. We have seen that when Federation or PSU voters had to choose between a Communist candidate and a Gaullist candidate, those who made a partisan choice divided in ways that are intelligible in the light of all the classic long-term indicators of partisan choice in France: religion, Gaullism, left-right location, perceptions of distance between self and party along the left-right dimension, and partisan attitudes. For centrists forced to choose between a Gaullist and a left-wing candidate, whether Communist or non-Communist, only partisanship and attitudes toward Gaullism serve to distinguish between the centrists who made one partisan choice or the other. And among Communists who had an opportunity to vote for a non-Communist leftist at the second ballot, only Gaullism distinguishes clearly between those who chose to do so and those who did not.

The subsets of voters that we have examined separately constitute a majority of the French voters who found themselves in forced-choice situations at the second ballot in 1967. They do not, however, include all the voters who could not repeat their first-ballot partisan choice. We did not, for example, discuss non-Communist leftists who were forced to choose between Gaullists and centrists (Type G districts), or between either of them and a Communist (Type D districts). Nor did we discuss the Gaullist voters in districts where there was no Gaullist candidate at the second ballot (as in Type C and Type E districts). We have not referred to the rightist or "other" voters who could not repeat their first-ballot partisan choices. And we have not mentioned the voters in districts where there was no leftist candidate at the second ballot (G and H districts).

It is time to take a more global look at the forces affecting French partisan choices at the second ballot by including all voters in a forced-choice situation, regardless of its particular nature. Here we shall consider three variables. The first two are partisan sympathies and perceived distances on the left-right dimension. We have already found that partisan sympathies can account for the partisan choices of both non-Communist leftists and centrists in certain forced-choice situations, and that perceptions of left-right distances can also account for the partisan choices made by the non-Communist leftists alone. We shall consider these two variables in tandem, much as we did in the last chapter. The third variable is Gaullism, the only one we have found to be operative among all three subsets of voters.

Partisan Preferences versus Left-Right Perceptions

Table 12-8 contains the mean party sympathy scores and the mean perceived distances from the voters' own left-right locations for the party chosen and the best available party rejected at the second ballot by all voters who cast valid ballots in forced-choice situations. Both factors register intelligibly. The voters who made partisan choices had, on the average, a moderately favorable view of the party for which they voted, and they had a distinctly unfavorable view of the "least disliked" party for which they did not vote. At the same time, they perceived the party for which they voted to be considerably closer to them in left-right terms, on the average, than the closest available alternative.

Although Table 12-8 does not indicate which of the two variables has the stronger effect on second-ballot partisan choices, a multiple regression analysis shows that partisan sympathies are somewhat stronger than perceptions of left-right distances. The multiple correlation coefficient for the two independent variables is $r = .60$. The partial correlation coefficient for net advantage in partisan sympathy is $r = .36$ and that for net advantage in perceived left-right distance is $r = .29$. As we know from the last chapter, the two independent variables are highly intercorrelated ($r = .57$ in the form employed here), but once again we find discrete partisan attitudes to be a stronger force than left-right perceptions in French electoral behavior.[10]

Unlike our findings in the last chapter, however, which showed that

Table 12-8. Mean partisan sympathy and mean perceived left-right distances for parties chosen and best available parties rejected by voters in forced-choice situations at second ballot, France, 1967.[a]

Attitude dimension	Party chosen	Party rejected
Mean partisan sympathy	56.1 (194)	33.0 (193)
Mean perceived left-right distance of party from voter	25.2 (162)	43.5 (154)

a. Case numbers in parentheses.

Table 12-9. Mean attitudes toward Gaullism, expressed in standard scores, by second-ballot partisan choice in forced-choice situations, France, 1967.[a]

Second-ballot partisan choice	Attitude toward Gaullism
Gaullist	.80 (51)
Centrist	.53 (19)
Leftist	−.32 (122)

a. Case numbers in parentheses.

electoral *participation* at the second ballot could be clearly accounted for by partisan sympathies but not by perceptions of left-right distances, we now find that although partisan sympathies are more potent than left-right distances, the latter do account to some substantial degree for partisan choice. There is nothing contradictory in these two sets of findings. Partisan attitudes account for voters' decisions to cast a valid ballot in forced-choice situations, but once they have decided to do so, perceived left-right distances count in determining the particular partisan choices the voters make, although not quite so much as partisan sympathies do. Participation and partisan choice are, in this sense, independent phenomena. The former depends essentially on partisan attitudes, whereas the latter depends on both partisan attitudes and perceptions of left-right distances.

Gaullism

Although there is some question as to the status of Gaullism as a long-term factor in French electoral behavior, there is no doubt about its power in 1967. Gaullism also left clear traces in the electoral behavior of forced-choice voters at the second ballot. Table 12-9 sets out the mean standardized scores relating to the Gaullist–anti-Gaullist dimension for all forced-choice voters, subdivided by their second-ballot partisan choice. The results are unambiguous. The voters who opted for Gaullist candidates were distinctly pro-Gaullist; those who voted for centrist candidates were also pro-Gaullist but less so than the previous group; and those who supported leftist candidates, whether Communist or non-Communist, were clearly anti-Gaullist. Gaullism, therefore, played an important role in French electoral behavior, both at the decisive ballot generally and within forced-choice situations at the second ballot in particular.

Candidate Estimates of the Vote Flow

We have already compared our sample estimates of the flow of the vote from the first to the second ballot with those computed by other researchers who employed different methods. Now we shall examine another set of estimates of vote transfers, those made by the candidates themselves.

At our interviews with candidates, we asked those who ran at the second ballot where they thought the votes came from that they gained between the first and second ballots, expressed as proportions of the voters for the various other parties running at the first ballot. Then, they were asked the same question concerning the origins of the votes that their opponents gained from one ballot to the other.[11] Candidates who were not eligible for the second ballot because they did not receive the required minimum proportion of votes at the first ballot, as well as those who voluntarily withdrew from the race, were asked what proportions of the people who had voted for them at the first ballot either voted for one or another party or abstained at the second ballot.[12]

Taking the replies that were complete and were expressed in proportions, we applied those proportions to the actual numbers of first-ballot votes cast for the relevant parties in each candidate's district, according to the official vote results.[13] That permitted us to compute, for several of the types of district listed in Table 12-1, the proportions of the first-ballot vote for each major party that the candidates of each major party estimated had shifted to each candidate at the second ballot. We are, therefore, able to compare the perceptions of the vote flow by each group of partisan candidates, in various types of electoral situation, with the flow of the vote as indicated by our mass sample estimates.

Table 12-10. Candidate (and mass sample) estimates of flow of vote from first to second ballot (percentages), France, 1967.[a]

(a) Districts where second-ballot competition was between Gaullists and Federation or PSU candidates (Type B districts: 26)

	Second-ballot vote		
First-ballot vote	Federation or PSU	Abstention or spoiled ballot	Gaullist
Communist			
Estimate of Communist candidates (14)	95	1	4
Estimate of Federation candidates (14)	93	1	6
Estimate of Gaullist candidates (16)	99	1	0
Mass sample estimate (42.9)	87	5	8
Centrist			
Estimate of Federation candidates (13)	42	53	5
Estimate of centrist candidates (17)	47	43	10
Estimate of Gaullist candidates (11)	46	48	6
Mass sample estimate (24.0)	38	12	50

Table 12-10. Continued

(b) Districts where second-ballot competition was between Gaullists and Communists (Type A districts: 27)

	Second-ballot vote		
First-ballot vote	Communists	Abstention or spoiled ballot	Gaullist
Federation or PSU			
Estimate of Communist candidates (9)	94	3	3
Estimate of Federation candidates (22)	78	10	12
Estimate of Gaullist candidates (11)	73	24	3
Mass sample estimate (64.2)	61	21	18
Centrist			
Estimate of Communist candidates (6)	31	47	22
Estimate of centrist candidates (20)	22	47	31
Estimate of Gaullist candidates (10)	25	51	24
Mass sample estimate (44.8)	9	39	52

(c) Districts where second-ballot competition was between Communists and centrists or among Communists, centrists, and Gaullists (Type C and Type D districts: 8)

	Second-ballot vote		
First-ballot vote	Communists	Abstention or spoiled ballot	Gaullist
Federation or PSU			
Estimate of Federation candidates (6)	80	5	15
Mass sample estimate (9.1)	75	15	10

a. Case numbers are in parentheses. Candidate Ns are unweighted; mass Ns are weighted.

Table 12-10 compares the estimates of the flow of the vote from the first to the second ballot, made by various categories of candidates in certain types of districts, with our own mass sample estimates of vote transfers for the same groups of districts. These mass sample estimates rest on the cumulative totals of the sample vote reported from all of the sample districts of each type, although case numbers are small for some types of district. The number of candidates of any partisan group whose estimates are compared with the mass sample estimate is never as large as the number of districts of the relevant type. This is because some candidates were not interviewed and, among those who were, some either did not answer the relevant questions or answered them in ways that could not be properly quantified. This is bound to have some distorting effect on the results, but we are reasonably confident that the distortion is not large, as the estimates of the flow of the vote to and from similar parties reported by groups of different partisan candidates tend to be quite uniform even when they are based on widely varying case numbers.

The candidates' estimates of vote transfers by Communist supporters in districts where the second ballot was a duel between a non-Communist leftist and a Gaullist, reported in part (a), are all fairly close to our mass sample estimates. To be sure, the candidates of all the major groups surveyed exaggerated the extent to which first-ballot Communist voters maintained leftwing discipline. But this was due mainly to the candidates' failure to recognize that there is an irreducible level of abstentions. If we were to add 6 percent to each group of candidates' estimates of the proportion of abstainers and spoilers, and reduce their estimates of the proportions of non-Communist leftist supporters and Gaullist supporters by the same amount proportionately, that would have virtually no effect on the reported estimates of the Gaullist vote, but it would bring the estimates of the non-Communist leftist vote much closer to our own sample estimates. Yet even without such adjustments, the candidates' estimates of the flow of the Communist vote from the first to the second ballot match our sample estimates fairly well, with those of the Federation candidates coming closest to our sample benchmarks and those of the Gaullist candidates being farthest from them. It is of more than passing interest that the candidates of the two main left-wing parties, the Communists and the Federation, had a sense that the Communist electorate was at least slightly vulnerable to the appeal of the Gaullists at the second ballot, whereas, somewhat ironically, the beneficiaries of Communist defections from the leftist alliance—the Gaullists— did not acknowledge this.

In the portion of part (a) containing the candidates' estimates of the vote transfers by centrist voters in districts where a Gaullist faced a non-Communist leftist at the second ballot, we find a tolerable match between their estimates and our sample estimates with regard to the proportions of centrist voters who shifted their support to the non-Communist left, but we find uniformly large differences between the candidates' estimates and the sample estimates of the proportions of centrists who transferred their support to the Gaullists or who abstained or spoiled their ballots.

Whereas the candidates tended to underestimate the second-ballot abstention rate of first-ballot Communist voters relative to our sample estimate, they overestimated the second-ballot abstention rate of centrist voters. Indeed, if we assume that the candidates' estimates of centrist abstention rates refer to *deliberate* abstentions, excluding any consideration of a base rate of abstention of some 6 percent (an assumption that is not illegitimate given the candidates' uniformly low estimates of Communist abstentions), and if we therefore add 6 percent to the candidates' estimates of the rate of nonparticipation, reducing their estimates for the other two electoral options proportionately, their estimates of the rate of centrist support for the non-Communist left would move still closer to our sample estimate, but their estimates of the nonparticipation rate would diverge even more widely from that estimate.

Moreover, the candidates' estimates of centrist vote transfers in favor of Gaullist candidates are also uniformly different from the sample estimate. The Federation candidates estimated the rate of Gaullist support among centrist voters to be no greater than their estimate of Gaullist support among Communist voters. The centrist candidates themselves estimated the flow of centrist support to the Gaullists to be five times less than our sample estimates. And, just as in their estimate of the flow of Communist support to the Gaullists, the Gaullist candidates, who were the main beneficiaries of centrist vote transfers, seem not to have been aware of the degree of their support among centrist voters.

In districts where the second-ballot competition was a duel between a Gaullist and a Communist, reported in Table 12-10, part (b), the candidates' estimates of vote transfers by non-Communist left voters varied considerably with the partisan attachments of the candidates. The Communists overestimated non-Communist left support for their party by about 50 percent, relative to the sample estimate. The Federation candidates also overestimated the attraction of the Communists for their first-ballot voters, but by a lesser extent; they had a more realistic view than the other main-party candidates of the appeal of the Gaullists to their first-ballot supporters. And, in a pattern that is becoming familiar, the Gaullist candidates underestimated the extent to which they drew support at the second ballot from the non-Communist left, although their estimates of Communist support and nonparticipation by that group match the sample estimates more closely than those of the other groups of partisan candidates.

In the same type of district, all the groups of candidates who were surveyed had similar perceptions of centrist vote transfers. They all overestimated Communist support among centrists, by comparison with our sample estimate, and they underestimated centrist support for the Gaullists, although on both scores the centrist candidates had a more "accurate" view of the behavior of their supporters than the candidates of the other parties did. Once again, the Gaullists were far from the sample estimate in this regard, this time by about 50 percent.

The last type of district for which we have relevant measures consists of those in which Communists faced centrists, or both centrists and Gaullists, at the second ballot (see Table 12-10, part c), although here case numbers for our sample estimate of vote transfers are very small. Federation candidates, the only group for which we have adequate data, estimated the second-ballot behavior of their first-ballot supporters in these districts in a way that matches our sample estimates quite closely.

Summarizing the candidates' perceptions of vote transfers between the two ballots in comparison with our mass sample estimates of these same transfers, we find three general characteristics. The candidates tended to overestimate the amount of centrist and non-Communist leftist support for the Communist party; they underestimated the extent to which these two groups of first-ballot voters shifted to the Gaullists at the second ballot; and, less important, they tended to ignore the fact that there is an irreducible proportion of abstentions. The "accuracy" of the perceptions of the candidates varied somewhat by party group, but on the whole their estimates tended to coincide.[14]

Conclusions

We have charted the flow of the vote from the first to the second ballot in districts with various configurations of partisan competition at the second ballot, and we have tried to account for the different choices made at the second ballot by people who made a common partisan choice at the first ballot that they could not repeat. We know that some voters, when faced with a forced choice, take refuge in abstention or deliberate ballot-spoiling. Others decide to make a new partisan choice. But those voters who have all supported one particular party at the first ballot commonly divide their support at the second. Some first-ballot centrist voters throw their support to the Gaullists, others to the left; some Federation voters shift to the Communists, others to the Gaullists; most Communist supporters vote for the Federation at the second ballot, but a small proportion prefer to cast their second ballots for Gaullists. And so on.

The factors influencing these partisan choices vary somewhat depending on the original partisan tendency of the voter. Federation voters who throw their support to the Communists in forced-choice situations differ from those who opt for the Gaullists, and they differ in predictable ways along all the familiar dimensions relevant to electoral choice generally in France: clericalism-anticlericalism, Gaullism–anti-Gaullism, sense of own left-right location, perceptions of partisan left-right locations, and degrees of felt party sympathy. Fewer operative influences affect the different partisan choices of centrist voters. For them, Gaullism and partisanship are the determining factors; neither the degree of clericalism nor left-right considerations appear to affect their partisan choices. For Communist voters, although we have very few cases of those who failed to support the left at the second ballot, Gaullism alone seems to account for these defections. Thus a complete and detailed presentation of the electoral forces at work in forced-choice situations at the second ballot would have to take original party attachments into account.

Because of our special interest in assessing the relative importance of perceived left-right distances and degrees of partisan sympathy as factors in the vote, we ran a test of their comparative influence on the partisan choices of first-ballot voters who also cast a valid ballot in forced-choice situations. Both forces influenced these voters' choice of a party, although there is reason to believe that of the two forces, which are highly correlated with each other, partisan sympathy is the stronger.

The flow of the vote between the ballots cannot be fully understood, however, without reference to those voters who abstained or deliberately spoiled their ballots at the second round of voting. More Federation voters took one or the other of those options than voted for Gaullists, for example, and an even larger proportion of centrists preferred abstention or ballot-spoiling to voting for a Communist. When we discussed participation versus nonparticipation (that is, abstention or ballot-spoiling) in the last chapter, we found that the decisive factor in determining whether or not people cast a valid ballot in forced-choice situations was partisan sympathy. In this chapter, that finding is confirmed at the level of separate blocs of partisan voters. It is displayed in starkest form among first-ballot Federation voters: the only difference between those who threw their support to the Communists at the second ballot and those who abstained or spoiled their ballots is that the latter were strongly anti-Communist, whereas the former looked on the Communists with some favor. Perceived left-right distances between the voters and the parties had little or nothing to do with that distinction. Similarly, the centrists who refused to choose between parties did not like either of the alternatives available to them.

It is apparent that one major force at work here is anti-Communism. How non-Communist voters behaved at the second ballot in 1967 depended overwhelmingly on whether the remaining leftist candidate was Communist or non-Communist. Four times as many centrists voted for the leftist candidate when he was not a Communist as when he was. Barely more than 60 percent of the non-Communist leftist voters threw their support to the Communists at the second ballot. But despite the importance of anti-Communism, due to the large number of voters it affects, it is not the *basic* operative force but rather the expression of partisanship and of the "unfriendly neighbors" phenomenon described in the last chapter.

In that chapter we pointed out that the French electorate generally sees less difference between parties in terms of their left-right locations than in terms of partisan sympathy. It is quite common for them to perceive two parties as being fairly close to each other on the left-right dimension, but to like one of them and dislike the other. Here that phenomenon is illustrated by the non-Communist leftists who refused to vote for either Gaullists or Communists. The same thing occurred at the opposite end of the political spectrum, where not one voter on the far right threw his support to a Gaullist at the second ballot. The practical consequences of this lack of cooperation on the right were slight compared with those that flowed from

the refusal of so many non-Communist leftists to support Communists, but
the underlying phenomenon is the same. Some voters simply loathe their
neighbors, at least when one defines neighborhoods as locations on the left-
right dimension.

The left-right dimension is not a wholly reliable basis for predicting
mass electoral behavior or even mass partisan attitudes because that dimension does not express all the forces that motivate people's electoral behavior.
A Socialist voter may feel that he is leftist and that his party and the Communist party are both about as leftist as he is, according to those economic,
religious, and group reference terms in which the mass electorate interprets
the left-right dimension. But that voter may also feel that the Communists
would throw people into jail, or that they are a bunch of Russian agents,
and neither of these notions is subsumed by the left-right dimension. Similarly, on that dimension a Catholic, free-enterprise admirer of Marshal
Pétain would not stand far from a Catholic, free-enterprise admirer of General de Gaulle. But "rightists" of the first type would not vote for Gaullist
candidates, and "rightists" of the Gaullist persuasion would not vote for
candidates who smacked of Pétainism.[15]

On the left, however, this neighbor-loathing phenomenon was not
symmetrical. Although a substantial minority of Federation voters refused
to throw their support to Communist candidates, Communist support for
Federation candidates was overwhelming. Some of the non-Communist leftist voters actually preferred Gaullists to Communists; others were at least
willing to run the risk that Gaullists would be elected rather than to vote
Communist. Communist voters, on the contrary, were willing to vote massively for the non-Communist left in order to defeat the Gaullists. The slogan of the allied left-wing parties in 1967, calling on the voters to support
"the single leftist candidate," drew a much more enthusiastic response from
the Communist than from the non-Communist electorate.

We saw in the last chapter that when French voters perceived certain
parties to be similarly located on the left-right dimension, it did not necessarily follow that they would think equally well (or ill) of these parties,
and, moreover, that this tendency for left-right perceptions to be independent of party sympathy was more marked among non-Communist leftists
than among Communists. This distinction is reflected here in the evident
reluctance of non-Communist leftists to support Communists, compared
with the broad willingness of Communists to support the non-Communist
left. A substantial proportion of non-Communist leftists were saying, in effect, of the remaining Communist candidate, "I know he's a leftist, but I
don't like him." Probably most Communist voters would have found that
position incomprehensible in 1967.

The evidence indicates that most *candidates*, regardless of party, would
also have found that position incomprehensible. They consistently overesti-

mated the proportion of non-Communist leftists that threw their support to the Communists. Indeed, they overestimated the extent to which all non-Communist voters shifted to the Communists and underestimated the extent to which they supported the Gaullists. This failure of the candidates accurately to chart the flow of the vote from the first to the second ballot has important implications for the representation process in France.

To the extent that a deputy tries to further the interests of his or her constituency, defined not in geographical terms but in terms of the electorate, a prior condition of success is to know who one's supporters are. This may be difficult enough under a simple single-ballot electoral system; it is even more difficult under the French two-ballot system. It is true, of course, that the proportion of a deputy's constituency that enters it via second-ballot vote transfers is comparatively small. Less than a fourth of the French voters are unable to repeat their first-ballot choice at the second ballot, and we have seen that a considerable fraction of these either abstain or spoil their ballots. But it is the net gains in vote transfers that provide the margins of victory at the second ballot, and their origins are a legitimate and necessary consideration in an examination of the French representation process. In the particular case we have examined here, it is evident that the most important implication for representative government lies in the failure of the Gaullist candidates to recognize the extent to which they drew support from centrists, non-Communist leftists, and even Communists. When we analyze in Part IV the extent to which French deputies may be said to represent their supporters, as opposed to all the voters in their districts, it will be helpful to keep in mind the different kinds of candidate misperceptions of the flow of the vote that we have traced in this chapter.

13

The Second Ballot: Candidate Behavior and Electoral Response

In discussing the second ballot we have dealt almost exclusively with the behavior of the voters: their electoral participation (Chapter 11), and the flow of the vote from the first to the second ballot (Chapter 12). The candidates entered the picture only briefly, when in that chapter we compared their perceptions of the flow of the vote with the estimates derived from our mass sample survey.

Obviously, the candidates are an essential element of the electoral process; their fortunes at the first ballot and their behavior between the ballots are decisive in shaping the partisan configurations from which the voters must choose at the second ballot. Some candidates are eliminated from the second ballot because they do not receive the requisite proportion of votes. Others, who are legally eligible to remain in the race, nevertheless withdraw, more or less voluntarily. Moreover, some of both of these types of drop-out candidates do nothing to affect the outcome of the second ballot, whereas others try to persuade their first-ballot voters to throw their support to another candidate. The efforts of those candidates to influence their voters may of course vary a great deal in nature and intensity.

The purpose of this chapter is to analyze the behavior of the candidates between the two ballots of the legislative elections of 1967. First we shall sketch out the patterns of behavior that were represented in our sample of candidates. Then we shall explore the underlying factors that account for variations in candidate behavior, both across the entire sample and for the subset of Federation candidates who were bound by national party policy to a leftist electoral alliance. Finally, we shall examine the response of the voters to candidate efforts to influence their second-ballot votes.

Patterns of Candidate Behavior

Our sample of candidates divided into three broad categories at the second ballot. About 10 percent ran in districts where the election was decided at the first ballot. For these candidates there was no second ballot and, consequently, no second-ballot behavior. They must therefore be excluded from several of the analyses that follow, but they will reappear later in this chapter. The remaining 90 percent divided almost equally between those who ran at the second ballot and those who did not. Of those who did not run, somewhat less than half were automatically eliminated from the race because they did not receive enough votes at the first ballot to be legally eligible for the second. The remainder were legally eligible to run at the second ballot but did not do so.

Conventional French political language distinguishes between two types of drop-out candidates. The operative words are the verbs *se désister* (to desist) and *se retirer* (to withdraw), along with their corresponding nouns, *désistement* (for which there is no adequate English translation) and *retrait* (withdrawal). The two terms differ as follows: to desist connotes dropping out in favor of another candidate, whereas to withdraw connotes dropping out without taking sides with any of the remaining candidates. Sometimes, when a drop-out candidate wants to emphasize his neutrality with regard to the remaining candidates, he describes his withdrawal as a *retrait pur et simple* (pure and simple withdrawal).

In real political life, however, there is not always such a clear-cut difference between a withdrawal and a désistement. Some candidates who withdraw may not care which remaining candidate wins the election. Others do care who wins but cannot bring themselves openly to support the lesser evil. Some of those candidates solve the problem by announcing their opposition to a remaining candidate without positively supporting an opponent of that candidate. Still others, confident that their supporters will spontaneously shift their support to the lesser evil in any case, simply withdraw without saying anything. Such subtleties apparently give some candidates the feeling that they have avoided the contamination of aiding political rivals, but, as we shall see later, they also risk failing to bring about the electoral outcome they desire.

Moreover, the terms withdrawal and désistement refer only to candidates who are eligible to run at the second ballot. Candidates who have been legally eliminated because they have not reached the required threshold of votes at the first ballot are called *éliminés* (eliminated candidates), but there is no conventional terminology to distinguish between an éliminé who supports another candidate at the second ballot and one who does not. The reason for this is almost certainly that the terminology relating to second-ballot politics originated when there were no strict rules governing the eligibility of candidates at the second ballot. When the single-member-district, two-ballot system was employed during the Third Republic (and even earlier), anybody who met the general legal qualifications for candidacy could run at the second ballot, even if he had not run at the first ballot. Prior to the Fifth Republic, there were no éliminés and hence no terminology relating to their behavior. None has developed during the Fifth Republic either, although the number of eliminated candidates has grown as the threshold for entry into the second ballot has been raised.[1] Indeed, little attention has been paid to the behavior of eliminated candidates, even though the electoral choices made at the second ballot by voters who have been liberated because their first-ballot choice was eliminated can have as important a marginal effect on the outcome of the election in a district as the choices made by voters whose preferred candidate either desisted in favor of another candidate or simply withdrew.

In order to avoid the potential ambiguities inherent in the stark division of the candidates who dropped out of the race more or less voluntarily between *désistés* and *retraités,* as well as to compensate for the absence of any fixed terminology to describe the behavior of éliminés, our interview protocol for the candidates included several questions designed to elicit as complete information as possible about their second-ballot activity.

Candidates who were eligible to run at the second ballot but who did not do so were asked whether they had desisted for another candidate; if they replied that they had not, they were then asked whether "nevertheless" (*tout de même*) they had helped another candidate between the two ballots. Candidates who were eliminated from the second ballot by the application of the 10 percent threshold were also asked whether they had supported another candidate. All candidates who indicated that they had desisted for or otherwise supported another candidate were then asked which candidate they had supported and what they had done to make their views known to their first-ballot voters.

This procedure turned out to be sound. Two-thirds of the drop-out candidates who were eligible to run at the second ballot told us that they had desisted for another candidate. Of the remaining third, fully a fourth responded to our follow-up question by reporting that "nevertheless" they had supported another candidate. In addition, more than a fourth of the eliminated candidates told us that they had helped another candidate between the ballots. The second-ballot behavior of the two basic groups of drop-out candidates, therefore, varied considerably. Among the drop-outs who were eligible to run at the second ballot, some three-fourths supported another candidate and only a quarter did not. Among the éliminés, those proportions were almost exactly reversed.[2]

The pattern of second-ballot electoral cooperation in 1967 was dominated by implementation of the alliance between the left-wing parties to support the single leftist candidate in each district who was best placed to win the seat. Literally all the candidates who told us that they had desisted for another candidate were leftists, and so were more than 60 percent of the éliminés who reported that they had supported another candidate.

The candidates who, while not desisting for another candidate, nevertheless helped one, as well as the remaining éliminés who supported another candidate, were a more heterogeneous group. They included Democratic Center candidates, some of whom supported leftists while others supported Gaullists; center-right candidates who tried to help the Democratic Center; independent Socialists who supported the Gaullists; Alliance Républicaine candidates who supported the left; and a few Gaullists who supported other candidates better placed to defeat the left.[3]

Most of the candidates who were eligible to run at the second ballot but who withdrew "purely and simply," as well as most of the candidates who were eliminated and did not try to help any remaining candidate, were Democratic Center candidates or—particularly among the eliminated—minor party candidates or independents. A small proportion of the "eligibles" who withdrew were Gaullists who had no chance of winning but who would have split the anti-leftist vote if they had remained. Another comparatively small fraction of the eliminated candidates who were inactive between the two ballots consisted of leftists in right-wing districts where no leftist candidate was eligible to run at the second ballot. But the most interesting group of candidates that neither ran at the second ballot nor helped another candidate consisted of non-Communist leftists who refused to help Communist candidates, despite the existence of a national electoral alliance between the left-wing parties. This phenomenon was sufficiently extensive to warrant special treatment later in this chapter. Here it is enough to say that the leftist parties' electoral alliance was neither welcomed nor fully implemented by all the non-Communist leftist candidates in 1967.

Candidate Perceptions of Drop-Out Candidate Behavior

So far we have referred only to the self-reported accounts of the between-ballots behavior of the candidates who dropped out of the race for one reason or another. But there were also about an equal number of candidates who *did* run at the second ballot. These candidates were all asked a series of questions concerning the drop-outs. First they were asked whether there had been any désistements in their favor and, if so, by which candidates, how these candidates had helped them between the ballots, and what they had done to make their views known to their first-ballot voters. Next the same candidates were asked whether there had been any withdrawals or eliminations that had worked to their advantage and, if so, by which candidates.

Finally, they were asked whether there had been any désistements in favor of their opponents at the second ballot and, if so, by which candidates, and also whether there had been any withdrawals or eliminations that they thought had worked to the advantage of their opponents.

Inasmuch as more than one candidate was interviewed in all but one of our sample districts, and three or more candidates were interviewed in the great majority of them, we had in hand a panorama of multiple perceptions of the same situations. Our objectives, of course, were to determine whether each candidate's self-reported behavior between the ballots was viewed in the same way by the other candidates, and, if candidate perceptions differed, in what ways and for what reasons they did so.[4]

As the data turned out, we might have spared ourselves this particular effort. The results pointed overwhelmingly to the concordance of the various candidates' perceptions of the second-ballot behavior of the drop-out candidates. In one sense, this massive evidence of agreement among candidates of a given district about who supported whom was disappointing. For as we were preparing the data and considering the structural factors that might affect the candidates' perceptions of what the other candidates were or were not doing, we arrived at several tentative propositions which, on their logic alone, appeared quite convincing.

For example, it seemed likely that there would be fewer perceptual conflicts relating to claims by drop-out candidates that they had helped other candidates than there would be in cases where drop-outs reported that they had *not* helped anyone else. On the one hand, if a candidate deliberately tries to help another one, he is almost surely going to do something that will be visible to others and will be perceived as being just what it is intended to be, help for another candidate. On the other hand, even a candidate who firmly believes that he is not helping another may nevertheless do something that might be interpreted by others as designed to help someone else.

Similarly, it seemed probable that harmony in candidate perceptions of the second-ballot behavior of others would vary with the type of drop-out candidate. Thus, unalloyed désistements would be more frequently confirmed than the more ambiguous category of withdrawals without désistement but with some support for another candidate. In the same vein, one would expect that such support, without désistement but after voluntary withdrawal, would be more clearly perceived by other candidates than would support given to other candidates by eliminated candidates, on the ground that voluntary withdrawal, being purposive, invites interpretation, whereas elimination, being automatic, does not arouse attention.

Lastly, it seemed that concordance of candidate perceptions of drop-out candidate behavior would depend greatly on whether or not the parties of the drop-out candidates had well-defined policies for second-ballot behavior.

On this reasoning, misperceptions would apply disproportionately to the behavior of Democratic Center candidates, who were in principle supposed to withdraw "purely and simply," and of other minor party or non-party candidates whose behavior, being generally unpredictable, might also be subject to a certain amount of perceptual confusion.

In fact, we found only the barest indications that such considerations were at work among our sample of candidates, affecting perceptions of the between-ballots behavior of the drop-out candidates. Our laboriously constructed scaffolding of hypotheses came crashing to the ground under the weight of real evidence.

What we had failed to recognize, of course, was that the logic underlying our hypotheses is more appropriate for people whose political attentiveness is casual and intermittent than for political elites who are highly interested participants in the very activities of which they are also full-time observers. In effect, our hypotheses simply posited the existence of filters of varying degrees of strength that would differentially affect the clarity of the perceptions of the persons peering through them. But that way of conceiving the problem becomes useless when the vision of virtually all the observers is sufficiently powerful to penetrate the strongest filter. And this is the situation in regard to candidate perceptions of the between-ballots behavior of drop-out candidates. Directly conflicting perceptions of who helped whom, on the part of the principals themselves, occurred in only a handful of cases, most of which involved Democratic Center or other minor party candidates. When asked about désistements, withdrawals, or eliminations that helped their opponents, candidates who survived into the second ballot sometimes confused désistements with helpful withdrawals or eliminations, but these were technical and not substantive perceptual "errors."[5] Gaullists who ran at the second ballot sometimes failed to recall that candidates of the minor PSU deliberately helped the remaining Federation or Communist candidate, but they almost never overlooked Federation support for a Communist, or Communist support for the Federation.

If, from one point of view, this broad perceptual agreement of the candidates is disappointing, from another it is of considerable theoretical importance because it clearly illustrates the powerful cognitive capacity of political elites. Later in this chapter, when we turn to mass perceptions of the second-ballot behavior of the candidates, we shall have occasion to contrast mass and elite perceptions of the same phenomena.

Conflicting Perceptions on the Left

Although we have emphasized the impressive concordance of candidate perceptions of the patterns of second-ballot behavior, one partial exception to that generalization needs to be mentioned. In a substantial proportion of the cases where a Communist candidate reported that the Federation candidate in his district had desisted in his favor, the Federation candidate flatly denied having desisted for anyone. These perceptual inconsistencies always took the same form. Whenever a Federation candidate claimed to have supported a Communist at the second ballot and that Communist candidate was also interviewed, the Communist always confirmed that he had been supported by the Federation candidate. But not all reports by Communists that they had been supported by the Federation candidate were confirmed by the relevant Federation candidates.

The explanation for these clear-cut perceptual conflicts is as simple as it is interesting. There is no reason to believe that either the Federation candidates who said that they had not desisted for the Communists or the Communists who said that they had done so were in error. The Federation candidates were referring to their personal inactivity and states of mind, and the Communists were referring to the Federation as a party and possibly also to local Federation officials other than the candidates themselves.

This interpretation is supported by the considerable precision with which the Communist candidates described how they had been helped between the two ballots. "By publication of a poster," said one Communist candidate, "by a press communiqué, a joint meeting." "They prepared a poster calling on people to vote at the second ballot for the single candidate of the left," said another. "They distributed a tract and mobilized their organizations, passing on the word to have people vote for the single candidate of the left." "There was the désistement of the candidate," another Communist candidate said, "and a Federation poster calling on people to vote for the candidate of [leftist] union—no one else—an appeal by the departmental councillors, and then appeals from the different important geographical areas." "There were posters, and leading figures from the Federation agreed to sign appeals in my favor," another Communist candidate told us. Yet in each case the relevant Federation candidate, who in fact withdrew from the race, said that he did not desist for the Communist candidate.

What we are dealing with here goes considerably beyond the comparatively simple problem of perception—the framework within which we have been discussing the candidates' accounts of one another's second-ballot behavior. What we are facing now is an important political phenomenon that deserves fuller examination: the manifest reluctance of a large proportion of the Federation candidates to cooperate with the Communist party at the second ballot despite the national electoral alliance that existed between the Communists and the Federation.

Tensions on the Left

One of the most striking findings that emerged from our analysis of the behavior of the candidates between the two ballots of the 1967 election was the widespread dissatisfaction among Federation candidates with the conditions imposed upon them by the national electoral alliance between the Federation and the Communist party. For the election of 1967, the Communist party, the Federation, and the PSU agreed that although they would compete with one another at the first ballot, they would mutually withdraw candidates at the second ballot in order to pool their strength in favor of the left-wing candidate in each district who was best-placed by the voters at the first ballot. There were differences from the start between the Communists and the Federation over how that general agreement should be interpreted. The Communists viewed it as a means of welding together an exclusively leftist political alliance, uncontaminated by any cooperation with centrist candidates. The Federation hedged on the notion of an exclusively left-wing alliance by emphasizing the primary need to defeat the Gaullists; this would leave the way open for the Federation to support centrist candidates in districts where no left-wing candidate had a chance to win the seat, in exchange for centrist support in districts where the Federation was a real contender. The pre-electoral alliance agreement left it to meetings of the parties between the first and second ballots to decide on the tactics to follow in particularly contentious cases.

This electoral alliance did not sit well with all non-Communist leftist politicians. Anti-Communism has always been a strong force among the non-Communist left, particularly but not exclusively in leftist districts where the non-Communists can defeat the Communists with centrist and right-wing electoral support, and also in areas where the non-Communist left has traditionally dominated the local councils by allying with the center and even with conservatives. Some Federation politicians refused to be candidates in 1967 under the conditions of the leftist electoral alliance. Several Socialist candidates were expelled from their party after the 1967 election for running against Communists at the second ballot even though the Communists had run ahead of them at the first ballot. These cases were exceptional, however. Discipline among the left-wing parties at the second ballot appeared to be at a historic peak at the 1967 election.

Our survey of candidates, however, indicates beyond a doubt that a large proportion of Federation candidates were reluctant personally to support Communist candidates at the second ballot. We have drawn attention to the refusal of Federation candidates to acknowledge that they desisted for Communist candidates at the second ballot even though the Communist candidates claimed that they had done so. But those cases, though important, do not by themselves convey an adequate sense of how widespread the discomfiture of Federation candidates was in 1967. Among those who were in a position to help Communist candidates at the second ballot, under the terms of the left-wing parties' electoral alliance, more than half either refused to do so or, if they did implement the alliance, did so minimally or otherwise indicated their dissatisfaction with the situation in which they found themselves.[6]

For example, among Federation candidates who dropped out of the race at the second ballot, almost 15 percent were in the category we have already discussed at some length: they did not perceive their withdrawals as désistements, even though the Communist candidates in their districts did so perceive them because of the help they received from the Federation. The proportion of reluctant Federation allies of the Communist party rises by another 3 percent if we add eliminated Federation candidates who claimed that they did not help any other candidate, even where the Communist candidate perceived the elimination as a désistement and reported specific Federation activities on his behalf between the two ballots.

The ranks of unhappy Federation candidates are enlarged by an additional 7 percent if we include those candidates who withdrew from the second ballot, who claimed that they did not desist for another candidate, and who did not help any other candidate, in districts where the Communist candidate confirmed that the Federation candidate had not desisted in his favor. In one such district, for example, the Federation candidate told us that he "withdrew without desisting for the Communist party candidate. I have always been opposed to Communism." Indeed, the Communist candidate in that same district told us that the Federation candidate had even campaigned against him.

Still another 7 percent of the drop-out Federation candidates acknowledged having desisted for the Communist candidate, but told our interviewers in unambiguous terms how repugnant they had found it to do so. One Socialist in northern France told us that he had desisted in favor of the Communist "to my regret," and that he had done "absolutely nothing to help him." Another Federation candidate, in the Paris region, told us that he had desisted for the Communist candidate "in spite of myself," and he too said that he had done nothing to help him.

A further 10 percent of the drop-out Federation candidates acknowledged having desisted for Communist candidates, and indicated that they had helped them, but at the same time they made it clear that they had tried to reduce their participation in the campaign for the second ballot to a minimum. A Socialist in a northern district, for example, desisted for the Communist candidate and informed his voters of his action by means of a poster, but he did not participate in the campaign for the second ballot. "They didn't ask me to," he said, "but I would not have participated if they had asked me to."

Finally, another 10 percent of the Federation drop-out candidates both desisted for Communist candidates and participated in the campaign, but they let us know that they did not approve of their party's alliance strategy, at least as applied to their districts. One candidate in the Paris region, after indicating that he had desisted for the Communist candidate and telling us what he had done to help him, volunteered the information that "these were not my sentiments but those of the Federation."

The attentive reader will note that we have reached the figure of 52 percent for the proportion of Federation candidates, among those who were in a position to help Communist candidates, who were manifestly unhappy about having to do so. This is a conservative estimate. We have rigorously excluded from the category of reluctant allies those Federation candidates who made comments that suggest criticism of their party's strategy in their districts, but which are not wholly unambiguous. Our estimate that more than half of the Federation drop-out candidates were displeased with the terms of the left-wing electoral alliance is rock solid.

Of course, the Federation candidates we have been discussing so far were those who had to pay the price of the left-wing electoral alliance. Some of them were annoyed simply because they believed that if they had stayed in the race they would have been elected. The other side of the coin was that Communist candidates dropped out of the race where they were out-distanced at the first ballot by the Federation candidates.[7] Some Federation candidates who were required by the alliance to drop out of the race might have won if they had remained, but there were also Federation candidates whose election was assured precisely because Communist candidates desisted in their favor.

Still, there were signs that the left-wing alliance did not operate entirely smoothly even with regard to Communist support for Federation candidates. Some 10 percent of the Federation candidates who ran at the second ballot gave clear indications to that effect: two-thirds of them told us that the Communist candidate did not desist in their favor or did nothing to help them,[8] and the remaining third were surprised that the Communist candidate actually desisted in their favor. And even among Federation candidates who were acknowledged beneficiaries of the alliance with the Communist party, there were unmistakable indications that they did not wholly welcome their allies. "They proposed joint meetings of militants of the two parties," one Federation candidate told us, "but, without refusing, I dodged the question." "The Communist party associated itself actively with my campaign," another said. "They gave instructions to their voters and put up posters, but I did not want any joint meetings."

It is even apparent that if the Federation beneficiaries of the left-wing alliance had not run ahead of the Communists in their districts, but had trailed them instead, they would have revealed similar doubts and hesitations about supporting Communists that we have already documented among the drop-out Federation candidates. One such victorious candidate told us that he had campaigned on the theme that he would not desist for another candidate at the second ballot (although there was little likelihood that that would be necessary, as the Communist party was comparatively weak in his district). Another Federation candidate who ran at the second ballot told us that "it would have been different if it had been the other way around. If I had invited my voters to vote Communist, it would not have worked so easily."

Altogether, about a fourth of the sample Federation candidates who ran at the second ballot gave some indication that the left-wing electoral alliance did not sit well either with them or with all their voters, even though these candidates, at least formally, were beneficiaries of the alliance. It will be recalled that among Federation candidates who dropped out of the race, a majority found the conditions of the alliance distasteful. If we take into account *all* the Federation candidates in our sample on whom the alliance had a directly operative effect, either because Federation candidates were required to drop out and leave the field open to Communists, or vice versa, we find that fully a third of them regarded the alliance as at least an embarrassment and more often than not a serious political error.

The unhappiness of so many Federation candidates with the terms of their electoral alliance with the Communists has a simple explanation: anti-Communism. This emerges with striking clarity when we compare the Federation candidates who did not support Communist candidates at the second ballot with those who did, along the same kinds of political measures that we employed in Chapter 11, in discussing mass electoral participation at the second ballot, and in Chapter 12, in discussing mass vote transfers from the first to the second ballot. These familiar measures include own left-right location, distance along the left-right dimension between the candidate's own location and his perception of the location of the various parties, and sympathy (or antipathy) for the various parties.

Table 13-1 sets out the mean scores on each of these dimensions for the two groups of drop-out Federation candidates, those who supported Communist candidates between the two ballots and those who did not. It can be seen at a glance that although there are differences between the two groups of Federation candidates in the expected direction on each dimension, those differences are less than overwhelming in every case but one. The one dimension that sharply distinguishes between them is sympathy for the Communist party.

The Communist supporters are somewhat to the left of the candidates who did not help the Communists; they perceive the Communist party to be slightly closer to them on the left-right axis, and they perceive the Gaullists to be somewhat farther from them on that same axis than do the candidates who did not support the Communists; and they are a bit more opposed to the Gaullists than the latter group is. But these are all differences of degree only; if they were the only predictors available to us, we would not want to rely on them to "explain" the difference in behavior between the two groups of Federation candidates. The only decisive factor is

Table 13-1. Mean scores on various attitude dimensions of drop-out Federation candidates, by support for Communist candidates at second ballot, France, 1967.[a]

Attitude dimension	Drop-out Federation candidates	
	Supported Communist candidates	Did not support Communist candidates
Own left-right location	18.0 (20)	26.0 (9)
Perceived distance of Communist party from own left-right location	−12.2 (20)	−17.6 (9)
Perceived distance of Gaullists from own left-right location	51.6 (18)	45.8 (7)
Sympathy for Communist party	62.8 (20)	31.4 (9)
Sympathy for Gaullist party	12.8 (20)	17.9 (9)

a. Numbers of cases in parentheses.

the difference between the attitudes of the two groups toward the Communist party. The Federation candidates who supported the Communists had, on average, a favorable attitude toward the Communist party, and those who did not help the Communists were distinctly anti-Communist. It is as simple as that.

This pattern of behavior, at the elite level, is precisely what we found when we investigated, in Chapter 12, the differences between those non-Communist leftist voters who supported the Communist party in forced-choice situations at the second ballot and those who refused to do so, either by abstaining or deliberately spoiling their ballots. We showed in Table 12-5 that the two groups resembled each other on several of the dimensions that have figured prominently in our analyses: own left-right locations, perceived left-right partisan locations, clericalism-anticlericalism, Gaullism–anti-Gaullism, and attitudes toward the Gaullist party.[9] The main difference between the two groups of non-Communist leftist voters lay in their attitudes toward the Communist party, just as it does for the two analogous groups of Federation candidates. The Federation candidates who abstained from helping Communist candidates at the second ballot were impelled by the same forces that motivated those non-Communist leftist voters who abstained from voting or spoiled their ballots in districts where the second-ballot choice was between a Communist and a Gaullist.

Candidate Behavior, Partisan Attitudes, and Left-Right Locations

The comparison we have just made between the second-ballot behavior of non-Communist leftist candidates and voters raises the larger question of whether there are similarities generally between the second-ballot behavior

of candidates and voters. In Chapter 11 we examined, for all first-ballot
voters who could not repeat their partisan choice at the second ballot, the
factors involved in their choice between voting for another candidate, abstaining, and spoiling their ballots. We found that the second-ballot electoral behavior of the people in forced-choice situations could be accounted
for by their attitude toward the parties in the form of degree of sympathy or
hostility, but not by their perception of the relative positions of the parties
on the left-right dimension. To what extent can the second-ballot behavior
of the candidates be explained generally in the same terms?

It is evident that the problem of the candidate who is eliminated from
the second ballot, or required by his party's electoral alliances to withdraw
from the race, is very similar to the problem of the voter who cannot repeat
his or her partisan vote. It is perhaps less obvious that there are direct parallels between the solutions available to the two groups of political actors—
voters and candidates. Forced-choice voters may vote for another candidate,
abstain, or register a protest by spoiling their ballots. The courses of action
open to "can't win" candidates, or to those who cannot win without risking
expulsion from their party for lack of discipline, are surprisingly similar to
those available to the forced-choice voters.

Just as forced-choice voters may vote for another candidate, so may
forced-choice candidates support another candidate.

Just as forced-choice voters may abstain, so may forced-choice candidates abstain. An eliminated candidate may simply "sit on his hands" and
do nothing during the second-ballot campaign. If, like the unhappy Federation candidates we discussed earlier, a candidate is technically eligible to run
at the second ballot but is required by his party to drop out in favor of a
candidate he does not want to support, he can minimally satisfy his party by
withdrawing, but do absolutely nothing otherwise to help his would-be
ally. In this sense, pure and simple withdrawal is analogous to abstention.

Finally, just as forced-choice voters can register a protest against their
party's electoral strategy by spoiling their ballots, forced-choice candidates
can refuse to adhere to their party's electoral policy. A candidate eligible for
the second ballot can drop out of the race but actively support a different candidate from the one supported by his party (and an eliminated candidate can do the same thing). We have already alluded to one case that
approximates this behavior, that in which a Communist candidate complained that the Federation drop-out candidate in his district had campaigned against him, and the Federation candidate himself, although he
did not specifically tell us that he had done so, made his anti-Communism
crystal clear.

A candidate can, of course, escalate his defiance of his party and actually
run at the second ballot against the candidate officially supported by his
party. There were such cases in France at the 1967 election, although none

appeared in our sample. Such a course of action is more serious and riskier than lower levels of indiscipline. But this only means that the range of protest measures available to a candidate is wider than that available to a voter, who can go no further than spoiling his ballot. Generically, both cases are protests against party policy.

We shall not try to "explain," in relation to the candidates, the three modes of mass behavior we examined in Chapter 11. There are too few candidates in the spoiler category to make that feasible. We can, however, examine the roots of the distinction between supporting and not supporting other candidates, and we shall do this in a way that permits us to exploit the maximum number of cases.

Happily, we not only have a record of the support or nonsupport of other candidates by the drop-outs in our sample, but we also have a record of the *hypothetical* support or nonsupport for other candidates of *all* the candidates in our sample, whether they dropped out at the second ballot or not. All candidates who dropped out of the race were asked, in the sequence of questions already described, whether they had helped another candidate and, if so, which one. Candidates who helped another were coded both for the support they gave and for their nonsupport of the other candidate or candidates who ran at the second ballot in their districts. If they indicated that they had not supported another candidate, they were then asked which party they would have desisted for (or simply helped, if they were éliminés) if they had decided to do so. Drop-out candidates were also asked which party or parties they would not have desisted for under any circumstances, and, if any parties were mentioned that they had not in fact already failed to support, these too were recorded as cases of nonsupport.

All other candidates, including those who ran at the second ballot and those who ran in districts where the election was decided at the first ballot, were also asked which party they would have desisted for if the circumstances had been such that "for some reason" they had decided to desist, as well as which party or parties they would not have desisted for under any circumstances. The record, therefore, includes for each candidate both "acts" of real or hypothetical support for other parties and "acts" of real or hypothetical nonsupport for other parties.[10]

The data set was then transformed so that the units of analysis were not candidates but rather acts of support or nonsupport for one or another of the four main competing political formations: the Communists, the Federation, the Gaullists (either pure UNR or Giscardian) and the Democratic Center.

Finally, in order to determine the relative contribution of partisan sympathies and sense of left-right distances to the candidates' between-ballots behavior, we ran a multiple regression analysis, with support for a given party versus nonsupport for that party as the dependent variable. Party sympathy as an independent variable was specified as the candidate's thermometer score for his own party less his thermometer score for the other party. Because of the tendency, noted in Chapter 4, for candidates generally to locate themselves to the left of the positions they assign to their own parties on the left-right dimension, we employed two alternate measures of left-right distance as the second independent variable. One measure was the unsigned distance between the candidate's self-ascribed left-right location and the location he assigned to the other party. The other was the unsigned distance between the location the candidate attributed to his own party on the left-right dimension and that which he assigned to the other party.[11]

The result of the analysis is summarized in Table 13-2. Almost 50 percent of the variance in the decision to support or not to support another party is accounted for by our two independent variables, and it is evident that partisan sympathies count for more than perceptions of left-right distances in determining the behavior of French candidates at the second ballot. And in this regard it makes virtually no difference whether one measures left-right distance in terms of the candidate's own personal location or in terms of the location he assigns to his party.

This analysis of candidate behavior is the closest match we can make to our analysis in Chapter 11 relating to mass electoral participation at the second ballot. The results are broadly the same in both cases. Partisan preferences account for mass participation at the second ballot; perceptions of left-right party differences do not. In the case of candidate behavior at the second ballot, perceptions of left-right distances count for something, but for less than partisan sympathies do. In critical choices both the French legislative elite and the mass electorate are moved by the same primary force of partisan attitudes.

This is a finding of considerable importance. In France the political vocabulary is dominated by left-right terminology, whereas partisan attach-

Table 13-2. Effects of perceived left-right distances and partisan sympathy on candidate behavior between the two ballots, France, 1967.[a]

Beta Perceptions of left-right distance	Beta Partisan sympathy	Multiple R^2
.29[b]	.47	.49
(429)	(429)	
.30[c]	.45	.48
(446)	(446)	

a. Number of candidate acts are in parentheses.
b. Difference between perceived locations of own party and other party.
c. Difference between perceived locations of self and other party.

ments are comparatively undeveloped at the mass level, and partisan entities, particularly in the center and on the right, are highly unstable. In such a context, the touchstone for political orientations at both the mass and elite levels would appear to be the left-right dimension. But we have seen, in a tentative fashion in Chapter 4 and more definitely in Chapters 10, 11, and 12, that that is not so at the mass level. As difficult as it is for much of the French mass electorate to form enduring, strong partisan attachments, partisan attitudes prevail over the left-right dimension as the source of mass electoral behavior.

We have also shown in Chapter 4, however, that the mass and the elite differ profoundly in their understanding of the concepts of left and right. The elite has a much more fully developed sense of the meaning of these terms than does the mass electorate, a substantial proportion of whom can assign no substantive meaning at all to them. And we saw further in Chapter 7 that there is a far closer linkage of left-right locations with policy positions on major issues among the elite than there is among even the most involved stratum of the electorate. In these circumstances, it would not be at all surprising to find that even though left-right orientations have limited functional utility for the typical French voter, they have considerable or even primary operational power for French parliamentary candidates. But this is not the case. In definitional and attitudinal terms, there is a vast difference between the elite and the mass with regard to the notion of a left-right dimension, but in *behavioral* terms there appears to be far less difference between them than one would reasonably expect to find. Partisan attitudes dominate elite electoral behavior just as they dominate mass electoral behavior.

Electoral Response to Candidate Behavior

When one candidate desists in favor of another, or otherwise tries to help another candidate, the objective is to persuade his or her first-ballot voters to throw their support to one of the remaining candidates at the second ballot. Does this strategy work? Are French voters normally aware of the second-ballot activities of drop-out candidates? If they are, does this have any effect on the way they cast their ballots at the second round of voting? And what about the voters who have supported candidates who survive into the second ballot? Do they know whether their preferred candidates have been supported by other candidates and, if so, does it have any effect on their behavior?

Candidate Behavior and Voter Awareness

In addition to asking the candidates about their activity between the ballots and their perceptions of the activities of the other candidates, we asked our sample of voters a series of questions designed to ascertain *their* perceptions of the activity of the candidates. Accordingly, all respondents who voted for a candidate at both the first and second ballots were asked whether the candidate for whom they had voted at the first ballot had also run at the second ballot. If they responded that he had not run at the second ballot, they were then asked whether that candidate had requested his voters to vote for another candidate or whether he had withdrawn "purely and simply." If the respondent replied that his candidate had supported another candidate, the respondent was also asked which candidate had been supported, whether or not he himself was satisfied with the endorsement made by the drop-out candidate, and—of course—for which candidate the respondent had voted at the second ballot.

Similarly, second-ballot voters whose first-ballot choices also ran at the second ballot were asked a parallel series of questions designed to elicit their awareness of whether their preferred candidate had been supported by another, their degree of satisfaction with any such endorsements, and whether they had repeated their vote for that candidate.

The first general point to be made with regard to the voters' perceptions of the candidates' activity relating to the second ballot is, as one would expect, that these differ considerably, in regard to levels of awareness, from those of the candidates themselves. We have already seen that the perceptions of candidates from the same district converge markedly concerning the second-ballot activity in that district. Except for comparatively rare cases that usually can be accounted for by special circumstances, the various candidates all perceive a given situation in the same way. It is not so for the voters. Their perceptions of candidate behavior at the second ballot are quite mixed.

Among the voters for drop-out candidates who gave clear and unambiguous support to other candidates, who in turn confirmed having received such support, almost 80 percent reported that their preferred candidate had supported another candidate at the second ballot and correctly designated either the name of that candidate or his party. From one point of view, that is a very large proportion of correct perceptions, and we have refrained from qualifying it with the modifier "only" for that very reason. But this "almost 80 percent" must be taken as a maximum estimate whose true value is almost surely quite a bit smaller. By restricting ourselves to ironclad cases of second-ballot support because they were fully confirmed by both principals, we have limited our case numbers. When we include all cases in which a candidate reported having supported another at the second ballot, whether or not that support could be confirmed directly by the alleged beneficiary, we not only run very little risk of including instances where there was not actually an endorsement of one candidate by another, but we also increase our numbers of mass cases substantially, thereby enhancing the stability of our estimate of the proportion of "aware" voters. Under these conditions, this estimate drops to slightly less than 70 percent. In other words, some 30 percent of the two-time voters whose first-ballot choice had dropped out of the race and thrown his support to another candidate were either unaware that their preferred candidate had helped another or, if they had some sense that he had done so, did not know which candidate he had helped.

Furthermore, in the cases where candidates had dropped out of the race without supporting another candidate, less than 80 percent of their first-ballot voters (who also voted at the second ballot) reported unequivocally that their preferred candidates had not helped another one. More than 10 percent of these voters simply did not know whether their first-ballot choice had thrown his support to another candidate, and another 10 percent thought that he had done so. As that last 10 percent were obviously guessing, it is not unlikely that a similar proportion of the voters who reported correctly that their candidates had not helped others were also guessing. That would bring our estimate of the proportion of "aware" voters down to some 70 percent, or the same level that we encountered with regard to voters whose candidates had supported someone else.

The second general point concerning voter perceptions of candidate activity between the ballots is that the first-ballot supporters of drop-out candidates appear to pay more attention to what is going on with regard to désistements than the supporters of the surviving candidates do. For the latter group the aggregate "awareness" level drops well below the 70 percent or so that we reported for the voters for drop-out candidates. Among the voters for those candidates who *received* support from other candidates at the second ballot, less than 40 percent reported that their candidate had been helped by another and also correctly identified the candidate (or the party of the candidate) who had helped him. Conversely, among supporters of second-ballot candidates who did not receive any help from other candidates, more than a fourth did not know whether or not their candidates had been helped by others, and a small fraction—some 2 percent—who were presumably guessing, reported that they had been endorsed by other candidates.

The crucial difference between these two groups—the 70 percent or so of first-ballot voters for drop-out candidates who were aware both that their candidate had thrown his support to another and who that other was, and the less than 40 percent of the first-ballot voters for second-ballot candidates who both knew that their preferred candidate had been supported by other candidates and by whom—is quite understandable. Voters who can repeat their first-ballot electoral choice do not need additional information as they approach the second ballot; but voters whose first-ballot choices drop out must reassess the situation and make a fresh decision. It is comprehensible that these voters should seek or be receptive to information from their pre-

ferred candidates, and that those who can repeat their choices should make
no particular effort to learn whether or not their choices have been endorsed
by other candidates.

Still, the extent to which the supporters of drop-out candidates are
aware of what these candidates recommend concerning their vote at the second ballot depends upon how clearly the candidates express their message to
the voters. There are two aspects to this consideration: the content of the
message and the amount of effort used in getting it across to the voters.

First, most drop-out candidates either frankly declare their support for
another candidate or remain silent and, therefore, neutral. As was mentioned earlier in the chapter, however, some candidates avoid making a
choice between these two positions. This failure to choose can sometimes
lead to arcane behavior well beyond the range of comprehension of most ordinary voters. One drop-out candidate told us that he had published a newspaper article between the ballots saying that one had to choose the lesser of
two evils, but without naming the candidate he supported. Another candidate, who reported that he had supported the Federation candidate, told us
that he had "hinted at it in the paper" and "contacted some friends." In one
district, a drop-out candidate told us that he had not supported anyone else,
but one of the remaining candidates, a Giscardian, claimed that the drop-
out had helped him "by communiqués that took a position in my favor
against the candidate supported by the Communists." The Giscardian's opponent at the second ballot summed up this situation nicely by reporting
that the drop-out candidate had desisted in favor of the Giscardian, "but
only in part." Case numbers are very small for the voters whose candidates
engaged in such subtle behavior, but we estimate that more than three-
fourths of them were ignorant of their candidates' "recommendations."

Second, voter awareness of drop-out candidates' behavior is affected by
how well the drop-outs communicate with their first-ballot supporters.
After asking drop-outs what they had done to inform their voters about
their positions, we divided the candidates who supported others into two
broad groups: those who said they had done nothing or who mentioned one
routine item, such as posters, tracts, or newspaper articles; and those who
mentioned two or more kinds of activity, including complete cooperation
with the surviving candidate. Among the first-ballot voters for candidates in
the first group, only some 40 percent were aware that their candidates had
supported another candidate and who that candidate was, whereas among
the voters for the more active group of candidates, almost 80 percent were
aware of their candidates' recommendations.

In this connection, we have confirmation that voters whose first-ballot
choices survive into the second ballot do not pay much attention to the activity of drop-out candidates. If they did, we would expect the accuracy of
their perceptions of the positions of those candidates to vary with the

amount of activity the candidates engaged in to communicate their sentiments to the voters. That, however, is not the case. The first-ballot voters for second-ballot candidates do not know much about what the other candidates are doing because they are just not looking their way.

Voter Awareness and Electoral Behavior

We have seen that far from all of the supporters of drop-out candidates are aware of those candidates' recommendations concerning how they should vote at the second ballot. Does that make any difference? Do the voters who know what their preferred candidates' recommendations are for the second ballot vote differently from those who do not?

The evidence indicates that it does indeed make a difference whether the first-ballot supporters of drop-out candidates know what the advice of those candidates is. Table 13-3 shows the reported second-ballot electoral behavior of the first-ballot supporters of those drop-out candidates who endorsed another candidate for the second ballot, broken down by whether the voters were aware of the specific endorsement made by their preferred candidate. We include the first-ballot voters for all candidates who supported another, however indirectly, and we also include the Federation voters in districts where the Federation candidate did not support the Communist, though the Communist said that he had and cited some kind of Federation activity on behalf of the Communist for the second ballot. Among the voters who were aware that their first choice had endorsed another candidate and who that candidate was, more than 80 percent responded by voting for the candidate who was recommended to them. Among those who were not aware that their preferred choice had endorsed another candidate, or who did not know which candidate he had recommended, less than 60 percent voted for the candidate endorsed by the drop-out.[12]

Table 13-3. Second-ballot vote of those first-ballot voters for drop-out candidates who endorsed another candidate, by awareness of endorsement (percentages), France, 1967.

	First-ballot voters	
Second-ballot vote	Aware of endorsement	Unaware of endorsement
Voted for endorsed candidate	83	58
Voted for another candidate or spoiled ballot	17	42
Total	100	100
Weighted N	(87.7)	(41.1)

Second-ballot endorsements, whether they reflect national electoral alliances among major parties or isolated cases of cooperation between candidates at the district level, can be fully effective only if the voters are aware of them. To some extent, it may be beyond the capacity of the parties and candidates to ensure that all their first-ballot supporters are aware of their second-ballot recommendations. The parties and candidates necessarily depend upon the attentiveness of the voters, and that, in turn, reflects variations in political involvement. But we have also seen that the parties and candidates themselves can affect their voters' awareness of their recommendations by avoiding ambiguity and making repeated efforts to get their messages across. When they do this, they have, according to our estimates, about a 25 percent greater chance of winning the votes they are aiming at than they have if they fail to communicate with their supporters.

We know from the analyses presented in Chapters 11 and 12 that participation and electoral choice at the second ballot by the first-ballot supporters of drop-out candidates depend heavily on the partisan attitudes of those voters toward the remaining candidates. We can approach this same phenomenon in another way on the basis of our respondents' evaluations of the endorsements made by their first-ballot candidates. It will be recalled that the people who reported that their preferred candidates had endorsed (or been endorsed by) others were asked whether they were satisfied with, dissatisfied with, or indifferent to those endorsements. How did relative satisfaction with the pattern of second-ballot endorsements affect the second-ballot vote?

Among those first-ballot supporters of drop-out candidates who were fully aware of their candidate's recommendation for the second ballot, and who were either satisfied with or indifferent toward that recommendation, well over 90 percent voted for the candidate who had been endorsed. Among the 20 percent of such aware voters who were dissatisfied with their candidate's endorsement, only some 30 percent voted for the candidate he recommended.[13] The 70 percent defection rate among voters dissatisfied with their preferred candidate's recommendation for the second ballot reflects the divisions among the first-ballot supporters of each major party that we charted in Chapters 11 and 12.

What about the voters whose first-ballot choices survive into the second ballot? Are they moved in any way by endorsements that other candidates make in favor of their own preferred candidate? We have already seen that less than 40 percent of them are aware that some other particular candidate has endorsed their own preference; but can we trace the effect of such endorsements on this limited group of voters? There is the possibility that some of them might be sufficiently outraged at their preferred candidate's willingness to accept the endorsement of another candidate to refuse to vote for him at the second ballot. For example, some of the Federation candidates in our sample made it clear that they did not want to be too closely associated with the Communist candidates who were supporting them for the second ballot, presumably out of concern that they might lose the votes of some of their anti-Communist supporters. In fact, virtually none of the people who were aware that their preferred candidate had been endorsed by another candidate indicated that they were dissatisfied with that endorsement. Some 80 percent of the relevant voters were satisfied that their candidate had been supported by another, almost 20 percent were indifferent toward the situation, and a bare 2 percent claimed to be dissatisfied. And practically no one among the people who were aware that their candidate had been endorsed by another failed to cast his vote at the second ballot for the same candidate he had voted for at the first. Whatever illogical or cynical second-ballot alliances there may have been in France in 1967, they had no visible effect on the second-ballot supporters of the candidates who benefited from them.

Conclusions

This chapter, like the two preceding it, has dealt with the unique French electoral institution of the second ballot. Unlike those two earlier chapters, which dealt primarily with the voters and only incidentally with the candidates, this one has focused on the candidates, although we have been concerned with the obviously important question of voter response to candidate activity as well.

We have examined the broad patterns of both forced and voluntary withdrawals of candidates from the second ballot, and we have seen that a political vocabulary that evolved in earlier times, when conditions were different from those in the late 1960s, is not wholly adequate for describing the full panoply of current practices. Nevertheless, there is broad agreement among the perceptions of candidates from the same district with regard to the support patterns between the drop-outs and the survivors in the district. Such conflicting perceptions or perceptual "errors" as occurred among the candidates can easily be explained by ambiguity in candidate behavior or by the technical distinction between a désisté supporting another candidate and an éliminé doing so.

We did encounter one form of ostensible perceptual conflict, however, that pointed the way to uncovering a political phenomenon of considerable importance. In a significant proportion of the relevant cases, drop-out candidates from the Federation told us that they did not desist in favor of the remaining Communist candidate, as the terms of the Federation-Communist electoral alliance required, whereas the surviving Communist candidate reported that such a désistement had taken place and then went on to describe in some detail how he had been helped by the Federation. In fact, there was no perceptual conflict in these cases. What happened was that the Federation candidate withdrew but did not personally help the Communist, although other representatives of the Federation on the district level did help the Communist candidate.

These specific cases of refusal on the part of Federation candidates to help Communists are illustrative of a much broader reluctance among Federation candidates to help their Communist allies at the second ballot. Close examination of Federation candidates who did help Communists as compared with those who did not indicates that the main distinction between the two groups was their particular attitude toward the Communist party. The Federation candidates who helped Communist candidates had a favorable attitude toward the Communist party, on the average, whereas those who refused to help Communists had an unfavorable view of the Communist party. In this respect, the behavior of Federation candidates paralleled the behavior of Federation voters. We saw in Chapter 12 that among various possible explanatory forces, it was anti-Communism that most clearly explained the refusal of Federation voters to support a Communist at the second ballot. And here we find that the same force accounts for the behavior of Federation candidates at the second ballot. Among Federation candidates, as among Federation voters, partisanship accounts for second-ballot behavior better than any other factor we tested.

Indeed, in a more general test, we found that across the entire field of candidates, partisan attitudes account for patterns of candidate support (and nonsupport) for other candidates at the second ballot better than do perceptions of the left-right locations of the parties. Here, too, we find an analogy with mass behavior that is directly relevant to one of the central concerns of this study. Candidates can find themselves in forced-choice situations at the second ballot just as voters can, and they have analogous options: support for another candidate, abstention from the contest, or protest. In Chapter 11, we reported that voter decisions concerning participation at the second ballot depend primarily on partisan attitudes, not on perceptions of left-right partisan locations. It would not have been unexpected, however, to find that candidate behavior at the second ballot depended mainly on perceptions of left-right distances between the parties of the candidates. After all, the notions of left and right have much more meaning for the elite than for the mass electorate, and left-right locations are linked to elite opinions on major political issues in a way that does not hold true for the electorate as a whole. But even for the candidates, partisanship is more powerful than sense of left-right distances in accounting for second-ballot behavior. Among both mass and elite, the critical decisions that must be made between the two ballots rest primarily on the degree of sympathy or antipathy they feel for the various parties.

Once drop-out candidates have decided to support other candidates at the second ballot, the extent to which their decisions are visible to the voting public depends on how directly and unambiguously they endorse particular candidates and on how much effort they expend in communicating their recommendations to their first-ballot supporters. For if both voters and candidates are broadly motivated by the same force—partisanship—in deciding how to act at the second ballot, it is also true that there are distinct differences between candidates and voters with regard to their levels of cognition. With few exceptions, the candidates know what other candidates are doing—including, of course, which drop-out candidate is supporting which surviving candidate. The candidates are so interested and attentive that they miss very little of what is happening in their districts. The situation is different for the voters, who are stratified by levels of political involvement to begin with, and whose perceptions are strongly affected by how clearly and frequently the candidates attempt to communicate with them. There are marked variations in the proportions of voters for drop-out candidates who are aware of the second-ballot recommendations of those candidates, depending on the nature and forcefulness of their recommendations.

The pay-off in terms of votes for the second-ballot candidates recommended by the drop-outs is real and substantial if these drop-out candidates take the trouble to communicate loudly and clearly with their first-ballot supporters. According to our estimates, there is an increased probability in the order of some 25 percent that the first-ballot supporter of a drop-out candidate will vote for the candidate who has been endorsed for the second ballot if that voter is aware of the specific endorsement made, compared with how that elector will vote if he either does not know whether his preferred candidate has supported another or, if he does know that, he does not also know which specific candidate has been recommended.

Of course, some attentive and aware voters will be dissatisfied with the recommendation made by their original, first-choice candidate and refuse to follow his advice. We have examined that phenomenon in both Chapter 11 and Chapter 12, and we have encountered additional evidence of it here as well. But this is a risk that accompanies all electoral alliances, whether they are nationwide or simply local. Free elections mean freedom of choice. Most voters, however, are prepared to follow the advice of their first-choice candidates. It is up to the candidates to render that advice unambiguously and emphatically.

PART III

The System
in Crisis

S o far, we have taken an extended excursion into what may be called "normal French electoral politics." We have traced the intricate process by which French voters select their representatives, keeping to the forefront the notion that an election is a means not only of choosing a deputy but also of conveying some sense of the direction which the electorate wants the course of public policy to take.

In the spring of 1968, first the students and then the workers, and probably unprecedented numbers of middle-class people as well, made it clear that "normal politics" is not the only way in which the people can try to communicate their discontents to their political leaders. They can also take to the streets, and that is precisely what happened in France in May 1968.

Part III will concentrate on this almost legendary episode in postwar French politics. The coverage will be brief, as befits an event that has already been treated more voluminously than any other in the history of contemporary France.

Our approach, which is contrapuntal, applies to two levels: the mass and the elite. On the first, or mass, level a leftward movement of impressive proportions developed from obscure beginnings. Temporarily blocked by the narrow right-wing victory of 1967, the frustrated leftists exploded in May 1968, in ways that we shall describe in demographic detail. But this outburst produced a countervailing, right-wing reaction, as evidenced by the extraordinary Gaullist electoral victory in June. Complex shifts took place in the pattern of political opinion as a result of the May upheaval, but the predominant change was a marked shift to the right, associated with the voters' proximity to the disorders. Hence our analysis makes central use of the left-right dimension. Although the importance of this dimension may be exaggerated in some cases, it may nevertheless be the main instrument with which the political elite interprets the policy implications of mass behavior.

On the second level, the parliamentary elite—particularly the unfortunate leftist candidates—understood clearly that the outcome of the June election was directly linked to the May disorders. There were, of course, more or less predictable variations in the candidates' interpretations of the student revolt, the strikes that followed it, and the links between the two main components of the mass upheaval, the leftward movement and the right-wing reaction. It is doubtful, however, whether anyone could have predicted the extent (borne out by our analysis) to which the candidates' perceptions of their constituents' opinions and behavior were colored by partisanship. The reader will encounter some staggering examples of gaps between perceptions and "reality" and will also find that some of these misperceptions are accompanied by elements of perceptual accuracy of a different order.

After we have examined the candidates' views of what the government should do in the event of another outburst of mass protest, as well as their opinions of rioting as a way of capturing the attention of the government, we shall be in a position to draw some conclusions about the fidelity of popular representation. Thus at the end of Part III we shall return to the central theme of this book. By then it will be clear that the events of 1968 can be read in either of two ways—as a legislative mandate for reform or as a mandate for law and order—depending upon whether one focuses on the May upheaval or on the June electoral backlash. Consequently it is necessary to examine the extent to which the deputies elected in June 1968 leaned toward one or the other of these two interpretations; for how they leaned at that time would have a great deal to do with how they acted as the people's representatives during the ensuing legislative term.

14

Revolt and Reaction: The Upheaval of May 1968 and the June Elections

During May and June 1968, France experienced a succession of events that was unprecedented in the annals of modern industrialized democracies. A small, localized student demonstration in Paris blossomed into a large-scale student revolt in virtually all of the university centers of France. Wildcat strikes and apparently spontaneous factory seizures followed, and soon France was in the throes of a nearly general strike that was to last for some two weeks. Massive demonstrations, notable for the high rate of participation by university-educated and managerial groups that are not customarily found among the ranks of street demonstrators, occurred in Paris and many other French cities and industrial centers. For a brief, intense, and emotionally charged period, routines were shattered, authority was flouted, hierarchies were ignored, and both hopes and fears were magnified well beyond their customary limits. That situation was altered when, at the end of May, President de Gaulle dissolved the National Assembly. What had appeared to many observers to be a revolutionary situation was abruptly transformed into an electoral competition.[1] Even more strikingly, the overt balance of forces shifted dramatically. The strikes and massive demonstrations represented a vast outpouring of opposition to Gaullist policies, and even, for many of the participants, to the Gaullist regime itself. But that unfavorable verdict, rendered in the streets, was overruled at the ballot box. The Gaullists won the greatest parliamentary majority in French republican history. The party of order was restored to power, and France went back to work.

Among those who returned to work with fresh vigor were the chroniclers and analysts of the upheaval itself. Soon a large number of books and articles appeared, offering a variety of interpretations of what came to be called "the events of May."[2] It is with some hesitation, therefore, that we present the reader with two more chapters dealing with these events. Nevertheless, we must do so, and for several reasons.

First and most important, although the initial design of this study of political representation considered the electoral process to be the sole means of communication between the mass public and the parliamentary elite, the demonstrations and strikes of May 1968 constituted a message from the French people that their legislative leaders could ignore only at their peril. We shall, therefore, take into account the extent to which the events of May influenced French legislative behavior during the years following their eruption. To do so properly, we need to examine these events in terms that lend themselves to such an analysis.

Second, and this reason is closely related to the first, it is important for any overall assessment of the effects of the May events that they be linked to the June elections that followed. Most chroniclers limit themselves to the events alone. Yet they are of a piece with the elections that they precipitated, in a way that is rich in irony. Ten nights of bitter confrontation between students and police in the Parisian Latin Quarter produced such massive anti-Gaullist reverberations across France that by the third and fourth weeks of May, half of the labor force was reported to be out on strike against the regime. Yet a scant four weeks later the totality of French voters, called to the polls to reconstitute the National Assembly dissolved on May 30 as a result of the crisis, gave the Gaullists the most resounding vote ever won by a single parliamentary grouping, right or left, in a century of French popular legislative elections. The apparent contradiction was of epic proportions; to many eyes, the sequence of events presents an astonishing puzzle. But fortunately, by a quirk of fate, we have both pieces of this puzzle locked within the waves of our panel study. Our data reflect not only the remarkable penetration and intensity of protest feeling and activity in the late days of May, but also the massive proportions of the shift to the Gaullists in the June elections. They provide, therefore, a unique base for examining how these two pieces fit together at the mass level.

Last, at a low level of theoretical importance but still of more than passing historical interest, we have empirical data concerning the incidence and character of popular participation in the demonstrations and strikes of May. The vast literature on the May events is, of course, primarily interpretive; the descriptions that exist are mainly "eye-witness" accounts of particular developments, often informative but inevitably partial.[3] The same fortuitous circumstances that enabled us to capture both the May revolt and the June reaction in terms of a common analytic thread also enabled us to estimate how many and what kinds of people filled the streets in May in what proved to be a futile effort to get rid of the Gaullists.

The May Revolt

The May revolt was unexpected. A few perspicacious individuals were concerned about the combustibility of France's burgeoning university student population,[4] or were generally skeptical about the stability of modern society.[5] But most professional observers of French politics were taken by surprise. *Le Monde*'s political commentator stated shortly before the greatest social upheaval in any modern democracy that France was bored.[6] Janet Flanner, writing as Genêt on May 1, in *The New Yorker* of May 11, said that "on May 30 President de Gaulle will have been in uninterrupted power for ten years. Pro or con, few Frenchmen think he should be disturbed." And in a book of ours that appeared early in 1968, we told our readers that "public demonstrations occurred frequently during the early years of the Fifth Republic but have been rare since 1963" (Pierce, 1968, p. 178).

The Coming of the Revolt

In retrospect, it is apparent that the French electorate moved suddenly and strikingly to the left between the fall of 1965 (just prior to the presidential election of that year) and the 1967 legislative elections. This leftward shift is only partly discernible through a simple reading of the returns from these two elections, which more or less bracket its trajectory. François Mitterrand won less than a third of the votes at the first ballot of the 1965 presidential election, at which he was the only left-wing candidate, but this comparatively poor leftist showing was masked by Mitterrand's taking of more than 45 percent of the vote at the run-off against de Gaulle. Mitterrand's second-ballot voters included anti-Gaullist centrists and even extreme rightists (Deutsch, Lindon, and Weill, 1966, p. 76); but if these are ignored, it appears as though the one leftist presidential candidate in 1965 was about as strong as all the leftist parties together in 1967. Yet in fact, there was a dramatic shift to the left in popular political outlook between those two dates, a shift that was the harbinger of the explosion of May 1968.

This leftward movement can be clearly traced in a series of mass surveys conducted by SOFRES between 1964 and 1967, at which the left-right self-placement of the respondents was regularly and uniformly charted. The SOFRES method of obtaining left-right self-placements differs from our own; SOFRES asks the respondents to locate themselves in one of several "baskets" with appropriate left-right labels, whereas we asked our respondents to locate themselves on a metric scale that also contained appropriate labels (see Chapter 4). But we found it comparatively simple to convert the SOFRES scores into our own measurement system.[7]

The result of this transformation of a series of SOFRES surveys between the middle of 1964 and the spring of 1967 appears in Figure 14-1. Between June 1964 and the fall of 1965, the mean left-right location of the
French electorate hovered around 53, on a scale where values above 50 are
rightist and values below 50 are leftist. Then, about the time of the 1965
presidential election, held in December, an abrupt shift to the left began to
take place. By January 1967 the national mean left-right location had fallen
to less than 46. It rose slightly at the time of the 1967 legislative elections,
but even taking this small rebound into account, the French electorate had
moved an average of some six points to the left in eighteen months. This is
a shift of impressive magnitude, of an order that one would not normally
expect to find in the absence of some powerful stimulus. This normal inertia, as we saw in Chapter 4, is due to the fact that about one-third of the
mass electorate consists of the marais—people without any interest in politics who place themselves at the midpoint of the left-right distribution. This
large group acts as a drag or anchor on the value of the mean left-right lo-

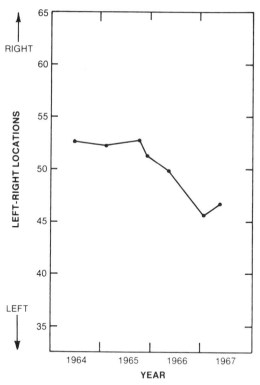

Figure 14-1. National mean left-right locations, France, 1964–1967.
SOFRES distributions converted into metric scores.

cation, so that a shift in the mean of some six points necessarily reflects wide changes of location among the more politically involved sector of the electorate.

We lack the data to explain precisely why this dramatic leftward shift in the political outlook of the French electorate took place when it did, but some elements of the situation suggest a plausible interpretation. Although the left did not do particularly well at the presidential election of 1965, for the first time since World War II the left-wing parties overcame their traditional rivalries by jointly supporting the candidacy of François Mitterrand. And Mitterrand's respectable showing at the second ballot, when he won more than 45 percent of the votes, legitimated and encouraged anti-Gaullist sentiments. De Gaulle won the election, of course, although his margin of victory was sufficiently narrow to undermine his lofty claims. French leftists had been frustrated electorally, but they simultaneously found more reason for hope than they themselves might have expected.

The developing sense of leftist solidarity and optimism was furthered by subtle changes in popular attitudes toward the Communist party, especially among the non-Communist leftists. Prior to the 1965 presidential election, Communists had been regarded with deep suspicion not only by a substantial majority of the electorate as a whole but also by large proportions of the non-Communist left. By 1966, the reservations of the non-Communist left toward the party had diminished noticeably (Duhamel, 1966).

There were two reasons for this. First, the Communist party, interested in ending its isolation (engendered by the Cold War) by allying with other leftist parties, began in 1964 to take various positions suggestive of growing attachment to "formal" democratic practices and even of a certain amount of independence from the Soviet Union. Above all, the Communists made their move toward left-wing solidarity in an uncommonly generous fashion by supporting Mitterrand for the presidency without making any programmatic or other demands on him. This conciliatory policy registered visibly throughout the mass public early in 1966, and particularly among leftists. Second, in the same year de Gaulle's foreign policy of independence from the United States and rapprochement with the Soviet Union reached its peak with French withdrawal from the North Atlantic Treaty Organization (including notice of the early removal from France of all American troops and NATO installations) and de Gaulle's visit to Russia.

While de Gaulle pursued détente with the Soviet Union, presumably to countervail U.S. influence in western Europe, France itself swiftly moved leftward. Even more than the Communists themselves, de Gaulle succeeded in removing the main obstacle to leftist unity: the perception that the Communist party was tied to a hostile foreign power. That perception was bound to change as the French government followed a policy that led other governments to wonder whether France was envisaging a reversal of alliances. As long as the French President appeared to be courting the Soviet Union, it could not easily be argued that to ally with or support the French Communist party was tantamount to giving aid and comfort to the enemy.[8]

The 1965 electoral scenario was replayed in 1967, this time in legislative terms. The left-wing parties were more unified electorally than they had been at any legislative election since the end of World War II. Once again they were thwarted in their bid for power, but this time their deep resentments could not be contained. When French students rioted in Paris early in May, to some extent in imitation of their American and German counterparts, a sympathetic wave of anti-Gaullism spread across the land to an extent that had no parallel in the United States, West Germany, or any of the other countries in which student confrontation politics had struck showers of revolutionary sparks. By the latter half of May, the crisis had reached such proportions that universities were closed nationwide, hundreds of factories were occupied by strikers, and some ten million workers, over half the national labor force, were reported to be out on strike. Major regions of the country had become almost completely paralyzed economically, and the final toppling of the Gaullist regime seemed imminent.

Participation in Demonstrations

Joining in political demonstrations was perhaps the most active form of rank-and-file participation in the May crisis and, by normal political standards, one of the most "difficult" or rare. Our data included reports on such participation. It is quite possible that these activities, though not illegitimate, may have been underreported. Nevertheless, even taking our survey estimates at face value, the rates of demonstration participation can be seen as considerable testimony to the degree of mass penetration achieved by the political ferment in May.

Our materials indicate that during this period about 8 percent of the populace went into the streets to express their political sentiments, most of them hostile to the Gaullist regime. This figure refers to the total electorate, including the old, the infirm, and many other types of people who could scarcely have participated in an active political movement. It projects to several million persons; that is, it is about equal to the number of French voters who would be expected to attend more conventional political meetings or rallies during the whole course of a normal election campaign.

Nevertheless, this 8 percent estimate is presented in its weakest form: several other considerations will serve to increase it subjectively. For example, although political ferment swept the whole of continental France from Lille to Marseilles and from Nantes to Strasbourg, the mounting of demonstrations was in the main an urban phenomenon. This means in turn that, unlike the situation with normal campaign rallies, there were many communes and even some whole election districts, usually rather rural in character, where a sympathizer could not have found a local or nearby demonstration in which to participate. Reflecting such differences, people living in cities of more than 50,000 were three times as likely to have taken part in a demonstration as those living in places of less than 5,000. Indeed, 60 percent of our respondents reported that there were no demonstrations in their immediate area, and the majority of such reports came from those living outside the larger cities, in places where the whole commune was specified as the "immediate area."[9] These reports do not establish that demonstrations were genuinely inaccessible to a person willing to travel a modest distance to participate in one. But our information on the geographic dispersion of the demonstrations implies that at least 33 percent, and perhaps as much as 40 percent, of the electorate were not within easy reach of such events. This suggests in turn that where demonstrations were reasonably accessible, they were drawing turnouts of close to 13 percent of the public. Again, this figure is only an average surrounded by a considerable dispersion of local values. In some of the "hottest" urban electoral districts, where demonstrations were most rampant, our sample estimates indicate participation rates of 30 percent or more, values which must be regarded as remarkable.

Who demonstrated? Some of the answers to this question are routine and therefore not surprising, although the social composition of the demonstrations may not have matched very well the expected composition of political rallies under normal circumstances. First, there was a strong gradient by age. Across the electorate as a whole, 17 percent of our respondents under thirty participated and the percentage must have been correspondingly higher in areas where demonstrations were relatively accessible. There was only slight participation by people over fifty. Conventional rallies would have shown a much higher median age.

Second, one finds the expected differential by sex: men were more likely to participate than women by about a 5–3 ratio, despite their minority status in the electorate. The demographic epicenter of participation lay among young males: the rate here was 30 percent, even ignoring demonstration accessibility, a consideration that, if taken into account, would move the effective rate much closer to 50 percent.

Although these age and sex lines would have been apparent to any casual viewer of the demonstrations, they are of interest here because they can be estimated as rates of selection from the appropriate pool for the country as a whole. In general accounts of the demonstrations, the social composition of the participating population has been presented from other points of view, particularly in terms of the ratio of students and intelligentsia to blue collar workers.

Because of the panel nature of our design, we cannot address this question of social composition in complete detail. The youngest segment of our panel was twenty-two years old in the spring of 1968. Nevertheless, the data present something of a double image. First, it is abundantly clear that the demonstrations appealed in the main to people of advanced education. *Rates* both of participation and of mere inclination to demonstrate among people of relatively high training (operationally, formal education beyond the secondary level) are three times as great as they are among those of more average, or working-class, educational backgrounds. If women are set aside, these rates are almost four times as great. Nearly half of all the males under twenty-nine with advanced training took to the streets.

At the same time, these propensity figures have no necessary bearing on the social composition of demonstrators encountered on the street, for the simple reason that common workers vastly outnumber people of advanced education in the French or any other social structure. Therefore, relatively low *rates* of participation by workers might still put them in the absolute majority. And this appears to have been roughly the case; for despite the fact that the demonstrations had an appeal which was sharply and inversely related to educational background, a majority of the actual demonstrators—although not an overwhelming majority (57 percent)—were of more limited education.

A glance at demonstration participation in occupational terms helps to focus the picture still more sharply. When we divide the work force into the six grades of occupational status discussed in Chapter 5 (see especially Figure 5–2), we find that in absolute numbers demonstration participation was overwhelmingly concentrated among the two groups of manual workers (skilled and unskilled), mainly those employed in the larger enterprises. But the participation *rate* among manual workers was not as high as among the two managerial groups (higher and lower). These groups include more than "managers," of course, and for some of the occupations included, such as business proprietorship, demonstration participation rates were at their lowest. But they were at their peak among top managerial personnel (*cadres supérieurs*), professional people (*professions libérales*), and educators (*professions littéraires et scientifiques; professions intellectuelles*). Among the (white-collar) supervisory nonmanual and lower nonmanual workers, by way of contrast, participation rates were very low. Finally, and departing from our occupational status categories, we should point out that demonstration participation was very modest in the agricultural sector generally, although it was impressive among wage-earning farm workers in particular.

Strike Participation

Politically significant though the rash of demonstrations was, it did not involve more than a small minority of the electorate. If the vote of June 23 had pitted all demonstrators against all non-demonstrators, even with "inclination to demonstrate" taken into account, the Gaullists would have won a still more stunning proportion of the vote.

The cause of the puzzle to which we alluded earlier—the outpouring of opposition to Gaullist rule, followed by a Gaullist electoral landslide—is imbedded in the widespread strikes which plagued the economy in the late days of May and into early June. Here, it was said, half the labor force, or 10 million Frenchmen, had stopped work in protest against the Gaullist regime. The newspaper figures were without question rounded and rough; our surveys provide somewhat more detailed estimates of the rate of work stoppage. In our sample, slightly more than 40 percent of the labor force indicated that they had been out on strike in connection with the disorders, a figure which projects to somewhat less than 8 million people. Furthermore, it should be kept in mind that such a figure does not mean 40 percent of the electorate, since very large numbers of French voters are not in the active labor force, and even the proportion of households in which the head of the unit is not in the labor force is rather substantial (among the retired in particular). Taking all these matters into account, only about 20 percent of the electorate were out on strike sometime during the disorders.

Nevertheless, the strike figures retain extremely significant magnitudes. It can be estimated that about one-third of all French households had at least one member participating in the strikes; and although the large majority of demonstration participants also struck, this latter figure would be a little higher still if demonstrations were added to the calculations. By any method of accounting, we see a society in grave crisis.

A survey is scarely needed to reveal the gross facts about the center of strike participation. The prime phenomenon on the labor front was the shutdown, often accompanied by occupation of the management offices, of large factories. Our survey mirrors this well: the highest strike rates in occupational terms—about 60 percent—occurred among workers in the largest enterprises. There was also some strike participation in small enterprises (under twenty workers), but the rates were less than half those among wage earners elsewhere. In the agricultural sector there was virtually no strike participation, and the urban-rural gradient in these behaviors was strong. Finally, strike participation rose among white collar employees in much the same way as did demonstration participation; that is, it centered heavily on the professions libérales (where relevant), and on the cadres moyens.

Somewhat less certain at the outset, however, was the way in which membership in various competing labor unions influenced strike behavior. Throughout the May–June days, the left-wing, Catholic-led CFDT (Confédération Française Démocratique du Travail) sought in various ways to distinguish itself from the Communist-led CGT (Confédération Générale du Travail), and generally gave the impression of more militancy. In particular, the CFDT leaders expressed solidarity with the demonstrating students far more explicitly than did the CGT leaders, who repeatedly warned their adherents about the dangers of "adventure" and "leftism."

There is nothing in our data, however, to suggest that CGT members were any less willing to strike than CFDT members. Our respondents were able to indicate whether they would have preferred to work during the strikes, as well as whether they had been out on strike. Although the number of people in our sample belonging to specified unions other than the CGT is very small, our data show that whereas there was an equivalent propensity to strike between CGT and CFDT households, there was, for strikers, a somewhat greater propensity to strike willingly among the CGT households.

One further point about demonstration and strike participation deserves comment. In 1967 we asked respondents whether they (or the head of the household, if the respondent was not the head) belonged to a union or a professional organization, and if they did, whether they had ever participated in a strike or a demonstration. Accordingly, we are able to assess the extent to which there was a fresh mobilization, as compared with a remobilization, within organized labor in May–June 1968.[10]

Of the households with organizational ties who had reported previous strike or demonstration participation, about half reported strike or demonstration participation in May–June; of those who had reported no previous strike or demonstration participation, about 30 percent reported strike or demonstration participation in the same period. Somewhat less than a third of the "organized" households, therefore, were led for the first time to become active in demonstrations or strikes during the 1968 upheaval.

The rate of participation in strikes was virtually the same for the reactivated as for the newly activated households, although the former displayed somewhat higher rates of participation in demonstrations alone and also of participation in both strikes and demonstrations. But among the strikers, the newly activated reported less unwillingness to strike than did the reactivated, possibly because of age difference. We are dealing here with small numbers of cases; but if our findings are representative, they mean that the freshly recruited strikers entered their new experience with more enthusiasm than the veterans.

District Variations in Prevalence of Disorder

The mere fact that both demonstrations and strikes tended to center in urban areas and to fade away toward the hinterland makes it clear that there were sharp variations between districts in regard to the incidence of disorder.[11] Across our sample districts, too, there is a considerable correlation between the incidence of strikes and demonstrations. More than 33 percent of our sample reported both strikes and demonstrations in their local areas. These areas we shall consider the set of "hot" districts, and although we only have about a one-tenth sample of all districts for 1968, this set includes such famous "hot spots" as Paris, Nantes, the lower Seine Valley, Lille, and Besançon. A slightly larger group of respondents (39 percent) reported the opposite: that neither strikes nor demonstrations took place locally. Those districts we shall label "inactive." Summing the two proportions shows that about 75 percent of the sample lived in either hot or inactive districts. In addition, a tiny handful of people reported local demonstrations without strikes. Virtually all of the remainder (about 25 percent) reported local strikes but no demonstrations, a logical result of the higher, more wide-spread incidence of strikes at that time in France. Therefore, if we wish to keep track of the contextual effects of the disorders, it will be useful to think in terms of these three main types of districts: "hot," "strike-only," and inactive.

It is not surprising that the hot districts tended to contain somewhat heightened proportions of leftist sympathizers, and of course within these districts the actual participation was disproportionately, but not exclusively, from the left, according to our "own left-right location" measurements of before. Less obvious, but pleasing, is the fact that in a general way those districts which had shown the most sharply polarized distributions on our left-right continuum in 1967 tended to become the hottest districts in 1968. Over all districts, a plotting of left-right polarization (as indexed by the standard deviation of own left-right locations) shows a total correlation with a continuous measure of district "heat" that is at best very weak and ragged. But at the highest end of the polarization and heat extremes a clear pattern emerges, almost as though thresholds of polarization levels were in-volved in propensity to disorder. To be specific, out of the seven sample dis-tricts that were the most polarized on the left-right continuum in 1967, six were among the eleven hottest districts in May 1968, and the seventh al-most made this classification as well.

Although before the disorders the hot districts were slightly more left-ist and much more polarized politically than the others, they did not lack the heavy admixture of the marais characteristic of all France. It is true that the marais is not typically visible politically, but because it is bound to fig-ure in election situations, we need to monitor its relationship to the disor-ders. This is particularly important for demonstration participation, where there is much more latitude for self-selection than in the case of strike par-ticipation, when a total factory is shut down and both militants and marais must go out on strike. Among the marais, rates of political participation other than voting are, as we have seen, very low indeed. There is little self-starting political interest or motivation in this group, and it would not be surprising if its demonstration participation had been at a low ebb in May and June. Nevertheless, the data attest to the opposite state of affairs: mem-bers of the marais were either remarkably likely or remarkably unlikely to participate, depending on whether demonstrations were going on close at hand or far away. In the hottest districts, their demonstration participation was substantial, not lagging far behind that of avowed leftist partisans. It is clear that although they were hardly politicized, they were quite willing to join in the excitement all around them, and consequently the crowds in the streets contained large numbers of people whose normal involvement in politics was thin or nonexistent. Outside the hottest districts, in areas where demonstrations were not close at hand, partisans of both left and right did reach some modest rates of participation—near the national norm of 8 percent—but marais participation in such areas fell away to almost nothing.

The June Elections

The great popular upheaval of May 1968 has received an enormous amount of attention. Nevertheless, the revolt was only one element of the massive dialectical process that shook France in the spring and summer of 1968. The other was the Gaullist landslide at the polls on June 23 and June 30. After the astonishing display of hostility to Gaullist rule through widespread strikes and demonstrations, the French voters turned to Gaullist candidates at the June elections in such numbers that for the first time in French Republican history a single party gained a majority of the seats in the popularly elected chamber. No account of the May crisis, particularly one that seeks to trace its overall impact on the representative process, can ignore the electoral backlash. It was Thermidor at the polls, and the National Assembly thus created was to shape French legislation for nearly five years after the revolt.

Shift to the Right

Earlier in this chapter, we described the sharp swing to the left of the French electorate between the presidential election of 1965 and the legislative elections of 1967, as registered in a series of SOFRES surveys which we converted into the currency of our own metric left-right measures. What happened as a result of the disorders of May 1968 was an even more abrupt *rightward* shift back to the level of late 1965, when François Mitterrand, as the only left-wing presidential candidate, had won less than 35 percent of the popular vote at the first ballot. Inasmuch as this sharp rightward mass movement is captured quite neatly within our own panel data, we can relate it directly to its electoral consequences in the form of the Gaullist landslide of 1968.

We pointed out in Chapter 4 that the self-ascribed locations of the French electorate form a distribution along the left-right continuum that has two key properties: a point of central tendency, and a degree of polarization or dispersion around that point. Both key features changed significantly in the wake of the May events, relative to their magnitudes in 1967.

When we had interviewed them in the late spring of 1967, the total set of persons whom we reinterviewed in 1968 had shown a mean left-right location of 48.3, a point slightly to the left of center. In the summer of 1968, after the disorders and the elections, the same set of people showed a mean location of 52.2, or a shift of almost four points to the right. Over the same period and for the same people, the polarization of the left-right distribution increased significantly. This implies, among other things, that the mean shift of some four points to the right was a net change concealing countercurrents of gross change. In other words, although some Frenchmen had been pushed to the left by events, those who moved to the right had shifted correspondingly by more than four points.

This net displacement to the right is displayed graphically in Figure 14-2, where we set out the distributions of the self-assigned left-right locations of all of our respondents who were interviewed in 1967 and 1968 and who attributed a left-right location (including 50) to themselves on both occasions. In 1967 the centrist bulge dominates the distribution, and leftists slightly outnumber rightists. In 1968, the centrist mode is diminished, the left is modestly reduced in numbers, and there is an evident increase in the ranks of the rightists.

Thus our data mirror well not only the ferment of May, set in motion by the anti-Gaullist student outbreak, but the Gaullist triumph at the polls in June. How are these two items related? Nobody can doubt that the strong social action in the streets of Paris and the factories of Nantes and other cities was responsible for the strong wave of social reaction at the polls

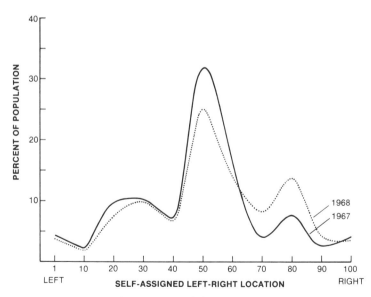

Figure 14-2. Mass self-locations on left-right continuum, France, 1967 and 1968. N = 526.

three weeks later. Questions arise only because the disorders were not wholly the work of a handful of student radicals, bent on revolution. What distinguished France from Berkeley and Berlin was the enormous resonance touched off across the land by the student confrontations in Paris. The most immediate sequel, of course, was at the provincial universities, where faculty and students rapidly occupied administration offices and took to the streets. Nothing like the same immediate and far-flung solidarity had been expressed at universities in the United States or Germany. More impressive still was the analogous response in the factories, whose populations (the workers) made up a far larger proportion of the national population. Although the workers' grievances and demands were patently distinct from those of the students at the outset, the speed with which the strikes spread, and more especially their astonishing spontaneity, seemed to attest to the fact that the students had released an impressive reservoir of pent-up anti-Gaullist sentiment in the land. In the late days of May, few political leaders, opposition or Gaullist, felt that the regime was any longer viable. Against such a backdrop the unparalleled magnitude of the Gaullist victory seemed ironic if not unbelievable.

Some of the apparent discontinuity between the May events and the June landslide can be traced to the gap between, on the one hand, public opinion as gauged by the actions of the politically visible and, on the other hand, public opinion as measured across the politically invisible, giving equal weight to each person, as in an opinion survey or a mass election. It takes only a very small fraction of a population to create and sustain major political disorder. In addition, whereas what has been called the "silent majority" dominates political outcomes at the polls, it rarely if ever engages in any other kind of directed political activity, and it is often quite out of tune with opinion in activist quarters. Although accounts in the press made it seem that half of grass-roots France was up in arms against the government, we have seen that only about a third of French households participated in the May activities in any noteworthy way, including work stoppages.

It is easy to find this gap between political visibility and political invisibility in our surveys, and to assess its effects on the sequence of events. Indeed, if we had to describe the center of the June reaction at the polls in political terms, we would point to the citizens of the marais. Although there was significant movement toward the right all along the left-right continuum, including movement by leftist sympathizers as well as by rightists, our data show that the people who did not relate themselves to this continuum, that is, the marais, made a very disproportionate contribution to the swing to the right electorally, by changing the direction of their 1968 votes as compared with those of 1967. They, the politically unanchored, were the ones who responded most impressively to the force of events. Some of their young members, of course, were swept into local demonstrations; by and large, however, their main days in the public sun were June 23 and June 30.

Left-Right Shifts and Proximity to the Disorders

Nevertheless, although the concept of differential political visibility makes a major contribution toward explaining the seeming discontinuity between the political events of May and June, the evidence suggests that it falls far short of a total explanation. It was not simply a matter of a minority of visible participants making loud noises in May, followed by a majority of invisible bystanders voicing their disapproval in June. From the start, there were compelling indications that the student riots and protests against the government were received with very considerable sympathy by the populace at large. A survey conducted in Paris by the Institut Français d'Opinion Publique (IFOP) on May 8 after several nights of student-police clashes showed the public expressing sympathy for the students' side of the conflict by an astonishing margin of 61 percent for to 16 percent against, with the remainder expressing no opinion. Yet a national survey begun at almost the same time but continued further into the month (May 14) displays a narrower margin of support for the students in the Paris region and an overall balance of opinion against the student demonstrations nationally. A survey in Paris on May 27 indicated that the distribution of opinion there had shifted against the students, by 50 percent to 42 percent, with only 8 percent without an opinion (*Sondages,* 1968, no. 2). Opinion, therefore, shifted rapidly in an adverse direction as the cries of student revolutionaries became increasingly sharp and gleeful. Meanwhile, the evidence also indicates that the industrial strikes, which began on May 14 with the occupation of the Sud-Aviation plant in Nantes, were greeted with considerable sympathy, and various other kinds of anti-Gaullist activities broke out in other sectors as well. In other words, although it is true that the "silent majority" played its characteristic role in the May–June sequence, many politicized French men and women changed their minds about the justifiability of the disorders as events ran their course in May. Thus, in June, the May events were repudiated not only by a frightened marais but also by politically aware voters who had welcomed them earlier.

This change of heart is best reflected in the 70 percent of our sample who refused, in the summer of 1968 (after the election), either to endorse or condemn in retrospect "those who launched the strikes and demonstrations," preferring instead the alternative statement that the authors of the disturbance "were justified at the beginning but carried things too far." This questionnaire item of ours was poor in one sense, for it made the intermediate response all too easy for the ambivalent respondent; but it does seem significant that in the wake of the vigorous election reaction in June, not even 20 percent of the sample were prepared to condemn the strike and demonstration leaders outright.

The rhetoric of the students, the expansion of the disorders, and the apparent incapacity of the government to restore order had led to widespread fears of civil war as the days passed. Although our earlier (1958) questionnaire items did not offer entirely comparable response alternatives, the 40 percent of our 1968 sample who reported having felt that the risk of civil war was "high" at the time of the disturbances, along with the additional 31 percent who felt there had been "some" risk, outstrip noticeably the proportion of the French electorate who had thought there was a risk of civil war in 1958, as measured by a national sample survey conducted after the dark days of May of that year had terminated the Fourth Republic (Dupeux, 1960, p. 133).

Concern over the possibility of civil war is distributed in our 1968 sample along two lines: first political predispositions (tendance); and second, relationship (proximity) to the disturbances. It is not surprising that concern was much greater among rightist than among leftist respondents, although the degree of fear expressed on the left was far from insignificant.

If, however, we subdivide our respondents further into subgroups according to their type of district (hot, strike-only, or inactive) as well as by their level of personal participation (in demonstrations, in strikes only, or none), the variations in patterns of concern about civil war become intriguing. The only subgroup that could be said to have had little concern about the risk of war was, as we would expect, the leftists in hot districts who had participated in demonstrations (about 10 percent of the electorate in such areas). But among the considerable majority of non-demonstrating leftists in the same districts, concern ran much higher than for all the leftists outside the hot districts. Moreover, although citizens of the marais outside the hot districts (particularly those who chose the position of 50 on our scale) showed generally less concern than the rightists—but, of course, more concern than the leftists—the members of the marais within the hot districts, including even those who had participated in the demonstrations, expressed greater concern than their rightist neighbors, and by a substantial margin! In sum, if we set aside the leftist demonstrators, fear of civil war ran higher in the hot districts despite their strong leftist complexion than in either of the other types of districts. Apparently, then, sheer proximity to the disorders was a potent determinant of fear of civil war—fear that affected all but the most active leftists, as well as both strikers and demonstrators who were not leftists. And in these hot districts it was the marais—even those who were swept into street action—who became most frightened.

A look at the other two types of districts, however, makes it clear that proximity is not the whole explanation, for higher levels of concern were registered in the relatively remote and inactive districts than in the strike-only areas. We commented earlier that public reaction to the strikes appears to have been relatively benign and sympathetic, in contrast to the growing distaste for demonstrations. It is true that in strike-only areas the majority of those rightists who did not participate in the strikes were more alarmed than were rightists in other areas. But apart from this subgroup (20 percent of the inhabitants), fear of civil war among the other 80 percent was almost absent. Leftist and marais citizens who did not strike or demonstrate were far less concerned than their counterparts living in hot areas. It seems likely that, for people in districts where local disorders occurred, fear of civil war seemed exaggerated, whereas in the more remote districts where people's reactions were prompted by the heightened reports from the mass media, fear was more widespread.

When we move from fear of civil war to attitudes expressed toward the demonstrators, we find about the same patterns over these same subgroups of partisans (left-right) and districts, with one exception. There is very clear negativism toward the demonstrators, if not fear of civil war, in the strike-only areas; if anything, the antagonism runs higher in those districts, although the left-right partisan polarization concerning the demonstrators runs strongest here as well.

Table 14-1 turns our attention to basic shifts in self-locations on the left-right continuum within our sample, although still within the same groupings of districts and respondents used for civil war fears and attitudes toward the demonstrators. The table is divided into quadrants according to whether or not (1) strikes or (2) demonstrations took place in the districts. (The upper right quadrant, reserved for districts which had demonstrations but no strikes, is so unpopulated that entries are not worth calculating.) The patterns we see in left-right changes in the table follow quite closely those described for civil war fears. Overall movement to the right is least in the strike-only districts and, indeed, is almost negligible for the nonpartici-pants of both leftist and rightist predispositions. The largest movement to the left occurs in the hot districts among leftist demonstrators (although the few respondents in other areas who also demonstrated show similar trends). These leftist demonstrators, though constituting less than 10 percent of the electorate, clearly account for the overall polarization of the left-right distribution after the crisis. But by contrast with these demonstrators in hot districts, their neighbors (including strikers) moved more sharply to the right than the national norm.

Turnover in the Partisan Vote

The notable rightward shift in mass left-right orientations between 1967 and 1968 was mirrored in a slightly attenuated shift in left-right partisan voting. As pointed out in Chapter 4, despite the rightward shift in self-locations between 1967 and 1968, there was impressive stability in the main

Table 14-1. Shifts of self-location on left-right continuum between 1967 and 1968, as a function of tendance and proximity to disorders, France.[a]

Degree of participation	Districts with strikes				Districts with no strikes			
	Left	50	Right	Total	Left	50	Right	Total
Districts with demonstrations								
Demonstrators[b]	-4.02 (22)	c	c	-2.36 (30)	c	c	c	c
Strikers only[d]	+11.91 (20)	+3.04 (15)	+4.62 (14)	+5.63 (48)	c	c	c	c
No participation	+0.59 (34)	+16.87 (24)	+7.28 (38)	+7.28 (98)	c	c	c	c
Total	+2.19 (75)	+10.76 (43)	+3.86 (55)	+4.85				
Districts with no demonstrations								
Demonstrators[b]	c	c	c	-5.70 (9)	c	c	c	c
Strikers only[d]	-1.19 (12)	+6.56 (5)	+10.07 (10)	+4.58 (27)	-4.55 (8)	0.00 (6)	c	-4.07 (16)
No participation	-0.16 (15)	+4.22 (16)	-0.67 (25)	+0.86 (57)	+3.14 (23)	+10.37 (54)	+7.39 (40)	+7.96 (117)
Total	-1.87 (31)	+4.87 (21)	+2.00 (40)	+1.35	+1.01 (31)	+8.60 (60)	+7.06 (44)	+6.28

a. + = shift to right; − = shift to left. Case numbers are in parentheses. Because of small case numbers, primary interest is in the marginal columns ("Total") and the "No participation" rows. Data are presented with regression effects corrected. Cell Ns do not sum exactly to marginal Ns because of fractional weighted frequencies and rounding.
b. Includes also those merely inclined to demonstrate, or persons of the same household.
c. Fewer than 5 cases.
d. Includes household members as well.

party locations assigned over those two years, at least by the mass population.[12] Yet there was an overall tendency in 1968 for the voters to locate the parties slightly to the left of where they had placed them (the same or equivalent parties) in 1967. Therefore, for the purpose of comparing left-right voting in 1967 and 1968, we have used the 1967 mean left-right party scores for both years, in order to have an identical measure. On this basis, for our respondents who were interviewed in both years, the mean left-right partisan vote at the decisive ballot in 1967 was 47.3 while in 1968 it was 50.1, representing a shift of 2.8 points to the right.

At first glance, it might appear surprising that the shift in the mean left-right vote between 1967 and 1968 was not so large as the shift in the mean of the underlying set of self left-right locations (2.8 as against 3.9). After all, the curve for the latter is heavily weighted at the center, and any undulation necessarily implies large gross shifts in left-right locations. The partisan vote expressed in left-right terms might well appear to be a more sensitive barometer of political change. Relatively few votes go to the parties for which the mean left-right vote scores approximate 50; the big electoral battalions are on the left and on the right, and one might expect that any net electoral shift in one direction or the other would produce a comparatively large change in the mean left-right vote.

But that overlooks the fact that the overwhelming majority of two-time voters repeat their partisan votes, even at an election that produces a landslide vote for one party. The constant voters are typically far more numerous than the third of the electorate who score themselves at 50 when asked to assign themselves a left-right location. Mean left-right vote scores are, therefore, less sensitive indicators of electoral change than mean left-right self-locations. In 1968, a relatively small shift in the mean left-right vote translated itself into an impressive Gaullist sweep.

That sweep took two forms: a striking increase in the vote for the Gaullists and their allies among the Giscardian Independent Republicans, compared with previous elections, and a healthy parliamentary majority for the pure Gaullists alone, which, when the Giscardians were added, amounted to an astonishing three-fourths of the entire Assembly. Before saying more about the size of this parliamentary majority, however, we should examine the shifts in the partisan vote that took place between the legislative elections of 1967 and 1968.

Table 14-2 sets out the turnover in the partisan vote, divided into the three broad categories of left, center, and right, for the respondents in our panel survey who cast a valid ballot at the decisive round of voting in both 1967 and 1968.[13] Almost 85 percent of them voted for the same partisan tendency at the two elections, but some 16 percent voted for a different tendency. Of these changers, almost 70 percent shifted their vote rightward, while the rest shifted their vote to the left.

Table 14-2. Turnover in partisan vote at decisive ballot, 1967–1968, among voters who cast valid ballots at both elections (percentages), France.[a]

Decisive vote, 1967	Decisive vote, 1968			Total
	Left[b]	Center[c]	Right[d]	
Left[b]	32	2	5	39
Center[c]	e	3	4	7
Right[d]	3	2	49	54
Total	35	7	58	100

a. N = 400.
b. Includes PCF, FGDS, and PSU.
c. Includes CD, PDM, and independent socialists.
d. Includes UNR, UDR, PDM-UDR, RI, and moderates (conservatives).
e. Less than 1 percent.

In the context of the May revolt and its impact on the political orientations of the electorate, we are most interested in the last two groups, those who changed their support dramatically. Case numbers are small, but the distinguishing characteristics of these two polar groups are highly suggestive. Those who abandoned the left for the right in 1968 were predominantly male, working-class centrists who admired de Gaulle. Those who took the opposite route from right to left tended to be young, poorly educated, uninvolved female leftists who had had a favorable view of de Gaulle in 1967 but who, after the May events, became sharply antagonistic to him. Of the various factors at work here, the dominant one is the attitude toward Charles de Gaulle.[14] In this special context we see a stark manifestation of the general electoral importance of the Gaullist–anti-Gaullist axis.

Conversion of Votes into Seats

For the student of mass political behavior, the most striking aspect of the 1968 legislative elections was the harvest of votes that the public disorders produced for the Gaullists and their Giscardian allies. From the perspective of parliamentary representation, however, the outstanding characteristic of the elections was the return to parliament of a governing majority of unprecedented size. If, in the broad sense, the Gaullists' gain in votes was impressive, their gain in parliamentary seats was nothing short of spectacular, as Table 14-3 indicates. Pure Gaullists (UDR-V[e]), Giscardians (RI), and a few dissident Gaullist candidates together won a bare majority of the votes at the decisive ballot in Metropolitan France in 1968, but the pure Gaullists alone won 60 percent of the metropolitan seats and, together with the Giscardians, the broad Gaullist bloc held almost 75 percent of the seats in the Assembly.[15] In 1967, the Gaullist bloc had won only some 44 percent of the

Table 14-3. Parliamentary groups in the National Assembly, 1967 and 1968 (Metropolitan and Overseas France).[a]

Parliamentary group	National Assembly seats	
	1967	1968
PCF	73	34
FGDS	121	57
PDM (centrist)	41	33
UD-V^e^ (Gaullist)	201	293
RI (Giscardian)	42	61
None (*non-inscrits*)	9	9
Total	487	487

a. These parliamentary groups include the deputies affiliated with them for administrative purposes.

votes at the decisive ballot; their slight majority of the seats in the Assembly was due to their dominance in Overseas France, as they did not have a majority of the seats for Metropolitan France. The Gaullists' gain in seats in 1968 was far greater proportionately than their gain in votes.

There is nothing unusual about a disproportion between partisan votes and legislative seats. Rae (1967) found that "electoral systems almost always award more than a proportionate share of the seats to the party which polls the largest single share of the vote" (pp. 72–73); that such a propensity is heightened by plurality or majority formula electoral systems, as opposed to proportional representation systems (p. 91); and that such systems further "tend to magnify changes in the popular support of parties when legislative seats are allocated" (p. 101). Nevertheless, Rae found the disproportionately favorable results for the Gaullist UNR in 1958 and 1962, the two Fifth Republic elections included in his study, to be "quite extraordinary, even by plurality formula standards" (p. 109). The disproportionate results for 1968 are similarly noteworthy, and they warrant a more general consideration of the vote-seat synapse in France.

Generalizations about the conversion of votes into seats in France are particularly difficult to make because the combination of a two-ballot electoral system and a multiparty system makes it hard to apply tests that are familiar to students of two-party politics. Some sense of the complexities of the situation emerges from the fine study by Bon and Jaffré (1978) of the relationship between the distribution of votes at the first ballot and the outcome of the second ballot at the district level. Bon and Jaffré show that there are regularities in the thresholds of first-ballot support that ensure either victory or defeat for leftist candidates, but that these thresholds vary from election to election and according to such factors as the balance of electoral strength at the first ballot between the Communist and non-Communist components of the left, whether the second-ballot leftist candidate is a Communist or not, and the size of the vote that is neither leftist nor Gaullist.

Despite the complexities of the French situation, however, it is possible to apply a simple predictive model. The progressive simplification of the multiparty system into two main electoral blocs between 1962 and 1978 makes it reasonable to treat the system essentially as a two-party system for purposes of estimation, although there are alternative ways of defining each of the two hypothetical parties. And even though electoral conditions differ at the first and second ballots, we can still rest this model on the votes cast at the decisive ballot.

Table 14-4 sets out the results of the application of a simple linear model of the relationship between seats won and votes received at the five legislative elections between 1962 and 1978. The 1958 and 1981 elections are omitted: the former because it antedates the development of the two main electoral blocs,[16] and the latter because the model was deliberately prepared prior to the 1981 election in order to determine how well it would predict that election's results in seats. The model takes the characteristic linear form, $y = a + bx$, where x represents the percentage of votes and y the percentage of seats won by a given party, a is the intercept, and b is the slope of the regression equation. The model is applied to the three different versions of a two-party system: left versus Gaullists, left versus all other parties, and Gaullists versus all other parties. It borrows heavily from Tufte (1973), who analyzed 132 elections in six two-party systems (including only votes re-

Table 14-4. Test of linear model relating votes cast and seats won at decisive ballot for hypothetical two-party systems at five French elections, 1962–1978, compared with actual two-party systems.

Party system	r^2	Swing ratio[a]	Advantaged party and amount of bias	
Hypothetical two-party				
Left vs. Gaullists (others excluded)	.99	3.52 (0.22)	Gaullists:	1.32
Left vs. all others	.74	2.10 (0.71)	All others:	1.12
Gaullists vs. all others	.63	2.20 (0.97)	Gaullists:	6.26
Actual two-party				
Mean of 9 series of elections examined by Tufte (1973)	.76	2.29 (0.35)		2.82

a. Standard error in parentheses.

ceived by the two major parties); and therefore we have cast our table in a form similar to that used by Tufte (1973, p. 543) and have included his mean values for the series he studied for comparative purposes.

Tufte (1973) refers to the slope of the regression equation relating votes and seats as the "swing ratio." Thus, at the decisive ballot and excluding all parties except those of the left and the Gaullists, a gain of 1.0 percent in the national vote for the left or the Gaullists typically produces a gain of 3.52 percent in seats for that party. The term "bias," also borrowed from Tufte (1973), refers to the percentage of votes greater or less than 50 that each of the two parties must win in order to win 50 percent of the seats. The bias is always symmetrical in a two-party system. If, as in the case of the left versus the Gaullists at the decisive ballot, the Gaullists are advantaged in that they need to win only 48.68 percent of the votes to win half the seats, the leftists are handicapped in that they must win 51.32 percent of the votes to win 50 percent of the seats.

The best fit among the three models is that for the left versus the Gaullists at the decisive ballot, which produces a strong correlation between votes and seats (although for only five cases) and a small standard error. It also shows an unusually highly leveraged swing ratio and a modest amount of bias in favor of the Gaullists.

This model omits parties that together won between 10 and 15 percent of the votes at three of the five elections considered, and almost 10 percent at another of those elections. At the same time, however, the proportion of votes won by "other" parties diminished monotonically from 1962 to 1978, while the proportion of straight fights at the second ballot between a leftist and a Gaullist increased during that same period even more strikingly than the "other" vote decreased. None of the fits are ideal, but the model of the left versus the Gaullists has at least the merit of expressing the end state of a developmental pattern.

When we take all factors into account and do not worry about significance levels, several tentative conclusions emerge. The most important is that the French electoral system is highly leveraged by international standards when only the left and the Gaullists are considered. There is some bias in favor of the Gaullists, but there is nothing unusual in its magnitude. Indeed, when one considers the next model, left versus all other parties, the left suffers even less of a handicap, and perhaps (on the basis of a logit model not shown) none at all. The real losers in the French system are the non-leftist, non-Gaullist parties. Not only does the leftist handicap diminish when they are taken into account, but the Gaullist advantage appears to soar when those "others" are included in the equation.

The linear fit for the left versus the Gaullists is all the more convincing because although this model was prepared before the 1981 legislative elections, which differed from the preceding ones in that the left decisively defeated the Gaullist bloc, it fits the 1981 elections more than tolerably well. At the decisive ballot that year, on a left-versus-Gaullists basis—and counting as Gaullist both the RPR (Rassemblement pour la République) and the UDF (Union pour la Démocratie Française), which ran together as the UNM (Union pour la Nouvelle Majorité)—the leftist parties won some 56 percent of the votes and 70 percent of the seats for Metropolitan France. According to the equation for the linear fit, they should have won 66.5 percent of the seats, a difference of 3.5 percent. In fact, comparing the actual percentage of the seats won by the left with that predicted by the model, the average error across the six elections involved (including 1981) is 2.7 percent, and the largest error is the 3.5 percent figure already cited for 1981.

These comments on the relationship between votes and seats in France may be summed up as follows: for the two main electoral blocs that competed between 1962 and 1981, the seat-vote ratio is highly leveraged; the system gave some slight advantage to the Gaullists during that period; and the ostensible complications of the two-ballot electoral system can apparently be overcome for analytical purposes by relying on the concept of the decisive ballot.[17]

Long-Range Impact of the Revolt

When Parisian students launched their revolt, they found France poised for a remarkably broad mobilization against the Gaullist regime. The unfolding developments rapidly elevated student leaders into positions of national and international prominence, and turned thought toward a romantic re-creation of a full-blown French Revolution. But even as this was taking place, the very rhetoric and tactics of the students were "turning France around." The budding revolt was soon crushed at the polls, though not because the French electorate had experienced any fresh burst of enthusiasm toward Gaullist policies: they went to the polls still dissatisfied with the broad lines of Gaullist governance, and basically sympathetic to the protest in the industrial sector. But in their voting they turned massively to Gaullism because the Gaullists appeared to be the sole force capable of providing the protection they wanted from the kind of incoherent disorder that the students seemed to be promoting. As luck would have it, the highly leveraged French electoral system transformed a real but modest electoral majority into an overwhelming parliamentary majority that left the Gaullists the masters of the new legislature.

Not only in Paris, but worldwide, a profound dislocation seems to have existed between, on the one hand, the students' strong and idealistic ethic of democratic participation in decisionmaking and, on the other hand, their rather remarkable ignorance as to what people outside the university want or are likely to put up with. There is little doubt that the social dynamics underlying the sequence of events in France also made a major contribution to the ascendancy of Ronald Reagan in California with his subsequent targeting of the education system there, as well as to the popularity around the end of the decade of such new American national figures as Spiro Agnew and George Wallace.

Although the same dynamic processes were also touched off elsewhere, the French situation was distinctive. Whereas events were writ large there, the time scale was so compressed that there was much less room for dispute about cause and effect. Events were magnified because, unlike most of the other campus revolts, the Paris uprising coincided with a period of much broader, public dissatisfaction with the political situation. This fact makes the defeat of the revolt more poignant, and provides eloquent testimony to the sheer power of the dialectic of reaction that came into play. When asked in the summer of 1968 whether the May–June crisis would tend to have good or bad effects on their personal situation, the French electorate responded in rather gloomy terms, and people of leftist dispositions were the gloomiest of all. Their defeat hung heavy over them.

In the latter part of this book we shall deal with the impact of the May revolt upon the behavior of the deputies who were elected in its wake in June, and we shall ask whether that early post-electoral gloom was justified by later events. Here we shall simply trace out, by means of measurements we made in the summer of 1969, the impact of the May upheaval on the left-right distribution of mass opinion in France. As we have already indicated, our survey of summer 1968 showed that the May events had succeeded in polarizing that distribution and in displacing its center of gravity to the right. Were these measurements merely recording a momentary spasm of reaction which would fade as soon as the routine of normal politics was reestablished, or was the shift to the right a more permanent change in the French political cleavage structure? On one hand, the referendum of April 1969 gave the French public a calmer situation in which to record its disenchantment with the leadership of de Gaulle, a disenchantment which, as we have implied, remained rather strong even during the voting of 1968, but which was at that time overridden by other concerns. On the other hand, the election of Georges Pompidou as President of the Republic in the summer of 1969 suggested that the Gaullist heritage remained alive and well.

Our assessments of the distribution of French left-right attitudes in the summer of 1969 indicate that the shift to the right of 1968 was no fleeting occurrence. On the contrary, virtually the same kind of substratum of right-wing support underlay Georges Pompidou's election as had sustained the Gaullist victory of 1968. Since we are primarily interested in individual change and its relative permanence, we have examined the subset of our respondents from whom we elicited left-right locations (including the 50-

point location) in 1967, 1968, and 1969. Among this subset of respondents the overall shift to the right between 1967 and 1968 was a bit stronger than it was among the larger group that had been interviewed only in 1967 and 1968, and so was the gain in polarization. In the 1969 measurement, the heightened polarization of 1968 subsided notably. But the *mean* of the distribution continued to be displaced to the right, at a point far closer to the 1968 mean than to that of 1967: more than 80 percent of the change from 1967 to 1968 was preserved in 1969.

The summer of 1969 was the latest date at which we were able to make our own direct measurements of the distribution of left-right opinion in France, but other evidence indicates that the displacement of the electorate to the right following the May events endured well into 1970. At the outset of this chapter, we referred to SOFRES surveys that included measures of mass left-right orientations, taken differently from ours but convertible into the same metric currency. Figure 14-4 displays the distribution of mean left-right opinion in France, as registered by the SOFRES surveys, across the entire period from 1964 to the middle of 1970. It can readily be seen that from the June 1968 election until the middle of 1970, when we stopped recording the distribution, it varied very little, but rather hovered around the point at

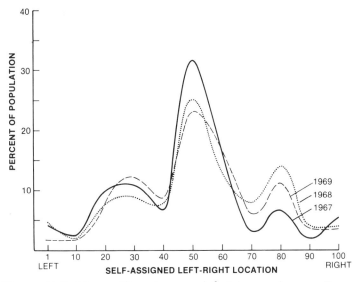

Figure 14-3. Mass self-locations on left-right continuum, France, 1967, 1968, and 1969. N = 349.

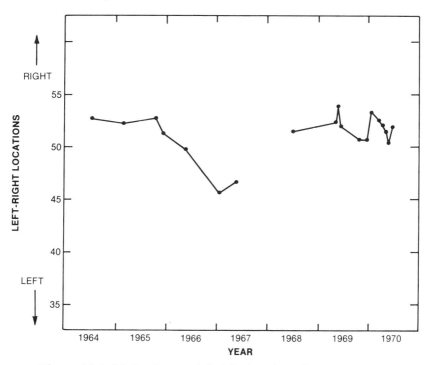

Figure 14-4. National mean left-right locations, France, 1964–1967 and 1968–1970. SOFRES distributions converted into metric scores.

which it had arrived in June 1968, as a result of the May upheaval. Naturally, one would not expect this new distribution of left-right opinion to last indefinitely. At some point, the influence of past events must weaken under the stimulus of new developments. But the May revolt clearly had a major impact on the distribution of political opinion in France that was striking in its magnitude, abruptness, and duration.

This shift in mass opinion produced a new National Assembly that was overwhelmingly weighted to the right. If there ever was a legislature in France that was elected to preserve law and order, it was the one chosen in 1968. Yet even minimal reflection upon the social revolt that had produced such an electoral reaction suggests that the message the French people had communicated during May and June was more complicated than that. The deep discontent with Gaullist rule displayed by the unprecedented May upheaval could reasonably be disturbing even to deputies whose electoral fortune had prospered as a result of the backlash to it. Later we shall see how the contrasting impulses toward repression and reform worked themselves out in the legislative process between 1968 and 1973, but first we must examine the more immediate reactions of France's parliamentary elite to the May revolt.

15

Elite Reactions to
The May–June Events

The dialectical events of May and June 1968, in the form of an unprecedented outpouring of mass discontent followed by an equally unexampled display of electoral support for social order, reverberated throughout the French parliamentary elite. The sample of major candidates for legislative office that we interviewed after the elections of 1968 enjoyed a privileged role as participant-observers during those convulsive events.[1] Some 85 percent of the candidates we interviewed had been on the scene in their districts during the upheaval,[2] and among those almost 20 percent volunteered that they themselves had participated in demonstrations, sit-ins, or meetings at factory gates. And the 1968 elections took place, of course, while memories of the May upheaval were fresh and emotions were still running high.

Our sample survey of the 1968 candidates is a rich source of information on how the May revolt appeared to the politicians who not only experienced it but also had to find ways to respond to it. In this chapter we shall set out the political elite's perceptions of the May–June events, and, insofar as possible, we shall show their contrapuntal relationship to events on the mass level as described in the previous chapter. We shall deal, in particular, with the 1968 candidates' views of the causes of the May upheaval, of the extent and nature of mass participation in the May events, of the effects of those events on their own electoral fortunes, and the broad "lessons" they appeared to have learned from the revolt. Evident throughout the entire account will be the capacity of partisanship to mold perceptions of reality. We would, of course, expect partisanship to affect, and to affect strongly, politicians' *interpretations* of politically relevant events; but in considering the May upheaval we shall also discover that the power of partisanship to shape the sheer *cognition* of events is nothing short of astonishing.

The Student Revolt

When the candidates were asked, at the outset of the interviews, what they thought was the underlying cause of the student revolt, almost 75 percent referred to some failure of the university system. No one defended the French universities, which were described by one Gaullist as "Kafkaesque." Virtually every grievance that has ever been expressed against French (or other) universities appears somewhere in our interviews with both Gaullists and opposition candidates: under-administration, lack of contact between students and professors, inadequate counseling, paternalism, overcrowded courses, and lack of appropriate facilities.[3]

The fundamental notion underlying these complaints was that the university system was badly outdated. Fully a third of the candidates, almost equally divided between the majority and the opposition, used terms such as *inadapté* (ill-adapted), *sclérose* (sclerosis), *vieillot* (antiquated), or *périmé* (outdated). In the opinion of a large proportion, perhaps even a majority, of the candidates at the 1968 election, the French university system had failed because it was inadequate to meet the needs of the students, the needs of the economy, even the needs of the modern world. A substantial fraction of the French parliamentary elite regarded the university system as an obsolete institution which had failed to adapt itself to the requirements of contemporary society, thereby frustrating and alienating enough students to produce the protest movement that eventually shook the political system to its foundations.

There was, furthermore, considerable agreement across partisan lines that the university system was inadequate in preparing students for jobs. Seventy-five percent of the opposition candidates and almost 40 percent of the majority candidates referred to student anxieties about finding jobs or to the lack of jobs for university graduates. These candidates, particularly those for the opposition, did not always make it clear whether the economy was not creating enough jobs for university graduates or whether the universities were not preparing students for the jobs that the economy was creating. But there can be no doubt that a majority of the 1968 candidates believed that student discontent arose from fear of not finding jobs.

In the light of this considerable display of cross-party consensus that the crying need of the French university system was closer links with the job market, one cannot help wondering whether the energy was misdirected that was expended during the summer and fall of 1968 in the preparation and adoption of what came to be known as the Faure Law. This law, which will be discussed in detail when we turn to the roll-call voting behavior of the deputies in the 1968–1973 legislature, established a framework for the reorganization of the French universities. Its guiding principles were to make the universities genuinely multidisciplinary centers of learning, to increase their autonomy from the Ministry of Education, and to enable students and junior faculty to participate in university decisionmaking. Not one of these principles has a direct connection with increasing the employment prospects of university graduates, or with rectifying the other complaints of the candidates; for although some of the members of our sample mentioned lack of participation by students in university governance, virtually none of them cited excessive disciplinary specialization or lack of university autonomy as major causes of student discontent.

Of course, the university reform bill that eventually became the Faure Law was prepared only after extensive consultations between the Ministry of Education and interested groups. The broad lines of the proposed reform, therefore, were crystallized by the time the bill came before the Assembly. And it was assumed that, once restructured, the universities would be in a much better position than they had been before to confront and solve problems, including the enlargement of job opportunities for the graduates. But the fact remains that the French political leadership failed to exploit a rare mood of cross-partisan consensus on the single specific issue of linking university education with employment opportunities.

There is no certainty, of course, that this widely shared preoccupation with the job market for university graduates could have been translated into concrete programs that both left and right would have found acceptable. As we have already indicated, there were ambiguities in the remarks the candidates made to us; some leftists may have felt, for example, that the capitalist system is inherently incapable of finding appropriate work for university graduates, however well that effort is organized. In 1976, in fact, when a French government did direct its attention to the specific problem of enlarging employment opportunities for university graduates, it met with a barrage of opposition on just that ground, and the effort was halted by lengthy student strikes.[4] All we can say with certainty is that our interviews with the parliamentary candidates after the 1968 elections indicate that they believed the students' main preoccupation was with jobs. The issues the government addressed were, by and large, not those that the candidates thought were on the students' minds.[5]

Although our sample of 1968 legislative candidates reached something approaching a "bipartisan" consensus about the obsolescence of the French university system, particularly in its failure to relate educational programs to employment prospects, most of the other remarks they made concerning the student revolt differed sharply on a partisan basis. Not surprisingly, opposition candidates concentrated their fire on alleged failures of the Gaullist regime, while Gaullists and their allies sought to deflect responsibility for the May outburst away from the regime toward other groups and forces. Indeed, much of the criticism that Gaullists directed against the university system may be interpreted as an attempt to shift blame for the upheaval away from the government. They seldom suggested that the government might have had some responsibility for the failure of the universities to satisfy the students. Instead, they tended to treat the university system as some force beyond their control; one Gaullist described it as "a difficult fortress to seize."

This is not to say that all Gaullists completely exonerated the regime, or that there were no points of overlap between the views of opposition candidates and supporters of the majority other than the one about the importance of jobs. But the diagnoses offered by the candidates were sharply differentiated by partisan attachment. Thus Gaullist candidates referred to subversion as often as they did to weakness in the university system as a basic cause of the student revolt, whereas less than 20 percent of the opposition candidates mentioned the role of various *groupuscules* (small groups) in preparing and leading the upheaval. Virtually every small far-left group in France was cited in this regard by someone: Maoists, anarchists, Trotskyites, the PSU, the "extreme-left," or simply "certain elements" determined "to create panic, confusion, and fear." No one suggested that the student revolt was caused by the *gauchistes* (ultraleftists) alone, unaided by other circumstances. Even Gaullists who were emphatic in their condemnation of extremists also indicated that a reform of the universities was overdue. But Gaullists were more than two and a half times as likely as opposition candidates to mention the incitement of ultraleftist groups as a basic cause of the revolt.

Similar partisan bias appears in the answers to our question about why the student revolt in France had been more severe than student revolts in other countries. About 20 percent of all the respondents, including almost 10 percent of the opposition candidates and some 25 percent of the Gaullist candidates, indicated that the French student revolt had *not* been more severe than student revolts elsewhere. As for the Gaullists who cited countries where they thought student discontent had been at least as serious as in France, all mentioned Latin American countries such as Mexico or Brazil, apparently unaware of the irony of their responses. But among the great majority (roughly 80 percent) of the candidates who accepted our implicit suggestion that the manifestation of student discontent had been more dramatic in France than elsewhere, three kinds of explanations predominated: those relating to French traditions, those relating to the nature of the Gaullist regime, and those relating to the government's behavior during the revolt. Each type of explanation was anchored in a distinctive partisan outlook.

Almost a third of the Gaullist candidates linked the severity of the student upheaval to the first explanation, French political traditions. One said that the French were setting an example, "as in 1789 and 1848"; another referred to the "romanticism of the barricades, the tradition of contentiousness"; still another evoked the French *fond de protestataire* (propensity for protest). One newly elected Gaullist singled out *présomption* (audacity) in the national temperament as the main explanation. "France is the country of intellectuality and adventure," he said. "The revolt took on its broad scope quite naturally. Other countries are confined by stricter discipline. In Spain it is the discipline of Catholicism. In the countries of the East it is Marxist discipline. In the Anglo-Saxon countries it is the discipline of Protestantism." But the Gaullists were as likely to place the accent on France as the country of liberty or democracy as the country of revolution. Whereas less than 10 percent of the opposition candidates spoke of French traditions in explaining the severity of the student revolt, and these were unanimous in recalling the revolutionary tradition of 1789, Gaullists sometimes highlighted the degree of liberty in France by referring to the harsh fate met by student protesters in other countries. One said that people had been sentenced to work camps in the German Federal Republic. Another said that Polish student leaders had been left to hang in public for three weeks: "That cooled off the protesters."[6]

The Gaullists' emphasis on historical traditions and national temperament as a major factor in the spread of the student revolt is consistent with their criticism of the universities. It tends to shift responsibility away from the regime, which they controlled, toward other forces beyond their reach. Indeed, it even suggests that a social outburst of the kind that occurred in May 1968 might have occurred under any circumstances. One unsuccessful Gaullist candidate said exactly that. His interpretation was that the groundwork for the revolt had been laid by the revolutionary current running through the works of Jean-Paul Sartre, Henri Lefebvre, and Herbert Marcuse, and that it would have taken place under any regime, even one headed by François Mitterrand.

By the same token, it is understandable that the candidates who gave the second explanation for the spread of the student revolt, attributing responsibility to the character and behavior of the Gaullist regime, were almost all from the opposition. Nearly 40 percent of the opposition candidates laid blame for the revolt's severity on the whole pattern of Gaullist rule. For those opposition candidates, the student revolt was not the expression of French tradition but rather a massive condemnation of the Gaullist regime, its policies and the social system on which it rested.

The third explanation, the government's conduct during the revolt, illustrates most clearly the different angles of vision of the majority and opposition candidates. More than a fourth of the candidates referred to the behavior of the government, and they were fairly equally divided between

Gaullists and their opponents. The Gaullists tended to claim that the student revolt had grown in magnitude because the government had not attempted to repress it by strong police measures. They often contrasted the government's restraint with stronger measures taken against student demonstrators in other countries, thereby reinforcing the theme of French liberty. The opposition candidates who thought that the revolt had spread because of the way the government had responded at its outbreak sometimes blamed the police, but there were few complaints about police excesses. More often, these candidates criticized the government for ineptitude, for not taking the students seriously, for dancing a "hesitation waltz," for not taking measures that would have brought some of the "provocative elements" to their senses. Some of the opposition candidates betrayed a note of exasperation at the government's failure to prevent the revolt from spreading: some criticized it for allowing a comparatively minor episode to turn into a major upheaval by not containing the movement early and resolving the problems that had caused it, while others argued that the disorders had actually been aggravated by government efforts to exploit them for political advantage.

Various other reasons for the severity of the student upheaval were also expressed. Some Gaullists pressed the familiar theme of provocation by extremists or other anti-Gaullists. Others claimed that dramatization by the media was responsible. Still others thought that the concentration of students, particularly in the Paris region, had inflamed the situation. One Gaullist, who said that the student revolt had been more severe in places where the students were concentrated in dormitory complexes (*cités universitaires*) than where they were not, drew an analogy between the student movement and such great religious movements as the Albigensian heresy and the Reformation. "The great currents of thought have appeared in monasteries, and the living conditions in the cités universitaires are analogous to those of monasteries: people in the same walk of life, with the same training, living in a closed world, strictly cut off from the outside world and having the leisure to discuss things with one another."

Finally, a small proportion of the candidates, whatever their views about the severity of the student upheaval, pointed out that what distinguished the French situation from others was that the student revolt in France had been followed by a massive strike movement on the part of the workers.

The Strike Movement

The first strikes by workers after the student protests began were reported to have been wildcat strikes, and the factory occupations that accompanied the early strikes were also reported as having occurred without the authorization of responsible agencies of the major unions. We wanted, therefore, to learn the views of the candidates about the apparent spontaneity of the strike movement.

We also wanted to ask the candidates about the length of the strike movement. The strikes lasted a long time by French standards, especially for such a generalized walkout, although there have been longer strikes in single industries or plants (Shorter and Tilly, 1974). We were particularly interested in the duration of the strikes because there was reason to believe that their length resulted from the efforts of the Communist-led General Confederation of Labor (Confédération Générale du Travail, CGT) to bring the movement under control.[7] The CGT's main rival union, the French Democratic Confederation of Labor (Confédération Française Démocratique du Travail, CFDT), which was led by Catholic trade unionists and seemed to have special ties of sympathy with the PSU, took a more militant stance during the May events than the CGT did, and there was a serious risk that the CGT might lose members to the CFDT. Moreover, Communist party behavior and declarations during the events indicated that the party was anxious to avoid contributing to, or appearing to contribute to, the creation of a revolutionary situation. In the circumstances of May 1968, characterized by escalating demagogy and the breakdown of organizational discipline, the efforts of the CGT to ensure control over its members and to give direction to the strike movement might well have contributed to prolonging the strikes.[8]

Accordingly, we asked the candidates for their views about both the spontaneity and duration of the strikes.[9] The particular question we asked violated accepted canons of questionnaire construction by referring to two separate subjects—spontaneity and duration—but that may actually have been an advantage, as it matched in complexity, and went some distance toward capturing, the texture of the event to which it referred. The question also gave the candidates an opportunity to present their reactions to the strike movement, and almost all of them did so, often at considerable length. They indicated both what they thought were the main reasons for, and the distinctive characteristics of, the strike movement.

Characteristics of the Strikes

Roughly a third of the candidates explicitly rejected the suggestion that the strikes had been spontaneous. About half of these candidates came from the Gaullists and the other half from the opposition. The opposition candidates were almost all Communists; in fact, almost 60 percent of all the Communists we interviewed denied that the strikes had been spontaneous.

In denying that the strikes had been spontaneous, the Communists interpreted spontaneity very differently from the Gaullists. Some Communists seemed to regard it as action without a cause, as though their Marxist background had accustomed them to think of all collective behavior in terms of underlying forces. "Nothing is spontaneous," one veteran Communist deputy told us. "Spontaneity never exists," said another, adding, "What looks like spontaneity to the naked eye loses that character on further analysis." Other Communists took a less philosophical approach, tending simply to interpret the sudden and massive strike wave as something that had been building up for a long time: "the fruit of a long maturation," as one said. Others even suggested that there was nothing particularly unusual about the May outburst, saying that there had been generally increased strike activity in recent years, thus likening the May explosion to earlier expressions of working class discontent.

The Gaullists interpreted spontaneity as the absence of organized leadership. They rejected the idea that the strikes had been spontaneous, believing instead that they had been launched by particular groups. Some said simply that the unions were responsible. A candidate from northern France claimed that factories had been closed by "rotating pickets" who went from one plant to another. Others were vaguer: the strike had been "orchestrated," "prepared for a long time," "launched by a small core," or *télécommandé.*[10]

Thus, in a fashion now familiar to us, Gaullists frequently attributed the strikes to the unions, revolutionaries, Trotskyites, or other small but determined groups, and opposition candidates placed responsibility either on the incompetence or neglect of the government or on grievous social and economic conditions for which the government was ultimately responsible. Nevertheless, a fraction of the candidates of the majority—that is, more than 20 percent of the Gaullists and their allies—expressed sympathy for the position of the workers. Low wages, long-standing disappointments, real social problems, and employment difficulties were all mentioned. Several Gaullist candidates were very critical of Gaullist rule in general. One spoke of a "society incapable of mastering the economy and ensuring an equitable distribution of income." Another spoke of "frustration in the face of a social system that they [workers and students] see no way of entering." Still another said flatly that the current form of Gaullism was "disagreeable." "These people," he added, referring to the Gaullists, "give the impression that they know it all and impose their views whatever anyone else thinks."

About a third of the Gaullists—but, of course, no Communist candidates and virtually no candidates of any opposition party—suggested that the Communist party and the CGT had thrown themselves into the strike movement in order to avoid being outflanked on their left. Few put it in such explicit terms, but that is the only conclusion that can be drawn from their comments. In the opinion of that group of Gaullists, the PCF and the CGT had no choice but to throw themselves into the fray if they were not to be overwhelmed by the extremists, Trotskyites, CFDT, or other groups to which they variously attributed the origin of the strike movement. As one newly elected Gaullist put it, the CGT "was obliged to go all out."

One veteran Gaullist deputy emphasized that the union-led strike movement had economic aims, as opposed to political ones, thereby agreeing with the equally experienced Communists who made the same point. "It was never a question of the workers and the CGT seizing power." One Socialist and one Gaullist even took the next step and credited the Communists or the CGT with helping to bring the whole upheaval under some kind of control: the CGT "threw water on the fire ... the CGT put the movement into reverse, for it prevented the workers from leaving the factories, which would have produced a revolution."

Links between the Student Revolt and the Strike Movement

When asked about the severity of the student revolt, about 10 percent of the candidates indicated that one of its distinctive characteristics was that it was followed by the large wave of strikes. The connection between the strike movement and the student revolt was a theme that we wanted to pursue independently in any case, and after asking the candidates about the spontaneity and duration of the strikes we also asked them how they thought the strike movement was linked to the student revolt.

More candidates perceived a connection between the two waves of popular discontent than regarded them as distinct from each other, and in roughly equal ratios among majority and opposition; but 50 percent of the opposition candidates replied directly to the question as compared with only some 30 percent of the majority candidates. It seemed that the question had more meaning for the opposition candidates, or that they had already reflected on it. The latter possibility is reinforced by the fact that more than 70 percent of the Communist candidates in our sample responded directly to the question, and we know that the issue of the stance to take vis-à-vis students and workers had been a matter of great concern to the Communist party during the May days themselves (Ross, 1982, ch. 7).

Consequently, the replies of the Communists are of particular interest. Some suggested a form of negative solidarity between the student and working-class movements arising from either repression or the existence of a common enemy in Gaullism or the state. One veteran Communist deputy told us in no uncertain terms that whereas the student movement was aimed at changing society radically, the unions did not have the same goal. But half of the Communists who responded directly to the question found a closer connection between the two movements than the Communist warnings about the dangers of "adventurism" that had been made during the revolt itself might suggest. Thus one Communist candidate told us that when the students put the government in difficulty the workers "profited" from that movement by launching their own. Another said that the student revolt "opened new perspectives" by showing the workers that they were not alone in their struggle, that "everyone was engaged" who sympathized with the students and the workers, even top management and engineers in the factories. Still another reported that the working class and the students were the social categories (*couches*) that were most sensitive to violations of democratic principles. One Communist candidate, who told us that the workers understood that the students' problem was their problem as well, also reported that students and workers had been united in his district during May, with students participating in meetings of workers. That was almost surely a deviation from the national norm, for the Communist-controlled CGT did its best to insulate the workers from student influence during the upheaval (Ross, 1982, pp. 190–194).

In fact, some non-Communist candidates, in arguing that the two movements were *not* connected, referred to the Communists' efforts to separate workers from students during the May days. One Federation candidate said that the students had sought out the workers but that the workers were reluctant to come to terms with them. A Gaullist told us that "it was enough to attend the meetings of the students at the Sorbonne and hear the speeches of the worker delegates denying the students on principle the right to meddle in union affairs." Still another Gaullist mentioned that the workers had not permitted the students to enter the Renault plants and emphasized that the students wanted to overthrow the regime, while the unions went on strike for economic goals.

Some candidates, usually Gaullists, returned to themes we have already encountered in slightly different contexts. Thus some indicated that both students and workers were led by the same kinds of groups, always described as extremists: Maoists, the ultraleft, the "Trotskyite network." Some referred to foreign connections: "political parties from abroad that are located to the left of the Communist party." "It's collectivism, Chinese-style revolution against capitalism," said one Giscardian deputy, who added that he had heard that the Chinese had given "800 million" to the students. Others emphasized the point, already mentioned, that the union leaders entered the fray in order to control their own followers. These candidates did not regard the strikes as economically motivated but rather as the only way for the working-class leaders to prevent their troops from deserting to the more radical groups that were leading the students.

About 10 percent of the candidates indicated that the students and the young workers on strike were linked by generational solidarity. Gaullists made that point twice as often as opposition candidates, perhaps because to do so was still another way of locating responsibility for the upheaval in the actors rather than in the surrounding circumstances.

On the whole, majority and opposition candidates alike tended to view the strike wave and the preceding student revolt as something more than a simple sequence of unrelated events, but not quite as two aspects of a common phenomenon. The student movement created the opportunity, provided the occasion, or produced the right psychological moment for the strike wave to occur. One word that was used by about 10 percent of the candidates, whether opposition or Gaullist, was "detonator" (or "match," or "spark"). In their view, the student movement had been the detonator setting off the explosion of strikes that quickly enveloped the country. The student movement opened a breach in the Gaullist regime into which the workers quickly jumped, whether out of imitation (because of shared griev-ances) or out of a perceived necessity on the part of the union leaders to channel and control a movement that threatened to engulf them.

Candidate Perceptions of Public Opinion

In discussing the student revolt, one candidate of the majority analyzed the situation in terms of the extent to which the government enjoyed public support. He argued that early in the student revolt the government's hands were pretty well tied because it did not have the backing of public opinion generally, and that even during the early part of the strike movement the government lacked popular support. In his view, that came only later, when the strikes became highly politicized.

Regardless of the merits of his argument, it is clear that this candidate "kept his ear to the ground." Because our entire study rested on that meta-phor, we were interested in all the candidates' assessments of the opinions of the voters in their districts during the mass upheaval. Accordingly, we asked them what proportions of their constituents they thought were in favor of, opposed to, or indifferent to the two groups that were the main participants in the revolt: the student demonstrators and the strikers.[11] We also sought their opinions as to how willingly the strikers in their districts had partici-pated in the work stoppages.[12]

The candidates' estimates of their constituents' attitudes toward the students and the strikers, and of the strikers' attitudes to their own partici-pation in the work stoppages can be measured against a corresponding set of independent estimates of "actual" district opinion derived from our 1968 mass survey. Among our measures of the three corresponding mass atti-tudes, the most reliable was almost certainly the one concerning the extent of unwilling (involuntary) participation in the strike movement. The mass respondents were asked to describe in detail their own work situation or that of the head of their household during the upheaval, and their responses enabled us to estimate with considerable accuracy the proportion of people who would have preferred to work during the May–June revolt but were prevented from doing so.[13] On the basis of this measure, we estimated that about one-fourth of the households reporting strike participation contained at least one person who was on strike against his will.[14]

Our estimates of district-level attitudes toward the students and the strikers rest on conventional thermometer scores registered with regard to "the strikers of May–June 1968" and to "the students."[15] The reference to the strikers is unambiguous; but in retrospect it is clear that we should have referred not simply to "students" but rather to "the student demonstrators," which is the term we used in eliciting the candidates' estimates of the amount of mass support for the students. Nonetheless, the specific designations of students and strikers in our thermometer question are less a source of ambiguity than is the absence of a time frame. Public attitudes toward the students and strikers changed during the course of the May–June upheaval,[16] but our thermometer question did not allow for this development. Our estimates of mass opinion, therefore, represent summary views ascertained some time after the heat of the May–June events had dissipated.

Table 15-1 reports the match between the candidates' estimates con-

Table 15-1. Mean candidate estimates of their constituents' revolt-related attitudes, compared with mass sample estimates, by candidate's left-right category (percentages), France, 1968.[a]

Constituents' revolt-related attitudes		Source of estimate		
		Mass sample		
	Leftist candidates	Leftists' districts	Rightists' and centrists' districts	Rightist and centrist candidates
(a) All 54 sample districts				
Unwilling strikers	13.6 (17)	35.6	19.7	62.7 (24)
In favor of strikers	60.2 (20)	36.1	36.9	24.5 (26)
In favor of student demonstrators	45.0 (17)	35.8	39.3	15.2 (23)
(b) Nine districts where competing candidates were interviewed				
Unwilling strikers	11.9 (9)		35.2	70.8 (9)
In favor of strikers	56.1 (11)		38.4	35.7 (11)
In favor of student demonstrators	39.9 (8)		44.3	16.6 (8)

a. Numbers of cases are in parentheses.

cerning the three items under consideration and the corresponding "actual" mass values, expressed as means across the districts represented, and broken down by the broad partisan affiliations of the candidates. All scores are in the form of percentages. For candidate assessments we have employed their estimates of the percentages of their constituents in favor of students and strikers, and for the "actual" district-level attitudes toward these two groups we have taken the percentages of district respondents that assigned them thermometer scores ranging between 51 and 100. Part (a) of Table 15-1 includes the scores for the maximal number of districts (fifty-four) for which we have valid data; part (b) contains the scores only for those districts for which we have valid data from both of the two main opposing candidates.

The overriding message of Table 15-1 is the power of partisanship to affect perceptions. In part (a) it is apparent that, for each of the three revolt-related attitudes, leftist candidates' perceptions differ enormously from those of rightist candidates, and that both of these differ, sometimes greatly, from the "true value" for the same districts as registered in our mass survey data. The most extreme case is that relating to unwilling strikers, in which the partisan distortions are all the more obvious because, by chance, the "true values" for the districts in which leftist candidates and rightist candidates were interviewed depart rather widely from the national mean. Accordingly, the comparatively low estimates for unwilling strikers made by leftists contrast sharply with the higher-than-average "actual" rates of involuntary strike participation in the leftists' districts, while the comparatively high estimates offered by rightists contrast sharply with an abnormally low "true value" for unwilling strikers in the rightists' districts.

This demonstration of the capacity of partisan attachment to shape the political elite's perceptions of reality may be brought into even sharper focus by examining the candidates' perceptions of involuntary strike rates not merely by broad partisan outlooks but by more specific party affiliations. Figure 15-1 reports the mean perceived percentage of involuntary strikers by the exact partisan attachments of the candidates. Rightist candidates reported large proportions, middle-of-the-roaders reported middling proportions, and leftists reported low proportions of involuntary strikers.

This is not to say that the candidates were not "objective" in their observations. We do not doubt that they actually "saw" what they reported. A handful of the candidates (four) took the trouble, in answering our question, to distinguish between the situation at the start of the strikes and toward the end.[17] One Communist candidate gave a particularly careful reply, distinguishing between the politicized large plants and the smaller ones where economic issues counted more heavily. Nevertheless, there is a product-moment correlation of .66 between the individual candidates' estimates of the proportion of involuntary strikers in their own districts and their self-ascribed locations on the left-right dimension.

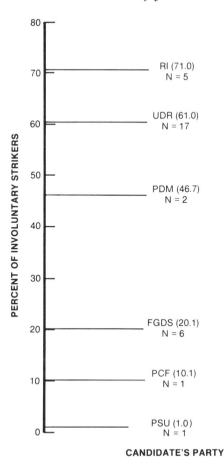

Figure 15-1. Mean candidate estimates of percent of involuntary strikers in their districts, by candidate's party, France, 1968.

   The impact of partisan attachments on perceptions of reality appears to be largely independent of the reality itself. As part (b) of Table 15-1 shows, for nine districts out of our sample of fifty-four we have valid replies to the question about involuntary strike rates from *both* of the leading candidates, one a leftist and the other either a Gaullist or a Gaullist-supported candidate. It should be kept in mind in this regard that, whatever the reality in each district concerning involuntary strike participation, the candidates' references had to be to an identical "objective" phenomenon. Yet the mean involuntary strike rates reported by leftist candidates was 11.9 percent as against 70.8 percent reported by their opponents from the same districts, a whopping difference of 58.9 percent. And our own mean sample estimate of the "true" value for those same districts is 35.2 percent! It is as though leftists and rightists were looking at the same object through opposite ends of a telescope.

In part (a) of Table 15-1, the candidates' estimates of the proportions of their constituents who were in favor of the students and the strikers provide further evidence of the way in which perceptions of political phenomena can be colored by partisanship. Overall, leftists thought that the student demonstrators and strikers were supported by some two and a half to three times as many people as rightists or centrists thought favored those two groups. The differences in the perceptions of leftists and their opponents narrow somewhat when we confine ourselves to the smaller number of cases that include only the competing candidates from the same districts (see part b), but it is still wide enough to illustrate the effect of partisanship on political perception. Indeed, across our entire set of candidates, the correlation between their left-right locations and their estimates of the proportions of people supporting the strikers is $r = .647$, while the corresponding correlation relating to perceptions of support for the students is $r = .553$.[18]

Despite these clear indications of partisan bias in perception, there is less absolute difference between the leftists' and rightists' perceptions of support for the students and the strikers than there is between their estimates of the incidence of involuntary strike participation, and there is also less distance between those estimates and the "true" values. We may take this to mean that there is a greater intrusion of reality into the candidate perceptions of public attitudes toward the students and strikers than into their perceptions of strike behavior. The reason for this may reside in the distinction between estimating the attitudes of *observers* of events and the attitudes of actual *participants* in the events. Our question about involuntary strikes referred to actors in the events. It is at least plausible that the intensity implicit in action accounts for the sharper polarization of the candidates' perceptions of the outlook of the strikers than of their perceptions of the voters' attitudes. Candidates sympathetic to the strikes might find it extremely difficult to believe that many of the strikers were not striking enthusiastically, while those unsympathetic to the strikes might find it almost impossible to acknowledge that most of the strikers were not acting under duress. When asked to assess the outlook of the broader public on these events, however, even such professional partisans are likely to take some account of the "real" balance of political forces and the fact that these rest on divergent views. As a result, their estimates of broad public opinion, though still biased on a partisan basis, are less biased than their estimates of the attitudes of the actors themselves.

It is apparent from Table 15-1 that however much their perceptions differed absolutely, both leftists and rightists believed that the strikers had more popular support than the students. That is not particularly surprising. Even though the magnitude of the 1968 walkouts was exceptional, strikes are a regular feature of French industrial relations, whereas large-scale student demonstrations are a comparative rarity. It is understandable that the French parliamentary elite in 1968 should have thought that there was more sympathy for the strikers than for the students. But by the same token, it is noteworthy that the 1968 candidates' estimates of the amount of popular support for the strikers departed considerably from the "reality." French political elites ought to be more practiced at gauging the amount of public support for participants in strikes, which are a common occurrence, than in estimating the public's response to massive student demonstrations, which are rare. Yet, on the whole, the candidates' estimates of support for the strikers were hardly more accurate than their estimates of the amount of public sympathy for the students. Overall, leftists did "better" than rightists in assessing support for the students, while rightists did "better" than leftists in their perceptions of support for the strikers. Indeed, among the smaller subsets of competing candidates from the same districts, the leftists *underestimated* the amount of sympathy for the students, while the rightists estimated almost exactly the amount of sympathy for the strikers.

In replying to our questions about the amount of public support enjoyed by the students and strikers, several of our elite respondents took the dynamics of the situation into account by distinguishing between the early and later days of the revolt, although not all of them furnished estimates that could be quantified. The replies of those who did offer precise figures, however, are of special interest.

According to seven of our respondents, more than half of whom were Gaullists, the mean proportion of constituents in favor of the student demonstrators at the outset of the revolt was over 70 percent, a substantially higher value even than the mean figure of 60 percent reported by the leftists as a whole. But in the opinion of those same seven candidates, by the end of the upheaval the level of popular support for the students had dropped to only about 15 percent. For that small subset of candidates, therefore, the evolution of popular opinion away from support for the students, to which we referred in the last chapter, was a salient element in their recollection of events—one which they took the trouble to specify.

An even smaller cluster of candidates also volunteered estimates of the amount of public support for the strikers both at the start and at the end of the strikes. These estimates rest on only four cases, but they express a decline from a mean proportion of 64 percent to one of 27 percent, a narrower range than that offered for the perceived shift in support for the students.

The conclusion that emerges from these two sets of dynamic perceptions is that the students squandered what was, at the outset, an overwhelming degree of popular support. The strikers, on the contrary, started out with somewhat less perceived support than the students, but although they too lost credit with the populace as the disturbances persisted, their level of mass support did not fall so low as did that for the student demonstrators.

Capturing Variability in District Opinion

We have suggested occasionally that one or another of the broad tendencies discernible among the 1968 candidates was more "accurate" in assessing the state of public opinion on the various revolt-related items for which we have independent estimates that can be used as a baseline for comparison. In view of the generally wide gaps between the mean estimates of the candidates and the "actual" mean proportions of voters holding relevant positions, it might seem sheer folly to probe into the matter further. On their face, the candidates' estimates of public opinion appear to be exclusively the result of wishful thinking. In point of fact, however, they reveal enough traces of perceptual "accuracy" to suggest that they represent something more than unadulterated romancing. Among the matters of opinion we have been discussing, this applies most clearly to the candidates' estimates of the proportion of unwilling strikers. It is also applicable, though in somewhat weaker form, to the estimates of the amount of popular support for the students. But it is demonstrably not applicable to candidate estimates of the degree of public sympathy for the strikers.

The kind of perceptual "accuracy" we are referring to here is correlational, in the sense that the variation in the district estimates of the candidates, across the group of candidates making such estimates, tends to match the variation in the "actual" scores across the corresponding set of districts.[19] From each candidate interviewed, we have estimates of the proportions of his constituents that were in favor of the students and that were in favor of the strikers, as well as of the proportions of strikers in his constituency that were on strike involuntarily. We also have independent estimates of these same proportions derived from a mass sample survey. The correlation between these two values gives us a measure of the extent to which the candidates as a whole ordered their estimates in the same way as the mass survey estimates of the same phenomena are ordered across our set of sample districts.

Because our mass sample estimates rest on comparatively few cases for each district, we would expect that in most cases a correlation resting in part on such small estimates would necessarily be attenuated. Fortunately, it is a comparatively simple task to make appropriate corrections, although the assumptions underlying those operations are by no means immediately transparent.[20]

The results of these analyses appear in Table 15-2, where we report, for each of our three revolt-related attitudes, the correlations between the candidates' estimates and the "true" values based on our mass sample estimates. The correlations are reported for leftists and rightists separately, as well as for the candidates as a whole.

Table 15-2. Correlation (*r*) between candidate estimates of constituents' revolt-related attitudes and "true" values, France, 1968.[a]

Constituents' revolt-related attitudes	All candidates	Leftists	Rightists and centrists
Unwilling strikers	−.02	.38**	.39 (.73*)
	(41)	(17)	(24)
In favor of student demonstrators	.09	.15 (.21*)	.28 (.38*)
	(40)	(17)	(23)
In favor of strikers	.04	−.01	.12
	(46)	(20)	(26)

a. Correlations marked with * have been corrected for small-sample attenuation. Those marked with ** are indeterminate after correction but approach 1.0. Those unmarked are raw correlations that have not been corrected because they are negative or trivial. Case numbers appear in parentheses below the correlations.

Across all candidates, the correlations are at or near the vanishing point for each of the three perceptual items, which is what we would expect given the wide differences between the absolute proportions reported by leftist and rightist candidates. When we take leftists and rightists separately, however, particularly for the item relating to involuntary strikers, and to a lesser extent for that regarding popular support for the students, the correlations advance notably, sometimes taking on values that are quite respectable even for the comparatively small numbers of cases registered. Therefore, as fanciful as the candidates' estimates of the proportions of unwilling strikers or student supporters in their districts may have been in an absolute sense, these estimates do capture at least modest amounts of the variability in the "objective" situation across the sets of districts involved.

It appears that a complex, but perfectly intelligible, perceptual process is at work here. On the one hand, both leftists and rightists tend to exaggerate, sometimes greatly, their estimates of the proportion of people holding a given attitude, in directions that conform to their own political sympathies. The two groups of opposing candidates will perceive the same objective phenomenon in very different absolute terms. But even though our opposing candidates are highly inaccurate in an absolute sense, these same candidates also share a kind of "feel" for their districts in a relative sense. The clearest example of this is that leftists uniformly exaggerated the amount of enthusiasm among the strikers, while rightists uniformly minimized it; but across districts, both leftists and rightists appear to have adjusted their estimates to conform to quite similar perceptions of the relative position of their districts on the matter. In districts where the proportions of involuntary strikers were "actually" high, both leftists and rightists missed the absolute mark by wide margins; but both groups of candidates in those districts tended to make estimates that were higher than those made by the candidates from districts where the proportion of unwilling strikers was "actually" lower. And in districts where our mass sample estimates pointed toward low rates of involuntary work stoppages, the candidates' estimates were also far from those absolute levels; but they tended on the whole to be lower than those made by the candidates from districts where our mass sample estimates were higher than the mean.[21]

We return to the question we raised earlier: would it be foolish to ask whether the leftists or the rightists were, on the whole, more accurate in their assessments of the revolt-related attitudes of their constituents? It now appears less vacuous to ask this question. As for accuracy in absolute terms, it should be recalled (from Table 15-1) that neither leftists nor rightists came close to the "true" values concerning unwilling strikers; the leftists' estimates of the proportions of people who supported the students were closer to the reality than those of the rightists, and the reverse was the case in connection with perceptions of popular support for the strikers. Now we find that although, in correlational terms, neither leftist nor rightist candidates were accurate in assessing the state of opinion toward the strikers, both groups of candidates were highly accurate concerning the proportions of unwilling strikers, and the rightists tended to be more accurate than the leftists with regard to constituency attitudes toward the students.

Some satisfaction may be derived from this fact. After all, the rightists won a landslide electoral victory in 1968. It would be less than cheering for holders of democratic values if that victory had been won by candidates who were in near ignorance of popular sentiments. As it is, we have demonstrated how powerful partisanship is in affecting elite perceptions in absolute terms. But reality plays a role along with wishful thinking in shaping politicians' perceptions of mass opinion. We cannot say with precision what cues transmitted the elements of the reality to the candidates concerning the two issues we have discussed here in some detail. But our correlational measures indicate that both leftists and rightists tended to perceive their districts similarly in relative terms with regard to involuntary strike rates and, to a lesser extent, concerning popular attitudes toward the students.

Another important point emerges from Table 15-2. The correlational measures indicate that the candidates had a clearer grasp of public attitudes toward the students than toward the strikers. That is not what we expected, although it is quite consistent with the fact, mentioned earlier, that absolute perceptions of support for the strikers were hardly more "accurate" than absolute perceptions of support for the students. We would expect our data to reflect the fact that French politicians are more experienced in judging the views of their voters toward strikers than toward rampaging students, but that is not the case.

The upheaval of May–June 1968 badly strained the French political elite's perceptual control. Like Charles de Gaulle himself, the parliamentary candidates at the 1968 election would not have exaggerated things too badly if they had also said, "In May, everything escaped me . . ." (Malraux, 1971, p. 28). But we have seen enough signs of perceptual accuracy on the part of these candidates to keep us from asserting that the mass revolt undermined their sense of district realities completely. Later in this chapter, we shall encounter another and more instructive case juxtaposing absolute perceptual error with considerable correlational accuracy.

Electoral Dynamics and Campaign Activities

In the last chapter, we charted in detail the relationship on the mass level between proximity to demonstrations or strikes, and shifts in left-right locations. Although the pattern of movements was complex, one of our findings was that people generally accepted the strikes, but that, except for confirmed leftists, they were driven to the right by their fear of the demonstrations. The candidates understood this, as we have already seen in this chapter in their perceptions of the absolute levels of mass support for the strikers and student demonstrators. There is also overwhelming evidence for it in the replies to other questions we asked the candidates about the 1968 election.

Impact of the Disorders on the Electoral Outcome

The clearest indication that the candidates considered the demonstrations to have been the decisive factor in determining the outcome of the 1968 election lies in their responses to our open-ended questions about the reasons for vote transfers between the two ballots. They were asked to describe the vote transfers they thought had taken place, as well as the reasons why the voters had shifted their support either to them or to their opponents.[22] Fully two-thirds of the candidates who replied to these questions spontaneously referred to the demonstrations or the violence, or the fear of them, and to the desire for order that they provoked. Ten times as many candidates referred specifically to the demonstrations and violence as to the strikes.[23]

The opposition candidates were particularly sensitive to the adverse effect of the demonstrations: fully 85 percent of them, as opposed to only some 40 percent of the majority's candidates, referred to the demonstrations or to the fear they had engendered. One after another, they told us how they had suffered electorally because of the atmosphere of fear that had permeated the election: "they were afraid"; "a reflex of fear"; "fear of disorder"; "fear of revolution"; "fear of sharing the wealth"; "fear of anarchy"; "fear of dispossession"; "fear of civil war"; "out of fear—that was all there was to it."

We were not surprised to hear leftist candidates complaining that the government's supporters had exploited this atmosphere, or even that they had deliberately created it. Although comparatively few of the majority's candidates (the Gaullists and their allies) attacked the strikers during the campaign, at least half of them heavily criticized the disorders. When asked what position they had taken toward the strikers, a mere 2 percent of the majority candidates told us that they had condemned them outright. Some 10 percent, however, said that they had emphasized the right to work. And more than 30 percent either told us that they had said little or nothing about the strikers during the campaign, gave us evasive answers, or said they had taken an equivocal position ("I affirmed the constitutional right to strike but also the natural right to work").[24] But fully 33 percent indicated that they either had given some sort of qualified support to the strikers (usually relating to raising the minimum wage or raising the low wages generally) or had refused to condemn the strikers even though they had opposed the disorders or the student extremists. Another 15 percent told us that they had not taken any position concerning the strikers but had opposed disorder. And the last 10 percent remarked that they had opposed the political character of the strikes, thereby suggesting (to us) that they would not necessarily oppose purely economic strikes.

This array of positions concerning the strikers is quite different from that represented by the opposition candidates' answers to the same question. Almost 70 percent of them told us simply that they had given unqualified support to the strikers, whereas no government supporter did so. And although almost an additional 25 percent said that they had both supported the strikers and opposed the disorder, their positions differed from the analogous ones taken by the majority candidates in being more supportive of the strikers. But it is clear also that the Gaullists and their allies were, on the whole, well attuned to the mood of the mass public. Despite the fact that they tended to make low estimates of the amount of public support for the strikers, they avoided alienating working-class voters unnecessarily and in some cases actually expressed sympathy for them. They sensed—quite rightly, as we have seen—that it was the demonstrations rather than the strikes that had turned the electoral trend in their direction, and it was on the disorder attendant upon the demonstrations that they tried to focus attention. The same strategy was, of course, not available to the left. They had to defend the strikers, and they could hardly make a paying issue out of opposing disorder when their own supporters were swelling the demonstrations with which the disorders were associated.

It is not surprising, therefore, that when asked to choose from a list of eight alternatives the one that they thought expressed the basic issue (*véritable enjeu*) of the election, 96 percent of the majority candidates selected "order versus anarchy." It is also noteworthy that 33 percent of the opposition candidates chose the same item.[25] In one way or another, opposition candidates as well as government supporters made it clear that they believed the May disorders accounted for the electoral outcome of June.

In addition, the candidates were sensitive to the way in which the May events blended with anti-Communism as an electoral theme. When discussing vote transfers between the first and second ballots, more than 25 percent of the majority candidates spontaneously cited anti-Communism as a reason for their electoral appeal. And among our forced-choice items describing the basic stakes of the election, the second most popular choice after "order versus anarchy" was "Communism versus anti-Communism," which was selected in equal proportions by candidates of the government and of the opposition. In 1967, a mere 7 percent of the candidates had selected "Communism versus anti-Communism" as one of the *three* basic issues of the election; in 1968, almost 40 percent of them selected that conflict as one of the *two* most important issues at stake.[26] The May events made the candidates aware of anti-Communism as an electoral force to a far greater extent than had been the case the year before. In discussing vote transfers, opposition and majority candidates alike made unprompted references to fear of Communism as part of the ambience of May. One Communist remarked ruefully that his party had "paid for the barricades that they had not built and the fires that they had not set."

Perceptions of the Magnitude of the Demonstrations

Given the importance that the candidates—particularly those of the opposition—attributed to the disorders in determining the outcome of the 1968 election, the candidates' perceptions of the magnitude of these disorders were of considerable interest to us. Just as we had ascertained the candidates' estimates of the attitudes of their constituents toward the strikers and student demonstrators, so we asked them what proportion of the voters in their districts they believed "had been led to participate in demonstrations, regardless of their political opinions." Table 15-3 reports the match between candidate perceptions and our independent sample estimates, in both absolute and correlational terms.

Once again we find the differentiation of responses by partisan affiliation. The leftists in our sample estimated that 29.5 percent of the voters in their districts, on the average, participated in demonstrations. The rightists and centrists, on the contrary, produced a mean estimate of 11.4 percent demonstration participation.

Up to a point, these divergent sets of absolute perceptions furnish another instance of political rationalization, analogous to those we have already encountered with regard to the candidates' perceptions of the degree of popular support for the strikers and student demonstrators and of the proportions of involuntary strikers. One can plausibly interpret the parti-

Table 15-3. Match between candidate and mass sample estimates of constituents' demonstration participation, in correlational and absolute terms, France, 1968.[a]

Type of estimate	Source of estimate		
(a) Correlational (*r*)	Leftist candidates .51 (.94*) (21)	All candidates .26 (.45*) (50)	Rightist and centrist candidates .20 (.33*) (29)
		Mass Sample	
(b) Absolute (in percent)	Leftist candidates 29.5% (21)	Leftists' districts 9.2%	Rightists' and centrists' districts 11.2%	Rightist and centrist candidates 11.4% (29)

a. Correlations marked * have been corrected for small-sample attenuation. Case numbers are in parentheses below the correlations and percentages.

san-based absolute differences in estimates of demonstration participation in terms of parallel efforts to bring the "facts" into harmony with the wish. The candidates of the majority parties and those of the opposition parties were in symmetrical situations of tension vis-à-vis the public at the time we interviewed them shortly after the 1968 elections. The Gaullists had just won a great electoral victory, but only after they had been subjected to a staggering outburst of mass hostility. The left had just suffered a major electoral defeat, but the unprecedented outpouring of mass discontent that preceded the election was an endorsement and vindication of their long years of opposition to the Gaullist regime. In such circumstances, it is understandable that the regime's supporters might unconsciously have wanted to minimize the evidence of the opposition to them, thereby allowing their electoral success to dominate their cognitive field. Conversely, it might have been psychologically satisfying to the leftists to make comparatively high estimates of demonstration participation. This would not only have magnified the number of people who were demonstrably their allies, but might also have made their disappointing electoral defeat more tolerable. By magnifying the number of demonstrators, the leftists would also have magnified the fear felt by their opponents, thereby accounting in the least unsatisfactory way for the severity of the left's electoral defeat. In this construction of events, the left lost badly at the election only because the demonstrations by their supporters had been enormous.

Yet, as plausible as this interpretation may seem, it is not the whole story. Considerable evidence indicates that the candidates' estimates of the magnitude of demonstration participation are more realistic than their estimates concerning the other revolt-related items we have considered. Before laying out that evidence, however, we should explain why we expected such evidence to appear.

The crux of the matter is that the class of perception involved in estimating demonstration participation is different from that involved in estimating public opinion. When we asked the candidates about public reactions to the strikers and the students, or about the proportion of unwilling strikers, we were asking them to assess constituents' *attitudes*. When we asked them to estimate the percentage of their constituents who had participated in demonstrations, we were asking them about their constituents' *behavior*. This question did not require an assessment of mental states, but rather, at least in principle, the description of an "objective" phenomenon. Candidates on the scene could directly observe the demonstrations themselves; candidates called away on other business, such as deputies attending parliamentary sessions in Paris, could rely on the observations of friends and associates back home. Those unable to observe events personally could rely on newspaper accounts in the local or even the national press.

At the same time, although demonstrations are "real," they are also notoriously difficult to quantify. Even wholly disinterested eyewitnesses can have difficulty estimating how many people are present at a large demonstration, and few if any of those caught up in the May explosion can have been wholly disinterested. The "presse d'information" on which nonobservers have to rely must acknowledge conflicting claims. We called attention earlier to the variation in estimates of the size of a given demonstration, depending upon who was doing the reporting (Pierce, 1968, p. 178).[27]

But the worst distortions in aggregate reporting are invariably made for propagandistic purposes. They are designed to impress or to denigrate, rather than to inform. We have no reason to believe, however, that our elite respondents were so motivated in replying to our questions. Some of the respondents in our candidate sample may have indulged in a bit of hyperbole, such as the Communist candidate who told us that "100 percent of the worker and peasant voters" in his district had demonstrated.[28] More often, though, the candidates responded quite carefully, sometimes indicating how many demonstrations there had been, or distinguishing between those by opponents of the government and those by its supporters, or pointing out that many of the young demonstrators were not voters. Some wishful thinking inevitably appears across our sample of estimates of demonstration participation. But these were clearly informed by objective considerations as well. A strong indication that reality impinged more on the candidates' estimates of demonstration participation than on the other revolt-related perceptions we discussed earlier is the fact that there was less partisan bias in these perceptions than in the others. Leftist candidates made larger estimates than rightists or centrists, on the average, but the correlation between the candidates' estimates of demonstration participation and their own left-right locations was $r = .46$, as opposed to the average of $r = .62$ across the three attitudinal estimates.

Nevertheless, some of the estimates of the number of demonstrators that were made by the 1968 candidates appear to be unrealistically high. For example, some 15 percent of the candidates who answered the relevant question reported that at least 50 percent of their constituents had participated in the demonstrations, whereas our estimates of "actual" demonstration participation, based on the mass survey, revealed not one district where one-half or more of the households reported at least one adult demonstrator. Even taking into account that our estimates understate the reality by omitting persons under twenty-two years of age (our mass sample includes only people who were twenty-one or older in 1967), that is a discrepancy of some importance. But although most of the "over-reporters" were leftists, some were rightists.[29] One Gaullist candidate from Marseilles, who told us that 50 percent of his constituents had demonstrated, added, "C'est exceptionnel," as though to indicate that he was aware of the improbability of his estimate.

Of course, in some of the hot districts it may well have looked as though everyone was out on the streets. This seems to have been the case at Nantes, which furnishes us with an illustration of how reality can at the same time wash out partisan bias and produce some exaggeration. One of the two main Nantes electoral districts was part of our sample, and each of its two leading opposing candidates reported that 80 percent of his constituents had participated in demonstrations.[30] Although we cannot make a stable estimate of the rate of demonstration participation for any individual district on the basis of our mass survey data, there can hardly be a doubt that the demonstrations at Nantes were huge relative to the size of the city's population. Anyone looking out on downtown Nantes on May 27, the day of the largest opposition demonstration, or on June 1, when the pro-government demonstration took place, would have seen an impressive number of people. Moreover, estimates in the press at the time quite adequately confirmed our candidates' own large estimates. Le Monde reported that 30,000 people participated in the May 27 demonstration and that from 25,000 to 30,000 people joined the Gaullist demonstration on June 1. The local press reported more extravagant figures for the same two demonstrations. It is impossible, of course, to find out exactly how many people demonstrated at Nantes. Other independent estimates vary widely.[31] But although it is likely that our candidates from Nantes exaggerated, that is less important than the fact that, if they did so, they did so equally, and in circumstances that give some plausibility to their estimates. Nantes was probably the hottest spot in France in May and June, and the estimates of demonstration participation by the candidates from Nantes were the largest made by any of the candi-

dates in our sample. Considerations of partisan bias do not apply here, however, because the opposing candidates reported the same figure. In this case,
subjectivity in perception was at its lowest and objectivity at its highest.

The correlational measures in part (a) of Table 15-3 confirm the existence of a high degree of realism in the candidates' perceptions of the magnitude of the demonstrations. The correlation, corrected for small-sample
attenuation, between our candidates' and our mass sample's estimates of
demonstration participation is $r = .45$. That is not a negligible value, and it
is statistically significant at the .01 level. The 1968 candidates as a group
displayed considerable relative perceptual accuracy in this behavior domain.

Furthermore, the correlational values for the leftist and rightist candidates separately are similarly impressive. They are in line with some of the
more robust correlations reported in Table 15-2.

If there is a certain similarity between the perceptual accuracy of leftists
and rightists concerning demonstration participation, on the one hand, and
the proportions of involuntary strikers, on the other hand, there was little
absolute congruence between "actual" proportions of involuntary strikers
and the estimates made by either leftists or rightists. In the instance of perceptions of demonstration participation, the estimate of the rightists came
close to our independent sample estimate, whereas that of the leftists departed widely from it, as indicated in part (b) of Table 15-3. To that extent,
it indeed appears that leftists were compensating for their electoral defeat by
magnifying the numbers of people who agreed with their criticisms of the
regime to the point of taking to the streets. But the accuracy that was lacking in the leftist's absolute estimates of demonstration participation was
made up for by their remarkable correlational accuracy. The rightists' and
centrists' perceptions were less impressive on a correlational basis, but the
absolute congruence between their estimates and our independent sample
estimates is striking. In different ways, leftists and rightists were influenced
by objective circumstances as well as by partisan rationalization. In gauging
demonstration participation, the 1968 candidates were trying to come to
terms with what had been a shattering experience for all of them, but they
did so within the gravitational field of reality. Our data have captured both
the distortion and the accuracy that were the result.

Conventional Factors in the Vote

The 1968 elections were dominated by recollections of the upheaval that
preceded them. Both our own data on the mass level and the perceptions of
the candidates indicate that the disorder attendant upon the mass demonstrations was decisive in determining the outcome. Yet we also know from
the last chapter that although the shift in votes from 1967 to 1968 was
enough to produce a landslide in seats for the Gaullists and their allies, the
overwhelming majority of voters did not alter their choice of party or ten-

dency. Traditional long-term factors in electoral choice, such as party identification, degree of attachment to the Catholic Church, and attitudes toward de Gaulle, played a role in shaping people's choices at the elections of
1968 as they had in 1967. How did the candidates perceive the impact of the
May revolt on the contribution of the more conventional factors to their
electoral drawing power?

In 1967 we had asked our sample of candidates to assess the relative importance of the following factors in helping them to win votes: their party
labels, their personal reputations, their positions concerning de Gaulle, the
activity of their party's workers, their positions on the major issues, and
their alternates (*suppléants*).[32] In 1968 we repeated the question in identical
form for the first four items, added an item relating to their positions concerning the strikers, and amended the item concerning issues to read: "your
position on the other major issues."[33] Figure 15-2 sets out in graphic form
the mean scores for each of the items asked in both years (including the
slightly altered question concerning issues), by year and by the broad left-
right political affiliation of the candidates. The higher the bars in the figure,
the greater the relative importance attributed to the factor by the candidates. The mean scores represented are based on all the candidates interviewed in 1967 and all those interviewed in 1968, and not simply on those
who were interviewed both times.[34] In reading Figure 15-2 it should be
borne in mind that winners tend to score all factors higher than losers do.

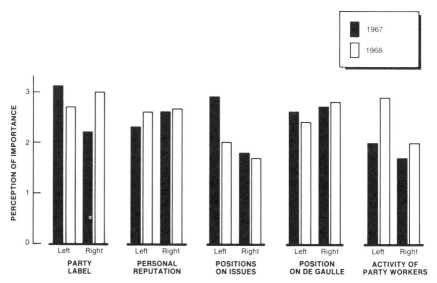

Figure 15-2. Candidate perceptions of importance of factors in the
first-ballot vote, by left-right political affiliation, France, 1967 and
1968.

That makes little difference for 1967, when the proportions of leftist and rightist winners among our sample of candidates were about the same, but it makes a substantial difference for 1968, when almost twice as many rightists as leftists in our sample of candidates were elected. One should not, therefore, compare the height of the bars for leftists and rightists for 1968. It is the relative changes in the heights of the bars between 1967 and 1968 for leftists and rightists separately that convey the message of Figure 15-2.

In 1967 the conventional factors in the vote that were perceived by the leftist candidates as having been most important were their party labels and their positions on major issues. They regarded their position toward de Gaulle as somewhat less important as an electoral drawing card, followed in descending order by their personal reputations and the activities of party workers. By 1968 that ordering of perceptions among leftists had changed. In that year they attributed most importance to the activity of their party workers, the item (among those we canvassed twice) to which they had assigned the least importance in 1967. They accorded somewhat less importance to their party labels in 1968 than they had in 1967, although that item still ranked comparatively high. The positions they took on major issues, however, suffered a sharp drop in perceived importance, from second place to fifth. Leftists thought their personal reputations were somewhat more important in 1968 than in 1967, while they assigned slightly less relative importance to their positions toward de Gaulle in 1968 than in 1967.

It is noteworthy that the two items which the leftist candidates thought had increased in both relative and absolute importance between 1967 and 1968—the efforts of their party comrades and their own personal reputations—are those that were most independent of the forces unleashed by the May upheaval. The "activity of party workers" refers simply to effort, which is wholly under the control of the people expending it, and, at least in principle, independent of the context in which it is expended. Personal reputation is a factor of a different order, but it is also *personal,* and in that sense must be distinguished from what is *contextual*—although obviously a politician's reputation is woven from strands of political as well as personal associations.

Conversely, the decline in the relative importance of party labels and issue positions for leftist candidates can be directly linked to the May revolt. They knew that their parties had declined in public esteem as a result of the disorders.[35] And the precipitous drop in the relative importance that they assigned to their positions on major issues reflects the belief that these customary issues had been submerged by the shock waves set loose by the May events. The leftist candidates surely did not think that their positions on the issues had changed from right to wrong between 1967 and 1968; they simply thought that in 1968 fewer people were listening to them. Their sense of the diminished electoral importance of their party labels and their positions on the issues reflected their generally gloomy outlook after their disastrous electoral experience, an outlook that was shared by the mass of leftist voters.

For the rightist (and centrist) candidates in 1967, their attitudes toward de Gaulle and their personal reputations were perceived as their most important drawing cards, followed by their party labels, their positions on the major issues, and the help of party workers, in that order. In 1968 there was one dramatic shift: party labels became the most important factor. This increase in importance for rightists roughly counterbalances the drop in importance for leftists. For the rightists, however, there was also an associated, if minor, move that suggests a unique interpretation of their increased appreciation of party. Their assessment of the relative importance of the activity of their party workers also increased, although not in the way it did for leftists. But it should be emphasized that the leftists, in assigning reduced importance to their party labels in 1968, were in no way abandoning their own traditional attachments to party, which have always been stronger on the left than elsewhere along the partisan spectrum. They were simply registering their understanding that the voters responded adversely in 1968 to the leftist parties generally. The rightists, on the contrary, may have been expressing a more basic change in outlook by upgrading the importance of party labels. That upgrading, taken in conjunction with the enhanced appreciation of party work, may actually have reflected a growing sense of the *enduring* importance of partisan affiliation.

Later we shall examine the extent to which the rightists' increased sense of the importance of party was translated into discipline in legislative voting in the Assembly that was elected in 1968. Here we shall simply add one note to reinforce the suggestion that the appreciation of party expressed by rightists in 1968 may have been more than a passing phenomenon. Figure 15-2 registers little change between 1967 and 1968 in the relative importance attributed to positions taken toward de Gaulle by leftists and rightists. This relative stability in perceptions accords poorly with what we know of the wellsprings of mass electoral behavior in 1968. In that year, attitudes toward de Gaulle were of greater importance as factors in the vote than they had been in 1967, even though they had been of major importance at that earlier election. The extent to which the electorate in 1968 polarized around Gaullism, to the immense advantage of the right, seems not to have been fully appreciated by those candidates who were the main beneficiaries of the phenomenon.

We have no way of plumbing the inner meaning of the rightists' failure to accord more relative importance to de Gaulle's drawing power in 1968 than they had in 1967. Taken together with their perception of the increased importance of their party label, however, it is a faint if uncertain harbinger of the later refusal of a significant fraction of the Gaullist leadership and their Giscardian allies to support de Gaulle at the 1969 referendum. Of course, they did not repudiate de Gaulle in 1968. But the May upheaval was a warning, and de Gaulle's own behavior during it showed signs of vacillation and misjudgment. Perhaps in a largely unconscious fashion, disenchantment with de Gaulle was gaining some hold on the right, and thoughts were already leaning toward consideration of his successor.

Popular Protest and the Representation Process

One result of the May upheaval was a change in the political agenda. The government formed after the 1968 election announced that it would prepare several reform measures. One of these, the Faure bill on university reform, had even been adopted by the National Assembly before our interviews with the 1968 candidates were completed. But neither this bill nor many of the other new measures had been on the legislative agenda before the May upheaval.

Later we shall give detailed consideration to the items on the new agenda, as well as to the effects of concern for those items on the degree of attention paid by legislators to older, and perhaps more enduring, issues. First, however, we need to assess the way in which the May upheaval affected the parliamentary elite's broad perspectives with regard to popular protest as a stimulus to political action.

Rioting as a Means of Political Pressure

The question we asked in order to elicit candidates' views on that extremely important matter was this: "As a result of the May–June events, some people think that rioting is the only real way of making sure that the government will pay attention to people's demands. Do you agree with this way of thinking or not, and why?"[36] This was not, of course, an easy question to answer within the confines of a brief interview situation. Although it was asked in a specific context, it relates to a permanent dilemma that has never been resolved in principle by political philosophers and that intermittently poses conscience-racking problems of concrete political choice. No government permits its citizens to riot, and no body of political philosophy suggests that rioting is an ideal form of political participation. But public disorder occurs with varying degrees of frequency in all democratic countries; and there are times when some people believe that although rioting may not be desirable as a general rule, it is nevertheless necessary in the circumstances and, in that sense, justified.

It is understandable, therefore, that some respondents gave ambivalent answers to our question, agreeing in a part of their response that sometimes the only way to capture the government's attention was to create a disturbance, but indicating in another part of their answer that they could not accept that formulation as a general proposition. "It all depends on the disturbance," one deputy said. "I think that when there is a very serious crisis, it is necessary to examine one's conscience. No, I think that it is obvious that one can adopt other methods." "I do not think so," another deputy said, "but it is true that French society is so conservative in every domain (the unions, the teachers, and so on) that there have to be shocks for people to become aware of such things as the problem of education." But less than 15 percent of the candidates gave us either mixed replies of this sort or more obviously evasive answers: the great majority of the candidates took unambiguous positions. Table 15-4 sets out the attitudes of the candidates toward the legitimacy of public disturbances, by majority and opposition.

The most intriguing aspect of Table 15-4 is the small degree to which the candidates' attitudes appear to be affected by partisan affiliation. As we shall see in a moment, some partisan differences are concealed within the broad categories of the table, but on the whole the similarities between the responses of majority and opposition candidates are more striking than their differences. A majority of both groups considered disorder to be unacceptable. More majority than opposition candidates replied ambiguously, but the percentages selecting that option are not large and the difference is not great. It is true that more than a fourth of the opposition candidates claimed that disorder was inevitable under Gaullist rule—that it was "the only way" for people to make themselves heard—while no majority candidate took that position. But three times as many majority candidates as opposition candidates, proportionately, agreed that disorder was an effective way of attracting the government's attention. If we combine the two groups that did not choose to emphasize the illegitimacy of disorder—that which held disorder to be inevitable and that which considered it effective—there is not much difference between majority and opposition.

We carefully considered why this was so when so many other sets of responses discussed in this chapter showed marked partisan differences. In-

Table 15-4. Candidate attitudes toward disorder as a means of political pressure, by majority and opposition (percentages), France, 1968.

	Type of candidate	
Candidate attitude	Majority	Opposition
Disorder is not legitimate	55	54
Mixed or evasive response	16	10
Disorder is inevitable under the Gaullist regime	0	26
Disorder is effective	29	10
Total	100	100
N	(32)	(24)

deed, the apparent anomaly is magnified in that the cases of partisan discrepancy we discussed earlier involved *perceptions,* which we might reasonably expect to converge if directed at the same phenomenon, whereas we are dealing here with *opinions* concerning a highly charged political problem on which one would expect wide divergence by partisan affiliation. In particular, we considered whether the formulation of our question, with regard to rioting *in general,* might have evoked a response on a fundamental philosophical level rather than on a level of current political positioning. In the end, we came to the conclusion that this was not so, because the most probable cause of an identical distribution of responses across government and opposition would be that the representatives of each group temporarily conceived of themselves as in the position of the other. In other words, for one fleeting moment opposition candidates might have imagined themselves to be in office facing hostile disturbances, while majority candidates similarly considered that they might one day be part of an opposition whose mass supporters had taken to the streets. There is, however, no evidence that either group made such a conceptual leap, and there is much evidence that our respondents were well anchored in the then current context of a Gaullist government and a leftist opposition.

The majority of the candidates, among majority and opposition alike, disagreed with the notion that rioting is the only sure way to gain the government's attention. If we break down the opposition candidates by their views on this matter, we find that the Communists, who were close to unanimous, were most likely by far to take that position, constituting some 70 percent of the opposition candidates who eschewed public disturbance. Among the majority candidates, however, it was the pure Gaullists who predominated. Some of the candidates (on both sides) who opposed disorder did not give their reasons for doing so, preferring instead to indicate the alternatives that they regarded as more appropriate means of political action: strikes, demonstrations, press campaigns, elections, channels of participation in the factories, and, most often, dialogue and discussion. Among those who did give reasons, there was some trace of agreement between Communists and Gaullists that violence is the work of minorities and does not produce lasting solutions to political problems. Further, some Communists argued that violence leads to repression and the isolation of the working-class movement, whereas Gaullists said that violence produces general disaffection and opens the way for all sorts of improper pressures and blackmail. Although the Communists' and Gaullists' reasons were not always the same, in the aftermath of May 1968 they broadly shared the view that public disorder was to be condemned.

In this regard more agreement is evident between Communists and Gaullists than between Communists and non-Communist leftists. Indeed, non-Communist leftists were less likely than either Communists or Gaullists to condemn disorder. Their modal response was that disorder was inevitable under the Gaullist regime because there was no other way for aggrieved groups to make their voices heard. More than half of the non-Communist leftists who gave unambiguous replies to our question took that position.

This difference in outlook between the Communist and non-Communist left does not mean either that the Communists approved of the Gaullist regime or that the non-Communists regarded violence as desirable. Communist candidates made their opposition to the Gaullist political system quite clear during the interviews, and non-Communist leftists who claimed that public disorder was inevitable under the Gaullist regime did not suggest that they preferred disorder to orderly political participation. On the contrary, some of them indicated that they regretted the situation they were describing. Yet in replying to an identical question, Communists chose to condemn disorder while the other leftists, although less unanimously, put the accent on condemning the Gaullist regime.

This difference in views almost surely reflects the habits and structures of two different kinds of parties. The Communist party, long habituated to operating with disciplined uniformity in every domain, carefully worked out its responses to the events of May as those events unfolded, and communicated them to party workers throughout the country (Kriegel, 1972, pp. 307–313). There is good reason to believe that the overriding tactical consideration of the Communists during May and June was to prevent disorder (Ross, 1982, pp. 193–194); for disorder would have ensured a platform for the left-wing extremists whom the Communists loathed. It would also have risked revitalizing the latent anti-Communism that the party had been trying hard to extinguish, a task with which it had had considerable success, thanks in no small part to de Gaulle's own behavior. Most serious of all, it could have led to a civil war from which the party could not have expected to emerge the victor.[37]

At the time of our interviews, therefore, the Communist party had taken a position on disorder that had been worked out, communicated to its sections, and implemented during May and June. When asked about the role of disorder in the political process, the Communist candidates replied almost without exception in accordance with their behavior during the upheaval itself. The party had opposed disorder during the revolt, and Communist candidates condemned disorder in its aftermath. Even a candidate who did not directly answer the question replied from the same perspective: "The workers did not start any riots."

In contrast with the Communists, the non-Communist leftists were a loosely structured group of political allies. There is no indication that the members of the Federation had any policy toward disorder in May and June similar to that of the Communists, but even if they had formulated one, it would not have led their candidates to give a nearly unanimous set of replies to our question about disorder as a means of political action. Federation candidates were simply not that disciplined. In discussing disorder, they divided according to their various personal estimates of its desirability, necessity, or inevitability. Some of them rejected violence categorically, as did almost all the Communists. More of them, however, gave precedence to their unfavorable views of the representativeness of the Gaullist regime and concluded that disorder was inevitable under that regime.

Perhaps the most interesting aspect of Table 15-4 is the cell showing that almost 30 percent of the candidates of the majority agreed to some extent that the only effective way to get a hearing from the government was to create a public disturbance. "I think that it was true." "They are not entirely wrong . . ." "Valid to a certain extent . . ." Often, the regime's supporters who took that position also expressed their regrets about the situation. "Unfortunately, it is true and I regret it," said one majority candidate. "A widespread opinion that is, alas, justified," another said. "Unfortunately, that is partly true," still another told us. "Alas! I am tempted to answer yes, alas!" said our last respondent of this type.

The position of these supporters of the regime was, to some extent, similar to that of the non-Communist leftists who told us that under the Gaullist regime there was no other way to get a hearing. When one Gaullist said, "The technocrats did not make any concessions," he was expressing a view not far from that of the leftist who told us that "with a regime that did not pay attention to any demands it was the only way to act." But there were also differences between the comments of the two sets of opposing candidates that reflected their basically different political affiliations and commitments. On the one hand, leftists tended to treat the situation that they thought made unrest inevitable as the result of Gaullist willfulness. "I am obliged to recognize that it is the regime that wants it," one leftist said of disorder. Another said that the government always wanted to ignore what it was told in parliament about the students or the workers or the farmers. The regime's supporters, on the other hand, tended to suggest that the disorders had come about because of Gaullist inadvertence.[38] "The government was lulled a bit into self-satisfaction . . . and it lost contact with the country," one Giscardian told us. "Errors were committed," said a Gaullist. The authorities, who "lack imagination," became mired in "daily routine," another majority candidate said. The opposition candidates thought that the situation was hopeless and condemned the regime as beyond redemption, whereas the regime's supporters thought that the situation was remediable and, though they criticized the regime, they could not very well condemn it.

Still, there were signs of strain within the governing majority. Barely half of the candidates of the majority who thought that one way of getting the government's attention was to create a disturbance were "pure" Gaullists. The others were Giscardians or centrists who had not been opposed by a Gaullist at the 1968 election. Politicians of these persuasions have regularly tried to distinguish themselves from the pure Gaullists even as they have allied with them, electorally or governmentally. At the same time, however, their critical stance in 1968 may have been another early warning, similar to that we mentioned earlier, of growing disenchantment with de Gaulle among his erstwhile supporters.

What to Do If History Repeats Itself?

The magnitude and duration of the May upheaval took the French political world by surprise. Neither the government nor the opposition parties expected such an event. In its early stages, it does not appear to have been taken very seriously by the government, and later, when the gravity of the disorders became evident, the authorities' hesitations, improvisations, and reversals of position indicated that they were quite unprepared for the realities of the situation. Similarly, the lack of coordination between the two main opposition groups, the Communist party and the Federation, left little doubt that they also had not anticipated such an outburst.

After the revolt had ended, but while it was still fresh in people's minds, it would have been quite normal for politicians to reflect on what the government ought or ought not to have done. Moreover, the fact that such an upheaval had taken place implied that similar events might occur again, thereby raising the question of what the government should do in that case. We were interested in our candidates' views on this score, and therefore we asked them what they thought the government should do in such a circumstance.[39] About a fourth of them failed to give a direct reply to the question. Some said that it was unlikely that such an event would occur again, at least in the near future; others insisted that the main thing for the government to do was to avoid such a recurrence; and a few took the reasonable but unhelpful position that the government should act according to the particular circumstances. But some three-fourths of our sample made specific recommendations as to what the government should do if such an upheaval should occur again.

Figure 15-3 sets out the frequencies for the response categories prescribing how to respond to social disorder, by the familiar classification of majority and opposition candidates. Unlike the situation depicted in Table 15-4 concerning the legitimacy of disorder, about which there was comparatively little differentiation by broad political affiliation, Figure 15-3 shows clearly the distinction between the views of the government's supporters and those of its opponents on the best response to disorder. This is particularly sharp at the two ends of the response scale, but some contrast appears in each response category.

Most of the responding majority candidates took what we may call the law and order position ("maintain order"). Their responses ranged from

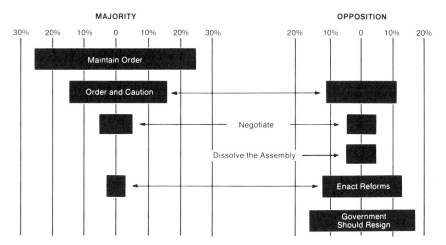

Figure 15-3. Frequency profile of candidates' prescriptions for handling future disorder, by majority and opposition, France, 1968.

that of the Gaullist who said, "Descendre dans la rue avec des mitraillettes" (Go into the streets with submachine guns), to simple and unalloyed references to maintaining order. The main thread running through these recommendations is the use of, or the threat of the use of, force. Such candidates, all of whom were government supporters, viewed mass protest exclusively in terms of maintaining public order. No opposition candidate took that position. At the opposite end of the scale, about a third of the responding opposition candidates, but not one majority candidate, said that in the event of a new outburst of mass discontent the government should resign. Some 40 percent of the Communist candidates took that position. Thus the Gaullist and Communist candidates, whose two parties were most likely to reject disorder as a means of political action, reacted very differently to our hypothetical replay of May 1968. Gaullists, on the one hand, tended to think of such a situation in terms of its ongoing effects. For most of them, it would represent an intolerable excursion outside the realm of legitimate political behavior, to be dealt with exclusively as a problem of public order. Communists, on the other hand, tended to think of a renewal of the May outburst essentially in terms of its causes. For many of them, such an event would signify the bankruptcy of the Gaullist government which should, therefore, resign.

A majority of the candidates who gave us valid responses recommended some course of action between these two extremes. The most popular intermediate response was the category labeled "order and caution." Its hallmark is recognition of the need to maintain order, combined with an indication that maintaining order alone is not adequate. One typical expression of this position is the recommendation to maintain order *and* to negotiate or enact reforms; others include references to maintaining order without bloodshed or to avoiding disorder without repression. Somewhat more majority candidates than opposition candidates, proportionately, took this position.

Similarly, the smaller number of those eschewing any reference to order but simply urging the government to negotiate contains somewhat more majority than opposition candidates proportionately. But the candidates who, instead of recommending negotiation, indicated that they preferred the government simply to enact reforms, were more likely to be opposition candidates than government supporters. Finally, a small proportion of opposition candidates, but (ironically) no majority candidates, recommended the course of action that de Gaulle had actually taken and that had proved to be so damaging to the parliamentary strength of the left: to dissolve the National Assembly.[40]

Despite the small number of cases with which we are dealing in Figure 15-3, the proportions of responses by majority and opposition candidates at each step of what approximates a scale running from repression to surrender are ordered in a fashion that fits our intuitive expectations. Still, one may stop and ponder for a moment the strong propensity of the candidates of the majority to approach the problem of mass protests essentially as a matter of maintaining order, as compared with their minimal inclination to deal with such a situation by enacting reforms. Even allowing for a certain understandable exasperation on the part of those candidates at the suggestion that there might be another spectacular outburst of the kind that had only recently rocked the regime, the distribution of responses among the majority candidates is more striking than the predictable contrasts between the responses of the majority and those of the candidates of the opposition.

That lopsided distribution of attitudes among the majority candidates concerning how to deal with mass protest has a bearing on the point with which we concluded the preceding chapter, dealing with the 1968 upheaval at the mass level. There we remarked that two different lessons could be derived simultaneously from the entire set of events running from the initial student outburst early in May to the Gaullist electoral victory in June. On the one hand, the widespread mass protests pointed toward the desirability of social reforms, while, on the other hand, the rightist electoral backlash pointed toward a popular desire for law and order. How the candidates who were elected to the National Assembly weighted these two readings of the situation would obviously provide the underpinnings for their behavior early in the life of the new legislature and possibly for its duration.

Legislative Perspectives on Repression and Reform

In shifting our focus from the 1968 candidates to the 1968 deputies, we find that the distinction between majority and opposition, which we have seen to be at the root of so many sharp differences in perceptions and political attitudes, is magnified in an absolute sense. Whereas candidates from the majority parties constitute some 60 percent of our sample of 1968 candidates, deputies from the same majority parties constitute some 75 percent of our sample of 1968 deputies,[41] just as they did in the Assembly actually elected in 1968 (and broadly described in the preceding chapter). This means that although we shall maintain for analytical purposes the distinction between majority and opposition that we have regularly employed in this chapter, such a distinction could have no practical meaning for the enactments of the legislature elected in 1968. In that legislature, which was controlled by a lopsided majority of Gaullists and their allies, the opposition deputies could have even less influence on the outcome of the legislative process than they had had before. The only population within which variations in attitudes toward reform and repression could have an operative effect on concrete legislative measures was the majority itself.

We saw earlier in this chapter that there was a certain amount of heterogeneity of outlook among the candidates of the majority on a number of questions. The topics we shall pursue further here with regard to the majority deputies' opinions are those concerning the causes of the student upheaval, the causes of the strike movement, and what the government should do in the event of another massive protest. For all three subjects, we simplified our measurement scales so that they ranged from −1 to +1, with 0 as the midpoint, and keyed them so that a negative score reflects an attitude suggestive of the need for reform and a positive score indicates a preoccupation with the need for maintaining social discipline (repression). Thus for the perceived causes of the student revolt, emphasis on the failures of the university or concern about job preparation is scored as −1, while emphasis on the role of the instigators of the revolt is scored as +1, with combined references scored as 0. An analogous scoring system was employed for opinions about the strike movement. With regard to what the government should do in the event of a new outbreak of mass protest, we modified the scale that appears in Figure 15-3 by omitting the categories of dissolution and resignation, which do not apply at all to the majority deputies, and by counting any reference to enacting reforms or negotiating with the protesters as −1, flat references to maintaining order as +1, and references to maintaining order but to avoiding violence as 0.

More important than our various measures, which are employed here only to convey a gross sense of differences within the set of majority deputies, is the kind of distinction among those deputies that might account for their differences in outlook with regard to reform and repression. In this regard, the most compelling factor we can think of is the distinction between the majority's reelected incumbents and the majority candidates who succeeded in overturning opposition incumbents. Our hypothesis is simply that the majority's deputies from comparatively safe seats—the victorious incumbents—would be less sensitive to the desirability of enacting reforms than those from marginal seats or, indeed, seats that had in the past easily returned leftists to the Assembly. Accordingly, we examined the mean scores on our selected measures separately for the majority's incumbents and for their newly elected deputies.

Figure 15-4 sets out the mean scores on our three measures for the two groups of majority deputies and, with regard to the causes of the student revolt and the strikes, for the opposition deputies as well. (The recoded scale concerning what the government should do in the event of another mass upheaval is not applicable to the opposition deputies because it does not include references to dissolution and the government's resignation, which so many opposition candidates recommended.)

The results indicate that there is a considerable difference in underlying outlook between the majority incumbents and the newly elected deputies with regard to the causes of the student revolt and the strikes, but that there is less difference between the two groups concerning how to handle another

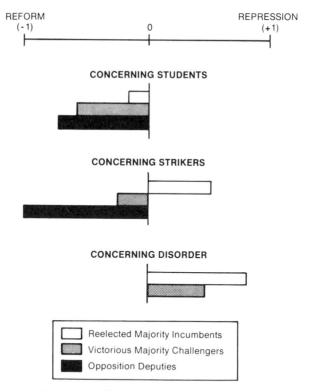

Figure 15-4. Deputy predispositions toward reform and repression, France, 1968.

mass upheaval. It does seem as though the newly elected majority deputies who had unseated opposition incumbents might be more receptive to reform measures than the reelected incumbents, at least with regard to students and workers. Of course, our measures are at best indirect, and—having been taken at the onset of the new Assembly—they might lose whatever force they had as that Assembly wore on. But even so, the newly elected majority deputies would logically appear to be the more likely representatives of the majority to be sensitive to the usefulness of reforms. More indulgent toward the students and the strikers than the victorious majority incumbents at the start of the new Assembly, they could be expected also to be more concerned about retaining their seats at the next election as the Assembly drew to its close. If any of the majority deputies were to draw the lesson from the May–June events that certain reforms were in order, it would be the newly elected deputies.[42]

Concerning how to handle a new mass upheaval, however, there was less difference between the two groups of majority deputies. For both groups, the mean scores were decidedly on the law and order side of the scalar midpoint. Although there was some prospect of reform, expressed more strongly by one group of majority deputies than by the other, there was little indication that majority deputies of any kind would treat mass protest in a general sense as anything other than a problem of maintaining public order.

Conclusions

We have traversed considerable ground in this effort to assess the reactions of the French parliamentary elite to the events of May and June 1968. The leitmotif of our analysis has been to investigate the elite's perceptions of more or less directly observable political phenomena, including states of public opinion in their districts, and then to set those perceptions against the "realities" insofar as it is possible to do so.

Broadly speaking, the results of this effort have been mixed. On the one hand, we have found that on one dimension after another the perceptions of the candidates at the 1968 election were strongly influenced, if not badly distorted, by partisan affiliation. That pattern holds true for presumably "objective" phenomena as well as in the realm of opinion and interpretation where one would normally expect partisan differences to be controlling. Ironically, the one major issue on which majority and opposition came closest to agreeing with each other—the illegitimacy of disorder as a means of political action—was a broad philosophical question on which politicians of different locations might normally differ widely.[43]

On the other hand, even though many if not most of the elite's perceptions amounted to rationalizations of party positions, those perceptions were also sometimes informed by a sense of reality. Thus, although the candidates' estimates of district-level demonstration participation often varied quite widely, depending upon whether the respondents were from the majority or the opposition, those estimates were tolerably tied to variations in district realities, particularly among opposition candidates. Moreover, those opposition candidates understood very well that they had been badly beaten at the election because of fears provoked by the mass demonstrations. And the majority's candidates understood that although they had been served beyond their dreams by the disorders flowing from the demonstrations, they should not make too much of an issue of the strikes, but perhaps even show some sympathy toward the strikers, if they were to maximize their electoral support.

Just as France's leftist voters emerged from the May–June events in a state of gloom and disappointment, so did the leftist politicians. They had, in effect, been beaten by rioting students over whom they had had no control, and were left in a helpless minority position in parliament. Neither the party labels nor the political arguments that they thought had served them well only a year earlier were enough to rescue them from ignominious defeat.

Within the reinforced and virtually impregnable Gaullist majority there was considerable indignation at the affront that the mass protests of May represented, as well as some gloating over the electoral results. But there was also a certain amount of caution, particularly among the newly elected rightist deputies who might not retain their parliamentary seats beyond a single term. And even well-entrenched incumbents could not ignore the fact that for almost a solid month students and strikers had appeared in unprecedented numbers to decry the Gaullist regime.

There was, therefore, on the part of the new parliamentary majority, a certain disposition toward reform, touching on the two groups that had been the principal actors of May 1968: students and workers. But if, in that sense, one can say that the newly elected power-holders showed signs of responding to mass appeals from the streets, there was little or no disposition among the majority to tolerate fresh outbursts of the same kind. If May was a cry for reform and June was an appeal for order, the indications at the outset of the new National Assembly were that it contained the potentiality for both. And it remained to be seen whether the May upheaval had sharpened in any general sense the elected deputies' sensitivity to their constituents' concerns in domains other than those directly related to the revolt.

PART IV

The Representation System

I n Parts I, II, and III we spent a great deal of time with both our voter sample and our elite sample. We have examined the political world of the voters, and have probed the mainsprings of their choices of candidates to represent them in the National Assembly. We have contrasted the social and ideational backgrounds of these two samples, and have also described their roles in and responses to the crises of 1968.

What remains is the subject of representation itself. Here we begin to exploit the fact that our two samples are not mere separate entities, but were selected on the basis of the tight functional interlock between them—constituents on the one hand, and their aspiring representatives on the other. In Part IV, we shall feature our linkage analyses tying popular opinion to policy outcomes in the National Assembly, through the intermediary of deputies elected to that body.

We shall start by relating classical theories about political representation to the actual structure of measurements available to us. The operationalization of representative relationships in the "diamond" form developed by Miller and Stokes will serve as our basic analytic framework, and the terms of this diamond will dictate much of the structure of the rest of this book. There will be, of course, a few necessary detours along the way. We shall discuss the complex folkways of the French National Assembly in generating the kinds of roll-call votes which serve as the ultimate policy outcomes of the representation process, and we must review the specific roll-call measures we shall use.

The actual discussion of representation will start out simply, describing the "basic bond" between constituency sentiments on the one hand and legislative outputs on the other. There is more than one class of sentiment that can be related to policy outcomes, however, and we shall canvass several of them, including the left-right composition of the district. There is also more than one way to conceive of a constituency, and we shall distinguish between that formed by the voters for the winning candidate and that formed by the voters for the losers. Methodological challenges will appear from time to time as we proceed. Good people have criticized the techniques we employ here, but we shall sturdily defend our positions. Others have worried about small district samples, but we shall show that size alone is not the decisive factor, and that in some circumstances small samples can furnish more reliable results than larger ones do in other circumstances. Gradually it will emerge that representation of a discernible kind is going on in the French system, thus precluding the possibility that chance alone is at work.

Moving around the Miller-Stokes diamond in order to find out how and why that representation is occurring, we shall explore elite knowledge of constituency opinion, as well as the factors—notably, the degree of homogeneity of the district and the way in which the representative conceives of his legislative role—that may affect the degree of accuracy of such knowledge. The notion of "party responsibility" as a representational theory will be assessed logically and examined empirically with the materials we have at hand.

Using the pioneering work of Miller and Stokes on the United States as a guide and basis for comparison, we shall explore the variation in the fidelity of district representation by issue domain, and by the marginality of the deputy's legislative seat. We shall also ask whether voters reward faithful district representatives by reelecting them, and punish less faithful ones with electoral defeat. And we shall not overlook the fact that in the late 1960s the French population employed not one but two channels of communication with the political elite: they struck, demonstrated, and even rioted; and they cast ballots for their chosen candidates. What effect did the 1968 revolt have on representation in France, with regard to both the immediate, revolt-related issues of education and union rights and the other more "normal" issues of public policy that we have included in our assessments of representation in France?

Finally, we shall try to learn which segments of the mass public are actually represented in France across the broad range of issues. If our findings on this score do not seem completely satisfactory, it will be because of intractable measurement problems. The distinctiveness of the French system of representation renders generalizations from it to the more generic case rather hazardous. The complexities of the French system make it difficult for all but the most involved and attentive citizens to employ the "normal" electoral process as a means of communicating unambiguously with their representatives. In addition, the dearth of directly comparable findings from other systems prevent us from offering more than a tentative conclusion regarding the location of the French representation system on the scale of representative virtue, relative to other modern democratic political systems.

16

---◆•◆---

Theories and Models
of Representation

Although, in the past two or three centuries, much has been published on the concept of political representation, this literature is riddled with confusion, as is attested by Hanna Pitkin's monumental effort to restore some order to the discourse (Pitkin, 1967). Commentators describe the same things in different terms, and different things in the same terms, so that constructive confrontation seldom occurs.

Throughout this book, and in Part IV in particular, we often use the phrase, "the nature of representation." The word "nature" is exceedingly vague in its referents; our use of it is deliberate, for it expresses the full complexity and multifaceted character of the notion of representation. At other times we refer to a "representation function," which sounds more definite at least superficially; and since we talk of this function as stronger (or firmer, or tighter) under some circumstances than others, the implication seems to be that we do *not* conceive of representation as an extremely complex, multifaceted, and perhaps irreducibly qualitative matter, but rather as something quite unidimensional, ranging in degree from a complete absence of representation through partial representation to perfect representation.

Our purpose in this chapter is to solve this apparent paradox, and to relate our solution to the classic controversies surrounding the concept of representation. We shall also state which of the many variants of the term "representation" we wish to address, and what bearing our specific measurements have on each definition. Finally, we shall show what the study of representation in a particular place at a particular time, as in France between 1967 and 1972, can add to our more general understanding of the nature of political representation.

An Initial Context

We should state, to begin with, that we are exclusively interested in "popular" political representation, in the context of "representative" legislative bodies, but not necessarily limited to such political agents alone. The qualifier "popular" means that what is being represented by the political agent is the will or interest of some public or constituency. In casual language, a given political agent may be said to "represent" all kinds of conceptual entities: he may, for instance, be a superb representative of "socialist values." That usage does not concern us here. When we use the term "representation" alone, it refers specifically to the will or interest of a constituency, not to some other entity or symbol. That constituency will and constituency interest can sometimes be discrepant presents a complication to which we shall return later in this chapter.

The focus on "interest" or "will" rules out as irrelevant some classes of statements that occasionally arise in discussions of representation, as, for example, that a certain "representative" body is manifestly not representative because its members are considerably more wealthy, better educated, and more skilled in parliamentary maneuver than their typical constituents. Such a body is indeed not representative in the sense of being an unbiased sample of the whole, but there is a marked difference between representativeness in a simple sampling sense and representation according to interest. To be sure, pure sampling considerations intrude into questions of interest representation in intriguing ways, as we shall see. But the statistically representative agent may represent constituent interests either superbly or poorly, and this may also be true of the statistically unrepresentative agent.

The focus on interest representation permits us to make summary judgments of a unidimensional kind as to the strength or weakness of the representative bond between the agent and the constituency. These judgments reflect a kind of "bottom line" arising from this relationship, and refer to the degree of congruence between constituency interest and representative action. Such congruence can indeed be seen as ranging in degree from nonexistent (or even perverse) through partial to perfect; and reasonable numerical indices of such a dimension can be constructed.

Any such measures are, of course, extremely summary. A vast number of configurations of intervening mechanisms, some of them mirror images of each other, can produce exactly the same summary degree of congruence. It is at this point that we begin to probe into the true complexities of the notion of representation, and although our treatment can be only partial, we shall indeed attempt to trace some of the main lines of the "nature" of this representation.

The need for the qualifier "political" in the term "popular political representation" is obvious, but it has one bite of a restrictive sort that should be emphasized. It properly suggests a context of direct conflict of interests. It is true that even a political representative may take some actions in furthering the interests of his constituency which involve no obvious opposition other than the inertias of nature. Our focus, however, will be exclusively on representation in a political context in which interests come into direct conflict, and where, for any major gambit, there is invariably a conscious opposition which is organized or organizable. This delimitation, coupled with the others already mentioned, rids us of many concerns which have unduly preoccupied theorists of representation, such as how an agent can be said to represent a senile person, or whether a postman represents the state when he drops a letter in our mailbox.

Up to this point, in describing the context in which it is appropriate for us to discuss representation, we have presented a number of simplifications, as compared with many classical discussions of the subject. Conversely, at least two important features of our context complicate the discussion: (1) each of our representatives is obliged to serve as agent not merely for one but for a multiplicity of other persons; (2) each of our representatives is obliged to represent this multiplicity of others not in a single action nor with respect to a single axis of dispute, but on a very broad range of axes of dispute.

These two further features of our context are not surprising or heterodox. They are common to most current legislative bodies, and are fundamental aspects of political representation. One functional *raison d'être* of the representative body is, of course, the difficulty of coping with large numbers of constituents in decisionmaking. The convenience of the first feature—the few representing the many—is achieved by multiperson constituencies with limited numbers of representatives. A special complication occurs, however, when the will of a constituency is badly but evenly split on some dispute in which the representative is expected to cast a vote "yea" or "nay." The second feature—issue multiplicity—is equally commonplace: most representatives in the public political arena are expected to decide on a very large number of policy matters, many of which are substantively unrelated to one another. Representation decisions that may be easy to make in one or two policy domains where constituency interests may happen to be massive and monolithic necessarily cover only a small fraction of the actions the representative is expected to carry out in the name of his constituency.

Both of these realistic complications will be of central concern to us later in this chapter. Before we turn to them, however, we shall review the conventional disputes about the proper or the existential nature of political representation.

Common Models of Representation

Although modes of popular representation appropriate to our context can assume a great variety of configurations, three modes that have been historically prominent will form the center of our treatment. The most celebrated normative controversy surrounding questions of political representation, the mandate-independence controversy, defines two of these modes in polar form. The third is the model of the responsible party.

The Mandate-Independence Controversy

The "mandate" view has deep roots in democratic values. It sees the representative as a "delegate" who is expected to act on explicit instructions from his constituency. In its extreme form, it expects the representative to limit his advocacies and his contributions to legislative decision to such instructions: he is a mere "errand-boy" serving as a passive conduit of constituency sentiments, required purely because the logistics of the situation prevents the total constituency from joining the assembly outright. In a less extreme form, the representative is allowed to use his own judgment to some degree, in part because instructions obviously cannot cover every action, and in part because there may be some matters, even weighty ones, on which the constituency for whatever reason fails to supply even general instructions. But the important point remains, even in this more realistic view, that instructions from the constituency, when they are forwarded, are preemptive over all other concerns.

The competing "independence" view received its classic statement from Edmund Burke in his speech to the electors of Bristol. Facing a public whose assumptions leaned toward the mandate view, he argued that once selected, the good representative exercises his own considered judgment or private conscience in his ultimate legislative decision, on the basis of the details of the legislative deliberation. Carried to an extreme well beyond Burke's statement, the independence view sees the representative as free of any particular obligations to his constituency per se: the constituency base of the selection process is merely an administrative recruitment device to find "a few good men," whose goodness and wisdom are affirmed by the esteem expressed in elections by peers who have seen them in action over a period of time. For Burke, the special obligation to the particular constituency remained, but the representative was a trustee of the true interests of the constituency, as God gave him to understand and reflect those interests. The point of his speech was that the representative's judgment as to those true interests might well diverge from time to time from the short-term will of the constituency; and when such divergences arose, the obligation of the representative was to follow the dictates of his conscience rather than the instructions of his district.

The popularity of the mandate-independence controversy has produced an extensive literature, some of it relatively creative, some of it relatively sterile. In the relatively creative view (which we share), the two poles delineated are most useful if taken as ideal types in the Weberian sense, neither of which can be expected to exist in pure form in terms of either the Real or the Good, yet which serve between them to define a continuum whereupon, in a more middling way, both the Real and the Good may profitably be located. The relatively sterile view is that which presumes that these poles are all-or-nothing matters, whether normatively or empirically.

Pitkin (1967, p. 155) recounts her frustration at the seeming force and good sense of arguments advanced by both mandate and independence advocates in the all-or-none mode, in view of the fact that these arguments were never designed to meet on any common ground. Enthusiasts of the independence model pointed out that representatives were specifically selected as experts by voting publics who had neither the time nor the inclination to steep themselves in the detailed considerations that must attend any kind of rational policy formation. Burke himself eloquently derided the notion of requiring such experts, after all the fact-finding, hearings, and deliberations had taken place, to vote exactly as their constituents might casually wish without benefit of this information. Advocates of the mandate view, on the other hand, asked how it could be said that any proper representation was taking place at all if the "trustee" voted repeatedly against the wishes of his district.

What both of these supposedly devastating critiques lack is any recognition of the fact that circumstances vary, and that it is likely that not only the Real but the Good varies with them. Some decisions must be taken under conditions of such emergency, or they involve such elaborate and arcane technical considerations that even the most devoted enthusiast of the mandate role does not care to argue with the necessity for a trustee, but shifts his argument to other grounds. Similarly, in real-life circumstances, there are some votes or chains of votes in which it would be so manifestly brazen to argue that the district's interest is somehow contrary to its obvious will, that even the most dedicated advocate of independence would not care to defend a sequence of contradictory votes by the representative, and hence prefers to focus his case on questions where special expertise is plainly more relevant. What all this means is that if we integrate over a multiplicity of real-life decisions made in legislatures, we are not likely to be dealing much at either pole, but somewhat closer to the middle, of the mandate-independence continuum—although exactly where will depend in significant degree upon normative beliefs as to the proper role for the representative.

To be more concrete, it is easy to rejoin as follows to the defense of the independence position. "Of course, the representative has been singled out from the constituency as an extremely well informed person and an agile parliamentarian. Of course, it is true that the average voter quite rationally does not want to dedicate equal amounts of time to becoming informed in detail about legislative gambits, even in an area of some modest concern to him, which most domains are not. Certainly there results something of an expert-client relationship. Yet, sparing the details, it is presumably true that the voter has some sense of the general thrusts of policy that he would prefer, among those options contested at the moment, as well as those he dislikes."

This matter is rendered most vivid by our study design. We would never have dreamed of asking our respondents their feelings about a series of detailed options having to do with the administrative and fiscal relationships between Paris and the Commission of the European Community in Brussels or the European Parliament in Strasbourg. Instead our questions were designed to assess whether the individual voter was eager to see a tighter European union effected, or whether he was reluctant about such a change. This is not a detailed compass bearing but a general question as to whether the ship of state should be steered roughly to the east or roughly to the west. The respondent may never have seen the inside of a ship, and is certainly vague about what specific operations are most likely to move the ship preponderantly in one direction or preponderantly in the other. That is, in fact, why he was encouraged to take on an expert who knew something about running ships. The respondent is not even much concerned whether the actual bearing is southeast by east, or northeast by east, or some other point, provided only that no west component appear. The fine tuning is again left to the good judgment of the expert.

Moreover, if the expert engages in some single maneuver which seems destined to thrust perversely toward the west, the voter may want to ask a challenging question or two. But he has ultimate respect for the expertise of the helmsman, and if it is explained that although the maneuver on the surface seemed to move the ship westward, it was only to arrive the faster at a speedier current carrying to the east, then the voter is likely to be tolerant of the greater experience of the expert. Only when the expert engages in a whole series of maneuvers, all of which seem destined to carry the ship westward and in fact have that result, may the voter come to wonder whether his expert is dealing with him in bad faith or is simply an incompetent navigator. It is only at this level of general thrust that our study materials can hope to evaluate the character of political representation in France, but we feel that this level is quite adequate to the task.

It is equally easy to rejoin to the mandate critique. "Of course, we should not want to maintain that some reasonable representation function pertained if, in some general and persistent way over a multiplicity of issues, representatives tended to vote contrary to the wishes of their constituencies. As a matter of fact, we are erecting a measurement apparatus capable of detecting that possibility if it should occur. It would register by our calibrations not merely as a lack of congruence between district sentiment and representative actions, but as a significant level of active incongruence. But we do not expect such findings, for (as we shall see later) there are a variety of reasons why such a truly perverse state of affairs would not emerge, even if there were no elections and all appointed "representatives" cared nothing for the will of the constituency they were designated to represent. A slightly more plausible question that might be asked from the mandate side involves the possibility that no association whatever emerges between district sentiment and representative decisions, rather than an actively negative relationship. In such an event, it might be asked whether the substantial costs of conducting popular elections at periodic intervals are worthwhile. But even this question, as we shall see, is embarrassingly extreme."

It seems worth recognizing from the outset, then, that all-or-none assumptions stemming from the mandate-independence ideal types bear little resemblance to anybody's reality or, for that matter, any serious idea of what is good. One can readily imagine that for an occasional specific legislator, on an occasional specific issue, a given roll-call vote might plausibly be described as quite purely "trustee" in the Burkean mold, or as quite purely "instructed-delegate." It would not be easy to be certain, since the discrimination is hard to make, save for those empirical cases where there is some major conflict between the dictates of the representative's conscience and the will of his constituency; and there is every reason to believe that such events are a minority of all the decisions he makes as representative. And for these cases of conflicting pressures, it would be hard to rule out the existence of some felt pressure from conscience or constituency, even if the other term ultimately won out. At the level of the specific decision for the specific representative, however, an all-or-none verdict might reasonably occur from time to time.

Yet when we crank upward one level of aggregation, to the set of votes cast over a period of time by a particular legislator, the likelihood that all of his votes are totally determined either by private conscience or by district instructions becomes vanishingly small. Some years ago a U.S. senator made a startling announcement, early in a six-year term. He pronounced that he was tired of demands from his constituency, and that he had decided he would not seek reelection four years thence. For the remainder of his term, he intended to make his congressional decisions entirely as he saw fit, and he would be much obliged to his constituents if they refrained from taking up his time by making any of their policy preferences known to him, since he did not retain the slightest interest in political sentiments in his constituency, and if any knowledge of these preferences was forced upon him, he would take great pleasure in assuring that their weight in any of his legislative decisionmaking was kept at absolute zero.

It is possible that for some period of time, even as long as the ensuing four years, the legislative record of this representative was quite purely Burkean. But in view of the fact that he made such a statement, it is extremely unlikely that his total legislative record, before as well as after, would class as purely Burkean. And given the astonishing nature of his pronouncement, it is quite clear that he was a limiting case, or extreme outlier, to begin with, relative to the world population of democratically elected representatives.

Pitkin (1967), working mainly with conceptual materials, concluded that there was a natural reason for the continued coexistence of both the mandate and independence views of representation, however contrary to each other they might appear, since both had their justifications as well as their vulnerabilities. Fenno (1978, p. 161), working from a rich and proximate inductive knowledge of a large number of elected representatives, has noted that justifications of particular legislative votes cast in terms of *either* district wishes *or* the dictates of private conscience are at least acceptable explanations for the voter, and often even stirring ones. And the implication is that neither justification is totally dishonest, in terms of the specific legislator vis-à-vis the specific vote.

The realistic fact of the matter is that most persons who achieve elective public office are also people who by virtue of their survival in a lengthy process of political "natural selection" have unusual confidence in their own capacities to digest facts and shape from them reasonably intelligent decisions, in the pure Burkean style. At the same time, there is overwhelming evidence that one of the abiding concerns—almost to the point of obsession—of these people is the hurdle of the next election (see Tardieu, 1937, for France; and for the United States, Mayhew, 1974, p. 13, or Fenno, 1978). Most of them, particularly those hidden in large legislative bodies, are sophisticated enough to know that very few of their roll-call decisions will ever be widely known in their constituencies, much less be seen as totally unjustifiable. But the possibility is always there—Friedrich's rule of "anticipated reactions"—and the concern is so acute that it is hard to imagine that constituency wishes, particularly if expressed with much vehemence, fail utterly to affect the thinking of even the staunchly Burkean legislator.

In short, then, if 0.00 means a representative's legislative record which is purely and unyieldingly Burkean, totally without regard for expressed district wishes, and 1.00 reflects a legislative record laid down at every step in response to perceived district instructions, we would be surprised if many political representatives in legislative bodies could be located much outside the limits of a narrower range, such as .30 to .70, or even .35 to .65.[1]

Presuming these quantitative surmises to have some merit, it follows that if we crank upward still another level of aggregation, to consider the coloration of legislative styles characterizing total legislatures, we would be obliged to conclude that because each legislature has its own variety of inhabitants, the summary figures for legislative bodies as wholes would tend to fall within some still narrower range, perhaps between .40 and .60.

Obviously, figures of this kind are fictions, or mere guesses at true values which are certainly unknown and quite conceivably unknowable. The principal point, nonetheless, should be clear. However useful the polar descriptions of the mandate-independence controversy may be as analytic tools, dependence upon them as true all-or-none realities is foolish. They define a heuristic continuum, but most of the "action" between them is likely to lie in a rather narrow middling range. This is a point that we posit as an empirical likelihood, rather than as a profession of normative preference. But at the same time it is likely that any reasonable normative preference will also lie significantly short of either zero or one, the reason being the ease with which any claim to the desirability of purity on this continuum can be reduced to absurdity (again, see Pitkin, 1967, p. 150). What is desirable rests in an obvious way on the details of the circumstances.

If it is true that few individual legislators are likely to lie outside the range of .25 to .75, and few total legislatures are likely to lie outside a range of .40 to .60 on our hypothetical scale, then one plausible conclusion might be that the differences between either individual legislators or total legislatures are so trifling that contrasts between them in this regard do not hold much intellectual excitement, however compelling the original ideal types might have been.

This is not at all the conclusion we wish to draw, however. We suspect that the mandate-independence distinction is of such conceptual importance, where problems of popular representation are concerned, that apparently small differences in legislative style, such as those within the range from .40 to .60, do have highly significant consequences with regard to the functioning of democratic systems.

This is a conjecture which we cannot prove, but which seems plausible enough to warrant the investment of a good deal of further work. We have, however, some shreds of evidence to support such a conjecture. For example, in another connection we have investigated attitudes toward popular representation in Brazil. It is apparent that Brazilian leaders, confronted by constituencies showing massive rates of illiteracy and an extremely limited awareness of national political life, are quite disdainful of suggestions that they should be closely attentive to constituency wishes.[2] This is not to say that constituency wishes are to be generally ignored, nor to maintain that in a situation of democratic elections Brazilian politicians would be totally immune to some margin of concern about keeping legislative records which would be resistant to attack. Perhaps, on our scale, a democratically elected

Brazilian Congress might rate the low but nonetheless substantial value of .35. The question is whether such a value, which is quite far from zero, portends significant differences in the nature of popular representation or policy outcomes, relative to a national legislature which shows a value of .60. We cannot demonstrate in any clear way that it does, but it is a hypothesis that seems worthy of continued pursuit.

Hence to a final point: if limited differences in terms of the mandate-independence controversy between legislators and legislatures do have some broader significance, then it is important that we develop instrumentation which can distinguish not only crudely between one and zero, but also much finer gradations as well. One of the purposes of this study has been to quantify and examine such finer differences.

A Third Model: The Responsible Party

Whereas the mandate-independence controversy defines in crystalline terms two polar models of the representation process, a third model cuts cross-grain to the axis defined by the first two alternatives. This is the doctrine of the responsible-party form of representation.

This doctrine assumes the kind of ongoing electoral process in which political parties are potent realities. It assumes further that these ongoing parties compete with one another by developing contrasting policy programs, which are widely publicized to prospective voters. Voters, thereby cognizant of such contrasts, will vote for whatever candidate is running as a representative of that program which is in some overall sense the closest to their own preference schedules. The final assumption, which cements in the term "responsibility," is that the candidate, however anonymous he may be, can in any event be counted on to pursue the program of the party under whose banner he is elected.[3]

When we say that such a doctrine cuts cross-grain to the mandate-independence controversy, we do not mean that it is neutral before these alternatives; quite to the contrary, the responsible-party model was delineated in an attempt to make mandate representation effective and efficient (see Kirkpatrick, 1971). The purpose of its advocates, who found the Burkean "independence" view of representation wholly abhorrent, was to let the public instruct; and the best means, they believed, was to require parties to commit themselves to a program which the voters could evaluate and which the winning party would be sacredly sworn to pursue. Thus the responsible-party doctrine runs athwart the mandate-independence controversy only in the sense that although it is all mandate, it raises questions about the means of representation in the mandate case. Most notably, it introduces the intervening mechanism of the political party.

Several ironies surround the historical evolution of the responsible-party model of popular representation. One is that it was in effect "discovered" after it had become something of a fait accompli in Great Britain, rather than existing in the minds of political philosophers before the fact. Another tantalizing irony, suggested by Eulau (1967), is the possibility that the eloquence of Burke's plea for the independence of the representative from constituency instructions stemmed from the fact that, at the time, Burke was aspiring to develop the first party caucus in Parliament, and he needed protection against the possibility that the demands of party responsibility and loyalty might require from time to time that he act directly contrary to the express instructions of the electors of Bristol!

We shall have more to say in a later chapter about the nature of the fit between a responsible-party model and the elements of the representation system assessed by the Miller-Stokes model. For now, it is worth noting that a limited part of the necessary workings of such a scheme can be seen from afar, without the need for a special study in depth. In the ideal responsible-party case, individual deputies always vote en bloc with their party caucuses, since it is part of the implicit contract with their supporters at the polls that they will do just this. The degree of party discipline in legislative voting is in most systems readily ascertainable, provided roll-call votes are recorded and caucus membership is known. In France, for example, because party discipline among deputies in the National Assembly is very strong, one key qualification for such a model already exists.[4]

At the same time, the presence of responsible-party features in a legislative system is as much a matter of degree as is behavior on the mandate-independence axis. Even in France, party discipline in roll-call voting falls discernibly short of perfection, and we shall later inquire whether these imperfections strengthen or weaken linkages between district sentiment and deputy behavior.

Moreover, caucus discipline is only one of several qualifications that must be met if a representation system is to match the ideal type specified by the responsible-party model. Another crucial qualification is that voters choose between competing party programs in casting their ballots. This qualification decomposes into a familiar chain of prerequisites, including one of voter awareness as to what those programs are. In Chapters 8 and 9 we inquired as to the clarity among the voters regarding the perceived linkages between the competing parties and candidates, on one hand, and the central policy disputes of the period, on the other. The answer was, as always, one of degree. Certainly some appropriate associations were present, but for a large majority of voters such perceived links were sketchy in the extreme. Thus if the superstructure of the representation process in France has certain architectural features that are clearly drawn to the specifications of the responsible-party model, it is uncertain that the foundations of the edifice are appropriate to it. This in turn leaves open what we may expect to find when we examine the overall representation function itself.

The three major models of the representation process that we have just described do not exhaust the possibilities, even at the level of the ideal type (see Luttbeg, 1968; and Sullivan, 1974). But they do fill in some of the most obvious reference points which we need to keep in mind as we consider the key elements in the representation process.

The Will to Represent

From the point of view of what have been called, by Wahlke, Eulau et al. (1962), legislative role styles or orientations, it would appear that the sine qua non for the representation process is some will on the part of the deputy to represent his constituency. We do not care for the moment what may generate such a motivation, whether it be an altruistic urge to serve his fellow man or a concern squeezed from him through fear of electoral reprisal. We have already suggested that almost every elected representative experiences at least some small concern about constituency representation. Even the seemingly aloof Burkean posture does not abjure a concern for constituency representation: it merely says that the good representative should attend to the constituency's interests as he sees them, and not necessarily to its expressed will, on those occasions when he believes these differ. One would certainly not expect the two to be diametrically opposed anything like half of the time. But the important conceptual point is the suggestion that if we became convinced that some specific legislator lacked even the smallest shred of concern for his constituency, as in the case of our retiring senator, then it would seem quite irrelevant to inquire further as to the nature of his constituency, its political sentiments, or other features of his relationship to it. It is in this sense that the presence of at least some marginal will to represent would appear to be a sine qua non for popular representation.

For certain definitions of representation, such an observation is true. It is almost true, but not quite, for our broader view of popular representation as a degree of congruence between constituency sentiment and representative behavior. It is not quite true because by our definition it is possible to have significant popular representation without any will to represent anything whatever on the part of the deputy. Such representation is possible even in the hypothetical case of the deputy who upon his first election leaves for the distant capital and thenceforth never receives any further news or communications from his district.

Inversely, it is possible, although unlikely, to have no trace of popular representation whatever in our sense of the term despite the presence of representatives who view their roles exclusively as instructed delegates, who invest unconscionable amounts of time in getting instructions from the home district, and who follow these instructions slavishly.

Admittedly both of these cases are oddities. They should surely not be taken as evidence that either presence or absence of a will to represent on the part of a deputy or, for that matter, a whole legislature, is inconsequential for popular representation. Such a will is, of course, of enormous importance. But tracking through these oddities on both sides is an excellent device for clarifying and justifying our definition of popular representation, particularly at its boundaries. And it can lay the groundwork for specification of the operational variables we shall later need to have in mind in order to evaluate intervening mechanisms in the representation process.

The Representative Malgré Lui

There is one intervening mechanism that can readily produce significant popular representation despite a representative who has a distaste for any effort to represent, but instead prefers to adhere religiously to the dictates of his own conscience. The mechanism is so plausible that it would take a kind of active perversity to avoid it. If the deputy has not been merely "parachuted in" to some totally alien electoral area (as is possible in the French system, among others), but rather is a native of it or at least has lived in it for some time, then the odds are that he will have internalized some of the outlooks on politics which are distinctive to his district. Even if he merely proceeds to "vote his conscience," without any reference to instructions or other current cues from his district, it is extremely likely that there will be some positive congruence between distinctive features of political sentiment in his district and his own legislative actions.

This variant on popular representation has sometimes been labeled "descriptive representation" (see, for example, Pitkin, 1967, ch. 4), and although we do not find the term very evocative, we shall adopt it to limit proliferation of jargon. Some authors have defined representation in ways which exclude descriptive representation from view entirely. In effect, from this point of view, if representation is not willful or intentional, then it does not "count" as popular representation at all.

We dislike such an exclusion. As a matter of fact, descriptive representation, in the degree it occurs, will register in our overall assessments of the popular representation function. But for once, instead of being obliged to shave a definition here and expand it there out of respect for the operational features of our measures, in this instance we are entirely pleased at a conceptual level that this registration will occur. We see no reason to want to sweep this form of representation under the rug. After all, it *is* one perfectly real form of representation: in fact, at an earlier time and under some relatively antique presuppositions, this variant was the beginning and end of what representation was supposed to be.

To be sure, it will be useful for us to make some quantitative discriminations in order to keep ourselves informed as to what portion of our popular representation function derives from such an unintentional or, as it were, "accidental" source. We are reasonably equipped to make such discriminations, and this is one important special case among several that we have in mind when we resort to such vague umbrella terms as "different intervening mechanisms" or "the nature of representation." But keeping this mechanism in plain view as one form of representation seems far preferable to using definitions which banish such unintentional representation from the field of view as being irrelevant to the general subject.

The Willing Representative Thwarted

The other odd case is much less plausible, but it is still worth mentioning. Given an elected representative determined to mirror constituency sentiments to the absolute letter, the problem often is how to learn what that district sentiment truly is. Social communication is ever problematic: and if we are talking about macrocosmic social communication (scores of thousands of constituents in each district), then we must remain aware that it suffers most of the frailties of microcosmic social communication, with a few others thrown in for good measure. This is not to imagine it likely that such a representative can find no constituents at all who are willing to instruct him on various matters. The question is whether the instructions the avid representative receives from some few, talking for the many, reflect accurately the true contours of district sentiment. In cases where these instructions are uncorrelated with actual district sentiment or, worse yet, are contrary to it, it follows that slavish obedience will produce a representative function which is null or worse. Thus the will to represent, taken alone, is less than a full assurance that popular representation will occur.

An Operational Model of the Representation Process

We are now ready to consider the portfolio of operational measurements that may shed light most efficiently on the issues surrounding the concept and practice of representation. As we have already explained at length, we interviewed a sample of the 1967 candidates, including a significant subset who won their elections and became deputies in Paris; and we also interviewed a sample of the rank-and-file voters in their constituencies. Then, after the upheavals of the spring of 1968, we returned to interview voters in a half-sample of the constituencies which had reelected their 1967 deputies, as well as voters in all the constituencies which had elected a new candidate. The question of efficiency in data specifications arises because all of these interviews were quite limited in length. Typically, they lasted about one hour; but some lasted longer, and sometimes much longer.

The minimal set of such measurements is laid out in the parent Miller-Stokes (1963, 1966) study of representation in the 1958–1960 U.S. House of Representatives. Although all sorts of measurements were taken in that study, just as in ours, four are central to the evaluation of the representation process with respect to any given issue domain. (The number of issue domains slated for investigation may vary, but the multiplier in information needs is a constant of four.) These four measurements are as follows:

(A) an expression of district sentiment on the issue, drawn from the mass interviews;

(B) a statement of the personal views, on the same issue, of each candidate competing for a seat in the district and, ultimately, of those elected to be deputies;

(C) a statement, usually drawn from the candidate or deputy interviews, of that politician's perception of district sentiment concerning the issue; and

(D) a summary expressing the roll-call record of the winning candidate or deputy on detailed chamber votes bearing on the issue.

It has become customary, again following Miller and Stokes, to organize these four measurements in the form of a diamond which is intended, at least in a crude way, to reflect differences in temporal priority, as shown in Figure 16-1.

It is important to understand what kind of model the Miller-Stokes paradigm is. It does not pretend to be a normative model like the three we have already discussed, which say in effect that the representation process ought to proceed in such and such a way. It is instead a form of litmus paper, or diagnostic model, which says that for a specific representation system observed at a given point in time, measures of these four parameters will enable us to say something useful about the nature of the representation which is occurring.

The model does not even demand that any discernible representation be occurring at all. Thus, for example, if the AD relationship (or what we

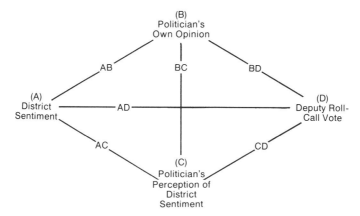

Figure 16-1. The Miller-Stokes "Diamond." Based on Warren E. Miller and Donald E. Stokes, "Constituency Influence in Congress," *American Political Science Review* 57:52.

shall call the basic representation bond) was observed in some special case to be essentially zero, then we would conclude that there was no representation with respect to that particular issue in the system in question at that time. In other words, the paradigm does not demand that there be representation in order to be useful: it purports to indicate whether some representation is occurring, in what degree, and by what pathways. It is an empirical tool, not a normative prescription.

The most interesting feature of this model is that different bonds across the diamond address quite different facets of our normative models of representation, and they do so in a remarkably efficient manner. Take, for example, the willing representative thwarted by his inability to gain accurate information about constituency opinions. By construction, he was a representative who voted whatever it was he thought his district wanted. What this means in terms of the diamond, integrated over a full legislature of such representatives, is that the CD bond must be set at 1.00, or a perfect correlation. We left the accuracy of his information as a variable, but imagined that it was so poor that his understanding of district sentiment was unrelated or perhaps even perversely related to actual district opinion. Again, integrated over a whole legislature of willing representatives so thwarted, the ailment would show up in terms of an AC bond which is at least null and perhaps even negatively related. Since in such a case the representation path is entirely confined to the ACD route, if the CD correlation is perfect by construction, then the basic representation bond, or the overall outcome represented by the AD linkage, will equal the value of the AC bond, which indexes the accuracy of the representatives' perceptions of district sentiment. If their information is so poor as to be utterly unrelated to actual sentiment, then the AD bond is also zero, and we are justified in imagining that no popular representation is occurring. If the information is worse than random, so that the AC bond is actually negative, then the AD bond will be negative as well, and we would conclude that the representation was working out not just poorly but quite perversely in an active sense.

We can trace out the relative configuration of values that the bonds in the diamond might take in terms of most of our other crucial ideal types of representatives. What is required of a legislature of pure Burkeans, for example, is that the BD bond stand at perfection (1.00). In such an instance, it does not matter how accurately such Burkean representatives gauge district sentiment, since in this instance, by construction, district sentiment is irrelevant. Some of these Burkeans may have devastatingly accurate assessments of their district, a fact which would push the AC bond toward perfection as well; or they may be quite unacquainted with their district sentiments, so that the AC bond would approach zero. In either event, it does not matter, since pure Burkeans propose in the final analysis to vote their own opinions on the issue.

What does matter, in this pure case, is the nature of the AB relationship, or the degree of natural fit between the representative's private opinion and the views of his constituency. This is important because if the BD relationship is perfect by construction, then the AD relationship, or the crucial assessment of the basic representation bond, is identical to whatever the AB relationship may happen to be. If the legislators in question are really pure Burkean, as we have imagined them to be, then we have arrived at one of our odd cases in which, from the legislator's own point of view at least, the nature of constituency sentiment is irrelevant. Nonetheless, if such representatives' own instincts resemble at all the distinctive perspectives of the constituency that spawned them, then even if such legislators were selected by some pure-chance mechanism to act as representatives for their district, we would have to imagine that their natural instincts would bear some relationship to constituency sentiment. In other words, the AB relationship would have some value greater than zero. This means in turn, in such a special case, that the AD relationship, which must be identical with this, is also greater than zero. In other words, some representation is occurring, even if the representative does not give a fig for what his constituents think. This is our case of the representative *malgré lui*.

Without pushing other scenarios, it should be clear by now that the Miller-Stokes paradigm is an extremely clever and useful diagnostic tool. It not only has the potential to detect the most famous ideal types of representation, should they ever occur in pure form in nature, but it has the capacity to indicate, on a finely graded scale, the relative degree to which one or another ideal type may be present in a situation. This is exactly what we need to describe the nature of popular representation in France, and we shall organize our presentation in ensuing chapters around this paradigm.

Nonetheless, the paradigm suffers certain limitations, and even though we propose to use it, it is important to notice what these limitations are. One limitation becomes evident even from a quick review of our three normative models of representation. The Miller-Stokes paradigm is exquisitely tailored to sort out those many controversies which arise in connection with the mandate-independence controversy. If we ask what it says about the party-responsibility model, however, the answer is reduced to the conditional and the partial. The paradigm clearly fails to illuminate the party-responsibility case in any high and instant relief. Yet it would be going too far to say that it is completely irrelevant for that model. On the one hand, certain configurations of observed values for the Miller-Stokes model do immediately blatantly disconfirm the presence of a party-responsibility system which is functioning properly. If we found such values, the party-responsibility hypothesis could be disposed of summarily. On the other hand, there are ranges of values along the various bonds of the model, any one of which would be quite reasonably congenial to the underlying operation of a pure party-responsibility system. Similarly, there are rather different configurations of values across the bonds as a set, any of which would be quite compatible with the functioning of a party-responsibility model.

Thus, however finely tuned the Miller-Stokes model may be to diagnose the mandate-independence axis, it is less discriminating with respect to the party-responsibility model. Therefore we shall supplement our use of this model with other kinds of analyses aimed at bringing the party-responsibility possibility into clearer focus.

Absolute versus Relative Congruence

The statistics conventionally used to express the relative strength of the bonds in the Miller-Stokes model are simple correlation coefficients, although for certain purposes standardized regression coefficients may be used as well. Such expressions of relatedness have the attractive property that they can be expected to "norm" between 0.00 and 1.00, where zero indicates no association whatever, and one indicates perfect association, in either a negative or positive direction.

The assumptions underlying these normed statistics are such that they index a *relative* kind of association or congruence, not an absolute kind. This is a distinction which does not exercise many scholars, because it would be a relatively rare data configuration from which one would draw vastly different conclusions according to which type of congruence was assessed. But because we are operating in a setting that is somewhat more likely to produce divergences than is true elsewhere, it is worth making the distinction entirely clear.

Let us erect a case involving representatives and constituencies where relative congruence is perfect but absolute *in*congruence seems frightening. We need scales for both the representatives and the represented which can be expressed in common, and it would be useful if they involved intuitively familiar units of absolute measurement. Let us use dollars to be spent for some government program. Over a full set of constituencies, the constituents most wildly enthusiastic about the program are willing to spend a million dollars of tax money for it, whereas in some other constituencies, hardly anybody wants to spend anything for it. In the legislature, enthusiasts feel that in order to give the program any fair chance, $100 million must be allocated to it. At the other extreme, resistant representatives find some attractions in the program, but would like streamlining and a pilot program first; so they want to spend $2 million on it. The mean preferred expenditure among voters is $7,000. The mean preferred expenditure among representatives is $60 million, a figure which in an absolute sense seems utterly incongruent with constituent preferences. What about the level of *relative* congruence between preferred means from constituency to constituency, paired with the specific dollar preferences of their representatives?

Thus far the data we have specified have foreclosed no possibilities, and the correlations indexing the level of congruence can range from a perfect positive association to a perfect negative one. The perfect positive relationship is easily realized if the lowest bidder in the legislature represents the constituency with the lowest mean preference, the highest bidder the constituency with the highest mean preference, and all the other pairings follow between these two proportionately (see Figure 16-2). In this case, *relative* congruence is perfect, but our sense of absolute incongruence is strong.[5]

How do we evaluate a case like this in terms of popular representation? On one hand, the dollar discrepancy is painful. On the other, it would be hard to argue that the perfect relative congruence is a meaningless datum with respect to representation processes, particularly as the same dollar discrepancy could co-occur with no association between representative and dis-

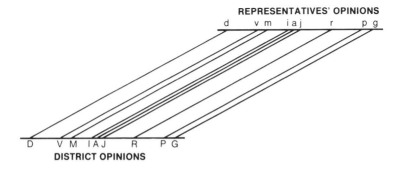

(a) Perfect relative congruence, but absolute incongruence.

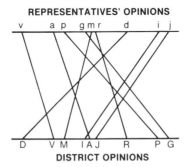

(b) Absolute congruence, but no relative congruence.

Figure 16-2. Absolute vs. relative congruence.

trict, or even with a perfect negative association. Indeed, in this case, one would suspect that the signs of relative congruence may be considerably more significant than the actual dollar discrepancy, since it would be easy to suppose that the public, unaccustomed to the orders of magnitude of dollars involved in public treasuries or in large-scale public programs, might have intended to talk like their representatives but were simply off by a few magnitudes. Perhaps if the same question had been reworded for the mass respondents in some belittling currency, such as cents per taxpayer per year, the response preferences, properly multiplied back, would have shown a very neat absolute fit with the representatives' preferences, as well as the perfect but relative one. Thus it is quite possible that the assessment of relative congruence may actually be more interesting, from the point of view of representation, than the question of absolute fit.

Of course, it is easy to construct the diametrically opposed example, in which the absolute fit is perfect in the aggregate between mass and elite (in our dollar example, identical means or even further moments of distribution), but the district-level relative congruence is either missing or is actually perverse. If the legislature votes to allocate exactly that mean figure, the most ardent champion of democratic theory can scarcely feel wronged, for the people are supposedly getting exactly what they want. Nonetheless, if the underlying relative congruence is absent or perverse, then the happiness of the outcome would seem to stem from processes which have nothing to do with the infrastructure of a popular representation system, including contests between competing candidates in local districts and continued district influence on the winning candidate. The coincidence of overall preference distributions between representatives and the represented may not be a complete accident, in view of the fact that both populations are living in the same time and place, with some common frames of reference which constrain such aggregate distributions to a high degree of fit. But the emergence of fit in such a case has totally bypassed the popular representation system, so that most observers would conclude that popular representation has not occurred.[6]

The virtue of providing two peculiar, polar-case examples of the divergence of absolute congruence from relative congruence is to edify the reader as clearly and as quickly as possible concerning the distinction between the two criteria. The danger in choosing such examples is the unintended implication that the two criteria may be at odds much of the time and thus may yield quite different impressions. Actually, there is little reason to suppose that the two diverge by very much with any frequency. We cannot, in our normal case, evaluate the possibility as incisively as we would like, for we are never measuring preferences with crisp dollar scales, but rather with self-locations on ordinal attitudinal scales where units have a good deal of the arbitrary about them. Yet there are usually some implicit anchors beneath the arbitrary categories that are likely to be taken for granted by both the mass and the elite respondents, such as the locus "where we are now" as a point of departure from which one can either push forward in a policy area or retreat in the opposite direction.

Individual versus Cross-District Fit

Achen (1978), in a perceptive critique of the use of measures of fit which standardize away absolute differences in scales, as does the correlation coefficient, has suggested three competing measures which capture different facets of the representation relationship, while still paying attention to the absolute scores assigned to the representative and the represented. One of these, a measure called "responsiveness," is essentially captured by the correlation coefficient or standardized regression coefficient, although Achen advocates the use of the corresponding expressions of regression with unstandardized coefficients, a practice which would provide an immediate tip-off (in the large intercept term) that our perfect relative congruence on the budgetary issue was coupled with a major discontinuity in absolute terms.[7]

The other two measures Achen suggests both hinge in a direct way on the actual absolute scale scores assigned to representatives and constituents on specific issue dimensions. They serve to highlight another frailty of the use of correlations to measure the degree of fit, a frailty closely related to the preceding limitation. Because correlations depend on variance, which is a group property, a correlational statement is somewhat shaped by features of the social context that may be extraneous for the kinds of conclusions we might like to draw. We stumbled over this difficulty earlier, when we wished to talk of the hypothetical Burkean legislator whose parliamentary vote must fit his private opinion. To express the matter in correlational terms fitting the Miller-Stokes model, we were obliged to insert a phrase like "across a whole legislature (of such types)," in order to say that the correlation would be perfect, since there is no such thing as a correlation between a single representative's opinion on an issue and his vote on that issue. And even this insertion is inadequate unless the social context provides variation in both opinion and votes.

We do not usually have trouble finding variation in political opinion in legislatures. But the dependence on the backdrop of the collectivity remains troublesome when we wish to make individual-level statements. And if we are confident enough about the adequacy of our measurement, there is a straightforward way to make such statements. If, for example, we wish to discuss the degree of fit between the opinion held by a specific representative and the corresponding opinion held by a single one of his constituents, then we can look at the simple difference between the representative's score of, say, 5, and the score of the constituent. If the constituent is also a 5, then the fit is perfect. If the constituent is a 4, the "distance" between them is 1; if he is a 3, the distance is 2, and so on. This measure of proximity depends on no other scores attributed to other actors.

Achen's second measure, which uses such distance scores, takes the mean of their squared values for any given constituency, as the measure of the *proximity* of a given representative to his constituency. His third measure, which concerns the *centrism* of a representative, is the difference between the representative's proximity score and the variance in district opinion, which happens to be the minimum proximity score that an agile representative could achieve by perfect positioning relative to the distribution of opinion in his constituency.

These three competing measures are interesting supplements to the social relativity of the currency of correlation or regression. They are quite unpalatable, of course, as Achen recognizes, unless the details of measurement for the representative and for the represented have been carried out in common terms, such as the same numerical scoring of the same response categories to the same stimulus items. Where our own linkage issues are concerned, some are neatly commensurate but others are not. In some instances, for example, mass respondents were asked closed, agree-disagree items, whereas elite respondents were asked open-ended questions; and the lengthy responses were later coded onto a continuum ranging from the most unqualified agreement to the most unqualified disagreement, usually in steps not easily relatable to the mass response categories.[8] We shall, however, use those linkage items which were elicited in identical ways at both levels to consider what differences in impressions about the nature of representation these more absolute formulations convey, relative to our normal currency of correlation and regression.

The Problem of District Heterogeneity

We said earlier in the chapter that one portentous aspect of our context is that each representative must represent not one other person, but many. In laying out some of the fundamental models of representation and considering what operations we may use to address them, we have built up a vocabulary which enables us to return to the problem of representation on a more abstract and formal level, to see just how portentous some of these features of our context are.

When, as is always the case, the representative has multiple constituents, it is likely that they do not speak to him in a single voice but that they show some heterogeneity of opinion. This is an aspect of the representation problem which classical theory very nearly ignores. A frequent counsel of despair in the literature, after the author's frustrating struggle with the metaphysics of the representation concept, is the observation that it is hard enough to see how an agent can represent even one other person, let alone a number of them at one time. Even Pitkin's (1967) extended treatment of the concept contains but a brief mention of the multiple-constituent problem.

To be sure, we cannot proceed to the multiple-constituent problem without a simplifying assumption concerning the representative's capacity to size up the wishes and situation of any single constituent with regard to any policy issue. This is unquestionably problematic, especially if the constituent himself is uncertain about that issue, or if the constituent is certain but there are features of his situation that might lead the representative to doubt that he understands his own best interests. Our starting assumption, however, is that the representative is able to arrive at what seems to be an acceptable summary of the will or interest of any constituent to whom he has access, with respect to any policy issue. Later we can relax this assumption of every constituent's clarity of position on a given issue.

We shall start with the very simplest version of such a nose-counting operation, one which is rather trivial, but which sets the stage for the layers of aggregation of the problem to which we shall later proceed. Let us suppose that there is a pending political issue on which the representative of a single constituency must cast a vote of the familiar binary kind—aye or nay, black or white. Each constituent is clearly of one conviction or the other—black or white. Let us make use of the familiar sampling metaphor, likening the constituency to an urn and each constituent to one of the black and white balls filling the urn.

For the single constituency, a simple continuum of possibilities is pertinent, represented by the proportions of black and white balls in the urn. The proportion is all that we shall vary for the moment, and the variation will be entirely orderly. Let us go to two polar cases.

In the first case, all the balls in the urn are black. This means perfect homogeneity of the electorate and therefore no "representation problem," if by that term we refer to some felt difficulty on the part of the representative. In every direction the representation "problem" is trivialized virtually out of existence. Since the representative himself was selected from this urn of black balls, he himself must be black. Thus even if he is more extreme than the classic Burkean, in insisting on private conscience without considering the district at all, he will vote black; and in the sense of descriptive representation he will perfectly represent his district although ignoring it completely. If, however, he is not a Burkean but instead is eager to represent the constituency's wishes, then his functional problem—discovering whether the constituency does indeed have some definable position or "instruction" on the matter—may not be solvable, for realistically he cannot assess all of the—say, 80,000—balls in the urn. (It is important to maintain this one realistic point of imperfect information.) But it is clear that this assessment step is at its formal minimum with respect to difficulty. If the representative has seen 800 balls with his own eyes, and they are all black, then his doubts about instructions are certainly minimal. But if he is socially sophisticated, his doubts do not go away because he knows that the balls in the urn are not randomly mixed, but rather are organized into strata and social network clusters. Thus it is possible that whereas the top 10,000 balls in the urn, including his own and all 800 of his contacts, are black, the lower 70,000 are all white. Further, if he is not only sophisticated but zealous, he may go out of his way to check other balls known to be lodged in other regions of the urn: those representing the local shop steward, the taxi driver, and so on. If all of these further contacts report not only that they too are black, but also that they themselves have never seen a white ball in the urn, then it may be the most comfortable legislative vote the representative ever casts.

At the opposite pole is the second case, in which the constituency urn contains an equal number of black and white balls. Here heterogeneity achieves its logical maximum, or homogeneity its logical minimum. If perfect representation is inevitable in the case of perfect homogeneity, here representation is undefined and impossible, at least if the delegate is expected to vote in a manner which pleases more constituents than it displeases. The last finger hold for descriptive representation despite a Burkean posture has vanished. The delegate seeking instructions can naturally try to avoid the impasse by abstaining, or can outflank it by redefining what his constituency is in terms of some subset, such as those who voted for him, who are much less likely to show an even split. But for the moment, such redefinition is not permitted. And if this representative sets out doggedly to canvass his constituency in the hope of finding some clear instruction, it will turn out that no sampling strategy will suffice: he must sort and count to the very last ball, and will still come away empty-handed.

We have delineated a continuum ranging from a case of perfect homogeneity at one pole to a case of perfect heterogeneity at the other, and since the latter is defined as the point where intraconstituency variance has achieved its maximum (decreasing to zero variance in the former case), there are obviously several quantitative indices that would express the locations of intervening cases. Since one pole defines representation which is inevitable and the other that which is impossible, it is easy to imagine that at intervening locations representation is correspondingly either more or less difficult to achieve, so that realistic details about district homogeneity are of great relevance for any understanding of representation. We shall argue exactly this, although one expansion of the argument needs to be made in the process. It may seem at first glance that our case is too preciously rigged in the exact 50–50 instance, even though we were looking for a logical pole. If there is even one black ball unmatched by a white one—a count, say, of

40,000 to 39,999—then the representative has his instructions and he is home free.

Such an argument has merit chiefly because in an ethos in which majority rule is used as a decision calculus, there is indeed a major step function at about 50–50. This is not only important, but it is clearly crucial. Nonetheless, if we turn the matter back to the broader range of functional problems surrounding the one representing the many, it is not clear that an excess of one ball in some 80,000 creates a dramatic change in the situation. Obviously, the change can be dramatized by saying (referring to any representation at all), "What was once impossible is now possible," and that, too, has the feel of a major step change about it. But for all practical purposes, the difficulties remain imposing. There is a faint edge for the operation of descriptive representation, but it is so vanishingly small as not to be there for any practical purpose. The delegate seeking instructions will be as confused by his partial samples as he was before, and even if he is moderately lucky he will have to sort and count to nearly the last ball, or perhaps to the very last ball, to be sure.

In short, it would seem indisputable that the difficulty of achieving representation is a potent, monotonically increasing function of district heterogeneity. This is, of course, tautologically true if success in representation is defined as the ratio of happy to unhappy constituents after the representative's vote has been publicized. But the same observation clearly embraces a lot of the intervening stages of the representation process, including the anguish of the representative himself.

Given its absolutely pivotal role in modifying the character of popular representation, the relative neglect of the heterogeneity-homogeneity dimension in earlier conceptual work on representation is rather surprising. Students of representation have been rectifying this neglect in the past decade or so. For example, Fiorina's modeling of legislator decisionmaking relative to constituency pressures is based on the distinction between "conflictual" and "consensual" districts, labels which refer to exactly the same dimension (Fiorina, 1977). Similarly, Fenno (1978, p. 4), after years of conversing with flesh-and-blood representatives about their home districts, notes that the most prominent dimension in these discussions is the representative's view of the homogeneity or heterogeneity of the district, and that no other dimension more "illuminates" his or her subsequent behavior.[9]

Several generalizations from the simple case are within immediate reach. Let us imagine, for example, that constituents' positions are not limited to black or white, but can vary in shades of gray between the extremes, with a midpoint case of indifference. Again, we can describe a pole of maximal heterogeneity in a univariate sense, which arises in the constituency that is still evenly divided but completely polarized, with no leavening shades of gray to intervene. The other case is that of no variance whatever:

there may be a wider variety of possible urns in this instance, since intervening shades are now permitted, but the important point remains that all balls in the given urn are of the same shade.

Although in most instances the representative must vote either aye or nay, he is not without a great variety of ways of responding to the degree of homogeneity of opinion in his constituency on the issue. If his district is homogeneous and extreme, he has all sorts of incentives not merely to vote for the issue, but also to be "out front" on the issue in every way he can manage. He can help initiate bills to epitomize the position, lobby for them with public pronouncements, twist the arms of indifferent colleagues, or trade vote promises with them, and the like. If the district is maximally heterogeneous on an issue—particularly one of exceptional public visibility—he can sit on his hands and wish it would go away, if he cannot himself go away at convenient moments.

The most interesting developments from the initial formal case, however, lie less in this direction than in the direction of aggregation from the single district, with its single representative, to an accumulation of such districts, each with its own distinctive index of homogeneity-heterogeneity, until the "constituency of the whole" is accounted for. Again, we can turn to some interesting limiting cases. The least interesting is the polar case in which all districts represented in the legislature are perfectly homogeneous internally and are identical in viewpoint even from one district to another, so that discrepancies (variance) between districts are zero, just as they are within districts. This is the limiting case of perfect consensus across the total population. A much more interesting polar case is one in which all districts are perfectly homogeneous internally, but nevertheless differ from one another. All variance in the total population lies across constituency lines, with none within. Another, diametrically opposed, configuration is one in which all opinion variance in the total population is, as it were, trapped within constituencies taken separately, and there is none between constituencies: all districts show exactly the same overall division of opinion, and each district is a perfect microcosm of the whole.

None of these absolutely limiting cases is likely to occur in nature in political systems of any size. "Real" representation systems are likely to lie somewhere in between. A familiar way of specifying the location of such intervening systems, if they lean more toward the intradistrict variance pole, is by a measure called eta, which is simply the ratio of the between-district variance to the total observed variance. That is,

$$\text{eta} = \frac{\text{between-district variance}}{\text{between-district variance} + \text{within-district variance}}$$

This eta measure is bounded from zero to one.

Why might such an expression be of interest? Remembering that we are still at the single-variable or single-issue level with respect to such an expression (since the "variance" referred to is univariate), we can imagine that any expression of this kind might itself take rather different values from one domain of policy conflict to another within a system. If the value of the *eta* statistic in a given issue domain, or policy area, is high, it signifies a domain in which effective representation comes easily because district differences tend to be clear. But if that value in a given policy area is low, suggesting that most districts agree, then we also need to know what the overall distribution of opinion in that domain may be. If districts resemble one another in displaying a rather lopsided margin for or against some policy proposal, then representation of the whole population is relatively easy and likely, although when district-by-district variation in the overall opinion division is really tiny, we shall not find much patterning of representatives' votes in terms of those district differences. The fact of the matter is, however, that political systems do not come to rest for very long on proposals that are easy for most participants to accept or to reject.[10] In the nature of things, much time and effort, not to say rancor, is expended on proposals that tend to divide combatants rather evenly. In such a case, with many districts nearly equally divided and differentiation between districts at a low ebb, the whole representation process becomes quite cloudy.

Axelrod (1970) has pointed out that the formal conflict-of-interest measure he uses works out in our context to be nothing more than the variance of an opinion distribution. He also hypothesizes that when each district in a representation system is a heterogeneous microcosm of national opinion variation (when eta is toward the low side), political competition tends to get worked out at the district level, and legislative debate is relatively moderate. When, however, each district is relatively homogeneous but between-district variance is high, political conflict at the local level is minimal and societal conflict is pushed upward to the system legislature, where representatives confront one another. Although each representative has clear instructions (or, in the sense of descriptive representation, a high probability of a clear and distinctive "conscience"), these instructions are diametrically opposed. The stage is set for very clear representation, but also for maximal legislative conflict.

It is for reasons such as this that differences in the nestings of opinion variance captured by the eta statistic are of intrinsic interest, not only with regard to the operations of the representative process, but also with regard to the more general tenor of national political life.

Territorial Differentiation of Issue Positions

Turning from formal theory to flesh-and-blood representation systems, we can legitimately ask whether, in such real systems, issues show sufficient variation in the eta statistic for these hypothesized differences in the tenor of representation by policy domain to be clearly discernible. For a variety of realistic considerations, it is likely that the empirical values of eta would lie somewhere nearer to the midpoint, for any given system, than to zero or one; and whether within such a range actual issue differentiation with respect to the eta expression is high enough to make much difference is a reasonable question.

Our study design permits us to arrive at a proper estimate of the eta statistic for each of the measures of political sentiment which we shall use as linkage issues to predict from district feeling to representative behavior. We find empirically that across eighteen issue measures (some overlapping in substance) chosen for their centrality in national political disputes of the period in France, the eta measures for all eighty-six districts of our design range from a low of .21 to a high of .41. Even this range, which is not large, can be a bit misleading due to a few outliers. A full half of the values observed lie between .277 and .306. In parallel estimations made for the United States in the later 1950s, or for West Germany about 1970 (Farah, 1980), values of eta for central political issues are again extremely common in the .28–.30 range. Of course these latter statements expressly aim at "middling" issues, and if we are interested in whether differences in etas associated with particular issues do have some broader consequence for the character of representation, then we are concerned to compare the relatively regional or sectional disputes displaying etas as high as .41 (for France), with those so regionally homogeneous as to show etas of only .21.

The first important point, however, is the suggestion that in these Western democracies, in the current period, within-district variation considerably outweighs between-district variation, but between-district variation can nonetheless be counted on to be much less than trivial. The second point is that the range of variation, as indexed by eta, is restricted for such issues most of the time. Perhaps it is too restricted for us to expect the majority of issues to show much differentiation in representation or to expect those variations in the locus of conflict suggested by theory.

At the same time, it is worth reflecting on how these etas arise, and why within-district variance tends to predominate in political systems of this kind. One thing that most democracies have in common is that the constituency, being in fact a geographical district, is *territorially* defined. Now if territory, in the "pure-geography" sense, were overwhelmingly correlated with political antagonisms, as it tends to be in the case of a so-called regional or sectional issue, then one might expect etas in territorially defined constituencies to increase very substantially. But pure geography is not obviously aligned with the axes of most issue disputes in such systems; and despite the recrudescence of irredentist movements around the marches of many modern states, it appears that purely regional issues have, over the past century, undergone a secular decline in intensity through the progressive "nationalization" of most political controversies (see Stokes, 1965).

If we ask when, in sheer flesh-and-blood terms, we have witnessed situations where the axes of political dispute have come into close alignment with pure geography, the American observer is apt to think of the controversy over the abolition of slavery which, in the mid-nineteenth century, precipitated the Civil War. It is well known, of course, that the correlation between pure geography and political positions on slavery did not even then achieve perfection. There were minorities, even of whites, scattered across the South, who were sympathetic to the abolitionist cause; and similarly, there were copperheads, or Southern sympathizers, residing in the North. Hence we cannot believe that the relevant eta statistics, if they had been known for the abolition issue in this period, would have approached unity, or complete district heterogeneity, unmixed with any residual within-district variance of opinion.

Nonetheless, it is fair to suppose that such relevant etas would have risen to very high levels on the abolition issue, particularly if blacks were considered to be excluded from the political system. And such a conjunction between the lines of policy cleavage and the territorial bases of the representation system did indeed force the bitterest debates upward into the halls of Congress, generating such a grievous polarization in that body that secession and civil war became the only modes of conflict resolution.

There are no twentieth-century political issues in the United States which could match the abolition question in geographical heterogeneity, although civil-rights controversies since World War II have provided a mirror of that earlier explosion. Some of the clarity of the earlier sectional polarization has been muffled by the progressive enfranchisement of blacks in the South, a trend which obviously heightens within-district variance of opinion on racial policy at the expense of between-district heterogeneity, and which has indeed resulted in greater conflict at the local level with correspondingly less conflict at the apex of the representation system. Nonetheless, regional differentiation on racial policy remained strong enough through the late 1950s and early 1960s to give shape to the Miller-Stokes (1963) conclusion that in the 1958–1960 House of Representatives there was significantly sharper popular representation in the domain of civil rights than in the domain of either social welfare or foreign policy.[11]

Of course, it is possible for the conjunction of political disputes with geographical terrain to occur without confrontations between large regional blocs when representation districts are drawn much more finely than major national regions, as they are in most countries. Another familiar configuration that lends itself to relatively high between-district differentiation (and high etas) is that involving disputes between city and countryside, since that distinction is once again defined in intrinsically geographic terms. Thus although there is in most systems a very significant intermediate leaven of districts sufficiently spacious to embrace both cities and large rural environs, the greatest metropolises contain not only many thoroughly urban districts but also, despite the advances of urbanization, some districts that are purely rural. In territorially defined representation systems, then, eta values computed by district for attributes like population density or "urbanicity" will necessarily be quite high.

The existence of such high etas does not in itself say much about political conflict, except as political issues arise on which urban and rural populations tend to have contrary viewpoints. Such issues, which are not wanting in most systems, include matters like farm subsidies and tariff questions, or more recently, the concentration of social welfare expenditures in inner-city areas. In somewhat more diluted form, one might add a range of "moral" issues, where cosmopolitan areas tend to form the cutting edge of social change and rural areas to be the rearguard of protection for tradition. But between the rapid shrinkage of farm populations and the increased access of national media to even the most remote rural areas, the tightness of the fit between urban-rural residence and political interests and viewpoints has suffered a visible decline in the twentieth century. Nonetheless, it is worth recognizing that, for the reasons our formal model has suggested, the coincidence of territorially defined representation districts with urban-rural differentiations has kept related issues much more at the "front and center" of legislative dispute than might otherwise be the case. The high etas betoken a kind of multiplier effect, where conflict at the apex of the representation system is concerned.

At the same time, the territorial definition of districts serves to reduce the rancor of legislative conflict concerning the perennial axes of dispute that coincide poorly with pure geography. Class conflict is an excellent example. To be sure, with the growth of large urban concentrations divided into increasingly fine geographic districts, the phenomenon of relatively pure "silk-stocking" districts pitted against relatively pure ghetto districts increases. Nonetheless, these remain extreme cases in most legislative systems, and a great majority of districts are internally quite heterogeneous in their social structure. District etas on social class measurements are thus subdued. In the same vein, the fair similarity of sex ratios across territorial representation districts, joined to the fact that viewpoints on sex roles are only moderately related to citizen gender in any event, produces very limited etas on issues involving women's rights. On all such matters, within-district dispute is likely to overshadow conflict at the legislative level. Finally, and despite a modicum of geographic differentiation in the case of districts built economically on defense industries, the whole realm of foreign policy is relatively sheltered from any stark polarization of viewpoints between districts.

During the past century, France has not been gripped by issues involving such depths of regional confrontation as those marking the abolition or civil-rights questions in the United States. Nonetheless, conflicting viewpoints between rural and urban areas, with Paris itself constituting a unique urban area, have become just as familiar as those in other territorially defined representation systems. If we look to other axes of dispute where geographic differentiation might be high for less obvious reasons, we are apt to think of sociological studies (for example, Boulard, 1950) that document the degree to which France is a geographical patchwork of zones, some of which are proclerical (where the practice of Catholicism is devout), and others which are at least secular, and sometimes animatedly anticlerical. This territorial differentiation shows up clearly in our own results: the highest eta for a nongeographical attribute, the value of .41 cited earlier, characterizes our measure of religiosity based on reports of frequency of Catholic church attendance.[12]

Otherwise, there is not much reason to expect France to differ notably from other modern states in the degree to which the lines of political dispute cut across purely geographic boundaries. Thus, for example, most *circonscriptions* (electoral districts) include some approximate microcosm of the national class structure, and hence etas for the classic issues of the socioeconomic left-right tendency are fairly moderate (around .30). And although there are exceptions (the eta for the importance of French independence of U.S. foreign policy, for example, is a surprising .35), the lowest etas across our set of linkage issues tend to cluster in the domains of foreign policy debate.

The Design of
Representation Systems

We have been arguing that the tenor of representation processes tends to vary across issue domains according to the degree that policy polarizations in the populace tend to coincide with the geographic partitioning of representative constituencies. In this discussion we have taken the fact of territorial constituencies as a given. From the viewpoint of Anglo-Saxon practice, as well as that of most of western Europe and of the many countries on other continents that have used Anglo-Saxon systems as models for their own political institutions, it is indeed easy to equate popular representation with geographic districts, just as though alternatives were impossible.

This is, however, a kind of myopia. Representation systems are consciously designed by political architects, and there are many ways to define a constituency. In fact, it would be possible, if not very plausible, to define such a system in order to maximize the entity indexed by the eta statistic. We noted earlier that the sexes and gender role attitudes are so well shuffled across gross geographic partitions that relevant etas by territorially defined constituencies are not likely to be very high. But why leave representation to mere geography? Why not say that women form one constituency and men the other, and that each will elect a representative or representatives to deliberate and formulate policies in areas of gender roles? If, however, the game is to maximize the etas, and, with them, the clarity of constituency instructions, this "treatment" may not be sufficiently potent; as we have noted, some women are strongly resistant to the advocacy of women's rights, and some men are highly sympathetic to these rights. But we can go further. We can say that citizens who favor women's rights, whatever their own gender, will constitute one constituency; citizens opposing such measures will form another; and those who are indifferent will form still a third. Thus in principle we can design constituencies in such a fashion as to bring the relevant eta all the way up to unity.

It should not necessarily be assumed at this point that high etas are a political desideratum. The question is a thoroughly normative one. On the one hand, the convinced populist democrat, who wants constituency instructions to be unmistakable in order to control errant representatives, is likely to want constituencies designed in such a way as to produce high etas. On the other hand, it can easily be argued that constituencies should be designed to keep etas modest, so that political conflict will be more evenly distributed between system levels instead of being exclusively concentrated at the apex occupied by the legislative arena. The choice of geographic districts as representation units seems to accomplish this end very nicely, although, since it is only one partitioning criterion among a very large number which would accomplish the same cross-cutting ends, it has an element of the arbitrary about it.

While our example of defining constituencies in ways which would maximize gender-role representation may seem fanciful, the design strategy is not at all unfamiliar in real-life representation settings. Even within the Anglo-Saxon tradition, persons selected or even elected to serve as representatives in many bargaining sessions, such as labor-management negotiations, are scarcely chosen with a view to particular pieces of terrain, but rather as known spokesmen or spokeswomen for one of the two conflicting interests. Such arrangements maximize etas by constituency: the likelihood of vigorous descriptive representation is assured, and "instructions," at least at the level of broad interests, are starkly clear in any event. If the two camps trying to bargain their way to agreement cannot achieve it—an outcome which is rather common—then a third party may be called in, now chosen quite specifically to *minimize* apparent predispositions toward the substance of the dispute.

Such representation designed around interest constituencies rather than territorial constituencies has not, of course, been historically limited to bargaining situations, but has also been common in national deliberative bodies. Indeed, this is basically the design strategy built into the corporatist state, as well as into numerous current Communist polities. Society is seen as an amalgam of interests whose differences must be ironed out by the state with its function of the authoritative allocation of values. Given such a view, it is entirely natural to convene assemblies of representatives of these interests to deliberate upon their reconciliation. Indeed, this could easily be claimed to be a much more natural procedure than selection by territorial units, save in polities where some of the main lines of interest cleavage are themselves sectional or regional, due to sharp economic diversity or regional clusterings of ethnic groups. Of course, there is no reason why, in systems of this design, regional or ethnic interests cannot be given an explicit part, along with labor, business, the church, landowners, and the other "estates" taken as constituencies.

Since representation based on interest constituencies will, in one sense at least, almost invariably produce clearer constituency instructions and more firmly assured descriptive representation than representation based on territory, it is interesting to consider why ardent democrats usually loathe such corporatist systems. Some of the reasons are historical accidents which reflect no necessary features of these designs. The most obvious is that corporatist representation has often tended to be carried out by executive appointment rather than by constituency election. This is obviously repugnant, almost by definition, to the observer with democratic convictions. But such selection of representatives from on high is not an intrinsic requirement of the design. Corporatist systems can and have functioned with more, as well as less, thorough within-constituency election mechanisms. Still, the democrat finds them dubious.

There are at least two major reasons, not entirely unrelated, which raise doubts as to whether such systems can be democratically or even "fairly" defined. One doubt springs from the difficulty of drawing up the list of recognized interest constituencies. There is obviously great latitude for unfair elite manipulation in that process. Some interests that to outside observers may appear to be lively and urgent, but which are threatening to the system architects, can simply be disposed of by leaving them off the list. Furthermore, even when the best democratic will prevails among the architects, defining such a list is an extremely ambiguous task because groups with discriminable political interests exist in very large number. Obviously the list must be restricted to a manageable set of relatively important interests, but how is "important" even to be defined?

Assuming that such a list can be completed, there remains the problem of establishing which set of individual citizens can be said to be members of each interest constituency and hence eligible to participate in the election of representatives. A pleasing feature of constituencies that are territorially defined is that, aside from a few fringe problems associated with mobility and multiple residences, geographic partitions place all citizens in mutually exclusive and exhaustive constituencies. Interest constituencies are much more awkward and unclear. Some citizens, for example, will have a legitimate claim to membership in two or more constituencies. And unless the list of interest constituencies is much more extensive than is customary in such systems, it is likely that a substantial minority of citizens will have no claim to any particular constituency membership, and thus will be virtually disfranchised. From the point of view of the democrat imbued with an ethic of "one man, one vote," the interest constituency design approaches the monstrous.

The second reason why the interest constituency design raises doubts stems from the fact that national legislatures are not special-purpose bargaining sessions convened to resolve a single conflict of interest. They are, instead, general-purpose deliberative assemblies expected to legislate on all manner of policy disputes.

The General-Purpose Assembly

The last feature of our context for studying representation is the standard legislature or parliament where representatives are called upon to exercise their judgment on a very wide variety of policy dimensions—indeed, the full range of concerns which the governance of the modern state requires. In view of this specification, it is likely that a territorial base for constituencies makes up for some of the disadvantages such a design might otherwise be thought to suffer, relative to the interest-constituency design of the corporatist model.

At this point we can return to a consideration of such phenomena as constituency heterogeneity or homogeneity in a much fuller way, that is, to the eta statistic we have used to index locations on a heterogeneity-homogeneity continuum, which in its conventional use is a unidimensional or single-interest expression. When Fenno's (1978) legislators complained of unusual heterogeneity in their districts, they presumably were talking in a fuller, multidimensional way. To be sure, if some single axis of policy dispute were of overriding concern to a particular constituency, but the within-district polarization on the issue was intense, then undoubtedly such a state of affairs would register with the troubled representative as a threatening degree of heterogeneity. But the multidimensional sense of disparate concerns, lighting on quite unrelated issue axes, is undoubtedly at stake in these complaints as well. The prototypic "heterogeneous" district is an amalgam of farmers in open country with one bundle of concerns, well-to-do suburbanites with a different set of sensitivities, and urbanites, perhaps split in turn into ethnic factions, who focus largely on still another domain of policy disputes. This is heterogeneity in a multidimensional sense, and one which obviously concerns representatives elected to any general-purpose assembly.

Pitkin has noted the degree to which Edmund Burke thought of representation in terms of a limited set of fixed and disembodied interests for the whole country, "of which any group or locality has just one" (Pitkin, 1967, p. 174). The constituency of Bristol, for example, represented the mercantile interest, and (in Burke's attendant concept of "virtual representation") it could represent that interest perfectly well for all the other centers of shipping and commerce in Britain, wherever they might be located. Similarly, other constituencies were seen as fit to represent the professional interest, or perhaps the agricultural interest.

Just as Burke's view of the representative role is hard to distinguish from a doctrine that has been labeled "paternalism" in Latin political cultures, so his view of the nature of interests and their desirable political expressions blends at most points with the assumptions that underlie the corporatist model of interest constituencies. Indeed, in some ways, the corporatist model might seem more consistent than the territorial model, since the primitivism of the single-interest assumption is less apparent if the constituency is limited to a particular interest group than it is when, as for Burke, the constituency is territorially defined. Bristol was not merely a dormitory for shippers and dockworkers, but a city with a complex occupational structure, including many members for whom mercantile issues had very little relevance.

Any general-purpose assembly deals with a large range of issues, virtually all of which touch directly on the vital interests of some segment of the society, but only a limited fraction of which mesh obviously into the concerns of a "shipping interest" or an "agricultural interest." It is because of this that the clarity of the representation process which an interest-constituency design can claim (as symbolized by high etas where its own immediate interests are at stake) begins to unravel badly beyond a certain point. The clarity of instructions from the interest constituency may be extremely high on the narrow range of disputes which are most relevant to it. But this clarity dies out rapidly in the remaining areas of dispute, which typically make up more than half of those to be handled, and which are largely irrelevant to this particular interest group and cross-cut its membership in unpredictable ways.

Advocates of the corporatist model of representation have a ready answer to such difficulties, and the answer is not particularly at odds with the fuller view of representation which Burke developed. It can be maintained that the society is an organic whole, and that any national political decision must by definition be of concern to the more parochial interest groups which form the parts and hence are dependent on the welfare of the whole. Thus there is no such thing as a decision which is irrelevant to an interest constituency, and Burke's admonitions to the representative to set aside local prejudices in favor of judgments of the interests of the nation as a whole follow the same line of thought admirably. Presumably, the good representative of an interest constituency is a source of inside information as to constituency needs and is an advocate of its interests on issues of the most vital relevance to it. On other issues, where other constituencies have much more at stake, his role is to sort out the conflicting advocacies and cast his weight for the resolution which seems to hew most closely to the interests of the nation as a whole.

This is not an unreasonable argument or prescription, although it does require an imposing level of faith that, amid the welter of conflicting claims, a line of national interest can be detected. It also largely disposes of the constituency, at least in areas outside those of most immediate concern to it, so that any notion of popular representation is greatly narrowed. This would not have troubled Burke, but it is one of the difficulties that the modern democratic observer is likely to have with the model.

Whatever attenuation of nongeographic interests will inevitably accompany a representation system defined on territorial lines, the mechanism does make itself available not only for some degree of popular representation in the "one man, one vote" sense on the full range of issues normally confronted by the assembly, but also vis-à-vis emergent issues that had not been conceived of when the representation system was designed. It is interesting, for example, to consider the difficulties which a burgeoning ecology movement might meet in a corporatist system, even one with a relatively capacious list of recognized interest constituencies. Such a system, constructed decades before currently relevant issues came into focus, would not contain a seat or seats in the assembly for representatives of ecological concerns per se; and given normal institutional inertias, the creation of such seats would not occur with any great speed, especially since the governors of such constituency reform would represent entrenched and long-standing interests which would find the new ecological advocacies unpalatable. Thus the surfacing of such an emergent issue would be feeble at best, dependent upon a maverick shipper here or a free-thinking farmer there who might be willing to take up the new interest as secondary to the one which had been central to his selection as a representative in the first place. In the territorial representation design, on the contrary, there is much less prefabrication of what the interests are and what the issues can be. The candidate campaigning for a general-purpose seat is encouraged to pick up whatever new alarums may be rising in the constituency and offer to represent them.

Two summary points can thus be made, each of which is important in its own right. One is that representation systems placed on a territorial base are subject to a certain kind of bias in both the representation process and the locus of conflict, a bias that hinges on the degree to which natural poles of conflicting interests tend to be aligned with pure geography. This is not necessarily a desideratum; it may even be seen as an ill. The other point is that, over and above such obvious blessings as administrative convenience and the embedding of the first stage of debate at the geographical grass roots, a territorial design is likely to be a highly reasonable general-purpose mechanism for the selection of representatives to a general-purpose assembly.

The Problem of the Subconstituency

We should not close this discussion without considering another problem which also involves the question of constituency definition. This problem is not unique to the territorial constituency, or district, although it is often more acute and pervasive in such a setting because the likelihood of within-constituency heterogeneity of opinion is higher there than in the interest-constituency case. Taking a set of such districts as a given, let us ask, "Who is to be represented?"

The classical answer is, of course, the totality of the district population, and our treatment up to now has supposed that this is the end in view. But it is not difficult, with a few simplifying restrictions, to force this answer into a logical impasse. If, returning to our simplistic model of constituencies as balls in an urn, we imagine an urn with a 51–49 majority of black balls, then the representative, forced to a binary choice, is by conventional assumptions expected to vote black. Yet such an action means that he not only is ignoring the wishes of almost half of his constituency, but is actively engaged in authoritative actions which directly contravene their wishes! There is no logical alternative: given the terms of the problem, it is impossible for him to cast a vote which represents not just some part of his district, but rather the district as a whole. This dilemma is built into every setting where within-constituency opinion is heterogeneous, although how pressing the dilemma is depends once again on the degree of heterogeneity.

Such logical difficulties have not pained democratic theorists very much, and rightly so, for representation of the totality of a district is commonly taken to mean representation of the majority of the district when heterogeneity is encountered. The notion of totality is at most operative in the denominator, as it were, to verify which option claims a majority of support. In fact, this tends to be the view of representation held casually by many citizens: the district is a testing ground for competing candidacies, and whichever candidate wins must naturally uphold the views of his supporting majority, which is to say, pursue advocacies directly contrary to the wishes of the losing minority in the district. From one point of view, this is nothing more than what majority rule is all about.

In real life, where the representative engages in many legislative actions in addition to casting binary votes, there are once again a variety of ways in which he can attempt to remain sensitive to the minority in his district who voted against him in the popular election. Even on an issue that is of high concern to both his own majority and the minority in the district, and where there is intense polarization, he will have to go along largely with the general thrust of majority wishes if he sees himself as a delegate. Nonetheless, he might examine the prospective calamities which alarm the minority in the legislative thrust he is following, and attempt through amendments and other maneuvers to minimize the likelihood that those particular calamities will be set off by the policy initiatives of the majority.

All the same, many situations will arise where such nuances are hard to find, and where the logic of the situation forces the representative to a sequence of behaviors in which he is working directly against the professed wishes of the opposing minority in his district. Fenno (1978) has noted that most of the representatives whom he observed operating in their home districts tended to think of those districts as a nested set of four concentric circles. The most capacious circle is, of course, the representative's geographic district taken as a totality, with its crucial property of relative homogeneity or heterogeneity. The next smaller circle is made up of his supporters at the polls who gave him office: his "re-election constituency." Within this circle there is in turn the circle of supporters who are active in providing him with support, or the "primary constituency." And finally, the smallest circle is made up of his immediate intimates, or entourage, the "personal constituency."

It does not take much thought to realize how much such a view of the local world eases the burden of representation, a task that usually would be utterly agonizing for the representative who saw himself as a delegate bound to promote the conflict of wills displayed by his district taken as a whole. Indeed, if our eta statistic is aimed at saying something about district heterogeneity in the first instance, and (by implication) saying something about ease of representation in the second instance, it should be self-evident that the level of etas for any given issue dimension is likely to undergo a major transformation if we shift from calculations based on the district as a whole to a new set where the constituency is redefined as the set of supporters who put the representative in office. On issues where districts as a whole are polarized, such a redefinition tends to reduce the within-constituency variance by a substantial percentage; and across districts we are pitting the leftist supporters of one candidate against the rightist supporters of his legislative opponent elected in another district, which means that the between-district variance is advancing absolutely at the same time.

Thus the eta statistic moves up very markedly from those relatively marginal ranges that may pertain for the district as a whole, to levels where popular representation is much more likely to be impressive. The parameter

which governs the degree of this advance is the background correlation between issue positions among the citizenry and their choice of candidates at
the polls. If on some given issue there is no correlation whatever between
voter viewpoints and their candidate selection, and this is true in each district, then there is no reason to expect the eta to mount as the constituency
is redefined down to supporters alone. But there is an opposing limiting
case in which the eta for all constituents taken as total districts is zero, but
the correlation between issue preference and candidate choice is perfect,
such that the eta limited to constituencies of supporters also becomes the
perfect value of unity. Between these polar cases, even small correlations
persistent in sign across districts between issue preferences and candidate
choice can act as a substantial multiplier on etas when constituencies are redefined from total districts to supporters alone. Within our French linkage
issues, for example, the etas reported earlier as ranging from .21 to .41 show
a new range from .35 to .66 when recalculations are done with electoral
supporters as the constituency.

Whether the good represesntative tries to take his total district as his
constituency, or merely the subset of those within his district that has provided him with electoral support, is a matter that we will leave to the
reader's judgment.[13] The important point is that any estimation of the nature of the popular representation function is likely to differ quite considerably according to which constituency definition is seen as the proper one.

Prospectus

Popular representation takes place in a context defined by electoral and legislative institutions, and these vary in significant ways even across the set of
superficially similar parliamentary democracies. In earlier chapters, we discussed at length the peculiarities of French electoral institutions, and how
they shape voters' choices. In the next chapter we shall set the other half of
the stage, reviewing the main distinctive practices of the French National
Assembly, the body to which all of our candidates have aspired, and in
which the winners have taken seats.

As the focus of this book is on popular representation, rather than on
the totality of legislative behavior per se, this review will be highly selective.
We recognize, of course, that many accounts of legislative decisionmaking
have been constructed which are intuitively compelling and empirically
persuasive (by such criteria as "variance accounted for"), but which do not
introduce the subject of constituency variation at all; instead they proceed
in terms of the pushes and pulls experienced in the day-to-day business of
party caucuses, legislative committees, and floor debates. In fact, it has been
cogently observed that legislative decisionmaking is "overdetermined," in
the sense that numerous classes of predictors, conceptually if not empirically

distinct, succeed rather impressively in accounting for the ultimate policy behaviors of individual legislators (Weisberg, 1978).

Nonetheless, some of the closest work examining the field of forces as actually experienced by real legislators, such as Kingdon's excellent study (1973, 1977), continues to stress the importance of the constituency in the representative's mind as he moves toward his voting decisions. In any event, while willingly recognizing that other forces bear on the legislator's decisionmaking, we still retain our fascination with whatever congruence there is between district sentiment and representative behavior, and the ways in which this congruence is played out through more proximal predictors, such as the representative's party affiliation.

17

The Deputies in
the National Assembly

Under the Fifth Republic, the French parliament, or legislature, occupies a position within the constitutional system that is quite different from the dominant role it played in earlier French democratic regimes. For example, under the Third Republic, which was founded and consolidated by men who were deeply suspicious of executive power, political practices were gradually institutionalized that subordinated the executive to the popularly elected lower house, the Chamber of Deputies. The President of the Republic, who was chosen by the parliament, was eventually reduced to the status of a figurehead, and the Premier and the cabinet were kept weak by frequent rotation in office. Ministerial instability became the hallmark of the system, which observers referred to as "government by assembly."

By 1946, when the Fourth Republic was established, there was considerable support among French political leaders for a stronger executive, but nevertheless the regime reverted to many of the characteristic practices of the Third Republic. Neither the party system nor the rules of the game were conducive to executive leadership. The new constitution was drafted on the assumption that postwar France would be governed by large, disciplined parties that would willingly support governments in their image. Procedural devices that might have strengthened the executive were either rejected or, like the constitutional provisions permitting the dissolution of the Assembly, so hedged with conditions that they were ignored by cautious governments or circumvented by ingenious deputies. The rules of the two chambers reflected the deputies' desire to retain their traditional prerogatives. When the party system became more fragmented and undisciplined groups more numerous, embattled governments were left with few defenses against pressures from the deputies except the threat of resignation. Ministerial instability prevailed, and the popularly elected lower chamber—now called the National Assembly—remained the chief locus of power.

Parliament disliked executive leadership, but it could not do without it entirely. Both the members of parliament and the government could initiate legislation, and although more than 75 percent of the bills introduced during the Fourth Republic were parliamentary bills (*propositions de loi*), more than 70 percent of the bills that became law were government bills (*projets de loi*).[1] But parliament only accepted leadership grudgingly. It adopted almost 250 laws a year, often legislating trivial details, but it failed to pass a large proportion of the measures proposed by the government. The Assembly had exclusive control over its own agenda and could obstruct the government simply by not considering its measures. The standing committees could also veto government bills by not reporting them to the Assembly. These committees frequently rewrote government bills; the rules of the chamber required the initial debate on a measure to focus on the text that emerged from committee rather than on the text that had originally been introduced; and measures were steered through parliament by the committees' *rapporteurs,* not by the ministers responsible for the proposals. Ministers could not move amendments, whereas deputies could. The Assembly did try to discipline itself in budgetary matters, but the only procedural device the government could use to prevent a measure from being drastically revised by a succession of amendments from the floor was to pose the question of confidence, which meant that the government would resign if its position was not upheld. In addition to shaping legislation, the Assembly also tried to direct the broad lines of national policy through the use of the interpellation, a debate on government policy followed by a vote on a motion expressing the Assembly's views on the subject. The interpellation was used less often and less destructively during the Fourth Republic than during the Third, but it was a means of harassing, warning, instructing, or reversing governments.[2]

De Gaulle and his followers set out to change all this when they founded the Fifth Republic in 1958. The President of the Republic was made independent of the legislature and was given substantial powers, including the right to exercise emergency powers, the power to dissolve the National Assembly once within any twelve-month period, and the power to hold referenda on certain subjects—all of which de Gaulle exercised within four years of becoming the first President of the Fifth Republic. In 1962, by questionable use of the referendum, the Constitution was amended to provide for the direct election of the President by universal suffrage, thereby, for the first time since the ill-fated Second Republic of 1848, giving the President an anchor in public opinion equivalent to that of the popularly elected legislative chamber. The Constitution conferred policymaking authority on the government, but that role could be preempted by the President if he could establish and maintain ascendancy over parliamentary opinion.

The powers of parliament were sharply circumscribed and the government was given primacy in the legislative process. The Constitution enumerates the subjects on which parliament may legislate; all remaining subjects may be controlled by government decree. This change, which was largely symbolic, injured the deputies' pride more than it affected their power, as no domain of importance over which parliament had legislated in the past was omitted from the list. More important was the distinction made between subjects on which parliament could legislate in detail and those on which it could determine only "the fundamental principles," leaving the details to government decree. Parliament could also delegate its legislative powers to the government for a given period of time, and it has done so at various times, including the period we are discussing in this book. Partly as a result of these constitutional rules, parliament enacts fewer than one hundred laws a year on the average, considerably less than the average annual output under the Fourth Republic.

A bicameral legislature was retained, consisting of the popularly elected National Assembly and the indirectly elected Senate.[3] The approval of both chambers is necessary to pass a law, unless the government decides that in a dispute between the two houses the position of the Assembly should prevail. All bills must be examined successively by the two houses and, if they are adopted in identical terms by both of them, they become law. If the two chambers do not agree on a measure, the government may require the appointment of a joint-conference committee (*commission mixte paritaire*) to try to work out an agreement between them. If the joint-conference committee is unable to do so, whether because it fails to reach agreement itself or because one of the chambers does not accept the measure the committee has agreed on, the government may ask the Assembly alone to make the final decision. Thus, the Constitution makes it possible for the government both to rely on the Assembly to enact measures that are opposed by the Senate and to allow the Senate to block measures favored by the Assembly but opposed by the government. In fact, most legislation is adopted by both chambers. During each of the two legislatures with which we are concerned in this study, the brief Third Legislature (1967–1968) and the more normal Fourth Legislature (1968–1973), 85 percent of the bills enacted into law by parliament were adopted by both chambers. Joint-conference committees were requested by the government for the remaining 15 percent of the bills considered, and in two-thirds of those cases the committees were successful in finding solutions that were acceptable to both the Assembly and the Senate. Less than 5 percent of the measures enacted during the Third and Fourth Legislatures were adopted by the National Assembly alone.

With the establishment of the Fifth Republic the legislative chambers lost control over their agendas. Members of parliament, as well as the government, retained the right to initiate legislation, but the Constitution requires that the agenda of each chamber give priority to government bills and to those parliamentary bills that the government has endorsed, in the order chosen by the government. In other words, no legislative business may be conducted without the approval of the government, although both chambers must be given time to ask questions of the government, to deal with matters involving the immunity of their members, and to conduct necessary internal business, such as the election of officers; and the National Assembly must always be given time for a motion of censure against the government.

Government control of the parliamentary agenda means that the committees (reduced in number to a maximum of six for each chamber) can no longer bottle up legislation by inaction. Moreover, the debate on government bills must take place on the government's draft and not on the committee's recommendations, although on parliamentary bills the committee draft remains the basis for debate. Amendments may be moved by the government, the committees, or members of parliament; ministers may rule amendments out of order if they have not previously been discussed by the appropriate committee, but this right is not usually invoked. The government's most powerful (and most resented) weapon against an onslaught of amendments rests on Article 44 of the Constitution, which permits the government to insist on a "package vote" (*vote bloqué*), a single vote on all or part of a bill incorporating only those amendments proposed or accepted by the government. Article 40 prohibits individual members of parliament from moving bills or amendments that would either increase public expenditure or reduce public revenue.

Interpellations were abolished in 1958. Members of parliament have the right to ask the government questions and these may sometimes be followed by debate, but neither house may take a vote to express its attitude toward the government or its position on a matter of public policy without the government's consent. The only exception to this rule is that the National Assembly may vote on a motion of censure against the government in certain conditions prescribed by the Constitution; motions of censure cannot be voted on in the Senate. The motion of censure is the instrument by which the Assembly is permitted to exercise ultimate control over the government. Adoption of a motion of censure requires the government to resign, but even in this regard the procedures give advantages to the government.

There are three ways in which the life of the government can be formally put at risk under the Constitution. First, the government may ask for the confidence of the Assembly on its program or its general policy, in which case the opposition of a majority of the deputies voting can defeat the government. Second, the government may ask for the confidence of the Assembly on a specific measure. In this case, one-tenth of the deputies may move a motion of censure against the government, but the motion must pass by a majority of all the deputies in order to bring the government down. If the motion fails to win the support of a majority of all the deputies, which the French call an "absolute majority," or if no motion of censure is introduced, the government is upheld and the measure is regarded as adopted. Third, one-tenth of the deputies may move a motion of censure whether or not the government has asked for the confidence of the Assembly, and the absolute majority rule applies in this case as well. But motions of censure uninvited by the government cannot be repeated indefinitely. If such a motion fails to pass, the particular deputies who introduced it may not move another uninvited motion of censure during the same session of parliament.[4] There is no limit, however, to the number of times the same deputies may introduce motions of censure in response to questions of confidence posed by the government on specific measures. If the Assembly censures the government, however, it runs the risk of being dissolved by the President while the government remains in office pending the outcome of the election. This is precisely what happened in the fall of 1962, when the Assembly adopted a motion of censure for the first and only time during the Fifth Republic. Moreover, the election of 1962 returned a majority in the image of the censured government, and the same Prime Minister was formally reappointed after the election.

The new constitutional system, with the balance of power tilted steeply in favor of the executive, was put under the control of the Constitutional Council, to which disputes over the constitutionality of laws and procedures were to be submitted for final decision, and which was required to scrutinize the rules of the chambers to ensure that they were in conformity with the Constitution. Under the Fifth Republic, the French parliament, "once among the most powerful in the world, became one of the weakest" (Williams, 1968).[5]

Still, it is important not to exaggerate. The French National Assembly is no rubberstamp: it has often been frustrated but it has seldom been cowed. Governments have often extracted reluctant support by using the procedural devices available to them, but their habitual supporters as well as the opposition deputies have openly complained, and there have been times when the government clearly thought it wiser to give the deputies their heads than to try to discipline them. The proportion of parliamentary bills relative to government bills enacted into law rose steadily, from 7 percent during the First Legislature (1958–1962) to more than 12 percent in the Second Legislature (1962–1967) and to almost 25 percent during the Third and Fourth Legislatures (1967–1973).[6] In this last period almost 15 percent of the parliamentary bills that were passed originated with the two opposition groups, the Communists and the Federation. During the same period the Assembly adopted thousands of amendments to legislative measures. About a fifth of these emanated from the deputies, another fifth from the government itself, and the remaining three-fifths from the committees (Assemblée Nationale, *Statistiques*). Figures such as these do not tell the whole story, of course. Much of the influence enjoyed by deputies is exercised informally, through party channels, or in the comparative privacy of parliamentary committees. The measurement of parliamentary influence is a delicate and subtle task. But even if it is indisputable that the National Assembly lost its political supremacy under the Fifth Republic, it is also true that it remains an indispensable element of the French political system, with power to refuse what the executive demands.

The pattern of legislative-executive relations is not only a matter of constitutional arrangements; it is also a function of the party system and of the particular configuration of party strengths at any given time. During the brief Third Legislature the Gaullists and their electoral opponents were almost evenly balanced in the Assembly, with the result that every vote counted in the most literal sense. During the Fourth Legislature, however, an entirely different parliamentary situation prevailed. The landslide electoral victory won by the Gaullists in 1968 produced a lopsided situation in the National Assembly. The Gaullist UDR alone had a clear majority of the seats, and the left-wing opposition parties, who were reduced to insignificant numbers, were temporarily demoralized. This comfortable Gaullist majority should have made the management of legislative-executive relations easier than during the tense Third Legislature, as the government could afford defections that would earlier have been fatal. But the circumstances of the election had produced strains that were bound to affect the relationship between the government and the Assembly. Deputies who interpreted their election as an invitation to reform obviously had different views from those who regarded it as a mandate to restore law and order. Furthermore, the euphoria in the ranks of the Gaullists was tempered by the sobering knowledge that their parliamentary dominance was fortuitous and not likely to be repeated; dozens of newly elected Gaullists would have to pick their way carefully if they were to have any chance of reelection.

When the UDR deputies, never magnanimous in victory, shouldered aside their erstwhile allies, the Independent Republicans, whom they no longer needed, this produced predictable antagonisms. But Georges Pompidou, who had to fight a national election when he ran for the presidency in 1969, was convinced that to win he needed the support not only of the

Gaullists but also of the Independent Republicans and centrists, whom he successfully wooed. After his election, the latter two groups were rewarded with more cabinet seats than the size of their parliamentary representation warranted, with the paradoxical result that within a year of its unparalleled electoral victory the UDR had less weight in the councils of government than it had had in previous legislatures. All this complicated what, on the surface, appeared to be untroubled legislative-executive relations. The Assembly that sat from 1968 to 1973, and which is the main basis of our study of French legislative behavior, was the least typical in French republican history. At the same time, the very context that made it unique created cross-currents of conflicting interests that were not very different from those that characterized more normal French assemblies.

The Composition of the Assembly

Between 1967 and 1973 there were 487 seats in the National Assembly: 470 for Metropolitan France and 17 for Overseas France (departments and territories).[7] Considerably more than that number of people sat in each of the two legislatures elected during that period, however, because of the comparatively large turnover in Assembly membership. In addition to turnover necessitated by the replacement of deputies who died or resigned because of ill health, appointment or election to other posts, political dissatisfaction, or scandal, the composition of the Assembly was affected by a constitutional provision prohibiting a member of the government from being also a member of parliament. In most parliamentary systems, including the earlier systems of the Third and Fourth Republics, members of parliament who are appointed to the government retain their seats in parliament. They vote just as the other members of parliament do, and when they leave the government they resume their roles as regular members. This has not been so in France under the Fifth Republic. A member of parliament who is appointed to the government must resign from parliament (or else from the government) within thirty days. As most members of the government come from the Assembly, that rule results in a considerable turnover among the deputies.

When seats are vacated in the Assembly, they are filled in one of two ways: either the deputy is replaced by his or her alternate (*remplaçant éventuel,* or, colloquially, *suppléant*), or a by-election is held, depending on the nature of the vacancy. Each candidate for the Assembly has an alternate whose name appears on the ballot along with the candidate's. When a candidate is elected and becomes a deputy, his or her seat is automatically filled by the alternate if the deputy either accepts certain positions, including a government post, or dies in office.[8] If a deputy resigns, however, or if an alternate who has become a deputy resigns or dies in office, the vacancy is filled at a by-election, except that no by-election may be held during the last twelve months of the maximum constitutional term of a legislature.[9] If a deputy who has resigned from the Assembly in order to join the government leaves the government later, he or she does not automatically return to the Assembly but, rather, must wait for an opportune by-election or the next general election to try to regain a seat.

A final potential source of turnover in the composition of the Assembly is the invalidation of electoral returns by the Constitutional Council, the quasi-judicial body which has, along with the other duties mentioned earlier, the task of settling electoral disputes. The Constitutional Council hears complaints of electoral irregularities, and when it determines that a complaint is well-founded, it unseats the deputy who was proclaimed elected and orders a by-election in the district in question. In most such cases, the unseated deputy goes on to win the by-election by a wider margin than that by which he or she had won the disputed election, and there is no change in the composition of the Assembly as a result. Occasionally, however, the winner of the contested election loses at the by-election and is replaced in the Assembly by the new victor.

Even though the Third Legislature lasted only a little longer than a year, a turnover of 6 percent of its members occurred during that period. Of the 487 deputies elected in the spring of 1967, 24 were appointed to the government, including Prime Minister Georges Pompidou, and were, accordingly, replaced by their alternates; four others died in office and were also replaced by their alternates; and one was unseated when the Constitutional Council annulled his election and his opponent at the by-election won his seat. A total of 516 people, therefore, served in the Third Legislature. Another way of looking at the turnover would be to compare the people who were serving in the legislature at the end of its term with those who were originally elected to the Assembly. This does not necessarily produce the mirror image of the gain beyond 487 people, partly because seats may be left vacant at the end of a legislature. Only 456 of the original 487 deputies elected in the spring of 1967 were still deputies when the Assembly was dissolved.

The case of the composition of the Fourth Legislature (1968–1973) is the same in principle as that of the Third, but it is far more complicated. Several of the deputies who had been appointed to the government early in the legislature, been replaced by their alternates, and then been dropped from the government ran successfully at by-elections and returned to the Assembly. (Three were later reappointed as ministers and were replaced by the same alternates who had replaced them earlier). Four deputies who had entered the Assembly as alternates died in office. Two of them had replaced ministers (one the Prime Minister) and in each case the minister ran for the vacant seat, won it, returned to the government, and was replaced again by a new alternate.

Most of the turnover in Assembly personnel resulted from appointments to the government. There were three governments during the Fourth Legislature, headed successively by Maurice Couve de Murville (1968), Jacques Chaban-Delmas (1969), and Pierre Messmer (1972). No government "fell" between 1967 and 1973 in the sense that it lost the confidence of the National Assembly; rather, the succession of governments reflected the extent to which the Prime Minister served only at the pleasure of the President. Shortly after the 1968 elections, de Gaulle replaced Prime Minister Pompidou (the architect of the Gaullists' great electoral victory) with Couve de Murville, who had been Foreign Minister for most of the Fifth Republic, and hence the faithful executor of de Gaulle's foreign policy. When Pompidou was elected President after de Gaulle's resignation, he replaced Couve de Murville with Chaban-Delmas, a deputy since 1946, mayor of Bordeaux since 1947, and President of the National Assembly since the inception of the Fifth Republic. Chaban-Delmas, who was more interested in domestic reforms than foreign affairs, pursued the creation of a "new society,"[10] while Pompidou himself tilted French foreign policy toward European cooperation. But Chaban-Delmas became entangled in controversy over his tax returns and Pompidou's European policy was not notably popular.[11] With the 1973 legislative elections on the horizon, Pompidou evidently thought it wise to seek refuge in Gaullist fundamentalism. In mid-1972 he replaced Chaban-Delmas with Pierre Messmer, who had been Minister for the Armed Forces from 1960 to 1969 and who symbolized fidelity to the policy of national independence, the core of Gaullist doctrine.

The appointment of each new Prime Minister was accompanied by changes in the composition of the government, and this succession of governments, along with the routine reshuffling of cabinet posts, contributed to turnover in the Assembly, as Table 17-1 indicates. In addition to the 487 who had originally been elected in 1968, 81 persons became deputies during the Fourth Legislature. Taking account of the four vacancies that occurred in 1972 but were not filled, only 402 of the original 487 deputies elected in 1968 were still in the Assembly at the expiration of its term in 1973.

It should be emphasized that many candidates elected to the Assembly never actually function as deputies during the life of a legislature. That is the case for deputies who are appointed to the government at the beginning of the legislature and remain there until the end of the legislative term, as well as for deputies appointed to the government at the beginning of the term who leave the government before the end of the term and are not able to return to the Assembly.[12] The twenty-four deputies who were appointed to the government in 1967 never actually sat in the Third Legislature, and twenty-five of the thirty deputies named to the government immediately after the 1968 election did not sit in the Fourth Legislature. Indeed, more than a dozen of the deputies elected both in 1967 and in 1968 never sat in either Assembly because they were appointed to the government immediately after each election and served exclusively as ministers.

Table 17-1. Changes in composition of National Assembly, Fourth Legislature, 1968–1973.

Year	Reason for vacancy	Mode of filling vacancy	Number of cases	Number of new personnel
1968	Appointment to government	Alternate	30	30
	Death of original deputy	Alternate	3	3
1969	Appointment to government	Alternate	19	19
	Resignation	By-election	6	1
	Election to Presidency of Republic	By-election	1	1
1970	Appointment to government	Alternate	1	1
	Death of original deputy	Alternate	4	4
	Death of former alternate	By-election	1	0
	Resignation	By-election	3	3
1971	Appointment to government	Alternate	5	3
	Death of original deputy	Alternate	3	3
	Death of former alternate	By-election	1	0
	Election to Senate	By-election	3	3
1972	Appointment to government	Alternate	9	8
	Death of original deputy	Alternate	1	1
	Death of former alternate	Not filled	2	0
	Resignation	Not filled	2	0
1973	Death of original deputy	Alternate	1	1
		Total	95	81

These various sources of change in the composition of the Assembly were reflected in our interviews with victorious candidates in 1967, in 1968, or in both years. Seven of the deputies whom we interviewed were ministers at one time or another between the election of 1967 and the termination of the Fourth Legislature in 1973, and—for varying lengths of time—these persons did not actually operate as deputies in the Assembly. In addition, two candidates who were interviewed died subsequently while in office.

The Parliamentary Group

The basic unit of party organization within the National Assembly is the parliamentary group. The deputies are authorized by the rules of the Assembly to organize themselves according to "political affinities," and the resulting groups are the parliamentary expression of the political parties.

The parliamentary groups are essential to the organization and operation of the Assembly. Appointments to the Assembly's committees are made by the parliamentary groups in numbers proportionate to each group's size, and if a deputy resigns from or is expelled from his or her group, the deputy automatically loses his or her place on the committee. The presidents of the groups are members of the Presidents' Conference (*Conférence des Présidents*), which allocates floor time to the groups in amounts roughly proportional to their size and prepares that part of the Assembly's agenda that is not controlled by the government.[13] When the President's Conference votes, the votes of the groups' presidents are weighted to reflect the sizes of the groups they represent. The presidents of the groups, or their authorized deputies, may demand that any vote taken by the Assembly (except those required under the rules of the Assembly to be held by secret ballot) be an open, recorded vote.[14]

The parliamentary groups are also important for the political decision-making process. They maintain communication among their members and organize their legislative work. They decide what position the group will take on a given measure, what their parliamentary tactics will be, who their spokesperson will be, and how they will vote. The president of a group may demand that a sitting of the Assembly be suspended for a group meeting, and it is quite common for groups to ask for a suspension in order to discuss their position when some unforeseen situation arises or toward the end of a debate when the moment of decision is approaching. Some groups have elaborate structures designed to permit the detailed examination of particular legislative domains by specialized study groups. Finally, the group structure provides a means by which ministers may communicate with their parliamentary supporters informally, apart from formal parliamentary debate.[15]

The minimum number of deputies required to form a group is thirty, and a deputy may belong to only one group. Under the rules, deputies may affiliate with (*s'apparenter à*) a group, with the permission of the group's officers, without actually joining it. Affiliated deputies do not count in calculating the minimum size of a group, but they do count for the allocation of committee places by proportional representation of groups. Although deputies who affiliate with groups usually select the group with which they are most in sympathy, for one reason or another they prefer to distinguish themselves from the group rather than joining it. Pierre Cot, the brilliant longtime fellow traveler who was elected on the Communist ticket in 1967, affiliated with the Communist group but did not join it. Sometimes affiliated deputies come from minor parties and are simply not numerous enough to form a separate group, as in the case of the four PSU deputies who affiliated with the Federation group in 1967. In 1967 and 1968, candidates from the defunct MRP who were elected as Gaullists affiliated with the Gaullist group, and so did several deputies from the heavily right-wing but not particularly Gaullist department of the Manche. Independent candidates elected with either obscure party labels or none at all often affiliate with a group instead of joining one: one such candidate who had defeated a

Gaullist in 1967 proceeded to affiliate with the Gaullist parliamentary group when he entered the Assembly. Finally, deputies from the overseas departments or territories often affiliate with groups rather than joining them; about one-third of the overseas deputies, including a Communist, did so in 1967.

Some deputies neither join nor affiliate with a parliamentary group. These deputies are referred to colloquially as *non-inscrits* (unregistered). Non-inscrits do not have the advantages of being represented in the Presidents' Conference, but they may serve on committees; after committee memberships have been allocated proportionately to the parliamentary groups, the remaining places on the committees are distributed to the non-inscrits. The characteristics of these deputies are similar to those of the affiliated deputies: some of them come from overseas districts, some belong to minor parties, some have received the endorsement of more than one party, and some are locally popular figures for whom a clear partisan attachment is not only unnecessary but could possibly be damaging. The non-inscrits can be very heterogeneous in political outlook. During the Third Legislature and at the start of the Fourth Legislature the non-inscrits consisted mainly of right-wing deputies, some centrists, and Aimé Césaire, the unbeatable left-wing deputy from Fort-de-France, Martinique. During the Fourth Legislature, a wide assortment of deputies moved for one reason or another from group membership or group affiliation into the ranks of the non-inscrits: at times there were more than thirty non-inscrits, enough to form a separate parliamentary group. Some of them seriously considered forming a separate group in 1971, in order to gain the advantages of group membership. The proposal came to naught, however, possibly because deputies ranging from Gaullist fundamentalists to François Mitterrand himself would have found it too difficult to produce a "political declaration" which they would all have been willing to sign—a basic requirement for the formation of a group (*Le Monde,* March 27, 1971).

Non-inscrits and affiliated deputies value their independence, but they are not unwilling to sacrifice it temporarily to aid fellow deputies in distress. The centrist group in the Fourth Legislature, Progress and Modern Democracy (PDM), contained some deputies who were very supportive of the governing Gaullist majority and others who were inclined to side with the opposition, indicating that although it may be difficult for deputies with different outlooks to prepare a statement they can all sign, it is not impossible. These two different tendencies managed to get along well enough in a single group until the fall of 1972, when four of the opposition supporters resigned from the group because they thought its position was too close to that of the governing majority. The resignations momentarily dissolved the entire group by reducing it to less than the minimum size of thirty members. But then three non-inscrits and one deputy affiliated with the Gaullists came to the rescue by joining the group, bringing its numbers up to the required minimum. On two later occasions when PDM deputies left the group, non-inscrits ensured the group's survival by joining it.

Electoral Parties and Parliamentary Groups

Each of the five main electoral formations that competed at the election of 1967 formed a parliamentary group after the election. The Communist party organized the Groupe Communiste, the Federation created the Groupe de la Fédération de la Gauche Démocrate et Socialiste, the centrists of the Democratic Center formed the Groupe Progrès et Dèmocratie Moderne, Giscard d'Estaing's Independent Republicans formed the Groupe des Républicains Indépendants, and the orthodox Gaullists created the Groupe d'Union Démocratique pour la Ve République.[16] For more than 90 percent of the deputies, the transposition from electoral party to parliamentary group was clear and direct. These deputies, whose electoral labels were unambiguous, joined the parliamentary group corresponding to their electoral party. For the remaining deputies the choice of joining a parliamentary group, affiliating with a group, or becoming a non-inscrit could not have been predicted on the basis of their electoral party alone, however reasonable their choices may appear to be in the light of other factors. This is true of all the decisions to affiliate with a group rather than to join it. The victorious joint MRP-Gaullist candidates merely affiliated with the Gaullist parliamentary group, but the lone joint Radical-Gaullist deputy joined it. And the four PSU deputies who affiliated with the Federation group in 1967 might well have chosen to remain non-inscrits instead. Sometimes deputies from a small party who are not numerous enough to form their own group prefer to be non-inscrits. As we shall see later in this chapter, after 1968 the Radicals sometimes affiliated with a Socialist parliamentary group and sometimes remained non-inscrits. And while some deputies with either obscure party labels or no labels at all may choose to be non-inscrits, others affiliate with or even join a group. Finally, some deputies do not join or even affiliate with the group that is the closest counterpart to the party label they have used (or are reported to have used) at the election. That was the case in 1967 with five Gaullist candidates who joined the Independent Republican group after the election, and with one Independent Republican candidate who joined the Gaullist group. Table 17-2 sets forth the correspondence between electoral parties and parliamentary groups at the opening of the legislature that was elected in 1967.

The same five electoral formations or groups that competed at the 1967 election also competed at the 1968 election, with some alterations of nomenclature, and each formed a parliamentary group again after the election. The Communist party and the Federation used the same party labels in 1968 as they had used in 1967, and the parliamentary groups they formed also bore the same names as they had in the previous legislature. The Gaullists and the centrists changed their party labels for the election, and they also changed the names of their parliamentary groups. The Gaullists fought the election under the banner of l'Union pour la Défense de la République (UDR); they called their parliamentary group the Groupe d'Union des Démocrates pour la République.[17] The centrists went to the hustings with the label of their old parliamentary group, Progrès et Démocratie Moderne (PDM), and they retained the same name for their group in the new Assembly. The Independent Republicans ran at the election with the label Union pour la Défense de la République–Républicains Indépendants (UDR-RI), and after the election they gave their parliamentary group the same name it had had before, Groupe des Républicains Indépendants. There were deputies in the new Assembly, as there had been in the previous one, who did not join any group but instead chose either to affiliate with one or to remain non-inscrits. The correspondence between electoral parties and parliamentary groups immediately after the 1968 election is shown in Table 17-3.

The structure of the parliamentary groups did not remain the same throughout the Fourth Legislature. Soon after the 1968 election the Federation, which had grouped together Socialists, Radicals, and the Convention, was dissolved; and each of those formations began planning its future strategy. At a Socialist party congress in July 1969 that party decided to form its own parliamentary group, and at the fall session of the Assembly the Federation group disappeared and was replaced by a Groupe Socialiste with, at the outset, forty-three members. The thirteen Radicals who had belonged to the Federation group first became non-inscrits and then, a few weeks later, affiliated with the Socialist group. As always, however, the Radicals were divided over whether to follow a leftist or a centrist strategy. Either way, the Radicals would have been happy to be associated with the Socialists; but although the leftists among them looked with approbation on close Socialist-Communist relations, the centrists did not. The Socialists had broken temporarily with the Communists after the left-wing electoral disaster of 1968 and, more important, after the invasion of Czechoslovakia in August 1968 by Russia and other countries of eastern Europe. The left-wing parties were badly divided at the time of the presidential election of 1969, when the three parties that had jointly supported François Mitterrand at the presidential election of 1965 each ran an unsuccessful candidate for the presidency: Jacques Duclos of the PCF, Gaston Defferre of the Socialists, and Michel Rocard of the PSU. By 1970, the Socialists had started to repair their relations with the Communists. This process accelerated after the middle of 1971, when François Mitterrand became the leader of the Socialists, and culminated in the summer of 1972 with the adoption of a common governmental program by the Socialists and Communists. The restoration of a

Table 17-2. Correspondence between electoral parties and parliamentary groups, Third Legislature, April 29, 1967.[a]

Electoral Party	Groupe Communiste	Affiliates	Groupe de la Fédération de la Gauche Démocrate et Socialiste	Affiliates	Groupe Progrès et Démocratie Moderne	Affiliates	Groupe d'Union Démocratique pour la Ve République	Affiliates	Groupe des Républicains Indépendants	Affiliates	Non-Inscrits	Total
PCF	71	2										73
PSU				4								4
Fédération												
Pure			2									2
SFIO			76									76
Radical			24									24
Convention			13									13
UDSR			1									1
Centre Gauche											1	1
Rassemblement Démocratique					1						1	2
Centre Démocrate												
Pure					9						1	10
MRP					12	1						13
Indépendant					6	2						8
UDSR					1							1
Rass. Dém.				1	5							6

												Total
CD & Fédération	71	2	116	5	38	3					1	235
Vᵉ République												
Pure							54	5	4			63
UNR							125	9				134
MRP								5				5
Radical							1					1
Rép. Ind.							1		34	3		38
Other									1		2	3
Dissident Gaullist											1	1
Other labels								1			2	4
No label						3						3
Total	71	2	116	5	38	3	181	20	39	3	9	487

a. Deputies from Overseas France who joined or affiliated with a group are assigned the closest corresponding electoral party.

Table 17-3. Correspondence between electoral parties and parliamentary groups, Fourth Legislature, September 24, 1968.[a]

Electoral Party	Parliamentary group										
	Groupe Communiste	Affiliates	Groupe de la Fédération de la Gauche Démocrate et Socialiste	Groupe Progrès et Démocratie Moderne	Affiliates	Groupe d'Union des Démocrates pour la République	Affiliates	Groupe des Républicains Indépendants	Affiliates	Non-Inscrits	Total
PCF	33	1									34
Fédération											
Pure			1								1
SFIO			42								42
Radical			13								13
Convention			1								1
PDM				29							29
UDR											
Pure						268	23	2		3	296
Rép. Ind.						2		55	3		60
Indépendant									1		1
PDM-Indépendant										1	1
Rassemblement Démocratique										1	1
Other										2	2
Other				1	3					2	6
Total	33	1	57	30	3	270	23	57	4	9	487

a. Deputies from Overseas France who joined or affiliated with a group are assigned the closest corresponding electoral party.

left-wing alliance split the Radicals. In the fall of 1970 most of the Radical deputies abandoned their affiliation with the Socialist parliamentary group and became non-inscrits. A year later, half of the Radical non-inscrits returned to the Socialist group, and, at the end of the legislature, nine Radicals were affiliated with the Socialist group while five others remained in the ranks of the non-inscrits.

Transfers between Groups

The shifts of individual Radicals between being affiliated with the Socialist group and being non-inscrits is an illustration on the partisan level of the kinds of transfers between groups that take place more or less continuously during the life of a French Legislature. The composition of the groups may also be affected, of course, by the replacement of deputies by their alternates or through by-elections, as well as by resignations or expulsions from particular groups.

Even during the brief life of the Third Legislature, there were thirteen changes in the composition of the parliamentary groups, not counting the routine movement into and out of the non-inscrits that occurs when deputy-ministers are replaced by their alternates.[18] In order to show the net effects of those individual-level changes, Table 17-4 sets out the group composition of the Third Legislature at three points in time: April 29, 1967,

Table 17-4. Changing composition of parliamentary groups, Third Legislature, 1967–1968.

Group	Date		
	April 29, 1967	May 18, 1967	May 30, 1968
Union Démocratique pour la Ve République	181	179	177
Affiliated	20	21	20
Fédération de la Gauche Démocrate et Socialiste	116	116	118
Affiliated	5	5	3
Communiste	71	71	71
Affiliated	2	2	2
Républicains Indépendants	39	41	41
Affiliated	3	3	2
Progrès et Démocratie Moderne	38	38	42
Affiliated	3	3	0
Non-Inscrits	9	8	9
Total	487	487	485[a]

a. Two seats were vacant at the close of the legislature.

the earliest date when the full complement of deputies had made their group choices; May 18, after the deputies appointed to the government had been replaced by their alternates; and May 30, the day on which the Assembly was dissolved.[19]

The Gaullist group lost two deputies to the Independent Republicans between April 29 and May 18, 1967, because the alternates of two Gaullist ministers were Independent Republicans; it lost one more deputy at the end of April 1968, when the election of a Gaullist was invalidated by the Constitutional Council and his seat was won by a candidate who joined the Federation group; and one Gaullist deputy resigned from the Assembly just before it was dissolved. The affiliates of the Gaullist group gained a non-inscrit by May, but lost a different member by the end of the legislature when a Gaullist affiliate also resigned from the Assembly. One conservative Federation deputy left the Federation group and joined the non-inscrits, while two deputies merely affiliated with the Federation group actually joined it. A deputy who was affiliated with the Independent Republican group joined it, and one of the group's members—a deputy from Overseas France—left it to join the PDM. The three deputies originally affiliated with the PDM group later joined the group itself. Lastly, a pair of moves that are invisible in Table 17-4 involves one non-inscrit who affiliated with the Gaullist group only to return to the ranks of the non-inscrits one week later. Of the parliamentary groups, their affiliates, and the non-inscrits, only the Communist group and its affiliates remained unchanged in size throughout the entire legislature.

Table 17-4 also illustrates the fragility of the parliamentary majority during the Third Legislature. When all the seats in the Assembly were filled, on April 29, 1967, the Gaullist and Independent Republican groups, plus their affiliates, held only 243 seats, one seat less than an overall majority of the Assembly. The situation was remedied in May when an overseas deputy shifted from the non-inscrits to the Gaullist affiliates, giving the Gaullists and their Independent Republican allies the narrowest possible arithmetical majority.[20] Of course, Gaullists and Independent Republicans could count on intermittent support from members of the PDM group and non-inscrits, but the government's control was precarious. Eighty-seven roll-call votes were taken in the Assembly during this legislature. The government managed to survive, but it was defeated on ten of these votes, and on six others a majority of the Gaullist deputies were on the losing side of the balloting.

Of course, more transfers occurred between parliamentary groups during the Fourth Legislature, which lasted more than four years, than during the Third. After applying a sterner test than we applied when computing transfers during the Third Legislature—that is, not counting switches between membership in a group and affiliation with the same group (as well as not counting temporary passage through the non-inscrits from one group to another)—we found that there were fifty-four individual transfers during the Fourth Legislature. It would serve no useful purpose to trace these in detail,[21] but it is illuminating to follow the changes in the overall composition of the groups across several dates during the life of the Fourth Legislature. These changes are shown in Table 17-5.

The four dates for which the group composition of the Assembly is shown are July 11, 1968, soon after the election; September 24, 1968, after the deputies who were appointed ministers in the first government formed after the election were replaced by their alternates; April 2, 1971, a time when most of the Radicals were holding themselves apart from the Socialists; and March 15, 1973, just before the close of the Legislature.[22]

The main trend noticeable in Table 17-5 is the reduction in the size of the Gaullist group and its affiliates. Between the start and end of the Fourth Legislature, they lost 7 percent of their members, most of whom transferred to the ranks of the non-inscrits. This erosion was due to a number of factors: unsuccessful Gaullist performance at by-elections; the resignation of Gaullist fundamentalists; the resignation or expulsion of left-wing Gaullists and others dissatisfied with the political stance of the group; intrigue; scandal;

Table 17-5. Changing composition of parliamentary groups, Fourth Legislature, 1968–1973.

	Date			
Group	July 11, 1968	September 24, 1968	April 2, 1971	March 15, 1973
Union des Démocrates pour la République	270	269	259	251
Affiliated	23	22	23	21
Républicains Indépendants	57	58	58	57
Affiliated	4	4	4	4
Fédération de la Gauche Démocrate et Socialiste	57	57	0	0
Affiliated	0	0	0	0
Socialiste	0	0	42	43
Affiliated	0	0	2	10
Communiste	33	33	33	33
Affiliated	1	1	1	1
Progrès et Démocratie Moderne	30	30	31	30
Affiliated	3	3	3	2
Non-Inscrits	9	10	31	31
Total	487	487	487	483[a]

a. Four seats were vacant at the close of the legislature.

and death or resignation from the Assembly occurring too late to allow for by-elections. Overall, the Gaullists and their affiliates lost twenty-one seats during the legislature. By the standards of most parliamentary systems, and surely by the standard of the Third Legislature of the Fifth Republic, this was a very large loss. It is a measure of the tremendous size of the Gaullists' parliamentary majority after the 1968 election that even after such attrition the Gaullist parliamentary group alone, not counting their affiliated members, retained a majority over all other groups in the Assembly and, counting the affiliates, an enviously large one. The luxury of being able to survive more than twenty defections comfortably between 1968 and 1973 contrasted sharply with the precarious situation of the Gaullists during the previous legislature.

Voting in the Assembly

There are five different methods of voting in the French National Assembly. In principle, the normal voting method is by a show of hands (*vote à main levée*). But if the outcome of such a vote is in doubt, a standing vote (*vote par assis et levé*) is taken. When either of these two methods is used, no record is kept either of the size of the vote or of how individual deputies voted. Votes are recorded, however, for two other types of votes taken in the Assembly. One is the ordinary open ballot (*scrutin public ordinaire*), and the other is the open ballot at the rostrum (*scrutin public à la tribune*). The fifth voting method is the secret ballot (*scrutin secret*), which is used when the Assembly acts as an electoral body, such as when it elects its president and, if the parliamentary groups cannot agree on allocating them without a vote, its other officers.[23]

We are, of course, interested only in the votes taken in the Assembly by both forms of open ballot (*scrutin public*). A vote by ordinary open ballot must be taken either if the President of the Assembly decides that one should be held or at the request of the government, at the request of the parliamentary committee which has primary responsibility for the measure involved, or at the written request of the president of a parliamentary group or his or her delegate, if that delegate's name has been previously communicated to the President of the Assembly. In fact, almost all requests for an open ballot are made by the presidents of the groups. There is no apparent pattern with regard to which group's president makes the request. Depending on the issue, one group may want a recorded vote more than the others; but we have no way of knowing how many groups might want an open ballot on any particular issue because the request of one group president is sufficient. An open ballot at the rostrum is required not only when the measure is one for which the Constitution requires a qualified majority for passage, such as constitutional amendments, but also for motions of censure.

The Assembly uses an electronic voting system for open ballots. At ordinary open ballots deputies vote from their desks by pressing the appropriate buttons. For open ballots at the rostrum, the clerk calls the roll and the deputies go to the rostrum, where, one at a time, they operate the electronic system. If that system is out of order, the deputies vote by placing voting cards in an urn. Each deputy's name is printed on his or her card; a white card signifies "for," blue "against," and red abstention.[24]

Except in cases where the Constitution provides for qualified majorities, a majority of the votes cast is required to pass a measure; the measure is defeated if there is a tie vote. The one type of qualified majority that figures prominently in the voting records which we shall employ later in this book is the motion of censure. Motions of censure have a special status in two respects. The first we have already mentioned: such a motion must be voted on affirmatively by a majority of all the members of the Assembly in order to be adopted. Second, when the deputies vote on a motion of censure, the vote is taken only among those in favor of censure. Opposing votes or abstentions are not asked for. The record of votes on censure motions contains only the names of the deputies who voted in favor of censure.

The record of the deputies' votes on open ballots, which we shall refer to as roll-call votes (although the roll is actually called only for open ballots at the rostrum) appears at the end of the verbatim account of the Assembly's proceedings for the day on which the votes were taken.[25] Once the balloting is closed, deputies may not change their vote; but it is not unusual for them to go on record indicating that their vote was recorded incorrectly. They do so by informing the President of the Assembly at the start of another sitting. The president makes a polite but firm set speech in return, reminding the member that the rules prohibit revision.[26] No change is made in the recorded vote, but the deputy's remarks to the effect that his vote was recorded incorrectly appear in the published debates.[27]

In principle, deputies must vote in person. The Constitution establishes this general rule but also states that proxy voting may be permitted in special circumstances provided that no one votes more than a single proxy; the circumstances in which deputies (and senators) may delegate their right to vote to another deputy (or senator) are spelled out in rather restrictive terms in an ordinance;[28] and the rules of the Assembly reflect these basic documents. In fact, the rules relating to voting in person have been regularly and openly flouted since 1962. Deputies vote for their absent colleagues, with the result that the records of roll-call votes may show that hundreds of deputies voted when only a handful were present in the chamber. Inasmuch as voting requires turning a key at each desk to activate the system, there is commotion in the chamber when a vote is taken as the deputies go from desk to desk recording the votes of their absent colleagues.

It is apparent that this procedure creates some problems for the study of roll-call votes that do not occur when legislators must either vote in person or deliberately pair, as in the British House of Commons or the United

States Congress. In the French case, there is room for slippage between a deputy's recorded vote and his or her actual vote intention. Although, on minor matters at least, it is likely that these informal procedures add somewhat to de facto parliamentary group discipline in French Assembly voting, on balance the French system of absentee voting does not pose serious obstacles to roll-call vote analysis. As we shall see, there is a high degree of voting discipline in the system, but there are also intelligible variations in that degree. Deputies do depart from group voting norms, and both formal and informal safeguards exist to ensure the faithful registration of the deputy's vote.

The formal requirement that deputies vote in person, except in special circumstances, has given rise to the recording in the official vote reports of two kinds of abstention from voting. One category of abstention is voluntary (*abstention volontaire*); the other is for persons who did not take part in the vote (*n'ont pas pris part au vote*). Deputies who are recorded as having abstained voluntarily were present when the vote was taken but chose to abstain. Deputies who are recorded as not having taken part in the vote were usually absent but did not delegate their vote to another deputy, and therefore no vote was cast for them—although it is possible that deputies so recorded were actually present but did not bother to vote.

Party Discipline in Assembly Voting

Decisions about the ongoing stream of legislation made in caucus by the parliamentary groups are absolutely central to the patterns of roll-call votes cast by individual deputies. This is not necessarily an extraordinary feature of the French National Assembly: substantial party discipline in voting is a standard feature of most of the world's legislative bodies, and therefore the U.S. Congress, with its relatively weak party discipline, is more to be remarked upon than the French situation.

Nevertheless, French legislative voting in recent years has shown a degree of party discipline which must be counted as strong in an absolute sense. In fact, no other single feature of the French institutional environment has weighed so heavily in our analysis of the National Assembly as a body chartered to represent the will of the French people. Indeed, it is a capital irony that whereas on the input side French political party formations are transient in their identities, and public attachments to them in the electoral process are highly fragile, legislative outputs are almost completely patterned and channeled by the party groups.

Extent of Party Discipline

Between the beginning of the Third Legislature in May 1967 and the termination of the Fourth Legislature in December 1972,[29] 445 votes (*scrutins*) in the National Assembly were formally recorded by the votes of individual deputies. For an Assembly of 487 seats, almost all of which were persistently occupied by either the elected deputy or his alternate, this means that about 215,000 individual ballots were registered in all.

Of these 215,000 votes, almost 196,000 were cast by members or affiliates of one of the five parliamentary groups in conformity with the modal preference of their caucuses—pro, con, or abstain.[30] We cannot, of course, attest that in each of these 196,000 instances the deputy's vote was a direct product of the caucus decision. In many of these cases the deputy's mind may have been made up in advance of any group discussion, or essentially foreordained by the knowledge that the motion at issue involved a government bill or an opposition amendment. But without inquiring as to the genesis of the individual decisions, the degree of within-group congruence of judgment can be stated as a behavioral fact, and it is impressive. Had each deputy been entirely sequestered from his fellows for the whole legislative period, and required to cast each of his votes according to his own lights, a pattern of within-party homogeneity would normally have emerged in any event. But it is also reasonably certain that such patterning in vacuo would have been far less marked. Within the living, communicating legislature, which provides not only friendly cues for the sympathetic seekers of guidance but also, at the fringes, an aura of sanction and stigma surrounding nonconformity, the pressures toward party homogeneity are strong, and are not breached without special reason.

Even our initial figures on the infrequency of nonconforming votes, suggesting that they are only nine votes in every hundred cast,[31] is in many senses an overestimate. For one thing, this summary takes as the individual deputy's parliamentary group membership the group with which he registered near the beginning of each of the two legislatures involved.[32] As we have seen, shifts of group membership in the middle of a legislative session do occur to some extent, and we may be registering some votes as defections relative to the modal position of the original parliamentary group that in fact conform to the position of the subsequent caucus.[33]

For another thing, our first summary figure of nine defections per hundred votes is based on all the members of the Assembly, and thereby includes willy-nilly the votes of the non-inscrits. By definition, all votes cast by non-inscrits fail to conform to a parliamentary group norm. This is not, of course, conceptually inappropriate, since the refusal to join a parliamentary group is in itself the most extreme form of refusing to accept party discipline. We would not think much of the party discipline of a legislature in which caucus members were 100 percent faithful to caucus decisions, but only one member in ten was willing to put himself within the caucus. In the French case, however, only two or three members per hundred chose to remain non-inscrits throughout each legislature, thus testifying to the general acceptance of the norm of party discipline in that body. And if we limit our calculations to persons who initially accepted the discipline of one or another parliamentary group, then the rate of votes which are not in conformity with the membership group drops from nine to only seven per hundred.

Even this figure is from some points of view a rank underestimate of the austerity of party discipline. It includes as "defecting" votes many marginal cases. For example, if a deputy is excused from a particular vote due to illness or absence and his caucus colleagues do not vote for him, he is registered as an involuntary abstention; and in our initial calculations this abstention counts as a vote *not* in conformity with the parliamentary group, if that group took a substantive position for or against the measure at issue, as it almost invariably would. Indeed, in this calculation any kind of abstention, including not only actual substantive reservations about the group position but other intrusions as well, is classified as a willful departure from the parliamentary group norm.

It is clear that the most striking form of dissent from these norms occurs when no abstention is involved, either on the part of the individual deputy (which is not an uncommon occurrence) or on the part of the group as a whole (which does occur from time to time but is rare). We might define this specific form of individual delinquency as a "substantively defecting vote." And if we do so, and total these votes across all 215,000 individual votes cast in the two legislatures, then we find that only about three and a half individual votes per hundred cast over the six-year period among initial members of parliamentary groups can be assigned to such a category.

What this figure means in reverse is that more than ninety-six times out of a hundred, there is no substantive defection in the roll-call vote cast by the initial members of parliamentary groups, relative to the position adopted in concert by members of the same caucus. This represents an extreme degree of determination. Then the mere knowledge of which of the five parliamentary groups has enrolled any given deputy at the outset is sufficient to predict his pattern of behavior in relation to policy outputs throughout a lengthy series of "decisions" over a period of several years, with only a small margin of error. From one point of view, such a high degree of determinism can be a source of dismay to the analyst, for it leaves little room for the challenge of explication. But it can also be treated as a source of welcome simplification in a process of representation which in most other respects is complex and often obscure. In later chapters we shall find certain points at which this simplification will enable us to ask further analytic questions about the quality of representation that we would not dare to address if we were faced with a more uncertain system of behaviors.

Although the degree of party discipline in Assembly voting is high, producing a strong sense of determinism about individual-level outcomes, we should not conclude that no uncertainty surrounds the aggregate pro-con outcome of legislative bills; and we certainly should not deduce that the vote decisions on these bills always look the same, give or take a few votes. Quite naturally, such uncertainty is at a maximum when the gross division of seats between government and opposition is near parity, as it was for the 1967–68 session; and it declines considerably when the majority becomes lopsided, as it was in the 1968–1973 Assembly following the May–June disorders. But despite this variation, the fact that individual deputies' votes can be predicted with a high level of success from knowledge of the positions of their caucuses says nothing in itself as to how each caucus will decide to vote on any given measure.

To be sure, a gross division between parliamentary groups sympathetic to the government and those in opposition is evident in almost any legislature, and with the government initiating legislative proposals and the opposition frequently suggesting amendments, the likely respective postures of the parliamentary groups from vote to vote are easy to predict. Nevertheless, this division, though apparent, cannot be counted on to reproduce itself endlessly over all votes brought to a roll call. In fact, given the possibility of an intermediate "abstention" posture, which caucuses can and do adopt upon occasion, the permutations of pro, con, and abstain alignments across even as few as five parliamentary groups are exceedingly numerous, and a surprising number of these occurred during the two legislatures we have in view. Of the 445 roll calls taken, a modest majority reveal two patterns, in which the center votes with either the two leftist or the two rightist groups. But another 32 alliance patterns can be found, and of these the vast majority occur more than once.

Thus, although party discipline is strong and aggregate outcomes tend to shift in rather solid blocs, the patterning of parliamentary group alignments cannot be taken totally for granted, and of course shifts in these caucus decisions are crucial to actual policy outcomes. Even for the most frequently occurring caucus alignments, which conform to the simple government-opposition dimension, the quantitative divisions arising from particular votes are less than perfectly repetitive, and not only because of the actions of the centrist PDM group, which sometimes sides with the government, sometimes abstains or suffers a sharp internal split, and sometimes sides with the opposition. Other sources of indeterminacy are the votes of a dozen or so non-inscrits, left out of the party discipline picture; the nearly twenty "substantively defecting" votes which can, on the average, be expected to arise in connection with the normal scrutin over the full Assembly; and a similar number of individual abstentions in the face of substantive caucus positions. When all of these sources of indeterminacy are combined, we find that a legislature marked by intense party discipline can sometimes behave like one whose aggregate vote outcomes swing with considerable amplitude from roll call to roll call.

Systematic Variations in Party Discipline

The most obvious source of variation in the behavioral record of fidelity to the postures of the parliamentary group is to be found in the character of the parliamentary group itself. The summary figures concerning defections that we have cited up to this point are of course averages across all five parliamentary groups, implicitly weighted by the size of membership. But these groups differ markedly in the levels of fidelity they ultimately achieve, and probably also in the levels they demand.

Figure 17-1 compares the rates of substantive defection in the two legislatures, partitioned by parliamentary group. Table 17-6 summarizes the same

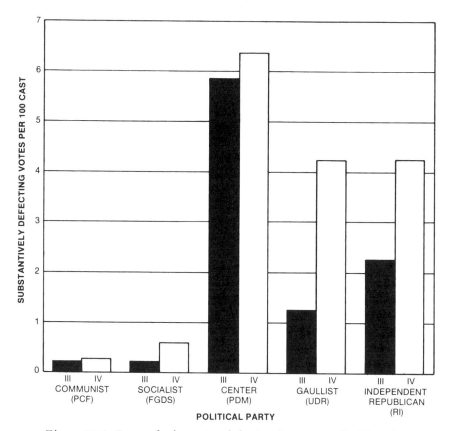

Figure 17-1. Rates of substantive defection from party discipline for the third (III) and fourth (IV) legislatures, 1967–68, 1968–1973, by parliamentary group.

Table 17-6. Rates of defection from parliamentary group position, by five parliamentary groups, Third and Fourth Legislatures, 1967–1973.

Parliamentary group	Rate of defection	
	Substantive defections[a]	All defections[b]
Communist (PCF)	0.3	0.5
Federation (FGDS)	0.6	1.6
Progrès et Démocratie Moderne (PDM)	5.8	13.6
Gaullist (UDR)	4.1	7.9
Independent Republican (RI)	4.0	9.6

a. Rates per 100 substantive votes (abstentions excluded) that conflict with substantive positions of the parliamentary group.

b. Rates per 100 votes that depart from group's modal position, whether pro, con, or abstain.

substantive defections as well as the rates of all kinds of defection from the modal position of the caucus (including abstentions) for both legislatures taken together. The intergroup differences are stunning. Whereas defections within the Socialist caucus are two or three times as numerous as among the Communists, those within the PDM caucus are almost ten times as numerous as those among the Socialists!

In general, groups of the left achieve a much greater level of party discipline than those of the right. In Figure 17-1 the high peak of defection reached by the PDM in the center is equally easy to grasp. We have already seen that the PDM was located, and conceived of itself, as a pivotal swing group between government and opposition. It swung its modal support back and forth according to the issue at stake. Even in the pre-disorder session, however, before the Gaullists won such a heavy majority of the seats that PDM support was of limited consequence, its power as a pivot was limited by its middle-of-the-road deputies. These deputies were middle-of-the-road for different configurations of reasons: although some, for example, preferred leftist alternatives on certain issues on which their peers had rightist inclinations, that situation could be reversed on other issues. Not only was the PDM a more difficult group to hold together than the others, but its appeals to party discipline were probably less effective because of its professed aims of ideological moderation and policy brokerage.

Another source of variation in party discipline that might similarly be called "constellational," depending as it does on the particular configuration of party groups and their relationships at a certain point in time, is suggested by the display in Figure 17-1. Although all five parliamentary groups showed at least some increase in substantively defecting votes in the Fourth Legislature as against the Third, this increase was proportionately greatest for the UDR. Of course, that Gaullist caucus, essentially representing the government, lacked an absolute majority in the initial session; it could only command such a majority by a razor-thin margin by mustering the full support of its Giscardian wing (RI), which had formed its own parliamentary group despite its Gaullist past. Because every vote from a UDR member was extremely precious, it is likely that pressure toward party discipline was intense. But the electoral revolution of 1968 produced a vast shift in the balance of power. The Gaullist UDR, without a single vote from any other parliamentary group (the Giscardian RI included), could afford a rate of substantive defections of 15 percent from within its own ranks and still command an absolute majority! Under such circumstances, it would not have been surprising if the urgency of complete party discipline had lost some of its intensity.[34]

Whereas Figure 17-1 suggests in crude form the existence of temporal variations in party discipline, Figure 17-2 plots these variations by parliamentary group across the six years of legislative sessions. There is again considerable variation in these rates for the same parties over time. We had half expected to find some secular increases in defection rates between the beginning and end of a legislative session, not only because defections were scored on the basis of the deputy's initial choice of parliamentary group, and the few later switches were not updated, but also because it would be reasonable to expect that, with the passage of time, the intrusion of new

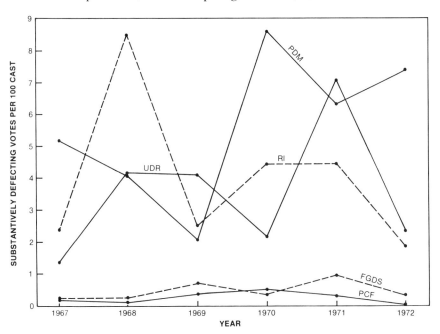

Figure 17-2. Rates of substantive defection from party discipline in National Assembly, by year and parliamentary group, 1967–1972.

"cross-cutting" issues not foreseen at the time of electoral alliance formation and parliamentary group election might cause the individual deputy's feelings of compatibility with his group to erode progressively. But Figure 17-2 gives little if any support to such an hypothesis, although the difference between the two sessions remains clear.

At the same time, Figure 17-2 does suggest a property of these defections whose existence was thoroughly reinforced by a more detailed scrutiny of the records. Although it remains true that strong and readily interpretable variation is tied up with differences between the parliamentary groups and their locations within the configurations of voting blocs in each session, it is also true that these defection rates are subject to fluctuations which must be seen as purely situational, in the most transient sense of that word. The high peaks registered by the RI in 1968, the PDM in 1970, and the UDR in 1971 are of this sort. They depend less on systematic features of the parliamentary groups, or their strategic positions in the legislative competition, than they do on the particular mix of topics which happened to arrive at the roll-call vote stage during the period of observation.

A more detailed description of the high tide of UDR defections in the 1971 roll calls will clarify this point. Early in the spring session of that year the government presented two bills directly addressed to the Paris region, one regulating the location of industrial sites and office buildings in the general area and the other modifying certain financial arrangements surrounding its public transportation system. These bills were anathema to virtually all the deputies from the Paris area, including a very substantial contingent of Gaullist deputies within the UDR caucus. The government succeeded in pushing these bills through the Assembly, and by the customary wide margins, but only with the help of non-Parisian members of other parliamentary groups. About 50 UDR deputies voted to reject these bills, even in the final summary votes (scrutin no. 198 and no. 216), with substantial numbers of others abstaining; and on some earlier amendments the UDR defections from the government's wishes soared even higher. On one amendment which gave the government one of its extremely rare defeats in the same session, 106 UDR deputies voted directly against the government position, and 10 more deputies abstained.

It is interesting in and of itself that the intrusion of such a regional issue (and very few of these appeared during these sessions) could be so potent in disrupting the normally strong imperatives of party discipline. Less important for our immediate purposes, but still intriguing, is the fact that such a regional issue happened to arise during the 1971 deliberations. In a six-year period we would expect many specific topics to pass through the agenda, and one of the interesting features of our calculations of defection rates is that they cover a wide "sample" of times and issues. But in addition, these two bills were the subject of an extraordinary number of specific roll-call votes. On the majority of bills, business is completed with no more

than three roll-call votes per bill. In the processing of these two similar regional bills, sixteen roll-call votes were recorded, or about one-seventh of all
the roll calls for the whole 1971 session. Therefore the noticeable bulge in
defections which is evident in the record at this point is due not just to the
emergence of this thorny topic but also to the extreme concentration of roll
calls that arose from it.

This variation in defection rates is, of course, highly situational. The
record would look very different if these two bills had been processed with
no more than a normal number of scrutins. A similar variation is apparent
at the level of the individual deputy's voting record. The voting record of
many Parisian Gaullists shows perfect or near-perfect fidelity to the positions of the UDR group over scores of specific topics, in all sorts of domains, during the six years of the Third and Fourth Legislatures. Yet
suddenly, on the two bills on the Paris region, these records register a dozen
or fifteen direct substantive defections all at once. Since defections are rare
to begin with, such totals imply that these faithful group members must be
as "maverick" as the tiny minority of deputies who depart from their parliamentary groups on ten or fifteen different specific topics at various points
throughout the same six-year period. This conclusion does not seem entirely
appropriate, but the oddity arises because of the degree to which defection is
a situation-specific phenomenon.

Given the obvious importance of specific topics in determining
whether defections will run high or low at various points in time, it is natural to wonder whether, in a more general way, certain broad types of roll-call
votes are more likely to stimulate defections than others. Although we have
not conducted exhaustive analyses on the subject, our evidence indicates
that this is the case.

The partitioning of scrutins by type, which produces the two most numerous contrasting categories, reveals a watershed between, on the one side,
overall or final votes on the total text of a bill, and, on the other side, roll
calls registered on the more specific amendments proposed to these texts. It
is not surprising that the number of votes on specific amendments or articles proposed as additions to texts is greater than the final votes on bills
taken as wholes. Yet the imbalance in frequency of the two types of vote is
not nearly so great as the logic of the situation might suggest. This is true
partly because the number of amendments officially offered by a deputy or
legislative committee to a given bill is usually much greater than the number that receive serious consideration (and vastly greater than the number
which, after debate, require a roll-call vote), and partly because roll-call
votes are often taken more than once on the same general text, due to the
procedure of multiple readings as well as revisions arising through the
joint-conference committees.

Although the differences are not dramatic, it is clear that votes on specific amendments show significantly higher rates of defection than those

scrutins that are taken on the final texts of total bills. After the smoke of detailed debate has dispersed, the global review of a bill seems to produce a return to tightened party lines on the final decision. Although this effect is visible for votes on nonfiscal texts, it is particularly apparent for government budget proposals, which produce large numbers of amendments on the most diverse topics. When the total budget is up for adoption or rejection, however, as occurred in some thirteen roll-call votes over the two legislatures, bloc voting becomes even more solid than usual. On this subset of votes, rates of substantively defecting votes by parliamentary group members fall off to 2.7 per 100, relative to a mean over all scrutins of 3.6; and the full summation of all forms of defection for these total-budget votes is a mere 3.3, relative to an overall mean of 7.0.

In still another sense, therefore, our initial raw estimates of global defection rates somewhat exaggerate their importance, even though these estimates are very small from an absolute point of view. In a general way, we would expect the passage or defeat of total bills to be more important legislative acts than the acceptance or rejection of specific amendments to such texts. To be sure, from time to time amendments are proposed which either tighten a bill so drastically, or emasculate it so completely, that their legislative fate is indeed crucial, fully as important as the fate of the bill itself. Nonetheless, such amendments are the exception rather than the rule, and it is unquestionable that the many-articled total texts have a broader "scope" as authoritative policy outputs than do revisions of wording of particular articles within such texts, which is almost invariably what amendments are.

Hence, although rates of deputy defection from parliamentary group positions are very small in the French Assembly even over the total corpus of roll calls, such figures exaggerate to some degree the incidence of defection to be expected for scrutins of the greatest scope.

Conclusions

In this chapter we have portrayed the impact of party discipline on the roll-call vote decisions of individual deputies in the French Assembly. In the process, we have indicated some of the circumstances under which the dictates of party solidarity appear to be stronger or less strong. We have found them stronger, for example: on the left than on the right; for noncentrist than for pivotal groups; under circumstances of tight party competition, in the sense of narrow likely majorities and increased uncertainty about outcomes; and on votes of broader scope. Within these broad lines of systematic variation, we have stressed a major component of variation in the impact of party discipline which is hard to describe as other than purely situational.

One possible line of systematic variation which we have not pursued so far concerns variations in defections arising from differences in viewpoint from deputy to deputy as to the proper conception of the representative role. In other words, although defection rates are absolutely low in the Assembly, it is quite possible that those that do occur come very disproportionately from a handful of mavericks who simply do not share the assumptions as to the virtues of party fidelity that are embraced by the vast majority of their peers. Or alternatively, it may be that the meager number of defections which do occur are haphazardly sprinkled across all deputies at stray points in time, and hence depend less upon different individual value systems than upon the highly situational interaction between a deputy's sensitivities and the specifics of a particular legislative measure. These possibilities will be considered in Chapter 21.

Our prime conclusions in this chapter are that party discipline in the Assembly is strong, and that when defections that are not the result of mechanical accidents in the recording of votes do occur, they are unlikely to be casual. Although it may seem unrealistic to describe any vote of any legislator as "casual," it would not be unreasonable to assume that, because of towering workloads and endless public distractions, in legislative systems where party cues are relatively weak some fraction of votes is cast with limited thought or information. Where the party cues are strong and a high cultural premium is placed on them, as is true in the French setting even among rightist parliamentary groups, the deputy operating under workload and information constraints may well contribute many rather casual votes to the support of his parliamentary group's position. But it is unlikely that he will cast votes contrary to the group position unless other special and even overweening considerations demand his attention. In the French Assembly, such defections—and they are few—are both deliberate and highly motivated.

18

The Basic
Representation Bond

Now that we have discussed the basic theories of representation in legislative bodies and examined the institutional peculiarities of the French National Assembly, we are ready to consider our own district-deputy linkage materials, with an eye to evaluating the nature of the representation process in France.

The full analysis model begins with the distribution of relevant political sentiments among voters in the local districts; it flows through a complex sequence of electoral choice to the decisionmaking processes in the Assembly, which rest partly on the representatives' will to represent, and their knowledge of, district preferences; and it terminates in a vote which either converts a government bill into the law of the land, modifies it, or defeats it outright.

In the remaining chapters of Part IV we shall be tracing out these processes that intervene between voter opinion and final legislative output. As a first analytic step, however, we shall short-circuit the full analytic model and ask what the nature of the empirical connection is between the initial input term and the final output term of the model. Regarding the intervening processes as something of a "black box," we shall first ask whether there is any discernible linkage between variations in public opinion at the district level and the final contributions which various deputies make to roll-call votes on relevant issues. This linkage (the AD connection in Figure 16-1) is what we shall call the basic representation bond.

In some ways this is a weak first step. On the one hand, if noteworthy connections are found, then, as we have already shown, a variety of competing intervening mechanisms may be involved. Any given level of linkage can be sustained in very different ways, and of course we are interested in specifying these mechanisms (the black box) in the French case. On the other hand, if we do not find reliable connections linking the inputs and outputs, we shall still want to explore the black box in order to diagnose whether all, or only one or two, of the expected intervening linkages are missing, or whether some intervening mechanisms actively bias outputs in a contrary direction from the inputs while others operate in a "positive" direction, leaving the final linkage in a neutral situation of stalemate.

Nevertheless, there are still a number of reasons for examining the basic representation bond first. The foremost is that this basic bond does define the ultimate nature of the representation function in France, whatever may go on in the intervening black box. If, for example, we find no sign of positive linkages on any front, this will suggest that the representation process in the French setting, at least as this is commonly construed in terms of theories of democracy and the popular will, is meaningless. No amount of diagnosis, or discovery of this or that positive intervening linkage, could overturn this basic fact.

It is true, moreover, that one of the primary findings in the parent Miller-Stokes (1963, 1964) work was that the strength of the basic representation bond differed quite markedly according to the policy domain at stake. Although various diagnoses as to the intervening mechanisms have captured a good deal of scholarly interest, these differences by policy domain showed through clearly in the basic representation bonds. Therefore, if parallel differences present themselves in the French case, we shall discover them in this chapter. And the early discovery of any such differences will provide useful guidance as to the most fruitful points of focus for subsequent explorations of the relative efficacy of intervening mechanisms.

Finally, and at an entirely practical level, this chapter will give us an opportunity to lay out our portfolio of measures of legislative output in the National Assembly during the 1967–1972 period, measures that will constitute our central dependent variables through the rest of Part IV. It will also provide a chance to consider in detail several competing measurement tactics which will set our analysis agenda for later chapters.

Summary Scales of Roll-Call Voting

Modern parliaments generate enormous quantities of official and semiofficial information as they pursue their business. These records—for example, the more or less verbatim debates, or the details of the internal organization of the relevant chambers—provide important interpretive information concerning the "throughput" stages of the legislative process. The central record of output is summarized by the official voting on those propositions and amendments that are sufficiently important or controversial to be brought to an individual-level tally for purposes of ultimate passage or defeat.[1]

During the two sessions of 1967–1972, a total of 445 votes were brought to such a roll-call stage. Only 87 of these roll-calls were recorded in the first (1967–68) session, before the dissolution of the Assembly during the May–June revolt, a fact which has several consequences for our ultimate operational treatment of the record. Although it is customary and utterly reasonable to set aside unanimous votes at the outset of analyses like ours because they offer no variation, the threshold for bothering to call the roll for votes is set rather high in the French system, with the result that unanimous votes are few. In fact, if we take a strict view of unanimity and require that all votes be cast "aye" or "nay," only three scrutins of the 445 recorded would qualify. If we take a looser definition and set aside blocs of abstentions, then an additional 12 votes were unanimous in the sense of having no minority "ayes" or "nays." Moreover, although the 1968–1972 session was noteworthy for its lopsided Gaullist majority, the vast preponderance of roll-call votes in the two sessions together—some 412 of 445—showed winning proportions of less than 85 percent, if abstentions are included. Thus the record still offers more than 400 roll-call votes that were at least moderately controversial.

Our basic task is to draw from this large corpus of votes a limited and manageable number of measures that summarize variations in individual deputy voting patterns on policy dimensions relevant to our interview materials concerning deputy policy attitudes and constituency opinion. Of course, there is no technical reason why we cannot examine relationships between district or deputy attitudes and the results of any single roll-call vote. In fact, we have examined some relationships of this sort, particularly for the first session, where the portfolio of votes on given topics is very limited. Nonetheless, our attitudinal items are rather general in scope, aimed at broad positions on one side or the other of major policy controversies, rather than at the details of a specific piece of relevant legislation. It may reasonably be assumed that, as we cumulate across the deputy votes cast on a number of pieces of legislation that differ widely in details but have in common a focus on some broader policy controversy, we are isolating the broad policy posture differences that form a reasonable parallel for our general attitude measures, and minimizing the intrusion of idiosyncratic concerns raised by the stray details of any specific measure. Therefore, quite apart from our practical desire to avoid the tedium of proceeding one by one across hundreds of roll-call votes, we believe it makes conceptual sense to arrive at compressed summary measures of deputy voting tendencies.

A major economy in this summarization task arises from the fact that many of the available roll-call votes, even certain of those judged as "important" by outside observers, lie on dimensions of controversy that were not included in our original skein of "linkage issues," and hence do not have any obvious a priori relationships with our interview materials. The original designation of these linkage issues took place in the winter of 1966–67 (although the return to the field in 1968 permitted some modest updating), and represented no more than reasonable conjectures as to what policy matters might dominate Assembly attention over ensuing years. Naturally, some of these surmises were outmoded by the sweep of events, so that certain controversies emerging in the later stages of the second session we had not foreseen at all, while a few of the originally constituted linkage issues declined in importance much more rapidly than we had anticipated.

Several of our preselected issues lost salience in this way. For example, two of the cognate foreign-policy items included in the mass and elite interviews involved: (1) the optimal degree of independence of French foreign policy from that of the United States; and (2) investment in the development of French nuclear weapons (*force de frappe*).

Although these two issues were treated as separate items in the interviews, they overlapped heavily in their genesis and substance. In the period preceding our study, President de Gaulle had startled much of France, as well as the world at large, by programming a major national commitment to the development of a deterrent nuclear arsenal. This move was merely one of the more dramatic in a series of gambits that de Gaulle adopted in an effort to forge a "third force" in the bipolar world created by the two nuclear superpowers, the United States and the Soviet Union. Gaining French admission to the "nuclear club" was one pragmatic means of reducing the country's dependence on the foreign policy maneuvers of the United States and NATO. Although such increased independence struck a positive chord in some segments of French society, the investment in nuclear weapons touched off a storm of domestic controversy in the middle 1960s which was sufficient to shake, if not break, the personal prestige that de Gaulle deliberately lent to the proposals. In 1966 it appeared that the force de frappe issue would remain a major one during the entire life of the new 1967 Assembly. It did occasion some lively debate in connection with the 1968 national budget discussions, but in view of the initial investments already made in the program, the question of follow-through investments became less and less controversial. In a rearguard action, the Communists did offer amendments to reduce or abolish the relevant appropriations during most annual budget debates up to the end of the session in 1972. Thus five direct roll calls are available, quite an adequate number (in principle) for our purposes, although all of them were heavily defeated and were not considered among the more important votes of the sessions. Meanwhile, although the broader question of the independence of French foreign policy from that of the United States may have given an overtone to other debates of the period, it was not the obviously dominant element in any roll-call vote.

Another predesignated linkage issue which failed to produce any significant harvest of relevant Assembly roll-call votes was the question of French foreign aid to underdeveloped countries. As usual, foreign aid allocations were bound into annual national budget proposals, and these budget proposals were voted on by the Assembly. But votes on the totality of the budget are not very informative with respect to more specific policy dimensions. Only twice were specific foreign-aid allocations isolated and challenged in special amendments that produced roll-call votes. Neither of these votes, which took place in the 1967–68 session, ranked as important in the annals of the period.

In several other instances—European integration, aid to church schools, and priority for economic development—there were as few as three roll-call votes of patent and direct relevance to the linkage materials drawn from our interviews. This number remains reasonably satisfying, however, since the votes involved were commonly judged to be among the most important of the sessions. Thus, for example, the "religious question" came before the Assembly only once in a pointed form leading to roll-call votes. This was in 1971, when the renewal of the Debré Act of 1959 governing the extension of state funds to the private religious schools was discussed and voted on. Although only three votes were recorded, the issue remained an emotional one, and the attendant roll calls were quite adequate to tap this dimension of policy controversy. In the same vein, whereas most of the controversial Gaullist emphasis on government investment in the nation's economic development was distributed through the structure of total budget proposals and rarely became isolated for special vote, there were three roll calls in this domain, including two major votes of approbation for Giscard d'Estaing's VIe Plan for "balanced growth," which stressed economic development through further industrialization (1970 and 1971).

At the other extreme, one of the two chief examples of an emergent controversy which had not figured at all in our designation of linkage issues involved the attention devoted by the Assembly, especially after 1969, to the legislative details of the push toward a decentralization, or "regionalization," of the French public administration. It is unlikely that positions in the attendant debates would have lent themselves to much unidimensional reduction in any event. By fits and starts over the course of the second session, the government developed its decentralization program, and of course the examination of such proposals in the Assembly produced the familiar lines of bifurcation along the government-opposition axis. This dimension, however, is present in a large number of votes on many assorted topics; and the considerations more properly specific to the decentralization debates involved a witch's brew of philosophies for or against aspects of local autonomy, mingled with regional and departmental sensitivities on highly particularized points. Therefore it is doubtful that any simple but robust dimension other than government-opposition could have been sifted from these deliberations, had we been foresighted enough to anticipate them.

We say that the decentralization issue was a primary example of an emergent controversy that we failed to anticipate. This may seem odd, in view of the fact that the unforeseen revolt of 1968 led directly to the dissolution of the first Assembly, and its widening repercussions were galvanic for much of the second session. But, as we have seen, the two main policy domains in the catalytic events of 1968—the structure and development of the education system, and the rights and roles of organized labor in the factories—had in fact been given some plausible representation as linkage issues even in our 1967 mass and elite interviewing. Moreover, what was undoubtedly the broadest "meta-issue" surrounding the revolt—the responsiveness of political elites to popular demands—was the very subject of our entire study. Hence, by the greatest of luck, we had taken a number of measurements appropriate to a "before-after" study of the central polarizations of the 1968 events. We shall naturally give uncommon attention to these most relevant linkage issues in subsequent chapters, and shall ultimately arrive at some conclusions as to the general impact of the 1968 revolt on the quality of popular representation in France.

In 1967 we had asked both mass and elite respondents two questions on the education system. One was in normal opinion form; the other was in the issue-importance or "agenda" form. Both questions focused on the degree of effort (for the elite, relative budgetary appropriations) the government should make to further the development of the education system. The questions were asked because even in late 1966 there were signs of tension in the education arena. Although the Gaullist government had taken a number of steps in the early 1960s to cope with the rapidly swelling tides of students seeking entrance to an already crowded higher education system, there was frequent criticism that the measures were inadequate. Hence the 1967 questions were asked on the assumption that the issue in this form might gain force. The university-based portion of the 1968 disorders represented just such a crescendo, although in the course of events there was an evolution from relatively generalized demands for greater government attention and resources for higher education, to a range of more specific but far-reaching proposals for one or another kind of basic structural reform of the education system.

In our mass reinterviews after the disorders, we asked more specifically about opinions concerning the desirability of governmental reform of the university system, as well as the importance of such reform on the public agenda. The corresponding items in the 1968 elite reinterviews probed the deputy's sense concerning the priority to be given the educational system in the national budget, and included direct questioning as to reactions to the government's reform proposals for the education system which were already being outlined by the Minister of Education, Edgar Faure. The Faure Bill was, in fact, at the virtual head of the agenda for the new session of the reconstituted Assembly, and in the heat of events was passed in October 1968, with no contrary votes and only thirty-nine abstentions, although somewhat greater differentiation of deputy opinion was evident in connection with amendment roll calls prior to final passage of the total bill. Still greater differentiation occurred when the 1968 Faure Act went through a revision process in 1971, generating five more roll-call votes.

The links between our 1968 mass and elite interview items on educational reform and priorities for the education system, on the one hand, and the Faure Bill debates as well as other votes on budgetary allocations for education, on the other, are entirely direct. Yet even our education items of 1967, for which we have much larger numbers of cases for both mass and elite, seem to have quite adequate relevance for the general controversy over the education system, even as it evolved in the wake of the 1968 events.

Much the same can be said of the fundamental policy issues involved in the other (labor) half of the 1968 disorders. Even in our 1967 elite interview we had asked our candidates their views as to whether the role of labor union representatives in industry and factory management should be expanded, reduced, or kept the same. As it happened, the demand for expansion of this role was central to the factory-based participation in the 1968 strikes and plant occupations. The 1967 mass item was slightly less focused on the question of *autogestion* (self-management) but it did ask respondents the degree to which they felt that the rights of labor unions should be more vigorously protected. These two 1967 items were repeated in 1968, along with an additional item of the agenda type, asked of both mass and elite samples, concerning the importance of recognition of unions at the plant level. Therefore, once again, all of these interview materials anticipated very nicely the primary issues crystallized by the disorders, and they can fruitfully be linked to the legislative decisionmaking that was prompted in the most direct way by the revolt, such as the major labor-union-rights reform legislation hurriedly brought before the Assembly by the government in the fall of 1968, aimed at giving the labor unions more extended participation in factory management. They can also be meaningfully related to a variety of other legislation arising through 1972 as other aspects of union rights came to be debated.

One other important class of legislation emerging in direct response to the disorders was not well covered in our predesignated linkage issues. This was the area of civil rights, brought into question by the confrontation politics of the period. From the spring of 1970 onward, the Gaullist government presented some repressive "law and order" bills to the Assembly.

Although ultimately passed by the dominant Gaullist majority, these measures provoked great public outcry, and one was later overturned as unconstitutional. These debates generated some sixteen nonredundant roll-call votes which lend themselves to a very fruitful scale captured as we passed. Regrettably, however, in view of the importance of these votes, we lack matching questionnaire items for them, and this must remain our major disappointment where foresight as to crucial policy domains is concerned.

After scanning all of the 445 roll-call votes for their relevance to our predesignated linkage issues, we arrived at a much more restricted pool of 123 roll calls spread across eight linkage domains. The distribution of these roll calls across substantive domains was grossly unequal. For example, 80 of the 123 votes fell into a general category of socioeconomic conflict, which had in turn several points of articulation with our interview materials, while the remaining 43 votes were much more thinly spread over the other seven linkage domains. But apart from civil rights and the decentralization issue, these 123 votes do include the vast majority of roll-call votes that were later singled out by observers as the most significant of the two sessions.[2]

The Tactics of Scaling

At a purely mechanical level, the procedure we normally used to combine votes over multiple roll calls in order to form summary scales can be described very briefly. For each roll call deemed suitable to contribute to a summary scale, "aye" votes and "nay" votes were scored as zero and two, properly keyed; and those abstentions arising for reasons other than absence from the Assembly were given the halfway value of one. Each summary scale is no more than the sum of such values across the set of roll calls seen as fit ingredients for it.

Although such a description is disarmingly simple, and permits the reader, once fortified with a list of roll-call votes (see Table 18-2), to replicate our scoring with great ease, it begs the question as to why certain roll calls from our original pool of 123 votes were "deemed suitable" for inclusion while others were not. And the considerations surrounding a decision for inclusion, consisting of a series of tests which any given roll call was required to survive, were as complex as the ultimate scoring rule was simple. Indeed, a memorandum describing the empirical properties of each substantive cluster of roll calls and indicating the bases for selecting each vote contributing to one or another of the final summary scales runs about the length of this chapter.[3] Obviously we cannot carry the reader through such a detailed description of the total structure of decisions surrounding each measure. Instead, we shall merely review here the basic postures which consistently informed these decisions.

Most of our decisions, including our choice of a relatively simple scoring mechanism rather than the more conventional Guttman scaling or factor analysis, were conditioned by the nature of deputy voting in the National Assembly, and particularly by the towering levels of party discipline in roll-call voting described in the last chapter. Such party discipline threatens to reduce any effort at an elegant "scaling" of Assembly votes to a rather trivial matter.

At the grossest level, one immediate consequence of great party discipline, along with the high frequency of votes pitting parties of the left against parties of the right, is the substantial number of roll calls which are virtually identical to one another, give or take a half-dozen votes out of a total of about 480. And these virtual identities can readily arise between pairs of votes that are utterly independent of each other in policy content. Of course, the fact that there is such a modal party vote configuration that reiterates itself across the most diverse kinds of content does not lessen the political importance of that configuration; if anything, its importance is the greater because of its prevalence. For this reason, we created one synthetic summary variable called a Pure Party measure, in which each deputy is merely assigned a scale score determined by the party caucus he attends, and the scores assigned to the respective parties approximate a central tendency across all voting configurations.[4]

Despite the obvious utility of such a synthetic variable, for most of our purposes we are interested in those departures from the modal party voting configuration on the part of both caucuses and individual defectors that are distinctive to our various linkage-issue domains. And where these aims are concerned, the presence of a modal party configuration which occurs often, almost irrespective of content, is one reason that we first winnowed the totality of our roll-call votes into a reduced set of "preliminary universes of content" (see MacRae, 1970, p. 24) defined by manifest issue substance, instead of applying scaling or clustering techniques to the whole corpus of votes blindly.

Even after this sorting was completed, however, the fact of extreme party discipline in the roll calls continued to exert a major influence on our subsequent procedures. Among other things, the coalescence of votes into large blocs, where the blocs themselves behave much of the time as though arrayed on a unidimensional continuum, means that there is often little challenge to Guttman scaling, at least over the Assembly as a whole. For example, Table 18-1 gives the modal position of each party caucus on each of the five votes falling into our pool of items on the force de frappe, arrayed in the form of a conventional scalogram.

At the level of these collectivities, the pattern is that of the perfect Guttman scale, despite the lack of extreme variation in the marginals of the roll-call votes. When the cumulative pattern of a Guttman scale is perfect, the normal additive Guttman scoring is identical to the simple additive scoring which we have used in forming our own summary measures. Hence

Table 18-1. Party positions on five roll-call votes concerning force de frappe.[a]

	Roll-call votes				
	1967–1968		1968–1972		
Party	#32	#33	#69	#340	#142
PCF	−	−	−	−	−
FGDS	−	−	−	−	0
PDM	−	0	+	+	+
UDR	+	+	+	+	+
RI	+	+	+	+	+

a. + = vote favoring force de frappe; − = vote against force de frappe; 0 = abstention.

the degree to which the cumulative pattern falls short of perfection at the level of the individual deputy, or the degree to which our simple scoring departs from Guttman scaling, hinges on the vote patterns shown by those few deputies who belong to no caucus, along with those who fail to vote with the modal position of their party.

We have already seen that for most votes most of the time, very few deputies fall into those last two categories. For example, over the Assembly as a whole on these five force de frappe votes, only 2.5 votes per 100 differ at all from the positions of the relevant party caucuses. Moreover, not all of these deviations need be construed as "error types" in the Guttman sense (that is, individual-level departures from perfect cumulativity). In fact, empirical examination shows that in this instance nearly half of the defecting votes conform to perfect scale patterns despite their deviation from the party position. In turn, this means that a coefficient of reproducibility assessing the degree of individual-level fit to a perfect cumulative pattern approaches .99.[5] And although conventions for allocating scores to error types can vary, it is likely that our final simple additive summary score for the force de frappe would show a product-moment correlation with any variant on Guttman scale scoring of the same items which, over the Assembly as a whole, would be above .99, and hence, for all intents and purposes, an identity. Thus our scoring is essentially the same as a Guttman scaling, save that its calculation is more efficiently described.

Naturally, the hierarchical structure of the force de frappe votes is neater than that in some of our other issue domains, or item pools. Yet most of the pools do approximate this situation. For the few which do not, a further stage of winnowing, which we are about to describe, can refine them to roughly the same point of clarity in terms of dimensional structure. Ultimately, for all of our pools of items the construction of a strong Guttman scale is almost child's play, *when we are operating over all parties in the Assembly at once.*

As MacRae (1970) has emphasized, however, we can make far more stringent demands on our data by pursuing our analyses within party groups. For work at this level, party groups which are polar and hence monolithic in their voting on particular issues are essentially discarded, and attention is focused on those parties near the pivotal point in the debate at hand, for which the defections from party discipline tend to be most numerous. Given significant rates of defection from such a party over a series of votes which seem to be substantively related, the question arises as to whether or not the defections seem to show reasonable cumulative patterns. This is, of course, a much sterner test of the data than is scaling over all parties at once, but it is the level at which our preparation of summary roll-call measures has proceeded.

Earlier we noted that after our numerous content domains or pools summing to 123 roll-call votes had been assembled, they were subjected to further testing and winnowing. Now we can state quite succinctly what these further tests were.

First, a few roll calls out of the 123 were excluded because they did little more than recapitulate our Pure Party measure. One could summarize across a very long series of such redundant measures and gain absolutely nothing in discrimination power over the scaling based merely on any single item in the set. Once beyond the Pure Party measure, our purpose was to detect departures from the modal configuration of party voting according to specific universes of content. Thus routine party votes added nothing to our measurement and were deleted.

Second, we excluded those votes for which reasonable within-party tests failed to show any substantial cumulative patterning of defections, and thus suggested a lack of unidimensionality. We state this criterion a bit indirectly, because reasonable within-party tests were not available for every one of our content pools. Such tests could only be conducted when members of some particular party caucus showed a reasonable margin of variation on at least two votes in the same item pool. In some instances—especially when the item pool was limited to two or three roll calls at the outset—these conditions were not present, and items were accepted for the final scaling without this kind of verification.

Third, careful attention was paid to the detection of those "ends-against-the-middle" votes which are the bugaboo of many cumulative scaling enterprises.[6] A vote was not considered to be in this category simply because the nominal position of Communist deputies coincided on a particular measure with the caucus position of a normally antagonistic group, such as the UDR or the Republicains Indépendants. Such an uncommon patterning might suffice to raise a caution flag, and lead to a more careful examination of the qualitative positions being taken in Assembly debate. In some cases, further examination would make clear that a routine

scoring of such a vote would put together strange bedfellows even with respect to the immediate substance of the debate, and would thus distort the
meaning of that scoring. But such was not necessarily the case merely because two parties, typically antagonistic, voted in the same direction on
some particular policy dimension.

Similarly, roll-call votes were not automatically discarded even when
ends-against-the-middle voting was detected. In a rare instance or two they
could be used profitably in scale construction. One such instance arose in
connection with the second (1971) debate over the Faure Law pertaining to
educational reform. This debate was a classic of the ends-against-the-middle
variety: the proposals of the Gaullist government for revisions of the Faure
Law were described by professional observers as being trapped between the
"grindstones" of the left and the right. Even the towering majority enjoyed
by the UDR in the Assembly suffered major erosion as Gaullist deputies defected from group discipline in response to either leftist or rightist critiques
of the revisions. Indeed, these votes gave us an excellent opportunity to sort
out three major wings of the UDR, provided the two types of antigovern-
ment votes could be reliably discriminated. Of the roll-call votes taken during the debate, some measures were pure leftist amendments, others were
pure rightist ones, and one or two more global votes fused both left and
right in a common opposition. Analyses of defections within the UDR,
coupling the known leftist and rightist votes with the more ambiguous
two-pronged votes, showed handsome cumulative patterns discriminating
party wings in the expected manner. Hence the discriminating information
was utilized in preparing a summary scaling for the Faure Law votes, and in
this exceptional instance different score values could accrue to the same defecting vote within the UDR.

Nevertheless, such a capacity to discriminate between wings within a
single party in an ends-against-the-middle vote was exceptional. More commonly, when such votes were detected, there was no means of discriminating between the wings on the basis of the voting record, and therefore a few
such votes were discarded from the original pool.

When MacRae advocated a focus on within-party roll-call scaling, the
purpose was typically to proceed with party-specific or party-controlled analyses. Thus it did not matter if scale currencies were party-specific also. But,
given our primary interest in linking broad variation in constituency sentiments with broad variation in deputy policy preferences, we expected to do
little analytic work that hinged on single Assembly parties taken separately.
If we have spent extended analytic time examining patterns of within-party
defection from group discipline, the purpose has been to achieve some satisfactory warrant for including various roll-call votes from our original pool
in the actual construction of our summary roll-call scales. Most of our scales
do capture some within-party variation in the modest degree permitted by

the raw materials, and these could be used for within-party analysis. The nature of our design, however, is such that we shall customarily be using the full range of cross-party variation, and hence the currencies for each scale must have meaning across the full gamut of legislative parties.

One way to summarize our scaling efforts is to say that we exercised great care in the editorial selection of roll calls within each of the content pools that had been established on the basis of our initial review of manifest substance. This care was exercised in order to assure that roll calls which would corrupt the meaning of each intended scale would be eliminated. Once we were satisfied with the unidimensional integrity of each winnowed pool, we proceeded to the additive scoring described earlier, which was very simply and straightforwardly accomplished except in the case of the ends-against-the-middle voting surrounding the revision of the Faure Law.

Actual Summary Scales Constructed

Following the general postures we have outlined, we winnowed our initial pool of 123 roll-call votes spread over eight content domains to a much more reduced set. In a few instances, it made sense to commission more than one summary scale in a particular content domain. Table 18-2 recapitulates in bookkeeping form the progress from the 123 roll-call votes employed as input, through the 54 winnowed votes, to the final output of 15 scales, with their tag-line identifications and the raw votes on which they were based. As the table makes clear, some of these scales are composites of subscales based on various partitions of broader issue domains.

The four simpler scales—two each from the domestic and foreign domains—require little further introduction. The *Economic Development Scale* rests on three votes, one taken in 1969 over the guaranteeing of loans for construction of major highways, and the other two, in 1970 and 1971, which were votes of approval for Giscard d'Estaing's VIe Plan for "balanced growth" with emphasis on stimulation of industrialization. The *Religion Scale* stems from three 1971 votes on the renewal of the Debré Act of 1959, defining the nature of state aid to religious schools. The *European Integration Scale* rests on a sequence of three 1970 votes involved in the French ratification of a decision of the Council of Ministers of the European Community giving Community institutions increased budgetary powers. The *Foreign Aid Scale* is by far the weakest in the whole set, being based on a mere pair of 1967 budgetary votes on aid to Algeria and to Greece. Moreover, in contrast to the case with all other scales, these two votes—the only roll calls available on the subject—were combined despite the lack of evidence of a cumulative relationship between the responses.

Coverage for the other four domains is more intricate. On the one hand, it was obvious to us from the outset that the area of socioeconomic issues, the classic domain of "left" and "right," would be complicated in

Table 18-2. Schema of sources for roll-call vote summary scales.

Content domain	Number of roll calls		Identification of roll-call votes remaining in winnowed pool, used for scalings[a]	Average reference lines per vote[b]	Designation of subscales	Designation of final summary scales
	Original pool	Winnowed pool				
General Government-Opposition	11	4 4	#8a, 16a, 80a, 87a #49, 144, 200, 315	151.6	Gov't.-Opposition II	Gov't.-Opposition
Domestic Socioeconomic Left-Right	28 Tax 19 Soc. Wel. 14 Housing 12 Union rights 5 Work 2 Pub./Priv.	11 6 3	#2, 20, 28, 85, 145–147, #266, 271, 335, 337 #30–32, 34, 36–37 #89, 205, 310	2.0 2.8	Income Distribution Droit syndical Union rights	Socioeconomic Left-Right
Economic Development	3	3	#66, 124, 243	17.7		Economic Development
Education	4 Budget 11 Faure	4 6	#35a, 48, 65, 157 #17, 244–248	5.3		Education Budget Faure Law Left-Right
Religion	3	3	#201–203	12.3		Religion
Foreign Force de Frappe	6	2 3	#32a, 33a #69, 142, 340	4.1	Force de Frappe I Force de Frappe II	Force de Frappe
European Integration	3	3	#125–127	2.3		European Integration
Foreign Aid	2	2	#42a, 43a	0.0		Foreign Aid
Total	123	54				

a. Roll-call votes show official numbering according to *Journal Officiel*; "a" after number indicates 1967–68 session.
b. Average number of lines devoted to roll calls in winnowed set of 54 in relevant annual issues of *L'Année politique*.

some degree by the sheer number of relevant roll-call votes on several specific issues. Indeed, we have seen that in our first provisional set of 123 votes some 80 votes fell into this category. On the other hand, reality helped us to simplify this large mass of votes, because the domain is characterized by uncommonly high levels of party discipline and the party positioning on most of the votes is enormously repetitive, with the Communists and Socialists consistently opposing the other three caucuses. Indeed, we estimated that if intercorrelations were mechanically run across this original set of 80 votes, more than two-thirds of these correlations would exceed .95.

In the face of this redundancy accompanying what was otherwise an embarrassment of riches where raw materials were concerned, we decided to make editorial selections by working from the other side of our linkage design, giving attention to the more specific facets of the generic socioeconomic debate emphasized in questions posed of constituents in the mass sample. The two most relevant items had concerned the issues of (1) the distribution of income; and (2) the rights of labor unions. A fitting match for the first item was found in the substantial series of votes focusing on the progressiveness of tax policy, and an *Income Distribution Subscale* based on eleven of the less redundant items in this area was prepared.

Meanwhile, because of the particular demands of the workers at the time of the May–June revolt, questions surrounding the second item, the prerogatives of labor unions, were very significant in this period. Indeed, one of the major responses of the government to the disturbances was the presentation, later in 1968, of a major bill expanding the legal rights of labor to participate in factory management. Although the left generally grumbled about the inadequacy of this government initiative, it could scarcely protest the measure but voted for it. Yet among the right and center parties there were rather violent objections to the permissiveness of the bill, and defections from party discipline reached a crescendo. Because of our particular interest in the impact of the May–June revolt on the representation process, it seemed worthwhile to capture deputy reactions to this crucial bill in the purest possible form. Thus one subscale was based on six of the eight votes generated during the passage of the bill, known as the *droit syndical*.

Although this subscale was useful in representing a direct and immediate response to the 1968 disturbances, the measure provided rather too little discrimination on the left. Therefore use was made of three other later votes bearing on union rights which produced more splintering of the left. When a standard scoring of these three votes was added to the scoring of the *Droit Syndical Subscale*, it produced a more generic *Union Rights Subscale* based on some nine roll-call votes.

Similarly, we may combine these two socioeconomic items, the Income Distribution Subscale and the Union Rights Subscale, in order to produce a

still more generic measure discriminating differences across the socioeconomic version of the left-right continuum. Just as the two component measures have specific counterparts in items in the mass questionnaire, so this
generic measure combining them in a *Socioeconomic Left-Right Scale* may
fruitfully be paired with measures from the mass sample concerning personal left-right locations.

Parallel complexities arise in the domain of education policy, and for
reasons which are also parallel. Although the mass sample in 1967 had been
queried concerning priorities to be given to further development of the
education system, it was not until after the disturbances of 1968 that a series
of measures reforming the education system were packaged as the Faure
Law. Our mass respondents were asked their opinions of such educational
reform only in 1968. In approaching this general area, we wanted to develop
roll-call scales which would reflect both the eagerness to expand the education system and the deputies' reactions to the Faure Law itself.

The most obvious manifestation of priority given to development of
the educational system arose from support of budgetary increases for that
system. Therefore, within the pool of education-related items, we first isolated a set of four instances in which questions of the size of the education
budget were voted upon directly. These items were used to constitute a first
Education Budget Scale.

Then attention was turned to eleven roll-call votes surrounding the
Faure Law. The first four of these votes, which, like the votes on the droit
syndical, were taken in 1968 in the direct wake of the May–June disturbances, produced the original passage of the legislation. As with the union
reform bill, passage was by an extremely wide margin, with no dissenting
votes and only a few abstentions. Yet at least one amendment produced
some discrimination, especially on the right. The other seven votes arose in
1971 in connection with a series of revisions proposed for the Faure Law.
These latter votes, coming at some remove from the pressures of the disturbances, were rather more hotly contested, and, as we remarked earlier in this
chapter, were subjected to volleys of criticism from both left and right.
Some amendments split the left, others split the right, and some produced
clear ends-against-the-middle voting. After careful analyses, we used six of
these votes (one from 1968 and five from 1971) to prepare a *Faure Law
Left-Right Scale,* designed to express deputy reactions to the Faure legislation
on a full continuum ranging from those who felt the measures were too liberal and permissive of student power, through those who accepted the proposals as an adequate response to the student portion of the 1968 revolt, to
those of more radical bent who felt the measures were an incomplete response. The preparation of such a scale required that at some few points the
same votes be given interpretations which were polar opposites, depending
upon the patterning associated with other items that lacked any ends-
against-the-middle ambiguity.[7]

Differential scales were constructed within two other domains for a rather different kind of reason. Our total original pool of 123 roll calls had been assembled promiscuously from both the 1967–68 and 1968–1972 legislatures (each of which we shall refer to for simplicity's sake as a session). As the scaling work proceeded, it turned out that most votes being used for particular scales came from one session or the other. Thus, for example, the foreign-aid items were taken exclusively from the first session, while most of the other scales were drawn exclusively from the second session. Apart from a single first-session vote for the education domain, only two issue domains—the government-opposition votes and those concerning the force de frappe—confronted us with a substantial mix of ingredient votes from both sessions.

The session differential was of some concern for the simple reason that the Assembly composition was not quite the same for the two periods. Of course, in establishing a scale score for the representative of a specific district over the two sessions, it is quite legitimate to imagine that one is dealing with a legislative seat which is constant, even if its occupants change with some regularity. In other words, in the handful of our districts represented in the first session by a Communist, but in the second session by a Gaullist, it is quite possible to follow the mechanical scoring of votes cast by the seat across the two sessions, thereby producing a summary scale score which is more or less in the middle between left and right to the degree that votes contributing to the summary come more or less equally from the two sessions. There is nothing at all wrong with such a solution of the scoring problem across sessions: indeed, for many conceptual purposes it is exactly what one would want. But upon occasion we were interested in making analyses within the first or the second session separately. For these purposes, we wanted to maintain some time discrimination in the summary scales most evenly divided between the sessions.

Therefore we created two separate subscales within the force de frappe domain, the first being based on two votes from the first session, and the second drawn from three votes in the second session. A third, summary *Force de Frappe Scale* was also created which obliterates the session differential by adding these two subscales together.

Very nearly the same strategy was followed in the case of the pool of government-opposition votes, a total of eleven over the two sessions. These are particularly important because they include all the votes of censure aimed by the opposition at the government, along with the results of votes of confidence requested by the government in response to its portfolio of policies. Their importance is dramatized by the amount of copy devoted to votes of this type in the summation of references in *L'Année politique* (see Table 18-2). In the first session, when the government majority was narrow, all six votes in the pool involved censure motions, whereas in the second session, when the opposition had no chance of bringing down the government, only two involved censure and the remaining three concerned motions of confidence. One attractive feature of this pool is that at least one such vote was taken in each of the six calendar years.

Although we wanted to represent these important votes with high fidelity, the six censure votes of the first session were readily reduced to four because three of them were separate readings of the same censure motion, and all members of our deputy sample, along with virtually all deputies more generally, cast the same vote at each reading. And for the second session, one vote was discarded from the five because none of the defections from party discipline occurred within our sample. This left four votes from each of the two sessions.

Our most summary *Government-Opposition Scale* simply sums across the eight relevant votes in the two sessions. For some purposes, however, this sum could be misleading, since most members of the PDM caucus behaved differentially across the two sessions, voting against the government three times of the four in the first session but supporting the government in all four votes in the second session. To isolate this time difference, a separate *Government-Opposition II Subscale* limited to the second session was created.

Review

We have now accounted, in at least modest detail, for all of the fifteen summary scales and subscales based on the roll-call votes of our deputies in the National Assembly. Naturally, some of these scales will turn out to be of much greater empirical interest than others. Nevertheless, it has seemed appropriate to describe the whole portfolio as it was originally created, before any empirical feedback became available.

It is not surprising that the positions on these fifteen summary scales and subscales are substantially intercorrelated. This result was virtually assured as a joint effect of infrequent departures from party discipline and the repetitiveness of caucus differences from one issue domain to another in the National Assembly. Table 18-3 presents these intercorrelations for all but three of the most redundant subscales, as calculated for the scale scores assigned to our 86 sample districts.

There are some rather low values in this matrix. But quite a number of them are associated with the Foreign Aid scale, which, as we have already noted, is in several senses the most weakly based of these measures. The trend of the intercorrelations is substantially higher for the bulk of the more generic and central scales. For example, setting aside the Foreign Aid measure, the central scale called Socioeconomic Left-Right shows an average correlation with all the other scales of .80. These high values occur despite the fact that component roll-call votes were specifically selected to maximize domain-specific differentiation in the summary scales.

Nonetheless, such high correlations do speak to an incontrovertible re-

Table 18-3. Intercorrelations for summary roll-call scales.

	Droit Syndical	Faure Law Left-Right	Economic Development	Religion	Income Distribution	European Integration	Socioeconomic L-R	Union Rights	Education Budget	Force de Frappe	Government-Opposition	Foreign Aid
Droit Syndical	—	.64	.29	.30	.32	.20	.50	.63	.32	.36	.27	.24
Faure Law Left-Right		—	.69	.73	.72	.44	.79	.80	.68	.66	.59	.33
Economic Development			—	.96	.96	.59	.94	.87	.88	.83	.80	.45
Religion				—	.99	.64	.96	.87	.91	.84	.78	.41
Income Distribution					—	.66	.97	.88	.92	.86	.79	.43
European Integration						—	.61	.53	.57	.57	.42	.05
Socioeconomic L-R							—	.97	.91	.87	.81	.46
Union Rights								—	.84	.83	.77	.47
Education Budget									—	.91	.85	.60
Force de Frappe										—	.86	.72
Government-Opposition											—	.68
Foreign Aid												—

ality concerning the repetitiveness of voting patterns in the Assembly, even across very disparate domains. If we have tampered with this reality by constructing scales which attempt to maximize differentiation by issue domain, we can see from Table 18-3 that the effort has not carried us very far. And this means in turn that frequently we shall want to ask domain-specific linkage questions less in terms of absolute indicators of congruence than in terms of incremental congruence between district sentiments and the modest *departures* of a particular roll-call scale from the most routinized configurations of party discipline. Indeed, it was for this purpose that we added the Pure Party summary measure mentioned above to our portfolio of deputy measures, so that it would serve as a foil, or a kind of baseline from which special effects in various issue domains could be evaluated.

Finally, it is worth noting that, at a technical level, each of our summary scale measures is linked more firmly to a particular legislative *seat* than to any given deputy occupying the seat. This is a distinction which will rarely be of concern, and we shall typically speak as though the pattern of roll-call votes was in fact the unique creation of specific deputies, since this is almost always the case. In a stray instance or two, however, a fraction of the relevant record was contributed by a *suppléant* (alternate), rather than by the actual deputy himself. Nevertheless, it is the association of a vote pattern with a specific seat that is of primary interest to us, since each seat is in turn uniquely associated with a constituency in a local district.

Gauging District Sentiment

In confronting the 445 roll-call votes of the National Assembly in this period, we were obliged to weed and compress the raw information to a heroic degree in order to arrive at a manageable set of measures for the output terms in the representation bond. In regard to the input term involving district opinions for our various policy domains, we faced no problem of sheer measurement bulk. If anything, our measures were quite sparse, consisting of responses to the not more than two dozen public policy questions that time permitted us to ask local voters.

We need not bother to explain these items at this point, since they concern two measures—the agenda measures of issue importance and the measures of policy positions—that we encountered earlier in this book (see especially Chapter 7). But we should consider the problems that are involved in using these responses to represent "district sentiment" in some aggregated, single-value form.

One problem concerns the items which are taken to reflect district opinion in any given policy domain. In the Miller-Stokes study, estimates of district sentiment were based on a summary scaling of two or three interview items, all lying within the same policy arena. In principle, the investigator, bound by stringent limits on interview time, is faced with a choice between multiple items aimed at a few issue domains, and fewer items spread across more domains. We deliberately chose the second alternative. In the case of one issue domain, European integration, and for special reasons unrelated to this book, we posed half a dozen questions: one, in agenda form, concerning the importance of moving toward an integrated Europe, and the other five addressing the desirability of different facets of integration, such as the combining of armed forces, economic unification, and so on. Once past this special case, only a few other domains were represented by as many as two separate items, and these invariably arose because the same domain was explored in the agenda form as well as in the policy-position form. Still other domains were represented by single items.

The analyses in this book have been carried out not only with district feelings represented by each relevant single item, but also with composite indices based on six items (European integration) or on item pairs where they are available. For simplicity's sake, we shall present most results by using the compounded indices, since the level of detail becomes quite confusing when results decomposed to the single-item level are displayed. But duplicating the analyses at the single-item level permits us to monitor any points at which the more summary composite results can be misleading.

And upon occasion, it will be important for us to retreat to the single-item form of analysis. One such occasion arises when we are making finer time-change comparisons between results using measures of district sentiment in 1967 and results using measures of sentiment in 1968. The problem with compound indices in this instance is that not all items forming composites in 1967 were repeated in 1968, and vice versa.[8]

For the European integration domain, with six items available, factor analysis was used to extract a principal component, and individual response patterns were then scored on the basis of factor loadings. Where only two items were available, as was true in most other cases, more elegant scaling was irrelevant, and the measures were compounded simply by adding the integer scoring of the two response arrays. In fact, the lack of more elegant scaling in these cases is probably of little moment, since at the individual level in the European integration case the same simple additive scoring of the six items shows a correlation of .996 with the elaborately achieved factor scores.

Once such individual scores are formed for the voters of diverse districts, a second problem concerns the way in which we aggregate these individual positions within the constituency to express some central tendency for overall district sentiment on the policy matter at stake. Variation inevitably exists within the district, whether we are dealing with responses to a single item or with index scores for a larger number of items. In the single-item case, some constituents agree strongly with the policy proposal, some disagree strongly, and the others take more moderate positions. Generally, where these single items are concerned, we have chosen to calculate district sentiment as a simple numerical mean formed over the response distribution, after assigning integer scores to the naturally ordered response categories.

This solution recognizes differences in intensity of reported feeling, so that even if two districts divide in the same proportions pro and con on an issue, a district with more "strong agree" responses and fewer "strong disagree" responses will appropriately score as slightly more favorable to the policy proposal than where the reverse is true. Although such a solution presumes a kind of equal spacing between ordered categories that is not strictly warranted, the means would actually vary only minimally under most plausible spacing assumptions; and this solution seems preferable to others, most of which would ignore the intensity information. Simple means were also drawn for the composite indices of domain opinion.

Small-Sample Attenuation of Estimates

By far the most vexing problem surrounding the estimation of district sentiment stems from the fact that the number of voter interviews within each district is limited. We actually took great pains in the original sample design to make each district sample "self-representing" and to avoid the situation in which some districts would generate only three or four interviews.[9] The ideal goal of the design called for equal numbers of interviews per district. Figure 18-1 shows the actual outcome, after accounting for some inevitable differences in response rate by district. Case numbers run from 10 to 35: only four of the 86 districts have fewer than 18 cases; and in 60 of the 86 the number of cases lies within the narrow range of 22 to 26.

Although this even distribution of cases will be helpful technically, we may still ask how a mere two dozen interviews can be expected to give any reliable picture of public feeling in districts composed of as many as 100,000 registered voters. Three facts offer us some immediate reassurance on this point.

The first is that although our estimate of sentiment in any given district is indeed subject to fair sampling variability, we can at least be sure that each estimate is unbiased. This assures us that if we repeatedly drew a large number of samples of this small size from each district, the means could be counted on to converge toward the true district value.

The second reassuring fact is that we shall never have any need to look at estimates for single districts taken alone. All of our analyses will involve multiple districts, often all eighty-six at once. Thus variability of estimates from one district to the next, provided the estimates themselves are unbiased, will tend to cancel out, thus leaving us with a reasonable view of the scene.

The third fact is that although the variability of these unbiased district estimates remains an annoyance, we can use sampling theory to tell us just

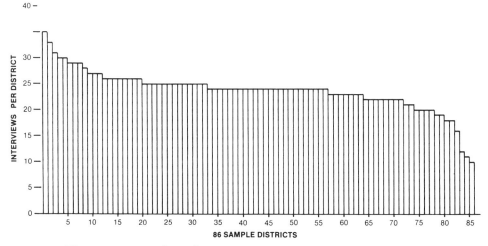

Figure 18-1. Number of interviews per district, 1967 mass sample.

how large this variability is expected to be for the case numbers either in any given district or accumulated across districts for the sample as a whole. This is comforting because it is easy to let our fears run away with us when error margins cannot be specified. Better yet, we can harness this information in more formal ways to correct some of our later analyses for the known effects of small-sample attenuation. For example, when we look at correlations between district sentiment and deputy roll-call voting, we know that we cannot expect a perfect correlation even if such perfection exists in reality, simply because of the shimmer of variability over our district estimates due to the small samples. But knowing what amount of variability to expect, we can calculate how much a perfect correlation will fall below 1.00; and using this lower value as a ceiling, we can adjust our observed correlations upward to remove the annoying attenuation.

The technical details of this correction are laid out in Appendix C. Here we shall give only a brief account of the verification procedure which we were able to carry out. This was based on one instance in which district parameters were already known, so that we could adjust our small-sample estimates of these parameters to see whether these corrections brought us closer to reality.

We knew from the official records what proportion of votes had been cast for each political party in each of our districts, and we had our own sample estimates of the same proportions, though based on very limited case numbers. We asked what outcome we could expect if we were to correlate our sample estimates with official results across all eighty-six districts. If our samples were very large indeed, we would expect to find very high correlations. This would not mean a perfect correlation, of course, because our interviews had merely elicited reports, not official vote totals. Our more general experience suggests that most respondents do remember their votes accurately and report them without distortion. Nonetheless, some few do not: the overreport of vote turnout is well known, for example, and occasional honest forgetting or active dissembling may occur. Hence we would have to expect some small margin of discrepancy between official vote totals and the reports which we would collect even if we interviewed every voter in the district. Thus we could not expect perfect correlations even with large samples, but certainly values up in the .90s.

But we did not have large samples, and this was bound to reduce further the expected correlations. Therefore we took this case of unusually full knowledge concerning party votes, and inquired as to how the calculated correlations would look once we had adjusted them to remove the known effects of small-sample attenuation.

Thanks to the multiparty system in France, we could form either a number of different correlations between district estimates and official vote proportions, or one correlation for each party that was represented across districts in the actual vote totals. We also could repeat this operation for either of two *tours* of voting, since these data are all published by district. When we lumped together the votes for obvious leftist and rightist parties for both our respondent reports and the official vote totals for each of the two tours in 1967, we discovered that the four "raw" or unadjusted correlations took very similar values, ranging from $r = .72$ to $r = .77$. Because these were rather high correlations, it was clear that even our small district samples were reflecting the known reality reasonably well, even though less than perfectly.

We could then process these raw correlations by estimating the proper attenuation correction necessary for each value.[10] These four adjusted correlations are presented in Table 18-4, which shows that the corrected values average close to .94, thus eliminating much of the shortfall from unity represented by the raw coefficients in the mid-.70s. Hence the outcome of the attenuation correction in this rare case where the district parameters were known looks very much as we would have expected. Once our small-sample variability was discounted, we arrived at correlations which seemed much more appropriate.

As we turn to other forms of district sentiment, we shall be dependent on our small-sample estimates alone. Nonetheless, this party-vote example gives us some empirical reassurance that our correction procedures are suitable to our situation. We shall in general be applying these corrections to our district linkage correlations. To maintain utter clarity about the matter, however, we shall follow the convention of attaching an asterisk to any correlation coefficient which has been adjusted for small-sample attenuation, as we have done in Table 18-4.

One important observation must be made about these corrected values. Although the estimates of ceilings of less than 1.00 on otherwise perfect correlations are theoretically sound, these estimates are no more than "long-run" expected values. Thus, if the truth were knowable, the actual ceiling that pertains in any special case would vary around this expectation. It is for this reason that we sometimes encounter correlations adjusted for attenuation that exceed the maximum defined value of unity. If such nonsense

Table 18-4. Correlations between district sample estimates and officially reported vote proportions, after correction for attenuation.

District samples vs. vote totals	Adjusted correlations
Percent of vote, parties of left, Tour I	.925*
Percent of vote, parties of left, Tour II	.891*
Percent of vote, parties of right, Tour I	.990*
Percent of vote, parties of right, Tour II	.929*

values were to push dramatically above unity, for example, to 1.85, we would have strong cause to doubt our correction model. Such obvious "errors" are rare, however; and in our data they typically produce only slight overruns, such as 1.02 or 1.03 (apart from a degenerate class of cases described in Appendix C, which we shall avoid). These slight overruns mean that the underlying correlation is indeed very high, approaching unity, and that the true ceiling placed on the correlation by our small samples must be a bit higher than we have calculated.

Given this special source of instability, it is probably wise to regard the adjusted correlations with some caution, putting rather less weight on second and third digits than is customary. Nevertheless, it should not be inferred from our example that the correction invariably brightens a raw correlation by some substantial increment. It is true that the adjustment is always "upward" in absolute value. But the same situation that calls for adjusting a raw correlation of .600 to .750*, which seems to be a very major change, will only change a raw correlation from .060 to .075*, a difference which is subjectively trivial. Thus the correction will not make a silk purse out of a sow's ear: there must be something of interest in the data before the correction adds much brightening.

The Basic Representation Bond

We have completed our review of the complex of raw materials which had to be assembled to examine the basic question as to the degree of congruence that exists empirically between variations in district sentiment and variations in roll-call voting in the National Assembly on the part of deputies formally committed to representing those particular districts.

Our materials are sufficiently rich to give us a large number of options as to which versions of these linkage correlations to display in taking a first comprehensive, yet simplified, glance at the nature of this basic bond. Not only do we have available both single-item predictors and the composites based upon some of them; we also have district measures for both 1967 and 1968, some few of which, though repetitions, have garnered different responses, and others of which diverge in manifest content; and we have roll-call summaries from both the 1967–68 and the 1968–1972 Assemblies as well. The permutations of linkages which we might examine become quite complex. The only certainties are that we want to use constituency estimates from all eighty-six of our districts, rather than the smaller subsets available to us later when deputy viewpoints must be factored in; and we want the expressions of district sentiment to refer to all respondents in a district, rather than to some subset, such as voters alone, or to other subsets that we shall examine later.

We have decided, for the first attempt, to use as predictors only data collected in 1967 at the district level. Later we shall examine changes occurring in representation due to the 1968 upheaval; but our 1968 measures are based on only 54 districts, rather than on the full 86 districts of the original sample. This decision to work from 1967 sentiment thus maximizes the case numbers underlying the linkage relationships. We shall use as dependent variables all of our roll-call summaries relevant for the 1967 district predictors, whether these legislative votes were cast in the first or second segment of the Assembly. Here the assumption is that whatever effect the reelection of 1968 might have had on the legislative voting record after 1968, a large majority of 1967 deputies were in fact returned to the Assembly in 1968, and hence it is reasonable to expect some empirical links between variations in district sentiment in 1967 and Assembly votes cast by the respective seats over the full five years which ensued.

As already mentioned, we shall further simplify matters by using composite summaries of district policy feeling where they are available to us. Generally, of course, our aim is to match a district measure of sentiment in a specific policy domain (such as education policy) with the corresponding summary scales of roll-call votes. At the same time, it is wise to include for each policy domain two other, more generic, barometers of district political sentiment. As we saw in Chapters 4, 5, and 10, both the voters' sense of their own left-right positioning and their attitudes toward de Gaulle lent significant coloration to their political choices in this period. These dimensions are generic in the sense that district variations in either of these predispositions might plausibly predict to almost any specific policy domain across the entire spectrum of national dispute, since most of these debates were defined between poles seen as leftist or rightist, or as Gaullist or opposition. Therefore, we shall keep track of congruence not only in terms of specific policy sentiments, but in terms of these more general predispositions as well.

Our first glimpse of the basic representation bond in France, as filtered through these many decisions, is presented for the various policy domains in Table 18-5. It is apparent that we receive an affirmative answer to the question whether there are discernible levels of positive congruence between many measures of district sentiment and variations in roll-call votes cast by the respective deputies in the National Assembly. These linkage correlations are never perfect, and the largest of them are only in the middling ranges. We knew from the outset, however, that there were enough sources of influence on Assembly voting other than district sentiment to prevent us from finding more than moderate levels of congruence, even after correction for small-sample attenuation. There are indeed a few stray negative correlations, but they are usually trivial in size; and there is no roll-call domain without at least some noteworthy positive congruence with one or more measures of district political sentiment. In a very general way, the cast of

Table 18-5. Linkage correlations: 1967 district sentiment by 1967–1972 roll-call vote summaries.[a]

Measure of district sentiment	Linkage correlations with roll-call vote summary			
	Specific issue	Left-right location	Gaullism	Roll-call vote
I. Generic debate				
Importance: Government Stability (1)	.15*	.41*	.20*	Government-Opposition
II. Domestic policy				
A. Social Welfare				
Income Distribution scale (2)	.20*	.37*	.10*	Income Distribution
Socioeconomic Left-Right scale (3)	.17*	.34*	.15*	Socioecon. Left-Right
Protect Union Rights (1)	.07*	.12*	.20*	Droit Syndical
Protect Union Rights (1)	-.01*	.30*	.20*	Union Rights
B. Church and State				
Public School scale (2)	.31*}	.39*	.11*	Religion
District Religiosity (2)	.36*}			
C. Education				
Education Priority scale (2)	-.07*	.47*	.21*	Education Budget
Education Priority scale (2)	-.06*	.36*	.08*	Faure Law Left-Right
D. Economic Development				
Importance: Economic Development (1)	-.10*	.26*	.03*	Economic Development
III. Foreign policy				
A. European Integration				
European Integration scale (6)	.15*	.34*	.14*	European Integration
B. Foreign Aid				
Foreign Aid scale (2)	.14*	.45*	.21*	Foreign Aid
C. Military Expenditure				
Force de Frappe (1)	.22*	.56*	.28*	Force de Frappe

a. Based on data from all 86 districts in which interviewing was carried out. Numbers in parentheses after each measure of district sentiment indicate the number of mass interview items contributing to the calculation. Asterisks denote correlations corrected for small-sample attenuation.

these results bears a reasonable resemblance to those found by Miller and Stokes for the United States.[11]

With this basic positive answer in hand, we shall resist any temptation to comment on many of the more detailed comparisons which Table 18-5 proffers. We are on the brink of manipulations of these linkage correlations (to be carried out in the next chapter) which will elucidate them in several nonobvious ways, and it would be premature to push them very far at this point. Nonetheless, if we stop with the broadest of comparisons, there are two or three further observations which can reliably be drawn even from Table 18-5.

The most noteworthy of these is the fact that, throughout the table, district variations in left-right coloration are more firmly associated with roll-call votes than are the specific policy sentiments most relevant to them. This raises the interesting possibility that our policy-specific measures may have little meaning in this context, independent of their participation in the broader left-right nexus. In other words, perhaps we could say as much about congruence from our left-right measures alone, without invoking the policy-specific items at all.

Although this hypothesis has some merit, it can be rejected in any extreme form. The background correlations between the more specific policy positions and left-right self-locations are in general less than overpowering, at least for the total citizenry, and they are often no more than trace associations. Thus, although the partial correlations between specific policy sentiments and roll-call votes are typically reduced relative to the zero-order correlations, those that are of any magnitude at all continue to show palpable signs of life when left-right district coloration is controlled.

Another way of asking the same question is to suggest that because of participation in a broader left-right nexus, the sizes of the zero-order correlations between specific policy items and their apparent roll-call matches are of a haphazard nature: for example, an "irrelevant" correlation linking education-policy feelings in the district with, say, roll calls on the force de frappe might have an even chance of being higher than the more "relevant" correlation between feelings on the force de frappe in the district and the force de frappe roll calls. We have also examined this possibility. For any given measurement of district sentiment, a substantial number of "irrelevant" correlations are possible, but only one (or at most, two) are truly "relevant." Although the "relevant" correlation is not in every case higher than all possible "irrelevant" ones, it often is so, and invariably it is well above the average across the set. In short, the specific policy measures seem to be tapping something appropriate beyond the left-right distinction, even though it is usually no more than at the margin.

Whatever autonomous life can be claimed for the policy-specific measures, there is no gainsaying the fact that they are persistently outshone in these linkage correlations by the more generic left-right variations. Since there are other ways in which these data might have fallen, this is a consequential message. However thin may be the understanding of many French voters concerning the policy significance of left-right differences across competing programs, and however secondary left-right criteria may be for them at the margin provided by the second tour, our data suggest that, at a systemic level, left-right cues and sortings may nonetheless serve as something of a central conveyor belt, maintaining a level of congruence between district preferences and deputy behavior. The data do not guarantee that this is so: the more specific party attachments and party cues provide a lively competing alternative. But we must wait to evaluate such possibilities. For now, it is important to keep the simple left-right predictor front and center in our ensuing chapters.

It is also clear that our other more generic dimension of preference—district variations in attitudes toward de Gaulle—has some strength as well, although these attitudes are obviously secondary in importance to the left-right attitudes, and they show linkages which are somewhat erratic.

One final comment about Table 18-5 is in order. Although it is premature to make any very strenuous comparisons between linkages from one policy domain to another, even though the display invites them, it is worth noting that the linkages within the domain of religion or church-state relations seem particularly firm. The correlations involved are not the very strongest in the table, taken one by one; but as a set they are impressive. The Religiosity measure (II,B) is our only domain-specific predictor which is not drawn from statements of policy preference. Instead, it is the same variable as that used in Chapter 5, but now aggregated to distinguish between "devout" districts and secular ones. Although domain-specific, this predictor shows substantial power, as does the equally specific Public School scale, which is based on church-state policy preference items. The reader will no doubt associate the relative strength of these linkages in the religious domain with the discussion in Chapter 5 of the underlying potency of the clerical dimension in French voting behavior, for these two findings are cut from the same cloth.

Conclusions

The presence of numerous correlations in Table 18-5 running in the directions to be substantively expected attests to the existence of a significant degree of congruence, from constituency to constituency in France, between the variations in policy sentiments and the roll-call votes that are ultimately cast in their behalf by their deputies to the National Assembly.

The sheer existence of these positive associations does not, however, tell us a great deal about their origin. The data do suggest a rather potent role for generic left-right predispositions and cues in helping to tighten these basic bonds. But these associations do not by themselves enable us to sift out the relative contributions of the various mechanisms—some resting on elite values and others depending on institutional forms—that sustain these relationships. Indeed, if we wish to deal with the stringent definition of representation that requires the deputy to have not only a conscious desire to heed the wishes of his constituents but also a practical means of doing so, then these associations fall well short of demonstrating that any such willful representation is occurring. They may be a necessary part of such a proof, but they are not sufficient. Some congruence of this kind will be visible, as we have seen, provided merely that deputies are sampled fairly by chance from districts that differ in their political sentiments.

An examination of the intervening mechanisms will, of course, be carried out in ensuing chapters. We shall be able to move more briskly now that we have laid out all the raw materials. As we begin to introduce intervening variables and to make other partitions of the data, our case numbers will generally dwindle. Crucial among the intervening variables is information drawn from personal interviews with the deputies and those candidates whom they defeated. In this chapter, needing only roll-call vote data, we have been able to deal with all of the 86 districts in our original design. But when we require information about deputy attitudes and perceptions of the constituency, we shall be reduced to the 66 of our 86 districts in which deputy interviews were successfully completed. Or again, if we begin to examine problems of temporal changes in representation before and after the 1968 dissolution of the Assembly, we shall be reduced to 54 districts, even in the ideal case, and fewer still for certain kinds of information.

There is, however, one further manipulation of the data underlying Table 18-5 which will permit us to harness all our districts. This manipulation will serve to "explode" the tabular information in rather dramatic and illuminating fashion, which is one reason why we have abbreviated the discussion of that table in this chapter. We shall arrive at this revised view of Table 18-5 at the end of the next chapter. We choose to "sneak up" on the matter, as it were, because it is important to arrive first at a finer understanding of the AB bond in the Miller-Stokes diamond (Figure 16-1), that is, the relationship between the deputy's personal convictions on policy issues and the political sentiments of his district.

19

Winners, Losers, and Their Constituencies

We shall now begin to decompose the basic representation bond between constituents and the legislative votes cast in their behalf—the AD bond, discussed in the last chapter—by taking account of the intervention of their duly elected representatives. The first leg of the decomposed relationship (that is, link AB in Figure 16-1) addresses the degree of similarity between the representative's own policy views and the relevant political sentiments of his district.

The Miller-Stokes model, of course, permits a representative to have a personal conviction on an issue which differs from the vote he may feel obliged to cast in a legislative roll call. Because of this latitude the AB bond can diverge in significant ways from the basic AD bond. Nevertheless, the nature of the AB relationship has been the object of an enormous amount of theoretical rumination and analysis, some of which we shall examine in this chapter.

What we want to know is, first, how close the representative's own views on given issues are to those of his constituents and, second, why they are more or less close. The second question is obviously complicated; but even the first, requiring a factual assessment of "closeness," is less than straightforward. Continuing to follow the Miller-Stokes model, we shall measure the tightness of the AB bond by the size of the correlation coefficient between the average sentiment across districts and the stated attitudes of their respective representatives.

Unfortunately, as we made clear in Chapter 16, numbers of this sort are dependent on collectivities: therefore it is impossible to define a correlation between the average sentiment on a given issue in a single district and the attitude position of its single representative. But when we have measured both of these positions on the same scale, we should be able to subtract one value from the other in order to arrive at an absolute, single-district assessment of closeness, or "proximity." A measure of this kind will read zero on a given issue when the representative's position and the average sentiment in his district exactly coincide. We shall look at this method of assessing closeness of representative conviction to district sentiment, and ask how it differs from estimates based on correlations.

No matter what mode of measurement we choose to adopt, theoretical questions tend to arise. How close is close? Suppose we find a certain representative who chooses for himself a left-right location of 33 in a district whose constituents choose locations averaging 49 (that is, one point left of dead center). Is the difference of 16 surprisingly large, or is it smaller than one might have expected?

The conventional way to give meaning to such a number is to establish a reference point in terms of which it will be obvious whether any given assessment of closeness is running large or small. There are several possible reference points, each of which addresses one of the fundamental theoretical issues underlying the question of political representation.

One reference point describes the kind of representation that would occur if deputies were chosen entirely at random from their constituencies, rather than by an elaborate mechanism of popular election. This is, of course, the phenomenon that Erikson and Luttbeg (1973) have called the "belief-sharing or consensus" mode of linkage, and which we described, following Pitkin, as "descriptive representation" in Chapter 16. We said there that such kinds of chance correlations in either the AB or the AD bond would be perfectly legitimate contributions to any representation process. Nonetheless, in order to probe the nature of representation more deeply, we should be able to isolate that portion of any observed representation function which chance alone would produce, without the mediation of elections. Very precise values can in fact be deduced as the proper correlation expectations for the random selection of deputies. These in turn provide pregnant reference points to give our observations of closeness deeper meaning.

Another possible reference point reaches to the very heart of democratic theory, for it is a cornerstone of that credo that the function of popular elections is to permit the people themselves (the electorate) to winnow out the candidate most palatable to them, rather than either to have such a representative appointed by a kind of dictator or to go without any representative at all. In a few lenient versions of that theory, the personal charisma of the leader, as appreciated by the constituency, is all that "palatable" need mean. In most versions of democratic theory, however, what is more or less palatable is closely hinged to competition over policy options: the aspiring representative is more or less "palatable" to voters in his district in the degree to which his personal policy positions, or at the very least, his party's program, either fits the policy sentiments of those voters or is an affront to them. Obviously, the AB bond is focused exclusively on the nature of that fit. And one prediction which seems absolutely fundamental says that, in general, we should expect a closer fit from elected than from rejected candidates.

In fact, we could even argue that if we could only measure the relative *degrees* of fit between all the voters in a jurisdiction (or district) and each candidate seeking their votes, then the size of the discrepancy in the fit between winner and loser(s) would be a quantitative measure of the effectiveness, and hence of the value, of the whole election process, at least with respect to a given jurisdiction and policy issue.[1] Of course, even if the winner were no closer to district sentiment than the losers, it would not prove that the election was valueless, since the sheer fact of popular election may clothe winners with a legitimacy which makes their governance more acceptable. But conversely, if winners were closer than losers, the discrepancy in fit could be taken as an answer to a mental experiment such as the following:

(1) Suppose all of the winners had lost: what difference would it have made to the quality of popular representation resulting from the election?

(2) Suppose that there had been no election at all, but instead a dictator had randomly selected one of the aspirants to office. How much difference would that have made to the representation function?

We cannot, of course, overlook the possibility that if the losers had been put in office, they might behave more like the winners than we might have expected from the initial differences in attitudes on policy issues. Although it is usually impossible to test such counterfactual possibilities, they seem to lie closer to our reach than usual in this instance. Thus, putting values on the basic functioning of elections could be an illuminating exercise.

Collective Representation

Before turning to the intradistrict questions that are the subject of this chapter, it is necessary to consider what Weissberg (1978) and others have called "collective representation." The whole notion of collective representation rests on a direct comparison between deputy attitudes and voter positions, which is exactly our subject here. Instead, however, of assessing fit by pairing districts with their specific representatives, Weissberg proposes assessing the fit more globally by comparing the average position on a given issue for all deputies in the legislature taken collectively with the average sentiment on the same issue for the electorate as a whole.

Provided one important condition is fulfilled, there is surely nothing difficult about producing such an assessment of fit. Indeed, such a picture of collective representation can be assembled in a matter of minutes, whereas most of our intricate district-level analyses have required many hours of work even after the raw materials were at hand.

The important precondition is that the issue positions of both deputies and voters must have been scaled in the same numerical terms, as in the case of identically worded issue questions. As we pointed out in Chapter 7, some of our issue items were asked identically of both the deputy and voter samples, but others were not. Unfortunately, the identical items did not form a balanced subset of all the issue dimensions covered. For example, all of the importance, or agenda, items were asked in identical form, but hardly any of the position issues were. This was regrettable because we found later that, for technical reasons, the importance items produced weaker results than the position items. We do have five items asked identically which gauge issue *positions,* but all five were addressed to a single issue domain: European integration. The main comfort in an otherwise odd subset of issues posed identically is the fact that the most important single issue item, the "super-issue" measured by left-right self-locations (see Chapter 4), was also carried out identically.

In short, then, in assessing collective representation we must limp along with a rather odd assortment of thirteen issue items instead of the full portfolio of twenty-six linkage measures displayed in the last chapter.

Not only is it very easy from a mechanical point of view to examine collective representation, but it is, as Weissberg has shown, of considerable theoretical importance to do so. Among other things, the discrepancy between deputies and voters calculated dyadically from district to district will always be at least as large as, and almost certainly larger than, the discrepancy calculated between the two taken as grand collectivities. This stems from a mathematical truth, but it has flesh-and-blood meaning in terms of what most would see as proper political representation. The fact is that minorities who go unrepresented by deputies from their own districts have an excellent chance of picking up representation from other districts where their views are in fact majoritarian. Thus an assessment of collective representation puts the best possible light on the fidelity of any representation function—a light which is entirely justified.

Another way of underscoring the importance of such an assessment of collective representation is to hark back to the differentiation we made in Chapter 16 between the absolute and relative congruence between deputy and voter opinion (Figure 16-2), which raised the possibility that the two opinions could be quite different from each other in an absolute sense, even though the *relative* congruence from district to district remained perfect.

The basic assessment of collective representation for our thirteen identical issues is shown in Figure 19-1. Although for the moment our main interest lies in the average views of deputies (winners) in the National Assembly, that is, of the subset of 66 candidates who won seats in the election (shown by black bars), the figure also shows the averages for the 206 losers (white bars), and the averages for the total candidate sample (cross-hatched bars). The relationships of all these elite positions to our mass sample can be seen at a glance, since all bars are expressed as deviations from the mass sample mean.[2]

The deviations of the elite means from the mean mass positions are not insubstantial, and they are very clearly patterned. First, the candidates put themselves, in general, well to the left of the mass sample. Second, almost without exception, they are more enthusiastic about European integration in all its facets than the average voter. And third, with the exception of one policy area, defense of public education, they attribute higher importance to the issues than do the rank-and-file voters.

Most of these sharp patterns will come as no surprise. In Chapter 7 we discussed at great length the problems caused to our measurements because the politically involved, and especially the political elites, tend to see all political issues as more absolutely important than do the mass of voters.[3] Neither this fact, nor the fact that losers see these issues as being somewhat less important than winners do, casts any aspersions on the quality of representation. Indeed, it is almost part of the moral compact of prospective deputies with the citizenry that they should take political issues more seriously than the electorate, since a fundamental reason for having political representatives is the need to transfer the labor of representation from the many, those who do not have the time, interest, or expertise to sift through the details of political controversies, to the few who do have this kind of involvement and thereby can serve as agents. From this point of view, good representation might be seen to require exactly the absolute discrepancies between mass, winners, and losers that appear in Figure 19-1. Any notion, for example, that losers might make better representatives than winners because they are slightly more like the electorate in having a limited interest in political issues is quite ridiculous on the face of it.

The still more blatant displacement of the whole elite sample toward leftist self-locations (to the left of center, close to 30) relative to the electorate as a whole, comes as no surprise either. In speaking of this marked left-seeking tendency of our elite respondents in Chapters 4 and 6, we concluded that although this was a symbolic matter of great historical interest, its current political consequences were limited. But in any matter of current political substance, the deputies to the right of this central tendency (that is, in the range 30–50) were behaving in legislative disputes exactly as the rightist

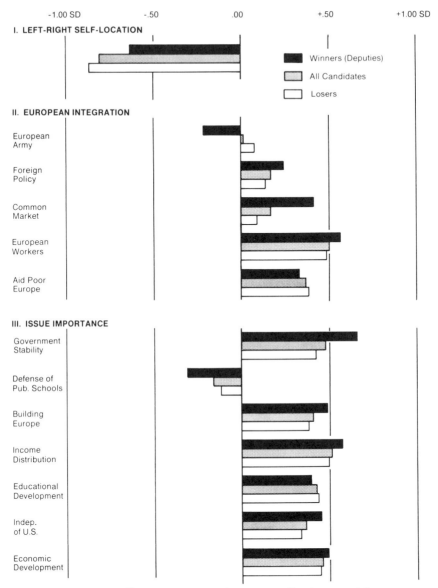

Figure 19-1. Collective representation: mean elite issue positions as deviations from mean positions for total electorate.

half of the political spectrum behaves in any country. They had a sharp and instinctive distaste for challenges to the status quo; they voted heavily against efforts to redistribute income; and they were keen on law and order in the wake of the 1968 disturbances. At the same time, however, it was clearly of importance to their political self-esteem to claim that they were respectably left-leaning, which is to say, safely within the 30–50 range of our 100-point scale of left-right self-locations.[4]

In view of all this, we need not be tempted to conclude that the huge deviations in the first panel of Figure 19-1 demonstrate that political representation was at its very worst in the France of the late 1960s as far as the super-issue of the left and the right was concerned. We would be most perplexed by such a conclusion in any event, since we have just completed a chapter on the basic representation bond in France which indicated rather eloquently that representation in legislative voting, as symbolized by the AD bond, was at its very best, not its very worst, in connection with the super-issue of left and right, relative to more specific political issue domains.

Fortunately, we can understand these apparently opposed outcomes because one measurement ("collective representation") addresses congruence in an absolute sense, whereas the other measurement invokes congruence in a relative sense. In other words, the empirical situation must bear some resemblance to panel (a) in Figure 16-2, because it seems that where the left-right dimension is concerned, relative congruence is substantial precisely when absolute congruence is embarrassingly low.

Then which version of congruence means *real* representation? We have no generic answer, nor, do we believe, is one possible. It all depends on what one means by representation. The whole construct is so time-honored that it is little short of annoying, after having said large theoretical things about the subject, to be asked, "Yes, but what mode of representation do you have in mind?" The question would be only niggling if the answer mattered very little, one way or the other. In the case at hand, however, the answer matters a great deal: for, according to which theoretical version of representation we have in mind, whether absolute or relative, we will arrive at nearly opposite conclusions concerning the super-issue of left-right differences.

Although we cannot answer the question in the general case, we certainly feel that in the specific case of left-right differences the high levels of *relative* representation say a good deal more than do the abysmal levels of *absolute* representation which characterize the remaining differences in Figure 19-1. This is so because the left-seeking tendency in the elite self-locations seems to be purely symbolic, without current substance. As we have already pointed out, many of the elites to the right of the elite mean (but still placing themselves in the left half of the spectrum) vigorously pursue configurations of policies that delight that fraction of ideological voters who place themselves to the extreme right of our scale (at 80 or 90). There is certainly nothing wrong with the substantive representation here, and its robust reflection in the AD bonds of the preceding chapter is more telling than the embarrassing displacement of the elites from the mass in their self-locations, when evaluated in terms of "collective representation" (Figure 19-1).

Of course, our diagnosis in this special case should not be taken as impeaching in any general way the theoretical interest of the concept of collective representation, or the utility of assessing it empirically. It simply adds another instance to that of the agenda issue in which relative congruence says much more about representation than absolute congruence does. In a sense, the problem in this case might be claimed to be one of measurement, but all of our issue-position measures yield no more than relative (ordinal) outcomes in any event, which raises the possibility that in some other cases we may learn more about the nature of representation by scrutinizing relative congruence. It is very fortunate that when we have identical measures we can monitor congruence in both senses.

Nonetheless, absolute congruence seems questionable as a criterion for the left-right issue, and we have already suggested that for the importance battery of items *absolute* congruence seems an absurd notion; it is probably subversive of good representation, since representatives are commissioned to be more involved in politics than their constituents. Yet as we switch to a context of *relative* congruence, good representation would seem to require that if a particular issue domain, such as the distribution of income, is of top priority in a given district, the deputy should also give it top relative priority. Thus even the importance items are likely to have greater significance if assessed in the more customary dyadic or district-level manner.

Representative Proximity to District Sentiment

When we turn back from experiments with collective representation to dyadic questions concerning the fit between district position and candidate postures on specific issues, it is clear that both absolute and relative metrics can again be used. Since they measure different facets of deputy-district congruence, they will usually give at least slightly different impressions as to the actual degree of fit. Happily, however, we need not commit ourselves to one or the other in advance, but can examine both.

Congruence Assessed by Correlations

Although in some ways assessments by correlations leap farther beyond the raw data, such procedures were first used by Miller and Stokes (1963) to estimate the closeness of the AB bond in their analytic diamond, and hence they stand as the conventional or traditional measure.

Basically, we want to know how strong the correlations are, from one issue dimension to the next, between deputies' positions and average sentiment in their districts. This kind of correlational statement is a very straightforward calculation. But we would like to continue comparing winning candidates with losing ones, and this requires an editorial decision or two. In many districts we interviewed, at the same time, several losing candidates of rather different ideological stripes. Do we want to throw all of these "odd fish" together in one calculation, or do we want to be more selective? Remembering the mental experiment as to what kind of representation would have occurred had the election results been reversed, we would be wise not to consider all the losers, many of whom had trivial support to begin with, but only the "serious" alternatives, such as those who were runners-up. To make a long story short, our examination of the data for a number of variant definitions of the loser group showed that although some sizable stray discrepancies exist, they tend to cancel out in ways that make our overall picture nearly identical, whichever definition of losers we choose. Hence we shall proceed with our largest pool of losers, that is, all those interviewed in our 86 districts.

Table 19-1 lays out these correlation values, as corrected for small-sample attenuation, over the set of thirteen identically posed issue items displayed in Figure 19-1. What is perhaps the most dramatic feature of the table, the high value linking the winner's (deputy's) own sense of left-right position with the average self-location in his district, reminds us immediately of our observation in the preceding section that, however poor the *absolute* fit, *relative* congruence for left and right self-location remains high.

We notice further that by any plausible way of operating on correlations, the winner-loser gap (our measure nominated to indicate the value of democratic elections) is more striking for left-right locations than for any of the other issue items in the table. We recall that, in left-right terms, winners already seemed closer to the electorate than did losers, even for the district-free data of Figure 19-1. This message seems the same as that one, but it is important to realize that technically it is *independent* of that earlier message, which hinged on absolute displacements of means for winners, losers, and the electorate. Nevertheless, assessing congruence by correlation implicitly sets all differences in means to zero (that is, wipes them out analytically) before it begins. Thus, although the substantive message is the same—winners are closer to constituents than losers, in left-right terms—the actual information is a fresh addition to what we had earlier ascertained.

The rest of Table 19-1 is somewhat more ragged. The average value of r^* for the winners' column is indeed positive, although not very impressive in magnitude (+.086). And the same average value for the losers is not

Table 19-1. Correlational measures of congruence between elite issue position and district sentiment.

Issue domain	Winners (66 deputies)	Losers (N = 206)
I. Left-right self-location	.483*	.041*
II. European integration		
French Army in European Army[a]	large, positive*	−.078*
France accept European foreign policy	−.112*	.096*
France remains in Common Market	.106*	.018*
Free movement, European workers	.233*	.186*
France aid poor Europe	.107*	−.158*
III. Issue importance		
Government stability	.196*	−.146*
Defense of public schools	−.257*	−.070*
Building Europe	−.078*	.174*
Distribution of income	.269*	−.183*
Educational development	.125*	.054*
Foreign policy independent of U.S.	.223*	−.034*
Economic development	−.269*	−.237*

a. Although it is clear that the corrected value for the European Army item among winners is positive in sign and large in magnitude (e.g., almost certainly greater than $r = .30^*$, and probably much larger), we cannot assign a precise corrected value. The reasons are technical and are discussed at the close of Appendix C on small-sample attenuation.

technically positive, although it is not very sharply negative (−.023). Thus we would tend to conclude somewhat less equivocally than before that winners are closer to constituents—now actually those of their own districts—than are their unsuccessful competitors.

Nonetheless, there is no gainsaying the fact that there is wide variation in pattern from issue to issue, and our eye naturally fixes upon some anomalies that seem quite dramatic, such as the strong reversal of sign which turns up in connection with the *importance* of European integration as an issue. Although this is one of the most striking counterintuitive features of the table, it seems to be somewhat offset by the fact that we do have five other items on European integration as a *position* issue, and although they are not univocal in themselves, they do destroy the possible conclusion that somehow European integration may have been an issue on which losers for some reason were more "representative" than winners.

Another case of significant reversal (winners more perversely linked than losers) that catches the eye concerns ratings of importance for the defense of the secular public schools. Here, in addition to the marked reversal, *both* winners and losers show negative correlations with opinion in their districts. This marked anomaly has a highly plausible explanation. We saw earlier (Figure 19-1) that this was the only issue to which elites attributed less importance than did voters, and we suggested (see note 3) that the down-pedaling of an issue which historically has been as rancorous and divisive among the mass public as this one was almost certainly intentional. We might go on to suppose that elite concern to minimize the issue would be strongest in those districts where the issue was most virulent, which is to say where common voters of both persuasions saw it as most important. Such a pattern could be expected to produce a meaningful negative correlation across districts between elite agenda ratings and those of their constituents. If we suppose further that winning candidates are more keenly attuned to all of these matters than are losers taken as a whole (many of whom have only casual links to the constituency or, for that matter, to mainstream political life in the nation), then the winner-loser reversal can easily be understood in the same terms.

Some of the other anomalies seem murkier in origin, and, in any event, it is not clear that they are of sufficient strength to warrant much detective work, particularly as we shall use another method of assessing this kind of elite-to-constituent similarity later. For now, these are the most noteworthy points in Table 19-1: the high winner-constituency link for left-right locations; the large winner-loser discrepancy on the same item; and the general cast of the table, which suggests to a modest degree that issue congruence with one's own district is higher for winners than for losers.

Proximity Assessed by Absolute Discrepancy

Achen (1977) has suggested that "correlations should be abandoned in the study of representation." Although there are several reasons for this view, the central one is that correlational indicators vary in size not only in response to factual differences in the strengths of structures but also in response to differences in the variances of the component variables from sample to sample, a kind of variance which under some circumstances may be seen as artifactitious.[5] In Chapter 16 we mentioned some noncorrelational measures that Achen (1978) suggests might be used in the study of representation. The substitute measure which is most relevant for our examination of the AB bond is a simple function of subtracting the position of the elite member on an issue from the positions of each of his district constituents.[6] We shall call this index the "absolute proximity" of the representative in his district, to differentiate it from relative congruence, for which correlation is a natural index.

This measure has all the advantages over correlations that Achen has laid out, but it also has a series of disadvantages which need recognition. We can summarize these rapidly, because we have already encountered them in dealing with collective representation, an assessment involving just the same kind of differencing of issue measures, although not carried out within districts.

First, it would seem foolish to engage in such a subtraction of elite from mass positions unless both were measured on the same scale. Most studies of representation lack such raw materials, but, fortunately, we can proceed on the basis of our misshapen subset of thirteen identical issue items. Second, because the numbers generated by such subtractions lack deliberately the kinds of normalization built into a correlation coefficient, they have hardly any intuitive meaning, and this creates an exposition problem. Third, these numbers, unlike statements of correlation, do not lend themselves easily to second-order manipulations parallel to partial correlation and regression, or path analysis.

Fourth, in discussing collective representation we became aware that for eight of our thirteen identically posed items (the seven importance issues and the left-right location), a statement of relative congruence was probably more meaningful than absolute proximity. This was so because the formation of absolute differences introduced stronger sources of extraneous variation than are typically encountered in correlational work; at the very least this was bound to be distracting, and at worst it could be actively misleading. Although it is true that this difficulty springs from the peculiarities of the specific matched items we have at hand, and is not a ubiquitous problem, we at least must remain aware that the Achen proximity measure, unlike our correlational measures of the AB bond, reintroduces in these cases exactly the same unwanted variation.

Keeping in mind these caveats, we shall examine the proximity measures averaged issue by issue across both our set of winners and our set of losers (see Table 19-2). Once again, we have transformed the obscure raw values into a recognizable standard-score currency. In this form, the signs in the two columns have to counterbalance. In ten comparisons of the thirteen, the intuitive expectation that winners would lie closer to district sentiment than their competitors is borne out. The three reversals tend to be rather weak in magnitude, and all occur in the third panel, where we most suspected that the Achen measure would encounter some variation extraneous or inimical to any plausible theory of representation that might be at stake.

There is some general correspondence between our two assessments of proximity (Tables 19-1 and 19-2), especially if we do not put too much weight on the third panel. In Table 19-2, among the European integration items, the only point at which the winner-loser contrast is relatively weak occurs for the same issue (a European foreign policy) which showed a reversal of winner-loser correlations in Table 19-1. The correspondence is more ragged for the weaker contrasts in the third panel, as we had reason to expect, but even there we find some matching contours. In both tables, there are three reversals of expectations, with losers seeming closer to their

***Table* 19-2.** Absolute proximity of elite issue position to district sentiment.[a]

Issue domain	Winners (66 deputies)	Losers (N = 206)
I. Left-right self-location	−.207	+.063
II. European integration		
French Army in European Army	−.239	+.072
France accept European foreign policy	−.132	+.039
France remains in Common Market	−.216	+.064
Free movement, European workers	−.199	+.060
France aid poor Europe	−.215	+.062
III. Issue importance		
Government stability	−.035	+.010
Defense of public schools	+.035	−.010
Building Europe	−.037	+.011
Distribution of income	−.013	+.004
Educational development	+.107	−.033
Foreign policy independent of U.S.	−.062	+.019
Economic development	+.097	−.029

a. Cell entries represent standard scores based on the mean and standard deviation of raw proximity values (mean squared "distances" from the elite position to each of his interviewed constituents) for all of our 272 candidates taken together. The smaller the algebraic value, the greater the proximity.

districts than winners. Two of these overlap, and one of them is the defense of public schools item, where we can understand the reversal, at least ex post facto. In the one instance where the reversals in each table do not match, the failure to reverse is by a relatively weak margin.

Although it has been interesting to compare the degrees of closeness that can be derived from the correlational measures of congruence and the measures of absolute proximity, we have not encountered information which would lead us to discard the correlational measure. This question has been a main motivation for making these comparisons, in view of the fact that for most of our position issues (other than left-right and European integration) we could not sensibly calculate absolute proximity in any event, for our interview items were posed in quite different forms and the arrays of responses, mass and elite, could only be expected to match in an ordinal or relative sense.

Of course, the Achen recommendation to avoid correlational measures of proximity was put forward mainly as a protection against the rather unlikely possibility of major distortions in variance. Losing some of the values of correlational treatment is a large price to pay for such assurance, especially because other less expensive safeguards, such as checking for variance anomalies, are readily available.

In our immediate situation, we have found that for eight of our thirteen identically worded issues the measure of relative congruence is obviously preferable to the Achen recommendation. For the other five position issues (all on European integration), there was no basis for such an a priori preference. But if we wanted to assess differences in the closeness of the winning deputy to his district across this set of five issues by both methods, the results would show a correlation of +.84. This leaves us a scorecard which says that the Achen proximity recommendation is, for our purposes, competitive with correlational measures only when the results it generates are not very distinguishable from those measures.

In sum, although we shall continue to have a healthy concern about the impact of substantively irrelevant variance discrepancies on our results, we shall not be embarrassed to use correlational measures freely. In fact, we shall use whichever type of assessment of the AB bond is more useful and less misleading in each instance.

A Note on Determinants of Proximity

Up to now we have been involved in a cross-issue analysis. We have used both the congruence measure and the proximity measure to examine how the closeness of actual or aspiring representatives varies from one issue to another. At the same time, we have kept track of the more generic differences in closeness between winning and losing candidates, and have arrived at the sense that, by and large, winners tend to be closer than losers to the views of their constituents.

It is an engaging notion, of course, that over a large number of issues there may be some types of representatives whose experience is such that their own political convictions are more closely attuned to those prevalent in their districts. An obvious prediction that we mentioned before—unfortunately, we lack cases to verify it—is that candidates "parachuted" into unfamiliar districts to run for office should not be expected to show the kinds of close natural fit with district opinion that are displayed by elites socialized into politics within the district.

More significantly for the theory of representation, it is often feared that deputies successful enough to win elections repeatedly will gradually take on the perspectives of the capital city and hence fall progressively out of tune with the local colorations of their districts, a trend which should show up in our proximity measures. An opposing argument suggests that the long-term representative survives because he becomes skillful at remaining in touch, and that he may be better attuned than the neophyte aspiring to office in the district.

To test these hypotheses about types of representatives, it is useful to have proximity measures which may be associated with individual elites, as the Achen type may be, but, at least conventionally, the more collective correlational measure may not.[7] Therefore we have taken the absolute proximity measures for individual elites as dependent variables in order to inquire after plausible sources of variation, from one aspiring representative to another, in the closeness of their own convictions to their constituents' views.

We had no more than begun our first provisional analyses of this type before we fell upon an astonishing result. We were asking, in an analysis of variance format, to what degree knowledge of the deputy's party would help to predict his proximity to his constituents, measured Achen-style, with respect to the super-issue of left-right locations. We unexpectedly found that, among our winners, we could predict over three-quarters of the variance in the absolute proximities (an eta of .879) from party membership alone. And among our larger and more variegated set of losers, we could still predict about 60 percent of the variance (an eta of .77). Although one rarely sees data of this clarity, especially when the dependent variable is an elegant second-order concept like the proximity of representative to constituency, the source of the finding is not obscure. It turns out that among deputies (winners), the mean squared distance of Communist and PSU members is nearly five times as great as the distance of the Gaullists or the Centre Démocrate, with the FGDS falling in between. The same substantive pattern occurs for losers as well.

In other words, what we are seeing here is a reprise of the now familiar fact that the elite left-right distribution is vastly shifted to the left, relative to the more centrist distribution of the voters. This means that the more leftist the party elite, the more magnified are the discrepancies between its self-locations and those of its local constituents. We have already suggested that this finding, although it may be of high interest to students of political culture and national symbolism, is of limited interest to the study of political representation.

We also have pointed out that proximity measures of the Achen type are peculiarly susceptible to this extraneous variation. What may have been lacking is a sense of the true force of the problem: this intrusive variation dwarfs almost anything else we might look at. We cannot get too excited about the discovery that experienced deputies are closer to their constituents in left-right terms than are losing candidates or even first-time winners, since we know that for other more prosaic reasons losers and first-time winners locate themselves to the left of our experienced deputies, and the sheer left-rightness of locations governs most of the variance in these proximities, in any case. Since our deputy sample is rather small, it is hard to control this variation to see what other determinants of left-right proximity may lurk in the background. Therefore we gave up on these analyses in proximity form, and moved on to the next theoretical question.

Descriptive Representation

Although we have been keeping track of contrasts in proximity between winners and losers, up to now we have not considered how our data look against the other baseline, that of the levels of congruence which could be expected if representatives were selected by chance within each district.

Let us review the reasoning which underlies this baseline. If from any given legislative district we put forward at random one person to serve as representative, we can say quite "precisely" (in a certain sense) what policy opinions we would expect him to hold. His individual opinions are expected to lie at the mean values for popular sentiment in his district on the various policy options of interest to us: that is, in a leftist district we are likely to draw a "representative" who is leftist; for a rightist district, we would be likely to draw a rightist representative; and for a centrist district, a centrist one.

It is because of this simple sampling principle that the phenomenon of descriptive representation becomes a very important model. It should be clear intuitively that the key parameter on which the levels of such representation are bound to depend is the one we made central in Chapter 16: the ratio of between-district variance to total variance. Where districts are internally homogeneous but very distinctive from one another, our odds of picking at random someone whose distinctiveness matches that of the district is very high. But if all districts have the same average opinion on an issue, then obviously there is no expectation of anything distinctive about any representative drawn from them.

If we turn away from the proximity measures of the AB bond to the vocabulary of correlation, then we can predict quite readily just what level of correlation would be generated for any given issue by chance drawings from the district. Here, however, we risk making a false step. We have just finished observing that the "expected" opinion of a randomly selected deputy is the mean opinion of the district from which he is sampled. We also explored in the last chapter the "basic representation bond," predicting an ultimate outcome—roll-call voting—from the mean opinion of districts. If the mean opinion of a district is also the expected opinion of any deputy selected at random from it, then we might conclude that the data we have already examined as the basic representation bond is nothing more nor less than the expected correlation between any randomly selected representative and what ultimately happens in terms of political representation for the district.

If this hasty conclusion were true, the whole subject of representation would become quite trivial. The implication would be that whatever degree or amount of representation occurs in a system is merely the amount that would occur by chance with random selection of deputies.

This implication is obviously not correct. It is true that the expected opinion of any given person drawn at random from a district is the mean opinion in the district; but if we actually proceeded to draw a large number of single-person samples, relatively few of our choices would turn out to lie at points indistinguishable from their district means. Now and again, random choice would thrust up a rightist citizen to represent a leftist district, and vice versa. Any such gross discrepancies between the means of district sentiment and the actual opinions of a single-case sample would greatly attenuate the correlations observed for the AB bond. More frequently, the discrepancy between the deputy and the district mean would be more moderate, but it would still help to attenuate the correlation.

What all this means is that although the opinion expected for any randomly chosen deputy is indeed the mean opinion in the district—a mathematical proposition of an existential sort which willy-nilly strikes a major blow on behalf of popular representation—this does not typically solve the *normative* problem of representation, because a sample of one is very small, and the odds of such a small sample matching district sentiment very closely are not reassuring.

Achen (1977) has not only provided an excellent discussion of the problem of descriptive representation, but he has also calculated for the Miller-Stokes study of representation in the United States the correlations between district sentiment and representative opinion to be expected from nothing more than random selection. Relative to such a null hypothesis, the correlations actually observed for the United States Congress are not very impressive. In one of three issue domains covered (social welfare policy) the observed and the expected correlations are essentially the same; and in the two others (foreign policy and civil rights) the observed value does clearly outrun the expected, although the expected values are substantial in their own right. Indeed, the expected correlation for civil rights (generally the most "active" issue domain in the Miller-Stokes results) is an impressive $r = .35$, conforming to our general rule (Chapter 16) that the more "geographic" (or "regional" or "sectional") the issue, the greater the proximity one would expect by chance selection alone.

Proceeding from this background, let us see what the same calculations produce from the skein of identical issues we have been exploiting (Table 19-3). The observed calculations are only given for actual deputies (winners), the group that concerns us here. But since the deputy figures come from Table 19-2, the loser correlations are available there as well.

We see first of all that the observed value for left-right self-locations vastly outruns the correlation to be expected if a sample of one were drawn from each district to sit in the National Assembly. The observed correlation is more than double the expected correlation, and we know that to make effective ratio comparisons of this kind we need to deal not with correlations but with their squares (that is, proportions of variance in common). Looked at in this fashion, our observed correlation for the left-right measure is over six times the level of congruence that would have been expected by the chance model of descriptive representation.

Table 19-3. Comparisons of observed correlations between district sentiment and deputy position with those expected by chance (descriptive representation I).

	Pearson correlations (*r*)	
Issue domain	Expected	Observed (deputies)
I. Left-right self-location	.192	.483*
II. European integration		
French Army in European Army[a]	.000	Large, positive*
France accept European foreign policy	.104	−.112*
France remains in Common Market	.219	.106*
Free movement, European workers	.221	.233*
France aid poor Europe	.222	.107*
III. Issue importance		
Government stability	.204	.196*
Defense of public schools	.195	−.246*
Building Europe	.256	−.078*
Distribution of income	.217	.269*
Educational development	.244	.125*
Foreign policy independent of U.S.	.271	.223*
Economic development	.214	−.269*

a. Although it is clear that the corrected value for the European Army item among winners is positive in sign and large in magnitude (e.g., almost certainly greater than $r = .30$*, and probably much larger), we cannot assign a precise corrected value. The reasons are technical and are discussed at the close of Appendix C on small-sample attenuation.

This is certainly an impressive figure, and we do not wish to obscure it by turning our attention rapidly elsewhere. Given the conceptual status of the left-right locations as a super-issue, the first row of Table 19-3 is by a wide margin the most important single set of entries, so that the large contrast is of inordinate theoretical significance.

One cannot look long at Table 19-3, however, without recognizing that, beyond the first row, the comparisons between observed correlations and those that might be generated by chance selection of representatives alone are bleak indeed. One is tempted to conclude that the "value added" to the fidelity of popular representation due to the intervention of popular elections must lie entirely along the lines of the left-right watershed, and that as soon as one "descends" to more specific political issues, there is simply no value added by elections at all: chance selection would do just as well.

Before we leap to any such wry conclusion, however, it is worth reviewing several persistent anomalies that hint that the conclusion itself is too glib. We should not wonder at the fact that left-right self-locations perform so well in this setting, but rather that the more specific policy issues, stereotypically related to them, do not. This is no anomaly: we have already seen (Chapter 7) that whereas those relationships with left-right positions are strong on the elite side, they are vestigial among common voters.

The first real anomaly arises as we note in the table that, among the specific issues, it is not simply a matter of an observed value here or there not exceeding chance; that is, we know that the chance values are no more than "expecteds." This means that there is nothing peculiar about finding observed values that fall short of the expected, even if they fall quite a distance short. All that we mean by the notion of an expected value is that, in the long run, observations will come to fall symmetrically around it. But even this could be a problem in evaluating Table 19-3, because it is not apparent that the observed values scatter symmetrically around the calculations of the expecteds; in general, it seems to be true for the winners that a majority of the observed values actually *lag behind* the values calculated as those expected by chance.

The second difficulty is compounded in a natural way out of the first. We may be taken aback at the apparent lack of discernment on the part of the voters (beyond the left-right super-issue), since they put forward "winners" who on many specific issues look less like the district than chance selections would have looked. It is implicit that almost any other choices the districts might have made would have shown greater proximity. But we already know that this is not true. It is certainly not unfair, if we are contemplating selection by pure chance, to lay losing candidates against such a baseline as well as winning ones. And however poorly Table 19-3 shows winners doing against chance (the left-right locations aside), it is clear from Table 19-2 that losers fare more poorly still.

How can all of our candidates register as less attuned to district sentiment than if they had been the products of chance selection? From this point on, we must proceed in a somewhat contingent style, because it is not entirely clear that there is any real puzzle here. Whatever is true of a lot of specific issues, we have already found that on the most capacious issue of all, that of left-right position, the congruence of winners and their districts does run vastly ahead of chance. That has to be the most important fact in Table 19-3, and perhaps we should leave the matter there.

Nonetheless, it does rankle to see so many candidates running on balance behind chance on these lesser issues. We have imagined that this may be more than accident, and hence worth trying to understand systematically. In this contingent vein, then, let us proceed.

Circumstances in which observed performance turns out to be "worse than chance" are often difficult to diagnose. Sometimes a source of active perversity can be located. Thus, for example, cats are notoriously poor experimental animals, often doing worse than chance, apparently because they are "wired up" to avoid doing what the experimenter wants them to do, in the degree they can perceive his intention. In many other situations, there is no obvious source of perversity, and our case is probably one of these. One can easily imagine elections being merely ineffectual, and failing to generate deputies whose views are congruent with their districts' majorities at more than a chance level. But in the degree that Table 19-3 suggests some actual shortfall below chance, it is hard to imagine that parties actively seek nominees who are more than normally discrepant from district sentiments.

In such a case, it is usually necessary to retreat to an examination of the realism of the chance model. The notion of random selection is of course totally unrealistic, but that is the key to arriving at a chance baseline, and we must stick with it. The other assumption of the model is that the sampling is done with equal probabilities across all (adult) members of the electorate. Of course this is very unrealistic as well, and here we can do some experimentation. We can vary the definition of the pool being sampled in ways that nudge it closer to reality. There is no point in pretending, in redefining the model, that we have not changed the substance of the problem in vital ways. But if our efforts at greater realism clear away the shortfall of our observations from even chance, we shall at least have located the nature of the problem.

We must limit ourselves to two such experiments, and we shall choose the two redefinitions of the pool that seem on a priori grounds likely to be most important, yet which will also be relatively independent of each other.

Limitations on the Pool: Education

Although there are no formal educational prerequisites for candidacy for the National Assembly, the odds of an illiterate person becoming a candidate are vanishingly small. In fact, we saw in Chapter 6 that in the 1967 sample the differences between deputies or candidates and the general electorate were at a maximum where formal education was concerned. Whereas two-thirds of our voters had no more than a primary school education, and only 6 percent had any higher education, two-thirds of our winning candidates had some higher education, as did more than half of all the other candidates.

That such gross discrepancies in education exist between deputies and their constituents need not imply the existence of attitudinal dissimilarities. None are to be expected, in fact, unless education is correlated with issue positions. And even then, for many specific issues, we cannot make any obvious predictions, although we would not be astonished to discover some. For some other issues, however, there are fairly routine predictions. We have already seen, for example, that persons highly involved in politics tend to attribute greater importance to any specific issue than is accorded by the common voter. Although formal education is not the same as political involvement, it is correlated with it, and it would therefore seem reasonable that the highly educated would give higher importance to specific issues than the poorly educated.

We would like to imagine that our deputies are being drawn by pure chance out of a pool defined by those with higher education in each district, in order to see whether this redefinition rids us of observed correlations which fail to match these new chance levels. Unfortunately, we cannot do this in any direct way because higher education is so limited in the electorate; in order to calculate the correlations to be expected by chance, we must have estimates of three different district parameters, which can only be based on our small samples in each district. Generally our small samples have been adequate, but now we are talking of basing estimates of these complicated parameters on the mere 6 percent of the voters who have enjoyed higher education. Whereas we have usually based our estimates on well over twenty interviewed persons per district, now the calculations for chance levels of congruence for the highly educated would have to be based on interviews with one and occasionally two persons as we move from one district to another. Obviously we cannot expect to get estimates of opinion variance from samples of one or two.

We do, however, have enough voters with higher education in our total sample of the electorate to get quite reasonable estimates of their opinions on our skein of issues. Thus we can find out whether our deputies and candidates as a whole tend to look more like these well-educated respondents than they do like the broader electorate. This puts us back into a "collective representation" format. Figure 19-2, which is designed as a parallel to Figure 19-1, makes this comparison easy.

The results are clear-cut. On almost every issue, all the candidates lie closer to the positions of the most educated 6 percent of the electorate than they do to the electorate as a whole. Moreover, whereas in Figure 19-1 losers were closer to the electorate than winners, that imbalance is redressed in Figure 19-2, which, if anything, tilts the other way. One way to summarize this information, since the discrepancies in both figures are expressed in a common currency, is to compare the average discrepancies underlying each one:

Average discrepancy on thirteen issues	*Winners*	*Losers*
Vis-à-vis total electorate	.440	.361
Vis-à-vis most educated 6 percent of voters	.246	.263

Remembering that large values mean greater dissimilarities and that the zero point on the proximity measure has high meaning, we can say that the shift in frame of reference from the total electorate to the thin stratum with the highest education cuts our sense of distance between winners and "constituents" nearly in half. The cut is not so dramatic for losers, who are some-

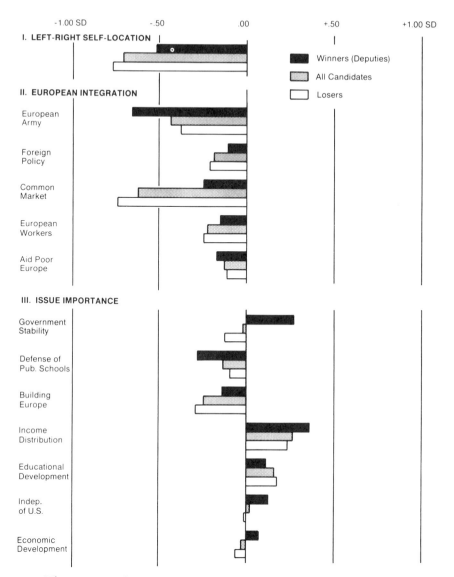

Figure 19-2. Elite issue positions as standard deviations from mean
position of voters with higher education.

what more like the full electorate in educational level, but there is still
nearly a one-third reduction in distance.

All told, this is impressive evidence that the restricted educational pool
from which representatives tend to be drawn does add to systematic dissimilarities between deputies and districts, and in a way that can help us understand why our estimates of relative congruence might have trouble keeping

up with chance levels (descriptive representation), when the chance model presumes random selection from among all district voters.

It is important to emphasize that we have *not* demonstrated that our deputies are really closer to district opinion than the earlier data suggested. The new sense of closeness is not, of course, between deputies and their constituents in total districts, but rather between deputies and a thin and surely unrepresentative subset of these constituents. Rather than demonstrating true closeness, then, we have only isolated one set of reasons why deputies are no closer than they are to the totality of their constituents.

It would be easy to leap from these last data to the cynical conclusion that popularly elected representatives are a very biased subset of their constituents and that they only "represent" their own kind. Though such a conclusion may come later, we must recognize that the current data do not necessarily refer to acts of representation, but rather to the private issue positions of the deputy, which he may honor only in varying degrees when faced with conflicting views from his constituents.

Nonetheless, in view of the marked educational advantages of legislatures in virtually every democracy, the impact of educational differences on issue positions becomes a haunting normative question. We shall discuss the stakes involved in our final chapter. For now, it is enough to point out that normative reactions must vary according to the nature of the issue involved. We have already agreed that if deputies regard political issues as more urgent than does the general population, the difference is probably benign. Also it is easy to imagine that, in many cases where substantive positions vary with education, the well-educated bring more relevant information to bear on the subject, and hence that their views are in some sense "wiser." At the same time, the specter of political issues is always with us—particularly class-related issues—on which the positions of the poorly educated are not merely uninformed but also reflect those problems of the underdog to which the well-educated elites are often very poorly attuned. It is at this point that governance by the highly educated alone can begin to pose serious problems of representation.

For the moment, we have demonstrated the massive restriction that educational background puts on the pool from which deputies may be drawn. The second major limitation, equally obvious, is that given deputies are not drawn randomly from pools of the well-educated, but are drawn by each of the diverse parties from pools limited by particular political persuasions. The introduction of this consideration is so basic as to require a separate section.

Subconstituencies of Supporters

In both the last chapter and this one we have been making the crucial assumption that the elected representative is obliged to represent his district as a whole, and not some limited subset of his constituents, even those who were kind enough to vote for him. In the last chapter, where we took our broadest view of the basic representation bond (AD), we operationalized "constituency sentiment" by taking mean attitude positions over all the people interviewed in a district, whether or not they had voted or how they had voted. Similarly, so far in this chapter we have examined the nature of the fit between the representative's own convictions and those of *all* of his district constituents.

Some highly respectable students of political representation regard this assumption as verging on the ridiculous. We discussed the reasons for this view at the end of Chapter 16: with binary legislative voting the norm, the deputy voting with his winning majority for a certain issue has to be voting against the people in his district who opposed that issue. We also discussed some halfway houses and nuances in the real-world legislative situation that can reduce the clarity of the imperatives somewhat, but there is no doubt that the belief that the good deputy represents his supporting majority, at least wherever there is a direct clash of wills, has much to recommend it.

The literature on representation is remarkably evasive, and perhaps even schizophrenic, on this question. On the one hand, although the classic normative discussions have avidly sought out the thorny legal, moral, and metaphysical issues underlying political representation, what is arguably the thorniest of all—the nature of the true constituency in territorial representation—has been mentioned only in passing. In most such treatments, it has been assumed that the deputy represents the district as a whole, an assumption helped along by a simplistic view of districts as consisting somehow of "single" interests, such as the "mercantile" interest.

On the other hand, much if not all of the more recent literature prefers to make another assumption and to regard the "constituents" of any given representative as those responsible for his victory at the polls. Clausen (1973), for example, points out that although the legally specified constituency may be the total district, the representative's perceived constituency is the set of voters who lent him support in the latest election, and in his analysis he keeps that definition central. We must confess that in treating "collective representation" we departed from Weissberg's treatment (1978) by comparing all deputies with all the electorate. In his own empirical work, he compares winning candidates with the *identifiers of their own parties* (Weissberg, 1978, p. 541n), and more recent scholars often follow suit (see, for example, Dalton, 1983).

We are indebted to the French government for our last example of this alternate assumption. The official statistics of legislative elections often include a bottom line indicating how many French citizens are "represented" in the new Assembly. This number is, of course, no more than a sum of those voting for winning candidates across all the nation's legislative districts. This sum is naturally much smaller than "40 million Frenchmen": given the multiparty system and frequent plurality victory of the period, along with a normal margin of nonvoters, the figure of those "represented" is usually a minority of the French electorate. The official implication is that the majority of voters must go without political representation until they have a chance to try again in the next legislative election![8]

This point is central because most scholars agree that the political heterogeneity of the constituency poses the most severe problem faced by the aspiring representative. This truth is as apparent in Fiorina's deductive model of the deputy's representational calculus (1974) as in Fenno's clinical observations of his interactions with his district (1978); that is why we made it the central theme of our theoretical discussion in Chapter 16. Of course, some geographical districts are tolerably homogeneous in their political opinions. The considerable majority, however, are not, and for these there is no surer or speedier way for the representative to "homogenize" his "constituency" politically than to define it as the base of his voting support, rather than as all the citizens of the district.[9]

In much of the rest of this chapter, we shall consider the difference it makes to our estimates of the fit between deputy convictions and constituency sentiment if, in defining the constituency, we substitute "own supporters" for the total-district concept which we used earlier. We could retrace all of our earlier steps, repeating each display in this revised form, but that would be tedious. What all of these displays would show, whether in terms of correlational congruence or absolute proximity, would not be surprising: deputies are very much closer to the policy attitudes of their own supporters than they are to those of the district as a whole.

We can now take another step in diagnosing the relationship between our data on the AB bond and the baseline of random selection. We have found indirect evidence indicating that one likely reason why issue congruence had trouble keeping pace at some points with the chance expectations of "descriptive representation" is that the pool from which actual candidates are drawn is limited to an educational elite.

The second limitation on the pool results from the fact that the parties put forth candidates, and that they do not find their candidates just anywhere in their districts, or just anywhere within the educated elite. Instead, candidates come from the partisan camps that are made up, roughly, of those people who have voted for the candidate. There are further realistic restrictions on these pools of possibilities, including the fact that candidates do not come automatically from the educated level of the voting base. Instead, they are very likely to have been active earlier in party affairs. In any event, we can imagine a chance model in which candidates are drawn at random from all voters in a partisan camp in a district; and then we can ask whether the observed selection process under these conditions performs better, relative to the chance baseline, than it did before when the "constituency" was the total district.

Unlike our earlier experimentation, in which we examined the education restriction on the candidate pool, we can arrive at these results directly, comparing observed correlations with those calculated from the chance model. This was not feasible with the education restriction, because if we had limited the pool to the educational category which was modal among our candidates, we would have been reduced to fewer than two cases of rank-and-file voters per district on the average. Where winners' and losers' supporters are concerned, however, we have close to ten cases per district on the average.

Are eight or ten cases enough? They are, but for reasons that seem to escape almost all scholars who are interested in representation. Even as perspicacious an observer as Fiorina, dealing with the Miller-Stokes 1958 study, seems to be uneasy that "such small samples" (per district) should be depended upon to yield estimates of constituent sentiments, "especially when constituencies are later broken down into majority-minority sectors" (Fiorina, 1974, p. 17). Since we are about to do this very thing for our own estimates, Fiorina's alarm is germane. It turns out, however, that such a breakdown does not produce *more* sampling error, but *less*.

If sampling error were solely a function of case numbers, then special alarm would be warranted. But a glance at any relevant formula reminds us that sampling error is a joint function of the case numbers *and* the variance of the variable with which we are working. As we move from all district members interviewed to those who supported the winner at the polls, it is clear, on the one hand, that, given some nonvoting, our case numbers are likely to be at least cut in half, a fact which will multiply any sampling error, ceteris paribus, by a factor of 1.41 (that is, the square root of two). But on the other hand, it is almost inconceivable that in the real world, a winnowing down to such a politically congenial subset of the district as those who voted for a particular candidate will not produce a very significant reduction in the absolute variance of attitude positions, relative to those variances for the total district. In fact, this is almost another way of saying what politics is all about. And as those variances shrink, sampling error shrinks with them, ceteris paribus. In the limiting case of a Communist cell giving identical responses to attitude questions, or of a group of Gaullist supporters responding unanimously to items about satisfaction with the behavior of General de Gaulle, the variance goes to zero (identical responses). And in such a circumstance, we can reduce our sample size all the way to one and still enjoy a sampling error which is at its logical minimum of zero.

In short, then, the operative question is whether the ballooning of sampling error as case numbers are reduced is less than, equal to, or more than the shrinkage of sampling error which is necessarily occurring as we winnow down further and further to more homogeneous subgroups in the district. On the basis of our extensive empirical experience with the representation design of a number of countries, the answer is quite unequivocal. In the French case, which is not at all out of the ordinary, the shrinkage in sampling error outruns the increase in sampling error by a clear margin, roughly two to one. This means that although we would be overjoyed to have twice as many, or a hundred times as many, cases per district as we have, it remains true that we are objectively better off making estimates with our majority-minority breakdown than we are with our estimates of total-district parameters, because the sampling errors tend to be visibly less.

Keeping all this in mind, we can construct Table 19-4, which looks essentially like Table 19-3, but which relates the attitudes of the deputies

Table 19-4. Comparisons of observed correlations between deputy position and sentiment of own voters, with those expected by chance (descriptive representation II).

	Pearson correlations (r)	
Issue domain	Expected[a]	Observed (deputies)
I. Left-right self-location	.487	.822*
II. European integration		
French Army in European Army[b]	.000	Large, positive*
France accept European foreign policy	.225	.836*
France remains in Common Market	.175	.364*
Free movement, European workers	.209	.190*
France aid poor Europe	.000	−.099*
III. Issue importance		
Government stability	.000	.188*
Defense of public schools	.000	.317*
Building Europe	.278	−.125*
Distribution of income	.173	.330*
Educational development	.020	.111*
Foreign policy independent of U.S.	.132	.343*
Economic development	.084	−.198*

a. The expected correlations for four of the thirteen items are listed as E(r) = .000. Such values arise in the following fashion. The algorithm for computing these values (see Achen, 1977) deduces the real variance as a residue, that is, what is left over in the observed variance after the error to be expected from sampling error alone (a theoretical calculation, based on the known numbers of cases in the several districts) is drawn off. In these four cases, where the structure is obviously very weak to begin with, the expected sampling error variance is already slightly greater than the variance actually observed, leaving no room for any true (that is, non-error) variance. If we proceeded blindly with the algorithm, we would be dealing with nonsensical terms such as negative variances. Therefore we have short-circuited the calculations at this point, and we report that there is no reason to expect any correlation in the chance selection case.

b. The corrected value for the European Army item is almost certainly greater than r = .30*, and probably much larger; the reasons why a precise value cannot be estimated are technical and are discussed at the close of Appendix C on small-sample attenuation.

(winners) to the constituency made up of their voters in the 1967 election. This table looks quite different from Table 19-3 in a number of vital respects.

Although there is some similarity between the columns of expected values in the two tables, it is not very strong; evidently, in moving from the total-district calculations to those for victorious supporters (defined at the decisive tour), a little sharpening has occurred as well as a lot of leveling. The most dramatic change is in the expected value for the left-right locations, which has risen from $r = .19$ to $r = .49$. Numerous other expectations in the first column show a leveling, however, and values that looked somewhat interesting for the total district now amount to little or nothing.[10]

These changes are not too surprising. We knew that the expectation for the left-right variable had to advance, and probably by a substantial margin, because this axis is most closely aligned with the partition we inserted as we shifted constituencies. What would happen to other specific issues not too closely tied to the left-right measurement was less clear, and some, though not all, of these other expectations have withered rather badly in the winnowed version of the constituency. When we treat issues as "equal" units (that is, do not give special weight to the left-right super-issue), the *expectations* for descriptive representation have declined somewhat from Table 19-3 to Table 19-4.

The observed (deputy) correlations, however, behave quite differently. With small exceptions, they generally increase in magnitude rather dramatically as we shift from the total district to the supporters of the winning candidate. The bellwether, as is often true, is the left-right measure, but several other measures advance as well. Overall, we see that whereas now and again the observed correlation for a specific issue does run behind the expected correlation, the trend is very clearly for the observed values to exceed this baseline.

Nevertheless, there is enough variability of results in Tables 19-3 and 19-4 to be somewhat distracting. Therefore it may be helpful to provide a crude summary of these tables by averaging their columns and showing the average r correlations for both winners and losers:

	Winners		Losers	
Constituency	Expected	Observed	Expected	Observed
Total district	.19	.11	.19	−.02
Own supporters	.14	.26	.10	.25

What do these last data tell us, and, equally important, what do they *not* tell us? First, it is important to understand that what happens to the data as we move from a total-district constituency to one which involves only winners (or losers) and their supporters is what has led Achen (1977) to warn us against correlations. Although the elite attitude measures are the same in the two forms, the mass distributions have changed, and at least for the more vital issues, such as left-right locations, the direction of change is obvious. As we stop pitting total districts against one another, but instead pit the leftist majorities from some districts against the rightist majorities from other districts, the left-right variance on the constituent side is bound to increase. This means that if certain other implicit terms are equal, our expected correlations should rise as well.

Achen sees this built-in increase as an artifact that should be expunged by shifting to some other kind of statistical vocabulary. We are satisfied with the contrary argument, which says that this kind of heightened variance is natural, not artifactual, and we actually want our summary statistics to reflect these variations in polarization, because in the final analysis they express the very heart and soul of the dynamics of political competition. More specifically, in the case just laid out, we have also said that redefining the constituency from whole district to own supporters is a great boon to the aspiring representative because it clarifies his world. His cue-giving environment suddenly takes on a sharpness of structure that was lacking when he was expected to represent everybody at once. And one thing that correlations are supposed to index conforms nicely to the construct of "degree of structure"—clear or fuzzy. If the redefinition of constituency touches off vital gains in the clarity of the structure within which the deputy is operating, then we would like to have our statistics reflect that natural fact, as correlations do, rather than having to take various evasive actions to erase this facet of change from the data artificially.

Second, the new data call for the same warning that we gave earlier in speaking of the apparent restrictions on the education pool from which candidates are drawn. These data show that just as the candidates are much closer in political posture to the well-educated in their districts, so also are they very much closer in their convictions to their own supporters than to their districts as a whole. Both of these "biases" are helpful in explaining why at some points even the winners do not measure up well against the yardstick of chance selection from the district as a whole. We must remember that Table 19-3 shows winners outrunning chance by a substantial margin on the super-issue of left and right: the shortfall, relative to chance, is restricted to our more specific issues, which would not be expected to be so powerful.

At the same time, our capacity to understand the biased nature of selection does not lessen the fact that, on specific issues, the winner's convictions and the sentiments of his total district show only a loose fit. This point may be of limited interest to those who do not feel that the representative is obligated to his total district, but it remains a property of the data.

Third, we should not overlook the fact, shown on our summary scorecard, that the attitudes of winning candidates and the relevant sentiments of their total districts, though only modestly congruent, still fit more closely than do the attitudes of losing candidates and district sentiments. It seems that the losing candidates, though showing very nearly the same levels of relative congruence with their own supporters as those shown by the winners, are even less in tune with their total districts, and that they fall more severely short of the chance yardstick as well.

Hence these further data continue to argue that the intervention of democratic elections does have an easily detectable function in improving the fit between representatives' views and district sentiments. To be sure, the selection of those representatives from the educated stratum of partisan camps is not calculated to tighten the fit in general. But it is clear from the evidence that elections generate a closer attitudinal proximity of the deputy to the total district than would have existed if the deputy had instead been drawn at random from the existing pool of candidates.

Supporter Subconstituencies and the Basic Representation Bond

The focus of this chapter has been upon the nature of the fit between the representative's own views and those of his electoral supporters, or of his total district, or of the total electorate (all variants on the AB bond); but we must resist the temptation to see this fit as some generalized commentary on the fidelity of political representation. It should not be so construed because the deputy's own convictions are but one station on the way to a legislative vote, and our final test for fidelity of representation involves the congruence between district sentiment and the ultimate legislative vote cast in its behalf.

When dealing with this AD bond in the last chapter, we assembled in Table 18-5 a general tableau showing for 1967 the strength of the linkages between district sentiments and ultimate roll-call voting for our basic skein of political issues. Although this table gives the most general picture we have of the character of representation in France in that year, we did not scrutinize it with exceptional care.

The first reason for this was that we were anticipating exploring the other bonds that intervene between the district and the legislative vote, such as the AB bond discussed in this chapter. Although we were glad to learn from Table 18-5 that there was some level of popular representation worth explaining in subsequent chapters, the main story seemed to be locked away, awaiting the decomposition of the data into the component bonds of the Miller-Stokes diamond, to which we were anxious to proceed.

The second reason was that it would be easy to partition Table 18-5 into another set of components so disparate as to raise questions as to the intrinsic value of the table. We do feel, however, that Table 18-5 has an important summary function, despite our analytic capacity to "explode" it into contrasting segments. Nonetheless, we shall be better equipped to sense that summary function after producing this "explosion," and now we are in a position to do so. This operation needs to be performed because Table 18-5 takes the constituency to be the total district, and we have just found that what the deputy should be expected to represent, from this point of view, is not the sentiments of a total district in all its heterogeneity, but rather the much more uniform issue positions of his own subconstituency of supporters.

What would Table 18-5 look like with the "constituency" term winnowed down to the set of supporters of the victorious candidates?[11] We can say in advance that when this shift in constituency definition is made, the linkage correlations of Table 18-5 do in fact spurt upward in magnitude some nine times out of ten, as they would be expected to do. Before turning to the actual data, however, we should develop one other point of comparison for such figures.

Throughout most of this chapter we have kept track of what is going on with respect to the AB bond for winners and losers differentially. The rationale for this procedure has been that we learn something thereby about the function of democratic elections, which screen a pool of candidates into winners and losers. More important, however, we are interested in the impact of such a triage upon the fidelity of the representation function.

When we turn back from the AB to the AD bond, we cannot mount these comparisons in the same way for the simple reason that the "D" term in the AD bond is represented by roll-call votes, which winners cast but losers do not. Therefore there is no way to ask how the AD bond would look for losing candidates, relative to winning ones.

There is, however, a cognate question which we *can* ask. If we were to inquire how well deputies support that fraction of their total districts that is made up of their own supporters, we would leave out the voters who opposed them. To put it another way, how faithfully does the deputy's record of legislative voting "represent" the position of opposition voters? One would not expect this representation to be very faithful. Logically, it should be some kind of "disrepresentation," or negative representation, if we assume that popular elections do have some active impact on the character of representation by districts. In actual fact, measuring the difference between the level of representation achieved by deputies with regard to their own supporters as against that achieved vis-à-vis opposing voters is another way of assessing how much difference the intervention of elections makes.

We shall proceed now to two displays of data which not only permit us to see by what margins the redefinition of the constituency from the total district to the supporter group increases our calculus of representation fidelity among winning candidates (deputies), but which also make clear the degree to which the entries of Table 18-5 typically bifurcate into strong representation of the winning candidates' supporters and absolute disrepresentation of the supporters of the losing candidates.

We shall accomplish this in the first instance through a tabular frame which, although it resembles Table 18-5, has entries which, instead of showing the basic representation bond (AD) for the total district or for the subconstituency of winning supporters, indicate the *differences in correlations* emerging when the correlations vis-à-vis the loser subconstituency are subtracted from the correlations vis-à-vis the subconstituency actually electing the deputy. In this format, positive values arise, as expected, when the relative congruence of roll-call vote and constituency sentiment is stronger in the predicted direction for winning supporters than for losing ones. Furthermore, the maximum value for such entries is not 1.00 but 2.00, as would arise if the correlation involving the winner supporters were +1.00 and that involving the losing supporters were −1.00.

Table 19-5 has been prepared with entries of this kind. Of the 39 entries, 38 are positive, and all but one or two others register very large differences between correlations for the winning as against the losing constituency. Although this table is not constructed to show it, most of the anomalies that disfigured parts of Table 18-5 are thoroughly rectified when we see the deputy's roll-call votes as cast not in behalf of his total district, but more in behalf of his supporting voters. Those anomalies of Table 18-5 were most pronounced in the column referring to specific issues, where four entries out of 13 were negative in sign. These negatives, though very limited in magnitude, were embarrassing, for they suggested that the deputies were voting systematically against the sentiments of their districts, or even in favor of the minoritarian views in those districts.

As we see from Table 19-5, however, this turns out not to be true on any issue, even on the weaker, single-item "specific" ones. More information is supplied by Figure 19-3, which, although it subsumes all of the information in Tables 18-5 and 19-5, helps to clarify what is going on. For all the linkages displayed in the tables, along with a number of others which are scale components or items of secondary relevance, this figure shows: (a) the level of the bond for the total district as constituency, represented by a short horizontal line across the vertical bar; (b) the level when the constituency is defined as the subgroup of winning supporters (top of black bar); and (c) the level for the loser definition of constituency (bottom of shaded bar).

In almost all the comparisons—some 57 of 63—the total-district level lies below that for the winners but above that for the losers, although there is no mathematical necessity that this should be so. And we see, furthermore, that in three of the four negative values in the specific-issue column for the total district (Table 18-5), the deputy's votes are representing his majority positively and the opposing minority negatively, despite the fact

***Table* 19-5.** Discrepancies in the AD bond as calculated with either winning or losing supporters as the "constituency."[a]

	Correlation discrepancies with roll-call vote summary			
Measure of district sentiment	Specific issue	Left-right location	Gaul-lism	Roll-call vote
I. Generic debate Importance: Government Stability	0.557*	1.231*	1.159*	Government-Opposition
II. Domestic policy A. Social Welfare Income distribution scale	0.521*	0.957*	0.977*	Income Distribution
Socioeconomic L-R scale	0.749*	0.982*	1.008*	Socioecon. Left-Right
Protect Union Rights	0.491*	0.634*	0.401*	Droit Syndical
Protect Union Rights	0.700*	0.951*	0.979*	Union Rights
B. Church-State Public School scale	0.847*	0.948*	0.981* ⎫	Religion
District Religiosity	0.768*	0.948*	0.981* ⎬	
C. Education Education Priority scale	0.586*	1.268*	1.295*	Education Budget
Education Priority scale	0.422*	0.778*	0.987*	Faure Law Left-Right
D. Economic development Importance: Econ. Devel.[b]	−.XXX*	0.847*	0.932*	Economic Development
III. Foreign policy A. European Integration European Integration scale	0.046*	0.723*	0.656*	European Integration
B. Foreign Aid Foreign Aid scale	0.840*	1.444*	1.550*	Foreign Aid
C. Military Expenditure Force de Frappe	1.253*	1.457*	1.525*	Force de Frappe

a. Cell entries are formed by subtracting the algebraic value of the correlation between constituency sentiment and roll-call vote, when "constituency" is taken to be made up of opposing voters, from the value when it is made up of winning supporters.

b. Although the cell entry for the specific issue is known to be negative, its magnitude cannot be reliably calculated for technical reasons discussed in the latter half of Appendix C.

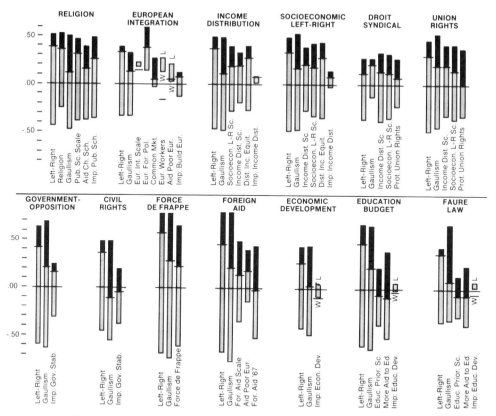

Figure 19-3. Levels of correlation between constituency sentiment and roll-call votes (the AD bond) for three definitions of constituency: winning supporters, losing supporters, and total district.

that the level of the AD bond for the total district dips into the negative region. The handful of deviations from these general patterns in Figure 19-3 include five cases in which the value for losers actually exceeds that for winners (noted in the figure with an "L" above a "W"), along with another case in which the winner value exceeds that for losers, but the total-sample correlation lies trivially outside the range defined by these poles. The former anomalies invariably involve single-item measures, rather than multi-item scales; and all but one of the cases permitting a check show that the parent multi-item scale performs according to intuitive expectations, even though one of its components may not. Moreover, these few anomalies tend to arise only when parent correlations are close to zero.

In short, then, Table 19-5 and Figure 19-3 give us solid assurance that representation is "positive" almost everywhere in the French system, even on the specific issues that looked rather unimpressive in Table 18-5. For example, whereas in that table the average correlation in the specific-issue column was only +.11*, it has forged ahead in Table 19-5 to a value of +.31*. Again, the Gaullism variable, which had a low average value of +.14* in Table 18.5, has surged forward even more dramatically to an average of +.55*, competing for attention with the left-right super-issue.

Throughout, the differences in representation between the winning and losing subconstituencies are awesome. In one sense this is not at all surprising, for it certifies that our measures have validity, especially as there is no artifact involved in these differences, and only political reality assures that they display the levels they do.

By now it is clear why we avoided making extended comments about Table 18-5 at the end of the last chapter. The total-district versions of the AD bond are surely of significance in their own right, including even those cases where the linkage appears negative. But foreknowledge that the total-district table is easily diffracted into the two contrasting subconstituency pieces puts a very different light on the matter. There is, of course, nothing illegitimate about either of the definitions of constituency, as we have seen. But it is obvious from our data, as well as from common sense, that it does matter a great deal which definition one adopts.

Summary

This chapter has centered on the fit between the deputy's views on controversial policies and the sentiments about them in his constituency, whether that constituency is the national electorate, the district in which he ran for office, or his local supporters at the polls. In the process, we have been obliged to explore various byways posed by measurement options. Our prime purpose, however, has been to use our examination of this fit as a means of addressing the most fundamental empirical question surrounding the democratic process: whether the intervention of popular elections in real-life settings actually produces greater fidelity in political representation.

This chapter has not given us the full answer. But we have been able to ask, first, whether deputies chosen by actual election show personal convictions more similar to those of their constituents than do candidates discarded by the same election process; and, second, whether winners thus selected show a closer fit with the distinctive sentiments of their constituencies than mere chance drawing from the same constituency would produce, under the standard term of descriptive representation.

The answer to that second question must run along two tracks. First, where the super-issue of left and right is concerned, elected deputies are a good deal more congruent with their constituencies than chance alone would indicate. This is true whether the constituency is defined as the total electoral district or only the subconstituency of supporters. Given the scope of the left-right dimension, this is probably the more important of our two answers.

The second answer goes below the left-right locations to many of the specific linkage issues. Here the attitudes of deputies do not on balance exceed chance expectations, and probably fall short of meeting them, *when the constituency is the total legislative district.* Since losing candidates do even worse, this difficulty in matching chance provoked us to a further explanatory analysis.

We were able to show that all of our candidates, but especially the winners, looked more similar attitudinally to the one voter in fifteen who had enjoyed higher education than to the rest of the electorate. By implication, this suggested that one reason for the failure of real elections to keep pace with a chance selection model was that the pool of candidates was actually limited in practice, if not in principle, to the more highly educated.

It also became clear that the pool was limited to partisan camps as well. When "constituency" was redefined as the candidates' own supporters at the polls, we found that even on specific issues both winning and losing candidates were more attitudinally similar to their constituents than a model of chance selection *from those constituencies* would predict.

In sum, then, popular elections in France in this period were achieving something beyond mere "descriptive representation," and they were doing so quite dramatically and unconditionally where left-right locations were concerned. They were also doing so for postures on most other political issues, although this can only be demonstrated clearly once it is recognized that candidates tend to represent subconstituencies of their supporters more than total districts.

More important still, we have encountered rather clear evidence that these popular elections tossed up as "winners" persons who were more "attitudinally representative" of their districts than the rejected candidates. Differences of this kind were negligible when we dealt with subconstituencies of the candidates' own supporters: losers were virtually as likely to resemble their own supporters attitudinally as winners were to resemble their victorious voters. But when the constituency was the total district, there was some observed congruence for winners but not for losers.

The pivotal importance of constituency definitions led us to return at the end of the chapter to the basic representation bond (AD) of the last chapter, to ask how it would look if supporters were used as the effective constituency. The degree of clarification was impressive, and a number of patterns which had been anomalous earlier came into more coherent focus. Furthermore, the gap between the kind of positive representation offered to his supporters by the winning candidate, relative to the "disrepresentation" implicitly given to the aggregate sentiments of opposing voters in the district, is impressive in its magnitude.

The question of "attitudinal representativeness" is well covered with the AB bond, but several other linkages remain to be investigated before we can move to more general conclusions. Two of these linkages are related to the question as to how the deputy forms his impressions of constituency sentiment, and that is the subject to which we shall now turn.

20

Elite Knowledge of Constituency Sentiment

In Chapter 16 we noted that the deputy who believes in voting his conscience and ignoring district sentiments might in fact "represent" those sentiments quite well in spite of himself, while another who believes in voting as his district instructs may represent it very poorly, again in spite of himself. The first syndrome is epitomized by the phenomenon of descriptive representation, which we probed empirically in the last chapter.

The most obvious way in which a delegate intent on following the wishes of his constituency to the letter may fail to do so is through some honest misunderstanding as to what those wishes are. If a few score referenda relating to key legislative issues were held within the span of a year in each home district, then such misunderstanding on the part of well-intended delegates would be quite inexcusable. But a steady flow of updated information on the evolution of constituent preferences is almost unobtainable, and its closest approximation, sample surveys conducted in local districts for the edification of the legislator, are not common and are a recent development. Under normal circumstances, the deputy only hears from a relatively large fraction of his district at election time, and then only about a bewildering bundle of issues wrapped obscurely in a single vote. Hence it is very difficult for him to size up true district opinion on more than a few issues.

Although it is likely that for modern territorial districts involving substantial heterogeneity, limitations on the accuracy of perceptions of district sentiment must be quite severe, it is clear at the same time that some modest accuracy is both important to the aspiring politician and a critical ingredient in any process of democratic representation. In campaign strategies surrounding competition for office, for example, one would expect accurate perceptions of the nature of the constituency and its wants to have a good deal of survival value—but this is a question that we can verify with our study data from losing as well as winning candidates.

More important still, such accuracy must logically place some kind of upper limit on the fidelity of representation which winning candidates can offer their constituents, once one gets past the healthy edge of representation arising from mere descriptive representation.

For these reasons it is desirable to investigate the levels of accuracy that pertain in our survey materials, and to arrive at a sense of some of the circumstances which may facilitate or impede accurate perceptions of those infinitely complex objects designated as legislative "districts." We are, of course, well equipped to do so. We asked all of our candidates not only what their personal convictions were with regard to our designated linkage issues, but also what the sentiments in their districts were on the same issues. These measurements of perceived district opinion form term "C" of the Miller-Stokes diamond (see Figure 16-1), and the question of perceptual accuracy invites us to compare this term with actual district opinion (term "A"), or, in other words, to examine the AC bond in the diagram.

Before turning to the actual analysis, we shall consider a few simple ideas which will guide our work. It is clear that the perception of district sentiment on the part of a candidate for office or an elected deputy is a special case, and an extremely important one, of a broader class of perceptions whereby political leaders (more generally construed) assess follower preferences; or, for that matter, of a still broader class of phenomena in which any kind of observer, including journalists or the voters themselves, size up the political temper of any aggregate of citizens, thereby "gauging public opinion." And, rather like a series of Chinese boxes, this broader class is again a special case of the more global phenomenon of social perception, which is in turn a special case of perception itself (see Clausen, 1977).

If all this is true—and it seems to be—then we would surely expect that any generic rules governing perception would hold in the special case where district sentiment is the object of the perception. Among the more trustworthy propositions of perception theory in psychology is the one which states that perceptual accuracy, or at least observer agreement as to stimulus properties (which is nearly the same thing), increases with the clarity of those properties, and degrades as those properties become ambiguous.

What do "clarity" and "ambiguity" mean when the special case of the object of perception is the state of political opinion in an aggregate? This question is complicated, and answers could be made along a variety of dimensions. The most obvious answer brings us back immediately to the matter of district heterogeneity or homogeneity. The state of opinion in a district would seem to be clearest as an object of perception when it is most homogeneous, either a view held unanimously by the constituents or a state of complete indifference. Ambiguity then would simply comprise attitudinal heterogeneity, perhaps indexed in the obvious ways with the variance of the opinion in the district, and perhaps dealt with in a more complicated fashion to take account of admixtures of indifferent constituents and those holding strong opinions pro or con.

When the stimulus object is clear, we would expect descriptions of it to be determined by the object: multiple judges should give the same description. As the object becomes increasingly ambiguous, variance in the description of it should increase, or, in other words, the reality determination of the descriptions should progressively decline. What accounts for the growing edges of variance that depart from pure reality? One source, of course, could be pure guesswork, which would create a random error term in the perceptions across multiple judges of the same object. But perception theory suggests that this is not all: that there are sources of systematic variance which, not being determined by the stimulus, are instead determined by what the particular judge brings to the assessment, often in the form of a personal need to see the object in a particular light. In Chapter 15 we found that some discrepancies in elite perceptions of the 1968 disturbances were of epic proportions, and that they seemed to be hinged to conflicting partisan angles of vision.

When the attitudes of others are perceived under conditions of stimulus ambiguity or of limited "true" information, an accompanying phenomenon that is commonly observed is *projection:* the observer tends to assume that the attitudes of others are closer to his own than they would objectively be if measured independently. In terms of our diamond paradigm, this would suggest that, as district opinion becomes less and less clear to the politician, the AC bond should weaken; but a part of the slack, beyond increases in pure error, should be taken up by the BC bond, involving the fit between the politician's own position and his perception of sentiment in the district. We shall take a brief look at this bond later in the chapter.

It would be quite inappropriate to suppose that stimulus clarity or ambiguity is the sole determinant of perceptual accuracy, especially in the specific case of aggregate opinion assessment. Such a proposition has arisen from laboratory work in which perceivers have been asked to "look at" objects of varying clarity. The only way to "look at" the object called district sentiment is to take a survey of its members with greater or lesser care. In our context, therefore, we are faced with questions of access to basic information which classic perception theory can simply ignore.

Let us suppose, for example, that opinion on some political issue is unanimous in the thirty-ninth circonscription in the Parisian area. We as naive outsiders are asked to judge what the distribution of opinion on that issue is in that district. Let us suppose, however, that we have no idea where the thirty-ninth circonscription lies in the area, or what kinds of people populate it. Except for our common-sense notion that a tract of contiguous land is being referred to, we bring absolutely no cues to the assessment.

This is by construction a case in which the stimulus object, being a unanimous view, is at its clearest, and hence misperception, ceteris paribus, should be at a minimum. But such rules of perception are in this instance overwhelmed by states of available information, and any response we make will by construction have to be pure guesswork. Therefore our judgment will have some of the predicted characteristics of a situation where information is less sparse but the distribution of opinions is heterogeneous.

Such an example is unrealistic because of its extremity. Nonetheless, deputies do not often get to "look at" opinion in their districts in the same way as the perceiver in the laboratory does, although now and then opinion polls may be taken which perform something of this "looking-at" function. For lack of more direct "seeing," they are obliged to piece together plausible constructions on the basis of rather limited cues. Most of those cues take the form of perceived associations of attributes, such as, "District X is mainly working class, so it is probably leftist." This much can sometimes be more directly observed in election outcomes. But other assessments of policy sentiment are undoubtedly made in the same associational way: "Since District X is leftist, it probably favors the protection of union rights or lay schools, since these are leftist positions." As we suggested in Chapter 7, it is likely that these associations between belief elements are perceived as being rather stronger than they are in reality.

We now have enough information on perception theory to proceed with our analysis. As we examine the accuracy of our politicians' perceptions, we shall find such sources of misperception as inadequate information, ambiguous stimuli, and the need to project one's own opinion onto the district, although such phenomena are not, of course, mutually exclusive.

Measuring the Accuracy of Perceptions of District Sentiment

The accuracy of politicians' perceptions rests once again on the notion of the "tightness" of a bond or linkage (in this case, the AC bond); and, as in the preceding chapter, this notion can be operationalized in two contrasting ways.

The intuitively obvious way would be to take an estimate of a district mean opinion on an issue offered by the candidate or deputy and subtract it from the mean value actually observed in the relevant district sample. A zero difference would mean perfect accuracy of estimate, and the procedure would give individual-level measures of accuracy that might be combined over multiple issues. The problem here is that such a method would require our elite informants to understand the ad hoc scale scores of our opinion measures in order to express their concept of the district mean in the same currency. This is, of course, too much to expect, although we do approximate such a procedure to arrive at parallel individual-level "absolute proximity" scores.

The second way of operationalizing the goodness of fit between politician perceptions and actual district sentiment, as employed in the Miller-Stokes paradigm, is by using correlational measures of relative congruence. This type of measurement has assets and liabilities which are closely akin to those reviewed in the last chapter. And once again, our choice between the two methods is bound to be influenced in some degree by the aptness of the currencies in which perceptions are measured, for simple subtraction makes rather strong assumptions about the commonality of the currency.

Measuring Perceptions of Distributions of Issue Positions

Granted that we did not want to ask our elite informants to estimate district means on various opinions in ad hoc scale scores, how did we proceed? The problem, of course, was that the informant had to describe not some "fixed point" at which an individual constituent was perceived to lie, but rather a *distribution* of positions in an aggregate. And we did indeed want something resembling distributional information, since we needed to know not only where the politician placed the central tendency of district sentiment, but also his sense of relative polarization of the issue in the district. But we had to collect this information in a minimum of time, since we had a number of linkage issues to cover.

Our solution in the case of left-right self-locations is in some ways prototypic of our procedures, at least for our "position issues." After we had asked our elite informants to locate the political parties as well as themselves on our left-right scale, we asked them, in another set of questions on the characteristics of their districts, to tell us what proportions of voters in the district they would classify as left, center, or right.

These three proportions, besides being fairly efficient to elicit, could be converted into a central tendency (mean) and a modicum of distributional information. Of course, we had no way of knowing how broad a range of responses the center would be imputed to encompass on our 100-point left-right scale. We assumed that this zone would include more than responses of "50" at the exact midpoint, numerous though those responses were. To find a defensible anchor, we took the average of the three perceived percent-

ages over all of our candidates as a group, and then divided our mass respondents according to their self-locations into three slices which would
match these proportions. Then within each of the three slices we calculated
an average left-right score. Happily, the mean observed for the middle slice
was 50.0, or the exact center of the nominal scale. For the left it was 24.0,
and for the right, 73.6. We then assumed that these were proper mean
values to weight by the percentages in each slice attributed by the politician
to his district.

In this fashion it was easy to calculate a "perceived mean" on the left-
right scale implied by the trichotomous percentages given by each elite informant, and to do so in the currency of our 100-point scale. Moreover, we
could also extract from the same percentages a crude estimate of the perceived variance or polarization of district voters on the same scale. Thus, for
example, an informant who estimated that 60 percent of the voters in his
district were center, with only 20 percent on each wing, would be perceiving a rather low-variance district in these terms, whereas the politician seeing a 45-10-45 array would be perceiving a district which was almost
maximally polarized.

Our elite informants were also asked to give us tripartite percentages
for each of our other position issues, indicating the proportion in their districts that they would expect to be favorable, unfavorable, or indifferent to
the stated issue. Regrettably, the full mass-attitude question was not read to
the elite. For example, although mass respondents were asked to agree or
disagree with the proposition that "the State should give aid to church
schools," the elite informants were asked simply what proportion in their
district would be for, against, or indifferent to "subsidies to church
schools." Although the fit here and elsewhere is certainly not embarrassing,
there is a potential for slight discrepancies, particularly in forming differences between perceived and observed district means.[1] Nevertheless, the
three percentages could once again be converted into an estimate of a mean
and a variance, just as in the case of the left-right distribution.

Although our position issues could be assessed in terms of three percentages, this tactic was of less value for the issue-importance items, since
there were no self-evident trichotomizations of the unipolar importance
scale. Therefore we did not try to get distribution information in these
cases, but simply asked the informants which importance rating would be
given "on the whole" by voters in their district. This single response is essentially the perceived mode of the distribution, but we shall treat it as a
mean nonetheless.

Our candidates were asked to characterize their districts in a variety of
other ways, including mix of ethnic backgrounds, degree of business lobby-
ing, and union activity. These open-ended questions shall not occupy us
here. But one such item asked the politicians how people in their districts

felt about religion. Responses could be coded into an ordinal array ranging from districts described as being dominated by a highly devout Catholicism, through a midpoint of indifference, to those with a generally antireligious atmosphere. We shall preserve this perceptual variable for some of our upcoming analyses, not only because it can be readily laid against district differences in voter reports of their own religiosity but also because of its manifest importance in the French context.

These are, then, our measures of perceived district sentiments. For seven issue-importance measures, eight specific position issues, left-right locations, and religiosity we have "point estimates" of perceived central tendency in the candidates' districts.[2] For the position issues and the left-right measure we also have point estimates of the variance of the distribution of district sentiment.

Measuring Perceptual Accuracy

With these measures of perception we can assess levels of accuracy in either of the two now familiar ways. We can subtract the perceived means or variances from their counterparts actually observed in the districts, or we can examine relative congruence of perceptions through the use of correlations. Which method is preferable depends in some degree on what we are trying to say, and also on whether we feel that the measurement scaling between the elite and mass sides is commensurate in an absolute sense or only in a relative sense.

We shall therefore employ both methods once again. But we must first establish one set of empirical anchors.

Reality Determination of District Perceptions

It would be delightful if, for any given perception of a district, we were able to state in some currency how much of the perception stems from the objective features of the district ("reality"), as distinct from all the other sources of potential variation in response, such as the needs of the perceiver or random error. We cannot, of course, do so with any exactitude, partly because for most of our district sentiments there is no hard-edged definition of "objective reality" to use as a yardstick.

Nevertheless, in almost all of the 86 districts in our study design—82, to be exact—we succeeded in interviewing more than one candidate. For these instances, then, we have two or more people describing to us the characteristics of what is objectively the same district. In as many as 63 of our districts we interviewed three or more candidates, hence furnishing even more "judges" of the same object. We can capitalize upon these multiple descriptions of the same object of perception to get some initial sense as to the degree in which "reality" dominates perceptions from one issue to another, by asking how convergent the testimony is from one "judge" to another.

Let us imagine the following trivial exercise. As we interview candidates from various districts, we ask them what percentage of the popular vote was won in their districts by the Communist party at the most recent election. What makes the exercise trivial is that we supply each respondent with a tabulation showing the Communist vote to three digits in every district in France, for the election in question. The respondent merely looks up his district in the table and reads back the answer. This procedure guarantees access to standardized information which symbolizes "reality." There still might be an occasional error, such as that made by an overconfident respondent who does not bother to use the table supplied, or by the one who reads the entry in the wrong row. But in principle, we would expect the results of interviews with many triads and tetrads of candidates from the same districts to show essentially no *within*-district variance: all of the observed variance would be that lying *between* districts. Thus, if reality totally dominated responses, we would expect an *eta* statistic to arrive at a perfect value of 1.00, indicating that pure district differences accounted for all of the variation in responses.

It is not hard to put our issue-perception materials into an analysis-of-variance format to ask this kind of question. The test is a rather severe one, for we are asking politicians who come by design from almost maximally different persuasions, to tell us what a district is like politically. Presumably we could get impartial observers to agree more closely.[3]

In Figure 20-1 we present the data in a graphic hierarchy of issue items. It is clear that reality is forcing a rather substantial level of convergence on these perceptions, despite the conflicting viewpoints of our "judges." At the same time, we must conclude that reality intrudes more forcefully for some issues than for others, and by a substantial margin. It is not hard to see why. Probably the most systematic feedback bearing on political attitudes which our candidates receive from their districts is that given by voting returns. It stands to reason that these returns would be seen as surer indicators of left-right coloration in the district than of any specific issue in the list. Therefore it may not come as a surprise that the left-right super-issue very nearly heads the list, where reality convergence is concerned. Similarly, there is probably clearer behavioral feedback about district religiosity tied up in such terms as church attendance and religious contributions than there is with respect to any of the other policy "sentiments." Therefore it is not surprising to find religiosity and the two church-state issues forming most of the rest of the top items in this kind of reality-determination hierarchy.

Somewhat more generally, we see that despite a considerable overlap in the two distributions, the importance items tend to produce less reality de-

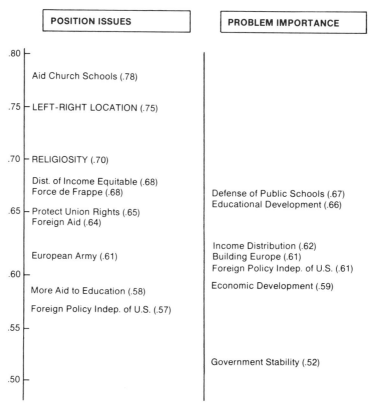

Figure 20-1. Intraelite agreement in judgments of district sentiments, by issue. Numerical entries are etas, formed by examining intradistrict variance in assessment of district sentiment by two or more candidates interviewed, relative to total variance. A high value means high agreement.

termination than the position issues, and the foreign issues give less determination than the domestic issues. In neither case does this seem surprising, for fewer cues were available in connection with those items and more had to be left to the imagination.

As a whole, then, the item hierarchy of Figure 20-1 makes a good deal of intuitive sense. We have presented it first so that it may serve as a backdrop for what follows. The basic message is that some perceptions are more thoroughly foreclosed by reality than others, at least for reasonable and thoughtful observers who are trying to give accurate descriptions. Although this hierarchy does not involve explicit accuracy measurements of the kind we are about to introduce, it seems to bear on questions of accuracy, and indeed, this item ordering will turn up again and again through the rest of the chapter.

Adequacy of District Knowledge

We shall now assess the accuracy of district knowledge on the part of our candidates, across the skein of linkage issues. This assessment will be basically "objective," but since we have reports from our elite informants as to their own confidence in their knowledge of policy sentiments in their districts, we shall begin with these subjective assessments of adequacy in perceptions.

Elite Confidence in District Knowledge

Despite a natural variation from one candidate to another, our elite informants felt reasonably confident about their readings of district sentiment. After we had grilled them with respect to many of the views in their districts, we asked, "Do you think you actually have pretty good knowledge of the opinion in your district on the type of issues that we have just now raised?" The question was open-ended, and invited them to comment as they wished.

More than one-third of those interviewed (some 35 percent) responded positively to the inquiry, without placing any conditions whatever on their knowledge. The great majority of the remainder also felt confident of their knowledge of district sentiment "in principle," although they placed some limitation—usually rather minor—on the extent of their familiarity. Longevity of exposure to the district, often in professional or governmental roles, was by a wide margin the major source cited for this confidence.

Only about one candidate in six (17 percent) admitted to feeling that he did not have very adequate knowledge of district sentiments. Such assessments tended to come from persons who pointed out their limited acquaintance with the district, including two or three who had actually been "parachuted" in to run for the Assembly seat. Some more permanent, local individuals complained of difficulties in finding mechanisms for "dialogue" with their constituents, however, and a few even mentioned the difficulty of keeping up with district opinion because it was so volatile.

Objective Assessment of Accuracy as Relative Congruence

One of the main advantages of our study design is that deputy impressions of opinion in their districts can be laid against independent measurements of that opinion. Since we can assess accuracy for a more complete set of issues by using correlational congruence than through proximities (which require identical wording), let us begin at that point.

Figure 20-2 is laid out in the same hierarchical form as that used for Figure 20-1. Three panels are presented, grouping (1) the means of the position issues; (2) the standard deviations of these issues (except for the reli-

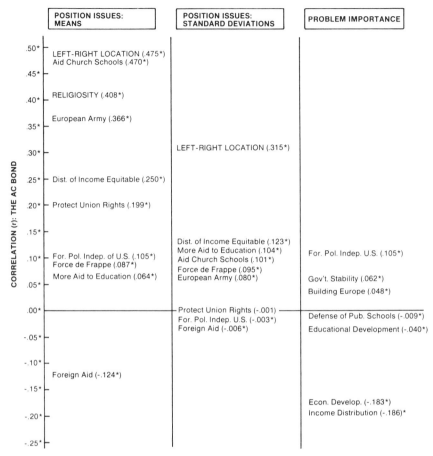

Figure 20-2. Relative congruence between elite estimates of district sentiments and values observed in the districts. Correlations (*r*) marked with an asterisk are adjusted for small-sample attenuation.

giosity item, measured in a different form); and (3) the battery of importance items. Height on the page indicates the level of correlation between the mean or the standard deviation implied by the candidate's description of the district opinion.

It is clear that very different levels of correlation pertain over the three panels. At the weak extreme (the third panel), correlations for the importance battery are arid indeed. Although two or three of the correlations, taken alone, would test out as significant, they scatter in both directions close to the zero-point, and it is easy to see the set as a whole as representing no more than a sampling distribution around zero, suggesting that even though candidates can be made to guess importance levels for their districts, they bring very little genuine information to the task, and collectively their estimates of these values match district reality at levels which do not exceed chance.

The picture is very different for the position issues (the first panel), where virtually all of the correlations are clearly significant and all but one (foreign aid) are in the intuitively expected direction.[4] Although the range of variation in correlation levels is very large in this panel, and some of the lower correlations are admittedly unimpressive, some of them do attain substantial magnitudes. And reminiscent of Figure 20-1, the super-issue of left-right, along with the religious cleavage, tops the list. There is not much doubt that highly meaningful cues on many of these position issues do emanate from the districts, contrary to the case for variations in problem importance.[5]

The second panel of Figure 20-2 displays rather middling levels of correlation, but ones which are of considerable interest in their own right. When we first decided to deduce from our elite informants' tripartite distributions of opinion for their districts some crude measure of variance, we did so with little expectation that any match could be found with the mass materials. It seemed a rather ambitious assumption that these political observers could sense not only central tendencies of district sentiment, but also dispersion or polarization. Yet our work on the changes brought about as a function of the 1968 revolt had shown the variance of left-right positions in districts to be a highly meaningful predictor of revolt participation (see Chapter 14), and of course such variance is the obvious indicator of political heterogeneity in the district.

Therefore we were pleased and intrigued to find that differences in polarization of districts in left-right terms do indeed appear to be perceived with more veridicality by their local political elites than is true of most of our other issue measures. Although the absolute levels of correlation are obviously not towering, they are a good deal more than trivial; in fact, they perform rather impressively. In addition, a majority of the rest of the position issues which can be assessed in these terms suggest that candidates have some meaningful glimmer of their variances as well.

Since most of these are domestic issues rather strongly correlated with left-right differences, it might be thought that perceptions of their heterogeneity are being induced toward weak significance simply as a derivative of those background connections with left and right. We have, however, examined our empirical measures of those background connections between left-right heterogeneity and polarization on other issues at the district level. Keeping in mind the looseness of belief system structure at the mass level (see Chapter 7), and assuming that our informants were merely generalizing to these issues from their perceptions of left-right polarization, it is not surprising that those connections are so weak that they can account for almost none of the observed accuracy in perceived heterogeneity on some of these other specific issues.

In sum, then, although these candidates may have real difficulty in predicting how their districts will respond to our problem importance ratings, their sense of the proportion of their districts registering as "indifferent" on a position (a specification which makes an important contribution to the dispersion of the perceived distribution of district sentiment) seems to mirror, though faintly, what is genuine about their districts.

Accuracy as Absolute Discrepancy

Although measures of absolute discrepancy are the most intuitively compelling indicators of perceptual accuracy, in practice they suffer several liabilities. One difficulty is that we must set aside more than a third of our measurements of perceptions as being in one sense or another incommensurate. (This is true of religiosity, and of the inferences about variance in sentiments.) There are also difficulties in interpreting some of the remaining discrepancy scores, because of the vastly different scale values being used. We have coped with this problem for presentation purposes by dividing our absolute discrepancy scores for a particular issue by a measure of the variance of the responses of the mass respondents to that issue. This not only tends to put the left-right measure into a currency approximating that of the other measures, but it also controls for artificial differences in variance arising from low ceilings on some of the measures.

Such an adjustment has been made in laying out Figure 20-3, in which we compare the accuracy values in relative congruence terms (from Figure 20-2) with those derived from absolute discrepancies, for those issues where the latter calculations make sense. Clearly the fit between the two measures is less than perfect, and in two or three comparisons of the sixteen there are rather substantial differences in the impression of accuracy created. Thus, for example, the specific position issue concerning aid for church schools (at locus .47, .48 in the figure) ranks as the second most accurate on the correlational measure, but it falls in the middle of the distribution of issues on the measure of absolute discrepancy. Again, the importance items on wealth distribution and economic development, the most inaccurately perceived in congruence terms, are up in the third quartile in terms of absolute discrepancy.

Nonetheless, there is a reasonable fit for most of the items, with the correlation underlying the scatter diagram for the sixteen measurements displayed arriving at a value of $r = -.65$, where of course the negative sign is the intuitively expected one. What all this means is that if we do not put too much weight on numerical details, we shall draw roughly the same story about issue differences in accuracy from both methods.

Not surprisingly, the rough story that both measurements register

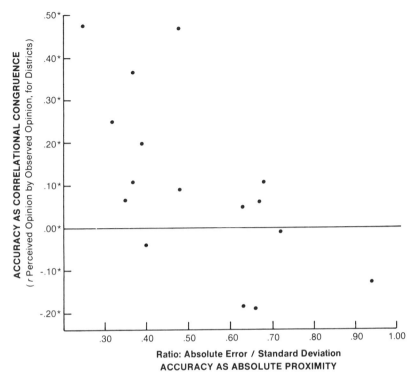

ACCURACY AS CORRELATIONAL CONGRUENCE (r Perceived Opinion by Observed Opinion, for Districts)

Ratio: Absolute Error / Standard Deviation
ACCURACY AS ABSOLUTE PROXIMITY

Figure 20-3. Accuracy of candidate perceptions of district sentiment on sixteen issues, compared for two measurement methods: absolute proximity (differencing) and relative congruence (correlational). Correlations (r) marked with an asterisk are adjusted for small-sample attenuation.

concerning which issues are being perceived more or less accurately bears more than a passing resemblance to the hierarchy established in Figure 20-1, which we took as a demonstration of the degree to which reality made an impress on the judgments involved. This is an obvious expectation, since it merely says that the less reality intrudes to force convergence of judgment among disparate observers, the greater the admixture of perceptual error relative to an independent measurement of the object. Hence the resemblance between the hierarchy of issues according to "reality" and according to perceptual accuracy mainly serves to reinforce our faith in the various statistical manipulations we have used to assess both terms. At the same time, the degree of fit between the two hierarchies is notably stronger when we measure accuracy as relative congruence than when we measure it with absolute discrepancies. Indeed, the correlation between congruence levels and "reality" for the sixteen issues measured in common between Figures 20-1 and 20-2 is

$r = .58$, whereas for the absolute discrepancy version of accuracy the same correlation is only $r = .24$ (sign corrected).

We have now completed our descriptive survey of variations in the accuracy of perceptions of district sentiments over our linkage issues, within the pool of elite political observers represented by our full candidate sample. Any conclusion which might suggest that these observers are either remarkably acute or remarkably misguided in their perceptions would have to rest on expectations for "reasonable" accuracy which elude us. The only handy external frame of reference against which these accuracy values might be assessed is the Miller-Stokes study in the United States in 1958. Their accuracy values are on a slightly different base, as they were not assessed by specific issue. But their relative congruence correlations corresponding to our Figure 20-2 were $r = .17$ for the social welfare domain, .25 for foreign involvement, and .74 for civil rights.

Such values are not totally out of line with our French levels, although they do seem to run on the high side; that is, we have no accuracy correlations which begin to approach the value of .74 for the U.S. civil-rights domain, and although there is internal variation, the French values for perception of foreign-policy matters do not seem to match the U.S. case either.

Where civil rights are concerned, we have emphasized repeatedly that the kind of regional heterogeneity in such attitudes—especially as they stood in the 1950s—would act to make their perception a rather simple matter, and surely that is what we are observing here. At the same time, there is a good deal of geographic heterogeneity in the left-right coloration of legislative districts in France. Moreover, the facts involved are ones on which our candidates key their attention avidly, and in the flow of popular elections they receive persistent updating information. Why should their perceptions show only about half as much variance shared with the "reality" measurement as is true for civil rights in the United States?

It is possible, of course, that civil-rights attitudes in that period were still much more starkly "territorial" than are district differences in left-right coloration in France. Nonetheless, we see the question in this form as legitimate, and it is one to which we shall return later.

The Constituency as Object of Perception

Ultimately we shall want to consider what makes some of our elite observers more accurate in their perceptions than others. First, however, we shall examine a few other "objective" properties of constituency sentiment that can affect the overall accuracy of these perceptions.

The Role of District Heterogeneity
in Obscuring Perception

Our data lend themselves to a test of the classic postulate that perceptual accuracy will erode as the stimulus object becomes more ambiguous. Presumably the deputy who takes an "instructed-delegate" view of his proper role as representative frequently asks himself what the majority opinion would be on the binary legislative vote at stake. It seems almost too obvious to require testing that such a judgment will come much more easily, with far less error, when the actual division of opinion in the district is enormously lopsided, than when it approaches a 50–50 division.

Our data go beyond this kind of test, inasmuch as we have not asked our elite informants merely where the majority stands in regard to a certain issue, but rather what the opinion division in the district may be. Thus the candidate facing a very divided (that is, "heterogeneous," "ambiguous") district can simply report that sentiment on that issue stands at 50–50, and receive high grades for perceptual accuracy. Nonetheless, it also seemed worth asking whether district heterogeneity (as represented by a high variance in individual opinions) continues to erode accuracy.[6]

The most direct test of the hypothesis requires correlating our measure of absolute accuracy with the observed standard deviations of the various issue items. Certain technical problems, such as low ceilings on the importance items, limit the number of issues for which such an operation makes sense. The bulk of the correlations, however, are in the expected direction: the greater the variability of issue responses, the lower the accuracy of their perception. The issue item with the fewest technical problems, the left-right positions, is also the most important substantively, and here the correlation is $r = .18$.

In short, we come away from this exercise with a sense that heterogeneity does operate to obscure perception, even in this severe form of the test, where high heterogeneity (attributing a 50–50 division of opinion to the district) can be graded as an accurate response. In this test, however, it would be too much to claim that the residual effects had much strength.

The Problem of Constituency Definitions

In the last chapter we discovered that our data were greatly clarified by shifting from the constituency as the total district to a definition which equated the constituency with the electoral supporters of the candidate. Is it possible that the reason our elite informants are no more accurate than we have found them to be is that, instead of offering descriptions of sentiments in their districts taken as totalities, they are really talking about opinions in their subconstituency of supporters? Such a definition would be a bit surprising, since our questions about district sentiment were imbedded in an interview segment obviously dealing with political leaders' total districts, including district diversities and the incidence of various kinds of pressure groups, such as unions, business groups, and agricultural organizations. Thus, by broad implication, the referent was always the full local citizenry.

Nevertheless, we can verify this question of referents, at least indirectly. Given the rather dramatic differences (seen in the preceding chapter) between the district as constituency and the subconstituencies of electoral supporters, it should be clear that a description of the one would be a very poor fit for the other. Therefore we can ask our data whether the descriptions we have accumulated are more accurate for the district as a whole or for the supporters only.

Here, as it turns out, the results are marvelously unequivocal, especially for the measure of inaccuracy as absolute discrepancy. We are rapidly disabused of the possibility that the candidates were trying to describe their own supporters, rather than the total district. The amount of absolute error in these accounts would increase very substantially if we were to pretend that the accounts were given for supporters.

Even the pattern of change as we substitute referents is intriguing. There is not much difference in accuracy of account as long as we limit our attention to the items for problem importance: the descriptions given would be about as accurate for electoral supporters as for the total district. But this is the subset of items for which there are rather limited reality cues to begin with (Figure 20-1), and where, in a relative congruence sense, descriptions do not show a collective accuracy much beyond chance (Figure 20-2). As soon as we shift to the subset of position issues, however, the estimates of inaccuracy mount very rapidly if we pretend that the descriptions pertain to supporters rather than to the district as a whole.

Absolute error increases with this shift of definitions in the case of all nine of our position issues, including the left-right locations. On the average, the error increases by not much less than one-third (29 percent). Moreover, the more clearly our earlier data suggested that an item was reality-determined, the greater the contrast in the error. Thus for our most sharply defined item, the left-right locations, absolute error averages 5.88 scale points if the referent is the total district, but it averages 14.93 (a figure nearly two and a half times as great) if we imagine that the descriptions were being given for the constituency of supporters, rather than for the total district.

Thus we can reasonably presume that our candidates were in fact attempting to describe their districts as totalities, and not their own more circumscribed subconstituencies of electoral supporters. This is no more than the perceptual task we had originally specified, but it is reassuring to know that these are indeed the referents, for that knowledge may affect our use of these estimates in other models.[7]

Despite this overwhelming internal evidence that our candidates are attempting to describe sentiment for the total district rather than for their own supporters, that evidence does not rule out a cognate possibility that has some intuitive plausibility. This is that, although our informants are indeed referring to the total district, they may make systematic errors of perception due to a tendency to exaggerate the numerical importance of their own supporters in the district. According to that model, the estimates offered for a district mean would tend to lie closer to the actual district mean than to the supporter mean; but they would nonetheless be systematically shaded off the district mean *in the direction of* the actual mean for supporters.

Any candidate imputing that a district mean lay in the zone between the actual district and supporter means would receive algebraic discrepancy scores in the two cases which were opposite in sign. If such attributions were made by any strong majority of our "judges," then we would expect to find negative correlations between the signed discrepancy scores formed when the referent was taken to be (a) the total district, on one hand, and (b) own supporters, on the other.

Here again the data are unequivocal. We not only fail to find such negative correlations, but the correlations which we do find are strong in magnitude as well as positive in sign. Singling out the left-right perceptions as the clearest diagnostic case, we find that many elite informants do indeed perceive the district to lie a little to the supporter side of its actual location, as though they were overestimating the weight of their own support in the electorate. This group, however, is considerably outnumbered by those who overestimate how distant the district as a whole is from the locations of their own supporters, thereby generating discrepancy scores of the same sign and of somewhat the same magnitude, and hence correlations of a substantial positive value between the two discrepancy scores. That correlation for the left-right attributions is a substantial $r = +.41$.

Thus we can readily reject the hypothesis that any major fraction of the absolute error in our elite informants' perceptions of their districts' sentiments arises from a tendency to overestimate the bulk of their own support. Such a pattern may add to absolute error in some cases, but the pattern itself is the exception rather than the rule.

The Constituency as Educational Elite

In the preceding chapter we found our politicians not only looking rather like their own supporters in attitudinal terms, but also looking more like the highly educated people they are than like the man in the street. In this chapter we have been able to reject outright the notion that in assessing district sentiment they tend to overestimate the presence and weight of their supporters in the constituency. This suggests a certain realism about the political heterogeneity of their districts, and a recognition that adverse elements are prominent in it.

But is it possible that, at a more subtle level, our candidates are prisoners of their most immediate social contacts, who tend, like themselves, to be relatively well educated people, so that their view of district sentiment is strongly displaced toward the distinctive attitudes of well-educated people, as though they overestimated their presence in the population?

As in Chapter 19, we lack enough cases of highly educated voters to test this possibility directly, district by district. We can, however, mount an indirect test by asking whether our candidate assessments of popular opinion on an issue tend to average out across the sample to a value which looks more like that characterizing our mass sample as a whole on that issue; or whether it looks more like the average value—typically, but not always, quite different—that characterizes the best-educated of our mass respondents, again over the sample as a whole.

After discarding those issues which show little differentiation by education, we still have left thirteen issues with a rather substantial gap between average positions for the mass and for the well-educated. Let us ask how often our candidate means fall within this gap, and when they do, where between the "brackets" they actually fall: closer to the mean for the educated, or closer to the total sample mean?

Over these issues, the mean attributed by our elite observers falls within the bracket of the two observed means seven times, to the far side of the mass mean four times, and to the far side of the mean for the highly educated twice. If we metricize the problem by taking account of actual distances defined by the space between the brackets (or beyond to either side) for each issue, then we find that on the average for our thirteen test issues, the location attributed by our candidates falls at a point 45 percent of the distance established by working from the actual mass mean at one pole toward the actual mean for the educated at the other. In other words, the average elite imputation falls just about halfway between the positions for the total sample and for the highly educated, although it is slightly closer to the mass mean.

Therefore, although there is indeed fair variability on the matter from one issue to the next, the conclusion here seems as inescapable as that in the preceding section: the positions taken by the most highly educated of the citizenry appear to act as a magnet to displace our elite observers' perception from the actual mass means they have been asked to estimate. If there were no such systematic attraction, then our observers' mean judgments across issues should scatter symmetrically around the true average positions for the total sample. They clearly do not; in fact, they tilt markedly in the direction of positions for the highly educated whenever the two actual means are at all discrepant.

Indeed, we can make some playful calculations of the following sort. Let us imagine that our elite observers know perfectly well that the attitudes of the well-educated in their districts differ from those of the less-educated on these issues. In fact, let us suppose that they are aware of the actual means for the most highly educated, as well as the actual means for the complement of the sample which is less educated. All they do not know is whether the well-educated stratum is 5 percent, or 35 percent, or 85 percent of the population they have been asked to assess. Under these conditions, a few elementary calculations show that the data already presented imply that our candidates are, on the average, seeing the highly educated as constituting 48 percent of the population, instead of the 6 percent they actually represent.

There is no need to emphasize that this figure is a fanciful one. But it is not obviously meaningless. Political elites interact disproportionately with the well-educated. If such observers gauged district sentiment as a straightforward summation of relevant messages received personally on a topic, and if we divided such message-givers into those highly educated and those less well educated, then we would probably not be astonished to know that half of the message-givers might be well-educated, even though such constituents amounted to a mere 6 percent of all constituents.

To summarize, then, we have been able to reject quite emphatically the possibility that our elite informants, in assessing district sentiment, systematically overestimate the weight of their own supporters' views. But indirect evidence suggests rather strongly that these assessments are systematically displaced from the actual mass means in the direction of the views of the most highly educated.

We have outlined one plausible scenario whereby such displacements could occur (the tendency to overweight one's personal contacts), but there is a competing scenario which is very distinct in concept if not in practice. In the preceding chapter we discovered that our informants' own convictions on these political issues tended to look a good deal more like those of the small top stratum of the highly educated than they did like those of the mass sample as a whole. Now we find that our informants perceive constituent opinion as colored in the same direction. Perhaps instead of misreading the frequency of the well-educated, our candidates are simply projecting some aspects of their own convictions onto their districts. Although in the long run we shall not be able to decide whether such an intrapsychic process or the social-interaction phenomenon is the better explanation for this general bias in perception, it is important to examine the psychological possibility in its own right, and we must return to district-by-district analysis to do so.

Influences of Own Position: The BC Bond

The perceiver brings to his judgments many predispositions which may affect his response. But the classic prediction, especially in relation to social attitudes, is that judgments will be influenced by the prior attitudes of the perceiver on whatever attitudinal dimension is at stake. This prediction involves the BC bond in the Miller-Stokes diamond, the linkage between the informant's own position on the issue and his perception of constituency sentiment with regard to it. Under most if not all circumstances, the expectation is that the correlation between own attitude and perceptions of district sentiment will be positive.

Naturally, a positive BC correlation could arise in ways which are quite independent of any tendency of the candidate to project his own attitude into his reading of district sentiment. Suppose that our informant has just done a sample survey and can tell us exactly how district sentiment is distributed. Suppose at the same time that his own attitudes are very close to those in the district, because in addition to the mechanisms of descriptive representation, he has won election as a result of this special proximity. Then his own attitude would be closely linked to his perception of district opinion, though not through the projection of his own attitude onto the district.

A first step in the isolation of possible projection influences is to ask whether there are links between own attitude (B) and district perceptions (C) which are independent of actual states of district opinion (A). This is no more than a statement of partial correlation or regression.

From one point of view such partial coefficients can be seen as rather conservative or minimal estimates of the amount of projection. Although some or even all of the overlap between the perceptions to be predicted from actual district opinion (A) and the informant's own opinion (B) may itself be due to projection, limiting the estimate to the partial coefficient ignores this possibility. From another point of view, the partial coefficients are not conservative. Phenomena other than projection could be intruding to tighten the BC bond independent of actual opinion, phenomena which might be detected with otherwise unmeasured variables. Or even if the BC bond is remarkably tight, it is always possible that causality is flowing in the other direction: the informant's own opinion has been shaped in the past by a knowledge of what district opinion is.

We cannot deal with all of these possibilities here. But we find that the simple BC correlations in our data are in fact positive in sign fifteen times out of sixteen tries, with the one exception being an insignificant $r = -.028$. Our informants *do* tend to give estimates of district sentiment which are relatively congruent with their own convictions on the matter at stake. Therefore we can ask how much of this correlation would remain if actual district sentiments were held constant, even though we realize we must interpret the results with some care.

Figure 20-4 reflects the most accessible two-factor model bearing on the way in which elite perceptions of district sentiments may be formed. We imagine that these perceptions are formed as some joint function of (1) actual district sentiment, and (2) the informant's own opinions. The height

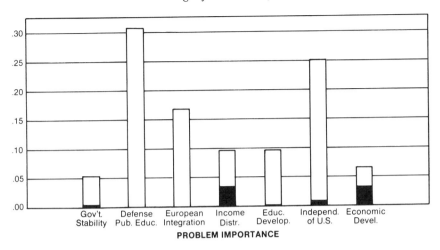

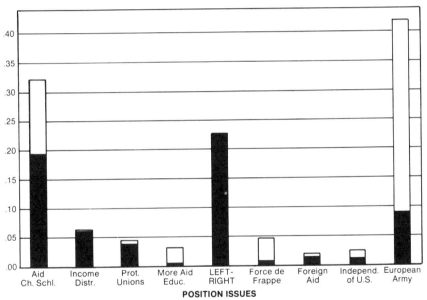

Figure 20-4. Accounting for variance in perceptions of district sentiment (C) on diverse issues, using as predictors actual district opinion (A) and informant's own position (B). Variance accounted for in (C) by (A) and (B) can be decomposed into three components: variance accounted for in common by the overlap of (A) and (B); variance accounted for by (A) net of (B); and variance accounted for by (B) net of (A). Total column length represents total variance accounted for; shaded area represents first two components; and white area represents the third component.

of each column in the figure refers to the total amount of variance in perceptions that is accounted for by these two factors jointly. The size of the
white area remaining at the top of each bar reflects the proportion of variance in perceptions that is accounted for by the informant's own opinions,
independent of the actual state of district sentiment. The black area at the
bottom of each column represents the variance accounted for by actual district opinion independent of the informant's own convictions, as well as the
proportion of variance accounted for by any overlap between own convictions and actual district sentiment.

Our ability to account for variance in perceptions through these two
factors, one of which is the "objective" reality, varies dramatically from one
issue to the next. Some of this variation, such as the high "reality determination" of the left-right locations or the aid to church schools, is by now
familiar. Our main concern here is with the proportion of this variance
which is uniquely "accounted for" by possible projection (the residual
white area in each column).

We see that over the seven problem-importance items, the data suggest
a dominant role for the projection of own convictions, in the elite statements about district priorities. The degree of determination from district
actualities, or any overlap between own position and district sentiment, is
scarcely more than trifling over these issues as a whole. At the opposite extreme are four of the five position issues bearing on domestic policy, where
the room left for potential projection is quite minimal. For the most important issue, that of left-right locations, this margin cannot be discerned in
the figure at all. Finally, the position issues referring to foreign policy seem
to fall between these extremes.

This general hierarchy of issue types reminds us of the array in Figure
20-1. At that point we noted that since there were very few reliable cues for
the candidate to use in assessing district priorities about issue importance,
much had to be left to the imagination. Figure 20-4 indicates rather dramatically how the imagination tends to fill in the vacuum: it is substantially influenced, it appears, by the perceiver's own convictions on the matter at
stake, just as classic theory predicts.

Earlier we urged caution in arriving at a judgment concerning the importance of projection, since in addition to the possibility of unmeasured
variables affecting the system, it is possible that our aspiring representative is
not projecting his own opinion on the district, but rather has been persuaded of his own position by a knowledge of district sentiment and the
reasons for it. Now that we have seen the data in Figure 20-4, let us consider
the relative plausibility of the projection hypothesis and the persuasion hypothesis in this special case.

First, it is important to keep in mind that the white areas in the columns of Figure 20-4 can refer to persuasion only in the degree that the per-

ception of district sentiment that is presumed to act causally on the candidate's own conviction is an *inaccurate* one; that is, the white area refers to the BC bond after actual district opinion (term "A") is statistically controlled. This means that any rater who knows actual district opinion accurately and is influenced by it in his own opinions contributes to the black areas in the columns, not the white.

With this point established, the persuasion hypothesis loses much of its credibility. Figure 20-4 implies that the white area, whether representing projection or persuasion, is at its maximum when we know on other grounds that the input of objective external cues is at its minimum. Under such circumstances, error increases because the judge has so little to go on. To argue, as the persuasion hypothesis requires, that the judge's own convictions are most deeply affected by his understanding of district sentiment when he is most thrown back on guesswork is not at all compelling. But of course it is under these conditions that projection is most to be expected. Therefore we do not hesitate to interpret the white areas in the columns of Figure 20-4 as primarily a phenomenon of projection.

In sum, then, we conclude that our estimates of district sentiments are shaped in some degree by projection of own preferences onto the district, but that the amount of that shaping varies dramatically from one type of issue to another. It can become large when reality cues are sparse, but it dwindles when such cues become more plentiful. In a limiting case like that of left-right orientations, there is no significant projection at all.

Reality and Left-Right Perceptions

The absence of detectable projection in perceptions of left-right coloration in the district robs us of one plausible set of reasons why the relative congruence of perceptions and objective truth are not higher in that instance, closer to the value of $r = +.74$ found by Miller and Stokes for the domain of civil rights in the United States in 1958.

It turns out, however, that one set of manipulations on the data can be carried out which will not only improve our sense of the accuracy of these left-right perceptions but will also confirm some of our suspicions as to how these perceptions are formed in the first place. We suspect that reports of left-right distributions in the district are the most accurate reports because they hinge on the hard data of recent election outcomes, a kind of information not typically available for any of the other forms of district sentiment (although religious practice has some similar characteristics).

Our measures of left-right sentiment in the district come directly from reports of self-locations from our mass respondents, rather than through some form of deduction from the votes they cast. Naturally, there is a considerable connection between these statements of left-right position and the votes cast by those who report them. People who place themselves on the left tend to vote Communist or Socialist, for instance. But, as we emphasized in Chapter 4, a very large minority of mass respondents, including many who vote, place themselves at the neutral midpoint of the left-right location. We have also seen that voters are capable of quite idiosyncratic views as to the left-right positions of the parties, even of those they prefer. For example, we can still find in our sample persons who are leftist in their own convictions, but who vote for a right-wing fringe party because they believe it is a leftist party. Finally, of course, in any given election there are various short-term influences on the vote which may persuade a genuine centrist to vote toward the left or right, especially in the atmosphere of compromise that prevails at the second tour.

When all of these dislocations are taken into account, there is room for substantial slippage between aggregated statements of left-right positions by district and the votes actually cast. If we once again assign the various parties single left-right positions based on the consensus view of them in the electorate (average locations), and look at the correlations between the "left-rightness" of the party voted for (so defined) and the voters' own reports of left-right location, the coefficients are substantial but not overwhelming, running in the low .60s, depending on the tour involved.

If the elite observer is gauging the left-right coloration of a district on the basis of recent voting returns, then we would expect him to weight some calculus of party left-right position with its proportion of votes. We can take our consensual party locations and multiply them by the actual fractions of votes cast for the various parties running in the district in the most recent (1967) election, to provide an alternate, vote-based measurement of left-right sentiment, district by district. If the calculations of elite observers are formed in the manner we expect, then such an alternate measure may provide a better "reality" check.

We find in fact that our measures of accuracy involving relative congruence do produce marked increases in values when the vote-based measure of district coloration is substituted for our more direct measure of self-reported locations. Figure 20-2 gives us a value of $r = +.48*$ using the direct measure, while the corresponding values using the vote-based measure run up into the low .80s. If we use the vote for the first tour, the corresponding value is $r = +.86$; for the second tour it is $+.79$. These numbers are very respectable, even relative to the Miller-Stokes value of $r = +.74$ for civil rights in the United States. Furthermore, we can inch them even higher by taking account of the further intervention in the judgmental task represented by the slightly different views of the candidates themselves as to how left, center, or right certain parties are.

This is frosting on the cake, however. The basic evidence is overpowering that our elites do hinge their estimates of left-right sentiment in their districts on a close knowledge of recent district voting patterns. Election results give them "harder" clues on which to base their estimates than is true for any of the other linkage issues, and although some idiosyncrasies intrude as elite observers convert vote divisions into the terminology of left and right, they are all working from the same reality and there is little latitude for projection.

Nevertheless, the translations from voting to left-right coloration do produce an erosion of accuracy in reports when we evaluate them in the terms in which they were requested—as statements of left-right tendencies. It is a nice point whether these inaccuracies arise because of our observers' naiveté as to the clarity of ideology in the electorate, or more simply because it is not easy to correct the vote distributions to take account of weakness of ideology. Nonetheless, the net result is a set of perceptions which, though only moderately accurate for left-right sentiments per se, is still as adequate as any in our skein of linkage issues.

Variations in the Availability of Information

Although we have found some warrant in our data for the effects of various phenomena central to perception theory, such as the tendency to fill in estimates of district sentiments with personal convictions where external information is limited, the most important conditions governing perceptual accuracy have to do with the availability of relevant information. From the point of view of psychological theory, the observation that perceptual accuracy might be governed by possession of relevant information would seem trivial, if not tautological. From our more institutional perspective, however, it is clear that some of our elite observers may be in a better position to receive information about district sentiment than others, and hence they are likely to give more accurate accounts of it. The hypothesis that long-term district representatives virtually living in their nation's capital tend to lose touch with district sentiment, as well as the opposite hypothesis that their long-term survival stems from their peculiar adeptness at keeping abreast of district feelings, are testable propositions about systematic variation in the distribution of information among key role occupants in the broader system. Similarly, it is not hard to imagine that different observers pursue different strategies in seeking information about their districts, and that some of these strategies may be more accurate and efficient than others. Propositions of this sort, which are of limited interest to the psychologist, are central to the study of representation. Indeed, the fact that having such information is tantamount to perceiving the district more accurately is the prime reason for asking about systematic differences in the flows of information to various of our elite respondents.

The Generality of Constituency Knowledge
or Ignorance

To presume that our elite informants are situated differentially with respect to flows of information about the district is to imagine that constituency knowledge is not entirely issue-specific: informants who tend to be more accurate than average in their perceptions of district sentiment on one issue will tend to be more accurate on other issues as well. If accuracy has any such generality for persons across issues, then we should find that our individual-level measures of discrepancy between perception and objective district issue postures should show positive correlations. Moreover, we would then be encouraged to winnow our data further, producing a single measure summarizing for individual informants their more generic level of accuracy across all issues.

The discrepancy intercorrelations tend quite clearly to be positive, although they are rarely very impressive in magnitude. Indeed, an initial factor analysis of the relevant matrix was a distinct disappointment. The structure that was revealed was very weak and unconvincing in its details. In these first efforts, however, those candidates who had been coded as saying that they did not know what constituency sentiment was on any particular item had been left out of the calculations as missing data, since it was not clear what discrepancy values to assign to them, and they were not numerous in any event.[8] But this treatment did not seem proper, given our quest for a knowledge-ignorance axis: clearly, people who confessed ignorance deserved to be an important part of the estimation. Therefore we resolved to code the handful of informants who gave such "don't know" responses at the maximally inaccurate value possible for the item in question. On this basis we carried out a second factor analysis.

This time a clearer structure emerged, although, contrary to our hopes, there was no single, dominant, knowledge factor. Instead, two fairly clear factors seemed present. One had loadings on all the issue-position items, while a second but quite distinct factor had loadings on all the problem-importance items. This pattern was not entirely reassuring, since the two types of questions had required different methods of calibrating inaccuracy, and, as we have seen, the problem-importance measures in particular have troubled us continuously with their measurement difficulties. Hence it seemed possible that in dealing with two factors, we might have adulterated one or both with some form of methods variance. Yet there was a modest but significant background correlation between the two factors, and so we decided to score individual candidates on each measure for further examination.[9]

In attempting to account for variation in these two summaries of perceptual accuracy we have looked at a variety of plausible factors related to the politician's situation which might help us to understand the differences registered. Working across four or five conceptual clusters of measures, amounting to more than a dozen variables, we find nothing that accounts for as much as 4 percent of the variance in either of our summary knowledge factors, although several predictors approach that level.

Moreover, as often as not, predictors which have importance for one of these two summaries of constituency knowledge do not have it for the other. For example, the closest thing we have to a criterion available for examining the meaning of these measures is the informant's own report of confidence in his knowledge of constituency sentiment, the variable discussed earlier in this chapter. We find that elite observers who claim greatest confidence in their feel for public opinion also show the greatest accuracy of knowledge for position issues in their districts, and the relationship ($r = +.16$) is one of the strongest where the position knowledge factor is concerned. Contrariwise, the confidence variable is only weakly related to the importance knowledge factor, and the sign of the relationship is negative! Although the two factors are by construction quite distinct, so that differential correlates are not surprising, such results are not easy to digest.[10]

However all this may be, we cannot be entirely surprised by rather lackluster relationships in predicting to these district knowledge factors, due to their base in our small-sample estimates of district properties. And we know that if we could correct them for attenuation, as we can our correlations, they would look brighter. Thus a predictor apparently accounting for only 3 or 4 percent of the variance in our knowledge factors might very well account for more than 6 or 7 percent if properly corrected. Hence we shall end this chapter with a consideration of these situational correlates of our district knowledge factors.

Experience as a Representative in Relation to District Knowledge

If we merely look at winners and losers in the 1967 election in terms of their accuracy scores from one issue to the next, the picture is very mixed. Winners are more accurate on some issues and less so on others, and this remains true whether we assess accuracy by absolute discrepancies or by relative correlations. Moreover, the differences are almost everywhere quite small. By both tests, the losers have the largest edge in accuracy where assessments of left-right are concerned; elsewhere the winners seem to have the edge, but by a very feeble margin. The safest conclusion is that winners and losers are very little differentiated where district knowledge is concerned.

Nonetheless, when we turn to our two summary knowledge factors, we do find them significantly related to three measures of longevity of election and parliamentary experience. In addition to a measure of the mere chronological age of our candidates, we know how long they have been active in direct political competition, based on a summation of the number of elections they have contested; and how long they have been *successful* in political competition, based on an indicator of the number of years they had spent in the National Assembly prior to the study in 1967. It is not surprising, of course, that these two latter measures are substantially intercorrelated ($r = +.67$), or that both correlate substantially with the first measure, age (in the $+.40$s).

Nor under these circumstances is it surprising that all three measures show relationships in the same direction with our knowledge factors, although this is in fact one of the very few times that these knowledge summaries share correlates of any strength.[11] The direction of these relationships suggests that the war-horses among our informants received poorer ratings on our accuracy summaries than did the fresher faces. The most telling of the relationships conceptually (between years in parliament and the position-issue knowledge factor) is also the largest: ($r = +.18$). Although this is not a towering value, we must keep in mind that it needs to be corrected upward for small-sample attenuation. And it seems to confirm the frequent suspicion that, in one sense or another, the successful representative does show modest signs of losing touch with his district.

It is interesting to speculate whether the successful long-term representative becomes increasingly vague about his district, or whether, although he has accumulated much more lore about the district than his younger competitors have, increasing fractions of that lore are out of date. These speculations have some grounding, for internal analyses have made clear to us the degree to which estimates of left-right locations in the district contribute to the general fact that the fresher faces show greater perceptual accuracy. This is important, because we have seen these assessments of left-right coloration to be the most reality-determined for all of our elite observers, and we have also adduced evidence of the calculus involved, using known vote returns.

Given these ingredients, the greater inaccuracy of the older deputies in assessing left-right tendencies in the district probably does not arise from ignorance of district voting returns, although the deputies with the lengthiest parliamentary experience undoubtedly do come from relatively "safe" districts where the details of the returns are less pressing. But it is not hard to imagine that the veteran of eight or ten elections in a given district might tend to integrate a decade or two of election returns in forming his impression of left-right coloration in the district, whereas younger observers, for whom the world was created yesterday, base their assessments on "the" election, that is, the one just past. On the one hand, if the election just past involved some short-term aberrations, as is often the case, the veteran observer may actually make better estimates with a longer time series in mind. On the other hand, if the left-right coloration of the district is evolving, as is often the case as well, the veteran may be working from outdated information. Since our criterion data were current statements, they may tend to favor the younger observers in either event.

Of course, this reasoning does not apply well to those issues which have arisen in a new form in the very recent past, such as the force de frappe in our period of French politics. Here the young also retain an edge in accuracy, relative to those representatives who are virtually living in Paris. In short, then, the notion of "losing touch" seems to find some confirmation in these data.

Channels of Communication

Another obvious set of expectations hinges on the notion that some channels of communication used by our candidates and deputies may reflect district sentiment more accurately than others. We asked all of our elite informants to tell us how important each of six such information sources was to them in forming their views of district sentiment. These sources included: newspapers; mail received; local party militants; professional organizations in the district; "personal contacts"; and information from the prefecture administration. We also asked whether the informant had ever used sample surveys as still another source of information about the district.

It would be handy for our analysis if dependence on these channels of communication fell into a few distinct patterns, especially if they divided empirically into the relatively "populistic" channels, such as mail, as opposed to the more elite channels, such as professional leaders and prefect administrators. Such patterns do not appear, however. There is some significant overlap between dependence on party militants and on professional organizations for district information ($r = +.33$), and lesser correlations are scattered elsewhere (personal contacts and mail, prefecture and newspapers, militants and mail), but generally preferences for these diverse channels are fairly idiosyncratic.

We do find, however, that our candidates' expressions of confidence in their capability to assess district opinion correlate rather differentially with dependence on particular channels. At the top of the list, mail and newspapers showed quite significant associations with generalized confidence in one's assessments (for both channels, $r = +.21$, with confidence). There is a middling association of this sort for "personal contacts" as well, but no reliable association at all for any of the other channels. It is quite possible that some of our candidates thought of mail and newspapers (with their reader opinion letters) as the two best channels of information about grass-roots sentiment, as opposed to information coming secondhand through such elite sources as professional leaders and party and civil officials. Putting a lot of emphasis on those two popular channels, they felt reassured in their assessment of district opinions.

But when we asked whether emphasis placed on certain of these channels could predict differentially to "objective" accuracy of assessment, as represented by our two knowledge factors, the answer was weakly positive at best. On the basis of our more reliable position-issue factor, the correlation with channel emphasis is nonexistent (usually very faintly negative, such as $r = -.015$) for six of the seven channels covered; and it is only a feeble positive ($r = +.09$) where dependence on newspapers is concerned.

This is another of the points at which the correlates of our two knowledge factors show some divergence. The correlation between newspaper dependence and our problem-importance knowledge factor is almost identical with that for the previous knowledge factor, and as with that factor, there is essentially no association between accuracy and emphasis on the prefecture, personal contacts, or sample surveys as ways of keeping abreast of district sentiment. But for the other three channels which show no association with the first knowledge factor—mail, militants, and professional organizations—there are quite substantial correlations (values of r from .17 to .19).

Not all of these results are easy to interpret, and even when we take account of small-sample attenuation, few of them are impressive enough to bear much weight. It seems likely that, in some modest degree, our candidates see their mail and newspapers as grass-roots information. It also seems likely that a stress on these channels is associated with slight increments of accuracy in district assessments (though not for mail where the position knowledge factor is concerned). Dependence on personal contacts, the use of sample surveys, and interest in information from the prefecture all seem uncorrelated with accuracy of assessment anywhere.

Other Correlates of Accuracy

Since our two knowledge factors frequently show rather different correlates, we should like to comment on two other points at which the correlations largely converge.

The first convergence is somewhat stray but amusing. The ardent leftist splinter party which intruded with some success in the 1967 elections was the radical PSU formation. At other points our data make clear that this new party was mainly visible to academics and intellectuals, particularly those in Paris, and it is likely that few of the candidates it sponsored in 1967 were long-term professional politicians. When we divide our candidate sample according to the party banners sponsoring their candidacies, we discover that across seven parties of any size the aspirants of the PSU show by far the greatest inaccuracy in gauging local opinion, and this is true with respect to *both* of our summary measures of constituency knowledge.

The second point of convergence is more central to our purposes. In another part of the questionnaire we attempted to get some sense of our elite informants' personal views regarding the desirable role of the representative. Some candidates showed more interest in letting the "instructions" based on popular sentiment in their districts influence their legislative decisions than did others, who expected to follow the counsels of party or private conscience. Although the differences are not dramatic, those more interested in voter views also showed higher accuracy scores, and once again on *both* knowledge factors. This finding is very suggestive, and we shall return to it in the next chapter, which is dedicated to the topic of role definitions among aspiring representatives.

Conclusions

The purpose of this chapter has been to explore the adequacy of perceptions of district sentiment on current controversies, as formed by politicians aspiring to represent those districts in parliament. We have tried to encase the discussion in a frame set by reality. If the lines of reality were everywhere unequivocal, then there would be no variability of perception, and questions concerning this part of the representation process would be trivial indeed. But legislative districts are very complex objects of perception, and information about the flux of public opinion within them is typically sparse, despite occasional loud but perhaps unrepresentative clamors.

In this chapter, therefore, we have examined variations in accuracy of perception across issues and also across individual "judges," as a function of their own political situations and convictions. The latter analyses produced some nuggets of interest, but systematic variation between candidates was rather outshadowed by variations in accuracy across issues domains.

Our assumption has been that issues vary in their "reality determination," or, roughly speaking, in the degree to which real cues about constituency positions are propagated for all observers to see. We tried to establish a hierarchy of our linkage issues in terms of such reality determination, by noting major differences in the degree to which elite observers of opposing political stripes converged in their assessment of sentiment in the same district. This hierarchy, presented in Figure 20-1, showed the left-right measure, religiosity, and religion-related issues as attracting the most convergent judgments. Elsewhere, the position issues seemed somewhat more convergent than the problem-importance items; and domestic issues seemed somewhat more convergent than foreign ones.

We then proceeded to more direct measures of perceptual accuracy, and found, indeed, that a hierarchy of issues arrayed by accuracy of perception (Figure 20-2) did offer much more than a passing resemblance to our hierarchy of reality determination. We noted that the attribute most accurately reported—the left-right coloration of the district—was also the attribute most routinely monitored in public data in the districts, in the form of repeated voting returns. We later introduced evidence which suggested that both reality determination and accuracy measurements would have increased substantially—putting the left-right assessments far in front of other things in the issue hierarchy—had we encouraged answers in the form of fractions of party strength, rather than the synthetic measure of left-rightness, which demanded somewhat idiosyncratic translations.

In much the same vein, it did not seem difficult to account for the high position in the hierarchy of items involving religiosity and the state-church question. Although no annual religious censuses are taken in legislative districts, the sharp geographic variation in religiosity has been highly salient since Chanoine Boulard's mappings of it after World War II (Boulard, 1950); and there are certainly behavioral indicators, such as church attendance and the fiscal health of the local parishes, which help to inform observers of the district situation. Aside from the very rare local demonstrations on one or two of our other issues, there is simply no source of information on district sentiment corresponding to those for religion and left-right coloration.

What, then, accounts for the rest of the hierarchy? The general hierarchy we saw for reality determination and perceptual accuracy should have produced in the reader a sense of déjà vu, for we have encountered something similar to it at a number of points in this book. We get something of the same hierarchy if we use the totality of our issue materials to predict to mass voting decisions (see Chapter 10). Similarly, our work in Chapter 7 on the ideological structuring of these issues hints again at a hierarchy quite reminiscent of the current ones. Most recently, we saw a similar hierarchy underlying our data on the strength of the basic representation bond in Table 18-5.

It turns out that we can create a similar hierarchy across our issues from a number of other starting points as well.[12] At least one of these would seem of obvious relevance to our current question of perceptual accuracy in describing district sentiments.

It will be recalled that some of our elite informants expressed doubt as to their ability to read district sentiment on many of these issues because district opinion was too unstable. We have a measure of one kind of stability available to us from our panel materials. We can, for example, form continuity correlations linking our voters' responses in 1967 to their responses to the same issue items in 1968. When we array the results in a hierarchy of relative stability, we find once again that this is a vague reprise of the old familiar hierarchy. With one or two exceptions, our candidates are generally most adept at assessing those sentiments which are most stable individually. The degree of association between the accuracy correlations and the continuity correlations is $r = +.61$. This pattern is reminiscent of that found in the Miller-Stokes data on a narrower base, where by far the greatest perceptual accuracy occurred in the case of civil-rights controversies, the same domain in which individual stability of issue attitudes was also at its maximum (see Converse, 1964).

Hence it seems that although a few issue axes are accurately perceived because cues about district opinions are formalized or promulgated, this is not true for most of the other issue dimensions. And here we can imagine that accuracy inches up somewhat when the faint and soft cues that do trickle in from the district have some redundancy because local positions on the issue are at least relatively stable.

In short, perhaps the most suitable generic description of the recurring hierarchy of issues is that it reflects what is basic, enduring, and central to popular politics in France, as opposed to what is secondary, or peripheral, or transient. We should not, however, leap to the conclusion that popular representation can only be faithful for these basic issues, although we may discover that to be the normal case.

In any event, as cues and stability diminish down the hierarchy of issues, more is left to the observer's imagination, and candidates fill the information vacuum in part with projections from their own convictions on the issues at stake. These tendencies contribute to another phenomenon, without being totally responsible for it: the estimates of voters' issue preferences seem to be systematically displaced in the direction of the rather distinctive preferences of the most highly educated stratum of the electorate.

Finally, we explored individual differences in accuracy of preference estimation across the elite informants. Though winners were not much more accurate in their perceptions of district sentiment than were losers, we did find some tendency for accuracy to be lower among successful party warhorses than among the fresher faces on the district scene, presumably because time spent away from the district in Paris erodes contact and up-to-date information in some degree. We did not find sharp differences in accuracy as a function of the differing channels of communication that were depended on for district information, although there was some sign that newspapers and mail were seen as grass-roots sources, and dependence upon such sources may increase accuracy faintly.

The last finding was left in an undeveloped state. It suggested that politicians whose views of the proper role for political representatives emphasized attention to district opinion were more accurate in their perceptions of district sentiment than were other aspiring representatives. This finding has intuitive appeal, of course, and it will be discussed in the next chapter within a broader consideration of varying views of the representative role.

21

Conceptions of
the Representative Role

In Chapter 16 we pointed out that the will to represent, or an intention to be "responsive" to constituency wishes on the part of the elected representative, is an ingredient crucial to the nature of the representation process. Indeed, some scholars would call it the sine qua non for judging that any representation worthy of the name is occurring. That is not our posture, for, as we suggested in Chapter 19, the kind of congruence which can be expected to arise as "descriptive representation" is by our lights a meaningful form of representation, even though it is in one sense unintended.

Nonetheless, as Eulau and Karps (1977) have stated, there is a basic distinction between passive congruence and active responsiveness. And it is a reasonable hypothesis that an intention to respond to constituency wishes is much more likely to be present when the actor sees such responsiveness as a reasonable expectation attached to the role of representative.[1] Such role conceptions are not an integral part of the Miller-Stokes diamond, although we stressed some propositions in Chapter 16 which implied that the parameters of the diamond would look rather different for representatives who conceived of their roles in mandate or Burkean terms.

Nevertheless, since separate measurements of such role conceptions are desirable in a study of this kind, we carried them out. Making such measurements was largely an act of faith, assuming as it did that our elite informants had consciously adopted a set of ideas concerning their appropriate behavior as political representatives. The likelihood that this was true of any but the few political philosophers among our candidates has often been questioned. There is little doubt, of course, that some representatives will pay more attention to their constituents at some times than at other times. But whether different philosophies underlie the differences between legislators can certainly be questioned.

Miller and Stokes found that although statements of role preferences given by their congressmen did produce the kind of differential diamond linkages for both the mandate and independent role conceptions that we suggested in Chapter 16, the differences were weak. Much sharper linkage differences in the same general directions were produced when behaviors of congressmen rather than their reports of role preferences were used as predictors. Thus those congressmen who invested more effort than others in learning about the state of opinion in their home districts seemed to give district opinion a stronger weight in their legislative voting, even though they fell short of expressing a clear "mandate" philosophy of representation.

At the same time, our elite informants were willing to respond to questions aimed at laying bare their conceptions of the representative role. It remains to be seen whether they did so with insight and accuracy, or whether they produced hasty rationalizations for their past behavior.

In any event, our purpose in this chapter is to review these reports of role conceptions, and to ask what difference, if any, they made to the behavior of our deputies in the National Assembly. Because of doubts as to meaningfulness of such role conceptions, we shall subject our operational measurements to more than normal scrutiny, questioning their reliability and apparent validity. Because of the strength of party discipline in Assembly voting (described in Chapter 17) we would expect to find strong reflections of these norms in the responses to our role items. We shall indeed find such strong reflections; but since they are expressed differentially, we shall need to ask whether it matters that some of our informants cherish these norms more than others.

Measures of Role Conceptions

Our questions about role conceptions were posed not only to sitting or former deputies, but also to aspirants running for office. Some of these questions were patterned directly after the legislative role items used by Miller and Stokes, whereas others were fashioned as supplements in order to depict the French case.

The questions fell into two sequences, deliberately somewhat redundant in their content; and because they might have seemed too "hypothetical" when posed in the abstract, we were eager to probe as far as possible into the experiential grounding of the responses we collected. It was easy to compose such questions for those respondents who had actually sat as deputies in the Assembly (coded as "ever-deputies"), but they could not be asked in exactly the same form of other candidates, including new winners (coded "never-deputies"). Thus it was necessary to introduce minor variants in question wording.

The first set of questions dealt with the handling of three forms of conflict, all involving, on one side, personal conviction or "private conscience," and, on the other side, either (1) the parliamentary caucus decision, (2) constituency preferences, or (3) the preferences of local party workers. Informants who had served as deputies were first asked whether or not they had experienced any such conflict in their legislative voting decisions. More than two-thirds (68 percent) of those with deputy service reported familiarity with the conflict between personal conviction or conscience and the first item, party caucus position. Nearly as many (63 percent) reported a conflict between their own conscience and the second item, preferences of voters in their constituencies. Far fewer (21 percent) reported any parallel conflict with the third item, local party leadership.

As an example, the conflict question addressing the first item was posed as follows in the two variant wordings:

For never-deputies	*For ever-deputies*
Suppose that as deputy you found yourself in the following situation: you wanted to vote in a certain way, but your parliamentary group decided to vote otherwise; what solution would you choose?	In the Assembly, have you ever found yourself in the following situation: your (parliamentary) group had decided to vote in a certain way, but you yourself wanted to vote otherwise? How have you resolved (would you resolve) such a problem?

Open-ended responses to these three conflict situations were transcribed and subsequently coded into a set of response categories, as indicated in summary form, with response distributions, in Table 21-1.

The primary impression created by the table is, of course, the depth of respect for the parliamentary group decision as the primary cue for the individual deputy. This is less marked among informants with actual deputy experience than it is among aspirants ("never-deputies"), though the difference is not very large. Yet even among the sitting and former deputies, responses are very heavily skewed in favor of the caucus position as the determining one in such cases of conflict. This is true even when the caucus position is paired against its apparently strongest competitor, the deputy's personal position. And on some other items, which did not involve the caucus explicitly, some of the same flavor shows through, in spite of the difference in question intention. For example, nearly one in five of our infor-

Table 21-1. Percentage responses of all candidates, by deputy status, to representative role-conflict items, 1967.

Responses to role-conflict items	Candidate status		Total elite sample
	Ever-deputy	Never-deputy	
(1) Party caucus vs. conscience			
Follow party discipline without reservation	37	45	43
Follow party discipline, but with reservations	23	23	23
It depends (mixed response)	2	3	2
Would abstain	4	3	3
Follow own conscience, but with reservations	5	6	6
Follow conscience, without reservations	22	18	19
Would resign	0	1	1
No caucus; or no discipline required	5	a	2
Such a conflict could not occur	2	a	1
Refuse or don't know	0	1	a
	100	100	100
(2) Constituents vs. conscience			
Would follow constituents without reservation	5	9	8
Follow constituents, but with reservations	5	8	7
It depends (mixed response)	7	3	5
Follow own conscience, but with reservations	1	6	4
Follow conscience, but tell voters why	15	20	18
Follow conscience, without reservations	43	30	34
Party discipline would reign in any event	17	18	18
Would try to convince voters first	0	1	1
Such a conflict could not occur	7	4	5
Don't know	0	1	a
	100	100	100
(3) Local party leaders vs. conscience			
Would follow local leaders without reservation	3	12	8
Follow local party leaders, with reservations	6	5	5
Would abstain	1	2	1
It depends (mixed response)	5	6	6
Follow own conscience, but with reservations	4	7	6
Follow conscience, without reservations	26	21	23
Depends on national congress, not local party	21	31	28
Never happens: no local party; not party member	32	16	22
Would resign	1	a	1
Refuse to say	1	0	a
Total	100	100	100
N[b]	(95–101)	(171)	(266–272)

a. Entries less than .05 percent.
b. Raw case numbers are shown, which vary slightly by panel according to varying numbers of "not ascertained." Percentages are based on weighted distributions.

mants sidesteps the constituent-conscience conflict by pointing out that party discipline would reign in any event. And nearly half of the respondents (more among deputies) sidestep the conflict posed between conscience and the positions of local party leadership, on grounds that more often than not refer again to party cues at the national level. For many, these other conflicts are simply not relevant: the main potential clash is that between party caucus and personal position, and even here the party caucus clearly carries the day.

We do not have to read much into the data of Table 21-1 to conclude that among these four potential sources of cues, the party caucus is a very strong first; personal conscience takes a moderate second place; and cues from constituents or local party leadership run a rather distant third and fourth.

The responses to the second set of questions mainly corroborate these impressions. Respondents were asked to rate the priority which is given (or, for aspirants, which *should* be given) to four sources of cues external to the self (or "own position") in forming Assembly vote decisions: the parliamentary group caucus position; the position of the local party; the position of a "majority of one's voters"; and a desire to support the position of the government. The structured responses offered to these priority questions ran from "absolute priority" through "strong" and "moderate" to "weak" and, finally, "none." Simple integer scoring was applied to these five response categories, and means were derived for the four types of cue, again for both "ever-deputies" and "never-deputies." Figure 21-1 summarizes these responses comparatively.

Again, we see that although our respondents are, on the average, willing to assign at least some priority to all four external considerations, the dominant ratings by quite a significant margin are given to the position of the parliamentary group caucus. The underlying data show that slightly over 50 percent of all informants accord that group "absolute" priority in decisionmaking, with only 7 percent assigning it either a weak priority or none at all. The latter proportion is not much greater than the proportion of respondents who either are deputies "non-inscrits" in any parliamentary group, or are candidates who are not members of any particular party. Barely more than 20 percent of the full elite sample assign absolute priority to the positions of the local party in their districts, and barely more than 10 percent accord this position of highest influence to the majority position of their constituents.

Although, once again, the differences are not large, informants who have never been deputies give persistently higher priority ratings to all four of these external sources of cues than are assigned by those with deputy experience. It seems clear that the latter view all of these sources of cues with more reserve, and it may not be too much to imagine that they are leaving

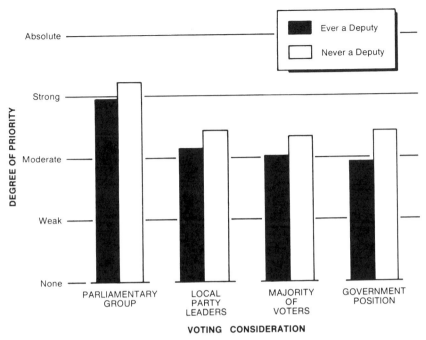

Figure 21-1. Average priorities assigned to each of four considerations in forming Assembly vote decisions, elite sample, 1967.

somewhat more room for the dictates of their own consciences than the aspirants think of doing.

By far the most disparate set of ratings underlying the group means presented in Figure 21-1 occurs in connection with the "desire to support the government" as a consideration in voting. The two most frequent responses to this item are the extreme categories of "absolute" priority and "none." Thus the moderate mean shown in the figure is somewhat misleading. It is clear that in the Assembly sessions held between 1967 and 1973 these particular ratings were entirely situational, with support of the government being very nearly coterminous with support of the positions of the UDR parliamentary group, the government party. The complete lack of interest in supporting the government per se comes quite naturally from the more determined leftist opposition, largely represented by the Communists and the FGDS. With a leftist government, these roles would almost certainly have been dramatically reversed.

In view of the overpowering strength of this obvious situational component, we shall pay little further attention to these government support ratings. We can benefit from a considerable simplification of our conceptualizations by setting this particular item aside.

We shall also set aside the local-party assessments as we move toward the main working variables that define representative roles. We had some initial interest in seeing how the French politicians would rate local-party inputs against some of the other possible influences on legislative voting decisions. Moreover, we could imagine that the local party, in the degree that it diverged from the national party positions, might be articulating home district interests. But it is clear now that such potential inputs were not accorded much importance by the actors involved, to whom a national-local discrepancy did not seem a very lively possibility. Therefore we shall profit from discarding this variable also.

Summarizing Representative Role Emphases

As we summarize the remainder of the data schematically in terms of the classic triad of forces bearing on representation—party caucus, personal conscience, and constituency—we can reasonably expect the French elite sense of relative representative responsibilities to look like the three-legged diagram in Figure 21-2, with the party entirely dominant (long leg), the dictates of personal conscience quite secondary (shorter leg), and the constituents a more distant third (shortest leg).

It is important to keep in mind that since Figure 21-2 is an aggregate summary, its details depend upon the particular population or mix of populations being summarized. For example, if we had some reason to exclude from our data all those deputies who are non-inscrits and all the candidates running for seats without party membership, the party leg would have to be lengthened to represent an even greater dominance over the other two po-

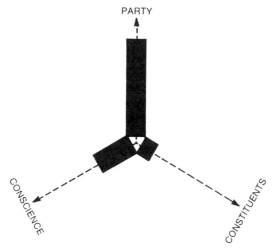

Figure 21-2. Schema of aggregated representative role emphases, France, 1967.

tential responsibilities. Or again, if Figure 21-2 were limited to informants with deputy experience, the party leg would have to be slightly shortened and the personal conscience leg slightly lengthened. Instead of excluding any information, however, we have begun by presenting the full portfolio of data from all of our elite respondents, to show how similar the large population of aspirants is to the population of deputies. It seems likely that the general contours of these role emphases, if not all the details, represent a reasonably characteristic and durable attitude of French elite culture, that having to do with the assumptions regarding popular representation in a democratically elected legislature.

Variations in Role Emphases by Party Group

It is easy to put a finger on one major source of heterogeneity in these role conceptions which is concealed by the aggregate summary portrayed in Figure 21-2. This springs to light when we partition our elite informants by party, whether in terms of the parliamentary group for the current deputies, or of the party under whose banner the various candidates ran in the election. Table 21-2 summarizes responses to the two primary conflict items among persons with deputy experience; the counterpart data for aspirants,

Table 21-2. Percentage responses of deputies, by parliamentary group, to role-conflict items, 1967–68.

Responses to role-conflict items	Parliamentary group				
	PCF	FGDS	PDM	UDR	RI
(1) Party vs. conscience					
Follow party	83	86	0	56	30
Depends	0	0	0	7	0
Abstain	0	0	12	7	0
Follow conscience	0	7	50	28	60
No group discipline	0	0	38	0	10
No such conflict possible	17	7	0	2	0
Total	100	100	100	100	100
N	(12)	(29)	(8)	(46)	(10)
(2) Constituents vs. conscience					
Follow voters	9	7	0	20	10
Depends	0	14	0	2	10
Follow conscience	46	31	100	67	80
Party discipline would reign	18	38	0	9	0
No such conflict possible	27	10	0	2	0
Total	100	100	100	100	100
N	(11)	(29)	(8)	(45)	(10)

which are not included, would look very similar, though not all of the differences would be so dramatic.[2]

The differences from party to party are very large, and the within-party homogeneity of response is suggestive of strong group norms. The few centrist PDM members show an almost total absorption with the personal conscience term; some actually pointed out that their caucus did not demand group discipline in voting. That assertion contained a certain amount of truth, although the voting patterns of group members were usually solidary enough to betray what might at least be called substantial intragroup communication and "coordination."

The Républicains Indépendants (RI) show some of the same tendencies, although they are less marked. Again, this is not surprising in view of the nature of this group which, like the PDM, was a "splinter" from a larger and more disciplined faction. It was made up of erstwhile Gaullists who wanted to be free from the pressure to rubber-stamp governmental programs which was exerted by the parent Gaullist caucus. Since both the PDM and the RI had come into being to express resistance to party discipline, it is not surprising that their own formally constituted caucuses displayed the weakest norms with regard to discipline.

Both of these groups were, however, rather small. Even in combination they represented only about 17 percent of the total membership of the 1967–68 Assembly and 19 percent of those in the 1968–72 period. Therefore they contribute only a modest coloration to the general role emphases summarized for the aggregate of French deputies in Figure 21-2. The broad contours of that diagram are primarily influenced by the three major party groupings, for all three of whom party discipline is of primary importance.

The two groups of the left—Communists and Socialists—gave very similar responses, and here party discipline was indeed supreme. In fact, from one point of view the detailed entries of Table 21-2 tend to blur that supremacy because those groups load heavily on "other" responses, including expressions of the impossibility of the postulated conflict, which, as we have seen, are often no more than alternate ways of recognizing the absolute primacy of party dictates. The members of the largest grouping, the Gaullists, are distinct from the left in placing less emphasis on party discipline, although on balance they also see party dictates as primary, conscience as secondary, and the preferences of local voters as least important.

The sharp contrasts in role choices from party to party underscore our earlier point that an aggregate summary such as that portrayed in Figure 21-2 depends on the populations in the data base. If we were to imagine a revised design for a French Assembly in which the PDM and RI held a majority, it is clear that the impressions produced would be quite different. But there is nothing intrinsically misleading about the figure in its present form, since it accurately reflects the specific admixture of French parties in the

1967–68 Assembly. More important, it is reasonable to presume that it also (at least roughly) reflects French parliaments over a much longer period, since despite some nominal changes, the admixture of a few dominant parties demanding considerable discipline, but flanked by splinter groups resisting that discipline, has been an abiding feature of the French legislative scene since World War II.[3]

To judge, however, that these empirically registered emphases deserve to be labeled "French" presumes not only that the responses collected would probably be characteristic of political elites in France over a longer period, but also that the patterns displayed are truly distinctive for *French* political elites. In other words, if the same configuration of emphases could be found in about any legislative system, we then could simplify matters by dropping the adjective "French" in describing the pattern. But if we look comparatively, there is rather clear evidence that these patterns are hardly universal.

Some Comparative Reference Points

Party discipline in legislative voting, which is extremely high in the French National Assembly, is notoriously low in the U.S. House of Representatives. Turning to the Miller-Stokes study of the U.S. body in 1958, we can ask whether there are parallel differences between the conceptions of the legislative role in these two institutions.

In some regards, there are uncanny similarities.[4] This is particularly noticeable in the case of conflict between personal and majority opinion in the local district: some 61 percent of U.S. congressmen report having faced such a conflict, as compared with 63 percent of French deputies. But with regard to the resolution of such a conflict, minor differences show up in some of the "noncontent" categories. Thus, for example, 4 percent of congressmen say that such a conflict is impossible, by comparison with 7 percent of the deputies. And again, almost 10 percent of congressmen say that they would in such an instance try to change opinion in their district before voting, whereas none of the deputies make such a response (although a few candidates do). If, however, we strip both distributions back to the majority of legislators on both sides who do choose one cue or the other, the congressmen show an 86-14 split in favoring conscience over district opinion, in striking agreement with an 85-15 split in the same direction among French deputies.

Such convergences do not, however, hold across all the representative role items. Since our particular interest lies in assumptions concerning the party factor, let us turn to these comparisons. The relevant Miller-Stokes item is a question which reads: "On most bills that come before the House, how important is it to you whether you vote the way the leadership of your party wants?" This item with its five response categories pairs less well with our open-ended item about party-conscience conflict than it does with our structured five-point rating item, which asks: "In deciding to vote in a certain way, what priority would you generally give to (the position of your parliamentary group)?"

Table 21-3 compares the two national legislatures in regard to the importance assigned to party for voting cues. Although there are slight differences in wording, both in the root questions and in the response categories, there is no mistaking the two distributions, for they are dramatically different. These system contrasts are the more impressive when seen against the backdrop of responses to the other two terms of the representation triad, where the conflict between voters and conscience is reported as being resolved almost identically between the two political systems. French deputies place great weight on party cues in voting while United States congressmen place little, and it does not seem rash to conclude that these discrepancies in role conceptions are cut from the same cloth as the behavioral differences in party discipline in roll-call voting in the two legislatures. In short, the verbal responses to our items seem to reflect what they should reflect, and with handsome fidelity.

We can add still another reference point by turning to the results published by Daalder and Rusk (1976), based on the same representative role-conflict items we have used, as posed to representatives in the lower house of the Dutch parliament in 1968.[5] When we adapt their tabulations to our simplified format, we find that responses to the item concerning conflict between conscience and voters are once again essentially identical to the French and American distributions, at least in their most important particu-

Table 21-3. Percentage importance assigned to party for voting cues by French deputies, 1967, and U.S. congressmen, 1958.[a]

Importance assigned by French deputies			Importance assigned by U.S. congressmen
Absolute	43	9	Very important
Strong	27	18	Quite important
Moderate	19	22	Somewhat important
Weak	5	18	Not very important
None	6	33	Not important at all
Total	100	100	
N (unweighted)	(98)	(154)	

a. For both data sets, small handfuls (less than 5% of each sample) of stray noncontent responses have been eliminated. Both arrays of percentages are computed on properly weighted data. The U.S. data are drawn from the Miller-Stokes study of representation, based on data available through the Inter-University Consortium for Political and Social Research (ICPSR).

lars. Some 57 percent of Dutch representatives report having experienced such conflict (versus 61 percent in the United States and 63 percent in France), and the split among content responses as to the direction of resolution of such conflict is 86-14 in favor of conscience (compared with the U.S. 86-14 or the French 85-15).

At the same time, Dutch responses to the conflict between party and conscience are visibly different from those in France and, as can best be told from less comparable items, they contrast with the responses of American congressmen as well. There are in the first instance more frequent reports of experience with such conflict in the Netherlands (80 percent, compared with 68 percent in France). And the basic split among content responses is 43-57 in favor of *conscience* over party dictates, as compared with the French split of 69-31 in favor of *party fidelity* over conscience.

If we mock up another schematic design using the three-legged form presented in Figure 21-2, but now restricting our attention to the deputies in France and adding somewhat presumptive designs for the sitting legislators in the other two countries, we arrive at the set of contrasts presented in Figure 21-3.[6] The only thing the three legislatures have in common is that their members appear to give rather short shrift in their legislative decision-making to the majority opinion of voters in their districts. The implications of even this commonality must be left clouded at the moment, since one argument for a high degree of party discipline is that it is a means of taking the voters into account with the greatest possible fidelity, although at a one-step remove.

But the differences are dramatic enough elsewhere—with the U.S. congressmen at one pole, the French deputies at another, and the Dutch repre-

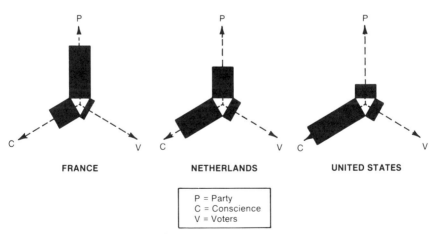

FRANCE   NETHERLANDS   UNITED STATES

P = Party
C = Conscience
V = Voters

Figure 21-3. Presumptive patterns of representative role emphases for legislators in three contrasting political systems.

sentatives somewhere in between with respect to the weight of party in role expectations—for us to reject out of hand any notion that the verbal reports of role emphases we have collected from our French informants are what any set of legislators in any political system would say. And most important, the Franco-American contrasts in these verbal responses fit admirably with the long familiar "objective" differences in behavior between the voting records of the two national legislators.

Individual Stability of Role Responses

We have now seen that our elite informants answer our questions about role conflicts in varying ways, ways that to some gross approximation seem to make sense given their behavior. Yet, as we noted at the beginning of the chapter, the mere capacity to elicit answers to questionnaire items does not mean that these role conceptions as stated reflect deep-dyed personal values that would remain constant for individuals over long periods of evolving legislative situations. At best, they may merely represent post hoc summations by an individual as to how he has watched himself behave under cross-cutting pressures in the recent past, and therefore they may have dubious predictive virtue for the future. Or, again, they may reflect less the underlying and abiding personal values than the group norms which are accepted and durable as long as one is affiliated with the group, but which have no normative appeal under other circumstances. Or, in the worst case, these role responses may have been offered very casually, and they may have little stability or reliability.

We are committed to probing further the meaning of the role responses we have collected. Both the fact that the French responses do seem to be distinctive, relative to those from other national legislatures, and the fact that dramatic but intelligible party differences open up within the French scene, suggest that the responses have some significant meaning for their donors. But such aggregate evidence of minimal coherence falls a good deal short of certifying that our role items are actually tapping basic individual differences in deep-seated political philosophies about representation.

Aggregate patterns such as these are actually compatible with radically different underlying situations, where any such stable individual values might be concerned. One way that a population can maintain a distinctive central tendency on measures such as these over a long period of time is for all population members to remain constant in their individual positions, in the way we take for granted if near-immutable personal values are involved. It is well-known, however, that such aggregate constancy—even a constancy which is very distinctive for one population relative to others—can also be maintained over long periods despite great amounts of individual-level fluctuation among population members. Our party members may in fact have no very fixed personal values on these matters, beyond a desire to respect what they see as the norms of their current groups. They may try to report those norms with as much accuracy as possible; yet if their individual responses were tracked over time, they might fluctuate in a kind of Brownian motion around the group norm, so that within the group there might be little or no personal stability at all.

Thus, although net constancy can reflect gross constancy, it can also conceal a great deal of gross change. And we would be likely to have rather different views of these role preferences, according to which pattern might pertain in our special case.

Fortunately, we are able to assess the degree of individual constancy in role conceptions which underlies the aggregate differentiation, because we have some fragments of cross-time data for our deputies in 1967 and 1968, and the same role items were asked of some deputies twice. This evidence is fragmentary in several senses. First, we have seen that we have only a small number of cases of such reinterviews ($N = 34$). Hence any estimates of response stability to be drawn from the reinterviews is itself subject to more sampling instability than we would like. We shall keep this instability in view by bracketing each estimate with confidence intervals (at a traditional .05 level).

A second difficulty in forming such estimates arises because we have dealt up to now with a kind of tripolar representative role variable. It is possible to prepare a set of nominal categories which summarize and differentiate the three polar types of role-preference configurations involved, and indeed we shall use such an omnibus descriptive measure. But for many purposes it is useful to have more orderly dimensionalized variables.

Therefore we have constructed two major component scales to express the main triad of potential role emphases. The first is a Party Discipline scale, running from no concern about party dictates to exclusive concern, with no attempt made at the low end of the scale to discriminate between legislators emphasizing private conscience and those favoring voters. It is based on three relevant items within each interview. It puts at one extreme the purest partisans, who accord their parliamentary group absolute priority in forming their voting decisions, who clearly choose party over conscience when the two are in conflict, and who find the voter-conscience item irrelevant on grounds that party discipline should carry the day in any event. At the opposing extreme are informants who give little or no priority to party dictates, who clearly choose conscience over party in case of conflict, and who make no mention of the primacy of party in response to the other item.[7]

The second measure is a bipolar Voter/Conscience scale, capturing the legislator's preference between these two possible reference points and ignoring whatever role he may accord to party dictates, although of course the purest partisans who fail to commit themselves on such a choice fall near the middle of this second scale. This variable is based on the voter-conscience conflict item, supplemented by the priority ratings according to voters in the decision equation.

We can evaluate the individual-level stability of these two scales, after a lapse of about a year on the average, for our deputies. For the Voter/Conscience scale the continuity correlation between the same measurements at two points in time is $r = .53$ (with a .05 confidence interval ranging from .24 to .74). This is not an overpowering magnitude, surely, but it is enough to suggest a degree of individual-level stability which goes beyond what a party difference in response would ensure by itself. For the Party Discipline scale, however, the cross-time correlation is a meager .30 (confidence interval from −.05 to .59). It seems intuitively that the sharp and largely constant party differences in discipline expectations, along with lack of much circulation between groups, would be enough to assure individual-level correlations at least this high, if not higher.

Closer examination of the paired values underlying the parent correlation of .30 for party discipline suggests a rather tantalizing property. On the one hand, a considerable majority of the thirty-three respondents involved, although well distributed across a nine-point scale, show either exactly the same score in both measurements, or a score differing by only one point. The degree of stability for these cases is impressive. On the other hand, a small handful of cases show an astonishing change ranging from three and one-half to five standard deviations—running nearly from one end of the scale to the other. If we had any right to delete the data from five of the thirty-three informants, the remaining correlation would approach .70, and be in a range where some assumption of abiding individual role values would be quite tenable. Of course we may not intrude on the data in this fashion; but it is fair to ask whether the few cases of dramatic change along the Party Discipline scale have other characteristics in common that set them apart from those informants with stable response patterns.

One of the five cases is rather transparent. It involves a deputy who remained non-inscrit in one session but took membership in a parliamentary group in the other. When a group member, he felt his proper role to be that of the faithful partisan. When non-inscrit, however, he would have had no reason to take the parliamentary group into account. This is an interesting case, as it helps to make clear the fundamental differentiation among what we would call (1) an abiding personal value, (2) an accurate situational measurement, and (3) pure unreliability. Clearly the responses in this case are situational: the informant is describing what he sees as appropriate role behavior *given* that he is a caucus member, or *given* that he has chosen to remain a nonmember. Presumably, however, his situational perspective is very stable.

In an effort to understand the sharp contrast between changers and nonchangers that we seem to find on the Party Discipline scale, we formed another hypothesis which seemed reasonable. Although all thirty-three of these respondents were deputies, at least by the time of the second measurement in 1968, a substantial number (thirteen) were novitiates, in the sense of having just taken seats in the Assembly for the first time at the point of either the first or the second interview. The most "experienced" of these freshmen thus had had only a few weeks of Assembly participation at the time of their first interview, whereas others were in their first weeks only at the time of their second interview. It seemed plausible that these new deputies were only in the early stages of crystallizing their personal values about the appropriate role of the representative vis-à-vis the parliamentary group. If so, the responses showing remarkable change might be concentrated among them. Because our case numbers were limited from the beginning, further partitions would produce unstable estimates, but the hypothesis seemed well worth checking in any event.

For all of its plausibility, the hypothesis was thunderously disconfirmed. The continuity correlation within the set of more experienced deputies ($N = 20$) recedes to a mere $r = +.20$ (confidence interval from $-.27$ to $+.68$). Among the novitiates, however, the correlation is $+.81$ (interval from $.47$ to $.94$)! Furthermore, despite the tiny case numbers, the difference between these correlation estimates is statistically significant, well within the conventional .05 level.

Although these results are thoroughly disconfirming of our hypothesis in its original form, it is not hard to think of a plausible scenario using the same general ideas which, though patently post hoc, might be compatible with these results. We had initially assumed that role expectations about party discipline might be only weakly crystallized until there had been a sufficient period of actual Assembly participation to forge more stable "real" attitudes. But it may be that such expectations, when stated in the abstract by an informant who has never experienced their real-life implementation, may also be extremely stable, up to the time when real challenges are encountered. The fact of the matter is that all of our novitiates of the 1967–68 period were close observers of political life, and many of them had been aiming for an Assembly seat for a considerable period of time. Hence it is easy to imagine that they had already crystallized some personal values as to how they would expect to interact with party discipline norms, either by accepting them enthusiastically or by expressing some resistance. And it is easy to imagine that these views would be highly stable as long as they remained untested values or assumptions about behavior.[8]

If such an interpretation has merit, then we can imagine that the legislative experience of our novitiates has simply been too brief to begin to put their untested values in flux, and that we should expect to find signs of such flux less among our new "freshman" cohort of deputies than among a "sophomore" cohort whose members have encountered continuing demands of reality that have forced their naive assumptions to change. At some later time, according to this scenario, we might expect them to return to a greater individual-level stability of responses.

Naturally, this more elaborate hypothesis puts even harsher demands on our feeble case numbers, and we do not have complete freedom in designating a subset of our deputies with, say, three years of experience rather than six. We can, however, look at those deputies in our sample who had had a first term of legislative experience and were headed into a second term in the 1967-68 period. There are only eight such cases in our sample of thirty-three repeated interviews. If, however, we proceed with this new trichotomization of the sample, we retain the same $r = +.81$ among the freshmen cohort; we find a new correlation of $+.45$ among our twelve long-term deputies; and, for the suspect set of sophomores lying "between" these oldest and newest groups, we find a correlation of $-.03$. Moreover, it turns out that four of the five cases of dramatic change in scores on the Party Discipline scale from one interview to the other are concentrated among these eight sophomore deputies.

The case numbers here are simply too few to take these data as any thorough confirmation of our revised, three-stage scenario. Although the difference in correlation between the freshman and sophomore cohorts is in fact highly significant in the statistical sense despite the limited case numbers, the coefficient for the most experienced deputies is in an intermediate range and cannot be reliably distinguished from either of the other two estimates. Nonetheless, the three-stage possibility must remain a lively hypothesis, and one worth more definitive testing in the future.

Further spice is added if we return to our other role scale, that pitting voters against conscience, where the total-sample continuity correlation was a more satisfying $r = +.53$, in order to ask the same questions about the phasing of experience. Our initial dichotomization of the sample shows a correlation of $+.16$ among freshman deputies, as opposed to $+.63$ for those more experienced. This difference does not quite achieve normal levels of significance (the p-value for the difference is under .15). But it is a rather strong trend, running in a direction which fits our original purely intuitive two-stage hypothesis, without any necessity for a third stage.

We might well rationalize all of these findings in a rather simple way. As we have noted, the norm of party discipline in legislative voting is so salient in France that one would expect most politicians aspiring to seats in parliament to have crystallized in advance some personal values—even if untested ones—about these norms. The voter-conscience axis, however, may involve issues that would be less salient before actual occupancy of the representative role. In this latter case, therefore, novitiates may come to the role with less crystallized attitudes, leaving our original two-stage surmise as the appropriate one, despite the fact that a three-stage process of prior crystallization, reality testing, and final firming up is necessary to explain the party-discipline patterns.

Another point of contrast between these two dimensions of representative role preference may be important as well. When the Assembly is in session, a legislator's party discipline is subject to more or less weekly evaluation of a tangible, objective kind. He either votes or does not vote with his caucus at any given time, and the public record is clear on the matter. There is no comparable scorecard for the other role dimension, and the deputy's gravitations between personal conviction and attention to district preferences are necessarily much more nebulous. Therefore it may well be that preferences about party discipline are more sternly tested by the hurly-burly of legislative reality, and hence more often in need of situational adjustment, than is true for the less frequent and more readily rationalized points of conflict between conviction and constituency.

To summarize, there is rather substantial individual-level stability on the voter-conscience axis, of an order which suggests that more abiding personal values are engaged. Role preferences concerning party discipline are less stable overall and have a more obvious situational component. At the same time, the very obviousness of the situational component begins to rule out the possibility that the lion's share of the instability observed in the party-discipline responses is due to the intrinsic unreliability or "measurement noise" of our instruments. The next section will amplify the evidence pointing in these directions.

Role-Preference Statements and Actual Role Performance

The validation of any measure rests on the demonstration that it in fact registers what it purports to measure. For attitudes, values, or other preferences, the proof of the pudding is often taken to be the degree of fit between verbal responses defining such preferences and other evidence as to actual choice of behavior. The assumption that attitudes are unreal except as they have some outcome in motor behavior is rather glib, and one to which we do not entirely subscribe, since there are any number of reasons, in addition to "unreal" attitudes, why relevant behaviors might not be carried out. However this may be, attitude-behavior correlations have an intrinsic fascination; and in our special case, we would certainly expect that legislators with different views of their representative roles would behave differently.

We have now defined three major poles for representative role preferences, involving the degree of felt responsibility or accountability to the dictates of (1) the party group, (2) voters in the local district, and (3) the private conscience. It is not equally easy to validate these dimensions. The chore of demonstrating by some external means that private conscience was or was not obeyed in some specific instance would seem about as easy as measuring the physical dimensions of the Holy Spirit. But as we have seen, evidence as to which deputies are being most doggedly faithful to the positions of their caucuses, and which are defecting, lies close at hand in the public record. It is natural, therefore, to ask how well our Party Discipline scale predicts to these trends in behavior.

Aggregated Behavior Prediction

At one level of aggregation, it is easy to show that the accuracy of prediction from our party-discipline attitudes to later fidelity of party voting is superb. In Chapter 17 we reported that there were very large differences, at least in a proportional sense, between the behavioral rates of defection from our five major parliamentary groups in the 1967–73 period. It is obvious from Table 21-2 that if we partition our informants by party group and take the means of Party Discipline scale scores within each group, we also find substantial differences. In fact, the correlation between the vector of five role-preference means and the corresponding vector of five behavioral defection rates is $r = +.88$.

We argued earlier that, since the strong internal discipline of the left, relative to party formations of the center and right, has been a feature of French Assembly voting records for decades, it is reasonable to expect that similar group differences in verbal statements of role preference, had they been measured repeatedly over the same long period, would have registered as well.

This is not to say that the norms of these party groups are perfectly constant. We have seen elsewhere that the Gaullist parliamentary group displayed notably higher rates of defection in member voting patterns during the second period of our study (the 1968–72 Assembly) than it had in the first period (1967–68). We interpreted this change as stemming from an unusual situational factor: the Gaullists had needed almost monolithic internal discipline to carry votes in the evenly divided 1967–68 Assembly, whereas they could afford remarkable defection rates and still win final outcomes in the second period.

Therefore it is of lively interest to note that among the deputies who provided us with two measurements of their party-discipline postures, one early in the 1967 session and the other very early in the 1968–1973 session, there is a slight overall decline in respect for party discipline by the time of the 1968 measure. Virtually all of this decline stems from a rather more brisk decline between the two years within the subset of Gaullist deputies.

In a relative sense, this decline is minor: although the Gaullist mean shifts a bit on the scale, it remains visibly less "disciplined" than the left and visibly more disciplined than the PDM. Even this minor relative movement, however, predicts admirably to the subsequent increases in actual defections in the Gaullist caucus, a matter which cannot fail to convince us once again of the apparent validity of the measurement.[9]

Predictions to Individual Behavior

All of these assessments remain at an aggregated level, however, and we must continue the validation procedure down to the level of the individual. This is desirable partly because this is the form in which attitude-behavior correlations are typically cast and partly because there remains a substantial amount of within-party variation on the Party Discipline scale, and we should know whether, when we hold group norms constant, such variation continues to seem meaningful.

Before proceeding to the data, we should explain that we have constructed two measures of the behavioral record of defection. The first is the obvious one: a simple proportion of the total votes on which the deputy deviated from the vote of his caucus. The solidity of this measure is a bit uncertain, because some specific topics were subjected to very large numbers of roll-call votes while others were represented by only a vote or two. It was clear that if a deputy was moved to vote against his party in one vote on a given topic, he would have a tendency to defect as well on other votes on the same topic. A good illustration of this was provided in Chapter 17 by the sixteen roll calls held on two bills dealing with regulation of the economy in the Paris region, in which some UDR members defected twelve or fourteen times. Such a spate of defections was enough to stamp these UDR members as substantial mavericks within the Gaullist camp, despite the fact that several of them voted religiously with their caucus on all other votes.

Because this conclusion did not seem proper, we constructed a second measure of the behavioral record which would take account of the lack of independence between defections on the same topic, considering any one of sixty-one topics to be the unit, rather than specific votes. Thus if a deputy defected once on a topic subjected to only two votes, a contribution of .50 was made to his total defection score, as compared with a contribution of .75 which would arise from twelve defections in a topic area voted on sixteen times. After a good deal of labor in constructing this second measure, we found that it correlated very highly with the first, simpler, measure, so that it matters very little which one is used as a behavioral criterion. But since the second version seems conceptually preferable, we shall cite our findings in terms of this "chunked-defection" measure.

Since we have data from two interviews as well as different behavioral records across sessions, there is some variety in the test correlations available to us. We shall focus on the version which utilizes all the data as fully as possible. For this version, the attitude predictors are drawn mainly from the 1967 interview, although they are averaged in with 1968 data in the limited number of cases where double reports are available; and the behavioral measure is the total chunked-defection record for the whole six-year period from 1967 through 1972.[10]

This version of the attitude-behavior correlation shows a value of $r = +.56$. This is a very respectable validation value, and one which stands in sharp relief against the initial continuity correlation of .30, which we reported earlier for the total Party Discipline scale taken alone over a period of a single year. Here the prediction "window" is a four- or five-year period after the measurement of the role preferences used as predictors.

When all of the empirical facts are put together, certain general conclusions emerge about the measurement of at least the party-discipline role preferences. The measurement itself cannot be too unreliable, despite the relatively low continuity correlation of .30. Moreover, it seems that such a low correlation must be due less to poor measurement than to accurately measured true change, a change which survived the great situational readjustments occasioned by the 1967–68 tumult in the French representational system.

Deputy Experience and the Behavior Prediction

Earlier we tried to explain the unexpected finding that role preferences about party discipline were much more stable among new deputies than among older ones, particularly the "sophomores." Normally, if one subpopulation has very stable attitudes while another has less stable ones, we would predict that an attitude-behavior correlation would be greater for the more stable population; and we would predict that the discrepancy in correlations between the populations would increase, the longer the span of time between attitude and behavior measurements. This would lead us to expect our attitude-behavior correlations to be higher for new than for old deputies, especially with time lags running out to five years.

But the three-stage scenario which we subsequently developed would imply the opposite prediction. According to that scenario, new deputies had very stable views of party discipline mainly because their legislative experience at the time of measurement was so brief that their views were no more than "untested values." It would follow that as their Assembly experience began to accumulate during the 1967–1973 period, their original untested assumptions would be undergoing more revision than would the assumptions of their more experienced peers. If this were the case, then we would expect their attitude-behavior correlations to be lower, not higher, than those for the veteran deputies.

Again, our case numbers are limited, but we have compared the attitude-behavior correlations for freshmen with those for more experienced deputies. The parent correlation of .56 subdivides into a freshman value of .50, as opposed to .57 for the more experienced majority. The difference is not large, and in view of our small case numbers, not statistically significant. But in view of the massive stability of party-discipline views among our freshmen deputies (continuity correlation of .81), we would not expect their attitudes to predict less well to behavior unless their views were changing more rapidly over the ensuing years than those of their senior colleagues.

Attitude-Behavior Correlations within Party Groups

Some of our earlier evidence suggested that a major source of the stability and patterning of party-discipline preferences is the existence of diverse party group norms on the matter, ranging from iron discipline on the left to somewhat more permissive norms on the center and right. Indeed, it would not be implausible to hypothesize that group norms are responsible for all of the stability and patterning that exists.

In terms of such a plausible model, we have imagined that within any party group, members might give party-discipline responses varying over time around the distinctive central tendency set by the actual group norm, but in a sort of random Brownian motion. Such a model would be compatible with all the data we have presented up to this point: the only source for the modest individual stability in responses we have observed would be stable membership in party caucuses with stable (and distinctive) norms on the matter. If such a model pertained, we would not expect any significant attitude-behavior correlations when group norms are held constant, that is, within the membership of any given party group. In such a case we would be obliged to conclude that, except for the choice of a party group, no idiosyncratic personal values concerning the nature of the representative role were involved and that respect for group norms was the whole explanation of these patterns.

The only barrier to performing a critical test between this model and a rival model in which individual values make some further meaningful input is, once again, limited case numbers. If our test correlations are unstable when we merely dichotomize our deputy sample into new and experienced deputies, it is not hard to see what would happen if we were to partition the parent sample into its five natural parliamentary groups. The relative sizes of these groups, however, particularly after the 1968 election, were extremely disparate. Thus for some caucuses we have tolerable case numbers; but for a couple of others the number of cases is less than five or six, and the computation of a correlation within such subsets is pointless.

For the version of the attitude-behavior correlation linking party-discipline preferences and actual rates of defection from caucus positions which produced our central value of $r = +.56$, we have some twenty-six cases, all of whom were members of the Gaullist caucus. Within this group, where all operated under a Gaullist norm, the attitude-behavior correlation remains at $r = +.49$. We can reject the null hypothesis of no internal correlation within that caucus at the .01 level.

In none of the other groups do we find an absolute correlation as high as in the Gaullist case, and since the case numbers for these groups are far fewer, there is no hope of establishing other significant within-party results. Yet we have inspected the test correlations formed within these other groups, and they average about $+.15$, despite some within-group limits on variation in views, especially on the left.

All told, we are content to conclude that the model which posits that group norms account for all of the observed behavior can be safely rejected. Clearly it is true that group norms, in their variations from party to party, have a potent influence on the stability and patterning of individual preferences as to observance of party discipline. Nonetheless, the data also seem to say that individual variation in premiums placed on party discipline exists even within specified parliamentary groups; and, as is far more important, this variation is demonstrably meaningful, in the sense that it predicts successfully that some party members will be more cavalier about observing party discipline than are other members who are operating under the same group norms. Thus it seems that individual values do add to the impact of group norms on the patterning of role-preference results.

Mass Views of the Representative Role

We have now achieved considerable assurance that our measures of role preferences among elite informants, especially those preferences having to do with party discipline, reflect real predictions. We shall shortly return to these elite attitudes to ask about some of the implications of the variations in role definitions. First, however, another aspect of the subject deserves our attention. We also know something about the French *voters'* notions of desirable representative roles, phrased in exactly the same terms that we have used to characterize elite assumptions about these roles. Obviously, in a work on political representation, it is useful to consider not only how aspirants to and holders of elective posts conceive of the role of representative, but also how that role is regarded by the people who are being represented.

We asked our mass sample in 1967 three questions about how "a good deputy" in the National Assembly should behave. Two of these questions asked how he should resolve party-conscience and voter-conscience conflicts in forming his policy decisions. The third, a parallel for the elite item concerning the degree of desire to support the government, asked whether a deputy should support the government to maximize benefits for his local district or remain aloof and free to criticize government actions. The simple distribution of responses to these items is presented in Table 21-4.

It is clear that the mass preferences concerning deputy role emphases show no congruence whatever with the elite distributions given in Table 21-1. For example, among those giving substantive responses, French voters choose conscience over party, 58–42, and voters over conscience, 69–31. These patterns do not bear even a passing resemblance to the elite views in any of the three countries shown in Figure 21-3, and least of all to those for France. The mass responses imply that voters should come first, personal conviction second, and party dictates third. This is the reverse of the French elite ordering, and the margins that lie between these rankings, in terms of percentage preferences, are very wide in most cases.[11]

It may not seem astonishing that voters in France feel that in cases of conflict their elected representatives should respond principally to voter opinion. But if there really is a developed philosophy among French political elites that voter opinion is best served when the representative is only a faithful delegate of the party group which "aggregates and articulates" mass opinion and sees to his election, then this philosophy has gained no currency whatever among the French mass electorate.

It is quite unlikely, of course, that the mass responses reflect any kind of well-developed political "philosophies." Indeed, it is dubious that the separate opinions expressed, even taken in isolation, stem from attitudes that are strongly crystallized. The large proportion of respondents who confess that they have no opinions are one symptom of feeble crystallization. Their likely instability, at least at an individual level, is another.[12] There is nothing particularly surprising about such weak crystallization. The issues of role performance, at least in the terms in which we have cast them, almost never surface into public debate. Hence there is little reason to suppose that most mass respondents would have had reason even to think of them in advance of the questionnaire situation. At the same time, although these data may not reflect considered opinion, it remains of interest that the elite values, which seem so clear-cut and prevalent, have had little apparent "take" at the mass level.

Mass Views of Representative Roles by Party Grouping

The most surprising aspect of this faint degree of "take" is that certain elite norms, if not the representative role debate itself, would seem to be part of the political lore that is accessible even at the mass level, particularly among the sympathizers of certain parties. For example, the policy discipline and absolute party loyalty classically demanded by the Communist movement, whether at the level of the local cell organization or the national congress, is

Table 21-4. Percentage preferences concerning deputy roles held by French voters, 1967.[a]

Party vs. conscience		Voters' views vs. conscience		Loyalty to government vs. conscience	
A good deputy should:		A good deputy should:		A good deputy should:	
Vote with his party	34	Do what voters want	57	Support government	29
It depends	4				
Vote own conscience	48	Vote own conscience	26	Keep distance	46
No opinion	14	No opinion	17	No opinion	25
Total	100		100		100
N	(1983)		(1981)		(1977)

a. Percentages are based on weighted data.

renowned. One can imagine politically inattentive French citizens being totally unaware of these hallmark norms, but unawareness on the part of voters supporting the Communist party at the polls is a different matter. Would we really expect a majority of Communist supporters in France to define the "good deputy" as one who ignores the dictates of his party in favor of his personal convictions or voter demands, when these terms are in conflict? It seems unlikely.

Therefore we have examined not only the deputy role preferences of Communist supporters in particular but also the patterning of these mass views by the party supporter group more generally. These data are presented in summary form in Table 21-5.[13]

As we see, there is some patterning by supported party. The differences are not overwhelming, particularly if we focus upon the two standard role measures and the three largest party groups (Communists, FGDS, and Gaullists). But the general contrasts between the left and the non-leftist parties are large enough to be significant. Even among Communist supporters we see that a majority still feel that good deputies should place the dictates of conscience, and certainly those of the voters, ahead of their parties. Nonetheless, the *relative* differences in emphasis that emerge among the

Table 21-5. Percentage mass preferences as to representative roles, by party of supporter, 1967.

	Party of supporter				
Role-conflict items	Communist (PCF)	Federation (FGDS)	Dem. Center (PDM)	Gaullist (UDV^c)	Ind. Rep. (RI)
In case of conflict, a deputy should follow:					
His party	48	49	28	40	31
His conscience	52	51	72	60	69
Total	100	100	100	100	100
His voters	72	71	57	67	60
His conscience	28	29	43	33	40
Total	100	100	100	100	100
In case of conflict, a deputy should:					
Support government	28	30	36	47	45
Keep his distance	72	70	64	53	55
Total	100	100	100	100	100

mass electorate mirror faintly but perceptibly the sharp differences that exist between members of corresponding parties at the elite level.

However all this may be, it remains true that the aggregate emphasis at the mass and elite levels, around which these parallel party variations occur, are not only grossly discrepant but, indeed, quite contradictory. This is vividly shown by the summary designs presented in Figure 21-4, which recapitulates the representative role emphases by party group at both elite (deputy) and mass (electorate) levels.

Among the deputies (upper row), the party differences in emphasis strike the eye immediately: all five patterns are distinct from one another. But a quick scan of the lower row, symbolizing the electorate, gives the impression that the five designs are nearly the same. It takes close examination to detect, for example, that the greatest stress is placed on conscience by supporters of PDM deputies, or that the respect for party dictates is strongest among supporters of leftist deputies.

The most striking fact of the whole display, however, is that the two rows bear no resemblance to each other in their general contour. In relative details, there is some congruence. Overall, there is none. Whereas the voters feel that the good deputy should be primarily oriented toward the wishes of voters and least concerned with party discipline, hardly any of the deputies see the voter as the most immediate concern, but instead they express primary loyalty to party dictates.

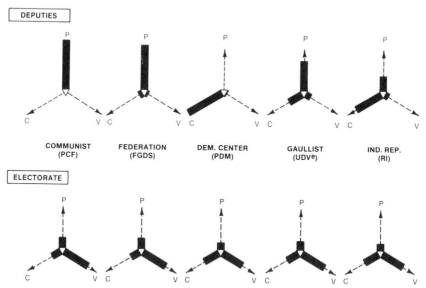

Figure 21-4. Elite and mass conceptions of deputy role, by political party.

Mass-Elite Linkages in
Representation Style

Thus it is clear that neither French deputies nor, for that matter, the more numerous aspirants to the Assembly, offer in the aggregate the conceptions of the representative role that their voters claim to see as desirable. It would be too strong to say that these mass conceptions of the representative role constitute "voter demands," since the main evidence on the mass side suggests that these opinions are poorly crystallized and lightly held. Nonetheless, it is worth asking whether there are any traces of *relative* linkage between voters and their deputies, even if absolute linkage is necessarily poor.

A modicum of such relative linkage is assured on the basis of the data already presented: that is, districts with large leftist majorities are likely to place a somewhat higher premium on party discipline than other districts. They are also more likely to elect leftist deputies, who in turn are much more likely than other deputies to revere party discipline. Thus some degree of voter-deputy linkage correlation must exist, at least where party discipline is concerned, though merely in terms of relative congruence.

We find such a meaningful correlation when the means of district preferences on the party-conscience items are paired with the Party Discipline scores for their elected representatives in the Assembly. The value for 1967 mass responses and 1967 Party Discipline scores for their own deputies is not trivial: $r = +.31$. When we make the same kind of pairing between district sentiments on the voter-conscience index, however, the correlation is a mere $r = +.02$.

Clearly the main linkage involves the party-discipline dimension, and, equally clearly, this moderate relative linkage can be traced back to the political parties with their varying norms about party discipline. A final question is whether, if party distinctions were ruled out, there would be any further sign of relative linkage on the party-discipline dimension or, for that matter, any sign of an emergent linkage on the voter-conscience dimension.

We have evaluated this final possibility by transforming the deputy scores on our two role scales to new values standardized by party on a national base. The scale value of each deputy is expressed afresh as a departure from the mean for his party among deputies nationally. When these party-standardized scores are correlated with district variations in mass responses to the representative role items, the coefficient for the party-discipline dimension shrinks from $+.31$ to $-.03$, and the coefficient for the voter-conscience pairings remains indistinguishable from zero.

Thus it seems fair to conclude that whatever relative linkage exists between districts and their deputies with regard to the virtues of party discipline is entirely mediated by variations in party norms, and that there is no relative linkage at all for the voter-conscience dimension.

Role Preferences and
Information Needs

Finally, we need to consider how differences in assumptions about the representative role affect the behavior of the deputy in the Assembly, in ways that go beyond respect for party discipline. One very simple but important hypothesis is that potential representatives will be more attentive to the opinions of voters in their districts if they conceive of district sentiment as an important input to their own legislative decisionmaking.

Such a proposition may seem close to tautological; however, it is less than certain that such an effect can be demonstrated because the deputy may have other reasons for being attentive to the state of district sentiment. For example, an aspirant who believes wholeheartedly in party discipline or the dictates of conscience may nonetheless try to stay close to district sentiment in order to make himself attractive to the district for election purposes, or even for the purpose of influencing it on policy matters.

Still, it seemed worth asking whether such an effect could be found. Although we lack any direct measure of attentiveness to district opinion, we do have measures of accuracy of perception of district sentiment (as explained in the last chapter); and it is a short further step to assume that the aspirant who is more attentive to local opinion will perceive it more accurately. It may be recalled that our most summary measures of perceptual accuracy came from a factor analysis of discrepancies between perception and actual opinion over more than a dozen linkage issues. In fact, two nearly independent accuracy factors were isolated, the first on the basis of perceptions of our problem-importance items, and the second on the basis of our position issues, including the left-right super-issue. The relative independence of these factors was brought home to us frequently in subsequent analyses, for the two factors more often than not had different correlates. Yet here and there they generated reasonably convergent results, including, as we pointed out, the association with representative roles.

Any analysis is somewhat cramped by the fact that most of our French elite informants stand pretty firmly in favor of either party discipline or private conscience as principal cues for their legislative decisionmaking: it is hard to find candidates who focus solely upon district opinion in the pure mandate sense. But it is relatively easy to show that the more unequivocally the candidate looks to partisan cues to the virtual exclusion of all else, or the more doggedly Burkean he is, the more inaccurate are his perceptions of district sentiment overall. This is shown in Figure 21-5, where we have taken the liberty of summing the scores for our informants on the two nearly independent accuracy factors. (In the component diagrams, pure Burkeans do more poorly on the problem-importance factor, while pure partisans do more poorly on the issue-position factor.)

Figure 21-5 makes it clear that accuracy of perception is greatest among

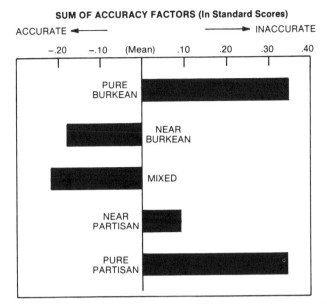

SUM OF ACCURACY FACTORS (In Standard Scores)

ACCURATE ◄────   ────► INACCURATE

Figure 21-5. Inaccuracy of perceptions of district sentiment (issue positions and problem importance), by representative role orientations.

those mixed types who do not commit themselves narrowly to the dictates of either party or conscience. We can presume that, in general, those most respectful of popular opinion as a competing cue tend to fall among these mixed types. We can get a purer test of that proposition, however, by limiting our attention to the item concerning the priority our candidates feel should be attributed to district opinion in roll-call vote decisions in the National Assembly. The association is not strong, but it is present in the expected direction and is so for both of the accuracy factors. Those giving greater priority to district opinion are also more accurate in their descriptions of both district issue positions ($r = +.07$, $p < .15$) and issue importance ($r = +.14$, $p < .02$).

In sum, then, although the French system does not generate politicians who feel that they should be delegates purely instructed by their districts, the data suggest that those who are least narrowly committed to party or conscience, and who believe most in district sentiment as a proper input to legislative decisionmaking, do in fact show greater accuracy in their assessments of that opinion, as logic would come close to requiring.

Conclusions

We have now completed our review, at a molecular level, of the major raw materials contributing to the process of political representation in France.

Seen in the legislative context of the National Assembly, these raw materials have included the state of district sentiment on policy cleavages of the day; the private convictions of local representatives on those same issues; the understandings of district sentiment on the part of those representatives; and finally (in this chapter), conceptions of the representative role, or the "will to represent."

We spent a substantial portion of this chapter evaluating our measurement of these role conceptions in terms of their nature and apparent validity. When such procedural dust had settled, however, it was apparent that the state of these role conceptions in France during the period of our study could be rather simply described as leaning heavily toward a view of party discipline as the appropriate posture of the good representative in the National Assembly.

This view was not, of course, unanimously held. A significant minority of our candidates and deputies seemed to prefer a rather Burkean view of the representation responsibility. There was also a fringe with enough concern about voter opinions to mitigate any unalloyed commitment either to party or to conscience. These mixed types were more accurate than their peers in assessing district opinion, and they, along with the Burkeans, appeared to account for a disproportionate share of that small quota of defections from party discipline that can be found in the legislative system of the National Assembly.

Acceptance of the norm of party discipline was less than unanimous in quite another sense as well. We saw that the voting population rejected party discipline as characteristic of the legislative decisionmaking of the "good deputy," and did so by a resounding margin. The voters instead preferred to have their representatives give primary heed to voter opinion and secondary attention to their own consciences, with party discipline falling in a weak last place. Relative disregard for party discipline occurs even among supporters of the most sternly disciplined of all of the French parliamentary groups, the Communist party.

Despite this distaste for party discipline among the public, and despite the minorities on the elite side who are themselves somewhat lukewarm about party discipline as the sine qua non for legislative decisionmaking, there is no question that the dominant view of the representative role among French political elites places a heavy premium on the sanctity of party solidarity in Assembly voting. And the dominance of this view is quite overpowering, as we saw in such a display as Figure 21-3.

Given the dominance of this allegiance to party discipline, it may seem a bit bizarre that we have devoted much time and labor to other parts of the full representation model, such as district sentiment on substantive issues and the accuracy of the representative's assessment of that sentiment. When most representatives themselves say that they would give tertiary attention, at best, to district opinion in arriving at their decisions as to the roll-call votes they will cast in the Assembly, why are these other terms worth any attention?

The reasons are two and utterly basic. One is, of course, a postulate that even a system of iron party discipline, provided it takes place within democratic assumptions, is an embodiment of a theory as to how popular representation is best achieved. We would be at a loss to know how to put this postulate to any empirical test without proceeding very much as we have with our study design, actually measuring public opinion on various issues and comparing it with the behavior of political representatives when determining the fate of those issues in the national parliament. Given such measurements replicated in a large number of different institutional settings, including some with extreme party discipline and some with very little at all, we can imagine arriving at some general conclusions as to ways in which party discipline does in fact amplify or attenuate the fidelity of political representation. But of course we could not formulate such conclusions if in the set of legislative systems with high party discipline we decided that independent measurements of public opinion were irrelevant.

The second reason is at a different level, but is ultimately intertwined with the first. It flows from the fact that in general our elite informants, including those whose responses give the most sacrosanct role to norms of party discipline, are intensely interested in public opinion and its fit with the positions of their own party caucuses, as well as with the flow of authoritative decisions from the Assembly. We can be sure of this for a number of reasons, none of which need imply that our informants are in the least dissembling even when they express the most exclusive allegiance to party discipline in forming their own decisions about roll-call votes.

Our questions tend to put these informants in the context of an ongoing series of roll-call votes, circumstances under which the party caucus will almost invariably have established a party position in advance. Many of them respond that under such circumstances they cannot be concerned with personal conviction or district opinions, or for that matter with any other competing source of decisionmaking cues, but rather will honor the requirements of party discipline and will do so without exception. That these assertions are true is well attested by the scarcity of defecting votes in Assembly roll calls.

This is not, of course, tantamount to a statement that they or their parties do or should ignore the state of public opinion in forming their programs. Indeed, there is a great deal of evidence that public opinion regularly competes with ideological consistency in the formulation of party programs and caucus decisions in the French political system, just as it does in most others. Some national party congresses lean more to ideology and others to the evolution of popular opinion, but few parties survive for long without a genuine concern for the fit between options chosen for party programs and the perceived demands and other postures of the electorate. Although the evidence is less public, it is certainly true that some of the pulling and hauling in attempting to decide caucus positions in all but ideologically certain circumstances depends upon what will seem most congenial to the public, or at least the portion of the public which that party sees as its central constituency. Moreover, it is likely that in the French system, as in the American, one of the most compelling excuses of the legislator for failing to observe party discipline on a given vote is that, in view of opinion on that issue in the home district, the party would risk losing the legislative seat in the next election if he were foolish enough to comply with caucus wishes, thereby flouting district preference on the matter.

What all this means is that at the elite level, the French representation system does indeed have certain elements familiar from the schemes for representation through "party responsibility." The prevalence and depth of respect for party discipline at the last stage of legislative decisionmaking—the final solidary front—is principal among these. But this element alone does not establish the French system in a party responsibility mold. And it surely does not mean that the other raw materials we have assembled, including individual convictions of the legislator or the distribution of opinion in his district, are irrelevant to the nature of political representation in the system. This will be seen more clearly as we put all of these raw materials together to give a broader view of the total representation process.

22

The Composite
Representation Process

We are now ready to put together the pieces we have assembled in recent chapters and to see the mosaic they produce. In Chapter 18 we discovered that a certain amount of popular representation was occurring in roll-call votes in the National Assembly, at least in the very precise and operational sense that positive congruence could be found between variations in district opinion and variations in the respective votes cast. We did not ask at that time what the intervening mechanisms were which might be producing that congruence. Was there a significant "will to represent" on the part of the representatives, or did such signs of positive congruence emerge merely through the phenomenon of descriptive representation? And what role was being played by the accuracy of elite perceptions of district sentiments?

We have been addressing these and other questions in a molecular way in the intervening chapters, and now it is time to stand back and gain some perspective on the process as a whole. When we do this, we are able to ask more searching questions as to the sensitivity of the basic representation relationship (the AD bond) to various intervening conditions. How does the fidelity of that basic relationship vary as a function of differences in the political issues at stake? Does it vary in the expected ways in response to differences in the will to represent? How is it affected by differences in the ways in which various representatives have come into office? How does it fluctuate in response to historical change, and by what mechanisms? Several broad questions of this kind will be considered in this chapter, and those which remain will be addressed subsequently.

Our main diagnostic tool will continue to be the Miller-Stokes diamond first presented in Chapter 16, although now we shall view it more
frequently as a whole than as a set of separate bonds. In Chapter 16 we
pointed out that this diamond was fine-tuned primarily to evaluate the nature of representation along the axis of the mandate-independence debate,
and we noted that one important competing view of representation—the
responsible-party model—did not fit the paradigm of the diamond in any
very obvious way. We saw in the last chapter that the strong party discipline observed in National Assembly voting has its roots in clear political
norms about the nature of the legislative role. Since party discipline in legislative voting is one of the absolute keystones of the responsible-party model,
we cannot discuss the broader representation process in France without
confronting this model in a much more detailed way, asking how well it fits
our data on the French situation and also how it intersects conceptually
with the parameters of the Miller-Stokes diamond. Subsequently we shall
turn to the data for the full diamond, and then we shall analyze the conditional variation in the configuration of parameters that it yields for the
French case.

The Responsible-Party Model
for Popular Representation

In Chapter 16 we saw that the normative doctrine of representation
through responsible parties included three essential requirements: (1) the
political parties present contrasting policy programs to the voters; (2) each
voter takes a survey across these program options and selects the "package"
of positions that best fits his or her personal preference schedule for these
issues; and (3) the elected party or representative doggedly struggles to promote each of the positions taken in the party platform. A mandate ethic for
representation is the guiding posture, and the political parties are seen as the
crucial agents for conveying popular wishes into enacted legislation. The
emphasis is upon the rationality of the voter and the accountability of elites
to their constituents.

Whereas the normative doctrine naturally sketches an "ideal type" of
representation, our empirical approach requires asking existential questions
of degree. Since the model of responsible parties levies a multiplicity of requirements, the fulfillment of each of these taken alone cannot be complete
but is bound to be a matter of degree. We can also define degree in terms of
the proportion of requirements that are satisfactorily fulfilled. But the logical structure of the model is such as to suggest that if one of its several requirements is not met, then the whole structure collapses as a rationale: the
chain is no stronger than its weakest link.

Our purpose now is to ask how closely the French representation system approximates the responsible-party model; and to ask in addition whether, and in what sense, the parameters of the Miller-Stokes model are of any use in such a diagnosis.

Our interest in the responsible-party model has been sharply whetted by the towering presence of party discipline in legislative voting in the Assembly. This discipline is not perfect—we might say reasonably that the requirement is only met at a 95–97 percent level—but it is very high, and party discipline is a sine qua non for any responsible-party system. The converse is, however, not true: the presence of nearly impeccable party discipline does not of itself ensure that a representation system is functioning in the responsible-party fashion.

The most obvious shortfall concerns the perceptions and decisionmaking of voters. From the bird's-eye view enjoyed by elites, parties may seem quite responsible and accountable; but from the grass-roots perspective of the voters, they (the voters) must be aware of the contrasting programs of the parties, which should be pivotal as they make their choices at the polls. The evidence we have examined on this score in earlier chapters, however, has certainly failed to provide any lusty confirmation of that requirement. For example, in Chapter 2 we found that only a limited minority of voters were even cognizant of many of the parties in the electoral system in France, and of course a knowledge of the program being proposed by a party is a much more advanced requirement than merely knowing that the party exists. Working from the issue side in Chapter 9, we found that between one-third and one-half of our voters would not venture to guess which of ten listed parties was most dedicated to particular policy goals, even though these goals, far from being obscure, were in each case taken from our list of the central and most familiar issues of the period. And among those who did perceive linkages between policy ends and particular parties, consensus as to which parties supported these ends was quite limited. Indeed, we commissioned a "clarity" index, combining both awareness of party relevance to issue positions and consensus as to the party most committed to the goal, which would be expected to register a value of 1.00 in a perfectly functioning responsible-party system. Over our skein of linkage issues, however, the index took meager values ranging from .12 to .30, suggestive of widespread ignorance and confusion over party positions on the main issues of the day.

Between this bleak evidence and our postulate that the functioning of a responsible party process can be no more complete than its weakest link, we are not encouraged to imagine that the French system matches such an ideal system at all well, however extravagant the party discipline in the legislature may be. Nonetheless, the matter is of sufficient importance to warrant closer scrutiny.

The Mass Side of the
Responsible-Party System

When Miller and Stokes (1963) made their pioneering examination of representation in the American Congress, they soon encountered a seeming paradox. There were clear signs of some positive congruence between district sentiments in issue domains and the roll-call votes cast by their representatives, *despite* the fact that two-thirds to three-quarters of the citizens interviewed did not appear to remember what candidates they had voted for, much less any issues for which these candidates might be expected to vote. How could such a paradox be resolved?

At least two answers lay close at hand. The first one, stressed by Miller and Stokes, was that the political party constituted the "missing link," so that although U.S. voters could scarcely remember what candidates they had voted for, much less the issue advocacies of these candidates, the printed ballot made it clear what *party* they were voting for. And although it would be too much to imagine that many voters would be well versed in the platforms of the two parties from one policy domain to another, the electorate would have some global images of the differences between the parties that could claim issue relevance. Thus, for example, one party was seen as being "the party of the common man" and the other the party of business and the wealthy. Of course, many voters had no such perceptions; and among those who did, there were some reversals of assignment as to which party was which. Yet the vast majority of voters with such perceptions agreed that the Democratic party was more for the common man than the Republican party. And hence it was not surprising that, down the road, an association grew up between Democratic or Republican voting at the polls and support or opposition to social welfare by representatives in the Congress, even if the voters knew nothing about the candidates save their party banners, which were printed on the ballot.

Although the level of functioning here is gross and dim, this scenario, evaluated theoretically, is clearly of a piece with the "responsible party" procedure. Furthermore, it emphasizes one forgiving aspect of a representation model which is otherwise quite harsh and demanding. Although the responsible-party doctrine expects a level of voter rationality which nowadays seems quite naive, it does display some respect for the limited attention and information of the voters, in that it does not require them to learn de novo at each election the idiosyncratic programs of the more or less new candidates between whom they must choose. Instead, all they must know are the basic differences between the programs of the two (or half-dozen) parties in the system. If these differences are at all abiding, as they are likely to be, the voters' progressive learning about them across elections can cumulate accurately, simplifying the acquisition process still further. One of the major points of the whole doctrine is that once the voters know this much, they cannot be tricked by some maverick candidate into voting incorrectly in programmatic terms.

A second resolution of the apparent Miller-Stokes paradox, entirely compatible with the first, has already been mentioned several times and is equally instructive. This involves the marvelous capacity of aggregation to conceal "noise" and confusion. Statements about the sizes of those limited minorities of American voters who were even aware of the identity of the candidates for whom they had voted are intrinsically disaggregated assessments. Statements of congruence between average district sentiment and legislative roll-call votes have, on the mass side at least, a highly aggregated base. Therefore some of the force of the paradox arises because, under the surface and hidden from sight, two different measurement currencies are being used.

The stark discrepancy between these currencies is best illustrated by a page from the history of the Miller-Stokes project itself. In a first provisional analysis, the issue sentiments of individual voters were correlated with the convictions and roll-call votes of their elected representatives. This was a disaggregated analysis. There were some fifteen hundred citizens and a hundred-odd representatives. The analysis was disaggregated because the sampling design had been geared to individuals, and congressional districts had been ignored. Therefore it was natural to deal analytically with some fifteen hundred examples of dyadic bonds between voters and representatives. The results were disastrous: there was a patchwork of insignificant correlations, ranging generally from $r = -.05$ to $r = +.05$.

This initial failure touched off a reconsideration of what data assembly would be most appropriate for the question. It was decided that instead of some fifteen hundred dyadic bonds linking individual voters to their legislators, theory required a level of aggregation such that the bonds should be reduced in number to a hundred-odd, linking each of the representatives to an aggregated statement of central tendency of opinion in their districts (namely, the mean of responses from each district). Once the currency was thus changed by a step of aggregation—and to our view, theory not only permits such restatement but requires it—then a substantial number of significant correlations (ranging even up into the .50s and .60s) began to emerge, although the actual data base had not changed at all. What had changed was the intervention of some "cleansing" aggregation.

We can even put some approximate values on the amount of cleansing which aggregation of individual dispersion into means by districts accomplishes, as suggested by the behavior of the *eta* statistic over our central political issues. There is some variability in the geographic maldistribution of the issues, and hence some variation in the details; but for the modal issue, about 90 percent of the total variance in individual responses lies within districts, and only about 10 percent between districts. Therefore, as we move from individual-level analysis to district aggregation, the change in currency is very dramatic. If there is some coherent signal which makes up three parts in 100 of individual variation, with the other 97 parts being some form of noise, then the signal is nearly undetectable under many circumstances, and it is bound to look absolutely feeble if it is detected. If, however, we artificially remove 90 parts of noise through aggregation and reconsider the signal, it will make up three parts in ten, or 30 parts in the revised base of 100; it will now be quite detectable and appear quite strong. Little wonder that users of aggregate voting data arrive at rather different impressions of such a matter as voter rationality, relative to users of sample survey data!

Although this description is a modest simplification of the problem, it helps to make vivid the ambiguities we encounter if we aspire to estimate the degree to which the French mass electorate functions in a responsible-party mode. Of course, it might occur that what we are calling the "coherent" part of the signal from the mass electorate (for example, consensual views about party policy positions) is in fact a very inaccurate reading of what the parties are trying to convey. In such a case we could agree that the voting mode fits the responsible-party model poorly, if at all. But suppose that the coherent part of the signal is quite accurate, although the signal-to-noise ratio is extremely feeble. Do we say that the functioning is perfect, or that it is pathetically weak? And if we say it is perfect, how shall we distinguish this case from others in which the signal is not only equally accurate but is stronger to boot?

A relevant example would be a case in which one of two parties espouses position A while its opponent espouses position B, and a sample of voters are asked what positions each of these parties adopts. Of 100 voters, let us say that 40 decline to answer on grounds that they have no idea what the positions are; and among the 60 who do attempt an answer, 31 get the alignment right and 29 get it wrong. In a highly aggregated sense, these voters have "on balance" called the alignment correctly. Nevertheless, we would not be overly impressed by how well the assumptions of the responsible-party doctrine were being met. And we would certainly want some way of discriminating between this case and another in which 90 of 100 voters describe the alignment correctly, with only six incorrect and four unable to say, in exactly the fashion captured by our clarity index of Chapter 9.

The empirical situation with our French data, as with the American data of Miller and Stokes, poses exactly this assessment problem. When we look at voter perceptions of party programs in disaggregated form, we find them fraught with ignorance and confusion. But if we set aside those who admit to being ignorant, and ask whether contrary perceptions are being minimized elsewhere, so that there is some edge of aggregate agreement, we can discern lines of judgment among the voters to the effect that the UNR emphasizes government stability and economic development, whereas protection of lay schools and concern over the distribution of income are more often than not attributed to the left. Since outside observers of the period would have pronounced these perceived linkages "accurate," it can be argued that voters as a whole are at least *perceiving* the world (as opposed to *behaving* toward it) in ways that are somewhat compatible with responsible-party assumptions. Yet these residual signals are certainly obscured by an enormous admixture of noise, and the question of actual voting choices, and their potential dependence on these perceptions of policy programs, poses a whole new set of problems.

Voting Choices and the Responsible-Party Model

Our work, described in Chapter 10, did not encourage us to expect voters to put enormous weight on party programs about current issues in making their decisions at the polls. Nonetheless, we decided to ask what the voting returns in our sample might have looked like if we had insisted on forcing our respondents to cast their votes in the terms laid out in the responsible-party model. We did not labor hard over this exercise, as we could see in advance that we would get nonsensical results in return. But it seemed useful to determine just how nonsensical they might be, as another means of assessing how well French voters approximate the model of responsible parties.

We proceeded in the following fashion. Although we lacked direct measures of the policy programs being promulgated by the parties at the time of the 1967 election, our candidate interviews had given us excellent samples of leading politicians in all of the major parties; and, quite naturally, variation in party affiliation accounted for rather substantial portions of the overall variance in policy positions. Therefore it seemed reasonable to consider a "party program" to be constituted by the mean positions of its elite sample members across our set of linkage issues. Because not all of these issues were posed in identical form, it was useful to recast the party positions as standard scores, based on the mean and standard deviation of the full sample of candidates. This gambit was also important in order to sidestep oddities such as the tendency among elites to assign themselves personal left-right positions considerably to the left of mass positions (see Figure 4-5).

With this operational definition of party programs in hand, we created standard scores for our mass respondents on all of the same linkage issues. Then, for each voter's position on each issue, we were able to say which of the programs of the five parties later forming caucuses in the 1967–68 session lay closest to his or her position on that issue; and thereby we were able to assign the individual a simulated party preference *with respect to that particular issue.* We then assigned a final simulated party vote on the basis of the party most often preferred, summed across all of our linkage issues. Although this procedure simplifies the system to five parties and assumes that the voter weights issues equally, it is not a gross distortion of the voter decision rules presumed by the responsible-party doctrine.

The summary distribution of this simulated vote across our mass sample is provided in Table 22-1, where it is compared with the relative proportions of the vote actually achieved by these parties in the first ballot of 1967.

At first the simulation looks quite apt for the Communists and the Democratic Center, but it soon becomes evident that these results are merely "lucky strikes." The general results are thoroughly absurd, with the smallest party in the actual system winning the simulated vote by a landslide of a magnitude never seen in the history of French democracy.

Of course, many details of this exercise may be questioned, including the fact that a disproportionate number of our linkage items concern European integration. Almost any reasonable rendering of the responsible-party assumptions seems to produce parallel absurdities, however. For example, having seen the power and generality of the left-right location measure, we might test the same decision rules using that measure alone. But to escape problems created by the severe left-leaning tendency of our elite informants, let us instead consider the party locations on the left-right continuum to be those ascribed on the average by the mass sample. Then we indeed reduce the ridiculous size of the Independent Republicans, but at the same time the small Democratic Center suddenly becomes the dominant party in the system, controlling just about one-third of the mass votes.

There is nothing truly perplexing in any of these nonsensical results: the simplest conclusion is that decisions at the polls by French voters do not, in general, bear a passing resemblance to the mechanisms presumed by the responsible-party doctrine. This conclusion becomes most obvious as we run through the relevant mechanisms at a disaggregated level, only summarizing subsequently, as we have done with these simulated votes.

The one remnant of that doctrine which remains viable at the mass

Table 22-1. Party vote simulated by decision rules of the responsible-party doctrine, compared with actual vote (percentages), 1967.

Party	Simulated vote	Actual vote
PCF	23.6	24.4
FGDS	3.6	20.8
CD	12.5	13.7
UNR	7.9	34.8
RI	52.4	6.3
Total	100.0	100.0

level, then, is the feeble signal betraying recognition of some of the main links between the most differentiated policy positions and specific parties. The feature of this signal which remains to be considered is that its presence seems to be strongly stratified by political attentiveness or involvement: that is, it would be possible for such recognitions to be distributed uniformly but feebly across the entire electorate. The data suggest, however, that the cognitive linkages presumed by the doctrine may instead be reasonably well developed for a thin stratum of the most involved voters—perhaps one in six or seven—while they are nearly nonexistent elsewhere, quite analogous to our findings about ideological structure in Chapter 7. This kind of differentiation renews the implicit question as to who gets represented, a question which we shall address in the final chapter.

If it is true, however, that a representation system is no closer to the responsible-party model than its weakest fulfillment of some component requirements, then our findings on the mass side of the interaction certainly cast the most severe doubt on the truth and utility of characterizing representation in France in such terms.

The Elite Side of the System

At this point it might seem desirable to argue that French political institutions and norms of political elites, including those requiring strong party discipline, are at least *designed* to offer the public a responsible-party system, even though the public may not be involved enough in politics to capitalize on the offer. But even this argument may be stronger than the case warrants.

Certainly accountability is now and again mentioned as one of the virtues of strict party discipline in National Assembly roll calls, in a vein which conforms painstakingly with the doctrine of party responsibility. But it is very far from clear that such accountability is the main reason for the strength of the norm. After all, this discipline has other well-recognized functions, such as the promotion of internal solidarity and the maximization of party bargaining power in legislative compromises and trade-offs.

Moreover, elite practices in French politics contain other elements besides party-discipline norms which seem as antithetical to a responsible-party doctrine as those norms are conducive to it. There is, in fact, some structural separation between the legislative party group by whom voting discipline is required and the electoral party which generates platforms and woos votes. This does not mean that the two structures are often at policy odds with each other, but such contradictions can occur. Indeed, historically there have been dramatic discrepancies, as when party coalitions formed for the purpose of maximizing mutual votes at the polls are subsequently ignored when it comes time to form a government, with different coalitions (and hence different mixtures of party programs) being actually installed in office. Of course, any such discontinuity between electoral parties and executive or legislative parties must be seen as absolute anathema from the responsible-party point of view. The fact that such potential for discontinuity co-occurs in the French system with strong party discipline once again leaves doubt that the discipline norms have grown up primarily to promote party accountability to the electorate.

Party Responsibility and the Miller-Stokes Assessments

Although evaluations of the degree to which certain requirements of the responsible-party doctrine are met empirically can reasonably include matters that lie quite outside the Miller-Stokes model, such as the intensity of party discipline in the legislature or the accuracy of voter perception of party programs, it is important to understand that estimates in the Miller-Stokes form are also relevant to any responsible-party doctrine.

This becomes obvious when we ask what we really want to know about the functioning of a system that has any responsible-party aspirations at all. Party responsibility, and hence accountability, is not, after all, the ultimate goal of the doctrine. The whole infrastructure prescribed by it is motivated by the goal that the public will should be conveyed upward and faithfully enacted into policy, in a mode which represents an intense commitment to a mandate theory of representation. The Miller-Stokes paradigm, of course, is tailored to assess how well an operating system is approximating the mandate ideal. It certainly is not geared to evaluate in detail the means advocated by the particular doctrine of party responsibility. But its relevance for assessing the general success of any means aimed at the goal of mandate representation is self-evident.

It may be easy to lose sight of these facts because we often think of the model of party responsibility as starting with party programs proposed to the voters from on high. But those who proposed the doctrine imagined that increased party accountability would increase public participation in party organizations as party programs were being developed. This means, among other things, that even though the party militant must ultimately accept the discipline of a party-wide decision, there is positive encouragement to try to push that final decision more to the left or more to the right according to one's own convictions before the fact—and to do that by any means available, including not only persuasion but also votes cast for more rather than less congenial leadership within one's party. The whole process is to be intensely democratized, in order that a mandate conception may be maximized.

In short, then, the doctrine of party responsibility can be construed as a testable hypothesis which says that the more closely a system is tailored to its requirements, the greater the fidelity of popular representation in it will be.

Party Discipline and the
Fidelity of Representation

We cannot test an empirical proposition of this grandeur with the materials at hand, which derive from only one system seemingly weak on a number of requirements of the doctrine at issue. Ideally, we would want data from a number of systems, some closely approximating the ideal type and others very discrepant from it, in order to ask about the truth value of this proposition.

Nevertheless, our French case does permit us to ask a narrower question: that is, whether the kind of strict party discipline demanded by the system seems to facilitate or impede the fidelity of representation we observe in it. We are able to address this question mainly because the discipline in roll-call voting which we have noted, though very strong indeed, is still less than perfect, and we introduced a variant in our coding of roll-call votes so that we could capture this discrepancy clearly.

Our main coding of roll calls, as reviewed in Chapter 18, simply reflects in the obvious way the actual votes cast by the occupant of each district. But we also registered the summary scale score for the district seat that would have pertained had the representative always cast his vote according to the dictates of his party caucus. It is not often easy in social science to deal with the "counterfactual"; but in this case our "maverick-free" coding expresses the legislative contribution that would have been associated with the district had party discipline been not just *nearly* complete, but *absolutely* complete, and it does so with indisputable accuracy despite the counterfactual nature of the assessment. One useful way to ask about the impact of party discipline upon the level of congruence between district sentiments and representative votes in the parliament is to see whether such congruence is weaker (or stronger) in the real-life case of slight defection or in the hypothetical case of flawless discipline.

The theoretical reasoning underlying this test is quite clear. The very strictness of party discipline in the French system argues that departures therefrom occur only under the pressure of rather strong forces. The most obvious forces running contrary to occasional party dictates would seem to be personal conscience and concern for local district opinion. There is little reason to imagine that acts of resistance to party discipline based on conscience would serve to increase the fidelity of district representation, relative to what perfect party discipline would produce. But resistance based on concern for district opinion should have exactly this effect, given reasonably accurate deputy perceptions.

Could actual votes be *less* faithful on the whole to district opinion than votes based on perfect party discipline? Yes, this could happen as well, and we should probably interpret it as a triumph for advocates of the responsible-party model: it would suggest that erosions of discipline from whatever source would tend to weaken the links of accountability on which the public depends, and thereby would lower the fidelity of representation. These are, then, the theoretical stakes which underlie our test.

Before proceeding to the main results, we should consider one logical corollary of the existing high degree of party discipline in Assembly votes, namely, that the difference between scale scores assigned on the basis of votes actually cast and those assigned on the basis of perfect party discipline is bound to be rather slight in the National Assembly. In any system of looser party discipline, with representatives departing frequently from the modal votes of their caucuses, substantial discrepancies could open up between a pure party scaling and actual votes, although we still would be obliged to expect a substantial positive correlation between the two calculations. But in the French case, with less than half a dozen out of every hundred votes cast in the Assembly representing a departure from caucus position, it may be asked whether the difference between the actual scaling and the hypothetical party scaling leaves any margin for analytic maneuver at all.

The margin is, in fact, very slight. It is greater, however, than might appear at first glance, because, as we noted earlier, in forming our roll-call scales we avoided multiplying pure party votes because of their redundancy. This kind of selection away from pure party lines serves in a modest way to produce some "decorrelation" between the two scalings for a particular domain, and thus to enhance the signal left by such sparse defections as did occur. Nonetheless, these intrusions do not go very far to lower the correlations between the two versions of each roll-call vote scale, and this means that our analytic leverage remains precarious indeed.

Across a dozen policy domains, the lowest correlation between the two competing vote scalings for our full complement of deputies is $r = .87$, and the next lowest is .91. The median correlation is .97, and the values rise as high as .995. Fortunately, in view of the ponderous care officially given to the accurate registration of roll calls and the extreme steps we ourselves have taken to verify our manipulation of them, we can consider these competing scales to be essentially error-free, so that a difference between a correlation of 1.00 and one of .97 cannot be dismissed as mere measurement noise, not worth the effort to scrutinize. But we surely cannot expect that our congruence correlations, predicting differentially from district sentiment to two such highly correlated dependent variables, will be able to differ from each other by more than a trifling degree.

Reviewing our congruence correlations expressing the basic representation bond (the AD linkage of Table 19-5) in these two alternate forms, the general trend of the evidence is that *defections from party discipline serve to increase the congruence between district sentiment and representative roll-call votes.* The differences are very modest, as they are bound to be. Nonetheless, if we set aside cases in which the basic AD correlation is less than $r = .07$ (on the assumption that we should focus our attention where some significant representation is occurring), then we can compare results between the two variant roll-call scales in twelve policy domains. And for ten of these twelve domains, average correlations between district sentiment predictors and the scales for the actual roll calls containing normal defections run *higher* than the counterpart correlations where defections are artificially ruled out.[1] To look at the matter another way, some sixteen predictor variables figure in one or more congruence relationships that are large enough to be treated as significant. For thirteen of these sixteen predictors, average congruence correlations are higher for the actual votes than for the perfect-discipline versions of the scales.

Thus the indication is that the limited defections from caucus discipline that do occur in the Assembly tend to increase the level of alignment between district sentiment and roll-call outcomes, and hence, by our lights, they serve to increase the fidelity of popular representation. It is naturally tempting to suppose that if party discipline in the Assembly were substantially weaker, so that defections were two or three times as common as they actually are, the gains shown by our congruence correlations would be even more vigorous. Strictly speaking, however, we cannot proceed to such a conclusion, since it is always possible that although the level of defection which we have observed acts felicitously to optimize congruence relative to pure party voting, further increases in defections might simply begin to lower congruence again. Nevertheless, the logic of the situation permits us to explore the levels of representation that would take place in the counterfactual case of perfect party voting, and it seems that one major implication of the pressures toward strict party discipline in Assembly voting is to lower the level of congruence between constituent opinion and representative performance.

Parameters of the Composite Diamond

Although more prefatory remarks risk being tiresome, we are keenly aware that the data which we are about to present in diamond form suffer certain limitations and ambiguities that are best made clear in advance. One or two of these will be quite self-evident, but they are worth mentioning nonetheless. Others would be unclear to those without an appreciation of the extreme complexity of the data set.

One limitation which is obvious, though regrettable, is that we shall be dealing only with the "constituency" operationally defined as the total district, rather than with the subset of electoral supporters in the district. In Chapter 18 we found linkages between total-district sentiment and legislative roll calls which were quite pallid for most specific issues, although somewhat stronger when the predictor was left-right sentiment in the district. Many of these pallid specific-issue relationships sprang into vivid relief when in Chapter 19 we changed the definition of the constituency from the total district electorate to the victorious supporters. It would be interesting if we could look at our diamonds in both of these forms in this chapter. But we cannot, for the simple reason that, although we asked our elite informants about sentiments in their total districts, we did not ask them parallel questions concerning sentiments among their own supporters. We would need the latter data to estimate full diamond parameters.

There is nothing wrong, of course, in looking at diamonds based on total districts. Indeed, some would see this as desirable conceptually, and the most obvious points of comparison—the Miller-Stokes estimates for three issue domains in the United States in 1958—are in fact cast in this form. A problem arises only because our data are clearly weaker and more volatile in this form than in the "winner" version from Chapter 19, for reasons we can easily understand; and it would be useful to be able to present diamonds with both constituency definitions. Unfortunately, however, we cannot.

Some of the ambiguities about the diamond estimates we shall present arise because these estimates are "averages" which conceal more heterogeneity than we would like. This heterogeneity takes two major forms: one form exists across items within issue domains; and the other exists in time, especially between the two legislative sessions.

Item Heterogeneity in Diamond Estimates

In preparing their diamond estimates, Miller and Stokes first combined two or three specific issue items into a scale for a more general issue domain, and then they used this compound as a measure of district sentiment. After so doing, they found rather large discrepancies in the configuration of values between the domains of foreign issues, social welfare policy, and civil rights (Miller and Stokes, 1963). They do not indicate whether the domain-distinctive patterns would have been clear for individual items taken separately.

In Chapter 18, for simplicity, we also combined multiple items into compound scales wherever possible in arriving at estimates of the AD bond. We intend to follow the same strategy in this chapter, for otherwise we would be swamped with bewildering arrays of numbers. At several points in the chapters between Chapter 18 and this one, however, concern about the identical wording of items, mass and elite, have carried us back to some work with individual issue items. In so doing, we have become aware of how our diamonds would look if based on single items in a domain, as compared with how they look when district sentiment is calculated as a single compound scale representing the domain. As might be expected intuitively, the coefficients estimated with compound scales usually look like crude averages of the values indicated by the component items estimated separately. The problem is that despite common membership in the same issue domain, the diamond estimates based on different individual items are sometimes quite discrepant. This means in turn that the conclusions we might reach about representation processes in particular domains might be more dependent on the happenstance of item selection than we would like.

In Figure 22-1 we provide, for edification, one of our more garish examples of such heterogeneity, a comparison of two single items: our position issue and our importance (agenda) issue addressed to the church-state debate over the schools. (Although the two questions were "keyed" in opposite directions as the items were posed, they have been adjusted to a common direction for this and other figures.) The right-hand sides of the two diamonds are reasonably consonant, despite the fact that the "B" and "C" measures (deputy's own position and his perception of district position) are quite different from one panel to the other. But the rest of the estimates are grossly discrepant. Had we used the first (position) measure alone, we would have concluded that in the domain of church-state relations, there is at least a moderate, though less than striking, level of popular representation (the AD bond). Had we used the second (importance) measure alone, we would have concluded that there was no representation at all.

In this case, we have already arrived at some understanding of these discrepancies. In Chapter 20 we suggested the lively possibility that many of our elite informants would have liked to "cool down" the religious issue by according it secondary importance, despite the fact that it was "hot" for their constituents. Because of the visibility of religiosity in districts where it is important, the politician cannot deny position differences, and indeed his own attitude is more likely to be "pro-church" if he is from a devout district than if he is not. But the importance of the matter *as a political issue* can be

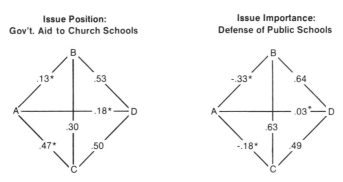

Figure 22-1. Two diamond estimates for the religious issue. Correlations (r) marked with an asterisk are corrected for small-sample attenuation.

subjected to denial and wishful thinking. We earlier presumed that the pressures toward denial simply increased as constituents accorded it more importance politically, thereby producing negative coefficients on the left side of the diamond and reducing signs of any faithful representation in the AD bond.

That we understand the discrepant profiles of Figure 22-1 does not, however, solve the underlying problem which such item heterogeneity poses if we wish to talk generally about the differences in the nature of representation from one policy domain to another. Miller and Stokes found major differences in diamond parameters *between* policy domains, and although they would not have found absolutely identical estimates for single-item components of their district sentiment scales *within* each domain, the implication has always been that within-domain variation in the estimates springing from specific item choice was modest relative to the stark between-domain variation. Such a pattern is much less clear for our French data. As we shall shortly see, there is some differentiation of parameters by domain, but it is more limited than in the American example, and within-domain heterogeneity risks competing with it in a number of the cases in which we have more than one relevant item. This leads to concern as to the robustness of our estimates of any domain-specific diamond parameters, especially when we have only a single-item measure available.

The remedy for this condition should flow from a proper diagnosis as to why the heterogeneity is occurring in the first place. One sensible generic hypothesis is that we are trying to combine specific measures of district sentiment that do not actually "belong together," despite self-evident membership in the same general policy domain. Indeed, the heterogeneous performances within the diamond paradigm may be taken as clear empirical proof that this is so.

This critique is easily pursued in the special case of the church-state debate items shown in Figure 22-1, where we are combining an item designed as a position issue with an item measuring agenda importance. The votes bound up in the roll-call scale (variable D) were *position* matters, not votes as to priority of consideration in an agenda sense. Hence, is it not reasonable that the district *position* shows some prediction to the roll-call outcomes, whereas the district sense of priority shows none at all?

This diagnosis is doubly appealing because throughout our work we have encountered signs that our agenda measures, however noble their intent, seem in practice to suffer some dilution in "true variance," relative to their position counterparts. Hence we might be better off to set aside the agenda measures entirely in our linkage work, even though this would limit us almost completely to single-item measures of district sentiment. We do not want to do this, however, unless we are sure that the diagnosis is accurate. Fortunately, if that diagnosis is apt, a number of corollaries should follow. The fact that none of these corollaries is confirmed leads us to doubt that item performance is heterogeneous within domains just because we are forcing together position items and measures of issue importance.

But let us examine some of these corollaries. Since all of our roll-call measures summarize disputes of position rather than agenda priority or importance, the most obvious corollary of the diagnosis would be that wherever we can pair a position item and an importance item in the same domain, the latter should have no apparent predictive value. Although this does occur in the church-state case, it does not occur in general. Where comparisons can be made, there may be slightly more life on the average in estimates using the position measures, as would be expected if there were some dilution in the agenda measures. But the difference is very limited, and the agenda item of a pair shows a higher correlation with the relevant roll call than the position item does, just about as often as the reverse is true, although the diagnosis implies that this should never happen.

Moreover, the diagnosis presumes that agenda importance in a domain is, from the point of view of the respondent, quite a different thing from substantive positions in the same domain. There is a real conceptual difference, of course, between these two matters, and now and again they may achieve some independence in practice. But much of the time there will be substantial overlap, as the church-state case makes clear. The position issue measures willingness to have the government subsidize parochial schools, and obviously taps an underlying clerical–anti-clerical dimension. The agenda version asks how important it is to defend the secular school system, typically meaning protecting it from intrusions by the church, including church claims on the education budgets of the state. It is hard to imagine that such an item fails to tap largely the same dimension.

Furthermore, the two sets of responses "go together" empirically. This is, as always, a matter of degree, for the compounding of specific items into sensible scales always depends on some evidence of internal consistency or covariation among the components. The problem is that the *degree* of covariation required to permit such compounding is less than obvious. We have already emphasized in Chapter 7 that none of the sets of responses to our various issue items is very tightly joined to any other set in the mass sample. Indeed, the intercorrelations are so low that some psychometric traditions might call into question the meaningfulness of any combination at all. Nevertheless, the crucial question is whether the correlations are low because of discrepant "true variance" or because of very low reliability of measurement. It is the former case which would argue against combination; under the latter circumstances the lower the correlations, the more urgent it is to drive out unreliability through item combination.[2]

Although interpretations of the details may vary, there is no doubt that observed correlations of the type we are dealing with in our mass sample are severely attenuated by a kind of measurement "noise" which surely behaves like unreliability. This being so, a particular premium is placed on doing as much item combination as makes substantive sense. This conclusion is reinforced in our case by the empirical awareness that whereas correlations among issue items are generally low for the mass sample, those between individual items in the same policy domain—usually but not always a position item and an agenda item—very typically run higher than the between-domain correlations.

To summarize this discussion, we have learned several lessons which have influenced the way in which we present our diamond data. For one thing, we shall indeed engage in item combinations. We also are so impressed with the degree of heterogeneity of results *within* policy domains, relative to that *between* policy domains, that we may feel it desirable to maximize our combinations in other ways, such as amassing all of our specific issues at once, regardless of domain, in order to get a very general impression as to the flow of representation in France. Miller and Stokes did not provide such a display, and properly so, for it was clear that the nature of representation depended mightily on the specific policy domain being assessed. In our case, however, the domain-specific variation is less marked; but within domains it seems to matter significantly what particular issue items have been selected for study. Under these circumstances, the best available hedge is not to overgeneralize from diamond parameters estimated for any single item, or even two- or three-item combinations, but rather to use all of our linkage issue items at once in some kind of combination. Although this still does not give us anything like a random sampling of the "issue universe" which pertained in France in the late 1960s, it does broaden the base of the estimates enormously, and it helps to clear away both domain and item-selection idiosyncrasies from the field of vision, in favor of a more general assessment.

Temporal Heterogeneity in Diamond Estimates

Our other source of heterogeneity arises because of the "seam" which events established in the middle of our study, dividing the legislative period into two different legislative sessions. Unfortunately, the transition from one legislative session to the other was not normal, but instead was marked by a rancorous dissolution of the chamber, ordered as a defensive reaction to a major national uprising, which itself was aimed at forcing French political elites to be more responsive to popular demands. Thus, although the first session (1967–68) occurred under "normal" conditions, during the second session inordinate pressures were being placed on the National Assembly to upgrade the speed and fidelity of its political representation.

For most purposes, as we have seen, it has been a great asset to have a "before-after" study of elite responsiveness under such dramatic circumstances. Surely we should use our data to examine the differences in the representation process as displayed in the two different sessions of the Assembly.

It turns out, however, that any such straightforward comparisons lie largely out of reach, at least for our data as presented in diamond form. In some small degree, this is because of the major disjuncture in the concerns addressed by the two legislative sessions. Much more centrally, the difficulty arises because the first of the two sessions was too brief to generate satisfying roll-call vote scales. Some of our vote scales (see Chapter 18) are based on data from the second session, and others mix parallel roll calls from both sessions. Almost none of the scales could be limited to the first session alone, for its voting record was too brief. It is ironic that most of our dependent variables, that is, the roll calls, come from the post-1968 period, whereas our independent variables, that is, our best measures of district sentiment, come from the pre-1968 "period" (1967). We did indeed reinterview constituents in 1968, after the crisis, and from these interviews we do have "after" measures of district sentiment, but we have them for only a little more than half of our districts. Hence, as we begin to assemble data to estimate any given diamond, we are torn between the temporal purity of using just "1968-only" district estimates and nearly doubling our data points by using 1967 information.[3]

Actually, there are more than just these two competing ways of estimating our diamond parameters, where temporal heterogeneity is concerned: 1967-only; 1968-only; and various defensible mixes both within and between the A and D terms. When these are crossed with the numerous options bound up in specific items and their various compounds, a large number of diamond variants can be constructed. Our strategy here has been to select from this embarrassment of riches, and our main rule has been to select the most "capacious" variant in any given policy-domain set. Capaciousness over items means, as we have seen, taking the maximum feasible compound scales, rather than specific items, to represent policy domains. Capaciousness in time means a kind of integration over the pre- and post-1968 periods. In this connection, we shall use our roll-call vote summaries as they are (heavily, but not exclusively, post-1968). Our measures of district sentiment will be drawn from the 1968 study for available districts, and from 1967 data otherwise.

Although this kind of integration over known temporal heterogeneity is not without its problems, we feel quite happy about it because before long we shall be able to address the key features of temporal heterogeneity directly. We shall not be able to look at separate diamond estimates for the two legislative sessions, but we can take another very satisfying route toward answering the question as to the impact of the 1968 disturbances on the nature of popular representation in France. At that point a judgment can be made as to the importance of the temporal change which our initial treatment will ignore.

Inconstancy of Bond Estimates

We have already displayed a number of individual bonds (AD in Chapter 18; AB in Chapter 19; and AC and BC in Chapter 20), and these will now become components in more complete diamonds. The coefficients presented earlier do not, however, agree exactly with their apparent counterparts in our displays here. Although the numerical discrepancies are usually minor, in a handful of instances they are quite blatant. These discrepancies are legitimate, but we should explain why.

Because the greatest discrepancies arise in connection with the AD bond, we shall simplify the discussion by focusing upon these. Comparisons may be drawn between the entries in the "Specific Issue" column of Table 18-5 and the same AD bonds in our fuller diamond representations in the remainder of this chapter. When we say that substantively parallel entries (between district sentiment in issue domain X and roll-call votes in that domain) are not identical in the two renditions, we do not mean that there is no connection whatever between parallel entries. In fact, for the most obvious set of some thirteen comparisons available, there is a correlation of $r = .88$ between the entries in Table 18-5 and their counterparts within the fuller diamonds. Yet it remains true that in none of the thirteen cases are the coefficients exactly the same, and in one case—the domain of foreign aid—the sign of the coefficient is actually reversed.

It is important to know whether these discrepancies are mere methodological artifacts or whether they have a theoretical rationale. Actually, there is room for methodological instability, because the estimates of Table 18-5 and those to be presented here are calculated on overlapping but detectably different data bases. For Table 18-5 we were able to use data from all 86 districts in our sample, rather than from just the subset of 66 districts in which we interviewed deputies. Our full diamonds must retreat to the 66 districts as a base for estimate, because two of the terms in the diamond—term "B" (deputy's own position) and term "C" (deputy's perception of district position)—are drawn from the elite interviews and are not known for the districts lacking such interviews. Since elite interviews are not needed for the calculation of the AD bond, there was little point, in Chapter 18, in not using our full complement of 86 districts.

Thus, on purely methodological grounds we would not expect estimates of the AD bond to coincide exactly for the 86- and 66-district cases. But they should not differ by more than a margin of sampling error that is unusually limited in size, because the 66 districts are in fact a proper subset of the 86 districts. We find no reasons to believe that they do differ by more than this small margin *on methodological grounds alone.*

They do differ, however, by somewhat more than this small margin, and for other reasons which are conceptual and easily understood. In Chapter 18 we wanted to know whether roll-call outcomes in the National Assembly were congruent, district by district, with variations in public opinion in the jurisdictions being "represented" by these roll calls. In effect, we were asking about the correlations linking district sentiment with legislative outputs of the district's lawful seat in the Assembly, without paying any attention to the individuals who might be occupying the seat at various times during the period of assessment. Our diamonds, however, focus upon the way in which specific individuals serving as elected representatives meld their own convictions and perceptions of district cues as acceptable influences on their legislative decisionmaking. For these purposes, we cannot confuse the vote contributions of different individuals, even though they may be representing the same district seat in the Assembly at different times.

In many studies of representation this issue does not arise, because the field of view is a single legislative session in which there is an identical mapping (except for mid-session deaths and retirements) between a list of seats and a list of individual representatives. But we have two sessions, and they were interrupted by an upheaval which shifted a substantial number of seats from left-wing to right-wing occupants. Indeed, the most striking discrepancy between the estimates of the AD bond in Chapter 18 and in the displays that follow did not arise primarily because of the differences between the 86- and 66-district estimates of exactly the same quantum, but because of the turnover in personnel. A change so gross as the change of sign for the AD bond involved in the domain of foreign aid occurred in this instance because foreign aid was the sole policy domain in which all of the relevant roll calls were cast in the first (the 1967–68) session. When the unit is the district seat, this time limitation becomes irrelevant, and such 1967–68 roll calls have been attributed to the districts involved even if they changed representatives in 1968. But when we traced the roles being played by individual representatives, we could not attribute to them the legislative votes cast entirely by other persons, who were usually their political opponents in the local district. This meant that, for foreign aid in particular, more than a quarter of the roll-call variable used in the 86-district "seat" formulation was wiped clean in recalculating the diamonds, leaving room for major displacements of estimate. The important point is that these displacements, although perhaps aesthetically annoying, are conceptually legitimate and, indeed, imperative, because the questions we are now asking, although they may appear to be the same as those asked in Chapter 18, are in fact distinguishable from them and therefore deserve to have distinctive answers.

The Completed Diamonds

We shall find it useful, in addressing our full diamonds, to focus upon summary diamonds averaging across all of the dozen or more policy domains. This is rather heterodox, relative to the Miller-Stokes treatment. But we have seen that these authors did not attempt such summaries because the major message of their data was that representation parameters varied dramatically from one policy domain to another. In the French case also there is some differentiation in parameters across policy domains; however, it is somewhat muted and is subject to rather lively within-domain variation as well. Therefore it is not unreasonable to average across our set of nearly a dozen domain-specific diamonds in order to establish a very gross, general picture of the French representation configuration. We shall do a certain amount of decomposition of this general picture by more specific issue domains in the next chapter.

We shall proceed in this fashion for another reason as well. If our French data fail to show the same crystalline and reliable contrasts in representation parameters from one policy domain to another that Miller and Stokes found for the United States, this does not mean that we lack a reliable watershed in our configurations of diamond estimates. Such a watershed exists, but it is of a different order. The contrasts are due to our need to decide whether to use the specific-issue attitudes or the "super-issue" of left-right location as the "carrier," or tracer, of the representation process. This should come as no surprise, for Table 18-5 made it clear that the left-right coloration of districts is repeatedly a better predictor of roll-call votes cast in behalf of the district than is district sentiment on the specific policies characterizing a domain, ironic though that may seem.

Just as we can erect a series of domain-specific diamond estimates where (a) district sentiment, (b) deputy position, and (c) deputy perception of district position are all addressed to a specific policy area, like income distribution or European integration, so also we can erect a second series of estimates where roll-call summaries vary as before from one domain to another, but where the earlier terms of the model refer to left-right measurements. Thus, district sentiment (term A) is based on the district mean for citizen left-right locations; deputy position (term B) is the deputy's chosen position on the left-right scale; and term C is his perception of the left-right coloration of his district. We speak here of a "series" of such estimates, and indeed we shall deal with thirteen diamonds assembled in this left-right form. It should, however, be emphasized that three terms of the four forming the diamond are constant across the set of thirteen, which means that only three of the six crucial coefficients in the diamond estimates are "free to vary" while the rest are constant. This stands in contrast to the issue-specific series, where all four diamond terms are fresh for each domain.

Figure 22-2 presents two summary diamonds. One, panel (a), shows simple averages of estimates over nine specific-issue diamonds; the other, panel (b), averages parallel estimates drawn from left-right diamonds which refer in turn to each of thirteen different roll-call vote summaries.[4] We have added to each coefficient a statement of standard deviation, in order to give some sense of the variation which the averages conceal. In the left-right diamond, three of these estimates (AB, AC, and BC) do not vary, for the reasons given in the preceding paragraph.

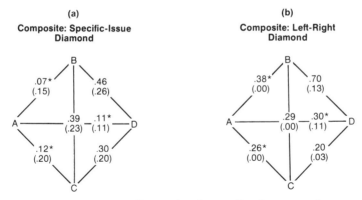

Figure 22-2. Composite diamond estimates for the composite representation process. Main entries along each bond are average correlation coefficients over matrices described in the text. Subordinate entries in parentheses are standard deviations for these averages. Correlations (r) marked with an asterisk are corrected for small-sample attenuation.

It can be seen at a glance that these two composite diamonds reflect rather different views of the broader representation process, with virtually no agreement on any of the separate bonds; and although each panel of the figure involves averages that conceal a certain amount of variation, many of the parallel bonds seem to have distributions that display restricted overlap. Finally, of course, the overall configurations of highs and lows in the two diagrams are dramatically different.

We have some understanding of the discrepancies between the left sides of these diamonds from our work in earlier chapters. Relative to panel (a), judgments about district sentiments on specific issues, the perceptions of left-right district coloration shown in panel (b) are heavily constrained by reality. Here the estimates are not only factually more accurate (higher AC bond), but are less colored by the deputy's own position (lower BC bond). In addition, the deputy is also much more like his district (higher AB bond), seemingly because elections winnow along left-right lines much more clearly than they do along lines of more specific issues, many of which have very limited redundancy in their alignments.

The new elements are the coefficients on the right side of each diamond, specifically the values of the BD and CD bonds. These bonds occupy a good deal of attention in the Miller-Stokes treatment. They are of interest from two theoretical points of view, neither of which pretends that there are not other major influences on the deputy's roll-call decisions, or requires that the two terms of deputy opinion and perception of district opinion be "uncaused" prime movers in the representation process. First, we may ask how much variation in roll-call voting can be jointly accounted for by these terms as measured. It can then be presumed that the remainder of the variation not accounted for is a statement of a maximum possible effect due to "other factors," independent of either deputy position or perceived district position. Second, we can ask what the relative importance of these two terms taken alone may be. This answer is of interest because it addresses the mandate-independence controversy in the most direct way. In an ideally functioning mandate system, the CD bond will account for whatever variance in roll-call vote either of the two diamond terms will account for, and any observed positive BD correlation will only arise spuriously, due to background BC links. In an ideally functioning independence system, however, the same central role of the two competitors (other factors aside) will be played along the BD bond, with any positive observed CD correlation being in the same sense "merely accidental."

As we can deduce from Figure 22-2, the answers to the first question vary according to the particular panel we inspect. The multiple correlation predicting roll-call vote from the two left-right terms (B, C) in panel (b) is +.70, whereas it is a mere +.48 for the specific-issue composite of panel (a). The first value compares reasonably with the parallel Miller-Stokes numbers for the United States, which were +.56 for the foreign-involvement domain, +.67 for social welfare, and +.86 for civil rights (Miller and Stokes, 1963). Thus, although there is rather stark differentiation by domain in the American case, the averages in our left-right panel are very close to the relevant average figured across the very disparate U.S. policy domains, which is likewise +.70. But the actual average which would provide a better conceptual correspondence—based on specific policy domains like those of the Miller-Stokes study—is a good deal lower.

Our first substantive conclusion is that "other factors" that bear on roll-call voting, yet are independent of the deputy's own position or of his perceptions of his district views, are in principle not grossly different in their overall impact in France and the United States, despite the French system of tighter party discipline. This conclusion, however, is not obvious *except as we recognize the potency of the left-right super-issue as a conveyor belt or transmission device across the whole spectrum of national policy disputes.* If we (like Miller and Stokes) had had nothing to work with save the specific issue measures, we might have concluded that "other factors" were much more violently intrusive in the French setting than in the American one. Had this been the case, moreover, it would have been easy to say just what these "other factors" were. Because party discipline is vastly more intrusive in the French case than in the American one, it would have been easy to conclude that it was at the center of the vague cluster of "other factors."

Happily, we need not make this error, because Figure 22-2 shows that once we hinge our understanding of the French representation process on the left-right measurements, there is no apparent difference between the representation systems of the two countries in regard to the "room" which is left over because of "other factors." However different these countries may be in many political particulars, the weight of the "other factors," independent of deputy's view and perception of district position in the general process of representation, is not one of them. Nevertheless, this judgment should not obscure the fact that if we work with measures from more specific policy domains, there is a considerable weakening of apparent representation. It is worth trying to get this kind of dilution into theoretical perspective.

It is obvious from a cursory inspection of the figure that the link between the deputy's own position and roll-call votes is mainly responsible for producing some semblance of representation in both panels. It is also obvious (particularly if we square the coefficients involved) that the major collapse in this link as we move from panel (b) to panel (a) is primarily responsible for the rather weak level of representation in the specific-issue diamond. What does this collapse mean substantively? Because the roll-call votes (term D) are packaged rather tightly by party, the difference in coefficients suggests that parties may be internally more homogeneous in regard to the left-right self-locations of their political leaders than in regard to the more specific issue positions of those leaders.

This is an interesting hypothesis in its own right, and it can be directly checked within our data. The operative question is the degree to which variation in the issue or the left-right positions of our deputies is accounted for simply by their party affiliation. The most useful statistic for this assessment is once again eta. Indeed, just as we showed earlier that the etas indexing maldistribution of issue positions from one legislative district to another are crucial barometers of the nature of representation that can occur from a mass perspective, so we can also show that *in a legislative system of high party discipline* the *etas* indicating the partisan heterogeneity of personal policy convictions will have a great effect on the size of the BD bond, and (other things being equal) on the fidelity of the AD bond as well.

Table 22-2 lays out these measurements, as they vary across the left-right locations and the specific-issue measurements contributing to the composite diamond in Figure 22-2. We have reason to be stunned at the dramatic variation evident here: at one extreme (the force de frappe), party location accounts for more than four-fifths (82 percent) of the variance in personal positions reported by our deputies, whereas for the issue of income distribution the corresponding value is only one-twentieth (5 percent).[5]

Closer examination suggests that homogeneity within the elites of the diverse French parties does indeed tend to be greater with respect to left-right self-locations than with respect to personal convictions on more specific issues. The pattern is not perfect: the left-right measure is not the highest but the second highest of the nine calculated. But it seems unlikely that its very high eta (.85) is accidental; and we can say that whereas party affiliations "account for" nearly three-quarters of the variance in these left-

Table 22-2. Variation in party heterogeneity of deputy policy positions, by issue position and left-right self-location.

Position	Number of items	Eta by party caucus
Specific issues		
Importance of government stability	(1)	.35
Church-school sum	(2)	.73
Income distribution sum	(2)	.22
Socioeconomic left-right sum	(3)	.32
Union rights sum	(2)	.56
European integration index	(5)	.78
Force de frappe	(1)	.91
Foreign aid	(1)	.30
Left-right self-locations	(1)	.85

right assignments, they account for less than one-third of such variance in positions within the "typical" (mean or median) specific-issue domain. And it is worth remembering that this strong ratio of "cleavage between parties" to "homogeneity within parties" is occurring on the left-right measure despite the tendency among these elites to crowd themselves toward the left in reporting their locations.

We can generalize the current argument further through the proposition that, in a legislative system featuring extreme party discipline in roll-call voting, the absolute magnitude of the BD bond will co-vary with the degree of party homogeneity in deputy convictions from one issue domain to the next. Indeed, we find that when our diamonds are disaggregated by issue domain, the etas of Table 22-2 "predict" variations in the sizes of the relevant BD bond at a very high level ($r = .947$). Of course, such a prediction remains absolutely contingent on the presence of party discipline in roll calls: lacking such discipline, there would be no special reason to expect any particular fit between party homogeneity in deputy convictions and the BD bond. Furthermore, we have not really "explained" the variations in the BD bond with the discovery of this relationship, since it merely pushes the theoretical question back to the circumstances under which party groupings will be more or less homogeneous in their issue positions.

Nonetheless, these observations do give us a better grasp of the logic governing the BD bond in a system of high party discipline, and as we return to the differences between the two composite diamonds of panels (a) and (b) of Figure 22-2, it is helpful to know that some of the discrepancy on the right side of these diamonds is in fact associated with weaker party differentiation on most of the specific issues.

Within both panels of Figure 22-2, the BD bond outweighs its CD counterpart. The imbalance, however, is much greater in the left-right diamond than in the specific-issue diamond. In fact, in the first diamond the CD bond is unusual in being absolutely greater, and by a significant margin, than the CD bond in the second diamond. The contrast is sharpened further if we remove the effects of the deputies' own positions before comparing the CD bonds in the two panels. In the left-right diamond, this partial correlation (CD·B) essentially vanishes, falling below .01, but for the specific-issue diamond it remains at +.15.

This is a satisfying result. Although in general the measures of left-right location seem to produce a more impressive level of congruence between district sentiment and ultimate roll-call votes (the AD bond), the transmission is primarily through election of ideologically appropriate deputies (term B), who, by displaying high intraparty homogeneity in left-right terms and high party discipline, create the conditions for such congruence. This pattern leans heavily toward the independence model of representation.

Yet when we turn to model measurements involving more specific issues, the conditions ensuring high AD congruence in the left-right diamond tend to erode. Deputies' convictions no longer fit so closely with district opinion, and although party discipline continues to hold sway, these personal opinions are seldom so neatly matched from one militant to another within the several parties. The erosion of these conditions does make vast inroads on the overall level of congruence observed in panel (a); but a little support arises in the lower half of the diamond in the stronger CD bond, a matter which is important because we are talking here of more specific issues.

This support does much less for the basic AD representation bond than it otherwise would because the deputies, who are not wholly accurate in their perceptions of district opinion on these more specific issues, engage in a fair amount of projection of their own opinions into the process, as we saw in Chapter 20. But the data do suggest that even in the highly disciplined atmosphere of the National Assembly, some whisper of representation according to a mandate or instructed-delegate model does occur, with deputies voting at the margin in limited accord with their views of district sentiment on specific issues.[6] And though this admixture is obviously weak, its detection does repay us for our pains in measuring citizen and deputy positions on more specific issues.

Another worthwhile question to be asked of our composite diamonds in Figure 22-2 requires us to treat them still more holistically. Is it possible to decompose the basic representation bond (AD) completely into contributions from either the deputy's own view (B) or his perception of district opinion (C)? Or does this system of relationships leave some of the AD congruence "unexplained" by these intervening variables, forcing us to concede that other, unmeasured terms must be making some further positive contribution to the observed levels of basic representation?

If we look first at the specific-issue diamond (panel a), we find that a visible AD bond would remain even after controlling away the effects associated with terms B or C (that is, $r_{AD \bullet BC} = +.07$). This indicates rather clearly that some unmeasured term or terms exist which are important in sustaining the basic representation bond even at the limited level we can observe with these issues. In view of everything else we know about the data, we are naturally led to suspect that an excellent candidate for this unmeasured variable might be the left-right self-locations of citizens and representatives.

If we turn again to panel (b), we discover that here, also, knowledge of district left-right locations (A) gives us a little more predictive leverage on the roll-call vote patterns—once the effects of the intervening left-right terms B and C are recognized—although slightly less than for panel (a), as though the unmeasured information is a bit less potent ($r_{AD \bullet BC} = +.05$). As before, we know that there are still unmeasured terms, this time of the kind involved in the specific issues relevant to particular roll calls. In short, although we are dealing here with artificial composite diamonds that do not invite overly precise numerical manipulation, we come away with an informal sense that once we have taken account jointly of the left-right super-issue and the more specific issues matched to each roll-call dimension, we would, in the average case, have achieved a fairly complete decomposition of these relationships. We would expect district sentiment to predict no more than negligibly to the relevant roll-call vote (if at all) on either left-right location or the specific-issue domain, after deputy positions and district perceptions within the specific-issue domain and on the left-right dimension had been taken into account.

We should emphasize that it is necessary to maintain a sense of perspective in considering the materials we have just presented. It is true that some modest utility can be discerned in our measurements of specific issues where the tracing of lines of popular representation is concerned. It is also true that there are signs, although muted ones, that our deputies take some cognizance of district opinion, or at least of what they think is district opinion, on these more specific-issue domains when they participate in roll-call voting. But neither of these truths should detract from the much stronger patterns in these composite diamonds when left-right positions are at stake, or from the fact that the apparent flows of influence in the diamond configuration suggest an independent trusteeship rather than a mandated-delegate type of representation.

Conclusions

We have carried this pair of contrasting composite diamonds about as far as is warranted in view of their unusually synthetic nature. They have been useful in providing a general view of the flow of the representation process in the National Assembly, at least as reflected in the diamond model. They have also helped us understand in some degree what we capture in that process when left-right measurements are used, as opposed to the more conventional measures made within specific-issue domains.

In arriving at conclusions, it is important to keep in mind that the data in our full diamonds take the "constituency" to be the total adult citizenry of a district, rather than the subset of those victorious supporters that some theories of democratic process would see as the only sensible definition of "constituency." But within the terms of this capacious definition, it is clear that the full diamonds show representation patterns that lie closer to the trustee than to the mandated-delegate pole.

The casual critic will not be surprised at this result, and indeed is likely to ask why it is necessary to mount a very large study in order to discover that in a legislative system with the high party discipline characteristic of the French National Assembly, the concern of deputies for opinion in their districts is limited and secondary. But analysis at this level is so casual as to miss the point. For one thing, it is glib to presume that a system of pure trusteeship or "conscience" voting and a system of high party discipline are more or less the same thing. In fact, once exposed, this equation seems quite questionable. We might bring the two sides of the equation into line by adding an ambitious series of further social, psychological, and political assumptions. But we would not take such steps implicitly, without considerable reflection.

At the same time, we can be equally casual in a different direction. We can say that party discipline must come first, even before local constituencies, if we are to have a system which is "accountable" to its members. This is a defensible proposition, of course, within the terms of a responsible-party model of representation. And if our discussion at the outset of this chapter has any merit, then we do not seek party accountability as an end in itself, but rather as a means to promote another more basic end which is very democratic: we seek a system of representation which is maximally responsive to the preferences of the governed. This point of view turns, therefore, on a distinctly delegate view of representation; and if we follow it to its logical conclusion, it is very doubtful that a system of such high discipline and hence "accountability" would show such weak traces of mandated flow across the composite diamonds.

However this may be, we are well aware that these diamonds are made up of gross averages which conceal a great deal of empirical variation. Some of this variation has important substantive meaning, while other parts of it present a troubling mix of substance and measurement artifact. The character of this variation will be considered in the next chapter.

23

—◆•◆—

Conditional Variations
in Representation

I n the last chapter we listed a group of questions about representation
which we planned to address before concluding Part IV. We have already approached some of the more holistic of these, such as the nature
of the fit between party discipline and the doctrine of party responsibility,
and the impact of party discipline on the flows of influence that we have
observed in our diamond paradigm—the pair of "synthetic diamonds" that
summarized broadly across all of our linkage issues.

A number of other questions remain, however, and they are very diverse in their substantive thrust. We have yet to examine the way in which
the representation patterns vary by issue domain. We shall also decompose
our data in a manner which permits us to view the temporal variation in the
character of representation, with primary emphasis on the impact of the uprisings of May and June 1968 upon the nature of popular representation
being provided by the National Assembly. Further questions will have to do
with the different ways in which deputies, through their conceptions of
their representative role, or through their varying relationships to their constituencies, may act to sharpen or dull the observed levels of fidelity in representation.

All of these questions deal with variation in representation due to differences in "conditions," whether these be issue domains or temporal periods or deputy composition. The basic emphasis will be placed on differences
in the fidelity of representation, which we shall continue to measure as the
degree of congruence reflected in the basic representation bond (AD). From
time to time, however, our theoretical concerns will be most clearly illu-

minated if we examine conditional variation more broadly across the relevant diamonds.

In this chapter, therefore, we shall proceed seriatim through diverse sources of potential variation, in sections that amount to minichapters. The first two of these will develop further the twin themes of item and temporal heterogeneity.

Variation by Issue Domain

As we have noted frequently, one of the main sources of the systematic variation in representation parameters revealed for the U.S. House of Representatives by the Miller-Stokes study (1963) was differences in issue domains. These results were as pleasing intuitively as they were clear-cut empirically. Fidelity of representation was weakest for the one issue domain out of three which referred to foreign rather than domestic matters. This seemed plausible: in that domain the items were remote from daily life, special expertise was required to evaluate policy options, and substantial portions of the relevant "intelligence" were classified. Little wonder then that representatives would give only limited attention to whatever they might divine of district opinion on such matters, preferring to keep them in their own hands. Domestic issues are, by definition, "closer to home," with almost everyone posing as an expert on policy effects. For these issues a further differentiation was reflected in the Miller-Stokes data: the fidelity of representation was higher on civil-rights issues involving racial cleavages than on social welfare policy. Once again, this seems plausible. Although ethnic antagonisms may be at the least inelegant and at the most frightening, it is easy to understand why grass-roots politicians, shrewdly assessing the power and fury of such prejudices, may find it necessary to suspend private judgment and merely make sure not to get on the wrong side of the home district.

The intuitive approach led us to expect a similar hierarchy to emerge within our French data. Our linkage issues contained a reasonable mix of both foreign and domestic issues. And although racial issues were not prominent in the French case, there was reason to suppose that the religious axis separating devout Catholics from persons of anticlerical feeling might represent a rough approach to the kind of pervasive intergroup hostility that is touched off by racial or ethnic differences in other countries.

Yet, as we have already indicated, that variation in representation across issue domains seems much less robust and less intelligibly patterned in our data than in the American data. In the first place, we have pointed out the heterogeneity in results dealing with separate issue items inside a given domain, using the religious domain, with state subsidies to church schools as an illustration (see Chapter 22).

More important, even in the case of the several major issue domains with the indices, we have not been impressed by any obvious *systematic* differences by type of issue between the levels of congruence represented (the AD basic bond). That is not to say that differences do not exist: they do, and they are rather large at certain points; but they defy any simple explanation. For example, fidelity of representation is not obviously higher for domestic than for foreign issues. The only obvious watershed in these results is the one which we examined closely in the last chapter: the dividing line between congruence assessed through specific issues and that measured by left-right locations.

In a general way, these comparisons showed higher representation bonds in the left-right than in the specific-issue diamonds. After reaching some understanding of this fact, we went on to suppose that when levels of representation tended to differ in the two currencies, they would also differ in a parallel way from one issue domain to another. Thus, if a specific issue showed high congruence relative to other issues in a left-right assessment context, that issue would also run absolutely lower, though still *relatively* higher, in the context of a specific-issue diamond assessment.

To add to the confusion, we did not find this kind of parallelism for different types of issues across the two modes of assessment. Instead, we came away with discordant impressions about the fidelity of representation according to whether we predicted roll-call votes through the left-right or the specific-issue diamonds. Indeed, over some nine issue domains which invited comparison, the correlation between the AD bond estimates turned out to be quite sharply negative ($r = -.41$). Furthermore, although any correlation hinged on a mere nine pairs of values is obviously unstable, it is quite possible that this negative correlation is meaningful in terms of our discussion of the two synthetic diamonds in the preceding chapter. In other words, it may be that there is a sort of compensation phenomenon going on: some issues are achieving high AD values because they are closely bound up with left-right differences and have high intraparty homogeneity as a corollary, whereas other issues, which lack these attributes and do not show up well in the left-right diamond, are "rescued" by tighter if more issue-specific bonds in the lower half of the diamond.

If we try to force some order on this cacophony by asking if there are a few issues about which both methods give convergent results, two or three do emerge. The most noteworthy is the force de frappe, which shows a relatively high AD bond whether we work from the left-right coloration of the district or from district sentiment on the issue itself.[1] There is no clear "loser" to match this "winner" at any great extremity, though if we had to pick a single issue on which the combined verdicts of the two methods suggested a weak AD bond, we would choose the domain of European integration. And these outcomes merely underscore the absence of a watershed between the foreign and domestic issues, since the high-fidelity and low-fidelity items are both classed among our foreign issues.

It can always be argued that "foreign issues" in the United States are much more remote from the citizen's own doorstep than they are in a country with the geopolitical situation of France. The foreign-issue domain in the Miller-Stokes study basically concerned the level of U.S. involvement around the world, and it ran from an internationalist pole to an isolationist one. The specific issues within the domain all involved some kind of commitment of U.S. resources, a fact that has one very clear "close to home" effect, namely, a demand of some magnitude on citizen taxpayers. Except for this implication, however, the foreign affairs arena is utterly remote, involving activity that takes place oceans away from home.

What we have coded as "foreign issues" for France, the argument would continue, are much more proximate. Participation in European integration would be, for example, a rather intimate question. Thinking about the more specific indicators, we find we are dealing with such charged domestic issues as the proper prices of products of the French dairy industry, or the question whether the French worker must risk competition with "guest workers," or whether sons conscripted into the Army must serve under officers of the neighboring power with whom hostilities have continued for several centuries. The closest parallel to the American issue of internationalism versus isolationism is the French item on foreign aid. But even here, the wording of the pivotal question on the mass side pitted foreign aid as such against more support for economically backward regions of France. No embellishment could have been better calculated to inject a prominent domestic flavor into what was otherwise a suitably "remote" foreign issue.

In short, it can be argued that we fail to find relatively weak levels of representation for "foreign" issues in the French setting because the referents are not so remote as their seeming parallels in the United States. Whether this substantive possibility is worth serious consideration or is merely a feeble attempt at a post hoc rationalization of some confusing results cannot be resolved here. It is worth noting, however, that in working with our linkage issues in Chapter 7 we expected manifest constraint and presumably internal organization to be weaker for the "foreign" issues than for the domestic ones, and aside from the force de frappe item, this expectation was upheld.

Even though we failed to find the watershed we expected when we divided our issue domains into domestic and foreign types, we did find some of the expected patterns within the set of domestic issues, although these were less than striking. We had anticipated that the religious issue might rank ahead of the other domestic issues in fidelity of representation, and for almost the same reason that the racial issue stood out in the Miller-Stokes study: well-informed politicians know that these issues are all-important to constituents, and that they as representatives must keep the peace on these matters with the home district, despite their own convictions.

It is reassuring, then, to discover that any reasonable combination of

estimates of the AD bond using both left-right predictors and district sentiment on specific church-school issues does show levels of representation
which are higher than those for any other domestic issue. Admittedly, this
advantage shown by the religious dimension is quite unimpressive, but it
exists in an absolute sense despite the fact that we are dealing here with the
two-item measure; and, as we saw in Chapter 22, the inclusion of the agenda
version of the religious issue considerably dulls most component relationships, including the AD bond. Therefore, if we were to deal with the most
defensible version of a simpler measure, the position item on church schools
taken alone, the level of representation would stand well above that for all
the other issues except the force de frappe. We are inclined to regard this
difference as meaningful, since we expected it long before we viewed the
data.

Nevertheless, this is at best a meager triumph, and it does not obscure
the fact that in our French data the variation in levels of representation
from one issue domain to another both is limited in magnitude and largely
lacks an obvious pattern, at least relative to the clarity of the Miller-Stokes
study. If there were no other vantage point from which our issue domains
seemed to perform in intuitively pleasing fashion, we might be tempted to
doubt the basic soundness of the measurement operations themselves; however, we are about to see that, in some contexts, differentiation in the nature
of measurement from one issue domain to another does appear to be highly
meaningful.

Impact of the 1968 Revolt on Popular Representation

When major segments of the French population rose up in wrath in the
spring of 1968 to proclaim violently that the national political elites of the
period were flagrantly unresponsive to popular policy demands, the two
segments most active in the revolt were (1) the university students, who
had been ignored for some time in their demands for much greater budgetary attention to higher education in the country, as well as for wide-rang-
ing structural reforms in the national university system; and (2) the
workers in large factories, who had also for some time been demanding a
larger role for their unions in the management of their industries.

Since elite unresponsiveness to popular wishes is the antithesis of the
kind of political representation our study was designed to examine, the
eruption of these dramatic events very soon after our first measurements had
been completed was in some ways regrettable, but in other ways it was fortuitous. The rebellion was regrettable because its very target—elite responsiveness—was central to our measurements. If we had been successful in
measuring that responsiveness, then the unexpected sequence of events

would have displaced those measurements to one side or the other in a variety of troubling ways. Among the lesser of these was the distressing fact that the deputies in the National Assembly, whom we had sampled and interviewed, had been precipitously thrown out, or at least subjected on very short notice to the gauntlet of a new election. The rebellion was fortuitous because it presented us with a very rare opportunity. It has long been recognized that the study by social scientists of the impact of dramatic but unexpected events has been greatly hindered because measurements taken in the wake of such events cannot be compared with comparable measurements made before the event. Thus, although the sudden intrusion of the 1968 revolt was bound to disrupt and confound our study, it also dropped into our laps the opportunity to produce a "before-after" study of a significant historical event.

We have already made some examination of our cross-time data at both the mass and elite levels, taken separately, in response to the events of May and June 1968 (see Part III). As yet, however, we have not examined the impact of these events on our most crucial "tracers," our numerous indicators of mass-elite representation linkages. If our measurements were at all successful, we would expect to find some rather lively changes in the configuration of representation parameters as a result of the revolt. And indeed, we warned the reader in the last chapter that lurking beneath the surface of the data was a good deal of temporal variation between the two sessions of the National Assembly, variation which for the moment we were going to sweep under the rug, but which we would return to later.

An ideal "before-after" study would have postponed the actual revolt until the middle of the five-year term of the Assembly for which deputies were supposedly elected in 1967. A revolt in 1970, for example, would have provided three years' worth of roll-call votes before dissolution, instead of the meager crop produced in less than one year. As it is, we lack any adequate roll-call record on central issues, as it might have stood in "normal" times, that is, before the revolt. We do have perfectly good measurements of popular attitudes on public policy disputes, and elite views of the same disputes and of their responsibilities as representatives, as they stood well before the revolt erupted. In fact, these are our most capacious measurements.

Because history did not provide much of a roll-call record before the Assembly was dissolved in the spring of 1968, we cannot draw neat comparisons between our representation diamonds in a given issue domain that are based on "before" measurements and parallel diamonds measured "after" the dramatic events. Fortunately, however, we have maintained some clear markers along the way so that we can sort out the effects of temporal variation, even if a neat confrontation of full "before" and "after" diamonds is not possible. Because these markers are of two different kinds, they result in two different analyses. Happily, the results converge in satisfying fashion, despite their quasi-independent origins.

Prediction from Post-Revolt District Sentiment

Up to now we have used our measures of pre-revolt district sentiment to predict to roll-call measures which are close to 80 percent post-revolt in their provenance. We have done so because our 1967 district measurements are drawn from nearly twice as many districts as those for 1968; and furthermore, within the fewer 1968 districts we have a lower average number of individuals, due to normal panel attrition. Our 1967 district data are therefore more robust, and by a substantial margin. But there is no reason why we should not examine a prediction to post-revolt roll calls from *1968* (hence, post-revolt) district positions. Obviously, the revolt brought some definite changes in district sentiments. A few of these changes may have been more absolute than relative, so that although the whole portfolio of districts moved some absolute distance in a common direction, relative district positions were preserved. But most of these changes—for various theoretically pregnant reasons, including the facts adduced in Chapter 14 showing that some districts were "hot" and others were not—resulted in a significant shuffling of relative positions as well, in a way that should affect our assessment of relative congruence between district position and ultimate roll-call behavior.

Let us suppose, then, that we want to compare the predictions we have already shown from 1967 district data to (largely) post-revolt roll-call votes with the predictions from 1968 data to the same roll calls, on the ground that these latter versions of district opinion are temporally more appropriate, even if they rest on fewer observations. What intuitive expectations would we bring to such new comparisons? Approaching the matter simply, we might expect that the observed levels of representation fidelity (the AD bond) would be much stronger when predicted from 1968 data than from 1967 data. In part, this expectation comes close to being a mere "technical adjustment": the 1968 or "post-revolt" sentiments are indeed more temporally appropriate, and hence should generate stronger relationships with post-revolt legislative behavior. But this relatively technical expectation should be strongly reinforced by a further substantive expectation.

The substantive expectation requires some explanation. Broadly construed, the uprising of the French population in May and June 1968 resulted from a sense of deep vexation that the established political elites of the country were not paying attention to popular demands and grievances. Yet total populations do not rise up in concert to make demands as generalized as this: such eruptions do not occur without narrower organization and more specific grievances. The more specific grievances consisted of two main salients (in the military sense): a concern among the workers for *autogestion* (self-management); and a concern among the students for university reform. The workers did not attribute to their demands much societal scope or generality, and indeed they were somewhat bemused to discover at the height of the revolt that the students wished to make some kind of common cause with them that they did not fully understand. The students, however, felt that although they had specific axes to grind concerning the financing of educational and structural reform in the university, they were at the same time speaking for the society as a whole. And the generic complaint concerned the unresponsiveness of the traditional elite political structures. Our own study suggests that our political elites were at least somewhat sensitive to this more generic criticism. In the degree that they did understand this traumatic message, we might expect to find that on purely substantive grounds, as well as technical ones, the apparent fidelity of representation was jerked upward by the intervention of the 1968 revolt. To put the matter baldly, the heat of the 1968 revolt should have touched off a sudden surge of elite responsiveness, which, with good luck, our measures should have reflected.[2]

When we look at actual comparisons, however, we find that the results run repeatedly in the opposite direction: almost everywhere, the AD bonds are considerably weaker when computed from the 1968 measures of district sentiment than they are when based on our "obsolescing" predictors from 1967 district responses.[3] This first impression is thoroughly confusing because it is so perverse: it implies that a popular revolt designed to increase elite responsiveness to public demands actually resulted in diminishing the fidelity of popular representation, at least as we have measured it.

This confusion does not last long if we scrutinize the results closely. In Figure 23-1 we have summarized the important data by depicting the arithmetic differences between AD bonds, according to whether district sentiment was measured before the revolt in 1967 or after the revolt in 1968. The bars of the graph which protrude downward indicate that the magnitude of the AD bonds declined when the 1968 measure of district opinion replaced the 1967 measure. The two panels of the figure reflect the fact that, as in the preceding chapter, we can assess AD bonds either with our generic measures of left-right sentiment or with the more specific issue measurements made in the domain of any given roll-call vote (the D term). (The second panel is truncated because a number of specific-issue measures applied in 1967 were not duplicated in the same form in 1968, so that inter-year comparisons are ruled out, although they can be made in all cases with left-right measures, as the first panel shows.)

As expected, the figure indicates that in most (but not all) cases the apparent fidelity of representation *declines* if we predict from post-revolt data. For anyone at all knowledgeable about the period, the clear exceptions are electrifying and highly meaningful. They fall in two areas of roll-call votes: those concerning union rights in general and *le droit syndical* in particular; and those concerning the Faure Law, dedicated to a reform of the national

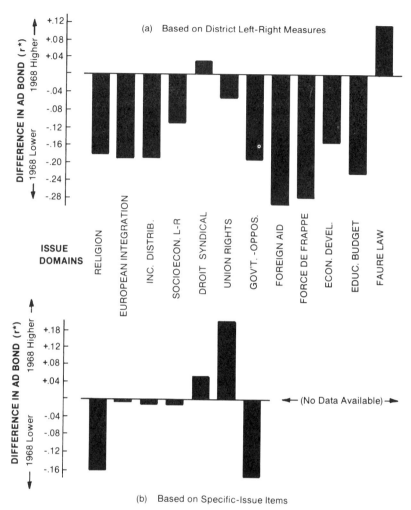

Figure 23-1. Comparison of AD bonds calculated on pre- and post-revolt district sentiment, by left-right and specific-issue measures, France.

education system. These two sets of roll-call votes are directly recognizable as the main legislative responses to the two primary thrusts of the whole revolt: unionists demanding fuller union powers, and students demanding educational reform.

That these two pieces of legislation stand out as especially "representative" for the period should not be surprising. In the summer and fall of 1968, as the newly constituted National Assembly began its labors in the traumatic wake of the revolt, the two pieces of legislation dealing with university reform and syndical law were the most impatiently awaited bills of the decade. Although they were being prepared by the conservative Gaullists who had been placed more solidly in power by the backlash of the 1968 election, there was general feeling in the press that the government authors of the new bills had better produce measures very conciliatory to the militants of both the union and university halves of the revolt if they wished to avoid further political damage.

The main surprise, then, is not that the impact of the 1968 revolt was to sharpen the fidelity of popular representation in the area of university reform and union rights; indeed, it is a pleasant confirmation to find that our complex and fragile data reflect this sharpening as clearly as they do. The surprise is that across a very broad front of public policy disputes less centrally involved in the disturbances, the impact of the revolt was to *corrode* levels of popular representation.

Such an outcome would probably have come as more of a surprise to the student militants than to the workers, if they recognized it. As we have suggested, the workers did not see themselves as the vanguard of broad-gauge societal change, as the university militants did. With the student example in front of them, the unions revolted in May 1968, dramatically and on a scale which was unprecedented, at least within this century, in the hope of attracting governmental attention to their demands for greater plant control, and they succeeded in winning major concessions. The university students, though pressing their own concerns relating to conditions within the university system, also saw themselves as the leading edge of broader societal reform, pushing the government into a new sensitivity to public demands. Although their interests were badly beaten at the polls in 1968, the students did indeed succeed (very much like the workers) in wresting from the national political elites a great deal of solicitude toward their immediate grievances. Despite a shocking loss of leftist seats in the Assembly, the students won from an otherwise unsympathetic Gaullist majority some major remedial legislation, which our data suggest was passed by representatives of the districts most concerned about the fate of the educational system.

The crowning irony, however, is that the tumult and the revisionist election did not heighten the fidelity of popular representation in any general way, as the students had professed to expect. Instead, it lowered it. In effect, the revolt and the election it necessitated thrust a gigantic lens between the governed and their governors. This lens greatly sharpened the image of the two major issues in the revolt. But it threw all the rest of the issues badly out of focus, at least where representation was concerned. If the students had intended to teach the Assembly a general lesson about the virtues of elite responsiveness, they failed, for the actual deputy response was a narrow and segmented one which, while reacting to the main demand, gave up major ground everywhere else.

Erasing the Revolt by Simulation

We arrived at this first set of conclusions by comparing the fidelity of the representation of district sentiment as it stood in 1968 with the same local opinion distributed as it had been in 1967. We can also take another route, partially independent of the first, which will produce a second reasonable assessment of the impact of the revolt on popular representation.

In the last chapter we exploited a fanciful coding of deputy roll calls, substituting for the votes we actually observed some other votes which would have occurred had all deputies observed party discipline all the time. We added still another set of hypothetical roll-call votes, this time to simulate what would have happened had the revolt not produced a dissolution of the National Assembly in May 1968. We did this in the obvious manner. The second, revisionist election had unseated more than one-quarter of the deputies in the 1967 Assembly, typically (although not always) replacing Socialist or Communist deputies with Gaullists. Our simulation, therefore, proceeded as though no seats had turned over; and the hypothetical votes we filled in as post-revolt roll-call choices by deputies who had actually been thrown out in 1968 were based on the assumption of pure party discipline.

It is important to be clear as to the conceptual status of this simulation. In the earlier case, when we pretended that our deputies sitting in both sessions of the Assembly voted pure party lines on all votes, we were rather smug about our capability to deal firmly with a counterfactual situation. The treatment was firm in the first instance because there was no ambiguity as to which binary choice party discipline required in each case; and in the second instance because the shifts of votes were so minor in their proportion that anticipation of them would have touched off no substantial changes in the bills presented or in the strategy of their presentation.

In our "no-revolt" coding of the roll calls we are also being counterfactual, but in a looser and more hesitant way. As before, we have no trouble in knowing how a seat belonging to a given party could have been expected to vote in every one of the post-revolt roll calls. But we are pretending that no revolt intervened, that no seats changed hands, and hence that the basic parameters of the legislative game, such as the proportion of seats the majority could count on, were also the same in the second session. These assumptions are of course very weak. There is every reason to believe that the succession of bills presented to the Assembly after the revolt had a different cast from that which they would have had if the revolt had not occurred, even though the identity of the governing party (the Gaullists) remained the same. This is true in part because, as we have already seen, the revolt itself turned government attention toward a different set of concerns; and in part because it is likely that the nature of the government bills presented to the post-revolt Assembly with its unprecedented Gaullist majority would have differed from the nature of the bills presented to a hypothetical post-1968 Assembly in which the government and its "majority" would have had a paper-thin margin. In short, then, our counterfactual simulation of a no-revolt situation is loose indeed. But it is nonetheless an object of perfectly respectable curiosity.

We find at the outset that the AD bonds associated with these simulated roll calls run higher on the average than any we have examined to date. Once again, this may clash with our simplest expectations, but the outcome only reinforces what we learned before: the presence of the new deputies, "substituted" into the Assembly by the revolt-generated election, serves to produce a major deterioration in the overall fidelity of representation, relative to what would have happened (conceivably) had the Assembly not been dissolved and its original cast of deputies not been changed.

The firmest point-by-point comparison of coefficients pits a No-Revolt Condition (using original 1967 district sentiment to predict to the full set of roll calls simulated for the 1967 deputies) with a Post-Revolt Condition (using actual 1968 district sentiment to predict to the roll calls actually cast by the post-revolt Assembly). If we form differences between parallel AD coefficients as we did before, then we find a pattern across issue domains which largely duplicates what we have seen in Figure 23-1, at least in a relative sense. The absolute levels of the coefficients are somewhat shifted: now *all* issues (instead of merely most of them) show deterioration in the Post-Revolt Condition, compared with the No-Revolt simulation. This includes, of course, the two issues most tightly bound to the revolt—the union issue and the Faure Law for university reform. But these two issues show differences between the conditions which are only trivial, whereas most other issues show a very marked deterioration. That most of the cross-issue variation in deterioration displayed in Figure 23-1 is simply mirrored in this partly independent set of calculations is witnessed by the fact that over the eighteen comparisons which can be made (using both left-right and specific-issue predictions), the correlation between the two sets of differences runs very high ($r = .85$).

Since both assessments of the impact of the revolt lead to the same general conclusions, it is important to consider how these results would modify some of the observations we made before, when we were operating without taking time change into account. There is little clear evidence that the intrusion of the revolt was responsible for the absence of expected differences in district-vote congruence between issue types, such as foreign and domestic issues, which we encountered earlier in this chapter. But it is worth pondering the more global finding that the revolt does seem to have attenuated the levels of representation fidelity we have been reporting for our AD bonds. This weakening was evident in the coefficients presented in our synthetic diamonds in the last chapter. And if we cast a side glance at the overall congruence levels found by Miller and Stokes for the United States at that point, some modest mental revisions are in order.

To be more precise, we suggested before that the levels of the AD bond observed in the context of pure left-right measurement seemed to approach a crude match with the Miller-Stokes magnitudes, but that when we used the more appropriate specific-issue predictions, the French values were very much lower than those found in the case of the three issue domains in the United States. Now we must reckon with the additional likelihood that the French values we were addressing—those based both on left-right location and on more specific issues—were tarnished in some degree by the intrusion of the 1968 revolt.

By how much? This question obviously cannot be given a hard answer, for there are limits to our counterfactual simulations. But we can at least ask how the AD bonds in the synthetic diamonds like those shown in Figure 22-2 would look if they were based on the No-Revolt scenario, instead of being calculated for the "real" deputies, including the 1968 replacements after the revolt. Under these circumstances, the AD bond for the left-right diamond would show an average of .50*, and the specific-issue counterpart would be .16*.[4] These values bring our sense of congruence levels still closer to those for the Miller-Stokes assessments, although the specific-issue versions still lag far behind. Common sense would suggest, however, that even our No-Revolt simulation understates normal levels of congruence, simply because a revolt did occur and did affect subsequent roll-call votes in ways that must leave even the simulated levels somewhat dulled.

The most important point remains, however, that although the revolt whetted popular representation in the two narrow issue domains associated most closely with the tumult, it served to attenuate the fidelity of representation everywhere else.

Representation and the Odds of Reelection

While we are dealing with matters of dynamics, or change over time, it is worth asking another classic question. Does the fidelity of representation which a deputy provides his district improve his chances of being reelected in the next election?

A good deal of clinical literature in recent decades has stressed the degree to which legislators in parliamentary democracies can become consumed with the imperative of reelection to another term (see, for example, Fenno, 1978). Indeed, all we need do is couple this concern with Friedrich's "rule of anticipated reactions" (1941), and we can generate mechanisms which keep legislators deeply fearful of doing anything which might upset constituents, however completely they may feel that normatively a legislator should follow his own conscience, in the fullest Burkean style. But at the core there is a reality question about the genuineness of penalties to be paid by the casual legislator who wanders too far from his district sentiments in his legislative decisionmaking.

Legislators inhabit at least two worlds, where relationships with the home constituency are concerned. One is the world central to this book, which involves casting votes "for" the district on matters of high national policy. Another world is frequently referred to as that of the "messenger-boy function," which keeps the legislator busy doing small favors for home folks which have little to do with the major axes of political debate. Here, at the broader end, the deputy may be more or less adept in the kinds of pork-barrel activities which funnel moneys and economic stimulation into the local district, pleasing some immediate beneficiaries enormously and offending virtually no one, or at least no one eligible to cast a relevant vote in the next election. At the finer end, the legislator can please constituents by short-circuiting problems they may encounter as clients of the administrative bureaucracy, or perhaps by submitting specialized "named" legislation in their behalf.

According to one theory, the deputy who is truly assiduous in performing such errands and local-interest work has little to fear in the way of electoral reprisal for broader policy stands: it is implicit in this theory that constituents feel only a weak concern for such broader matters, if in fact they are watching at all. From this point of view, the way to make friends and ensure reelection is by unremitting attention to local service.

We are not in a position to make any comparative evaluation between these imperatives of meticulous errand-running and palatable policy decisions. But of course our paradigm is ideally conceived to ask whether re-election penalties can be detected where deputies seem to contribute legislative decisions in directions which are rather more remote than usual from the center of gravity of policy sentiment in their districts.

In contemplating an actual test, two practical problems confront us. First, as we have seen, there were too few roll-call votes in the pre-revolt session of the Assembly to permit us any reasonable reading as to variations by deputy in the fidelity of district representation. This is, however, a trivial problem: it means that we shall not use the 1968 legislative election as our test of survival for incumbents. Rather, we shall turn to the election of 1973 instead.

The second practical problem is more forbidding, but quite within reach of solution. The data as we have analyzed them up to this point do not lend themselves to the kind of test we have in mind because they are too finely disaggregated in one direction, and too crudely aggregated in another. They are too finely disaggregated by specific issue. We can say a given deputy was close to the sentiment in his district on issues a, d, e, g, and h; was moderately close on issues c, i, and k; and was not close at all on issues b, f, j, l, and m. But this level of disaggregation is enormously ponderous and, ultimately, quite confusing. What we really need is a more global statement as to differences between deputies in broad "tendencies" toward dis-

trict policy compatibility in legislative votes over a large range of issue domains at once. In short, here we must arrive at much greater aggregation.

Where we must disaggregate in order to arrive at a more efficient test is
at the level of the Assembly and the deputy. Up to this point, in dealing
with questions of fidelity of representation we have worked with our AD
bonds in a correlational vein, so that we operate with all deputies at once
whether the context is comparisons across issues or between pre-revolt and
post-revolt actors. Of course, if we had some effective way to divide our
deputies into two groups according to their behavioral concern for casting
legislative votes to fit district preferences, then we could contrast the correlational output of an AD or fuller diamond form between the two groups
so partitioned. But the numbers within each subset would begin to be quite
small (33 districts on the average for 1967 data, and about 16 for 1968
data), thus increasing the instability of estimates considerably. And in any
event, what we really want to employ is some estimate of district fidelity
disaggregated all the way down to the individual deputy, not just to a crude
dichotomization of the Assembly sample.

We can solve both of these problems more or less at once, although it
will require some mildly heterodox statistical procedures to do so. Any
statement of the Pearson product-moment correlation coefficient (r) of the
type we have been using to index the magnitude of our AD bond and
others in our diamonds can very legitimately be seen as a measure of average
covariation across a set of observations paired for individuals.[5] In our immediate circumstance some deputies contribute high positive values to the prospective correlation, while others contribute very weak positive values or
even negative ones, thereby serving to drag down the magnitude of the final
summary correlation. There is no reason, of course, why these individual
contributions to the final correlation cannot be intercepted and used as indicators in their own right. Thus it is quite easy to disaggregate our AD
correlations in order to assign working values to specific deputies that indicate whether these individuals are casting legislative votes which, on a given
issue X, fit district sentiment more or less closely than the average.[6]

If we can disaggregate our data with this kind of ease, we also can continue on a step to arrive at the kind of reaggregation that seems warranted
as well. Suppose we now have a statement of the relative contribution
which a given deputy makes to some specific AD bond, whether he or she is
voting closer than or less close than "average" to the mean value of district
sentiment. If we wish a more global (that is, a less issue-specific) statement
about the deputy and the compatibility of his legislative behavior with district sentiment, then it is not inappropriate to draw some average of such
relative values calculated over a large variety of issues, including, for example, domestic and foreign.

It is exactly these averages of individual contributions to AD bond covariation which will be our dependent variables in this section and at other

points later on. In view of the way in which we have organized our data explicitly up to this point, however, we shall keep separate in our cross-issue aggregation two versions of the dependent variable: (1) average contributions to those AD bonds calculated by using our left-right measurements repetitively; and (2) contributions averaged across all of our relevant specific issues (in the "capacious" form of those measurements used, for example, for Figure 22-2).

The degree of fit between these two versions of our preferred dependent variable is of natural interest, and it is not entirely clear what we should expect. If we christened both variables with the same name, such as "relative congruence of legislative votes with district sentiment," then it might be expected that they would show substantial intercorrelations, being apparently no more than noisy measures of the same underlying trait. But, given their indirect parentage, we know that these two measures indeed must be "noisy"; and if they showed strong intercorrelations (say, $r = .75$ or above) we would do better to combine them, since most of the unshared variance would have to be pure measurement error. Moreover, there was more than a hint in our investigations of the synthetic diamonds of the preceding chapter that representation might proceed by more than one route, and that progress along either of these two particular routes might be compensatory for blockages along the other route. If so, then we should not be startled to find that our two derived measures of individual-level AD congruence might actually be negatively correlated. In such a case, there surely would be no point in merging the two estimates.

Happily, we can examine the nature of the fit empirically, once we have calculated the two individual-level contributions to the AD bond, one based on specific-issue congruence, the other on congruence gauged mainly with left-right measures. The observed correlation here is modestly positive, being $r = +.34$. A value this high under circumstances in which there may be some alternative compensatory mechanisms operating to increase the fidelity of representation at the level of the individual deputy by more than one route is reasonably reassuring, and it might not be entirely farcical to combine the two versions of the measure to solidify the element which they appear to have in common. At the same time, the correlation is certainly limited, and this leads us to feel that for the most part we should keep the two versions of the variable separate.[7]

With all this said, we can now proceed directly to a test of the theoretical question at hand: among deputies in the Assembly, does greater congruence of votes with district sentiment increase the probability of reelection in any discernible way? Our best answer is that it does, and of course in the direction we would expect intuitively. When we use the weaker congruence calculation based upon specific-issue measures, we find a reasonable "tendency" for reelection to accompany high district congruence, although the levels of association are not dazzling over our limited number of 64 deputies who sought reelection in 1973. (We find here that $p < .10$, a value which may not look embarrassing, but the true value is closer to .10 than to .09!) We retrieve the same substantive result from our congruence measure based on left-right locations, although here the case for statistical significance is considerably more impressive ($p < .001$).

In fact, using the stronger version, we can make other statements about the nature of the relationship. For example, we can say that for deputies who cast legislative votes which were one standard deviation more congruent than "normal" with sentiments in their home districts over the 1967–1972 period (a distressingly relative localization) the odds of reelection in 1973 were very close to four chances out of five ($p = .79$). But for those deputies whose votes were one standard deviation *less* congruent than the average, the odds of reelection were only about 50–50. This odds gradient is, therefore, fairly steep, and it would seem that the incentives to deputies to tighten the congruence of their voting with opinion in the home district are strong indeed.

Sadly, such a conclusion rests squarely on the assumption that there is something causal about the empirical association just demonstrated. There may be, but that is far from certain. Some plausible rival hypotheses exist, including at least one which has an interesting theoretical pedigree.

We can move most directly to these other theoretical possibilities if we first consider another way of looking at the fact that our deputies who were losers in the 1973 election tended to come disproportionately from among those deputies who were abnormally distant from their district sentiment in the general cast of their legislative votes. This competing view recognizes that the post-revolt election in 1968 was one of abnormal "surge" to the right, which ensconced a substantial number of rightists in the Assembly from districts that usually tended to produce narrow leftist wins. These one-term marginal rightists would naturally bulk large among incumbents losing their seats in the 1973 election, and, quite possibly because of the reasons for their 1968 victory, would tend to include also a disproportionate share of deputies uncommonly distant attitudinally from the issue preferences of their districts.

It is important to realize that this rival hypothesis does nothing to change the fact that, in our data, deputies who are less congruent with their districts are less likely to be reelected, a finding which overflows with conceptual significance. Indeed, from one point of view, the fact that the 1973 election took place after a peculiar surge in left-right voting in 1968 does not mean that relatively leftist districts did not throw out incumbents at a great rate in 1973 *exactly* because those incumbents were reflecting district sentiments much more poorly than their more "normal" (that is, leftist) competitors would have. Nonetheless, setting the empirical association in this perspective does change its flavor somewhat. Instead of election defeat as punishment for flawed representation, perhaps there is some dynamic which for other reasons puts low-congruence deputies into seats which are electorally "marginal," and high-congruence deputies into "safe seats." It turns out, of course, that a great deal of ink has flowed in both directions about a hypothesis of this kind.

Representation and the Marginality Hypothesis

Fiorina (1974) has provided a very useful review of the status of the marginality hypothesis, beginning with the work on representation by Julius Turner (1951). Turner was one of the first to offer some empirical evidence of actual constituency representation, evidence that was about as impressive as it could be, considering that it was somewhat indirect. Turner worked from a view of the core social and demographic base of each of the two major parties in the United States, in order to define a set of sitting representatives who might be thought of as representing districts "atypical" of their nominal party. He found that these representatives tended to show much less party loyalty in their congressional voting than did representatives of districts more typical of their party base. He inferred that, since the legislative votes of these mavericks could not by definition be seen as cued by party loyalty, but seemed instead to be cued by the countervailing nature of the home district, the configuration yielded strong circumstantial evidence of the presence of an effort to represent the home district in the legislature.

Thus was born, in effect, the "atypicality" hypothesis, which was tested rather more rigorously by MacRae in his seminal study of the Massachusetts House of Representatives (1952). His careful working of the data within this rather narrow setting did indeed seem to provide impressive support for Turner's speculations about atypicality. MacRae, however, raised another possibility, which Fiorina calls the "marginality hypothesis." He argued the substantial plausibility that deputies from "marginal" districts might be less loyal to their parties in their legislative voting than representatives with "safe" seats. This could be so, the reasoning went, because, in the Turner mode, disloyalty to party hinted at special loyalty to district wishes, and we can easily see that deputies in marginal seats might be especially concerned to please their districts, whatever their parties might dictate.

Intuitively, this is a very powerful hypothesis, because its motivational base seems so impeccable. After all, deputies who are the favorite sons of local voting blocs powerful enough to have won their seats historically by large margins obviously need not suffer anything like the levels of rational apprehension about reelection that are experienced by deputies in marginal seats. This does not mean that these occupants of safe seats can do absolutely as they please, without any concern whatever for local sentiment or the vicissitudes of reelection fights. But if fear of electoral reprisal is any concern whatever of these elected representatives—vast bodies of testimony and evidence confirm that it is—and we needed to find some means of gauging where this concern is more or less acute, we obviously would turn to one of the indices as to the safeness or marginality of the seat occupied. Thus, if just one more link is supplied, that is, if apprehension about re-election pushes the rational deputy to solicitude about district sentiment and to more extensive efforts not to offend it in his own legislative votes, then we can easily understand that we might discover deputies in marginal seats displaying greater congruence with district sentiment in their legislative behavior than tends to be found among deputies blessed with more secure seats.

The actual MacRae test of the hypothesis required still another logical link, since he was obliged to work operationally with party loyalty in legislative voting, instead of more directly with congruence between voting and district. Thus the intuitive plausibility of the argument did depend, as is so often the case, on a series of presumed links. Nonetheless, MacRae felt that he was able to show a meaningful (negative) association between seat marginality and at least party loyalty. He felt moreover that this association existed over and above the clear effects of atypicality, although here his demonstration was considerably weakened by the high collinearity between "atypicality" and "marginality": virtually all of the sharply atypical seats were also marginal ones, and seats which were "safe but atypical" hardly appeared in nature. This raises the question as to whether atypicality and marginality are really separable entities, and whether the demonstrable effects of atypicality on party loyalty are not better understood in the MacRae light as a consequence of marginality and of heightened anxiety about reelection.

However this may be, the marginality hypothesis in the form developed by MacRae came to be dramatically disconfirmed by the data collected for the Miller-Stokes study of the 1958 U.S. House of Representatives. Here, of course, there was much more direct measurement of constituency sentiment. And Miller (1964) reports quite striking data to suggest that it is the representatives from *safe* seats, not marginal ones, who are most likely to put some weight upon perceived constituency sentiments in forming their decisions about legislative votes.

Although this finding—noteworthy for its strength in the Miller-Stokes data—directly contradicts the MacRae surmise and, for that matter, what would seem to be an "obvious" motivational expectation, it does not in any way contradict any empirical findings. For although MacRae dealt with empirical data, his actual operationalizations involved party loyalty in legislative voting; and the kind of sensitivity to constituency pressures which he suspected was provoked by marginal seats was "read" in the data as a weakening of party loyalty in legislative votes. As we shall see in our own data, findings of the MacRae sort (safe seats showing greater party loyalty) and of the Miller sort (safe seats showing greater congruence with district sentiment) are not mutually incompatible by any strict construction.

As Fiorina helps us to understand, the MacRae party-loyalty finding is not at all obscure intuitively. After all, it is likely that occupants of safe seats belonging to a given party tend at any point in time to define the policy center of gravity of that party, and to influence, or even more directly "govern" (in party caucuses they control through their seniority), what the "party line" actually is. Naturally, if these safe-seat occupants tend to set the party line, it is not surprising that they vote for it with greater fidelity than do the more transient occupants of marginal seats who presumably are acting under a more discordant set of cues, including their own convictions on issues. Thus we can undergird findings relating party loyalty to marginality with a sound intuitive understanding.

Findings of the Miller sort, however, have no such easy rationale: indeed, we would be prepared to expect the reverse on the basis of our motivational discussion. Fiorina erects a justification for many of the more specific Miller results. Some of these justifications follow in a very direct and satisfying way from Fiorina's own formal modeling of the calculus of the representative who tries to behave vis-à-vis his district in such a way as to ensure reelection. A few of the Miller results remain very perplexing, however, and Fiorina's efforts at justification in these latter instances are by his own admission rather strained. Before we begin to survey some of these complex patterns, it is worth asking whether such results—including Miller's most counterintuitive ones—can be discerned in our own French data.

The Marginality Hypothesis under French Conditions

The ways in which we might operationalize the notion of the "safety" or "marginality" of legislative districts are somewhat more numerous for the French case than they are for two-party systems. Nevertheless, we have arrived at a reasonable ranking of all of our eighty-six districts in terms of their relative marginality by using official results from the highly "normal" election of 1967, and proceeding thenceforth in stages.[8]

Even though our main focus here is upon the hypothesis linking marginality or competitiveness of district to fidelity of representation, it is useful at the outset to ask about the older Turner-MacRae hypothesis tying party discipline to marginality in a negative direction. As we have seen, actual defections from party discipline are rare enough in the Assembly to provide no more than a test at the extreme margins; however, we can resort to our role materials of Chapter 21 for a fuller variable depicting role concern over party discipline. And if among our deputies we correlate that variable with our measure of district marginality, we do indeed find some association of the kind classically expected. The safer the seat, the greater the expressed concern about the maintenance of party discipline in legislative voting, although the magnitude of the association is pretty limited ($r = .10$).

If minimization of concern about party discipline in legislative voting were the same thing as heightened concern about responding to district wishes, as early versions of work in the area assumed, then the existence of such an association, even the meager one just reported, would mean in turn that empirically, in France, concern about district wishes runs higher in more marginal districts, just as MacRae had argued. But, as we noted earlier, quite a number of other concerns besides cues from the home district can limit devotion to party purity. Therefore it is important to test the association between seat marginality and responsiveness to the home district more directly. Fortunately, we are well equipped for such a test.

We can proceed by either of two routes. By far the simpler route works from the measure of individual responsiveness to district wishes devised for the preceding section by decomposing AD correlational bonds, as calculated either for specific-issue diamonds or for left-right diamonds. This quantity would seem to be a reasonable reflection of the notion actually at stake in the MacRae version of the marginality hypothesis; and all we need to do is to examine the nature of its association with our measure of district marginality. We find that for both measures the direction of association is the same, which is not surprising in view of the fact that they are fairly intercorrelated. Nonetheless, the correlation registers as only trivial for the weaker or noisier measure based on specific-issue AD bonds ($r = +.03$), while for the stronger measure based on left-right links it is an impressive $r = +.42$. The direction here is to be read as responsiveness increasing with seat safety. Hence these first results fit the Miller findings for the United States and run against the original MacRae marginality surmise.

The second route is a very elaborate one which has the disadvantage of distracting us with an almost endless richness of comparison. This route depends upon the replication for the French case of the key data display in the Miller original. This display (Figure 3 of Miller, 1964) was set up in four-fold table form, although each of the four "cells" of the table was itself a "diamond" of full representation estimates. First the legislative districts covered by Miller's study were dichotomized into those relatively "safe" and those "marginal" or electorally competitive. Then the "A" term, which normally summarizes average district sentiment, was decomposed into two subconstituencies, the supporters of the majority (winning) and minority (losing) candidates. Thus the diamond configuration was presented for majority versus minority candidates where seats were "safe" and where they were marginal.[9] Finally, this fourfold display of diamonds was repeated three times, once for each of the three policy domains featured in the Miller-Stokes study (social welfare, civil rights, and foreign policy). Fortunately, we will be permitted some modicum of simplification because, although the general fidelity of representation varies sharply over these three domains, the most noteworthy points of comparison between given bonds within the diamonds repeat themselves faithfully (albeit at different absolute levels) across all three policy domains. We can retain these crucial differences, therefore, even if we average across policy domains for the Miller display.

Such a possibility of averaging is most congenial to us on the French side in view of the fact that we are dealing with nearly a dozen policy domains. When we average our French data, we can keep this complex data display within bounds, although we shall continue to find it useful to separate diamonds based on specific issues from those based on left-right measurements. It makes sense to compare these two sets of averages not with the most dramatic special cases which come to view in certain domains in the American case, but rather with the same kind of cross-policy central tendencies, especially since such averaging will hide little of what is important in the American data with regard to the marginality hypothesis.

In short, then, we can produce data displays which are essentially replicates of the Miller figures, or at least of their averaged form. We do so in the three parts of Figure 23-2, including in 23-2A the French specific-issue averages; in 23-2B the averages based on left-right diamonds; and in 23-2C the averaged Miller data from the United States.

We shall not attempt to comment on all of the comparisons which Figure 23-2 offers. Instead we shall focus here on those particulars which are of most concern to us vis-à-vis the marginality hypothesis, beginning with a general survey of the variation which is being concealed in the French and American cases as we take averages of coefficients over a number of issue domains within each country (ten for France, three for the United States). Given the sharp variation by issue domain with which we are familiar from the U.S. data, we might imagine that more variability underlies the American summaries. Yet the standard deviations are not grossly dissimilar between the two countries, as may be seen if we average the five shown for each set of specific-issue diamonds. (These averages are drawn from the indicated regions of Figures 23-2A and 23-2C.)

Constituency	France		United States	
	Safe	Marginal	Safe	Marginal
Majority	.24	.22	.23	.19
Minority	.20	.22	.16	.22

Indeed, we see signs of roughly the same patterning of greater and lesser variability of estimates underlying our averages across the fourfold "conditions" of the analysis design. Therefore we can begin to look at the averages with some assurance that their bases are not highly discrepant from country to country.

Of the many comparisons available between conditions and countries,

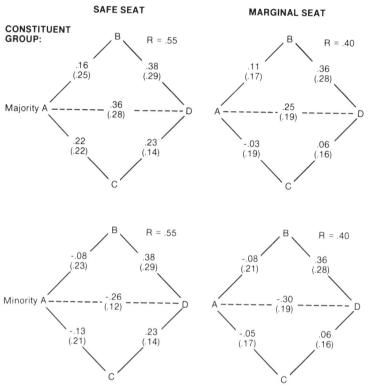

Figure 23-2A. French representation by seat marginality and majority preference as estimated by averaging specific-issue diamonds, France, 1967–1972 (following Miller, 1964). Main entries for each linkage are coefficients averaged over ten relevant specific-issue diamonds. The standard deviation for each average is given in parentheses. Following Miller (1964, table 3), the three coefficients involved with term A are merely zero-order product-moment correlations uncorrected for attenuation. The BD and CD entries are based on normalized regression coefficients produced by predicting D jointly from B and C.

two pairs in particular are central to the marginality hypothesis—the same two that drew the greatest attention from Miller originally and Fiorina subsequently. The first pair directly compares the AD bonds, and the second compares the magnitudes of the BD and CD bonds. As Miller reported originally, the American data argue quite dramatically through both comparisons that the representatives from *safe* constituencies provide the greatest fidelity of representation to their home constituents, especially the majority which elected them. This conclusion is bulwarked by much larger AD bonds for safe-seat representatives than for those from more competitive

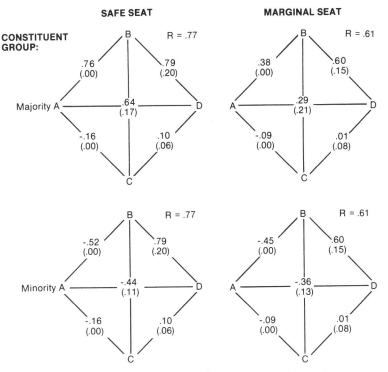

SAFE SEAT   **MARGINAL SEAT**

Figure 23-2B. French representation by seat marginality and majority preference as estimated by averaging left-right diamonds, France, 1967–1972 (following Miller, 1964). Constructed from data parallel to those used for Figure 23-2A. Standard deviations for three coefficients not involving term D are zero because terms A, B, and C are the same for all diamonds.

districts, and also by signs that "safe" representatives give much greater weight to perceptions of district sentiment in their legislative voting than do representatives from marginal districts (that is, the size of the CD bond, relative to the BD one, is very much greater for safe than for marginal districts). These twin fndings, as Miller summarized them, "clearly confound any general expectation that sharp electoral competition binds representative and represented more tightly together" (Miller, 1964, p. 365).

Our French data, though in a general way and in more muted tones, reproduce these central but counterintuitive findings. This is clearest for the comparisons of the AD bond: although details vary between the two countries, there is no doubt that the lion's share of whatever popular representation is occurring takes place for representatives of safe seats and vis-à-vis their electoral majorities. This contrast holds even for the weaker specific-

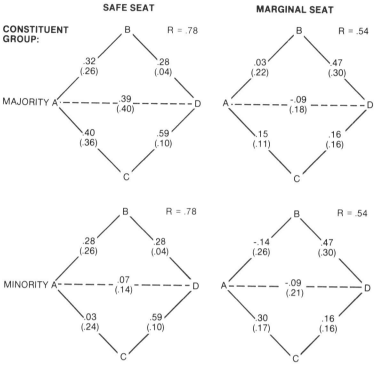

Figure 23-2C. U.S. representation by seat marginality and majority preference as estimated by averaging three specific-issue diamonds (as presented by Miller, 1964). Main entries for each linkage are coefficients averaged over the relevant diamonds for the policy domains of social welfare, civil rights, and foreign policy (see Miller, 1964, table 3). The standard deviation for each average is given in parentheses. Coefficients involved with term A are merely zero-order product-moment correlations, uncorrected for attenuation. The BD and CD entries are based on normalized regression coefficients produced by predicting D from B and C.

issue diamond; and for the left-right diamond it approaches being as dramatic as in the American data. These results in particular recapitulate what we learned as we followed the simpler route using our correlation-based measures of individual congruence or responsiveness.

The other part of the central Miller results—that is, the comparisons of the BD and CD bonds—comes through a little less clearly on the French side, but it seems to find some replication there nonetheless. As we pointed out in the last chapter, in the French system the main flow of deputy decisionmaking presumes groupings into political parties of relatively like-minded politicians, who generate a strong BD bond by close party discipline. This does not mean that signs of more direct district representation cannot be found at all. But it does mean that, at least relative to the American case, the system leans toward heavier BD and weaker CD bonds.

Once this general displacement is accepted, we do not have to strain to see parallel patterns between the French case and the American data. In both French formulations, the ratio of the CD coefficient to its BD partner is larger—betokening greater attention to district wishes—for deputies in safe seats than it is for those whose districts are more competitive. The effect is clearer, however, in the specific-issue data, and this is appropriate if, as we came to believe in the last chapter, the left-right diamonds tend to reflect the mainstream "party-discipline" form of legislative decisionmaking while the modest elements of true constituency influence shine through more clearly in data that are based squarely on specific issues.

Beneath the synthetic data of Table 23-2 the parallels with the American data continue, insofar as the marginality hypothesis is concerned. Thus, for example, within the American data the central marginality patterns are at their sharpest for the domain of civil rights, where overall district representation reaches its maximum as well. We earlier suggested that the closest conceptual American equivalent for the civil-rights question in France was the clerical-anticlerical dimension. And the relevant specific-issue diamond does indeed conform most dramatically to the Miller patterns: the AD bond is, for example, $r = +.71$ for deputies from safe districts, but $-.01$ within the competitive districts. Moreover, the contrasts between the BD and CD bonds fall as they should. For the safe-seat "condition" the CD bond reaches its maximum for all observed issue domains ($r = +.73$), and this value for the zero-order relationship is at exact parity with the size of the BD bond. As we turn to standardized regression coefficients controlling away the effect of the other determinant (B or C predicting to D), the coefficient for the BD leg is slightly higher than for the CD leg (.43 to .41), but the corresponding values in the marginal-seat condition are a very different .50 to .19.

All told, then, our French data in their own way lend major confirmation to those main results from the Miller analyses which seemed so counterintuitive. This does not mean we have done anything to clarify *why* they occur, beyond the suggestions made by Miller and by Fiorina. But the fact of replication in such a different institutional setting does serve to suggest that they are well worth diagnosing. Before we consider competing diagnoses, however, let us turn to some of the secondary comparisons that have attracted attention, including a major one which does *not* replicate well between the two bodies of data.

Miller expresses astonishment that there is no sign of any positive agreement between constituency sentiment and legislative votes cast by representatives from competitive districts even if one defines his own *majority* as the constituency, not to mention, of course, the minority constituency in the same types of districts. According to some theories, such minority constituencies are expected to receive more attention and hence less "disrepresentation" in marginal districts than in safe ones, chiefly because they are more of an electoral threat in such areas. However this may be, one would expect the representative from a marginal district to show signs of congruence at least with his majority, even if the MacRae version of the marginality hypothesis is wrong. In fact, however, the Miller results show no such congruence for either constituency, and the impression is given that the representative receiving conflicting cues from the heterogeneous district merely goes his own way and does as he pleases.

Fiorina has equal trouble with this facet of the data. Although he offers useful diagnoses that flow from his own modeling of representation strategies, they do not clearly account for such absence of agreement between representatives of competitive districts and their own majorities: in fact, they would lead to opposite conclusions. Fiorina goes on struggling with ways of encompassing these findings, but he is not very successful.

It is interesting, therefore, to find that this is the main aspect of the American results which clearly fails to replicate in the French data. Although the AD bond with majority wishes tends to run lower for deputies from competitive than from safe districts, it still appears clearly positive in both the specific-issue and the left-right formulations. Furthermore, the magnitude of the AD bonds for the stronger left-right diamonds shows a pattern unlike that in the American data: starting with a maximum at the upper left, there is a steady clockwise progression to a minimum at the lower left. There is nearly the same pattern in the weaker specific-issue diamonds, although it breaks down by a trivial margin at the end of the circuit.

This is a very intelligible pattern, and understanding it may be helpful in our subsequent diagnoses as to what is going on in these displays more generally. Our understanding is enhanced if we think in terms of a trivially primitive version of these AD correlations. Let us consider the state of affairs that would pertain if we had one set of districts whose citizens are in majority "Yes" on an issue, and another set of districts whose citizens are in majority "No." Let us imagine that the several elected representatives within each set behave as pure delegates, rigidly instructed by their majorities, as they are asked to vote "Yes" or "No" in the legislative chamber.

If we were to dichotomize districts according to their majority, and then erect a fourfold table showing how the representatives of each district type voted, which is essentially what is involved in the assessment of an AD bond, we would find by construction the kind of pattern which signals a perfect association (+ 1.00): there would be zeros in the off-diagonal cells.

If we then asked about the association of these deputies' votes, not with their majorities but with their minority constituencies, the zeros would shift to the main diagonal, the off-diagonal cells would be full, and we would have a perfect negative association ($-$ 1.00). Of course in this elemental case we would not even bother to redo the calculation, because it is redundant: knowledge of the association with the majority determines the association with the minority. And this is not simply because we have postulated a perfect association. In other words, if we suppose that only four-fifths of the deputies from each type of district comply with their majorities, so that the AD bond shows an association of $+$ .60, then we can say with confidence that the association of votes with minority sentiment would be $-$ .60.

The important point is, of course, that in such an elemental case a mirror-image relationship pertains between calculations based on majority and minority sentiment, and this is a logical necessity rather than any exciting substantive discovery. This "logical necessity" does not dictate what level any given AD bond will be, nor does it say that safe seats will show greater congruence than marginal ones. But it does say that for such a primitive data assembly the kind of pattern we described as "clockwise" for our French data of Figure 23-2 is rather to be expected: if deputies enjoying safe seats vote more frequently and intensely for their majority constituents than marginal deputies do, then by the same token they more frequently and intensely "disrepresent" their local minority opposition than do those from more competitive districts.

We can see from our French displays that such mirror-image expectations are a good deal less than logical necessities, a conclusion which is more dramatic in relation to the American data. How has the logical imperative become submerged in these displays? It cannot have disappeared totally, and an underlying logic lurks in the background that must leave some imprint on even these data. But the information being assembled is much more complex than that involved in our pair of "elemental" binary variables. District sentiment is measured as a matter of degree on each of a number of attitude items, and then typically combined into some larger aggregate. Similarly, the roll-call variable, though based on binary choices, is also summed across a number of votes, so that consistency or extremity or "relative purity" of approach is being gauged as well. Minority sentiment is no longer merely the direct complement of majority sentiment: a deputy of "delegate" proclivities might vote the same way, if, on some composite issue scale ranging from 1 to 10, his majority supporters scored a mean of 7.6 and the minority 4.5, as he would if the majority were 2.8 and the minority 2.4.

In short, the range of possible configurations has expanded mightily, liberating the problem from the simple redundancy of the most primitive version. At the same time, one of the sources of intrusion on redundancy is methodological artifact, such as, for example, the sensitivity of correlations to peculiarities in comparative variances. And although we cannot tell what an AD coefficient calculated for minority sentiment will look like simply by knowing the majority-constituent value, we have to recognize that in the typical intradistrict relationships, which are necessarily the basic building blocks for all of these data, the deputy who does more for his majority is likely to be doing less for his minority constituents, provided only that the two blocs are in active opposition.

These simple lessons do not in themselves resolve our diagnostic problems about the marginality hypothesis and why it is that, in both the American and French data, deputies from safe seats appear much more responsive to district opinion, despite theoretical reasons associated with election risk which would lead us to expect just the opposite. In fact, we have noted already that this finding is both conceptually and empirically independent of the "mirror-image" or "complement" effect between majority and minority sentiment just reviewed. Nonetheless, for data displays such as those in Figures 23-2A through 23-2C it is worth keeping these deep-background imperatives firmly in mind, because they provide a base expectation along the majority-minority axis of the display, even if they say nothing about the safe-marginal axis of the same displays.

Some Diagnoses of the Marginality Effect

Even though both Miller and Fiorina puzzle over the failure of marginal-seat representatives to show signs of positive policy congruence with at least their majority supporters, we shall not worry about that pattern further, since it is not replicated in our French data. But the basic marginality finding does not only replicate, but replicates handsomely, and is counterintuitive as well. Hence we should consider further some of the ways in which it may be understood.

Both Miller and Fiorina offer interpretations, although they are somewhat independent of each other. Miller singles out most centrally the fact that occupants of safe seats have generally enjoyed much longer tenure in office and thus have had more opportunity to become aware of district preferences. He points to data showing safe-seat occupants to be more accurate in their perceptions of district sentiment (see the AC bond, Figure 23-2C), and notes that in their direct reports, too, they claim greater confidence in their knowledge of district opinion than do their counterparts in more marginal seats. Since a "general correlate" of lack of confidence in such knowledge is greater reliance by the representative on his own preferences in forming roll-call decisions, the marginal representative would seem to be a victim of such felt ambiguity.

Fiorina, starting with the same observation of more accurate district perceptions on the part of safe-seat occupants, introduces a different causal note. He suggests that the difference between safe and marginal districts may correspond quite closely with a difference between districts where opinion is relatively homogeneous and those where it is heterogeneous. This seems to be a reasonable suggestion: certainly what makes districts seem homogeneous politically is that they are heavily pro (or con), rather than more evenly divided between these conflicting tendencies. And if such an equivalence actually holds, greater accuracy in safe-seat perceptions follows directly. Moreover, Fiorina showed earlier with his modeling of a representation calculus that under reasonable assumptions about the mix of election strategies (vote "maximization" versus mere maintenance), representatives even of safe districts can be expected to vote with their dominant constituency groups a disproportionate amount of the time.

It is likely that both of these diagnoses have some merit, although our data suggest certain amendments. For example, Fiorina's contention that perceptual accuracy should be greater in more homogeneous districts is of course entirely congenial with our point of view, and one for which some limited evidence exists in our data (see Chapter 20). The supposition that "safe" districts correspond to homogeneous ones is less certain, however. If opinion can only be binary, as in the choice between two candidates, then the equivalence is nearly a truism, since the variance of a proportion (the normal definition of heterogeneity) is at its maximum when the proportion is .50. But when a more extended continuum of opinion positions is possible, does it necessarily follow that safe districts are more homogeneous ones?

It has seemed worth checking this proposition directly within our data, since we have what might well be an ideal "test variable" in our left-right locations. This variable is ideal, first, because for those French respondents sensitive to the meaning of left-right differences, even small distances on our hundred-point scale (such as that between zero and twenty, or twenty and forty) appear to have considerable meaning. Furthermore, the aspect of these measurements at issue in Fiorina's surmise is their intradistrict variance, and we have found at several points in earlier chapters that differences in district-level variance (or "polarization") for the left-right locations of citizens have substantial predictive power.

When we look at the relationship between the marginality or safety of seats by district and district left-right variance, however, we find an association which is in the direction expected by Fiorina, but one so trivial in magnitude ($r = +.03$) as to be utterly incapable of supporting other chains of reasoning necessary to account for any effects observed in connection with marginality.

Some of the other suppositions underlying these diagnoses encounter mixed results in our data as well. For example, there is no problem in linking length of parliamentary service with seat safety, even if the latter is only defined in terms of the single election of 1967: the correlation in our French case is $r = .42$. Furthermore, it is true in our data, as in the American, that the more senior deputies express greater confidence in knowledge of district opinion than do the junior deputies, although the association is not overwhelming ($r = .22$). But, as we may recall from Chapter 20, once we made the effort to measure accuracy of district opinion in a satisfying way, there was no sign that the more senior deputies were actually more accurate in their district perceptions. In fact, the modest observed relationships went in the opposite direction, as though the longer the deputies served in Paris, the more out of touch with district opinion they became.[10]

There is another point of view from which the data configurations of Figures 23-2A–23-2C in general, and the key marginality effect in particular, may be fruitfully viewed, even though strictly speaking there is no actual "explanation" involved. For the most part, in both the French and American displays the safe-seat diamonds show correlations which are higher in *absolute* magnitude than their counterparts in competitive (marginal) districts. Over the two French panels there are only two exceptions, and one tie, out of sixteen such independent comparisons. The picture is more mixed in the American panel, with three exceptions in eight trials, although even here the magnitudes associated with the exceptions are on balance visibly smaller than is true for the comparisons which fit the rule.

We have already discarded the Fiorina suggestion about intradistrict variance differences between safe and marginal seats. But there is another potential source of variance difference between the two subsets of these samples which is rather obvious. This is the great likelihood that for many bipolar political variables (and most policy cleavages are indeed bipolar), citizens in and deputies from safe districts constitute a higher-variance subgroup than the complementary subgroup of citizens and deputies from more competitive districts. This is easily seen in the abstract if we imagine any generic policy continuum "unfolded," as in part (a) of Figure 23-3: the marginal seats by definition lie in the middle, and the safe seats are toward the extremes. Hence on this variable or, to a lesser degree, any linearly related variable, the "folding over" of the variable to combine safe-seat extremes produces a higher-variance group than the complement in the middle. And, for any given bivariate data featuring linear relationships, it is to be expected that extreme-case analysis, dropping out data from the murky middle group, tends to enhance correlation magnitudes.

We need not leave it to guesswork that such variance differences exist between our two groups of safe and marginal seats. We have examined the univariate variances for the A, B, C, and D terms which have been used to form the more specific diamonds later averaged for Figure 23-2. Despite the stray instances in which the ratio of the safe-seat variance to the marginal-

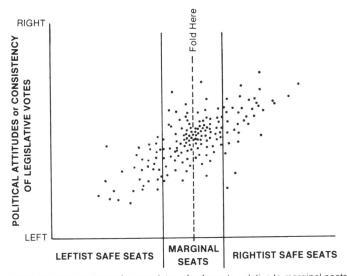

(a) Likely higher variance for correlates of safe seats, relative to marginal seats

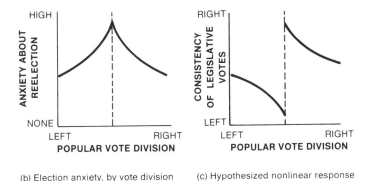

(b) Election anxiety, by vote division

(c) Hypothesized nonlinear response to electoral anxiety taken alone

Figure 23-3. Three hypothetical correlates of seat marginality, France.

seat variance is slightly less than one, indicating that the variance is actually higher in competitive districts, the ratio runs well beyond one in most instances. In fact, the patterns averaged by type of term are instructive:

Term	*Average ratio*
A. District sentiment variables	1.12
B. Deputy issue positions	1.17
C. Deputies' perception of district	1.08
D. Legislative votes in assembly	1.51

Even the lowest entry here shows that the variance in district perceptions among deputies from safe seats is running 8 percent greater on the average than that among deputies from marginal districts. This is not in itself
a huge difference; and, furthermore, we should hasten to add that the variance discrepancy is lower for the two terms involving the home district (A
and C) than for the two other terms involving deputy attitudes and behaviors. Indeed, this latter pattern smacks of a familiar finding (see, for example, McClosky, 1960), which shows that political differentiation in attitudes
is sharper at the elite than at the corresponding mass level; and these data
may also hint that if elite attitudes amplify differences in mass political attitudes, elite behaviors may proceed to amplify them a great deal more, since
the "action" term, D, shows an inflation of variances which is three times
greater than that for even the elite attitudes, which are already inflated.

We find this kind of discussion helpful in understanding the contrasts
between representation parameters by seat marginality, as shown in Figure
23-2. Nevertheless, it is extremely important to be aware of what a discussion at this level does and does not accomplish. It does *not*, for example,
show that the contrasts between safe and marginal seats in the figure are
mere artifacts of method. At the very least, the effects which we address here
are associated with conventionally linear relationships which are in an
equally conventional degree somewhat "fuzzy." And if the underlying relationships are passably linear, then we have indeed ruled out empirically the
original version of the marginality hypothesis, which supposed anxiety
about reelection to move in a very nonlinear fashion over any unfolded
continuum (as it may well do), along the lines shown in part (b) of Figure
23-3, and which also supposed that heightened responsiveness to district coloration would tend in corresponding fashion to produce legislative voting
which might look rather like part (c) of Figure 23-3. Our results, which are
relatively linear, clearly disconfirm such a pattern. Yet to have proved that
we are seeing many results here which follow from conventional linear relationships does not in itself help us to understand why they are linear.

Here the diagnosis may be fairly simple, despite the seductiveness of
the expectation that tight electoral competition might keep the representative intensely solicitous about district wishes. That whole line of thought
presumes that most representatives would prefer not to worry about district
preferences, and hence that, once electoral pressures were alleviated, most
representatives would run amok and vote in all kinds of strange ways.
Fiorina challenges such an assumption, and we are inclined to do the same.
What the fuzzy linear relationship says, in gross, is that deputies from more
extreme districts tend to vote in parliament in more extreme patterns than
do deputies from more middling districts, who cast votes in more middling
ways. This need not be a shocking finding, once we recognize that deputies
from "safe" districts, which tend to fall toward one or the other political
extreme, may themselves feel rather "set" in the same outlook, and hence

little inclined to toy with different political postures simply because they may feel free of a certain level of electoral pressure. Indeed, they may well give unusual credit to the perceptions they harbor about district opinion simply because that opinion has so often shaped their own, and because there is no countervailing local position which is well articulated and which they might hesitate to ignore totally in their legislative votes. Although this diagnosis may not be entirely satisfying, it at least has the advantage of fitting the observed data to a reasonable degree.

A Postscript on Legislative Roles

In Chapters 16 and 21 we indicated that the mix of conceptions of the representative role in any given legislature should affect the fidelity of popular representation reflected in its legislative decisions. Most particularly, we would expect that legislatures dominated by Burkeans would show less apparent responsiveness than legislatures dominated by politicians with a delegate view of the representative role. Hence role conceptions should be another major source of conditional variation in the quality of popular representation.

We have no intention of exploring this argument a second time. We already know that voter opinion is not seen as crucial to legislative decisionmaking by most deputies in the French National Assembly. But at the margins we have continued to note signs that attention is given to district sentiment, particularly in circumstances where there is some visible independent life to the CD bond in our broader diamonds. These circumstances arise mainly in connection with the measurements of more specific issues. We had not arrived at all of these relevant measures by Chapter 21; but now that we have, it is worth asking whether our earlier role measures predict to some of these more complex outcome measures in the ways that common sense suggests they should.

One of the main new measures available to us now that we have moved to the right side of the diamond paradigm can be derived directly from the CD bond, which reflects the degree to which the legislative vote of the representative is congruent with his perception of sentiment in his district. Just as earlier in this chapter we decomposed the AD bond into a set of greater or lesser individual contributions to the correlations involved, so now we can decompose the CD bond in the same way, arriving at individual-level measures which index the degree to which, over all of our issue domains, particular deputies tend to add to or detract from the "average" observed levels of the CD bond. This higher-order measure should say something about the deputy's attentiveness to district opinion in forming legislative decisions, at least as he conceives that opinion. It is a natural measure to lay against role conceptions of voter importance.

In Table 23-1 we present the zero-order correlations (r) between this

Table 23-1. Predicting individual contributions to the CD bond from variation in deputy role conceptions, information sources, and other characteristics, France, 1967.[a]

	Basis of CD measure	
Deputy characteristics	Specific-issue variables	Left-right variables
Role conceptions		
Importance of voters to decisions	.30	.33
Role summary: voters vs. conscience	.28	.26
Information sources		
Newspapers	.28	.26
Mail	.07	.13
Militants of local party	.20	.16
Professional organizations	.00	−.09
Personal contacts	−.37	−.14
Prefecture	−.27	.07
Survey results	−.01	−.08
Other deputy characteristics		
Length of residence in district	.18	.12
Years served in parliament	−.03	−.03
Proportion of district urban	.16	.20
Degree to which seat is safe	.25	.22

a. Entries are zero-order correlations (r).

measure of contribution to the CD bond and the most relevant variables referring to the conception and implementation of representative roles in the legislature, as well as additional measures which have become important to us in this chapter. As with our earlier individual-level AD measure, we have kept separate the versions of the CD measure based on specific-issue and left-right diamonds. (These two measures correlate at the level of $r = +.55$, suggesting a reasonable overlap in what the two variables measure.)

We see in the first panel that the CD measures behave as they should, relative to the two most relevant role conceptions: that is, the more importance the deputy accords to voter positions as a desirable force in his legislative decisionmaking, and the greater weight he accords to voters relative to his own conscience in such decisions, the stronger his personal contribution to positive CD bonds in our various diamond displays.

The second panel refers to our battery of questions asking the deputies how much weight they would tend to place upon various sources of information in assessing policy sentiments in their districts, and whether, more factually, they had ever used sample surveys. The sample survey item seems to lack any association with the CD measure. There is a plausible pattern

vis-à-vis the other preferred channels for information about district sentiment, however. Deputies who appear behaviorally to place most weight on
their perceptions of district sentiment in legislative decisionmaking are least
respectful of information about that sentiment gleaned from personal contacts, professional organizations, and probings carried on at the prefecture
level (more or less, the county building). They prefer to depend more upon
newspapers, mail, and information supplied by local party militants. These
latter sources could hardly be seen as providing unbiased information about
popular opinion. Mail and letters to the editor tend to come from the more
educated and attentive segments of the citizenry; and although some local
party workers may indeed have their ears to the ground, that cannot be
taken for granted in any given case. Nonetheless, all three of these sources,
preferred by those deputies who give greatest weight to district opinion,
would appear to have more popular authenticity and less pure elite parochi-
alism than would be supplied by the deputy's immediate personal contacts,
professional associations, or the seat of regional government. Therefore
these data have a further satisfying plausibility about them that addresses
the variation in the way deputies implement their representative roles.

The third panel assesses correlations with other deputy characteristics,
including some which offer a further postscript to our comments on the
marginality hypothesis in this chapter. Most important, we see that the safer
the deputy's seat, the stronger the individual contribution to a positive CD
bond in our diamond figures. This is, of course, no more than a recapitula-
tion (by other means) of the finding which was apparent in Figure 23-2, but
it is interesting to see how strong the association is in this individual-level
form. Although we have seen that there is a substantial correlation between
seat safety and years of service in parliament, this display again discourages
any assumption that the CD bond is heightened because of length of deputy service and hence greater familiarity with the district: sheer seniority in
the Assembly is essentially uncorrelated with the CD measure, and this remains true despite the fact that pure length of residence in the district does
show some positive correlation with it. Besides the role variables, the
strongest correlates of the CD measure involve seat safety, a finding that
justifies the attention we have paid to that hypothesis.

Summary

The purpose of this chapter has been to explore a number of potential
sources of variation in the general fidelity of popular representation in the
National Assembly, as well as the variation in attentiveness of these elites to
public opinion in their voting decisions.

One of the most publicized sources of such variation in the American
case—that arising from differences between types of issues—failed to emerge

in an intelligible way. Variation does exist in the French case, but it is often as lively across issue items drawn from the same domain as it is across domains. Even after various forms of within-domain averaging were used, there was still no sign of the expected finding that foreign issues, relative to domestic issues, showed lowered fidelity of representation. The sole expectation of this kind which survives with any clarity is that the religious issue, as embodied by debates over governmental support to church schools, does seem to be somewhat analogous to the civil-rights policy domain in the United States. For this domain, political elites seemed more than normally concerned to mirror local preferences in their legislative decisions.

As soon, however, as we turned to temporal variation in the fidelity of representation, as captured by the extension of our study across the 1968 revolts and the attendant dissolution of the National Assembly, we had no trouble finding intriguing patterns dependent on the identity of particular issues. In general, it appeared that the net impact of the disturbances was to focus subsequent representation on the two policy areas which were manifestly at the center of the storm: the demand for university reform among the students and the demand for greater union control among the factory workers. For these two areas, the fidelity of representation sharpened in the wake of the revolt. For all other domains, the levels of representation seemed clearly to deteriorate, relative to the levels which appeared to pertain before the uprising.

We then proceeded to ask another very natural question: does fidelity of representation on the part of the individual deputy increase his odds of reelection? We found it fairly easy to mount a test of this hypothesis, and the result was positive. But we felt obliged to inquire after the proper interpretation of the finding, since other dynamics could have contributed to or even governed the result.

In particular, we needed to consider the possibility that occupants of legislative seats which were safe from much intense electoral competition would tend in a general way to represent their constituents more faithfully than members with competitive seats. This possibility demanded consideration despite the fact that it was both somewhat counterintuitive and contrary to the assumptions made by MacRae (1952) and others. However, Miller (1964) had established it as a finding for the United States. In the central particulars, our French data reflected these American patterns. Our French deputies were much less likely to see their roles as being directly and immediately responsive to district opinion than was true of their American counterparts, a fact which meant that signs of attentiveness to such opinion were in general rather muted in our data. Nonetheless, fidelity of representation was visibly greater for members with safe seats than for those with marginal ones, and the weight of the CD bond in decisionmaking was larger there as well.

We could not discard the possibility that our deputies actually did increase their odds of electoral survival by heightened responsiveness to the policy sentiments of their districts. It was clear, however, that such odds would be more favorable, ceteris paribus, for the deputy occupying a safe seat (an outcome less manipulable in the short term than responsiveness to district sentiment); and it was also clear that safe-seat occupants were more likely to win reelection. It may ultimately be possible to distinguish between these determinants of reelection, but at our present level of crude discrimination the key factors are too intercorrelated to enable us to make a firm differentiation.

Finally, we followed up on our earlier discussions of the representative role by asking about the conditional variation in representation which might ensue, as measured by some of our more complex indicators of performance. Once again, the main tests were generally positive: deputies who professed uncommon interest in what common voters thought, relative to the dictates of their own consciences, tended across all issue domains to contribute disproportionate strength to the CD bond, or the link between their perceptions of policy sentiment in their districts and their ultimate roll-call voting patterns.

Since macrocosmic representation of the kind being examined here involves an enormous complex of relationships, many other potential sources of variation in deputy responsiveness could be explored; however, we have covered most of those which have been of persistent concern in the literature. But there is another question, and perhaps one of the most basic, which looks for variation in representation from still another angle of vision. This question has hovered over our text at many points, and it deserves to be addressed more directly in the last chapter of this book. The question is, "Who gets represented?"

24

The Nature of
Representation in France

Throughout this long book, we have reported many narrow research findings at various levels of investigation, all of which were inspired by a desire to understand the nature of political representation in France. These findings may be likened to threads in a tapestry. Now the time has come to add the final strand to that tapestry and to examine its recurring patterns.

One central question remains which is pivotal to an understanding of the way in which the French democratic system of representation operates. This question, in simplest form, is, "Who gets represented in such a system?" The answer of the hypothetical democrat who might have designed this mode of popular representation would be, of course, that everybody is represented, and equally so. Perhaps that is true, but it is reasonable to suspect that in practice some constituents may be "more equal than others." Thus, in summarizing the nature of French representation, we must take account of such potential biases. In Chapter 19 we found that, technically speaking, the supporters of the winning deputies get far more faithful representation in the National Assembly than either the supporters of the losing candidates or the constituency as a whole. This answer, however, is rather obvious, and it comes close to being tautological. Are there not other answers, revealing other lines of bias, which show that popular representation in France caters more closely to some types of constituents than to others?

We shall find that, as we pursue this question, the design of our study does not permit us to propose answers that are as unequivocal as we would like. But it does offer some illumination, which will be a useful preface to our final viewing of the tapestry that depicts popular representation in France.

Who Gets Represented?

The extant literature, some of our own findings, and common sense all converge upon two prime hypotheses as to what kinds of constituents may have disproportionate influence upon the ultimate workings of any democratic representation process. According to these hypotheses, more faithful representation can be won by constituents who are of high social status or who are highly involved politically. Indeed, a cynic might argue that "the district," as the typical representative sees it, is nothing more than an expressive public made up of those who rank high in both status and political involvement.

The reasoning behind these hypotheses is utterly straightforward. The two most distinctive characteristics of the sitting representative, relative to any randomly selected citizen of the same polity, are that he is immensely involved in politics and that he tends to be of rather high social status. Similarly, the constituents with whom the representative most often discusses politics are much more politically involved and of higher status than the average citizen.

This is not to say that the representative is totally insulated from the opinions of the less politically involved or of the lower strata of society. As a matter of fact, one of the great wisdoms of a democratic system is that elected officials are likely to be keenly aware that the political sentiments they hear expressed on the daily round always have the potential for being dramatically unrepresentative. Thus, whether representatives are motivated more by the ideal of public responsiveness or by the fear of electoral reprisal, they are among the few professional elites who must distrust the sentiments of their personal entourage and try to assess opinion more broadly, or "at large." In the light of these pressures, our hypotheses about bias in representation take on new meaning, and we need to ask how adequately representatives "correct" for the obvious status and involvement biases of their close personal world. If the correction is less than adequate, then we should expect to find that the representation system caters disproportionately to those of status and involvement. That there are strong system incentives to implement such a correction, in the form of reelection needs, leaves the bias hypothesis open to challenge. But there is certainly no countervailing hypothesis which posits that the representation system may grant undue influence to the downtrodden and politically apathetic.

Various strands of the data reported in earlier chapters help to increase our interest in the question at hand. In Chapter 19 we discovered that whenever issue sentiments at a national level differed in systematic ways as a function of the status characteristic of educational attainment, our representatives' own convictions fitted those of the well-educated better than those of the average citizen. Nevertheless, this finding, clear though it was, did not answer our present question about representation bias, because we were speaking at the time of representatives' personal convictions on the issues, and not about their role behavior as public officials. Of course, representatives have the same inalienable right to personal opinions as anybody else; and these need not dominate their behavior as representatives, especially if they sense that their own opinions are highly unrepresentative. But this finding does reveal clearly that unless representatives intentionally avoid basing their "representing behaviors" on their own opinions, we should find clear signs of a bias in representation fidelity which disproportionately favors higher-status opinion.

We have also encountered parallel clues where political involvement is concerned, especially when viewing the process of representation as a kind of communication system in which representatives need to understand district sentiment on particular issues through very limited cues. In Chapter 7 we divided our common citizens into three strata on the basis of their self-reported political-involvement levels, and found that much of the cognitive coherence needed by representatives in order to "read" local sentiment on the basis of a cue such as the left-right trends in voting patterns was monopolized by the 15 percent of the electorate that were most intensely involved. As long as we thought of constituencies as being limited to this attentive stratum, a surge of leftist voting could be crudely translated into corresponding sentiment with regard to more specific issues, such as the force de frappe or union rights or the issue of lay schools. For the other 85 percent of the electorate, such a leftist surge had almost no interpretation at all in terms of other more specific issues, simply because knowing that a voter in this less-involved majority of the constituency was leftist told representatives next to nothing about any other issue positions they might favor.

This does not mean that voters in these less attentive strata cannot make their voices heard on the more specific issues that exercise them. Of course they can; and when they do, there is no reason to imagine that these more specific signals will not be faithfully received. But in most constituencies, most of the time, such specific-issue mobilization will not achieve much intensity; and even when it does, the frank inability of representatives to deduce what other sentiments need representation, out of the vast majority of remaining issues not bound up in the temporary mobilization, spells trouble for general-purpose representation of the less-involved strata of the constituency. Thus we might expect the less-involved constituents to receive less faithful representation not only because they are less likely to "have the ear" of the representative from day to day, but also because the political claims they generate are, in the aggregate at least, awash in "noise" and idiosyncratic patterns of preference that are difficult to decode from the sparse clues which are normally available. Hence the representative does not receive any clear mandate from this portion of the constituency, but responds instead to the more focused and coherent signals from the highly involved.

For a final set of theoretical considerations, let us review the nature of the background relationship between status and political involvement. It is well recognized that at most times and places people of higher status are also more politically involved. From this point of view it might be asked whether we are really proposing to deal with two tests of representation bias, or with only one.

At this point we should beware of exaggerating the closeness of the relationship between status and political involvement. It is true that at the individual level within our mass sample, there is a solid correlation ($r = .32$) between the capacious measures of social status and those of political involvement which we intend to use; but this means that there is only about a 10 percent overlap between the variances of these two measures. Even granting that both measures contain some error variance which could not be expected to overlap, such figures do leave substantial room for independent effects of the two variables on any bias in representation.

Such a possibility is of keen theoretical interest because social status is a relatively ascribed characteristic, whereas political involvement is a relatively achieved one. The difference is, of course, no more than a matter of degree. Although some individuals manage to climb or fall significant distances up or down the status ladder over the course of their lifetimes, dramatic short-term change of this kind is relatively rare. One major component of status, for example, is educational attainment, and this characteristic is essentially fixed for adults. Political involvement, on the contrary, is a motivational matter and can be entered into or discarded in the very short term. To be sure, the kind of political involvement which puts a person into a position of some influence in a political organization is not likely to be generated overnight. But most political groups are permeable to those willing to invest relatively short periods of energy and loyalty.

The counterpoint between social status and political involvement may perhaps best be described by the proposition that in most democratic systems, persons can wield a level of political influence through political activation which can make up for major deficits in social status. The most handsome treatment of this subject at a macrocosmic level is included in the cross-national studies of Verba, Nie, and Kim (1978), which trace out the ways in which societal institutions dedicated to the political mobilization of lower-status voters, such as politically oriented labor unions, can serve to reduce the correlation between social status and political participation well below the values which seem to pertain in polities like the United States, where unions are less militant in national politics and less tightly bound up in the party system.

For all of these reasons, it is stimulating to consider whether the French representation system tends not only to favor majority constituents, but also to give special weight to the opinions of either higher-status constituents or of those who are more politically involved.

Some Operational Difficulties

It would be relatively simple to design an excellent test for these representation biases. We could recompute new mean values for district sentiments limited to those of our constituents who are the most involved or to those of highest status. Then we could ask whether our index of the basic representation bond—the correlations involving the AD term—tends to run higher for such an exalted slice of the constituency than it did for our original total constituency. We might also calculate the same correlations for both the less-involved and the lower-status strata, to verify that they do indeed fail to match the levels of representation fidelity found for the higher groups.

The final specification necessary for this ideal test would tell us how large an upper fraction of the constituency should be isolated in order to make such an examination. There is, of course, no fixed rule here, although experience with these matters suggests that we might find the liveliest effects by isolating a rather thin top stratum. In earlier chapters, for example, when we divided our sample of citizens into high-, medium-, and low-involvement groups (see, for example, Figures 7-1 and 7-2), we have profitably made the top group a mere 15 percent of the population, instead of one-third. We would have preferred to have made this stratum thinner still, say, 5–10 percent, but we did not because of small case numbers. This level of fractionation would also be equally telling where representation bias is concerned.

It is obvious that we cannot undertake such an ideal test because our case numbers within districts are far too small for further fractionation.[1] The only way in which we can hope to glimpse bias contrasts is by merely dividing each of our district samples into more or less exact halves, thus giving us ten or twelve cases to represent the upper and lower strata of each district. We shall rapidly discover that in some instances even these numbers are too low for stable estimates, but nonetheless we can achieve enough reliable contrasts to make it worth our effort.

Mounting the Test

For two reasons it was important to select our most capacious variables bearing on status and political involvement. First, at a theoretical level, we wished to use as strong and stable measures of each construct as possible, and this meant selecting multi-item indices. Second, on a more practical level, it was important to have a highly differentiated set of scores on each of the two diagnostic variables in order to permit exact halvings of each district sample, without the confusion that would be generated if there were a large number of ties in scores at the prospective point of partition.

For political involvement, our basic measure, used in Chapter 7, fulfilled these specifications well. And for social status we reconstructed the three classic status measures—the educational attainment of the respondent, the relevant *family* income, and the occupational status of the head of the household—in such a form as to express percentiles of the population from high to low. After these relativistic measures had been put into a common currency, our final status scores for individuals were simply averages of the three percentiles. These scores ranged in practice from the fourth percentile (a respondent with no education in the household of an unskilled laborer earning less than 400 francs a month), to well up in the ninety-seventh percentile (university or grande école education, professional or high managerial occupation, and family income over 4,200 francs per month).

Our halving of each constituency along these status or involvement lines was a relative matter; that is, we might have divided our respondents into high and low groups by splitting them all at the fiftieth percentile and letting the chips fall where they might at the district level. Had we done so, we would undoubtedly have found "silk-stocking" districts in Paris or Lyons where two-thirds or more of the constituents would have qualified for the higher-status "half" of their districts, as well as backward and rural districts in which the reverse would have been true. Such departures from the parity of distribution by district would greatly have eroded the efficiency of our case numbers, which were already thin. But in any event, it is theoretically more appropriate to see status as a district-relative matter. For the purposes of the substantive hypothesis at issue, the representative from a poor district is not without some constituents who have more status and political clout than others, and it is fair to imagine these to be simply those locals who are *relatively* high in status or involvement, even though they may by national standards be rather low in both respects.

Results

After our data had been restructured in this fashion, there were two levels of results. The first level told us what comparisons were safe to look at, given the thinness of our case numbers. Some of these first, or "possibility," results are in themselves theoretically illuminating provided we understand the issues involved. Therefore we shall take a brief look at them.

In all of our major examinations of the representation function up to this point we have operated in a two-ply fashion, predicting legislative roll-call vote outcomes first from district sentiments on specific issues, and second from district left-right coloration. Both versions are of interest in their own right, although it is clear that representation has generally been better tuned in an absolute sense to the gross cue of left-right than to finer issue-specific reactions within the district, despite the visible impacts of the latter. Therefore we regret the discovery that after our district samples have been divided in half along other than majority-minority lines, we can no longer make representation contrasts by using left-right constituent locations as an effective predictor.

The reasons are not difficult to understand, especially for the involvement comparisons. Our "telescope" loses its resolving power both as case numbers for each district decline *and* as differentiation between districts declines. We were able to withstand 60 percent declines in case numbers in the majority-minority comparisons of Chapter 19 because they were more than offset by greatly heightened between-district differentiation: data from rightist majorities in some districts were pitted against those from leftist majorities in other districts, thus greatly sharpening between-district contrasts and retaining remarkable resolving power.

The involvement contrasts are quite different intuitively. If we think about the matter, we shall expect contrasts in left-right means between districts to be *somewhat* sharp for the politically involved (although less so than for majority voters). But for those who are apathetic about politics, and hence either fail to choose any left-right self-location or tend to place themselves in the exact middle (neutral) position of our scale, between-district differentiation might fall off drastically. We are, in effect, comparing the marais of one district with the marais of another, and our data show that these contrasts between districts are very muted.

Worse yet, when we are dealing with left-right self-locations rather than positions on specific issues, we suffer exaggerated case losses, because more than 20 percent of our respondents overall give no content locations. These losses are already troubling for the highly involved, as they reduce our effective cases per district from eleven or twelve when we use specific issues to about ten for the left-right measure. And among the uninvolved, who are still less likely to claim a left-right location, the average number falls to eight. When this latter decline is coupled with a general collapse in between-district differentiation for the uninvolved, it is not surprising that our data send clear signals of imminent "garbage" results.[2] If we force these data to speak in any event, the numbers, which are full of sound and fury (including AD correlations that rove from large negative quantities to values greater than the permissible limit of 1.0), signify little or nothing.

The long and short of it is that we must discard as uninterpretable all AD-bond results in which the A term consists of the left-right positions of the politically uninvolved in our sample districts. We find, furthermore, that district differentiation is frequently less sharp when calculated for the higher-status half of our district samples than for the lower-status half—less sharp than the differences between the halves defined by involvement, as we might expect, given the background association between status and involvement. But the weakened differentiation coupled with case loss on the left-right measure pushes the high-status results involving left-right self-locations also below the minimum for intelligibility. The results involving left-right predictors which remain sturdy enough for examination are thus those for the lower-status half, on one hand, and for the higher-involvement half, on the other. This is, of course, the wrong comparison, and therefore these results are worth no more than a fleeting glance.

All of this turns our attention to the second round of results—the AD calculations in which the predictors are all the specific-issue sentiments in the districts. We are in a little better shape here because there is less missing data than for the left-right locations. It is not surprising, however, that in one or another of our four key "conditions" (high status, low status; high involvement, low involvement), a specific issue may also show insufficient district differentiation to yield minimal results, thereby sapping our interest in at least its paired value, even if not in the results of the three remaining conditions, which usually remain intelligible. After this self-winnowing takes place, we are left with five issue domains in which meaningful AD bonds can be calculated for every one of the four key conditions, thereby permitting symmetric comparisons. If we limit our attention to the two involvement conditions, we can read comparisons over seven issues.

These comparisons are summarized in Table 24-1. The configuration is simple and clear: fidelity of representation, as reflected in a heightened AD bond, is very considerably higher for the upper-status half of the constituency than for the lower-status half. This fits the direction that we had predicted on obvious intuitive grounds, although the differences may be rather

Table 24-1. "Who gets represented?" Fidelity of representation in constituencies varying in social status compared with that in constituencies varying in political involvement.[a]

Number of issues	Social status		Political involvement	
	High	Low	High	Low
Average over five policy domains	.28*	.12*	.14*	.14*
Average over seven policy domains	—	—	.17*	.15*

a. Cell entries are the mean correlation coefficients (r), corrected for small-sample attenuation, between average sentiment within the upper and lower strata of each district taken separately, and the parallel index of roll-call votes in that policy domain cast on behalf of the district. Reasons for missing entries are explained in text.

greater than we had any reason to expect. Nevertheless, although we had anticipated that the involved portions of constituencies would achieve closer representation than the uninvolved portions, neither of the views which we can take of this proposition lends any support to that expectation. Indeed, we are surprised that the results are as flat as they are, given that there is a modest overlap between high-status and involved constituents in each district.

When we pair off these results and lay them against our theoretical introduction, they suggest rather strongly that, in the domain of popular representation at least, the energy bound up in political involvement does not make up for the influence on policy outputs that is exercised by the higher-status segments of the community. We say "in the domain of popular representation" because we do not for a moment quarrel with the other findings, most notably those of Verba, Nie and Kim (1978), which show that institutional forms can mobilize lower-status persons and thus help to minimize, if not erase, the status differentials in political participation that are so striking in systems that have been left, as it were, "to nature." There are, of course, no inherent contradictions between their results and ours. Nonetheless, although it is true that political involvement is an achieved characteristic which can help equalize political participation, this need not mean that equalized political participation produces, in any simple way, equal influences on policy outputs. A sobering note struck by our findings is that such equalizations at one stage of the process may not result in equalizations at later stages.

Although we respect the above results and expect them to take a deserved place in the literature, we regard them somewhat conditionally. If we explain the conditions which we suspect may pertain, it will become clear why we devoted so much space to introducing these findings.

The comparisons that should ideally have been included in Table 24-1, but that are missing from it for methodological reasons, are the corresponding coefficients based on predictions made, not from sentiment on specific issues, but from general left-right preferences. We were very eager to inspect those comparisons. One large and abiding difference that has suffused all of our linkage results is that, in general, our roll-call results by district seem much better attuned to gross differences in the left-right coloration of our constituencies than to district variations in specific issue positions. If we reflect upon why this is so, we can begin to understand why it is frustrating not to be able to add these comparisons to Table 24-1.

We have presumed that these differences in the levels of apparent fidelity of representation have resulted because there are in effect two types of representation in operation. Of course, in real life these types, which are invariably matters of degree, are often hard to distinguish; however, as ideal types, they can be shown to be very distinct. The key issue involves the grossness or the fineness of the popular control mechanism. The gross version of the system involves generic, overall cues such as left-right position: these cues are fed into the black box of elections and deliberative bodies with the abiding instruction, "When it comes to deciding what left-right means on much more specific issues, you deputies figure it out, and vote accordingly." With this gross version as a guide, it is obvious what the finer control mechanism presumes. It does not leave the finer coding to representatives and party factions: instead it gives the system meaningful and highly specific issue-by-issue instructions. The difference lies in whether people are expressing political demands in large, prefabricated packages or in detailed instructions. It is not unlike the critical difference over which legislatures and executives classically squabble: granted that the executive may exercise a veto power over legislation, how finely may he do so? Can he veto specific items in a bill, or do the governing rules require him to gauge the bitter against the sweet, and either accept a mixed package as a whole or reject it as a whole?

If we look at the general run of our linkage data from this perspective, it is not at all surprising, for any number of reasons, that the fidelity of representation seems to be substantially greater for the gross version of the control system than for its finer counterpart. Reasons for this difference have cropped up in almost every chapter of this book. For example, in the early chapters our data suggested that simplifying cues like partisanship and left-right locations offered substantial fractions of the French electorate a way to reduce political information costs, as well as some rational relief from the strenuous information requirements presumed if each policy domain had to be sorted through in detail. To take another example, in Chapter 20 it became apparent that much of what a deputy can know most accurately about district sentiment is carried over one rather gross channel: election returns, with all of the limitations in message about highly specialized policies which mere shifts in party support or the left-rightness of the district imply. Whether we think of the message as sent, or the message as received, it is scarcely surprising that gross inputs from the broad electorate register with greater fidelity than do inputs about details, which, in the most obvious way, go far beyond the carrying capacity of the channel.

With this general rule in mind, however, it is not hard to imagine that the finer control system must operate through less constricted and thus higher-capacity channels than do mere election results; and it is not any harder to imagine that these finer-grained channels are likely to involve the kind of week-to-week personal contact which tends to benefit at least those constituents of higher status. This fact in itself does not explain why, as Table 24-1 implies, the more involved are not comparably benefited. But it does lead in the most direct way to other conjectures. The two most obvious are that biases in representation fidelity hinged to ascribed power are less noteworthy in the gross control system than in the fine control system; and that sheer motivation, as represented by high investments in political interest, are more likely to exert a greater equalizing influence on the gross system than on the fine-control system.

It is at this point that we need the grosser left-right predictions which are the counterparts of those in Table 24-1, in order to verify our reasoning. Unfortunately, however, they are not available, because of low case numbers and minimal district differentiation. We can consider our most recent hypothesizing as worthwhile grist for future work, but we cannot evaluate it here.

Meanwhile, we have identified one major condition that should be placed on the results of Table 24-1. The patterns in the table are striking enough in their own right, but it is possible that they would not be duplicated in counterpart results for the gross-control representation system, as indexed by left-right predictors. Nonetheless, the table retains its keen interest, since most work on representation flows from assumptions which focus on a "fine-control" system. It gives an answer to our central question, one of the most fundamental that can be posed to a large-scale representation system: "Who in the system is best represented?" It indicates that in this period in France, at least, persons of higher social status appear to have received representation that was more carefully tailored policy by policy to their concerns than to those of their lower-status counterparts. Apart from the attendant fact that political involvement does not appear to make up for shortfalls in status in achieving more "customized" service, this finding is probably not surprising. But establishing it within the terms of our current measurements is of considerable value, and must be regarded as the key element of our concluding assessments of the representation process.

The Distinctively French Context

In giving a title to this chapter, we were obliged to choose between "The Nature of Representation" and "The Nature of Representation in France." The difference is consequential. Have we been discussing the way in which the representation process happened to work out in one major industrialized democracy in the 1960s and 1970s? Or can our observations be generalized more readily to any exemplar of the kind of political system with general-purpose elections and assemblies which we originally described as our setting in Chapter 16?

It is quite natural for us to hope that both purposes have been served, even though prudence has led us to the more modest version of the chapter title. But it is not always easy to establish the appropriate scope of such generalizations, particularly in a study focusing on a single country. We have been fortunate at some points to have at our disposal other studies of representation cast in more or less the same mold, such as the Miller-Stokes study for the United States of 1958 and European work done on a parallel base.[3] These external reference points give precious background to any judgments of generality, and we have tried to use them. Nonetheless, large chasms must be leaped by some act of faith in order to reach our ultimate judgments of generality.

Without any illusions as to the difficulties involved, we have felt that sifting between what is uniquely French and what is likely to pertain in a more general sense to the functional problems of large-scale political representation systems offers us a worthwhile, if perhaps not entirely safe, framework within which to review and summarize the major findings of this book.

It is important to note at the outset that this sorting of findings is scarcely an either-or matter, with outcomes seen as either generic or as some distinctive peculiarity of the French polity. In fact, we shall argue that there is a crucial halfway house between these two kinds of simplistic answers, which may well be the most richly documented of all in our findings. Results of this mixed kind give us hope that we have learned something generic about representation because the idiosyncracies of the French situation—history, institutions, and political culture—have permitted us to discern it.

Distinctiveness is, of course, a matter of degree. The strict party discipline in the French National Assembly that has been crucial for our examination of representation is in one sense distinctive. But it is hardly unique in modern parliamentary democracies; and much that we have said about it would be relevant for a number of other legislative systems as well.

The same would apply, with appropriate nuances, to the importance of religious attachments in shaping mass political choices in France. This phenomenon appears in various guises in other countries as well, though it is by no means universal. We have been able only to suggest some of the ways in which the presence of this "cross-cutting" line of cleavage may affect a representation process in which the legislative agenda is overwhelmingly populated with issues that have no direct relevance to religion. It may well be the case that the fidelity of constituency representation suffers because of *both* the great number of nonreligious issues that regularly preoccupy the deputies *and* the specifically religious issues that occasionally surface, due to the admixture of religious and other forces that motivate the electorate in choosing its representatives. Testing that proposition is beyond our capacities here, but the possibility that it is to some degree correct has major implications for the representation process in other countries as well as in France.

To find unique elements, we may be driven to the historical juncture at which our study took place. Here two elements have impacted most clearly on our results. One was the lengthening shadow of Charles de Gaulle, lending its own imposing coloration and relief to the French politics of the period. To be sure, de Gaulle was but one of several charismatic leaders to dominate politics in the early years of postwar Europe: Churchill in England, Adenauer in West Germany, and de Gasperi in Italy. But in the end he had dominated more completely and for a longer time than any of the others. How the de Gaulle presence may have influenced the character of popular representation during the period of our study, beyond the obvious fact that he had authorized the institutions of the Fifth Republic which were necessarily our context, is not and cannot be entirely clear. But it is worth noting that the pervasive influence of de Gaulle as a political figure may well have been amplified by the tendency in French culture, itself somewhat distinctive, to deal in personalized politics more than in faceless party apparatuses.

The other unique feature was, of course, the outbreak of the upheavals of May and June 1968. On the one hand, these upheavals cannot be construed as unique, for social turmoil and confrontation politics were erupting all over the West in this period. Uprisings in Berlin, civil rights and peace protests in the United States, and the "hot autumn" of 1968 in neighboring Italy were some of the other expressions of the same general international mood. On the other hand, the uprisings in France were indeed unique for this period, because of their combination of magnitude, duration, geographic scope, and sheer destructiveness.

Although the imprint of de Gaulle upon our findings concerning the nature of representation in France is ambiguous, there is no ambiguity about the imprint of the uprisings. Even at a superficial level, these events produced a dissolution of the Assembly, and multiplied our original study design by the requirement that we go back for an "after" measurement, thereby turning a complicated study into one still more complex. But this enriched design has permitted us to trace out some of the implications of the revolt for the representation process in a way that surpasses normal political history.

We saw the intrusion of the revolt more as a blessing than a curse, as far as our theoretical interests in representation were concerned. There is no doubt that this glimpse into a system in deep political crisis, especially a crisis over elite responsiveness to popular demands, was an unexpected dividend. The trajectories of popular uprisings have rarely been well documented at the level of motivations and understandings of the situation on the part of plausible samples of the participants, central and secondary. These motivations and perceptions are normally the stuff of endless and arguable imputation on the part of those reconstructing the physical record; and it is useful to have more systematic information about them.

Of course, some of the record surrounding the 1968 uprising has long been visible, thanks in no small measure to voting statistics. Few sequences of events bring to mind so quickly the possibility that in social events, as in physical ones, "action produces reaction." If the "action" in the equation—the initial student and worker revolt—had parallels in other countries in the same epoch or, for that matter, in France at other times following the launching of routine democracy in 1870, it outstripped all parallels in its sheer magnitude. Therefore it is appropriate that the "reaction" or backlash, as measured in popular votes, clearly outstripped any parallels in other nations in the late 1960s, or any domestic disturbance in France in the preceding century. This one sequence does not in itself guarantee the details of any mechanical analogy; for, as we have seen, support for the action was remarkably widespread, and reaction and backlash only appeared after the protest had escalated to an excess of anarchy and destruction. The mechanical analogy says that reasonable protest will always escalate to gross irresponsibility, which may or may not be true.

This action and reaction was evident in the public record quite apart from our study. What our materials add is some illumination of perceptions across conflict lines, and more especially, a detailed assessment as to the impact that such a violent assault against the representation system had on the way in which popular representation was subsequently managed. Here our chief finding is double-edged. *In spite of the electoral reaction,* the explosiveness of the uprising produced a great concern to placate and conciliate, even on the part of the victorious and vindicated right. This meant that the most immediate grievances of the students and workers were given priority treatment by the National Assembly, and "responsiveness" was focused exclusively upon those particular demands. Our study shows that this constriction of responsiveness produced a measurable decline in actual responsiveness across the rest of the broad front of political concern in the French nation in the period around 1970.

This is a finding which, if unforeseen, at least carries with it a compelling plausibility. We could never have discovered it without the aid of the unique French uprising. At the same time, we have paid a significant price for this fortuitous gain in knowledge, because our work has been confounded with the intrusion of the crisis. Originally we were interested in broad comparisons between the nature of representation in France and its nature in other countries. Few direct comparisons were available, although we did have fairly clear counterparts in the Miller-Stokes data for the United States. As a first step toward a broader empirical theory of these matters, it would have been interesting to see whether a legislative system featuring tight party discipline like that of the National Assembly reflected popular sentiment in home districts more or less faithfully than the relatively undisciplined system of the U.S. Congress.

Although we would probably have wanted to use the size of the basic representation bond (AD) as our ultimate measuring stick, we would not have been able to arrive at any definitive matching of "bottom lines" for the two systems, because for each of them fidelity measured in this form does vary quite extravagantly by issue domain. Therefore we would have been left with rather more vague impressions, integrating over a large number of AD values in each system, and then comparing results. If we were to do so for the data displayed in this book, we would probably conclude that the AD bonds we have seen for France appear to run a bit lower on balance than those registered by Miller and Stokes for the United States. This modest deficit is visible *despite* taking into account the most robust French communication channel, the gross cues of left and right. Yet our motivation to put weight on these cross-national comparisons was greatly weakened because our analysis of crisis-generated effects demonstrated that the uprising and the second election it occasioned tended to *diminish* the fidelity of representation over most issue domains while at the same time sharpening fidelity in the two instances most related to the grievances. This means in turn that we had no way of assessing whether a shortfall in representation on the French side depended on long-term structural differences or, more simply, on the fact that we caught the system in crisis.

In sum, then, the historical juncture did not ruin our design, because we seem to have learned very plausible and important things from it. Nonetheless, our original purpose would have been well served if we could have carried out observations under more routine conditions as well.

Besides these major imprints of the immediate historical juncture, which were unique, we encountered other quite distinctive features of French political culture and institutions. One cultural trait which may be unique to France is the political elite's peculiar penchant for leftist self-locations. Although this marked anomaly required some adjustments in measurement strategy, there was no reason to believe, once we were within a mode of relative congruence assessment, that it intruded upon the generality of our representation results. Another distinctive cultural trait involved constrictions on intergenerational transmission of partisanship, harking back, as well as we could tell, to inhibitions concerning political communications from parents to children. It is likely that this distinctive syndrome has had effects on the nature of representation, and we shall spell these out later. Moreover, we adduced a certain amount of evidence which implied that the distinctiveness of this trait appears to be dying out, although its effects on the representation process certainly continued during the period of our study.

French Institutions of Representation

Several institutions govern the terms of popular representation in any democratic polity, ranging from laws regulating the conduct of elections to procedures established for the comportment of political parties and legislative bodies. Indeed, the attendant machinery is so multifarious that it represents less what anthropologists call a "culture trait" than what must be called a "culture complex." Few of the more unitary elements in this complex, such as single-member districts or parliamentary caucuses, are likely to be unique. Most are familiar variants of standard practices, although one or two such elements, like the system of run-off voting which we dissected in Chapters 11, 12, and 13, are relatively distinctive to the French system. What tends to be more distinctive for any polity, however, is the broader architecture of the system, the actual configuration of individual elements. In this holistic sense the French system is certainly distinctive.

Modern systematic political science has been the target of much criticism on grounds that it had become engrossed in individual political behavior and had abandoned political institutions as objects for scholarly assessment. The interest in microbehavior was real enough, as was the shift of focus away from institutions; but these were less a sign of disinterest in institutions than a search for "a place to stand," a vantage point from which to assess institutions more effectively. When political institutions are consciously designed de novo, as they often are, they are shaped to accomplish certain system goals by channeling actor behavior in ways deemed beneficial for the polity. Even when, as in the case of most modern party systems, they have not been designed from scratch, but have "just grown," they have become institutionally encrusted and regulated to fit other political institutions in prescribed ways. The degree to which these institutions accomplish their intended goals is always subject to controversy; and one means of assessment is to ask not only whether they shape behaviors in the ways intended but also whether they seem to entrain unintended consequences.

We know in a general way what modern institutions of democratic representation have been designed to achieve: some routinized means of projecting a modicum of popular voice on policy decisions. Whether the component parts of such institutions actually operate in concert to achieve such goals is, however, an empirical question, and one which has been our main concern.

Therefore we have tried to keep the presence of national political institutions to the front and center as we have worked; and we did so from the outset, when we began by focusing attention on the common French voter and his view of his political system. Our frequent resort to comparative cross-national data has been most helpful in keeping clear the impact of French national institutions and culture on the behaviors we are studying. One powerful way of summarizing a persistent theme of this book is to observe that repeatedly—in Chapters 2, 3, 8, 9, and elsewhere—we have been able to suggest empirically that often, though not always, what appear to be oddities in French political behavior within the representation process are merely deflections which have institutional roots. For example, since American, or British, voters seem to respond in very similar ways to common institutional situations, differences in behavior seem to be less a product of intrinsic contrasts in "national temperament" than of contrasts in human institutional design. As we begin to pin down the impacts of these designs on actual representation behaviors, we have a vantage point from which to assess the component institutions more effectively.

With these thoughts in mind, and also with a desire to look at the French institutions of representation holistically instead of merely retracing our steps, we find ourselves face to face with one fundamental fact: that in the grand architectonics of the French political system, it is the political party that is the "designated vehicle" for political representation. The party is the central collective entity which dictates a program of policy preferences to be supported in the legislature. The voter lucky enough to select a winning candidate has in effect bought a share of a party caucus vote, and his or her representation, infinitesimal as it may be, has thereby been assured.

The party is also, from the point of view of representation, the crowning glory of the French system in at least two other respects: first, there are many parties; and, second, new parties are relatively easy to launch in response to new challenges. In two-party systems, the choices of competing programs, even when the system escapes from its built-in pressures toward Tweedledum and Tweedledee, are as restricted as they can be without crushing out competition altogether. The voter who has an idiosyncratic pattern of policy preferences over the dozen or more highly distinctive policy domains that are routinely canvassed by a multipurpose legislature is inevitably forced to accept the bitter with the sweet; neither of the two parties is likely to express the voter's preference with any exactitude, and the choice will be the lesser of two evils. Furthermore, in a two-party system, parties are not easily replaceable in order to keep pace with societal change. Indeed, in such systems the phenomenon of "realignment" is typically ponderous and self-evident, with younger party cadres often struggling to revise old party goals and platforms which are still being espoused by the old guard. This massive creaking of two-party systems is scarcely necessary in France, because rather dramatic changes in the profiles of policy alternatives can easily result from short-term party fissions, fusions, and full-blown party replacement.

It would be too much to suppose that this constellation of design features in France arose historically with the sole aim of providing the French voter with a remarkably delicate instrument for popular representation. Nevertheless, from an elite point of view, the system would seem to have this kind of potential: voters are offered a remarkable panoply of party choices, expressing a great variety of policy combinations, and this rich menu of alternatives is updated with uncommon frequency. Moreover, as we established in the latter part of Chapter 7, deputies in the French system can expect to assess district sentiment more accurately on the basis of party vote proportions than on the vaguer impressions of district left-right tendency. And finally, the norms of party discipline within the National Assembly would seem to assure that voters' policy preferences at the polls will be directly projected, at least approximately, into legislative outcomes. In short, the design of this complex of institutions would seem, from the elite's viewpoint, to be a rational voter's delight, and one capable of a level of fine-tuning which is quite impressive in view of the ponderous size of national systems of political representation.

Nevertheless, none of our data have suggested that the fidelity of representation in France is uncommonly high, relative to other systems of rather different and more parsimonious design. Once again, we cannot put as much weight on this overall verdict as we would like, in part because of the crisis period during which the assessment was made. We also have little base for such a comparative judgment once we get beyond the constituency defined as the total district, although some of our data in Chapter 23 using minority and majority constituencies continued to suggest moderately lower levels of representation fidelity for France than for the United States. In any event, we have seen no reason to imagine that representation in France runs *high* relative to our meager outside reference points. And it has not been difficult to understand why this is so, although ferreting out the details has required us to pay almost tedious attention throughout our work to the tracing out of several levels of interaction between the voters and the French parties.

This tracing has laid bare a crowning irony of the French representation system. Although elite institutions seem well designed to provide for fine-tuned responsiveness to popular demands centering upon the political party as vehicle, the French voter seems on the whole to be rather less clearly oriented to the party system than is typically found in other well-developed democracies.

This point must be developed with great care, because there is no question that our findings are rather subtle with respect to the overall role of parties in the French representation system, when we consider the views of our mass sample. Where party objects are most salient for some voters, either as foci for emotional loyalties or as general reference points (see Chapter 10), responsiveness to lines of partisanship may be fully as keen as in any other system, and perhaps even more so. Indeed, the vast bulk of our data, seen in the multiplicity of tests carried out in Parts I and II, suggests that party identifications as well as more transient party cues tend to outweigh the grosser cues provided by left-right orientations as long-term guides for issue position-taking and candidate selection at the polls.

This is not to say, however, that left-right cues are not thoroughly helpful as organizing devices for the French voter: of course they are, and much of our linkage work in Part IV has emphasized how much the gross left-right organization of the system promotes representation, relative to the effects transmitted through the more specific issues. But the parties cannot be tightly drawn into these latter comparisons; and where direct comparisons can be made, party cues seem to carry the day over left-right symbols. It is certainly not true in any general way that left-right orientations can be counted on to make up fully for the modest confusion which swirls about the party system in the minds of the common voter, because of the system's size and volatility. And although those who profess some sense of left-right location outnumber those who profess abiding party attachments, these professed left-right locations are considerably less stable than are partisan feelings. Finally, even the greater prevalence of left-right orientations over partisan ties is in several ways rather illusory: many who offer left-right locations can say little about what these mean, and the most common response from the electorate as a whole is to self-locate at the neutral point on the left-right continuum. Moreover, many who lack partisan orientations are not part of the active electorate. Although such people are somewhat aided in their observations of the system by some vague sense of left-right landmarks, their low participation means that for the active voters the difference between subscription to parties and to left-right locations is much smaller than meets the eye.

Thus it is fair to argue that, on balance, partisanship is more important than left-right position in the workings of the mass half of the French representation system, just as it is fair to argue that those French voters who do have reasonably developed partisan loyalties are governed in their political decisions at least as clearly by these attachments as are citizens in other modern democratic systems. But neither argument is incompatible with the true source of irony: overall, party identifications in the American sense seem to be less fully developed in the French political culture than in the American; the rich galaxy of parties is, for many French voters, partially obscured by ignorance; and even for the parties that are known, the salience of these parties as points of orientation seems lower than in some competing systems. It is these facts which seem most responsible for preventing the French representation system from living up to the kind of potential which its design at the elite level would seem to offer, and which leaves our assessments of the basic representation bond in France somewhat tarnished.

The force of these propositions came home to us most clearly in Chapters 8 and 9, where we dealt with voter perceptions of candidates and parties at the polls, with specific emphasis on the basic feature of any policy representation process, the voters' mental associations between parties and candidates as objects of choice, as well as the issue positions which they might be expected to advocate. There is no question that some French voters are avidly interested in politics, that their knowledge of the party system is extensive, and that their sense of party-issue linkages is impeccable. Moreover, we were not surprised to find that more French voters link issues with parties than with candidates (despite a party clue attached to almost all candidates); and that these associations showed considerably greater clarity than was the case for candidate-issue linkages. Nevertheless, although party-oriented voters exist in France and lend no small measure of structure to the representation system, we also found that, in a general way, candidates are more salient to voters than are parties. And the existence of this large admixture of candidate-oriented voters, who do not form issue links as clearly as party-oriented voters do, goes a long way toward explaining why the sensitive potential of the distinctive French representation system is not even moderately approached.

Thus we have the irony of a representation system which, examined from the top down, is hinged on the political party and is almost ideally organized to represent the fine grain of popular opinion; and yet which, viewed from the bottom up, is not exploited in any thoroughgoing way because orientation to the details of the party system is quite stunted relative to what is found in most other comparable polities. Some of the limited attention to party agencies seems to be due to what we have called the unique aspects of the French political culture that de-emphasize parties, including the inhibitions surrounding communication of partisan preferences from parents to children. But the final touch of irony appears when we recognize that the very elements of the French representation design that make it such a sensitive instrument also put it out of the reach of the common man. The difference between the potentiality and the reality of the system is rather like that between an organ, with its great banks of keys and cross-cutting stops and pedals, and a simple four-note horn. The two instruments make vastly different demands, in both knowledge and practice, upon the user. This metaphor is helpful in emphasizing that our work with the French representation system indeed addresses the most basic and generic issues involved in the theory of representation as it relates to the large-scale, multipurpose national legislatures.

The Generic Problem of
Popular Representation

It is fitting, finally, to consider how the peculiarities of French political culture highlight some of the generic problems of system design which arise in attempting to maximize the fidelity of popular representation in a large-scale national decisionmaking system.

One way to conceive of such a system is as a communication device in which information is expected to flow, more or less faithfully, up and down.

Of course, communication is not the only important factor in such a system; as we have seen, concepts such as "the will to represent" are pivotal as well. Nonetheless, we can conduct a substantial amount of analysis by using only the abstract terms that relate to communication. This is why we have emphasized the concept of the fit between the "message as sent" and the "message as received." Clearly, one of the first requisites of any effective communication system is that these two types of message not be estranged from each other by some form of distortion. And this in turn puts an information burden upon those at both ends of the communication: knowledge is needed about what messages can be sent through the system and what symbols best convey them, in order to minimize the possibility of misunderstanding.

The French representation system has the virtue of permitting a wider range of messages to be sent than is possible in the simpler two-party systems; it also has the liability of making high information demands upon its users, assuming that they wish to exploit it fully. When we see the French system in this light, we find that three other propositions dealing with general communications systems are applicable.

The first has to do with redundancy, or the repetition of the same messages through the system. Redundancy is important in ensuring that the messages that are sent are received; and the higher the channel capacity of the system—that is, the more numerous and various the messages that it can transmit—the more important redundancy is in ensuring the reception of particular messages. We have seen the effects of redundancy at many points in our work, particularly toward the end of Chapter 20, where we noted that our linkage issue domains seemed to array themselves repetitively in the same rough kind of hierarchy of stability and familiarity. It is the old familiar linkages, endlessly reiterated over many years, that receive the widest recognition among the public, just as the old familiar issues are the ones on which elite recognition of mass preferences is likely to be most accurate.

The second proposition hinges on the possibility of coping with a complex communication system by using it in what might be called a "reduced form." A simplistic two-party system permits a given vote to transmit only a binary message, although of course abstention can be seen as a third statement. The channel capacity of a 10-party French system or a 31-party Dutch system is enormous by comparison. At the same time, the sheer variety of options puts high information demands upon the user. If these information demands are too much for some casual users, there is nothing to prevent them from simplifying the system in their own minds by focusing on two principal parties, presumably ones about which information is most prevalent, and then proceeding to engage in decisionmaking that is the same as that engaged in by the voter in a two-party system. On this basis, it could be argued that a more complex party system would always be preferable to a two-party one, since nothing would be lost by casual voters, and much would be gained if they could send more discriminating messages by first paying the information costs necessary to learn what the total system had to offer.

There is, of course, a good deal to recommend this viewpoint. Certainly we have seen evidence suggesting that substantial numbers of French voters do live in a political landscape which does not seem to extend phenomenologically beyond two or three of the major parties, whatever other fine-grained alternatives are available to them. The only countervailing consideration is the possibility that casual voters feel in some degree confused by and therefore psychologically excluded from normal system participation because they cannot readily follow the politics of the unfamiliar parties. Very early in this book we saw that the kaleidoscopic party system itself appears to inhibit normal party attachments, and that the level of popular dissatisfaction with the number of parties in the system runs very high.

The third proposition, which is similar to the first two, can be stated very succinctly. The heavier the information demands placed on voters by a representation system, the more sharply stratified will representation become, with the most knowledgeable few exerting an inordinate amount of direct control, relative to the less knowledgeable many. We are speaking, naturally, of the kind of control and influence over the representation system that would register in our data, ignoring for the moment the high likelihood that the more knowledgeable voters exert control through other types of political channels as well. And this proposition brings us back to the concerns with which we began this final chapter.

Throughout this book we have seen many instances of what might be called a stratification of political cognitions, whether we were talking of differential awareness of the party system, of ideological organization of the perceived political world, or of perceptual clarity concerning links between the several parties and policy postures on specific issues. Wherever we looked, the apparent stratification was marked, and of course all three of these cognitive terms are important in directing political choice and expression toward the fulfillment of personal viewpoints, and hence, ultimately, representation. Much of the structure of French public opinion seems to derive differentially from a rather thin stratum of the most attentive citizens, and clearly the lack of attention to political matters that characterizes most voters substantially excludes them de facto, if not de jure, from a great deal of fine-tuned representation.

We have distinguished between the kind of fine-tuned representation which responds to district sentiments concerning specific issues and that which responds to the grosser cues of left-right location. Although we lacked the materials necessary to demonstrate the following hypothesis, we suggested that the less demanding left-right cues might broaden the accessibility of representation in at least its crude form. Much of our earlier linkage work, by showing that substantially greater levels of representation fidelity are associated with left-right predictors than with specific-issue ones, lends a certain credibility to this assertion. We actually were able, however, to demonstrate an increase in the levels of achieved representation on specific issues in proportion to the degree of formal education, if not of political involvement. This configuration provides some support for the presumption that the more complex the information requirements, the more sharply stratified will be the achievement of representation through common institutions.

Because large-scale political systems with mechanisms of multipurpose representation must rest upon the prevailing conditions of information and choice, all of these systems, to some extent, manifest differential representation. The question, as usual, is one of degree. And however delightful a representation instrument the French system may be for those equipped to play upon it, it seems to fall short of its potential for much of the electorate much of the time.

Appendices
Notes
Bibliography
Index

Design and Implementation of the Mass Interviewing

The First Mass Survey of the French Electorate, 1967

The sequence of studies reported in this volume was initially planned by the authors in the autumn of 1966 as a single representation study with interlocked mass public and political elite components, to be carried out in connection with the French national legislative elections scheduled for March 1967. The mass and elite components were to be "interlocked" in the sense that portions of the electorate to be sampled were to stand in an unambiguous functional political relationship to the particular political elites to be interviewed. More specifically, they were to reflect the actual constituents of the representative role for which the elite respondents were vying as candidates. Since the representative function in France, as in most other democracies, is defined on a territorial base, the key initial procedure in the study design concerned the selection of a manageable sample of legislative districts (*circonscriptions*).

The Sample Design: Selection of Districts

We discovered that SOFRES, the sample survey agency in Paris, had already drawn for other purposes a sample of legislative districts which fitted our needs almost perfectly. From the districts which constituted metropolitan France (but excluding Corsica) in 1966, a stratified probability sample of 84 districts had been selected by SOFRES.

The lines of stratification for this selection were both political and geographic. The districts forming the original universe were initially divided into three strata based on the results of the first ballot of the 1965 presidential election in each district:

(1) 289 districts in which de Gaulle had led Mitterrand in the popular voting, and Mitterrand had in turn led Lecanuet;

(2) 103 districts in which the order of finish had been Mitterrand first, de Gaulle second, and Lecanuet third; and

(3) 66 districts in which de Gaulle had led, with Lecanuet second and Mitterrand third.[1]

Each of these three initial strata was subdivided according to further characteristics of recent French political history. In particular, the well-populated first stratum was subdivided into seven classes, following the percentage of votes gained by the UNR in the district at the first ballot of the legislative elections of 1962. The third stratum was also subdivided according to the same criterion, but into only three roughly equal substrata, out of respect for its limited size. The second initial stratum, which had preferred the leftist candidate Mitterrand, was subdivided into five groupings according to the proportion of votes received by the Communist party in the 1962 elections. Thus the legislative districts of France were divided into fifteen strata, each displaying a marked degree of political homogeneity, as far as recent political inclinations were concerned.

Within each of these strata, component districts were arranged in a fashion which took account of geographical proximity, and then individual districts were selected by systematic sampling with a random base, so that geographic dispersion was maximized. Each district was given a probability of selection proportional to the number of its citizens registered for the presidential elections of 1965.

The care which had gone into the probability selection of the 84 districts, the sampling rate for the districts (about one out of every five), and the dominant political stratification criteria all combined to recommend this particular sample of districts to our use. There was only one inconvenience: after the SOFRES sample had been drawn, certain legislative districts around Paris, swollen by rapid population growth, had undergone subdivision in a reapportionment prepared for the 1967 elections. It was not difficult, however, to reconstitute the sampling for the affected area in a manner which properly took account of new district boundaries and the expanded universe of 467 Metropolitan districts (excluding Corsica). This adjustment produced a revised sample of 86 districts, which formed the basis for this study.

The Sample Design:
Selection of Mass Respondents

Designation of the 86 sample districts automatically defined the set of political candidates contesting the 1967 election, and hence the identity of the elite interviews. On the side of the mass public, however, further sampling stages were necessary to designate specific citizens for interviewing. The nature of the design required that respondents be selected within each district in such a fashion that all 86 of these microsamples be as representative of their surrounding district as possible. On the one hand, economic constraints on interviewer travel naturally made it impossible to select anything like a random (and randomly dispersed) sample of the citizenry in the district. On the other hand, it would have been less than desirable to attempt to represent the total district in each case with no more than a single geographic cluster of respondents from some narrow area within the district.

Therefore, within each district the communes, which can range in size from small towns to large cities, were subdivided into rural and urban strata, according to whether or not the population agglomeration surrounding the town hall (*mairie*) was less or more than 2,000 persons, according to the 1962 national census. Within the urban stratum, one commune was selected with probabilities proportional to its population size. Within the stratum of rural communes, two cantons (roughly equivalent to U.S. counties) were selected by the same methods, and then two communes were drawn from within each canton. Although some purely urban districts contained no rural communes, this procedure in the typical case arrived at a designation of five communes per legislative district. Since voter registration lists are maintained at the level of the commune, the selection of individuals for interview was then carried out directly by a systematic sampling from these lists, without further geographic clustering. Since communes are considerably more heterogeneous microcosms of the society, both politically and socially, than, for example, the residential neighborhoods or census tracts often used as penultimate sampling stages in the United States, the result of these operations was 86 samples of individuals, each of which could yield unbiased estimates of the district populations without a great exaggeration of sampling variability due to local clustering in relatively homogeneous micro-areas.

In view of our need to have the small mass sample from each district provide the most adequate possible estimates of district properties and district opinion, sampling fractions were handled over the course of the selection stages in such a fashion as to yield a roughly equal number of interviews (24) from each of the 86 districts. Although differential response rates from district to district subsequently produced some actual inequalities in interview yield per district, the number of interviews was in fact more rectangularly distributed across districts than would have been the case if such precautions had not been taken (see Figure 18-1). Overall, however, each individual registered on a voting list in Metropolitan France had about one chance in 14,000 of being included in the mass sample.

A word must be said about the use of voting lists as a final sampling frame. Unlike the situation in the United States, voter registration lists in France encompass in principle a quasi totality of the adult population enjoying French citizenship. Although, of course, aliens are not included, the lists are supposed to be sufficiently complete to provide an excellent summary of the French electorate for political sampling purposes. In fact, however, they are less than ideal as a sampling frame for the simple reason that their current accuracy and inclusiveness at any point in time—even close to an election—is subject to fair local variability. This in turn leads to difficulties in establishing a significant response rate, as we shall see in the next section. Yet the alternate means of arriving at a sample of individuals in France tend to be even less attractive. Small-area sampling with the exhaustive listing of dwelling units within areas for purposes of probability selection was not practiced in France at the time of our 1967 study, on grounds that residential patterns, especially in urban areas, are such as to make address-listing both difficult and misleading. As a replacement, "random walk" routines were supplied to interviewers within small areas, which if properly carried out could be hoped to produce much the same results. But since our experience with permitting the interviewer this much latitude in the ultimate selection of individual respondents in situ has generally been poor, we chose the voting lists as the least of all evils, because of its greater susceptibility to control and verification.

Conduct of the Field Work

Mass interviewing for the 1967 study was begun late in April, or some six weeks after the second ballot of the March legislative elections. It was essentially completed by the end of June.[2]

For reasons implied above, interviewers were required to interview the respondent designated from the voting lists without substitution, and callbacks were used to help implement the process. After the study was completed, however, the 2,046 valid interviews constituted only 63.0 percent of the predesignated respondents. Taken as a normal response rate, this figure is very low, although its base in somewhat indifferently kept voting lists renders it rather difficult to compare with response rates in some other settings, where anything much less than 80 percent is usually seen as unsatisfactory.

The category of nonresponse which is of greatest concern is the direct refusal of a designated respondent to be interviewed. This is also the category of nonresponse which has the least obvious connection with the voting-list sampling frame. Nevertheless, the overall refusal rate of about 10 percent, though perhaps a bit high, is not wildly out of line with recent experience in the United States. Moreover, we note that the refusal rate among women is about 40 percent greater than for men. One reason why women refuse to cooperate with a political interview is their perception that political interest is a domain for the male, usually their husbands. Since French women have had the suffrage only since World War II, it seems quite possible that this sex-role assumption remains stronger in France than in the United States, and makes some contribution to an increment of refusals.

A second category of nonresponse—absences from the home—accounted for another 13 percent loss from the original sample names. This figure is somewhat high, relative to our experience in the United States. It may reflect fewer callbacks with a sample which was less highly clustered into narrow geographic areas than most sample survey designs can afford to be in the United States.

If these had been the only sources of nonresponse, the response rate for the survey would have been over 77 percent, a marginal but not unfamiliar figure in the United States, particularly in recent years. But two other sources added another 14.2 percent to the overall nonresponse rate: people who had moved from the address given in the voting lists (8.0 percent); and a somewhat more heterogeneous remainder (6.2 percent), including mainly such causes of nonresponse as death or the discovery that the individual listed was unknown at the address. Much of this margin of loss can be seen as peculiar to the obsolescences of the voting-list sample frame. Dwelling-unit samples in the United States, for example, only encounter movers as a source of nonresponse when the house is temporarily vacant between occupants, a rather uncommon event. In the French case, however, a new family in a dwelling unit constitutes a nonresponse. Similarly, deaths cannot possibly figure as nonresponses in dwelling-unit samples, and for a respondent not to be known by the residents is equally impossible. In other words, a very large portion of the high rate of nonresponse must be directly attributable to voting lists that were less than current.[3]

The meager response rate for predesignated individual respondents does not guarantee that the representativeness of the sample is badly flawed. It merely increases the possibility that it might be biased with respect to our estimations concerning the state of the French electorate in 1967. Whether or not it is in fact seriously biased depends on the degree of correlation between the reasons for nonresponse and the political variables being canvassed in the study. If there is no such correlation, the sample estimates can be seen as unbiased. The truth of this matter is typically unknown, although encouraging comparisons of the sample with known population parameters can be helpful in reducing concern.

Weighting of the Sample

Before we consider such parameter comparisons, however, one other facet of the nonresponse rate must be exposed. Although the overall rate of nonresponse was 37 percent, this rate showed sharp variation both by region and by the location of the sample point on an urban-rural gradient. With regard to the latter, a lower response rate in larger urban agglomerations than in small towns and rural areas is a pattern very familiar to survey researchers in a multitude of industrialized countries. But the urban-rural gradient in responses for our French study seems particularly steep. For the Parisian agglomeration in the region of the Seine it attains a maximum which just passes 50 percent nonresponse. In rural areas of some regions, such as the Loire, the nonresponse actually falls below 20 percent. Interestingly, the large increment of nonresponse in Paris cannot be attributed to political concealment expressed as refusals to cooperate: the refusal rate for Paris is actually *lower* than the national average. Most of the increment in Parisian nonresponses arises from respondents who have moved, a type of problem that is peculiarly tied to the voting-list base and is most likely to become problematic with residentially mobile populations.

Although it is not hard to understand this increased nonresponse rate in such areas, the degree of increase is sobering for the representativity of the sample. The sample was designed to represent the population of Paris in its proper proportion to rural areas of the country. If, however, half of the Parisian respondents cannot be located or otherwise fail to respond, while three-quarters of small-town and rural respondents cooperate, we obviously have a substantial biasing of the sample toward rural overrepresentation. Therefore, though we may continue to hope that, within more or less rural areas, the reasons for nonresponse are uncorrelated with our political variables, it is obviously desirable to reweight the sample to take account of known variations in response rate.

We have performed such a reweighting for our 1967 sample. Each individual's response has been given a weight which is an inverse function of the response rate at his or her particular sampling point. Thus in areas where response rates were below average, observations were weighted greater than unity. Where response rates were relatively full, individual observations have a weight of less than one. The net effect is that the sample reflects the original, theoretically accurate, distribution of cases across regions and types of places. With very rare exceptions, which have been noted, all estimates in the text of this study are based on the weighted, rather than the raw, frequencies.[4] In case this fact should be unsettling to the reader, we should note that over a large range of univariate comparisons between the weighted and unweighted versions of the data, the discrepancies between the two were rarely more than miniscule. This fact implies in turn that the areal bases of variation in nonresponse are essentially uncorrelated with the political variables with which we are dealing, which is to say that the reweighting was scarcely worth the bother. But since the weighting had been calculated, and since it is conceptually superior under the circumstances, we have employed it consistently in reporting results.

Comparisons with Known Parameters

The low response rate in the 1967 sample leaves us particularly eager to see how well the sample estimates compare with known national parameters. Unfortunately, there are few parameters available for our purposes, and some of these, such as occupation, are themselves unduly influenced by differential coding practices on the part of various agencies, so that observed discrepancies in distributions cannot be unequivocally assigned to sampling variation.

Of the demographic variables commonly monitored by the French census agency INSEE,[5] those for which coding ambiguities are at a minimum are sex, age, and certain aspects of residential location (region, size of place). These residential variables, however, formed a part of our initial sample design, and our reweighting of the data back to an exact fit with the design specifications makes comparison with the parent census data rather artificial. The age and sex variables, however, are free to show sampling variations. As indicated in Table A-1, the proportions per sex in the sample are in excellent agreement with the census data; but where age is concerned, the very young—especially those 21–24—are underrepresented. This is not a surprising outcome. The voting lists from which the sample was drawn are not kept rigorously up-to-date, and there is undoubtedly some lag in getting new cohorts entered. Moreover, young people in their twenties show a very high rate of residential mobility, so that those who have been registered undoubtedly figure disproportionately in our forms of nonresponse that arise from such mobility (for example, respondent moved, unknown at address). Partly because of residential mobility and the registration confusions it brings, cohorts newly entered into electorates typically vote at rates which are quite low compared with those of their elders. Thus if we keep in mind that our sample is geared more toward representing the registered French electorate than the adult population as a whole, the discrepancies by age are not particularly oppressive. Indeed, as Table A-1 also indicates, our sample's estimates of the age distribution among people over thirty could scarcely be finer.

We can also inspect in Table A-1 the comparisons made available by a rather coarse categorization of occupational groups. Here, although there is some risk of definitional discrepancy, the fit between the two distributions is reasonably good. There is some overrepresentation of people in the highest levels of the urban status hierarchy, and some underrepresentation, though to a lesser degree, of rural occupations. Probably the former effect is the only one that exceeds reasonable sampling error, and it is not clear that it would do so if we had parameters based on the registered electorate rather than on the adult population as a whole. It is likely that the very youngest people are underrepresented on the voting lists, along with the transient portion of the population, and both of these groups tend to inhabit lower-

Table A-1. Demographic comparisons of 1967 mass sample with relevant national census estimates (percentages).

Demographic group	Census estimates (INSEE)[a]		1967 Mass sample estimates	
Sex				
Male	47.5		47.1	
Female	52.5		52.9	
Total	100.0		100.0	
Age group	Pop. 21 and over	Pop. 30 and over	Pop. 21 and over	Pop. 30 and over
21–24	7.9	—	4.5	—
25–29	9.5	—	7.1	—
30–39	20.9	25.3	22.4	25.4
40–49	17.8	21.5	19.1	21.6
50–59	16.5	20.0	17.3	19.6
60–69	15.3	18.6	17.4	19.6
70 plus	12.1	14.6	12.2	13.8
Total	100.0	100.0	100.0	100.0
Occupation				
Male				
Indust., gros commerçants, prof. lib., cadres sup.	5.6		9.3	
Artisans, petits commerçants	7.3		8.3	
Cadres moyens	5.8		7.0	
Employés	6.3		9.1	
Ouvriers, service	34.8		31.1	
Agriculteurs exploitants	11.8		10.8	
Salariés agricoles	4.5		2.3	
Divers	2.9		1.1	
Non-actifs	21.0		21.0	
Total	100.0		100.0	
Female				
Indust., gros commerçantes, prof. lib., cadres sup.	1.1		3.5	
Artisanes, petites commerçantes	3.9		5.0	
Cadres moyens	3.4		4.5	
Employées	8.1		7.4	
Ouvrières, service	13.4		12.2	
Agricultrices exploitantes	6.9		4.1	
Salariées agricoles	0.6		0.3	
Divers	0.7		0.5	
Non-actives	61.9		62.5	
Total	100.0		100.0	

a. All statistics, which are estimates for the population age 21 and over, as of the beginning of 1967, are based on data from the French Institut National de la Statistique et des Etudes Economiques (INSEE).

status occupations. Another artificial contribution to the slight bias toward higher-status occupations comes from a tendency on the part of a few respondents to describe lower-status occupations in a glamorous way which can produce a miscoding, an effect that the census estimates may avoid more successfully than we did. Nevertheless, the sample seems to mirror the employment status and occupational structure of the French electorate reasonably well.

For any survey dedicated to politics and elections, another set of national parameters is available which is in many ways the most critical of all. Perhaps the central variable in our mass study is the vote our respondents cast in the 1967 election, and of course the official totals of votes cast for various parties nationwide is a matter of public record. In view of the sometimes loose relationships between specific candidates and particular national parties or coalitions of parties in the 1967 election, however, some edge of coding indeterminacy, not unlike that encountered in assigning occupation, remains for these comparisons. Basing our assignment of official votes as completely as possible upon decisions made by others for public sources, and trimming away the portions of the national vote that our sample does not purport to represent, such as Corsica and the overseas territories, we have arrived at the official distribution of the first-ballot vote displayed in Table A-2. In addition to these results for continental France, Table A-2 gives the official first-ballot results for the 86 districts of our sample. Because these first-ballot results differ only marginally from those for all of continental France, the latter alone will be considered in comparing our sample estimates with the official results.[6]

Several cautionary notes should be struck before examining these comparisons between our sample estimates and the official returns. First, it is a common characteristic of all post-election surveys that the report of voting turnout appears inflated, and our sample is no exception. The official results show that 81 percent of the registered voters turned out for the first ballot, while about 91 percent of our sample reports having cast a vote. This is a somewhat stronger overreport than is often found: an increment of 7 percent would be a more customary value. Nonetheless, certain factors peculiar to the French situation could be expected to increase the apparent over-report. For example, the names of some persons actually deceased do remain on the rolls, as our interviewers found, and these persons are counted "officially" as nonvoters, although they are not counted in this way in our sample. Similarly, the people on the move who leave their names on election rolls also count as nonvoters officially, but they are not included in our sample estimates. The main effect, however, is probably generated by a reluctance to admit not having lived up to the citizen responsibility of voting. Some of the people who did not know how they voted, as well as some of the refusals, may well represent actual nonvoters.

Second, some people always refuse to divulge their party or candidate

Table A-2. Percentage comparisons between 1967 mass sample estimates and official returns for first ballot, 1967.

	Official returns		1967 mass sample
Vote	Metropolitan France[a]	86 sample districts[b]	86 districts
Party			
Communist (PCF)	22.6	22.7	20.0
PSU	2.2	2.2	2.1
Federation (FGDS)	18.9	19.3	19.9
Independent Socialist	0.4	0.9	0.4
Democratic Center (CD)	12.7	13.3	11.0
Ve Rép. (excluding RI-V^e)	32.2	32.6	36.9
RI-V^e	5.4	4.6	6.1
Dissident Gaullist	0.4	0.5	0.5
Alliance Républicaine (AR)	0.3	0.4	0.3
Miscellaneous	4.9	3.5	2.8
Total	100.0[c]	100.0[c]	100.0
Nonvoters			
Abstentions (% of registered voters)	19.0	19.0	11.5
Refused	—	—	14.5
Don't know	—	—	2.6
Not ascertained	—	—	4.0
Void or blank ballots (% of those voting)	2.2	2.2	1.2

a. Results are for 467 legislative districts: Metropolitan France with Corsica excluded, or the domain which forms the universe for the sample design in this study.

b. Results are for the same 86 districts which form the frame for the mass sample.

c. Official returns for partisan vote are expressed as percentage of valid ballots.

choice, even when they maintain that they have voted. The rate of refusal in our sample (14 percent) is mountainous by comparison with similar election studies in many other countries. In the United States, for example, refusal rates are usually less than 3 percent of voters. But high rates of refusal to divulge voting choice are very characteristic of France. Although we would naturally have preferred to have a sample with a lower refusal rate, the rate we experienced is not unusual for France; compared with many studies done there, it is actually good. Thus a substantial refusal rate seems unavoidable, and the question remains whether the distribution of the vote among persons who do reveal their choice fits well with official returns. In this regard, we are extremely pleased with the comparisons in the upper portion of Table A-2.

The largest discrepancy in the vote distribution is an overreport in our mass sample of the vote for the Gaullist Ve République. Although this discrepancy is modest proportionally, it undoubtedly reflects a social desirability element in the report of the vote. The Ve République, as the dominantly popular party in the system in 1967, was probably not concealed as frequently as were other party votes; it may actually have drawn some dishonest, "bandwagon" reports as well. Some honest misperceptions of Democratic Center candidates as being truly Gaullist may also have contributed to the surplus.

The main underreport, apart from the Democratic Center, occurs in the case of the Communist party. Again, an underreport of Communist voting is completely taken for granted in French political surveys. Indeed, the noteworthy feature of our underreport is not that it exists, but rather that it is as small as it is. Throughout the postwar period and into the 1960s, sample interview reports of Communist voting typically ran 35 to 50 percent below the known parameters based on the official count of secret ballots, and sometimes even further below those parameters. Thus our own sample estimate, which approaches 90 percent of the true Communist vote, is especially pleasing. Nevertheless, there is no reason to imagine that this report is any special certification of the quality of our sample or our interviewing. In the middle 1960s many factors, including Gaullist foreign policy, were creating a sense of rapprochement with eastern Europe in general and Moscow in particular. In the course of these events, the French Communist party, long treated as a political pariah by the majority of French political leaders and common citizens, regained a considerable degree of social respectability. In many ways, this rapprochement reached a local peak in 1967, and we have assumed that the tenor of the times produced a relatively faithful report of Communist choices. We shall see that under the stresses of 1968, this fidelity in the report of voting for the extreme left suffered some temporary erosion.

To summarize this brief treatment of the methodological adequacy of the 1967 mass sample, it appears that it may be considered at the very least an adequate representation of the French voting public of that year, and by the standards of most earlier political surveys in France, it is a remarkably good one. The underlying response rate is far from handsome. But a large proportion of the special difficulties seems to reside in the limited accuracy of the voting lists, and these special difficulties appear to be essentially uncorrelated with either the major demographic characteristics (except for age, at one extreme), or, more important, with the political substance of the study.

The Second Wave of
Mass Interviews, 1968

The 1967 mass and elite surveys had not been planned as the first wave of a panel study. Indeed, it was only when General de Gaulle dissolved the National Assembly on May 30, 1968, and set new elections for June 23 and June 30, that the possibility of returning to the field to reinterview our 1967 respondents first came under serious discussion.

The timing was extremely awkward. In view of the events occurring in France during the month of May, it seemed imperative to get a second-wave interview into the field as rapidly as possible after the second ballot on June 30. This need for haste was compounded by the fact that August is the month of vacations for most of the French citizenry, including many on the staff of SOFRES who would be conducting the new survey. On one hand, we knew that it would be physically impossible to complete the fieldwork during the month of July, and that some interviewing would have to be laid over until September. On the other hand, it seemed important to complete as much of the mass interviewing as possible while the events of May and the ensuing elections were fresh in the public mind.

At the same time we found ourselves, in the first week of June 1968, with no funds available for such a second wave, and a precious fortnight was spent aggregating emergency support from the University of Michigan Council for International Programs. It was only as these funds became assured that we could authorize any serious preparations for fieldwork. In view of the late start, the first mass interviews could not be taken until July 16. Although the SOFRES staff worked with great diligence for the remainder of the month, only about one-third of the interviewing was completed during July. Some further interviews were collected, at a reduced pace, during August, but more than 40 percent of the work had to wait until September. The last three respondents were not interviewed until early October.

The funding which we were able to secure in haste was patently inadequate to permit a full second round of interviews, being scarcely more than half of the necessary sum. Therefore we drew a random, stratified half-sample of our original 86 districts as a primary target for our second-wave interviews at both the mass and elite level. In addition, the representation design made it important to reinterview at the elite level in those districts where the deputy elected in 1967 had been replaced by a new contestant as a consequence of the unexpected 1968 election. A certain portion of these "deputy change" districts naturally fell into our half-sample of 43 districts selected for second-wave interviewing. Among the 43 districts not selected for the second wave, however, 11 additional districts witnessed a change in deputies as a result of the 1968 Assembly election. Therefore we returned also to these 11 districts for reinterviewing at both the mass and elite level in 1968.

To summarize, the second wave of mass and elite interviews was carried out in 54 of the original 86 districts. Of the 54 districts, 43 represent a proper sample of the French electorate, and over the course of this study most estimates of the state of French public opinion as it stood after the 1968 elections have been based on this restricted but proper sample. Another way of looking at the matter is to suggest that the second wave involved a 100 percent reinterviewing in all districts that changed deputies between 1967 and 1968, but only a 50 percent reinterviewing among those districts that returned the same deputy to the National Assembly as a result of the new elections. By assigning twice as much weight to the latter districts as to the former, representativity was restored to the entire set of 54 districts. Occasionally, therefore, when it seemed particularly important to maximize the actual cases for 1968, we assigned a weight of 1.294 to the 31 districts of our 54 where the incumbent won in 1968 and a weight of 0.647 to the 23 districts where the incumbent lost. The individual 1967 weight of each 1968 respondent was then multiplied by his or her district weight to produce a final 1968 weight for each 1968 respondent. Again it should be noted that the weighting system in no way inflates case numbers.

The stringent limitations on funds meant that it was impossible to follow people who had changed their place of residence between 1967 and 1968.[7] This fact, along with our lack of original planning for a panel design and the harried circumstances under which the fieldwork was conducted, meant that the response rate for the second wave of the panel was precariously low. Out of the 1,032 respondents interviewed in 1967 in the 43 districts of our half-sample, only 578 yielded valid reinterviews in 1968. In the 11 supplementary districts experiencing a turnover of deputies, 158 respondents were reinterviewed out of an original pool of 269 persons in the 1967 sample. The overall response rate, calculated on the original pool of successful 1967 interviews, was thus only 57 percent.[8] If this figure is corrected for those 1967 respondents known to have died before the 1968 interviewing, the response rate reaches 58 percent.[9] In Table A-3 we summarize the various reasons for failure to reinterview, as assembled by the SOFRES staff.

Of course, no panel study maintains contact with all of its original respondents, and the difficulties are particularly severe when the time lapse between waves amounts to many months and the sample is made up of a mobile and far-flung national population. Nonetheless, our experience with similar samples in the United States suggests that, under more propitious circumstances and with proper financing, some 75 percent of the set of original respondents might reasonably have been reinterviewed after the time interval that elapsed between the first two waves of the French study, or perhaps some 65–70 percent if persons shifting their residence were not to be pursued. Therefore our second-wave response rate must by any reasonable standards be considered low.

The obvious queston is, "To what degree are our second-wave results flawed by the considerable panel attrition we encountered?" Since the case

Table A-3. Sources of panel mortality, second wave of mass interviews, 1968 (percentages).

Source		Percent of non-interviews	Percent of total 1967 sample in 54 districts
Death		4.0	1.7
Had moved from address		12.8	5.5
Unknown at address		1.9	0.8
Lengthy absence[a]		23.2	10.0
Interviewed incorrect respondent		9.2	4.0
Refusal		48.9	21.0
Due to illness	4.7		
Prior questionnaire too long	15.6		
"No change in opinions"	1.9		
"Political reasons"	13.9		
No explanation given	12.8		
	48.9		
Total		100.0	
Successful reinterview			57.0
Total			100.0

a. Often summer vacations where callbacks were impractical.

shrinkage was already marked, due to the deliberate reduction of the design to a half-sample, the further inroads of panel "mortality" mean that our 1968 results must admit to a much greater sampling error than characterizes our large initial sample. Indeed, it is for this reason, among others, that we have depended primarily upon the 1967 sample for most of our estimates of the abiding characteristics of the French electorate. Yet what we most need to know is whether our dropouts in 1968 were an unusual subset of the original pool of respondents, thus causing the results from the 1968 survivors to give a biased set of estimates of the political situation in France as of that year.

It would be possible for a panel to suffer very substantial attrition without biasing results in this sense. People who continue with such a panel obviously differ in systematic ways from people who disappear from view. Among other things, they have not died, moved, or become seriously ill, and they are less likely to have resented being interviewed earlier. Bias, however, enters the picture only in the degree that one or another reason for dropping out of the panel is correlated with the characteristics being assessed by the particular study. If there is no correlation, there is no bias.

The analysis of nonresponse bias in secondary waves of a panel study is enormously enhanced, relative to the analysis of nonresponse in single-stage interviews, by the fact that a great deal is known about the missing respondents: they have already provided one full interview. It is therefore easy to compare all of the most relevant attributes of the dropouts with those of the remainder of the original pool. Long-term panel studies of the electorate in the United States have suggested that bias accruing even from very substantial panel mortality is remarkably limited. The main line of systematic differentiation, in terms of political variables, which separates dropouts from survivors centers upon the degree of interest in things political. Citizens who pay little attention to politics tend to find an hour-long interview on the subject a source of some embarrassment, and although they may have unwittingly fallen into a first interview, they are forearmed against a second. This means that over the successive waves of a panel study there is a slow but steady drift toward a set of survivors who are somewhat more interested in politics than the parent population they are expected to represent. Yet it cannot be emphasized too strongly that even this source of bias is extremely small, very nearly within the limits of variation that could be mistaken for sampling error over as many as four or five waves in a four-year period. Naturally, if political interest is an "epicenter" for panel attrition in political surveys, it follows that subsequent waves of such studies must also be biased in terms of the numerous characteristics that are correlated with political interest, such as levels of formal education. But if attrition along lines of political interest is itself very weak, as has been our experience, then the bias in education will be much weaker still, because that attribute is only modestly correlated with political interest. This has indeed been our empirical experience in the United States: the upgrading of political interest in successive panel waves is itself quite faint; and concomitant changes in the educational composition of the panels, though discernible, are infinitesimal by comparison with the percentage differences typically required by sampling theory to draw reliable inferences. In other words, experience with panel surveys of this political type in the United States suggests that most of the reasons why persons drop out of panels are essentially uncorrelated with the central variables of the study. Only one class of such reasons, contributing in no more than a limited way to the overall attrition, is so correlated, and this is impatience with the specific political substance of the interview.

With these observations as background, we may approach the second or 1968 wave of our study in order to assess the bias which might be expected from the considerable mortality which it suffered. There are several ways to make such an assessment, all of which depend in some sense or other upon comparisons between 1968 survivors and dropouts with respect to their original *1967* characteristics, which are known in detail on both sides. We find it most relevant to the kinds of inferences to be made from the 1968 data to put the query in the following form. Let us suppose that instead of the actual 1967 sample of more than 2,000 persons which we interviewed, we had fallen upon the self-selected subset of persons who were later to yield our 1968 data. By how much, and in what direction, would our estimates of the 1967 situation be distorted?

To answer this question we have canvassed a very large number of the specific variables in the 1967 study, comparing the distributions of persons who were subsequently to become 1968 survivors with the distributions generated by the total 1967 sample. In particular, we have made a haphazard selection of about 100 nominal and ordinal variables in the 1967 study, and another 25 variables of pseudo-interval status, for special examination. Where the nominal and ordinal variables are concerned, we have calculated the percentage difference for each code category between estimates yielded by the 1968 survivors and those from the full 1967 sample. Over some 623 code categories within the 102 nominal and ordinal variables, the average displacement of the 1968 survivors in 1967 characteristics is 1.45 percent. For the pseudo-interval variables, estimates of 1967 means based upon the subset of 1968 survivors taken alone depart on the average by only .04 standard deviations from the means produced by the total 1967 sample.

Psychologically, these discrepancies appear small indeed. They suggest, for example, that if we had succeeded in interviewing all of our original 1967 respondents in all of our original 86 districts, our estimates of any given 1968 percentage would not on the average differ from what we see in our 1968 wave by as much as 1.5 percent. In fact, however, there are points of view from which such differences are not, strictly speaking, small. For example, the discrepancy of 1.45 percent cited above is no more than an average value, and this means that some code categories among survivors show deviations from the parent sample which exceed 3 or 4 percent. More important still, it can be shown that if we had drawn our panel of 1968 survivors by purely random methods from the original 1967 respondents, it is highly unlikely that we would have found average percentage differences between code categories as great as the 1.45 percent encountered. The expected average difference under such circumstances, taking rough account of the proportionate size of the code categories being examined, would be much less than 1 percent. Thus if we did not already know that the dropouts had systematic qualities, the data themselves would warn us of the fact.

However all this may be, discrepancies of the magnitude observed remain far smaller than might gloomily be supposed in view of the low reinterview rate of 57–58 percent. And it is obvious that, given our sample size, we would put no inferential weight even on percentage differences that exceed the average discrepancy by three or four times. Thus it is unlikely that any substantive conclusions drawn from the 1968 data will be seriously misleading as a result of the extensive panel mortality, although it is sensible to treat those data with an increment of caution.

We can forearm ourselves still further against the possibility of being misled if we pay close attention to whatever substantive patterning can be discerned in the discrepancies between survivors and the original pool of respondents. A fair portion of the observed discrepancies, including some of the largest ones, form hardly any coherent pattern. Thus, for example, we occasionally find a marked difference occurring in one of the interior categories of an ordinal variable. If survivors show an increment of 5 percent in the "weak agree" category of a five-point Likert scale, but the increment is largely offset by a 3 percent decrement in the more extreme "strong agree" category, the departure seems to be an anomaly without clear interpretation, and one which would intrude very little on analytic conclusions. Since the categories of most of our variables enjoy a natural order, we look for true patterns in which a decrement at one end of the ranking is matched by an increment at the other end, signaling some significant correlation between the variable and panel survival. Where such patterns do emerge within single variables, we then look to see whether other variables of the same general intent show parallel discrepancies. In point of fact, such repetitive patterns turn out to be rare and rather feeble when they do occur for our 1968 survivors. But they are worth mentioning, to indicate what we are missing.

Based on our experience with such panels elsewhere, we first checked to see whether our 1968 survivors taken alone would have given us higher estimates of the political involvement of the electorate in 1967 than those drawn from the full 1967 sample. Our most summary five-item index of political involvement was useful for such comparisons, and Table A-4 shows

Table A-4. Comparative estimates of 1967 political involvement for original sample and subsequent 1968 panel survivors (percentages).

Involvement index[a]	Total 1967 sample[b]	1967 index for subset of 1968 survivors in half-sample of districts
5	16.4	16.4
4	38.8	40.1
3	17.5	20.9
2	15.1	13.9
1	6.0	5.3
0	6.2	3.4
Total	100.0	100.0
Weighted N	(1984.7)	(554.1)

a. 5 = highest involvement; 0 = lowest involvement.
b. Includes all 86 original districts.

the expected difference, in some degree. The discrepancies are somewhat irregular and, indeed, quite trivial over much of the range. The main discrepancy, approaching 3 percent, turns up in the least involved fringe of the
original sample. It is as though about three-quarters of the 1967 sample had
coped with the questionnaire reasonably well, but the least involved quarter
had found it sufficiently onerous, embarrassing, or both, to resist a second
participation. We would assume that this resistance was expressed in complaints about the length of the first interview, as well as in some of the unexplained dropouts. The mean discrepancy per category in the two above
distributions (1.58 percent) does slightly exceed that calculated over our
hundred-odd test items (1.45 percent), but it is not as great as we expected.

Almost one-quarter of our items show greater average discrepancies
than the involvement index. A substantial portion of these more discrepant
items, however, has a rather direct link with political involvement as well.
One set of persistent discrepancies emerges in connection with our measurement of recognition and recall of the French political parties. For seven
of the nine parties, average discrepancies per category run ahead of those for
the involvement index (3.20 percent to 2.27 percent), and the direction is
always the same: our 1968 survivors are always more likely than the 1967
respondents to be able to name a party, or at least to recognize it when
prompted. Parallel discrepancies turn up regularly in other items where pure
political knowledge is at stake. Eight percent more of the subset of 1968
survivors were able in 1967 to supply the name of the winning candidate in
their local district than was true of the parent sample as a whole, and an
increment of 6.5 percent knew which party had presented that candidate.
Almost 7 percent fewer survivors were *unable* to name any candidates running in the district, by comparison with the levels in the original sample.
These discrepancies account for virtually all of the most marked single-cate-
gory divergences in our comparisons. Moreover, although the magnitudes
of difference tend to be much smaller, lesser proportions of survivors occupy
such null categories as "don't know" and "no opinion" over a much wider
range of items. Such an epicenter of panel mortality in political-information
items nicely substantiates our initial assumption that the second interview
would tend to be avoided most avidly by respondents who felt ignorant
during the course of the first experience.

Given this modest bias along lines of information and involvement,
other associated differences are quite predictable. About 4 percent more of
the survivors claim to have voted in all past elections. Survivors are also
more partisan: about 4 percent fewer have no party identification, and an
increment of 4 percent express a "very close" attachment to the chosen
party. By the same margin, survivors are more likely to report always having
voted for the same party. Certain demographic differences follow as well, although in general these tend to be more restricted than one might suppose.

Survivors show a slight (2 percent) increment in proportion of males, and a faint trend toward higher social status.

All told, it is likely that political attentiveness accounts for the lion's share of the modest systematic bias which marks the second wave of our panel. Nonetheless, we would be remiss not to consider the possibility of other sources of bias and, in particular, those which might give an apparent advantage to left or right in the second wave. In Table A-5 we array some of the comparisons between survivors and the full sample on a number of pseudo-interval measures in the 1967 sample which bear on any possible partisan drift. The upper rows of data (A) bear on perceptions of the left-right locations of the several major French party groupings. These perceptions, which need not betray any information about the respondents' own left-right sympathies, are included merely as a "neutral" frame of reference to provide some sense of the deviations that do arise on measures of this sort when the partisanship of the individual is not at stake. As we see, the departures among the survivors are generally very small and haphazard in their left-right direction where these perceptual measures are concerned.

The remaining rows of data bear more or less directly on the partisan displacement of the survivor sample, and they present a rather mixed picture. The "thermometer" measures (B) suggest a small but somewhat consistent rightist coloration in the evaluative reactions of the survivors, by comparison with the parent sample: only attitudes concerning the business-labor cleavage intrude as exceptions. Moreover, self-locations on the left-right continuum (C) show a rightist displacement for survivors as well. But the most crucial variables, the two 1967 votes expressed as left-right means (D), fail to confirm this pattern. The behavior of survivors is almost identical to that of the original pool, although such tiny differences as do exist are inclined to the left.

It is of interest to examine the more detailed partisan distribution of the 1967 vote as registered among the survivors. Moreover, the officially tabulated party distribution of the vote in 1968 provides one important external parameter for further evaluation of the 1968 survivors in the actual year of the second wave. All of these comparisons are laid out in Table A-6. If we first consider the discrepancies between the 1968 survivors and the 1967 parent sample in the estimation of the 1967 vote, we can see why the survivors do not show a rightist displacement in the mean value for the left-right scoring of the vote. Survivors do underrepresent the Communist vote at the far left more than was true in the parent sample. But much of this loss is made up by Federation votes, which are still classed as considerably farther to the left of center than the Gaullist groupings lie to the right. Overall, the mean discrepancy per party category between the survivors and the parent sample is 1.45 percent, or exactly the figure we earlier found as an average over all 102 of our test variables. In the same terms, the original

Table A-5. Comparison of 1967 means on left-right perceptions and thermometer scores for original sample and subsequent panel survivors.

Respondent perceptions	1967 mean for total 86-district sample	1967 mean for subset of 1968 survivors in half-sample districts	Deviation of survivor mean in SD units from parent sample mean	Partisan direction of survivor bias
A. Estimates of left-right positions of parties				
SFIO	30.7	30.2	.03	Left
Alliance Républicaine (AR)	73.3	72.1	.03	Left
Centre Démocrate (CD)	55.5	55.8	.02	Right
PSU	26.4	27.6	.07	Right
Républicain Indépendant (RI)	63.0	62.6	.02	Left
MRP	59.0	60.3	.07	Right
PCF	12.7	12.0	.04	Left
Parti Radical	37.1	36.0	.06	Left
UNR	68.8	69.3	.02	Right
FGDS	26.6	26.3	.01	Left

B. Affect expressed toward political objects (thermometer)

Labor unions	66.9	67.1	.01	Left
Mitterrand	51.1	50.1	.04	Right
Clergy	53.9	55.1	.05	Right
PCF	42.0	40.1	.07	Right
SFIO	51.2	50.5	.03	Right
De Gaulle	62.0	63.7	.07	Right
UNR	51.1	52.4	.05	Right
Big business	39.1	38.6	.02	Left
Tixier-Vignancour	33.8	35.3	.07	Right
MRP	44.2	46.0	.09	Right
PSU	46.3	45.9	.02	Right
Pompidou	48.0	49.6	.06	Right
C. Own left-right location	47.5	48.9	.06	Right
D. Left-right scoring Tour I vote	46.9	46.7	.01	Left
Tour II vote	46.6	46.6	.001	Left

Table A-6. Percentage comparisons between second-wave sample and official returns for 1967 and 1968 national votes.

1967 First Ballot

Vote	Official returns[a]	Total sample (86 dists.)	1968 survivors (43 dists.)
Party			
Communist (PCF)	22.6	19.8	17.9
PSU	2.2	2.2	2.4
Federation (FGDS)	18.9	19.8	22.1
Independent Socialist	0.4	0.4	0.7
Democratic Center (CD)	12.7	9.9	11.5
Ve Rép (less RI-V^e)	32.2	36.9	36.2
RI-V^e	5.4	5.8	7.7
Alliance Républicaine (AR)	0.3	0.3	0.1
Miscellaneous	5.3	5.3	1.4
Total	100.0	100.0	100.0
Nonvoters			
Abstentions (% of Regis. voters)	19.0	9.1	6.9
Refused	—	14.0	11.2
Don't know	—	2.6	1.5
Not ascertained	—	4.5	3.1
Null or blank (% of those voting)	2.2	1.1	1.3
Weighted N		(2007.0)	(554.1)

1968 First Ballot

Vote	Official returns[a]	1968 sample (43 dists.)
Party		
Communist (PCF)	20.1	12.7
PSU	3.9	3.5
Federation (FGDS)	16.4	18.9
PDM	10.4	13.7
UDR (non-RI)	37.3	37.2
UDR-RI	6.3 }	10.4
RI (non-UDR)	1.5 }	
Mouvement pour la Réforme	0.2	0.3
Technique et Démocratie	0.4	0.7
Miscellaneous	3.5	2.6
Total	100.0	100.0
Nonvoters		
Abstentions	19.9	9.1
Refused	—	11.8
Don't know	—	0.8
Not ascertained	—	0.8
Null or blank	1.7	1.5
Weighted N		(554.1)

a. Results are for the 467 legislative districts of Metropolitan France, excluding Corsica.

1967 sample departs from the official parameters by an average of 1.28 percent. The survivors, however, diverge from those parameters by a significantly greater mean figure (2.20 percent), although a fair amount of this discrepancy arises from the behavior of the nondescript "miscellaneous" category.

As for the vote parameters in 1968, the main feature of the comparison is the gross underrepresentation of Communist voting by respondents who survived to the second wave. At first glance, it appears that Communist voters dropped out of the panel in droves in 1968, a possibility which would explain some of the earlier rightist coloration of survivors noted for the thermometer and self-location measures (Table A-5). But this suspicion does not bear up under examination. The 1967 comparisons between survivors and the parent sample do show some small attrition of Communist voters. But the large drop in 1968 cannot be due to panel mortality, because the 1968 sample and the 1967 survivors are the same people, and they reported substantial Communist voting in the earlier year. It is likely that the 1968 drop in reported Communist votes has a ready explanation. As we have already noted, Communist voting was very markedly underreported in French political samples throughout the long period when the party was widely regarded as a pariah by much of the electorate, but the greater acceptance of the Communist party in the mid-1960s eliminated much of this underreport. The disorders of May and June 1968, however, led to a new fear campaign against the extreme left by the government. Under these conditions, it would not be surprising if Communist voters had retreated to their older habits of concealment. For a small margin of them, this may have meant refusal to participate in the second wave of our panel. Yet most continued with the interviewing, while representing their vote as "Federation" or refusing to divulge it at all. Even with this substantial underreport, the average party-category discrepancy of 1.98 percent from the official parameters is less than the survivors showed in their 1967 vote report, compared with 1967 parameters.

The balance of evidence in Tables A-5 and A-6, along with indications from other items in the questionnaire, has led us to the conclusion that whatever partisan bias can be said to have entered the second wave is faint, but that it probably gives a slight edge to the right in general and Gaullism in particular, at least among those survivors who frequently report political opinions. Individuals who do record a vote but who fail to locate themselves on the left-right continuum or to give many thermometer ratings may redress the balance considerably. For many purposes, however, we should recognize that a weak rightist coloration lingers more often than not in the attitudinal responses.

Demographically, we have already noted a slight increment of males and a tiny upgrading of social status among survivors, which appear to be a normal consequence of increased selection along lines of political information and involvement. Two other discrepancies in the social characteristics of the survivors that are large enough to mention may be associated with the slight rightist coloration of the second wave. First, survivors are somewhat more likely to live in the larger cities (over 100,000 population). This fact taken alone may well reflect chance variation in the selection of the 43 districts of the half-sample. But it is also true that survivors show some increment of persons who grew up in small communities, with the implication that migrants to the larger cities are slightly overrepresented among the 1968 survivors. Second, survivors are somewhat more likely to be practicing Catholics, with the increment in religiosity which that fact entails. Beyond these points, however, no other noteworthy demographic discrepancies were apparent to us.

If we may summarize what is known about bias in the second wave introduced by panel mortality, the most important point is that the 1967 properties of our 1968 panel survivors approximate much more closely those of the full 1967 sample than the response rate of less than 60 percent might imply. It remains true that one can detect small signs of systematic bias, largely involving the increased survival of the politically attentive. Therefore it is worth keeping in mind that our 1968 wave will overestimate political information, although the differences are so small in any absolute sense that the reader would stand in danger of mentally overadjusting if he were to place major emphasis on this fact. There is also a chemical trace of a rightist bias, although at points it seems elusive. All things considered, if we restrict our attention to the major contours of data from the second wave, it can be considered a very adequate representation of the French electorate in 1968, apart from the renewed Communist vote concealment that the events of that year appear to have stimulated.

The Third Wave of Mass Interviews, 1969

Our 1969 fieldwork, involving the third wave of mass interviews, was motivated by the intrusion of the spring referendum which led to the retirement of de Gaulle and the subsequent presidential elections. Since there was no change in the composition of the National Assembly, the purpose of the third study was to permit a dynamic mapping of individual change at the mass level across the whole sequence of public consultations begun in 1967. Its relevance for the legislative representation aspects of the original design was therefore limited, and no elite interviewing was carried out. Furthermore, there was no point in conducting any reinterviews on the mass side in the 11 supplementary districts studied in 1968 because of a change of deputies. Therefore the 1969 study rests exclusively on the same 43-district base as that which underlay the panel data from the second wave.

Most panel studies display a steady attrition of case numbers over succeeding waves. Of course, such a pattern is foreordained if the design does not call for renewed pursuit of original respondents who have failed to participate in an intervening wave. Yet such a steady decline in numbers is typical even when earlier dropouts are solicited again.

The third wave of the French panel study is an exception, although hardly a mysterious one. Although it, like the second wave, arose unexpectedly, our concern about a fresh onslaught of panel mortality led us to handle the situation somewhat differently. For one thing, in 1968 the gravity of the May–June crises had drawn us into the field at breakneck speed, since it seemed important to capture a picture of the situation before the tensions and aggravations began to erode in the public memory. There was no comparable crisis in 1969, and we did not feel hurried in preparing for the study. Ideally, we would have conducted the interviewing in the month or two just after the presidential elections. This, however, would have reintroduced all the difficulties of such work during the vacation period. Since a major portion of our interest lay in assessing the temper of opinion after the country had returned to a politics which was more routine relative to the 1968 crisis, we were content not to resume interviewing until late September 1969, even though we were aware that popular recollection of votes cast in both the April referendum and the June elections would lose some fidelity as memories of behavior faded. The interviewers entered the field in the closing days of September, and a vast majority of the interviews (over 80 percent) were collected in October. Most of the remainder were completed in November, although a few stragglers were pursued into December and early January.

Response Rates

This delay provided much more adequate lead time for preparation than had been available in 1968, and more resources were thrown into the effort to preserve panel cases. Although we did not attempt any systematic pursuit of 1967 respondents who had moved their place of residence, we did return to many of the 1968 dropouts, and we had enough success with them to surpass a simple offsetting of the inevitable new losses. As a result, our 1969 panel response rate regained precious ground. In the half-sample of 43 districts in 1968, we had reinterviewed some 56 percent of our original respondents after slightly more than a year's lapse of time (ignoring corrections for deaths). In 1969, after more than a two-year lapse, we succeeded in reinterviewing 61.5 percent of that original half-sample. The latter figure is not systematically below parallel experience in the United States for a two-year interval, at least under conditions where movers are not followed.

In Table A-7 we recapitulate the final disposition of all respondents successfully interviewed in 1967, in terms of their district location and presence or absence in the second and third waves. We see that, of the total

Table A-7. Internal structure (N) of panel reinterviews, 1968 and 1969.

Interviews			Number of reinterviews	43-district half-sample for panel	11-district supplement: deputy change	32-district remainder (not in panel)
'67	'68	'69				
X	X	X	Two	491	1[a]	0
X	X		One: 1968	87	157	0
X		X	One: 1969	144	0	1[a]
X			None	310	111	744
	Total cases, 1967 sample			1032	269	745
	1968 crude reinterview rate			56.0%	58.8%	—
	1969 crude reinterview rate			61.5%	—	—

a. Stray cases of movers into the 43 districts who could be reinterviewed without special effort.

round of 1969 reinterviews, just under one-quarter were conducted with respondents not included in the intervening second wave. If of the original 1967 pool we had reinterviewed the full 56 percent recontacted in 1968 plus another 5 percent missed in that year, there would be only very limited room for change in our 1968 account of bias arising from panel mortality. But there was a certain amount of turnover in the reinterviewed group, which left some latitude for change in the complexion of this panel bias between the waves.

At the same time that we endeavored to improve our panel response rate in 1969, we also decided to collect a small fresh sample from the 43 districts as a control group for comparison. We hoped that such a sample would not only provide a check on how far our panel might have drifted from a true representation of the electorate through successive attrition, but would also yield an assessment of any contamination that the panel might have suffered as a result of repeated interviewing. For reasons not entirely clear, save for the extreme pressures we exerted toward a respectable response rate, the yield of interviews from the fresh sample was higher than that which had been achieved in the original 1967 sample. Of 565 addresses drawn randomly from the voting lists in our half-sample of 43 districts, 384 interviews were completed, for a response rate in the fresh sample of 68.0 percent. Thus we have a small but relatively good sample of the French electorate in 1969, uncontaminated by earlier interviewing.

Assuming that the 1969 panel had not deteriorated too much, our best estimate of the situation in the French electorate in 1969 would involve a simple combination of the panel and the fresh sample, all from the 43-district half-sample. This combination yields more than 1,000 cases, as opposed to the 384 cases of the fresh sample taken alone, or the 637 panel cases, and is indeed the basis for our nonpanel estimates of 1969 parameters. Of course, for any estimates involving individual change in the 1967–1969 period, we are restricted to our panel sample. In either event, it is important to know how sound the third-wave panel is.

We can evaluate it from two different points of view. We can conduct comparisons between 1969 survivors and the original 1967 pool with respect to 1967 characteristics. Or, alternatively, we can examine the fit between the fresh sample and the panel with respect to 1969 estimates. In point of fact, we have done both.

Sample Bias due to Panel Mortality: 1969

When we compare the 1967 responses of 1969 survivors with the pool of 1967 respondents from which they were drawn, the general impression is one of arrested deterioration. Average percentage discrepancies per code category, calculated as before over a large number of variables, run if anything slightly lower than in the case of the comparisons involving 1968 survivors, although the difference is minimal. The 1969 data parallel to those given in Table A-5 for the 1968 survivors show some interesting contrasts. Where the "neutral" perceptual task of locating the several political parties on a left-right continuum is concerned, we find a substantial (30 percent) reduction of discrepancies from the parent mean among 1969 survivors, relative to the 1968 discrepancies. Where the more affective data from the thermometer measure are concerned, the discrepancies remain about the same size, and show about the same slight rightist coloration for 1969 as for 1968 (see Table A-5).

Nevertheless, the respondent's own left-right location in 1967 among persons about to become 1969 survivors is displaced almost .09 standard deviation units to the right from the mean of the parent sample. Although this is still scarcely a major divergence in absolute terms, the important point is that the displacement to the right is visibly increased over that observed for the 1968 survivors. Yet when we turn to the left-right scoring of the two 1967 ballots, we repeat the experience of Table A-5: the means for 1969 survivors are displaced by .02 and .001 to the *left* for the first and second elections.

Comparisons between 1969 survivors and the 1969 fresh sample are somewhat limited because the interview schedule in 1969 was relatively short, and more especially because case numbers in the control sample are so few. Thus, for example, if we compute the kind of average percentage difference per category that we used to assess discrepancies earlier, we would expect such differences to run about three times greater than in the preceding comparisons purely because of increased sampling variability. Such an average difference calculated over a range of variables between the two 1969 samples does in fact run visibly higher than it did for the 1968 and 1969 comparisons on 1967 characteristics; but instead of being triple the size, it is a good deal less than double the size. It still outruns what might be expected from chance alone; yet the proportion of discrepancy which must be assigned to some kind of bias, as opposed to random sampling variability, is very much smaller.

More detailed examination of the points where discrepancies occur confirms this judgment. There are larger percentage discrepancies scattered through the comparisons, but they create less sense of a substantive pattern than emerged from our work with the 1968 survivors. Thus, for example, one of the main signs of bias earlier was the slightly heightened involvement, evident especially in information levels, shown by survivors relative to the original 1967 pool of respondents. The 1969 survivors show the same bias, when compared with 1967. But when compared with the fresh sample, the expression of political involvement in 1969 differs little and, if anything, is actually *lower* than among the new interviewees (see upper part of Table A-8). Moreover, despite earlier findings, the fresh sample shows a slightly more advanced education distribution than do the panel survivors of the same year. Unfortunately, the 1969 interview lacks much in the way of information-level measures for comparison. And, despite the lesser education

Table A-8. Percentage comparisons between 1969 survivors and fresh sample on simple measures of involvement and Gaullism, 1969.

Measure	Fresh sample	1969 panel survivors
Interest in politics, 1969		
"Est-ce que vous vous intéressez à la politique?"		
Beaucoup	6.8	5.0
Assez	14.6	13.8
Un peu	35.9	39.2
Pas du tout	42.4	40.7
Other	0.3	1.3
Total	100.0	100.0
N	(384)	(637)
Satisfaction with de Gaulle, 1969		
"Dans l'ensemble, étiez-vous satisfait ou mécontent du Général de Gaulle comme Président de la République?"		
Très satisfait	21.1	23.3
Plutôt satisfait	41.4	50.6
Plutôt mécontent	18.2	20.1
Très mécontent	10.2	5.9
Other	9.1	7.1
Total	100.0	100.0
N	(384)	(637)

and involvement of the 1969 survivors, they do report higher levels of vote turnout than is shown by the fresh sample. This limited but rather clear contamination effect in turnout report has appeared in all the other political panel surveys we have encountered. In general, then, although we know that panel mortality has selected toward heightened political attentiveness, we must conclude that a fresh sample of almost 400 cases could through sampling variability alone give even higher estimates.[10] This fact speaks to the limited size of the involvement bias among our panel survivors more generally. As we observed earlier, that bias is clearly present, but it would be easy to exaggerate it.

The other pattern of faint bias noted among the 1968 and 1969 survivors—a slight coloration by Gaullism, clericalism, and the right generally—receives the expected confirmation in the 1969 comparisons with the fresh sample. At the level of a simple tabulation, this can be seen in the lower part of Table A-8. It also is visible as the main source of minor discrepancies in means on our various pseudo-interval measures, as displayed in Table A-9. It should be remembered that because of the much smaller sample sizes in this table, we should expect larger discrepancies here than in the counterpart table of the preceding section (Table A-5), at least to the degree that the earlier discrepancies represented pure sampling error, rather than some other bias. There is an increase, although it is not frightening in most cases. Nonetheless, the small Gaullist and clerical biases do show through.

The most striking difference evident in these comparisons arises at the central point, in connection with own left-right location, confirming the earlier comparisons with 1967 for 1969 survivors. At the same time, outside information leads us to queston which of the two 1969 samples is the more accurate. Ordinarily we would assume that the fresh sample, though smaller, gives a less biased estimate, particularly in view of our familiarity with the rightist coloration among survivors due to panel mortality. SOFRES, however, was measuring left-right self-locations with its own measure over this period, and equivalences set up between that measure and our own suggest an estimate for our measure in this time period of about 50.8, or a value in between our two samples but closer to that for our panel survivors. Indeed, if we were to combine our fresh sample and our survivors, thereby arriving at more than 1,000 cases, our estimate would become 50.4, or very close to the SOFRES value. Therefore there is a very lively possibility that although our survivors do overrepresent the right, the small fresh sample by chance overrepresents the left, and we are best advised to combine the two whenever possible.

Finally, we shall turn our attention to some comparisons of our 1969 samples in terms of the various vote reports, where other external parameters are available. Here a variety of comparisons are possible, involving the original 1967 vote for 1969 survivors, or any of three votes cast by the fresh

Table A-9. Comparisons between 1969 survivors and fresh sample on means of affect and left-right placement measures, 1969.

Measure	Fresh sample	1969 panel survivors	Survivor means displaced	
			SDs	Direction
1969 affect toward				
Unions	62.7	63.5	.04	Left
Teachers	68.5	67.9	.03	a
Clergy	54.4	58.1	.16	Right
Americans	49.2	49.5	.01	a
PCF	33.7	33.9	.01	Left
de Gaulle	59.4	63.1	.14	Right
Poher	47.7	49.1	.06	a
UDR	50.9	53.9	.12	Right
Duclos	37.5	36.8	.03	Right
Students	52.7	51.9	.03	Right
Russians	41.8	40.1	.07	Right
Army	53.0	56.0	.13	Right
Pompidou	58.2	60.3	.08	Right
Strikers	41.6	41.4	.01	Right
1969 left-right location of				
Pompidou	68.5	69.2	.04	Right
Poher	55.4	55.8	.02	Right
Duclos	15.6	15.3	.02	Left
Deferre	31.9	31.2	.04	Left
Rocard	29.4	27.8	.09	Left
Krivine	10.6	10.1	.03	Left
Ducatel	46.0	47.3	.06	Right
1969 own left-right location	47.1	52.4	.24	Right

a. Not applicable.

sample and the survivors as of 1969. Moreover, since some of our panel-based estimates in this study have depended on three waves taken together, that is, on that subset of the 1969 panel survivors who had been interviewed in 1968 as well as 1967, we include their vote totals in the respective elections as a special category.

Table A-10 provides a retrospective glance at the reported voting behavior on the first ballot of the 1967 legislative election that is central to this book, which may fruitfully be compared with Table A-6, covering the 1968 survivors. It is clear that the fidelity of the 1967 report is lower than that provided by the full 1967 sample, and by a margin greater than likely sampling error. Yet, if anything, both 1969 panel groups are slightly closer to the official 1967 returns than were the 1968 survivors. Thus again the general message is one of arrested panel deterioration.

Table A-10. Percentage comparisons between 1969 panel survivors and official returns for first ballot, 1967.

Vote	Official returns[a]	3-wave sample[b]	All 1969 panel survivors[c]
Party			
Communist (PCF)	22.6	17.1	16.8
PSU	2.2	2.7	3.0
Federation (FGDS)	18.9	21.7	22.5
Independent Socialists	0.4	0.7	0.6
Democratic Center (CD)	12.7	12.8	13.0
Ve Rép. (excluding RI-V^e)	32.2	35.8	34.6
RI-V^e	5.4	7.6	7.4
Alliance Républicaine (AR)	0.3	0.2	0.1
Miscellaneous	5.3	1.4	2.0
Total	100.0	100.0	100.0
Nonvoters			
Abstentions (% of registered voters)	19.0	6.7	7.3
Refused	—	10.2	12.6
Don't know	—	1.5	1.2
Not ascertained	—	3.4	2.9
Void or blank ballots (% of those voting)	2.2	1.3	1.7

a. Results are for the 467 legislative districts of Metropolitan France (Corsica excluded).
b. Weighted N = 486.2
c. Weighted N = 632.2

In view of the superb initial report of the 1967 vote, and its adequate reflection among later panel survivors, the comparable data for the 1969 ballots come as something of a shock (Tables A-11 and A-12). Both presidential ballots are seriously misreported, and the recall of the April referendum even falls in the wrong direction. The bias is Gaullist in all three cases; and if we had lacked the data from the fresh sample, we surely would have concluded that the slight, known rightist bias in the third panel wave had somehow been disastrously amplified in the reporting of these votes. We have, however, the indispensable clue from the fresh sample that this is not the case. The Gaullist bias does continue to mark the survivors, but it is relatively small, particularly if we recall the earlier evidence suggesting that the fresh sample itself may have a slight overrepresentation of the left. All the evidence combines to make it clear that if we had taken a totally new survey in 1969, we would probably have suffered much the same flawed vote report. The problem is not one of panel attrition.

Another frightening hypothesis is easy to reject. This is that both the 1969 fresh sample and the 1969 survivor group share the same serious inter-

Table A-11. Percentage comparisons between official 1969 presidential election results and our 1969 sample estimates.

(a) First ballot				
Vote	Official returns[a]	3-wave sample[b]	All 1969 panel survivors[c]	Unweighted fresh sample[d]
Candidates				
Pompidou	43.8	53.0	52.1	49.9
Poher	23.4	23.5	4.2	4. 25.7
22.6				
Duclos	21.6	15.8	13.7	16.1
Defferre	5.1	3.4	4.2	4. 25.7
3.0	4.5			
Ducatel	1.3	0.6	0.6	1.4
Krivine	1.1	0.9	0.7	0.7
Total	100.0	100.0	100.0	100.0
Nonvoters				
Abstentions	21.7	8.2	7.3	9.6
Null or blank ballots	1.3	—	—	—
Refused	—	4.9	6.1	10.2
Don't know	—	4.8	4.3	2.9
Not ascertained	—	—	0.1	1.3

(b) Second ballot				
Vote	Official returns[a]	3-wave sample[b]	All 1969 panel survivors[c]	Unweighted fresh sample[d]
Candidates				
Pompidou	57.6	68.6	65.5	64.8
Poher	42.4	31.4	34.5	35.2
Total	100.0	100.0	100.0	100.0
Nonvoters				
Abstentions	30.9	18.2	17.1	18.2
Null or blank ballots	6.5	7.0	6.2	4.4
Refused	—	4.3	5.1	8.1
Don't know	—	1.1	1.2	1.0
Not ascertained	—	—	0.4	2.3

a. For the 467 legislative districts of Metropolitan France (Corsica excluded).
b. Weighted N = 486.2.
c. Weighted N = 632.2.
d. Unweighted N = 384.

Table A-12. Percentage comparisons between official 1969 referendum results and our 1969 sample estimates.

Vote	Official returns[a]	3-wave sample[b]	All 1969 panel survivors[c]	Unweighted fresh sample[d]
Yes	46.8	54.8	54.6	52.1
No	53.2	45.2	45.4	47.9
Total	100.0	100.0	100.0	100.0
Abstentions	19.3	8.7	7.6	7.0
Null or blank ballots	2.7	4.4	4.5	2.6
Refuse	—	4.3	5.5	8.6
Don't know	—	4.7	5.3	6.3
Not ascertained	—	0.2	0.2	1.0

a. For the 467 legislative districts of Metropolitan France (Corsica excluded).
b. Weighted N = 486.2.
c. Weighted N = 632.2.
d. Unweighted N = 384.

nal flaws. This is not very plausible: demographic comparisons which have known parameters (not discussed in detail) range from acceptable to excellent for both 1969 groups. If, however, the argument shifts to some pervasive flaw uncorrelated with social structure but highly correlated with basic political dispositions, a flaw which happens to be largely shared with the fresh sample, then it is easily disconfirmed not only by the weight of all the political-attitude evidence throughout the 1967–68–69 sequence, but most notably by the fact that our 1969 survivors had, in 1967, given a very adequate account of their voting behavior in that year.

Clearly then, there is a grave flaw in the vote report, but it occurs in common for both the survivors and the fresh sample; and it is localized to the 1969 ballots, rather than being pervasive either in time or in its extent to other political dispositions. There really is no mystery about what is going on. In all countries where elections have clear winners, a "bandwagon effect" is evident in post-election surveys so that voting for the winner is overreported. As is also well known, the degree of this overreport mounts progressively as the election recedes in the public memory. The bandwagon phenomenon has not commonly been noted in relation to French elections, but most people familiar with the problem have assumed that this is simply because the normal French legislative election does not have clear winners in such an obvious, public way as, say, an American presidential election does. To be sure, the French press headlines as "winners" the parties that have managed to raise their vote, for example, from 8 percent to 13 percent over a pair of elections. But because of the multiparty fractionation of the vote distribution at the legislative election, "winners" in any social-majority sense of the word simply do not exist. Among the nearest recent approximations are the votes culled by the Gaullists in 1968 or even 1967, and we have already implied that the modest overreport of these votes in those years has to some degree a bandwagon source.[11] But this overreport was small by comparison with what we find in the 1969 presidential election. We assume this was simply because, first, the clarity of the victory (30–35 percent of the vote) was much less in 1967; and, second, our post-election survey took place rather quickly after the election, thereby minimizing the bandwagon problem. In 1969, however, there was a clear winner in Pompidou, and our interviewing had been delayed until four months or more after the election and until six months after the referendum.

This explanation accounts quite easily for the reports of two ballots of presidential voting. When we asked our 1967 respondents—a large sample without the later Gaullist bias, which reported its 1967 legislative vote perfectly—how they had voted in the 1965 presidential election first ballot, over 60 percent reported that they had voted for the ultimate winner, de Gaulle, although the known parameter for his vote was only 45 percent. Thus the bandwagon effect after some fourteen or fifteen months was about a 15 percent increment in percentage points, as compared with the increments of between 6 and 11 percentage points in the reports of Table A-11, after a lapse of about four or five months. This is a rather routine registration of bandwagon reporting.

The explanation does not, however, address quite squarely the report of the April referendum. In this instance, the "nays" won, provoking de Gaulle's retirement. Yet the public recollection six months later produced a victory for the "yeas." There is little precedent for analyzing such a situation, particularly in view of the clear Gaullist victory which had intervened between the April referendum and the vote report of the fall. It seems likely, however, that the intervening Gaullist glow was contaminating the referendum report, and if some of our autumn respondents had lost track of what "yes" and "no" meant substantively, as is quite likely, a tendency toward acquiescence in an ambiguous situation would also help to account for an exaggeration of the affirmative vote. It is to be remembered that all of these bandwagon effects co-occur with a substantial overreport of the vote, and the two phenomena are undoubtedly related: people who have not in fact voted, but who either hesitate to admit the fact or, more honestly, fail to remember, say that they have voted and tend very disproportionately to record what is remembered as the popular choice. In any event, it is ironic that the referendum on which de Gaulle had staked his position, and lost, was remembered by the public mind as accumulating to a positive vote a bare six months later.

The fact that we can understand the misreport of the 1969 votes does not mean that they are not an inconvenience. We have been obliged to limit the analytic weight placed on these reports, although we have employed them in some degree for various panel estimates. Fortunately, the voting which is central to this study is the selection of representatives to the National Assembly, and the evidence we have shown suggests that this vote is more accurately reported.

Aside from the faulty indication of 1969 voting, all the data seem to indicate that the 1969 panel survivors continue to be an adequate representation of the French electorate. The modest panel deterioration visible between 1967 and 1968 was apparently brought to a stop by our successful efforts to increase the response rate in 1969. At the same time, where parameter estimates of the 1969 state of affairs are concerned, it appears that a combination of the 1969 panel survivors and the fresh sample is likely to provide the most satisfactory base.

The Structure of
the Elite Sample

The First Wave, 1967

The Sample Design

The logic of the design for the 1967 mass sample implied that all candidates in the 86 districts of the sample frame would be interviewed. Because cost considerations made that impossible, various candidates were removed from the potential sample population at the start.

There were 400 officially registered candidates in the 86 districts of the sample frame. Of these, 47 were removed because they had received less than 5 percent of the valid votes cast at the first ballot in their respective districts. Another eight were removed because they had received the votes of less than 10 percent of the registered voters in districts where the election was decided at the first ballot. These two operations reduced the potential sample base to 345 candidates.

In addition, Communist party candidates were deliberately underrepresented. This was done for two reasons. First, we were uncertain whether we would be successful in obtaining interviews with Communist party candidates.[1] Given the possibility of their systematic refusal to be interviewed, and our need to make most efficient use of our limited resources, we thought it wiser to underrepresent Communist party candidates than to plan for their full representation and then have to reduce the size of the sample among the other groups of candidates whose willingness to be interviewed was more likely.

This procedure commended itself to us for a second reason as well. In view of the historic record of Communist party discipline, we had reason to believe that on many items in our interview schedule there would be greater homogeneity among Communist party candidates than among the candidates of other parties. On matters on which there was a fixed party position, for example, we did not expect to find much variation among the personal opinions of the candidates.

We did not, however, want to underrepresent the Communist party in an extreme fashion. It was possible that Communist candidates would willingly grant interviews (which, in fact, turned out to be the case). And our interview schedule did contain items on which their responses could be expected to vary, perhaps as much as those of the candidates of any other party. For example, our questions concerning the candidates' perceptions of district opinion might very well discover a variance among Communist party candidates which would be interesting and important to explore. Therefore, although we did underrepresent Communist party candidates, we nevertheless interviewed enough of them to ensure that our analysis of the replies would be significant. In other words, we followed a form of minimax strategy.

This strategy turned out to be eminently satisfactory. By applying a test to determine the relative degree of intra-Communist homogeneity across several classes of variables, we have found that although homogeneity is unusually great on certain items, it is less so on others.

In testing the assumption of relative Communist homogeneity, it is clear that we are interested in the degree of dispersion in Communist responses, or their standard deviation. The question is, "With what other non-Communist measure of dispersion should they be compared?" Clearly there is little point in comparing them with the standard deviation for our candidate sample as a whole, or even with that of our non-Communist sample, because many items in the study show greater or lesser degrees of party differentiation across all parties; that is, variation *within* all parties is frequently much smaller than the total variation across the sample, since the latter variation accumulates *between*-party variation as well.

Therefore we assessed relative Communist homogeneity by comparing the standard deviation of Communist responses (where that statistic is meaningful) with the standard deviations on the same items within each of the four other party groupings in our sample which are of sufficient size to yield stable estimates of dispersion: the 71 candidates of the Fédération de la Gauche; the 73 candidates of the Ve République; the 52 candidates of the Centre Démocrate; and the 19 candidates in the "Other" category.[2] We then recorded where our Communist candidates placed in a ranking of all five partisan groups for homogeneity, based on the relative size of the standard deviation within each group, over a number of variables. We also computed, for each of the same items, the proportion of the standard deviation for the group at the median that was represented by the standard deviation within the Communist group. Some of these data are summarized in Table B-1.

In general, the relative homogeneity of responses among Communist candidates follows our commonsense expectations almost perfectly. If we leave missing data aside, the Communists present an absolutely monolithic front with regard to their own issue positions on certain policy controver-

Table B-1. Homogeneity of responses by Communist candidates, relative to those given by four other candidate groupings, 1967.

Class of items	Number of items	Communist rankings on homogeneity					Communist SD ÷ SD for median group
		Most homo-geneous	2nd	3rd	4th	5th	(Average over items)
Own issue positions	13	8	2	2	1	0	.51
Importance of various information channels	5	5	0	0	0	0	.74
Priorities for decision sources (deputies)	4	1	1	1	1	1	.77
Estimates of importance accorded various issues by constituency	6	3	1	0	1	1	.84
Estimated left-right locations of 14 political groupings	14	6	3	3	0	2	.92
Own sense of importance of issues	7	4	0	0	2	1	.97

sies, particularly those surrounding the role of workers in industry, the distribution of wealth, and some items involving the claims of church schools on state aid. Indeed, no other group shows such perfect homogeneity on any one class of items. Even here, however, the homogeneity among our Communist candidates is less than perfect, particularly on such issues as educational reform and certain aspects of European integration. Nevertheless, on their own issue positions, the variation among Communist candidates is about half of the value displayed by the median group in terms of partisan homogeneity.

Reasonably enough, as we move outward from the issues of public policy on which the party line prevails, relative Communist heterogeneity increases. This is not to say there are no other points at which the Communists present a solid front. For example, when asked what influences would affect their voting decisions in the National Assembly, Communist deputies were unanimous in according absolute priority to cues from their parliamentary group. Similarly, they were unanimous in attributing the highest personal priority to the issue of a more equitable distribution of income in the country. But as Table B-1 indicates, especially in the last column, the relative homogeneity of Communists is somewhat less for other kinds of behavior and perceptual variables.

All things considered, the data support our sampling decisions very handsomely. Beyond a narrow set of "party line" policy issues, it is not true that to have interviewed one Communist candidate is to have interviewed them all. On the one hand, significant differences do exist between the political perspectives and reality assessments of individual Communist candidates. On the other hand, the set of Communists interviewed are, on balance, more homogeneous than the other major partisan groupings. Thus it was a justifiable efficiency to undersample them somewhat.

The sample of Communist party candidates was drawn as follows. The 345 candidates remaining after the preliminary elimination included 82 Communists. We reduced that number to 77 by removing five more names—those of candidates in districts where there was no left-wing candidate at the second ballot. From the 77 remaining names, we drew a subsample of 50 names.[3] Our 1967 sample of 313 candidates, therefore, included 50 Communists and 263 representatives of other parties.

In fact, interviews were held with six Communist candidates and one Federation candidate who fell outside this sample, but who, of course, were within our 86 sample districts. These interviews were saved and coded so that the precious information they contained could be used. Not only were all but one of these "accidental" interviews taken with the already underrepresented Communist group, but four of them (including that with the Federation candidate) were taken with candidates from the categories we had excluded at the start in the interest of economy; to include them serves to enhance the representativeness of the candidate sample. Three of the six Communist candidates who were accidentally interviewed were among the 27 whose names could have been, but were not, drawn for our subsample of 50 Communists, and one of these three was a victorious candidate, who therefore augmented the number of interviews we were able to take with Communist deputies.

Response Rates

The interviews were conducted by SOFRES' most experienced interviewers during the summer and fall of 1967. About 70 percent of the interviews were taken by the end of July, some 90 percent had been completed by the end of September, and the remainder were conducted in October and November.

The overall response rate of 85 percent among the candidates in our sample was very satisfying. As Table B-2 indicates, this rate ranged from a high of 93 percent for Federation candidates to a low of 64 percent for PSU candidates. The Communists, about whose willingness we had been uncertain, displayed no particular propensity to avoid being interviewed.[4] We secured interviews with 39 of the 50 Communist candidates in our subsample, for a response rate of 78 percent, and the fact that we were able to conduct a total of 45 interviews with Communist candidates produced a response rate of 80 percent, as indicated in Table B-2.

The response rate among victorious candidates was slightly lower than that among the candidates as a whole. Some 26 percent of the candidates in

Table B-2. Response rates for candidate sample, by party, 1967.

Party	Number of candidates in sample	Number of interviews	Percent of sample interviewed
Communist (PCF)	56[a]	45[a]	80[b]
PSU	14	9	64
Federation (FGDS)	76[c]	71[c]	93[d]
Democratic Center (CD)	61	50	82
Ve République	86	73	85
Other	27	24	89
Total	320[e]	272[e]	85[f]

a. Includes six accidental interviews.
b. 78 percent if accidental interviews are excluded.
c. Includes one accidental interview.
d. No change if accidental interview is excluded.
e. Includes seven accidental interviews.
f. No change if accidental interviews are excluded.

our sample were victors at the election; 24 percent of our interviews were taken with winners. The breakdown of interviews taken among deputies of the various parties appears in Table B-3. Of the large groups, the Federation was again the one which was most accessible to our interviewers. It was among the Democratic Center and the Communists that the response rates of deputies were lowest, but there is no reason to believe that any group systematically avoided granting interviews.

Determining Partisan Affiliations

We have already alluded to the minor difficulties we encountered in classifying candidates according to party affiliation. For countries such as the United States or Great Britain, which have comparatively simple party systems, the problem of indeterminacy of party affiliation seldom arises. In the case of the French system, however, the degree of certainty with which individual candidates can be assigned to particular partisan groups, or even to broad political tendencies, varies considerably. There is seldom if ever any difficulty in determining who the candidate of the Communist party is in any district, but there are also candidates who run *sans étiquette* or with some locally oriented or highly general party label which does not correspond to any national political party or even to any parliamentary group.

In one sense, the problem of classifying candidates reduces itself to the degree of fineness of discrimination among candidates with which the classifier will be satisfied. The fewer and the larger the categories which one creates (including "miscellaneous"), the less error there will be in the technical sense. By the same token, however, the less useful the classification system will be for analytical purposes, that is, for throwing light on

Table B-3. Response rates among winning candidates, by party, 1967.

Party	Number of winning candidates in sample	Number of interviews	Percent of sample winners interviewed
Communist (PCF)	11[a]	7[a]	64[b]
PSU	1	1	100
Federation (FGDS)	20	19	95
Democratic Center (CD)	7	4	57
Ve République	41	34	83
Other	1	1	100
Total	81[a]	66[a]	81[c]

a. Includes one accidental interview.
b. 60 percent if accidental interview is excluded.
c. No change if accidental interview is excluded.

how, and how accurately, the electorate discriminates among the candidates that are presented. Because one of our main objectives was to learn as much as possible about how the public identifies the candidates, we sought as fine a classification of their partisan affiliation as could reasonably be produced. Three main sources of information were available to us for this purpose: the volume of electoral results published by the Ministry of the Interior; the daily Paris newspaper, *Le Monde,* particularly the issues of March 7, 1967, and March 14, 1967, in which electoral results for each district were reported for the first and second ballots of the election, respectively; and the interviews which were held with candidates in our sample.

Prior to the election, the Ministry of the Interior published a volume, in a limited edition, which contained a district-by-district list of candidates (République Française, Ministère de l'Intérieur, 1967a). After the election the ministry published another volume, containing the same information as the earlier one, but also including the electoral results by district, as well as various other items of useful information concerning the election (République Française, Ministère de l'Intérieur, 1967b). The district-by-district lists of candidates which appear in both volumes cite the *étiquettes* (party labels) of some but not all of the candidates. The labels attributed to the candidates were supplied by the candidates themselves and, in that sense, they are highly reliable. But candidates are not legally required to indicate what their party affiliation is, and many of them do not do so. There is, therefore, no official list of all the candidates including their party labels as they have supplied them.

The results published by the Ministry of the Interior do, however, assign each candidate to one of nine categories established for the purpose of reporting the electoral results by district. Five of these categories refer to discrete political formations: the Parti Communiste, the Fédération de la Gauche Démocrate et Socialiste, the Gaullist Comité d'Action pour la Ve République, the Centre Démocrate, and the Alliance Républicaine pour les Libertés et le Progrès. The other four categories refer to comparatively broad tendencies: extreme left, miscellaneous left, miscellaneous moderates, and extreme right. It is, therefore, possible to learn how the Ministry of the Interior assessed the broad partisan affiliation or political location of those candidates who did not supply the authorities with any étiquette.

The official volume, however, does not contain any overall breakdown by partisan origin of the candidates of the three umbrella organizations: the Gaullist Ve République, the leftist Federation, and the centrist Democratic Center. Each of these political formations was a kind of confederation which endorsed candidates from several parties or groups. The candidates who ran under the Ve République label came from the orthodox Gaullist Union pour la Nouvelle République (UNR), or from M. Valéry Giscard d'Estaing's Gaullist conservatives, the Républicains Indépendants, or in some cases from the Radical party or from the recently defunct Mouvement Républicain Populaire (MRP); while still others did not have any particular partisan attachments apart from their endorsement by the Ve République formation. Federation candidates included some from the Socialist party (SFIO), the Radical party, the Convention des Institutions Républicaines (CIR), as well as some without any well-marked partisan background. The Democratic Center was an even more heterogeneous grouping than the Ve République or the Federation. It included candidates from the MRP, anti-Gaullist conservatives more or less affiliated with the Centre National des Indépendants, candidates from the virtually undefinable Rassemblement Démocratique, Radicals who opposed the leftward orientation of the larger number of Radicals who had joined the Federation, and a host of more or less center-right candidates without any well-known, specific political affiliation. Because the partisan labeling of the candidates often does not appear in the volume of the Ministry of the Interior, we turned for it to the distinguished Paris daily newspaper, Le Monde.

Le Monde published a detailed account of the results of the first ballot of the 1967 election in the issue of March 7, 1967, and a detailed account of the results of the second ballot in the issue of March 14, 1967. Both issues contain unofficial vote totals for each candidate, by district, and the latter issue also contains, for most of the districts, a brief description of the maneuvering of the parties and candidates between the two ballots; most important, both issues supply an étiquette for virtually every candidate.

The designation of party labels by Le Monde is very detailed. Candidates endorsed by the main umbrella organizations—the Ve République, the Fédération, and the Centre Démocrate—are often described in hyphenated form to indicate their specific partisan origin. Ve République candidates are variously described as UNR–Ve République, Républicain Indépendant–Ve République, MRP–Ve République, Radical–Ve République, or simply Ve République. Fédération candidates are designated as SFIO-Fédération, Radical-Fédération, Convention-Fédération, or just Fédération. Centre Démocrate candidates are also variously described: some are simply designated as MRP–Centre Démocrate or Independant–Centre Démocrate. Still others have such labels as Rassemblement Démocratique, soutien Centre Démocrate.

In addition to providing a breakdown of the party affiliations of the candidates of the broad political formations, *Le Monde* also assigns specific labels to candidates whom the Ministry of the Interior includes only among the broad, general categories of its summary statistics. For example, *Le Monde* specifically labels the candidates of the Parti Socialiste Unifié (PSU) and the Independent Socialists, whom the ministry groups together with the extreme left category, as well as the dissident Gaullists, whom the ministry classifies among the miscellaneous moderates.

The fine distinctions made by *Le Monde* among Ve République candidates, candidates of the PSU, Independent Socialists, and dissident Gaullists made it possible for us to provide the somewhat detailed comparison between the 1967 mass sample and the official returns for the first ballot in 1967 which appears in Appendix A (Table A-2). The breakdown of party labels by *Le Monde* also served as the basis for constructing candidate weights, which will be discussed later in this appendix.

The richest source of information available to us about the partisan affiliations of the candidates was the interviews which were conducted with the candidates themselves. Early in the interview schedule, the candidates who had been reported in *Le Monde* as affiliated with the Gaullist Comité d'Action pour la Ve République, the Fédération de la Gauche Démocrate et Socialiste, or the Centre Démocrate were asked to specify the party label they had used most often to identify themselves to the voters in their districts. From the start of our inquiry, it had appeared important to us to ascertain how the candidates endorsed by these umbrella organizations preferred to identify themselves to their constituents. Each such candidate had a range of options open to him. He could emphasize the broad electoral formation which endorsed him, the specific party with which he might be affiliated, both the broad electoral formation and his particular party, or some other preferred description. Indeed, in the effort to learn how uniformly even the Communist party's candidates had presented themselves to the voters, we asked them which party label they had used most often to identify themselves to the voters in their districts.

Additional questions designed to elicit how the candidates perceived themselves in partisan terms were asked near the end of the interview. All candidates were asked which political party they belonged to, and those who cited the Centre Démocrate, the Ve République, or the Fédération de la Gauche Démocrate et Socialiste were then asked to specify the party within that grouping to which they belonged.

Further, they were asked if they had always belonged to the political party they had cited, and, if not, which party or parties they had belonged to previously. In that way we were able to learn the former political affiliations, as well as the current political affiliation, of the candidates.

In the great majority of cases, the information about party affiliations and party labels supplied by the candidates who were interviewed concurred with the political designations assigned to them by *Le Monde,* as well as with the étiquettes published by the Ministry of the Interior. There were, however, some discrepancies. We cannot describe them in detail, for we do not want to risk identifying our candidates, but we can give some illustrations of the differences. We have already mentioned that two candidates whom we had classified as Centre Démocrate on the basis of *Le Monde* informed the interviewers that they were not Centre Démocrate candidates. Furthermore, one candidate in our sample was labeled by *Le Monde* as MRP–Centre Démocrate, but he made no reference to the MRP in his interview. Three others were reported simply as Centre Démocrate by *Le Monde,* but one of these told us that he used only MRP as a party label, and the other two said that they used both the MRP and Centre Démocrate as party labels. Similarly, two other candidates who were reported only as Centre Démocrate told us in their interviews that they used Indépendant as their party label, one of them exclusively and the other in conjunction with Centre Démocrate.

Although most of the discrepancies we encountered involved candidates either actually or allegedly affiliated with the Centre Démocrate, some concerned candidates from other groups. One candidate reported by *Le Monde* only as Fédération told us that he used both SFIO and Fédération as party labels; another who was reported in the same terms told us that he belonged to the SFIO. Still another candidate who was reported as Radical–Fédération made no mention of the Radical party when asked about his party label and party affiliation, but said that he belonged to the Convention. Among the Gaullist candidates, we discovered two whom *Le Monde* labeled only as Ve République, while the information furnished in their interviews indicated that they should be classified as Républicains Indépendants.

In our own classification of the candidates who ran in our 86 sample districts, we preserved most, though not all, of the distinctions so carefully recorded by *Le Monde.* Our objectives in this regard will be explained more fully below, when we discuss the left-right scoring of the candidates; the main point is that the particular categories we wanted to retain were those which we could reasonably expect the voters to perceive along a left-right dimension. In assigning candidates to our code categories, however, it was occasionally necessary for us to resolve conflicts in the accounts of the party affiliations of the candidates that were available to us.

Our general rule was to adhere to the party labels assigned to the candidates by *Le Monde* as long as no strong contraindications were supplied by the candidates themselves in their interviews. Specifically, this meant that when *Le Monde* assigned only a broad confederal label—such as Centre Démocrate—to a candidate, but that candidate told us that he had employed a more specific party label (either exclusively or in conjunction with the confederal label) to identify himself to his constituents, we departed from the *Le Monde* label and assigned the more specific party label to that candidate. For example, those who were classified by *Le Monde* as Centre Démocrate only, but who told us that they commonly used either MRP alone or both MRP and Centre Démocrate in communicating with their constituents, were classified by us as MRP–Centre Démocrate. We did not, however, diverge from the confederal labels supplied by *Le Monde* when they omitted specific party affiliations that were known to us but apparently not communicated to the voters by the candidates. For example, one candidate who was classified by *Le Monde* simply as Fédération told us that he belonged to the SFIO. The party label he used, however, was Fédération. We followed *Le Monde* in this case. If *Le Monde* did not perceive the candidate as SFIO, and he himself did not use it as his party label, his constituents would not have been likely to perceive him as SFIO.

How the candidate was likely to be perceived by his constituents was more important to us than what he actually was politically in objective terms. One candidate who was supported by the Centre Démocrate told us that the support he received from it was given against his will and that he did not use the Centre Démocrate label. We decided, however, that this candidate should be coded within the large Centre Démocrate family, in a category appropriate to the other information he supplied. The Centre Démocrate had obviously put its stamp on him in some fashion that was visible not only to the candidate himself but also to *Le Monde,* and it was not unreasonable to assume that the voters would also have regarded him as affiliated with the Centre Démocrate.

Sometimes *Le Monde* not only assigned a confederal label to candidates who we thought could be more precisely designated, but it also assigned a party-specific label to candidates who we thought should be described only by a confederal label. For example, one candidate who was classified by *Le Monde* as MRP–Centre Démocrate told us that he used only Centre Démocrate as a party label and made no reference to having belonged to the MRP; therefore we classified him simply as Centre Démocrate.

Quite a few of the candidates to whom *Le Monde* assigned party-specific labels did indeed inform us that they either belonged to or had in the past belonged to those parties; but instead of referring to their precise party affiliations during the campaign, they employed only the broad confederal labels appropriate to them. There was no ideal solution to this problem. If we had retained the specific labels assigned by *Le Monde* we would have ignored the fact that, for one reason or another, the candidates themselves had preferred not to rely on them to identify themselves to their constituents. If we had assigned the general labels used by the candidates, however, we would have been overlooking the fact that each of those candidates did indeed belong to the party attributed to him by *Le Monde,* as well as the possibility that this information might have been generally available to their constituents. Indeed, some of it was, since some of the candidates were incumbents associated with a national party. And although we knew how the candidates had described themselves, we did not know how the local press or even the candidates' supporters had described them. In the end, we decided to assume that at least some of the information available to the press would also have reached the public. In cases where *Le Monde* assigned a specific party label to a candidate, and the candidate either belonged to or had previously belonged to that party, we followed *Le Monde,* even if the candidate did not use his specific party as a label during the campaign.

There were other situations which made the assignment of party affiliations difficult. Some candidates did not use any party label at all; others referred not to a party but to a parliamentary group; and still others employed sets of descriptive terms unrelated to any political party or parliamentary group. In each of these cases, we assigned party positions to the candidates, on the basis of the information available to us, in ways which we believed to be reasonable, but which necessarily reflected elements of uncertainty.

Left-Right Scoring of the Candidates

The main reason for assigning precise party affiliations to candidates in our sample districts was that we needed to assign a location on the left-right scale to as many of them as possible. The left-right scores which we assigned were based, in the overwhelming majority of cases, on the mean left-right locations attributed to the parties by the respondents in our mass sample. In other words, we knew where the voters in our sample located most of the parties, and we only needed to match the candidates with those parties in order to give them partisan locations on the left-right scale.

We knew, on the basis of our survey, the mean left-right location assigned to ten national parties or political formations: the Parti Communiste, the PSU, the Fédération de la Gauche of Mitterrand, the Parti Socialiste (SFIO), the Parti Radical, the Centre Démocrate of Lecanuet, the MRP, the Républicains Indépendants of Giscard d'Estaing, the UNR, and the Alliance Républicaine of Tixier-Vignancour. This list contains three parties which ran candidates independently (Communists, PSU, and Alliance

Républicaine); two broad electoral federations (Fédération de la Gauche of Mitterrand and Centre Démocrate of Lecanuet); and five specific parties associated with broad electoral federations (SFIO and Radicals for the Fédération; MRP for the Centre Démocrate; and UNR and Républicains Indépendants for the Comité d'Action pour la Ve République).

Candidates who ran directly for the three discrete parties were, of course, assigned the mean left-right scores which our respondents attributed to those parties. Candidates whom we had classified simply as Fédération or Centre Démocrate were scored at the mean attributed to those groups by our sample. Within those two electoral formations, we scored the candidates to whom we had been able to assign a specific partisan background at the means assigned to those specific parties by our respondents. Candidates for the Fédération who were SFIO were scored at the mean assigned by our respondents to the SFIO; those who were Radicals were scored at the mean location our survey revealed for the Radicals. Similarly, candidates for the Centre Démocrate with an MRP background were scored at the mean for the MRP.

There was one large electoral confederation for which we had no left-right measure from our respondents—the Comité d'Action pour la Ve République—just as there were principal components of the other two broad electoral formations for which we had no similar left-right measure: the Convention des Institutions Républicaines within the Federation, and the Indépendants within the Centre Démocrate. We handled those problems as follows. All Ve République candidates were divided into two categories: the first made up of those who were Républicains Indépendants; and the second consisting of all the others, whether they had run simply as Ve République, as UNR, as "Gaulliste," or under some other kind of label—or even without any label.[5] Candidates in the first category were, of course, coded at the left-right location of the Républicains Indépendants of Giscard d'Estaing, and those in the second were coded at the mean left-right location assigned to the UNR.

The candidates whom we classified as Convention-Fédération were assigned the same left-right location as the candidates whom we classified simply as Fédération. Our reasoning here was that the Convention candidates expressed whatever imagery was associated with the Fédération that gave it an identity apart from its main components—the Socialists and the Radicals—just as directly as did those candidates whom we classified as Fédération.

We relied on a different technique in assigning left-right locations to those candidates who were Indépendant–Centre Démocrate. We did not have any mean assessment of the left-right location where the electorate placed Indépendants, but we did have grounds for estimating where that location should be. The left-right scale which the interviewers showed to the respondents in order to help them understand what was meant by the question asking them to place the various parties and themselves on a left-right scale contained a number of points which associated a figure with a verbal description of that location on the scale. For example, the figure 1 at the left end of the scale was labeled "Extrême Gauche," the figure 20 was labeled "Gauche," the figure 50 was labeled "Centre," and so on (see Figure B-1). The figure 60 was associated, less directly, with the label "Droite Modérée."[6] Now there is no fixed definition which one can attribute to the label "Indépendant" in the context of the 1967 election. For some candidates it could mean past or current association with the Centre National des Indépendants (CNI), once the principal conservative party in France. The CNI was eclipsed by the UNR and the Républicains Indépendants, but it continued to exist in 1967 and some of its adherents were affiliated with the Centre Démocrate. Alternatively, Indépendant could mean simply "independent" in the sense of being independent of any specific party. Historically, however, French independents have been associated with more or less conservative groups and policies, which knowledgeable commentators on French politics have often described as "moderate." Accordingly, it seemed reasonable to locate the Indépendant–Centre Démocrate candidates, as well as candidates associated with the CNI, at that point on the left-right scale—60—which casual viewers of the scale would be likely to associate with the Droite Modérée.

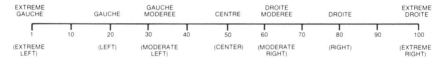

Figure B-1. Echelle gauche-droite (left-right scale).

We used the designated points on the left-right scale to estimate the locations of other candidates as well. Candidates who were simply "Centre Gauche" were placed at 30, which the scale associated with "Gauche Modérée." It was at that point also that we decided to place those candidates who were Independent Socialists. Those few candidates who we thought should be identified as reflecting the right or left wing of a party, such as left-wing Gaullists or non-Federation Radicals, were coded halfway between the location of their party and the location of left or right on the scale. One label, Rassemblement Démocratique, we interpreted in terms of the parliamentary group of that same name which had been formed in the 1962–1967 National Assembly. The deputies who formed that group included "various moderates, Radicals, and center left" (*Le Monde,* April 14, 1967). The location of the group as a whole, therefore, appeared to be sufficiently indeterminate for us to code it at 50, and to locate individual candidates associated with that label at the election halfway between 50 and whatever more precise affiliations could be assigned to them.

Other particular decisions had to be made. The Rassemblement Européen de la Liberté, an extreme right-wing group whose leaders regarded the Alliance Républicaine as too moderate (Williams, Goldey, and Harrison, 1970, p. 209), was coded at 89. We did not code that group at 100, the literal point for the extreme-right, because the extremity of a scale was not likely to be the mean location to which any group of voters would assign even an extremist party. Instead, we moved in from 100 by as many points as the mean location assigned by the voters to the most extreme left party (the Communist party) differed from the fixed scale score of 1 for the extreme left.

With one exception, dissident Gaullists were placed at 74, the location appropriate to right-wing Gaullists. That location was consistent with the assumption that Gaullist dissidence primarily reflected discontent with Gaullist policy toward Algeria, an attitude shared by the Alliance Républicaine. The one exception was a Gaullist dissident who told us that he was a left-wing Gaullist.

The full listing of party labels assigned to the candidates in our 86 sample districts, and their corresponding locations on the left-right scale, appears in Table B-4.

Table B-4. Left-right scoring of candidates, 1967.

Score	Candidate's party label
12	Parti Communiste Français (PCF)
26	Fédération; Fédération-Convention; Parti Socialiste Unifié (PSU)
30	Centre-Gauche; Socialiste Indépendant
31	Fédération-SFIO
37	Fédération-Radical
44	Gaulliste de Gauche; Gaulliste Dissident de Gauche
53	Centre Démocrate–Centriste; Centre Démocrate–Rassemblement Démocratique
55	Indépendant Centriste
56	Centre Démocrate (CD)
58	Radical de Droite; Centre Républicain
60	Centre Démocrate–MRP; Centre Démocrate–Indépendant; Républicain Indépendant (non-Giscardien); Indépendant; Centre National des Indépendants (CNI); Sans Etiquette–MRP; Sans Etiquette–CNI
63	Républicain Indépendant (Giscardien)
69	Union pour la Nouvelle République (UNR)
73	Alliance Républicaine (AR)
74	Gaulliste Dissident

Weighting Systems

Just as it appeared advisable to weight the 1967 mass sample in order to re-move the effects of variations in response rate by the urban-rural character of the sampling points, so it appeared advisable to weight the elite sample in a way that would counteract differences between the proportions of candi-dates interviewed from the various partisan formations. Accordingly, we created two sets of weights applicable to the elite sample. One set applies to the entire population of candidates interviewed and appears in Table B-5. The other set applies only to the subset of sample interviews taken among the victorious candidates (deputies) and appears in Table B-6. The weights employed throughout the analyses in the text have depended upon the rele-vant sample population. When analyzing the candidates, we employed the candidate weights. When analyzing only the deputies, we employed the deputy weights.

A distinctive feature of both the candidate weights and the deputy weights is that they were not calculated in a manner designed to equalize response rates within each partisan group with the proportion of each such group in the *sample*. Rather, we weighted in order to equate the set of re-sponses within each partisan group with the proportion of the total *universe* of each corresponding partisan group. The base figure for determining the candidate weights, therefore, is the total number of candidates who won at least 5 percent of the valid ballots in districts in continental France,[7] not the total number of candidates in the sample population. Similarly, the base fig-ure for determining the deputy weights is 467, the number of deputies from continental France in 1967, not the number of deputies in the sample popu-lation.

We have already referred to our desire, when creating weights for the 1967 mass sample, to avoid employing a weighting system which would ar-tificially inflate the reported number of interviews to an exaggerated level. We were motivated by the same consideration when we created the candi-date weights and the deputy weights. Indeed, the weighted Ns for both candidates and deputies slightly understate the actual number of interviews obtained.

It should be noted that the deputy weights distinguish among the component elements of the Federation groups, but the candidate weights do not. We did not try to discriminate, for purposes of weighting, among the component groups either of the Federation or of the Democratic Cen-ter, even though we went to considerable trouble to distinguish among them for the purpose of placing the candidates on a left-right scale. There were enough discrepancies between the party affiliations of the candidates as assigned by the press and as described in the interviews to persuade us that if we tried to classify too finely in the weighting we might risk distorting the resulting weighted Ns. Although we were reasonably confident of the pre-

Table B-5. Candidate weights, 1967.

Party or group	Candidate population[a]		Candidates interviewed			
	Number	Percent	Number	Percent	Weight	Weighted N
Communist (PCF)	463	24.1	45	16.5	1.5	67.5
Unified Socialist (PSU)	73	3.8	9	3.3	1.2	10.8
Federation of the Democratic and Socialist Left (FGDS)	411	21.4	71	26.1	0.8	56.8
Democratic Center (CD)	364	18.9	50	18.4	1.0	50.0
Gaullists (exclusive of Independent Republicans)	402	20.9	61	22.4	0.9	54.9
Independent Republicans (RI)	65	3.4	12	4.4	0.8	9.6
Dissident Gaullists and Republican Alliance (AR)	31	1.6	4	1.5	1.1	4.4
Independent Socialists	11	0.6	4	1.5	0.4	1.6
Other	103	5.3	16	5.9	0.9	14.4
Total	1923	100.0	272	100.0		270.0

a. Total number of candidates receiving at least 5 percent of the valid ballots in districts in Metropolitan France, excluding Corsica, as reported in République Française, Ministère de l'Intérieur, *Les Elections législatives de 1967* (Paris: Imprimerie Nationale, 1967).

Table B-6. Deputy weights, 1967.

Parliamentary group	Deputy population[a]		Deputies interviewed			
	Number	Percent	Number	Percent	Weight	Weighted N
Communist (PCF)	72	15.4	7	10.6	1.4	9.8
FGDS						
SFIO	76	16.3	12	18.2	0.9	10.8
Radical	24	5.1	5	7.6	0.7	3.5
Convention	16	3.4	2	3.0	1.1	2.2
Affiliated (including PSU)	5	1.1	1	1.5	0.7	0.7
Progress and Modern Democracy (PDM)	40	8.6	4	6.1	1.4	5.6
Union of Democrats for the 5th Republic (UD-V^e)	187	40.0	28	42.4	0.9	25.2
Independent Republicans (RI)	40	8.6	6	9.1	0.9	5.4
No group	7	1.5	1	1.5	1.0	1.0
Total	467	100.0	66	100.0		64.2

a. Deputies from Metropolitan France, excluding Corsica, at the start of the legislature elected in 1967. The breakdown of the FGDS group by parties of origin is based on *Le Monde*, March 18, 1967.

cise partisan locations of the candidates in our 86-district sample, we could not be sure of the partisan affiliations of the entire universe of candidates, and, of course, we would have had to know these in order to establish a highly differentiated classification of candidates for weighting purposes. Accordingly, we weighted the candidates only by electoral groups about whose composition we were reasonably certain.

When calculating the deputy weights, however, we were working with a smaller total population of comparatively well-known political backgrounds, and it was possible to break down the Federation parliamentary group into its constituent subgroups. We chose not to do so for the centrist group of Progress and Modern Democracy (PDM), however, as the heterogeneity of its members was great and its size comparatively small.

Parliamentary Experience and Electoral Situations

The candidates interviewed naturally reflected a wide range of parliamentary experience and specific electoral situations. Table B-7 shows the past parliamentary experience of the candidates interviewed as against their specific situations at the election of 1967.

Table B-8 provides a complete partisan breakdown of the prior parliamentary experience and the 1967 electoral fortunes of all 272 candidates who were interviewed in 1967.

The Second Wave, 1968

The Sample Design

Just as we were prevented by severe financial constraint from returning in 1968 to reinterview all of our 1967 mass survey respondents, so we could not attempt to obtain a full set of interviews in 1968 with all the major

Table B-7. Parliamentary experience by 1967 electoral situation of candidates interviewed, 1967.

Parliamentary experience	1967 electoral situation				
	Elected	Defeated[a]	Desisted or withdrew	Eliminated from second ballot	Total
Incumbent	42	11	1	1	55
Former deputy	3	11	6	2	22
Senator or former senator	4	4	0	0	8
No previous parliamentary experience	17	58	57	55	187
Total	66	84	64	58	272

a. Either in districts where the election was decided at the first ballot, or at the second ballot.

Table B-8. Candidates interviewed, 1967, by party, parliamentary experience, and electoral situation.

	PCF	PSU	FGDS				Centre Démocrate				RI-V^c	AR	Diss. Gaul.	Ind. Soc.	Other	Totals
			SFIO	Rad.	Conv.	Fed.	MRP	Ind.	CD	V^c Rép.						
Elected[a]																
Incumbent	3		5	4			1	1	1	16	2					33
										(6)	(3)					(9)
Former deputy										2					1	3
Senator or former senator			1	1						2						
New	4		6	1	2				1	3				1		17
Defeated[b]																
Incumbent			1				1	2		5	2					11
Former deputy	2			1	2			1		4					1	11
Senator or former senator					1				2	1				1		4
New	8		5	1	2	1			3	17	4		1	1	1	44
	(5)	(1)	(1)	(2)	(1)	(1)	(2)								(1)	(14)
Desisted or withdrew																
Incumbent				1				1								1
Former deputy	2	1		1	1			1								6
New	17	8	2	9	4				9	4		2	1	1	2	57
Eliminated from 2nd ballot																
Incumbent														1		1
Former deputy							1	1								2
New	4		2		4	2	5	1	9	4	1		1		8	55
Totals	45	9	31	13	19	8	9	8	33	61	12	2	2	4	16	272

a. Figures in parentheses refer to cases where the election was decided at the first ballot.
b. At second ballot or where election was decided at the first ballot.

candidates in our original 86 sample districts—a set comparable to the nearly complete set of interviews that we had conducted in 1967. Instead, it was necessary to limit our efforts according to a stern set of priorities.

Our overriding concern was to ensure that we would have interviews with a representative sample of deputies in the legislature elected in 1968 in order to carry out our intended study of the relationship of the deputies' roll-call votes to their own personal opinions, their perceptions of the opinions of their constituents, and the actual opinions of their constituents on related subjects. Originally, we had hoped to conduct this analysis on the basis of several years' roll-call votes by deputies elected in 1967. This expectation was frustrated in 1968 by the dissolution of the National Assembly that had been elected in 1967, after only 87 roll-call votes had been taken. Accordingly, our top priority was to try to interview (or reinterview) the winning candidate in each of the 43 districts in which we also reinterviewed our 1967 mass respondents. This set of elite interviews was intended to provide us with a fresh record of the deputies' perceptions and personal opinions which could be compared with the fresh set of opinions on the same or related subjects which was being obtained by our second wave of mass interviews, conducted within the random, stratified half-sample of our original 86 districts.

Our second priority was to enlarge our record of parliamentary opinion in 1968 by also carrying out interviews with the winning candidates in the 11 districts of the original sample of 86 which did not fall within the 43 half-sample districts, but in which the incumbent deputy did not return to office (and in which we also reinterviewed our 1967 mass respondents).[8] By adding this second level of interviews, we were attempting to obtain a full record of both parliamentary and public opinion in a representative sample of districts in which there was a turnover of deputies in 1968. And by combining the 1968 interviews of winning candidates with the interviews taken in 1967 with candidates who were elected in 1968 but not reinterviewed in 1968, we would have a full record of certain items of information for the entire 86 district sample of deputies elected in 1968, even though that information would have been collected in two different years.

Although our two top priorities involved interviewing 1968 winners, who would sit as deputies for the life of the newly elected legislature, our interest in relating their subsequent legislative behavior to the electoral process required us also to interview the most prominent 1968 losers. Accordingly, our third level of priority was to interview the 22 incumbent deputies who lost their seats in 1968, 12 of whom fell within the 43 half-sample districts and 10 of whom fell outside them. Our fourth and last priority was to obtain interviews with eight candidates in the 43 half-sample districts who had not been in the 1967 elite sample, but who were important runners-up in 1968 in that they were all leading challengers at the second ballot in their districts. To this last group, we added three other candidates who had been runners-up in their districts in both 1967 and 1968.

All told, therefore, we sought interviews in 1968 with 87 major candidates, of whom 54 had won, 22 had been defeated as incumbents, and the remaining 11 had been unsuccessful second-ballot challengers. Of the 87, 48 had already been interviewed in 1967, but the remainder had not been in the 1967 sample.

The Response Rate

Most of the interviews were conducted in September and October 1968, but about a dozen were held in November and December. The response rate (66 percent) was not so satisfying as that of 1967, but this overall rate concealed some wide variations. More than 70 percent of the 48 candidates whom we approached for a second interview (all but two of whom had been winners either in 1967 or in 1968, or in both years) agreed to be reinterviewed,[9] and the response rate was slightly higher among the major candidates who fell into our sample for the first time in 1968.[10] The category of candidates whom we were least successful in interviewing consisted of the dozen candidates who had also been in our 1967 sample but from whom we did not obtain interviews at that time. Only two of these candidates were interviewed in 1968; almost all the others explicitly refused to grant an interview. To some extent, therefore, the lower response rate in 1968 was due to the fact that the sample contained a relatively large number of candidates whom we had failed to interview in 1967 and who may therefore be regarded as refractory.

The breakdown of interviews by party (see Table B-9) indicates that the response rate was highest for the candidates of the non-Communist left, next highest for the Communists, third highest for the pure UDR and In-

Table B-9. Elite response rates by party, 1968.

Party or group	Number of candidates in sample	Number of candidates interviewed	Percent interviewed
Communist (PCF)	16	11	69
PSU	1	1	
FGDS			
SFIO	9	7	75
Radical	4	2	
Convention	2	2	
Progress and Modern Democracy (PDM)	7	3	43
UDR	41	26	64
Independent Republicans (RI)	7	5	
Total	87	57	66

dependent Republican candidates, and lowest for the PDM candidates. It appears from these figures that the candidates of the opposition parties, which had suffered a severe electoral defeat in 1968, were by no means reluctant to be interviewed.

A similar phenomenon is revealed in Table B-10, which displays the full set of 1968 interviews by interview status, party, and 1968 electoral situation. It can be seen that, as in 1967, the response rate for the entire set of candidates was higher than the response rate for the winners alone. In one sense, this is the result that would normally be expected. On the whole, deputies are probably busier than most other people, and it is understandable that even when willing to be interviewed, they may find it difficult to arrange time for an interview.

In the circumstances of 1968, however, after a massive turnover of seats, it would not have been surprising if defeated incumbents had been more reluctant than the winners to be interviewed. That did not turn out to be the case. The response rate for defeated incumbents was not so high as it was for unsuccessful non-incumbent challengers (although we are dealing here with small numbers), but it still was higher than the rate for the winning candidates.

Weighting Systems

Given the relatively small size of our 1968 elite sample and the even smaller number of interviews obtained, we made no attempt to weight the respondents by party in order to render the entire set of interviews proportional to the actual partisan distribution of the leading 1968 candidates or of the 1968 deputies. But for both the entire sample of 1968 candidates and the group of winners within that set, we applied weights to compensate for the fact that we had sought interviews in every district where there was a turnover of deputy, but in only half of the districts where the incumbent was returned. Accordingly, when the entire set of 1968 candidates was analyzed (as in Chapter 15), we assigned twice as much weight to the candidates from districts where the incumbent was returned to office as we did to those from districts where there was a turnover of seats. Similarly, when working with the 1968 winners only, we gave twice as much weight to those from the 43-district half-sample as we did to those from the 11 additional districts among our 1968 total of 54. In keeping with our practice of avoiding inflated Ns, we assigned weights of 1.294 or 0.646 to the 1968 candidates, as appropriate; and similarly, but more simply, we assigned weights of 1.2 or 0.6 to the subset of 1968 winners.

We also combined the interviews taken in 1967 or 1968 with deputies who served in the 1967 legislature or the 1968 legislature (or both) in order to give us the largest possible set of deputies for each legislature. As shown in Table B-6, 66 deputies were interviewed in 1967. In 1968, we were able to interview four more persons who had served as deputies in the 1967 legisla-

Table B-10. 1968 elite interviews by interview status, party, and electoral situation in 1968.

Sample of 87 candidates	Interviewed in 1968 only					Interviewed in 1967 and 1968								Total	Percent
	Communists	SFIO	PDM	UDR	Ind. Rep.	Communists	PSU	Fed.-SFIO	Fed.-Rad.	Fed.-Conv.	PDM	UDR	Ind. Rep.	Total	Percent
Deputies from half-sample of 43 districts		1	1	4		3		2			1	9	4	25	61
Winners in 11 other sample districts where incumbent turnover				5								3		8	
Defeated incumbents in 12 districts of half-sample	1					2	1	1	1	2				8	68
Defeated incumbents in 10 districts outside half-sample	2					2		2	1					7	
Non-incumbent challengers at 2nd ballot in 8 districts of half-sample	1		1	5	1									8	82
Major non-incumbent challengers in 3 districts outside half-sample		1					1							1	
Total	4	2	2	14	1	7	1	5	2	2	1	11	5	57	66

Table B-11. Combined deputy weights, 1967.

Parliamentary group	Deputy population[a]		Deputies interviewed			
	Number	Percent	Number	Percent	Weight	Weighted N
Communist (PCF)	72	15.4	10	14.3	1.1	11.0
FGDS						
SFIO	76	16.3	12	17.1	1.0	12.0
Radical	24	5.1	5	7.1	0.7	3.5
Convention	16	3.4	2	2.8	1.2	2.4
Affiliated (including PSU)	5	1.1	1	1.4	0.8	0.8
Progress and Modern Democracy (PDM)	40	8.6	5	7.1	1.2	6.0
Union of Democrats for the 5th Republic (UD-V[c])	187	40.0	28	40.2	1.0	28.0
Independent Republicans (RI)	40	8.6	6	8.6	1.0	6.0
No group	7	1.5	1	1.4	1.1	1.1
Total	467	100.0	70	100.0		70.8

a. Deputies from Metropolitan France (excluding Corsica) only.

Table B-12. Combined deputy weights, 1968.

Parliamentary group	Deputy population[a]		In Half-sample of 43 districts			In remaining 43 districts			Total	Percent	Weight	Weighted N
	Number	Percent	1967	1968	1967 & 1968	1967	1968	1967 & 1968				
Communist (PCF)	33	7.1			3				3	4.5	1.6	4.8
Federation (FGDS)	57	12.2		1	2	5			8	12.1	1.0	8.0
Progress and Modern Democracy (PDM)	31	6.6	2	1	1	3			7	10.6	0.6	4.2
Union of Democrats for the Republic (UDR)	279	59.8	4	2	9	16	5	1	37	56.2	1.1	40.7
Independent Republicans (RI)	60	12.8	1		4	2		1	8	12.1	1.0	8.0
No group	7	1.5		2				1	3	4.5	0.3	0.9
Total	467	100.0	7	6[b]	19	26	5	3	66	100.0		66.6

a. Deputies from Metropolitan France (excluding Corsica) only.
b. Includes one alternate who replaced a deputy elected in both 1967 and 1968 who had been interviewed in 1967.

ture. Three of these were Communists and the fourth was a member of the group for Progress and Modern Democracy (PDM). Accordingly, we added these four 1968 interviews to the 66 already obtained in 1967, and reweighted the responses by parliamentary group in order to make the enlarged set of 70 interviews proportionate, by group, to the actual distribution of seats in the 1967 legislature. This operation is displayed in Table B-11. As we compare Table B-11 with Table B-6, we see that the addition of the four 1968 interviews operated to bring the weights closer to unity.

The parallel weighting operation for the deputies who served in the 1968 legislature is displayed in Table B-12. These weights show more dispersion than do those for 1967. Fortunately, the group for which the weight is most extreme—the Communist party—is also the group which displays the greatest homogeneity of response, as was indicated in Table B-1. Weights uniformly closer to unity would obviously have been a more desirable outcome, but considering that our sample size was small to begin with, that we are weighting to render our results by group proportionate to the group distribution of the actual universe and not to the group distribution of the sample population, and that several of the groups of the universe are themselves relatively small percentages of the total, the outcome is as satisfying as could be expected.

Left-Right Scoring of the Candidates

The problems of determining the party affiliations of the candidates and scoring them on the left-right scale were essentially the same for 1968 as they had been for 1967. But we interviewed fewer candidates in 1968 than in 1967—an average of one candidate per sample district instead of more than three—although, as we have already indicated, those interviewed in 1968 were mainly winners or defeated incumbents. The smaller numbers meant, however, that in only a few cases could we rely on the candidates' own descriptions of the party labels they had used during the campaign. Accordingly, in determining the party affiliations of the candidates, we were more dependent on public sources of information than we had been in 1967.

The Ministry of the Interior published a volume containing the results of the 1968 election, which listed all the candidates, but like the parallel volume for 1967 it did not contain the party affiliation of all the candidates (République Française, Ministère de l'Intérieur, 1968). Therefore, as in 1967, we relied mainly on the detailed reporting of the results of each of the ballots which appeared in *Le Monde* (June 25, 1968, and July 2, 1968). *Le Monde* again distinguished between Gaullist candidates from the orthodox Gaullist party, this time the UDR, and those from the Independent Republicans of M. Giscard d'Estaing, and it distinguished among the various constituent elements of the Federation: the SFIO, the Radical party, and the Convention. *Le Monde* distinguished less frequently among the partisan origins of the candidates of Progrès et Démocratie Moderne (PDM) than it had done for the candidates of the Centre Démocrate in 1967. And, as in 1967, *Le Monde* provided much valuable information about multiple party support for individual candidates, unusual or local party labels, and distinctions between official candidacy and support.

Within the limits of this reduced information base (relative to that of 1967), we followed the same principles in assigning partisan affiliations to the candidates that we had applied in 1967. If an interviewed candidate from any of the main confederations—Gaullist, Federation, or PDM—told us that he had used a more specific party label during the campaign than was reported in *Le Monde,* we assigned that specific label to the candidate. If *Le Monde* indicated a specific partisan origin for a candidate, and that party affiliation was confirmed by the candidate, we followed *Le Monde,* even if the candidate did not indicate that he had used it to identify himself to his constituents. As a result, Gaullist and Federation candidates were coded as finely for 1968 as they had been for 1967, but PDM candidates were coded less finely. We considered attributing more precise party affiliations to PDM candidates not interviewed in 1968 who had run as Democratic Center candidates in 1967, and whose specific partisan origins had been known to us then either from interviews or from *Le Monde,* but we rejected that course on the ground that we had no basis for assuming that these candidates identified themselves to their constituents in 1968 in the same way as they had done in 1967.

Certain arbitrary, but reasonable, decisions had to be made for 1968 as for 1967. Unlike the situation in 1967, the Gaullists did not run in every district in 1968. In some districts they merely supported candidates that were invested or endorsed by one or more other parties. These candidates were coded separately in the appropriate categories. One candidate who told us that he ran under the Centre Démocrate label was coded as PDM.

We also had less information with which to score the 1968 candidates on the left-right scale than we had had for 1967. For that year, we had known the mean left-right locations that were assigned by the respondents in our 86-district sample to ten national parties or political formations. For 1968, we only knew the mean left-right locations attributed by the respondents in our 43-district half-sample to six political parties or formations: Progrès et Démocratie Moderne de Duhamel, PSU, Républicains Indépendants de Giscard d'Estaing, Parti Communiste, UD Ve République, and Fédération de la Gauche.[11] In addition, we could rely on those designated points on the left-right scale shown to the respondents which were labeled "Gauche Modérée," "Droite Modérée," and so forth.

Communist and PSU candidates were scored at the mean figure assigned to each of these parties by our 1968 sample electorate. Independent Republicans were scored in the same fashion, and all other Gaullist candidates were assigned the score for the UD Ve République. Federation candidates who did not have a more precise partisan affiliation were scored at the mean assigned by our sample to the Federation. This score was less than one-half of 1 percent to the left of the score assigned to the Federation by our sample for 1967. Inasmuch as we had a breakdown of Federation candidates by party origin in 1968, but no left-right locations for the SFIO or the Radical party (as we had had for 1967), we assigned scores to SFIO-Fédération candidates and to Radical-Fédération candidates that were to the left of the scores for those candidates in 1967 by the same proportion as the Federation was perceived by the electorate in 1968 to be to the left of its location in 1967. Convention-Fédération candidates were scored at the same place as simple Fédération candidates, as had been done for 1967.

We have already pointed out that PDM candidates were, on the whole, less finely coded for 1968 than for 1967. Very few candidates in our sample districts could clearly be identified as PDM-Indépendant or PDM-MRP. As a result, we were not particularly troubled by the absence of a sample estimate of the left-right location of the MRP, a party which in any case had been defunct by 1967 and was already of low visibility to the electorate in that year. We coded the small number of PDM-Indépendant and PDM-MRP candidates in our sample districts at the same point: the scale location for Droite Modérée (60).

Other candidates with multiple endorsements were coded at the mean of the mean left-right location of the relevant parties.

A list of the party labels which we assigned to the candidates who ran in our 1968 sample districts, along with the left-right locations of these labels, appears in Table B-13.

Table B-13. Left-right scoring of candidates, 1968.

Score	Candidate's party label
10	Parti Communiste Français (PCF)
25	Fédération; Fédération-Convention
27	Parti Socialiste Unifié (PSU)
30	Fédération-SFIO; Union des Républicains (Independent Socialists)
36	Fédération-Radical
40	Progrès et Démocratie Moderne–Centre Gauche
44	Gaulliste de Gauche
50	Progrès et Démocratie Moderne (PDM)
58	Progrès et Démocratie Moderne–Union pour la Défense de la République
59	Union pour la Défense de la République–Progrès et Démocratie Moderne–Indépendant
60	Progrès et Démocratie Moderne–Indépendant; Progrès et Démocratie Moderne–MRP; Républicain Indépendant (Giscardien); Action Paysanne et Sociale
67	Union pour la Défense de la République (UDR)

APPENDIX C

Correction of Correlations
for Small-Sample Attenuation

Any correlation formed between fixed characteristics of our sample districts—for example, between the pattern of roll-call votes cast by each Assembly seat associated with each district and estimates of mass constituency properties, such as issue attitude means—must naturally be laid against conventional statistical criteria concerning the sampling distribution of the correlation coefficient. Such a routine evaluation takes cognizance of the fact that we interviewed only within a proper sample of 86 legislative jurisdictions. Thus the N appropriate for statistical inference is at most 86, and at times it dwindles to 66 (where such a correlation depends on the presence of a deputy interview) or 54 (for the 1968 interview design).

The Attenuation Correction

Entirely distinct from the problems entailed by the sampling of districts is a second level of stochastic "blur" created by the fact that we did not interview all voters within our sample districts, but only a very small sample (averaging 23 or 24 persons per district). Although means and proportions reflecting mass constituency attributes based on these small samples provide unbiased estimates of actual district parameters, the small-sample basis for these estimates leaves them quite unstable. This additional source of sampling error means that even if we knew that one fixed characteristic of our districts correlated perfectly in the real world with some district parameter estimated from our small samples, we could not expect to find a perfect correlation in our observed data based on these samples. In effect, there would be some value less than 1.00 which would represent an expected "ceiling" value on such a correlation, given the fact that observations on one of the two variables are afflicted with a special increment of small-sample error.

If we can calculate such an expected value for the "ceiling" from our knowledge of the sample design, then we can make the upward corrections on any of our observed correlations that are necessary to discount the advanced error margins associated with the limited size of our voter samples in each district. Fortunately, standard sampling theory enables us to arrive at excellent estimates of what these small-sample error margins must be expected to be in any given district; and we can pool these estimates across districts to arrive at a statement of the total error variance in a set of observations of sample means or proportions directly attributable (at least as an expected value) to our small constituency samples.

The corrections used in this book for small-sample attenuation follow directly from parallel corrections devised by Donald E. Stokes for the purposes of the Miller-Stokes study, although minor variations in sampling design in our study, as well as considerations of convenience, have led to slightly different computational details. Following Stokes, let x_i be the actual mean of the small-sample variable for the ith district ($i = 1, 2, \ldots, I$) as such a parameter might be determined from a full enumeration of district members. Let X_i be the mean observed in our small sample of the ith district. Then

$$X_i = x_i + e_i, \tag{1}$$

where e_i is the error resulting from the sampling of members of the ith district.

When the observed values by district $X_1, \ldots, X_I$ are correlated with another district-level variable y whose values $y_1, \ldots, y_I$ are not subject to a corresponding error due to small-sample estimates, we arrive at the observed correlation r_{Xy}, and wish to deduce from it the true value r_{xy} which we could expect to pertain had we enumerated rather than sampled each district.

We can assume without loss of generality that x, X, and y are expressed as mean deviates. Then multiplying y times each side of equation (1) and summing across districts yields:

$$\sum_{i=1}^{I} X_i y_i = \sum_{i=1}^{I} x_i y_i + \sum_{i=1}^{I} e_i y_i. \tag{2}$$

By the definition of the correlation coefficient, this is equivalent to

$$I r_{Xy} s_X s_y = I r_{xy} s_x s_y + I r_{ey} s_e s_y. \tag{3}$$

Given the sample design, we can assume that $E(r_{ex}) = E(r_{ey}) = 0$, so that the final term drops out, and we have

$$r_{Xy} s_X = r_{xy} s_x, \tag{4}$$

or

$$r_{xy} = \frac{r_{Xy} s_X}{s_x}. \tag{5}$$

Since the variance of a linear combination is equal to the same linear combination of the variances of its terms, it follows from equation (1) that

$$s_X^2 = s_x^2 + s_e^2. \tag{6}$$

Substituting for the unobserved s_x in (5) then gives

$$r_{xy} = \frac{r_{Xy}s_X}{\sqrt{s_X^2 - s_e^2}} = \frac{r_{Xy}}{\sqrt{1 - \left(\frac{s_e}{s_X}\right)^2}}. \tag{7}$$

Thus an expected value for the correlation coefficient r_{xy} can be computed from the observed (and attenuated) correlation r_{Xy} by introducing a divisor or attenuation coefficient, α, which depends on the ratio of s_e to s_x, as estimated from our sample data:

$$\alpha = \sqrt{1 - \left(\frac{s_e}{s_X}\right)^2}. \tag{8}$$

The relevant model for estimation of the crucial variance components from our sample data is provided by a random-effects one-way analysis of variance. Within the terms of such a model, the mean sum of squares within groups (districts), or MSSW, is an unbiased estimate of the true error variance, σ_e^2. The mean sum of squares between groups, or MSSB, is an unbiased estimate of the true error variance plus the true variance associated with differences between districts. Hence:

$$\alpha = \sqrt{1 - \frac{\text{MSSW}}{\text{MSSB}}}. \tag{9}$$

This estimation model assumes random sampling, both of groups and of individuals within groups. Our sample design fulfills these conditions to within a very reasonable approximation.[1] A second assumption is that "errors," or within-district variations, are independent both of district membership and of each other. Although we cannot be sure that our data do not violate this assumption, there is no obvious reason to believe that they do. A third assumption concerning the normality of distributions of both error and district differentiations is also fairly approximated.

A final assumption necessary for the efficient application of an estimation equation like (9) is that case numbers by district are equal. Unlike the Miller-Stokes study, our French data collection, which was designed from the start as a representation study, aimed at equal case numbers per district. In practice, of course, because of modest variations in response rate by district, as well as minor variations in the incidence of missing data for specific variables, case numbers depart in some degree from absolute equality. The divergence from equal case numbers becomes more marked in the 1968 reinterviewing, due to further variations by district in panel attrition.

Nevertheless, this departure from equal case numbers remains modest enough to produce little distortion relative to the parent model. For example, for a characteristic set of content responses on one of our issue items, the mean N per district is 23.29, with a standard deviation of 3.6 responses per district. Application of the standard formula for effective "cell" size for variance component estimates when cell sizes are in fact unequal changes the district N from 23.29 to 23.28. This is an utterly trivial difference for our purposes.

Pathologies of the Attenuation Correction

Although it has been resurrected only in recent years by political scientists and sociologists, the correction of correlations for one or another form of attenuation—usually for test unreliability—has a rather ancient history in psychometrics. Such corrections were in vogue for a while, and then fell into disrepute in the later 1940s and the 1950s because of the frequency with which "corrected" correlations greater than 1.00 were being reported.

It is worth understanding such frailties of the correction clearly, for whereas it is true that we are using such a correction in a different context, our estimates are subject to pathologies which are entirely parallel, and must be kept in mind.

There is nothing surprising about corrected correlations running above 1.00, because the solution for α, the putative "ceiling" for an observed correlation given attenuating error, is no more than an expected value, and a mere estimate of it at that. In other words, in any given case we may underestimate or overestimate α, with systematic consequences for our corrected coefficients. If we underestimate α badly, and are dealing with a situation where true underlying correlations are very strong, we may well generate "corrected" correlations that surpass 1.00, embarrassing though that may be. Indeed, if we simulate a situation in which we have a batch of perfect underlying correlations attenuated by levels of error which we can estimate, and we do so, then about half of our "corrected" values will lie above 1.00 and the other half below.

What a correlation corrected to a value above 1.00 tells us, then, is that the true correlation is very high, and that we have underestimated the value of α, as we shall do approximately half the time. In such uncertain terrain, it is important that we keep our wits about us. In particular, we need to know something about the sampling variability of our estimates of α. We would have to look at our corrected results quite differently, according to whether we knew that the relevant α's had probable errors of .002, .020, or .200. The last possibility, though quite frightening, cannot be ruled out under some circumstances.

Relative to most attenuation corrections in the literature which are for test or measurement unreliability, our correction for small-sample limitations is on fairly firm ground; that is, the correction in the unreliability case will be adequate or inadequate, robust or volatile, according to the firmness of the estimate of the reliability coefficient for the test or measure at stake.

Now it is well known that any such reliability estimates in psychometric work have a major element of the presumptive in them. There are, for example, different ways of arriving at such estimates, none of which is seen as ideal. Hence, although it probably is worth making such corrections for measurement unreliability, particularly where the reliability is almost certainly low, there is a good deal of ad hoc about the details of the procedure, and corrected coefficients running above 1.00 should surprise nobody.

In our case, the estimated ceiling derives from sampling theory, and the basic calculation to be used is not up for dispute, as it is with empirical estimations of reliability. Nonetheless, the α remains no more than an expected value, and, as conditions vary, the implied sampling variability around the estimate can be smaller or larger. Unfortunately, the sampling distribution of α is unknown. Through experimentation and practical use, however, we have achieved a rather clear view as to when our α's must be considered less trustworthy. The magnitude of our α's is, of course, a joint function of case numbers in our districts and of η, the index of between-district heterogeneity. In most of our practical applications, the (average) Ns are remaining fixed at a bit better than 23 per district. What is varying is the degree of between-district heterogeneity from one political issue to the next. With the N fixed, we can plot the way α varies as a function of η (see Figure C-1).

From this figure it is obvious that when an observed η falls much under .25, the magnitude of the α can vary in appalling degree with only very small changes in the η's. This raises curiosity as to the variability of the η statistic itself, although unfortunately once again, its sampling distribution is unknown. In pursuing the problem we have done some Monte Carlo experimentation with the stability of our η's by such means as comparing η's from various randomly selected within-district half-samples. These results are in general quite reassuring: the η's look like rather inert estimates.

Nonetheless, it seems true that η's themselves begin to destabilize as they move downward below .25 toward .20, and this growing edge of instability, coupled with the enormous volatility of α's against changes in η in these regions becomes frightening indeed. Fortunately, the η's with which we are dealing are typically in the range from .28 to .35 when we are working with total district samples, and they advance upward quite dramatically for issues when within-district partitions into winning and losing constituencies are made (see Chapter 19). Hence we are generally on fairly solid ground where the stability of our correction estimations is concerned.

One or two issues, however, fall well below that range and put us on very thin ice indeed. The most troubling example by far concerns the issue of some merger of the French Army with a European Army, where between-district variation is so feeble that we have an η of only .21. This converts to an α of less than .17, which means that we should not expect to

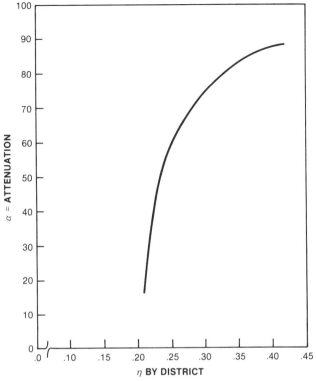

Figure C-1. Illustration of the variation in *alpha* (attenuation coefficient) as a function of *eta,* for Ns averaging 23 per district.

find correlations between district means on the European Army item and other variables surpassing this very low value. But we do find such correlations almost immediately (although again, not always): for example, the correlations between deputy position on the European Army and own-district sentiments thereon is observed to be $r = .195$. Correcting this value in our standard way for small-sample attenuation, the correlation would be transformed to a nonsense value of $r = 1.17*$. If such nonsense values had been frequent in our work, or if the reasons for their emergence in special cases had been obscure, we would have discarded the method completely, despite its obvious relevance.

We have almost never encountered such oddities, however, and where we have, the association with weak-η issues is overpowering: the culprit is almost always the European Army item with its η of .209, although the next most fragile item—European foreign policy, with an η of only .231 and an expected α of .454—is now and again problematic. Only two other of our nineteen single-item issues have η's less than .27, or α's less than .66, when total districts are taken into account. Although partitioning into winning and losing subconstituencies advances the η's into higher ground, the Ns are also cut by more than half, producing strains toward further attenuation. The net effect here for most issues is to put our corrections on firmer ground despite the diminution in Ns. But, for a few issues, and typically those which were weak-η issues to begin with, the gain in η (the European Army item advances from .21 over total districts to .26 among losers, and .31 among winners) is more than offset by the shrinkage in cases. This means that estimates of α that were already too precarious to trust for the total-district comparisons become simply ridiculous.

In some of our work, the problems posed by single items like the European Army are not pressing, because we are able to use more summary indices. Thus, despite inclusion of the European Army item in it, our European Integration Scale shows a healthy η of .31 (α of .77) even for total-district estimates. In some contexts, however, such as that of Chapter 19, it becomes important to work with single items. At such times, we avoid agitating the reader with nonsense values where they would appear. For example, in Table 19-1 we simply indicate that the AB bond for deputies on the European Army item is large and positive, which it certainly must be: even if our estimated α of .17 is such a grotesque underestimate that a truer value would be .50, the observed correlation would still be $r = .39^*$, a value which in the context of the table is surely large and positive. If the underestimate were any less gross, the corrected value would grow correspondingly larger.

APPENDIX D

Questionnaires

Mass Survey Questionnaire, 1967

Bonjour Madame, Monsieur. J'appartiens à la SOFRES et je fais un sondage pour connaître l'opinion des Français sur quelques grandes questions d'actualité. L'opinion de *tous* les Français nous intéresse, même de ceux qui n'ont pas d'opinion ou qui n'ont pas le temps de s'informer!

Voulez-vous avoir l'amabilité de répondre à mes questions.

Vous êtes bien M_____ né(e) en _____
  (nom et prénom)   (l'année de naissance indiquée sur la feuille de route)

Q.1. Pour la France, selon vous, quel est le problème le plus important à l'heure actuelle?

Q.2. Diriez-vous que, dans l'ensemble, vous êtes très satisfait, assez satisfait, peu satisfait, ou pas du tout satisfait de:

(*Tendre liste-réponse*)

(a) vos conditions de logement.

(b) du revenu de votre foyer.

(c) du travail que vous faites (ou, si vous ne travaillez pas, du travail que fait le chef de famille).

(d) des possibilités qu'ont les enfants de nos jours de recevoir toute l'instruction dont ils ont besoin.

Q.3. Est-ce que, depuis 1958, le gouvernement a pris des mesures qui ont eu pour vous des conséquences favorables? [Oui; Non (passer à Q.4).]

Q.3bis. Lesquelles?

Q.4. Et a-t-il pris des mesures qui ont eu pour vous des conséquences défavorables? [Oui; Non (passer à Q.5).]

Q.4bis. Lesquelles?

Nous allons maintenant aborder ensemble un certain nombre de jugements sur lesquels les avis diffèrent. Si vous n'avez pas d'opinion sur un point ou un autre, dites-le; cela nous intéresse également.

Q.5. Etes-vous satisfait ou mécontent du Général de Gaulle comme Président de la République? [Très satisfait; Plutôt satisfait; Plutôt mécontent; Très mécontent.] (*Tendre liste-réponse*)

Q.6. Si vous comparez les institutions de la IVe République et celles de la Ve, sans tenir compte de la personnalité du Général de Gaulle, diriez-vous que les institutions de la Ve République sont bien meilleures, plutôt meilleures, pareilles, plutôt mauvaises ou beaucoup plus mauvaises?

Q.7. Pour chacun des problèmes suivants, pouvez-vous me dire si vous le considérez comme très important, assez important, peu important ou pas important du tout?

(*Lire les thèmes; tendre liste-réponse*)

(a) La stabilité gouvernementale, est-elle très importante, assez importante, peu importante ou pas importante du tout?

(b) La défense de l'école laïque?

(c) La construction de l'Europe?

(d) Une répartition équitable des revenus entre les différentes catégories de Français?

(e) Le développement de l'enseignement?

(f) L'indépendance de la France par rapport aux Etats-Unis?

(g) Le développement économique du pays?

Q.8. Voici un certain nombre de jugements sur ces problèmes.

Voudriez-vous nous donner votre opinion, en disant si vous vous estimez d'accord ou non? Et, comme avant, si vous n'avez pas d'opinion, cela nous intéresse aussi.

(*Lire les phrases; tendre liste-réponse*)

(a) L'Etat doit aider les écoles libres—êtes-vous entièrement d'accord, plutôt d'accord, plutôt pas d'accord, ou pas du tout d'accord?

(b) La force de frappe est nécessaire si la France veut garder son rang de grande puissance.

(c) Dans la répartition du revenu national les ouvriers sont vraiment défavorisés.

(d) L'Etat devrait faire un plus gros effort pour l'enseignement.

(e) Plutôt que d'aider les pays sous-développés, le gouvernement ferait mieux d'aider les régions françaises en difficulté.

(f) La politique extérieure de la France doit être entièrement indépendante des Etats-Unis.

(g) Les droits des syndicats devraient être mieux défendus.

Q.9. On parle depuis longtemps de l'unité de l'Europe. Croyez-vous que l'unité de l'Europe aurait, à l'heure actuelle, des effets bons ou mauvais sur

(*Lire les thèmes; tendre liste-réponse*)

[Très bons; Plutôt bons; Plutôt mauvais; Très mauvais; Pas d'effet.]

(a) la situation économique de la France?

(b) la prospérité de votre profession (ou, si vous ne travaillez pas, la profession du chef de famille)?

(c) votre bien-être personnel?

Q.10. A quel point seriez-vous d'accord ou non avec les mesures suivantes? Seriez-vous entièrement d'accord, plutôt d'accord, plutôt pas d'accord ou pas du tout d'accord?

(*Lire les thèmes; tendre liste-rèponse*)

(a) Que l'armée française soit fondue dans une armée européenne?

(b) Que le gouvernement français accepte une politique étrangère commune pour les six pays du Marché Commun?

(c) Que la France maintienne son adhésion au Marché Commun?

(d) Que les Français puissent s'installer et travailler n'importe où en Europe et qu'inversement les ouvriers et entreprises "étrangères" puissent venir s'installer en France?

(e) Que le gouvernement français utilise une partie des impôts pour aider les régions les plus pauvres de l'Europe?

Q.11. Est-ce que vous vous intéressez à la politique beaucoup, assez, un peu, pas du tout?

Q.12. Pendant la campagne électorale, avez-vous regardé à la télévision les émissions concernant la politique? [Oui, la plupart; oui, quelques-unes; oui, mais seulement une ou deux; non.]

Q.13. Pendant la campagne électorale, est-ce que des candidats ou des représentants des candidats ont pris contact personnellement avec vous (soit en venant vous voir, soit en vous téléphonant)? [Oui; Non (passer à Q.14).]

Q.13bis. Les candidats ou les représentants de quels candidats? (*Ne rien suggérer.* Cocher d'après votre fiche de renseignements sur les candidats de la circonscription)

[Candidats: A, B, C, D, E, F, G, H, I, *autres* (préciser).]

Q.14. Pendant la campagne électorale, avez-vous essayé de convaincre des personnes de votre entourage de voter dans le même sens que vous?

(*Si oui,* demander: souvent ou quelquefois?) [Oui, souvent; oui, quelquefois; non.]

Q.15. Parmi ces différentes choses, quel a été, selon vous, le véritable enjeu des dernières élections législatives. Que mettriez-vous en 1er? (*Tendre liste-réponse*)

Q.15bis. Et en 2e?

Q.15ter. Et en 3e?

(a) la ville contre la campagne.

(b) le Communisme contre l'anti-Communisme.

(c) de Gaulle contre les partis.

(d) les catholiques contre les laïques.

(e) l'initiative privée contre l'intervention de l'Etat dans le domaine économique.

(f) la Ve République contre la IVe République.

(g) la gauche contre la droite.

(h) les partisans d'une Europe unie contre les adversaires de l'Europe.

(i) le gouvernement contre l'opposition.

(j) la classe ouvrière contre les capitalistes.

(k) le pouvoir personnel contre la démocratie.

Q.16. Pour défendre les intérêts des gens comme vous, sur qui comptez-vous le plus? (*Tendre liste-réponse*) [Syndicats, organismes professionnels; partis politiques; les élus.]

Q.17. Croyez-vous que dans la vie politique française à l'heure actuelle, les partis devraient jouer un rôle très important, assez important, peu important ou pas important du tout?

Q.18. Compte tenu de tout ce que les partis représentent, à votre avis, existe-t-il *beaucoup* de différences entre les partis, *quelques* différences, ou *peu* de différences?

Q.19. Selon vous, le nombre des partis politiques existant actuellement en France est-il trop faible, convenable, ou trop grand?

Q.20. Combien de partis croyez-vous qu'il devrait y avoir?

Q.21. Quels sont tous les noms de partis politiques que vous pouvez me citer? (*Ne rien suggérer*, mais insister pour avoir les noms; cocher dans la 1ere colonne du tableau ci-dessous)

Q.21bis. Et sur cette liste, y a-t-il d'autres partis que vous connaissez et que vous n'avez pas pensé à me citer? (*Tendre la liste des partis;* puis cocher dans la 2e colonne.)

Q.21ter. (A poser pour tous les partis cités à Q.21 et Q.21bis)
Sur cette échelle qui va de l'extrême gauche à l'extrême droite (*tendre la liste avec l'échelle*), où placeriez-vous ... (compléter en citant le nom du parti)?
(Si un chiffre n'est pas cité, demander, "Ce qui correspond à quel chiffre?" et noter le chiffre cité dans la 3e colonne.)

PARTIS	Q.21	Q.21bis	Q.21ter
Parti Socialiste SFIO	Y	X	__ __ __
Alliance Républicaine de Tixier-Vignancour	Y	X	__ __ __
Centre Démocrate de Lecanuet	Y	X	__ __ __
PSU	Y	X	__ __ __
Républicains Indépendants de Giscard d'Estaing	Y	X	__ __ __
MRP	Y	X	__ __ __
Parti Communiste	Y	X	__ __ __
Parti Radical	Y	X	__ __ __
UNR	Y	X	__ __ __
Fédération de la Gauche de Mitterrand	Y	X	__ __ __
Autres Partis, en notant leurs noms tels qu'ils sont cités			
_____	Y		__ __ __
_____	Y		__ __ __

Q.22. Et vous-même, si vous aviez à vous placer sur cette échelle, où vous placeriez-vous? (*Tendre à nouveau la liste avec l'échelle*; et noter le chiffre cité)

Q.23. On oppose souvent partis de gauche et partis de droite. A votre avis, en quoi consistent les différences les plus importantes entre la gauche et la droite?

Q.24. Parmi les partis politiques suivants [Parti Communiste, Fédération de la Gauche de Mitterrand, SFIO, Parti Radical, MRP, Centre Démocrate de Lecanuet, UNR, Républicains Indépendants de Giscard d'Estaing, PSU, Alliance Républicaine de Tixier-Vignancour], quel est celui qui, selon vous, lutte le plus pour assurer:

(*Lire les phrases; tendre liste-réponse*); (*une seule réponse par ligne*)

(a) la stabilité gouvernementale?

(b) la défense de l'école laïque?

(c) la construction de l'Europe?

(d) une répartition équitable des revenus entre les différentes catégories de Français?

(e) le développement de l'enseignement?

(f) l'indépendance de la France par rapport aux Etats-Unis?

(g) le développement économique du pays?

Q.25. A votre avis, un bon député doit-il, à l'Assemblée Nationale, voter comme son parti lui ordonne de le faire, ou bien doit-il prendre ses décisions lui-même sans tenir compte des positions de son parti?

Q.26. Il est déjà arrivé que les électeurs exigent de leur député qu'il agisse contre ses propres convictions. Dans ce cas, pensez-vous que le député doit faire ce que les électeurs demandent, ou ce qu'il désire lui-même?

Q.27. Selon vous, un député doit-il soutenir le gouvernement pour en obtenir des advantages pour sa circonscription, ou bien doit-il garder ses distances à l'égard du gouvernement pour conserver sa liberté de critique?

Q.28. Il y a des personnes et des groupes qui influencent le gouvernement ou l'opinion publique. Nous aimerions savoir quels sont vos sentiments à leur égard.

Voulez-vous mettre une note de 0 à 100 aux personnes ou groupes que je vais vous citer en fonction de la sympathie que vous éprouvez pour eux:

(*Tendre la liste avec l'échelle de sympathie*)

100 signifie que vous avez beaucoup de sympathie,

  0 signifie que vous ne les aimez pas du tout,

 50 signifie, soit que vous n'êtes ni pour ni contre eux, soit que vous ne connaissez pas grand chose sur eux.

Quelle note donneriez-vous:

(*Citer les noms un à un*)

(a) aux syndicats?

(b) à M. Mitterrand?

(c) au clergé?

(d) aux Américains?

(e) au Parti Communiste?

(f) au Général de Gaulle?

(g) aux petits commerçants?

(h) au Parti Socialiste SFIO?

(i) aux Allemands?

(j) à M. Lecanuet?

(k) à l'UNR?

(l) au Grand Patronat?

(m) aux Russes?

(n) à M. Tixier-Vignancour?

(o) au MRP?

(p) à M. Giscard d'Estaing?

(q) aux fonctionnaires?

(r) aux Anglais?

(s) au PSU?

(t) à l'armée?

(u) à M. Pompidou?

(v) au Parti Radical?

Q.29. Depuis que vous êtes électeur, diriez-vous que vous avez voté *à toutes* les élections législatives et présidentielles, *à la plupart, à quelques-unes, ou à aucune?* [Aucune, passer à Q.31.]

Q.30. Aux élections législatives, avez-vous voté pour le même parti ou la même tendance toujours, la plupart du temps, ou bien avez-vous voté pour des partis différents?

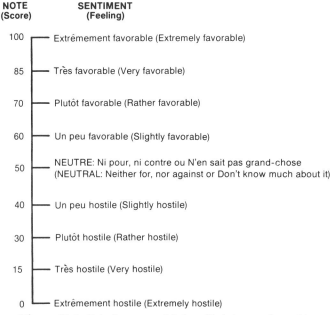

Figure D-1. Echelle sympathie-hostilité (*sympathy scale*).

Q.31. Dans l'ensemble, que jugez-vous le plus important lorsque vous votez: le candidat dans votre circonscription, le parti lui-même, ou le chef du parti? (*Ne rien suggérer*) [Le Parti, Le Chef, Le Candidat, Le Programme, Le Parti et le Chef également, Le Parti et le Programme également, Le Chef et le Programme également, Le Candidat et le Programme, Le Candidat et le Parti, Le Candidat et le Chef.]

Q.32. Quel est le parti dont vous vous sentez habituellement le plus proche? (*Une seule réponse, en la notant telle qu'elle vous est donnée par l'interviewé*) [Aucun, NSP, passer à Q.34.]

Q.32bis. Diriez-vous que vous vous sentez très proche de ce parti, assez proche, ou pas très proche?

Q.32ter. Qu'est-ce qui vous plaît surtout dans ce parti?

Q.33. Vous êtes-vous senti à certains moments, plus proche d'un autre parti? [Oui; Non (passer à Q.34).]

Q.33bis. Quel parti était-ce? (*Une seule réponse, en la notant telle qu'elle vous est donnée par l'interviewé*)

Q.34. Y a-t-il des partis pour lesquels vous ne voteriez en aucun cas? [Oui; Non, NSP (passer à Q.35).]

Q.34bis. Lesquels?

Q.35. Avez-vous voté au *premier tour* lors des élections législatives de *Novembre 1962* pour élire les députés? [Oui; Non, NSP (passer à Q.39).]

Q.36. Avez-vous voté dans cette circonscription? [Oui, poser Q.36bis, puis Q.39; Non, poser Q.37.]

Q.36bis. Pour quel candidat ou parti avez-vous voté? *Attention,* je dis bien au *premier tour* des élections de 1962.

Q.37. Dans quelle circonscription avez-vous voté?

Q.38. Vous rappelez-vous pour quel parti ou pour quel candidat vous avez voté? *Attention,* je dis bien au *premier tour* des élections de 1962.

A TOUT LE MONDE

Q.39. Avez-vous voté lors *du premier tour* de l'élection présidentielle, le 5 Décembre 1965? [Oui; Non, NSP (passer à Q.41.)]

Q.40. Pouvez-vous m'indiquer pour quel candidat vous avez voté; *attention,* je dis bien au premier tour? (*Tendre liste-réponse*) Pour répondre, il vous suffit de citer la lettre correspondant au nom du candidat.

[J—M. Marcel Barbu; K—Le Général de Gaulle; M—M. Jean Lecanuet; O—M. François Mitterrand; P—M. Pierre Marcilhacy; W—M. Jean-Louis Tixier-Vignancour.]

Nous allons parler maintenant des dernières élections de Mars 1967.

Q.41. Pouvez-vous me citer les noms des candidats qui se sont présentés ici, dans votre circonscription, *au premier tour,* le 5 mars 1967? (*Ne rien suggérer*)

[*Enquêteur:*
—Noter dans la 1ere colonne, les noms ou à défaut toutes les autres précisions servant à identifier les candidats.
—Pour chacun des candidats identifiés, poser Q.41A et Q.41B et noter les réponses dans le tableau ci-dessous.
—Si l'interviewé n'a identifié aucun candidat, passer directement à Q.41C.]

Q.41A. (Pour chaque candidat identifié): De quel parti ou tendance était-il?

Q.41B. (Pour chaque candidat identifié): Avez-vous lu ou entendu quelque chose à son sujet?

[*Enquêteur:* Comparer les candidats identifiés à la liste complète des candidats de la circonscription (voir fiche de renseignements):
—Si l'interviewé a identifié tous les candidats, passer à Q.42.
—Si l'interviewé *n'a pas identifié tous* les candidats, poser la question Q.41C.]

Q.41C. Et quels sont les partis ou tendances représentés *au premier tour* dans votre circonscription que vous n'avez pas pensé à me citer? (*Noter les partis ou tendances cités* dans la 2e colonne du tableau ci-dessous)

Q.42. Un certain nombre d'électeurs n'ont pas voté au premier tour. Vous-même, avez-vous voté au premier tour? [Oui (passer à Q.43); Non.]

Q.42bis. Pourquoi?

Q.42ter. Si vous aviez voté, pour quel candidat auriez-vous voté? Pour répondre il vous suffit de citer la lettre correspondant au nom du candidat. (*Tendre liste-réponse*) (Candidat A, B, C, D, E, F, G, H, I) [Passer à Q.44.]

Q.43. Pourriez-vous me dire pour qui vous avez voté au premier tour? Pour répondre il vous suffit de citer la lettre correspondant au nom du candidat. (*Tendre liste-réponse*) [Candidat A, B, C, D, E, F, G, H, I.]

Q.43bis. Est-ce que ce candidat a soutenu ou s'est opposé à l'action du Général de Gaulle?

Q.44. Dans votre circonscription y a-t-il eu un 2e tour [poser Q.45], ou bien le député a-t-il été élu dès le premier tour [passer à Q.54]?

Q.45. Vous-même, avez-vous voté au 2e tour? [Oui (passer à Q.46); Non.]

Q.45bis. Pourquoi?

Q.45ter. Si vous aviez voté, pour quel candidat auriez-vous voté au 2e tour? (*Tendre liste-réponse*) [Candidat A, B, C, D, E, F, G, H, I.] [Passer à Q.54.]

Q.46. Voulez-vous me rappeler si le candidat que vous avez préféré au premier tour s'est représenté au 2e tour? [Il s'est représenté au 2e tour (passer à Q.49); il ne s'est pas représenté au 2e tour (poser Q.47); n'a pas voté au 1er tour (passer à Q.52).]

Q.47. A-t-il appelé ses électeurs à voter pour un autre candidat ou bien s'est-il retiré purement et simplement? [Il a appelé ses électeurs à voter pour un autre candidat (poser Q.47bis); il s'est retiré purement et simplement (passer à Q.48).]

Q.47bis. Pour quel autre candidat a-t-il appelé ses électeurs à voter? (*Ne rien suggérer:* vérifier le nom du candidat cité sur votre fiche de renseignements et cocher à la lettre correspondante) [Candidats A, B, C, D, E, F, G, H, I.]

Q.47ter. En avez-vous été satisfait ou mécontent, ou bien cela vous a-t-il laissé in-différent?

Q.48. Vous-même, pour quel candidat avez-vous voté au 2e tour? (*Tendre liste-réponse*) [Candidat A, B, C, D, E, F, G, H, I.] [Passer à Q.53.]

Q.49. Est-ce qu'un autre candidat s'est désisté en sa faveur; c'est-à-dire qu'un autre candidat s'est retiré en appelant ses électeurs à voter pour le candidat que vous avez préféré au premier tour? [Oui, un autre candidat s'est désisté en sa faveur; non, un autre candidat ne s'est pas désisté en sa faveur (passer à Q.51).]

Q.50. Quel était l'autre candidat qui s'est désisté en sa faveur? (*Ne rien suggérer;* vérifier le nom du candidat cité sur votre fiche de renseignements et cocher à la lettre correspondante) [Candidat A, B, C, D, E, F, G, H, I.]

Q.50bis. En avez-vous été satisfait ou mécontent, ou bien cela vous a-t-il laissé in-différent?

Q.51. Estimiez-vous alors les chances d'être élu de votre candidat, c'est-à-dire celui pour qui vous avez voté au 1er tour, excellentes, bonnes, plutôt bonnes, médiocres, ou nulles?

Q.51bis. Avez-vous voté pour lui? [Oui (passer à Q.53); Non.]

Q.51ter. Pourquoi n'avez-vous pas voté pour lui?

Q.52. Pour quel candidat avez-vous voté au 2e tour? (*Tendre liste-réponse*) [Candidat A, B, C, D, E, F, G, H, I.]

Q.53. En définitive, pour laquelle de ces raisons avez-vous surtout voté pour ce candidat au 2e tour? Est-ce parce qu'il vous plaisait, parce que vous ne vou-liez pas que ses adversaires soient élus, ou pour une autre raison? (*Une seule réponse*)

A Tout le Monde

Q.54. Voici une liste des candidats qui se sont présentés au premier tour dans votre circonscription. (*Tendre la liste*) Parmi ces candidats, quels sont ceux qui vous semblent lutter le plus pour assurer:

(*Lire les thèmes*)

(a) la stabilité gouvernementale?

(b) la défense de l'école laïque?

(c) la construction de l'Europe?

(d) une répartition équitable des revenus entre les différentes catégories de Français?

(e) le développement de l'enseignement?

(f) l'indépendance de la France par rapport aux Etats-Unis?

(g) le développement économique du pays?

Q.55. Parlons maintenant du candidat qui vient d'être élu dans votre circonscription. Pouvez-vous me dire quel est son nom? [Oui (indiquer son nom); Non.]

Q.55bis. Pouvez-vous me dire quel est son parti? [Oui (indiquer son parti); Non.]

[*Enquêteur:* Vérifier sur votre fiche de renseignements si les réponses données à Q.55 et Q.55bis sont exactes. Si elles ne sont pas exactes ou si l'interviewé n'a pu se rappeler soit le nom, soit le parti, dites: "Il est toujours difficile de se rappeler ces choses;

je vois ici que son nom est _____,

et qu'il est du parti _____.]

Q.56. Est-ce qu'il a soutenu ou s'est opposé à l'action du Général de Gaulle?

Q.57. Savez-vous s'il siégeait dans la précédente assemblée comme député de cette circonscription? [Il siégeait comme député de cette circonscription, (poser Q.58); il siégeait mais comme député d'une autre circonscription, il ne siégeait pas (passer à Q.60).]

Q.58. Vous rappelez-vous quelque chose que M_____ (nommer le député) a fait pour les électeurs de votre circonscription? [Oui (poser Q.58bis); n'a rien fait, ne se souviens pas (passer à Q.59).]

Q.58bis. Qu'a-t-il fait?

Q.59. A-t-il fait quelque chose pour vous personnellement ou pour votre famille? [Oui (poser Q.59bis); n'a rien fait (passer à Q.60).]

Q.59bis. Qu'a-t-il fait?

Maintenant, parlons un peu du gouvernement.

Q.60. Certains pensent que parmi les gens qui nous gouvernent, il y en a qui ne sont pas très honnêtes. Et vous, pensez-vous qu'il y en a un bon nombre, quelques-uns seulement, ou à peu près aucun d'entre eux qui ne sont pas très honnêtes?

Q.61. Croyez-vous que les gens qui nous gouvernent donnent une chance égale à tous, qu'il s'agisse de gros bonnets ou de gens ordinaires, ou croyez-vous qu'ils accordent plus d'attention aux gros bonnets?

Q.62. Croyez-vous que les gens qui nous gouvernent gaspillent l'argent de nos impôts ... [une grande partie, une certaine partie, ou pas beaucoup]?

Q.63. Jusqu'à quel point, selon vous, peut-on faire confiance aux gens qui nous gouvernent pour agir comme il faut ... [à peu près toujours, la plupart du temps, quelquefois, ou pratiquement jamais]?

Etes-vous d'accord ou pas d'accord avec les opinions suivantes?

Q.64. Je ne crois pas que le gouvernement se préoccupe beaucoup de ce que les gens comme moi pensent.

Q.65. La politique et le gouvernement semblent parfois si compliqués que les gens comme moi ne peuvent vraiment pas comprendre ce qui se passe.

Q.66. En général, les députés que nous élisons perdent vite contact avec le peuple. [D'accord, pas d'accord, ça dépend des députés.]

Q.67. Lorsque vous discutez avec quelqu'un, vous arrive-t-il de vous laisser convaincre, ou bien tenez-vous ferme sur votre position?

Q.68. A votre avis, les jeunes doivent-ils être laissés à l'école aussi longtemps que possible, même si cela implique des sacrifices financiers pour leur famille? [Oui, doivent être laissés à l'école; non, ne doivent pas.]

Q.69. D'une façon générale, diriez-vous qu'on peut faire confiance aux gens, ou au contraire qu'on ne prend jamais assez de précautions avec certaines personnes?

Q.70. En gros, quelle réputation est préférable selon vous: la réputation de savoir travailler avec les autres, ou celle de se tirer d'affaire tout seul?

Renseignements Signalétiques

Eh bien, M_____, je vous remercie, j'ai presque terminé, je vais vous demander maintenant quelques renseignements pour le classement des réponses.

Q.71. Actuellement, exercez-vous une profession?

Oui	1
Non, chômeur	2
Non, retraité	3
Non, ménagère	4
Non, étudiant	5 (passer à Q.75)
Non, autres raisons (préciser)	6

[*Enquêteur:*
—Si l'interviewé ne travaille pas mais a auparavant exercé une profession, passer à Q.72.
—Si l'interviewé *n'a jamais* exercé de profession, passer à Q.77.]

Q.72. Quelle est (quelle était) votre profession: Expliquez-moi précisément ce que vous faites. (Noter en détail, puis coder)

Agriculteur exploitant	1	(passer à Q.73)
Salarié agricole	2	

Industriel, gros commerçant   3 ⎫
Profession libérale   4 ⎬ (passer à Q.75)
Petit commerçant, artisan   5 ⎭
Cadre supérieur   6
Cadre moyen, employé   7
Ouvrier   8
Personnel de service   9
Divers   0

Q.72bis. Etes-vous fonctionnaire? [Oui (passer à Q.75); Non.]

Q.72ter. Est-ce que vous travaillez dans une petite, une moyenne, ou une grande entreprise? [Petite entreprise, c'est-à-dire moins de 20 salariés; moyenne entreprise, c'est-à-dire entre 20 et 200 salariés; grande entreprise, c'est-à-dire plus de 200 salariés.] [Passer à Q.75.]

Q.73. (*Pour les Agriculteurs Seulement*)

Appartenez-vous à un syndicat ou une organisation agricole? [Oui; Non (passer à Q.77).]

Q.73bis. Lequel (ou laquelle)?

Q.74. Connaissez-vous la position de ce syndicat (cette organisation) sur le problème de l'unité de l'Europe? [Oui; Non (passer à Q.76).]

Q.74bis. Diriez-vous qu'il (elle) est très favorable, plutôt favorable, neutre, plutôt hostile, ou très hostile à l'unité de l'Europe? [Passer à Q.76.]

Q.75. Etes-vous syndiqué? [Oui; Non (passer à Q.77).]

Q.75A. A quel syndicat appartenez-vous?

Q.75B. Avez-vous idée de la position de votre syndicat sur le problème de l'unité de l'Europe? [Oui; Non (passer à Q.76).]

Q.75C. Diriez-vous qu'il est très favorable, plutôt favorable, neutre, plutôt hostile, ou très hostile à l'unité de l'Europe?

Q.76. Vous est-il arrivé de participer à une grève ou à une manifestation?

A TOUT LE MONDE

Q.77. Etes-vous le chef de famille? [Oui (passer à Q.84); Non.]

Q.78. Actuellement le chef de famille exerce-t-il une profession? [Oui; non, chômeur; non, retraité; non, ménagère; non, étudiant (passer à Q.82); non, autres raisons (préciser).]

[*Enquêteur:*
—Si le chef de famille ne travaille pas mais a auparavant exercé une profession, passer à Q.79.
—Si le chef de famille *n'a jamais* exercé de profession, passer à Q.84.]

Q.79. Quelle est (quelle était) la profession du chef de famille? Expliquez-moi précisément ce qu'il fait. (Noter en détail, puis coder) [Agriculteur exploitant, salarié agricole (passer à Q.80); industriel, gros commerçant, profession libérale, petit commerçant, artisan (passer à Q.82); cadre supérieur, cadre moyen, employé, ouvrier, personnel de service, divers.]

Q.79bis. Est-il fonctionnaire? [Oui (passer à Q.82); Non.]

Q.79ter. Est-ce-que le chef de famille travaille dans une petite, une moyenne ou une grande entreprise? Petite entreprise, c'est-à-dire moins de 20 salariés; moyenne entreprise, c'est-à-dire entre 20 et 200 salariés; grande entreprise, c'est-à-dire plus de 200 salariés. [Passer à Q.82.]

(*Pour les Agriculteurs Seulement*)

Q.80. Le chef de famille appartient-il à un syndicat ou une organisation agricole? [Oui; Non (passer à Q.84).]

Q.80bis. Lequel (ou laquelle)?

Q.81. Connaissez-vous la position de ce syndicat (cette organisation) sur le problème de l'unité de l'Europe? [Qui; Non (passer à Q.83).]

Q.81bis. Diriez-vous qu'il (elle) est très favorable, plutôt favorable, neutre, plutôt hostile, ou très hostile à l'unité de l'Europe? [Passer à Q.83.]

Q.82. Le chef de famille est-il syndiqué? [Oui; Non (passer à Q.84).]

Q.82A. A quel syndicat appartient-il?

Q.82B. Avez-vous idée de la position de son syndicat sur le problème de l'unité de l'Europe? [Oui; Non (passer à Q.83).]

Q.82C. Diriez-vous qu'il est très favorable, plutôt favorable, neutre, plutôt hostile, ou très hostile à l'unité de l'Europe?

Q.83. Est-il arrivé au chef de famille de participer à une grève ou à une manifestation?

A TOUT LE MONDE

Q.84. A quelle classe sociale diriez-vous que vous appartenez? (Noter la réponse telle quelle vous est donnée par l'interviewé)

[*Enquêteur: Si la réponse ne fait pas allusion à la classe moyenne ni à la classe ouvrière,* poser Q.85; sinon passer directement à Q.86.]

Q.85. Si vous aviez à choisir entre la classe ouvrière et la classe moyenne, que choisiriez-vous?

Q.85bis. A quelle sorte de gens pensiez-vous quand vous avez dit ... (citer la réponse faite à Q.85)?

Q.85ter. A quelle sorte de gens avez-vous pensé quand on a parlé de ... (l'autre classe non citée à Q.85)? [Passer à Q.87.]

Q.86. A quelle sorte de gens pensiez-vous quand vous avez dit ... (citer la réponse faite à Q.84)?

Q.86bis. A quelle sorte de gens pensez-vous quand on parle de ... (l'autre classe non citée à Q.84 soit la classe ouvrière, soit la classe moyenne)?

Q.87. Quel est le dernier établissement d'enseignement que vous avez fréquenté comme élève ou étudiant(e)? Est-ce un établissement d'enseignement primaire; primaire supérieur; secondaire; technique, commercial; ou supérieur (université, grande école)? [Si n'est jamais allé à l'école, passer à Q.88.]

Q.87bis. Pendant les années d'enseignement primaire, étiez-vous dans une école libre ou une école laïque? [Ecole libre; ecole laïque; les deux; cours privé non libre; autres écoles: (préciser).]

Q.88. *Situation de famille:* êtes-vous marié, veuf, célibataire, ou divorcé?

Q.89. *Sexe.*

Q.90. *Age:* quel âge avez-vous?

Q.91. Depuis combien de temps habitez-vous cette commune? [En années.]

Q.92. Où avez-vous vécu pendant la plus grande partie de votre enfance: dans une grande ville, dans sa banlieue, dans une ville de moyenne importance, dans une petite ville, un village, dans une ferme isolée?

Q.92bis. Dans quel département?

Q.93. Pendant votre jeunesse, quand vous aviez entre 10 et 18 ans, quelle était la profession de vos parents ou de ceux qui vous ont élevé?

(*Noter en détail puis coder*)

Agriculteur exploitant

Salarié agricole

Industriel, gros commerçant

Profession libérale

Petit commerçant, artisan

Cadre supérieur

Cadre moyen, employé

Ouvrier

Personnel de service

Divers.

Q.94. De vos parents (ou de ceux qui vous ont élevé) pendant votre jeunesse, diriez-vous plutôt qu'ils étaient *très à l'aise, simplement à l'aise,* qu'ils *ne vivaient pas mal à condition de faire très attention,* ou que la vie était *difficile* pour eux?

Q.95. Vous rappelez-vous si votre père à cette époque s'intéressait à la politique? [Beaucoup; moyennement; peu; pas du tout.]

Q.96. De quel tendance ou parti était-il (votre père) à l'époque?

Q.97. Avez-vous entendu votre père parler de ses préférences politiques à cette époque? [Oui, souvent; oui, quelquefois; non, jamais.]

Q.98. Quelle est votre religion? [Catholique; Protestante; Juive; Autre; Aucune.] (Si aucune, passer à Q.99)

Q.98bis. (Poser selon la réponse à Q.98): Allez-vous à l'église (au temple ou à la synagogue) . . . au moins une fois par semaine, souvent dans l'année, quelquefois, rarement, ou jamais?

Q.99. Voici une liste de revenus mensuels (*tendre liste-réponse*). Nous désirons savoir dans quelle tranche de revenus vous situez votre foyer, en comptant toutes les rentrées d'argent dans le foyer telles que les salaires, allocations familiales, pensions, revenus, recettes, etc. Pour répondre, il vous suffit de citer la lettre correspondante:

A. Moins de 400 F.   (Moins de 40 000 anciens francs)

B. De 400 à 800 F.   (De 40 000 à 80 000 anciens francs)

C. De 801 à 1 100 F.   (De 80 001 à 110 000 anciens francs)

D. De 1 101 à 1 400 F.   (De 110 001 à 140 000 anciens francs)

E. De 1 401 à 1 700 F.   (De 140 001 à 170 000 anciens francs)

F. De 1 701 à 2 100 F.   (De 170 001 à 210 000 anciens francs)

G. De 2 101 à 2 600 F.   (De 210 001 à 260 000 anciens francs)

H. De 2 601 à 3 200 F.   (De 260 001 à 320 000 anciens francs)

I. De 3 201 à 4 200 F.   (De 320 001 à 420 000 anciens francs)

J. Plus de 4 200 F.   (Plus de 420 000 anciens francs)

Elite Survey Questionnaire, 1967

Q.1. Je voudrais d'abord vous poser quelques questions au sujet de l'activité que vous avez déployée dans votre circonscription pendant la campagne électorale de 1967, c'est-à-dire à partir du mois de Février. Avez-vous fait campagne tous les jours; presque tous les jours; la plupart du temps; seulement une partie du temps; quelques jours seulement? [Autre (préciser).]

Q.1A. Avez-vous essayé, vous ou vos amis politiques, d'entrer *personnellement* en rapport avec les électeurs, soit par téléphone, soit pas des visites? [*Oui:* uniquement par téléphone, le plus souvent par téléphone mais aussi par des visites, a peu près autant par téléphone et par des visites, le plus souvent par des visites mais aussi par téléphone, uniquement par des visites, autrement (préciser); *non.*]

Q.1B. Qu'avez-vous fait d'autre pour avoir des contacts avec vos électeurs? [A organisé des réunions publiques; a pris contact avec des ouvriers dans des usines; s'est rendu sur d'autres lieux de travail (préciser); a organisé des réunions pour certains groupes (préciser quels groupes); autres (préciser).]

Q.2. Dans votre campagne du premier tour, sur quels thèmes avez-vous le plus insisté?

Relance (Si l'interviewé a répondu "le programme de son parti," demander sur quels aspects du programme il a particulièrement insisté)

Q.3. Quelles catégories sociales ou quels groupes professionnels avez-vous surtout cherché à atteindre pendant votre campagne électorale du premier tour?

Relance (Si l'interviewé a répondu "tous les groupes," demander quels groupes plus précisément)

Q.4. A votre avis, auprès de quelles catégories d'électeurs avez-vous recueilli *le plus* de voix au premier tour?

Q.5. Et auprès de quelles catégories avez-vous recueilli *le moins* de voix au premier tour?

Q.6. Voici différents éléments qui ont pu vous aider à obtenir les suffrages de vos électeurs au premier tour. Pour chacun d'eux, diriez-vous qu'il a été décisif, très important, assez important, peu important, ou pas important du tout? (*Tendre liste-réponse*)

(a) Votre étiquette politique.

(b) L'activité des militants qui vous ont aidé dans votre circonscription pendant la campagne électorale.

(c) La réputation de votre suppléant.

(d) Votre réputation personnelle.

(e) Votre position sur les grands problèmes politiques.

(f) Votre position envers le Général de Gaulle.

Q.7. Y a-t-il des journaux—régionaux ou nationaux—qui vous ont soutenu? [Oui, ils m'ont soutenu moi personnellement; oui, ils ont soutenu le parti qui me présentait (poser Q.7A); non (passer à Q.8).]

Q.7A. Lesquels? (Noter les noms très précisément)

Q.8. D'un autre côté, est-ce qu'il y avait des journaux qui étaient contre vous? [Oui, contre moi personnellement; oui, contre le parti qui me présentait (poser Q.8A); non (passer à Q.9).]

Q.8A. Lesquels? (Noter les noms très précisément)

Q.9. Est-ce que vous estimez que la presse a fait à votre candidature, et à votre campagne, une place suffisante? [Oui, estime que la presse a fait une place suffisante; non, estime que la presse n'a pas fait une place suffisante.]

(A Poser aux Candidats Ve République)

Q.10. Vous étiez candidat Ve République. Ce terme rassemblait plusieurs nuances politiques. Pendant votre campagne, quelle étiquette avez-vous utilisée le plus souvent pour vous faire connaître des électeurs de votre circonscription?
(Ne rien suggérer)
Ve République seule
UNR seule
UNR et Ve République
Républicain Indépendant seul
Républicain Indépendant et Ve République
MRP seul
MRP et Ve République
Radical seul
Radical et Ve République
Gaulliste
Autre (préciser).

(A Poser aux Candidats Fédération de la Gauche Démocrate et Socialiste)

Q.10.1. Vous étiez candidat Fédération de la Gauche Démocrate et Socialiste. Ce terme rassemblait plusieurs nuances politiques. Pendant votre campagne, quelle étiquette avez-vous utilisée le plus souvent pour vous faire connaître des électeurs de votre circonscription?
(Ne rien suggérer)
Fédération seule
SFIO seule
SFIO et Fédération
Radical seul
Radical et Fédération
Convention des Institutions Républicaines (CIR) seule
Convention et Fédération
Autre (préciser).

(A Poser aux Candidats Centre Démocrate)

Q.10.2. Vous étiez candidat Centre Démocrate. Ce terme rassemblait plusieurs nuances politiques. Pendant votre campagne, quelle étiquette avez-vous utilisée le plus souvent pour vous faire connaître des électeurs de votre circonscription?
(Ne rien suggérer)
Centre Démocrate seul
MRP seul
MRP et Centre Démocrate

Indépendant seul
Indépendant et Centre Démocrate
Radical seul
Radical et Centre Démocrate
Rassemblement Démocratique seul
Rassemblement Démocratique et Centre Démocrate
Autre (préciser).

(*A Poser aux Candidats du Parti Communiste*)

Q.10.3. Pendant la campagne électorale, quelle étiquette avez-vous utilisée le plus souvent pour vous faire connaître des électeurs de votre circonscription? (Si la question n'est pas comprise, demander: vous êtes-vous présenté à eux le plus souvent sous l'étiquette PCF, ou avez-vous employé d'autres termes, comme, par exemple, "Candidat de la Gauche"?) [Parti Communiste Français PCF; autre (préciser).]

(*A Poser aux Candidats dans les Circonscriptions Où l'Election A Eté Faite au 1er Tour*)

Q.11. Nous savons que dans votre circonscription le problème des désistements ne s'est pas posé. Mais s'il s'était posé, et que—pour une raison quelconque—vous aviez pris la décision de vous désister, pour le candidat de quel parti l'auriez-vous fait?
(*Ne rien suggérer*)
    (Si la personne interrogée répond en donnant le nom d'un candidat, écrire ce nom)
Q.12. Et pour quel(s) parti(s) ne vous seriez-vous désisté en aucun cas?
(*Ne rien suggérer*)
    (Si la personne interrogée répond en donnant des noms de candidats, écrire ces noms)

PASSER À Q.24

(*A Poser aux Candidats Eliminés du 2e Tour*)

Q.13. Avez-vous apporté votre aide à un autre candidat dans votre circonscription entre les deux tours? [Oui (poser Q.13A); Non (poser Q.13B).]
Q.13A. Lequel?
    (*Ne rien suggérer*. Cocher dans la 1ere colonne du tableau ci-dessous puis passer à Q.13C)
Q.13B. (*Si Non à Q.13*)
    Si, pour une raison quelconque, vous aviez apporté votre aide à un candidat d'un autre parti, pour qui l'auriez-vous fait?
    (*Ne rien suggérer*). Cocher dans la 2e colonne du tableau ci-dessous puis passer à Q.14)
Q.13C. (*Si Oui à Q.13*)
    Qu'avez-vous fait pour l'aider? Comment avez-vous fait pour faire partager vos sentiments à vos électeurs du premier tour?
Q.14. Et pour quels partis ne vous seriez-vous désisté en aucun cas?

(*Ne rien suggérer*)

(Si la personne interrogée répond en donnant des noms de candidats, écrire ces noms)

Q.15. Nous voudrions avoir votre opinion sur les transferts de voix entre les deux tours parmi vos électeurs. A votre avis, comment se sont partagés, en gros, au 2ᵉ tour, les électeurs qui avaient voté pour vous au 1ᵉʳ tour? En quelle proportion ont-ils voté pour tel ou tel parti ou se sont-ils abstenus?

Q.15A. Il semble que les transferts de voix ont été assez différents selon les circonscriptions. Pour quelles raisons pensez-vous que les choses se sont passées comme vous venez de le dire, dans votre circonscription au 2ᵉ tour?

Relance (Si l'interviewé a répondu, "Ils ont suivi les consignes qui leur étaient données par les candidats ou les partis," demander pourquoi ils ont suivi ces consignes)

Q.15B. Entre les deux tours, sur *quels thèmes* ou *problèmes nouveaux* a-t-on particulièrement insisté: en quoi la campagne électorale pour le 2ᵉ tour a-t-elle été différente de celle du 1ᵉʳ tour dans votre circonscription?

PASSER À Q.24

(*A Poser aux Candidats Qui Se Sont Désistés ou Retirés au 2ᵉ Tour*)

Q.16. Parlons maintenant du 2ᵉ tour. *Après avoir pris connaissance des résultats du 1ᵉʳ tour,* aviez-vous tout d'abord envisagé de vous maintenir au 2ᵉ tour? [Oui (poser Q.16A); Non (passer à Q.17).]

Q.16A. Finalement, pourquoi avez-vous décidé de ne pas vous maintenir?

[*Enquêteur:* Si l'interviewé a répondu à Q.16A que c'était une décision prise par son parti à l'échelon national, poser Q.16B et Q.16C. Sinon, passer à Q.17.]

Q.16B. Pensez-vous que cette décision de votre parti était raisonnable sur le plan de votre circonscription?

Q.16C. Pourquoi?

Q.17. Est-ce que vous vous êtes désisté pour un autre candidat?

Q.17A. Pour quel candidat vous êtes-vous désisté?

Q.17B. Qu'avez-vous fait pour l'aider? Comment avez-vous fait pour faire partager vos sentiments à vos électeurs du 1ᵉʳ tour?

PUIS PASSER À Q.17G

Q.17C. Avez-vous tout de même apporté votre aide à un autre candidat dans votre circonscription entre les deux tours? [Oui (poser Q.17D); Non (passer à Q.17F).]

Q.17D. Lequel?

Q.17E. Qu'avez-vous fait pour l'aider? Comment avez-vous fait pour faire partager vos sentiments à vos électeurs du 1ᵉʳ tour?

PUIS PASSER À Q.17G

Q.17F. Si, pour une raison quelconque, vous aviez pris la décision de vous désister, pour quel parti l'auriez-vous fait?

(*Ne rien suggérer*)

(Si la personne interrogée répond en donnant le nom d'un candidat, écrire ce nom)

Q.17G. Pour quel(s) parti(s) ne vous seriez-vous désisté en aucun cas? (*Ne rien suggérer*)

   (Si la personne interrogée répond en donnant des noms de candidats, inscrire ces noms)

Q.18. Nous voudrions avoir votre opinion sur les transferts de voix entre les deux tours parmi vos électeurs. A votre avis, comment se sont partagés, en gros, au 2e tour, les électeurs qui avaient voté pour vous au 1er tour? En quelle proportion ont-ils voté pour tel ou tel parti ou se sont-ils abstenus?

Q.18A. Il semble que les transferts de voix ont été assez différents selon les circonscriptions. Pour quelles raisons pensez-vous que les choses se sont passées comme vous venez de le dire, dans votre circonscription au 2e tour? *Relance* (Si l'interviewé a répondu, "Ils ont suivi les consignes qui leur étaient données par les candidats ou les partis," demander pourquoi ils ont suivi ces consignes)

Q.18B. Entre les deux tours, sur *quels thèmes* ou *problèmes nouveaux* a-t-on particulièrement insisté: en quoi la campagne électorale pour le 2e tour a-t-elle été différente de celle du 1er tour dans votre circonscription?

PASSER À Q.24

(*A Poser aux Candidats Qui Se Sont Présentés au 2e Tour*

Q.19. Parlons maintenant du 2e tour. *Après avoir pris connaissance des résultats du 1er tour,* aviez-vous tout d'abord envisagé de vous retirer ou de vous désister au second tour? [Oui (poser Q.19A); Non (passer à Q.20).]

Q.19A. Finalement pourquoi avez-vous décidé de vous maintenir?

   [*Enquêteur:* Si l'interviewé a répondu à Q.19A que c'était une décision prise par son parti à l'échelon national, poser Q.19B et Q.19C. Sinon, passer à Q.20.]

Q.19B. Pensez-vous que cette décision de votre parti était raisonnable sur le plan de votre circonscription?

Q.19C. Pourquoi?

Q.20. Si, pour une raison quelconque, vous aviez pris la décision de vous désister, pour quel parti l'auriez-vous fait? (*Ne rien suggérer*)

   (Si la personne interrogée répond en donnant le nom d'un candidat, écrire ce nom)

Q.20A. Pour quel(s) parti(s) ne vous seriez-vous désisté en aucun cas? (*Ne rien suggérer*)

   (Si la personne interrogée répond en donnant des noms de candidats, inscrire ces noms)

Q.21. Replaçons-nous dans la situation qui existait au lendemain du 1er tour. A ce moment-là, quelles étaient, à votre avis, vos chances de l'emporter au second tour: étaient-elles excellentes, bonnes, plutôt bonnes, médiocres, ou nulles?

Q.22. Y a-t-il eu des désistements en votre faveur? [Oui (poser Q.22A); Non (passer à Q.22E).]

Q.22A. Lesquels?
(Si la personne interrogée répond en donnant des noms de candidats, écrire ces noms)

Q.22B. Certains de ces désistements étaient-ils inattendus? [Oui (poser Q.22C); Non (passer à Q.22D).]

Q.22C. Lesquels?
(Si la personne interrogée répond en donnant des noms de candidats, écrire ces noms)

Q.22D. De quelle façon ce (ou ces) parti(s) vous ont-ils aidé entre les deux tours? Comment ont-ils fait pour faire partager leurs sentiments à leurs électeurs du 1er tour?

Q.22E. Y a-t-il eu d'autre part des retraits ou des éliminations qui ont plutôt joué en votre faveur? [Oui (poser Q.22F); Non (passer à Q.22I).]

Q.22F. Lesquels?
(Si la personne interrogée répond en donnant des noms de candidats, écrire ces noms)

Q.22G. Certains étaient-ils inattendus? [Oui (poser Q.22H); Non (passer à Q.22I).]

Q.22H. Lesquels?
(Si la personne interrogée répond en donnant des noms de candidats, écrire ces noms)

Q.22I. Y a-t-il eu des désistements *en faveur de vos adversaires?* [Oui (Poser Q.22J); Non (passer à Q.22M.]

Q.22J. Lesquels?
(Si la personne interrogée répond en donnant des noms de candidats, écrire ces noms)

Q.22K. Certains de ces désistements étaient-ils inattendus? [Oui (poser Q.22L); Non (passer à Q.22M).]

Q.22L. Lesquels?
(Si la personne interrogée répond en donnant des noms de candidats, écrire ces noms)

Q.22M. Y a-t-il eu enfin des retraits ou des éliminations qui ont plutôt joué en faveur de votre (ou vos) adversaire(s)? [Oui (poser Q.22N); Non (passer à Q.23).]

Q.22N. Lesquels?
(Si la personne interrogée répond en donnant des noms de candidats, écrire ces noms)

Q.22O. Certains étaient-ils inattendus? [Oui (poser Q.22P); Non (passer à Q.23).]

Q.22P. Lesquels?
(Si la personne interrogée répond en donnant des noms de candidats, écrire ces noms)

Q.23. Nous voudrions avoir votre opinion sur les transferts de voix entre les deux tours dans votre circonscription.

D'abord, à votre avis, d'où provenaient les voix que vous avez gagnées du

1er tour? En quelle proportion les électeurs de tel ou tel parti ont-ils voté pour vous au 2e tour?

Q.23A. Il semble que les transferts de voix ont été assez différents selon les circonscriptions. Pour quelles raisons pensez-vous que ces électeurs ont voté pour vous au 2e tour plutôt que pour votre—ou vos—adversaire(s)?

Relance (Si l'interviewé a répondu, "Ils ont suivi les consignes qui leur étaient données par les candidats ou les partis," demander pourquoi ils ont suivi ces consignes)

Q.23B. D'autre part, d'où provenaient, à votre avis, les voix que votre— ou vos—adversaire(s) ont gagnées du 1er au 2e tour? En quelle proportion les électeurs de tel ou tel parti ont-ils voté pour votre adversaire au 2e tour?

Q.23C. Pour quelles raisons pensez-vous que ces électeurs ont voté pour votre adversaire au 2e tour plutôt que pour vous?

Relance (Si l'interviewé a répondu, "Ils ont suivi les consignes qui leur étaient données par les candidats ou les partis," demander pourquoi ils ont suivi les consignes)

Q.23D. Entre les deux tours, sur quels *thèmes* ou *problèmes nouveaux* avez-vous particulièrement insisté: en quoi votre campagne électorale pour le 2e tour a-t-elle été différente de celle du 1er tour?

A TOUT LE MONDE

Q.24. Parmi ces différentes choses, quel a été, selon vous au fond, le véritable enjeu des dernières élections législatives?

Que mettriez-vous en premier?

Et en 2e?

Et en 3e?

(*Tendre liste-réponse*)

(a) La ville contre la campagne.

(b) Le Communisme contre l'anti-Communisme.

(c) De Gaulle contre les partis.

(d) Les catholiques contre les laïques.

(e) L'intiative privée contre l'intervention de l'Etat dans le domaine économique.

(f) La Ve République contre la IVe République.

(g) La gauche contre la droite.

(h) Les partisans d'une Europe unie contre les adversaires de l'Europe.

(i) Le gouvernement contre l'opposition.

(j) La classe ouvrière contre les capitalistes.

(k) Le pouvoir personnel contre la démocratie.

Q.25. Sur cette échelle qui va de l'extrême gauche à l'extrême droite (*tendre l'echelle*) où placeriez-vous les principaux partis?

(*Ne pas suggérer de partis*)

(Essayer d'obtenir des chiffres précis)

Q.26. Et vous-même, si vous aviez à vous placer sur cette échelle, où vous placeriez-vous?

Q.27. A votre avis, en quoi consistent les différences les plus importantes entre la gauche et la droite?

Relance

Q.28. Pour chacun de ces problèmes politiques, pouvez-vous me dire si vous le considérez comme *très* important, *assez* important, *peu* important, ou *pas du tout important?*

(*Tendre liste-réponse*)

(a) La stabilité gouvernementale.

(b) La défense de l'école laïque.

(c) La construction de l'Europe.

(d) Une répartition équitable des revenus entre les différentes catégories de Français.

(e) Le développement de l'enseignement.

(f) L'indépendance de la France par rapport aux Etats-Unis.

(g) Le développement économique du pays.

Q.29. Pour chacun de ces mêmes problèmes politiques, quelles seraient, à votre avis, les réponses que donneraient dans l'ensemble les électeurs de votre circonscription? [Très important, assez important, peu important, pas du tout important.]

[Si la personne interrogée répond, "Les mêmes que moi," coder ici (passer à Q.30).]

(a) La stabilité gouvernementale.

(b) La défense de l'école laïque.

(c) La construction de l'Europe.

(d) Une répartition équitable des revenus entre les différentes catégories de Français.

(e) Le développement de l'enseignement.

(f) L'indépendance de la France par rapport aux Etats-Unis.

(g) Le développement économique de pays.

Q.30. Pourriez-vous me dire, avec précision, quelle est votre position sur les questions suivantes:

A. La question de la force de frappe nationale?

Relance

B. La question de la priorité à donner à l'enseignement dans les dépenses de l'Etat?

Relance

C. La question de l'aide aux pays sous-développés?

Relance

D. La question de l'indépendance de la politique étrangère française à l'égard de celle des Etats-Unis?

Relance

Q.31. A quel point seriez-vous d'accord ou non avec les mesures suivantes? Seriez-vous entièrement d'accord, plutôt d'accord, plutôt pas d'accord ou pas du tout d'accord?

(*Lire les thèmes; tendre liste-reponse*)

(a) Que l'armée française soit fondue dans une armée européenne.

(b) Que le gouvernement français accepte une politique étrangère commune pour les six pays du Marché Commun.

(c) Que la France maintienne son adhésion au Marché Commun.

(d) Que les Français puissent s'installer et travailler n'importe où en Europe et qu'inversement les ouvriers et entreprises étrangères puissent venir s'installer en France.

(e) Que le gouvernement français utilise une partie des impôts pour aider les régions les plus pauvres de l'Europe.

Q.32. J'aimerais avoir votre avis sur la question des subventions de l'Etat à l'école libre. Etes-vous entièrement d'accord, plutôt d'accord, plutôt pas d'accord, ou pas du tout d'accord avec les propositions suivantes?
(*Tendre liste-réponse*)

(a) L'Etat devrait donner des subventions aux écoles libres pour leur permettre de faire face à toutes leurs dépenses.

(b) L'Etat devrait donner des subventions aux écoles libres uniquement pour payer les salaires des enseignants.

(c) L'Etat devrait donner des subventions seulement aux parents des élèves de sorte que ceux-ci puissent les reverser selon leur choix aux écoles libres ou aux écoles publiques.

(d) Aucune subvention de l'Etat ne devrait, en aucun cas, être attribuée à l'école libre.

Q.33. Quelle est votre opinion sur le rôle des représentants syndicaux des travailleurs dans l'entreprise? Pensez-vous que leur rôle devrait être développé, réduit ou qu'il devrait rester ce qu'il est actuellement?

Q.34. Et sur la question de la répartition des revenus entre les différentes catégories sociales? Pensez-vous que la répartition actuelle entre les différentes catégories sociales est à peu près équitable? [Oui (passer à Q.35); Non.]

Q.34A. Quelles sont les catégories sociales que vous jugez défavorisées?

Q.35. Les circonscriptions sont très diverses en ce qui concerne leurs caractéristiques économiques, professionnelles, religieuses, et sociales. Je voudrais vous poser quelques questions au sujet de votre circonscription.

A. Quelle est l'activité économique principale dans votre circonscription?

B. Quelle est l'attitude des gens à l'égard de la religion?
Relance

C. Y a-t-il une forte activité syndicale?

D. Est-ce qu'on s'intéresse beaucoup à la politique dans le milieu des affaires ou de l'industrie?
Relance

E. Y a-t-il un syndicalisme agricole actif?

F. Y a-t-il des minorités importantes, par exemple des rapatriés ou des Algériens musulmans, ou d'autres ouvriers étrangers, etc.?

G. Votre circonscription présente-t-elle d'autres caractères originaux?

Q.36. Dans votre circonscription, les rivalités politiques, relèvent-elles plutôt des oppositions entre partis, ou plutôt des rivalités entre fortes personnalités? [Plutôt oppositions entre partis; plutôt lutte de personnalitiés (passer à Q.37A); les deux.]

Q.37. Entre quels partis les rivalités sont-elles les plus accentuées?

[*Enquêteur:* Si réponse "Les deux" à Q.37, poser également Q.37A; sinon passer à Q.38.]

Q.37A. Quelles rivalités personnelles sont les plus accentuées?

Q.38. Quels sont les conflits ou les problèmes économiques et sociaux les plus sérieux dans votre circonscription?

Q.38A. Ces problèmes sont-ils plus sérieux, moins sérieux, ou à peu près semblables à ce qu'ils étaient il y a environ 10 ans?

Q.39. Dans votre circonscription, les rivalités politiques dont nous venons de parler sont-elles plus ou moins directement liées à ces problèmes économiques et sociaux ou bien au contraire sont-elles indépendantes? [Elles sont liées aux problèmes sociaux (poser Q.39A); elles sont indépendantes des problèmes sociaux (passer à Q.40).]

Q.39A. De quelle manière sont elles liées à ces problèmes économiques et sociaux?

Q.40. Si vous deviez répartir, en gros, les électeurs de votre circonscription entre la gauche, la droite, et le centre, quel pourcentage attribueriez-vous à chacune de ces tendances?

[*Enquêteur*: (Si le total ne fait pas 100%, signalez-le à l'interviewé).]

Q.41. Pourriez-vous évaluer, en pourcentage, la proportion des électeurs de votre circonscription qui sont pour, ou contre, ou indifférents aux options politiques suivantes:
(*Tendre liste-réponse*)
(a) Les subventions aux écoles libres.
(b) La force de frappe nationale.
(c) Une répartition plus équitable des revenus entre les ouvriers et les autres couches sociales.
(d) Un plus gros effort pour l'enseignement.
(e) L'aide aux pays sous développés.
(f) Une politique étrangère indépendante de celle des Etats-Unis.
(g) La défense des droits des syndicats.
(h) L'intégration de l'armée française dans une armée européenne.

Q.42. Pensez-vous que vous avez en fait une bonne connaissance de l'état de l'opinion dans votre circonscription sur le genre des questions que nous venons d'évoquer ci-dessus?

Q.43. Pour connaitre l'état de l'opinion dans votre circonscription, quelle importance attachez-vous aux sources d'information suivantes: beaucoup d'importance, assez d'importance, peu d'importance, ou aucune importance?
(*Tendre liste-réponse*)
(a) Les journaux.
(b) Votre courrier.
(c) Les militants locaux de votre parti.
(d) Les organisations professionnelles.
(e) Des contacts personnels.
(f) L'administration préfectorale.

Q.43A. Avez-vous quelquefois utilisé des sondages? [Quelquefois; une seule fois; jamais.]

Q.43B. Y a-t-il d'autres sources d'information que vous considérez comme importantes dans votre circonscription? [Oui (poser Q.43C); Non (passer à Q.44).]

Q.43C. Lesquelles?

Q.44. Maintenant, nous voudrions connaître vos sentiments à l'égard des partis politiques. Voulez-vous mettre une note de 0 à 100 en fonction de la sympathie que vous éprouvez pour eux:

(*Tendre liste-réponse*)

100 Signifie: beaucoup de sympathie

  50 signifie: indifférent

   0 signifie: antipathie complète

Quelle note donneriez-vous aux ... (citer les noms un à un)

(a) Parti Communiste?

(b) Parti Socialiste (SFIO)?

(c) UNR?

(d) MRP?

(e) PSU?

(f) Parti Radical?

(g) Républicains Indépendants?

(h) Indépendants du Centre Démocrate?

(i) Alliance Républicaine de Tixier-Vignancour?

(*A Poser aux Candidats Qui Se Sont Présentés sous une Etiquette Autre Que:* Parti Communiste, Fédération de la Gauche Démocrate et Socialiste, Centre Démocrate, Ve République, PSU)

Q.44A. Pour quelles raisons avez-vous choisi l'étiquette sous laquelle vous vous êtes présenté?

A Tout le Monde

Q.45. Vous est-il arrivé avant 1967 de poser votre candidature à des élections législatives et de ne pas être élu? [Oui (poser Q.45A); Non (passer à Q.46).]

Q.45A. Quand, et dans quelle circonscription?

Q.46. Quelles sont les circonstances qui vous ont amené à être candidat la 1ere fois que vous vous êtes présenté aux élections législatives?

(*A Poser aux Députés Sortants et Anciens Députés*)

Q.47. A l'Assemblée, vous êtes-vous jamais trouvé dans la situation suivante: votre groupe avait décidé de voter d'une certaine façon, et vous vouliez, vous, voter d'une autre façon?

Q.47A. Comment auriez-vous ou comment avez-vous résolu ce problème?
Relance

Q.48. Vous êtes-vous jamais trouvé dans la situation suivante: vous vouliez voter d'une certaine façon, et vous croyiez que la majorité de vos électeurs désirait vous voir voter d'une autre façon?

Q.48A. Comment auriez-vous ou comment avez-vous résolu ce problème?
Relance

Q.49. Vous êtes-vous jamais trouvé dans la situation suivante: vous vouliez voter d'une certaine façon, et les instances locales de votre parti désiraient vous voir voter d'une autre façon?

Q.49A. Comment auriez-vous ou comment avez-vous résolu ce problème?
Relance

Q.50. En prenant la décision de voter d'une certaine façon, quelle priorité donniez-vous généralement aux considérations suivantes: priorité absolue, forte priorité, priorité moyenne, faible priorité, aucune priorité?
(*Tendre liste-réponse*)
(a) Désir de soutenir le gouvernement.
(b) La position de votre groupe parlementaire.
(c) La position de votre parti dans votre circonscription.
(d) Votre estimation de la position de la majorité de vos électeurs.

Q.51. Je voudrais vous demander quelle est votre experience comme député. Vous spécialisez-vous dans un domaine politique particulier? [Oui (poser Q.51A); Non (passer à Q.52).]

Q.51A. Lequel?

Q.51B. Est-ce un choix personnel, ou cela a-t-il été décidé par votre parti? [Choix personnel; décidé par votre parti (passer à Q.52); les deux.]

Q.51C. Pourquoi avez-vous choisi ce (ou ces) domaine(s)? (Plusieurs réponses possibles) [Parce qué cela vous intéresse; parce que cela relève de votre compétence professionnalle; parce que c'est important pour votre circonscription; autre raison (préciser).]

Q.52. Comme député, quand le Parlement est en session, quel pourcentage de votre temps consacrez-vous:
(a) aux problèmes nationaux?
(b) aux problèmes de votre circonscription?

Q.52A. Et le reste du temps, quel pourcentage de votre temps consacrez-vous:
(a) aux problèmes nationaux?
(b) aux problèmes de votre circonscription?

Q.53. A l'Assemblée, appartenez-vous à des groupes d'études, associations ou amicales parlementaires, groupe régional ou autre intergroupe parlementaire? (Plusieurs réponses possibles) [Si non, passer à Q.55.]

Q.53A. Lesquels plus précisément?

Q.54. Est-ce que vous consultez ces groupes avant de décider comment voter sur les mesures qui les intéressent? [Oui, toujours; oui, la plupart du temps; oui, mais rarement; non.]

(*A Poser aux Anciens Députés, aux Députés Sortants, et Egalement aux Nouveaux Députés*)

Q.55. Etes-vous Président d'un Conseil Général, Maire, ou Conseiller Municipal? [Oui, Président d'un Conseil Général; oui, Maire de _____; oui, Conseiller Municipal pour Paris; oui, Conseiller Municipal pour Province: non, rien de tout cela (passer à Q.56).]

Q.55A. Des différentes fonctions que vous occupez, quelle est celle qui vous permet le mieux de rendre service aux électeurs de votre circonscription?

[Votre rôle de Député; votre rôle de Maire; votre rôle de Président de Conseil Général; votre rôle de Conseiller Municipal pour Paris; votre rôle de Conseiller Municipal pour Province.]

Q.56. Dans votre circonscription, quelles sortes de gens vous écrivent le plus fréquemment?

Q.56A. Et quelles sortes de gens viennent vous voir le plus fréquemment?

Q.57. Dans votre circonscription, avec quelles sortes de gens avez-vous le plus de contacts réguliers? Quelles sont leurs fonctions?

Q.57A. Est-ce que vous consultez ces gens avant de décider comment voter sur les mesures législatives auxquelles ils s'intéressent?

Q.57B. Dans votre circonscription, avec quelles sortes d'organisations avez-vous le plus de contacts réguliers?

Q.57C. Est-ce que vous consultez ces organisations avant de décider comment voter sur les mesures législatives auxquelles elles s'intéressent?

Q.58. Lisez-vous *régulièrement* des journaux français ou étrangers quotidiens ou hebdomadaires, je dis bien régulièrement? [Oui, des journaux français; oui, des journaux étrangers; oui, les deux; non (passer à Q.59).]

Q.58A. Lesquels?

[Si la personne est un Ancien Député ou un Député Sortant, passer à Q.68.]

(*A Poser Seulement aux Nouveaux Députés*)

Q.59. Je voudrais vous demander comment vous concevez votre tâche de député. Avez-vous l'intention de vous spécialiser dans un domaine politique particulier? [Oui (poser Q.59A); Non (passer à Q.61).]

Q.59A. Lequel?

Q.60. Est-ce un choix personnel ou cela a-t-il été décidé par votre parti? [Choix personnel; décidé par votre parti (passer à Q.61); les deux.]

Q.60A. Pourquoi avez-vous choisi ce (ou ces) domaine(s)? (Plusieurs réponses possibles) [Parce que cela vous intéresse; parce que cela relève de votre compétence professionnelle; parce que c'est important pour votre circonscription; autre (préciser).]

Q.61. Quel pourcentage de votre temps pensez-vous que vous devrez consacrer, quand le Parlement est en session:
　(a) aux problèmes nationaux?
　(b) aux problèmes de votre circonscription?

Q.61. Et le reste du temps, quel pourcentage pensez-vous consacrer:
　(a) aux problèmes nationaux?
　(b) aux problèmes de votre circonscription?

Q.62. Appartenez-vous à des groupes d'études, associations ou amicales parlementaires, groupe régional, ou autre intergroupe parlementaire? (Plusieurs réponses possibles) [Si non, passer à Q.64.]

Q.62A. Lesquels plus précisément?

Q.63. Seriez-vous disposé à consulter ces groupes avant de décider comment vous voteriez sur les mesures qui les intéressent? [Oui, toujours; oui, la plupart du temps; oui, mais rarement; non.]

(*A Poser aux Nouveaux Députés et Egalement aux "Autres" Candidats*)

Q.64. Supposez que vous vous trouviez comme député dans la situation suivante: vous désireriez voter d'une certaine façon, mais votre groupe parlementaire déciderait de voter autrement; quelle solution adopteriez-vous?
Relance

Q.65. Supposez que vous vous trouviez comme député dans la situation suivante: vous désireriez voter d'une certaine façon, mais vous estimeriez que la majorité de vos électeurs désire vous voir voter autrement; quelle solution adopteriez-vous?
Relance

Q.66. Supposez que vous vous trouviez comme député dans la situation suivante: vous désireriez voter d'une certaine façon, mais les instances locales de votre parti désireraient vous voir voter autrement; quelle solution adopteriez-vous?
Relance

Q.67. Lorsqu'un député prend la décision, à l'Assemblée, de voter d'une certaine façon sur telle ou telle question, quelle priorité doit-il donner, à votre avis, aux considérations suivantes: priorité absolue, forte priorité, priorité moyenne, faible priorité, aucune priorité?
(*Tendre liste-réponse*)
(a) Désir de soutenir le gouvernement.
(b) La position de son groupe parlementaire.
(c) La position de son parti dans sa circonscription.
(d) Son estimation de la position de la majorité de ses électeurs.

A Tout le Monde

Pour terminer, je voudrais maintenant vous poser quelques questions personnelles qui nous aideront dans le classement statistique des réponses.

Q.68. Où avez-vous vécu pendant la plus grande partie de votre enfance: dans une grande ville, en banlieue, dans une ville de moyenne importance, dans une petite ville, un village, dans une ferme isolée? (Noter la réponse précise, puis coder)

Q.68A. Dans quel département? (Ou pays, si en dehors de la France)

Q.69. Quand vous étiez jeune, votre père s'intéressait-il à la politique? [Beaucoup; moyennement; peu; pas du tout.]

Q.70. De quelle tendance ou parti votre père était-il à l'époque?

Q.71. Quel était le niveau d'instruction de votre père? [Pas d'études; primaire; primaire supérieur; technique ou commercial; secondaire; supérieur.]

Q.72. Quelle était la profession de votre père?
(*Noter en clair, puis coder*)
Agriculteur exploitant
Salarié agricole
Industriel, gros commerçant
Profession libérale
Petit commerçant, artisan
Cadre supérieur
Cadre moyen, employé

Ouvrier

Personnel de service

Divers.

La politique (préciser).

Q.72bis. Etait-il fonctionnaire?

Q.73. Quand vous étiez à l'école primaire, étiez-vous dans une école libre ou une école laïque? [Ecole libre; école laïque; les deux; cours privé non libre; autres écoles (préciser).]

Q.74. Quel est le dernier établissement d'enseignement que vous avez fréquenté comme élève ou étudiant? Est-ce un établissement . . . ? [Pas d'études, primaire, primaire supérieur, secondaire, technique ou commercial (passer à Q.75); supérieur (poser Q.74A).]

Q.74A. Dans quelle localité avez-vous fait vos études supérieurs?

Q.74B. Dans quelle faculté ou grande école?

Q.74C. Vous êtes-vous notamment spécialisé dans une branche et si oui laquelle?

Q.75. Quelle était votre profession lorsque vous avez commencé à vous engager activement dans la politique?

(*Noter en clair, puis coder*)

Agriculteur exploitant

Salarié agricole

Industriel, gros commerçant

Profession libérale

Petit commerçant, artisan

Cadre supérieur

Cadre moyen, employé

Ouvrier

Personnel de service

Divers.

Q.75. Exercez-vous toujours cette profession? [Oui; oui, mais à temps partiel (passer à Q.77); non.]

A.76. Que faites-vous actuellement?

(*Noter en clair, puis coder*)

Agriculteur exploitant

Salarié agricole

Industriel, gros commerçant

Profession libérale

Petit commerçant, artisan

Cadre supérieur

Cadre moyen, employé

Ouvrier

Personnel de service

Divers

Politique.

Q.77. Avez-vous des liens personnels avec un journal ou un hebdomadaire diffusé régulièrement dans votre circonscription? [Oui; Non (passer à Q.88).]

Q.77A. Lequel (ou lesquels)?

Q.77B. Quels sont ces liens? Etes-vous propriétaire; directeur; éditeur; rédacteur; journaliste; autre (préciser)?

Q.78. Quels sont les postes administratifs ou les postes du secteur semi-public
(HLM, Caisse de Sécurité Sociale), les plus importants que vous avez occupés pendant ces cinq dernières années?

Q.79. A quel parti politique appartenez-vous?
[Centre Démocrate, Ve République, Fédération de la Gauche Démocrate
et Socialiste (poser Q.79A); Parti Socialiste (SFIO), PSU, Parti Communiste, Parti Radical, Républicains Indépendants de Giscard d'Estaing, MRP,
UNR, CNI, Alliance Républicaine de Tixier-Vignancour, *Autre* (préciser)
(passer à Q.79B).]

Q.79A. Et à l'intérieur de . . . à quel parti plus précisément?

Q.79B. Avez-vous toujours appartenu à ce parti politique? [Oui (poser Q.79C);
Non (passer à Q.80).]

Q.79C. Quel âge aviez-vous quand vous avez commencé à vous sentir proche de
ce parti? [Passer à Q.81.]

Q.80. A quel(s) parti(s) apparteniez-vous auparavant?

Q.80A. La première fois que vous vous êtes senti proche d'un parti, quel âge
aviez-vous?

Q.81. Qu'est-ce qui vous a fait adhérer au parti auquel vous appartenez actuellement?
(Si l'interviewé a répondu, "Le programme de mon parti," faire une relance. "En particulier, avec quels aspects du programme aviez-vous le plus
de sympathie?")

Sexe de l'interviewé.

Pour terminer avez-vous des observations à faire sur l'un ou plusieurs des sujets
que nous venons d'aborder?

Mass Survey Questionnaire, 1968

Introduction
Bonjour Madame, Monsieur.
Vous êtes bien M_____ né(e) en _____
(nom et   (l'année de naissance indiquée
prénom)   sur la feuille de route)

J'appartiens à la SOFRES et je fais un sondage pour connaître l'opinion des
Français sur quelques grandes questions d'actualité. L'année dernière, vous avez
eu l'amabilité de répondre à mes questions. J'aimerais à nouveau vous interroger.
L'opinion de *tous* les français nous intéresse, même de ceux qui n'ont pas d'opinion ou qui n'ont pas le temps de s'informer!

[*Enquêteur:* Si la personne est réticente, signaler que le questionnaire
est beaucoup plus court que l'année dernière.]

Q.1. Pour la France, selon vous, quel est le problème le plus important à l'heure
actuelle?

Q.2. Diriez-vous que, dans l'ensemble, vous êtes très satisfait, assez satisfait, peu
satisfait, ou pas du tout satisfait:

(*Tendre liste-réponse*)

(a) de vos conditions de logement?

(b) du revenu de votre foyer?

(c) du travail que vous faites (ou, si vous ne travaillez pas, du travail que fait le chef de famille)?

(d) des possibilités qu'ont les enfants de nos jours de recevoir toute l'instruction dont ils ont besoin?

Q.3. Pour chacun des problèmes suivants, pouvez-vous me dire si vous le considérez comme très important, assez important, peu important, ou pas important du tout?

(*Lire les thèmes; tendre liste-réponse*)

(a) La stabilité gouvernementale est-elle très importante, assez importante, peu importante, ou pas importante du tout?

(b) La défense de l'école laïque?

(c) La construction de l'Europe?

(d) La reconnaissance de la section syndicale d'entreprise?

(e) La réforme de l'Université?

(f) Le développement des mesures sociales?

(g) La lutte contre le chômage?

Q.4. Voici un certain nombre de jugements sur ces problèmes. Voudriez-vous nous donner votre opinion, en disant si vous vous estimez d'accord ou non, et si, comme avant, vous n'avez pas d'opinion, cela nous intéresse aussi.

(*Lire les phrases et tendre liste-réponse*)

(a) L'Etat doit aider les écoles libres: êtes-vous entièrement d'accord, plutôt d'accord, plutôt pas d'accord, ou pas du tout d'accord?

(b) Il vaut mieux pour la France réduire ses dépenses militaires plutôt que de garder son rang de grande puissance.

(c) Dans la répartition du revenu national, les ouvriers sont vraiment défavorisés.

(d) L'Etat devrait réformer l'Université.

(e) Les droits des syndicats devraient être mieux défendus.

(f) L'unification économique du Marché Commun devrait être accélérée.

(g) L'Etat devrait accroître son budget pour les mesures sociales.

Q.5. Etes-vous satisfait ou mécontent du Général de Gaulle comme Président de la République? (*Tendre liste-réponse*) [Très satisfait; plutôt satisfait; plutôt mécontent; très mécontent.]

Q.6. A votre avis, le Général de Gaulle a-t-il eu raison d'évoquer le Québec libre l'année dernière lorsqu'il est allé au Canada? [Oui; Non.]

Maintenant, parlons de la période qui a précédé les élections législatives. Parlons des événements de mai-juin.

Q.7. Pour vous tenir au courant pendant ces jours-là, avez-vous lu les journaux: Souvent, de temps en temps, rarement, ou jamais? Avez-vous:

(*Tendre liste-réponse*)

(a) lu les journaux?

(b) écouté les nouvelles à la radio?

(c) regardé les actualités à la television?

(d) parlé avec des camarades de travail?

(e) parlé avec des voisins?

(f) lu les tracts des syndicats ou d'autres organisations?

(g) observé les événements directement?

Q.8. Il y a des opinions diverses au sujet des ouvriers et des étudiants qui ont déclenché les grèves et les manifestations. Quelle est l'opinion la plus proche de la vôtre: ceux qui ont déclenché les grèves et les manifestations ont eu raison; ont eu tort; ont eu raison au début mais après sont allés trop loin?

Q.9. Avez-vous cru, par moment, pendant ces jours-là, qu'il y avait un fort risque de guerre civile; quelques risques de guerre civile; peu de risque de guerre civile; ou pas de risque du tout de guerre civile?

Q.10. Y a-t-il eu des entreprises en grève ici à . . . (citer le nom de la commune)? [Oui; Non.]

Q.10bis. Y a-t-il eu des manifestations ici à . . . (citer le nom de la commune ou, pour les villes de plus de 100,000 habitants, dire: "dans votre quartier")? [Oui; Non.]

Q.10ter. Vous-même, avez-vous été amené à participer à de telles manifestations? [Oui; Non.]

(Noter les commentaires faits par l'interviewé)

Q.11. Pendant cette période, est-ce que la vie de . . . (citer le nom de la commune ou, pour les villes de plus de 100,000 habitants, dire: "dans votre quartier") a été très perturbée; assez perturbée; peu perturbée; ou pas du tout perturbée?

(Noter tous les commentaires faits par l'interviewé)

Q.12. Pendant ces jours de crise, quelles personnalités dans votre localité ont pris publiquement position à l'égard des événements? Par exemple: *Le député* de votre circonscription, a-t-il pris position . . . ?

(*Noter la réponse ci-dessous, puis lire les thèmes un à un*)

(a) Le député de vote circonscription?

(b) Le maire de votre commune?

(c) Le clergé?

(d) Les dirigeants syndicaux?

(e) Les enseignants?

Q.12bis. Y a-t-il d'autres personnes de votre localité qui ont pris publiquement position? [Oui; Non (passer à Q.14).]

Q.13. Lesquelles?

(Noter la réponse telle qu'elle vous est donnée par l'interviewé. Faire préciser la fonction; noter la fonction et le nom. Noter tout groupe cité: Conseil Municipal . . . etc.)

Si la *réponse* donné est *précise*—par exemple, l'interviewé vous cite des noms de personnes ou de groupes—poser *Q.13bis*. Si la *réponse* donnée est vague— par exemple, "tout, beaucoup de monde,"—*passer à Q.14.*]

Q.13bis. Qui d'autre encore?

A Tout le Monde

Q.14. Finalement, quelle est votre opinion quant aux effets de cette crise sociale sur votre situation personnelle? Pensez-vous qu'elle va avoir de bons effets; de mauvais effets; ou pas d'effets du tout?

Q.15. Il y a des personnes et des groupes qui influencent le gouvernement ou l'opinion publique. Nous aimerions savoir quels sont vos sentiments à leur égard.

Voulez-vous mettre une note de 0 à 100 aux personnes ou groupes que je vais vous citer en fonction de la sympathie que vous éprouvez pour eux:
(*Tendre la liste avec l'échelle de sympathie*)
100 signifie que vous avez beaucoup de sympathie,
  0 signifie que vous ne les aimez pas du tout,
  50 signifie, soit que vous n'êtes ni pour ni contre eux, soit que vous ne connaissez pas grand chose sur eux.
Quelle note donneriez-vous:
(*Citer les noms un à un*)
(a) aux syndicats?
(b) à M. Mitterrand?
(c) au clergé?
(d) aux pieds noirs?
(e) au Parti Communiste?
(f) au Général de Gaulle?
(g) aux Chinois?
(h) à la Fédération de la Gauche Démocrate et Socialiste?
(i) à la police?
(j) à l'UD Ve République?
(k) à M. Giscard d'Estaing?
(l) aux étudiants?
(m) à M. Bidault?
(n) à Progrès et Démocratie Moderne de Duhamel?
(o) à l'armée?
(p) à M. Mendès-France?
(q) à M. Pompidou?
(r) aux grévistes de mai-juin 1968?

Q.16. Est-ce que vous vous intéressez à la politique beaucoup; assez; un peu; pas du tout?

Q.17. Avez-vous jamais *écrit* ou *parlé* à votre député pour lui donner votre opinion sur un sujet auquel vous vous intéressez? [Oui, a écrit et parlé; oui, a écrit; oui, a parlé; non.]

Q.18. Depuis que vous êtes électeur, diriez-vous que vous avez voté *à toutes* les élections législatives et présidentielles, *à la plupart, à quelques-unes* ou *à aucune?* [Si aucune, passer à Q.20.]

Q.19. Aux élections législatives, avez-vous voté pour le même parti ou la même tendance toujours; la plupart du temps; ou bien avez-vous voté pour des partis différents?

Q.20. Compte tenu de tout ce que les partis représentent, à votre avis, existe-t-il *beaucoup* de différences entre les partis, *quelques* différences, ou *peu* de différences?

Q.21. Quel est le parti dont vous vous sentez habituellement le plus proche?
(*Une seule réponse en la notant telle qu'elle vous est donnée par l'interviewé, même si la réponse ne fait pas allusion à un parti ou est nettement hostile aux partis*) [Aucun, NSP, Refus (passer à Q.23).]

Q.22. Diriez-vous que vous vous sentez *très* proche de ce parti, *assez* proche, ou *pas très* proche?

Q.23. Y a-t-il des partis pour lesquels vous ne voteriez en aucun cas?
[Oui; Non; NSP (passer à Q.24).]

Q.23bis. Lesquels?
(Noter la réponse telle qu'elle vous est donnée par l'interviewé, même si la réponse ne fait pas allusion à un ou des parti(s).]

Q.24. Avez-vous voté au *premier* tour lors des élections législatives de mars 1967 pour élire les députés? *Attention:* Je dis bien aux élections de mars 1967.
[Oui; Non (passer à Q.26).]

Q.25. Pour quel parti, ou pour quel candidat, avez-vous voté? *Attention:* Je dis bien au *premier* tour des élections de 1967.

Q.26. Parmi les partis politiques suivants [Parti Communiste; PSU; Fédération de la Gauche; Progrès et Démocratie Moderne; UD Ve République; Républicains Indépendants de Giscard d'Estaing], quel est celui qui, selon vous, lutte le plus pour:
(*Lire les phrases et tendre liste-réponse; tourner la liste au hasard; une seule réponse par ligne*)
(a) la stabilité gouvernementale?
(b) la défense de l'école laïque?
(c) la construction de l'Europe?
(d) la reconnaissance de la section syndicale d'entreprise?
(e) la réforme de l'Université?
(f) le développement des mesures sociales?
(g) réduire le chômage?

Parlons maintenant des élections de cette année, celles de juin 1968.

Q.27. Pendant la campagne électorale, est-ce que des candidats ou des représentants des candidats ont pris contact, personnellement, avec vous, soit en venant vous voir, soit en vous téléphonant? [Oui; Non (passer à Q.28).]

Q.27bis. Les candidats ou les représentants de quels candidats?
(*Ne rien suggérer.* Cocher d'après votre fiche de renseignements sur les candidats de la circonscription)
[Candidats: A, B, C, D, E, F, G, H, I, J, *autres* (préciser).]

A Tout le Monde

Q.28. Parmi ces différentes choses, quel a été, selon vous, le véritable enjeu de ces élections. Que mettriez-vous en 1er?
(*Tendre liste-réponse, tourner la liste-réponse au hasard*)

Q.28bis. Et en 2e?
(a) Le Communisme contre l'anti-Communisme?
(b) De Gaulle contre les partis?
(c) La Ve République contre la IVe République?
(d) L'ordre contre l'anarchie?
(e) Le gouvernement contre l'opposition?
(f) La classe ouvrière contre les capitalistes?
(g) Le pouvoir personnel contre la démocratie?
(h) La gauche contre la droite?

Q.29. Je vais vous citer les principaux partis qui ont présenté des candidats à ces dernières élections législatives. Sur cette échelle qui va de l'extrême gauche à l'extrême droite (*tendre la liste avec l'échelle*), où placeriez-vous chacun de ces partis?

Où placeriez-vous ... (compléter en citant le nom du parti):
(a) Progrès et Démocratie Moderne de Duhamel?
(b) PSU?
(c) Républicains Indépendants de Giscard d'Estaing?
(d) Parti Communiste?
(e) UD Ve République?
(f) Fédération de la Gauche?
(Si l'interviewé ne cite pas un chiffre, demander, "Ce qui correspond à quel chiffre?" et noter le chiffre cité)

Q.30. Et vous-même, si vous aviez à vous placer sur cette échelle, où vous placeriez-vous?
(*Tendre à nouveau la liste avec l'échelle*)

Q.31. Pouvez-vous me citer les noms des candidats qui se sont présentés ici, dans votre circonscription, *au premier tour,* le 23 juin 1968?
(*Ne rien suggérer*)

[*Enquêteur:*
—Noter dans la 1ere colonne, les noms ou à défaut toutes les autres précisions servant à identifier les candidats.
—Pour chacun des candidats identifiés, poser Q.31A et Q.31B et noter les réponses dans le tableau ci-dessous.
—Si l'interviewé n'a identifié aucun candidat, passer directement à Q.31C.]

Q.31A. (Pour chaque candidat identifié): De quel parti ou tendance était-il?

Q.31B. (Pour chaque candidat identifié): Avez-vous lu ou entendu quelque chose à son sujet?

[*Enquêteur:* Comparer les candidats identifiés à la liste complète des candidats de la circonscription (voir fiche de renseignements).
—Si l'interviewé a identifié tous les candidats, passer à Q.32.
—Si l'interviewé *n'a pas identifié tous* les candidats, poser la question Q.31C.]

Q.31C. Et quels sont les partis ou tendances représentés *au premier tour* dans votre circonscription que vous n'avez pas pensé à me citer? (Noter les partis ou tendances cités dans la 2e colonne du tableau ci-dessous)

Q.32. Un certain nombre d'électeurs n'ont pas voté au premier tour. Vous-même, avez-vous voté au premier tour? [Oui (passer à Q.33); Non.]

Q.32bis. Si vous aviez voté, pour quel candidate auriez-vous voté? Pour répondre, il vous suffit de citer la lettre correspondant au nom du candidat.
(*Tendre liste-réponse*) [Candidat A, B, C, D, E, F, G, H, I, J.] [Passer à Q.34.]

Q.33. Pourriez-vous me dire pour qui vous avez voté au premier tour? Pour répondre, il vous suffit de citer la lettre correspondant au nom du candidat.
(*Tendre liste-réponse*) [Candidat A, B, C, D, E, F, G, H, I, J.]

Q.34. Est-ce que ce candidat a soutenu ou s'est opposé à l'action du Général de Gaulle?

Q.35. Quelle a été la position dc cc candidat à l'égard des grévistes de mai-juin: a-t-il pris position *plutôt en faveur* des grévistes, *plutôt contre* les grévistes, ou *n'a-t-il pas pris position?*

A TOUT LE MONDE

Q.36. Dans votre circonscription, y a-t-il eu un 2^c tour [poser Q.37], ou bien le député a-t-il été'elu dés le premier tour [passer à Q.52]?

Q.37. Vous-même, avez-vous voté au 2^c tour? [Oui (passer à Q.38); Non.]

Q.37bis. Si vous aviez voté, pour quel candidat auriez-vous voté au 2^c tour? (*Tendre liste-réponse*) [Candidat A, B, C, D, E, F, G, H, I, J.]

Q.38. Voulez-vous me rappeler si le candidat que vous avez préféré au 1er tour s'est représenté au 2^c tour? [Il s'est représenté au 2^c tour (passer à Q.43); il ne s'est pas représenté au 2^c tour (poser Q.39); n'a past voté au 1er tour (passer à Q.48).]

Q.39. A-t-il appelé ses électeurs à voter pour un autre candidat, ou bien s'est-il retiré purement et simplement? [Il a appelé ses électeurs à voter pour un autre candidat (poser Q.40); il s'est retiré purement et simplement (passer à Q.42).]

Q.40. Pour quel autre candidat a-t-il appelé ses électeurs à voter? (*Ne rien suggérer;* vérifier le nom du candidat cité sur votre fiche de renseignements et cocher la lettre correspondante) [Candidat A, B, C, D, E, F, G, H, I, J.]

Q.41. En avez-vous été satisfait ou mécontent, ou bien cela vous a-t-il laissé indifférent?

Q.42. Vous-même, pour quel candidat avez-vous voté au 2^c tour? (*Tendre liste-réponse*) [Candidat A, B, C, D, E, F, G, H, I, J.] [Passer à Q.49.]

Q.43. Est-ce qu'un ou plusieurs autres candidats se sont désistés en sa faveur; c'est-à-dire se sont retirés en appelant leurs électeurs à voter pour le candidat que vous avez préféré au premier tour? [Oui, un autre candidat s'est désisté en sa faveur; oui, plusieurs candidats se sont désistés en sa faveur; non, aucun candidat ne s'est désisté en sa faveur (passer à Q.46.]

Q.44. Quels étaient ce ou ces candidats qui se sont désistés en sa faveur?

[*Ne rien suggérer,* vérifier le nom des candidats cités sur votre fiche de renseignements et cocher dans la 1ere colonne du tableau ci-dessous. Pour chaque candidat cité par l'interviewé, *poser la Q.45* et cocher la réponse dans le tableau ci-dessous.]

Q.45. Avez-vous été satisfait ou mécontent de ce désistement ou bien cela vous a-t-il laissé indifférent?

Q.46. Estimiez-vous alors les chances d'être élu de votre candidat, c'est-à-dire celui pour qui vous avez voté au 1er tour: excellentes, bonnes, plutôt bonnes, médiocres, ou nulles?

Q.47. Avez-vous voté pour lui? [Oui (passer à Q.51); Non.]

Q.48. Pour quel candidat avez-vous voté au 2^c tour? (*Tendre liste-réponse*) [Candidat A, B, C, D, E, F, G, H, I, J.]

Q.49. Est-ce que ce candidat a soutenu ou s'est opposé à l'action du Général de
Gaulle?

Q.50. Quelle a été la position de ce candidat à l'égard des grévistes de mai-juin?
A-t-il pris position *plutôt en faveur* des grévistes, *plutôt contre* les grévistes, ou
n'a-t-il pas pris position?

Q.51. En définitive, pour laquelle de ces raisons principales avez-vous (ou auriez-
vous) voté pour ce candidat au 2e tour: est-ce parce qu'il vous plaisait, parce
que vous ne vouliez pas que ses adversaires soient élus, ou pour une autre
raison?
(*Une seule réponse*)

A Tout le Monde

Parlons maintenant de M _____ (*nommer le candidat élu dans la circonscription*), *le candidat qui vient d'être élu dans votre circonscription.*

Q.52. Savez-vous s'il siégeait dans la précédente assemblée comme député de cette
circonscription? [Il siégeait comme député de cette circonscription (poser
Q.53); il siégeait mais comme député d'une autre circonscription; il était
sénateur; il ne siégeait pas (passer à Q.55).]

Q.53. Vous rappelez-vous quelque chose que M _____ (nommer le
député) a fait pour les électeurs de votre circonscription? [Oui; n'a rien fait
(passer à Q.54).]

Q.53bis. Qu'a-t-il fait?

Q.54. A-t-il fait quelque chose pour vous personnellement ou pour votre famille?
[Oui; n'a rien fait (passer à Q.55).]

Q.54bis. Qu'a-t-il fait?

A Tout le Monde

Q.55. Croyez-vous qu'un député qui n'est pas originaire de votre département
pourrait représenter votre circonscription aussi bien qu'un député qui l'est?

Q.56. Votre député, est-il originaire de ce département?

Q.57. Voici une liste des candidats qui se sont présentés au premier tour dans
votre circonscription (*tendre la liste*). Parmi ces candidats, quels sont ceux
qui vous semblent lutter le plus pour:
(*Lire les thèmes; une seule réponse par ligne*)
(a) la stabilité gouvernementale?
(b) la défense de l'école laïque?
(c) la construction de l'Europe?
(d) la reconnaissance de la section syndicale d'entreprise?
(e) la réforme de l'Université?
(f) le développement des mesures sociales?
(g) réduire le chômage?

Q.58. Maintenant, parlons du gouvernement. Certains pensent que parmi les
gens qui nous gouvernent, il y en a qui ne sont pas très honnêtes. Et vous,
pensez-vous qu'il y en a plusieurs, quelques-uns seulement, ou à peu près
aucun d'entre eux qui ne soient pas très honnêtes.
Etes-vous d'accord ou pas d'accord avec les opinions suivantes?

Q.59. Je ne crois pas que le gouvernement se préoccupe beaucoup de ce que les gens comme moi pensent.

Q.60. La politique et le gouvernement semblent parfois si compliqués que les gens comme mois ne peuvent vraiment pas comprendre ce qui se passe.

Q.61. En général, les députés que nous élisons perdent vite contact avec le peuple. [D'accord, pas d'accord, ça depend des députés.]

Enfin, voici une opinion d'un autre genre.

Q.62. D'une façon générale, diriez-vous qu'on peut faire confiance aux gens, ou au contraire qu'on ne prend jamais assez de précautions avec certaines personnes?

Renseignements Signalétiques

Eh bien, M _____, je vous remercie, j'ai presque terminé; je vais vous demander maintenant quelques renseignements pour le classement des réponses.

Q.63. *Sexe.*

Q.64. *Age:* quel âge avez-vous?

Q.65. Depuis combien de temps habitez-vous cette commune? [En années.]

Q.66. Où avez-vous vécu pendant la plus grande partie de votre enfance: dans une grande ville, dans sa banlieue, dans une ville de moyenne importance, dans une petite ville, un village, dans une ferme isolée?

Q.66bis. Dans quel département?

Q.67. Actuellement, exercez-vous une profession?

Oui.

Non, chômeur.

Non, retraité.

Non, ménagère.

Non, étudiant.

Non, autres raisons (préciser).

Enquêteur: Si l'interviewé ne travaille pas, demander s'il a exercé une profession auparavant.

—Si oui, passer à Q.69.

—Si non, passer à Q.73.]

Q.68. Pendant la période des événements de mai-juin, avez-vous travaillé normalement ou non? [Oui, a travaillé normalement (passer à Q.69); Non.]

Q.68bis. Pendant cette période-là, les gens se sont trouvés dans des situations diverses. Vous-même, quelle a été votre situation à ce moment-là?

(*Tende liste-réponse*)

Pour répondre, il vous suffit de citer les lettres correspondant à votre situation.

A. J'ai fait grève moins d'une semaine.

B. J'ai fait grève une semaine ou plus.

C. Je ne pouvais pas aller travailler (manque de transport).

D. Je voulais travailler mais mon entreprise était occupée ou fermée par un piquet de grève.

E. Je n'avais pas ce qu'il fallait pour travailler (manque de matériaux ou d'outils, manque de personnel, manque de clients, etc.).

Autres raisons (préciser).

(*A Tous Ceux Qui Exercent ou Qui Ont Exercé une Profession*)

Q.69. Quelle est (quelle était) votre profession? Expliquez-moi précisément ce que vous faites (faisiez).
(*Noter en détail, puis coder; ne pas accepter des descriptions vagues, comme "arti-san"*)
Agriculteur (poser Q.70)
Salarié agricole (passer a Q.70bis)
Industriel, gros commerçant
Profession libérale
Petit commerçant, artisan
Cadre supérieur   } (passer a Q.71)
Cadre moyen, employé
Ouvrier
Personnel de service
Divers.

Q.70. Etes-vous (ou étiez-vous) propriétaire-exploitant, fermier, métayer ou sa-larié?
Q.70bis. Quelle est (ou était) la superficie de votre exploitation? (Ecrire le chiffre cité, puis coder) [Moins de 12 hectares, de 12 à 39 hectares, de 40 à 199 hectares, 200 hectares et plus.]
Q.71. Etes-vous (ou étiez-vous) patron, fonctionnaire, ou salarié?
(*Une seule mention*)
Q.72. Combien d'ouvriers ou d'employés avez-vous (eu) sous votre responsabi-lité dans votre travail? *Ne comptez pas les membres de votre famille.*
(Ecrire le chiffre exact, puis coder) [De 0 à 3, de 4 à 9, de 10 à 24, 25 et plus.]

A TOUT LE MONDE

Q.73. Etes-vous le chef de famille? [Oui (passer à Q.82); Non.]
Q.74. Actuellement, le chef de famille exerce-t-il une profession?
Oui.
Non, chômeur.
Non, retraité.
Non, ménagère.
Non, étudiant.
Non, autres raisons (préciser).

[*Enquêteur:* Si le chef de famille ne travaille pas, demander s'il a exercé une profession auparavant.
—Si Oui, passer à Q.77.
—Si Non, passer à Q.81.]

Q.75. Pendant la période des événements de mai-juin, le chef de famille, a-t-il travaillé normalement ou non? [Oui, a travaillé normalement (passer à Q.76); Non.]

Q.75. bis. Pendant cette période-là, les gens se sont trouvés dans des situations diverses. Quelle a été la situation du chef de famille à ce moment-là?
(*Tendre liste-réponse*)
Pour répondre, il vous suffit de citer les lettres correspondant à la situation du chef de famille.
A. Il a fait grève moins d'une semaine.
B. Il a fait grève une semaine ou plus.
C. Il ne pouvait pas aller travailler (manque de transport).
D. Il voulait travailler, mais son entreprise était occupée ou fermée par un piquet de grève.
E. Il n'avait pas ce qu'il fallait pour travailler (manque de matériaux ou d'outils, manque de personnel, manque de clients, etc.).

Autres raisons (préciser).

Q.76. Pendant ces jours-là, le chef de famille, a-t-il été amené à participer à une ou plusieurs manifestations? [Oui, à une; Oui, à plusieurs; Non.]

Q.77. Quelle est (ou quelle était) la profession du chef de famille? Expliquez-moi précisément ce qu'il fait (ou faisait).
(*Noter en détail, puis coder; ne pas accepter des descriptions vagues, comme "artisan"*)
Agriculteur (poser Q.78)
Salarié agricole (passer a Q.78bis)
Industriel, gros commerçant
Profession libérale
Petit commerçant, artisan
Cadre supérieur   } (passer a Q.79)
Cadre moyen, employé
Ouvrier
Personnel de service
Divers.

Q.78. Est-il (ou était-il) propriétaire-exploitant, fermier, métayer ou salarié?

Q.78bis. Quelle est (ou était) la superficie de son exploitation? (Ecrire le chiffre puis coder) [Moins de 12 hectares, de 12 à 39 hectares, de 40 à 199 hectares, 200 hectares et plus.] [Passer à Q.80.]

Q.79. Est-il (était-il) patron, fonctionnaire ou salarié?
(*Une seule mention*)

Q.80. Combien d'ouvriers ou d'employés a-t-il (avait-il) sous sa responsabilité dans son travail? *Ne comptez pas les membres de sa famille.*
(Ecrire le chiffre exact, puis coder) [De 0 à 3, de 4 à 9, de 10 à 24, 25 et plus.] [Passer à Q82.]

Q.81. Pendant la période des événements de mai-juin, il y a eu des manifestations; le chef de famille, a-t-il été amené à participer à une ou plusieurs de ces manifestations? [Oui, à une; Oui, à plusieurs; Non.]

A Tout le Monde

Q.82. De vos parents (ou de ceux qui vous ont élevé) pendant votre jeunesse, diriez-vous plutôt qu'ils étaient *très à l'aise, simplement à l'aise,* qu'ils *ne vivaient pas mal à condition de faire très attention,* ou que la vie était *difficile* pour eux?

Q.83. Vous rappelez-vous si votre père à cette époque s'intéressait à la politique beaucoup, moyennement, peu, pas du tout?

Q.84. De quel tendance ou parti était-il (votre père) à l'époque?
   (*Noter la réponse* telle qu'elle vous est donnée par l'interviewé)

   [*Enquêteur: Coder le caractère du domicile de l'interviewé*— appartement, maison particulière, ferme non isolée, ferme isolée. L'interviewé habite-t-il à la même adresse qu'en avril-mai 1967?]

Elite Survey Questionnaires, 1968

Interviews were conducted in 1968 both with candidates who had already been interviewed and with candidates who were being interviewed for the first time. For the convenience of the interviewers, and to minimize errors, a separate interview schedule was prepared for each category of candidates, although there was a substantial overlap in the content of the two sets of questionnaires. These interview schedules are reproduced below in combined form. An asterisk precedes questions which were asked only of candidates being interviewed for the first time. A dagger precedes questions which were asked only of candidates being reinterviewed. The numeration of questions is not, therefore, faithful to that of either of the original questionnaires.

†*Introduction*

Je me permets de vous poser, à nouveau, quelques questions que je (qu'on) vous ai (a) posées l'année dernière et au sujet desquelles les opinions ou les faits ont pu changer depuis. Je vais vous poser aussi quelques questions au sujet des événements de mai-juin. Parlons d'abord des événements de mai-juin.

*Introduction

Je me permets de vous poser quatre catégories de questions: au sujet des événements de mai-juin; de l'élection; de votre circonscription; et des grands problèmes politiques permanents. Parlons d'abord des événements de mai-juin.

Q.1. A votre avis, quelle a été la cause profonde de la révolte des étudiants?

Q.1A. D'autres pays ont aussi connu des soulèvements d'étudiants, mais ceux-ci ont été moins importants qu'en France. A votre avis, pourquoi la révolte des étudiants a-t-elle été plus importante en France qu'ailleurs?

Q.2. Comment peut-on expliquer le caractère spontané et la longue durée du mouvement de grèves parmi les ouvriers?

Q.3. A votre avis, de quelle manière le mouvement de grèves s'est-il trouvé relié à la révolte des étudiants?

Q.4. Combien de temps avez-vous passé dans votre circonscription entre le déclenchement de la révolte des étudiants et la dissolution de l'Assemblée Nationale?

Q.5. Pendant cette période-là (entre le déclenchement de la révolte des étudiants et la dissolution de l'Assemblée National), avez-vous essayé de faire connaître aux électeurs de votre circonscription votre position envers les grévistes? [Oui (poser Q.5A); Non (passer à Q.6).]

Q.5A. Qu'avez-vous fait pour communiquer avec eux?

Q.6. Pourriez-vous évaluer, en pourcentage, la proportion des électeurs de votre circonscription qui est favorable, défavorable, ou indifférente:
(a) aux grévistes de mai-juin?
(b) aux étudiants qui ont manifesté?

Q.6A. Parmi les électeurs de votre circonscription, à peu près quel pourcentage, à votre avis, a été amené à participer à des manifestations (quelles que soient leurs opinions politiques)?

Q.7. Y a-t-il eu des entreprises en grève dans votre circonscription?

Q.7A. Parmi les actifs de votre circonscription, à peu près quel pourcentage, à votre avis, a fait grève:
(a) moins d'une semaine?
(b) une semaine ou plus?

Q.8. Y a-t-il eu des entreprises occupées ou fermées par des piquets de grève dans votre circonscription? [Oui (poser Q.8A); Non (passer à Q.9).]

Q.8A. Parmi les gens qui étaient en grève dans votre circonscription, à peu près quel pourcentage, à votre avis, ont voulu travailler mais ne pouvaient pas le faire parce que leurs entreprises étaient occupées ou fermées par des piquets de grève?

Q.9. Dans votre campagne électorale quelle position avez-vous pris à l'égard des grévistes de mai-juin?

Q.10. Pendant votre campagne électorale, quelle étiquette avez-vous utilisée le plus souvent pour vous faire connaître des électeurs de votre circonscription?
(*Ne rien suggérer:* noter la réponse telle qu'elle vous est donnée par l'interviewé, puis coder)

Parti Communiste Français (PCF)
PSU
Parti Socialiste (SFIO)
Parti Socialiste (SFIO)–Fédération   } [passer à Q.11.]
Parti Radical
Parti Radical–Fédération
Convention (des Institutions Républicaines; CIR)
Convention–Fédération

Fédération (de la Gauche; FGDS) [Poser Q. 10A.]
Centre Progrès et Démocratie Moderne (PDM)
UDR
UDR–UDV^e   } [passer a Q.11.]
Gaulliste
UDR–Républicain Indépendant
Républicain Indépendant
Autre [Passer à Q.10C.]

Q.10A. Avez-vous indiqué assez souvent le parti politique auquel vous appartenez à l'intérieur de la Fédération? [Oui (passer à Q.10B); Non (passer à Q.11.]

Q.10B. Lequel?
Parti Socialiste (SFIO)
Parti Radical
Convention (des Institutions Républicaines; CIR)   } [passer à Q.11.]
Autre (préciser).

Q.10C. Pour quelles raisons avez-vous choisi cette étiquette?

Q.11. Quelles catégories sociales ou quels groupes professionnels avez-vous surtout cherché à atteindre pendant votre campagne électorale du premier tour?
Relance (Si l'interviewé a répondu "tous les groupes," demander quels groupes plus précisément)

Q.12. A votre avis, auprès de quelles catégories d'électeurs avez-vous recueilli le plus de voix au premier tour?

Q.13. Et auprès de quelles catégories avez-vous recueilli le moins de voix au premier tour?

Q.14. Voici différents éléments qui ont pu vous aider à obtenir les suffrages de vos électeurs au premier tour. Pour chacun d'eux, diriez-vous qu'il a été décisif, très important, assez important, peu important, ou pas important du tout?
(Tendre-liste-réponse; lire les thèmes)
(a) Votre étiquette politique;
(b) L'activité des militants qui vous ont aidé dans votre circonscription pendant la campagne électorale;
(c) Votre réputation personnelle;
(d) Votre position à l'égard des grévistes de mai-juin;
(e) Votre position sur les autres grands problèmes politiques;
(f) Votre position envers le Général de Gaulle.

Q.15. Y a-t-il des journaux—régionaux ou nationaux—qui vous ont soutenu? [Oui, ils m'ont soutenu moi personnellement; oui, ils ont soutenu le parti qui me présentait (poser Q.15A); non (passer à Q.16).]

Q.15A. Lesquels? (Noter les noms très précisément)

Q.16. D'un autre côté, est-ce qu'il y avait des journaux qui étaient contre vous? [Oui, contre moi personnellement; oui, contre le parti qui me présentait (poser Q.16A); non (passer à Q.17).]

Q.16A. Lesquels? (Noter les noms très précisément)

†Q.17. Estimez-vous que la presse a fait à votre candidature et à votre campagne, une place suffisante? [Oui, estime que la presse a fait une place suffisante; non, estime que la presse n'a pas fait une place suffisante.]

(A Poser aux Candidats dans les Circonscriptions où l'Election A Eté Faite au 1er Tour)

Q.18. Nous savons que dans votre circonscription le problème des désistements ne s'est pas posé. Mais s'il s'était posé, et que—pour une raison quelconque—vous ayez pris la décision de vous désister, pour le candidat de quel parti l'auriez-vous fait?

(*Ne rien suggérer:* si la personne interrogée répond en donnant le nom d'un candidat, écrire ce nom)

Q.19. Et pour quel(s) parti(s) ne vous seriez-vous désisté en aucun cas?

(*Ne rien suggérer:* si la personne interrogée répond en donnant des noms de candidats, écrire ces noms)

PASSER À Q.24

(*A Poser aux Candidats dans les Circonscriptions où l'Election A Eté Faite au 2ᵉ Tour*)

Q.20. Nous savons que pour vous le problème des désistements ne s'est pas posé. Mais s'il s'était posé, et que—pour une raison quelconque—vous ayez pris la décision de vous désister, pour le candidat de quel parti l'auriez-vous fait?

(*Ne rien suggérer:* si la personne interrogée répond en donnant le nom d'un candidat, écrire ce nom)

Q.20A. Et pour quel(s) parti(s) ne vous seriez-vous désisté en aucun cas?

(*Ne rien suggérer:* si la personne interrogée répond en donnant des noms de candidats, inscrire ces noms)

Q.21. Y a-t-il eu des désistements en votre faveur? [Oui (poser Q.21A); Non (passer à Q.21C).]

Q.21A. Lesquels?

(Si la personne interrogée répond en donnant des noms de candidats, écrire ces noms)

Q.21B. De quelle façon ce (ou ces) parti(s) vous a-t-il aidé entre les deux tours? Comment a-t-il fait pour faire partager ses sentiments à ses électeurs du 1ᵉʳ tour?

Q.21C. Y a-t-il eu d'autre part des retraits ou des éliminations qui ont plutôt joué en votre faveur? [Oui (poser Q.21D); Non (passer à Q.22).]

Q.21D. Lesquels?

(Si la personne interrogée répond en donnant des noms de candidats, écrire ces noms)

Q.22. Y a-t-il eu des désistements en faveur de vos adversaires? [Oui (poser Q.22A); Non (passer à Q.22B).]

Q.22A. Lesquels?

(Si la personne interrogée répond en donnant des noms de candidats, écrire ces noms)

Q.22B. Y a-t-il eu enfin des retraits ou des éliminations qui ont plutôt joué en faveur de votre (ou vos) adversaire(s)? [Oui (poser Q.22C); Non (passer à Q.23).]

Q.22C. Lesquels?

(Si la personne interrogée répond en donnant des noms de candidats, écrire ces noms)

Q.23. Nous voudrions avoir votre opinion sur les transferts de voix, entre les deux tours, dans votre circonscription. D'abord, à votre avis, d'où provenaient les voix que vous avez gagnées du 1ᵉʳ au 2ᵉ tour? En quelle proportion les électeurs de tel ou tel parti ont-ils voté pour vous au 2ᵉ tour?

Q.23A. Il semble que les transferts de voix ont été assez différents selon les circonscriptions. Pour quelles raisons pensez-vous que ces électeurs ont voté pour vous au 2ᵉ tour plutôt que pour votre (ou vos) adversaire(s)?

Relance (Si l'interviewé a répondu, "Ils ont suivi les consignes qui leur étaient données par les candidats ou les partis," demander pourquoi ils ont suivi ces consignes)

Q.23B. D'autre part, d'où provenaient, à votre avis, les voix que votre (ou vos) adversaire(s) a gagnées du 1er au 2e tour? En quelle proportion les électeurs de tel ou tel parti ont-ils voté pour votre adversaire au 2e tour?

Q.23C. Pour quelles raisons pensez-vous que ces électeurs ont voté pour votre adversaire au 2e tour plutôt que pour vous?

Relance (Si l'interviewé a répondu, "Ils ont suivi les consignes qui leur étaient données par les candidats ou les partis," demander pourquoi ils ont suivi les consignes)

A Tout le Monde

Q.24. Parmi ces différentes choses, quel a été, selon vous au fond, le véritable enjeu des dernières élections législatives?

Que mettriez-vous en premier?

Q.24A. Et en deuxième?

(*Tendre liste-réponse*)

(a) Le Communisme contre l'anti-Communisme

(b) De Gaulle contre les partis

(c) La Ve République contre la IVe République

(d) L'ordre contre l'anarchie

(e) Le gouvernement contre l'opposition

(f) La classe ouvrière contre les capitalistes

(g) Le pouvoir personnel contre la démocratie

(h) La gauche contre la droite.

Q.25. Sur cette échelle qui va de l'extrême gauche à l'extrême droite, où placeriez-vous chacun de ces partis? (*Tendre l'échelle*)

Où placeriez-vous . . . (compléter en citant le nom du parti)

(Si l'interviewé ne cite pas un chiffre, demander, "Ce qui correspond à quel chiffre"? et noter le chiffre cité)

(a) Progrès et Démocratie Moderne

(b) PSU

(c) Républicains Indépendants

(d) Fédération de la Gauche

(e) Parti Radical

(f) Parti Communiste

(g) UDR

(h) Parti Socialiste (SFIO).

Q.26. Et vous-même, si vous aviez à vous placer sur cette échelle, où vous placeriez-vous?

*Q.27. A votre avis, en quoi consistent les différences les plus importantes entre la gauche et la droite?

[*Relance*]

Q.28. Pour chacun de ces problèmes politiques, pouvez-vous me dire si vous le considérez comme *très* important, *assez* important, *peu* important, ou *pas* important *du tout?*

(*Tendre liste-réponse; lire les thèmes*)

(a) La stabilité gouvernementale.
(b) Le développement économique du pays.
(c) La défense de l'école laïque.
(d) La construction de l'Europe.
(e) Une répartition équitable des revenus entre les différentes catégories de Français.
(f) La reconnaissance de la section syndicale d'entreprise.
(g) La réforme de l'Université.
(h) L'indépendance de la France par rapport aux Etats-Unis.
(i) Le développement de l'enseignement.
(j) La lutte contre le chômage.
(k) Le développement des mesures sociales.

Q.29. Pour chacun de ces mêmes problèmes politiques, quelles seraient, à votre avis, les réponses que donneraient dans l'ensemble les électeurs de votre circonscription?

(Tendre liste-réponse; lire les thèmes)

(Si la personne interrogée répond, "Les mêmes que moi," coder ici [passer à Q.30])

(a) La stabilité gouvernementale.
*(b) Le développement économique du pays.
(c) La défense de l'école laïque.
(d) La construction de l'Europe.
*(e) Une répartition équitable des revenus entre les différentes categories de Français.
(f) La reconnaissance de la section syndicale d'entreprise.
(g) La réforme de l'Université.
*(h) L'indépendance de la France par rapport aux Etats-Unis.
*(i) Le développement de l'enseignement.
(j) La lutte contre le chômage.
(k) Le développement des mesures sociales.

Q.30. Pourriez-vous me dire, avec précision, quelle est votre position sur les questions suivantes:

A. La question de la force de frappe nationale?
Relance

B. La question de la priorité à donner à l'enseignement dans les dépenses de l'Etat?
Relance

C. La question de l'aide aux pays sous-développés?
Relance

D. La question de l'indépendance de la politique étrangère française à l'égard de celle des Etats-Unis?
Relance

E. La question de la réforme de l'Université?
Relance

F. La question de la priorité à donner aux mesures sociales dans le budget de l'Etat?
Relance

Q.31. A quel point seriez-vous d'accord ou non avec les mesures suivantes?

Seriez-vous entièrement d'accord, plutôt d'accord, plutôt pas d'accord ou pas du tout d'accord?

(*Lire les thèmes; tendre liste-réponse*)

(a) Que l'armée française soit fondue dans une armée européenne.

(b) Que le gouvernement français accepte une politique étrangère commune pour les six pays du Marché Commun.

(c) Que la France maintienne son adhésion au Marché Commun.

(d) Que les Français puissent s'installer et travailler n'importe où en Europe et qu'inversement les ouvriers et entreprises étrangères puissent venir s'installer en France.

(e) Que le gouvernement français utilise une partie des impôts pour aider les régions les plus pauvres de l'Europe.

Q.32. J'aimerais avoir votre avis sur la question des subventions de l'Etat à l'école libre. Etes-vous entièrement d'accord, plutôt d'accord, plutôt pas d'accord, ou pas du tout d'accord avec les propositions suivantes?

(*Tendre liste-réponse*)

(a) L'Etat devrait donner des subventions aux écoles libres pour leur permettre de faire face à toutes leurs dépenses.

(b) L'Etat devrait donner des subventions aux écoles libres uniquement pour payer les salaires des enseignants.

(c) L'Etat devrait donner des subventions seulement aux parents des élèves de sorte que ceux-ci puissent les reverser selon leur choix aux écoles libres ou aux écoles publiques.

(d) Aucune subvention de l'Etat ne devrait, en aucun cas, être attribuée à l'école libre.

Q.33. Quelle est votre opinion sur le rôle des représentants syndicaux des travailleurs dans l'entreprise? Pensez-vous que leur rôle devrait être développé, réduit, ou qu'il devrait rester ce qu'il est actuellement?

Q.34. Et sur la question de la répartition des revenus entre les différentes catégories sociales? Pensez-vous que la répartition actuelle entre les différentes catégories sociales est à peu près équitable? [Oui (passer à Q.35); Non.]

Q.34A. Quelles sont les catégories sociales que vous jugez défavorisées?

Q.35. Revenons pour un instant aux événements de mai-juin. Si des événements semblables éclataient encore une fois, qu'est-ce que le gouvernement devrait faire, à votre avis?

[*Enquêteur:* Si l'interviewé répond que ça n'arrivera pas, notez-le, et demandez: "Mais si cela arrivait, que pensez-vous que le gouvernement devrait faire?"]

Relance

Q.36. Certaines personnes tirent comme leçon des événements de mai-juin que l'émeute est le seul moyen efficace d'assurer que les autorités publiques fassent droit à des revendications. Etes-vous d'accord ou non avec cette manière de penser, et pourquoi?

Relance

*Q.37. Les circonscriptions sont très diverses en ce qui concerne leurs caractéristiques économiques, professionnelles, religieuses et sociales. Je voudrais vous poser quelques questions au sujet de votre circonscription.

A. Quelle est l'activité économique principale dans votre circonscription?

B. Quelle est l'attitude des gens à l'égard de la religion?

Relance

C. Y a-t-il une forte activité syndicale?

D. Est-ce qu'on s'intéresse beaucoup à la politique dans le milieu des affaires ou de l'industrie?

Relance

E. Y a-t-il un syndicalisme agricole actif?

F. Y a-t-il des minorités importantes, par exemple des rapatriés ou des Algériens musulmans, ou d'autres ouvriers étrangers, etc.?

G. Votre circonscription présente-t-elle d'autres caractères originaux?

Q.38. Dans votre circonscription, les rivalités politiques relèvent-elles plutôt des oppositions entre partis, ou plutôt des rivalités entre fortes personnalités? [Plutôt oppositions entre partis (poser Q.38A); plutôt lutte de personnalités (passer à Q.38B); les deux.]

Q.38A. Entre quels partis les rivalités sont-elles les plus accentuées?

[*Enquêteur:* Si réponse "Les deux" à Q.38, poser également Q.38B; sinon passer à Q.39.]

Q.38B. Quelles rivalités personnelles sont les plus accentuées?

Q.39. Quels sont les conflits ou les problèmes économiques et sociaux les plus sérieux dans votre circonscription?

Q.40. Dans votre circonscription, les rivalités politiques dont nous venons de parler sont-elles plus ou moins directement liées à ces problèmes économiques et sociaux ou bien au contraire sont-elles indépendantes? [Elles sont liées aux problèmes sociaux (poser Q.40A); elles sont indépendantes des problèmes sociaux (passer à Q.41).]

Q.40A. De quelle manière sont-elles liées à ces problèmes économiques et sociaux?

Q.41. Pensez-vous que la majorité des électeurs de votre circonscription savent si vous êtes originaire ou non du département qui comprend votre circonscription?

Q.41A. Habitez-vous effectivement votre circonscription? [Oui (poser Q.41B); Non (passer à Q.42).]

Q.41B. Depuis combien de temps habitez-vous cette circonscription?

Q.42. Si vous deviez répartir, en gros, les électeurs de votre circonscription entre la gauche, la droite et le centre, quel pourcentage attribueriez-vous à chacune de ces tendances?

[*Enquêteur:* (Si le total ne fait pas 100%, signalez-le à l'interviewé).]

Q.43. Pourriez-vous évaluer, en pourcentage, la proportion des électeurs de votre circonscription qui sont pour, ou contre, ou indifférents aux options politiques suivantes:

(*Tendre liste-réponse*)

(a) Les subventions aux écoles libres.

*(b) La force de frappe nationale.

(c) Une répartition plus équitable des revenus entre les ouvriers et les autres couches sociales.

*(d) Un plus gros effort pour l'enseignement.

*(e) L'aide aux pays sous-développés.

*(f) Une politique étrangère indépendante de celle des Etats-Unis.

(g) La défense des droits des syndicats.

*(h) L'intégration de l'armée française dans une armée européenne.

(i) La réduction des dépenses militaires.

(j) La réforme de l'Université.

(k) L'accélération de l'unification économique des pays du Marché Commun.

(l) L'augmentation du budget de l'Etat pour les mesures sociales.

Q.44. Pensez-vous que vous avez en fait une bonne connaissance de l'état de l'opinion dans votre circonscription sur le genre des questions que nous venons d'évoquer ci-dessus?

Q.45. Pour connaître l'état de l'opinion dans votre circonscription, quelle importance attachez-vous aux sources d'information suivantes: beaucoup d'importance, assez d'importance, peu d'importance, ou aucune importance?

(*Tendre liste-réponse*)

(a) Les journaux.

(b) Votre courrier.

(c) Les militants locaux de votre parti.

(d) Les organisations professionelles.

(e) Des contacts personnels.

(f) L'administration préfectorale.

Q.45A. Avez-vous quelquefois utilisé des sondages? [Quelquefois; une seule fois; jamais.]

Q.45B. Y-a-t-il d'autres sources d'information que vous considérez comme importantes dans votre circonscription? [Oui (poser Q.45C); Non (passer à Q.46).]

Q.45C. Lesquelles?

Q.46. Maintenant, nous voudrions connaître vos sentiments à l'égard des partis politiques. Voulez-vous mettre une note de 0 à 100 en fonction de la sympathie que vous éprouvez pour eux.

(*Tendre liste-réponse*)

100 signifie: beaucoup de sympathie

  50 signifie: indifférent

   0 signifie: antipathie complète

Quelle note donneriez-vous aux ... (citer les noms un à un)

(a) Parti Communiste?

(b) Parti Socialiste (SFIO)?

(c) UDR?

(d) Fédération de la Gauche?

(e) PSU?

(f) Parti Radical?

(g) Républicains Indépendants?

(h) Progrès et Démocratie Moderne?

*Q.47. Vous est-il arrivé avant 1967 de poser votre candidature à des élections législatives et de ne pas être élu? [Oui (poser Q.47A); Non (passer à Q.48).]

*Q.47A. Quand?

*Q.48. Quelles sont les circonstances qui vous ont amené à être candidat la première fois que vous vous êtes présenté aux élections législatives?

(*A Poser aux Députés Sortants et aux Anciens Députés*)

Q.49. A l'Assemblée, vous êtes-vous jamais trouvé dans la situation suivante: votre groupe avait décidé de voter d'une certaine façon, et vous vouliez, vous, voter d'une autre façon?

Q.49A. Comment auriez-vous ou comment avez-vous résolu ce problème?
    Relance

Q.50. Vous êtes-vous jamais trouvé dans la situation suivante: vous vouliez voter d'une certaine façon, et vous croyiez que la majorité de vos électeurs désirait vous voir voter d'une autre façon?

Q.50A. Comment auriez-vous ou comment avez-vous résolu ce problème?
    Relance

Q.51. Parmi ces questions (*tendre la liste*), en voyez-vous qui pourraient vous placer dans la situation d'avoir à voter selon les désirs de la majorité de vos électeurs plutôt que de voter selon votre propre jugement? [Oui (poser Q.51A); Non (passer à Q.52).]

Q.51A. Lesquelles?
    (*Cocher pour chaque question citée par l'interviewé*)
    (a) Les subventions aux école libres.
    (b) Le budget militaire.
    (c) L'aide aux pays sous-développés.
    (d) Le rôle des syndicats dans l'entreprise.
    (e) Le budget de l'enseignement.
    (f) La politique étrangère.
    (g) La réforme de l'Université.
    (h) Le budget des mesures sociales.
    (i) L'unification économique des pays du Marché Commun.
    (j) La répartition des revenus entre les différentes catégories sociales.

Q.51B. Pourquoi ces questions plutôt que les autres?

Q.52. Vous êtes-vous jamais trouvé dans la situation suivante: vous vouliez voter d'une certaine façon, et les instances locales de votre parti désiraient vous voir voter d'une autre façon?

Q.52A. Comment auriez-vous ou comment avez-vous résolu ce problème?
    Relance

Q.53. En prenant la décision de voter d'une certaine façon, quelle priorité donniez-vous généralement aux considérations suivantes: priorité absolue, forte priorité, priorité moyenne, faible priorité, aucune priorité?
    (*Tendre liste-réponse*)
    (a) Désir de soutenir le gouvernement.
    (b) La position de votre groupe parlementaire.
    (c) La position de votre parti dans votre circonscription.
    (d) Votre estimation de la position de la majorité de vos électeurs.

Q.54. Je voudrais vous demander quelle est votre expérience comme député.

Vous spécialisez-vous dans un domaine politique particulier? [Oui (poser Q.54A); Non (passer à Q.55).]

Q.54A. Lequel?

Q.54B. Est-ce un choix personnel, ou cela a-t-il été decidé par votre parti? [Choix personnel (poser Q.54C); décidé par votre parti (passer à Q.55); les deux.]

Q.54C. Pourquoi avez-vous choisi ce (ou ces) domaine(s)? (Plusieurs réponses possibles) [Parce que cela vous intéresse; parce que cela relève de votre compétence professionnelle; parce que c'est important pour votre circonscription; ou pour une autre raison (préciser).]

Q.55. Comme député, quand le Parlement est en session, quel pourcentage de votre temps consacrez-vous:
(a) aux problèmes nationaux?
(b) aux problèmes de votre circonscription?

Q.55A. Et le reste du temps, quel pourcentage de votre temps consacrez-vous:
(a) aux problèmes nationaux?
(b) aux problèmes de votre circonscription?

Q.56. A l'Assemblée, appartenez-vous à des groupes d'études, associations ou amicales parlementaires, groupe régional ou autre intergroupe parlementaire? (Plusieurs réponses possibles) [Si non, passer à Q.58).]

Q.56A. Lesquels plus précisément?

Q.57. Est-ce que vous consultez ces groupes avant de décider comment voter sur les mesures qui les intéressent? [Oui, toujours; oui, la plupart du temps; oui, mais rarement; non.]

(A Poser aux Anciens Députés, aux Députés Sortants, et Egalement aux Nouveaux Députés)

Q.58. Etes-vous Président d'un Conseil Général, Maire, ou Conseiller Municipal? [Oui, Président d'un Conseil Général; oui, Maire de _____; oui, Conseiller Municipal pour Paris; oui, Conseiller Municipal pour province (poser Q.58A); non, rien de tout cela (passer à Q.59).]

Q.58A. Des différentes fonctions électives que vous occupez, quelle est celle qui vous permet le mieux de rendre service aux électeurs de votre circonscription? [Votre rôle de Député; votre rôle de Maire; votre rôle de Président de Conseil Général; votre rôle de Conseiller Municipal pour Paris; votre rôle de Conseiller Municipal pour Province.]

Q.59. Dans votre circonscription, quelles sortes de gens vous écrivent le plus fréquemment?

Q.59A. Et quelles sortes de gens viennent vous voir le plus fréquemment?

Q.60. Quels genres de services êtes-vous appelé le plus souvent à rendre personnellement à vos électeurs?

Q.61. Dans votre circonscription, avec quelles sortes de gens avez-vous le plus de contacts réguliers? Quelles sont leurs fonctions?

Q.61A. Est-ce que vous consultez ces gens avant de décider comment voter sur les mesures législatives auxquelles ils s'intéressent?

Q.61B. Dans votre circonscription, avec quelles sortes d'organisations avez-vous le plus de contacts réguliers?

Q.61C. Est-ce que vous consultez ces organisations avant de décider comment voter sur les mesures législatives auxquelles elles s'intéressent?

Q.62. Est-ce qu'il vous est arrivé d'intervenir auprès des ministères pour mieux servir les intérêts de votre circonscription? [Oui (poser Q.62A); Non (passer à Q.63).]

Q.62A. Quels ministères, en particulier?

Q.62B. Est-ce que cela arrive souvent, de temps en temps, ou rarement?

Q.63. Lisez-vous *régulièrement* des journaux français ou étrangers quotidiens ou hebdomadaires, je dis bien régulièrement? [Oui, des journaux français; oui, des journaux étrangers; oui, les deux (poser Q.63A); non (passer au guidage).]

Q.63A. Lesquels? [Journaux français; journaux étrangers.]

[*Guidage:* Si la personne est un ancien député ou un député sortant, passer à Q.72.]

(*A Poser Seulement aux Nouveaux Députés*)

Q.64. Je voudrais vous demander comment vous concevez votre tâche de député. Avez-vous l'intention de vous spécialiser dans un domaine politique particulier? [Oui (poser Q.64A); Non (passer à Q.66).]

Q.64A. Lequel?

Q.65. Est-ce un choix personnel ou cela a-t-il été décidé par votre parti? [Choix personnel (poser Q.65A); décidé par votre parti (passer à Q.66); les deux.]

Q.65A. Pourquoi avez-vous choisi ce (ou ces) domaine(s)? (Plusieurs réponses possibles) [Parce que cela vous *intéresse*; parce que cela relève de votre compétence professionnelle; parce que c'est important pour votre circonscription; ou pour une autre raison (préciser).]

Q.66. Quel pourcentage de votre temps pensez-vous que vous devrez consacrer, quand le Parlement est en session:
(a) aux problèmes nationaux?
(b) aux problèmes de votre circonscription?

Q.66A. Et le reste du temps, quel pourcentage pensez-vous consacrer:
(a) aux problèmes nationaux?
(b) aux problèmes de votre circonscription?

Q.67. Appartenez-vous à des groupes d'études, associations ou amicales parlementaires, groupe régional ou autre intergroupe parlementaire? (Plusieurs réponses possibles) [Si non, passer à Q.68.]

Q.67A. Lesquels plus précisément?

Q.67B. Seriez-vous disposé à consulter ces groupes avant de décider comment vous voteriez sur les mesures qui les intéressent? [Oui, toujours; oui, la plupart du temps; oui, mais rarement; non.]

(*A Poser aux Nouveaux Députés et Egalement aux "Autres" Candidats*)

Q.68. Supposez que vous vous trouviez comme député dans la situation suivante: vous désireriez voter d'une certain façon, mais votre groupe parlementaire déciderait de voter autrement; quelle solution adopteriez-vous?
Relance

Q.69. Supposez que vous vous trouviez comme député dans la situation suivante: vous désireriez voter d'une certaine façon, mais vous estimeriez que la majorité de vos électeurs désire vous voir voter autrement; quelle solution adopteriez-vous?
Relance

Q.69A. Parmi ces problèmes politiques (*tendre la liste*), en voyez-vous qui pourraient vous placer dans la situation d'avoir à voter selon les désirs de la majorité de vous électeurs plutôt que de voter selon votre propre jugement? [Oui (poser Q.69B); Non (passer à Q.70).]

Q.69B. Lesquels?

(*Cocher pour chaque réponse citée par l'interviewé*)

(a) Les subventions aux écoles libres.

(b) Le budget militaire.

(c) L'aide aux pays sous-développés.

(d) Le rôle des syndicats dans l'entreprise.

(e) Le budget de l'enseignement.

(f) La politique étrangère.

(g) La réforme de l'Université.

(h) Le budget des mesures sociales.

(i) L'unification économique des pays du Marché Commun.

(j) La répartition des revenus entre les différentes catégories sociales.

[*Enquêteur:* Pour chaque réponse citée, poser Q.69C.]

Q.69C. Pourquoi ces problèmes plutôt que les autres?

Q.70. Supposez que vous vous trouviez comme député dans la situation suivante: vous désireriez voter d'une certain façon, mais les instances locales de votre parti désireraient vous voir voter autrement, quelle solution adopteriez-vous?

Relance

Q.71. Lorsqu'un député prend la décision, à l'Assemblée, de voter d'une certaine façon sur telle ou telle question, quelle priorité doit-il donner, à votre avis, aux considérations suivantes: priorité absolue, forte priorité, priorité moyenne, faible priorité, aucune priorité?

(*Tendre liste-réponse*)

(a) Désir de soutenir le gouvernement.

(b) La position de son groupe parlementaire.

(c) La position de son parti dans sa circonscription.

(d) Son estimation de la position de la majorité de ses électeurs.

A TOUT LE MONDE

Pour terminer, je voudrais maintenant vous poser quelques questions personnelles qui nous aideront dans le classement statistique des réponses.

*Q.72. Où avez-vous vécu pendant la plus grande partie de votre enfance: dans une grande ville, en banlieue, dans une ville de moyenne importance, dans une petite ville, un village, dans une ferme isolée? (Noter la réponse précise, puis coder)

*Q.72A. Dans quel département? (Ou pays, si en dehors de la France)

*Q.73. Quand vous étiez jeune, votre père s'intéressait-il à la politique? [Beaucoup; moyennement; peu; pas de tout.]

*Q.74. De quelle tendance ou parti votre père était-il à l'époque?

*Q.75. Quel était le niveau d'instruction de votre père? [Pas d'études; primaire; primaire supérieur; technique ou commercial; secondaire; supérieur.]

*Q.76. Quelle était la profession de votre père?

(*Noter en clair, puis coder*)

Agriculteur exploitant
Salarié agricole
Industriel, gros commerçant
Profession libérale
Petit commerçant, artisan
Cadre supérieur
Cadre moyen, employé
Ouvrier
Personnel de service
Divers
La politique (préciser).

*Q.76A. Etait-il fonctionnaire?

Q.76B. De vos parents (ou de ceux qui vous ont élevé) pendant votre jeunesse diriez-vous plutôt qu'ils étaient *très à l'aise, simplement à l'aise,* qu'ils ne *vivaient pas mal à condition de faire attention,* ou que la vie était *difficile* pour eux?

*Q.77. Quand vous étiez à l'école primaire, étiez-vous dans une école libre ou une école laïque? [Ecole libre; école laïque; les deux; cours privé non libre; autres écoles (préciser).]

*Q.78. Quel est le dernier établissement d'enseignement que vous avez fréquenté comme élève ou étudiant? Est-ce un établissement...? [Primaire, primaire supérieur, secondaire, technique ou commercial; supérieur (poser Q.78A, B, C).]

*Q.78A. Dans quelle localité avez-vous fait vos études supérieures?

*Q.78B. Dans quelle faculté ou grande école?

*Q.78C. Vous êtes-vous notamment specialisé dans une branche et si oui, laquelle?

*Q.79. Quelle était votre profession lorsque vous avez commencé à vous engager activement dans la politique?
Agriculteur exploitant
Salarié agricole
Industriel, gros commerçant
Profession libérale
Petit commerçant, artisan
Cadre supérieur
Cadre moyen, employé
Ouvrier
Personnel de service
Divers.

Q.80. Exercez-vous toujours cette profession? [Oui; oui, mais à temps partiel (passer à Q.82); non.]

Q.81. Que faites-vous actuellement? Quelle profession exercez-vous actuellement?
(*Noter en clair, puis coder*)
Agriculteur exploitant
Salarié agricole
Industriel, gros commerçant
Profession libérale

Petit commerçant, artisan
Cader supérieur
Cadre moyen, employé
Ouvrier
Personnel de service
Politique
Divers.

Q.82. Avez-vous des liens personnels avec un journal ou un hebdomadaire diffusé régulièrement dans votre circonscription? [Oui (poser Q.82A); Non (passer à Q.83).]

Q.82A. Lequel (ou lesquels)?

Q.82B. Quels sont ces liens? Etes-vous propriétaire, directeur, éditeur, rédacteur, journaliste, autre (préciser)?

Q.83. Quels sont les postes administratifs ou les postes du secteur semi-public (HLM, Caisse de Sécurité Sociale), les plus importants que vous avez occupés pendant ces cinq dernières années?

Q.84. La première fois que vous vous êtes senti proche d'un parti politique, quel âge aviez-vous?

Q.85. A quel parti politique appartenez-vous?
(*Ne rien suggérer*)
Centre Démocrate (CD)
Centre Progrès et Démocratie Moderne (PDM)
UDR
Ve République
Fédération de la Gauche Démocrate et Socialiste (FGDS)
Parti Communiste (PCF)
PSU   (passer à Q.85B)
Parti Socialiste (SFIO)
Parti Radical
Républicains Indépendants
MRP
Indépendants
Autre (préciser)
Aucun parti (passer à Q.87).

Q.85A. Et à l'intérieur de . . . à quel parti plus précisément?

Q.85B. Quel âge aviez-vous quand vous avez commencé à vous sentir proche de ce parti?

*Q.85C. Avez-vous toujours appartenu à ce parti politique? [Oui (passer à Q.86); Non.]

*Q.85D. A quel(s) parti(s) apparteniez-vous auparavant?

Q.86. Qu'est-ce qui vous a fait adhérer au parti auquel vous appartenez actuellement?
(Si l'interviewé a répondu, "Le programme de mon parti," faire une relance. "En particulier, avec quels aspects du programme aviez-vous le plus de sympathie?")

Q.87. Quel âge avez-vous?

Sexe de l'interviewé.

Pour terminer avez-vous des observations à faire sur l'un ou plusieurs des sujets que nous venons d'aborder?

Mass Survey Questionnaires, 1969

Interviews were conducted in 1969 with three classes of respondents: (1) persons who had previously been interviewed in both 1967 and 1968 and who were, therefore, being interviewed for the third time; (2) persons who had previously been interviewed in 1967 but not in 1968 and who were, therefore, being interviewed for the second time; and (3) persons who fell into a fresh sample of respondents who were being interviewed for the first time.

One interview schedule was used for the first and second groups, and a different schedule was used for the third group. The latter contained certain questions, marked with an asterisk, which were not asked of the first two groups in 1969 as they had already been asked in an earlier interview. Questions applying to the first and second groups, but not to the third, are marked with a dagger. As in the case of the 1968 Elite Survey Questionnaires, the 1969 Mass Survey Questionnaires are reproduced below in combined form. The numeration of questions is not literally faithful to that of the original questionnaires.

Introduction

* Bonjour Madame, Monsieur. J'appartiens à la SOFRES et je fais un sondage pour connaître l'opinion des Français sur quelques grandes questions d'actualité. L'opinion de *tous* les Français nous intéresse, même de ceux qui n'ont pas d'opinion ou qui n'ont pas le temps de s'informer!

  Voulez-vous avoir l'amabilité de répondre à mes questions.

  Vous êtes bien M _____ né(e) en _____
  (nom et prénom)   (l'année de naissance indiquée sur la feuille de route)

† Bonjour Madame, Monsieur.

  Vous êtes bien M _____ né(e) en _____
  (nom et prénom),   (année de naissance indiquée ci-dessus).

J'appartiens à la SOFRES et je fais un sondage pour connaître l'opinion des Français sur quelques grandes questions d'actualité. Vous avez déjà eu l'amabilité de répondre à nos questions. J'aimerais à nouveau vous interroger. L'opinion de *tous* les Français nous intéresse.

  [*Enquêteur:* Si la personne est réticente, signaler que le questionnaire est beaucoup plus court que celui de l'année dernière.]

Q.1. Pour la France, selon vous, quel est le problème le plus important à l'heure actuelle?

Q.2. Diriez-vous que, dans l'ensemble, vous êtes très satisfait, assez satisfait, peu satisfait, ou pas du tout satisfait:
(*Tendre liste-réponse*)
(a) de vos conditions de logement?
(b) du revenu de votre foyer?
(c) du travail que vous faîtes (ou, si vous ne travaillez pas, du travail que fait le chef de famille)?
(d) des possibilités qu'ont les enfants de nos jours de recevoir toute l'instruction dont ils ont besoin?

Q.3. Pour chacun des problèmes suivants, pouvez-vous me dire si vous le considérez comme très important, assez, important, peu important, ou pas important du tout?
(*Lire les thèmes; tendre liste-réponse*)
(a) La stabilité gouvernementale est-elle très importante, assez importante, peu importante, ou pas importante de tout?
(b) La défense de l'école laïque?
(c) La construction de l'Europe.
(d) La reconnaissance de la section syndicale d'entreprise?
(e) La réforme de l'Université?
(f) Le développement des mesures sociales?
(g) La lutte contre le chômage?
(h) Une répartition équitable des revenus entre les différentes catégories de Français?
(i) Le développement de l'enseignement?
(j) L'indépendance de la France par rapport aux Etats-Unis?
(k) Le développement économique du pays?

Q.4. Voici un certain nombre de jugements sur ces problèmes. Voudriez-vous nous donner votre opinion, en disant si vous vous estimez d'accord ou non, et si, comme avant, vous n'avez pas d'opinion, cela nous intéresse aussi.
(*Lire les phrases et tendre liste-réponse*)
(a) L'Etat doit aider les écoles libres: êtes-vous entièrement d'accord, plutôt d'accord, plutôt pas d'accord, ou pas du tout d'accord?
(b) Il vaut mieux pour la France réduire ses dépenses militaires plutôt que de garder son rang de grande puissance.
(c) Dans la répartition du revenu national, les ouvriers sont vraiment défavorisés.
(d) Les droits des syndicats devraient être mieux défendus.
(e) L'unification économique du Marché Commun devrait être accélérée.
(f) L'Etat devrait accroître son budget pour les mesures sociales.
(g) La force de frappe est nécessaire si la France veut garder son rang de grande puissance.
(h) L'Etat devrait faire un plus gros effort pour l'enseignement.
(i) Plutôt que d'aider les pays sous-développés, le gouvernement ferait mieux d'aider les régions françaises en difficulté.
(j) La politique extérieure de la France doit être entièrement indépendante des Etats-Unis.

Q.5. En ce qui concerne le Général de Gaulle, pourriez-vous me dire ce qui vous plaît, ou vous plaisait en lui? Et ce qui vous déplait, ou vous déplaisait en lui?

Q.6. Dans l'ensemble, éticz-vous satisfait ou mécontent du Général de Gaulle comme Président de la République? (*Tendre liste-réponse*) [Très satisfait; plutôt satisfait; plutôt mécontent; très mécontent.]

Q.7. Il y a des personnes et des groupes qui influencent le gouvernement ou l'opinion publique. Nous aimerions savoir quels sont vos sentiments à leur égard.

Voulez-vous mettre une note de 0 à 100 aux personnes ou groupes que je vais vous citer en fonction de la sympathie que vous éprouvez pour eux. (*Tendre la liste avec l'échelle de sympathie*)

100 signifie que vous avez beaucoup de sympathie,

   0 signifie que vous ne les aimez pas du tout,

   50 signifie, soit que vous n'êtes ni pour ni contre eux, soit que vous ne connaissez pas grand chose sur eux.

Quelle note donneriez-vous:

   (*Citer les noms un à un*)

   (a) aux syndicats?

   (b) aux enseignants?

   (c) au clergé?

   (d) aux Américains?

   (e) au Parti Communiste?

   (f) au Général de Gaulle?

   (g) à M. Poher?

   (h) à la police?

   (i) à l'UDR?

   (j) à M. Duclos?

   (k) aux étudiants?

   (l) aux Russes?

   (m) à l'armée?

   (n) à M. Pompidou?

   (o) aux grévistes de mai-juin 1968?

Q.8. Est-ce que vous vous intéressez à la politique beaucoup; assez; un peu; pas du tout?

Q.9. Compte tenu de tout ce que les partis représentent, à votre avis existe-t-il *beaucoup* de différences entre les partis, *quelques* différences, ou *peu* de différences?

*Q.9A. Depuis que vous êtes électeur, diriez-vous que vous avez voté à *toutes* les élections législatives et présidentielles, *à la plupart, à quelques-unes,* ou *à aucune?*

*Q.9B. Aux élections législatives, avez-vous voté pour la même parti ou la même tendance toujours, la plupart du temps, ou bien avez-vous voté pour des partis différents?

Q.10. Quel est le parti dont vous vous sentez habituellement le plus proche? (*Une seule réponse, en la notant telle qu'elle vous est donnée par l'interviewé, même si la réponse ne fait pas allusion à un parti ou est nettement hostile aux partis*)

Q.11. Diriez-vous que vous vous sentez *très* proche de ce parti, *assez* proche, ou *pas très* proche?

Q.12. Y a-t-il des partis pour lesquels vous ne voteriez en aucun cas? [Oui; Non (passer à Q.13).]

Q.12bis. Lesquels?
[Noter la réponse telle qu'elle vous est donnée par l'interviewé, même si la réponse ne fait pas allusion à un ou des parti(s).]

Q.13. Avez-vous voté au *premier* tour lors des élections législatives de juin 1968 pour élire les députés? *Attention:* Je dis bien aux élections législatives de juin 1968. [Oui; Non (passer à Q.15).]

Q.14. Pour quel parti, ou pour candidat, avez-vous voté? *Attention:* Je dis bien au *premier* tour des élections législatives de 1968.

Q.15. Avez-vous voté au dernier *référendum,* en avril 1969? [Oui; Non (passer à Q.18).]

Q.16. Et de quelle manière, avez-vous voté au référendum? [Oui; Non; nul; blanc.]

Q.17. Pourriez-vous nous expliquer pourquoi vous avez voté de cette façon?
Parlons maintenant des élections présidentielles, celles de juin 1969.

Q.18. Pendant la campagne électorale, est-ce que des candidats ou des représentants des candidats ont pris contact, personnellement, avec vous, soit en venant vous voir, soit en vous téléphonant? [Oui; Non.]

Q.19. Pouvez-vous me citer les noms des candidats qui se sont présentés à l'élection présidentielle, au *premier* tour?
(*Ne rien suggérer*)

[*Enquêteur:*
—Noter les noms, ou à défaut toute autre précision servant à identifier les candidats dans la première colonne du tableau ci-dessous. Respecter l'ordre dans lequel l'interviewé a cité les noms.
—Pour chacun des candidats identifiés, poser Q.19A et noter les réponses dans la 2e colonne du tableau ci-dessous.
—Si l'interviewé n'a identifié aucun des sept candidats (voir fiche de renseignements), passer aux instructions ci-dessous.]

Q.19A. (Pour chaque candidat identifié): De quel parti ou tendance était-il?

[*Instructions à l'enquêteur:*
—Si l'interviewé *n'a pas cité tous les candidats au l^{er} tour des élections présidentielles,* dire avant de poser Q.20: "Il est assez difficile de se souvenir des noms de tous les candidats."
—Si l'interviewé *a cité tous les candidats au l^{er} tour des élections présidentielles,* poser directement Q.20.]

Q.20. Maintenant, je vais reprendre les noms des candidats au premier tour de l'élection présidentielle. Sur cette échelle qui va de l'extrême gauche à l'extrême droite (*tendre la liste avec l'échelle*), où placeriez vous chacun de ces candidats?
Où placeriez-vous M _____ (compléter en citant le nom du candidat)?

(Si l'interviewé ne cite pas un chiffre, demander, "Ce qui correspond à quel chiffre?" et noter le chiffre cité)

(a) Pompidou
(b) Poher
(c) Duclos
(d) Defferre
(e) Rocard
(f) Krivine
(g) Ducatel

Q.21. Et vous-même, si vous aviez à vous placer sur cette échelle, où vous placeriez-vous?
(*Tendre à nouveau la liste avec l'échelle*)

Q.22. Un certain nombre d'électeurs n'ont pas voté au premier tour. Vous-même, avez-vous voté au premier tour de d'élection présidentielle? [Oui (passer à Q.24); Non.]

Q.23. Si vous aviez voté, pour quel candidat auriez-vous voté? Pour répondre, il vous suffit de citer la lettre correspondant au nom du candidat.
(*Tendre liste-réponse*)

A. Pompidou ⎫
B. Poher   ⎬ (passer à Q.25)

C. Duclos ⎫
D. Defferre
E. Rocard ⎬ (passer à Q.29)
F. Krivine
G. Ducatel ⎭

Q.24. Pourriez-vous me dire pour qui vous avez voté au premier tour? Pour répondre, il vous suffit de citer la lettre correspondant au nom du candidat.
(*Tendre liste-réponse*)

A. Pompidou ⎫
B. Poher   ⎬ (passer à Q.25)

C. Duclos ⎫
D. Defferre
E. Rocard ⎬ (passer à Q.29)
F. Krivine
G. Ducatel ⎭

Q.25. Le candidat que vous avez préféré au 1er tour s'est représenté au 2e tour. Est-ce qu'un ou plusieurs des candidats éliminés ont donné des consignes à leurs électeurs pour le 2e tour? [Oui; Non (passer à Q.31).]

Q.26. Quels étaient ce (ces) candidat(s) qui ont donné des consignes à leur électeurs?

[*Enquêteur:*
—Cocher le nom de chaque candidat cité par l'interviewé dans la 1ere colonne du tableau ci-dessous.
—Reprendre le 1er nom cité par l'interviewé et poser successivement à propos de ce candidat les Q.27 et 28. Cocher les réponses dans les colonnes correspondantes du tableau ci-dessous.

—Procéder de même pour chaque autre candidat cité par l'interviewé à Q.26.

—Puis passer à Q.31.]

Q.27. Monsieur ... (Duclos, Defferre, etc., selon le cas), qu'a-t-il recommandé à ses électeurs? [Voter Pompidou; voter Poher; abstention; bulletin nul ou blanc; autre consigne (préciser laquelle ci-contre).]

Q.28. Avez-vous été satisfait ou mécontent de cette recommandation, ou bien cela vous a-t-il laissé indifférent? [Satisfait; mécontent; indifférent.]

(Après avoir posé Q.28 pour la dernière fois, passer à la Q.31)

Q.29. Le candidat que vous avez préféré au 1er tour ne s'est pas représenté au 2e tour. A-t-il donné des consignes à ses électeurs pour le 2e tour? [Oui; Non (passer à Q.31).]

Q.30. Qu'a-t-il recommandé à ses électeurs?

(*Ne rien suggérer*) [Voter Pompidou; voter Poher; l'abstention; un bulletin nul ou blanc; autre consigne (préciser laquelle).]

Q.30bis. Avez-vous été satisfait ou mécontent de cette recommandation, ou bien cela vous a-t-il laissé indifférent? [Satisfait; mécontent; indifférent.]

A Tout le Monde

Q.31. Vous-même, avez-vous voté au 2e tour? [Oui (passer à Q.33); Non.]

Q.32. Si vous aviez voté, pour quel candidat auriez-vous voté au 2e tour?

(*Tendre liste-réponse*) [A. Pompidou, B. Poher (passer à Q.34); n'aurait pas voté, bulletin nul ou blanc (passer à Q.35).]

Q.33. Pour quel candidat avez-vous voté au 2e tour?

(*Tendre liste-réponse*) [A. Pompidou, B. Poher (poser Q.34); bulletin blanc ou nul (passer à Q.35).]

Q.34. En définitive, pour laquelle de ces raisons principales avez-vous (ou auriez-vous) voté pour ce candidat au 2e tour? Est-ce parce qu'il vous plaisait; parce que ne vouliez pas que son adversaire soit élu; ou pour une autre raison?

(*Une seule réponse*)

Q.35. Pouvez-vous me dire qui est le député qui représente votre circonscription à l'Assemblée Nationale? [Oui; Non (passer à Q.38).]

Q.36. Quel est son nom? (Ecrire le nom—ou à défaut toute autre précision—cité par l'interviewé)

Q.37. De quel parti ou tendance est-il?

Q.38. A-t-il pris publiquement position en faveur d'un candidat au 1er *tour* de l'élection présidentielle? [Oui; Non (passer à Q.40).]

Q.39. En faveur de quel candidat a-t-il pris position?

[*Enquêteur:* Les questions 40 et 41 *ne doivent pas* être posées pour les interviews faites à Paris Ville.]

Q.40. Le maire de votre commune a-t-il pris publiquement position en faveur d'un candidat au 1er *tour* de l'élection présidentielle? [Oui (poser Q.41); Non, le député est maire (passer à Q.42).]

Q.41. En faveur de quel candidat a-t-il pris position?

A Tout le Monde

Q.42. Voici la liste des candidats qui se sont présentés au premier tour de l'élection présidentielle (*tendre la liste*). Parmi ces candidats, quels sont ceux qui vous semblent lutter le plus pour:
(*Lire les thèmes*) (*Une seule réponse par ligne*)
(a) la stabilité gouvernementale?
(b) la défense de l'école laïque?
(c) la construction de l'Europe?
(d) la reconnaissance de la section syndicale d'entreprise?
(e) la réforme de l'Université?
(f) le développement des mesures sociales?
(g) réduire le chômage?
(h) une répartition équitable des revenus entre les différentes catégories de Français?
(i) le développement de l'enseignement?
(j) l'indépendance de la France par rapport aux Etats-Unis?
(k) le développement économique du pays?

Q.43. Maintenant, parlons du gouvernement. Etes-vous d'accord ou pas d'accord avec les opinions suivantes: Je ne crois pas que le gouvernement se préoccupe beaucoup de ce que les gens comme moi pensent.

Q.44. La politique et le gouvernement semblent parfois si compliqués que les gens comme moi ne peuvent vraiment pas comprendre ce qui se passe.

Q.45. En général, les députés que nous élisons perdent vite contact avec le peuple. [D'accord, pas d'accord, ça dépend des députés.]

Q.46. Enfin, voici des opinions d'un autre genre. D'une façon générale, diriez-vous qu'on peut faire confiance aux gens, ou au contraire qu'on ne prend jamais assez de précautions avec certaines personnes?

Q.47. A votre avis, les jeunes doivent-ils être laissés à l'école aussi longtemps que possible, même si cela implique des sacrifices financiers pour leur famille? [Oui, doivent être laissés à l'école; Non, ne doivent pas.]

*Q.47A. En gros, quelle réputation est préférable selon vous: la réputation de savoir travailler avec les autres, ou celle de se tirer d'affaire tout seul?

Renseignements Signalétiques

Eh bien, M _____, je vous remercie, j'ai presque terminé; je vais vous demander maintenant quelques renseignements pour le classement des réponses.

Q.48. *Sexe.*

Q.49. *Age:* quel âge avez-vous?

Q.50. Depuis combien de temps habitez-vous cette commune? [En années.]

*Q.50bis. Où avez-vous vécu pendant la plus grande partie de votre enfance: dans une grande ville, dans sa banlieue, dans une ville de moyenne importance, dans une petite ville, un village, dans une ferme isolée?

*Q.50ter. Dans quel département?

Q.51. Actuellement, exercez-vous une profession? [Oui; non, chômeur; non, retraité (passer à Q.52); non, ménagère; non, étudiant; non, rentier; non, autres raisons (poser Q.51bis).]

Q.51bis. Avez-vous exercé une profession auparavant? [Oui; Non (passer à Q.55).]

Q.52. Quelle est (quelle était) votre profession? Expliquez-moi précisément ce que vous faites (faisiez).

(*Noter en détail, puis coder*) [Agriculteur (poser Q.52A); salarié agricole (passer à Q.52B); industriel, gros commerçant; profession libérale; petit commerçant, artisan; cadre supérieur; cadre moyen, employé; ouvrier; personnel de service; divers (passer à Q.53).]

*Q.52A. Etes-vous (ou étiez-vous) propriétaire-exploitant, fermier, métayer ou salarié?

*Q.52B. Quelle est (ou était) la superficie de votre exploitation?

(Ecrire le chiffre cité puis coder) [Moins de 12 hectares, de 12 à 39 hectares, de 40 à 199 hectares, 200 hectares et plus (passer à Q.54).]

Q.53. Etes-vous (ou étiez-vous) patron, fonctionnaire ou salarié?

(*Une seule réponse*)

Q.54. Dans votre travail, avez-vous ou aviez-vous des ouvriers ou employés sous votre responsabilité? *Ne comptez pas les membres de votre famille.* [Oui; Non (passer à Q.55).]

Q.54A. Combien d'ouvriers ou d'employés avez-vous (eu) sous votre responsabilité? *Ne comptez pas les membres de votre famille.*

(Ecrire la chiffre exact, puis coder) [0, 1, 2, 3, 4, 5, 6, de 7 à 9, de 10 à 24, 25 ou plus.]

Q.55. Etes-vous le chef de famille? [Oui (passer à Q.60); Non.]

Q.56. Actuellement, le chef de famille exerce-t-il une profession? [Oui; non, chômeur; non, rétraité (passer à Q.57); non, ménagère; non, étudiant; non, rentier; non, autres raisons (poser Q.56bis).]

Q.56bis. A-t-il exercé une profession auparavant? [Oui; Non (passer à Q.60).]

Q.57. Quelle est (quelle était) sa profession? Expliquez-moi précisément ce qu'il fait (ou faisait).

(Noter en detail, puis coder) [Agriculteur (poser Q.57A); salarié agricole (passer à Q.57B); industriel, gros commerçant; profession liberale; petit commerçant, artisan; cadre supérieur; cadre moyen, employé; ouvrier; personnel de service; divers (passer à Q.58).]

*Q.57A. Est-il (ou était-il) propriétaire-exploitant, fermier, métayer ou salarié?

*Q.57B. Quelle est (ou était) la superficie de son exploitation?

(Ecrire le chiffre, puis coder) [Moins de 12 hectares; de 12 à 39 hectares; de 40 à 199 hectares; 200 hectares et plus (passer à Q.59).]

Q.58. Est-il (était-il) patron, fonctionnaire ou salarié?

(*Une seule réponse*)

Q.59. Dans son travail, le chef de famille a-t-il (ou avait-il) des ouvriers ou employés sous sa responsabilitié? *Ne comptez pas les membres de sa famille.* [Oui; Non (passer à Q.60).]

Q.59A. Combien d'ouvriers ou d'employés a-t-il (ou avait-il) sous sa responsabilité dans son travail? (*Ne comptez pas les membres de sa famille*).

(Ecrire le chiffre exact, puis coder) [0, 1, 2, 3, 4, 5, 6, de 7 à 9, de 10 à 24, 25 ou plus.]

A Tout le Monde

Q.60. On parle souvent des différentes classes sociales. La plupart des gens disent qu'ils appartiennent soit à la *classe moyenne,* soit à *la class ouvrière.* Vous-même, avez-vous le sentiment d'appartenir à l'une ou l'autre de ces classes? [Oui; non, ni l'une, ni l'autre (passer à Q.60ter).]

Q.60bis. Laquelle? [Classe moyenne; classe ouvrière (passer à Q.61).]

Q.60ter. Si vous aviez à choisir, diriez-vous que vous appartenez à la classe moyenne ou à la classe ouvrière?

*Q.61. Quel est le dernier établissement d'enseignement que vous avez fréquenté comme élève ou étudiant(e)? Est-ce un établissement d'enseignement primaire; primaire supérieur; secondaire; technique, commercial; ou supérieur (université, grande école)?

*Q.62. Pendant les années d'enseignement primaire, étiez-vous dans une école libre ou une école laïque? [Ecole libre; école laïque; les deux; cours privé non libre; autres écoles (préciser).]

*Q.63. *Situation de famille:* êtes-vous marié, veuf, célibataire, ou divorcé?

*Q.64. Pendant votre jeunesse, quand vous aviez entre 10 et 18 ans, quelle était la profession de vos parents ou de ceux qui vous ont élevé? (*Noter en détail puis coder*) [Agriculteur exploitant; salarié agricole; industriel, gros commerçant; profession liberale; petit commerçant, artisan; cadre supérieur; cadre moyen, employé; ouvrier; personnel de service; divers.]

*Q.65. De vos parents (ou de ceux qui vous ont élevé) pendant votre jeunesse, diriez-vous plutôt qu'ils étaient *très à l'aise, simplement à l'aise,* qu'ils *ne vivaient pas mal à condition de faire très attention,* ou que la vie était *difficile* pour eux?

*Q.66. Vous rappelez-vous si votre père à cette époque s'intéressait à la politique? [Beaucoup; moyennement; peu; pas du tout.]

*Q.67. De quel tendance ou parti était-il (votre père) à l'époque? (Noter la réponse telle qu'elle vous est donnée par l'interviewé, même si la réponse ne fait pas allusion à un ou des partis)

*Q.68. Avez-vous entendu votre père parler de ses préférences politiques à cette époque? [Oui, souvent; oui, quelquefois; non, jamais.]

*Q.69. Quelle est votre religion? [Catholique; Protestante; Juive; autre; aucune (passer à Q.71).]

*Q.70. (Poser selon la réponse à Q.69): Allez-vous à l'église (au temple ou à la synagogue) au moins une fois par semaine, souvent dans l'année, quelquefois, rarement, ou jamais?

*Q.71. Voici une liste de revenus mensuels (*tendre liste-réponse*). Nous désirons savoir dans quelle tranche de revenus vous situez votre foyer, en comptant toutes les rentrées d'argent dans le foyer telles que les salaires, allocations familiales, pensions, revenus, recettes, etc. Pour répondre, il vous suffit de citer la lettre correspondante:

A. Moins de 400 F.   (Moins de 40 000 anciens francs)
B. De 400 à 800 F.   (De 40 000 à 80 000 anciens francs)
C. De 801 à 1 100 F.   (De 80 001 à 110 000 anciens francs)
D. De 1 101 à 1 400 F.   (De 110 001 à 140 000 anciens francs)
E. De 1 401 à 1 700 F.   (De 140 001 à 170 000 anciens francs)

F. De 1 701 à 2 100 F.	(De 170 001 à 210 000 anciens francs)
G. De 2 101 à 2 600 F.	(De 210 001 à 260 000 anciens francs)
H. De 2 601 à 3 200 F.	(De 260 001 à 320 000 anciens francs)
I. De 3 201 à 4 200 F.	(De 320 001 à 420 000 anciens francs)
J. Plus de 4 200 F.	(Plus de 420 000 anciens francs)

RS.1. *Enquêteur:* Coder le caractère du domicile de l'interviewé—appartement, maison particulière, ferme non isolée, ferme isolée.

†RS.2. L'interviewé, habite-il à la même adresse qu'en juillet-septembre 1968? [Oui (fin de questionnaire); Non.]

†RS.3. *Enquêteur:* Indiquer ci-dessous la commune et le département où habite actuellement l'interviewé.

Notes

Introduction

1. Portions of the parent study developed for the United States at the Survey Research Center of the University of Michigan have been reported by Miller and Stokes (1963) and Miller (1964). Versions of the study have been developed for Britain, Sweden, the Netherlands, Italy, Japan, Australia, West Germany, and Canada.

2. A much more detailed account of each of these data collections, along with descriptions of some of their more important technical properties, is provided in Appendices A and B. Copies of the actual interview schedules are given in Appendix D.

1. The Framework of French Politics

1. For the politics of this early postwar period, see Goguel (1952, ch. 1) and Wright (1948). The text of the Bayeux speech is in *L'Année politique, 1946* (1947).

2. René Pleven, Minister of Foreign Affairs in the last government of the Fourth Republic prior to de Gaulle's return to power, was reported to have said at the last cabinet meeting: "We are the legal government. But what do we govern? The Minister for Algeria cannot enter Algeria. The Minister for the Sahara cannot go to the Sahara. The Minister of Information can do nothing but censor the press. The Minister of Defense is disobeyed by the army" (quoted in Williams and Harrison, 1960, p. 68).

3. The Socialist Minister of the Interior at the time, Jules Moch, wrote that "Prague, in 1948, haunted my sleepless nights as much as Madrid, in 1936" (1958, p. 10).

4. There were other attempts to form new parties, but none was successful. The Union Démocratique et Socialiste de la Résistance (UDSR) aspired to become a major party, but although it contained leaders of undeniable talent (including François Mitterrand), it remained a splinter party and is usually combined in electoral statistics with the Radicals, with whom it generally allied for electoral purposes. Some of de Gaulle's supporters tried to launch a Gaullist party (the Union Gaulliste) in 1946, but the General did not encourage the effort.

5. This was due in large part to a contrived electoral law that enabled the Third Force parties to win a disproportionately large share of the parliamentary seats relative to their popular vote, at the expense of the Communists and Gaullists. Proportional representation had been employed for the elections of 1945 and 1946. The electoral law was changed for the 1951 election in order to give an advantage to the Third Force parties, which could ally with one another, over the Communists and Gaullists, who could not. Allied parties could run competing lists of candidates, but when the ballots were counted, any party or group of allied parties which won a majority of the votes in an electoral dis-

trict won all the seats in the National Assembly for that district. In the case of a victorious alliance, the seats were distributed among the allied parties in proportion to the number of votes contributed by each of the allied parties to the total number of votes received by the allied parties combined. If no party or group of allied parties won a majority of seats in the district, the seats were distributed among all the parties which competed in the district in proportion to the number of votes they received. As this electoral law applied to multimember districts which had from two to ten seats, it provided a considerable parliamentary bonus to parties which could simply file a statement of alliance and which together could command a majority of the votes in a district. In one district of the Nord, for example, where Socialists, MRP, Radicals, and conservatives were allied, they won 53 percent of the votes and all ten seats; while in another district of the Nord, the same four parties won 40 percent of the votes, and received only four of the ten seats for the district. Allied parties won majorities, and consequently all the seats, in a third of the districts. One blatantly discriminatory feature of the electoral law was that the winner-take-all provision did not apply in Paris, where the RPF was particularly strong, or in the Paris suburbs, where the Communists were particularly strong. The Third Force parties were afraid that their Gaullist and Communist opponents might sweep all the seats in those areas, so there they required a proportional representation system (and one which, unlike the system used where applicable in the rest of France, favored the smaller parties).

6. For a fuller discussion of the 1956 election, see Pierce (1957).

7. The best single work on the Poujadists is Hoffmann et al. (1956).

8. The provision for alliances in the electoral law that had worked so well for the Third Force parties in 1951, by magnifying their parliamentary strength relative to their electoral support, had little effect in 1956. The split among the Radicals and the antagonism between the Socialists and the MRP prevented broad alliances from being made, and few alliances won the majorities needed to win all the seats in a district. Accordingly, almost all the seats were distributed on the basis of proportional representation, accounting for the sharp increase in the number of Communist deputies.

9. This ambiguity appears in the first sentences of his speech at the Forum during his visit to Algiers after returning to power in 1958: "I have understood you. I know what has happened here. I see what you wanted to do."

10. Exact comparisons with 1956 are impossible because the multimember electoral districts used with proportional representation in 1945 and 1946, and with the quasi-PR/quasi-winner-take-all system of 1951 and 1956 (see above, n. 5), were abandoned in 1958, and France returned to its classic two-ballot, single-member-district system known as the *scrutin uninominal à deux tours*. For a description of this system, see below, n. 11.

11. Under this electoral system, Metropolitan France is divided into single-member electoral districts, of which there were 465 for the elections of 1958 and 1962, 470 for the elections of 1967 and 1968, 473 for the election of 1973, and 474 for the elections of 1978 and 1981. Any candidate who wins a majority of the valid ballots cast wins the seat for the district, provided that his majority includes at least 25 percent of the total number of registered voters for the district. If no candidate wins such a majority, there is a run-off ballot one week later. In fact, the great majority of the seats are won at the second, run-off ballot. During the Fifth Republic (through 1981), the proportion of metropolitan seats won at the first ballot has ranged from a low of 8 percent in 1958 to a high of 35 percent in 1981, with a mean across seven elections of less than 20 percent. Thus, the second ballot is crucial, and we will discuss mass and elite behavior at the second ballot at some length in Chapters 11–13.

Any candidate who ran at the first ballot may run at the second ballot, provided he won a certain proportion of the vote at the first ballot. For the elections of 1958 and 1962, this qualifying proportion was 5 percent of the votes cast at the first ballot; for the elections of 1967 and 1968, the qualifying proportion was raised to 10 percent of the registered voters at the first ballot, and it was raised further to 12.5 percent of the registered voters for the elections of 1978 and 1981. A candidate may run at the second ballot without having met this condition, however, if there is only one candidate in the district who does satisfy it. This exception is made to ensure that there will be at least two candidates at the second ballot. Candidates who do not qualify for the second ballot are automatically eliminated. Not everyone who qualifies for the second ballot necessarily runs at the second ballot. Under this electoral system allied parties withdraw in one another's favor at the second ballot in the attempt to pool their electoral support. Usually allied parties withdraw in each district in favor of whichever one of their candidates won the most votes at the first ballot; sometimes, however, they support a candidate even if he did not win the most votes of all the allies' candidates at the first ballot, if he seems most likely to win at the second ballot. The Communist party made a certain number of such "gifts" to their allies in 1962, 1967, and 1968. Alliances are not necessarily formal or nationwide. Tacit agreements may be made among parties with respect to a limited number of districts. Sometimes a party does not have an explicit national policy, but simply leaves the decisions about alliances to its local candidates, who may make different kinds of alliances in different districts.

12. In 1962 this party was officially known as the UNR-UDT because of a recent merger of the Union for the New Republic with a smaller, more leftist Gaullist organization called the Union Démocratique du Travail (UDT).

13. The method of electing the French president is similar to, but not identical with, the method of electing French deputies (see above, n. 11). A majority of the valid ballots cast is required for election. If no candidate wins a majority, there is a run-off ballot two weeks later. Only two candidates may run at the second ballot. The Constitution provides that the two candidates who may run at the second ballot must be those, among the candidates who want to run at the second ballot, who received the most votes at the first ballot. If the two front-runners at the first ballot want to compete at the second ballot, they and only they may do so. If one of them decides to withdraw from the race, his place may be taken by the candidate who received the third largest vote at the first ballot, and so on. In fact, at each of the presidential elections held under this electoral system through 1981, a second ballot has been necessary and the two front-runners at the first ballot have run at the second ballot.

14. The only exception was the presidential election of 1969.

15. It was particularly tumultuous in the United States, where civil strife contributed to the electoral withdrawal of Lyndon B. Johnson, who only four years earlier had won the greatest victory to date of any presidential candidate in the twentieth century; in West Germany, where a "great coalition" gave birth to an "extraparliamentary opposition" and paved the way for the transition from Christian Democratic to Social Democratic rule; and in Great Britain, which was faced once again with bitter sectarian strife in Northern Ireland.

16. De Gaulle's withdrawal from public life in 1969 was his third and last; he died the following year.

17. The Assembly elected in 1956 was cut short by the collapse of the Fourth Republic, and that elected in 1958 by de Gaulle's dissolution when it censured his government for agreeing to hold a referendum on direct presidential elections. If the National Assembly is not dissolved earlier by the president, its term expires at the start of the regular April parliamentary session of the fifth year following its election, and new elections must be held during the sixty days preceding that expiration date.

18. See Chapter 17.

19. Ministère de l'Education Nationale (1969, pp. 20–21).

20. On the May revolt generally and the leftward shift in particular, see Chapter 14.

21. Most of the leaders of the largest French union organization, the Confédération

Générale du Travail (CGT), are high ranking members of the Communist party. The general secretary of the CGT in 1968 was Georges Séguy, who was also a member of the political bureau of the Communist party.

22. Ironically, the Baden commander was General Jacques Massu, who had played a prominent role in Algeria when the revolt there toppled the Fourth Republic. Goguel (1984) argues persuasively that de Gaulle had overcome his earlier discouragement before he went to Baden to see Massu.

23. See Chapter 14 for a discussion of the relationship between votes and seats under the French electoral system.

24. The French Constitution does not provide for a vice-president. Upon the death or resignation of the President, the President of the Senate becomes interim President of the Republic, with restricted powers, only until the election of a new President, which normally must take place between 20 and 35 days after the presidency becomes vacant.

2. French Voters and Their Party System

1. In the actual Rose-Urwin data, the two major parties in the United States show a vote variability over time which actually exceeds that for France. But the statistics presented for the United States are based on presidential election results rather than on voting for the national legislatures, as is the case for the other eighteen countries. When congressional voting is substituted for the presidential results to bring the United States to a comparable base with other countries, its instability falls back close to the cross-national average.

2. It is ironic that the first systematic study of mass voting behavior—André Siegfried's classic *Tableau politique de la France de l'Ouest sous la Troisième République* (Paris: Armand Colin, 1913)—was carried out in France and conveyed the impression to more than one generation of scholars that French voting patterns displayed a remarkably long-term stability. In point of fact, Siegfried himself was impressed by the high variability of party labels in the 1870–1910 period he covered, and his amazement with signs of stability arose from the basic political tendencies beneath these superficial cues. More recent analyses of data from the Siegfried period, and on a national rather than regional base, have suggested that the clear lines of stability present are nonetheless more feeble than those within United States voting data from the same period. See Converse (1969, pp. 459–485).

3. See Appendix A for a discussion of this phenomenon in relation to the French referendum and presidential election of 1969.

4. The constancy estimates for the United States were sufficiently similar for the two pairs of successive elections to justify our cumulating the estimates.

5. Originally, for our party constancy calculations we erected three sets of criteria for party continuity, at different levels of stringency. Obviously, whenever a party continues under the same name for successive elections, very few coding decisions need to be made. But when a party leadership continues and merely changes the party name between elections, should it be considered to be the same party or a different one? Where the elite party system and the contest over policy outputs are concerned, few would contest that it is the same party. Where the voter is concerned, however, problems of recognition arising from the name change, and lack of awareness that the party remains otherwise identical, raise more of an issue. In our most stringent coding, even a name change was considered to have produced a different party. But we also used progressively looser criteria for two other codings. In the loosest form, parties were considered to be identical at two points in time despite name change if there had been no more than minor adjustments in leadership composition or coalition membership. Thus, for example, the PDM of Duhamel in 1968 was considered to be the same party as the Centre Démocrate of Lecanuet in 1967.

We wish to emphasize that all of our constancy results are based on this loosest criterion of party continuity, as is the estimate of the 1967–68 net change in Figure 2–1. The remainder of the French calculations in Figure 2–1 merely attempted to apply the same loose criterion to earlier elections. Still looser criteria than we used are of course possible and are occasionally used. Thus, for example, it might be argued that the Gaullist UNR of the late 1950s was "really" equivalent to the MRP of the immediate postwar period, because of ideological similarities and obvious transfers of many early MRP votes to the later UNR. Yet pursuing the logic this far quickly smoothes away the phenomenon of rapid party change in France, and that, for our purposes, is quite self-defeating. Therefore, even our loosest criterion remains somewhat stringent.

6. The controlling operation in this case has been accomplished by accumulating the French individual stability values at each level of offering constancy, weighting them by the proportions of American voters who encountered each level. Thus the French values express what might have been expected from the French sample if the constancy of election offerings had been like those for corresponding situations in the United States. The United States values vary slightly from comparison to comparison even when the election "condition" referred to was the same, since varying U.S. cases were dropped for lack of any match on the French side at particular levels of constancy of election offerings.

7. Since we know that some respondents failed to register recognition of parties that they subsequently seemed well aware of, it is tempting to imagine that our recall and recognition measures give a systematic understatement of levels of information about the existence of various parties. This may well be true for the recall measure, since it would have been hard for a respondent to pretend to know more parties than he actually had in mind. The recognition measure, however, is very vulnerable to overestimation, since there was no check on the accuracy of the individual's report that he did in fact recognize further parties on the list provided. Since it is an abiding concern of respondents in the interview situation to minimize appearances of ignorance, there is probably some artificial inflation of these accounts as well as circumstances which act to deflate them erroneously.

8. Figure 2–3 ignores the fact that a few stray parties not included in our list of ten were also named, particularly by those persons with full "cognitive maps" of the party system.

9. For example, we deliberately included on our list of ten parties two which had been prominent in earlier French politics but had become more or less defunct by the time of the 1967 legislative elections. These were the MRP and the Radical-Socialist parties. For them the ratio of recognition to recall was unusually high, especially among older voters, since there was some tendency to define these parties out of the domain of recall, although recognition was not difficult.

10. This calculation is drawn by taking the individual voter's perception of each of the ten parties as a single unit of observation.

11. Multiple mentions of factors affecting vote decisions were permitted, if not encouraged. A bit less than 2 percent of the electorate stressed joint attention to parties and programs, and party knowledge among these respondents was far higher than in any other group.

12. If "don't know" respondents are included in the calculations, the eta, or the association between party knowledge and the number of parties seen as optimal, is .41.

13. One useful virtue of an analysis in this format is that we can expect individual-level factors to be independent of all system-level factors.

14. It should be said, however, that a variety of items tapping attitudes toward the party system were deliberately excluded from consideration, despite knowledge that they correlate with the party recognition variable rather strongly. Although these variables indeed represent individual-level differences, their causal status relative to party knowledge is entirely ambiguous: many of them may as well be results of greater or lesser knowledge

of the party system as causes of it. We might also note that all statements in this passage concerning variance accounted for refer to a conventional linear additive prediction model.

3. Party Loyalties in France

1. Some of the principal treatments of the subject include Campbell et al. (1960, esp. chs. 6–7); Campbell et al. (1966, esp. chs. 2–3).

2. Almond and Verba (1963). The five countries studied are the United States, Great Britain, Germany, Italy, and Mexico.

3. In sample surveys of the 1950s, reports of Communist voting vastly underrepresented the known voting strength of the party. Similarly, in the 1958 study the proportion of persons revealing an identification with the Communist party was only one-fifth of its national voting strength, although the corresponding proportion for most other parties was 45–65 percent. In our 1967 study, however, the percentage reporting a Communist vote did not fall much short of the proportion in the official vote statistics (see Appendix A). At the same time, the proportion of admitted Communist identifiers amounted to 53 percent of the proportion of national voting strength, or a figure not much below the proportion of identifiers to actual voters displayed on the average by other parties.

4. The panel survival rate in 1969 was better than that in 1968, and the 1969 estimates also include an infusion of 35–40 percent "fresh" interviews with new respondents. See Appendix A.

5. For further comments on these effects during May and June 1968, see Chapter 14.

6. In the tabulation, "Some political position" refers to mentions of left-right locations, political leaders, and groups other than political parties.

7. This statement may seem surprising in view of conclusions drawn by Inglehart and Hochstein (1972) and Cameron (1972) that French party identifications had advanced massively in the first ten years of the Fifth Republic. These investigators were working in common with an IFOP study conducted in July 1968, comparing the party identification distributions with those we had collected in 1958 (Converse and Dupeux, 1962). It seemed that 25 percent more French voters were willing to express some abiding identification than had been true in 1958. But the data collection methods used were quite different from those we had used in 1958 and largely repeated in 1968, including the presentation of a list of parties to help the voter remember what specific party he or she was so enthusiastic about. These authors recognized that the sum of methods differences could only work to inflate the proportions of identifiers artificially at the second time point, but they rejected the possibility that these artifacts might account for all of the differences. The evidence, however, points to the fact that their contrasts *must* be completely a methods matter, since our 1968 data, which were collected in exactly the same weeks as theirs, yet with methods standardized, show very limited change. It is our best guess that although the presentation of a list would obviously act to inflate the proportion of specific-party responses, this is probably not the only reason for differences in findings. Both our 1958 and 1968 surveys paid for extra training on the specific interview schedule, whereas the 1968 IFOP study was a typical low-cost operation with minimal study-specific interviewer training and quota sampling. In the absence of special training, interviewers could be expected to perform in routine ways, which included in this period of market research a distinct pressure not to accept noncontent responses. The theory was that every respondent had true preferences on everything, and the difference between a good interviewer and a poor one was that the good interviewer would succeed in coaxing the respondent to reveal some "content" response, however reluctant he or she might be to make one. Indeed, in some polling houses, ratios of null responses accepted were for-

mally used to evaluate interviewer performance. Given these pressures, it is not hard to imagine why the IFOP distributions for 1968 look different from ours. It is easy to imagine interviewers "translating" vague and tortured statements of orientation into specific-party categories on the list, and more generally refusing to take "none" for an answer by making clear that it was an unacceptable response and requesting another try by the respondent.

8. In the two-party American case, nonidentifiers are placed in the independent middle, between the two party poles. There is no comparable organization of the data when dealing with multiple parties.

9. To compute correlations for stability of location across multiple parties, it is necessary to introduce some scheme for ordering those parties. The scheme which we use consistently here and elsewhere is the set of left-right locations of the parties provided by our respondents themselves. This procedure is discussed in Chapter 4.

10. Converse, Dupeux, and Meisel (1967).

11. Campbell et al. (1960, pp. 161–165). For a full development of the model, see Converse (1969).

12. Norpoth (1978) also finds that proportions swell in the lower left cell of his corresponding turnover table for West Germany (based on three observations) when he counts as "variable" identifiers people who move in or out of a party identification, as opposed to those actually changing identifications. Leduc (1981) finds an even greater swelling when this change is made for the three-wave Netherlands data.

13. The fractionalization index ranges from a value of 0.00, where all politically sentient members of a polity are in the same party, to a value of 1.00, or a hypothetical polity so fractionalized that each person is a complete political party unto himself or herself. Our Figure 3-4 is drawn with a baseline of .48, or about the lowest value which represents any political competition at all. Below this value, we have a single party so dominant that it will almost never lose an at-large vote, at least by any normal majority criterion.

14. To isolate the verdict from turnout variations, the data presented are limited to two-time voters. When nonvoting is added to the denominator as an instance of inconstancy, all proportions of repeaters decline, but the patterns remain essentially the same.

15. Since we have deliberately contrasted extremely new and extremely old parties in Figure 3-6, the function for the total sample does not invariably lie between the two lighter lines, although that is generally the case.

16. The relevant literature here is massive. Some of the most central early references include Hyman (1959) and Greenstein (1965). More recently, the most incisive work has been provided by Jennings and Niemi (1974, 1981) for the United States; and in a more comparative perspective, Jennings, Allerbeck, and Rosenmayr (1979) and Allerbeck, Jennings, and Rosenmayr (1979).

17. As Niemi (1973) has pointed out, parent-child correlations with respect to partisanship tend to run high (by about .10) when the "parent" datum is no more than the child's report of parental partisanship. The Jennings-Niemi work has greatly profited from independent reports from both parent and child.

18. The full discussion of the 1958 findings is presented in Converse and Dupeux (1962).

19. Roig and Billon-Grand (1968). See also the excellent article reviewing this book by Greenstein and Tarrow (1969, pp. 95–137).

20. Data kindly furnished by SOFRES.

21. On the basis of his studies of French bureaucratic organization and behavior, Crozier (1964) has argued that Frenchmen tend to avoid face-to-face hierarchical relationships because the strain involved in such confrontations is excessive for both the superior and the subordinate. The reason, he suggests, is that Frenchmen conceive of authority as

absolute; when they hold authority they tend to exercise it absolutely, and when they are on the receiving end they expect it to be wielded absolutely. Direct confrontations are avoided wherever possible by both parties: by the superior because he will regard any resistance to his authority as an intolerable affront, and by the subordinate because he will regard the superior's exercise of authority as an intolerable humiliation.

22. The primary problem in comparison arises because the 1967 interviewers left an unusual number of responses to the father's partisanship question blank. Technically speaking, this absence of any response is typically to be coded as "not ascertained," on the assumption that by accident the interviewer skipped the question. When such nonresponses are few—and they rarely amount to more than 1 or 2 percent of a sample—they are usually excluded from calculations. In this instance, however, they approach 10 percent of the total sample, despite the fact that respondents have answers recorded for neighboring questions—also about their fathers—at normally high rates. Moreover, closer analysis shows that 96 percent of these nonresponses are associated with cases in which the father "never" talked about his preferences, and almost 80 percent fall into the two lower-right-hand cells of Table 3-2, where the likelihood of some perception of father's partisanship is at a very low ebb. Therefore, it seems probable that most of these "not ascertained" codes represent interviewer failures to record what was said when the respondent could not answer the question. We have proceeded with this assumption for the estimates given in the text. If we had not done this, but instead had excluded these "not ascertained" codes from the percentage calculations, then a full 44 percent of the "ascertained" portion of the 1967 sample would have reported some partisan perceptions of their fathers.

23. The study cited by Cameron (1972), though probably not comparable methodologically, generated an estimate of 43 percent of children knowing parental partisanship for 1968.

24. Even this result is contingent upon other decisions. The first basic question has to do with equivalences between party formations from one election to the next. Usually we required either strict identity or coded percentages as party change. But it happened from time to time that two smaller parties simply coalesced between two elections, or two wings of a prior party ran candidates separately at the next election. On the very rare occasions when these fusions or fissions were totally straightforward, the groupings were seen as equivalent, rather than as different parties. The second question has to do with the variable spacing between election pairs. Actual transitions varied between spans of five months and spans of five years, and common sense suggests that for reasons having nothing to do with system volatility, more party change will accumulate over a five-year span than over five months. This intuition is handsomely supported by the data for the eleven postwar transitions: the correlation between transition spans and degree of change in party support (percentage difference sums) is $r = .84$. The results we cite are not from raw data, but are based on residuals after differences due to span times are removed.

4. *La Gauche et la Droite*

1. For an intriguing discussion of the symbolism that has been attached to "left" and "right" over the millennia, see Laponce (1970b).

2. For parallel discussions, see Percheron and Jennings (1981). An excellent general statement of the potential interplay between party and left-right cues is provided by Inglehart and Klingemann (1976).

3. See Figure B-1 in Appendix B for the left-right scale that we used in all our mass and elite surveys. The scale was labeled in identical fashion for each survey.

4. Voters were asked for party locations in two stages, rather than the single stage employed for elite respondents. They were first asked to name and locate the parties

which occurred to them spontaneously. Then they were presented with a full list of main parties and asked to locate others which they could recognize in addition to those already rated. This process, which yielded our earlier measures of "party visibility," produced a distinction which will continue to be of interest to us in this chapter.

5. Since 1967, when our first measurements were taken, several publications involving similar inquiries have appeared. Jean Laponce has done imaginative empirical work on the left-right dimension with more selective French and Canadian subpopulations (Laponce, 1970a). Reports involving further countries include Barnes and Pierce (1970), Barnes (1971), Klingemann (1972), and Inglehart and Klingemann (1976).

6. The continuous distributions presented in Figure 4–3 are of course smoothed ones: that is, respondents tended to choose party locations in terms of rounded numbers like 20 or 35 or 60, and not intervening values like 17 or 33. Judicious grouping around the commonly used values and a slight smoothing have produced the final graph.

7. This is a splendid example of an intriguing form of imperfect information that we have discussed elsewhere (Converse, 1964). The actor has a superficial knowledge of "what goes with what," but lacks the information as to the "why" of the matter that would permit him to assign newly cognized objects in the same terms.

8. The detailed steps underlying the construction of these regions are included in our treatment of political regionalism in Chapter 5.

9. One way of expressing the degree of regional differentiation in any variable is to state the proportion of total sample variance that is "caught" between regions, as opposed to within-region variance. Although averages of self-locations do differ quite widely (roughly, from 42 to 54) over the nine regions, only about 3 percent of the total variance in these self-locations can be attributed to regional differences. Aside from the Alliance Républicaine, the comparable figure for perceived party locations varies around 1 percent.

10. Our discussion here has been limited to the question of aggregate stability of assigned locations, excluding the *individual* stability of those judgments. Since we reinterviewed the same persons, we could assess individual stability as well. But for this kind of question—a judgment as to a "fixed" external object—there is no reason to expect any massive *correlation* between individual judgments over time, particularly if the absolute values assigned to any given party show minimal variation, and if what limited variation exists is no more than momentary judgment error. In point of fact, the cross-time correlations at the individual level for three parties described identically in our 1967 and 1968 surveys are modestly positive (between .20 and .40), or about what we might intuitively expect.

11. Inglehart and Klingemann (1976) report French data from 1973 in which 78 percent provide left-right self-classifications, a value almost identical to ours for 1967, despite the use of a single-question format.

12. This term also stems from the seating arrangements of the revolutionary Convention of 1792–93. Variously translatable as "marsh," "swamp," or "morass," it was a derisive term referring to the group that sat and voted in a centrist position between the Girondins on the right and the Jacobins on the left, who were also designated "the Mountain" because their leftist ranks extended to the highest rows of the amphitheater. In current usage it refers to those who are neither left nor right, although Deutsch, Lindon, and Weill chose it for their indifferent center because it evokes the 'fluidity, the inconsistency, and the absence of stable orientations" that distinguish these voters (1966, p. 21).

13. Employing a different measure of own left-right location, Cayrol, Parodi, and Ysmal (1973, pp. 83–86) found a similar tendency among French deputies elected in 1968 not to want to appear to be conservative.

14. The sole exception occurs in connection with the Radical party, which in this period was already centrist and moribund. This exception seems trivial.

15. McClosky, Hoffman, and O'Hara (1960). The original finding has been replicated in a variety of settings, with extensions such as those proposed in Farah and Miller (1974).

16. This second variation on a centrist preference at the mass level emerges quite clearly in seven of the ten possible party comparisons, and the three exceptions are quite readily understood. These exceptions are the three least visible parties in the system: the PSU, the Alliance Républicaine, and the Républicains Indépendants. In all of these cases, as we have seen, lack of familiarity among nonsympathizers leads to much guesswork as to their locations, producing mean estimates that are drawn in toward the center. Of course, persons identified with these parties do not suffer the same guesswork, and this produces the exceptional case in which adherents actually locate their own parties at positions slightly more extreme than the mass sample as a whole, contrary to the usual symptom of a centrist preference.

17. Since in later chapters we shall depend heavily upon the elite self-locations in left-right terms as well as the mass ones, it might be asked whether they are not "spoiled" or misleading because of their dramatic displacement to the left. On the contrary, these responses are very robust, and if interpreted *relatively*, as correlations are, they maintain their meaningfulness completely.

18. This code had originally been inspired by our earlier efforts to estimate the "levels of conceptualization" of American voters, as reported in Campbell et al. (1960, ch. 10), although it provides a discernibly different measure. The original measure surveyed a much larger volume of qualitative judgments about politics volunteered by respondents, in order to detect indirectly what ideological dimensions or other frames of reference seemed to characterize their thinking about politics. The current measure, instead, directs the respondent to the left-right or liberal-conservative distinction in an explicit way, and probes his understanding of the difference. The first measure is aimed at active use of ideological concepts, while the second one attempts a more lenient assessment of recognition and understanding. For an application of both measures jointly across the mass publics of five Western nations, see Klingemann (1979).

19. These similarities are not surprising. Although France was not included, Klingemann has reported extensive comparative work with the level-of-conceptualization variable in four countries of western Europe and the United States. Although some national differences do emerge—a greater ideological "potential" in Germany and Austria than in the United States or the other European countries, for example—the similarities remain impressive. In particular, there is little support for any conventional impression that European electorates are in general much more ideologically sensitive than is the American electorate (Klingemann, 1979, esp. pp. 245–247).

20. Substantial numbers of those giving "ideological" responses also mentioned these group associations. For purposes of codings such as those displayed in Figure 4-6, however, these respondents are assigned to the top category. More generally, priorities are given to any responses higher in the code scheme.

21. This five-item index will serve as our standard measure of political involvement in this book. In simple additive fashion it combines the following variables: (1) whether or not the respondent voted in the current year; (2) report of long-term vote frequency; (3) political interest; (4) strength of partisanship; and (5) perception of party differences.

22. Such an index is merely the sum of differences in parallel percentage values in the two distributions, or the total amount by which one distribution would have to be changed in order to match the other.

23. We emphasize this point because of the frequency with which investigators examining belief system constraint or attitude stability isolate some portion of a mass sample, such as the college-educated, label it an "elite," and then complain because the

differences predicted in Converse (1964) emerge only faintly if at all (see Achen, 1975, or Judd and Milburn, 1980). In any event, political involvement is a much more effective criterion variable than education, probably for the same reason that our genuine political elites differ much more markedly in political involvement from the most attentive 15 percent of the mass population than they differ from them in educational achievement.

24. It should be kept in mind that the continuity correlation for party identification is calculable only if there is some way of scoring all the parties. The scoring used here is the consensual left-right assignment of the parties, which may seem to introduce a left-right frame of reference "through the back door" to help in evaluating the stability of party identification. This is unlikely to create any serious artifacts, however, since party identification continuity is examined without any contamination from the respondent's own statement of left-right location or, for that matter, from his idiosyncratic views of party location.

25. Case numbers, already sparse for our two crucial test groups, dwindle further for the second tour votes taken alone, because of districts with only one tour of voting.

5. Class, Religion, and Gaullism

1. The literature is vast. See in particular Alford (1963); Lipset and Rokkan (1967); Lijphart (1971); Rose (1974); and Michelat and Simon (1977).

2. In assigning class self-perceptions, we have discarded the relatively small number of rural class references, as well as the "don't knows," the refusals, and the not ascertained. In later references to broad distinctions between perceived middle-class and perceived working-class status, we have combined references to the bourgeoisie and the middle class.

3. The ordering of the 1958 parties that we employ here is based on a socioeconomic dimension, itself the mean of two socioeconomic dimensions on which a panel of experts rated the parties in 1958. The parties were also ordered on a religious dimension in 1958, and we shall rely on that ordering later in this chapter.

4. The 1969 survey included the third wave of our panel study, plus a fresh random sample of voters, which together yielded 1021 cases. See Appendix A.

5. Butler and Stokes employed these questions: "There's quite a bit of talk these days about different social classes. Most people say they belong to either the middle class or to the working class. Do you ever think of yourself as being in one of these classes?" (If thinks of self in these terms) "Which class is that?" (If does not think of self in these terms) "Well, if you had to make a choice, would you call yourself middle class or working class?" Our rendering of this sequence of questions was as follows: "On parle souvent des différentes classes sociales. La plupart des gens disent qu'ils appartiennent soit à la classe moyenne, soit à la classe ouvrière. Vous-même, avez-vous le sentiment d'appartenir à l'une ou l'autre de ces classes?" If yes: "Laquelle?" If no: "Si vous aviez à choisir, diriez-vous que vous appartenez à la classe moyenne ou à la classe ouvrière?"

It will be recalled that in 1967 we ascertained the respondents' subjective class simply by asking them which social class they belonged to and assigning the array of responses either to the bourgeoisie, the middle class, or the working class. By far the largest number of responses were precisely "working class" and "middle class," but we nevertheless had to assign a variety of other designations to our broad categories. The more constraining question which we asked our respondents in 1969 made it possible for us to test the reliability of our 1967 coding of subjective class in terms of our panel respondents' self-assignment to either the middle class or the working class in 1969. In 1969, 68 percent of the respondents whom we had assigned to the middle class in 1967 told us that they were in the middle class. Among the respondents whom we had classified as working class in 1967, 78 percent replied that they were working class in 1969.

6. A summary of the way in which the categories of occupational status were created for British respondents appears in Kahan, Butler, and Stokes (1966). We are grateful to those authors for making their complete code for occupational status available to us so that we could undertake an equivalent coding of our own occupation data.

7. We have substituted "middle class" and "working class" for Alford's use of "nonmanual occupations" and "manual occupations" respectively.

8. The lower managerial group is the least populated of the French occupational groups (Weighted $N = 25.2$), but we find a similar leftist bulge among the same category for 1967, for which the number of cases is more than twice as large.

9. Too much should not be made of the absolute proportions, as the survey question involved a forced choice among several alternatives; but the relative proportions are significant.

10. See Q.98 and Q.98bis of the 1967 questionnaire, in Appendix D.

11. See Q.28 of the 1967 questionnaire.

12. The respondents were asked to state their degree of agreement or disagreement, in Likert-scale format, with the following two statements: "L'état doit subventionner les écoles libres" (The government should subsidize parochial schools); and "Le danger clérical existe toujours" (The danger of clericalism always exists).

13. The 1967 question elicited the degree of agreement or disagreement with the statement, "L'état doit aider les écoles libres" (The government should help parochial schools).

14. If correct, the slight trend that appears in Table 5–4 would support McHale (1969, p. 311) in his assertion that "the religious cleavage is still a factor in French electoral politics, although its importance has declined somewhat under the Fifth Republic."

15. This is true not only when one groups people by occupational background on the basis of a simple division between nonmanual and manual occupations (as in Figure 5–3), but also when one groups them into the Butler and Stokes (1969) categories of grades I–III and IV–VI, thereby taking into account that a majority of the people from lower nonmanual occupational backgrounds (Grade IV) perceive themselves as belonging to the working class. It is also true when one dichotomizes on the basis of a simple distinction between subjective middle class and subjective working class.

16. For a brief summary of the central theories, see Rae and Taylor (1970, pp. 12–14, 85–90).

17. The first group consists of Catholics who attend church once a week or more, or who often attend church; the second consists of Catholics who sometimes attend church or rarely attend church; and the third consists of Catholics who never attend church and of persons without any religion.

18. It is well known that women outnumber men among the more devout churchgoers, and that men outnumber women among the people who are indifferent to religion or religious practice in France. But that gender difference in popular attitudes toward religion in no way affects the strength of the relationship between religion and political preferences within sex groups. There is virtually no difference between men and women in the strength of the relationship between religion and religious practice and party identification.

19. The relevant literature is voluminous. We cite here only Siegfried (1913) and Goguel (1981, 1983a, 1983b).

20. The regional map of France that appears in this chapter, whose regions are the same as those shown in Table 5-5, was not prepared in the manner described, for it includes all 467 continental electoral districts and not merely the 86 districts of our sample. In preparing the map, we ascertained the proportions of the vote cast for François Mitterrand at the first ballot of the 1965 presidential election in each of the nine sample regions we created on the basis of our left-right measures, and then we assigned the districts

outside our sample to the regions on the basis of similarity in the proportions of votes cast for Mitterrand. The vote for Mitterrand, who was backed by all the leftist parties in 1965, when the configuration of parties had been essentially the same as it was in 1967, is as good an aggregate measure of leftist support as any. In most cases we aggregated the presidential vote to the level of the *département*, but although each region is a contiguous area, department boundaries were not respected in every case.

21. For the purposes of this analysis and others appearing later in this chapter, we have created an overall indicator of socioeconomic status by combining our measures of subjective class and household occupational status with measures of education and family income. Also, we are now employing our most powerful indicator of religious attitudes, consisting of a clerical-anticlerical scale based on both our measure of religion and frequency of church attendance and our measure of affect toward the clergy as registered on a standard "thermometer" scale.

22. The proportion in each case is based on the sum of the total variance accounted for by each of the two variables in question. The convention is slightly flawed in that the common variance is counted twice; but that discrepancy is preferable to excluding the common variance entirely, which would be the result if we summed the partial variance contributed by each of the two variables. Inasmuch as we are trying to determine how the two variables "fit" together within each region, it is reasonable to take into account not only their relative strengths but also their interaction with each other. The correlation between clericalism and average socioeconomic status is nowhere above $r = .33$; therefore, little distortion results from counting the common variance twice in computing our denominators, while there is some gain in allowing the variation in that correlation from region to region to have some marginal effect on our results.

23. The region which is most "out of order" in its ranking in Figure 5-5 compared with its ranking in Table 5-5 is the Bassin Parisien, where the relative importance of clericalism in left-right voting is rather less than would be expected of one of our most clerical and rightist regions. One possible explanation for its anomalous ranking is that it has less geographical integrity than any of the other eight political regions we constructed, as a glance at the map in this chapter will show. It forms a ring encircling the Paris region, and Paris must surely operate as a barrier to whatever intraregional communications contribute toward giving regions their distinctive political outlooks. In short, the Bassin Parisien may not be a political region at all.

24. Both the *Sondages* (1963, no. 3) and Michelat (1965) scales of Gaullism are slightly contaminated for association with parties because they include attachment to the Gaullist UNR as a scale item, but the effect is slight since the scales contain six and nine items respectively.

25. We shall return to the events of May-June 1968 in Chapter 14, where the scene is presented from the side of the mass electorate, and again in Chapter 15, which analyzes the reactions of the parliamentary elite to those events.

26. Our pro-Gaullist–anti-Gaullist dimensions for 1967 and 1968 are analogous to our clericalism-anticlericalism measure. While the latter combines religion, frequency of church attendance, and degree of sympathy for the clergy as measured on the thermometer scale, the former combines a five-point scale of satisfaction with de Gaulle and degree of sympathy for de Gaulle as registered on the same thermometer scale. For convenience we shall refer to the axis as Gaullism, but the reader should bear in mind that this expresses the full range of attitudes toward de Gaulle, negative as well as positive.

6. *The Candidates*

1. For details concerning the elite sample, see Appendix B.
2. A small fraction of those had served as senators.

3. A similar distinction between incumbents and former deputies, regardless of length of parliamentary service, will appear in Chapter 8, relating to candidate visibility.

4. Cayrol, Parodi, and Ysmal (1973) report that more than one-half of the deputies elected in 1968 had a relative who had held a political office of some kind.

5. De Gaulle was reported to have said, after looking over the list of the some 200 UNR deputies elected in 1958, that he had found 48 on whom he could count, come what might (Jean Ferniot, 1958). In fact, only some 30 metropolitan deputies were to leave the party between 1958 and 1962 (Charlot, 1967, p. 196).

6. The separate partisan rates were 100 percent for the PSU candidates, 95 percent for the Communist candidates, and 82 percent for the Federation candidates. Cayrol, Parodi, and Ysmal (1973) report that early political socialization was more evident among the leftist deputies elected in 1968 than among the others.

7. Fathers' parties mentioned that still existed in 1967 and for which we obtained the candidates' perceptions of their location on the left-right dimension were assigned the mean score attributed to them by the candidates as a group; thus the Communist party was assigned a score of 6, the Socialist party was given a score of 23, the Radical party was assigned a score of 34, and so forth. Tendencies that were mentioned were assigned their scores on our standard left-right scale; the left was counted as 20, the center 50, and the like. Parties mentioned for which we had no left-right locations as perceived by the candidates were assigned locations chosen on the basis of our best estimate of their probable placement. Thus "whites" were assigned 80; "nationalists," royalists, and Bonapartists were assigned 90; and Vichyites and fascists were assigned 99, to give some illustrations. This scoring of miscellaneous groups is, of course, arbitrary; but it is not unreasonable and, in any event, applies to comparatively few references.

8. Left-right locations were assigned to the parties or tendencies of the mass electorate's fathers by the same method employed for the candidates, except that in this case the scores assigned to existing parties were based on the mean locations attributed to them by the mass electorate, not by the candidates.

9. On a grouped basis similar to that employed by Deutsch, Lindon, and Weill (1966) and described briefly in Chapter 4 of this book, Cayrol, Parodi, and Ysmal (1973, table 12, p. 90) cross-tabulate the left-right locations of the French deputies elected in 1968 with the deputies' perceptions of the left-right locations of their fathers. On the basis of these data, reported in a table with six left-right categories for the deputies and seven for their parents, we note that 16 percent of the 289 deputies for whom there were matching data placed their fathers to their left, while almost 40 percent placed them to their right. Somewhat more than 40 percent placed their fathers in the same left-right category in which they placed themselves, not including another 4 percent who did so but who—being of the extreme-left—could not have placed either themselves or their fathers further to the left if they had been of a mind to do so.

10. Two-thirds of the candidates who ran in the Paris region had been raised in the region, if not in the same department.

11. The Assembly elected in 1967 contained a total of 11 women out of a full complement of 487 members (Metropolitan France and Overseas France included).

12. Conversely, we include under "small business" both *artisans,* who differ from *industriels* in that they employ only five or fewer employees, and *commerçants,* who employ fewer than three people. See INSEE (1962, pp. 19 and 21).

13. The occupational classification of the mass sample includes the former occupation of retired heads of households.

14. Under official French coding conventions, members of parliament are classified as *cadres supérieurs,* or top management (see INSEE 1962, p. 27). But we have so classified only those deputies who told us that their occupation was politics, or being a deputy. We also included in that category a handful of candidates who, although not deputies at the

time they were interviewed, had been deputies previously, and who reported that they were retired members of parliament without indicating that they had any other occupation.

15. In Table 6-9 we also report the later occupations of the few respondents who told us that they had had no occupation when they first became politically active.

16. It was not always ascertained unambiguously whether a candidate had been a wage earner or a small independent craftsman; for example, when a candidate indicated only that he had been "an electrician," he could have been either. We imagine that among the Communists the candidates who answered in that fashion had in fact been workers, but we cannot be sure.

17. Eighteen percent of the former workers among the Communist candidates were white collar employees in 1967; only 12 percent were still workers (or retired workers).

18. Eligibility for service in parliament is governed by Ordinance No. 58-998 of October 24, 1958, and its later modifications by Ordinance No. 58-1027 of October 31, 1958, and by Ordinance No. 59-224 of February 4, 1959. Late in 1971, after a Gaullist deputy had been implicated in fraudulent real-estate dealings, parliament extended the list of occupations incompatible with parliamentary service by adding directors or administrators of corporations that raise investment funds from the public or of profit-seeking companies engaged in real-estate promotion or the construction of apartments for sale.

19. These proportions, and others we shall report in this analysis, are based on small case numbers, but we are dealing with a true elite sample and we have confidence in the results.

20. Teachers in the state-run educational system are civil servants in France. The requirement that they take leave while serving in parliament applies to all levels, elementary, secondary, and higher, except that university professors who hold chairs or are directors of research are exempted from the rule.

21. There is obviously a similarity, although not identity, between our notion of the professional politician and Sartori's claim that the professional politician "is a man for whom the alternative to politics is unemployment" (1961, p. 596).

22. The Communist party reminds its deputies of their humble origins (and contributes to the party's treasury) by requiring them to contribute their salaries to the party and, in return, paying them the equivalent of a skilled worker's wages.

7. Policy Attitudes of Mass and Elite

1. In retrospect, we were probably too timid about asking our elite respondents to answer precisely the same items. In subsequent contexts, such as Brazil, we have been bolder, and with considerable success. Nevertheless, the collection of more open-ended material from the elite sample permits a coding along further dimensions than that assessed by the structured questions asked of the mass sample.

2. French political commentators have related issue position scales to left-right locations at least since the early twentieth century. Siegfried (1948) cites several amusing examples, including this item relating to the navy, apparently drawn from a satirical manual for candidates at the election of 1906:

Left:	No boats
Center Left:	Small boats (submarines)
Center:	Average-size boats (destroyers)
Center Right:	Big boats (cruisers)
Right:	Great big boats (battleships)

3. The nonlinear form casts responses to all European integration items as a joint function of both own left-right location and its square root.

4. The main empirical work actually employing a separate "elite" sample, which has frequently been cited as a disconfirmation, was reported by Luttbeg (1968). The "elite" in this case, however, was purely local: persons prominent in politics in two small Oregon cities. Moreover, the data do show differences between this "elite" and the more normal cross-section samples in the two cities which are in the direction predicted and appear to be statistically significant. The only reason the study is cited as a disconfirmation is that Luttbeg felt the differences should be larger. A later publication (Luttbeg, 1971), based on different and in some respects more relevant data, is billed as a confirmation, but this amendment is usually left uncited.

5. We should point out again, as we did originally, that the correlation coefficient is far from an ideal indicator of constraint, since that indicator is an individual construct while the correlation coefficient hinges completely on such collective properties as variance and covariance. Indeed, in some analytic settings where variance is artificially reduced, it would make no sense whatever to use coefficients of association as indicators of constraint, as Barton and Parsons (1977) have explained. We proceed with such coefficients, however, because the alternatives, which are rare, have their own peculiar liabilities, including less ready communication. This use presupposes that the variances on these policy matters arise in a natural setting of political competition when editorial choice leans toward the more controversial issues.

6. In both figures, dashed lines between the mass and elite data points are used to indicate instances in which quite parallel but not identical items were asked. Although the role of labor unions and the distribution of income were discussed with elite respondents, the form of these items differs too much to make comparisons worthwhile. The reader should keep in mind, in contemplating both of these figures, that although the percentages of the electorate partitioned by the involvement cutpoints are as shown at the bottom of these graphs, it remains true that missing data on all items, and particularly the left-right self-locations, occur more frequently among the least involved 28 percent than among the top 15 percent. Thus the parity of case numbers underlying these relationships is greater for top and bottom than may appear.

7. It should be remembered that this is a progression in r (the Pearson product-moment coefficient) and not in r^2. It is obvious that an advance to the square of these expressions would largely ruin our sense of majestic progression.

8. The reader should be assured that neither of the earlier submatrices discussed was characterized by a large negative correlation entry. This appears only in the agenda item submatrix, where negative correlations abound once the items are properly keyed for content.

9. It is important to understand that the class of measurement situations in which responses to form can compete with responses to content, especially among those not too familiar with the content, is probably very large indeed. Other well-recognized instances include mechanical agree-disagree question formats that attract "yea-sayers" and "nay-sayers" who inflate inter-item correlations for reasons that have nothing to do with item content, or attitude constraint as normally construed. It is, of course, imperative to include item reversals in order to detect the intrusion of such artifacts. Indeed, without any diagnostic aids it is quite possible that difference in attitude constraint as a function of content familiarity can be utterly obscured where responses to form can inflate correlations as well. This is true because those unfamiliar with the content, and hence likely to show less true constraint, are also those more likely to respond to item form, so that the empirical patterns are offsetting in a way which is undetectable if reversals are not included.

10. The third factor in the elite case is unintelligible, and the fourth factor appears to involve pro- and anti-Gaullism.

11. We stretched our identity criterion very slightly to include one position issue,

that on aid to church schools. For other position issues the elite sample was asked an open-ended question, and ultimate coding categories differ from those in the mass sample. For the church school item, however, the question was in closed form for both samples, the response categories were the same, and the questions themselves were almost identical.

12. This is not, of course, to insist that all policy attitude formation must follow one or the other of these two routes. In fact, we assume that many policy attitudes are formed without knowledge of what would be appropriate for either type of cue. But it is likely that some attitude formation does in fact proceed along one or the other of these routes; and it is also likely that differences in relative prevalence between the two should show up in differences in the tightness of linkage with either party identification or left-right position.

13. The classic reference here is Robinson (1950). See also Alker (1969).

14. Such a state of affairs is not, however, different from some other realistic models in which the representative knows what he knows about opinion in his district exclusively from direct communication with a few constituents who are, more or less by definition, the politically informed and involved.

15. The rationale and method for this correction are laid out in detail in Chapter 19 and in Appendix C.

16. This value is considerably larger than the .015 cited earlier in this chapter, because that figure was limited to the subset of mass linkage issues for which there were exact matches with elite items and codings. Four of the issue position items excluded from that prior calculation (force de frappe, church schools, union rights, and distribution of wealth) show much stronger links with left-right positions than most of the items included in the calculation. This exclusion does nothing, however, to confound the point made earlier in the mass-elite contrasts, for as Figures 7-1 and 7-2 suggest, if left-right linkages for these items run higher in the mass sample, they advance much higher still for the inexact-match counterparts in the elite sample.

17. This exception is the portion of the linkage issue intercorrelation matrix for the mass respondents involving the agenda or issue importance items which, as we have seen, show correlation magnitudes that are artificially inflated relative to the elite responses.

8. Candidate Visibility

1. Description by party was not counted as a correct identification of a candidate in the absence of the candidate's name. But a correct description of a candidate in the absence of a name was counted as accurate identification if the descriptive category employed was sufficiently precise (e.g., "the mayor of X" as opposed to "someone from X"). We accepted accurate descriptions in lieu of names because of a conversation we had years ago with the late V. O. Key, Jr., who told us he was once asked his Congressman's name and could not recall it, even though he knew almost everything else about him.

2. The index was formed by awarding two points if an accurate name or description of the candidate was given, two further points if the respondent said that he or she had read or heard something about the candidate, and two further points if the exact party or tendency of the candidate was supplied along with an accurate name or description (reduced to *one* further point if only a rough approximation of the candidate's party or tendency was supplied along with the name or description). A score of zero was entered for those candidates running in a respondent's district for whom the respondent failed to supply an accurate name or description; knowledge of the candidate's party without an accurate name or description of the candidate added nothing. The index, therefore, ranged between 0 and 6, with scores of 0, 2, 4, 5, and 6 possible.

3. We must be tentative on this score because of the small number of former deputies in our sample of interviewed candidates who were returned to the Assembly in 1967.

We have only one pure case of the kind, plus two other cases of candidates who were elected to the Assembly in 1962 but gave up their seats shortly after the election to become ministers. Their mean visibility score is virtually identical with that of the victorious incumbents in 1967, however, and it has a comparatively small standard deviation.

4. See note 3 above.

5. For purposes of this analysis, our sample of eighty-six districts was divided into three groups, according to the proportion of the population living in urban areas, on the following bases: least urban, 00–29 percent; middle range, 30–69 percent; most urban, 70–100 percent.

6. It should be pointed out, however, that the candidates from the most urban districts were the most satisfied with the adequacy of the press coverage of their campaigns, while there was almost no difference in the levels of satisfaction reported by the candidates from the other two kinds of districts.

7. Average candidate visibility is the sum of the candidate visibility index scores assigned to each voter (as described in note 2) divided by the number of candidates who ran in the voter's district.

8. Also see Figure 2-4.

9. We should remind the reader that total party visibility is the sum of the separate party visibility scores which are assigned to each voter and which are computed differently from the candidate visibility scores (see Figure 2-4).

10. When the respondents reported their vote at our survey, they were not required to recall their vote unaided; they were shown a list of the candidates who had run in their district, with their party affiliations, and were asked to indicate which candidate they had voted for by designating a letter preceding the candidate's name. This made it possible for the respondent to indicate which candidate he or she had voted for without having to mention the candidate's name, a useful device in interview situations where third persons may be present. See Q.42ter, Q.43, and Q.48, in Appendix D.

11. The small group of people who voted for candidates not affiliated with national parties have been excluded from the calculation.

12. The U.S. surveys were oriented toward learning what proportions of the voters knew *both* the name of the candidate *and* his party and what proportion of the voters knew neither of those items. Accordingly, in the case of respondents who gave incorrect answers, it is not possible to tell from the coded data who supplied an incorrect name and who supplied a correct name but the wrong party. Therefore, it is not possible to build a candidate visibility index for the United States identical to the one we constructed for France. It is possible, however, to determine the proportion of such ambiguous cases, and we shall return to this point later.

13. There was a slight difference in the way in which the "heard or read" part of the candidate visibility battery was included in the French and U.S. questionnaires. In France, respondents were only asked whether they had heard or read about a candidate if they had already named or accurately described the candidate. In the United States, after the respondents were asked the names and parties of the candidates, they were all told the names of the candidates and then asked if they had ever heard or read about them. The only bias that might derive from these different ways of including the "heard or read" component would be an inflation of affirmative answers regarding having heard or read in the United States, due to increased confidence on the part of respondents whose identification of one or more candidates was confirmed by the interviewer.

14. As mentioned earlier, we accepted accurate descriptions of the French candidates, as well as correct names, while only correct names were accepted at the U.S. surveys. That methodological difference does not account for the cross-national difference in visibility levels, however, as only 3 percent of the correct identifications of French candidates were based on descriptions as opposed to names.

15. The lack of stability in French party nomenclature, particularly but not exclusively in the center and on the right, poses problems of equivalence with the simple American system, whose two main parties have borne the same names for more than a century. For France, we accepted as correct (1) all appropriate party labels (such as either UNR or Gaullist, either Federation or Socialist), (2) incorrect party labels provided they were supplemented by appropriate left-right designations, and (3) appropriate left-right designations in the absence of a name. Left-right designations were accepted only where no opposing candidate could also be similarly designated.

Overall, almost 90 percent of the responses we counted as correct party assignments took the form of party labels, with the remainder divided about equally between cases of incorrect party labels accompanied by correct left-right tendencies and correct left-right tendencies only. As usual, there was variation among parties. Among the people who identified Communist candidates and correctly designated their party, 98 percent mentioned a party label; almost 95 percent did so for UNR (Gaullist) candidates; almost 90 percent did so for Federation candidates; and more than 80 percent did so for Democratic Center candidates. Among the partisan groups for which there are substantial cases, the Giscardian Independent Republicans fared poorest in terms of party labels; barely more than half of the relevant respondents assigned them a party label while almost as many relied on left-right designations.

16. The 1978 U.S. Election Study also contains a measure of candidate *recognition*, parallel to the measure of party recognition that we employed. Jacobson (1980) and Mann and Wolfinger (1980) make good use of the recognition measure in studies which are designed to explore candidate evaluation as a determinant of the vote, and which are therefore confined to actual voters, as opposed to our consideration of the entire electorate. Much as we would like to have a measure of candidate recognition for France, along with our measure of candidate recall, we take issue with Mann and Wolfinger's statement that candidate recall is a "faulty measure" (1980, p. 622). It may be inadequate or inappropriate for some purposes, but there is nothing intrinsically "faulty" about it as a measure of political knowledge.

17. The flat results for 1978 may be due to the very low turnout for the congressional elections of that year. So few people bothered to pay any attention to the election that, among those who did, it is likely that the proportion of involved voters was sufficiently large that most of the people who knew something about any of the candidates knew something about most of them, regardless of their location in some conventional hierarchy of prestige.

18. To the extent that Kingdon's (1967) "congratulation-rationalization" effects, whereby winners tend to emphasize their personal roles in their victories while losers tend to assign blame elsewhere for their defeats, are at play here, we would expect some exaggeration in assignment of electoral importance to personal reputation among successful incumbents.

19. We would, of course, be more cautious in our insistence on the importance of party in U.S. congressional elections if we were dealing with data from more recent years, but the reported congressional vote coincided with the voters' party identifications more closely in 1958 than at any other election between 1956 and 1978 (Mann and Wolfinger, 1980, table 1).

20. "Decisive" and "very important" are counted as 3; "quite important" and "somewhat important" count as 2; "not very important" counts as 1; and "not important at all" counts as 0.

21. In Chapter 2 we reported that when one controls for institutional differences there is little difference between French and U.S. voters in their propensity toward constancy in partisan electoral choice.

9. Issues, Parties, and Candidates

1. This does not, of course, exclude the possibility that candidates and parties may base their electoral appeals on left-right imagery, as in the efforts to seek support for "the single candidate of the left" that played such a large role in campaigns for the second ballot during the period under study here.

2. The question relating to party-issue linkage was Q.24; the question concerning candidate-issue linkage was Q.54.

3. In case readers may think that the large proportions of respondents registering "don't know" on these questions result from some technical flaw in the administration of our survey, we should point out that IFOP asked a similar question in national sample surveys conducted in January and February 1967, and that the range of proportions recorded as "ne se prononcent pas" (do not say) was between 31 percent and 49 percent, depending upon the issue. See *Sondages* (1967, no. 3).

4. We include "don't know" as a valid response, but exclude references to "all the parties" or to more than one party. The last two responses will be analyzed separately later in this chapter.

5. See Chapter 2 for a fuller discussion of party visibility.

6. The measure, called the probability of dyadic agreement, is equal to the sum of the squared decimal shares of the electorate choosing each of the parties. This probability is, therefore, $\sum_{i=1}^{n} S_i^2$, where S is the proportion of voters selecting any party as the party linked to the issue. We have borrowed the measure from Rae (1967, pp. 53–58).

7. The measure of clarity for each linkage issue is simply the joint probability that any voter will link an issue with some specific party and that any two voters will associate the same party with that issue. We can consider the extent of party linkage for a given issue as a conditional expression of the first probability, and the consensus score for that issue as the second probability. Our clarity measure for each issue, therefore, is the product of the proportion of voters that associates the issue with an individual party, expressed in decimal form, and the consensus score for that same issue.

8. As in the case of our corresponding analysis of party-issue linkage, we have reduced the set of respondents for this aspect of the analysis of candidate-issue linkage to those people who gave a valid reply (including "don't know") to all seven of the questions concerning candidate-issue linkage. That limits the number of cases to less than 60 percent of the sample, but it ensures that all proportions are drawn from a common base.

9. When the respondents were asked which party they thought had fought hardest for each of the various linkage issues, they were shown a list of ten national parties from which they could choose. When they were asked which candidate they thought had fought hardest for each of the same issues, they were shown a list of the candidates who had run at the first ballot in their districts, along with the candidates' party affiliations. Therefore, respondents who know nothing about the candidates that would enable them to associate them with a given issue, but who did have knowledge about the issue positions of the parties, could have selected candidates as standing for certain issues simply because of their party labels.

There is some indication that this did, in fact, happen. Substantial proportions of people who could not name or describe any candidate who had run in their districts nevertheless linked candidates with issues. The proportions of people in the category that did so ranged from 26 percent to 40 percent, depending upon the issue. It is possible, of course, that seeing the name of a candidate jogged some respondents' memories and that their responses were based on that secondary recollection. As Chapter 2 explained, significant numbers of people who did not spontaneously recall the names of certain parties claimed to recognize them after they had been reminded of them, and the same phenomenon could undoubtedly have occurred with regard to candidates. But we do not find so many people linking issues with parties among those who did not spontaneously recall the name of any party that ran in their districts as we find people linking issues with candidates among those who did not recall the name of any candidate who ran in their districts. The proportions of people whose memories might have been jogged into associating issues with parties ranged from only 14 to 27 percent, depending on the issue, and were uniformly lower, for every linkage issue, than the corresponding proportions of people whose memories might have been jogged into associating issues with candidates. It would appear, therefore, that for some of the people for whom all of the candidates running in their districts were invisible before they were shown a list of the candidates and their parties, the crucial reminder was not the name of the candidate but the candidate's party label, and that on the basis of the party label they linked particular issues with candidates.

We could have prevented our respondents from making such a transference by showing them a list containing only the names of the candidates who had run in their districts, without any indication of the parties with which those candidates were affiliated. That would have permitted us to measure the extent of pure candidate-issue linkage, uncontaminated by any admixture of party-issue linkage. But that would also have created an artificial situation which would have cast doubt upon the utility of our measure. Except in the comparatively few cases where candidates deliberately eschew any party label, the candidates are presented to the voters in conjunction with their partisan affiliation. The ballot that the voter casts at the decisive moment of electoral choice contains, in almost every case, both the name of the candidate and the name of that candidate's party. When candidates are more visible to the voters than their parties, it is not because the voters do not have the opportunity to link the candidates with parties. That linkage is made regularly by the press and other elements of the campaign media, and it is made on the very ballot form that the voters cast. If we had separated the candidates' names from their parties when we asked our respondents which candidate they thought had fought hardest to achieve various policy goals, we would have obtained a measure of candidate-issue linkage that would not have been directly relevant to the situation in which French voters actually find themselves. By posing our candidate-issue linkage questions in the form that we chose, we came closer to matching the actual situation of the voter when casting a ballot. Our measure of candidate-issue linkage, therefore, produces more reliable estimates of the extent to which the voters associate the candidates with various issue positions than the alternative, exclusive candidate-issue linkage measure would have done.

10. We have made that estimate by assuming that the proportions of people linking issues with candidates, even though all the candidates running in their districts were invisible to them, should be no larger than the proportions of people linking issues with parties even though all the parties running in their districts were invisible to them. Overall, the figure works out to about 2 percent of the entire electorate.

11. This measure is based on the number of times respondents who answered all seven candidate-issue linkage questions and all seven party-issue linkage questions replied, "Don't know." See note 8 above.

12. The correlation between candidate-issue linkage and political involvement is almost identical with that between party-issue linkage and political involvement. A table relating level of political involvement to the number of policy domains with which the voters linked candidates would strikingly resemble Table 9-1.

13. This fraction of the electorate, of course, contains the most abstainers; so the probabilities of misinterpreting the messages sent by the electorate to the parliamentary elite at election time are reduced in that sense.

14. Remember that when our respondents were asked which party they thought had fought hardest for each policy, they were shown a list of ten national parties from which

they could choose, and that when they were asked which candidate had fought hardest to achieve each policy, they were shown a list of the candidates who had run in their districts. Not every national party ran a candidate in every district, of course, so that any respondent who cited a party in association with an issue when that party had not run a candidate in the respondent's district could not be consistent in his or her choice of party and candidate. All such respondents have been excluded from the calculation of consistency rates reported in this chapter, as have the voters who could not possibly be consistent because they linked a given issue with a candidate who did not belong to a national party.

15. The data relating to party-issue linkage also appear in Table 9-4.

16. The exceptions are defense of the secular schools, which proportionately as many voters among the least involved as among the medium-involved associate with more than one candidate (although proportionately more than twice as many among the most involved do so), and an independent foreign policy, for which no coherent pattern exists.

17. In determining consistency, all Federation candidates and parties were regarded as equivalent, and so were all Democratic Center candidates and parties. For example, a voter who linked an issue with a Federation-SFIO candidate and with the Radical party was counted as consistent. Similarly, a voter who linked an issue with a Democratic Center candidate and with the MRP as a party was also counted as consistent. On the contrary, cross-linkage of an issue with a UNR candidate and with the Independent Republican party, or the reverse, was not counted as consistent. This practice is in line with the rules we have followed for determining consensus over party-policy linkages and which we shall follow in connection with consensus over candidate-policy linkages.

18. More technically, clarity is the joint probability that a voter will associate an issue with an individual candidate (or party) and that any two voters who have done so will associate the issue with the same candidate (or party).

19. The filter was Q.31, which asked, "On the whole, what do you consider most important when you vote: the candidate in your district, the party itself, or the party's leader?" That question was a reliable indicator of various forms of expression of attachment to political parties (see Chapter 3). It is also a valid, if not particularly powerful, indicator of electoral orientations. When subdivided according to replies to the question, putative party-oriented voters cited parties more frequently when they reported how they had voted than the putative candidate-oriented voters did, while candidate-oriented voters cited candidates more frequently than the party-oriented voters did. (Both groups of voters, however, cited parties more frequently than candidates when describing how they voted.) Moreover, more party-oriented voters than candidate-oriented voters, proportionately, could spontaneously recall the party for which they had voted, but not the candidate; while a larger proportion of candidate-oriented voters than of party-oriented voters could recall the candidate for whom they had voted but not the party.

10. The First-Ballot Vote

1. We do not include here either Rosenthal and Sen (1977), whose model of French legislative voting employs aggregate data, or the growing body of interesting work within the political economy domain (Rosa and Amson, 1976; Lewis-Beck, 1980, 1983; Hibbs and Vasilatos, 1981; and Lafay, 1981).

2. In combining groups, where party identification was missing we substituted the mean left-right party identification score for all respondents who had a true party identification; where own left-right locations were missing, we substituted a score of 50.

3. Belsley, Kuh, and Welsch (1980, pp. 112–113) outline a procedure for diagnosing degrading collinearity that can be implemented by use of the TROLL program for ordinary least squares (Center for Computational Research in Economics and Manage-

ment Science, Alfred P. Sloan School of Management, Massachusetts Institute of Technology, June 1982). This program, which computes and prints the regression diagnostics (condition indexes and variance-decomposition proportions), was run for Group 1, Groups 1 and 2 combined, and Groups 1 through 4 combined. In no case did the conditions for degrading collinearity appear. We are grateful to Colin K. Loftin for calling this program to our attention, and to Brian L. Wiersema for his invaluable assistance in running it.

4. See note 2.

5. There is some question whether, in comparing our results with those of Fiorina (1981), we should refer to our values for the entire body of 1967 voters or to some subset of them, say Groups 1 and 2 combined, which embrace about two-thirds of the active 1967 electorate. Fiorina (1981, pp. 157 and 161) reports the number of cases on which each of his several analyses rests, and he indicates that he minimized the amount of missing data by counting instances of "no opinion" or "don't know" as valid neutral scores on certain variables, but he does not report the proportion of the actual voters that is covered by each application of his model. Our independent estimates of those proportions, based on the U.S. Election Panel studies for 1956, 1958, and 1960, and for 1972, 1974, and 1976, which Fiorina employed, point to an average coverage of somewhat more than 80 percent of the persons who voted for congressional candidates. If this estimate is accurate, it would appear that when comparing our results with those of Fiorina, there is at least as good reason to employ the figures for our Group 1, or for Groups 1 and 2 combined, which include more than two-thirds of the voters, as those for Groups 1 through 4 inclusive, which embrace virtually the entire body of voters. Both Groups 1 and 2 contain the crucial party identification variable, and since together they include almost as large a proportion of the actual voters as does Fiorina's model, it is not illegitimate to consider only those two groups when assessing the relative power of our long-term model. For Groups 1 and 2 combined, the applicable indicators account for some two-thirds of the variance in the left-right vote.

6. We rely on from two to four variables; Fiorina employs from seven to fifteen, with a mean of eleven.

7. Lindon and Weill (1974) neither report case numbers nor indicate how they handled missing data.

8. We determined "correctness" by running a scatter plot including the full range of predicted values and the actual left-right vote for the entire population of Groups 1 through 4 inclusive, and then establishing cut-off points on the scale of predicted values that optimized correctness in prediction.

The ranges of values considered correct for each range of left-right voting scores (and the major parties included in the latter) are as follows:

Range of predicted values	Number of cases	Scores on dependent variable	Major parties included
11.64 – 25.11	199.4 (14.6%)	12	Communist party (PCF)
25.12 – 47.31	534.9 (39.3%)	26 – 37	Federation (FGDS)
47.32 – 57.84	228.9 (16.8%)	44 – 60	Democratic Center (CD)
57.85 – 71.11	399.2 (29.3%)	63 – 74	UNR (Gaullists); Independent Republicans (Giscardians)

9. There is some room for ambiguity in our predictions where more than one party has the same left-right vote score (as in the case of the Federation and the PSU), but such occurrences are infrequent.

10. The Federation of 1967 no longer existed in 1973, when Lindon and Weill

(1974) tested their model, and the Democratic Center had been succeeded by the Mouvement Réformateur.

11. It is true that partisanship can affect attitudes toward de Gaulle (Converse and Dupeux, 1966), and also, probably, sentiments of left-right location. But where that occurs, party identification is likely to be strong enough to affect the partisan vote as well, and it is precisely the existence of such powerful attachments in France that we are putting into question.

12. This data set was chosen because 1980 was the first presidential election year when the U.S. National Election Study was based on a congressional district sample frame. A presidential year is more desirable than an off-year for testing models of congressional voting (at least for our purposes), because information flow relative to congressional candidates is much higher in presidential years than in off-years, as we showed in Chapter 8.

13. The scores are 0 for Strong Democrat; 1 for Weak Democrat; 2 for Independent-Democrat; 3 for Independent; 4 for Independent-Republican; 5 for Weak Republican; and 6 for Strong Republican.

14. We ran the same tests for collinearity on the U.S. data as we ran on the French data, with similarly negative results.

15. Across five regressions on the dichotomized 1967 vote, the average multiple R^2 is .639 and the average standardized beta for party identification is .563, compared with mean values of .669 and .620, respectively, for five regressions on the complete scale of 1967 votes. No beta for party identification fell below its counterpart in the "matching" U.S. analysis.

16. Actually, the categories of Democratic and Republican leaners regularly included in the standard U.S. summary measure of party identification represent a form of residual partisanship. But taken in that sense, residual partisanship is normally regarded as a long-term force in the United States.

17. Party sympathy scores, as measured by a "feelings thermometer," are less stable than left-right party identifications. For our 1967–1968 panel of respondents, the zero-order correlation for party identification is $r = .83$, compared with an average of $r = .65$ across sympathy scores for six political objects among people with a party identification, and with $r = .48$ among persons without a party identification. The six objects included de Gaulle, Mitterrand, Giscard d'Estaing, Pompidou, the French Communist party, and the Gaullist UNR-UDR. The mean correlations for the two purely partisan objects are $r = .67$ and $r = .39$ for voters with and without a party identification, respectively.

18. Because attitudes toward European integration have a curvilinear relationship with left-right locations, scale scores on that dimension were squared (see Chapter 7).

19. Party sympathy was measured by using the "feelings thermometer." Respondents were shown a vertical scale with nine graduated markings ranging from 0 to 100; each mark was labeled with a term designating an appropriate degree of sympathy or hostility (see Appendix D for Q.28 of the 1967 questionnaire). The respondents were read a list of political objects, including the names of the main political parties, and they were asked to indicate what grade on the scale they would give to each object. They were told by the interviewers that a grade of 100 meant that they had a lot of sympathy for the group, that 0 meant they did not like it at all, and that a grade of 50 meant either that they were neither for nor against it or that they did not know much about it. The scores given by each voter to the various parties reflect that voter's order of preference among them at the moment. The individual thermometer scores can, of course, be used to establish the mean affect of various groups of voters for each particular party. Such sympathy scores were not obtained for every party, but measures of affect were ascertained in exactly the same fashion for several leaders of parties for which we did not obtain similar measures, and sympathy for the leaders was substituted—as appropriate—for sympathy for their parties.

Accordingly, the rightist "parties" included in the analysis were the Gaullist UNR, Giscard d'Estaing (substituting for the Independent Republicans), and Tixier-Vignancour (substituting for the Alliance Républicaine). For the left the procedure was more complicated but rested on the same principles. Direct sympathy scores were applied for the Communist party and the PSU. We have no Convention (CIR) or Federation sympathy scores, but we do have such scores for the Socialist party (SFIO), the Radical party, and François Mitterrand. When the Federation candidate was a Socialist (or a Radical), we first searched for a Socialist party (or Radical party) sympathy score, but if there was none, we used the score for Mitterrand (if available). For straight Federation candidates or Federation candidates from the Convention, we used the sympathy score for Mitterrand.

11. The Second Ballot: Electoral Participation

1. The main difference between the two-ballot systems of the Third Republic and the Fifth Republic is that anyone could run at the second ballot during the Third Republic, whether or not he had been a candidate in the same district at the first ballot. Under the Fifth Republic, no one may run at the second ballot if he has not received a certain minimum proportion of the votes at the first ballot in the same district. The two-ballot system is also used in France for the election of municipal councillors, departmental councillors (conseillers généraux), most senators, and the President of the Republic.

2. It should be repeated that because our universe was restricted to continental France, it excluded Corsica, where two of the three seats were also won at the first ballot in 1967. Among our sample of 86 districts, 10 seats were won at the first ballot in 1967.

3. In 1958 and 1962, the required minimum was 5 percent of the votes cast at the first ballot. In 1967, 1968, and 1973, the qualifying minimum was 10 percent of the registered voters in the district. In 1976 the threshold was raised to 12.5 percent of the registered voters.

4. Two other studies of the 1967 French elections (Mothe, 1967; Lancelot and Weill, 1970) produce estimates of second-ballot abstention rates among first-ballot voters in a position to repeat their votes that are quite different from our own estimate of a base rate of 6 percent, almost surely because of methodological differences.

5. It might be countered that reports of null ballots do not necessarily represent protest votes; they might simply conceal abstentions or failure to recall for which party the respondent had voted. There is good reason, however, to believe that they do represent annoyance at the limited choice of candidates presented at the second ballot. All the reports of spoiled second ballots from our respondents came from people who had voted at the first ballot but who were unable to repeat their vote at the second ballot. If reports of spoiled ballots were, to a considerable extent, merely evasive replies, we would expect to find them randomly distributed among all classes of voters, instead of being concentrated in the category of voters with the most obvious motivation to spoil their ballots.

6. Party sympathy was measured on the thermometer scale as described in Chapter 10, note 19, including the substitution of sympathy scores for certain party leaders in the absence of direct sympathy scores for the parties themselves.

7. The partition was based on replies to a question, asked of second-ballot abstainers, concerning why they had not voted. About one-third of the voters who could not repeat their first-ballot choice at the second ballot replied that they had abstained because there was no suitable candidate running at the second ballot. These persons were classified as deliberate abstainers. All the other abstainers, most of whom claimed that some obstacle had prevented them from going to the polls, were classified as random abstainers. A third kind of abstainer—the chronic abstainer who fails to vote at either the first or second ballot—is not included in our analysis because we are considering only people who voted at the first ballot.

8. It would be more satisfying if the spoilers liked the best available parties even less than the deliberate abstainers did. It takes more effort to spoil a ballot than to abstain, and it would be reasonable to expect the spoilers to be more hostile to the available choices than the abstainers are. On our measures, however, the opposite is the case.

9. We excluded the main outlier from the calculation of the mean; an average of 38.4 points separates the mean degree of sympathy Alliance Républicaine identifiers showed for Tixier-Vignancour as compared with their next preferred political object, the Radical party, which they actually disfavored.

10. When we generate the mean scores on the left-right variables referred to in Table 11-2 for the deliberate abstainers and the random abstainers separately, we do find support for the notion that perceived left-right distances account for the abstention of the deliberate abstainers. We are down to an N of 7 in this subgroup, however, and we cannot generalize from such a limited finding when the larger group of ballot spoilers does not also appear to be acting on the basis of left-right perceptions.

11. We thought it possible that the left-right distances analysis departed from the expected results because of the inclusion of the marais, those people who classify themselves at 50 on the left-right scale, but who have so little interest in politics that virtually no political meaning is associated with their self-classification. Accordingly, we replicated Table 11-2 excluding the marais, but the results were basically unchanged. On the marais, see Chapter 4 and Deutsch, Lindon, and Weill (1960).

12. The correlations are literally negative: the smaller the left-right distance between the voter and the party, the greater the voter's sympathy for the party.

13. Because we do not have direct sympathy scores for the Federation, the Independent Republicans, or the Democratic Center, we have substituted the sympathy scores for Mitterrand, Giscard d'Estaing, and Lecanuet. We do not believe that such a resort to "functional equivalents" is a serious source of error. The sympathy scores, for which we employ mixed objects, give us the better results, and the left-right distances, for which we have uniform measures, create the puzzle to be solved. See note 6.

14. There is some irony here, as the left-right locations that Rosenthal and Sen assign to the various French parties derive from our own 1967 survey. Rosenthal and Sen base their analysis on aggregate electoral data. In order to test spatial models, they require empirically based single-dimensional locations that they can assign to the various parties and their voters. The party preference data they employ are based on estimates we produced by a Coombsian unfolding analysis of 1958 French survey data (Converse, 1966). The partisan left-right locations they employ are based on the mean perceptions of the location of the French parties on the left-right dimension as reported by our 1967 mass sample. Therefore, our findings concerning French electoral participation at the second ballot are in accord with those of Rosenthal and Sen when both they and we base our analyses on partisan preferences, even though they employ 1958 data derived in one fashion and we employ 1967 data derived in another way; and our findings diverge from theirs when both they and we not only base our analyses on the left-right locations of the parties but also employ, to a considerable extent, the same set of empirical data!

15. The phrase appears regularly. This particular citation is from Fauvet (1973).

16. Nor do they vary intelligibly when we repeat the analysis, confining the abstainers to those who abstained deliberately.

17. We are unable to make a proper test of the effects on participation of the number of second-ballot candidates for the set of voters who could not repeat their first-ballot choices, because of small case numbers for voters in districts where there were more than two candidates at the second ballot, as opposed to districts where there were only two candidates.

18. In 1958, 10 percent of the runners-up did not also run at the second ballot; in 1962 and 1967 the proportion was 12 percent; and in 1968 it was 8 percent. The propor-

tion dropped sharply in 1968 because the Gaullists won many seats at the first ballot in that year in districts where a second ballot is usually necessary and where the runner-up is usually a rightist or centrist who drops out at the second ballot. In 1958 and 1962 the front-runner dropped out in one district.

19. Rosenthal and Sen wrote before the elections of 1973, but everything that has been said here about the elections of 1967 and 1968 also applies to those of 1973, 1978, and 1981. It should be added that because the legislative elections from 1967 to 1978 were characterized by second-ballot competition between two big electoral blocs, there was little variation across those elections in the number of candidates who ran in each district where there was a second ballot. The mean number of candidates at the second ballot was 3.1 in 1958 and 2.4 in 1962. For the elections of 1967 and 1968 it was 2.2, and for those of 1973 it was 2.1. At the election of 1978 there were only two candidates in all but one of the districts where there was a second ballot, and in 1981 there were straight fights in all of them.

12. The Second Ballot: The Flow of the Vote

1. In Table 12-1 and in the analysis that follows, Federation and PSU candidates are grouped together, and centrists include all Democratic Center candidates, center-left candidates, and independent Socialists. Gaullists include all candidates endorsed by the Comité d'Action pour la Ve République, whether UNR, Independent Republican, or of another specific partisan background. The right includes Alliance Républicaine candidates, dissident Gaullists, and conservatives not otherwise assigned. The category "Other" includes a few candidates who generally have center-right attributes, but whose exact partisan location could not be determined.

2. Case numbers are pitifully small for districts where there was no left-wing candidate at the second ballot (Types G and H), but our estimates suggest that in those districts the Communists' abstentions and ballot-spoiling exceeded the non-Communist leftists', while non-Communist leftists were much more likely than Communist supporters to vote for a non-Gaullist party in the absence of a leftist candidate. This suggests that although the Communist vote at the second ballot was essentially pro-leftist, rather than merely anti-Gaullist, some non-Communist leftists were motivated at least as much by anti-Gaullist sentiments as by pro-leftist views.

3. The results are basically unchanged if we group the few cases of "Other" voters included in Table 12-1 with the centrists, whom they tend to resemble.

4. Some of the findings of this survey were reproduced in Duhamel (1968).

5. Some of the findings of this article were reported in Duhamel (1967).

6. There are some differences in the composition of the categories used in the three sets of estimates that are compared in Table 12-4. Both IFOP and we ourselves combine Federation and PSU voters in a single category, while Lancelot and Weill refer only to the "non-Communist left," which may be a somewhat more inclusive grouping. IFOP uses the Democratic Center as a separate category, whereas we enlarge it slightly into the "center" (as described in note 1), and Lancelot and Weill enlarge it still further into a category they label the "non-Gaullist right." The latter difference might produce some distortion in the comparison of the various estimates.

A potentially more serious difference between the categories to be compared concerns the handling of abstentions and spoiled ballots. We distinguish between abstentions and spoiled ballots; Lancelot and Weill combine the two into a single category; and IFOP makes no mention of spoiled ballots but refers only to abstentions. Yet it is with respect to abstentions and spoiled ballots that some of the largest differences between the various estimates occur. Our estimates of abstentions and spoiled ballots are higher than those of either IFOP or Lancelot and Weill. This, of course, is not particularly surprising.

We mentioned in Chapter 11 that our estimates of the proportion of abstentions among people who could repeat their first-ballot partisan choice at the second ballot were generally higher than those made by IFOP and by Lancelot and Weill for the same classes of voters. There is no reason why we should not also expect our estimates of nonparticipation to be higher than theirs among voters who could *not* repeat their first-ballot choice at the second ballot.

7. Clericalism and Gaullism are the compound measures described in Chapter 5.

8. In view of the weakness of social class as a predictor of the vote, as reported in Chapter 5, we did not expect it to register strongly in the context of the second ballot. It does not do so, at least in the conventionally expected direction. Non-Communist leftist voters who supported the Communists at the second ballot came from higher-status occupational backgrounds than did those who voted for the Gaullists, and those who voted for the Communists were more likely to regard themselves as middle-class (as compared to working-class) than those who supported the Gaullists.

9. This type of non-Communist leftist voter also comes from a higher-status occupational background than the other two types and is more likely to regard himself or herself as middle-class than as working-class.

10. The difference between an *r* of .36 and one of .29 might appear trivial, but since the proper comparison is actually between those two values squared, the former is 50 percent larger than the latter. Multiple regression with a dichotomous dependent variable such as ours (voted leftmost or rightmost) is inappropriate if the distribution of that variable is badly skewed, but in this case the mean is .65, which is within acceptable limits.

11. See 1967 candidate questionnaire, Q.23 and Q.23B, in Appendix D.

12. See 1967 candidate questionnaire, Q.15 and Q.18, in Appendix D.

13. In some cases we converted verbal statements into proportions on an arbitrary but reasonable and uniform basis; for example, we consistently interpreted "very few" to mean 5 percent.

14. It is unlikely that the candidates' estimates were influenced by the results of the IFOP survey conducted between the two ballots, to which we referred earlier in this chapter (see Table 12-4). The basic publication containing the IFOP data did not appear until after almost all the candidates in our sample had been interviewed, although the data may have appeared earlier in the press. In any case, although sometimes the candidates' estimates of the flow of the vote are closer to the IFOP estimates than to our sample estimates, sometimes they diverge more widely from the IFOP estimates than they do from our own. Moreover, it is clear from the completed interview schedules that the candidates considered the matter on the district level, rather than on the national level.

15. We have no empirical evidence of Gaullist refusal to vote for traditional rightists because our sample did not contain a district where a rightist ran at the second ballot but a Gaullist did not.

13. The Second Ballot: Candidate Behavior and Electoral Response

1. For the election of 1958 and 1962, the threshold was 5 percent of the votes cast in the candidate's district. For the elections of 1967, 1968, and 1973, it was 10 percent of the registered voters in the candidate's district. Prior to the election of 1978, the required minimum was raised still further to 12.5 percent of the registered voters in the candidate's district.

2. Remember that our sample of candidates underrepresents those who were eliminated from the second ballot because we removed candidates who received less than 5 percent of the valid ballots in their respective districts. Inasmuch as most of those were

obscure candidates without major party affiliation, it may be that an even larger proportion of them than of our sample of eliminated candidates did not help another candidate between the ballots. Nevertheless, a rough estimate of their probable behavior, based on a comparison by party label with the known behavior of candidates with the same party labels in our sample, suggests that our sample estimate is not far off the mark for the entire relevant population.

3. Second-ballot support for Gaullists by Giscardians, and vice versa, was excluded by the fact that these two groups did not oppose each other at the first ballot.

4. This procedure also enabled us to confirm, to a certain extent, the reports of behavior by, or in relation to, candidates who were not interviewed and who could not, therefore, give us their own accounts. Because of our deliberate undersampling of Communist candidates, they represent a disproportionately large number of uninterviewed candidates; but both because of the broad net we cast in this series of questions and for other reasons that will become clear later in this chapter, we are satisfied that the accounts we received relating to uninterviewed Communist candidates would not have been contradicted by them in any significant way.

5. After all, the difference between a désistement and frank support by an eliminated candidate for another candidate is simply a matter of the proportion of votes won by the drop-out candidate. Even privileged observers may not recall whether a drop-out candidate was in one category or the other.

6. For this analysis, we have excluded Federation candidates in districts where there was no second ballot or where there was no leftist candidate at the second ballot.

7. The Communist party even withdrew its candidates in 13 of the metropolitan districts where they ran ahead of the Federation at the first ballot, but where they believed a Communist candidate had little or no chance of winning at the second ballot, though a non-Communist might do so. Several of the beneficiaries of this Communist largesse were close collaborators of François Mitterrand (Cayrol, 1971, pp. 246–247). The strategy was successful, with the left winning 10 of the 13 seats, for a net gain of 9. Some of the drop-out Federation candidates in our sample expressed their regret that they had not been recipients of such "gifts."

8. These reports could not be directly confirmed because the Communist candidates in the same districts were not interviewed.

9. We do not have a measure of attitudes toward General de Gaulle (or toward the clergy) for our candidate sample that we could use for direct comparison with the mass sample.

10. Real support could pertain to only one party; real nonsupport could pertain to as many as two parties. Up to two mentions of hypothetical support and up to three mentions of hypothetical nonsupport were coded. These limits were set empirically.

11. This scoring system meant that our few minor party and nonparty candidates, for whom no relevant thermometer or left-right scores were available, were excluded from the analysis. For technical reasons we also excluded the few stray cases in which the Alliance Républicaine was the object party.

12. Table 13-3 does not include abstentions at the second ballot. For technical reasons, only first-ballot voters who also voted at the second ballot were asked whether their first-ballot choices had endorsed or been endorsed by another candidate; so we do not know whether or how the two groups of voters considered in Table 13-3 divided with regard to abstentions at the second ballot. There is no reason to expect skewing in either one direction or the other, however. It is possible that random abstentions among the group of "aware" voters would be augmented by those of people who did not like the recommendation their first-choice candidate made, but the "unaware" group, which we can expect to contain a larger share of uninvolved voters than the other group, would also be likely to produce a larger proportion of abstentions.

13. Only votes for candidates and spoiled ballots are included; abstentions are excluded. See note 12 above.

14. Revolt and Reaction: The Upheaval of May 1968 and the June Elections

1. André Malraux (1971) reported that in December 1969 de Gaulle had told him, "In May, everything escaped me. I no longer had a grip on my own government. Certainly, that changed when I was able to appeal to the country, when I said: 'I am dissolving the Chamber.' "

2. In a useful analysis, Bénéton and Touchard (1970) reported that more than 120 books on the May crisis had been published in France, not to mention special issues of journals and journal articles.

3. No doubt every reader has his or her favorite account. In the empirical domain, we particularly enjoy Deledicq (1968), which contains essays on the student revolt written by 116 University of Paris science students who went to class on May 9 for a mid-term examination in mathematics and were asked instead by their instructor (Deledicq) to write down their thoughts on the developing events. For a fine general interpretation, see Hoffmann (1974, ch. 6).

4. Jacques Narbonne apparently predicted in 1963 that the French universities would explode in 1968 (Tournoux, 1969, pp. 43–44; and Alexandre, 1969, pp. 16–17).

5. Raymond Aron (1968, p. 128) wrote that "the indifference which so many citizens show toward their state and their rulers in countries where there is representative government . . . probably attests to a latent uneasiness which might suddenly explode in a crisis of wild passions."

6. Pierre Viansson-Ponté in *Le Monde,* March 15, 1968.

7. We performed this conversion for each SOFRES survey by cumulating cases inward from the two extremities of our metric left-right scale for 1967, and recording the points at which we reached the proportions reported by SOFRES as being extreme-left and left, and extreme-right and right, and then taking the weighted mean of these four groups plus the group that placed itself at the center. We are grateful to SOFRES for making their data available to us.

8. Another result of the growth in respectability of the Communist party between 1964 and 1967 was the greater willingness of Communist voters to acknowledge their political sympathies in 1967 as compared with earlier (and later) years. In French national sample surveys prior to 1967, Communist votes were typically underrepresented by from 35 to 50 percent. In our 1967 survey, the Communist vote was underrepresented by only some 10 percent, a clear indication that for the first time in postwar France Communist supporters felt comfortable enough to report their true partisan sympathies to strangers (see Appendix A).

9. In cities of more than 100,000 population, respondents were asked whether a demonstration had occurred in their *quartier* (neighborhood).

10. It is possible, of course, that some households which reported no previous participation in strikes or demonstrations in 1967 actually engaged in such activity between the date of the 1967 interview and the events of May–June 1968, but we have no way of knowing how many may have done so.

11. Earlier we cited etas for geographically based groups, as a measure of the ratio of between-district to within-district variance. When our sample is split into its component electoral districts, etas for most political attitudes and behaviors are closely grouped around .30. Where the May–June disorders are concerned, however, variables dealing with local incidence of disturbance move up into a range of from .45 to greater than .60.

12. Interestingly enough, as noted in Chapter 4 the sense of relative left-right loca-

tions of the several political parties among our *elite* respondents did show greater responsiveness to the fine grain of political events in the May–June period. Thus, for example, placements for the PSU, which strongly sympathized with the revolt, were shifted to the left, while the normally more extreme-left Communists, whose leaders were hesitant about revolt support, were subsequently located less to the left than they had been in 1967.

13. Remember that the decisive ballot may be either the first or the second ballot, depending on whether a candidate wins a majority of the votes at the first ballot.

14. Changes in left-right voting between 1967 and 1968 were more closely associated with changes in attitude toward de Gaulle than with changes in self-ascribed left-right locations. Moreover, as one would expect, these voting changes occurred mainly among voters who were not firmly anchored in the party system. Among the third of our respondents who had the same party identification in 1967 and 1968, there was little change in the vote and, hence, little correlation between vote change and changes in left-right locations or attitudes toward de Gaulle. Among the remainder of the electorate, however, the segment that accounts for most of the shift to the right in the vote, changes in attitudes toward de Gaulle were associated more closely than changes in left-right locations with changes in the left-right partisan vote. The great Gaullist electoral victory of 1968 was due in large part to a surge in favorable attitudes toward de Gaulle among people without any party identification.

15. See Chapter 17 for a detailed discussion of the composition of the 1967 and 1968 legislatures.

16. In 1962, 49 percent of the second-ballot contests were straight fights between a candidate from the leftist bloc and a candidate from the Gaullist bloc. In 1967 the proportion rose to 66 percent; in 1968 and 1973 it was 73 percent; and in 1978 and 1981 it was virtually 100 percent.

17. Readers may be interested to know that the application of the "cube law" is not ruled out in France. It would take us too far afield to make that demonstration here, but it will be done in another study. See also Didier (1978).

15. Elite Reactions to the May–June Events

1. Fifty-seven leading candidates (all of whom were either incumbents or principal challengers) were interviewed within a sample frame of 54 electoral districts. Thirty-three of them were winners, and 34 of the 57 had also been interviewed in 1967. See Appendix B for a complete discussion of the 1968 elite sample.

2. The incumbents were in their districts, on the average, about fifteen of the twenty-eight days between the outbreak of the student revolt and the dissolution of the National Assembly. The challengers were on the site several days longer, but the patterns of local presence varied greatly between incumbents and challengers. Virtually all of the former spent some time in their districts during the revolt, and most of them spent as much time there as their duties in Paris permitted. The challengers, on the other hand, tended to spend either *all* their time in their districts, if they lived in them, or *none* of it, because they lived and worked elsewhere (usually in Paris) and were only later "parachuted" into the districts where they ran for office.

3. Almost half of the Gaullists and their allies found fault with the university system; among opposition candidates the proportion was almost two-thirds.

4. The depth of the distrust that the left felt toward the government in 1976 is clearly expressed in *L'Année politique 1976* (1977, p. 43). After indicating that the main purpose of a reform initiated by the Gaullist minister for the universities was to adapt university programs to the needs of the economy, the summary continued as follows: "Well and good, but when one considers the hostility of many students to economic lib-

eralism, one can easily understand that such subordination of university job placement to the requirements of a liberal economy does not appear as progress but rather as 'reaction,' in every sense of the word."

5. There is some evidence to suggest that the candidates' perceptions were correct. Almost 60 percent of the student essays reproduced in Deledicq (1968) refer to student concern about finding jobs after graduation.

6. Following student demonstrations, courses in certain subjects were suspended at the University of Warsaw from March 30 to May 11, 1968.

7. For a timely piece on the overlap between the CGT leadership and membership in the Communist party, see Adam (1968).

8. We had suggested that interpretation earlier, in Pierce (1973, pp. 132–133, 273). More recently, Ross (1982, ch. 7) has confirmed it generally if not in all details.

9. The question was, "How can one explain the spontaneity and the length of the strike movement among the workers?"

10. A survey of plants struck in May 1968 indicates that in only a few were the workers hostile to their local unions. In most cases surveyed, the local unions either were in control from the start or gained control soon after the first walkout. In the main, the strikes were spontaneous only in that they had not been planned in advance and were not directed by the national union organizations. See Erbès-Séguin (1970) and Shorter and Tilly (1974, p. 141).

11. See Q.6 of the 1968 candidate questionnaire.

12. The question (Q.8A) was as follows: "Among the people who were on strike in your district, about what percentage, in your opinion, wanted to work but could not do so because their places of work were occupied or closed by pickets?"

13. Our sample estimates rest on Q.68 of the 1968 questionnaire, which asked whether the respondents had worked normally during the May–June events. If they responded that they had not worked normally, they were asked a follow-up question, Q.68bis, that took the form of a card listing four situations from which the respondent was asked to select his or her own. The four situations included: "I went out on strike"; "I could not go to work (for lack of transportation)"; "I wanted to work but my firm was occupied or closed by pickets"; and "I did not have what I needed to work (lack of material or tools, lack of personnel, lack of clients, etc.)." Each alternative was designated by a letter, and the respondent was asked to cite the letter corresponding to the alternative that described his or her work situation. This was done to minimize any embarrassment the respondent might have felt about describing his or her situation directly in front of any persons, other than the interviewer, who might have been present. If none of the listed situations described that of the respondent, he or she was asked to state what the situation had been. When the respondent was not the head of household, similar questions (Q.75 and Q.75bis) were asked in the same form with regard to the head of household.

14. That estimate is in minimal terms. Almost another fourth of striking households could conceivably have contained at least one person whose work stoppage was forced by circumstances.

15. Q.15 of the 1968 mass questionnaire.

16. In the last chapter we called attention to the voters' overwhelming assessment that the people who launched the strikes and demonstrations "were right at first but then went too far."

17. In these four cases, the average estimate was 11 percent for the start of the strikes and 69 percent for the end of them. For Table 15-1, when dealing with respondents' replies given in the form of a range, we scored the means of the proportions cited. Also, when the respondents made verbal rather than numerical estimates, we scored "very few," "infinitesimal," and "insignificant" as 5 percent; "the majority" as 55 percent; and "all" as 100 percent.

18. Literally, the correlations are negative, as the further right the candidate, the smaller the proportion of perceived supporters for students and strikers.

19. Later in this book we shall rely heavily on correlational measures in order to assess the degree of congruence between candidate-specific information and district-specific information. These operations will extend into other domains the kind of analysis we are reporting here concerning the candidates' perceptions of the revolt-related attitudes of their constituents as well as their constituents' actual behavior. This form of correlational analysis raises a number of important methodological questions. We prefer, however, to postpone that discussion until Chapter 16, where it will be linked directly to various stages of what amounts to a large-scale use of such analysis. We shall, therefore, defer the more fundamental explanation and defense of our use of correlational analysis, limiting ourselves here to two essential points in order to make our method clear.

20. These assumptions are discussed in detail in Chapter 18 and Appendix C.

21. Naturally, determinations of "accuracy" become even more difficult to make when one subdivides districts according to "low" and "high" objective scores, for then candidates who err in one direction or the other because of wishful thinking will tend, solely by accident, to be "accurate" in their perceptions in one or the other set of districts.

22. See the Q.23 series of the 1968 candidate questionnaire. A different type of analysis of replies to some of the same questions appears in Chapter 12.

23. Because such a large proportion of seats was won at the first ballot in 1968, questions about second-ballot vote transfers were inapplicable to a large percentage of our respondents. Consequently, the analysis here rests on small numbers of cases (13 for the majority and 16 for the opposition). The responses, however, are differentiated so sharply along theoretically relevant dimensions that we have full confidence in the findings.

24. One centrist told us, appropriately, that he had taken a "pivotal" position ("une position charnière, si vous voulez").

25. The other seven items included: Communism versus anti-Communism, de Gaulle versus the parties, the Fifth Republic versus the Fourth Republic, the government versus the opposition, the working class versus the capitalists, personal power versus democracy, and the left versus the right. The same question was asked of the mass sample of voters, who also chose "order versus anarchy" more often than any other alternative.

26. In 1967, however, the candidates had been offered eleven alternatives, whereas in 1968 they were offered only eight.

27. *Le Monde* (May 15, 1968) reported that the protest march from the Place de la République to Place Denfort-Rochereau in Paris included 200,000 people, according to the prefecture of police, and almost a million, according to the claims of the participating groups. On June 1, 1968, the same paper reported that the organizers of the pro-Gaullist march from the Place de la Concorde to L'Etoile claimed that a million people participated; the police estimate was, again, 200,000. The methods used by the police to estimate the size of demonstrations are discussed in *Liaisons* (March 1975), cited in *Le Monde*, October 9, 1976. For a method of handling conflicting estimates, see Prost (1966).

28. That estimate works out to 77 percent on the basis of the distribution of the work force in the candidate's district. INSEE, the national French statistical office, prepared a great deal of demographic data on a district-level basis at the time of the 1967 election, and we have used these data in translating verbal estimates into quantitative scores wherever it was possible to do so.

29. In about one-third of the districts where both candidates estimated demonstration participation, the rightist reported a larger figure than the leftist. Correspondingly "wrong" estimates (in terms of partisan bias) were almost never made by the competing candidates concerning their constituents' *opinions*.

30. One such estimate included everyone who took part in *réunions* and *rencontres*.

31. Four major demonstrations took place in Nantes, the first three opposed to the government (May 13, May 27, and May 31) and the fourth in favor of the government

(June 1). The main chronicler of events in Nantes, who writes as an eyewitness and is sympathetic to the government's opponents, reports that more than 20,000 people participated in the first demonstration, about 40,000 in the second, and 30,000 in the third, and that the prefect estimated that there were 20,000 participants in the pro-government demonstration (Guin, 1969, pp. 52, 89, 104, and 110). A more conventional historian, who believes that reports of demonstration participation at Nantes were much exaggerated (and who cites Guin in his bibliography), estimates that the participants in these same four demonstrations numbered 15,000, 20,000, 10,000, and 17,000 respectively (Dansette, 1971, pp. 259, 267, and 338–339). Neither author specifies how he arrived at his estimates. The local paper, *Presse-Océan,* reported figures of 20,000, 30,000–40,000, 30,000, and 30,000 at the time of the events themselves, although in the case of the last, pro-Gaullist demonstration, it said that "some people say even more, others, less."

32. See Chapter 17 for a discussion of the role of alternates.

33. See Q.6 of the 1967 questionnaire and Q.14 of the 1968 questionnaire.

34. The smaller panel of candidates that was interviewed twice shows the same kinds of shifts in the relative importance of the various factors in the vote between 1967 and 1968 that are registered in Figure 15-2 (although there is some variation in the magnitude of those changes), except for the rightist candidates' perception of the relative importance of their position concerning de Gaulle. In the figure, that factor gains slightly in importance among rightists between 1967 and 1968; within the panel, it loses slightly in perceived importance.

35. Among mass respondents interviewed both in 1967 and 1968, the mean sympathy scores in 1967 were 50 for Mitterrand, 40 for the Communist party, and 50 for the Socialist party. In 1968 they were 33 for Mitterrand, 31 for the Communist party, and 42 for the Federation.

36. See Q.36 of the 1968 questionnaire for the original French version.

37. René Andrieu, the editor-in-chief of the Communist daily newspaper, *L'Human-ité,* wrote in the issue of May 22, 1968, that "civil war is not a country fair and does not necessarily lead to socialism." The context was a debate with Jean-Paul Sartre over Communist behavior in 1945, but it is difficult to believe that the remark was not intended to explain Communist behavior in 1968 as well. Cited in *Le Monde,* May 23, 1968.

38. One pure Gaullist, however, told us that "those who had the means of enacting reforms did not want to do so." He did not indicate who these people were.

39. The exact question was, "Let us return for a moment to the May–June events. If similar events were to occur again, what do you think the government should do?" See Q.35 of the 1968 candidate questionnaire.

40. Actually, the President may not dissolve the National Assembly for twelve months following an election provoked by a presidential dissolution, so that option would not have been available until June 1969. Parliament may dissolve itself, but that eventuality would hardly have been likely given the lopsided majority held by the Gaullists and their allies. In this regard it should be pointed out that, as far as it is possible to tell, when the candidates in our sample discussed the hypothetical recurrence of a mass upheaval they assumed that the government at the time would be Gaullist. This was a perfectly reasonable assumption for them to make in the entire context. There is some irony, however, in the fact that later, in May 1983, students and other groups created disturbances in the streets because of their opposition to the policies of a leftist government.

41. We refer here only to the deputies in our sample who were interviewed in 1968. A great many of the deputies who were interviewed in 1967 but not in 1968 were also elected to the Assembly in 1968, and they will be included in our later analyses of behavior during the legislature elected in 1968. See Appendix B for details concerning the elite samples.

42. Both groups of majority deputies appear to have been more sympathetic to the students than to the strikers, but that is almost surely more an artifact of our measures

than the reflection of a real difference in outlook. We have already seen how easy a target the university system was for candidates of all political stripes when they discussed the causes of the student revolt. We also know that even rightist candidates perceived more popular support for the strikers than for the student demonstrators, and that many majority candidates took pains not to antagonize the workers during the electoral campaign. Moreover, in discussing what the government should do in the event of another upheaval, the majority deputies were harder on the students than on the strikers. It is the difference in scores between groups of majority deputies on the same issue that matters here.

43. Even in this case, however, the broad agreement between majority and opposition was due to partisan discipline among the Communists, who were nearly unanimous in opposing disorder.

16. Theories and Models of Representation

1. Eulau (Wahlke, Eulau, et al., 1962) distinguishes a third type of representational role, in addition to those of delegate and trustee. This is the "politico," who is responsive to both mandate and independence orientations, according to the circumstances. We do not try, either here or in our later chapter on representative roles, to disengage explicitly such a role mix, although in terms of the hypothetical continuum just established, it should be clear that the politico type would include those representatives centering around .50. In this formulation, the exact fraction of politicos in a given legislature would directly depend on the details of operational definitions, such as the range of eligibility around the midpoint, and the extremity of the marginal distributions on items defining the poles. In the study of state legislatures being reported, the trustee orientation is by some margin the predominant one, with politicos being considerably more numerous than pure delegates. Role types here were discriminated according to responses to two open-ended questions concerning how the representative viewed his job, relative to his perceptions of his constituency's view.

2. This cluster of attitudes on the part of political elites in Latin cultures is often dubbed, particularly by outsiders, "paternalism." The term is more than faintly pejorative. It refers to a set of motivations among the elite that couples benevolence toward the constituency with a conviction that the constituents are too ill-informed to distinguish their long-range interests from their momentary whims, a task which must therefore be performed by their leadership. The relevant slogan, also pejorative, is "Papa knows best." The Burkean view of mass-elite relationships, though utterly vulnerable to charges of "elitism," generally avoids the blatantly pejorative connotations surrounding the descriptor "paternalism," perhaps because of its appeal to the higher authority of the individual conscience. Some profound philosophical divide may separate the Burkean view from what is called in other settings "paternalism," but if so, it escapes us.

3. We shall limit our description of the responsible-party model to the few assumptions most important to a theory of political representation. As a result of the historical context in which concern for responsible parties arose, the actual model contains other intellectual baggage as well. Classic statements of the model include Schattschneider (1942), Burns (1949), the Committee on Political Parties of the American Political Science Association (1950), and Ranney (1954). The historical context led to an association of the doctrine with two-party systems. But, as critics have pointed out, the conditions necessary for such programmatic parties to arise are more likely to be found in multiparty systems of the French type (see Epstein, 1967); and from our point of view the model is potentially relevant to systems of any number of parties greater than one. The development of the notion of the "people's mandate" in Great Britain is authoritatively treated in Emden (1959).

4. Signs of strong party discipline in legislative voting are a necessary but not suffi-

cient condition for responsible-party functioning. In the French case, for example, Macridis (1963, p. 171) has noted that the party caucus or legislative *groupe* in the National Assembly sometimes acts quite independently of the campaign party which had organized the electoral effort and publicized the party "program."

5. In Chapter 15 we encountered several instances of relative congruence along with severe levels of absolute incongruence in connection with elite perceptions of constituent opinions and behavior during the upheaval of May–June 1968.

6. A dissenting view, developed by Weissberg (1978), will be examined in Chapter 19.

7. We shall not, in fact, present unstandardized coefficients, although we shall scrutinize them. The conceptual point being made—that when impressions gleaned from unstandardized coefficients and standardized ones diverge, it is the unstandardized ones which are more revealing—is impeccable. All that this leaves out is the general unintelligibility of unstandardized coefficients to readers who have not spent months engrossed in the research and who are not familiar with the meanings of scale differences in the absolute units used. When the units are familiar, such as dollars spent or years of education achieved, the unstandardized coefficients are certainly helpful. Or when a portfolio of measurements with roughly the same absolute metric and roughly the same variances is being used, then unstandardized coefficients may be vaguely intelligible even to those who have not spent time absorbing the details of the metrics used, although this is typically the case in which impressions created by standardized coefficients are least likely to diverge from those suggested by unstandardized ones. When the scale units are arbitrary and are set in grossly different denominations, as ours are, then the presentation of unstandardized coefficients becomes an expositor's nightmare unless one is willing to believe, as some seem to, that recognitions that came hard to the investigator are innate to the casual reader. Most troublesome are those who glibly publish unstandardized coefficients without even adumbrating the kinds of explanations of scaling details, score ranges, and such matters which the overachieving reader must start with in order to make any sense whatever of the data displayed. There has to be a better way. To us, the obvious means of having the best of both worlds is to publish primarily in standardized coefficients, as a minimal service to the reader interested in what is going on, while using investigator familiarity with the scaling details to monitor the results in unstandardized vocabulary, and to call the matter to the reader's attention at those exceptional points where the messages of the unstandardized coefficients diverge from those published. This will be our practice.

8. When faced with incommensurate scalings of this kind, one's instinct is to render them commensurate by simply converting the two response distributions into the common currency of standard scores. Such a maneuver is in part self-defeating, however, since the limitation of correlational statements prompting this whole discussion is the edge of social relativity induced by the fact that the correlational calculation implicitly standardizes the scores of each of the variable pairs relative to its population distribution. The use of standard scores retreats to exactly the same form of relativity.

9. Of course, the representatives' perceptions of what constitutes district heterogeneity are much more embracing than our simple, single-issue case. We shall consider our multiple-issue context in its own terms later.

10. The likeliest exception to this rule involves the case of the "passionate minority," where there may be a lopsided 70-30 split on a policy proposal, but the 30 percent minority feels much more intensely about its position than the majority feels about its own assumptions. If one has made more extended measurements (as we have), so that intensity of opinion is registered as well as mere binary direction, then the case remains conflictual because the *mean* of the opinion distribution is perilously near the middle even if the simply yes-no proportions are not; and it is a case where opinion variance is higher than one might normally expect in view of that lopsided yes-no distribution.

11. Achen (1978) has reanalyzed the Miller-Stokes data in ways which he believes serve to challenge this conclusion as to the relative clarity of representation on questions of civil rights. But the feeble links which he shows between representatives and their constituents on civil-rights opinions are merely what remain after Southern representatives have been discarded from the analysis. Since Southern representatives and their constituencies make up something like half of the polarization being discussed by Miller and Stokes, the attenuation of the remaining relationships when this natural between-district variance is set aside is hardly surprising, and it rather misses the point. Nonetheless, the sharp decline in relationships when one of the two contesting regions is ignored helps to dramatize the degree to which the original findings were, in fact, shaped by such regional polarizations.

12. This measure was used in Chapter 5. Although it is not a measure of issue opinion in the sense of our other linkage issues, it is a potent indicator of differences in district religious sentiment, and we shall use it later in a manner coordinate with the other measures of district feeling.

13. As Fenno (1978) notes, the representative may well have his eye on something more than the set of voters who supported him in the preceding election. He tends to see the electorate in the district in terms of at least three layers: those who he assumes will always vote for him, those who sometimes will, and those who never will. Being more interested in *prospective* support than in the support which is a fait accompli, and desiring to maximize that prospective support, he has a keen interest in maintaining a favorable image among the "sometimes" supporters of the preceding election, while also trying to appeal to those who did not vote for him in the preceding election but might consider doing so in the future. Although we did collect some information on perceptions of this kind, when we refer to the "supporter" constituency we shall generally mean the set of voters operationally defined as having cast their vote for the candidate in question.

17. The Deputies in the National Assembly

1. *Proposition de loi* is sometimes translated as private member's bill. That term, derived from British parliamentary practice, seems too restrictive in the French context, where propositions de loi are often introduced by partisan groups as well as by individuals. Therefore, parliamentary bill seems a more appropriate translation. There is no problem with *projet de loi,* which is purely and simply a government bill.

2. For an authoritative account of the parliament of the Fourth Republic, see Williams (1964, chs. 16–20).

3. Senators are chosen by departmental electoral colleges that range in size from about 270 to more than 6,000 electors. The electors include the deputies and departmental councillors for each department, plus delegates chosen by the municipal councils of the department. The number of delegates varies with the size of the town. For towns with 9,000 or more inhabitants, all the municipal councillors serve as electors; towns of more than 30,000 inhabitants are entitled to an additional delegate for every 1,000 inhabitants in excess of 30,000. In the largest departments, which have five or more senators, the election is by proportional representation; in the remaining departments, there is a two-ballot majority system.

Senators serve for nine years, and one-third of the seats are renewed at triennial elections. The Senate is smaller than the Assembly: after the senatorial elections of 1965, there were 274 senators; after the 1968 elections there were 283. A 1976 law enlarged the Senate gradually, to 295 seats in 1977, 304 in 1980, and 315 in 1983.

4. Because there are two regular parliamentary sessions per year, one in the fall and the other in the spring, the restriction is not severe. Special sessions are also possible.

5. See also Guichard-Ayoub et al. (1965); Gicquel (1968); Williams and Harrison (1971).

6. For the first two legislatures, see Gicquel (1968, p. 311n.). For the Third and Fourth Legislatures, see the annual volumes of Assemblée Nationale (*Statistiques*), published by the Secrétariat générale de l'Assemblée nationale.

7. Three seats for Metropolitan France were added for the election of 1973, and still another for the elections of 1978 and 1981.

8. The Norwegian parliamentary system has for a long time incorporated these two elements of the French system, which were introduced under the Fifth Republic: the requirement that members of the government not be members of parliament, and the alternate system for replacing members of parliament. The Norwegian and French arrangements differ in detail, but both have the same basic properties.

9. Ordinance No. 58-1065 of November 7, 1958, says, "The powers of the National Assembly expire at the opening of the regular April session in the fifth year following its election."

10. Chaban-Delmas' adviser for social affairs was Jacques Delors, who was to become Finance Minister after François Mitterrand's election to the presidency in 1981.

11. In the spring of 1972 Pompidou organized a referendum on the admission of Great Britain, Denmark, Ireland, and Norway to the European communities. The government's position in favor of admission won handily, but a third of the registered voters abstained.

12. During the thirty-day grace period given to members of parliament appointed to the government in order to decide whether they will enter the government or stay in parliament, they may not participate in any votes.

13. As of October 23, 1969, the other members of the Presidents' Conference were the President and the six Vice-Presidents of the Assembly, the presidents of the six standing committees, and the *rapporteur-général* of the Finance Committee.

14. Voting in the Assembly is discussed in more detail later in this chapter.

15. There are few detailed studies of the operation of French parliamentary groups. For the Communist group, see Maisl (1969). For the Gaullist group, see Charlot (1971).

16. The orthodox Gaullist party at the time was officially named the Union pour la Nouvelle République–Union Démocratique du Travail (UNR–UDT). In November 1967 the party changed its name to Union des Démocrates pour la Vᵉ République (UD-Vᵉ), and in December the party's parliamentary group in the Assembly changed its name to Groupe d'Union des Démocrates pour la Vᵉ République.

17. In the fall of 1968 the party changed its name again, this time to Union des Démocrates pour la République, which happily retained the initials UDR.

18. When ministers are replaced by their alternates, the alternates almost always pass through the non-inscrits before joining or affiliating with a parliamentary group.

19. For all roll-call analyses of the Third Legislature reported in this book that relate votes in the Assembly to the parliamentary groups, we take the composition of the groups as of May 18, 1967, as the base. It would have been futile to use the composition of the Assembly at an earlier date; the replaced ministers would have appeared only as missing data, and it was not technically feasible to alter the composition of the groups frequently in our record of roll-calls in order to match the actual changes in the composition of the groups that took place throughout the legislature.

20. The majority was heavily dependent on overseas deputies during the Third Legislature. The Gaullists and Independent Republicans held only 230 seats from Metropolitan France at the start of the legislature, while the Federation, Communists, PDM, and non-inscrits held 240. But Gaullists or Independent Republicans held 13 of the 17 overseas seats from the start, and that figure rose to 14 in May. Before the end of the legislature, however, one overseas deputy switched from the Independent Republicans to PDM, as already mentioned.

21. About one-third of the 54 switches involved the Radicals' movements in and out

of affiliation with the Socialist group, but we have not included in that total the initial move of the Radicals from the Federation group to affiliation with the new Socialist group when the Federation group disappeared.

22. The base date for the distribution of deputies across parliamentary groups that we use for relating the groups to voting in the Assembly during the Fourth Legislature is September 24, 1968.

23. The National Assembly has six vice-presidents, twelve secretaries, and three *questeurs*, who direct the financial and administrative services of the Assembly. These officers are supposed to be chosen in a way that will reflect the political configuration of the Assembly.

24. This method was used for taking open votes before electronic voting was introduced.

25. *Journal Officiel de la République française. Débats parlementaires, Assemblée nationale.*

26. The following exchange, from the *Journal Officiel de la République française, Debats parlementaires, Assemblée nationale* (October 1967, p. 3636), which occurred on October 17, 1967, illustrates the procedure:

M. Bernard Chochoy. I request the floor for a clarification concerning a vote.

M. le président. M. Chochoy has the floor.

M. Bernard Chochoy. My dear colleagues, for the vote taken Friday afternoon on the Finance Committee's amendment number 11 to Article 15 of the first part of the budget, I am recorded by error as having voted 'against.'

I wish to state, Mr. President, that I voted 'for' and I request that the correction be made.

M. le président. My dear colleague, inasmuch as Article 68 of the rules prohibits any correction of a vote after the balloting is closed, I can only formally acknowledge your statement.

As the electronic device only registers the impulses it receives, and the precision with which it records them is accompanied by extreme sensitivity, there is reason to believe that the vote recorded in your name is the result of the involuntary, faulty operation of your voting machine at the time of the vote in question.

M. Bernard Chochoy. The machine malfunctioned.

M. le président. Of course.

27. All of the work relating to roll-call votes that appears later in this book rests on votes as officially recorded. Because these votes are the actual output of the legislative system, we made no effort to track down individual corrections.

28. Ordinance No. 58-1066 of November 7, 1958.

29. The Assembly elected in 1968 did not sit in 1973, although new elections were not held until March of that year.

30. For these immediate calculations, the two forms of abstention are treated as equivalent: that is, when the modal position of a parliamentary group on a scrutin was a particular form of abstention, the member who registered another form of abstention is still considered as having voted in a fashion congruent with his group.

31. In this chapter and those that follow, we have deliberately chosen to index the degree of party discipline or intragroup cohesion in voting in terms of the simple proportion of votes conforming to caucus norms, rather than using some of the other indices of legislative group cohesion that have been popular in the political science literature. The most familiar of these, the Rice index of cohesion, along with its recent variants, is inappropriate since it assumes a two-party legislature, although it was used by Wilson and Wiste (1976) for the French National Assembly between 1958 and 1973. The index proposed by Lowell at the turn of the century, making use of the proportion of roll-call votes in which nine-tenths of a group's members vote on the same side of an issue, is applicable to the French case and has been widely used since its invention. But the nine-tenths cut-

off point strikes us as needlessly arbitrary, and the simpler statement of the proportion of conforming votes communicates more rapidly, although it must be kept in mind that any such figure calculated over all roll calls is no more than an expression of central tendency, which can conceal variation from vote to vote. For a review of the relevant considerations involved in such a choice, see MacRae, Jr. (1970, ch. 6).

32. See notes 19 and 22 above.

33. Of course, mirror-image errors would be possible as well, although the odds are very high that they would be much less frequent. We have deliberately limited our calculations to group memberships as formally registered near the outset of each session, in part because we are interested in the stability of these influences in the longer term. Thus, in extremis, a legislature could show a perfect intraparty homogeneity of roll-call votes, but one which would be quite spurious if each legislator were free to choose the caucus he preferred for the purpose of each new issue.

34. Although the Gaullists were a single group at the caucus level, rather than a coalition of groups, they had gone well past the point of the "minimal winning coalition"; and therefore, as Riker's "size principle" would predict, their internal cohesion declined. See Riker (1962).

18. The Basic Representation Bond

1. Although, as we saw in the preceding chapter, there is a little discrepancy between the official record of individual votes and deputy intentions due to alleged errors in the voting process, our quantitative treatment in the whole of Part IV rests on the official record of individual roll-call contributions. This procedure has been followed not only for practical reasons but also because the official record is exempt from latter-day correction and represents the ultimate will of the Assembly in its governance function.

2. One indicator of the relative importance of particular roll-call votes that is "objective," in the sense of being created independently of our own investigation, is the length of the descriptive references (line count) made to various votes in the relevant annual volume of L'Année politique. The 123 votes taken as an initial pool for our summary scales received an average of 11.8 lines of descriptive comment per vote, relative to an average of 3.1 lines devoted per vote across the remaining 306 votes of the session. These summary statistics are a bit misleading, since censure motions and votes of confidence draw comments at a volume which is an order of magnitude greater than that for virtually all other types of proposals, and all such votes have been included in our pool of 139 votes. Even setting roll-call votes of this type aside as a special case, however, the remaining items in our selected pool occasioned nearly twice the volume of content as those not included.

3. A copy of this memorandum will be mailed to any interested reader upon request.

4. For the purposes of this synthetic variable, Communists were scored 1, the Federation 2, the PDM 7, and both UDR and RI 9.

5. A coefficient of reproducibility of .90 is usually considered to be an adequate fit, given this number of items and the limited range of variation displayed in these marginals.

6. The prototype of such a vote is the case in which opposition to a centrist budgetary appropriation proposal is made up of a mixture of certain "nays" cast because the sum proposed is seen as too lavish and of others cast because it is seen as inadequate. It is obvious that the consideration of all such "nays" as equivalent for the purposes of contributing to a scale of, say, fiscal conservatism would be thoroughly inappropriate.

7. For the sake of conventionality, we also constructed a companion scale from the same Faure Law items, which made no such interpretive leaps but rather considered as equivalent all votes hostile to the law, from whichever extreme they came. As might be

expected, however, this Like Faure Law measure performed very poorly in subsequent analyses, relative to the Faure Law Left-Right summary scale. It tended to show essentially the same contours of expected relationships, but they were severely tarnished in magnitude, just as we would expect if scaling were carried out mechanically despite an ends-against-the-middle admixture to the voting. For simplicity's sake, we have omitted this flawed roll-call scale from our presentation.

8. Another potential difficulty that might be suspected, given the heterogeneity in sizes of item bases, is that our European integration index, based on six items, is much more reliable than some of our single-item measurements, and hence results cannot be compared across domains. Where composites are used, we shall tag each variable with the number of component items (1, 2, or 6) to keep the reader aware of the differences. Nevertheless, our experimentation with multiple-item indices as compared with their single-item components suggests that the problem is not a serious one. If reliability were accruing at a rapid rate as we move from one European integration item to a composite of six such items, then in practice linkage correlations involving the six-item index should be as high as, if not higher than, the best single-item correlation in the set. This is not, however, what we observe. Although in all instances the correlation involving the composite does outrun by a small margin the average of single-item correlations in the set, the difference is modest indeed, and the correlation involving the composite is invariably less than the best (or the better) of the single-item components. Clearly the greater problem is that results are more dependent upon the specific item or items drawn from the hypothetical universe of all possible items representing the policy domain than we would like.

9. The rectangular distribution of larger case numbers, along with the self-representing samples at the district level, take care of the difficulties addressed by Erikson (1978) in his revision of some of the original Miller-Stokes estimates for the United States.

10. The calculations are presented in detail in Appendix C.

11. For their three issue domains, Miller and Stokes publish two different sets of figures corresponding to our basic representation bond. The first, the raw correlations initially presented (Miller and Stokes, 1963, p. 49), were as follows: for civil rights, .57; for social welfare, "approximately 0.3"; and for American foreign involvement, −0.09. A later revision of the same piece (Miller and Stokes, 1966, p. 359) provides values corrected for attenuation, and hence more parallel to our own, of "about .65*," "approximately .4*," and "less than .2*,"respectively (our asterisks added). It should be kept in mind that the Miller-Stokes linkage correlations involve two years of congressional roll-call votes, whereas the French data refer to a five-year period of roll calls, interrupted by one reelection.

19. *Winners, Losers, and Their Constituencies*

1. Naturally, one would need to find equally compelling ways to summarize across issues for any given jurisdiction, and across such jurisdictions to total electorates, if one wished to assess the overall value of a particular election.

2. Thus, for example, the mean position in the total electorate sample on the question of the Common Market is 1.91, and for our total candidate sample the mean is 1.74. This is a difference of 0.17, in the direction of greater support for the Common Market. Whether that is a big or a small difference will be totally obscure to anyone who does not know the details of the measurement. What is important is the variation underlying such means. On one hand, if all voters fell in the range from 1.86 to 1.96 on the Common Market item, then a candidate mean as remote as 1.74 would be shocking. On the other hand, if voters are scattered over a range of 100 points, then a difference of means between voters and candidates of a mere 0.17 may be an utterly trivial displacement. To convey

this kind of relative information, the means on the elite side have been rescaled as deviations from the mass means, expressed in units of standard deviation of the mass distribution. Thus, in the Common Market case, a raw difference of 0.17 turns out to be a difference of 0.17 SDs of the voter distribution, because for this particular issue it happens that one standard deviation in the voter sample is just about one raw scale score. For the left-right measure, however, one standard deviation is 23 raw units. Our standardized conversion in Figure 19-1 permits evaluation of the discrepancies across issues in common terms.

3. Even the one exception to this rule which comes through clearly in Figure 19-1, that concerning the priority to be given issues of governmental allocations to public and Catholic schools, is no mystery to students of French politics. Around the turn of the century the political system was nearly torn asunder by a gripping and embittered debate over the role of church and state in the education of children. In the wake of World War II, there were signs of widespread collusion among political elites of quite different ideological stripes to convince the public that the issue of church schools was not the most important one normally faced by the French government, however sharply this debate continued to resonate in the mass public. Our agenda items reflect these patterns admirably, as the church-school issue is the only one which the elite sees as less important than the common voter does.

4. One additional contrast in the left-right panel of Figure 19-1 stems from the fact that here, unlike the situation with ten of the other twelve comparisons, losers are less like the mass electorate than are winners. They are still more sharply displaced to the left, a deviation which is in fact the largest in the whole figure. This is perfectly intelligible: we have seen that the 1967 election took place in a period when many political observers felt that the Gaullists might at last have become vulnerable, a perception which undoubtedly encouraged an outpouring of candidates from some of the smaller splinter formations of the left, including many without any realistic chance of success.

5. The fact at stake here is undeniable, but the lesson to be drawn from it is highly arguable. There is no doubt that egregious problems of inference arise when correlational summaries are used in study settings where the investigator has intruded in some way—usually by innocent decisions of study design—to produce artificial truncations in the variance of the variables he is correlating. The textbook reductio ad absurdum is the investigator who decides that the varying height of children is not strongly correlated with chronological age because the correlation he discovers in his sample of fourth-grade children is in fact quite weak. Here of course the restriction of the sample to a single grade puts ridiculous limits on the variance of chronological age, so that little correlation can be expected and any that is observed is next to meaningless, at least as providing any estimate as to how age and height co-vary in general among children. Achen himself (1978) appears to take seriously an example nearly as absurd as this when he contests the Miller-Stokes estimates of the strength of representation in the domain of civil rights with figures calculated after he had made a decision to set aside the South, a maneuver which obviously emasculated the main lines of representational conflict that made the Miller-Stokes findings substantively interesting. A less obvious, and hence more insidious, version of investigator-induced variance oddities occurs when samples that are analytically partitioned into subsamples by way of controlling some factor consequently produce, in unnoticed ways, very disproportionate variances across partitions for the working variables that are to be correlated.

If correlations could never be used without such investigator-induced artifacts, it might be a subject for concern, although that is not obviously true. Aside from these investigator sins, however, there remain distinct differences from sample to sample in what we might think of as "natural" variation occurring for the same conceptual variables. In our context, for example, we know that positions on some issues are more polarized at some times and places than they are at others. A fine example is the polarization produced in our left-right self-locations by the 1968 disturbances, as registered in a substantial advance in the variance of the measure (see Chapter 14). This difference can have its effects on correlations formed for the two samples, but in no way can this be seen as an artifact induced by the investigators: the heightened variance is clearly a property of the real world, and one that we would do well to keep in view if we wish to describe that world. Under these circumstances a blanket ban on the use of correlations would be quite foolish. The sensible question becomes, "What features of the real world is the analyst attempting to isolate and highlight?" For some purposes the correlation statement will be just what is needed; for other purposes it will obscure and confound what is sought. The rule here, as always, is not to try to drive nails with a saw or turn screws with a hammer.

6. The actual measure as proposed and as implemented here involves the mean squared difference between the scale position of the elite and each of his (sampled) constituents. See Achen (1978), p. 484, equation 4.

7. Actually, since a correlation coefficient can be seen as a mean of individual contributions to covariation, it is possible to assign meaningful quantities of this sort to individuals, and we shall do so later. This is unconventional, however, and of course does not escape from the collective frame of reference surrounding correlations.

8. Here, of course, the argument concerning the virtues of collective representation becomes worthwhile. It points out that minorities in some districts profit from the representation given them by majorities in other districts (Weissberg, 1978).

9. This need not mean, of course, that the representative loses interest in all the persons in his district who failed to participate in his winning majority at the last election. According to all the renditions of the deputy's calculus, saturated as it is with concern for reelection, he would be delighted to do anything which might be irresistibly attractive to those who were not quite up to voting for him the last time, especially if he did not thereby offend any of his earlier supporters. These are small increments at the margin, however, and we shall not obscure the situation badly if we operationalize the main reference point for the deputy as being those voting for him at the last election.

10. Although the left-right super-issue is not the only one for which expectations sharpen considerably as we shift from the district to supporters as a constituency, it is the only one given in Tables 19-3 and 19-4. We have limited these tables to those of our linkage issue items which are identical matches. Among our remaining position issues, three others show major increases in the expected correlations as the constituency is narrowed in this fashion: (a) aid to church schools, $E(r)$ from .14 to .38; (b) force de frappe, $E(r)$ from .15 to .41; and (c) distribution of income, $E(r)$ from .18 to .37. Gains at these points are not surprising, as these are three of the position issues that are most closely associated with left-right variation.

11. Here and elsewhere in Part IV, the term "supporters" when used without further modification refers to members of the electorate voting for the candidate in question at the *decisive* election. Because of the two tours of voting in the French system, it would be possible to define different subsets of supporters, such as those voting for Candidate X at the first tour, as opposed to those voting for him at the second tour. Of course the differences in average sentiment between the two operational definitions would be trivial, and it would be quite tedious to double the length of our exposition by treating supporters differentially by tour. Here we are glad to economize once again by using the concept of the *decisive* tour—the vote that actually assured the winners of office, whichever tour it may have been.

20. Elite Knowledge of Constituency Sentiment

1. The weakest fit of the eight perceived position issues occurs on the foreign-aid item. Most of the position issues posed of the electorate were in the form, "The government should . . ."—with a single option mentioned. The option was then given in abbre-

viated form to elite informants, to draw their estimates of proportions for, against, and indifferent. The foreign-aid item for the voters, however, gave more of a double option: "Rather than aiding the underdeveloped countries, the government ought instead to help the regions of France in difficulty." Here the elite informants were asked to estimate proportions for and against "aid to underdeveloped countries" only. One can sense a shaky fit here, and indeed it turns out that the matching of these items gives atypical results.

2. Our basic skein of linkage position issues only numbers seven. The eighth is a measure of the specific issue involving the merger of the French Army with the European Army. This item was added because the larger battery of European integration items, used so heavily in the preceding chapter, was not part of the formal linkage-issue structure. For these perceptions, the European Army variable was added to "represent" the battery.

3. Moreover, there are some technical problems with the analysis format which arise because the number of districts ("conditions") is large relative to the number of cases, which are sparsely and unequally scattered across the districts. For these reasons we should not place enormous weight on the absolute ranges of the summary numbers (etas) involved, but rather should give primary attention to the relative positioning of the several issue items, since the sparse distributions are naturally a constant over all comparisons.

4. It is interesting that the one negative coefficient, which is weakly significant here, is for the same issue (foreign aid) for which we noted earlier a rather poor fit between the description offered elites and the actual wording of the mass question. See note 1 above.

5. Another mild anomaly in Figure 20-2 is the level of correlation of the European Army item, which seems remarkably high for such a foreign-policy issue. Actually, the proportion of candidates who frankly reported that they "did not know" how district sentiment would run for the European Army (and hence who were not included in the calculation for Figure 20-2) is about double that for any of the other issues in the figure. Where the European Army is concerned, 15 percent "did not know." Thus the appearance of high knowledge levels for the item is somewhat misleading.

6. Karps (1978) has noted in another connection that in the Miller-Stokes data set there is at best a feeble and uncertain relationship between district heterogeneity and accuracy of perception of district positions within the main linkage-issue domains being used in the study. For his tests, however, he used a general-purpose measure of district heterogeneity referring to the variety of religious, ethnic, and racial groups reported by legislators for their districts. Here we are dealing with issue-specific measures of such heterogeneity.

7. We would clearly not want a model of the Miller-Stokes form in which the constituency terms were a mix of total-district and supporter definitions. In the last chapter we achieved some clarification by substituting supporter means for district means as the "A" term of the diamond. Yet we cannot expand the model further in that direction without measuring candidate perception of supporter sentiment, not just total-district sentiment. In subsequent investigations of the model we might be well advised to make such measurements.

8. The "don't know" responses amount to less than 1.5 percent on the average for the problem-importance items, as well as for the left-right locations taken alone. Their incidence goes up somewhat for the remaining position issues, and the proportions are more variable. For the European Army item, nearly 15 percent of our elite informants said that they did not know what the district sentiment would be. This is almost double the "don't know" proportion for any other item. Nevertheless, the average proportion for the rest of the position items remains at 6 percent. These discrepancies between the importance and the position items may contribute to the fact that when the "don't know" responses are scored as highly ignorant, the ignorance factor for the position issues seems the more robust.

9. The two factors were generated by an oblimin rotation. The factor composed of

the importance items captured 21.0 percent of the total variance of the seven relevant discrepancy variables. The other factor stemming from the issue-position and left-right placement scores garnered 32.2 percent of the total variance in those items.

10. Such discrepant findings would be less unsettling if we could trust the meaningfulness of one of these knowledge factors more than the other. If we must make a choice, we find several reasons to prefer results from the position-issue knowledge factor, including the finding just mentioned.

11. The three longevity variables laid against the two summary knowledge factors generate six correlations. All have the same sign, and only one—the years in the Assembly by the importance knowledge factor—is below an r of .10, dropping to $r = .034$.

12. It might be well to emphasize that we are talking throughout about *resemblances* between hierarchies, and not identities between them. Although some of the resemblances are less close than others, the sheer recurrence of even the same vague hierarchy from many different starting points is worth comment.

21. Conceptions of the Representative Role

1. The literature on the role of the representative is voluminous, and we shall cite here only those works which have a direct bearing on our own. Pitkin (1967) gives the leading philosophical examination of the issue, and Pennock and Chapman (1968) explore it from a variety of viewpoints. Wahlke et al. (1962) pioneered the empirical study of representative roles on a comparative basis. Hunt (1969) and Woshinsky (1973) explored legislative roles in France from perspectives that are somewhat different from ours. Cayrol, Parodi, and Ysmal (1971, 1973, 1976) have examined the conceptions of the representative role held by French deputies in the 1968–1973 legislature both in a broader fashion and in a way that closely parallels our own. Loewenberg (1972) discusses the use of role concepts briefly but aptly. He points out that "the influence of the legislative role system on the output of the legislature has not been explored," and argues that the linkage of legislative roles with legislative behavior "seems necessary if this concept is to be employed profitably in the formulation of theory for comparative research." Our development here attempts to respond to just such a demand.

2. Because of the small case numbers involved when the limited deputy sample is divided five ways, we have taken the liberty in Table 21-2 of dealing with a summation of responses between the 1967 and 1968 deputy interviews, despite the fact that nearly a quarter of these responses come from 1968 reinterviews with deputies whose 1967 responses are also counted. Since statistical significance is not a pressing issue and we are interested in the types of answers to these items that are made by French deputies of differing party stripes, this modest overlap is of little consequence, save for the bolstering of response numbers.

3. Cayrol, Parodi, and Ysmal (1971, 1973, 1976) interviewed 407 of the 487 sitting members of the National Assembly elected in 1968 during the period between October 1969 and June 1970. Although their exact items and coding of open-ended responses differed from ours, they did assess perceptions of deputies concerning conflicts between conscience and voters, and between conscience and party (not "parliamentary group," which was our parallel cue). Overall, they found greater weight being given to personal conscience relative to voter wishes, just as we did for the 1967 deputies. But they found more deputies from 1968 indicating they would follow their consciences than their parties, whereas we found the opposite for 1967 deputies. This discrepancy does not seem too worrisome, because leftist deputies, most attached to group discipline, represented about 40 percent of the legislature elected in 1967 but less than 20 percent of the Assembly elected in 1968. Moreover, the response rate in the later study was higher in the three

centrist and rightist groups, and especially so for the Républicains Indépendants and PDM deputies, those least oriented to group discipline. It is not clear whether these response rate differences were weighted away, or whether the non-inscrits, who were least interested in discipline, were included in the summaries.

4. At this point we shall largely set aside the responses generated by our Assembly candidates who failed to win a seat, since the easiest cross-national comparisons are formed with other sets of current legislators rather than with mere aspirants.

5. Barnes (1977) has also published data from parallel items posed of a sample of deputies in the Italian parliament. Although the published data are not presented in a form which permits close comparisons with those displayed here for France, the United States, and the Netherlands, it is quite apparent that priorities assigned to competing cues from party, conscience, and constituents look much more like the French distributions than like those from the other two countries. If anything, the party factor may be even more dominant among Italian deputies than among the French.

6. As in Figure 21-2, the schematic designs here are data-based; that is, the total lengths of the three shaded legs or bars are made equal for each design; and the relative lengths of these bars are calculated from the ratios of content response proportions to the two role-conflict items. The presumptive element in Figure 21-3 arises from the fact that the U.S. question involving the influence of party discipline is not in the same form as that available for the other two countries. Thus some rough extrapolation from the French design and the contrasts in Table 21-2 had to be employed.

7. The component items of both scales show the kinds of moderate intercorrelations, in the intuitively obvious directions, that usually characterize items of this overlapping kind.

8. Asher (1973) has shown that in the U.S. Congress, for example, the view of freshman congressmen as to appropriate cues for their roll-call voting choices becomes more complex over a period of early experience that can be as short as four months.

9. Cayrol, Parodi, and Ysmal (1976) also examine their role data by party group. The results look much like ours save for the Gaullist UDR, where they found the majority of post-1968 UDR deputies favoring conscience over party dictates. Thus it is of some interest that our data taken in 1967 and again in the summer of 1968 show a trend among Gaullist deputies away from adherence to discipline toward placing greater weight on private conscience at the intersection of these two legislatures. The Cayrol data, elicited from fifteen months to two years later, may simply reflect a continuation of this trend, and a continuation which fits the eroding Gaullist discipline over the course of the 1968–72 legislature.

10. It should be evident that the few deputies non-inscrits in any parliamentary group drop out of all of the ensuing calculations, since the votes they cast cannot be coded as either loyal or defecting vis-à-vis a chosen party caucus. For the quasi-totality of the deputies interviewed who *are* group members, four other votes are removed from the calculations for one parliamentary group. These are instances in which the pivotal PDM exactly split its votes, so that the evidence as to which verdict represented a party line is moot.

11. Barnes (1977) has presented parallel mass data for the Italian electorate. The mass responses to the voter-conscience conflict look very much like those for France, with preference for voter wishes strongly outdistancing concern for deputy conscience. On the party-conscience conflict, however, a majority of Italian voters expect the deputy to follow party dictates rather than own conscience, contrary to the French case.

12. Because we did not repeat these representative role items in our subsequent mass reinterviews, we have no stability estimates for them for the French electorate. But Thomassen (1976) reports stability correlations for these items, replicated on the Dutch electorate in the 1970–72 period, which fall in the .20–.26 range (r) for time lapses of a year.

This may not appear very much lower than the value of .30 we cited for the party-discipline scale among French deputies. But the best comparisons are made with the squares of these coefficients; and in such terms, one can say that while the elite party-discipline responses are not impressively stable, the mass responses are only about one-half as stable as the elite measures. In addition, on the elite side there are obvious grounds to expect gripping pressures toward situational change, occurring at a fair rate and with fair incidence, to reduce the stability of party-discipline responses. There are no counterpart daily pressures on the mass side, and it is likely that the instability is not only greater but of quite a different order. Where these pressures are less concrete and persistent on the elite side, as with the voter-conscience dimension, responses are almost six times as stable as are their parallel terms for the mass electorate.

13. Party support groups here, as elsewhere, are constructed on the basis of votes cast at the decisive ballot of the 1967 election. Voters whose chosen candidates won seats in the Assembly are assigned groups according to which of the five parliamentary groups the deputy chose to join at the beginning of the 1967 session. Voters whose candidates lost are assigned a bit more crudely to the parallel set of five electoral party groupings, according to the best evidence available as to the party banner under which the candidate ran.

22. The Composite Representation Process

1. It is worth noting that one of the two exceptions occurs in connection with the domain of income-distribution policies, where defections from party discipline are so few that the two competing roll-call scales show a correlation of .995. The next highest correlation between the alternate scales is an r of .987, a value which begins to leave more of a margin for real discrimination.

2. It is under these circumstances, and for these reasons, that any diamond estimates involving survey responses (terms A, B, and C) may be in some degree dependent on the numbers of items combined into the scales being used. Indeed, although we said earlier that diamond estimates from a compound scale tend to look like a crude average of results from each component taken separately, most of the time the absolute magnitudes of the coefficients run above the levels of such an arithmetic average, and occasionally they run above the level of the highest estimate, as is the case at a point or two with the church-state domain. Although a correction for this artifact could in principle be achieved, there are attendant complications with which we cannot cope here. We shall therefore do the next best, which is to alert the reader in tabular presentations as to the numbers of items underlying each scale.

3. Another solution to this problem of temporal heterogeneity would have been to use roll-call data from the legislative session *preceding* our 1967 election and interviews, rather than those after it. This would have conformed to the usage of the parent Miller-Stokes study, in which the roll-call votes were drawn from the 85th Congress of 1956–1958, or *before* the interviews with the public and the candidates competing in the 1958 congressional election. We have a distinct preference for our own order, as implemented here, especially for contrasts involving winning and losing candidates in the mode of Chapter 19, since the intellectual question being posed has to do with policy outputs shaped by a legislature which in turn has survived election. Nevertheless, the other temporal order still addresses questions of sheer congruence between district opinion and deputy choice. And in some cases, such as with passing issues like the force de frappe, it would give us a richer and in some ways more "normal" set of legislative decisions to summarize. Such analyses must await another study, however.

4. We have more diamonds in the left-right form than in the issue-specific form because of an occasional ambiguity as to particular issue-specific diamonds. For example, we

have measures of how expansive voters and districts would be with budgets for public education. We also have a roll-call summary of votes on government bills for education budgets. The problem is that it is not entirely clear how to score the fit between these terms. In general, the right supported these government propositions while the left opposed them, so that an intelligible left-right diamond is easy to assemble. But the left, by a margin which was exceedingly small, tended to express more enthusiasm over government spending on education than did the right. It is probable that when the left opposed these budgets, the reasons were often that they were seen as inadequate allocations. We do not, however, know this to be the case: some leftists may have seen them as too large. Hence it is hard to handle the outcome save as a government-opposition (or left-right) matter.

5. Other analyses suggest that party variation in attitudes toward income distribution is limited by somewhat the same factors as those that make most party elites prefer to see themselves as distinctly to the left of their normal ideological bedfellows. Most deputies claim to want a much more even distribution of income than exists, so that the basic variability of response is restricted. The same postures also blur party lines to some degree for the composite variable entitled "socioeconomic left-right."

6. Of course, the data underlying Figure 22-2 include traces of defections, which, as we saw earlier in this chapter, serve to improve the congruence between roll calls and district opinion.

23. Conditional Variations in Representation

1. Throughout this study, the force de frappe responses have behaved with unexpected "strength." We found in Chapter 7 that they are more highly correlated with left-right self-locations than one would anticipate, given some commonsense assumptions and the performance of other foreign issues. Similarly, in Chapter 20, district sentiments about the development of a nuclear strike force are perceived by elites with much greater accuracy than would seem warranted by the novelty of the issue and the lack of obvious local cues with regard to citizen feeling on it. At the risk of reiteration, let us note that all of these cognate anomalies may stem from the fact that our measurements were made in a period when General de Gaulle, the dominant mover and "issue" in national politics, had singled out the force de frappe as his prize personal cause. As a result, feelings about Gaullism may have become more tightly bound up with this issue than with any other, thus giving it a visibility and a connotational clarity that was unusual and, perhaps, transient. Since Gaullist favor and disfavor could be read in election returns from the district level with almost the same clarity as left-right coloration, such associations would help explain the perplexing accuracy of perceptions on the matter. And the strong assimilation of the issue of Gaullism to basic left-right differences as well as to the government-opposition roll-call votes on the force de frappe may help to explain its strength in the other contexts as well. In sum, perhaps the force de frappe issue behaves as it does mainly because it became a proxy for voter polarization over Gaullism.

2. So far, we have summarized a substantive point that is partly technical, which argues that AD bonds calculated from 1968 predictors should be stronger than the same bonds predicted from 1967 district data. There is one further argument, however, which may seem contrary. This hinges on the fact that our 1968 district data are intrinsically weaker, that is, they are based on fewer districts and fewer individual observations within districts. Nevertheless, these considerations would not lead us to expect reduced AD bonds as a result. The fewer observations per district could produce this result, but our correction for small-sample attenuation is a highly specific countermeasure designed precisely to remove any relevant artifacts from the data. And although the fact of fewer districts is regrettable, the cost to be paid is in heightened sampling variability of estimate, not in any inevitable bias of estimates toward attenuated correlations.

3. Once again, as we begin to talk of precise measurement, it is important to emphasize that our measurement base must necessarily change. In Chapter 18 we dealt with a sample of 86 districts, within which interviews had been conducted in 1967 and for which roll-call votes in the National Assembly were available. In Chapter 22, when we turned to estimates of the full diamond of representation parameters, we were obliged to retreat to some 66 districts for which deputy interviews as well as mass ones were available. Now, as we introduce our 1968 data, we suffer a further attrition: we have estimates of district sentiment for only 54 districts, and even this number is, from a sampling point of view, not fully efficient because only some 43 districts provide a randomly selected view of the Assembly. Although the additional 11 districts, selected with certainty from the original sample of 86 districts because legislative seats changed hands in them, can be counted upon to add to this view in a very useful way, they are of less than perfect sampling efficiency because of their certainty of selection. If we wished to use 1968 data in diamond form, we would reduce our number of districts still further, because we would then be required to have personal interviews with deputies as of 1968. This need would reduce our effective number of districts from 54 down to a number like 32 (a number a shade imprecise because of the death of a deputy in mid-session).

4. These values cannot be tightly compared with those in Figure 22-2 because of slight changes in base, including the fact that there is no useful simulation of votes for the foreign-aid issue, since the relevant roll-call votes all occurred in the 1967 session. Loose comparisons are not, however, greatly misleading.

5. This is most obvious in the alternate formula for r appropriate when the variates x and y have already been converted to standard scores. Then

$$r = \frac{\sum xy}{N}.$$

Here it is clear that r has the structure of an average, which is to say, the sums of a quantum over N cases, subsequently divided by N. The quantum is the product of x and y expressed as standard scores. Where three standard scores are jointly positive or jointly negative, the contribution to r is highly positive. Where they differ in signs, the contribution is negative and tends to drag down any expected positive correlation. We propose to intercept and employ these individual contributions.

6. Once again, it is important to note that we write these lines despite full recognition that correlational assessments have been put under rather severe attack in recent years because the values they display are intrinsically dependent on properties of the total population figuring in them (such as univariate variances), and hence have been condemned as at the very least theoretically uninteresting, and more often as being both misleading and prescientific (see Achen, 1977). It is painful, in the face of such a barrage, not only to work liberally with correlation coefficients but even to hint at imputations of values to individuals that take on meaning solely because of the group backdrop against which these individuals are operating, such as distributions of attitudes and behaviors in contrasting populations. Let us state as plainly as possible that we are aware that the values we are about to assign to individual deputies in this context are completely population dependent. Thus we may give a value to a deputy which makes him appear unusually compatible with sentiments in his district, even though he might register as quite the opposite if we could somehow extract him and his district as a joint unit from France in the 1967–1972 period, and transplant the unit to, say, the Land of Oz in 1900. This may be a limitation so sobering that we have no right to proceed at all. But we are of the view that individuals like our deputies have not only absolute personal properties, but also relational properties with other segments of their social surroundings; and that if this relationship to the social surroundings were to change dramatically, as a move to Oz suggests, then their behavior would change as well, and the reason for our interest in the

case would be lost. Indeed, the prime purpose of our study has been to examine these highly complex relationships, including the location of individuals (citizens or deputies) within relevant population distributions of attitudes and behaviors, whether they are more or less polarized (which matters enormously); and more especially, to examine the joint fit of such distributions, as well as the location of individuals within those joint fits. These are all highly relational concerns, and hence ones which are not badly served by relative statistics that locate the individual at some point in a population distribution, be it univariate or bivariate. In short, our sins may be mountainous, but for better or worse, we do not claim innocence.

7. Let us rapidly confirm for the sophisticated reader, however, that the deputy-level measure of congruence based on specific-issue calculations is rather noisier (suffers a larger proportion of error variance) than the measure based on the left-right locations. This should have been apparent from the relative levels of correlation summarized in the synthetic diamonds of Chapter 22, which seem much more robust for the left-right measures.

8. In the first stage, we focused upon all of our districts which were so "safe" as to have been decided by a majority victory in the first tour of voting. Within this subset, districts were ordered by the relative size of the majority captured. Beyond these safest seats, the districts requiring a second or run-off tour were sorted out. In many cases these districts devolved into a two-way race in the second balloting, but in a number of cases they remained at least triangular. To arrive at a further ranking of marginality, we in effect dealt in the second stage with the size of the margin enjoyed by the victor *relative to his closest competition,* that is, the candidate finishing second. This seemed to be the most reasonable operationalization of seat "safety" for the multiparty case, although rival possibilities exist.

9. The operational definition of "safe" and "marginal" in the Miller study is based on representative reports, rather than on objective summations of vote margins in the district, such as we have used. Two advantages of subjective reports are that respondents were asked to integrate over a number of elections ("Over the years has the district been a safe district, a fairly close district, or what?"), and that the reports reflect anxiety levels of the representatives, which may be firmer predictors to their efforts at representation than the "objective" data on the chances of defeat. Nevertheless, our objective definition meshes more solidly with past literature on the subject. In any event, we are willing to assume that the subjective reports and objective conditions are massively correlated, and that we are looking, in what follows, at what is largely the same partitioning of districts for the two countries.

10. This essentially negative finding must be laid against the correlational evidence from the French portions of Figure 23-2 which show safe-seat occupants assessing district opinion with greater relative congruence than deputies from marginal districts, just as in the American case. However this may be, and despite the substantial association between seat safety and seniority, it does not appear that seniority is the appropriate intervening variable to explain the safety-accuracy association.

24. The Nature of Representation in France

1. If we wanted to recast district opinion on a base of the most involved 10–15 percent of each district sample, our estimates of means would rest on two or three cases. Such estimates would suffer enormous sampling error. Indeed, the reader may recall that when we wanted to partition our district samples into winning and losing voters in Chapter 19—giving us eight or ten cases per district estimate—we were relieved to discover that we were dealing with politically homogeneous subgroups, relative to our total-district estimates, because this meant that our sampling error was actually *less* despite more than halving our case numbers. This was, however, a highly unusual circumstance. For

the projected partitions by status and political involvement, there is little or no gain in policy homogeneity, so that even halving the samples incurs greatly increased error over either the total sample or majority-minority partitions.

2. The advance caution signal which we have used throughout is alpha, our estimate of the factor necessary to correct our observed correlations for small-sample attenuation. Alpha performs this function well, because it is itself the appropriate joint function of case numbers and between-district differentiation. It is clear from an inspection of Figure 1 in Appendix C that alpha begins to collapse with rapidly increasing speed well before all district differentiation has disappeared, just as it does with case decline. The interaction of the two is, of course, a potent multiplier indeed. For the purposes of this analysis, we have discarded analytic results when alpha falls below .50. This threshold was easy to choose because our data showed a major disjuncture at this point: of all the comparisons we wished to attempt, 38 alphas fell between .50 and .81. Six fell at .38 or below (down to .21). There were no instances between .38 and .50, which suggested a very natural floor for qualification.

3. See, for example, some of the data presented in Chapter 21. Other excellent studies of representation exist in a similar format, including Barnes (1977) for Italy, and Farah (1980) for West Germany. Close comparison with these other studies has not always been easy, however, either because their designs are truncated or because of the absence of published tabulations on matters that interest us.

A. Design and Implementation of the Mass Interviewing

1. We report the number of districts in each category as communicated to us by SOFRES in their report on sampling procedures. These total to 458 districts, while in fact the total should be 462 (465 Metropolitan districts less the three districts for Corsica). The discrepancy escaped our notice until this appendix was prepared, much too long after the survey was conducted for SOFRES to be able to account for it. At the time we contracted with SOFRES, however, we were fully satisfied with their sampling procedures, and the worst-case hypothesis (assuming actual omission of four districts from the universe) would have imposed a zero probability of selection upon less than 1 percent of the districts.

2. Interviewing began on April 21, 1967, and was terminated on July 28. Nearly 33 percent of the interviews were conducted in April, 53 percent in May, 11 percent in June, and 2 percent in July. The date of interview was not ascertained for 3.8 percent of the interviews.

3. In retrospect, it has occurred to us that it might be worthwhile to use voting lists in France not only as a designation of respondents but as an index of dwelling units. When the respondent is at the expected address, he or she is interviewed. But when he or she has moved from an address or has died, a random procedure would be used to select respondents from among the current occupants.

4. One of the liabilities of a weighting scheme is that weighted frequencies cannot readily be drawn within the canons of statistical inference for unweighted raw observations. To minimize this problem, we selected a weighting transformation which left the total weighted N (2007.0) very close to, but slightly less than, the raw N of 2046. This means that the weighted frequencies filled in for various tables in this study are roughly equivalent in magnitude to the underlying raw frequencies for the tables, except in rare cases where the sample is partitioned along regional or urban-rural lines, or along the lines of some variable strongly correlated with these variables.

5. Institut National de la Statistique et des Etudes Economiques.

6. The official results were obtained from République Française Ministère de l'Intérieur, *Les Elections législatives de 1967* (Paris: Imprimerie Nationale, 1967). There is

some discrepancy between the official coding and our own coding (based on *Le Monde* of March 7, 1967, and March 14, 1967) of the party affiliation of certain candidates, almost exclusively in the Democratic Center and Miscellaneous categories. The official results for 1968 which appear in Table A-6 were obtained from the equivalent source for the elections of that year: République Française Ministère de l'Intérieur, *Les Elections législatives de 1968* (Paris: Imprimerie Nationale, 1969). The comment about candidate coding for 1967 applies also to 1968, for which our own coding relies on *Le Monde* of June 25 and July 2, 1968.

7. In view of the district-based design, we would not in any case have been interested in pursuing persons who had moved out of our sample districts. Ideally, however, we would have liked to reinterview those 1967 respondents who had merely shifted residence within one of our districts.

8. It should be remembered that this figure does not include nonresponses from the original pool of addresses approached in the 1967 survey.

9. The number of deaths to be expected over this time lapse would slightly exceed the figure for known deaths.

10. In other words, since we know the 1969 survivors to be slightly more involved and educated than the 1967 pool, but find them still lower on both counts than the fresh sample, we must either conclude that the original 1967 sample happened to underestimate these terms, or that the 1969 fresh sample overestimates them, or some combination of the two, as a matter of simple sampling variability. This is so because the fresh sample, like the 1967 sample, cannot be subject to bias either from contamination or from panel mortality. Moreover, its response rate was relatively good. Therefore, discrepancies must be due to the sampling variability of a small sample.

11. These words were written well before the Socialist victory of 1981.

B. The Structure of the Elite Sample

1. In 1964, for a study of opinions among several sectors of French elites, Macridis and his colleagues contacted ten French Communist political leaders but received no "positive answers" from them and none were interviewed. Their total of 147 interviews with French elites included only two with members of the Communist party, both within the category of trade unions and professional associations. See Deutsch et al., 1967, pp. 10–13, 19, 36–38, and 312.

2. The inclusion of a residual category for comparison can be subject to some dispute, since we would have a priori expectations that such a category would show unusual heterogeneity. On balance, it is indeed the most heterogeneous category. It does, however, have a center-right coloration, and it was included partly because it shows more homogeneity than one would expect. In a few instances, for example, it is the most homogeneous of the five categories.

Two of the candidates classified as Centre Démocrate for this analysis were subsequently classified as "Other," after an inspection of their questionnaires failed to reveal any connection with the Centre Démocrate, although the press indicated that they had received Centre Démocrate support.

3. The names were drawn randomly by district: each name had an equal probability of being selected. Probability of selection was not proportional to the population of the districts; therefore, the Communist sample may overrepresent the less populous districts relative to the more populous ones.

4. Just as our 1967 mass survey coincided with a high point of Communist party acceptance, which enabled us to achieve a panel estimate of the Communist vote that approximated the actual Communist vote, so does our survey of candidates appear to have coincided with a period of growing interest in survey research methods on the part of

Communist party leaders. See, for example, the account of a panel discussion by Communist leaders on the sociology of political forces in *Le Monde,* April 19, 1967. At the end of the interview schedule, all of our respondents were given an opportunity to comment on the questionnaire through the medium of this question: "In conclusion, are there any comments you would like to make on any of the subjects we have discussed?" About 60 percent of the respondents either had no comment to make or made only perfunctory remarks. Seven candidates, however, chose to make distinctly unfavorable comments about the questionnaire, and four of these were Communists. Three times as many Communists, however, volunteered favorable remarks about the interview.

5. The only exception was one Gaullist candidate who told us that he used "UDT-Gaulliste de Gauche" as a label; we coded him for that location. Gaullists with an MRP background were coded at the left-right location of the UNR, not of the MRP. It seemed to us that MRP politicians who joined the large, decade-old Gaullist movement of the Fifth Republic acquired a new political affiliation in a way which could not be attributed to the MRP politicians who joined the new Centre Démocrate.

6. Strictly speaking, "Droite Modérée" applies to the space between 60 and 70 on the left-right scale and, symmetrically, "Gauche Modérée" applies to the space between 30 and 40. When the scale was reproduced, these two labels were displaced slightly to the left, with the result that respondents viewing the scale casually might reasonably associate "Droite Modérée" with 60 and "Gauche Modérée" with 30. Rather than tidy up this labeling for subsequent uses of the scale, we retained it at each wave of our interviews, with both the voters and the candidates.

7. In view of the accidental interviews taken among candidates who received the votes of less than 10 percent of the registered voters in districts where the election was decided at the first ballot, we did not further reduce the candidate population by the number of candidates in that category for the purpose of calculating the candidate weights.

8. In 10 of these 11 districts there was a turnover of party control in 1968; in the other one the incumbent did not run again, but the seat was held by the same party.

9. Several of the candidates we interviewed in 1967 had asked to see the results of our survey. We were unable to oblige them in 1968 with any published piece, but we prepared a brief analysis of some of the elements of the 1967 elite survey especially for the candidates from whom we requested a second interview, so that they could see a sample of the kind of work we were intending to do. Care was taken to avoid displaying types of data that might contaminate the most central of the 1968 responses.

10. One deputy whom we planned to reinterview was replaced in the Assembly by his alternate (*suppléant*) before he could be interviewed. The alternate was interviewed instead, and this is classified as an initial interview.

11. The listing here follows the manner in which the parties and groups were presented in the 1968 mass survey questionnaire.

C. Correction of Correlations for Small-Sample Attenuation

1. Before pooling the within-district estimates of sampling error variance, the Stokes treatment introduces a multiplier reflecting the highly clustered design of Survey Research Center national samples. Although in the French case a stratified random sampling of legislative districts produces an efficiently clustered design, the within-district samples drawn systematically from voter registration lists come very close to representing simple random samples of the districts involved. Thus the design effect multiplier of 1.40 employed by Stokes is inappropriate. It is unlikely that a corresponding multiplier for the French design would exceed 1.02 for within-district estimates, and therefore we have ignored this correction.

Bibliography

Achen, Christopher H. 1975. "Mass Political Attitudes and the Survey Response." *American Political Science Review* 69:1218–1231.

————1977. "Measuring Representation: Perils of the Correlation Coefficient." *American Political Science Review* 21:805–815.

————1978. "Measuring Representation." *American Journal of Political Science* 22:475–510.

Adam, Gérard. 1968. "Eléments d'analyse sur les liens entre le P.C.F. et la C.G.T." *Revue française de science politique* 18:524–539.

Alexandre, Philippe. 1969. *L'Elysée en péril.* Paris: Fayard.

Alford, Robert R. 1963. *Party and Society: The Anglo-American Democracies.* Chicago: Rand McNally.

Alker, Hayward R., Jr. 1969. "A Typology of Ecological Fallacies." In Mattei Dogan and Stein Rokkan, eds., *Quantitative Analysis in the Social Sciences,* ch. 4. Cambridge, Mass.: MIT Press.

Allerbeck, Klaus R., M. Kent Jennings, and Leopold Rosenmayr. 1979. "Generations and Families: Political Action." In Samuel H. Barnes, Max Kaase, et al., *Political Action: Mass Participation in Five Western Democracies,* ch. 16. Beverly Hills, Calif.: Sage.

Almond, Gabriel A., and Sidney Verba. 1963. *The Civic Culture.* Princeton, N.J.: Princeton University Press.

L'Année politique (since 1944–45). Paris: Editions du Grand Siècle, Presses Universitaires de France, and Editions du Moniteur.

Aron, Raymond. 1968. *Progress and Disillusion: The Dialectics of Modern Society.* New York: Praeger.

Asher, Herbert B. 1973. *Freshman Representatives and the Learning of Voting Cues.* Sage Professional Papers in American Politics 04-003. Beverly Hills, Calif.

Assemblée Nationale. *Statistiques.* Annual volumes published by the Secrétariat général de l'Assemblée nationale.

Aver, Evelyne, Constant Hames, Jacques Maître, and Guy Michelat. 1970. "Pratique religieuse et comportement électoral à travers les sondages d'opinion." *Archives de sociologie des religions* 29:27–52.

Axelrod, Robert. 1970. *Conflict of Interest.* Chicago: Markham.

Bachrach, Peter, and Morton Baratz. 1962. "Two Faces of Power." *American Political Science Review* 56:947–952.

Barnes, Samuel H. 1971. "Left, Right and the Italian Voter." *Comparative Political Studies* 4:157–175.

————1977. *Representation in Italy: Institutionalized Tradition and Electoral Choice.* Chicago: University of Chicago Press.

Barnes, Samuel H., and Roy Pierce. 1971. "Public Opinion and Political Preferences in France and Italy." *Midwest Journal of Political Science* 15:643–660.

Barton, Allen H., and R. Wayne Parsons. 1977. "Measuring Belief System Structure." *Public Opinion Quarterly* 41:159–180.

Belsley, David A., Edwin Kuh, and Roy E. Welsh. 1980. *Regression Diagnostics: Identifying Influential Data and Sources of Collinearity.* New York: Wiley.

Bénéton, Philippe, and Jean Touchard. 1970. "Les interprétations de la crise de mai-juin 1968." *Revue française de science politique* 20:503–544.

Bon, Frédéric, and Jérôme Jaffré. 1978. "Les règles d'élection au scrutin majoritaire." *Revue française de science politique* 28:5–20.

Boudon, Raymond. 1977. "The French University since 1968." *Comparative Politics* 10:89–119.

Boulard, Fernand. 1950. *Essor ou déclin du clergé français.* Paris: Editions du Cerf.

Brown, Steven R. 1970. "Consistency and the Persistence of Ideology: Some Experimental Results." *Public Opinion Quarterly* 34:60–68.

Brulé, Michel. 1966. "L'Appartenance religieuse et le vote du 5 décembre 1965." *Sondages* 2:15–19.

Budge, Ian, Ivor Crewe, and Dennis Farlie, eds. 1976. *Party Identification and Beyond: Representations of Voting and Party Competition.* London: Wiley.

Burns, James McGregor. 1949. *Congress on Trial.* New York: Harper.

Butler, David, and Donald E. Stokes. 1969. *Political Change in Britain: Forces Shaping Electoral Choice.* New York: St. Martin's.

———1976. *Political Change in Britain.* New York: St. Martin's. Second College Edition.

Cain, Bruce E., and John Ferejohn. 1981. "Party Identification in the United States and Great Britain." *Comparative Political Studies* 14:31–48.

Cameron, David R. 1972. "Stability and Change in Patterns of French Partisanship." *Public Opinion Quarterly* 36:19–30.

Campbell, Angus, Philip E. Converse, Warren E. Miller, and Donald E. Stokes. 1960. *The American Voter.* New York: Wiley.

———1966. *Elections and the Political Order.* New York: Wiley.

Campbell, Angus, and Henry Valen. 1961. "Party Identification in Norway and the United States." *Public Opinion Quarterly* 25:505–525.

Campbell, Bruce A. 1971. "French Elections and Voter Stability: A Model of Voting Behavior for the French National Electorate." PhD dissertation, University of Michigan.

Campbell, Peter. 1958. *French Electoral Systems and Elections since 1789.* London: Faber and Faber.

Capdevielle, Jacques, Elisabeth Dupoirier, Gérard Grunberg, Etienne Schweisguth, and Colette Ysmal. 1981. *France de gauche, vote à droite.* Paris: Presses de la fondation nationale des sciences politiques.

Cayrol, Roland. 1971. "La campagne de la gauche." In Centre d'étude de la vie politique française, *Les Elections législatives de mars 1967.* Cahiers de la fondation nationale des sciences politiques 170. Paris: Armand Colin.

Cayrol, Roland, Jean-Luc Parodi, and Colette Ysmal. 1971. "L'image de la fonction parlementaire chez les députés français." *Revue française de science politique* 21:1173–1206.

———1973. *Le Député français.* Fondation nationale des sciences politiques, Travaux et recherches de science politique 23. Paris: Armand Colin.

———1976. "French Deputies and the Political System." *Legislative Studies Quarterly* 1:67–99. Originally published as "Les députés français et le système politique," *Revue française de science politique* 25:72–105.

Charlot, Jean. 1967. *L'Union pour la nouvelle République: Etude du pouvoir au sein d'un parti politique.* Cahiers de la fondation nationale des sciences politiques 153. Paris: Armand Colin.

————1971. *The Gaullist Phenomenon.* New York: Praeger.

Clausen, Aage. 1973. *How Congressmen Decide: A Policy Focus.* New York: St. Martin's.

————1977. "The Accuracy of Leader Perceptions of Constituency Views." *Legislative Studies Quarterly* 2:361–384.

Committee on Political Parties of the American Political Science Association. 1950. *Toward a More Responsible Two-Party System.* New York: Holt, Rinehart and Winston.

Converse, Philip E. 1964. "The Nature of Belief Systems in Mass Publics." In David Apter, ed., *Ideology and Discontent.* New York: Free Press of Glencoe.

————1966. "The Problem of Party Distances in Models of Voting Change." In M. Kent Jennings and Harmon Zeigler, eds., *The Electoral Process.* Englewood Cliffs, N.J.: Prentice-Hall.

————1969a. "Of Time and Partisan Stability." *Comparative Political Studies* 2:139–171.

————1969b. "Survey Research and the Decoding of Patterns in Ecological Data." In Mattei Dogan and Stein Rokkan, eds., *Quantitative Ecological Analysis in the Social Sciences,* pp. 459–485. Cambridge, Mass.: MIT Press.

————1970. "Attitudes and Non-Attitudes: Continuation of a Dialogue." In Edward R. Tufte, ed., *The Quantitative Analysis of Social Problems.* Reading, Mass.: Addison-Wesley.

————1975a. "Public Opinion and Voting Behavior." In Fred I. Greenstein and Nelson W. Polby, eds., *Handbook of Political Science,* vol. 4, ch. 2. Reading, Mass.: Addison-Wesley.

————1975b. "Some Mass-Elite Contrasts in the Perception of Political Space." *Social Science Information* 14:49–83.

Converse, Philip E., and Georges Dupeux. 1962. "Politicization of the Electorate in France and the United States." *Public Opinion Quarterly* 26:1–23.

————1966. "De Gaulle and Eisenhower: The Public Image of the Victorious General." In Angus Campbell, Philip E. Converse, Warren E. Miller, and Donald E. Stokes, *Elections and the Political Order.* New York: Wiley.

Converse, Philip E., Georges Dupeux, and John Meisel. 1967. "Continuities in Popular Political Culture: French and Anglo-Saxon Contrasts in Canada." Paper prepared for the International Conference on Comparative Electoral Behavior.

Converse, Philip E., and Roy Pierce. 1979. "Representative Roles and Legislative Behavior in France." *Legislative Studies Quarterly* 4:525–562.

Crewe, Ivor. 1976. "Party Identification Theory and Political Change in Britain." In Ian Budge, Ivor Crewe, and Dennis Farlie, eds., *Party Identification and Beyond: Representations of Voting and Party Competition,* ch. 3. London: Wiley.

————1981. "Why the Conservatives Won." In Howard R. Penniman, ed., *Britain at the Polls, 1979: A Study of the General Election.* Washington and London: American Enterprise Institute for Public Policy Research.

————1983. "Why Labour Lost the British Elections." *Public Opinion,* vol. 6, no. 3, pp. 7–9, 56–60.

Crewe, Ivor, Bo Särlvik, and James Alt. 1977. "Partisan Dealignment in Britain, 1964–1974." *British Journal of Political Science* 7:129–190.

Crozier, Michel. 1964. *The Bureaucratic Phenomenon.* Chicago: University of Chicago Press.

Daalder, Hans, and Jerrold G. Rusk. 1976. "Perceptions of Party in the Dutch Parliament." In Samuel C. Patterson and John C. Wahlke, eds., *Comparative Legislative Behavior,* ch. 6. New York: Wiley.

Dahl, Robert A. 1966. *Political Oppositions in Western Democracies.* New Haven and London: Yale University Press.

Dalton, Russell J. 1983. "Political Parties and Political Representation: Party Supporters and Party Elites in Nine Nations." Paper presented at the Annual Meeting of the American Political Science Association, Chicago.

Dansette, Adrien. 1971. *Mai 1968.* Paris: Plon.

Davis, Otto A., Melvin J. Hinich, and Peter C. Ordeshook. 1970. "An Expository Development of a Mathematical Model of the Electoral Process." *American Political Science Review* 64:426–448.

Deledicq, André, ed. 1968. *Un Mois de mai orageux: 113 étudiants parisiens expliquent les raisons du soulèvement universitaire.* Toulouse: Edouard Privat.

Deutsch, Eméric, Denis Lindon, and Pierre Weill. 1966. *Les Familles politiques: Aujourd'hui en France.* Paris: Les Editions de Minuit.

Deutsch, Karl W., Lewis J. Edinger, Roy C. Macridis, and Richard L. Merritt. 1967. *France, Germany, and the Western Alliance: A Study of Elite Attitudes on European Integration and World Politics.* New York: Charles Scribner's Sons.

Didier, Chantal. 1978. "La Sur-représentation de la majorité en France et en Grande-Bretagne." Doctoral dissertation, University of Paris II.

Dogan, Mattei. 1960. "Changement de régime et changement de personnel." In Association française de science politique, *L'Etablissement de la cinquième République: Le Référendum de septembre et les élections de novembre 1958.* Cahiers de la fondation nationale des sciences politiques 109. Paris: Armand Colin.

Downs, Anthony. 1957. *An Economic Theory of Democracy.* New York: Harper.

Duhamel, Alain. 1966. "L'Image du parti communiste." *Sondages* 1:57–71.

———1967. "Les transferts de voix, notamment à gauche, varient selon les régions et les candidats du second tour." *Le Monde,* September 2.

———1968. "Le transfert de voix au second tour des dernières élections législatives." *Le Monde,* November 7.

Dupeux, Georges. 1960. "D'une consultation à l'autre: Les réactions du corps électoral." In Association française de science politique, *L'Etablissement de la cinquième République: Le Référendum de septembre et les élections de novembre 1958.* Cahiers de la fondation nationale des sciences politiques 109. Paris: Armand Colin.

Duverger, Maurice. 1965. *Political Parties: Their Organization and Activity in the Modern State.* New York: Wiley.

Emden, Cecil S. 1959. *The People and the Constitution: Being a History of the Development of the People's Influence in British Government.* Oxford: Oxford University Press.

Epstein, Leon. 1967. *Political Parties in Western Democracies.* New York: Praeger.

Erbès-Séguin, Sabine. 1970. "Le Déclenchement des grèves de mai: Spontanéité des masses et rôle des syndicats." *Sociologie du travail* 12:177–189.

Erikson, Robert S. 1978. "Constituency Opinion and Congressional Behavior: a Reexamination of the Miller-Stokes Representation Data." *American Journal of Political Science* 22:511–535.

Erikson, Robert S., and Norman R. Luttbeg. 1973. *American Public Opinion: Its Origins, Content, and Impact.* New York: Wiley.

Eulau, Heinz. 1967. "Changing Views of Representation." In Ithiel de Sola Pool, ed., *Contemporary Political Science: Toward Empirical Theory,* ch. 3. New York: McGraw-Hill.

Eulau, Heinz, and Paul D. Karps. 1977. "The Puzzle of Representation: Specifying Components of Responsiveness." *Legislative Studies Quarterly* 2:233–254.

Eulau, Heinz, John C. Wahlke, William Buchanan, and LeRoy Ferguson. 1959. "The Role of the Representative: Some Empirical Observations on the Theory of Edmund Burke." *American Political Science Review* 53:742–756.

Eurobarometer 5 (May 1976). *Revenues, Satisfaction, and Poverty.* Principal Investigators: Jacques-René Rabier and Ronald Inglehart. Commission of the European Communities and Center for Political Studies, University of Michigan. ICPSR (Inter-University Consortium for Political and Social Research) edition, 1978.

Farah, Barbara G. 1980. "Political Representation in West Germany: The Institution and Maintenance of Mass-Elite Linkages." PhD dissertation, University of Michigan.

Farah, Barbara G. and Warren E. Miller. 1974. "A Comparative Analysis of Dimensional Structures: Political Ideology in American Masses and Elites." Paper presented at the Annual Meeting of the American Political Science Association, Chicago.

Fauvet, Jacques. 1973. "Le Changement et le pari." *Le Monde,* March 3, pp. 1 and 14.

Fenno, Richard F., Jr. 1978. *Home Style: House Members in Their Districts.* Boston: Little, Brown.

Ferniot, Jean. 1958. "L'U.N.R., qui est-ce?" *L'Express,* December 4, pp. 8–11.

Fiorina, Morris P. 1974. *Representatives, Roll Calls, and Constituencies.* Lexington, Mass.: D. C. Heath.

————1977. *Congress: Keystone of the Washington Establishment.* New Haven, Conn.: Yale University Press.

————1981. *Retrospective Voting in American National Elections.* New Haven, Conn.: Yale University Press.

Friedrich, Carl J. 1941. *Constitutional Government and Democracy.* Boston: Little, Brown.

Gicquel, Jean. 1968. *Essai sur la pratique de la Ve République: Bilan d'un septennat.* Paris: R. Pichon and R. Durand-Auzias.

Goguel, François. 1946. *La politique des partis sous la IIIe République.* Paris: Editions du Seuil.

————1952. *France under the Fourth Republic.* Ithaca, N.Y.: Cornell University Press.

————1965. "Analyse des résultats." In François Goguel, ed., *Le Référendum d'octobre et les élections de novembre 1962.* Cahiers de la fondation nationale des sciences politiques 142. Paris: Armand Colin.

————1967. "Les Elections législatives des 5 et 12 Mars 1967." *Revue française de science politique* 17:457–458.

————1968. "Les Elections législatives des 23 et 30 juin 1968." *Revue française de science politique* 18:837–858.

————1970. *Géographie des élections françaises sous la troisième et la quatrième République.* Paris: Armand Colin.

————1981. *Chroniques électorales: La quatrième République.* Vol. 1 of *Les Scrutins politiques en France de 1945 à nos jours.* Paris: Presses de la fondation nationale des sciences politiques.

————1983a. *Chroniques électorales: La cinquième République du général de Gaulle.* Vol. 2 of *Les Scrutins politiques en France de 1945 à nos jours.* Paris: Presses de la fondation nationale des sciences politiques.

————1983b. *Chroniques électorales: La cinquième République après de Gaulle.* Vol. 3 of *Les Scrutins politiques en France de 1945 à nos jours.* Paris: Presses de la fondation nationale des sciences politiques.

————1984. "Charles de Gaulle du 24 au 29 mai 1968." *Espoir* 46:3–14.

Goguel, François, Alain Lancelot, and Jean Ranger. 1960. "Analyse des résultats." In Association française de science politique, *L'Etablissement de la cinquième République: Le Référendum de septembre et les élections de novembre 1958.* Cahiers de la fondation nationale des sciences politiques 109. Paris: Armand Colin.

Greenstein, Fred I. 1965. *Children and Politics.* New Haven, Conn.: Yale University Press.

Greenstein, Fred I., and Sidney G. Tarrow. 1969. "The Study of French Political Socialization." *World Politics* 22:95–137.

Guichard-Ayoub, Elaine, Charles Roig, and Jean Grangé. 1965. *Etudes sur le Parlement de la Ve République.* Paris: Presses Universitaires de France.

Guin, Yannick. 1969. *La Commune de Nantes.* Cahiers libres 154. Paris: Librairie François Maspero.

Hauss, Charles S. 1978. *The New Left in France: The Unified Socialist Party.* Westport, Conn. Greenwood Press.

Hibbs, Douglas A., Jr., and Nicholas Vasilatos. 1981. "Economics and Politics in France:

Economic Performance and Mass Political Support for Presidents Pompidou and Giscard d'Estaing." *European Journal of Political Research* 9:133–145.

Hoffmann, Stanley. 1963. "Paradoxes of the French Political Community." In Stanley Hoffmann et al., *In Search of France*. Cambridge, Mass. Harvard University Press.

————1974. *Decline or Renewal? France since the 1930s*. New York: Viking Press.

Hoffmann, Stanley, et al., with the collaboration of Michel Des Accords. 1956. *Le Mouvement Poujade*. Cahiers de la fondation nationale des sciences politiques 81. Paris: Armand Colin.

Hunt, William H. 1969. "Legislative Roles and Ideological Orientations of French Deputies." Paper presented at the Annual Meeting of the American Political Science Association, New York.

Hyman, Herbert. 1959. *Political Socialization*. Glencoe, Ill.: Free Press.

Inglehart, Ronald, and Avram Hochstein. 1972. "Alignment and Dealignment of the Electorate in France and the United States." *Comparative Political Studies* 5:343–372.

Inglehart, Ronald, and Hans D. Klingemann. 1976. "Party Identification, Ideological Preference, and the Left-Right Dimension among Western Mass Publics." In Ian Budge, Ivor Crewe, and Dennis Farlie, eds., *Party Identification and Beyond: Representations of Voting and Party Competition*. London: Wiley.

INSEE (Institut national de la statistique et des études économiques). 1962. *Code des catégories socio-professionnelles*, 4th ed. Paris: Imprimerie Nationale.

Jackson, John E. 1975. "Issues, Party Choices, and Presidential Votes." *American Journal of Political Science* 19:161–185.

Jacobson, Gary C. 1980. "Congressional Elections, 1978: The Case of the Vanishing Challengers." Paper prepared for the Conference on Congressional Elections, Rice University and the University of Houston, Texas, January 10–12.

Jennings, M. Kent, Klaus R. Allerbeck, and Leopold Rosnmayr. 1979. "Generations and Families: General Orientations." In Samuel H. Barnes, Max Kaase, et al., *Political Action: Mass Participation in Five Western Democracies*, ch. 15. Beverly Hills, Calif.: Sage.

Jennings, M. Kent, and Kenneth P. Langton. 1969. "Mothers versus Fathers: The Formation of Political Orientations among Young Americans." *Journal of Politics* 31:329–358.

Jennings, M. Kent, and Richard G. Niemi. 1968. "The Transmission of Political Values from Parent to Child." *American Political Science Review* 62:169–184.

————1974. *The Political Character of Adolescence*. Princeton, N.J.: Princeton University Press.

————1981. *Generations and Politics*. Princeton, N.J.: Princeton University Press.

Journal Officiel de la République française: Débats parlementaires, Assemblée nationale. 1967–1973.

Jouvenel, Robert de. 1914. *La République des camarades*. Paris: Bernard Grasset.

Judd, Charles M., and Michael A. Milburn. 1980. "The Structure of Attitude Systems in the General Public: Comparisons of a Structural Equation Model." *American Sociological Review* 45:627–643.

Kaase, Max. 1976. "Party Identification and Voting Behavior in the West German Election of 1969." In Ian Budge, Ivor Crewe, and Dennis Farlie, eds., *Party Identification and Beyond: Representations of Voting and Party Competition*, ch. 5. London: Wiley.

Kahan, Michael, David Butler, and Donald Stokes. 1966. "On the Analytical Division of Social Class." *British Journal of Sociology* 17:122–132.

Karps, Paul D. 1978. "Representation and Political Participation: What Nexus?" Paper presented at the Annual Meeting of the American Political Science Association, New York.

Kingdon, John. 1967. "Politicians' Beliefs about Voters." *American Political Science Review* 61:137–145.

————1973. *Congressmen's Voting Decisions.* New York: Harper & Row.

————1977. "Models of Legislative Voting." *Journal of Politics* 39:563–595.

Kirkpatrick, Evron M. 1971. " 'Toward a More Responsible Two-Party System': Political Science, Policy Science, or Pseudo-Science?" *American Political Science Review* 65:965–990.

Klingemann, Hans D. 1972. "Testing the Left-Right Continuum on a Sample of German Voters." *Comparative Political Studies* 5:93–106.

————1979. "Measuring Ideological Conceptualizations." In Samuel H. Barnes, Max Kaase, et al., *Political Action: Mass Participation in Five Western Democracies,* ch. 8. Beverly Hills, Calif.: Sage.

Kriegel, Annie. 1972. *The French Communists: Profile of a People,* trans. Elaine P. Halperin. Chicago: University of Chicago Press.

Lafay, Jean-Dominique. 1981. "The Impact of Economic Variables on Political Behavior in France." In Douglas A. Hibbs, Jr., and Heino Fassbender, eds., *Contemporary Political Economy: Studies on the Interdependence of Politics and Economics,* pp. 137–149. Amsterdam: North-Holland Publishing Company.

Lancelot, Alain, and Pierre Weill. 1970. "Les transferts de voix du premier au second tour des élections de mars 1967: Une analyse de régression." In Centre d'étude de la vie politique française, *Les Elections législatives de mars 1967.* Cahiers de la fondation nationale des sciences politiques 170. Paris: Armand Colin.

Laponce, Jean A. 1970a. "Note on the Use of the Left-Right Dimension." *Comparative Political Studies* 2:481–502.

————1970b. "Dieu—à Droite ou à Gauche?" *Canadian Journal of Political Science–Revue canadienne de science politique* 3:257–274.

LeDuc, Lawrence. 1981. "The Dynamic Properties of Party Identification: A Four-Nation Comparison." *European Journal of Political Research* 9:257–268.

Lewis-Beck, Michael S. 1980. "Economic Conditions and Executive Popularity: The French Experience." *American Journal of Political Science* 24:306–323.

————1983. "Economics and the French Voter: A Microanalysis." *Public Opinion Quarterly* 47:347–360.

Lijphart, Arend. 1971. *Class Voting and Religious Voting in the European Democracies: A Preliminary Report.* Occasional Paper no. 8, Survey Research Center, University of Strathclyde, Glasgow.

Lindon, Denis, and Pierre Weill. 1974. *Le Choix d'un député: Un Modèle explicatif du comportement électoral.* Paris: Editions de Minuit.

Lipset, Seymour Martin, and Stein Rokkan. 1967. *Party Systems and Voter Alignments.* New York: Free Press.

Loewenberg, Gerhard. 1972. "Comparative Legislative Research." In Samuel C. Patterson and John C. Wahlke, eds., *Comparative Legislative Behavior: Frontiers of Research,* pp. 3–21. New York: Wiley.

Luttbeg, Norman R. 1968. "The Structure of Beliefs among Leaders and the Public." *Public Opinion Quarterly* 32:398–409.

————1971. "The Structure of Public Beliefs on State Policies: A Comparison with Local and National Findings." *Public Opinion Quarterly* 35:114–116.

MacRae, Duncan, Jr. 1952. "The Relation between Roll-Call Votes and Constituencies in the Massachusetts House of Representatives." *American Political Science Review* 46:1046–55.

————1958. "Religious and Socio-Economic Factors in the French Vote, 1946–56." *American Journal of Sociology* 64:290–298.

————1967. *Parliament, Parties, and Society in France.* New York: St. Martin's.

————1970. *Issues and Parties in Legislative Voting: Methods of Statistical Analysis.* New York: Harper & Row.

Macridis, Roy C. 1963. "France." In Roy C. Macridis and Robert E. Ward, eds., *Modern Political Systems: Europe.* Englewood Cliffs, N.J.: Prentice-Hall.

Maisl, Herbert. 1969. "Le Groupe communiste à l'Assemblée nationale française (1962-1967)." In Pierre Ferrari and Herbert Maisl, *Les Groupes communistes aux Assemblées parlementaires italiennes (1958-1963) et françaises (1962-1967).* Paris: Presses Universitaires de France.

Malraux, André. 1971. *Les Chênes qu'on abat . . .* Paris: Gallimard.

Mann, Thomas E., and Raymond E. Wolfinger. 1980. "Candidates and Parties in Congressional Elections." *American Political Science Review* 74:627-632.

Markus, Gregory B. 1983. "Dynamic Modelling of Cohort Change: The Case of Political Partisanship." *American Journal of Political Science* 27:717-739.

Markus, Gregory B., and Philip E. Converse. 1979. "A Dynamic Simultaneous Equation Model of Electoral Choice." *American Political Science Review* 73:1055-70.

Martin, David. 1978. *A General Theory of Secularization.* New York: Harper & Row.

Mayhew, David R. 1974. *Congress: The Electoral Connection.* New Haven, Conn.: Yale University Press.

McClosky, Herbert, Paul J. Hoffman, and Rosemary O'Hara. 1960. "Issue Conflict and Consensus among Party Leaders and Followers." *American Political Science Review* 54:406-427.

McHale, Vincent E. 1969. "Religion and Electoral Politics in France: Some Recent Observations." *Canadian Journal of Political Science-Revue canadienne de science politique* 2:292-311.

Michelat, Guy. 1965. "Attitudes et comportements politiques à l'automne 1962." In François Goguel, ed., *Le Référendum d'octobre et les élections de novembre 1962.* Cahiers de la fondation nationale des sciences politiques 142. Paris: Armand Colin.

Michelat, Guy, and Michel Simon. 1971. "Classe sociale objective, class sociale subjective, et comportement électoral." *Revue française de sociologie* 12:483-527.

————1977. *Classe, religion, et comportement politique.* Paris: Presses de la fondation nationale des sciences politiques and Editions Sociales.

Miller, Warren E. 1964. "Majority Rule and the Representative System of Government." In Erik Allardt and Yrjö Littunen, eds., *Cleavages, Ideologies, and Party Systems: Contributions to Comparative Political Sociology.* Helsinki: Westermarck Society. Reprinted in Erik Allardt and Stein Rokkan, eds., *Mass Politics: Studies in Political Sociology.* New York: Free Press, 1970.

————1976. "The Cross-National Use of Party Identification as a Stimulus to Political Inquiry." In Ian Budge, Ivor Crewe, and Dennis Farlie, eds., *Party Identification and Beyond: Representations of Voting and Party Competition,* ch. 2. London: Wiley.

Miller, Warren E., and Donald E. Stokes. 1963. "Constituency Influence in Congress." *American Political Science Review* 57:45-56. Reprinted in Angus Campbell, Philip E. Converse, Warren E. Miller, and Donald E. Stokes, *Elections and the Political Order.* New York: Wiley, 1966.

Ministère de l'Education National. 1969. *Tableaux de l'éducation nationale: Statistiques rétrospectives, 1958-68.* Paris.

Moch, Jules. 1958. "De Gaulle, d'hier à demain." *La Nef,* July-August.

Le Monde. Paris. 1965-1973.

Mothe, Philippe. 1967. "Sondages et simulation entre les deux tours." *Sondages* 3:89-99.

Niemi, Richard G. 1973. "Collecting Information about the Family: A Problem in Survey Methodology." In Jack Dennis, ed., *Political Socialization: A Reader in Theory and Research.* New York: Wiley.

Norpoth, Helmut. 1978. "Party Identification in West Germany: Tracing an Elusive Concept." *Comparative Political Studies* 11:36-61.

Le Nouvel Observateur. Paris. May 28, 1973; June 10, 1974; April 24, 1978; June 1, 1981; July 4, 1981.

Page, Benjamin I., and Calvin C. Jones. 1979. "Reciprocal Effects of Policy Preferences, Party Loyalties, and the Vote." *American Political Science Review* 73:1071–89.

Pennock, J. Roland, and John W. Chapman, eds. 1968. *Representation.* New York: Atherton Press.

Percheron, Annick. 1982. "Religious Acculturation and Political Socialization in France." In Suzanne Berger, ed., *Religion in West European Politics.* London: Frank Cass.

Percheron, Annick, et al. 1978. *Les 10-16 Ans et la politique.* Paris: Presses de la fondation nationale des sciences politiques.

Percheron, Annick, and M. Kent Jennings. 1981. "Political Continuities in French Families: A New Perspective on an Old Controversy." *Comparative Politics* 13:421–436.

Pierce, Roy. 1957. "The French Election of January 1956." *Journal of Politics* 19:391–422.

———1968; 2d ed., 1973. *French Politics and Political Institutions.* New York: Harper & Row.

———1981. "Left-Right Perceptions, Partisan Preferences, Electoral Participation, and Partisan Choice in France." *Political Behavior* 3:117–136.

———1983. "Untangling French Voting Behavior: Pierce Replies to Rosenthal." *Political Behavior* 5:247–250.

Pierce, Roy and Philip E. Converse. 1981. "Candidate Visibility in France and the United States." *Legislative Studies Quarterly* 6:339–371.

Pitkin, Hanna. 1967. *The Concept of Representation.* Berkeley: University of California Press.

Pompidou, Georges. 1982. *Pour rétablir une vérité.* Paris: Flammarion.

Priouret, Roger. 1947. *La République des partis.* Paris: L'Elan.

Prost, Antoine. 1966. "Les manifestations du 12 fevrier 1934 en province." *Le Mouvement Social* 54:6–27.

Public Opinion, August-September 1980.

Putnam, Robert D. 1973. *The Beliefs of Politicians: Ideology, Conflict, and Democracy in Britain and Italy.* New Haven, Conn.: Yale University Press.

Putnam, Robert D., Robert Leonardi, and Rafaella Y. Nanetti. 1979. "Attitude Stability among Italian Elites." *American Journal of Political Science* 23:463–494.

Rae, Douglas W. 1967. *The Political Consequences of Electoral Laws.* New Haven and London: Yale University Press.

Rae, Douglas W., and Michael Taylor. 1970. *The Analysis of Political Cleavages.* New Haven and London: Yale University Press.

Ranney, Austin. 1954. *The Doctrine of Responsible Party Government.* Urbana, Ill.: University of Illinois Press.

République Française, Ministère de l'Intérieur. 1967a. *Liste des candidats aux élections législatives, 5-12 Mars 1967.* Paris: Imprimerie Nationale.

———1967b. *Les Elections législatives de 1967.* Paris: Imprimerie Nationale.

———1968. *Les Elections législatives de 1968.* Paris: Imprimerie Nationale.

Riker, William H. 1962. *The Theory of Political Coalitions.* New Haven, Conn.: Yale University Press.

Robinson, William S. 1950. "Ecological Correlations and the Behavior of Individuals." *American Sociological Review* 15:351–357.

Roig, Charles, and Françoise Billon-Grand. 1968. *La Socialisation politique des enfants: Contribution à l'étude de la formation des attitudes politiques en France.* Cahiers de la fondation nationale des sciences politiques 163. Paris: Armand Colin.

Rosa, Jean-Jacques, and Daniel Amson. 1976. "Conditions économiques et élections: Une analyse politico-économétrique (1920–1973)." *Revue française de science politique* 26:1101–24.

Rose, Richard, ed. 1974. *Electoral Behavior: A Comparative Handbook.* New York: Free Press.

Rose, Richard, and Derek Urwin. 1970. "Persistence and Change in Western Party Systems since 1945." *Political Studies* 18:287–319.

Rosenthal, Howard. 1967. "The Popularity of Charles de Gaulle: Findings from Archive-Based Research." *Public Opinion Quarterly* 31:381–398.

————1981. "Untangling French Voting Behavior: Tales of Aggregation." *Political Behavior* 3:363–369.

Rosenthal, Howard and Subrata Sen. 1973. "Electoral Participation in the French Fifth Republic." *American Political Science Review* 67:29–54.

————1977. "Spatial Voting Models for the French Fifth Republic." *American Political Science Review* 71:1447–66.

Ross, George. 1982. *Workers and Communists in France: From Popular Front to Eurocommunism.* Berkeley: University of California Press.

Särlvik, Bo, and Ivor Crewe. 1983. *Decade of Dealignment: The Conservative Victory of 1979 and Electoral Trends in the 1970s.* Cambridge: Cambridge University Press.

Sartori, Giovanni. 1961. "Parliamentarians in Italy." UNESCO, *International Social Science Journal* 13:583–599.

Schattschneider, E. E. 1942. *Party Government.* New York: Holt, Rinehart and Winston.

Schleth, Uwe, and Erich Weede. 1971. "Causal Models on West-German Voting Behavior." *Sozialwissenschaftliches Jahrbuch für Politik,* vol. 2, pp. 73–97. Munich and Vienna: Gunter Olzog Verlag.

Shively, W. Phillips. 1972. "Party Identification, Party Choice, and Voting Stability: The Weimar Case." *American Political Science Review* 66:1203–25.

Shorter, Edward, and Charles Tilly. 1974. *Strikes in France, 1830–1968.* London: Cambridge University Press.

Siegfried, André. 1913. *Tableau politique de la France de l'Ouest sous la Troisième République.* Paris: Armand Colin.

————1930. *Tableau des partis en France.* Paris: Bernard Grasset.

————1948. "Les problèmes de la nomenclature politique." In Fondation nationale des sciences politiques, Centre d'études scientifiques de la politique intérieure, *Colloque de sociologie électorale.* Paris: Domat-Montchrestien.

Sondages: Revue française de l'opinion publique. 1962–1973.

Stokes, Donald E. 1965. "A Variance Components Model of Political Effects." In John M. Claunch, ed., *Mathematical Applications in Political Science.* Dallas, Texas: Arnold Foundation, Southern Methodist University.

Stokes, Donald E., and Warren E. Miller. 1962. "Party Government and the Saliency of Congress." *Public Opinion Quarterly* 26:531–546. Reprinted in Angus Campbell, Philip E. Converse, Warren E. Miller, and Donald E. Stokes, *Elections and the Political Order.* New York: Wiley. 1966.

Suleiman, Ezra N. 1974. *Politics, Power, and Bureaucracy in France: The Administrative Elite.* Princeton, N.J.: Princeton University Press.

————1978. *Elites in French Society: The Politics of Survival.* Princeton, N.J.: Princeton University Press.

Sullivan, John L. 1974. "Linkage Models of the Political System." In Allen R. Wilcox, ed., *Public Opinion and Political Attitudes.* New York: Wiley.

Tardieu, André. 1937. *La Profession parlementaire.* Vol. 2 of *La Révolution à refaire.* Paris: Ernest Flammarion.

Tate, Neal C. 1980. "The Centrality of Party in Voting Choice." In Peter H. Merkl, ed., *Western European Party Systems: Trends and Prospects,* pp. 367–401. New York: Free Press.

Thomassen, Jacques. 1976a. *Kiezers en Gekozenen in een Representatieve Demokratie.* Alphen: Samsom.

———1976b. "Party Identification as a Cross-National Concept: Its Meaning in the Netherlands." In Ian Budge, Ivor Crewe, and Dennis Farlie, eds., *Party Identification and Beyond: Representations of Voting and Party Competition,* ch. 4. London: Wiley.

Tournoux, J. R. 1969. *Le Mois de mai du Général.* Paris: Plon.

Tufte, Edward R. 1973. "The Relationship between Seats and Votes in Two-Party Systems." *American Political Science Review* 67:540–554.

Turner, Julius. 1951. *Party and Constituency: Pressures on Congress.* Baltimore, Md.: Johns Hopkins Press.

Verba, Sidney. 1971. "Cross-National Survey Research: The Problem of Credibility." In Ivan Vallier, ed., *Comparative Methods in Sociology: Essays on Trends and Applications.* Berkeley: University of California Press.

Verba, Sidney, Norman H. Nie, and Jae-on Kim. 1978. *Participation and Political Equality.* Cambridge: Cambridge University Press.

Viansson-Ponté, Pierre. 1963. *Les Gaullistes: Rituel et annuaire.* Paris: Editions du Seuil.

Wahlke, John C., Heinz Eulau, William Buchanan, and LeRoy C. Ferguson. 1962. *The Legislative System: Explorations in Legislative Behavior.* New York: Wiley.

Waterman, Harvey. 1969. *Political Change in Contemporary France: The Politics of an Industrial Democracy.* Columbus, Ohio: Charles E. Merrill.

Weisberg, Herbert F. 1978. "Evaluating Theories of Congressional Roll-Call Voting." *American Journal of Political Science* 22:554–577.

Weissberg, Robert. 1978. "Collective vs. Dyadic Representation in Congress." *American Political Science Review* 72:535–547.

Williams, Philip M. 1964. *Crisis and Compromise: Politics in the Fourth Republic.* London: Longmans.

———1968. *The French Parliament: Politics in the Fifth Republic.* New York and Washington: Praeger.

Williams, Philip M., David Goldey, and Martin Harrison. 1970. *French Politicians and Elections, 1951–1969.* Cambridge: Cambridge University Press.

Williams, Philip M. and Martin Harrison. 1960. *De Gaulle's Republic.* London: Longmans.

———1971. *Politics and Society in de Gaulle's Republic.* London: Longmans.

Wilson, Frank L., and Richard Wiste. 1976. "Party Cohesion in the French National Assembly, 1958–1973." *Legislative Studies Quarterly* 1:457–490.

Woshinsky, Oliver H. 1973. *The French Deputy: Incentives and Behavior in the National Assembly.* Lexington, Mass.: D. C. Heath.

Wright, Gordon. 1948. *The Reshaping of French Democracy.* New York: Reynal & Hitchcock.

Index